BACK TO BASICS

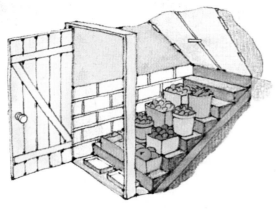

Edited by Abigail R. Gehring

BACK TO BASICS

A Complete Guide to Traditional Skills

Skyhorse Publishing

BACK TO BASICS

Skyhorse Publishing books may be purchased in bulk at special discounts for sales promotion, corporate gifts, fund-raising, or educational purposes. Special editions can also be created to specifications. For details, contact the Special Sales Department, Skyhorse Publishing, 307 West 36th Street, 11th Floor, New York, NY 10018 or info@skyhorsepublishing.com.

Skyhorse® and Skyhorse Publishing® are registered trademarks of Skyhorse Publishing, Inc.®, a Delaware corporation.

www.skyhorsepublishing.com

10 9 8 7 6

Library of Congress Cataloging-in-Publication Data

Back to basics: a complete guide to traditional skills/edited by Abigail R. Gehring.

    p. cm.

  Includes bibliographical references and index.

  ISBN-13: 978-1-60239-233-5 (hardcover)

  ISBN-10: 1-60239-233-1 (hardcover)

  1. Home economics—United States—Handbooks, manuals, etc. 2. Sustainable living—United States—Handbooks, manuals, etc. 3. Handicraft—United States—Handbooks, manuals, etc. 4. Life skills—United States—Handbooks, manuals, etc. I. Gehring, Abigail R.

TX23.B33 2008

640.973—dc22

                                        2007037522

Printed in China

The editors are grateful for the assistance provided by the following organizations and individuals:

Barry Acker
The A. I. Root Company
John Bell, Ph.D.
Frank Berte
Bil-Mac Installations
Kent Bloomer
Caswell-Massey Co. Ltd.
Chamber of Commerce, Ashville, N.C.
Chr. Hansen's Laboratory, Inc.
Cumberland General Store
Kenneth Davies
Nigel Dickens
Easter Wholesale Fence Co. Inc.
Farm Pond Harvest
Fence Industry
Finnish Consulate General
Fire-Glow Distributors, Inc.
Michael Frerking
Garden Way Catalog
Gothard, Inc.
Green Mountain Cabins, Inc.
Haddon Tool

Independent Power Developers, Inc.
R.A.J. Jungreis
Sharon Kahkonen
L. T. Kreutzig
Klaus Kroner
Rev. Henry Lewis
Michael Linn, Ph.D.
L. H. MacDaniels, Ph.D.
Randolph Martin
Miccio Laboratory, Inc.
Museum of New Mexico
Norman Neuerberg
Northeastern Solar Energy Corporation
G. H. Oberly, Ph.D.
Pacific Gas and Electric Co.
Karen Schlesinger
Shelburne Museum
Stanley Sheldon
Bruce Sloat
Julie Sopher
June Sprigg
Paul Stark, Jr.
John Tompkins, Ph.D.
Theodore Torrey, Ph.D.
Neil Welliver
Heinz Wutscher, Ph.D.

Contents

About This Book

Back to Basics is a book about the simple life. It is about old-fashioned ways of doing things, and old-fashioned craftsmanship, and old-fashioned food, and old-fashioned fun. It is also about independence—the kind of down-home self-reliance that our grandparents and great grandparents took for granted, but that we moderns often think has vanished forever, along with supermarket tomatoes that taste good, packaged bread that does not have additives, and holidays that are not commercialized.

At its heart *Back to Basics* is a how-to book packed with hundreds of projects, step-by-step sequences, charts, tables, diagrams, and illustrations to help you and your family reestablish control over your day-to-day lives. The book is organized into six main sections. The first deals with shelter, the second with energy, the third with raising food, the fourth with preserving food, the fifth with home crafts, and the sixth with recreation. The subjects presented lead in logical sequence along all the way stations on the road to self-sufficiency. An added feature, "Sources and resources," lists suggestions for further reading plus names of suppliers of hard-to-find equipment.

Practical, useful information is provided on just about every skill and handicraft under the sun. You will learn how to make your own cheese, raise your own chickens, harvest your own honey, generate your own electricity, and brew your own applejack. You will be able to try your hand at blacksmithing, broom-making, and stone masonry. You will discover how to make soap, tan a hide, build an igloo, heat with wood, smoke a salmon, and create your own cosmetics. Some projects are difficult and demanding—building a log cabin or installing a solar water heating system are tasks for someone with experience, skill, and a strong back. But most of the jobs are well within the capabilities of the average person, and many are suited for family participation, especially for the kids.

While *Back to Basics* is a book for doing, it is also a book for dreaming. There is no need to run out and start baking adobe bricks in order to enjoy learning the ins and outs of adobe construction. (It might even set you thinking about putting up your own adobe home someday.) Similarly, your imagination is apt to be fired by the interviews with folks around the country who are already practicing the skills and crafts described in *Back to Basics*. Among others, you will hear from a husband-and-wife team who built a log cabin in Alaska, some suburban kids who raise goats and pigs in their backyard, a city worker who specializes in urban gardening, and a New Hampshire artisan who is keeping alive the Indian art of building birchbark canoes. There are also descriptions of bygone ways of doing things: the technique of pitsawing, the Indian way of smoking a deer hide and making jerky, the inner workings of a water-powered gristmill. These—along with the historical background of each skill and charming old prints that illustrate many of them—make for fascinating reading.

Americans are a contradictory people. No nation has ever moved farther from the harsh realities of wilderness existence. Yet, paradoxically, no nation has clung more tenaciously to its early ideals—to the concept of personal independence, to the mystique of the frontier, to the early pioneers' sense of rugged self-reliance. It is as if somewhere, deep in the American spirit, there has always lurked a distrust of the very technology that we, more than any other people, have spawned. Perhaps this distrust was an accident, but perhaps it was fate; for in the light of recent events that have called into question our easy dependence on modern technology, it seems to have been prophetic. Americans have long yearned for a return to basics; now, suddenly, it has become a necessity. *Back to Basics* can do much to guide the way.

—*The Editors*

Part One

Land: Buying It—Building on It

A house, we like to believe, can be a noble consort to man and the trees. The house should have repose and such texture as will quiet the whole and make it graciously one with external nature.
—*Frank Lloyd Wright*, The Natural House

The homes of the settlers conformed naturally to the great architect's precepts. People built slowly in those days, over generations, and they understood their land as only those who spend their lives on it can. Their building materials were the very stuff of the earth around them—trees from their woods, rocks from their fields, adobe mud beneath their feet—so it was small wonder that their homes blended well with the surrounding countryside. Above all, they built their homes themselves, and so each mitered beam, each length of floorboard, each hand-riven shingle took on a special meaning of its own. In *Land: Buying It—Building on It* the process of creating a home the traditional way is described, from the acquisition of a site to the construction of the house to the installation of walls and outbuildings. Some of these jobs are difficult; others are within the capabilities of the average person. All help impart a personal touch to a house. In the final analysis that is the ingredient that makes a house a home.

Buying Country Property

Realizing the Dream
Of Owning a Place
In the Country

With careful planning and a modest investment almost anyone can turn the dream of owning a small farm or a few acres of country land into a reality. And with some effort this land may provide a significant portion of life's amenities: wood for the fireplace, fresh produce for the table, a pond for fishing or swimming—even waterpower to generate electricity. But as with any other major purchase, care and caution are required.

The first step is to have, in general terms, a strong notion of what it is you want. Those desiring year-round warmth will obviously have different priorities than those who wish to see the seasons change. Prospective part-time farmers will look for one kind of land, whereas weekend sojourners will look for another. Whether you enjoy isolation or prefer neighbors nearby is another consideration to ponder. And, of course, there is the matter of money: how much you can afford to put down, how much you can pay each month for a mortgage and taxes. Once you have made these decisions, pick an area or two to investigate. Get the catalogs of the Strout and United Farm real estate agencies, and look for ads in the Sunday paper real estate section. Also subscribe to local papers from the regions of your interest; these may provide lower priced listings plus information on land auctions.

When a property appeals to you, investigate— first by phone and then in person. When looking, do not neglect small matters, such as television reception, the contours of the land, and the style of the farmhouse; but never lose sight of your ultimate goals or basic priorities, and gauge the property in that light.

Abandoned farms, like the one at right, often offer the greatest value. Not only has the land already been cleared—though it may have become overgrown— but there are outbuildings and a residence in place, though these may require considerable renovation. In addition, the owners of the property are likely to be particularly interested in selling, since they have already moved away.

Some buildings, like this one, are beyond repair. However, a dilapidated building may make a beautiful piece of property less expensive. In addition, it offers the opportunity to build a dream home from scratch.

To Buy or Not to Buy: Resist That Impulse

Once you have found a piece of property that appears to meet your needs, resist the temptation to come to terms. This is the time for an in-depth investigation rather than a purchase. After leaving the parcel, think about it, talk about it, try to remember its contours, and list all the things you do not like as well as the things you do. If after a week or so the land still is appealing, arrange to spend an entire day tramping about it.

Walk slowly about the property in the company of your family. Among the subjects of discussion should be these: Is the ratio of meadow to woodlot about what you have in mind? Does the woodlot consist of hard or soft woods? (The former are generally more valuable as timber and fuel.) Is the meadow overlain with ground cover, indicating some fertility? Is it swampy? Is there a usable residence on the property? If not, can you afford to build? Is there a road that cuts across the property into a neighbor's driveway? If so, there is likely to be an easement on the parcel, conferring on the neighbor the right to cross at will. If there is no electricity, gas, or telephone service, ask yourself honestly how well you can get along without these conveniences. And if your goal is to be a part-time farmer and full-time resident, check into employment possibilities in the area.

If the answers to most of these questions are satisfactory, then begin a more formal survey of the property. For those who plan to grow vegetables, grains, or fruits, the question of soil fertility becomes a major factor in any ultimate decision. Take a spade and dig down—way down—in several widely scattered places. Ground that is adequate for good crops will have a layer of topsoil at least 10 inches deep; 12 or 15 inches deep is better. The topsoil should be dark, and when handled it should feel soft, loose, and crumbly to the touch. If the topsoil seems rich enough and deep enough, make doubly certain by taking several samples to the nearest county agent; he can analyze it for acidity (pH) and mineral content and tell you what crops are best to grow on it. Another way of discovering what crops the soil will support is to find out what the neighbors are growing. If the farm over the fence has a healthy stand of corn, and a thriving vegetable garden, the chances are good that the land you are looking at will also accommodate those crops.

When walking the land, look for evidence of soil erosion. Gullies are a sign of erosion, as are bared roots of trees and bushes. Parched, stony, light-colored soils indicate that erosion has carried off the rich topsoil. If you are only planning a small kitchen garden, erosion and lack of topsoil can be repaired. But if extensive cropping is your goal, the cost of restoring scores of acres to fertility may be beyond your reach.

Check the drainage capacity of the land. If the subsoil is so compacted or rocky that it cannot quickly absorb water, then the plants you sow are likely to drown. Also bear in mind that poor drainage can make it difficult to install a septic system, since sewage will tend to back up or rise to the surface. Inspect the property in the wake of a heavy rainstorm. If the surface is muddy or even very spongy, it is a sign that the drainage is poor. Dig several widely spaced holes in the ground, each one about 8 inches around and 3 to 4 feet deep. Check the soil near the bottoms. If it is hard-packed and unyielding to the touch, chances are it is relatively impermeable to water. Or pour a bucket of water on the ground, wait 10 minutes, and dig to see how far the water has penetrated. For the most accurate information, a percolation test by a soil engineer is necessary.

If you are planning on building a house, carefully inspect possible construction sites. The land for the house should be reasonably flat, with easy access to a public road. Do not overlook the site's relationship to the winter sun. A house with a northern exposure, particularly if it is on a slope, is likely to cost considerably more to heat than one with a southern exposure that can take advantage of the warming rays of the low-lying winter sun.

Finally, there is the all-important matter of water—the lack of a reliable source of water for drinking and irrigation can make an otherwise desirable site worthless. The subject is discussed in detail on page 12.

In all events, try to delay a commitment until you see the land in all seasons; both the blooms of spring and the snows of winter can hide a multitude of evils.

Decoding the real estate ads

Composite view of typical country property (right), together with a real estate advertisement (inset) of the type that might appear in the classified section of a newspaper or as part of a catalog of realty listings, serves to illustrate the gap that sometimes exists between description and reality. The phrase "Approx. 12 acres" may mean just about anything at all but likely indicates that no accurate survey has been made. "Handyman's delight" is most often a euphemistic way of saying that the house and outbuildings are wrecks, as an on-site inspection would reveal. "C. 18th cent, details" probably reflects an unsupported belief that the house may be as much as 200 years old. The reference to state land carries the implication that the area is protected from overdevelopment, but the ad does not state that a road cuts across the property to permit loggers access to the state forest. Oddly, but not atypically, the ad fails to point out a number of positive aspects. Though the phrase "Riv. vu" indicates the presence of running water nearby, the fact is that both a stream and a pond exist on the property. Nor does the ad reveal that there is an excellent woodlot and that the farmhouse is in close proximity to a public highway, allowing for easy access. For all its deficiencies, the ad does awaken interest, but only by visiting can you judge the property accurately.

COUNTRY CLASSIC
No. 4731 . . . Approx. 12 acres, $61,000. Handyman's delight. Though 12 rm. hse. needs work. Riv. vu & orig. c. 18th cent. details offer pos. luxury country living. Land adjoins state forest. All sports nearby. Grow own vegs., fruit.

Buildings Are Important But Water Is Vital

In assessing country property the most important single consideration is the availability of an adequate supply of fresh, potable water. With water virtually anything is possible; without it virtually nothing. Consider, for example, that a single human being uses between 30 and 70 gallons per day; a horse between 6 and 12; a milk cow about 35; and a 500-square-foot kitchen garden, if it is to thrive, must have an average of 35 gallons of water per day. Even if the property is to be used only as a country retreat, a family of four will require a bare minimum of 100 gallons every day for such basic needs as drinking, washing, cooking, and sanitation. In short, complete information about water availability is an imperative when assessing country property. This is not to say, however, that a piece of land should, in all cases, be rejected if the existing water supply is inadequate, since in most instances a water system can be developed (see pp.54–57). Nevertheless, this can be an expensive, laborious, and time-consuming effort, and it is far more satisfactory if a water system is already in place.

Existing systems. If there is a well or other water source, along with plumbing in the house, in the out buildings, and at the fields, test the system out as completely as possible. Try all of the taps: one at a time, several at once, all at once. Is the flow sufficient for your purposes? Does the water pressure drop significantly when several taps are on at once? Has the water been tested for potability and for minerals, particularly salt? Water with even a relatively low salt content may be useless for drinking or irrigation. Remember that a fast flow in spring may become but a trickle in the dog days of summer. This is another reason to visit a property in different seasons before purchase.

Aboveground water. A river, stream, brook, or pond on the property may provide adequate water, particularly for irrigation. A freshwater spring bubbling up from the earth can usually provide drinking water, but again, such sources may dry up during the summer. If you plan to use a river or pond for recreational purposes, such as swimming or fishing, make certain that pollutants from logging operations, sewage treatment plants, and factories are not being dumped upstream. Pollutants, of course, can make the water unusable for irrigation as well. Check with local and state authorities on the amount of water you may take from a watercourse.

Plants that provide clues to water in dry country

Rushes and cattails are a sign of marshland or of water very near the surface.

Pickleweed indicates the presence of salty water at or just below the surface.

Saltbush indicates water near the surface, but the quality may be poor.

Mesquite indicates that water is to be found from 10 to 50 ft. beneath the ground.

Reeds signify the existence of good quality water very close to the surface.

Black greasewood generally means that mineralized water exists 10 to 40 ft. down.

Rabbit brush will grow only where there is water no more than 15 ft. below the ground.

Elderberry shrubs are a fairly good sign that there is water about 10 ft. down.

Also make sure that the source is properly positioned to allow you to get the water from where it is to where it will be needed. A stream below a building site and garden plot will be useful only with the installation of pumps. Even one above these areas may require siphons and considerable piping if it is to be useful.

Marshlands. Though marshes and swamps indicate a high water table and, under the proper conditions, a possible pond site, they are considered negative factors by most builders, since they provide breeding grounds for mosquitoes and other insect pests and the land is useless for construction unless drained and filled.

Public water supplies. In a number of rural areas water is supplied by an outside utility company. Some utilities are owned by the government, others are owned privately with rates established by law, and still others are associations of landowners who have pooled their resources to bring water in from distant sources so that they can irrigate their lands and provide for themselves and their livestock. Hookups to any of these water utilities can be expensive and, in the case of the landowners' associations, impossible to obtain. It may be, however, that the owner from whom you are obtaining the land already has shares in the local cooperative

water association. If so, make sure that the transfer of these shares is included as part of the purchase price and that you know in advance the amount of water to which your shares will entitle you.

Water rights. The fact that a parcel has water either aboveground or underground is not necessarily a guarantee that the owner has the right to exploit the resource. In some states even underground water must be shared. Before purchasing any property, have your lawyer check on your water rights.

Sources and resources

Books

Nash, George. *Old Houses: A Rebuilder's Manual.* Needham Heights, Mass.: Prentice Hall, 1979.

Orme, Alan D. *Reviving Old Houses: Over Five Hundred Low-Cost Tips and Techniques.* Avenal, N.J.: Random House Value, 1994.

Poore, Patricia, ed. The *Old House Journal Guide* to *Restoration.* New York: NAL-Dutton, 1992.

Sherwood, Gerald E. *How to Select and Renovate an Older House.* New York: Dover, 1976.

Sizing Up the House and Barns

The extent and condition of improvements play a large role in determining the worth of any piece of property. Direct access to a county highway via well-maintained internal roads is a major factor when considering a piece of land. A house, barn, and other outbuildings in good condition, the presence of primary utilities, and a central heating system all add to the market value of any parcel. When assessing improvements, look beyond the appearances and into such matters as structural soundness, electrical service capacity, the age of the heating system, and the relationship of the house to the winter sun.

First examine the house as a whole. Is it big enough for your needs? Does it afford sufficient privacy? Does it appear to be well maintained? Very important is the placement of the house. To take full advantage of the low-lying winter sun, it should present a broad front to the south and have a large proportion of its window openings facing south. Look at the windows themselves. Are storm windows and tight-fitting screens installed? Make notes as you move along the outside of the house and as you inspect the inside. Check for wood rot both inside and out, using an ice pick to jab at the beams and supports. If the pick goes in easily,

there is probably wood rot, an expensive condition to repair. Look for signs of termites and carpenter ants, particularly along the baseboards of the ground floor and in the exposed joists in the basement. Also check the main fuse box to see if the electrical service is sufficient for your needs (modern service is at least 100 amps at 240 volts), then inspect the water heater as to age and capacity. A four-person family requires a 30-gallon gas water heater or a 50-gallon electric model. As you move from room to room, look up and down as well as around. Stains on the ceilings or evidence of recent plastering may mean roof leaks; horizontal stains on the lower part of basement or ground floor walls indicate flooding. Finally, hire a building engineer for an in-depth analysis. The deficiencies he finds may not necessarily be overwhelming, but they could provide you with a strong bargaining position for lowering the price by thousands of dollars.

Many people considering a move to the country seek out the charm of 18th- or 19th-century structures. Real estate agents recognize this and often emphasize that a house is one or two centuries old. Generally, it is best to verify such claims. Some tips on what to look for in dating a house are given below.

Clues to a building's age

Irregular lath marks on beams indicate building dates from 18th or early 19th century.

Accordion lath marks (rarely seen) were produced by a technique not used after 1830.

Straight lath marks, regularly spaced, indicate post-1850 construction.

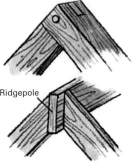

Ridgepole

No ridgepole on roof (top) usually means pre-1800; presence of ridgepole indicates later date.

Hand-sawed beams, with irregular, slanted saw marks, date from before 1750s.

Vertical cuts in regular patterns usually indicate lumber was sawed before 1860.

Curving saw marks point to post-1860s construction–the more even, the later.

Blunt wood screws with no taper were not made after 1840. Hand-cut notches in heads can give clues to age of screws.

Tapered screws with pointed ends were made after 1840. Notches in heads were cut by machine rather than by hand.

Wrought nails, with square, tapered shanks and hand-forged heads bearing hammer marks, were made before 1800.

Cut nails, sliced from a sheet of iron, were not made before 1800. They are still manufactured for use in flooring.

Benchmarks for the buyer

Major points to consider when contemplating the purchase of a piece of country property are listed below. Use them as a checklist to avoid costly mistakes.

Contract of sale. The contract describes the terms under which the property is being sold. It should include a description of all encumbrances on the property and should be made contingent upon a successful title search and the ability of the buyer to secure adequate financing. Have your lawyer draw up the contract of sale rather than accept a real estate agent's standard form.

Easements. If land has no direct access to a highway, make sure you have an easement (legally binding right-of-way) across intervening properties. Know also if neighbors have an easement on the property you plan to buy.

Eminent domain. Many public and quasi-public agencies have the right to condemn land (with compensation to owners) for roads, drainage canals, dams, airports, school construction, power lines, rights-of-way into bordering state-owned property, and the like. Check with the local planning board to ascertain if any condemnation proceedings are contemplated.

Land contracts and mortgages. Land contracts are the least advantageous means of buying land because the seller or financing agency holds title until the purchase is fully paid off. The title holder may, during this interval, encumber the property by using it as collateral; the purchaser can lose the land if the title holder fails to make payments. Mortgages in which the buyer has title to the property and uses it as collateral offer greater protection against foreclosure.

Mineral and other encumbrances. The seller or an earlier owner may have sold or reserved the right to exploit minerals, timber, or even the water on the land. These encumbrances, if properly recorded, are legally binding.

Survey. Check with county recorder to determine if a legally binding map of the property has been made. If not, insist that a licensed surveyor draw such a map, preferably at the seller's expense.

Taxes. Check with local authorities to find out the amount of taxes (property, school, water, sewer) on the property you contemplate buying. Also try to determine if these taxes have been rising rapidly in recent years. Some states tax standing timber, mineral deposits, and water rights. Make sure there are no liens for unpaid taxes on the property.

Title search and insurance. Have your lawyer or a title insurance company check records to make sure you are buying land free of liens and encumbrances. Purchase title insurance—a one-time expense—that will guarantee the accurary of the title search.

Water rights. Contract of sale should include clause in which seller guarantees a minimum water supply. Make sure the clause is in accordance with state laws on water rights.

Zoning laws. Check with the local zoning board to be certain you may use your land in the manner you intend. Also check building and health codes for the same purpose.

Planning Your Home

The Key Ingredient In Home Design Is You

A well-designed home, like a well-tailored garment, should fit your taste, needs, and pocketbook. In years gone by, homesteaders achieved this goal by designing and building their own houses. One reason they were successful was that they were guided by traditions handed down over the centuries. Another was that their homesteads evolved over many years, each generation altering and enlarging the original to suit its particular needs so that the house slowly became better and better.

Nowadays, the best way to ensure that the home you build will have the right feel for you and your family is to take an active part in the design process. This is true whether you intend to put up a vacation cabin, a family residence, a retirement home, or a full-fledged homestead. Learn about design, look at as many homes as you can, and if you plan to hire an architect, shop carefully before you choose one.

Choosing a Building Site

The main house—even if it is just a cabin or cottage—is almost always the focal point of any site development plan, and the first step in designing it is to decide where it will be located. To choose a site intelligently, you should have a good idea of how you want to live. Do you favor a secluded home far from the road? Are you interested in a sweeping vista? Do you plan to put up a sprawling one-story structure or a more compact two-story house? (The former is useful if stair climbing presents a problem for anyone in the family; the latter is generally more energy efficient.) Do you foresee the need for future additions and, therefore, a larger site? Do you require a full basement? (If you do, avoid a site that will require expensive blasting of bedrock.)

Next, examine what your property has to offer. Consider the general lay of the land, the bearing strength of the ground (see *Preparing the Site*, p.21), the

Log home is well protected by trees against fall or winter winds. If built in a hot climate, log homes can be built on piers to allow air to circulate beneath.

Frame dwelling in the Northeast has sloping roof to allow snow to slide off easily in the winter. Having the barn attached to the main house makes it easier to care for the animals in poor weather.

Stone cottage has an eyebrow dormer to allow extra light into the second floor. Like brick, stone is fireproof and maintenance free. Attic helps retain heat, partially compensating for poor insulating ability of stone.

Adobe house in the Southwest has thick walls that offer excellent insulation against incessant heat of the sun. Adobe's structural weakness limits house to one story; its vulnerability to rain rules out use in any but the most arid regions.

soil's ability to absorb rainwater and sewage, the frost depth, the availability of drinking water, the height of the water table, the amount of annual sunlight, and the direction of prevailing winds. Pay particular attention to accessibility. How far is a proposed site from existing electric and telephone service lines? How many feet of driveway will have to be installed to provide access to the nearest public road? Of all development costs, road building is often the most extreme. In general, a well-chosen building site should suit the terrain and provide adequate drainage away from the foundation. For this reason, gently sloping ground is usually best but not always necessary, since pole or pier foundations that compensate for uneven ground can often be constructed.

Energy efficiency is becoming a basic element in site selection just as it was in the past. Significant savings

in heating can be realized by building on the lee side of a rise or by locating the building site downwind from a stand of trees. A site that takes advantage of the low winter sun—even if the home is not designed for solar heating—can reap major long-term energy savings.

Most sites require some shifting of earth. Because of the labor and expense involved, thorough planning is a must. The goal is to move as little earth as possible. Of the three methods of leveling—cut, fill, and a combination of the two—the last is easiest and most economical.

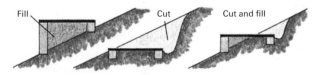

Cut-and-fill leveling technique requires least movement of soil.

Using the Lay of the Land to Advantage

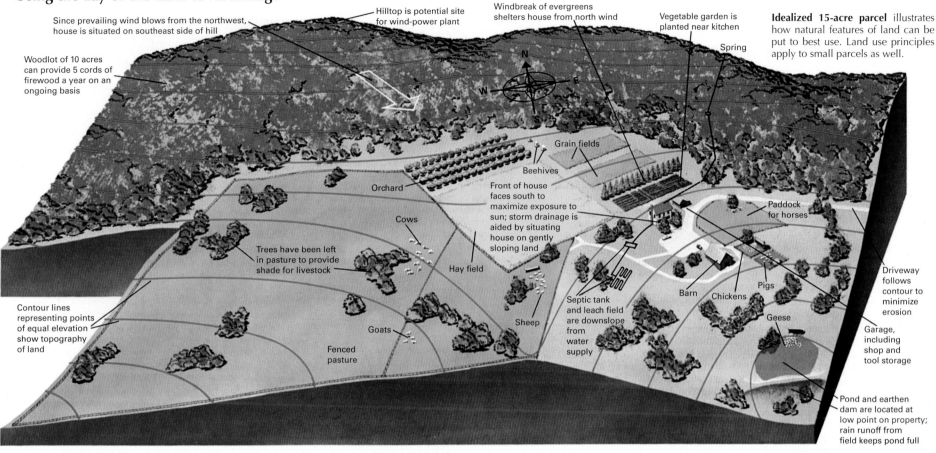

Since prevailing wind blows from the northwest, house is situated on southeast side of hill

Hilltop is potential site for wind-power plant

Windbreak of evergreens shelters house from north wind

Vegetable garden is planted near kitchen

Spring

Idealized 15-acre parcel illustrates how natural features of land can be put to best use. Land use principles apply to small parcels as well.

Woodlot of 10 acres can provide 5 cords of firewood a year on an ongoing basis

Grain fields

Beehives

Orchard

Front of house faces south to maximize exposure to sun; storm drainage is aided by situating house on gently sloping land

Paddock for horses

Cows

Trees have been left in pasture to provide shade for livestock

Hay field

Septic tank and leach field are downslope from water supply

Barn

Chickens

Pigs

Driveway follows contour to minimize erosion

Contour lines representing points of equal elevation show topography of land

Goats

Sheep

Geese

Garage, including shop and tool storage

Fenced pasture

Pond and earthen dam are located at low point on property; rain runoff from field keeps pond full

A detailed map can be an invaluable planning aid. To make your own map, you will need a plane table (a board mounted on a tripod is best, but a card table will do), straight pins, a ruler, a spirit level, and a 10-foot pole marked in feet and inches. Start by drawing the outline of your property on a large sheet of paper; if you do not have a boundary map, you can get one at the town assessor's office. The remainder of the job consists of plotting as many distinct features as possible. If your property is relatively open, you can also find the height of each point and sketch in equal-altitude contour lines. When mapping, concentrate on features that will tie the map together, such as a road, a stream, a hedgerow, or an old stone wall. Either pace off the distance to each feature or else take sightings on it from two different locations: the intersection of the two lines of sight will pinpoint the feature.

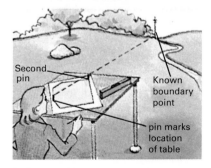

1. Set up table at a corner of your property line, insert pin at corresponding point in map outline, and adjust table so it is horizontal. Then sight from pin to another known boundary point, align map along line of sight, and insert second pin.

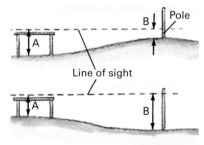

2. Sight from first pin to other distinct features. Have assistant pace off distance to each point. Then have him hold measuring pole while you sight to it. Height of table (A) minus height from base of pole to line of sight (B) equals height of point.

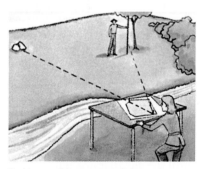

3. Move table to one of the points you have already mapped, reorient map as in Step 1, and map more points as in Step 2. By setting up table at a number of locations, you can map enough points to sketch in the topography of your land.

15

Getting Your Ideas Down On a Sheet of Paper

Settling on a design for a home reflects a series of compromises between the ideal and the possible. The most fundamental compromise involves size: the expense of building a home is directly proportional to the number of cubic feet of interior space it contains. In addition, a larger home requires more energy to heat and cool and is more expensive to maintain.

One way to cut down on cubic feet without sacrificing comfort or floor area is to keep the ceilings low. Typically, a traditional two-story farmhouse will have 8-foot ceilings on the ground floor and 7-foot ceilings upstairs where the bedrooms are located. Another energy saver is an attic. The heat that rises to the peak of a cathedral ceiling is almost totally wasted. An attic not only eliminates this waste but also functions as a jumbo-sized insulating space, moderating the temperature both summer and winter.

Space in houses divides three ways: communal (living room, dining room, recreation room), private (bedroom, studio, study), and service (kitchen, bathroom, garage, laundry, closets). The allocation of these spaces into rooms depends on the needs and tastes of the family. When sketching your designs, pay particular attention to the way the different spaces interact. Traffic flow between areas should be smooth, and a private space should never lie in the flow between two communal areas. Service areas generally function as appendages to communal or private areas. The kitchen, for example, must be adjacent to the dining room, and the bathrooms should be convenient to the sleeping quarters. Separation can be important; a noisy family room should be far away from an area used for studying.

Home design should take into account future needs. A growing family will either have to build extra space into the original house or plan on future additions. The escalating cost of building materials argues for the first alternative, but any excess space will mean unnecessary heating bills, property taxes, and mortgage payments until the day that it is put to use. Plan your addition so that it meets the following criteria: it should not interfere with natural lighting or spoil the view; it should not conflict with local zoning requirements; and, in the case of a second floor addition, the original structure should be strong enough to support it.

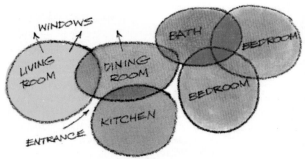

Layout of space can begin with a series of informal "bubble" sketches. Each bubble represents a particular use of space. The more of these diagrams you draw, the nearer you are likely to come to sensing the best floor plan. You should also make a point of visiting and examining as many homes as possible.

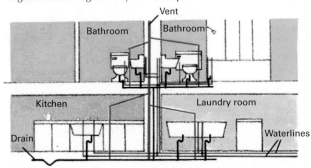

Clustering of utilities, such as waterlines and drainpipes, in one area of the house is advisable from point of view of economy, ease of installation, and ease of maintenance. In a typical layout the kitchen sink and laundry room are placed back to back with a bathroom located above.

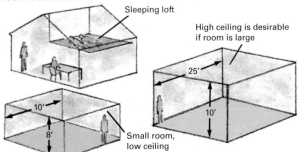

Room size should be suited to function—large and spacious for a main communal area, small and cozy for a den or child's bedroom. Cathedral ceilings are attractive, but they waste heat. A sleeping loft can reduce heat loss in a room with a cathedral ceiling without destroying the ceiling's dramatic impact.

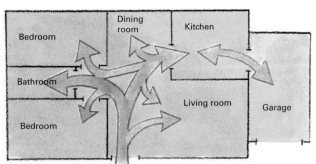

Sketch of floor plans, with rooms in approximately correct proportion, follows space layout. With such sketches, defects in the location of doorways and patterns of personal movement can be discerned. Bathroom in sketch shown, for example, might be considered too long a walk from kitchen.

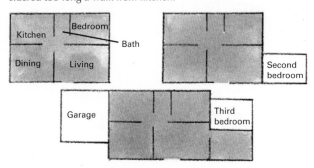

Build small and add on later is often preferable to building everything at once, particularly for a growing family. As the years pass, you will know more accurately whether you need that extra bedroom or studio. However, the initial design should take possible additions into account.

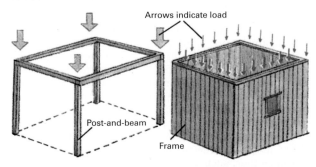

Frame construction and post-and-beam construction are the two principal building methods. In the former, house weight is borne by all segments of each wall; in the latter, by separate posts. Frame construction costs less and is more widely used; post-and-beam permits larger spaces, bigger windows.

Drawing Accurate Floor Plans

After a basic layout has been developed, the next step is to draw carefully scaled floor plans. Try to base room dimensions, ceiling heights, and the widths and lengths of floors on increments of 4 feet insofar as possible. This is because standard sheets of plywood and other building materials are sold in 4- by 8-foot sheets. In addition, keep in mind the following design criteria:

Closets. Minimum depth for a closet is 2 feet.

Counter space. Allow 2 feet from the wall for kitchen counters, since most kitchen equipment protrudes about that amount.

Doors. Interior doors are generally 2 1/2 feet wide; the front door should be 3 feet wide.

Hallways. Widths run from 2 feet up to 4 feet and more. The longer the hallway, the wider it should be.

Kitchen aisles. Small is not necessarily convenient. A minimum aisle width of 4 feet is recommended when equipment is laid out along parallel walls; increase this dimension to 5 feet if the kitchen is U-shaped.

Room dimensions. The ratio of room length to width should be no more than two to one. Overall size varies from 5 feet by 5 feet for a small foyer to 20 feet by 30 feet or larger for a living room. In general, the bigger the room, the higher the ceiling should be.

Walls. Allow a thickness of 1/2 foot for both interior and exterior walls. If the walls are masonry, allow 1 foot.

When drawing plans for a two-story house, trace the structural elements of the ground floor, then use the outline to draw the rooms on the second floor.

Architects and Other Outside Aids

A home is the most expensive possession that a family is ever likely to own. On the average, it takes a healthy, energetic couple a year or more of full-time labor to put up a relatively modest house, and even then they will almost surely have to hire workmen for site clearance, grading, and excavation. With so much time, labor, and money invested, it is vital that the house plans be accurate and sound. In most cases this means that outside design aid will have to be enlisted.

The most straightforward way to get help is to hire an architect. A good architect does not come cheaply—a fee of 10 percent of the cost of a home is not unusual. One way to save money is to have the architect make only a basic sketch, then let a contractor work out the practical details. This procedure still gives you the benefit of the architect's ability to establish lighting, space relationships, flow patterns, and environmental harmony.

When choosing an architect or contractor—or for that matter when doing your own designing—there is no substitute for examining actual houses: no floor plan or

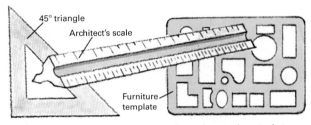

45° triangle
Architect's scale
Furniture template

Inexpensive tools can aid in drawing floor plans and vertical views. A triangle makes it easy to draw lines at right angles; an architect's scale lets you choose from 12 different scales that automatically convert feet to inches; and a furniture template helps you indicate such items as chairs, sofas, and shelves.

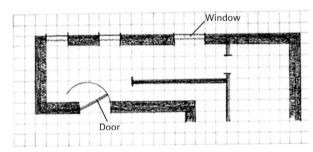

Window
Door

Quadrille paper with four or five squares to the inch is handy for sketching floor plans. If the side of each square in sketch is set to 1 ft., the area of each room can be quickly determined by counting the number of squares it encloses.

Model of house can be constructed out of foam core board or corrugated cardboard. Carefully draw the outlines of floor plans, house sides, interior walls, and roof on the cardboard, then cut out pieces along outlines, including doorways and windows, and put the model together with rubber cement or transparent tape. With a little imagination you can place yourself in each room, sense how it feels, and make design adjustments. By setting the model outdoors on a sunny day (or simulating the sun with a high intensity lamp) you can tell how much natural lighting can be expected.

rendition can replace the real thing. Visit all the homes you can (most homeowners will be happy to show you around if you explain your purpose), and note which homes give you a good feeling and which leave you with a negative impression. Try to spot the features you like or dislike; sometimes the difference between a desirable and undesirable home comes down to nothing more than carpeting, wallpaper, or furniture. Before you pick an architect or contractor, quiz him closely; especially if you are interested in energy efficiency, solar heating, or other special technology. Do not rely on verbal assurances alone. Rather, ask the architect or contractor to show you examples of his work.

An alternative to hiring an architect is to purchase standard plans. Magazines containing floor layouts and artist's renderings are available at building supply dealers and magazine stores. After choosing a plan, you can order complete blueprints for a few hundred dollars.

Sources and resources

Books and pamphlets

Ching, Francis D.K. *Building Construction Illustrated*. New York: Van Nostrand Reinhold, 1991.

DeCristoforo, R.J. *Housebuilding: A Do-It-Yourself Guide*. New York: Sterling Publishing, 1987.

DiDonno, Lupe, and Phyllis Sperling. *How to Design & Build Your Own House*. New York: Knopf, 1987.

Kern, Barbara, and Ken Kern. *The Owner-Built Homestead*. New York: Scribner's, 1977.

Ramsey, Charles G., and Harold R. Sleeper. *Architectural Graphic Standards*, 7th ed. New York: John Wiley, 1993.

Shemie, Bonnie. *Houses of Wood: Northwest Coast*. Plattsburgh, N.Y.: Tundra Books, 1994.

Sherwood, Gerald H. and Stroh, Robert C., eds. *Wood Frame House Construction: A Do-It-Yourself Guide*. New York: Sterling Publishing, 1992.

Uniform Building Code. Whittier, Calif.: International Conference of Building Officials, 1994.

Wagner, Willis H. *Modern Carpentry*. South Holland, Ill.: Goodheart-Willcox, 1992.

Walker, Les, and Jeff Milstein. *Designing Houses: An Illustrated Guide*. Woodstock, N.Y.: Overlook Press, 1979.

Wood Frame House Building. Blue Ridge Summit, Pa.: TAB Books, 1991.

Preparing the Site

Carving Your Homestead From the Wilderness

A small cabin on a minimal foundation normally needs little site preparation. For a larger home, however, the work of clearing the land, leveling a building site, developing an access road, excavating, and laying a foundation sometimes requires as much labor, time, and expense as erecting the house itself. Pioneer settlers, lacking power machinery, searched for building sites that required a minimum of preparation. Though such sites are scarce today, the loss is more than offset by modern techniques and equipment that permit the development of lands that the pioneers would have been forced to pass up.

Planning and Preparation

The job of site development starts in the winter, when trees are bare and the features of the terrain are clearly visible. This is the time of year to lay out your plans in detail. It is also the time to cut and haul away any trees that have value as lumber or firewood.

Start actual clearing as soon as possible after the spring thaw, when the ground is firm and dry: land cleared later in the year seldom develops enough ground cover to prevent erosion. The initial stages require only hand tools—a chain saw, an ax, and a brush hook. Later, heavy equipment must be brought in for grading and excavation. A rented gasoline-powered chipper is useful for shredding brush; the chips make excellent mulch for gardening, landscaping, and erosion control. If you have the time and energy, hand clearing has advantages over machinery: far greater numbers of trees and shrubs can be left undisturbed, and there will be less damage to the natural features of the surrounding area. Hand clearing also saves money and gives you additional time to plan the final construction.

Surveying the site, grading the land, and excavating the foundation and drainage field are jobs for professionals unless you happen to have experience in this type of work. A home is too important to risk the consequences of trial-and-error learning, so assess your abilities fairly before you begin.

The Four Stages of Site Development

1. Start clearing in winter by cutting down trees that are on the building site. Winter is the best season for logging, since wood is driest and snow on the ground eases the job of hauling. Leave 3-ft. stumps to ease the job of removing them later.

3. Erect batter boards to mark building lines and excavation boundaries. Simple foundation trenches can be dug by hand, but a powered backhoe with an experienced operator is usually more economical in the long run.

Batter board

2. Wait until spring, when the ground is fully thawed, to pull stumps. Use animals or a mechanical aid, such as a winch, unless they are to be removed by bulldozer. Ordinary cars and trucks do not have enough traction for the job.

4. Pouring a foundation is the last step before construction begins. You will need plenty of assistance, since the job is long and difficult even if you hire a cement mixer. For maximum strength the entire footing should be poured at one time.

It takes two to survey. The assistant (right) will point to a spot. When that spot is in line with the surveyor's scope, the assistant will measure its height above ground. That height, minus the height of the scope, will give the ground elevation where the pole stands.

Sources and resources

Bureau of Naval Personnel. *Basic Construction Techniques for Houses and Small Buildings Simply Explained*. New York: Dover, 1972.

Church, Horace K. *Excavation Handbook*. New York: McGraw-Hill, 1980.

DiDonno, Lupe, and Phyllis Sperling. *How to Design and Build Your Own House*. New York: Knopf, 1987.

Nichols, Herbert L. *Moving the Earth: The Workbook of Excavation*. New York: McGraw-Hill, 1988.

Clearing the Land and Building an Access Road

The job of site development starts with clearing the land and constructing an access road. There was a time when this work was accomplished with the sweat and muscle of animals and men, but today the fastest and cheapest method is to hire a bulldozer run by an experienced operator. Prepare in advance for the job of clearing by marking features that might affect the grading of the site and access road on your development map. Also rent a builder's level and measuring rod; you will need them to make sure that the building site and access road are graded to the proper angles.

Tree removal should be thought out carefully. Generally speaking, stands of native hardwoods are more valuable than evergreens and should receive priority if a choice has to be made to cut one type or the other. An exception would be a case where dense evergreens can serve as a windbreak or where diseased hardwoods may eventually fall and damage the house. Trees less than 4 inches in diameter, along with brush and undergrowth, usually can be cleared away with little worry. Consult a forester, however, before removing large numbers of bigger trees; he can help you work out a plan for gradual removal that will allow the remaining growth to adjust to altered water-table characteristics. Use paint or plastic ribbon to distinguish trees that are to be removed; mark trees that are to be saved with paint or ribbon of another color. Trees that are cut should be carried away as lumber or sawed into firewood and left to season. Stack firewood nearby, between standing trees; it will be easier to haul after it is seasoned.

Access roads should be 10 feet wide or more—a wide road will last longer than a narrow one because wear and tear is spread over a larger surface. Grade all curves to an inside radius of 30 feet for a car, 45 feet if large vehicles, such as oil trucks, will use the road. A turnaround at a garage or dead end should be a minimum of 30 feet by 40 feet. Drivers must have at least one car length of unobstructed vision at all points along the road, so foliage should be kept low along curves. Similarly, trim trees and shrubs far enough back from the shoulders to prevent them from interfering with traffic. Try, however, to leave a screen of foliage for soil control, privacy, and encouragement of wildlife.

If a road is being put in on a steep slope, do not cut it directly uphill. Instead, traverse the slope by following the contour lines. Slope gradients should be no more than 10 percent (a 1-foot rise for every 10 feet in length) to minimize vehicle strain and road damage from braking and wheel spinning. In order to prevent landslides, embankments should be smoothed back to their angles of repose—the point at which a given material ceases to

slide downhill of its own accord. (See p.21.) Incorporate gutters, ditches, and culverts into the roadway to minimize erosion, mud formation, and frost heaving.

Road surfaces of dirt, gravel, or crushed rock are adequate in most parts of the country although occasional routine maintenance will be necessary. Regrading and smoothing require little more than hard work and often can be accomplished with the simple homemade equipment shown below.

Drainage ditches and culvert pipe carry storm runoff away from roadway and help prevent washouts caused by water streaming down from hillsides. Additional protection against erosion is provided by making center of road higher than edges. The standard crown for a dirt road has a rise of 1/2 in. per foot of road width.

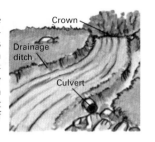

Homemade tools for grading

Fresno scraper, for moving loose dirt and gravel, is made from 55-gal. drum cut in half with ends left intact. Bolt or weld a blade of 1/2-in.-thick steel along bottom edge, and add braced handle made of 2 x 4's or thick poles.

Buck scraper smooths high spots left by fresno. Use sturdy 2 x 12's for buckboard, 1/4-in.-thick steel for blade, strap iron for bracing. Handle is bent iron pipe. Operator stands on trailer board, applies pressure to handle to regulate blade.

Taking elevations with a builder's level

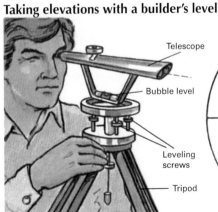

1. Mount builder's level on tripod and adjust until bubble is stable throughout 360° rotation of telescope. Measure height of scope above the ground.

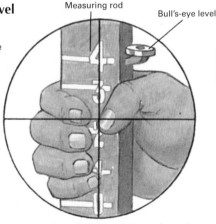

2. Have assistant hold measuring rod at point where elevation reading is desired, then sight rod through scope. Rod marking, minus scope height, is elevation.

3. Take elevations of surrounding points by rotating telescope; tripod must remain fixed. In each case, subtract scope height from rod reading to obtain result.

Laying the Groundwork Gets You Started

Setting Corner Stakes and Batter Boards

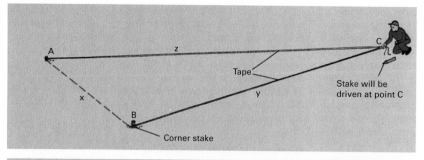

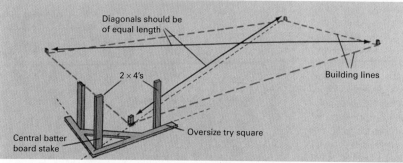

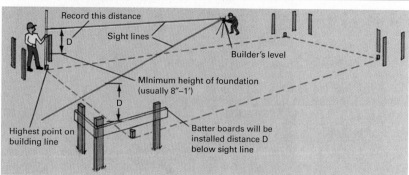

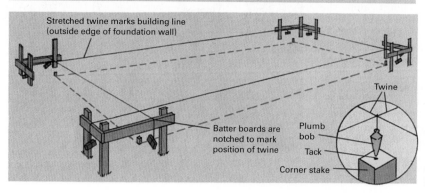

After the building site has been cleared and leveled, actual construction can begin. The first step is to set up accurate building lines to mark the structure's perimeter. Once that is accomplished, the area can be excavated for the foundation. Start by setting the corner stakes, which identify the exact locations of each corner of the proposed building. Make these stakes of 2 × 2 lumber, 2 to 3 feet in length, and sharpen their ends symmetrically to keep them from twisting when driven into the ground. Drive the first stake so that it is centered over the spot selected for the first corner of the building. Locate the second corner by measuring from the first, then drive another stake into the ground at that spot. The two stakes define the corners, length, and position of one side of the building. The other corners and sides can now be found by measuring out from the established corners according to the ground plan of the building. Each time a new corner is established, drive a stake into the ground to mark it. Square or rectangular structures require only four corner stakes. If the building is L-shaped or has additional projections, stake out a central rectangle, then lay out the extensions.

Precise right angles are essential throughout. One method of achieving them, explained in Step 1 at right, is to use the Pythagorean theorem. Another way is to build an oversize try square in the shape of a right triangle; construct it from a metal angle iron or from lumber carefully selected for straightness. Place the square at a known corner of the site so that one arm lies along the established straight line and the other arm extends at right angles to it in the direction of the corner location you wish to find. Measure along this arm to establish the new corner.

The corner stakes are usually removed during excavation, since their locations normally place them in the path of any foundation trenches that must be dug. In order to keep a permanent record of their location, horizontal boards known as batter boards are set up on stakes several feet outside the site at each corner. The boards are then notched with saw cuts so that strings stretched between them will intersect directly over the corner stakes. Batter boards are used to record other information as well, such as excavation boundaries and footing widths, and are generally left in place throughout most of the building process.

1. Locate corner stakes at right angles to known building lines with help of Pythagorean formula. Stakes A and B mark corners of known line x. Length of side y is specified in plans. Compute length of z by adding together square of side x and square of side y; z equals the square root of sum ($z = \sqrt{x^2 + y^2}$). Now attach tape equal in length to z to stake A and another tape equal in length to y to stake B. The point on the ground where both tapes are stretched tight when held together is correct spot for C.

2. Complete corner stake layout by using methods described in Step 1 to locate remaining stake. Check final rectangle by stretching tape between diagonally opposite stakes: both diagonals should be equal. Next step is to erect batter boards. Set central batter board stakes 6 ft. behind corner stakes along extended diagonals. Use homemade oversize try square built of metal or lumber to locate the remaining batter board stakes, and drive them about 6 ft. from each central stake, making sure they are parallel to the building lines.

3. Horizontal 1 × 6's complete the batter board assemblies. Set up a builder's level, and have an assistant hold a measuring rod at the highest corner stake. Sight to the rod, and record the difference (D) between the rod reading and the minimum height of the foundation above grade. Next, have the assistant hold the rod alongside each batter board stake in turn. In each case sight to the rod, subtract the distance D, and mark the stake at that point. Nail on the 1 × 6's with their top edges touching the marks.

4. Record location of building corners by stretching twine between batter boards so that their intersections fall directly over the centers of the corner stakes. Achieve precise alignment by hanging plumb bob from intersections as shown. (Use thumbtacks to mark centers of stakes.) Make saw cuts in batter boards to establish twine locations permanently, and note on boards which corner each cut represents. Stretch twine and make cuts to record other information, such as excavation boundaries.

Excavating for a Firm Foundation

Excavation for the foundation can begin as soon as the building lines are established. Be sure to dig deep enough so that the base, called the footing, will be safely below the level of frost penetration. Freezing ground expands and can crack an improperly laid foundation. Local building authorities can provide you with precise specifications for building safe foundations in your area. You should also consult a government soil engineer who will analyze the type of ground upon which your site is located and determine its weight-bearing ability, drainage characteristics, and other factors that influence the kind of foundation best suited to that spot.

Power shovels and backhoes are the most efficient and economical tools, for excavation unless the amount of digging is very small. Try to hire equipment and operators by the job rather than by the day or hour so that you do not have to pay for wasted time due to problems and delays that are not your fault. Be sure that the plans for digging are fully understood by the excavator beforehand, and be there yourself when the work is performed. To lessen the chance of cave-ins, which are not only potentially dangerous but also time-consuming to repair, have the scooped-out earth placed at least 2 feet from the rim of the excavation. Topsoil should be stripped from the site and piled in a separate area to prevent it from becoming mixed with the subsoil. (Mixing would change the vitally important drainage

and weight-bearing characteristics of the subsoil. The topsoil can be used later for landscaping.) The excavation itself should extend at least 3 feet beyond the building lines to give space for such work as manipulating building forms and laying concrete block. Do not backfill the excavation until the entire foundation is laid and the floor of the building has been attached; only then will the foundation walls be well enough braced to eliminate any danger of collapse. It is also important that the excavation be no deeper than called for in the plans, since refilling to the correct level does not restore the weight-bearing capacity of the original undisturbed soil upon which the foundation rests.

There is always plenty of trimming to be done with hand shovels, so be safety conscious. Do not let debris collect in and around excavations. Use a ladder to avoid jumping in and out of trenches, and do not work so near a partner that you risk injuring each other with your tools. Brace all trenches more than 4 feet deep with boards placed vertically along the banks. For added strength, especially if heavy equipment is used nearby, install crosspieces that span the width of the trench between the vertical boards. If possible, slope the sides of the excavations back to their angles of repose. Watch for cave-in signals: cracks developing nearby or earth trickling down the sides. And check the site carefully after heavy rains or a weekend break.

Common types of foundations

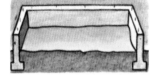

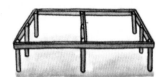

Perimeter foundation made of poured reinforced concrete, masonry block, or stone is strong, provides basement or crawl space, and conforms to most codes. Excavation and formwork are often necessary, usually requiring heavy equipment.

Wooden pole foundation made of logs, ties, or telephone poles leaves underside of building exposed but requires little excavation and is good for steep sites and remote areas. Pole foundations are not suitable on soft ground.

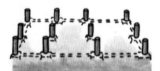

Concrete slab foundation of reinforced concrete also serves as basement or ground floor and is especially suited to passive heat storage in solar designed buildings. Steep site or high water table may preclude use.

Concrete pier foundation is inexpensive and needs little excavation. Piers are suitable on steep sites but do not provide the anchoring strength of perimeter or slab foundations. Piers can be either precast or poured.

Bracing for trenches

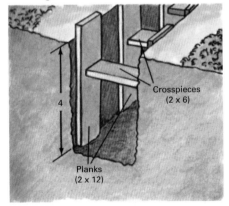

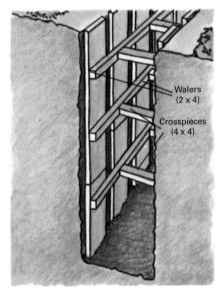

Light bracing (above) consists of vertical planks placed at 3- to 5-ft. intervals, held apart by crosspieces. For heavy bracing (right) set planks almost side by side. Horizontal walers tie planks together and distribute pressure. Nailing is not necessary; wedging holds boards tight.

Suitability of various soils for building

Soil description	Value as foundation material	Frost action	Drainage	Angle of repose
Gravel	Excellent	None	Excellent	
Gravel-sand-silt mix	Good	Slight	Poor	40°–55°
Gravel-sand-clay mix	Good	Slight	Poor	
Sand	Good	None	Excellent	
Sand-silt mix	Fair	Slight	Fair	50°–60°
Sand-clay mix	Fair	Medium	Poor	
Inorganic silt	Fair	Very high	Poor	
Organic silt	Poor	High	Impervious	55°–70°
Clay	Very poor	Medium	Impervious	
Peat or organic soil	Not suitable	Slight	Poor	40°–45°

Foundation is only as strong as the earth beneath it; chart gives key characteristics of common soils. Frost action refers to amount of frost heaving that can be expected.

Converting Trees Into Lumber

Processing Your Timber Into Hand-Hewn Beams And Top-Grade Lumber

Horsepower is often the best way to log rugged timberland.

Making your own lumber is practical and economical. You not only save the cost of buying wood but of having it delivered. You can cut your lumber to the sizes you need rather than shaping your projects to the sizes available. And you can use your timber resources to the fullest, harvesting trees when they are mature, converting the best stock into valuable building or woodworking material, and burning imperfect or low-quality wood in your fireplace.

Most important of all is the quality of the wood you get. Air-dried lumber of the type demanded over the years by furnituremakers, boatbuilders, and other craftsmen is rare and expensive—lumbermills today dry their wood in kilns rather than wait for years while it seasons in the open. The lumber you cut and stack yourself can match the finest available and in some cases may be your only means of obtaining superior wood or specially cut stock at a reasonable cost. You may even be able to market surplus homemade lumber to local craftsmen.

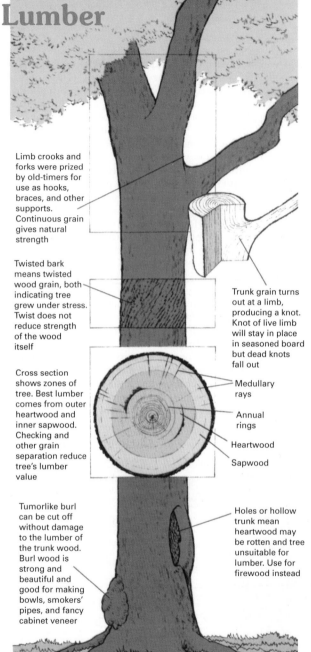

Limb crooks and forks were prized by old-timers for use as hooks, braces, and other supports. Continuous grain gives natural strength

Twisted bark means twisted wood grain, both indicating tree grew under stress. Twist does not reduce strength of the wood itself

Trunk grain turns out at a limb, producing a knot. Knot of live limb will stay in place in seasoned board but dead knots fall out

Cross section shows zones of tree. Best lumber comes from outer heartwood and inner sapwood. Checking and other grain separation reduce tree's lumber value

Medullary rays

Annual rings

Heartwood

Sapwood

Tumorlike burl can be cut off without damage to the lumber of the trunk wood. Burl wood is strong and beautiful and good for making bowls, smokers' pipes, and fancy cabinet veneer

Holes or hollow trunk mean heartwood may be rotten and tree unsuitable for lumber. Use for firewood instead

For best lumber and greatest yield per log, select trees with smooth, straight trunks at least 1 ft. in diameter. Trees that have branches at the top only are best, since limbs cause knots in finished boards. Avoid hollow trees or trunks with splits; both probably signal extensive interior decay.

The Lumbermen's Tools

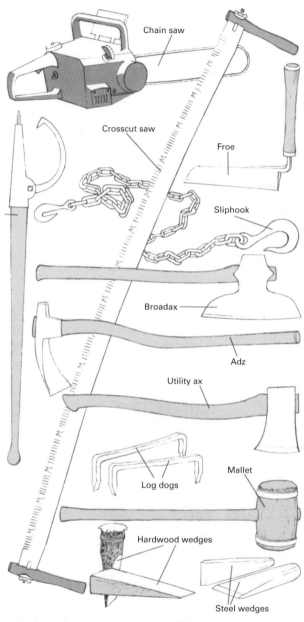

Chain saw

Crosscut saw

Froe

Sliphook

Broadax

Adz

Utility ax

Mallet

Log dogs

Hardwood wedges

Steel wedges

Many home-lumbering tools are available from hardware stores. Some, however, such as froes, broadaxes, and adzes, are manufactured by only a few firms and are difficult to find. Wooden mallets can be homemade; log dogs can be fashioned from steel reinforcing rod (rebar) sharpened at both ends.

Logs and Logging Techniques

Once a tree has been felled and trimmed of limbs (see *Wood as a Fuel*, p.84), it is generally hauled elsewhere for conversion into boards. Trunks that are too long or heavy to move must be bucked into sections. Make your cuts near crooks or defects to preserve good board wood. Log lengths may range from 2 to 16 feet, depending on intended use and your ability to haul them.

A good deal of lumbering is still done with horses, especially in hilly areas inaccessible to motor vehicles or where there is a risk of environmental damage. Horses are ideal when only a few trees are being culled or where forest growth is dense. In flat country a four-wheel-drive vehicle with tire chains can be more efficient. Buy a good tree identification handbook (see *Sources and resources*, p.24), and use it to identify your trees so that you will know what you are cutting. Pay particular attention to bark characteristics, since logging is often done in winter, when there are no leaves. (Logs can be moved more easily on snow, and winter-cut logs season better.)

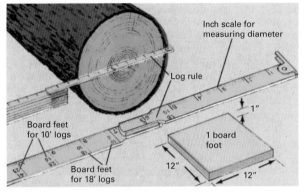

Use a log rule to estimate board feet. Varying scales exist, each yielding slightly different results; the Doyle rule shown above is typical. To use a log rule, determine length of log, measure diameter at small end, then read board feet directly from tables on rule corresponding to those measurements.

Tips on bucking

Plan bucking cuts to avoid wasting wood. Group defects together to minimize scrap; allow only enough extra length for trimming logs to final board dimensions.

Hauling logs

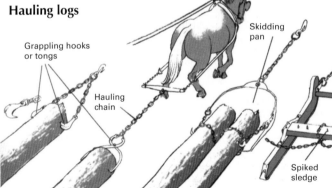

Horses and oxen are versatile haulers, good in deep woods or over rough terrain. Shovellike skidding pan or heavy sledge with spikes holds log end and eases the job. Tongs or hooks on hauling chain grip the log. Keep the animal moving forward slowly and steadily, and avoid following routes that take you along the side slopes of hills. Never haul logs down an icy or steep grade; instead, unhook the log at the top of the slope and let it roll or slide down.

Using a vehicle

Four-wheel-drive vehicle that has tire chains and power winch is efficient but less maneuverable than a draft animal. Keep the vehicle away from deep mud, heavy snow, and thick woods. Use a pulley chained to a tree to maneuver logs around sharp turns. Pad the chain to prevent damage to tree trunk.

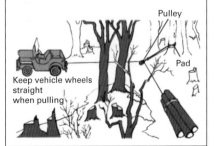

Common woods for lumber

Beech is hard, strong, heavy, and shock resistant. It is good for furniture, floors, and woodenware and can be steam bent. Beeches grow in all states east of the Mississippi River.

Black cherry, or wild cherry, is medium weight, strong, stiff, and hard. Straight-grained cherry is excellent for making furniture or cabinets. It grows in the eastern United States.

Black walnut is medium weight, has beautiful grain, is easy to work, and is strong and stable. Reserve this wood for special paneling and furniture. It grows throughout the United States.

Douglas fir is light, easy to work, and very strong. A leading structural wood (building timber, plywood), it is also used for Christmas trees. It grows on the Pacific Coast and in the Rockies.

Eastern red cedar is light, brittle, easy to work, and decay resistant. It grows in the eastern two-thirds of the country and is used for fence posts and as mothproof closet or chest lining.

Eastern white pine is light, semisoft, easy to work but strong, and has been used for everything from clapboards to furniture since colonial days. It grows mostly in the northeastern United States.

Northern red oak is tough and strong but heavy and hard to work. It is excellent for use in timber framing and as flooring. It grows in the northeastern third of the United States.

Shagbark hickory is strong, tough, and resilient, making it ideal for tool handles and sports equipment. It can be steam bent. Hickory grows in most of the eastern and central United States.

Shortleaf or yellow pine is a tough softwood with good grain. Formerly used for sailing ship masts and planking, it makes good clapboards. It grows in the southeastern United States.

Sugar maple, excellent for furniture, floors, and woodenware, is hard, strong, easy to work, and extremely shock resistant. It grows in New England and the north-central United States.

Western white pine, similar to Eastern, resists harsh weather and is a good board wood for house frames and panels. It grows best in the mountains of the northwestern United States.

White oak is similar to red but stronger and more resistant to moisture. It can be steam bent and is often used in boats. It grows in the eastern United States from Canada to the Gulf.

White spruce is light, strong, and easy to work. It can be used for house framing and paneling but is not decay resistant. It grows in the northern United States from Maine to Wisconsin.

Yellow birch is heavy, hard, and strong, with a close, even grain. It is excellent for furniture, interior work, and doors. It is easy to work. It grows in the Northeast and the north-central states.

All About Boards, Beams, Shingles, and Shakes

Making lumber is simpler than most people realize. A chain saw and lumbermaking adapter are almost indispensable accessories if you plan to make boards. The chain saw can also be used to make beams and heavy building timbers, but you may wish to hew these by hand instead. The broadax is the traditional tool for hand-hewing; however, an ordinary utility ax costs less, is more widely available, and will perform almost as well. Of course, axes and chain saws are potentially dangerous tools and should be used with extreme caution. To split shakes and shingles, a special tool called a froe is needed. Froes are available from a few specialty hardware suppliers or they can be made by a blacksmith from a discarded automobile leaf spring. The key to making shingles is not your tools but the wood you use. Choose only straight-grained wood of a kind noted for its ability to split cleanly, such as cedar, oak, and cypress.

Seasoning is probably the most important step in making your own lumber. During this stage the wood is slowly air dried until ready for use. Freshly cut lumber must be stacked carefully to permit plenty of air circulation between boards; at the same time it must be protected from moisture, strong sunlight, and physical stresses that can cause warping. Done properly, drying by air produces boards that are superior in many ways to the kiln-dried stock sold at most lumberyards. Air drying is a gradual process that does not involve the high temperatures used in kiln drying, and the wood cells are able to adjust to the slow loss of moisture without damage, toughening as they dry and shrink and actually becoming stronger than when fresh. Moreover, sap and natural oils, which do not evaporate as quickly as water, remain in the wood for long periods of time, further assisting curing. Air-dried lumber is not only strong but also durable, attractive, highly resistant to moisture damage, and well conditioned against seasonal shrinkage and swelling caused by changes in humidity.

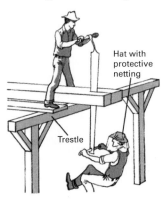

Pitsawing was once the standard method for making boards, and it can still be used. Place the log on trestles or over a pit. The upper man stands on the log, starts the saw cut with short strokes, then continues cutting by pushing the saw blade down from shoulder height (a heavy saw works best). Lower man guides saw and returns blade but does no actual cutting.

Hat with protective netting

Trestle

How to Slice a Log

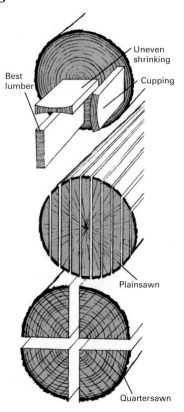

Uneven shrinking

Best lumber

Cupping

Plainsawn

Quartersawn

Quality of lumber varies depending upon what part of the tree it comes from. Innermost heartwood is relatively weak; use it only for heavy timbers and thick planks. Best boards come from surrounding area. Avoid using extreme outer sapwood next to the bark. Lumber cut so that rings are perpendicular to the sawn sides of the board when viewed from the end is less likely to warp. Boards whose ends show curving lines tend to cup as they dry.

Two basic ways to cut boards are plainsawing (slicing through the full diameter of the log) and quartersawing (cutting the log into quarter sections before ripping it into boards). Plainsawing yields the widest boards and the most lumber per log; quartersawing yields less lumber, but boards are of higher quality.

Lumbermaking With a Chain Saw

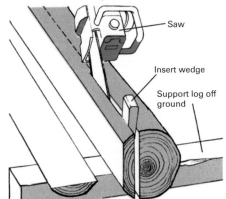

Saw

Insert wedge

Support log off ground

Chain saw can be used without guide to rip logs into boards, but skill and practice are needed to cut long lengths. Raise log off ground to avoid blade damage and kickback; wedges in cut prevent blade from being pinched.

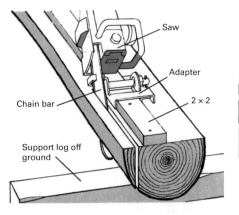

Saw

Adapter

Chain bar

2 × 2

Support log off ground

Simple adapter attaches to chain bar; 2 × 4 nailed along length of log acts as guide for making straight cuts. Support log off ground; attach and test entire assembly before starting saw. Reposition board after each cut.

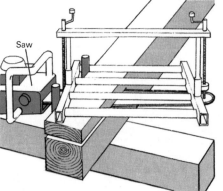

Saw

Portable chain-saw mill, best manned by two men, cuts horizontally, permitting operation with log on ground. Rollers keep saw blade level and adjust vertically to make boards of different thicknesses. Mill fits any chain saw.

Sources and resources

Books
Collingwood, G.H., and Warren D. Brush. *Knowing Your Trees*. Washington, D.C.: The American Forestry Association, 1984.
Constantine, Albert, Jr. *Know Your Woods*. New York: Scribner's, 1975.
Hoadley, R. Bruce. *Understanding Wood*. Newtown, Conn.: Taunton Press, 1987.
Schiffer, Herbert, and Schiffer, Nancy. *Woods We Live With*. Atglen, Pa.: Schiffer Publishing, 1977.
Seymour, John. *The Forgotten Crafts*. New York: Knopf, 1984.
Sloane, Eric. *An Age of Barns*. New York: Henry Holt & Co., 1990.
Sloane, Eric. *A Museum of Early American Tools*. New York: Ballantine Books, 1985.
Soderstrom, Neil. *Chainsaw Savvy*. Dobbs Ferry, N.Y.: Morgan & Morgan, 1984.
Underhill, Roy. *The Woodwright's Shop*. Chapel Hill, N.C.: University of North Carolina Press, 1981.
Wittlinger, Ellen. *Noticing Paradise*. Boston: Houghton-Mifflin, 1995.

Hand-Hewing a Beam

Squaring a log into a beam is easier if you use green freshly cut timber. You can also save a lot of extra labor by hewing the logs where they have fallen instead of hauling them to a separate site. Before you begin, be sure to clear the area of all brush and low-hanging branches that might interfere with your ax work.

Choose logs that are only slightly thicker than the beams you wish to hew. Judge this dimension by measuring the small end of the log. Place the log on wooden supports (notched half-sections of firewood logs will do)

with any crown, or lengthwise curve, facing up. The two straightest edges of the log should face the sides. Do not remove the bark; its rough surface helps hold the ax to the mark and also diminishes your chances of striking a glancing blow with possibly dangerous results. It is not always necessary to square off all four sides of a log. Old-time carpenters often hewed only two sides, and sometimes, as in the case of floor joists found in many old houses, they smoothed off only one. Rafters, in fact, were often left completely round.

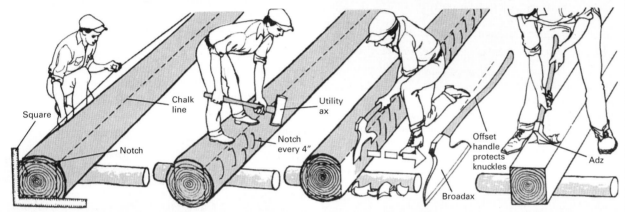

1. Scribe timber dimensions on log ends. Cut notches for chalk line; attach line and snap it to mark sides.

2. Notch logs with utility ax. Make vertical cuts at 4-in. intervals to depth of chalk line marks.

3. Hew sides with broadax. Keep ax parallel to log, and slice off waste by chopping along chalk marks.

4. Smooth hewn surface with adz if desired. Straddle beam and chop with careful blows of even depth.

Splitting shingles and shakes

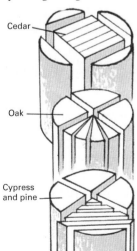

Billets are log sections from which shakes and shingles are split. Use straight-grained logs, 2 ft. or more in diameter, with no knots. Cut logs into 11/2 to 2-ft. lengths for shingles; for shakes use 21/2- to 4-ft. lengths. (Longer clapboards can also be split but only from exceptionally well-grained timber.) To make cedar billets, split off outside edges of log section to form squared block. Split block in half, then halve each piece again. Continue until all pieces are of desired thickness. With oak, split the log first into quarters, then radially. Discard heart and outermost sapwood. Cypress and pine are quartered, like oak, then split along the grain at a tangent to the growth rings.

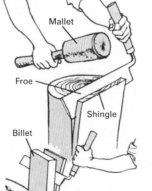

To make shingles with a froe, rest billet on a stump. Drive froe blade into top of log using a heavy wooden mallet or homemade maul. Twist blade to split wood by pulling handle toward you.

To make wood shakes (oversize shingles), brace billet in fork of tree or other improvised holder. Stand behind upper limb of fork, drive froe into wood, and twist blade to start split. Then slide the froe farther down into the crack while holding the split wood apart with your free hand. If the split starts to shift off-center, turn wood around so that opposite side of billet rests against upper limb of fork, and continue twisting with froe.

Seasoning and Stacking Lumber

Commercial lumber mills season new wood in ovens, called kilns, to dry it quickly. Seasoning wood by exposing it to the open air will do the job as well or better, but the process takes much longer—at least six months for building lumber and a year or more for cabinetmaking stock. A traditional rule of thumb is to let wood air dry one year for every inch of board thickness.

The best time of year to begin seasoning new lumber is in the early spring, when the dryness of the cool air coupled with the windiness of the season combine to produce optimal drying conditions. A spring start also permits the curing process to continue uninterrupted for as long as possible before freezing winter temperatures temporarily halt evaporation. Set aside or build a sheltered area such as a shed (it may be no more than a roof set on poles) to protect the wood from harsh weather and direct sunlight. Seal the ends of each newly cut board with paint or paraffin to prevent checking, and stack the lumber in one of the ways shown below so that it receives adequate ventilation and support. Place the poorest quality pieces on the top and bottom of the pile, where weather damage and warping is greatest. Date and label each stack for future reference.

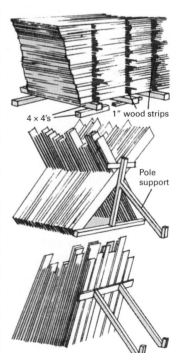

Flat stack lumber that will remain undisturbed for long periods. Place 4 × 4's on floor or on ground treated with pesticide. Lay boards side by side, 1 to 2 in. apart, then stack in layers separated by 1-in.-thick wood strips.

Pole stack saves labor and space, requires less foundation, and allows lumber to shed rainwater. Lean boards against pole support so they are nearly vertical, crisscross pieces for maximum exposure of surfaces.

End stack is used only for nearly seasoned wood because it provides limited air circulation. Lean boards against wall or frame with spaces between boards at bottom. Boards can be removed without disturbing pile.

Building a Log Cabin

An American Symbol, Whether Pioneer Shack Or Kit-Built Mansion

Log cabins have long symbolized the American pioneering spirit and love of independence—and with good reason. Made from inexpensive, locally available materials, they are well suited to homesteaders of any era. For the early settlers, most of whom were neither woodsmen nor carpenters, they provided sturdy, economical housing that did not demand expert skills or require scarce materials and tools. In colonial days trees were plentiful and free. A rough cabin of logs and split lumber shakes or shingles could be put up quickly by one or two people using little more than an ax. Such a structure would last a lifetime; some survive after more than two centuries. Nowadays, cabins are still comparatively economical to build, and with the help of modern techniques and materials they can be made to last even longer. When putting up a log cabin from scratch, the greatest investment remains time and labor rather than trees and tools. But another option also exists: instead of cutting and peeling your own logs, you can buy an entire log cabin kit complete with precut logs.

Traditional log-building methods were brought here from Scandinavia. The first American log cabins were probably built by Finnish colonists at New Sweden, near the mouth of the Delaware River, in 1638. By the 1800s log cabins were common from the Atlantic to California and from Alaska to the Southwest. Only a few decades ago cabins were still being built by traditional methods in backwoods areas of the United States and Canada. The chain saw, however, has ended the need for many centuries-old skills, and few men exist today who can notch logs with an ax as skillfully as their grandfathers once did.

Most early log cabins consisted of only one room. Ease of construction plus availability of timber contributed to the enormous popularity of log cabins in colonial America. In turn, log cabins helped make possible the settlement of lands from New England west to the Great Plains.

Hewn-beam cabins are a refinement of the round-log style. Flush notches permitted installation of exterior siding. The interior was often plastered over as well, hiding the log work completely.

Choosing Trees and Preparing Logs

Evergreens—pine, fir, cedar, spruce, and larch—make the best cabin logs. You will need about 80 logs for an average one-room cabin. Should you decide to cut your own, be sure of your logging skills and your ability to transport the logs out of the forest. Select trees that are about equal in age, thickness, and height. Look for stands that are dense but not crowded and are located on level land. Avoid trees with low limbs. Good building logs should be between 8 and 14 inches in diameter. Once you select a size, all should be approximately the same. Logs should be straight and free of structural or insect damage. Allow at least 4 feet extra per log so that the ends can project beyond the corner notches.

Cutting is best done in winter when the sap is out of the wood: the logs weigh less, season faster, and resist decay better. In addition, hauling is easier and less damage will be done to the environment, since the ground will be frozen and foliage will be at a minimum.

Logs with the bark removed dry faster and are less susceptible to insect damage. Peeling logs with a drawknife or spud (see opposite page) is easiest when logs are freshly cut. Stack logs off the ground to prevent warpage and decay. Let them season three to six months.

A note on safety

Working with logs requires you to be alert and safety conscious. The building site is likely to be uneven, and both materials and equipment are heavy and awkward to handle. Tools such as axes and chain saws are dangerous, especially in inexperienced hands. Wear protective clothing, boots, and safety glasses. Do not take chances.

The Tools You Will Need

Proper tools make the job of building a log cabin much easier and help achieve a high level of craftsmanship. Shown at right are some of the tools needed. In addition, you should have an assortment of basic carpenter's tools, including a handsaw, chisels, measuring tools, and sharpening equipment. A small winch can save a good deal of sweat and strain, and you will also need a chain or a stout rope. Traditional log-building tools are usually hard to find and expensive if bought new or from antique dealers. Begin collecting the ones you will need well in advance. Farm auctions, flea markets, and tag sales are possible sources. If you are buying a chain saw, get one with an instant chain brake and a 16- to 20-inch bar. Learn how to use it safely, keep it sharp at all times, and always wear protection for your ears and eyes.

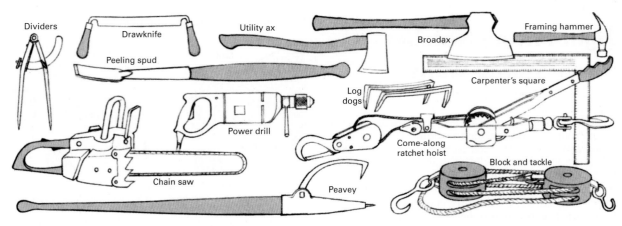

Log builders' tools: a basic kit includes such old-fashioned tools as a broadax as well as modern implements.

Foundation and Siting

Although the pioneers often built their cabins directly on the ground, it is better to build on a raised foundation for protection against both termites and damp rot. The crawl space beneath the floor can be used for storage, wiring, plumbing, and under-the-floor insulation. One type of foundation, shown at right, consists of reinforced concrete piers strategically placed around the perimeter of the building and beneath important floor girders. Other possibilities are the concrete slab foundation or stone masonry block foundations of the type shown on page 38 (Building With Adobe) and on page 46 (Building a Stone House). Stone is the traditional foundation material. Piers can be of wood rather then concrete. Use log posts of black locust or treated cedar set into the ground on stone or concrete pads.

Locate your cabin in a sheltered, well-drained area, and design it to take advantage of the sun's changing angle throughout the seasons. Make batter boards to mark the corners of the site and stretch string between them to form the exact outline of the foundation. Consult standard building texts for complete advice.

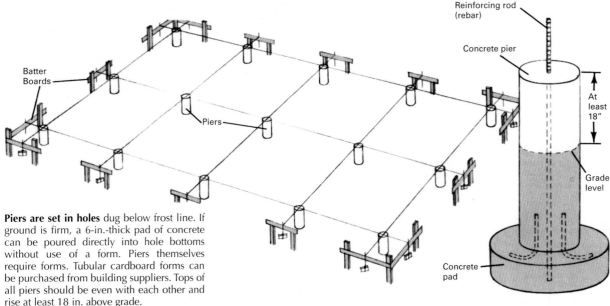

Piers are set in holes dug below frost line. If ground is firm, a 6-in.-thick pad of concrete can be poured directly into hole bottoms without use of a form. Piers themselves require forms. Tubular cardboard forms can be purchased from building suppliers. Tops of all piers should be even with each other and rise at least 18 in. above grade.

Sill logs are notched flat and drilled so tops of piers will seat firmly and take rebar anchors. Compensate for log taper by alternating wide and narrow ends when building walls. Termite flashing should also be inserted in any area where this insect poses a problem. Concrete piers can be faced with stone to make them attractive; leave wooden piers exposed.

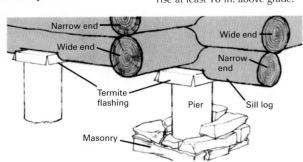

Ordinary garden hose with 6 in. of clear tubing in each end can be used to find equal heights above grade level at widely separated points. Attach one end of hose to reference point, the other to new location. Fill end near reference point with water until water reaches mark. Water level at the other end will then be at same height.

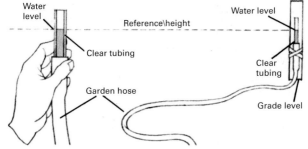

27

Tight-Fitting Notches Mean Sturdy Walls

Well-made notches lock wall logs in place and prevent water from collecting inside the joints. They involve as little cutting away of wood as possible to avoid weakening the logs. Many builders spike the logs together at the joints, but spiking is not necessary for the types of joints shown here. Except in chinkless construction, shown on page 33, notches are generally cut so that a 1- to 2-inch gap remains between parallel logs. This makes chinking easier and more durable.

Round notch is easy to make and very effective, especially when combined with the chinkless construction method. It is a Scandinavian technique and represents one of the earliest notching styles. A sturdy pair of wing dividers with a pencil attached to one leg is essential for scribing a perfect joint. To make the notch, follow the step-by-step procedure shown at right.

V-notch is one of the favorite styles in the Appalachian Mountains. It can be cut with only an ax—the fit is accomplished by trial and error. By adding a carpenter's square to your tools, perfect first-try joints can be made.

Chamfer and notch, probably of German origin, is a more complex notching style but has the advantage of holding the logs in two directions. It is often found on hewn-beam cabins. Since there is no projection beyond the notches, the logs form a flush corner that can be easily covered with clapboard siding. In many parts of the country this notch is called the half-dovetail.

Scribing and cutting a round notch

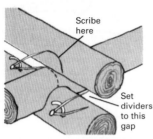
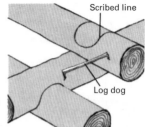
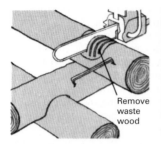

1. Place log at corner. Set dividers to space between logs. Scribe top log on both sides by drawing dividers over surface of lower log.

2. Roll log over and pin in place with log dogs. If you are unable to buy log dogs, you can fashion your own from rebar (reinforcing bar).

3. Rough out notch with chain saw or ax. Deepen center and trim edges to scribed line with chisel. Roll log back into place.

4. Finished notches shed water, since they are cut only in underside of logs. Ends of logs should project about 1 1/2 ft. beyond corners.

Hewing a V-notch with ax and square

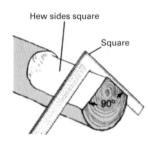
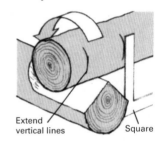
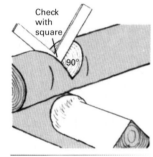

1. Mark 90° angle on butt of log, then hew peak with ax or chain saw by removing wood outside of lines. Keep sides straight. Check accuracy of cut with carpenter's square.

2. Place next log on peak and mark notch width by extending vertical lines upward. Then roll log 180° toward center of wall and pin in place with log dogs.

3. Cut V-notch by hewing wood from between side marks. Maintain 90° cut, and roll log into proper position occasionally to check notch for solid fit.

4. V-notch on underside of one log fits over peak of log below. Experienced woodsmen can cut the joint by eye, but using a square improves accuracy.

Cutting a chamfer and notch

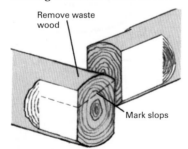
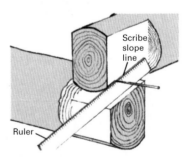
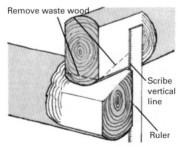
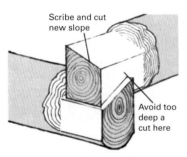

1. Hew sides of log parallel. Then mark slope to angle from top of one side, about one-third of way down other side. Remove wood with ax.

2. Place second log on top of first as shown, its end flush with side. Hold ruler along bottom log and scribe slope line on both sides of top log.

3. Hold ruler against vertical face of lower log and scribe line on upper log so that it intersects slope line. Scribe both sides and end of log.

4. Hew or saw wood from scribed area. Avoid too deep a cut. Carefully trim for a snug fit, then scribe and cut new slope in top log as before.

5. Chamfer-and-notch style is intricate—careful measuring and skillful cutting are required. Results, however, are attractive and durable.

Windows and Doors, Then Roof and Floors

The initial step in building a cabin is to prepare the site. Construction of the foundation, walls, and roof comes next. One of the final jobs is to install the windows and doors. Although windows and doors are among the last items completed, they must be planned from the first to ensure that the rules of sound building design are followed. One rule is that wall openings for doors and windows should be located away from corners. Another is that the openings must not penetrate either the sill log or the top plate. Normally at least two logs should span the space above a doorway or window, although in a small cabin with no upper loft the log below the plate can be partially cut away.

Cut out door and window openings after the walls are completed or prepare them for cutting during the building process. Kit homes save on lumber by using logs that have been precut to conform to the precise window and door openings specified in the plans. Once the wall is up and the openings are made, use rough-cut commercial lumber to build the frames. Since the bottom of a door frame serves as a threshold, it should be made of a hardwood, such as oak. Notch and flatten the top and bottom logs, and then fit in the frame by one of the methods shown below. Be sure to slope the flattened surface of the bottom log toward the outside so that water can drain away. Allow several inches for settling between the frame and the top log, and chink the gap with fiberglass insulation protected by metal flashing as shown below. It is best to have the doors and windows on hand when the wall openings are cut.

Installing a splined frame

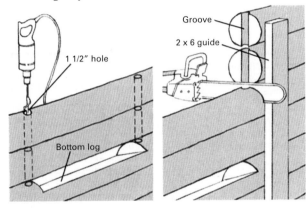

Flatten log that will be at bottom of window, and mark width of frame on it. As each log is laid in place, bore 1 1/2-in. holes through it (left). Bore outside of the mark on both sides of the opening. When top of frame is reached, attach 2 × 6 guides and saw down through each log (right), cutting through the edge of the holes nearest the opening to form vertical grooves.

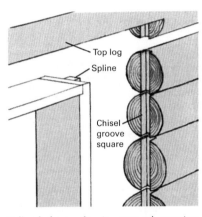

Splined frame fits in grooved opening. Chisel groove square or trim with tip of chain saw. Assemble frames and nail 1 1/2-in.-sq. strips along outside edges. Work frame into place before attaching top log. Caulk gaps with sealer.

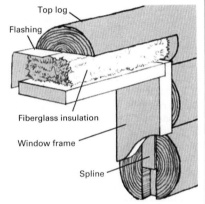

Log walls may settle up to 4 in., so provide an extra space allowance above openings. Fill the gap with fiberglass insulation that compresses as logs descend. Install protective copper flashing on the top log above the insulation for weather seal.

Fitting a nailed frame

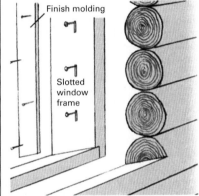

Nailed frame can be fitted after wall is completed. Saw out opening to match frame dimensions. Allow extra room at top. Assemble frame and nail it onto log ends through slotted frame sides to allow settling. Caulk with sealer.

Putting a Floor in Your Cabin

Unless your cabin is set directly on the ground, the floor must be supported by joists. These are beams spanning the distance between sill logs or between sills and a center floor girder if the distance between sills is more than 10 feet. The girder, like the sills, must be supported by the foundation. Notch the sills (and girder) to take the joist ends after the second round of logs is in place. All notches must be carefully cut to the same depth.

Logs for joists should be 6 to 8 inches in diameter and be hewn flat on top. Joists of 2 × 10 commercial lumber can also be used. They generally produce a more level floor and are just as strong as logs. Space joists at even intervals, between 16 inches and 2 feet apart center to center. The flooring itself consists of two layers: a subfloor and a finish floor. The subfloor can be made of 1 × 8 tongue-and-groove lumber, 3/4-inch plywood, or particle board. Traditionally, the finish floor is made of wide pine planks; hardwood, such as oak or maple, will wear better, however. Fasten the finish floor with cut nails for an authentic appearance. Or simulate a pegged floor by countersinking screws and concealing them beneath dowel plugs. Tar paper is often placed on the subfloor to prevent dampness. Insulation beneath the subfloor will cut down on heat loss.

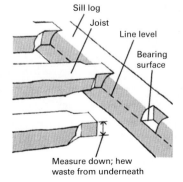

Notch joists carefully into sill logs for a level floor. Use string and a line level to ensure that bearing surfaces of all sill notches are at the same height. When cutting the ends of joists, hew top surfaces flat, then measure down from the top and trim excess from beneath. Commercial 2 × 10's can also be used as joists.

Raising the Roof Beams

Two traditional roof styles—rafter and purlin—are illustrated at right. Rafter-style roofs require ceiling joists or tie beams to prevent the walls from spreading outward, since the vertical load of the roof exerts downward pressure at an angle on the cabin sides. Purlin roofs produce no spreading even under tremendous snow loads because vertical pressure is not transferred at an angle but instead is supported directly beneath by long horizontal logs resting on the end walls of the cabin. Although tie beams are not required for the walls when a purlin roof is used, they are generally installed anyway as parts of the trusses that support the purlins themselves. Without trusses the purlins of any but small cabins may sag under their own weight.

The first step in making either style of roof is to install plates—large logs similar to sills that are notched to take the ceiling joists, tie beams, or truss supports. The plates should also be notched to take the rafter ends unless extra, courses of wall logs are to be added to form a second-story loft.

Gable ends rise to a peak at each end of the cabin. In a rafter-style roof they can be built after the rest of the roof is completed. One type of gable consists of horizontal or vertical log sections spiked together and trimmed to the angle of the roof pitch. Another kind, shown at right, is built like an ordinary exterior frame wall. Panel the exterior of the gables with lumber siding or log slabs. Gables for a purlin roof (also illustrated at right) are made of horizontal log sections spiked one on top of another and notched to take each purlin as it is set in place during the building sequence. Afterward, the angle of the roof pitch is marked and the log ends are trimmed off with a saw, as illustrated on page 35.

Rafter-style roof with framed gable ends

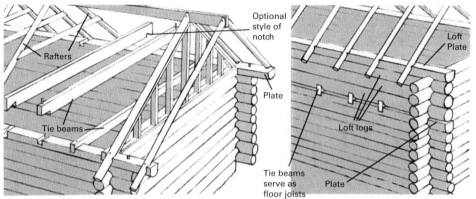

In rafter-style roofs, plates are spiked or pegged in place (far left). Install tie beams in plate notches cut on 2-ft. centers. For rafters use logs or 2 x 8 lumber spaced 2 ft. apart. Notch rafters and spike to plate. Nail tops to ridgepole, or assemble rafter pairs on ground and erect as units. Logs can be added above plates (near left) to increase attic space.

Purlin roof with log gable ends

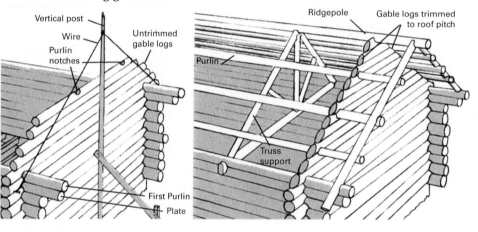

Roof pitch determines purlin location. Cut vertical posts to height of roof peak and set them against center of end walls (far left). Stretch wire from posts to wall sides as a guide when installing purlins and trimming final angle of gable ends. Allow for the fact that purlins will be set in notches that are half their diameters. Support purlins with trusses every 12 ft. (near left).

Details of rafter installation

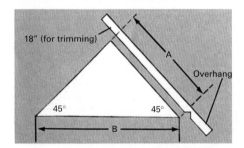

Traditional angle of roof pitch is 45°, steep enough to shed snow from roofing. To determine rafter length (A), divide length of end wall (B) by 1.4, then add additional 18 in. for trimming (more if an eave overhang is desired).

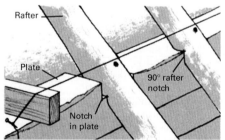

Cut right-angle notch in each rafter where it attaches to the plate. Vary the depth of the notches to compensate for variations in rafter thicknesses. If the plate is uneven, notch it to equalize depths, using level line as guide.

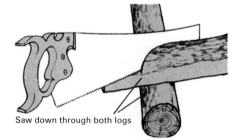

To match rafter ends at peak when ridgepole is not used, overlap each pair and saw both at once. Before cutting, make sure plate-notched ends are set correct distance apart. Nail 1x 6 collar tie across joint for extra strength.

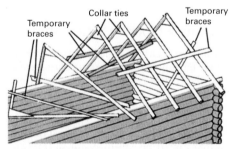

Raise preassembled rafter pairs by resting ends on plate logs, then pushing peak upright with pole. Spike rafters to plate at notches; brace until decking is installed. Permanent braces are required in windy or heavy snow areas.

Raising the Walls

After the foundation has been laid and the sill logs and end logs that form the base of the cabin have been set in place, the next step is to raise the walls. Decide before starting how the floor will be built (see p.30), whether or not to use the chinkless method of stacking the logs described on page 33, and also whether you will use short precut logs to frame the window and door openings as the walls go up, or saw out these openings later from the solid walls as builders of traditional cabins usually do.

The basic steps in constructing the walls are hoisting the logs into position, aligning them so that they are vertical and at right angles to each other at the corners, and notching them so that they lock permanently in place. Since logs weigh several hundred pounds each, lifting is best done with mechanical assistance. Two traditional methods are shown below. Plenty of manpower helps too—not just to make the job easier but to make it safer as well. Once a log is up it should be carefully positioned for notching with the help of carefully aligned sighting poles driven into the ground a short distance from each corner. Sight along the log's length to make sure its center is lined up with the poles.

After a log is in place for notching, scribe it at both ends, roll it over, and use log dogs to fasten it to neighboring logs while you cut the notch. For safety, always roll logs toward the center of the wall. Most logs have a crown, or slight bow along their length. This should face upward on the finished log so that as the cabin settles the logs will flatten and their fit will improve. To keep walls level, alternate the wide and narrow ends of the logs as shown. Use a plumb bob to check verticals and an oversized square made from 2 × 4 lumber to make sure corners form right angles.

Hoisting logs into place

Hauling logs to the top of the wall is a major undertaking. One common system uses a block and tackle hung from the top of a gin-pole tripod. Another combines a block and tackle for mechanical advantage with poles for leverage. Instead of a block and tackle, a so-called come-along ratchet hoist can also be used. It is slow but can be operated safely by one person. A come-along can also be used to draw wall logs tightly together.

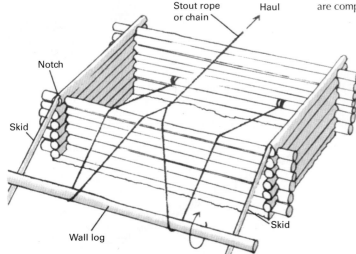

Inclined skids, a pioneer device, can be used to roll logs upward. Skids should form a 30° angle and be notched at ends to hold them in place on the wall. Tie ends of rope to a wall log already in place; pass center of rope under the log being raised. Tie another rope to center of first rope, and haul on free end to roll log up ramp. Have two persons guide the log, and never stand between the skids when hauling the log upward.

Alternate courses to keep the walls level

Precise leveling of log walls is not necessary. Compensate for the natural taper of logs and prevent the accumulation of large errors by laying each course of logs so that the thick ends join the thin ends. Alternate the thick and thin ends vertically as well to avoid high corners when the walls are completed.

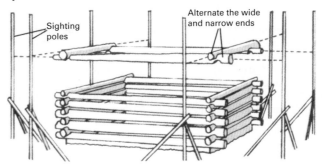

Working with short logs

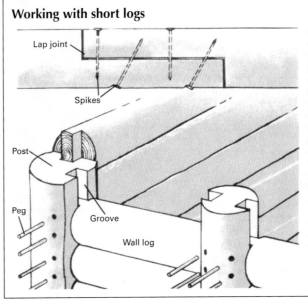

Short logs can be lapped and spiked together end to end (left above) provided the joint does not occur over a wall opening or beneath a joist or beam requiring support. Many kit homes make use of this joint. The French-Canadian pioneers introduced the *piéce-en-piéce* construction method (left below). Slotted vertical posts are used to anchor short horizontal logs notched to fit the grooves. *Piéce-en-piéce* construction is excellent for building long walls, even with small diameter logs. Be sure to provide a firm foundation. Horizontals may be pegged after settling is completed.

The Finishing Touches: Shakes and Chinking

Rafters stand a few inches above the sills they rest upon, with the result that there are narrow spaces between the top of the wall and the underside of the roof. These spaces are generally filled with short segments of lumber known as snowblocks, or birdstops. Fit them as shown in the illustration at upper right, either between rafters or on each side of the plates. In warm areas the gaps are often screened without being plugged in order to provide increased ventilation.

Most cabin roofs are surfaced with wooden shakes or shingles, materials that can either be purchased in a lumberyard or made by hand (see *Converting Trees Into Lumber,* p.25). Standing-seam sheet-metal roofing or asphalt shingles may also be used; both are long-lasting, durable, and attractive. Shakes are slabs of wood split from straight-grained, knot-free sections of logs. They should be about 1/2 inch thick and 18 to 30 inches long. Shingles are thinner and less rough-hewn than shakes. Both are traditionally made from cedar, oak, or cypress and must be completely seasoned before use; otherwise splitting will occur at the nailing points as the wood shrinks. Shakes and shingles are sold in lots called squares. Each lot contains four bundles, and each bundle will cover 25 square feet of roof. Nail shakes and shingles along the roof in overlapping rows.

Old-fashioned roofs were not insulated. The shakes or shingles were nailed directly to the purlins running the length of the roof or fastened to rows of furring strips nailed horizontally across the rafters. Skins or rugs were sometimes placed on the floor of a full loft to retain heat in the lower room; the upper story remained cold. Modern roofs are decked over, sealed with a moisture barrier to prevent condensation, and completely insulated with urethane, styrofoam, rock wool, or fiberglass. Openings for the chimney, stovepipe, and vent stack should be flashed with aluminum or copper to prevent leaks. There are several methods of constructing insulated roofs; two of the most common are shown below. Insulation requirements vary according to climate zones (see *Making Your House Energy Efficient,* pp.76–81).

Covering the Roof

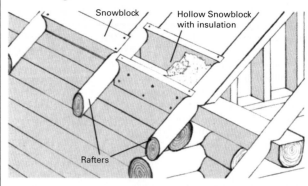

Snowblocks, also called birdstops, seal gaps between rafters along the wall tops. Trim log sections or lumber to size; bevel to match roof pitch. Insulation can be placed as shown. In warm climates screening is often installed instead of snowblocks.

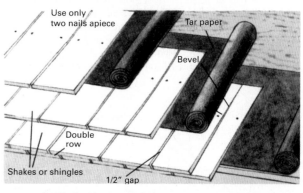

Start roof with double row of shakes (or shingles) at bottom. Overlap each row, leaving exposed only a third of length of shakes beneath. Space shakes 1/2 in. apart and use only two nails per shake. Tar paper between rows reduces leakage.

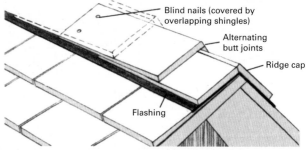

Use galvanized nails to fasten shingles at ridge cap. Alternate the butt joints of top course shingles and blind-nail them as shown. For added moisture protection install metal flashing over roof peak beneath final row of shingles.

Two Ways to Insulate

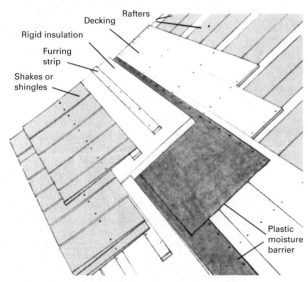

Rigid insulation is more expensive than the soft type but requires less lumber when it is being installed. Nail pine decking boards across rafters. Cover with plastic moisture barrier. Lay insulation board over plastic. Nail 1 x 3 furring strips through insulation to rafters. Cover with shakes, shingles, or metal.

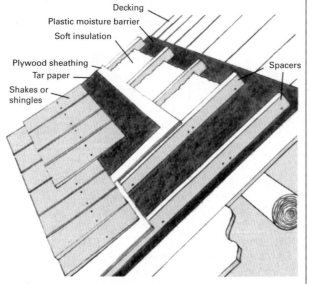

Soft insulation is laid in channels between spacers and is protected by plywood sheathing. Allow airspace as shown. Lay plastic moisture barrier atop decking and toenail 2-in.-thick spacers through decking to beams. Install insulation and sheathing, and cover with shakes, shingles, or other roofing.

Chinking the Gaps

Unless you have used the chinkless construction technique shown at right, your most important finishing-up job will be to chink the gaps between logs. Traditionally, chinking was done with clay and had to be repeated frequently until the logs were completely settled. Fiberglass insulation, temporarily covered with strips of plastic and later chinked permanently with mortar, saves labor and requires little additional maintenance.

Once the cabin is weathertight, other finishing projects may be completed at leisure. These include wiring, plumbing, any interior partitions, wood stoves, fireplaces, and chimneys. Interior log walls can be covered with two coats of clear urethane varnish for a durable, washable finish. Spray the exterior of the cabin with preservative every two to three years.

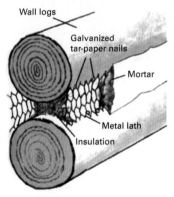

Wall logs
Galvanized tar-paper nails
Mortar
Metal lath
Insulation

First step in chinking is to pack insulation between logs, cover it with metal lath, and seal it temporarily with strips of clear plastic sheeting. After logs have seasoned (up to one year) apply mortar over lath. Use one part sand, three parts Portland cement, plus a handful of clay or lime for a stickier mix. Repair chinking periodically as logs settle.

Tips on wiring

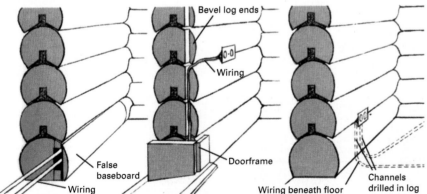

Bevel log ends
Wiring
Doorframe
False baseboard
Wiring
Wiring beneath floor
Channels drilled in log

Plan ahead for wiring. Chinkless construction and wiring that runs beneath floors or drops from above may require boring holes through logs during assembly. Wiring can also run behind baseboards and between logs. Bevel log ends to run wires vertically behind a doorframe molding. Check local codes and have an electrician supervise.

Chinkless construction

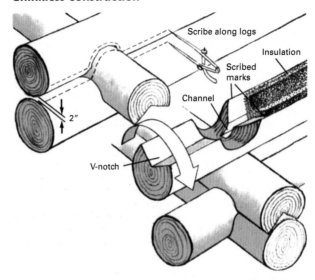

Scribe along logs
Insulation
Scribed marks
Channel
2"
V-notch

Chinkless notching eliminates gaps between logs, making periodic chinking with clay or mortar unnecessary. Extra building time is needed, however, since each log must be grooved and filled as it is laid in place. First, cut round notches in ends of top log to approximate fit, allowing a gap of about 2 in. between it and lower log. Then, with dividers or log scribing tool, scribe both sides of log, transferring contours of bottom log to underside of top log. Finish cutting the round notches to the newly scribed lines, then make V-notch and channel along the length of the log, using the scribed lines as a guide. Pack channel with fiberglass insulation, and roll log into place on wall.

Sources and resources

Books

Berglund, Magnus. *Stone, Log and Earth Houses.* Gloucester, Mass.: Peter Smith, 1991.

Hard, Roger. *Build Your Own Low-Cost Log Home.* Charlotte, Vt.: Garden Way Publishing, 1985.

National Plan Service, Inc. *Country Rustic Home Plans.* Bensenville, Ill.: National Plan Service.

Pearson, David. *Earth to Spirit: In Search of Natural Architecture.* San Francisco: Chronicle Books, 1995.

Underhill, Roy. *The Woodwright's Shop: A Practical Guide to Traditional Woodcraft.* Chapel Hill, N.C.: University of North Carolina Press, 1981.

Organizations

Log House Builder's Association of North America. 22203 S.R. 203, Monroe, Wash. 98272.

A Husband-and-Wife Team Takes On Alaska's Challenge

In Alaska, where the Hutchinsons built their log cabin from scratch, weathertight walls really count in the winter. Full heating needs for the entire cabin are supplied by a single wood-burning stove.

"My husband has lived outdoors a lot and has built log cabins before, but this one was my first, and when we began it I was a little bit afraid because I didn't know much about carpentry. I wondered whether I would be strong enough or disciplined enough to finish the job. My biggest fear, as funny as it may seem, was that the cabin would fall down! Thank goodness it never did. In fact, once you get the feel of working with logs, building a cabin is a lot like building with the little toy log sets that kids have.

"It took us about three years to build the cabin because the building season up here is so short. We had no unforeseen disasters and no injuries, except for a cut finger. I peeled logs and did anything else I could to help. Let me tell you there really were a lot of logs. I got so I hated the sight of them. The hardest task for my husband, I guess, was installing the ridgepoles for the roof. That was very tricky.

"We had a few arguments, mostly over some of his building ideas. He wanted to cut vents close to the ceiling to let out moisture, and he also wanted to leave space above and below the interior partition walls so that heat from our single wood stove would circulate throughout the cabin. In spite of the way I felt then, I have to say now that his ideas really turned out well. The vents work fine and the stove keeps the entire cabin warm even in the coldest weather.

"A log cabin really has a lot of charisma. It's very warm and mellow and feels like a home right from the start. I'm very proud of what we've done. People stop by to look at the cabin and ask us questions about how we made it, and I get a feeling that we've accomplished something. I believe it's like a work of art, at least that's the way I like to think about something we've worked so hard on—a real work of art."

Cabins in Kit Form Ready to Assemble

If you want to build a log cabin but lack the manpower, skills, or time needed to start from scratch, your answer may be a log cabin kit. Seasoned logs, already peeled, notched, and cut to sizes that conform to standard designs or to your own custom plans, are available from a growing number of commercial log-home manufacturers in this country and Canada. These kits are available in varying degrees of completeness, from a simple shell of precut wall logs and roof beams to an entire house in packaged form. Prehung windows and doors, finished flooring, roofing materials, heating, plumbing, and even kitchen fixtures may be included.

Arrange to have your kit delivered after the foundation is completed, but place your order well in advance. Manufacturers usually suggest that you leave at least six months between your order and the delivery date. All pieces come individually marked to correspond with a coded set of plans and step-by-step building instructions that are included with the kit. The logs are uniform in diameter and are usually milled flat on two sides to make construction easier. Most manufacturers peel the logs by machine, but a few provide hand-peeled logs for greater authenticity. Logs are notched and spiked together as in traditional cabin building, and some manufacturers also include special steel rods for strengthening the corners. Modern caulking or spline material is often used for weather sealing between the logs and around door and window frames. Floors and roofs generally incorporate standard-sized commercial lumber to simplify the construction job. If the design of your cabin calls for exposed roof beams, however, log rafters and purlins are available as well. These are usually supplied uncut; final notching and trimming are done at the site.

Compared with a conventionally framed house, the major potential savings in a log cabin kit are in labor costs, since the buyer can do much of the work himself. Though the cost of materials for both types of construction is about the same, log buildings require less finishing work—such as insulation, paneling, and painting—and less upkeep than equivalent frame houses.

A sense of warmth, comfort, and security is part of the rustic charm that radiates from the interior of this kit log home.

Taking Delivery and Getting Started

1. Be on hand when your kit arrives; delivery date is usually guaranteed. Give driver complete directions to the site beforehand and make sure access road can handle trailer truck. Have extra help on hand to unload logs. Stack logs near the site in piles according to size or as plans direct. Protect logs from weather.

2. Set center girder and sill logs in place first, anchoring them to top of foundation wall according to building instructions. Note that flat side of sill log faces in. Strip of 1-in.-thick fiberglass insulation acts as sill sealer. Sills and girder must be level in order for floor joists to be accurately installed.

3. Floor joists and framing follow standard building practices. Subfloor of 3/4-in. plywood is installed with grain of outer plies running at right angle to joists. Use 9d common or 8d threaded nails spaced 6 to 7 in. apart. Stagger adjacent panels so that butt joints occur over separate joists to distribute load evenly.

4. Mechanical aids make light, fast work of raising wall logs. Here, manufacturer-supplied hoisting equipment is being used by a professional building crew. Logs can also be placed by hand or with the aid of a block and tackle. Most kits make use of many small logs that are easier to handle.

Walls and Partitions

Pull logs in toward the center to ensure a square fit. Use a come-along ratchet hoist for extra pulling power. Steel rods with special coupling nuts included with kit add strength to corners by binding logs vertically.

Spike logs together at 8-ft. intervals, using 8- to 10-in. spikes and a 6-lb. sledgehammer. Begin spiking at one corner, and work all the way around the house, laying up one course of logs at a time before proceeding higher.

Plastic splines installed between logs as walls are raised eliminate the need for further chinking. Some kit manufacturers supply caulking compound instead of splines. Grooves to fit the splines are cut beforehand by machine.

Interior walls are standard stud frame type, useful for enclosing wiring and plumbing. For ease of construction assemble frames on the ground, then tilt into place and nail directly to log walls and subfloor.

Ceiling and Roof

Ceiling joists are precut and prenotched; hoisting them into place usually requires assistance. Joists are then spiked in place.

Short lap-jointed logs are sometimes used as joists. These are supported at the joint by a double-framed interior wall.

Gable logs are spiked in place but left untrimmed. Scrap lumber nailed along the gable serves as saw guide for correct roof pitch.

Trim log ends flush with saw guides, using chain saw. For safety, saw through one log at a time; discard waste end before continuing.

The finished cabin

Rafters may be supplied in log form or as dimension lumber. Most manufacturers precut the angle of the peak ends but leave notching and cutting the final length of each rafter up to the builder. The rafters are either spiked to a ridgepole erected between the gable ends or are assembled in pairs on the ground and then spiked to the top of the wall. Usually a minimum of 18 in. is left below the rafter notches. The extra length is needed to form overhanging eaves.

With the roofing on and doors and windows hung, the house is virtually complete. Other finishing jobs can be done after you move in. Inside walls may be left untreated, or coat them with clear urethane to make them washable. Spray the exterior with preservative every few years to retard decay. A new cabin takes a year or more to fully season. Expect to have to caulk or chink seams occasionally as logs continue to dry and settle.

Building With Adobe

Creating a Homestead Out of Sun-Dried Mud

Adobe, or sun-dried mud, is among the most ancient and widely used building materials. The ingredients for making adobe—soil, water, and straw—are cheap and abundant, and the bricks themselves are easy to make, easy to use, and durable. Perhaps most important, adobe is an energy saver. Thick-walled adobe homes provide interior environments that are thermally stable, resisting both the penetrating heat rays of the sun during the day and the outward flow of warmth from within during cool nights.

Adobe is an arid-climate material; unless it is specially treated, it tends to decompose in humid conditions. But in regions to which it is suited, adobe brick will last almost indefinitely. Remains of adobe structures 700 years old and more still stand in parts of Arizona and New Mexico. The famous Taos Pueblo of New Mexico, an enormous adobe complex, has been the home of unbroken generations of Indians since long before their first encounter with the Spanish conquistadores in 1540. With such a long history it is not at all surprising that the architectural style of adobe that evolved over the centuries—a blend of ancient Indian technology with later Spanish stylization—is both in harmony with nature and perfectly adapted to the resources of the region.

Sources and resources
Books
McHenry, Paul G. *Adobe: Build It Yourself*. Tucson, Ariz.: University of Arizona Press, 1985.
Stedman, Myrtle, and Stedman, Wilfred, eds. *Adobe Architect*. Santa Fe, N. Mex.: Sunstone Press, 1987.
Periodicals
Adobe Journal. Adobe Foundation, P.O. Box 7725, Albuquerque, N. Mex. 87194.
Organizations
Local organizations offer periodic adobe workshops. The following schools have taught regular courses in adobe for several years: New Mexico State University, Las Cruces, N. Mex. 88003 Yavapai College, Prescott, Ariz. 86301.

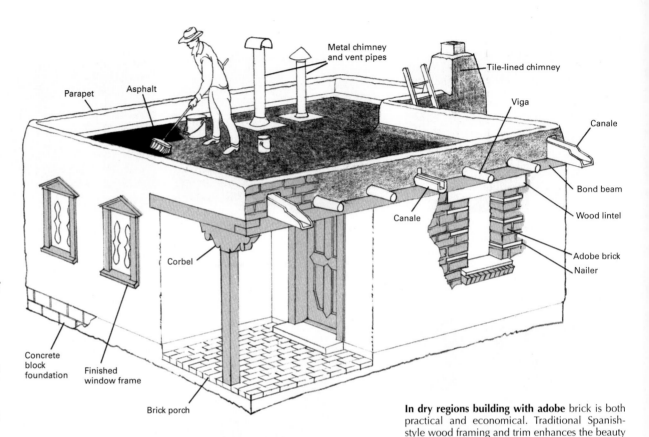

In dry regions building with adobe brick is both practical and economical. Traditional Spanish-style wood framing and trim enhances the beauty of the thick earthen walls.

How to Tell If Your Soil Is Suitable for Adobe

The ideal soil for making adobe has little or no organic matter and contains sand, silt, and clay in roughly equal proportions. The ingredients work much like ordinary concrete: the sand and silt act as filler, the clay as binder. Too much filler results in bricks that crumble easily; too much clay results in bricks that crack as they dry. Organic soil is not acceptable, since the bricks will be weak and harbor vermin.

The knack for choosing adobe soil is not hard to acquire. Start by looking at different soil samples: squeeze them and smell them to detect organic content. Next, perform the tests shown at right. The tests are easily done and will give the approximate proportions of sand, silt, and clay. If you find some likely adobe, check further by digging samples from several spots, mixing them thoroughly to obtain an average profile. Further tests using sample bricks are shown on the next page. As a final step, have a commercial laboratory perform a detailed composition analysis. This will probably be required by the local building code in any case.

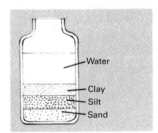

Put **handful of soil** in a jar of water, shake thoroughly, and allow to settle 24 hours. Coarse sand will settle at the bottom, silt in the middle, clay at the top. Proportions should be roughly equal, with at least 25 percent clay. Organic material will float; very little should be present.

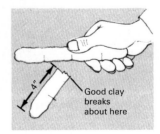

Mix soil with a little water and roll into cylinder 3/4 in. in diameter and 8 in. long. Soil should not stick to hands. Cylinder of good adobe soil will break at between 2 in. and 6 in. when held out straight. If it breaks at less than 2 in., add clay. If it breaks beyond 6 in., add sand.

Making Adobe Brick

The traditional way of mixing adobe—in a hand-dug pit—is simple but physically demanding. Much labor can be saved by using a rotary tiller to dig up the soil and a power cement mixer to blend it with water and straw.

There are two ways of casting adobe bricks: gang mold and cut slab. In the former method each brick is separately cast; in the latter a large slab is cast and then cut into bricks. With either method bricks should be at least 4 inches thick and of manageable weight. The most commonly used dimensions are 4 by 10 by 14 inches (about 35 pounds) and 4 by 12 by 16 inches (about 50 pounds). Newly formed bricks must dry uniformly;

otherwise they will crack. For this reason, wet brick should be protected from uneven exposure to wind and sun. Cover new bricks with burlap after the forms are off, and turn the bricks on edge as soon as they are firm. Cure bricks at least 10 days before stacking them. Do not make bricks when temperatures fall below freezing.

Local building codes usually call for laboratory tests of adobe to determine moisture absorption, compression, and breaking strength. The last two tests can be approximated as shown below. Experiment with sample bricks made of different soil mixes and keep accurate records to help determine the best formula.

Cement mixer can be bought or rented. Commercial 4-cu.-ft. size makes 8 to 10 bricks per load. Place chicken wire over mixer's mouth to screen oversize material. Add about 8 gal. water, about 250 to 300 lb. of dirt (30 to 40 lb. per brick), and a double handful of straw cut into 2-in. lengths.

Gang-mold method

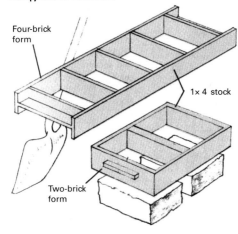

Four-brick form

1 × 4 stock

Two-brick form

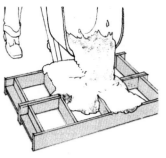

1. Before use, form should be cleaned and soaked in motor oil. Pour mix into center of form (it should flow easily, barely sticking to hoe), then spread it outward with hands.

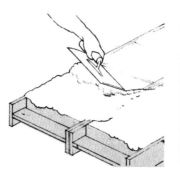

2. Smooth off top by drawing trowel or 2 × 4 across form with sawing motion. Remove form promptly to prevent sticking. Brick should sag downward no more than 1/4in. if mix is correct.

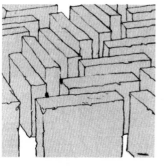

3. Dry bricks on edge as soon as they are firm enough to stand (one to three days). Herringbone bracing pattern keeps rows from toppling. Cure bricks until they are hard—10 days or longer.

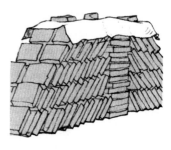

4. Stack bricks against central column to distribute weight evenly. Cover top to protect from rain but leave sides open. For long-term storage, stack on wooden platforms, cover sides with plastic.

Cut-slab method

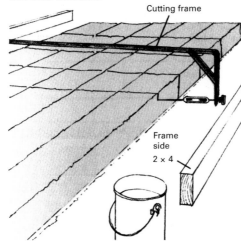

Cutting frame

Frame side
2 × 4

Wooden frame is set directly on packed level ground. Frame is 4 in. deep and sized to yield several mixer loads of bricks. Sides must be at least 1 1/2 in. thick and should be clamped together with bars. After mud is poured and smoothed, score surface to brick dimensions, knock down frame, and cut as shown with piano wire stretched across wooden or steel frame. Turnbuckle facilitates tightening the wire.

Testing the strength of your bricks

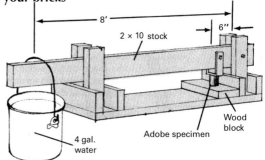

8'

2 × 10 stock

6"

4 gal. water

Adobe specimen

Wood block

Compression strength can be measured with homemade device. Use pipe sections to cast 2-in.-long, 2-in.-diameter adobe cylinders. After standard curing, place cylinders in oven at 150° F for two hours to ensure uniform drying. Cap bearing faces with plaster of paris. Test shown applies pressure of 300 lb. per square inch—a safe figure for adobe.

Modulus of rupture test determines breaking strength of cured brick. Suspend four-week-old sample brick between two others. Brick should support 160-lb. man. Brick should not break if dropped from shoulder height; adobe that fails test normally needs additional clay. Building codes require that tests be verified by laboratory.

A Strong Foundation For Massive Walls

Building an adobe house requires careful planning, but actual construction is comparatively simple. The building site and concrete foundation should be prepared according to standard building methods. Walls are constructed by laying the adobe blocks like ordinary bricks; adobe mud, without the straw, serves as mortar. Adobe does not hold nails, so wooden inserts must be set in place as construction proceeds. After the walls are up a continuous bond beam of wood or concrete is set in place to tie the walls together and distribute the weight of the roof. Floors are generally made of brick or adobe, although concrete slab floors or wooden floors laid atop joists anchored to the foundation are also used. Decide plumbing and electrical arrangements prior to construction. Also determine the locations of fireplaces beforehand; fireplaces made of adobe are heavy and require thick foundation slabs.

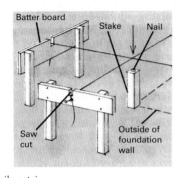

Use either transit or builder's level to lay out site plan. Helper holds vertical rod to stake out corners precisely and to determine grade levels if excavation is required. Batter boards are then set up near corners of site and notched with a saw. String stretched between notches outlines foundation.

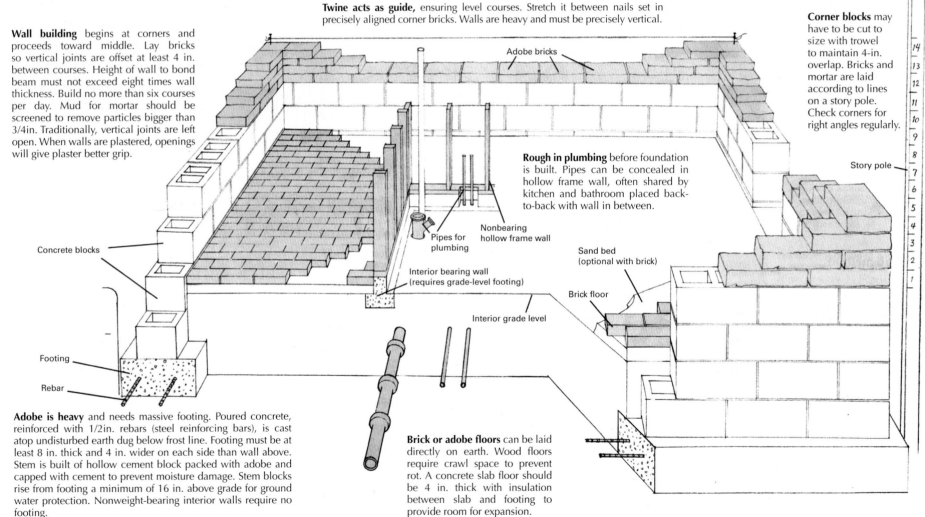

Twine acts as guide, ensuring level courses. Stretch it between nails set in precisely aligned corner bricks. Walls are heavy and must be precisely vertical.

Wall building begins at corners and proceeds toward middle. Lay bricks so vertical joints are offset at least 4 in. between courses. Height of wall to bond beam must not exceed eight times wall thickness. Build no more than six courses per day. Mud for mortar should be screened to remove particles bigger than 3/4in. Traditionally, vertical joints are left open. When walls are plastered, openings will give plaster better grip.

Adobe bricks

Rough in plumbing before foundation is built. Pipes can be concealed in hollow frame wall, often shared by kitchen and bathroom placed back-to-back with wall in between.

Corner blocks may have to be cut to size with trowel to maintain 4-in. overlap. Bricks and mortar are laid according to lines on a story pole. Check corners for right angles regularly.

Story pole

Concrete blocks

Pipes for plumbing

Nonbearing hollow frame wall

Interior bearing wall (requires grade-level footing)

Interior grade level

Sand bed (optional with brick)

Brick floor

Footing

Rebar

Adobe is heavy and needs massive footing. Poured concrete, reinforced with 1/2in. rebars (steel reinforcing bars), is cast atop undisturbed earth dug below frost line. Footing must be at least 8 in. thick and 4 in. wider on each side than wall above. Stem is built of hollow cement block packed with adobe and capped with cement to prevent moisture damage. Stem blocks rise from footing a minimum of 16 in. above grade for ground water protection. Nonweight-bearing interior walls require no footing.

Brick or adobe floors can be laid directly on earth. Wood floors require crawl space to prevent rot. A concrete slab floor should be 4 in. thick with insulation between slab and footing to provide room for expansion.

Doors, Windows, Beams, and Wires

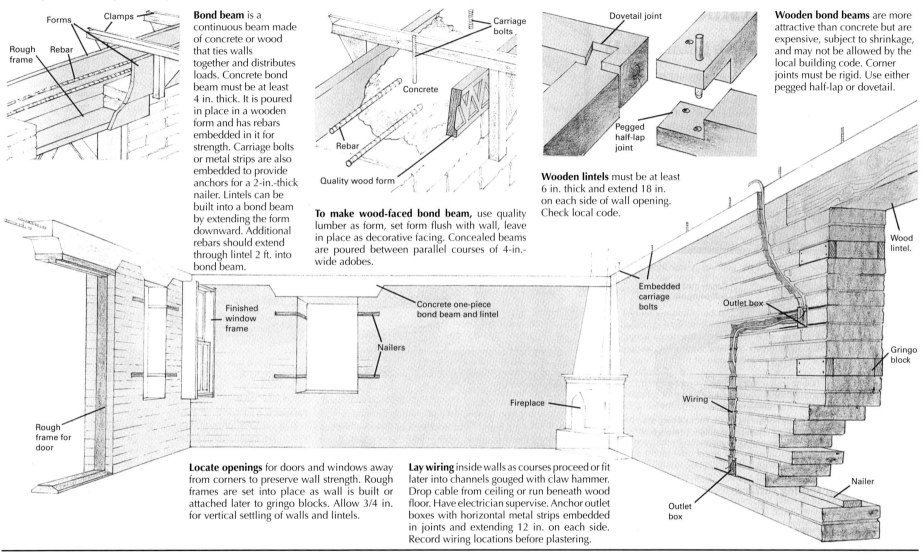

Bond beam is a continuous beam made of concrete or wood that ties walls together and distributes loads. Concrete bond beam must be at least 4 in. thick. It is poured in place in a wooden form and has rebars embedded in it for strength. Carriage bolts or metal strips are also embedded to provide anchors for a 2-in.-thick nailer. Lintels can be built into a bond beam by extending the form downward. Additional rebars should extend through lintel 2 ft. into bond beam.

To make wood-faced bond beam, use quality lumber as form, set form flush with wall, leave in place as decorative facing. Concealed beams are poured between parallel courses of 4-in.-wide adobes.

Wooden bond beams are more attractive than concrete but are expensive, subject to shrinkage, and may not be allowed by the local building code. Corner joints must be rigid. Use either pegged half-lap or dovetail.

Wooden lintels must be at least 6 in. thick and extend 18 in. on each side of wall opening. Check local code.

Locate openings for doors and windows away from corners to preserve wall strength. Rough frames are set into place as wall is built or attached later to gringo blocks. Allow 3/4 in. for vertical settling of walls and lintels.

Lay wiring inside walls as courses proceed or fit later into channels gouged with claw hammer. Drop cable from ceiling or run beneath wood floor. Have electrician supervise. Anchor outlet boxes with horizontal metal strips embedded in joints and extending 12 in. on each side. Record wiring locations before plastering.

Providing surfaces for interior nailing

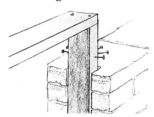

Rough frames afford surfaces for attaching doors or window frames. Use 2 × 4's or wider. Recess frames into notched adobe bricks. Drive 16d nails partway into frame at joint lines before blocks are laid to anchor mortar.

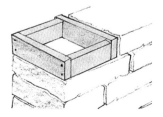

Gringo block—a wooden box made of 2 × 4's—is a simple, traditional way to provide a nailing surface. Set it in place of brick at nailing point and fill it with adobe. Use two on each side for windows; three on each side for doors.

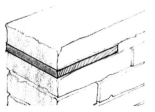

Nailing surface of another kind is made by fitting 1-in. stock into mortar joints. Such horizontal nailers can be used either as gringo blocks or as fastening surfaces for shelves and wall hangings or as framing for interior walls.

From Floor to Roof: The Final Steps

Since roofs and ceilings must be designed with the load-bearing capacities of walls and foundations in mind, it is essential to have professional assistance when planning them. This is particularly true for old-style earth roofs; although they provide excellent insulation and economy, they are extremely heavy. Asphalt or tile roofs are lighter and offer greater architectural freedom. A roof must also protect the walls from water runoff. This is accomplished by channeling roof drainage into protruding gutters called *canales*.

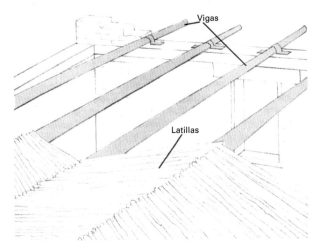

Classic adobe ceiling uses large peeled logs called *vigas* to support narrower peeled saplings called *latillas*. Natural taper of *vigas* creates drainage slope. *Latillas* are nailed in herringbone pattern to accommodate differences in *viga* diameters.

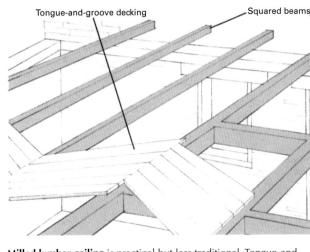

Milled lumber ceiling is practical but less traditional. Tongue-and-groove decking provides extra insulation and eliminates shrinkage gaps. Milled beams are even, so decking can span several beams. Beams are often adzed by hand for texture.

Canales

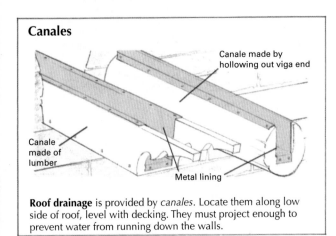

Roof drainage is provided by *canales*. Locate them along low side of roof, level with decking. They must project enough to prevent water from running down the walls.

Details of roof construction

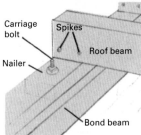

Roof beams can be anchored to nailer or straps embedded on top of concrete bond beam. Use spikes or bolts if bond beam is wooden.

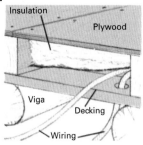

Two-ply roof incorporates insulation and makes wiring easier. Interior surface is of standard decking. Use 1/2-in. plywood for exterior.

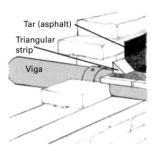

Parapet is traditional; fit and seal bricks carefully around *vigas*. Triangular wooden strip along perimeter supports dished roofing.

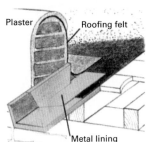

Grade roof to drain off water; line *canales* with rustproof metal. Seal roof seams and joints by hot-mopping with tar. Inspect frequently.

Your choice of roofing surfaces

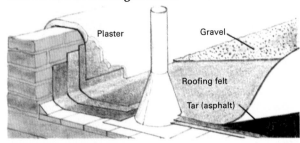

Hot-mopped roof consists of three or more layers of treated felt mats sandwiched between coats of asphalt. Felt is dished upward at sides. Cover final tar layer with light-colored gravel to reflect heat and protect asphalt from direct sunlight.

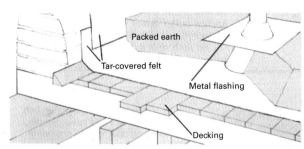

Packed earth of high clay content is traditional roofing material. Recommended thickness of earth is 6 to 8 in. Install it over hot-mopped felt for best results. Foundation, walls, and *vigas* must be massive to accept extra weight.

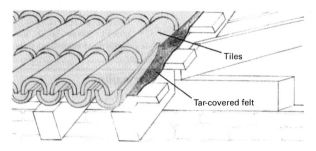

Peaked tile roofs are common where average rainfall is high. Standard trussed-roof building techniques are used. Trusses may be left exposed, or a ceiling can be installed to create an attic. The cost of tile is high, but permanence of roof offsets expense.

Interior and Exterior Plastering

Plastering protects and beautifies adobe walls. Mud with a high clay content is the traditional plastering material (it is still used by southwestern Indians), but it requires more frequent maintenance than modern stucco compounds and is more vulnerable to moisture damage.

The first step in exterior plastering is to nail galvanized chicken wire to the wall with rust-resistant 16-penny nails. Next, trowel on a primary, or scratch, coat, pressing it into joints and gaps for a strong bond. Just before the scratch coat hardens, roughen it with a rake so that the following coat (called the brown coat) will have something to grip. The brown coat is troweled on smooth and left to dry and cure at least 10 days before a finish coat of thin stucco—colored if desired—is applied.

Neither chicken wire nor a scratch coat is needed for interior plastering. Use fibered gypsum plaster mixed with sand for the first coat; unfibered gypsum plaster and sand for the second. This finish will not rub off on clothes. Since plastering is messy, interior work is best accomplished before the floor is laid. If wood is to be plastered, first cover it with 15-pound asphalt felt and strips of metal lath to keep the wood dry and prevent the plaster from cracking as the wood swells and shrinks.

Floors

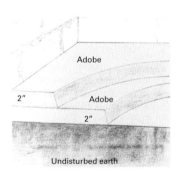

Adobe mud for floors should be 20 percent clay and have extra straw mixed in. Make floor at least 4 in. thick, built up of packed 2-in. layers. If cracks form, fill with adobe. Traditional floor sealant is ox blood. A modern alternative is boiled linseed oil.

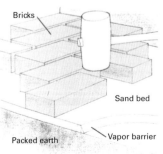

Brick floors are laid in 1-in.-thick bed of sand atop surface of packed earth. Treat earth with insecticide, then cover it with plastic vapor barrier. Tamp bricks into place with mallet. Fill cracks by sweeping floor with fine sand. Finish with commercial sealers and wax.

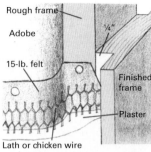

Frames of doors and windows are notched with 1/4-in. groove so that they overlap plaster rather than butt against it. This helps reduce cracking. Baseboard is similarly notched. Install felt and metal lath at wall openings to protect the edges.

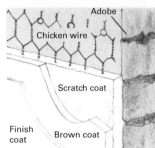

Exterior walls require chicken-wire backing and three coats of plaster. Total thickness is about 3/4 in. Plaster should extend below grade level for even detail. Inside walls need only two coats of plaster and no wire.

Fireplaces

Adobe holds heat well, making it ideal for fireplaces. Fireplace exterior can be anything imagination allows. Shape bricks with dull hatchet and masonry saw; finish with mud spread over chicken wire. (Technical aspects of fireplaces are discussed in *Fireplace Construction and Design*, pp.62–65.)

Anita Rodriguez, Enjarradora

Maintaining an Adobe Tradition

In Taos, New Mexico, Anita Rodriguez is an expert in *enjarrando*—the craft of plastering with adobe. Above is an adobe home in Taos with an *horno*, an ancient type of oven.

"When I was a child in Taos, where I was born, nearly all the buildings were adobe. Now they have been replaced by technological construction, but I have never forgotten the lovely soft shapes of earthen walls or the fireplaces that were in every home. It is hard to exaggerate the beauty and harmony of that vanished town.

"In this part of the country for over 500 years the craft of finishing adobe has traditionally belonged to women. The Spanish word for such a woman is *enjarradora*. In English this means only "plasterer," but *enjarradoras* also build fireplaces, lay mud floors, and paint walls with clays of various colors by an ancient method called *alisando*.

"A friend who knew my interest in adobe asked me to build her a fireplace. Someone else happened to see it and asked me to build another one, and that's how I got started. Today I am a professional *enjarradora*. One can only learn *enjarrando* from *enjarradoras*. The techniques are passed on in a strictly oral tradition that has never been written down. I learned from Hispanic *enjarradoras* who were generous to me with their knowledge; and while I was teaching school at Taos Pueblo, I too passed my knowledge along to other women.

"With the interest in environment and the emphasis on energy saving, there is a revival of interest in adobe construction. It is particularly good for buildings with solar heating. Adobe walls are excellent insulators. They trap heat in winter and keep the interior cool in summer.

"Working with adobe is hard physical labor. Ten years of *enjarrando* have not made me look like Charles Atlas, but I work with men all day and know that women are much stronger than people think they are. The work has given me a sense of my roots. I identify with my culture and I don't want it to die."

Building a Stone House

A Home Made of Rock: Beauty Plus Strength

People have a natural love for stones. Children climb on them, collect them, and skim them over ponds. Our most magnificent structures are made of rock, as well as some of our most ancient. To this day, a house made of stone provides a special feeling of security, comfort, and coziness.

For years stone houses were made by expert masons using the time-tested technique of laying each rock individually in place. More recently, however, the slipform method has become popular, especially among do-it-yourselfers. A slipformed house can be built for less than two-thirds the cost of a similar home made of wood and will compare favorably with mason-built stone houses in terms of durability and attractiveness.

Stone home has exposed interior walls and beams. The combination of rustic materials and modern accents create a unique and comfortable living space.

Choosing Your Stone

There are many variables to keep in mind when selecting building stones. Perhaps the most important consideration is availability: stone is heavy and if good stone cannot be found locally, shipping costs can be prohibitive. Stone for building should be durable and waterproof, qualities that depend not only on the type of rock but also on climate. Limestone, for example, is among the most durable of construction materials in arid areas but will weather rapidly in a wet climate. Attractiveness is also important. Ideally, stone buildings should fit in with the prevailing architecture and blend with the local topographical features as well.

The chart at right gives some of the common rock types and their suitability as building stone. However, you can tell a lot about a stone without knowing what type it is. Start by examining it carefully to determine its features. Compare its weight, texture, and appearance with other stones. Good building stone is heavy and therefore less likely to absorb moisture. Break open a sample with a sledgehammer. The rock should be difficult to fracture and should break into rough-textured, irregular chunks. Stone that crumbles or splits easily along flat planes is probably weak and porous. Though

the stone may still be suitable for building under many conditions, water may seep in, hastening erosion and causing cracking in freezing weather.

Streambeds, mines and quarries, rocky pasturelands, lakeshores, and abandoned stonework are all likely sources for building stone. Maps published by the U.S. Geological Service show locations of abandoned mines and quarries. In suburban areas talk to contractors who may be involved in demolition work. In the country ask local farmers; you may find all the rock you need free for the hauling. If the stone is not on your property, be sure to talk to the owner before you take any, and always put the emphasis on working safely.

Suitability of rock types for building

Rock type	Durability	Water resistance	Workability
Basalt	Excellent	Excellent	Difficult
Gneiss	Good	Good	Moderate
Granite	Excellent	Good	Moderate
Limestone	Fair	Poor	Easy
Marble	Good	Excellent	Moderate
Sandstone	Fair	Fair	Easy
Schist	Good	Good	Moderate
Slate	Good	Excellent	Easy

Fieldstone is loose surface rock. It is rough textured and worn from exposure to nature and the passage of time.

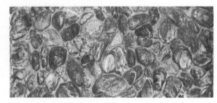

Creek stone is polished smooth by running water. Its unusual character lends it to decorative uses, such as fireplace facings.

Quarried stone is cut from massive outcrops. Its surfaces are freshly exposed, sharp, clean, and regular.

Principles of Traditional Stonemasonry

For centuries the only way to erect a stone house was to lay the stones individually like bricks. The skill of the stonemason involved selecting the proper stone to lay in place and then adjusting the stone to fit securely, either by shaping it to fit or by filling in around the stone with specially chosen smaller rock fragments called shims.

The first stone structures were dry, that is, built without mortar. Later, clay, lime, or cement was used to set the rocks in place. In either type of masonry, structural integrity depends on the same two forces—gravity and friction—and the key to building enduring stonework has always been to make full use of both forces. For gravity to do its job, keep the stones' bedding surfaces horizontal or canted slightly inward toward the center of the wall. Maximize friction by creating as much contact between stones as possible. Follow the old rule "one over two and two over one" so that each stone rests across at least two stones beneath; gravity then locks the stones together and unifies the structure. Maintain solid bedding surfaces by shaping or shimming any stones that fit poorly. Shaping is done with a hammer and chisel. Shimming is done by inserting small pieces of filler rock in spaces between stones, thereby providing support and increasing surface contact. However, do not use shims as wedges to hold stones in place. If you do, the wedged stones may eventually work free. The best use of shims is for leveling and stabilizing the bedding surfaces, always with the goal of keeping them as horizontal as possible in order to make the fullest possible use of the force of gravity, which pulls straight down.

Mortar eliminates much of the shaping and shimming needed in dry-wall construction. It does not, however, glue the stones together. Portland cement, the active ingredient in mortar, cures as hard as stone and automatically provides a perfect seat for the rocks as they are laid, filling the smallest gaps.

For maximum structural integrity each stone should weigh straight down on the ones beneath it (left). Stones in a mislaid wall (right) tend to slide out; the higher the stones are stacked, the greater the tendency to crumble. Shape the stones with hammer and chisel or use small fragments as shims to keep bedding planes horizontal or tilted slightly inward.

Shaping the stones to fit

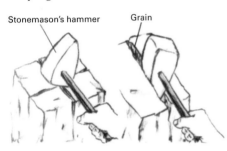

Large rocks should be broken into random chunks with a sledge or stonemason's hammer. Use the wedge-shaped end of the mason's hammer to split the stone along the grain.

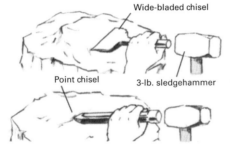

Wide-bladed chisels are used when scoring, smoothing, and splitting soft stone. A point chisel is employed when working with hard stones where impact must be concentrated.

When hewing stone, chip rock away gradually to avoid breaking entire block. Place stone on bed of sand and score with chisel. Chip off small pieces using flat face of hammer. Work from edge toward line with steady blows. On hard rock you may have to hammer quite a while before cracking begins. Wear safety goggles to prevent injury from rock chips.

Mortaring the stones in place

1. Mortar proportions are one part portland cement to three parts sand. Add only enough water for a firm mix.

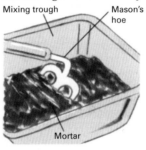

2. Stones should be clean and surfaces wet. Shape stone and test for fit before laying down bed of mortar.

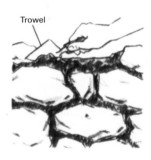

3. Lay mortar on bedding face with a trowel. Do not smooth. Use only enough to provide firm support.

4. For effective seating drop stone in place from a few inches above. Once stone is set, do not move it farther.

5. Scrape off excess mortar and pack it into vertical joints. Use a trowel; mortar will irritate skin.

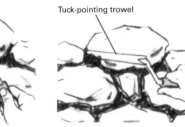

6. Use tuck-pointing trowel to trim mortar. Clean stones with cleaning compound from building supply dealer.

The Slipform Method Of Casting Walls

Slipforming is a method of building with stone that does not require advanced masonry skills. Rather than shaping, shimming, and mortaring each stone into place individually, loose stones are simply packed into removable forms and cemented together by filling in around them with concrete. In a slipformed wall an entire layer, or course, is built as a unit. A number of forms are connected end-to-end and filled. While the mix hardens, a second chain of forms is placed on top of the first and also filled. When the bottom layer has set, those forms are removed and reattached above the second to form a third layer. In this way wall building proceeds vertically like a game of leapfrog. Properly done, the results are excellent. A slipformed wall is sturdy, weatherproof, and almost indistinguishable

from old-style mortared masonry—and can be put up in half the time it would take to lay it stone by stone.

For ease of handling, forms are usually 18 inches deep and about 8 feet long. Stones to fill them should also be of manageable size—no more than 50 pounds each—and have at least one fairly flat face. Stockpile a wide variety so that you will have plenty to choose from. Cast the walls at least 14 inches thick. Place stones in the form with their flat faces against the side that will become the exterior wall. Try to follow the "one over two, two over one" rule that holds for mortared masonry so that gravity will help bind the stones together.

Stone is a poor insulator and, in addition, joints between stones tend to develop small leaks. As a result, most slipformed walls are built so that the stones extend no more than two-thirds of the way through the wall from the exterior to the interior. The inside face is smooth concrete. Furring strips are usually embedded in the concrete, and the wall is finished with insulation and paneling. If you want your interior wall to be of stone, place a 2-inch layer of solid insulation in the

middle of the form and fill in on either side with stones and concrete. This type of wall will be thermally sound as well as leakproof.

Apply a coat of oil to the slipforms before using them so they can be removed more easily later on. As you pour the concrete, tamp it down, striking the forms occasionally with a hammer to dispel air bubbles. Your aim should be to surround each stone with 1 to 2 inches of concrete. It is vital that the bonding between successive layers be strong and weathertight. Try to complete an entire course on a single pour to avoid vertical through-seams, which will weaken the walls. Horizontal seams tend to form on the top of a course. To keep them from allowing moisture into the house, slope the top of each pour downward to the outside. Do not cap the courses with concrete; instead, finish each course with stones that protrude vertically, so they will mesh with those in the next layer. Surfaces that have cured for more than 48 hours may require application of a commercial bonding agent or a paste of portland cement and water before the next layer is poured on top.

Good Concrete Is the Secret of Slipforming

When building slipformed stonework, the quality of the concrete is most important. Concrete is made up of portland cement, sand, and gravel. For slipforming, 1/2-inch-diameter gravel is best. Recommended proportions are one part cement, three parts sand, and four parts gravel. Proper water content is the secret of strong concrete. There must be enough water so that the mixture can be worked and the chemical reaction that hardens the cement can go to completion. Too much water results in weak concrete. Generally, for a batch

of concrete mixed from one sack of cement (94 pounds), 5 gallons of water are needed. Adjust this figure to accommodate the moisture content of the sand and gravel. To obtain good results when you are mixing by hand, use the method shown below. With a power mixer, blend the dry ingredients first, then add water gradually until a workable mix is obtained. It helps to have an experienced person on hand when you make your first batch.

Concrete must not dry too fast. Water evaporating from the mix while it cures has the same effect as adding

too little water at the start. Nor must ordinary concrete be exposed to freezing temperatures for at least a week after it has been poured. The chart describes different types of portland cement, each suited to a particular building condition. Type I is suitable for all but severe conditions. Type III is excellent for slipforming because its rapid setting time allows forms to be removed sooner. So-called air-entrained cement will trap microscopic air bubbles as it hardens, causing it to resist frost damage. Use Type III A in all areas where heavy freezing occurs.

Types of cement and where to use them

Type I	**General purpose:** Moderate-weather building conditions in areas where light to moderate freezing will occur	
Type IA	**General purpose, air-entrained:** Moderate-weather building conditions in areas where heavy freezing occurs	
Type III	**High strength, early set:** Early or late season building conditions in light to moderate freeze areas where conditions require rapid concrete setting and early form removal	
Type IIIA	**High-early, air-entrained:** Early or late season building conditions in heavy freeze areas where conditions require rapid concrete setting and early form removal	

The measuring box

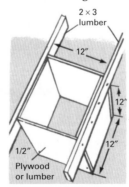

2 × 3 lumber

12"

12"

12"

1/2"

Plywood or lumber

Measuring box for dry ingredients has a 1-cu.-ft. capacity. Box has no bottom. Sides are 1/2-in. plywood or 3/4-in. lumber with 2 × 3 boards for handles. Join parts with screws, not nails, for extra strength. When mixing concrete, place box in mixing trough, fill, and lift up. Each filling equals one unit of a particular ingredient.

Mixing the components

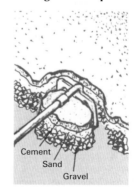

Cement
Sand
Gravel

To mix concrete by hand, first wet the mixing trough. Spread correct proportions of ingredients in layers over three-quarters of the bottom; then pour water into remaining area. To mix, pull sections of dry material forward into water with mason's hoe and blend until proper consistency is reached.

Assembling the Forms

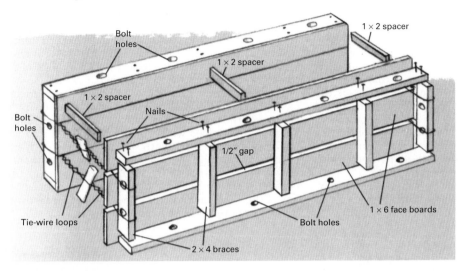

Build your own slipforms using 1 × 6 boards or sheets of 1/2-in. plywood for the faces. Nail them to 2 × 4 braces as shown. Leave 1/2-in. gaps between face boards or drill holes in plywood so that tie-wire loops can be threaded through to hold the sides together. Bore holes in end, top, and bottom braces to bolt forms together end-to-end and in vertical layers. You will need enough forms to assemble two end-to-end chains the length of the wall section being poured. The forms will be stacked one on top of the other leapfrog fashion as the wall is raised. For efficiency and economy use standard commercial lumber sizes for forms, and make them interchangeable by planning walls to be even multiples of form dimensions.

Getting Ready to Build

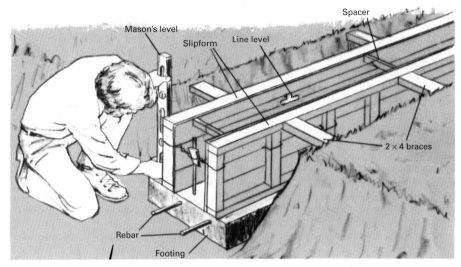

Reinforced concrete footing poured below frost line ensures firm base for heavy masonry walls. Footing should be 4 in. wider on each side than width of wall and at least 10 in. thick. Set forms in place along footing marked with a chalk line. Make tie-wire loops by inserting light wire through holes or between boards and tying around vertical braces. Twist loops tight with nails while inserting 1 × 2 wood spacers cut to width of wall to maintain correct dimensions. Use mason's level, and line level to make sure forms are plumb. Adjust by tapping forms with hammer. If additional support is needed, nail extra braces across the tops of the forms or prop the sides with 2 × 4's set in the ground as shown in the illustration.

Filling the Forms

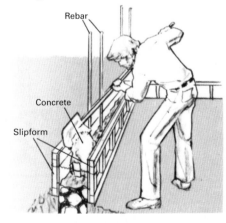

Place stones 2 in. apart with flat faces against form. If rebar (steel reinforcing bar) and furring strips are being used, install them now. Pack remaining area with concrete and tamp well, allowing the concrete to flow beneath stones.

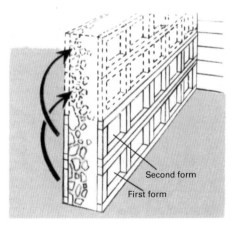

While masonry cures in first form, second form is placed on top and filled. After 48 hours first form is removed and placed atop second form as its contents continue to cure. Clip tie-wires flush; they will remain embedded in the wall.

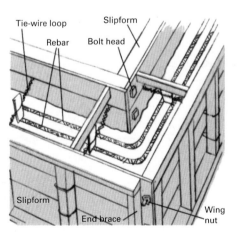

Corners are built as a unit with special forms that can be bolted together at right angles. Lay a 6-ft. length of 3/8-in. rebar, bent at a right angle, into corners every 10 in. vertically. Use cornerstones that have two faces at right angles.

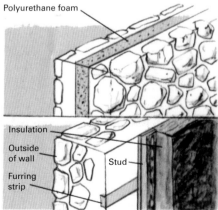

Stone is cold unless insulated. Sandwich-type wall (top) with core of 2-in. polyurethane foam provides exposed stone inside house. Or embed treated furring in wall as it is built, then attach studs, insulation, and paneling.

Movable Slipforms: An Old-fashioned Home Using Modern Methods

Stone houses have the quality of blending into the landscape, especially if they make use of stone gathered from the building site itself. Plan a house that will harmonize with the environment. Choose an area of well-drained solid ground upon which to build, since masonry will crack if settling occurs. Stone walls are not easily modified, so plan your house large enough to accommodate any anticipated needs for more space in the future, and take into account plumbing, heating, and electrical arrangements. Wall openings for these systems are far easier to incorporate during the construction process than to drill afterward.

Begin by collecting stone. The more you have on hand the better. Unless you plan to pour a concrete floor along with the foundation, it is a good idea to stack the piles of rock in the center of the site. That way you will have less distance to carry the stone and will be able to keep all possible choices in view. Store bags of cement where they will stay absolutely dry, stacked on wooden platforms with an airspace beneath and covered with plastic. Cover sand also if rain is frequent.

Build enough forms to be able to "slip" them properly. This means having on hand as many forms as are needed to construct a wall section two courses high. Ideally, you should build enough forms to reach between natural openings in the wall plus special forms for corners or odd shapes. Remember to make forms from standard lumber and to plan wall dimensions in multiples of form sizes. That way you will not have to construct a number of different forms and can use them interchangeably.

You might design your house with low walls for greater ease in handling stone. Extend windows and doors all the way to the top plate to eliminate the need for lintels. Frames are studded with nails on the outside and laid up directly in the forms, with spacer blocks on each side to prevent concrete from being pushed behind them if they are not as thick as the wall itself. Use heavy timber joined with pegged lap joints. Soak the frames and any of the wood that will make permanent contact with masonry in preservative to prevent dry rot.

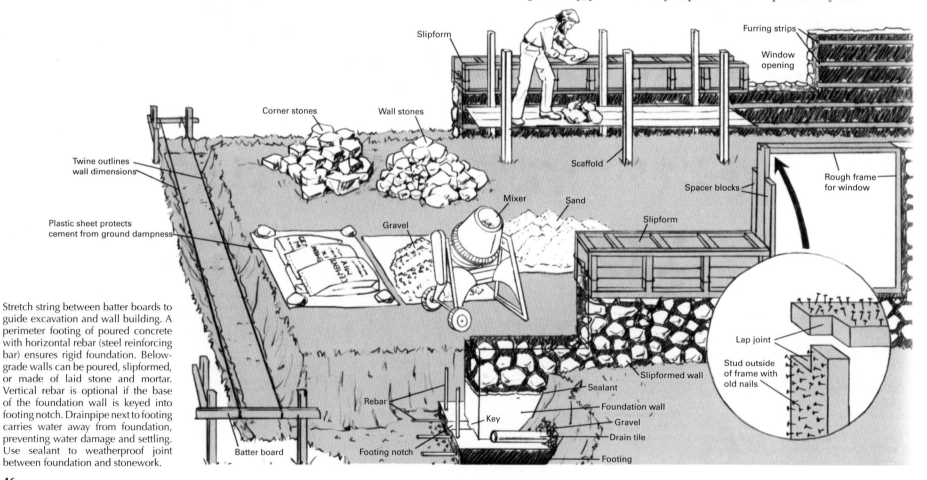

Stretch string between batter boards to guide excavation and wall building. A perimeter footing of poured concrete with horizontal rebar (steel reinforcing bar) ensures rigid foundation. Below-grade walls can be poured, slipformed, or made of laid stone and mortar. Vertical rebar is optional if the base of the foundation wall is keyed into footing notch. Drainpipe next to footing carries water away from foundation, preventing water damage and settling. Use sealant to weatherproof joint between foundation and stonework.

Skylight

Cathedral celing

Truss-type roof supports

Gable end

Sandwich-type insulated stone wall (retains fireplace heat)

Furring strips embedded in wall (later paneled)

Crawl space

Hardwood finish floor

Subfloor

Floor joists

Foundation wall

Joist header board

Packed sand

Undisturbed earth

Slipformed stone wall

Sandwich-type wall, with stone face inside, stores heat from fireplace or sunlit windows. Paneled stud walls permit easy installation of shelves, plumbing, and wiring. Flagstone or slate floors are laid at ground level. Wood floor is raised, since crawl space is needed to prevent rot. Gable ends are wood. Roof may be simple truss type. Since slipformed walls can withstand the outward thrust of the rafters, few tie beams are needed. This allows architectural freedom to include such features as the skylight and cathedral ceiling.

Sources and resources

Books
Basic Masonry. Menlo Park, Calif.: Sunset Books, 1995.
Burch, Monte. *Brick, Concrete, Stonework*. Saddle River, N.J.: Creative Homeowner, 1980.
McClintock, Mike. *Alternative Housebuilding*. New York: Sterling Publishing, 1989.

Raising a Barn

Timber-Frame Method, Now Centuries Old, Still Means Quality

Sturdy old barn is a testament to old-time craftsmanship. Gambriel roof was a favorite style among thrifty farmers because of the increased interior space it provided. The original shingles have been replaced with more modern roofing, but the frame remains sturdy, largely due to the amazing durability of post-and-beam construction.

Farm families have long valued a sturdy barn as much as a comfortable home. Barns are a symbol of the farmer's relationship with the land and of his personal goals and values. Eric Sloane, the noted historian and artist of Americana, describes the sturdy old barns of New England as the "shrines of a good life." Their simple, honest lines and lasting strength seem to reflect the farmer's steadfast love of the soil and enduring belief in a secure and bountiful future.

Care, pride, and dedication go into the construction of a good barn. Very often details of craftsmanship hidden high in the hayloft are likely to be of finer quality than those displayed in the parlor of the family house. Old-fashioned barns had massive, carefully fitted frameworks of hand-hewn timbers, joined together with stout wooden pegs instead of nails. This construction method, called timber frame, or post and beam, had its roots in medieval European architecture. In spite of the time, labor, and skill necessary, the great-grandfathers of today's farmers built

in this style because of its proven ability to last, even though the faster, cheaper, and easier method called stud framing—building as we do today with 2 × 4's and nails—was available to them as early as the 1830's.

Stud framing requires the additional strength provided by wall sheathing and siding. A timber frame, however, is self-supporting. The heavy posts and beams—the principal frame members—are joined together at right angles, then braced with additional diagonal timbers notched into them. The result is a strong and stable triangular support. Barn siding, necessary only to enclose the structure, is usually made of low-cost lumber, such as rough-cut 1-inch pine boards, nailed vertically to the frame.

Sections of a barn frame are generally built on the ground in units called bents. When all the bents are completed, they are raised upright and joined together to form the completed frame. Because the bents are so massive, community effort is usually required when the barn is ready to be

erected. In fact, part of the beauty of an old-fashioned barn lies in the spirit of community friendship it reflects. A hundred years ago an entire town might turn out on the "raisin' day" of a barn like the one shown above; to raise a small barn, such as the one described on the following pages, a dozen or so friends should suffice.

Sources and resources

Books

Benson, Tedd. *Timber-Frame Home*. Newtown, Conn.: Taunton Press, 1996.

Fitchen, John. *The New World Dutch Barn*. Syracuse, N.Y.: Syracuse University Press, 1968.

Halsted, Byron D., ed. *Barns, Sheds and Outbuildings*. Battleboro, Vt.: Alan C. Hood, 1977.

Kelley, J. Frederick. *Early Domestic Architecture of Connecticut*. New York: Dover, 1963.

Sloane, Eric. *An Age of Barns*. New York: Henry Holt & Co., 1990.

Wallas, Elliott. *The Timber Framing Book*. Kittery Point, Maine: Housesmith's Press, 1977.

Building plans and measured drawings

Historical American Building Survey. Library of Congress: Photoduplication Service, 10 First St. SE, Washington, D.C. 20540.

Organization

Early American Industries Association. P.O. Box 2128, Empire State Plaza Station, Albany, N.Y. 12220.

Tools Should Be Big and Sturdy

Timber-frame construction requires heavy-duty tools. Chisels should be the strongest type available, with socket ends to prevent the handles from splitting under repeated malleting. Three blade widths are helpful: 1 inch, 11/2 inch, and 2 inch; the overall length of the chisels should be at least 15 inches. You will also need a six- or eight-point crosscut saw, a 11/2 to 2-inch auger (or brace and bit), a mallet, a sledgehammer, a hatchet, measuring tools, and a level. A chain saw is valuable, and if electricity is available, a great deal of sweat can be saved with a sturdy power saw and a rugged electric drill. Keep edged tools sharp for safety, accuracy, and ease of use.

In the 19th century, carpenters had special tools designed expressly for timber framing. As a result, framing a barn back then was easier in many ways than it is now. You may be fortunate enough to locate some of these valuable old tools at specialty tool stores, farm auctions, or through advertisements in collectors' magazines.

A minimum kit

Barn-framing tools shown here can be obtained at most quality hardware stores. In addition, you will need several standard carpentry tools, including a claw hammer, pry bar, and jack plane. To give framing timbers an authentic ax-hewn appearance, use hand tools on exposed surfaces, and limit the use of power tools to hidden areas.

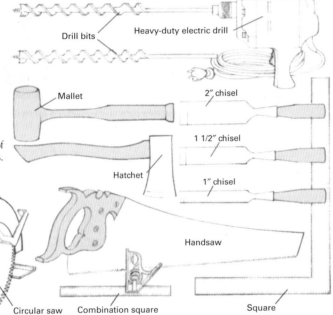

Drill bits
Heavy-duty electric drill
Mallet
2" chisel
1 1/2" chisel
Hatchet
1" chisel
Handsaw
Circular saw
Combination square
Square

Old-fashioned specialties

Old-timers had a tool for every job. Mortising was done with a special ax or with a combination of boring machine, corner chisel, and slick (for smoothing). Frames were pounded together with a 40-lb. beetle. Pegs were shaped by driving them through a steel sizer. Pikes helped in raising the barn sides upright.

Peg sizer
Boring machine
Mortising ax
Auger
Corner chisel
Slick
Beetle
Pike

Some Tips on Timber

Seasoned hardwoods-usually oak or chestnut-are the traditional timbers for frames. Pine, hemlock, fir, or spruce can also be used, provided that all vertical posts made of these weaker woods are at least 6 inches square and that horizontal beams measure at least 6 inches by 8 inches. Seasoned wood is best, but framing timbers can be green if allowances are made for later shrinkage. Try to obtain the timber from trees felled during the winter months. Winter-cut wood contains less sap, so seasoning is faster, shrinkage is less, and the wood is more resistant to decay. You may choose to hew your own beams (see *Converting Trees Into Lumber*, pp.22–25), or you can order them from a sawmill. Stack lumber off the ground and protect it from wet weather. Insert 1 × 2 boards between layers to allow air circulation.

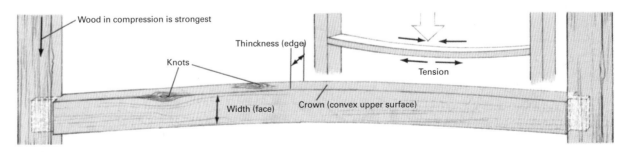

Wood in compression is strongest
Thickness (edge)
Knots
Tension
Width (face)
Crown (convex upper surface)

Wooden members can support the greatest loads when stress is along the direction of the grain, as in the vertical post at far left. Horizontal beams sag because stress crosses grain. Compression, which forces wood together along beam's top surface, creates tension along the bottom, stretching wood apart. For maximum horizontal strength, place beam on edge with its natural arc, or crown, facing upward, like an arch. However, if large knots are present on the concave edge rather than the crowned edge, place that edge up instead so that the knots will be pressed into the wood, not loosened and forced out by tension.

Timber-Frame Joinery: Like Giant Furniture

Timber framing is cabinetmaking on a grand scale. Except for size, the frame of an old-fashioned barn hardly differs from that of a traditional blanket chest, cabinet, or bureau of drawers; each is basically the framework of a box. Even the individual elements of construction are the same.

The principal joint used in both barn framing and furniture framing is the mortise and tenon. This joint has been used by carpenters and cabinetmakers since ancient times because of its great strength and simple construction. When accurately cut, fitted, and pegged together, a mortise-and-tenon joint will be virtually as

strong as the wood from which it is made. The technique of making mortise-and-tenon joints for timber-frame structures differs from that used when working on a piece of furniture. The tools are larger, the timbers are harder to maneuver, and the entire process must take into account the greater physical forces at work as well as the sheer weight of the materials involved.

Old-timers recognized that a tight fit was the key to a sound, long-lasting joint and summed it up in the motto "Measure twice, cut once." They made and fitted each joint individually, paring the sizes to the last sliver of wood, then took the joint apart until the barn was ready for assembly. Since no two joints were quite alike, the pieces were marked to avoid mistakes on raising day. Roman numerals were used as labels because they were easy to cut with a chisel; they can often be seen inscribed in the sturdy timbers of 19th-century barns.

Wooden pegs and well-made joints hold frame of barn together.

Making a Mortise-and-Tenon Joint

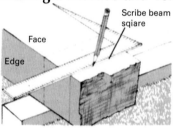

1. Make tenon first. Scribe rough end of beam square on all sides, then measure off tenon length and scribe it on all sides. Tenon length should be half thickness of receiving timber.

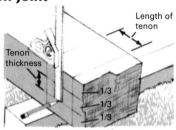

2. Place beam on its side. Use combination square as gauge to mark tenon thickness on both edges of the beam. Tenon thickness should be one-third the width of the receiving timber.

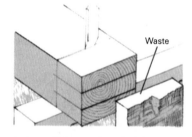

3. Saw off the rough end of the beam, being careful to cut along all four squaring-off lines. Then connect the ends of the tenon-thickness lines with a combination square.

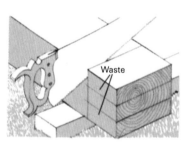

4. Saw the tenon shoulders next. Cut must be square. For accuracy, score line with chisel, and begin cutting with saw tilted back. Rock saw forward as rear thickness line is reached.

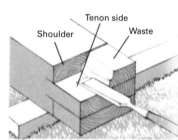

5. Remove waste from tenon sides. Use either ripsaw, chisel and mallet, or a sharp hatchet. To use hatchet, begin chopping at end of beam near surface; work along grain.

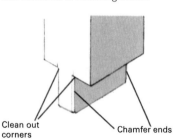

6. Smooth tenon and shoulder with an extra-sharp wide-bladed chisel or a block plane. Take special care to clean out corners. Chamfer (bevel) ends to ease final assembly.

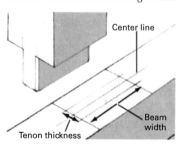

7. To lay out mortise, place tenoned piece across timber and scribe width of beam. Remove, then scribe center line, adding tenon-thickness dimensions on either side as shown.

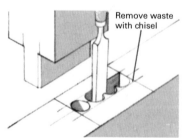

8. Bore out waste with bit slightly smaller than mortise width. Use tape on bit for depth gauge, and hold drill at precise 90° angle to work. Bore the two end holes first.

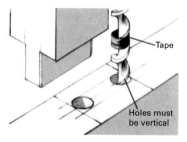

9. Smooth mortise sides with wide-bladed chisel and mallet, and carefully square corners. Use exact-sized chisel to trim mortise ends. Be sure walls remain square and vertical.

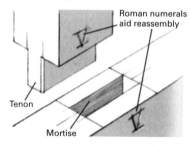

10. Check final fit by measuring both mortise and tenon; some trimming is usually necessary. Mark each piece to aid later assembly (chiseled Roman numerals are traditional).

From Beams to Bents

Before a barn raising can begin, mortised posts and tenoned beams must be fastened together and then braced with diagonal timbers to form bents, the basic units of barn construction. Styles of bents vary; in all cases, however, they consist of combinations of posts, beams, and braces—nothing else.

Each joint should be pegged, not nailed. Wooden pegs are stronger and longer lasting than nails, screws, or bolts, and, unlike metal fasteners, they will never rust. In addition, the pegs shrink and swell in harmony with the surrounding timbers, producing very tight joints with little or no splitting during moisture changes. Pegs should always be made of harder wood than the timbers that they join; oak and black locust are best. They must be made of completely seasoned wood; otherwise they can shrink and loosen in their holes. Ideally, a peg will tighten with age as the wood around it shrinks.

Braces, which make the framing rigid, must be installed carefully so that the structure remains square. The best way to ensure precision is to fit the braces after the main timbers have been joined and pegged.

Making pegs

Whittle hardwood pegs by shaving corners to form rough octagon. Diameter is one-third tenon length.

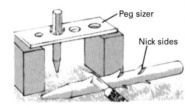

Stock can be driven through steel peg sizer instead. Notches in sides of finished pegs give tighter fit.

Fitting braces

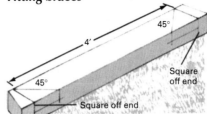

1. Mark 45° angle at one end of timber and scribe across ends. Mark length of brace, then scribe second 45° angle.

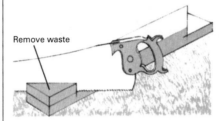

2. Measure, then saw halfway through brace by cutting along angle lines. Remove triangular waste sections with chisel.

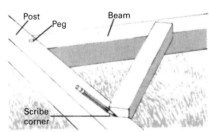

3. With post and beam pegged at 90° angle, hold brace in place and scribe outline of corner on each timber.

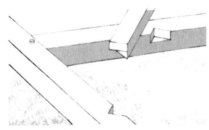

4. Scribe depth of notch on inside edge of timbers, then remove waste with chisel. Fit the brace; drill and peg securely.

Drawboring

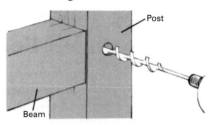

1. Driving pegs through offset holes draws joints tight. Begin with joint assembled; bore through one side of mortise only.

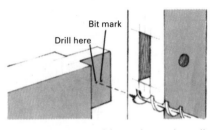

2. Remove tenon and locate bit mark. Drill hole through tenon, centered a fraction of an inch closer to its shoulder.

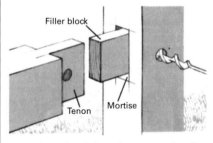

3. Replace the drill in the mortised timber and continue boring through the other side. Use filler block to steady bit.

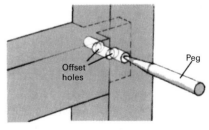

4. Reassemble joint. Insert a long peg with a tapered point, and drive it in until full thickness of peg travels through both timbers.

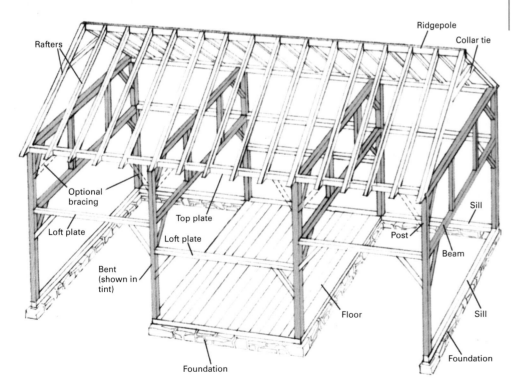

Timber-frame barn is less complicated than it appears. It is basically a series of bents joined together.

Building Your Own Old-fashioned Barn

Four-bent barn built on the windward side of a gentle slope.

Even if you are not a farmer, a small barn has dozens of practical uses. The four-bent barn shown here could be used as a two-car garage; it could also be a workshop or studio, and the two lofts overhead provide a generous bonus of storage space. Trees suitable for use as framing timbers may be available on your own property. If they are, you can try your hand at hewing them square yourself (see *Converting Trees Into Lumber,* pp.22–25). If you have a chain-saw mill for making boards, you can also saw out your own dimension lumber for the roof and siding. Otherwise have the beams and boards cut to your specifications at a sawmill.

Before you begin to build, take time for careful planning and site preparation. Barns that are designed only for storage and farm use seldom come under building code restrictions, but those that are modified for living usually do, so check with the building inspector. In any case, you will want to be certain of the terrain and drainage characteristics of the building site, and you should also consider the changing angle of the sun throughout the seasons as well as any tendency of the site to harbor extra cold or dampness. Barns need plenty of ventilation, so look for an area that receives a constant breeze, such as the windward side of a hill. A traditional spot for hay and livestock barns is just beyond the crest; not only does this location provide good ventilation, but the rise forms a natural ramp that allows the hay to be easily unloaded at either the main floor or loft level. At feeding time the farmer can take advantage of gravity by pitching the hay down, out a rear door, to animals sheltered below in the protected barnyard at the base of the hill. Observe the locations of barns in your own area; you may discover unique and useful building customs that are based on local ingenuity. Also, several books given in the sources and resources section on page 48 contain useful photographs and information about siting.

Barn foundations are traditionally made of fieldstone and are laid dry (without mortar). Mortared stone, reinforced concrete, or concrete block can also be used. The foundation wall should reach below frost level for protection against damage from repeated freezing and thawing and should rise at least 18 inches above grade. After the foundation is laid, anchor the sill beams to it. When the major framing timbers have been notched and numbered for joining, the barn is ready to raise.

If you want to raise the barn the traditional way, hold a raising bee. Invite friends, neighbors, and their families to share the work, then celebrate afterward with food and drink. In bygone days a raising bee was the only way to get the barn up, since most barns were too big for one family to raise, and machinery was not available.

Construction Plans for a Small Barn

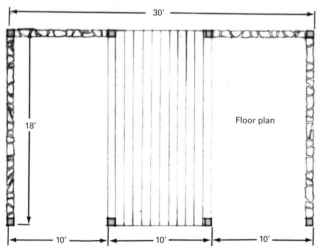

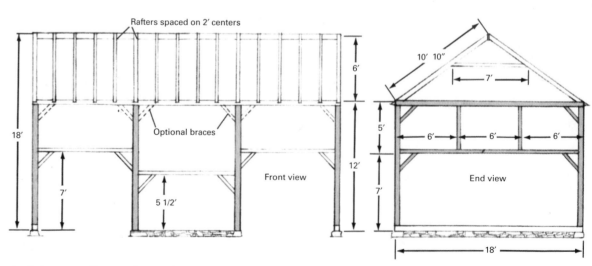

Specifications can be adjusted to suit individual needs, especially if you hew the timbers yourself, as the builder of the barn pictured here did. Before building this or any barn, seek professional advice to be sure that timber sizes and span lengths are correct for the conditions and type of wood being used. Braces are especially important. For extra strength include as many as possible.

Raising Day

1. Preservative-treated sills, already in place, are mortared to a fieldstone foundation wall. Base of wall must be below frost level.

2. Bents are assembled on raising day. Prenotched, numbered timbers are first pegged together, then braces are cut and fitted.

3. Assembled bents are moved to their proper locations and laid flat, ready to be hoisted into place by the raising crew.

4. Everyone works together to raise the bent into place. Two people check to see that the posts are seated properly.

5. The first bent propped, a second bent is raised while several people guide the fitting of the horizontal beams between.

6. Photograph shows how tenons on horizontal beams fit into mortises in posts. Joints will be pegged later.

Installing the plate

Hoisting each of the top plate beams is a two-stage task. First a beam is raised to crew members stationed partway up; they in turn raise the beam to a group on top. Several block-and-tackle devices slung from the bents can also be used. Be careful when working aloft with heavy timbers.

The finished barn

Rafters and siding are final steps. Conventional roof with ridgepole is easy to erect and economical. Use 1-in. rough-cut pine for siding.

Completing the roof sheathing and putting down shingles are the only jobs remaining. Two coats of barn red give finished structure traditional look.

Developing a Water Supply

Reaching Downward To Tap the Reservoirs Beneath Our Feet

Water is one of the elementary staples of life, and the existence of a dependable supply of drinking water is probably the single most important factor in determining whether a homesite will be livable or not. Virtually all the water we use arrives as rain and collects either on the surface of the ground or beneath it. Most of the privately owned residential water supply in the United States comes from wells. Aboveground sources, such as ponds, lakes, reservoirs, and rivers, supply the remainder, almost always for large-scale users, such as heavy industry and population concentrations in urban and suburban areas.

Digging for water is a centuries-old practice with significant sanitary benefits. Due to natural filtration, well water is relatively pure, whereas water in ponds and streams is highly susceptible to bacterial pollution from human and animal waste. But digging wells manually is hard, sweaty work and at depths greater than 10 to 20 feet can be extremely dangerous as well.

Modern methods of well construction, which rely on boring and driving equipment, water pumps, and drilling machinery, avoid most of the danger but still take time, work, and money. In addition, they remain almost as chancy as ever when it comes to striking water. Old-time dowsers and water witches—people who seem to have a special knack for locating subsurface water—are still consulted, but recourse to common sense, a knowledge of local geology, and a professional well digger's experience are likely to prove better guides. Assistance in finding and developing a well on your property can also be obtained from your state's water resources agency.

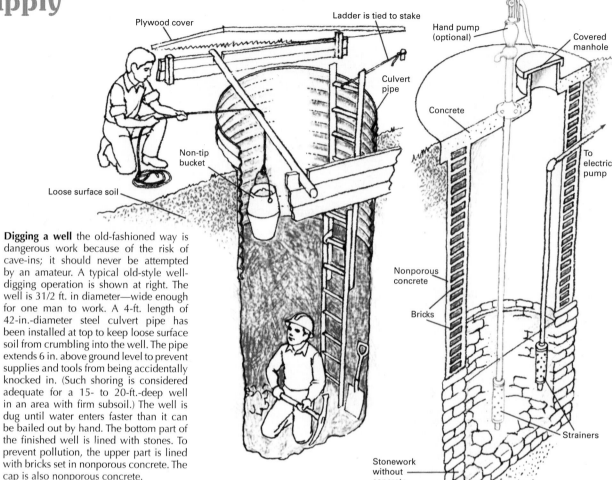

Digging a well the old-fashioned way is dangerous work because of the risk of cave-ins; it should never be attempted by an amateur. A typical old-style well-digging operation is shown at right. The well is 3 1/2 ft. in diameter—wide enough for one man to work. A 4-ft. length of 42-in.-diameter steel culvert pipe has been installed at top to keep loose surface soil from crumbling into the well. The pipe extends 6 in. above ground level to prevent supplies and tools from being accidentally knocked in. (Such shoring is considered adequate for a 15- to 20-ft.-deep well in an area with firm subsoil.) The well is dug until water enters faster than it can be bailed out by hand. The bottom part of the finished well is lined with stones. To prevent pollution, the upper part is lined with bricks set in nonporous concrete. The cap is also nonporous concrete.

Old wells were dug with a pick and shovel. When the water table was near the surface and the well shallow, a long counterweighted pole with a bucket at one end sufficed to lift the water up. For deeper wells (they were sometimes dug down 100 ft.), a windlass was used to crank up each bucketful of water. When not in use, such wells should be covered as a safety measure and to keep out dirt and debris.

Where to Find Water

Of the rain that falls on the land areas of the world, the major part collects in lakes and rivers, some evaporates, and the rest, called groundwater, filters slowly into the earth. In many areas groundwater is the most dependable water—often the only water—available.

The top of a groundwater reservoir is known as the water table, a level that moves up and down according to the rate at which water is being taken out and replenished. In some locales the water table is a few feet from the surface—a relief to well drillers; elsewhere, the table is so far down even drilling becomes impractical.

Groundwater is frequently confined within rock formations, where it forms an aquifer, or underground stream. If the aquifer originates from a high elevation, the water may be under enough pressure to bubble up spontaneously to the surface when a drill bit reaches it. This type of natural flow is called an artesian well and does not require a pump. Water tables also break the surface, creating seeps, springs, swamps, and ponds.

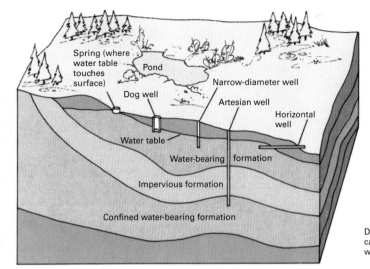

Variety of water sources (left) is equaled by the variety of ways water can be tapped. Because of the complex structure of aquifers, wells quite close to each other can nevertheless differ markedly in output.

Wells draw the water table down in their vicinity, sometimes causing neighboring wells to dry up. In the example shown below, well A was dug first, creating a dry cone-shaped volume around it. Next came well B, which produced water until well C was put in.

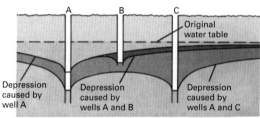

Small-Diameter Well Construction

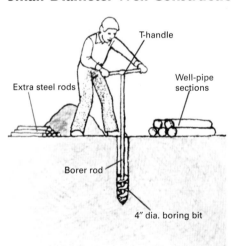

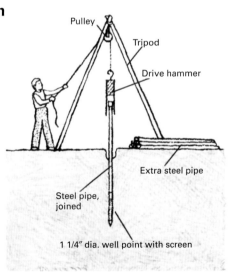

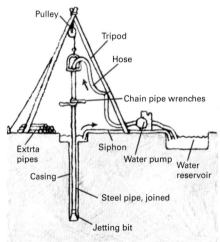

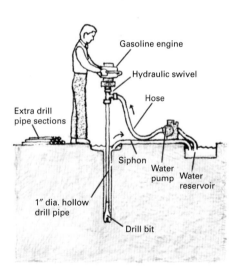

Bored well can be put in with inexpensive hand tools. First a 1-ft.-deep hole is driven with a pick or crowbar, then the borer introduced. As the borer penetrates, segments are added to its rod to accommodate increased depth. Periodically, the borer must be lifted to empty the hole of loosened cuttings. Boring is impractical for wells deeper than 50 ft. Moreover, if a large stone or a rock formation is met, the operator has to abandon the hole and start again elsewhere. After water is encountered, the well pipe and water intake are installed.

Driven well is put in by hammering a pipe directly into the earth. The point of the pipe is screened to keep dirt out, since it will serve later as a water intake. The pipe is hammered in by repeatedly dropping a heavy weight on it. Well depths of up to 150 ft. can be achieved with equipment like that illustrated. To check for the presence of water, lower a weighted string down the pipe, then raise the string and examine the end to see if it is wet. Once water is detected, drive the pipe down another 20 to 30 ft. to guarantee water supply.

Water-jetted well can be put in fairly rapidly with a pump that forces water down a pipe. The water pressure jars the soil loose and forces it up the well hole to the surface. As the well deepens, the pipe should be rotated periodically to help keep it vertical. The mud in the upward flowing water helps to line the well wall and prevent crumbling. A casing, installed as the well is being jetted, will further reinforce the wall. If no rock formation is encountered along the way, a strong pump can jet a 1-ft.-diameter well to a depth of 300 ft.

Drilled well can penetrate thousands of feet below the surface; the depth is limited only by the power of the drilling engine and the quality of drill bit used. For very hard rock, diamond-tipped bits are required. A hand-held, 3-horse-power drilling unit like the one shown can reach a depth of about 200 ft. A water pump is used to wash soil and rock cuttings to the surface and to cool and lubricate the bit. After the hole is drilled, the hole is reamed to a diameter of 3 in., and the well pipe and screen (or submersible pump) are installed.

Aboveground Storage In Pond or Cistern

Of the various types of surface water the most valuable for a home water supply is a spring. Springs can be thought of as naturally occurring artesian wells, the water being pushed to the surface by gravity. A mere trickle can support the water needs of a home if it is collected in a cistern or holding tank. A spring's flow can be measured by timing how long the spring takes to fill a 5-gallon container. For example, if the container takes 30 minutes to fill, the spring will provide 10 gallons an hour, or 240 gallons of water a day—enough to support a small homestead. Remember, however, that springs can run dry at certain times of the year.

In some areas the most practical way to obtain drinking water is to channel rain falling on a roof into gutters that lead into a cistern. In a region of moderate rainfall (30 inches per year), a roof with a surface area of 1,000 square feet will collect an average of 50 gallons of water per day, enough for a two-person household with modest water needs. Since rainfall varies over the year, the cistern must hold enough water to cover expected dry periods. For example, a 50-gallon-per-day requirement could be supported for 30 days by a cistern that is about 6 feet on each side and 5 1/2 feet deep. Cisterns up to five times this size are practicable.

For large-scale water storage a pond is usually the best alternative. Ponds are excellent for such major uses as irrigation, livestock maintenance, and fish farming. In addition, they attract and support wildlife and provide water for fire protection if located within 100 yards or so of the structure to be protected. A pond can be a simple excavated hole if the water table at the site is close to the surface, or an earth embankment can be built to collect runoff. Unless the pond is also intended for power generation (see *Waterpower*, p.98), you should not attempt to impound a running brook. (There are legal restrictions that govern the development and use of waterways, and, in addition, a large and expensive spillway may have to be constructed.)

The probability is high that water from ponds, brooks, and similar aboveground sources will not be healthy enough to drink, particularly if livestock have direct access to the water source or if the source is located in areas suffering from pollution, such as mining regions. If necessary, water can be purified with ceramic filters or by chlorination. In emergencies the water can be boiled.

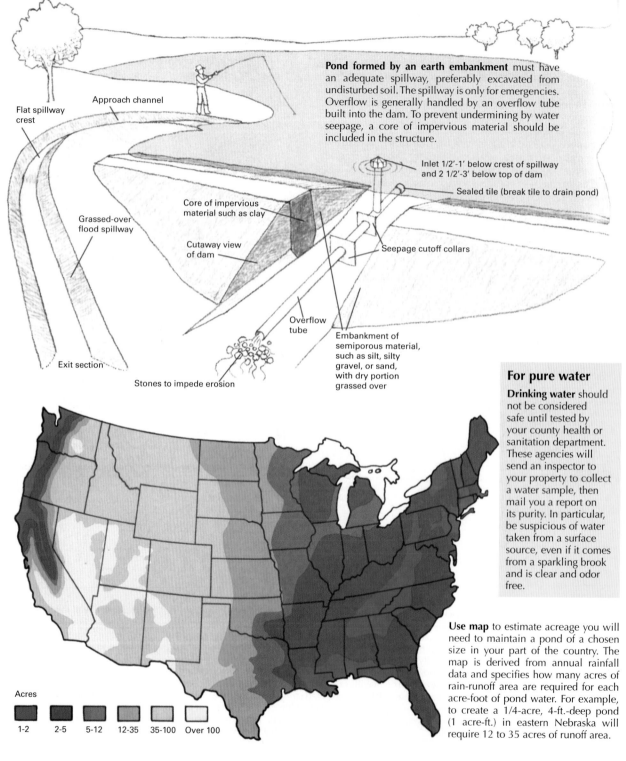

Pond formed by an earth embankment must have an adequate spillway, preferably excavated from undisturbed soil. The spillway is only for emergencies. Overflow is generally handled by an overflow tube built into the dam. To prevent undermining by water seepage, a core of impervious material should be included in the structure.

Flat spillway crest

Approach channel

Inlet 1/2'-1' below crest of spillway and 2 1/2'-3' below top of dam

Sealed tile (break tile to drain pond)

Grassed-over flood spillway

Core of impervious material such as clay

Cutaway view of dam

Seepage cutoff collars

Overflow tube

Embankment of semiporous material, such as silt, silty gravel, or sand, with dry portion grassed over

Exit section

Stones to impede erosion

For pure water

Drinking water should not be considered safe until tested by your county health or sanitation department. These agencies will send an inspector to your property to collect a water sample, then mail you a report on its purity. In particular, be suspicious of water taken from a surface source, even if it comes from a sparkling brook and is clear and odor free.

Acres

1-2   2-5   5-12   12-35   35-100   Over 100

Use map to estimate acreage you will need to maintain a pond of a chosen size in your part of the country. The map is derived from annual rainfall data and specifies how many acres of rain-runoff area are required for each acre-foot of pond water. For example, to create a 1/4-acre, 4-ft.-deep pond (1 acre-ft.) in eastern Nebraska will require 12 to 35 acres of runoff area.

Ways to Collect and Store Rainwater and Spring Water

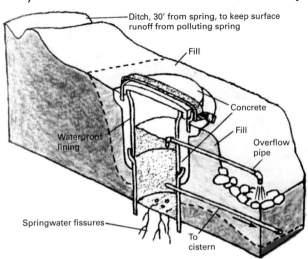

Ditch, 30' from spring, to keep surface runoff from polluting spring
Fill
Concrete
Fill
Overflow pipe
Waterproof lining
Springwater fissures
To cistern

Spring water collection structure, formed primarily of concrete, helps stabilize water flow and protects water from surface contamination. Take care when excavating to avoid disturbing the fissures; otherwise the flow can be deflected.

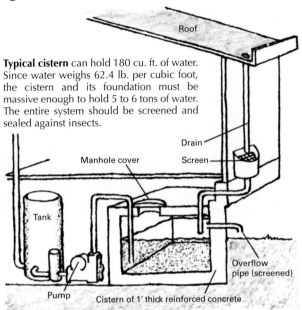

Typical cistern can hold 180 cu. ft. of water. Since water weighs 62.4 lb. per cubic foot, the cistern and its foundation must be massive enough to hold 5 to 6 tons of water. The entire system should be screened and sealed against insects.

Roof
Drain
Screen
Manhole cover
Tank
Pump
Cistern of 1' thick reinforced concrete
Overflow pipe (screened)

Springhouse is made of stone and built into the hillside to keep the interior cool in all seasons.

An old-style springhouse

Inlet from spring
Water for drinking
10" dia. vent
Milk cans
Silt-settling trough
Trough
Shelf
Cheese
12" thick stone walls
Outlet

Springhouse of the type built last century put a spring to work to keep food cool. Such perishables as milk and butter were placed in containers, and the containers were set in a trough through which cool spring water flowed, keeping the food at refrigeratorlike levels even in summertime.

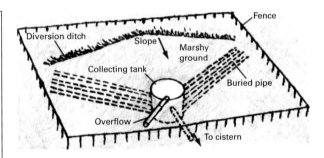

Fence
Diversion ditch
Slope
Marshy ground
Collecting tank
Buried pipe
Overflow
To cistern

Marshy area can be tapped for water with a system of perforated or open-joint pipes draining into a tank. Pipes are buried in packed gravel faced by a plastic barrier on the downslope side to help concentrate water near them.

Sources and resources

Books and pamphlets
Campbell, Stu. *Home Water Supply: How to Find, Filter, Store, and Conserve It.* Charlotte, Vt.: Garden Way Publishing, 1983.
Manual of Individual Water Supply Systems. Washington, D.C.: Environmental Protection Agency, 1987.
Matson, Tim. *Earth Ponds: The Country Pond Maker's Guide.* Woodstock, Vt.: Countryman Press, 1991.
Wagner, Edmund G., and J.N. Lanoix. *Water Supply for Rural Areas and Small Communities.* Geneva, Switzerland: World Health Organization, 1959.

Saunas and Hot Tubs

Using Warmth and Ritual For Total Relaxation

The beneficial effects of a warm bath have been recognized for thousands of years. The sauna, a hot-air bath followed by a quick cool-down, originated before the birth of Christ. In pre-Columbian North America, so-called sweat baths, remarkably similar in detail to the sauna, were a common custom among Plains Indians, and the Japanese have long practiced communal hot-water bathing. Recently, Americans have begun to take an interest in communal heat baths, primarily because of the sense of shared contentment they provide. The interest has focused on the traditional Finnish sauna, along with a new development: the hot tub.

Saunas today are much like those used in Finland for centuries. The hot tub is an American idea, conceived a few years ago by Californians who converted discarded wine vats into bathing units. Both saunas and hot tubs should be used with care, however. Hot tubs should be kept below 103°F and saunas below 170°F. Pregnant women and persons with heart conditions should avoid them altogether.

A-frame sauna is located next to a serene lake with a stunning view. Taking a sauna is not so much a way to get clean as it is a means of achieving profound emotional relaxation. The ritual of the sauna begins with a "perspiration bath" in hot dry air. Next comes a brief steaming, followed by a beating with leafy birch twigs. Then the bathers wash, plunge into the snow or into a cold lake, and dry off. The final phase is a period of rest and relaxation, preferably in the open air.

Make Your Own Hot Tub

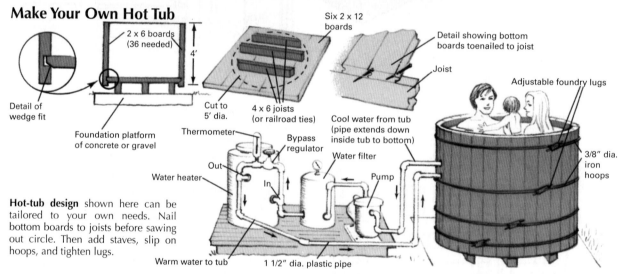

Detail of wedge fit

2 x 6 boards (36 needed)

4'

Foundation platform of concrete or gravel

Cut to 5' dia.

4 x 6 joists (or railroad ties)

Six 2 x 12 boards

Detail showing bottom boards toenailed to joist

Joist

Thermometer

Out

Water heater

In

Bypass regulator

Water filter

Pump

Cool water from tub (pipe extends down inside tub to bottom)

Adjustable foundry lugs

3/8" dia. iron hoops

Warm water to tub

1 1/2" dia. plastic pipe

Hot-tub design shown here can be tailored to your own needs. Nail bottom boards to joists before sawing out circle. Then add staves, slip on hoops, and tighten lugs.

American Indian sweat lodge

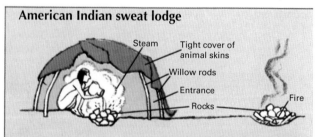

Steam

Tight cover of animal skins

Willow rods

Entrance

Rocks

Fire

Plains Indians had a kind of sauna of their own-the sweat lodge-long before Europeans arrived on the scene. Warmth was provided by hot rocks carried into the lodge. Water poured on them made steam. Like the Finns, the Indians ended the bath with a plunge into a river or a roll in snow.

The wine vat is the prototype of all true hot tubs. A tub the size shown here holds about 500 gallons, or 2 tons, of water. To sustain such a load requires strong wood and a stable foundation. For the benefit of bathers, the wood should not be resinous or splintery. Spruce or cedar are good choices, but redwood is the best.

The bottom of the tub should be as watertight as possible. Ask the lumberyard to mill either tongue-and-groove or shiplap joints on the bottom boards; then coat the joints with roofing mastic along the lower edges and nail the boards to the joists. Use 8d galvanized finishing nails. Drive them at an angle, countersink them, and top them with mastic. To make the tub sides, bevel both edges of each stave between three and five degrees off right angle and notch them near their lower ends to fit the bottom boards. Coat the outer halves of the edges and the bottom of each notch with mastic, then tap the staves in place one by one around the tub. The last stave will have to be trimmed to fit. Put the hoops loosely in place, then tighten them, starting with the lowest hoop (which is placed where the staves join the bottom).

The capacity of most home hot-water systems is too small to fill a hot tub. For continuous high temperatures and clear water while bathing, use a heater, filter, and pump, rigged as shown. These items are best purchased as a group from a supplier dealing in hot-tub equipment.

Building a Sauna

To conserve heat, a sauna should be as compact as possible, especially the bathing area. The ceiling should be low, the windows small and double paned, and the doorway low and narrow. For a quick exit in case of an emergency, have the door open outward.

Saunas are invariably made of wood. Frame construction is the most economical, but log construction is more traditional and deemed superior because of the ability of logs to retain and reradiate heat. (For log construction techniques, particularly the chinkless style often used for saunas, see *Building a Log Cabin*, pp.26–35.) For a frame sauna, start with a poured cement slab foundation, or use concrete piers and bolt the sills (large foundation lumber) onto them. Beveled siding, tongue-and-groove boarding, or plywood can be used on the exterior, with wood shingles on the roof. The wood should not be painted or varnished; instead, impregnate exterior woodwork with preservative, or use durable lumber, such as redwood. Install a minimum of 4 inches of foil-faced insulation in the roof and walls. The foil should face the sauna's interior. Since exposed metal can burn the skin, all implements and handles should be wooden, and all nails should be countersunk. Round off bench edges with sandpaper, and use duckboards-movable slatted flooring—to protect feet from a cool floor.

A wood-burning stove is traditional, but an oil, coal, gas, or electric heater can be used instead. (To install a wood stove, see *Heating With Wood*, p.86.) The heating stones around the stove should be dense enough to store a large amount of heat and should not crack when heated; cobblestone-sized pieces of granite or lumps of peridotite, a dark igneous rock, are often used.

The high air temperatures in a sauna are bearable because the air is fairly dry and because bathers can take the heat in stages, first on the bottom benches where temperatures are lower, then on the higher benches. For breathing comfort, water should be ladled onto the stones now and then to add a bit of moisture to the air. After 15 or 20 minutes the bather cools off in an icy lake, new fallen snow, or a cold shower.

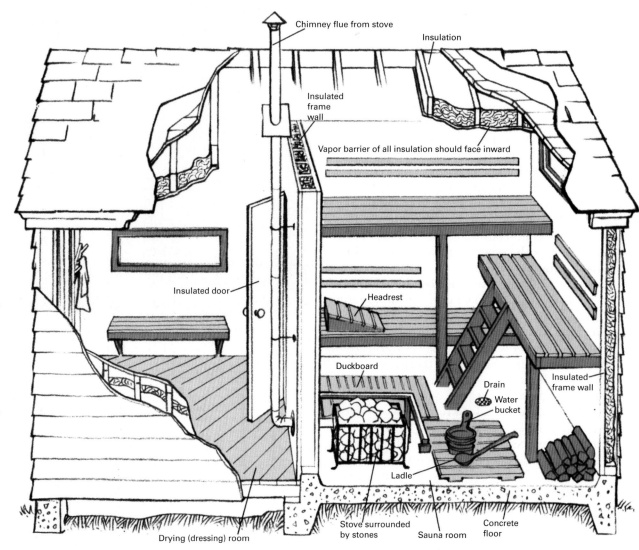

Chimney flue from stove

Insulation

Insulated frame wall

Vapor barrier of all insulation should face inward

Insulated door

Headrest

Duckboard

Drain

Water bucket

Insulated frame wall

Ladle

Drying (dressing) room

Stove surrounded by stones

Sauna room

Concrete floor

Sources and resources

Books and pamphlets

Cowan, Tom, and Maguire, Jack. *Spas and Hot Tubs, Saunas and Home Gyms*. Saddle River, N.J.: Creative Homeowner, 1988.

Herva, M. *Let's Have a Sauna*. Washington, D.C.: Sauna Society of America, 1978.

Nelson, Wendell. *Of Stones, Steam and the Earth: The Pleasures and Meanings of a Sauna*. New Brighton, Minn.: Finnish America, 1993.

Sherwood, Gerald, and Stroh, Robert C., eds. *Wood Frame House Construction: A Do-It-Yourself Guide*. New York: Sterling Publishing, 1992.

Interior walls of the sauna should have a natural timber surface, and neither oil, varnish, paint, nor wax should be applied to them. The wood selected for the benches and interior paneling should be durable and should show high resistance to splitting and splintering in order to withstand the wide swings in temperature to which it will be subjected. Eastern white pine or sugar pine are often used for the interior paneling, since both have a pleasant resinous aroma that adds to the sauna experience. For the benches, however, a nonresinous wood should be selected because contact with the resin is irritating to the skin; white cedar or western red cedar are good choices.

Saunas often have auxiliary rooms in addition to the main sauna room; the sauna shown here has a dressing room attached. The extra room has supplementary uses, such as providing a place to hang up the wash or acting as a guest room for overnight visitors. Benches in the sauna can be any size or shape imagination suggests but should always be built to provide at least two distinct bathing levels, and preferably three, on which bathers can recline full length. Bench seats should be slatted to improve heat circulation and designed to permit access to the floor beneath them so that cleaning will be easy. If the benches are movable, cleaning becomes simpler yet.

Sanitation

Disposing of Waste Without Wasting Water

Modern sanitation methods, such as flush toilets, septic tanks, leach fields, and sewerage treatment plants, have come to be taken for granted. Not only is their vital role in preventing the proliferation of contagious bacteria all but forgotten, but their imperfections are often ignored, particularly the enormous amount of water they consume. In addition, the sheer volume of waste that now pours into our lakes and rivers is beginning to overtax the ecosystem, destroying wildlife and polluting the waters.

In recent years attention has begun to focus on new kinds of waste disposal devices that greatly reduce water consumption and at the same time convert the waste into nonpolluting material. Some new types of toilets have cut water usage to 2 quarts per flush, others go further, doing away with the flush method entirely. Among the latter are toilets that incinerate the refuse, toilets that partly decompose the refuse through anaerobic (oxygenless) digestion—outhouses are a somewhat primitive example—and toilets that turn the refuse into high-quality compost via aerobic decomposition. Some of the newest approaches are finicky to operate, and others are costly to install; but most hold promise for saving water and energy while reducing pollution.

Sources and resources

Books and pamphlets
Hartigan, Gerry. *Country Plumbing: Living With a Septic System.* Putney, Vt.: Alan C. Hood Publishing, 1986.
Kruger, Anna. *H Is for EcoHome: An A to Z Guide to a Safer, Toxin-Free Household.* New York: Avon, 1992.
Wagner, E.G., and J.N. Lanoix. *Excreta Disposal for Rural Areas and Small Communities.* Geneva: World Health Organization, 1958.
Whitehead, Bert. *Don't Waste Your Wastes—Compost 'Em: The Homeowner's Guide to Recycling Yard Wastes.* Sunnyvale, Tex.: Sunnyvale Press, 1991.
Wise, A.F., and Swaffield, J.A. *Water, Sanitary and Waste Services for Buildings.* New York: Halsted Press, 1995.

Primitive but functional outhouse is still standing from the early 1900s. Familiar crescent moon ventilating hole once meant "For ladies only."

Incinerating Toilets

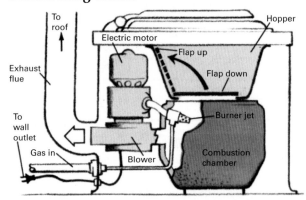

Refuse is converted to sterile, odorless ash in incinerating toilet. When top lid of seat is lifted, flap beneath the seat opens and a cycle timer is set. When lid is closed again, the flap drops down and refuse burns for about 15 min., after which unit is cooled by blower. Burner is fueled by natural or LP (liquid propane) gas. Hopper should be washed once a week and ash removed from combustion chamber with a shovel or vacuum cleaner. Toilet is effective but relatively costly to run and cannot take overloading—as might happen if the owner were to host a large party.

Pit Privies

Pit privy, or outhouse, must be located where it will not pollute the water supply. Place it downhill from any spring or well and be sure that the water table, even at its highest level, is several feet below the bottom of the privy's pit. A pit with the dimensions shown will last about five years if used continuously by a family of five. Once the pit fills up, it must be covered and the privy moved to a new site. Though safe and sanitary if properly constructed, pit privies tend to be smelly. They are also uncomfortable to use, especially in winter.

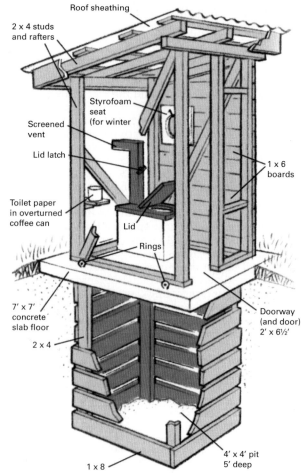

Privy is built on precast concrete slab to stop rodents and divert rain from pit. Rings cast in slab permit entire structure to be hauled by tractor to a new site when pit becomes full.

Composting Toilets

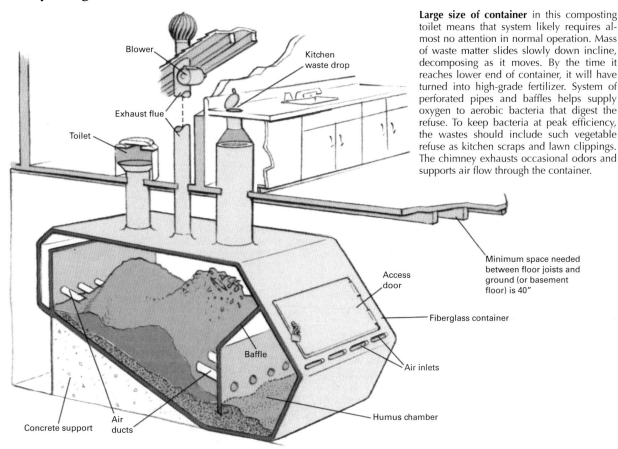

Large size of container in this composting toilet means that system likely requires almost no attention in normal operation. Mass of waste matter slides slowly down incline, decomposing as it moves. By the time it reaches lower end of container, it will have turned into high-grade fertilizer. System of perforated pipes and baffles helps supply oxygen to aerobic bacteria that digest the refuse. To keep bacteria at peak efficiency, the wastes should include such vegetable refuse as kitchen scraps and lawn clippings. The chimney exhausts occasional odors and supports air flow through the container.

Unlike outhouses, composting toilets are just about odorless. Their chief requirement is a steady supply of air to maintain the aerobic (oxygen-loving) bacteria that feed on the refuse inside the fiberglass composting container. These bacteria function best between 90°F and 140°F—temperatures considerably higher than normal room temperature. A properly designed container can lock in the warmth generated by the bacteria themselves, helping to maintain the ideal temperatures.

In principle, a composting toilet does not require energy to operate. In practice, however, this is likely to hold true only in warm climates. In colder areas, during the winter, the composter will generally draw warm air from the house interior, venting it to the outdoors. In extremely cold regions, such as Maine, northern Minnesota, and Alaska, the composter may even require an auxiliary heater to maintain the proper composting

temperature. Occasionally, a blower must be added to the exhaust flue to prevent odors from seeping into the house via the toilet seat or kitchen waste access port.

A composting toilet must usually be supplemented with a small standard septic tank and leach field to handle greywater (water from the bathtub, washer, or sink). Generally, a composting system is most economical where water is in short supply or where soil and topography combine to limit the effectiveness of more conventional waste disposal systems.

To offset the rather high cost of commercial models, some homeowners have tried building their own composting containers out of concrete block or other material. The job is difficult and can lead to problems, such as compost that does not slide properly and solidifies in the tank. Should that happen, the container must be broken open and the compost chipped out.

Other Toilets

A number of new waste-disposal devices have recently appeared on the market. Most are for special needs, such as a vacation home or in arid climates.

Chemical toilets employ a lye solution to destroy bacteria; the waste must be emptied and disposed of periodically. They are safe but have a tendency to give off an offensive odor.

Freezer toilets are odor free but require an energy-consuming compressor to freeze the waste; like chemical toilets, they must be emptied at intervals.

Vacuum toilets are fairly expensive. They work like waterless flush toilets, using special plumbing and a pump that sucks the waste into a collecting chamber.

Nonaqueous flushing systems imitate conventional toilets, but instead of water they recycle treated oil. Like vacuum toilets, these systems are expensive.

Greywater disposal

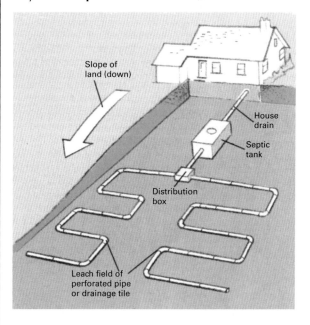

Typical septic system has a 200-cu.-ft. holding tank and a 120-ft. leach field. The field consists of pipe made of clay tile or perforated fiber buried 1 1/2 to 3 ft. deep. The tank can be concrete, fiberglass, or asphalt-lined steel, with an access port to pump out accumulated sludge. Dimensions of system can be reduced one-third if waterless toilets are used. Excavation for system can be by hand, but the job is more easily handled with mechanized equipment, such as a backhoe.

Fireplace Construction and Design

The Welcoming Hearth: Rumford Rediscovered

The theory of fireplace design is almost entirely the work of a single man-Benjamin Thompson, better known as Count Rumford, an American Tory of the colonial period who eventually fled to England. Rumford's findings, particularly his discovery that a wide, shallow firebox radiated the maximum amount of heat into a room, revolutionized fireplace design in the early 1800s. The introduction of cast-iron stoves, however, followed later by an almost universal conversion to oil, gas, or coal central heating, changed the role of the fireplace from that of a vital home-heating device to a mere status symbol; along the way many of Rumford's precepts were forgotten or ignored: in an age of limitless energy fireplace efficiency no longer seemed important.

Nowadays, Rumford's ideas are enjoying a renaissance. Although the Uniform Building Code restricts total adherence to Rumford's principles, it is still possible to construct a fireplace that comes close to the energy-efficient ideal. With a Rumford-style fireplace the fellowship and security that a blazing open hearth inspires can be enjoyed at a minimum cost and with a maximum of home-heating warmth.

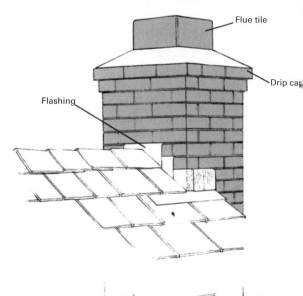

How a Fireplace Works

Fireplaces are basically hollow towers constructed out of strong, long-lasting, heat-resistant materials, such as stone, brick, adobe, or metal. They can be designed in a myriad of shapes and sizes; but no matter what they look like on the outside, all fireplaces are virtually alike inside, consisting of four basic units. These are the base, firebox, smoke chamber, and chimney. The hollow core of the chimney is called the flue.

The base is simply the platform upon which the upper sections of the fireplace rest. It should be solid and massive in order to support the weight of the heavy masonry above it. The firebox, built atop the base, is where the fire is set. Most fireboxes are lined with a special type of brick, called firebrick, which will withstand high temperatures. The design of the firebox should allow heat generated by the fire to be radiated outward into the room, while at the same time preventing heat from escaping up the chimney in the form of hot gases. The funnel-shaped smoke chamber is erected directly above the firebox. It serves as a transition unit, channeling the smoke from the fire below into the flue above. The final unit, the chimney, carries the smoke and hot gases away and passes them into the atmosphere.

In order to work efficiently, the firebox, smoke chamber, and chimney should be built in correct proportion to each other. The smoke chamber should have a smooth interior surface and should slope inward from its base toward the chimney opening at an angle no greater than 30 degrees from vertical. The area of the chimney opening itself should be about 10 percent of the area of the firebox opening. In addition, the size of the fireplace must fit the proportions of the room. Air drawn by the fire has to be replaced. In a small room the strong draft of a large fireplace will suck warm air out of the room and send it up the chimney. To replace this warm air, additional air will be drawn into the room, most likely from outdoors through cracks around the windows and doors. Not only is this wasteful but the room may actually be cooler than it would have been with a smaller fireplace that drew less air.

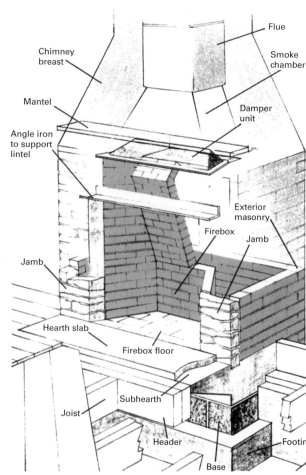

Traditional-style fireplace (right) has the shallow heat-radiating firebox characteristic of the Rumford design. This feature is the main reason for its excellent heating ability. The firebox and other elements of the Rumford design, including a wide smoke chamber, can be incorporated into almost any style of fireplace from modern to traditional. In general, the width of the front opening should be restricted to no more than 42 in.; anything wider will result in lower efficiency for most rooms.

Sources and resources

Books and pamphlets
Brann, Donald R. *How to Install a Fireplace*. Briarcliff Manor, N.Y.: EasiBild, 1978.
Edwards, Alexandra. *Fireplaces*. San Francisco: Chronicle Books, 1992.
Manroe, Candace O. *For Your Home: Fireplaces and Hearths*. New York: Little, Brown & Co., 1994.
Orton, Vrest. *The Forgotten Art of Building a Good Fireplace*. Dublin, N.H.: Yankee Books, 1969.

Planning a Rumford Fireplace

Determine the size and overall shape of your fireplace by making drawings and scale models of various design possibilities, then taking the time to analyze each. The location of a fireplace should not interfere with household traffic, and its exterior should harmonize with the surroundings. It is also important to realize that many fireplace components—bricks, flue tiles, dampers—are manufactured in standard sizes and that your designs must take these fixed dimensions into consideration. For example, the Rumford-style fireplace whose construction is shown here uses a standard 10-inch-wide cast-iron damper and standard-sized terra-cotta flue tiles; neither was available in Rumford's day.

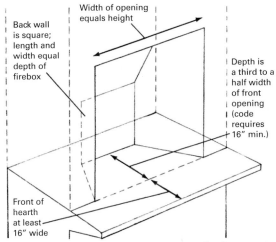

Rumford firebox (above) is designed for maximum radiation. Front opening is square. Ideal firebox depth is one-third the width of front opening but at least 16 in. deep in order to satisfy Uniform Building Code requirements.

Smoke chamber (right) should begin at least 8 in. above lower edge of lintel. Damper is centered over firebox floor so that smoke can travel vertically into smoke chamber. The chamber itself tapers gradually to the same dimensions as the chimney flue opening.

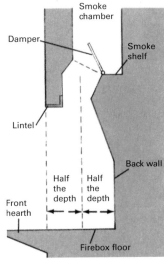

Tools and materials

Tools for fireplace building are the same as those used in other stone and concrete work. Some of the more specialized tools are shown below. Among materials you will need are cement, sand, and concrete block for the footing, base, and hearth; firebrick for the firebox; ordinary red brick for the smoke chamber, exterior, and chimney; and terra-cotta flue tile for the chimney interior. Some special mortar and concrete mixes are also necessary (see chart at right).

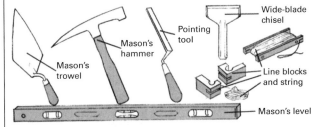

Building a fireplace requires only a few basic masonry tools.

The bricklayer's art

Practice applying mortar and raising walls before actually starting to build. Sequence shows proper way to "butter" the end of a brick with mortar for firm bond. Dip bricks in water before buttering them. Remember that mortar is caustic and abrasive. It should not be worked by hand or come in contact with bare skin.

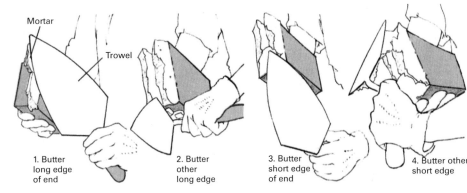

1. Butter long edge of end
2. Butter other long edge
3. Butter short edge of end
4. Butter other short edge

Mixing guide for concrete and mortar

Uses	Portland cement	Sand	Gravel	Hydrated lime
Footings	1	3	4	
Hearths	1	2	3	
Laying brick	1	6		1
Laying stone	1	3		
	1	4 1/2		1/2
Smoothing inside of smoke chamber	1	4		1

Chart shows correct proportions for mixing both concrete and mortar to suit different applications. Two blends are shown for laying stone; the second one is a stiffer mix than the first, but both are of equal strength. For all formulas mix the dry ingredients first, then add water until smooth.

Raising a brick structure

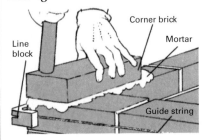

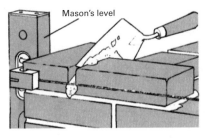

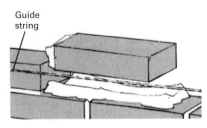

1. Lay corner bricks first. Set each one atop mortar base so that outside corner touches plumb line. Hold brick in place with one hand; level it by tapping the edges with trowel handle.

2. Set second brick in place on mortar base 3/8 in. from corner brick. Align by tapping with trowel handle. Carefully fill gap between bricks with mortar, taking care not to disturb corner bricks.

3. Lay succeeding bricks in a similar fashion, but butter one end of each before installing it. Work from corners toward the center; keep bricks in line with guide string held by line blocks.

From Footing to Flue: Building a Fireplace

Exact fireplace dimensions are impossible to specify, since each must be designed for the room it is to heat. Typical hearth openings, however, are 32 to 38 inches square, and from these initial opening dimensions the rest of the fireplace can be designed proportionately according to the rules and considerations given on pages 62 and 63. Strict adherence to Rumford's principles is not necessary in order to derive most of the increased heating ability of a Rumford-style fireplace. Wherever possible, choose dimensions that will allow you to use bricks and concrete blocks without extra shaping.

Use high-temperature mortar for the firebox sides and back. Make the mortar by mixing 1 pound of fireclay per 6 ounces of water, or buy premixed air-setting refractory cement at a boiler or kiln repair shop.

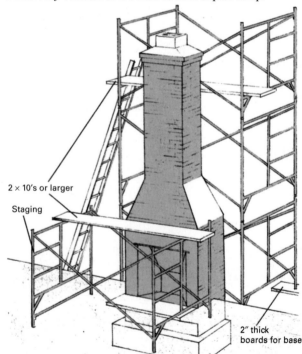

Rent modular staging from a construction supply center. When putting it up, make sure it is level and plumb. Support the legs on wide boards 2 in. thick. Check often to detect sagging.

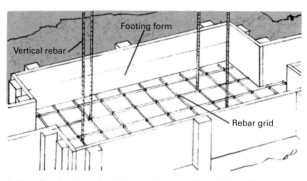

1. Install rebar (steel reinforcing bar) grid and, if code requires, vertical rebar as well. Make grid by wiring lengths of 3/4-in. rebar together to form 8-in. squares. The concrete footing should be 12 in. thick and extend 8 in. beyond dimensions of chimney breast on all sides. Footing must lie below frost line.

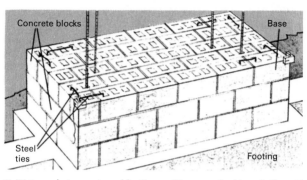

2. Distance between top of footing and bottom of subhearth (Step 3) should be divisible by thickness of concrete blocks used for base plus their mortar joints. Construct base atop footing. Drop plumb lines; use line blocks to keep courses level. Install 1/4-in. horizontal steel ties every 18 in. between courses.

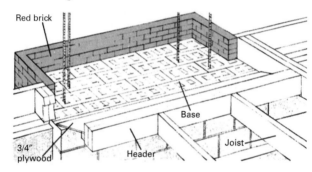

3. Subhearth must extend at least 16 in. in front of firebox. Prepare for its pouring by laying two courses of red brick around exterior of base. Joists and headers serve as remainder of form with 3/4-in. plywood as bottom. Concrete blocks that enclose rebars should be packed with concrete; fill others with rubble.

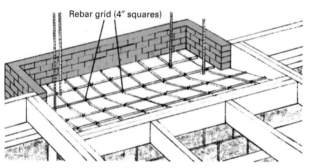

4. Allow 24 hours for mortar on double layer of bricks to set. Lay down grid of 1/2-in. rebar, elevated with brick scraps so that mesh will be in center of slab. Pour concrete 4 in. thick at thinnest (interior) edge, then level and smooth. Upper surface of subhearth should come no higher than level of subfloor.

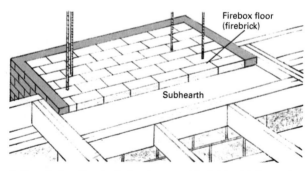

5. Form firebox floor by laying dampened firebricks tightly together on bed of mortar spread on rear of subhearth. Do not mortar joints between bricks. Ideally, top surface of firebrick should be flush with finished house floor. Front hearth slab, installed after all work is done, can rise 1 in. higher to trap ashes.

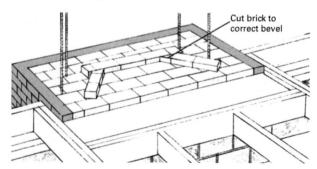

6. Mark firebox dimensions on firebox floor and begin laying firebrick for firebox sides and back. Cut bricks to size with mason's hammer or use a power saw with a masonry blade. Lay one course at a time, working from the back toward each side. Mortar joints must be less than 1/4 in. thick.

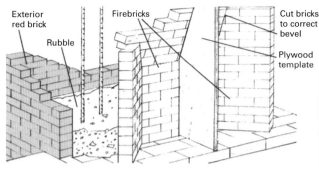

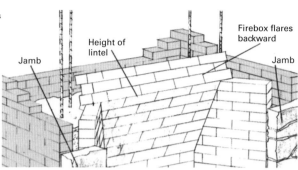

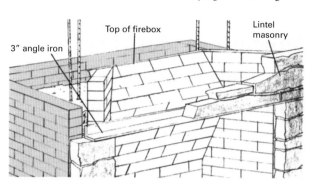

7. Use plywood template cut to angle of firebox back in order to lay slanted bricks. Hold template in place against each brick as it is laid: mortar must harden somewhat before template can be removed. Continue to build up exterior brickwork, filling in around and behind firebox with rubble.

8. To accommodate standard 10-in.-wide damper, flare top of firebox backward, beginning above lintel height, so that basic Rumford design is not affected. Next, build up jambs on each side (stone can be used instead of brick). There must be at least 8 in. between the firebox sides and the house walls.

9. Lay up jambs so they are level at lintel height, then install 3-in. angle iron to support lintel masonry. Continue to lay material above the lintel until it is on the same level as the top of the firebox. Smooth the interior surface of the lintel masonry with a coating of mortar.

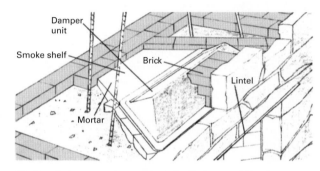

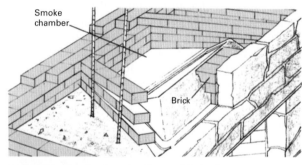

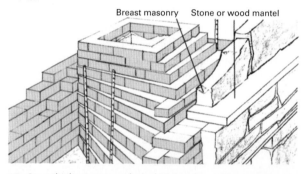

10. Install damper unit on top of the firebox and lintel masonry. Position it so that smoke can rise vertically into chimney when damper is open. Build up the exterior masonry and rubble until both are even with top of firebox, then smooth the area behind firebox with mortar to form smoke shelf.

11. Build smoke chamber of ordinary brick. Set the courses stepwise so that each extends about 1 in. beyond the course below and tapers to the size and shape of the chimney flue. Be sure to allow clearance for damper to function without binding. Smoke chamber should slope inward at no more than 30° angle.

12. Smooth the interior of smoke chamber with mortar as you proceed. When front slope provides enough space, install mantel atop lintel masonry, and construct chimney breast behind mantel. Breast masonry should be same material as jambs and lintel if exposed or ordinary brick if hidden behind wall.

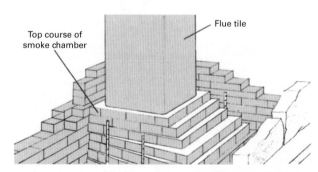

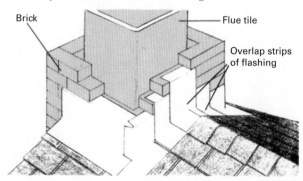

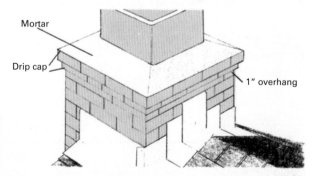

13. Spread mortar on top course of smoke chamber and install flue tile. Check that tile sides are plumb, shimming them with brick scraps if necessary. Scrape away any mortar inside flue. Lay up courses of exterior brick, setting in the sides until 6-in. gap surrounds flue. Fill gap with rubble.

14. Continue building chimney by adding additional flue tiles and bringing up exterior masonry and rubble fill. Where chimney penetrates roof, install metal flashing between courses, overlapping each piece 4 in. Copper is the best material for flashing, although galvanized steel or aluminum may be used.

15. Finish chimney with drip cap made by overlapping two courses of brick so that each overhangs the one below by 1 in. Spread mortar on top; smooth and bevel surfaces so they shed water. For protection from cross drafts chimney height should be 3 ft. higher than any other point within a 10-ft. radius.

Stone Walls and Brick Pavements

Mortarless Masonry: The Natural Alternative To Concrete and Tar

Stone is one of nature's finest building materials. It is plentiful, free, attractive, and enduring. Long before mortar was developed, stone was used to build walls, walks, roads, towers, and monuments. Some of these structures, like Stonehenge in England or the great monolithic statues of Easter Island, have withstood the ravages of time for millennia. In America mortarless stone construction is chiefly associated with New England. There, colonial farmers made a virtue of necessity by using stones from their rocky fields for everything from walls to root cellars.

The principles of mortarless, or dry wall, construction have remained unchanged over the centuries: walls must be perfectly vertical, their individual stones should overlap each other, and the base of the wall should be as wide or wider than the top. Materials have remained largely unchanged, too, although brick has been added to the dry mason's repertoire and is especially useful for walkways, driveways, and patios.

Almost any size, shape, or variety of rock can be used for dry wall construction. Old foundations, loose rubble from an abandoned quarry, a rock-strewn field, or the bed of a stream are likely sources of building stones. If it is not your property, be sure to get the owner's permission before removing any rock. And never attempt to quarry rock without professional help; rock is massive (170 pounds per cubic foot for granite) and can break unexpectedly.

Old stone wall is constructed from fieldstone. The turnstile allows ramblers to explore the moors more easily.

Stone masonry is an art when practiced by a dedicated craftsman. In the richly variegated wall shown above, stones have been carefully placed for strength as well as beauty: the largest rocks are at the base with stone decreasing in size as the wall gets higher. Like all dry walls, it has a certain amount of flexibility, or "give," making it relatively immune to frost heaving.

Tools and Supplies

The tools and equipment needed for dry wall stonemasonry tend to be simple and rugged. Most, if not all of them, will already be part of your home stock of tools; others can be purchased as the need arises: there is little point in investing in special chisels and a set of steel wedges, for example, if you are not going to split stone.

Whatever tools you buy, be certain their quality is high. Rocks can be enormously heavy, and sudden, unexpected failure of a piece of equipment can cause serious injury. You should also be sure to purchase and use the three items most connected with safety: heavy-duty steel-toed work shoes, a pair of sturdy leather work gloves, and safety goggles with plastic lenses to wear whenever you chip, shape, or otherwise dress stone.

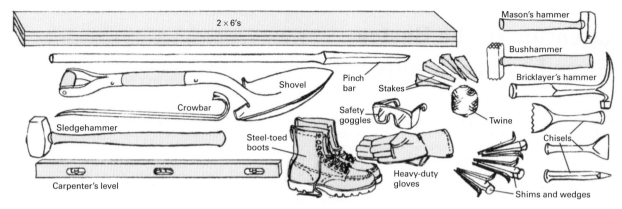

Most stonemason's tools are available in any good hardware store. Sturdiness is vital, but avoid tools that are too heavy for you.

Moving and Lifting Large Stones

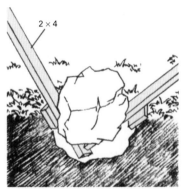

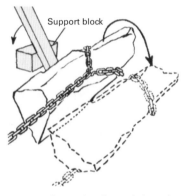

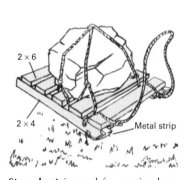

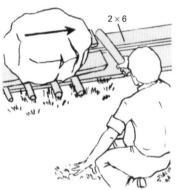

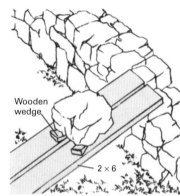

Pair of 2 × 4's, worked in opposition, are employed as levers to raise large stones. Pry first with one, then the other, until one can be used as a ramp. Do not stand in hole with rock when raising it.

Large rocks can be dragged short distances with a chain hooked up to a winch, vehicle, or draft animal. After attaching chain, flip rock over; tension of chain will keep rock from digging into earth.

Stone boat is good for moving large rocks. Make the boat's bed of 2 × 6's, the runners of 2 × 4's. Line the front of each runner with a metal strip. Tie boulders to the bed to prevent them from rolling off.

Boards and rollers serve as a temporary roadway over limited distances. Pick rollers up from rear, lay them down in front of advancing rock. Effort can be saved by levering the rock forward from behind with a 2 × 4.

Stones can be rolled up ramp to wall top. Wooden wedges keep stones from slipping back. Make ramp out of long boards so that the slope will be gradual. Before moving a stone, measure it to be sure it will fit wall.

Shaping Stone

Shaping, or dressing, stone can be tough, exhausting work and should be avoided if possible. Moreover, the rough, natural surface of a rock will add much to a wall's character and beauty. Occasionally, however, a bit of dressing is essential. Use a chisel to chip off an unwanted protuberance on a flat side, a mason's hammer to dull a jagged edge, or a bushhammer to powder a point. Brute force blows with a sledgehammer can pulverize a lump or even an edge, but they may also split the rock. If a rock is too large to handle, it can be split. Whenever you split or shape rock, be sure to wear your goggles—a flying stone chip can blind you.

To split a rock that has a stratified (layered) structure, mark a line along the grain, then chip on the line with the sharp end of a mason's hammer until a crack starts to form. Widen the crack gradually by driving wedges into it at several points. When the crack is wide enough, pry it apart with a crowbar.

Granite and other rocks with uniform textures are difficult to split. Start by drilling holes about 6 in. apart along the split line with a narrow-bladed chisel that is rotated after each blow. Next, hammer thin wedges into the holes. Follow these with progressively larger wedges until the rock cracks in two.

Attention to the Basics Gives Lasting Results

There are three types of dry walls: freestanding, breast, and retaining. Breast walls are simply rock pavements laid into sloping ground to prevent soil erosion. Retaining walls are similar to freestanding walls except that they require dug-in foundations and are open on only one side—the other side butts against an earth terrace. Both retaining walls and dry walls are held together by friction and gravity. Friction is maximized by laying each stone so that it makes the greatest possible surface contact with the greatest number of stones around it. Since gravity works in only one direction—straight down—the wall must be perfectly vertical. If it is, the overlapping weights of the individual stones will effectively knit the structure together along its base line. If the wall is out of plumb and leans, it eventually will be reduced to a pile of rubble. When constructing either a freestanding or retaining wall, set up stakes and stretch a line between them at the planned wall height. Along with a carpenter's level, the string and stakes will act as guides to keep the wall even and vertical.

Principles of a Freestanding Dry Wall

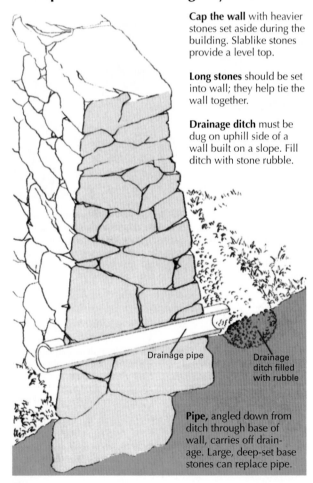

Cap the wall with heavier stones set aside during the building. Slablike stones provide a level top.

Long stones should be set into wall; they help tie the wall together.

Drainage ditch must be dug on uphill side of a wall built on a slope. Fill ditch with stone rubble.

Drainage pipe

Drainage ditch filled with rubble

Pipe, angled down from ditch through base of wall, carries off drainage. Large, deep-set base stones can replace pipe.

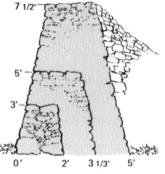

Interior rocks are always level

Cross section shows rocks placed so that each major stone bears on at least two others beneath it. Note chunky rocks wedged inward by small slivers driven beneath them. Use small stones in interior only; set largest stones at base.

Proper wall width depends on height. Minimum width of base is 2 ft. For walls higher than 3 ft., width of base should be two-thirds of height, and wall should be tapered upward symmetrically so that center line is plumb. For attractive appearance top the wall with flat slabs.

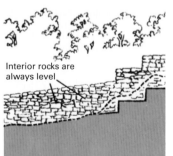

Keep wall level across uneven ground. Cut trenches through small rises or build up base to fill small depressions. Wall running up a gentle slope can have a sloped top, but interior rocks must be laid level. When slope is steep, wall should be built in stepped sections, each with a horizontal top.

Retaining and Breast Walls

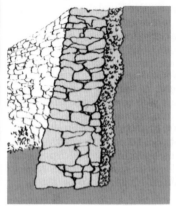

Retaining walls buttress earth terraces. They are wider than other dry walls with bases that are set well into the ground (2 to 3 ft.). Occasionally they are designed to lean slightly into the terrace. If a retaining wall is more than 2 ft. high, its base should be wider than its top but only on the open side. Pebbles between soil and wall help water drain through openings. Pipes or drainage holes in the wall should angle down toward the open face and be designed to prevent undermining of the wall by runoff. The ground in front of the wall should slope down to help carry off water.

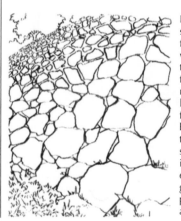

Breast walls help stabilize soil on slopes. Build wall from bottom up. If the wall is so high that the entire slope cannot be paved from ground level, pave as much as you can, then allow several weeks for bottom section to set before doing higher portions. Use chunk-type rocks set level with each other in holes spaced as close to each other as possible. Fill gaps with soil topped with pebbles. Grass seed can be added.

Sources and resources

Books
Adams, J.T. *The Complete Concrete, Masonry, and Brick Handbook.* New York: Chapman & Hall, 1983.
Concrete and Masonry Construction. Washington, D.C.: U.S. Department of Labor, 1993.
Fields, Curtis P. *The Forgotten Art of Building a Stone Wall.* Dublin, N.H.: Yankee Inc., 1971.
Kern, Ken, and others. *Stone Masonry.* New York: Scribner's, 1977.
Sunset Books, eds. *Walks, Walls and Patio Floors.* Menlo Park, Calif.: Lane Publishing, 1993.
Vivian, John. *Building Stone Walls.* Charlotte, Vt.: Garden Way Publishing, 1979.
Periodicals
Gluckin, Neil Dana. "A Legacy of Brick Underfoot," *Americana,* 29 West 38th St., New York, N.Y. 10018. March–April 1978.

Paving With Brick or Stone, Alternatives to Blacktop

Driveways and walks made of inlaid brick or stone have proved their worth over the centuries. They are durable, attractive, and, unlike blacktop or concrete, allow the ground to breathe: moisture and nutrients can seep down to the roots of trees, and earthworms and other subsoil creatures can continue to live undisturbed.

Brick is probably the easiest material to work with. Standard 8- by 4- by 3-inch bricks can be laid in an almost infinite variety of patterns or employed to fill precise areas with special motifs. In addition, the flat, even shape of the bricks allows tight gap-free packing.

Cobblestones—rocks smoothed by streams into roundish chunks the size of baseballs—are more lasting than bricks but make a very rough surface that is hard on the feet and almost impossible for bicycles. Belgian blocks and other dressed stone blocks are durable but expensive. Flagstones, useful and attractive for walks and patios, are too fragile for driveways.

Mortarless paving relies on a smooth underbase and the friction of individual pieces rubbing against each other to stay together. The edges of such paving should be held by some kind of frame, otherwise the outermost stones will gradually tumble away. In colonial times slabs of stone sunk upright were used to line pavements. Cinder-block slabs and railroad ties have been used in more recent days. For walks, patios, and short driveways, 1 × 4's, treated to prevent rot, will do the job. Moreover, these same edging boards can double as building frames.

Building sand makes an excellent underbase. The sand suppresses weeds, improves drainage, and infiltrates cracks, helping to lock the bricks together, yet letting them move with the earth. The result is a lasting, maintenance-free driveway.

Laying a brick walkway

1. Lay out a width of paving at one end of the walk by setting a row of bricks side by side. Drive stakes, each a frameboard width out, on either side of bricks. Measure distance between the stakes, then drive another pair at the other end of walk the same distance apart. Stretch twine between each stake and its opposite at other end of the walk on the outside surface of each stake.

2. Dig along twine lengths, making vertical side trenches about 6 in. deep. Drive a series of stakes along the inside edge of each twine. Nail frameboard to the inside faces of the stakes, then dig out center of area.

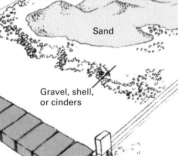

Stake
Twine
Sand
Gravel, shell, or cinders
Row of bricks marks width of driveway

Tamp down sand vigorously after it is poured

Smoothing board with arched bottom

Frameboard

Stakes to which frameboard is nailed

3. Fill excavation 1 1/2 in. deep with gravel, shell, or cinders. After tamping, add 2 in. of sand or use 4 in. of sand alone. Smooth the sand with an arched board—it improves drainage by making the walk higher in the center. When cutting the arch in the board, allow 1/2 in. of crown for each 2 ft. of pavement width.

4. Start at one end of the excavation and begin laying bricks, always working from one side to the other. Tap each brick into place with a hammer cushioned by a block of wood. The bricks should fit snugly and be even with each other. Odd shapes in a pattern are filled with pieces split from a whole brick. Use a pointed tool to score a line on the brick, then tap the piece with a hammer. Like scored glass, it should snap cleanly.

5. When bricks are in place, cover surface with 1/2 in. of sand, sweep it into the cracks, and hose down with a fine spray of water from a hose held some distance away. If necessary, repeat the process until all cracks are filled. Fill in and cover trench and framing with soil. Stay off the paved surface for several weeks, then repeat sweeping and spraying process. In shady locations weeds can be discouraged by allowing moss to grow in the cracks. Herbicides can also be used, but do not install plastic sheet under the brick to inhibit weeds. It will interfere with drainage and increase the chances of frost damage in colder areas.

Interlocking paving patterns are the most durable. Straight, or running, bond (left), herringbone (center), and basketweave (right) are classic examples. For driveways, two rows of thick, flat-topped rocks are sometimes added as auto wheel tracks.

Gravel and stone pavements

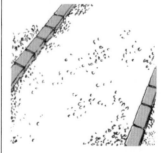
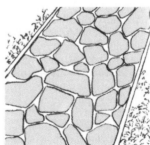

Gravel (or pebble, shell, or cinder) paving should be at least 5 in. thick. Usually wood or concrete framing is used, but occasionally the paving is edged with bricks buried vertically in the ground so that only 1 to 2 in. of each brick extends above the surface. Edging helps keep the gravel in place.

Stone paving is laid like brick. Use slabs or chunks 3 to 4 in. thick that have at least two parallel flat sides. Thick cobbles and big irregular chunks require an extra-thick sand base. Match adjacent rocks carefully to fit as closely as possible. Never lay a stone with a sharp bump on exposed side.

Fences

Building Fences for Beauty As Well as Practicality

The poet Robert Frost took exception to the old country notion that "Good fences make good neighbors." But there is no disputing the fact that good fences can be useful and attractive. Fences keep livestock in and pests out; they prevent small children from wandering off; they serve as boundary markers, windbreaks, sunshades, and privacy screens. And while some fences are merely utilitarian, others are true adornments: a rambling split-rail fence or an old-fashioned zig-zag can be every bit as pretty as the countryside in which it is set.

Choosing a Fence to Fit Your Needs

Choosing a fence is an exercise in common sense. First, you should decide exactly what functions the fence is to serve, then you should consider such factors as cost, appearance, and durability. If the main purpose of the fence is privacy, it should be tall and free of gaps. So-called stockade fences made of upright poles fulfill this requirement as do tightly spaced picket fences and fences of woven redwood slats. If you want to enclose a play area, the fence should be strong enough to re-sist the wear and tear of children and tall enough and tightly woven enough to prevent their squeezing out or climbing over. It should also be free of dangerous projections and open enough to let you keep an eye on the kids. A welded wire fence would meet these requirements.

In rural sections barbed wire is an economical way to fence in livestock. The barbs are dangerous, however, and their use is forbidden in most residential areas. A better choice, especially for smaller lots in built-up locales, would be a split-rail fence. Not only will it do the job, but it is safe and attractive as well. In addition, split-rail fences are easy to erect, require little lumber, and are longer lasting and more maintenance free than most fences. (A picket fence, for example, requires peri-odic painting and is relatively fragile.)

Fences require planning. To calculate the amount of wire or boards you will need and the number of fence posts that you will have to set, mark off the corners of

the fence line with stakes and measure the distances between; the sum of these measurements is the amount of fencing you must obtain. In order to figure the correct number of posts, allow one for each corner and a pair for each gate. Along a straight fence line posts are usually spaced at 16-foot intervals for woven wire, at 12- to 14-foot intervals for barbed wire, and at 5- to 8-foot intervals for board or rail fences, depending on the lengths of lumber available. When laying out a wire fence around a curve, space the posts more closely.

Take special care when building a fence along a prop-erty line. Unless you and your neighbors agree on legal provisions, you will have to make certain that the fence is on your own land. Zoning laws often stipulate that a professional boundary survey be made.

Choosing a Fence to Fit Your Needs

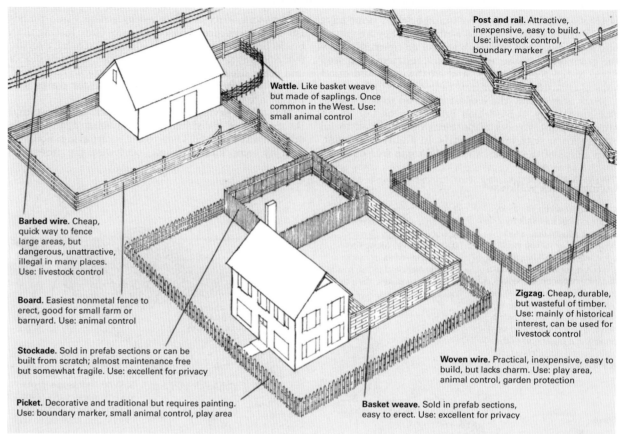

Post and rail. Attractive, inexpensive, easy to build. Use: livestock control, boundary marker

Wattle. Like basket weave but made of saplings. Once common in the West. Use: small animal control

Barbed wire. Cheap, quick way to fence large areas, but dangerous, unattractive, illegal in many places. Use: livestock control

Board. Easiest nonmetal fence to erect, good for small farm or barnyard. Use: animal control

Stockade. Sold in prefab sections or can be built from scratch; almost maintenance free but somewhat fragile. Use: excellent for privacy

Picket. Decorative and traditional but requires painting. Use: boundary marker, small animal control, play area

Zigzag. Cheap, durable, but wasteful of timber. Use: mainly of historical interest, can be used for livestock control

Woven wire. Practical, inexpensive, easy to build, but lacks charm. Use: play area, animal control, garden protection

Basket weave. Sold in prefab sections, easy to erect. Use: excellent for privacy

Fence styles have evolved throughout the centuries into a panorama of varieties designed to suit specific needs.

Life expectancy of fence posts

Wood type	Untreated	Treated
Birch	2-4 yr.	10-20 yr.
Black locust	20-30 yr.	Not needed
Cedar	15-20 yr.	20-30 yr.
Douglas fir	3-7 yr.	15-18 yr.
Elm	4 yr.	15 yr.
Hickory	5-7 yr.	15-20 yr.
Maple	2-4 yr.	15-20 yr.
Oak	5-10 yr.	15-20 yr.
Osage orange	20-25 yr.	Not needed
Pine	3-7 yr.	20-30 yr.
Redwood	10-15 yr.	20-30 yr.
Sassafras	10-15 yr.	20-25 yr.
Spruce	3-7 yr.	10-20 yr.

Making Post-and-Rail Fences

The familiar split-rail fence is an updated version of the rustic post-and-rail fences built by homesteaders out of timber cleared from their lands. Like the picturesque zigzag fence, a split-rail fence can be built by anyone who has timber and some simple tools.

Split-rail fences are economical to construct: they require relatively little lumber, they can be built from wood you harvest yourself, they require no hardware to hold them together, and they can be left unpainted—weathering will eventually turn the wood a soft silver-gray that blends unobtrusively with the landscape. Any of the woods shown in the chart on page 70 can be used, although the difficulty of splitting certain woods, particularly elm, can add considerably to the work.

When splitting rails, you will find it easier to work with green freshly cut logs rather than seasoned timber. Also, since wood tends to split more readily in cold weather, try to do your rail-splitting in the winter and early spring. You will need an 8-pound splitting maul or sledgehammer and three or four sturdy wedges. Old-fashioned wooden wedges as well as wedges made from steel can be used, but you will need at least one steel wedge in order to make the initial opening. Poles can be employed rather than split rails if plenty of 3- to 4-inch-diameter timber is available; the fence will still be attractive, and a good deal of labor can be saved. Milled 2 × 4's also can be used as rails, but the fence will cost more and lose much of its rustic charm. When working with either split rails or poles, use a saw to taper the ends of the rails so they will fit side by side in the slotted posts. It is not necessary to taper the 2 × 4's; simply place the rail ends one on top of the other in the slots.

For posts try to select a longer-lasting variety of wood, and be sure to treat the belowground portions by soaking them in creosote or other commercial preservative, such as pentachlorophenol. Digging post holes is usually done by hand with a clamshell-type post-hole digger, but gasoline-powered augers are also available on a rental basis. In soft ground, fence posts can be sharpened with a chain saw and simply hammered directly into the earth with the aid of a post maul or sledge.

The number of tiers of rails that you should install depends on the use to which the fence will be put. For a boundary fence or for penning such small animals as sheep, a two-tiered fence is sufficient. Larger livestock require three to four tiers. The vertical distance between rails, and between the bottom rail and the ground, should be about 15 inches. Some livestock owners staple a strand of barbed wire across the top of the posts, inside the fence, to keep heavy animals from rubbing against rails and dislodging them or loosening the posts.

Splitting the rails

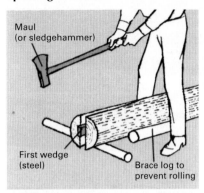
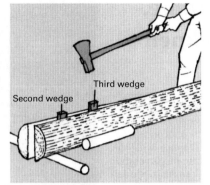
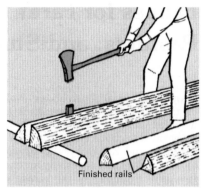

1. Use straight-grained logs with 9- to 12-in. diameters. Drive wedge into butt end to open a 2-ft.-long crack.

2. Lengthen crack by driving additional wedges until log splits along entire length. Work to keep crack centered.

3. Lay split trunks flat side down. Then split each half into quarters (finished rails) by repeating Steps 1 and 2.

Setting the posts and assembling the fence

1. Use 5- to 6-in.-diameter logs for posts. To make slots for rails, bore groups of 2-in.-diameter holes in upper parts of logs, and trim away waste with a heavy chisel and mallet.

2. Post holes should be 2 1/2 ft. deep or one-third length of post, whichever is greater. Set post in hole on gravel base. Fill with layers of earth and gravel; concrete capping is optional.

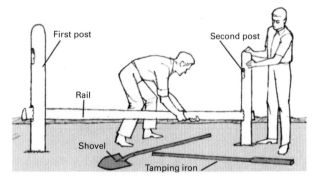

3. Set the first post, and tamp soil firmly around it using an iron bar or tamping iron. Place second post in its hole; fill but do not tamp. Install rails between posts.

4. Tamp firmly around the second post. Continue assembling the fence by setting the next post loosely in place, installing the rails, then tamping the soil around the post, and so on.

Fences for Farm, Home, Pastures, and Stockpen

Many traditional fence styles evolved as by-products of the land-clearing process, which produced enormous amounts of timber suitable for fencing. In heavily wooded sections of the country, such as Tennessee, Virginia, and Kentucky, the zigzag rail fence was the most popular type, especially for enclosing pastureland. Beautiful examples of the zigzag still stand in Cades Cove in the Great Smoky Mountains National Park. For small stockpens designed to contain sheep or pigs, portable wattle fences were common. Built of saplings, shoots, or branches, the wattle fence was a holdover from the settlers' European heritage, since fence timber had long been scarce in the Old World. The stockade fence was originally a protective structure around forts and settlements; the relatively flimsy modern version serves mostly as a fence for privacy.

Barbed wire and, later, woven wire replaced wood for use by settlers who reached the treeless prairie states. Not only was barbed wire less expensive than scarce lumber, it was far easier to install. It came into such widespread use among cattlemen and sheepmen that historians claim its invention in 1870 deserves more credit than the six-gun for the taming of the West.

Post and rail wood fencing systems use the least amount of wood, making them well suited for larger, more open areas of land. Zigzag fencing is made of overlapping tiers of split rails with a 1-ft. overhang. The rails zigzag, creating a 120-degree angle at each bend. No hardware is needed for zigzag fences, but they use much more lumber than post and rail fencing.

A variety of wooden fences

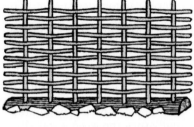

Wattle fence is constructed of woven saplings. Uprights are set in base of flattened logs. Fence can be permanent or built in portable 8-ft. panels. Pile stones on base logs for added stability.

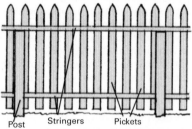

Post   Stringers   Pickets

Picket fence is made with 2 × 4 stringers nailed to 4 × 4 posts. Pickets are 1 × 3 slats nailed to stringers at the top and the bottom. The tops of pickets are generally pointed for style as well as to shed water.

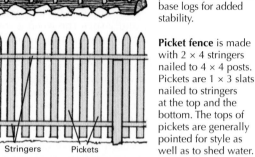

Stringers

Stockade fence is built like picket fence, but stakes are longer and more closely spaced. Stakes can be round or half-round. Stakes can be nailed to stringers or woven together with wire.

The art of stringing barbed wire

Barbed wire is used for fencing in horses and cattle. Popular types of wire are 12-gauge (heavyweight), with 4-point barbs, and 14-gauge (lightweight), with 2-point barbs. Use heavyweight wire for small areas, since small fences receive more pressure from animals; use lightweight wire for open pastures.

Barbed wire is stretched between posts, then stapled in place. A reel is needed for safety and to keep the wire from tangling; a stretching device makes the wire taut. Installers should wear thick gloves and should stand with a fence post between themselves and the wire during the stretching operation.

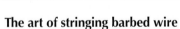

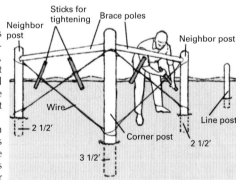

1. Corners are braced by fitting poles and wires between corner posts and neighbors on either side. Wires should be twisted tight. Corner posts are set deeper than others—about 3 1/2 ft.

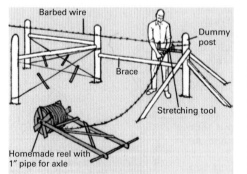

2. Fencing is stretched between corners, using stretcher tool or block and tackle, then stapled to line posts. Temporary brace and dummy post (set 18 in. deep) support corner post during stretching.

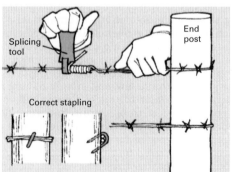

3. Final step is to splice each wire around last post. Each strand is drawn tight against post, stapled in place, then wrapped back on itself and twisted several times, using pliers or splicing tool.

Gates and Stiles
For Getting Through

Fences, whose primary job is to bar passage, must still be designed to permit legitimate movement. Gates of one sort or another are the most common solution to the problem, but for livestock fences around large pastures, an old-fashioned stile—a device that bars animals but lets people through—can suit the purpose admirably.

Decorative gates for yard and garden fences may need to be only wide enough for a person to pass through, but

a minimum width of 4 feet is required for gates that must accommodate such devices as lawnmowers, wheelbarrows, and garden machinery. Gates in farm and pasture fences should be 12 to 16 feet wide in order to admit livestock and large machinery. Regardless of size, the gate and its support must be strongly built, since it will receive more wear and tear than any other part of the fence. To prevent sagging and lessen stress on the far end of a gate, a diagonal brace of wood, wire, or steel cable is usually installed between the gate's low corner at the hinge side and its high corner at the far end. Gateposts must be sturdy, firmly set, and absolutely vertical. To keep them from loosening, shore them with lumber, strategically placed boulders, or poured concrete slabs.

Stiles: an old idea that still works

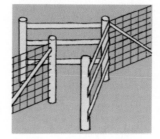 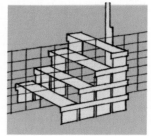

Zigzag stile is built into fence. Openings in stile should allow a man through but bar livestock.

Stepladder stile can be added to completed fence. Single set of horizontal boards acts as stairs both up and down.

Planting sturdy gateposts

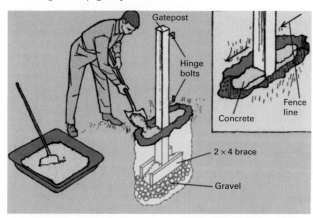

Gatepost at left is braced by 2 × 4's at base and cap of concrete at top. Nail 2 × 4 braces to bottom of post, set in hole with braces parallel to fence line, and fill with earth to within 1 ft. of surface. Then pour slab, using about 1 cu. ft. of concrete.

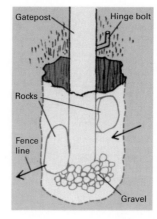

Boulder-braced gatepost (right) is kept in place with rocks—the bigger the better. Place them firmly against the post parallel to the fence line.

Lightning protection

Wire fences with nonmetal posts are a lightning hazard unless metal ground rods are installed. Make ground rods from 8- to 10-foot lengths of 1-inch-diameter pipe. Attach them within 150 feet of each end of the fence and at 300-foot intervals in between. The rods should extend 6 inches above the fence posts and be sunk into the ground far enough to be in constant contact with moist soil. Attach the ground rods to the wire side of the posts.

Ground rods safeguard people and animals against lightning.

A strong and simple gate

Heavy-duty gate, 6 ft. wide, is made of 1 × 6's fastened together with 3/8-in.-diameter carriage bolts. Sandwich three horizontal members between cross braces and vertical end boards. Use heavy steel strap hinges to attach the gate to the post, and string wire diagonally from the top of the gatepost to the end of the gate. Install a turnbuckle in the wire to adjust tension. Gate can be doubled in size by increasing the length of each horizontal board and adding a second pair of cross braces and end boards.

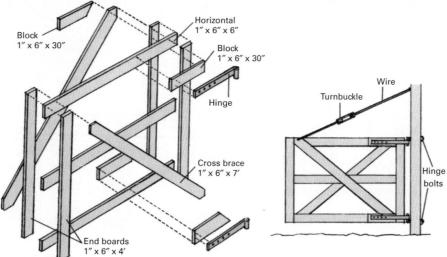

Sources and resources

Books and pamphlets
Barnett, Jim. *Walks, Walls and Fences*. Saddle River, N.J.: Creative Home-owner, 1996.
Fences and Gates. Menlo Park, Calif.: Sunset-Lane, 1996.
Martin, George A. *Fences, Gates and Bridges: A Practice Manual*. Brattleboro, Vt.: Alan C. Hood, 1992.
Snow, Diane. *How to Design and Build Fences and Gates*. San Francisco: Ortho Books, 1985.

73

Part Two

Energy From Wood, Water, Wind, and Sun

The era of cheap and abundant energy is recognized to be over.
—James Schlesinger, Former Secretary of Energy

The energy joyride—that brief delusion of 20th-century man that the supply of cheap fuel was limitless—came to a sudden stop in 1973 with the Arab oil embargo and subsequent price rises. But long before then, farsighted individuals had been advocating a change to what have come to be called alternate energy sources: waterpower, wind power, solar energy, wood, and other nonfossil fuels. Conservation was one reason, saving money was another, but equally important were ecological considerations, for the growing use of oil and coal was polluting the earth, the air, and the oceans. *Energy From Wood, Water, Wind, and Sun* is both an overview and a detailed look at small-scale applications of these "new" sources of energy. The techniques needed to use them in the home are described as well as the methods for determining if a particular system—be it wood stove, waterwheel, windmill, or solar heater—makes good economic sense for the individual homeowner.

Making Your House Energy Efficient

Energy-Saving Measures That Cost Least

The most effective way to save money on fuel bills is to use less fuel. At one time this philosophy was taken as a matter of course in America. Heavy shutters helped homeowners keep their houses warm in winter, cool in summer. Shrubbery was planted with an eye to protecting the home from weather and not used merely for decoration. Chimneys ran through the center of the house rather than along the exterior. Homes were compact, not sprawling, and designed to draw family members together not only for conversation but also to share body heat. In many farm homes even animal heat was used occasionally by sharing living quarters with a goat or cow, or by housing large animals in a space alongside or beneath the family's living quarters. The need to save fuel influenced customs and manners too. Bundling, the practice of permitting unmarried couples to occupy the same bed without undressing, allowed courtships to proceed with a minimal cost in firewood.

With the advent of the energy crisis, many old practices are being revived. These techniques, when combined with modern insulation and weather stripping, allow us to immunize our homes against the vagaries of the weather to a degree unimagined by our ancestors.

Sources and resources

Books and pamphlets

Davis, Joseph C., and Walker, Claxton. *Wage the Energy War at Home*. White Plains, N.Y.: Emerson, 1978.

Energy-Efficient Windows. Washington, D.C.: U.S. Department of Energy, 1994.

Guide to Making Energy-Smart Purchases. Washington, D.C.: U.S. Department of Energy, 1994.

Residential Solar Heating Collectors. Washington, D.C.: U.S. Department of Energy, 1994.

Tomorrow's Energy Today. Washington, D.C.: U.S. Department of Energy, 1994.

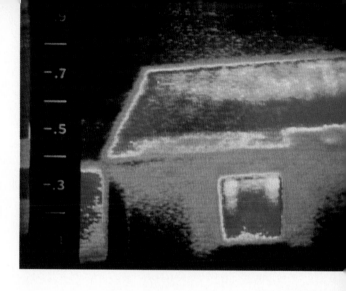

Thermographs of your house will show you where heat is being lost and how great the loss is. Bright yellow areas are locations of greatest heat loss, while red, light blue, and dark blue indicate progressively less loss. Typically, the poorly insulated roof shows up as a major source of leakage. Thermographs are taken at night to avoid misleading effects due to daylight, and a professional firm must be hired to take them because of the high cost (many thousands of dollars) of the special infrared scanner that is used. If you are planning to have new insulation and weather stripping installed in your home, ask the contractor if he will provide a thermograph. Some companies use before-and-after thermographs as a diagnostic tool and may include them free of cost.

Where heat leaks out and cold leaks in

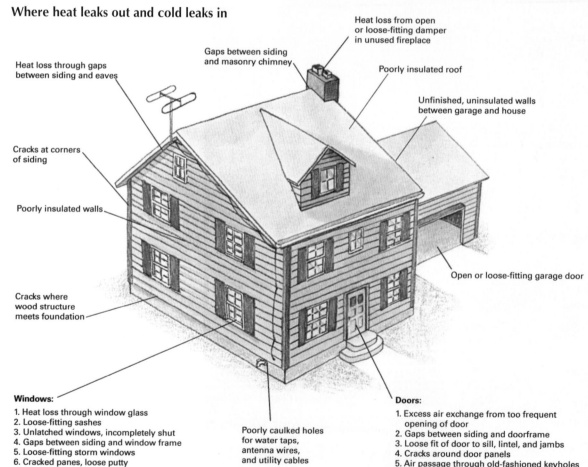

Heat loss through gaps between siding and eaves

Gaps between siding and masonry chimney

Heat loss from open or loose-fitting damper in unused fireplace

Poorly insulated roof

Unfinished, uninsulated walls between garage and house

Cracks at corners of siding

Poorly insulated walls

Cracks where wood structure meets foundation

Open or loose-fitting garage door

Windows:
1. Heat loss through window glass
2. Loose-fitting sashes
3. Unlatched windows, incompletely shut
4. Gaps between siding and window frame
5. Loose-fitting storm windows
6. Cracked panes, loose putty

Poorly caulked holes for water taps, antenna wires, and utility cables

Doors:
1. Excess air exchange from too frequent opening of door
2. Gaps between siding and doorframe
3. Loose fit of door to sill, lintel, and jambs
4. Cracks around door panels
5. Air passage through old-fashioned keyholes

Reducing Air Infiltration

Every house has gaps and cracks through which outdoor air can enter and indoor air escape. In most houses air exchange takes place at a rate of one to two changes in an hour. Inevitably, this turnover of air causes a substantial loss of heated air in wintertime.

Caulking and weather stripping are the basic means for reducing this loss. Properly applied, they can lessen the air exchange rate by 50 percent and cut fuel bills by 5 to 20 percent, depending on how leaky your house is.

Caulking is used to seal construction cracks in the body of the house, such as those between window frame and siding. The usual way to apply caulking is with a caulking gun loaded with a cartridge of caulking compound. When the trigger is pressed, a continuous bead of compound is squeezed out, like toothpaste from a tube. The compound is also sold in a ropelike strip that can be pressed into place. Caulking is not a modern development. In pioneer days homesteaders would plug leaky cabins with such materials as moss, mud, clay, and pitch-impregnated rope. Today's caulking compounds are superior. They are easier to apply, last longer, and insulate better. Oil-based compounds are still very common. Others include acrylic latex types that permit cleanup with water before they set. Butyl compounds are more flexible and stick to more materials.

Weather stripping is used to seal gaps between moving parts, such as those between a window sash and frame, and at door closures. To minimize wear, match the weather stripping to the motion of the parts. For compressive contact, as in a door closing, use felt or foam. For a sliding motion select a tough plastic or metal strip. Whatever type you buy, be sure it is thick enough to fill the gap. Foam stripping is available with a wood backing or with a self-stick adhesive backing. Where considerable compression is likely, as in a front door closure gap, use an open-cell foam, such as urethane. For light compression use a closed-cell type, such as vinyl. Adhesive-backed weather stripping bonds best when the temperature is above 50°F. During cold weather warm the surface to which the stripping is to be applied with a heat lamp or hair dryer. In some cases inexpensive felt stripping can be used for sliding as well as compressive contact. Where sliding motion is involved, the felt must be mounted carefully so that contact pressure is adequate but not excessive, since friction shortens the felt's useful working life. Felt stripping is usually held in place by tacks or staples. Wherever possible, with any type of stripping, make a trial fit with a short length before doing the complete job. Check that the seal is snug enough to block drafts but not so tight that the window cannot open or the door catch fail to hold.

Caulking

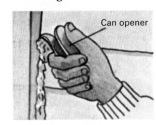

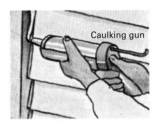

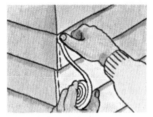

Before caulking, clean away any crumbling old caulking, flaking paint, and dirt with either a putty knife or the point of a can opener.

Apply caulking in continuous bead, working it into cracks. To flow freely, caulking must be warm. In winter keep it indoors until you use it.

Rope-type caulking is less messy than cartridge caulking and does not require a gun to apply. Press caulking firmly into cracks.

Stuff large gaps more than 1/2 in. wide with oakum, fiberglass insulation, or other insect-proof material before sealing with caulking.

Weather stripping

Windows can be sealed against the weather in a number of ways. The most effective method is to tack specially designed strips of spring metal in the channel between sash and jamb. You can also nail rolled vinyl along sash border. Adhesive-foam strip can also be attached along border; it is simple to install but should not be used where window sash rubs against window frame.

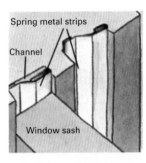

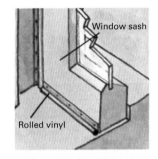

Doors as well as windows can be weatherproofed by various methods. Adhesive-backed foam along the jamb is easy to install but wears out quickly. Longer lasting is a strip of foam rubber with wood backing nailed to fit snugly against the door when closed. More durable yet is a strip of spring metal.

Maximum toughness is a requirement for weather stripping put in between door and threshold. A sweep nailed to the door bottom works well if there is no carpet or rug to interfere with it. More troublesome to attach are channels of metal with vinyl inserts that you can screw either to the threshold or to the door bottom to seal space between door and threshold. Unless the threshold is worn out or absent entirely, it is preferable to attach a channel to the door bottom.

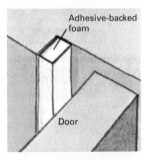

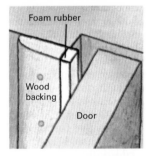

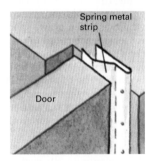

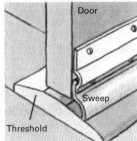

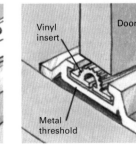

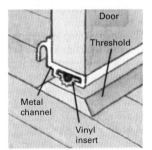

Keeping Heat In (And Cold Out)

One of the most effective ways to save energy in the home is by adding insulation. The concept is simple: keep the flow of heat through walls, ceilings, floors, and roofs to a minimum. As the chart shows, different materials have a wide range of insulating abilities. Among traditional building materials, only wood—and that in thicknesses found in log cabins—is an effective insulator. The

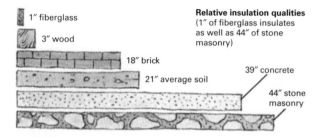

1″ fiberglass

Relative insulation qualities (1″ of fiberglass insulates as well as 44″ of stone masonry)

3″ wood

18″ brick

21″ average soil

39″ concrete

44″ stone masonry

chart also indicates that stone masonry is a particularly poor insulator; a castle may be magnificent to look at, but it is a chilly place in which to live.

Because heat rises, the attic and roof are the first targets for insulation. Next in importance are walls and windows, then crawl spaces and basements. Insulating materials are rated in terms of their R value: the higher the R value, the more insulation they give. Typically, R-30 insulation might be used for an attic and R-20 insulation for the outside walls. However, the optimum values for your house can depart significantly from these. When selecting insulation, a key point to be aware of is that doubling the amount of insulation (using R-60, for example, instead of R-30) will not double fuel savings. More likely you will achieve barely enough savings to compensate for the cost of the added insulation.

When putting in insulation, it is important to install a vapor barrier to prevent moisture from condensing in the insulation. Blankets (rolls of insulation) and batts (precut lengths of blanket) often come with a vapor barrier already attached in the form of a waterproof layer of plastic or aluminum foil. Always install the barrier so that it faces toward the interior of the house. In older homes a vapor barrier can be created by applying two coats of paint to the inside of walls to be insulated, and sealing penetrations. If there is wallpaper, remove it before painting.

Floors and walls

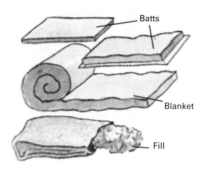

Batts

Blanket

Fill

Insulation comes in different forms for different purposes. Batts and blankets fit well between joists and studs; loose fill and pumped-in foam are used for areas more difficult to reach.

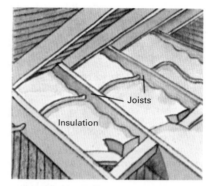

Joists

Insulation

To insulate attic floor, select batts or blankets so that they fit snugly between attic joists. Place batts with vapor barrier face down. Be sure not to cover any attic vents or light fixtures.

Joist

Fill

Loose fill works well on attic floors. Use a board or garden rake to spread it evenly. If joists are boarded over, hire a contractor to drill holes into boards and blow fill into spaces between joists.

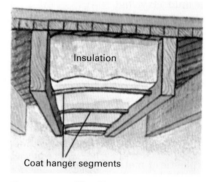

Finished homes with wood-frame walls can be insulated with loose fill or foam that is blown or pumped in through holes drilled into outside walls. This job is best handled by professionals.

Insulation

Coat hanger segments

Floors over cold cellars are worth insulating. Press batts or blankets between joists, vapor barrier facing up, and secure with wire mesh or pieces of coat hanger cut to fit between joists.

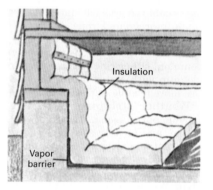

Insulation

Vapor barrier

Crawl spaces can be insulated with batts or blankets. Note: Because of possible frost heaving, always provide proper perimeter drainage.

Windows

Shutters are a traditional means for containing house heat. Leave them open during daylight hours so that sunlight can get in; close them at night to keep heat from radiating out through windows. Slatted shutters are used in summer for shade.

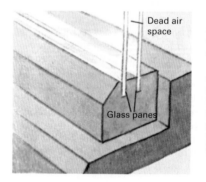

Dead air space

Glass panes

Double-pane windows (and storm windows fitted over existing windows) reduce heat loss by creating a layer of dead air between the panes that acts like insulation. For maximum benefit, windows should fit tightly and joints should be fully weatherproofed.

Pipes, ducts, and heaters

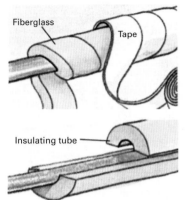

Fiberglass

Tape

Insulating tube

Hot-water pipes to distant faucets often waste heat. Wrap pipes with 1/2-in.-thick fiberglass and seal with plastic tape or else install ready-to-use foam-type insulating tubes with self-sealing aluminum backing. Insulation also protects pipes from freezing. If used on cold-water pipes, it will keep water cool in summer and stop pipes from sweating.

Duct

Fiberglass

Mask to protect against fiberglass particles

Exposed heating and air-conditioning ducts in unused cellars or attic spaces raise fuel bills unnecessarily. To cut down on the waste, first seal joints and other leaky spots with aluminum-foil tape or silicone caulk. Then cover ducts with 2 in. of blanket-type fiberglass or similar insulation.

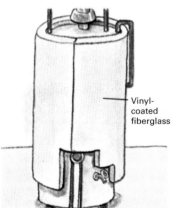

Vinyl-coated fiberglass

Hot-water heaters can waste fuel the year round. Special insulating material of 2-in.-thick fiberglass with a vinyl outer coating should be used. Wrap entire heater in material except for bottom and controls. Complete water-heater insulation kits are available that can be slipped on, then trimmed to size.

Heat-Saving Vestibules

For years vestibules have been looked on solely as repositories for umbrellas, galoshes, dirty boots, old toys, and snow-covered children's togs. Lately, they have been rediscovered as the heat-conserving structural devices they were originally meant to be, and many owners of homes that lack vestibules are having them installed or building them onto their houses themselves.

A vestibule saves heat and increases the comfort of your house in two ways. First, it acts like an oversize storm door to provide a barrier between the front door and the outside. Second, it serves as an air lock, cutting to a minimum the transfer of cold air indoors as you enter or leave the house. And the same qualities that make a vestibule an efficient heat saver in winter also conserve energy in the summer, when the air conditioner is on. As an added bonus, a well-designed vestibule is an attractive addition to any home.

If you are thinking of adding on a vestibule, design it to blend in with the overall look of the house. The vestibule should have room for a bench and enough space for coats, overshoes, and other such items. Otherwise it need not be large—in fact, the smaller it is, the more efficiently it functions as an air lock.

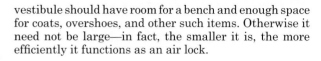

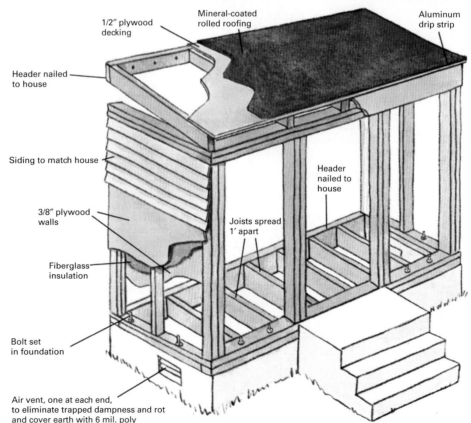

1/2″ plywood decking

Mineral-coated rolled roofing

Aluminum drip strip

Header nailed to house

Siding to match house

3/8″ plywood walls

Fiberglass insulation

Joists spread 1′ apart

Header nailed to house

Bolt set in foundation

Air vent, one at each end, to eliminate trapped dampness and rot and cover earth with 6 mil. poly

This version of a vestibule uses 2 × 4's for structural members. Inside dimensions are 40 in. by 84 in. Prefabricated door and window units will save time and work. You can use a conventional storm door with a small window on each side or a fenestrated door with matching stationary windows, as in the picture. Door is hung on studs made of doubled 2 × 4's. A solid masonry foundation extending below the frost line is essential. The depth of the frost line for your area can be obtained from a local weather bureau. In many localities you can simply dig a trench the width of the vestibule wall and fill it with concrete. The foundation should protrude at least 8 in. above the ground. Install wiring before putting in inside wall.

Protecting Your Home With Trees and Earth

Winter winds, like a forced-air cooling system, can cause substantial heat loss from a house. The loss is due to various effects: lowered air pressure, conduction, and evaporative cooling. These combine to produce a temperature drop called the windchill factor. The chart at right shows how large the factor can be. For example, if during January the average outdoor temperature in your area is 10°F, an average wind speed during the same period of 10 miles per hour will make it seem like –9°F—a net difference of 19 degrees. If your house stands fully unprotected from the wind, the drop of 19

degrees that it is therefore subjected to might be virtually eliminated if you can find a way to block the wind. As an estimate of how much fuel such a step might save, check your fuel bills for January and for a month in which the average outdoor temperature was 19 degrees above January's temperature. The difference between these costs would be the saving for January. Such savings can range up to 30 percent in a year.

Various methods exist for keeping wind away from a house. One of the most esthetically pleasing is a strategic placement of trees and shrubbery to block the wind. Planted near the house, trees can also shade it in summer and save on air-conditioning costs. Walls, trellises, and parapets can also be built onto or near the house to deflect air currents. When planning a new structure, consider the shape of the land—slopes and hills strongly affect the way the wind blows.

Windchill

Wind speed	Temperature when there is no wind				
	50°F	30°F	10°F	–10°F	–30°F
5 mph	48	27	7	–15	–35
10	40	16	–9	–31	–58
15	36	11	–18	–45	–70
20	32	3	–24	–52	–81
25	30	0	–29	–58	–89
30	28	–2	–33	–63	–94
35	27	–4	–35	–67	–98
40	26	–6	–36	–69	–101

When the wind blows at speeds listed in left-hand column, your body—and outside walls of your house—will react as if the temperature were as given in the remaining columns.

1. Winter

2. Summer

3. Autumn and winter

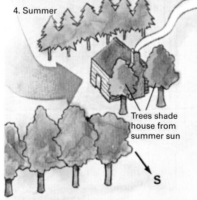

4. Summer

Trees shade house from summer sun

S

Trees and shrubs can be planted in a variety of ways to redirect the wind. If the cold winds of winter arrive mostly from one direction, a single line of evergreen trees will do a good job of blocking them (Fig. 1); more rows at other angles to the house may be needed if the wind is variable. In the summer, however, these same trees may interfere with cooling breezes. One solution (Fig. 2) would be to plant a row of deciduous trees (trees that shed their leaves in autumn) to deflect summer winds onto the house. Once autumn arrives and the leaves have fallen (Fig. 3), the evergreens will function as before to protect the house. Deciduous trees are also valuable as shade trees (Fig. 4) to keep the rays of the hot summer sun off the house. Their advantage over evergreens is that sunlight will be able to get through during the winter to warm the house.

A thoughtful, step-by-step approach to planting windbreaks is advisable. Wind patterns can vary considerably during the year. In many cases, not until the windbreak is in place can you be sure what its net effect will be. Phone or write your state energy office or local utility company for further information. Local agricultural extension offices can help and may provide you with lists of additional resources.

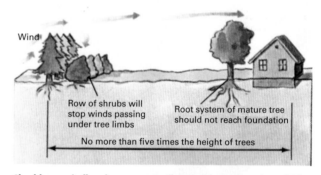

Wind

Row of shrubs will stop winds passing under tree limbs

Root system of mature tree should not reach foundation

No more than five times the height of trees

Shrubbery windbreaks are most effective when planted no farther from the house than five times the height of the windbreak (150 ft., for example, for a windbreak with 30-ft.-high trees). The trees should be far enough away from foundations and sewer pipes to prevent root damage. The distance can be inferred from tree size; root systems of mature trees usually extend about as far as the trees' branches.

Structures that impede air flow past the house, such as fences, walls, and parapets, can also serve as windbreaks. Even a trellis—which is normally used to support vines—or a similar wind-spoiling attachment serves this purpose.

Underground Houses

Houses that are built into the earth or beneath it are virtually immune to fuel shortages. This is because very little fuel is necessary to keep them heated comfortably above the surrounding temperature of the earth in which they are buried, a temperature that stays remarkably close to 55°F the year round.

This impressive fuel-saving advantage is offset, however, by the desire of most people for open space and sunlight rather than the cavelike atmosphere of an underground dwelling. Moreover, since subsurface structures are surrounded by tons of earth, some individuals worry that the walls may collapse or that escape may be difficult in case of fire or other emergency.

Many underground houses have been built in this country. Those that have been are often only partly buried. This type of design can still achieve major fuel savings if the layout of the house permits the residents to live aboveground during the warm months of the year and belowground during the cold months. Even if a house is embedded more deeply in the earth, its design can still achieve a degree of airiness by incorporating skylights, sunken courtyards, and aboveground panels that deflect the sun's rays down light shafts. Another variant is to build the house into the side of a hill. That way one or more walls can be left exposed to let in sunlight and provide views of the countryside.

There are a number of special problems associated with underground structures. Erosion of the earth that covers the house must be kept in check. Usually this can be done by planting grass or shrubs that stabilize the soil. The shrubs should have short roots so they will not penetrate the walls or ceiling. An underground building must have enough strength to sustain the heavy load of earth pressing down on the dwelling. To achieve extra strength, underground houses are often built in the shape of a circle or octagon, designs that achieve a relatively even distribution of load. Roofs reinforced with steel beams and heavy concrete walls are also used.

Extra effort has to be made to keep belowground homes dry. Even with a waterproof vapor barrier around the structure that blocks moisture from the earth, the house must cope with condensation that accumulates inside. Surface houses have enough openings to let interior dampness quickly evaporate. Underground houses, however, need special ducts and blowers to keep them dehumidified. The problem is similar to the one many homeowners experience with their basements; but while a small portable dehumidifier will handle the moisture problem in the average basement, a much larger system is needed to control the humidity in an underground home.

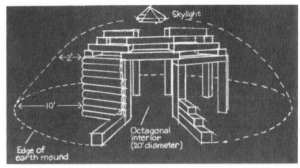

Traditional Navaho hogan is the basis for the design of this octagonal log-supported home in the Southwest. The logs rest on footings of stone and form the roof as well. The structure is covered by a mixture of earth and pumice. A vapor barrier of asphalt paint and stucco protects the logs from moisture.

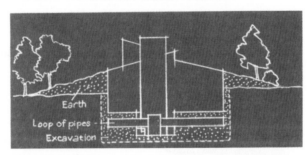

This New England structure is essentially a two-story house buried halfway in the earth. A sunken courtyard-greenhouse, like a solar collector, supplements the fossil-fuel heating system. In winter, heat is extracted by a heat pump from a deeply buried air pipe; in summer, cool air is pumped inside the same way.

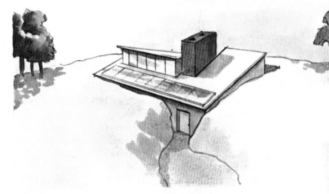

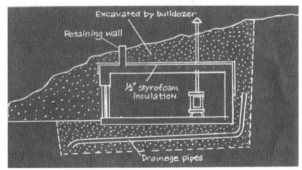

Built into the side of a hill, this Midwest home is nearly impervious to the effects of wind, storms, and tornadoes. An asphalt coating waterproofs the concrete roof and walls, which support more than 1 million lb. of earth. Drainage tiles below footings channel away water that collects there as a result of soil seepage.

Wood as a Fuel

A Reliable, Renewable Home-Heating Fuel

Wood, as the old saying goes, warms two times: when you cut it and when you burn it. The saying sums up the chief virtues of heating by wood—healthy exercise, comforting warmth, and the homey pleasure of a wood fire. In addition, wood is widely available and economically competitive with fossil fuels. And if you gather your own firewood, the savings can be tremendous, cutting your yearly fuel bill from hundreds of dollars to practically nothing.

Felling, bucking, splitting, and stacking a full cord of wood is a vigorous day's work for even the heartiest individual.

Managing a Woodlot

A woodlot can supply wood indefinitely if the quantity you take out of it each year is no more than the amount replaced by natural growth over the same period. As a rule of thumb, 1 acre of woodland can produce 2/3 cord of hardwood each year. (A cord is a stack measuring 4 feet by 4 feet by 8 feet; it is illustrated in the picture above.) If you own or have access to 10 acres of woodland, you should be able to harvest 6 to 7 cords a year—enough to heat an average three-bedroom house.

The better you manage your land, the less acreage you will need. Woodlot management is like tending a garden, except it takes longer to see the results—years instead of months. In execution, it is a program of selective cutting based on the age and condition of each tree and how closely one tree grows to the next. As in gardening, experience is the greatest asset.

The first trees to cut down are those in an advanced state of decay and those damaged by disease or insects. These conditions are usually obvious, even to the inexperienced eye. As an exception, a tree with damage only to its leaves might be left for another season to see whether or not it is able to recover. Also, an occasional dead tree should be left standing as a home for wildlife. After damaged trees have been removed, harvest trees that have no potential value as lumber or trees that crowd others and inhibit their growth. Your county agent and state forester can both provide additional information on tree harvesting. The state forester may also be willing to go over your woodlot, marking the trees that should be culled.

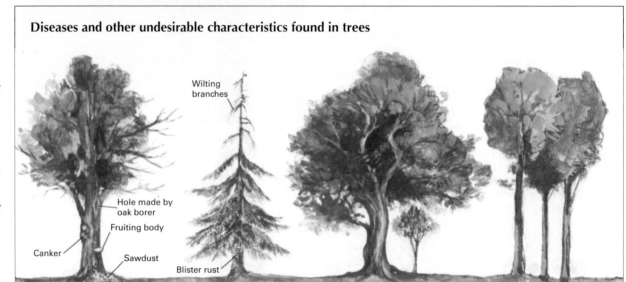

Diseases and other undesirable characteristics found in trees

Wilting branches

Hole made by oak borer

Fruiting body

Canker

Sawdust

Blister rust

Fruiting body or a canker (an open wound caused by rot) on the trunk of a hardwood tree indicates serious disease. Damage by insects is typified by holes left by oak borers and a sawdustlike residue at the base of trunk that results from infestation by certain types of bark beetles.

Disease that often afflicts evergreen trees is blister rust. Wilting branches may indicate an attack by weevils, while extrusions of pitch from the trunk of the tree are signs that pine beetles are present. Even slight symptoms may mean extensive internal damage.

Wolf trees are trees that take up large amounts of space and are too twisted and gnarled to have value as lumber. Due to advanced age they grow very slowly, robbing smaller trees of sunlight and nutrients and underutilizing the sunlight that they do absorb.

Cull trees from groups that grow too closely together. Saplings, for example, should be about 6 ft. apart, trees with trunk diameters of 12 in. should be 18 ft. from each other. Sell straight, tall, unblemished trees to a mill, since they are worth more as lumber than as fuel.

Obtaining Wood

The cost of fuel wood depends very much on where you live and on the type of wood you are buying. In cities and treeless parts of the country you will probably have to pay much more for wood than in forested regions; and in either locale a cord of hardwood (generally more desirable for burning) is likely to be priced considerably higher than the same amount of softwood.

Wood is usually sold either by the cord or by the face cord. A cord is a stack of split or unsplit logs that measures 4 feet by 4 feet by 8 feet, but the amount you actually get in a cord will depend on how the wood is piled—in the old days some woodcutters developed an uncanny ability to stack cordwood with a maximum of airspace and a minimum of wood, and the practice, regrettably, has not entirely died out. The so-called face cord is not a cord at all but rather any pile that measures 4 feet high by 8 feet long. The width of the pile can be almost anything; sometimes it is no more than 12 inches and it is rarely more than 2 feet.

Wood is sometimes sold by the truckload. A 1/2-ton pickup will hold roughly 1/3 cord of wood. When buying by volume, keep in mind that the heat value of wood is directly indicated by its dry weight. Unfortunately, when wood is still wet, it is not always easy to estimate the amount of water in it. Try to avoid woods with a high resin content; resin adds to creosote buildup in a chimney (see *Heating With Wood*, p.91).

On many occasions you can obtain fuel wood at nominal cost or for free. Public parklands and forests, town dumps, and lumber mills are sources for such wood. Even private owners may let you on their land to clear dead or unusable timber.

Sources and resources

Books and pamphlets

Drying Wood With the Sun. Washington, D.C.: U.S. Department of Energy, 1983.

Harris, Michael. *Heating With Wood*. New York: Carol Publishing, 1980.

Hogencamp, Robert. *Heating With Wood*. Washington, D.C.: U.S. Department of Energy, 1980.

Sharpe, Grant W., et al. *Introduction to Forestry and Renewable Resources*. New York: McGraw-Hill, 1995.

Smith, Robert A. *The Backyard Woodcutter: A Guide to Preparing Your Own Firewood*. Bristol, Wis.: Huron Group, 1994.

Thomas, Dirk. *The Harrowsmith Country Life Guide to Wood Heat*. Buffalo, N.Y.: Firefly Books, 1992.

Energy Source	Unit	Dollar Cost for Equal Net Heat: Each Column Shows the Fuel Unit Prices to Obtain Heat at the Same Cost Per Btu.									
Heating Oil #2	gal.	$2.00	$2.10	$2.20	$2.30	$2.40	$2.50	$2.60	$2.70	$2.80	$2.90	$3.00
Propane	gal.	$1.25	$1.31	$1.38	$1.44	$1.50	$1.57	$1.63	$1.69	$1.75	$1.82	$1.88
Kerosene	gal.	$1.76	$1.97	$2.06	$2.16	$2.25	$2.34	$2.44	$2.53	$2.62	$2.72	$2.81
Natural Gas	therm	$0.96	$1.46	$1.53	$1.60	$1.67	$1.74	$1.81	$1.87	$1.94	$2.01	$2.08
Electricity	kWh	$0.00	$0.06	$0.06	$0.07	$0.07	$0.07	$0.08	$0.08	$0.08	$0.08	$2.09
Seasoned Wood	cord	$267.35	$280.72	$294.09	$307.45	$320.82	$334.19	$347.56	$360.92	$374.29	$387.66	$401.03
Wood Pellets	ton	$236.31	$248.13	$259.94	$271.76	$283.57	$295.39	$307.20	$319.02	$330.84	$342.65	$354.47

This table compares prices of heating fuels on a Btu to Btu basis. Btus are units of heat energy. This approach is necessary because heating fuels are purchased in different kinds of units, such as gallons, therms, cords and kilowatt-hours (kWh), each containing a different amount of Btus. This table also factors in the different typical efficiencies of the heating systems that use the various fuels. The result is a more meaningful price comparison of the usable heat.

Find the price closest to the price for whatever fuel you are currently using. The alternative fuel you are considering will cost less per usable Btu if you can get it at a price LOWER than its price in the same column as the price for the fuel you are currently using. On the other hand, if the alternative fuel you are considering will cost you MORE than its price in the same column as the price you are paying for the fuel you are currently using, the alternative fuel will cost you more per unit of usable energy than the fuel you are currently using.

Characteristics of different kinds of firewood

Wood species	Approx. weight of 1 cord (in pounds)	Value of air drying	Resistance to rot	Ease of splitting
Shagbark hickory	4,200	Little	Low	Intermediate
Black locust	4,000	Little	High	Intermediate
White oak	3,900	Some	High	Intermediate
American beech	3,900	Some	Low	Difficult
Red oak	3,600	Some	Medium	Intermediate
Sugar maple	3,600	Some	Low	Intermediate
Yellow birch	3,600	Some	Low	Intermediate
White ash	3,500	Little	Low	Intermediate
Cherry	2,900	Little	High	Easy
American elm	2,900	High	Low	Difficult
Sycamore	2,800	High	Low	Difficult
Douglas fir	2,800	Variable	Medium	Easy
Eastern red cedar	2,700	Variable	High	Easy
Tulip (yellow poplar)	2,400	High	Medium	Easy
Hemlock	2,300	High	Low	Easy
White pine	2,100	Variable	Medium	Easy
Basswood	2,100	High	Low	Easy
Cottonwood	1,900	High	Low	Intermediate

Use the table at left when choosing firewood and making cost comparisons. When you buy by the cord, heavier wood gives more value per dollar, since weight is equivalent to heat. To find out how many pounds of wood of a particular species you get in a cord, look down the weight column. The figures assume that the wood has been air dried (20 percent of its weight remains water).

Before drying wood, check the column on value of air drying. Some woods have too little water in them to benefit much from drying; others should be dried six months or longer.

Dealers often describe the wood they are selling as hardwood. In general, hardwood is heavy and softwood is light. The division is only approximate, however. Some hardwoods are light, some softwoods heavy.

Tools and Techniques For Harvesting Wood

The best way to get fuel wood is to cut it yourself. Every step in the process—from felling the tree to bucking it into usable lengths to splitting and stacking it—provides vigorous outdoor exercise that is healthful and satisfying. With proper equipment and convenient access to the forest area in which you are working, you can harvest a cord of wood a day. A week or two of heavy work and you should have enough wood split and stacked to heat a reasonably well insulated house for one year (more wood will be needed, of course, in the colder parts of the nation, less in warmer climates).

Felling and bucking with a two-man saw can be quiet and sociable, but the efficient chain saw is the best choice for heavy work—it can cut through wood 10 to 30 times faster. Some chain saws run on gasoline, others on electricity. Gasoline models, although more expensive, are better for most purposes, since the electric versions require an extension cord (impractical in the deep woods) and are not as powerful. Chain saws can be dangerous. Make sure the model you get has all the available safety features, and read the instruction book carefully before using it. Chain saws are also noisy; operate them with consideration for your neighbors.

All your woodcutting tools, including the chain saw, should be kept sharp. Dull edges require much more labor and create hazards. Your chain saw will stay sharp longer if you avoid cutting through dirt-encrusted logs or allowing your saw to dig into the earth beneath a log. There are several signs of a dull chain saw: the chips become smaller, more force is required to make the saw bite into the wood, the wood smokes due to increased friction, and the saw does not cut straight.

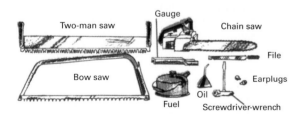

The blade of a bow saw is cheap. Replace blade when it gets dull. You can sharpen cutters on a chain saw, but be sure to use proper file and file guide and to follow instructions in your owner's manual. If in doubt, take chain saw to your dealer.

Chain-saw operator is in process of making a 45° angle face cut, the second of three cuts made when felling a tree.

Felling a Tree

To get a tree to fall where you want, first make a notch on the side facing the desired direction of fall. This is done with two cuts: first the undercut, then the face cut. A third cut, the backcut, is then made at a slight angle downward, approaching the undercut about 1 inch above it. Leave an inch or two of uncut wood to act as a hinge to encourage the tree to tilt in the direction you want. If the tree does not fall of its own accord, push it with a long pole or peavey. Do not cut through the hinge.

Felling a tree can be dangerous. A side may be rotten, the tree may twist or bounce off another tree, or the trunk may rip loose and kick back in the direction opposite to its fall. Dead branches may also fall on you. For these reasons it is vital to have at least one, preferably two, clear escape routes and to get out of the way as soon as the tree begins to fall.

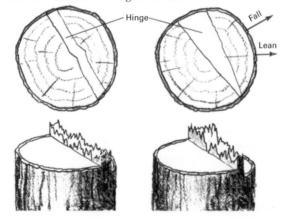

Pivoting technique lets you coax a tree to fall the way you want, even if it leans another way, provided the difference is not too great. Make backcut so that hinge is thicker at one end than the other. As tree falls, trunk will cling to wider end of hinge, causing it to pivot in that direction. Practice this technique in open woods before you try it in a tight spot.

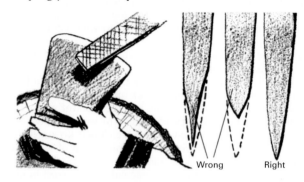

Sharpen ax with carborundum file or use ax stone lubricated with light oil (avoid motor-driven grinders). Maintain original blunt taper. Do not try to take out every nick; you will only remove more metal than is necessary, shortening life of ax.

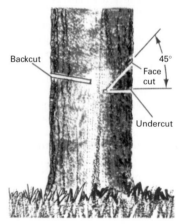

A notch cut about one-third of way into trunk guides tree to fall in direction of notch. Set backcut higher than point of notch to prevent tree from falling backward. Tree will fall as planned unless it is leaning in some other direction. You can follow a similar cutting procedure with an ax, though control of fall will not be as precise.

Chain saw may bind when making backcut into a large tree. You should have a wood, plastic, or aluminum wedge with you to free the saw. Knock wedge into backcut until pressure is eased, then resume sawing. (By using more than one wedge you can also encourage the tree to fall in the direction you want.)

From Tree to Firewood

Winter is the best time for felling and bucking. The underbrush is thin, you sweat less, and there are no biting insects. Also, it is easier to spot dead trees and to choose safe paths of fall and good escape routes. Should there be snow on the ground, you will be able to slide logs about with less effort. On the average, a tree with a diameter of 12 to 14 inches will yield about 1/4 cord of wood. One to two dozen such trees will probably satisfy the heating requirements of your house for one season.

When you cut a tree down, make sure the area is clear of people, particularly children. If the tree is near a house, attach a strong rope high up on the trunk and apply tension so that the tree will fall in a safe direction. You can get the rope up by weighting one end with a rock and throwing it over a limb. To apply tension, you can either have a helper pull on the rope from a safe distance or else attach the rope to another tree.

Once cut, a tree may hang up on another tree instead of falling all the way to the ground. If you cannot pry it loose with a peavey, tie a rope to its trunk and use a block and tackle attached to another tree to pull it loose.

When you remove a limb from a felled tree, make it a practice to stand on the side of the trunk *opposite* to the limb; that way you will minimize the risk of cutting your foot with the saw or ax. During the bucking operation (sawing the tree into logs), the weight of the tree as it sags can pinch your saw blade and bind it. The pinching is caused by compression, either along the top side of the fallen tree trunk or the bottom side. With practice, you will learn into which side to cut to avoid binding. When binding does occur, hammer a wedge into the cut to free the saw. The wedge should be made of wood, plastic, or other soft material to avoid damage to the saw.

Limbing and bucking

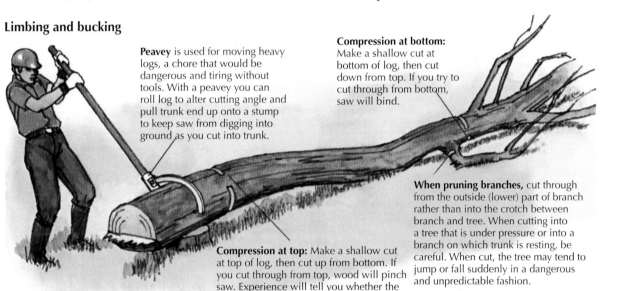

Peavey is used for moving heavy logs, a chore that would be dangerous and tiring without tools. With a peavey you can roll log to alter cutting angle and pull trunk end up onto a stump to keep saw from digging into ground as you cut into trunk.

Compression at bottom: Make a shallow cut at bottom of log, then cut down from top. If you try to cut through from bottom, saw will bind.

When pruning branches, cut through from the outside (lower) part of branch rather than into the crotch between branch and tree. When cutting into a tree that is under pressure or into a branch on which trunk is resting, be careful. When cut, the tree may tend to jump or fall suddenly in a dangerous and unpredictable fashion.

Compression at top: Make a shallow cut at top of log, then cut up from bottom. If you cut through from top, wood will pinch saw. Experience will tell you whether the compression is in the top or bottom of log.

Splitting and stacking

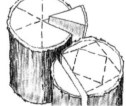

When splitting logs with an ax or splitting maul, proceed as if cutting a pie (left). However, if wood is twisted and fibrous (like elm), split it into tangential segments.

Heavy logs are better split with a sledgehammer and steel wedge. Never use the ax as a wedge or its poll (blunt end) as a hammer. You will ruin the ax.

Splitting screw, which attaches to the rear axle of a car, is one of several splitting devices on the market. Be sure to follow the manufacturer's instructions when using it.

One way to stack wood so that pile does not topple is to build up the ends log cabin style, as shown here. To protect from rain, place cordwood with bark up.

Sawbucks, cutting cribs, and woodsheds

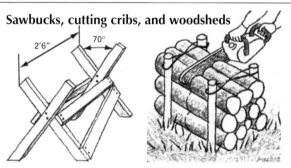

2'6"   70°

Sawbuck holds log so that it will not shake or shift as you cut. Make sawbuck taller than necessary; use it, then trim it to most comfortable height.

Cutting crib lets you cut many logs at once. An easy way to make one is to drive four posts into ground, then rope tops together so posts do not spread.

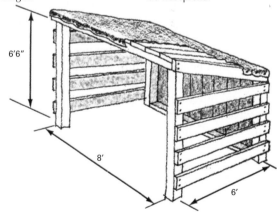

6'6"   8'   6'

Woodshed can be made from scrap lumber. Protect stored wood from rain and snow, but allow enough air circulation inside to dry the wood. Store wood off the ground.

Heating With Wood

Wood-Burning Stoves: Plenty to Choose From Whether Old or New

Like the sun itself, a hearth fire or wood-burning stove radiates heat directly onto the human body. When you and your family cluster by the fireside on a frosty winter evening or gather near the cheery warmth of your stove, you will experience a satisfaction and comfort that modern central heating fails to equal. You will also be enjoying the only form of indoor heating that the human race has known for thousands of years.

Though they are charming and sometimes a bargain to operate, wood-burning devices require attention. Fuel must be replenished, draft regulators and dampers have to be set, ashes must be removed, and the chimney must be cleaned out. Though drudgery for some, many people take pleasure in these chores, enjoying the direct hand they have in the control of their environment.

If you have never tried heating your home with wood, proceed gradually. For example, you might start with one stove, installed to heat one room, leaving the rest of the house to be heated by a more conventional system; in this way you can learn the virtues and idiosyncrasies of wood burning and be able to plan intelligently any expansion of its use. You may discover, for example, that wood burning might work well in conjunction with a solar energy installation, the former doing most of the job in midwinter, the latter handling the load in spring and autumn.

Making it easier for you is the wide array of wood-burning devices on the market today, most of good design, high efficiency, and excellent workmanship. With these at your disposal, you are likely to find the right stove for your situation whether you look for economy, esthetic pleasure, or a combination of the two.

Stoves of the Past

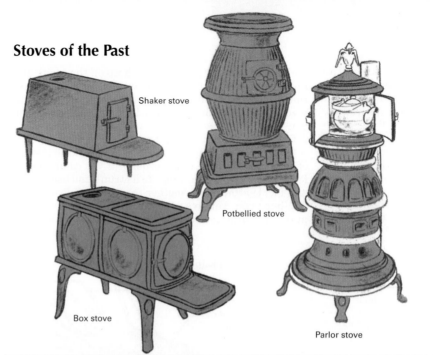

Shaker stove

Potbellied stove

Box stove

Parlor stove

Stoves have been used to warm homes for centuries, but until recently, particularly in America, they took second place to fireplaces. In the 19th century, however, the development of techniques to produce cheap cast-iron plate helped iron stoves become the most popular home-heating devices. Hundreds of firms marketed stoves in a fantastic variety of shapes.

Iron stove design began with the box and the cylinder. A famous early version was invented by Franklin (see below). Despite the merits of his stove, it was soon supplanted by models that stood on legs and could be placed anywhere in the house rather than being tied to an existing fireplace or requiring special floor construction. At their peak iron stoves could boast of ashpits, built-in chambers for teakettles, secondary combustion chambers, and a lively baroque decor.

Ben Franklin's improved fireplace

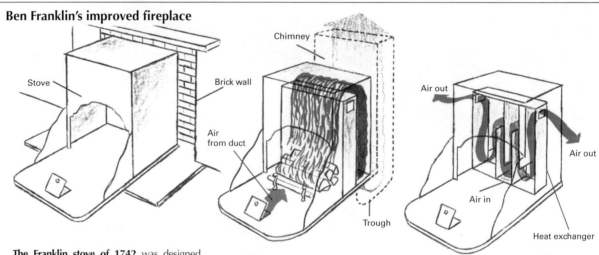

Stove

Air from duct

Chimney

Brick wall

Trough

Air out

Air out

Air in

Heat exchanger

The Franklin stove of 1742 was designed expressly to improve on the notorious inefficiency of old-time fireplaces. It was an immediate success, gaining popularity during Franklin's lifetime and influencing stove design for years to come. Note, however, that the original Franklin should not be confused with what are now called Franklin stoves; the two types have little in common.

Fireplaces waste heat by sucking heated air from the room and sending it up the chimney. To circumvent this, Franklin blocked the chimney opening with a brick wall. To let smoke exit, he fitted a trough beneath the wall so that the smoke from his stove could exhaust under and up behind the wall. A damper inside the stove controlled the rate of exhaust. Fresh air was drawn from whatever space was under the floor (a cellar, for example) via a duct cut through the floor; the duct opened onto the fire.

To improve the stove's efficiency, a baffled heat exchanger was placed between the fire and the back of the stove. Air to the exchanger was channeled from under the floor in the same way as the fresh air for combustion was channeled. The air in the heat exchanger absorbed heat from the fire and exhaust, passing out into the room via two ports, one on each side of the stove.

Modern Stoves

Recent developments in stoves have been mainly technological, an attempt to design a stove that will squeeze the last calorie of heat out of the wood being burned. Although there are many models on the market, no one stove can be singled out as generally superior to the rest. The best stove for you will depend on your personal taste, the purpose for which the stove is to be used, and on how the stove is installed and operated.

From the standpoint of efficiency, a good stove should not draw any more air than that needed for the wood and the gases given off by the wood to burn. Fireplaces, for example, for all their appeal and hominess, do not obey this rule. They gulp large amounts of unneeded air. In many homes, this air comes down the furnace and water heater chimney to create a potentially dangerous situation. Building codes or home insurance agents may require installation of a make-up or combustion air vent. To minimize this problem with stoves, many manufacturers make them airtight, meaning that the stoves are so well sealed and free of chinks that the air flow can be adjusted to the exact rate needed. You can even starve the fire of oxygen and make it go out. An incidental advantage of airtight stoves is that they can be left untended for many hours, even overnight, while continuing to generate warmth at a fairly constant rate.

Another attribute of a good stove is that it transfers heat to the house rather than letting it go up the chimney. To accomplish this, a system of chambers or baffles is usually built into the stove. The hot air, smoke, and gases are channeled through the chambers or past the baffle walls. These, in turn, absorb the heat and radiate it into the room. There are a variety of stove modifications using this principle, some as simple as the single horizontal baffle-plate design used in such European stoves as Lange, Jøtul, Trolla, and Morsø; others with complex air-flow arrangements supported by secondary air inlets, as in the American-made Defiant, Tempwood, and Ashley stoves.

As an added convenience, some stoves have a built-in thermostat; you set it for a particular temperature and the thermostat takes over, opening and closing the draft regulator (adjustable air inlet) to control the rate at which the fire burns. On stoves without a thermostat it is up to you to adjust the regulator to get the desired burn rate; you will learn by experience how to set it. To maintain a fire overnight, the regulator should be opened only a crack. Note, however, that slow burn rates can result in creosote buildup in the chimney (see *The Creosote Problem*, p.91).

Some home heating units combine a wood-burning furnace with a conventional hot air system of the sort used with natural gas or oil burners. These have the advantage of heating the entire house with a single unit instead of with a number of stoves or fireplaces distributed in different rooms. Also, wood can be stored and dried in the basement, next to the furnace, minimizing handling and keeping the rest of the house free of wood chips. Countering these advantages, however, is the kind of heat provided; most people find the radiant heat of a stove more comfortable than warm air from a register.

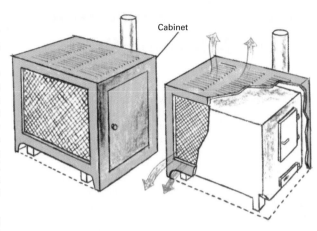

Circulator-type stoves, such as those made by Ashley and Rite-Way, are fabricated from steel plate and feature a cabinet (optional with some units) that surrounds the stove proper. Air between stove and cabinet heats up and is circulated out into room either naturally by convection or by a blower. A thermostatically controlled draft regulator is part of the design. Well-made units approach other airtight stoves in efficiency, but the warm air produced by the cabinet-enclosed models is generally not as pleasant as heat from radiant stoves.

Wood-burning furnaces (see picture below) are essentially overgrown circulator stoves; their larger size is needed to accommodate the heating requirements of an entire house. They are normally installed in the cellar, just as an oil burner would be, and blow heated air through ducts to the rooms above.

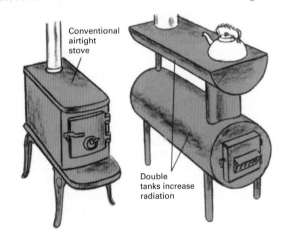

Airtight stoves have top ranking for fuel savings, simple construction, ease of use, and long life. The design has been popular in Scandinavia for some time, and now American manufacturers, such as Fisher and Sunshine, make airtight units as well. One version, by Sevca, is built from a pair of empty propane tanks and features a separate smoke chamber above the fire chamber that extracts heat from the exhaust smoke and reradiates it into the room before it is lost up the chimney. The flat shelf shown offers a warming surface for the teakettle.

Labels on image 1: Conventional airtight stove; Double tanks increase radiation

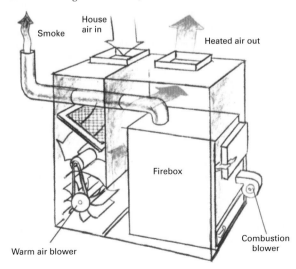

Labels on image 3: Smoke; House air in; Heated air out; Firebox; Combustion blower; Warm air blower

Franklin stoves as made today are only remote descendants of Ben Franklin's original design. The modern version amounts to a straightforward cast-iron stove, with doors in front that open to let you view the fire—a feature Franklin himself strove to keep. With doors closed the stove gains in efficiency but not up to the level that well-made airtight stoves attain.

Selecting and Installing A Wood-Burning Stove

Choose a stove whose capacity matches the heating requirements of the space you intend to heat. A stove that is too small will have to be refueled frequently and still may not generate enough warmth. An overly large stove can be even worse, causing overheating on all but the coldest days, and more creosote build up from general use.

Manufacturers usually specify the heating characteristics of a stove in terms of the number of rooms or the number of cubic feet of space the stove can heat. In a few cases they give the heat output in BTUs per hour. An average-sized room contains about 1,500 cubic feet. When the temperature outside is at the freezing level, you should be able to heat such a room with a stove that puts out 15,000 BTUs per hour. Of course, there are many variables to consider. How well insulated and weatherproofed is your house? (The better your house retains heat, the smaller the stove you will need.) Is your home laid out ranch style or does it have a compact two-story design? (It is easier to heat a compact house than a sprawling single-level home.) What sort of wind velocities are typical in winter? (The more wind, the bigger the stove you will require.) Above all, you must consider the severity of the winter in your area. A stove that will function admirably in Maryland or Arkansas may work only marginally in New York, Kansas, and eastern Oregon and be totally inadequate in northern Maine, Minnesota, Montana, or Alaska.

Though a central location for the radiant heat unit is advisable, other considerations such as chimney location may take precedence. Bear in mind that you will frequently be transporting firewood into the house; the trail of dust, mud, and wood chips that usually follows a trip from woodpile to stove can become a nuisance. To shorten the trail, place the stove near the doorway through which the wood will be brought or install a through-the-wall woodbox.

Buying a used stove

Not very long ago it was easy to find a discarded cast-iron parlor stove or cooking range. Now, however, these have become treasured antiques, and unless you are lucky they will cost you as much as a new stove.

Besides being attractively designed, old stoves were made to last; however, many were built to burn coal rather than wood, so their fireboxes tended to be

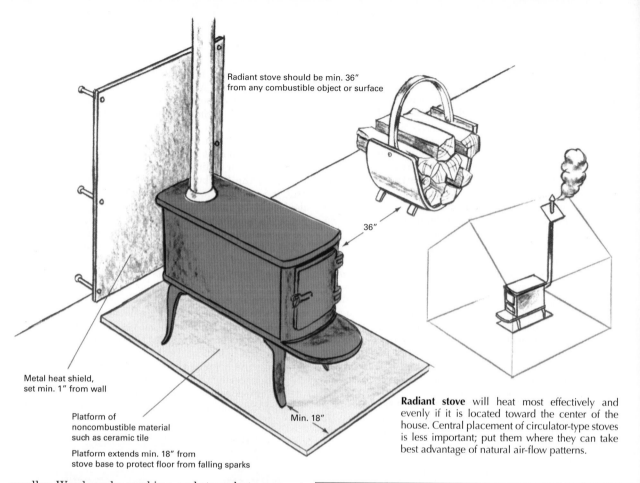

Radiant stove should be min. 36″ from any combustible object or surface

36″

Metal heat shield, set min. 1″ from wall

Platform of noncombustible material such as ceramic tile

Min. 18″

Platform extends min. 18″ from stove base to protect floor from falling sparks

Radiant stove will heat most effectively and evenly if it is located toward the center of the house. Central placement of circulator-type stoves is less important; put them where they can take best advantage of natural air-flow patterns.

smaller. Wood can be used in a coal stove, but you must cut it into shorter pieces and load the stove more often.

If you come across a stove you like, examine it carefully for cracks, particularly in the firebox. Cracks are responsible for inefficient operation and will cause the room to smoke up when the stove is started. Sometimes a cracked firebox can be fixed by welding or brazing, but this must be done by a specialist—repairing cast iron is a very tricky business. Cracks found in other parts of the stove, where the operating temperature does not rise as high, can be chinked with stove putty.

Before buying an old stove, be sure you will be able to replace essential parts, such as grates and doors, that happen to be warped, broken, or missing. There are a number of stove works around the country able to provide parts or cast new ones for you. Be wary of stoves that show signs of extensive rust. Surface rust can be removed with a wire brush followed by the use of stove black, but if vital inner parts are corroded, you may find it difficult or impossible to repair them.

One style of woodbox

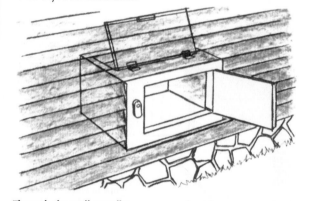

Through-the-wall woodbox conserves heat because you do not have to open house door to fetch each load of wood. Keep interior of box dry to help prevent insect infestation and wood rot. Weatherstrip both doors.

Chimney Installations

A properly designed and installed chimney will produce a strong, even draft through the stove without any back-puffing (smoke coming out of the stove). Backpuffing occurs when the chimney has the wrong capacity or too many bends in the way of the smoke path. The capacity of a chimney is determined by its height and inside diameter; the higher and wider the chimney, the more capacity it has. When the capacity is too small, the stove will smoke whenever you try to raise its heat output by opening the draft regulator beyond a certain point. When the capacity of the chimney is too large, smoking can also occur, since the rising smoke-saturated air loses too much heat to the chimney surface. As a result, the air rises more slowly, generating a back pressure whose effect is visible as backpuffing. Backpuffing can also result from inadequate clearance at the chimney top; a chimney should be at least 3 feet higher than any object within 10 horizontal feet of it.

Usually, smoke problems arise only when you connect to an existing chimney. Typically, a masonry chimney may have too large a capacity; a metal chimney, too small a capacity. Do not connect to a chimney already used by another stove or fuel burner. When installing a new chimney, match the inside diameter of the chimney to the diameter of the stove's exhaust flue.

A safe installation is vital. You risk burning down your house if an uninsulated stovepipe touches or passes near a part of the house made of wood or other flammable material. Manufacturers of prefabricated chimneys give installation guidelines, but check building code requirements for your area also.

Using a fireplace chimney

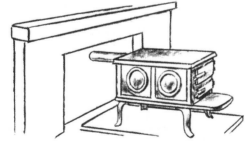

To connect a stove to an existing fireplace chimney, remove fireplace damper and frame. Install stainless steel liner in chimney and extend above the chimney. Seal with sheetmetal where liner exits damper throat. Fill between liner and masonry chimney with hi-temp insulation or cement slurry. Seal top of liner with sheetmetal and add proper cap. Connect the stove collar.

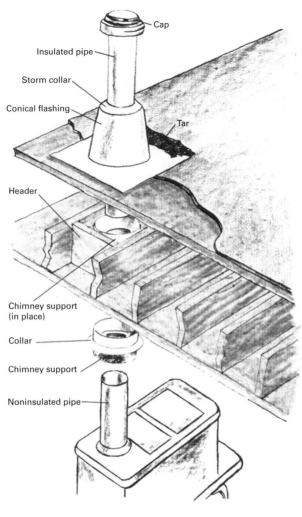

Special spacer made of noncombustible material must be used to support any stovepipe that passes through a frame wall. A useful addition is to install T-sections with soot pockets and cleanouts in place of ordinary 90° bends in stovepipe.

Installing a prefab chimney

1. Set stove in desired position, then use plumb bob to find center of hole that will be cut in ceiling for chimney. Ideally, chimney should pass through gap between roof beams. To locate beams, tap ceiling.
2. Draw a square on ceiling around center mark just large enough to accommodate chimney support (for example, 11 by 11 in. for 7-in.-diameter flue).
3. Cut square out of ceiling with compass saw.
4. Drill guide hole up through roof at one of four corners of square opening.
5. Working on top of roof, use guide hole to help draw and cut out a square hole centered on hole in ceiling below but 3 in. larger in each dimension (14 by 14 in. for the example here).
6. Saw through any beams that block 11- by 11-in. opening.
7. Cut headers to fit opening, then nail them in place between roof beams. Drive in nails at 45° angle.

8. Lift chimney support into hole in ceiling from below. Fasten support to adjacent beams and headers by hammering eightpenny nails through collar of support into beams and headers.

9. Lower insulated pipe section into chimney support from roof. (The section simply rests in support; conical flashing placed later will restrain section from toppling.)

10. Apply liberal amount of roofing tar to roof around 14- by 14-in. hole. Slip conical flashing down onto tarred area.
11. Add additional section of insulated pipe; then tighten band that locks sections together.
12. Put on storm collar and cap.
13. Nail rim of flashing to roof; then add more tar along flashing edges.

14. Seal gap between storm collar and pipe with caulking compound. (The purpose of the compound, and the tar around flashing edges, is to seal installation from inclement weather.)

15. Install noninsulated stovepipe by pushing it up from below into chimney support. Then attach stovepipe bottom to exhaust flue on stove.

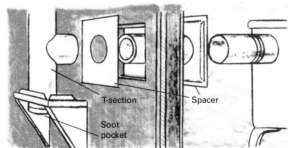

Starting and Operating A Wood-Burning Stove

To start up a fire in a wood stove, place a pile of kindling (thin slivers of quick-burning wood) over crumpled newspaper and top the pile with several light pieces of split wood. Open the draft regulator (and chimney damper if the stove has one), ignite the paper, and shut the stove door. After a few minutes, when the fire is going well, add larger and heavier pieces of wood—enough to fill almost the entire combustion chamber of the stove if you want a long burn. To avoid troublesome starting, use wood that is dry and fully seasoned.

As soon as the larger pieces of wood have caught fire, close the draft regulator two-thirds of the way or more. The further you close it, the slower the burn rate and the longer the fire will last. Remember, however, that a slow fire tends to increase creosote buildup (see facing page).

With a little trial and error in setting the stove's regulator, you will learn how to correct for external factors such as outside temperature, presence or absence of sunlight, and degree of wind chill. On very cold days, for example, you will find that the draft up the chimney is stronger than usual because the difference between inside and outside temperatures is greater. The result may be an excessively fast burn rate. To compensate, you should close the draft regulator or chimney damper a bit more than you would normally. Of course, if your stove has a thermostatically controlled regulator, these adjustments are made for you automatically.

Even with a well-designed chimney, a stove may occasionally backpuff. If this happens as you fire up the stove, try closing the draft regulator a bit. If backpuffing tends to occur when you add fuel, open up the regulator a minute or two before opening the stove door; increasing the draft will carry the smoke up the chimney.

Smoking can also be a sign of creosote buildup in the chimney; since this condition promotes chimney fires, it should be eliminated. Poor chimney design is another cause of smoking (see *Chimney Installations*, p.89). Finally, tight house construction and/or kitchen and bath exhaust fans can make a fireplace or non-airtight stove backpuff by restricting the air supply. Opening a nearby window a crack to increase air flow into the house will probably clear up the difficulty.

Draft reversal

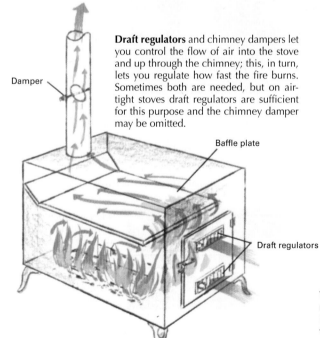

Draft regulators and chimney dampers let you control the flow of air into the stove and up through the chimney; this, in turn, lets you regulate how fast the fire burns. Sometimes both are needed, but on airtight stoves draft regulators are sufficient for this purpose and the chimney damper may be omitted.

Damper

Baffle plate

Draft regulators

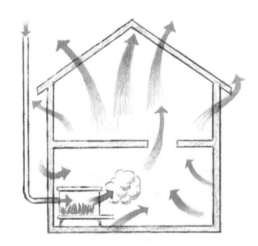

Warm stove air sometimes chooses a path through the house rather than up the chimney. Air then flows down chimney and into room. This is called draft reversal and is more common with exterior chimneys. To counteract the effect, open a window near stove. Also, before starting fire, ignite wad of paper in stovepipe. Once chimney is warm, air will go up it.

Making your own stove

Small wood stove can be made from a 15-gal. closed-head heavy gauge grease drum after cleaning drum of any residue of grease. Tolerances need not be precise. One weld and some furnace cement to hold stovepipe flange to stove top are needed. All other parts bolt on. Cut rectangular openings for fuel loading and ash removal; then cut doors from sheet metal to overlap the openings 1/2 in. all around.

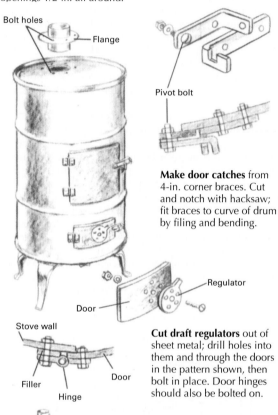

Bolt holes

Flange

Pivot bolt

Make door catches from 4-in. corner braces. Cut and notch with hacksaw; fit braces to curve of drum by filing and bending.

Door

Regulator

Stove wall

Filler

Door

Hinge

Cut draft regulators out of sheet metal; drill holes into them and through the doors in the pattern shown, then bolt in place. Door hinges should also be bolted on.

Kits for converting oil drums into stoves usually include legs, door assembly with draft regulator, and a 6-in. stovepipe flange. The picture shows a 55-gal. drum with parts bolted on. (For a longer stove life, a discarded water-heater tank might be substituted for the oil drum illustrated.)

Safety

Anything that is flammable—curtains, clothing, paintings, furniture, wall hangings—can catch fire if it is repeatedly heated to 300°F or above. Since a stove will soon bring nearby objects to this temperature, it is vital to adhere to the standard set by the National Fire Protection Association by keeping flammable materials at least 3 feet away from any wood-burning device.

Chimney fires are another hazard. Creosote, a wood by-product, tends to accumulate on chimney walls and may be touched off by sparks or flames from the stove. A chimney fire generally has a crackling or roaring sound. As the fire's intensity increases, the stovepipe may vibrate violently and turn red hot. If the chimney is well built, and all metal chimney joints have at least three screws, the fire will likely die out without causing any damage. In some cases, however, it may become so hot that it ignites nearby wall lathing, wooden beams, or other structural members. In addition, chimney fires occasionally send clouds of sparks onto the roof, setting the roof aflame.

The first step to take in the event of a chimney fire is to stop the flow of air to the fire. This is easily done on an airtight stove by closing all draft regulators. With a fireplace, you should have a large metal cover available that can quickly be put over the fireplace opening. With a leaky stove, a sopping wet blanket thrown over it may serve to stop the flow of air through the leaks. Have a bucket of water ready to wet the blanket down, since the moisture may quickly steam off and leave a dry blanket to catch fire. As soon as you can, check the roof for sparks and wet it down with a hose if there is any sign of danger. If the chimney passes through upper floors of the house, inspect all areas adjacent to the chimney. You should certainly have several fire extinguishers handy in the event the fire starts to spread. Above all, if there is any hint that the fire is spreading beyond the confines of the chimney, call the fire department at once.

The best defense against a chimney fire is prevention. Clean your chimney regularly and operate your stove or fireplace so as to minimize creosote buildup. Details are given at right. Almost as important, you should make certain your chimney is in good running order. You will need to inspect it carefully to determine its condition. Do not assume that it is adequate simply because it has been in service for a number of years. Old stovepipes may not meet present-day requirements. If the chimney is made of brick, its flue may be cracked, the mortar may be partially disintegrated, or the chimney may have been built without a flue liner. If you have any doubts about the safety of a chimney, contact your local fire department; it can save you money and heartache.

The Creosote Problem

Creosote is a substance deposited on chimney walls by smoke flowing up the chimney. Chemically, creosote is a mixture of unburned organic compounds. When hot, it appears as a dark, viscous liquid. When it cools, it forms a solid, tarry residue that may later turn to a black ash that seems to grow from the inner surface of the chimney in leaflike flakes. Creosote can burn, making it a fire hazard. It may also build up to such a point that it partially or completely blocks the air flow up the chimney, making the stove smoky and hard to light.

Contrary to what one might expect, the more efficient a stove is, the more apt it is to produce creosote. Leaky, inefficient stoves burn hot and fast, and the chimney walls become so hot that creosote does not have a chance to form on them.

If your chimney becomes clogged frequently by creosote, you may be running the stove at too low a burn rate. A smoldering overnight fire sends a lot of creosote-forming smoke up the chimney. To get an overnight burn with a minimum of creosote, run your stove hot, until the wood in it has been mostly reduced to charcoal, before closing down the draft regulator to its nighttime position. Of course, some heat will be wasted during the initial high burn period (unless the stove is adjacent to a large thermal mass, such as a heavy masonry wall, that absorbs heat and reradiates it back into the room overnight). A daytime approach, especially useful in the fall and spring when less heat is needed, is to make small, hot, quick-burning fires rather than cool, slow-burning ones. You will have to refuel the fire often, but combustion will be more complete.

Hot creosote will drip down the chimney. Ideally, it will flow into the stove and be burned up. But if the stovepipe is a poorly joined metal one, the creosote may drip out of the joints and make a disagreeable mess. To discourage this, it is preferable to install the stovepipe and chimney sections with crimped ends inserted downward. This arrangement is typical of European chimneys but the opposite of traditional American practice.

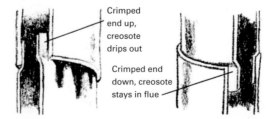

Crimped end up, creosote drips out

Crimped end down, creosote stays in flue

If your chimney runs straight up, you can inspect for creosote buildup by holding a mirror inside the stove when the stove is cold. Hold the mirror at a 45° angle directly under the flue opening. You can estimate the amount of creosote by the amount of daylight you can see. If you have a metal chimney with turns, T-sections installed at appropriate locations will permit you to check most of the chimney.

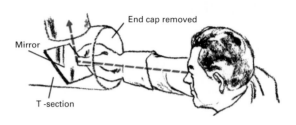

Mirror

End cap removed

T-section

A simpler but less reliable estimate can be made by tapping the stovepipe with a finger; the tap will produce a tinging sound if the pipe is clear but a duller, heavier sound if the pipe walls are laden with creosote.

Cleaning a chimney

The chimney on an airtight stove can become clogged in as short a time as two weeks if the stove is used carelessly. On the other hand, a stove used regularly and properly in a cold climate may need its chimney cleaned no more than once a year.

Cleaning a chimney is a messy job, and many prefer to hire a chimney sweep to do it. Some stove owners try to avoid the job by running a very hot fire once or twice a week to burn out accumulated creosote. The method is not reliable, however, and in addition such fires may eventually damage the chimney and break down its insulating properties. Chemical preparations are available that help disintegrate creosote when they are thrown on the fire. But first check with a stove or chimney dealer to make sure the preparation will not damage the chimney liner.

The best cleaning method is to lower a stiff chimney brush through the top opening. Work the brush up and down to knock soot and creosote down the stove pipe and into the firebox where it can be cleaned out. The stove should be cold. It also should be shut tight, otherwise clouds of soot may waft into the room. To better seal the doors, lap several pages of newsprint over the opening and close the doors onto the paper and latch them shut. (For the same reason, when cleaning a fireplace chimney, cover the fireplace opening as tightly as you can.) Never use tire chains in a burlap bag. This can easily break tile or cement lined chimneys and internal mortar joints. Oldtimers sometimes tied a rock to the top of a small evergreen tree and lowered the tree upside down by rope from the top of the chimney.

Fireplaces: Warm, Charming... And Inefficient

A fire glowing and crackling in a fireplace generates an aura that no other type of heating can equal. The aroma of burning wood, the play of light and shadow, the warmth from the flaming logs evoke a sense of peacefulness, security, and contentment. It is no wonder that wood-burning fireplaces are prized features of homes and apartments. At the same time, there is no denying that the heating efficiency of most fireplaces is low—less than 10 percent in many cases compared with upward of 60 percent for the best airtight stoves.

Much can be done, however, to improve the performance of even the oldest and most wasteful fireplace. Among the simpler steps is to make more effective use of the damper—a pivoted metal plate that can be adjusted to control air flow in the chimney. When the fire is burning, open the damper just enough to keep the fire from smoking. This will reduce the amount of heated room air lost up the chimney. It is also important to close the damper completely when the fireplace is not in use. This simple precaution, observed winter long, may reduce your overall heating costs significantly. The reason is that with the damper open enough warm air can be lost up the chimney to turn the fireplace into a heating liability rather than an asset. However, do not close the damper when the fire is still smoldering; otherwise

To start the fire, first pile kindling (thin pieces of dry wood that burn quickly) on balls of crumpled newspaper placed between the andirons. Top the kindling with light pieces of split wood and two or more logs. Open the chimney damper and ignite the newspaper. **Caution: Never pour kerosene or other flammable liquid on the wood to help start the fire.**

you will wind up with a house full of smoke and noxious gases. To prevent heat loss up the chimney when the fire is low but not yet fully out, place a tight-fitting cover made of sheet metal over the fireplace opening. Few manufacturers make these covers, but it is easy enough to cut one out yourself.

Fireplace efficiency can also be boosted with the help of special equipment. One useful accessory is the tubular convection grate illustrated on the next page. Also described on the next page is a heat-saving fireplace that convects air around the firebox via ducts

or enclosed spaces and then sends the heated air back into the room. Prefabricated units often incorporate this design. Modern masonry units, too, frequently use the same approach. To some degree, however, these improvements change the character of the fireplace, making it somewhat like a circulator-type stove and diluting the esthetic appeal that makes a fireplace attractive. Another effective device for raising fireplace efficiency is airtight glass doors fitted over the fireplace opening. These doors cut down on the amount of warm air lost up the chimney but also isolate the fireplace from the room; you can see the fire, but you lose intimacy with it.

Most people eventually develop their own techniques for building fires, yet there are nuances that are sometimes overlooked. When the logs are too close, not enough air will flow between them to support efficient burning; when they are too far apart, the logs will not absorb enough heat from adjacent logs to reach combustion temperature. Adjust the spacing for minimum smoke and maximum burn rate. A poker and tongs will come in handy for this chore.

A common problem is a fireplace that backpuffs smoke into the room when the fire is started. An effective remedy is to hold a wad of burning newspaper directly under the chimney flue before lighting the main fire. This prewarms the walls of the chimney, making it more apt to draw properly. If the problem persists, the house may be overly airtight (see *Draft reversal,* p.90). Open up a nearby window an inch or two until the fire is burning well. Check the furnace and water heater draft hoods to make sure replacement air is not also being pulled down their chimneys. If it is, contact your gas utility or state energy office for advice. (An inadequate chimney, poorly designed fireplace or house exhaust fans, may also be to blame.)

Implements and accessories for the fireplace

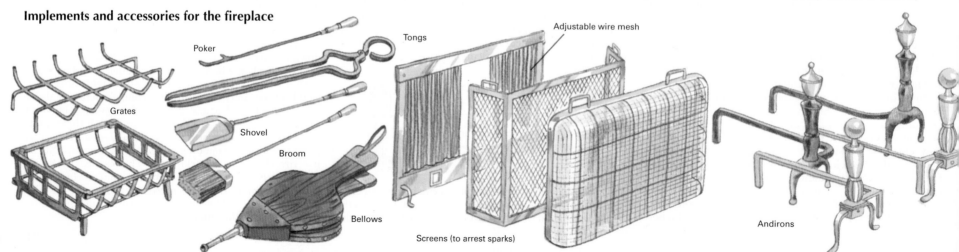

Grates

Poker

Tongs

Adjustable wire mesh

Shovel

Broom

Bellows

Screens (to arrest sparks)

Andirons

Equipment for Improved Efficiency

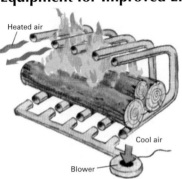

Heated air

Cool air

Blower

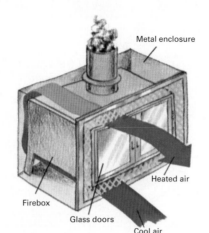

Metal enclosure

Heated air

Firebox

Glass doors

Cool air

Tubular convection grate, used in place of an ordinary grate or and-irons, serves as a ready-made heat exchanger for a fireplace. The fire heats the air inside the tubes, causing it to flow by convection out of the top openings. Efficiency is increased, since warm air goes into the room rather than up the chimney. A blower attached to the bottom openings of the tube will speed heat transfer.

Freestanding fireplace is easier to install than a built-in unit. Like a metal stove, it radiates heat in all directions. However, without masonry to slow heat transfer, the fire must be tended more often than with a masonry unit.

Prefabricated fireplace uses a special metal firebox so well insulated that the unit can be installed with "zero clearance," that is, directly next to wooden framing. Prefabricated fireplaces often come with airtight glass doors in front to reduce heat loss and a system of air ducts and spaces to circulate room air around the firebox and then out into the room again by convection. Like any wood-burning heater, performance is improved if the chimney is installed entirely inside the house.

Masonry and ceramic stoves

Large masonry and ceramic stoves evolved over the years from continued attempts to improve fireplace efficiency. Originally developed in Europe, and later imported to the New World by the Pennsylvania Dutch and other early settlers, the stoves are vastly more efficient than the old-fashioned fireplace. (Their obvious advantages helped inspire Ben Franklin to design his famous fireplace stove.) Shown at left is a massive Russian-style brick stove featuring a serpentine arrangement of exhaust ducts to capture the heat before it can escape up the chimney. The stove is built entirely within the house. It is fired for a brief time with a very hot fire and damped only after the wood has burned down to smokeless coals. The heat from the fire is absorbed by the masonry, which slowly reradiates it into the room. From one firing enough heat can be stored in the masonry to warm a room for two days, and the heat given off remains remarkably even for that period. Since the fire burns hot, little creosote forms in the exhaust, making the stove one of the few wood-burning devices that can be left untended for long periods without collecting creosote.

Making your own bellows

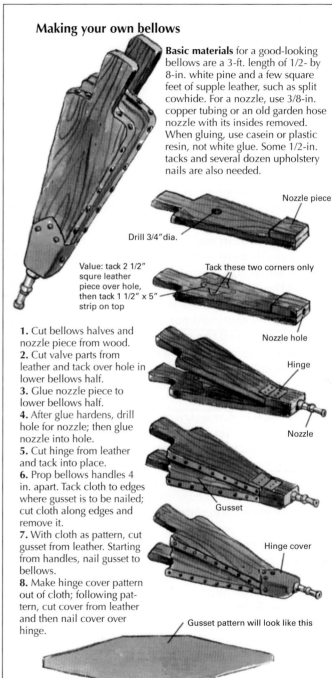

Basic materials for a good-looking bellows are a 3-ft. length of 1/2- by 8-in. white pine and a few square feet of supple leather, such as split cowhide. For a nozzle, use 3/8-in. copper tubing or an old garden hose nozzle with its insides removed. When gluing, use casein or plastic resin, not white glue. Some 1/2-in. tacks and several dozen upholstery nails are also needed.

Nozzle piece

Drill 3/4" dia.

Value: tack 2 1/2" squre leather piece over hole, then tack 1 1/2" x 5" strip on top

Tack these two corners only

Nozzle hole

Hinge

Nozzle

Gusset

Hinge cover

Gusset pattern will look like this

1. Cut bellows halves and nozzle piece from wood.
2. Cut valve parts from leather and tack over hole in lower bellows half.
3. Glue nozzle piece to lower bellows half.
4. After glue hardens, drill hole for nozzle; then glue nozzle into hole.
5. Cut hinge from leather and tack into place.
6. Prop bellows handles 4 in. apart. Tack cloth to edges where gusset is to be nailed; cut cloth along edges and remove it.
7. With cloth as pattern, cut gusset from leather. Starting from handles, nail gusset to bellows.
8. Make hinge cover pattern out of cloth; following pattern, cut cover from leather and then nail cover over hinge.

Waterpower

Streams and Rivers Provide Energy Free for the Taking

The use of waterwheels to free human beings from heavy labor is almost as ancient as the use of draft animals. The earliest applications of such wheels were to raise water from wells and to turn millstones to grind grain. Later, waterwheels were adapted to provide power for other processes to which a slow, ponderous, unceasing rotary motion was suited. In early America, textile factories and sawmills were generally built on riverbanks to take advantage of waterpower.

With the advent of steam power in the 19th century, the massive, wooden waterwheel became obsolete, and water did not again compete as a power source until the invention of the high-speed turbine for generating electricity. This development not only led to huge hydroelectric installations but also made small, private hydropower installations possible.

A personal hydroelectric power source has the potential to sustain every household energy need and provide an unexcelled level of independence. Having enough water flow is less a problem than one might imagine, particularly in hilly areas where hundreds of thousands of potential hydroelectric sites remain untapped. With a drop of 50 feet from water source to turbine, for example, a brook small enough for a child to jump across can provide enough power for a single-family dwelling. However, bear in mind that the smaller the installation, the higher will be the construction cost for each kilowatt generated. Scaled against the cost of power from a public utility, it may be 10 to 20 years before a small installation pays back its initial expense, though rising fuel costs may substantially shorten the payback period.

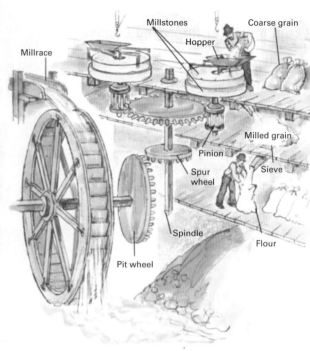

Old-fashioned gristmills could grind 5 to 10 bushels of grain an hour. The miller poured the grain into a hopper from which it trickled down through the eye of the upper millstone onto a bed stone. As the 1/2-ton upper stone rumbled over the bed stone, it scraped off husks and pulverized the grain. The husks were then separated with a sieve, leaving flour.

Traditional Waterwheels

Breast wheel

Undershot wheel

Tub wheel

Individuality and variety marked the waterwheels of the past. Their diameters ranged from 3 ft. to 20 ft., and they incorporated every conceivable water-flow scheme. The most efficient type was the overshot wheel shown above, but if the water source was not high enough, a breast wheel or undershot wheel was employed. Of low efficiency, but simplest to build because it used no gears, was the tub wheel. A typical large wheel made 10 to 20 revolutions per minute; with wooden gearing this could be stepped up to 10 times the rate. A number of traditional waterwheels are still in operation in America, turning out the stone-ground meal so highly prized by home bakers.

Modern Waterpower Systems

Waterpower achieves its greatest usefulness when it is converted into electricity. Lighting fixtures, heating systems, small appliances, cooking ranges, and machinery of all sorts are some of the common applications. The conversion is made possible by electrical generators that transform rotary motion into electric current.

Though not originally designed for the purpose, old-fashioned waterwheels can actually be used to run generators, but not without overcoming a major obstacle: electrical generators do not operate efficiently except at high speeds, on the order of 1,500 revolutions per minute. To reach these speeds, a large step-up in the waterwheel's rate of rotation is required, somewhere in the vicinity of 100 to 1. Wooden gears simply will not work—friction alone would destroy them. Instead, rug-

ged, well-made gears or pulleys are required that are not only highly efficient but also capable of handling the huge forces present in the shaft of a waterwheel. Heavy-duty tractor transmissions have been adapted for the purpose and can provide several years of service. The design and construction of a system that will last 20 years or more calls for a high level of mechanical ingenuity plus persistence and luck in finding the appropriate used or abandoned equipment.

Gearing problems can be circumvented by using a turbine instead of a waterwheel. Turbines are devices that convert water flow directly into high-speed turning motion. Little in the way of supplementary gearing is needed to achieve generator speeds. In addition, turbines are much smaller than waterwheels of the

same power output, hardly larger than the generators with which they are coupled. Turbines run with a high-pitched whine—not as soothing as the rumble and splash of the old mill wheel—and some are subject to cavitation (wear caused by air bubbles).

Before you buy a turbine, you should measure the characteristics of your stream, particularly its head, so you can match the turbine to them. ("Head" is the vertical drop the water makes from the point where it is diverted from the stream to the point at which it reaches the power-generating equipment.) Pelton wheels, for example, perform best under high head conditions; propeller turbines, the reverse. "Flow"—the volume of water carried by the stream past a stationary point each second—is also a factor in turbine design.

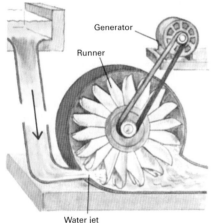

Pelton turbines operate best with heads of 50 ft. or more. The high-velocity jet of water that results from such heads spins the bladed runner up to generator speed without the need of additional gearing. Pelton runners can be any size from 12-ft. diameters for megawatt installations down to 4- to 18-in. diameters for home installations. Very little flow is required to run a small Pelton turbine, in some cases no more than the water issuing from a modest spring. The need for a high head, however, restricts installations to hilly or mountainous locations. Also, springs tend to dry up during some parts of the year and freeze up during other parts, so care must be taken to select a water source that will provide year-round power. A recent improvement in impulse turbines is to orient the jet at an angle to the blades, as in Turgo turbines. These units are smaller and faster than Peltons.

Cross-flow turbines work well when the head is greater than 3 ft. Water from a rectangular orifice passes through a barrel-shaped runner in such a way that the water strikes the ring of blades on the runner two times. This turbine is a relative newcomer; it has not yet been built in megawatt sizes but shows a great deal of promise for use in small installations. Moreover, it is simple enough for a person with a home machine shop to make; yet it can match the performance of the other turbines shown on this page, whose fabrication requires a high level of technology. It works well over a wide range of water flow, is relatively free from problems caused by silt and trash, and is not affected by cavitation. To improve efficiency, the rectangular orifice can be partitioned and parts of it closed off during periods of low flow. Some step-up gearing may be needed for optimum generator speed.

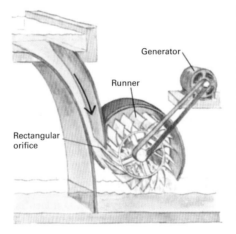

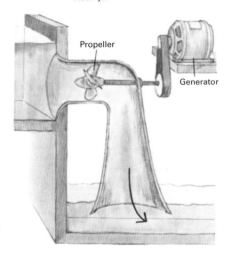

Propeller turbines are most effective at relatively low heads of from 3 ft. to 30 ft. The propeller is completely submerged and is impelled more by the dead weight of the water than by the water's velocity. In high-head installations, propeller turbines suffer wear from cavitation. In addition, they work well only over a narrow range of speeds, so care is required to match the size of the turbine to the available stream flow. For example, when flow drops to 50 percent of a propeller turbine's optimum, the power output will drop by about 75 percent, and when the flow drops to 30 percent, the output becomes nil. To overcome this limitation, some large hydroelectric installations use several turbines in tandem, shutting down one or more whenever the flow lessens. Others employ Kaplan turbines, which have automatically adjustable blades that compensate for flow changes.

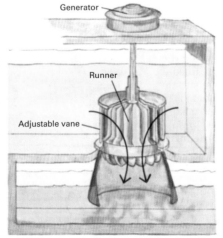

Francis turbines can be used over a wide range of heads 4 ft. and more. As with a propeller turbine, the runner is immersed in the head water, which is guided onto the blades of the runner by a ring of adjustable vanes. The Francis turbine is highly efficient at its optimum flow but easily damaged by grit and cavitation. It is frequently used in large hydroelectric stations and is relatively expensive. As with propeller turbines and other interior-flooded turbines, a draft tube beneath the unit with its bottom rim immersed at all times in the tail water (the water flowing out of the power station) is a valuable adjunct: as water drops from the turbine runner down the draft tube, it sucks more water down with it, adding to the effective head of the system. This added head can be of substantial importance whenever the overall head of the remainder of the installation is small.

Finding Out How Much Your Stream Can Do

To determine the amount of power available in a stream, it is necessary to measure the water flow and make calculations from these measurements. This is not a hard job, since a rough estimate is usually all that you will require. Generally, wide seasonal variations in flow put a limit on the degree of precision that makes sense when measuring a stream. Changes on the order of 100 to 1 in the volume of water carried by a stream are not uncommon from one part of the year to another. In the Southwest, large rivers as well as smaller streams often dry up completely for long periods of time.

The key information that your measurements should provide is whether or not a stream will yield enough kilowatts of electricity to make its development worthwhile. You will also want to get an idea of how large the equipment has to be to generate these kilowatts and what type of installation should be used.

A rough estimate, however, may fail to provide sufficient precise data to determine how the installation should be constructed or what specifications the turbine and generator should have. For greater precision professional surveying instruments may be needed; but before involving yourself at this level of complexity, consult the turbine supplier with whom you expect to do business. He should know the degree of accuracy required.

A stream should be measured several times during the year so that its overall potential can be estimated and the power-generating equipment tailored to the variations in flow. The measurements will have value even when the flow is so large that only a small fraction will satisfy your power needs. It is particularly important to measure a stream near its low point during the year. Also, potential flood level should be ascertained if equipment is to be installed near enough to the stream so that it could be destroyed by a flood. When a dam is to be constructed, knowledge of flood potential is crucial.

If you are not familiar with your stream's annual ups and downs just by living near it, contact the nearest U.S. Geological Survey Water Resources Office (a branch of the Interior Department) for information on water runoff in your area. The information is free and likely to include rainfall and river flow data going back many years. If a stream is too small to have been directly measured by the office, a knowledge of local water runoff will help you form a profile of its behavior.

What You Must Measure

To find out how much power a stream can deliver, you must know three key measurements: the stream's head, its velocity, and its cross-sectional area.

Head refers to the vertical fall between the water source and turbine. In other words, it is the difference in elevation between the point where the water will be diverted from its natural streambed to the point where the water will be piped into the turbine.

Velocity refers to how fast the stream flows.

Cross-sectional area is a product of the width and depth of the stream.

To make the measurements, follow the procedures outlined on this page and the next. Once the three quantities are determined, multiply them together to obtain a power product. The greater the product, the greater the power available.

Measuring head

Head is measured in step-by-step fashion proceeding downstream from the water source to the planned hydropower location. You will need an assistant to help you make the measurement plus the following equipment: a carpenter's level, a camera tripod or similar support, an 8-foot-long pole, and a tape measure.

Set up the tripod near the water source and place the carpenter's level on the tripod's table. Adjust the table to the horizontal, then vary the tripod's height until the sight line along the level's upper surface is lined up with the water source. Next, have your helper hold the pole vertically at a location downhill from the tripod so that you can sight from the other end of the level to the

pole. Call out instructions as you sight toward the pole, and have your assistant make a chalk mark on the pole at the point where the sight line intersects it.

Now set up the tripod and level downhill from the pole at the location where the sight line, looking back uphill toward the pole, will intersect the pole at a point near its base. The assistant should now mark the new point of intersection, measure the distance between marks, and jot the measurement down. Once this is done, both chalk marks can be erased and the pole set up at a new location downhill, where the entire procedure is repeated. Once the power site is reached, add up the figures you have jotted down and you have the head.

When the stream is tiny

Flow from a spring can be measured by funneling it into a 5-gal. container and timing how long the container takes to fill. For example, if it takes 20 seconds, the flow is 5/20 gal. per second, or 0.035 cu. ft. per second (multiply by 0.14 to convert gallons to cubic feet). Flow, measured by a container, is the equivalent of the velocity times area, factors that are separately measured in larger streams. Water behind the embankment should not change elevation during the period of measurement.

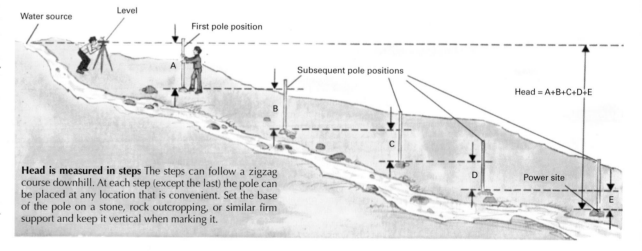

Head is measured in steps The steps can follow a zigzag course downhill. At each step (except the last) the pole can be placed at any location that is convenient. Set the base of the pole on a stone, rock outcropping, or similar firm support and keep it vertical when marking it.

Measuring velocity

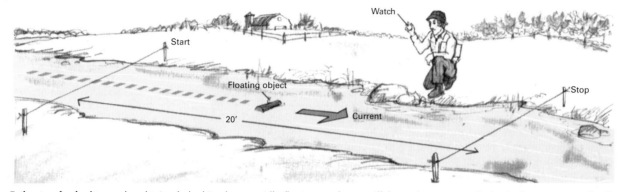

Estimate of velocity can be obtained clocking how rapidly floating objects move down the center of the strem. Select a portion of the stream that is reasonably straight and without obstructions, turbulence, or eddies. Tie strings across the stream at two locations spaced 20 ft. apart, with each at right angles to the direction of flow. Toss a cork, or other object that floats, into the center of the water upstream of the first string and time how many seconds it takes for the stream to carry the cork from one string to the other. Divide this amount into 20 ft., multiply the result by 0.7,

and you will have the stream velocity in feet per second. (The factor of 0.7 is necessary to reflect the fact that portions of the stream flowing along the banks and near the bottom move more slowly than the surface of the stream where the measurement is made.) As an example, suppose the cork took 10 seconds to traverse the 20-ft. distance from string to string. Dividing 20 by 10 and multiplying by 0.7 gives a velocity of 1.4 ft. per second. For greater accuracy, repeat the measurement several times, then average the results.

Measuring area

Cross-sectional area of a stream must be measured at the same location at which you measured the stream velocity. Mark off one of the strings in equal intervals. Six to 12 intervals should be enough, depending on the size of the stream. Measure the depth of the stream at each of the marked points on the string, record each measurement, and calculate their average after all the measurements have been made by adding the figures together and dividing by the number of measurements. Multiply this result by the width of the stream, measured from bank to bank, and you will have the area.

As an example, suppose your stream measures 6 ft. across and you have marked your string at five points, each 1 ft. apart with depth measurements at each marker 1/2, 1, 11/4, 3/4, and 1/2 ft. respectively. The measurements add up to 4 ft.; 4 ft. divided by five gives an average of 4/5 ft.; and 4/5 ft. multiplied by six results in an area of 4.8 sq. ft.

What the Power Can Do

After measuring the head, velocity, and area, multiply together the numbers you have obtained and divide the result by 23. You will then have the usable stream power in kilowatts. Expressed as a formula, the calculation is:

$$\text{Power in kilowatts} = \frac{\text{Head in feet} \times \text{Velocity in ft./sec.} \times \text{Area in sq. ft.}}{23}$$

The divisor, 23, is in the formula to make the answer come out in kilowatts and to reflect an overall system efficiency of 50 percent.

For example, for a head of 10 feet, a stream velocity of 1.4 feet per second, and a cross-sectional area of 4.8 square feet, the usable power output is:

$$\text{Power} = \frac{10 \times 1.4 \times 4.8}{23} = 2.92 \text{ kilowatts}$$

To find out how much electricity is available to you over a period of a month, multiply the figure you have obtained for power by 720—the number of hours in an average month. In the example above the 2.92 kilowatts (if this output is constant) would provide 2.92 × 720 = 2,104 kilowatt-hours per month.

The computation is similar if a container is used to measure flow (see facing page). Just take out velocity and area from the formula and substitute the flow measurement in their place.

Power capability

The amount of kilowatt-hours per month that can run the appliances listed:

300 kilowatt-hours will run all those in **A**

700 kilowatt-hours will run all those in **A** and **B**

1,500 kilowatt-hours will run all those in **A**, **B**, and **C**

8,000 kilowatt-hours will run all those in **A**, **B**, **C**, and **D**

A
Coffee pot
Hair dryer
Lights
Mixer
Record player
Refrigerator
Sewing machine
Television set
Toaster
Vacuum cleaner
Washing machine

B
Clothes dryer
Electric blankets
Electric range
Food freezer
Iron

C
Air conditioner
Hot water heater
Porable electric heater

D
Electric heating system

Making the Calculations

Once you determine a stream's power, you can estimate its usefulness. One way to do this is to compare the kilowatt-hours stated on your electric bill with the stream power you have calculated; you will then have a quick estimate of the proportion of your needs the stream will be able to satisfy. For the comparison use a bill with a monthly charge that is high for the year.

Another way to estimate what the stream can do is to use a capability chart like the one above. In an approximate way the chart indicates the number and type of appliances various power outputs can handle. It assumes that the use of these appliances will be fairly evenly distributed over each month and also assumes that a storage system, such as a bank of batteries, is used in the power system to take care of peak power demands (see *A Power System for Hilly Areas*, p.100).

One measurement of the stream is not likely to be enough to make a reliable estimate. Because stream flow varies, measure the stream's velocity and area at several times during the year (over the course of a number of years if possible) and use the lowest measured power to estimate usefulness.

Leading the Water To the Powerhouse

A small dam—one up to 4 feet high and 12 feet across—can often be built of locally available materials such as earth, stones, or logs. Such a dam can provide a dependable supply of water at an intake to a race (a canal for diverting water from a stream to a power station) or at a penstock (a pipe that serves as a race).

To moderate the effects of monthly and seasonal variations in stream flow, larger dams can be built. These will store excess water and release it during periods of low flow, providing more dependable power year round. Also, larger dams offer additional head (vertical drop from pond surface to turbine), a factor that can be critical in locations where the terrain is flat.

As the dam is made larger, however, its design becomes more and more complex and the number of potential problems increases. Particularly serious are cracks that may develop because of the varying stress and strain characteristics of the materials used in constructing the dam. In addition, rock formations under the dam may permit unexpectedly large amounts of groundwater seepage that threaten the dam's stability. As a result, dam builders must proceed with extreme caution. A failed dam can be awesomely destructive.

The best way to design against flooding is to obtain rain runoff data for the stream's watershed going back a substantial number of years. If such data are not available, the dam's construction must incorporate a large safety factor. Extra safety precautions must also be taken in earthquake-prone areas. If you are considering building a dam and have any doubts about the design of either the dam or its race, consult a professional engineer. In addition, you should check local regulations governing structures that affect stream flow. For dams above a certain size, a permit must be filed and limitations on construction observed. For further information, write to your state's water resources agency.

When building a dam and race, the area to be flooded, plus a marginal strip around the area, must first be cleared of trees and bushes. This is to prevent any undesirable tastes and odors that may later result from the decay of the plants. The foundation site of a dam itself should, at the very minimum, be cleared of all soil (earth containing organic matter). If a rock fill or concrete dam is to be built, the site should be dug down to bedrock, hard clay, or other stable formation.

While construction is in progress, it will be necessary to divert the course of the stream. One way to do this is to dig a temporary channel around the construction site. Another method, useful for small streams, is to build a wooden flume that straddles the dam, carrying the water overhead while construction proceeds beneath. A third solution is a drainpipe installed under the dam works. By fitting the pipe with a valve, it can be made a permanent part of the structure for use in emergencies. However, such pipes may crack and silt up with the passage of years, so they should not be relied on as the only flood control device.

A Low-Head, High-Flow Power Site

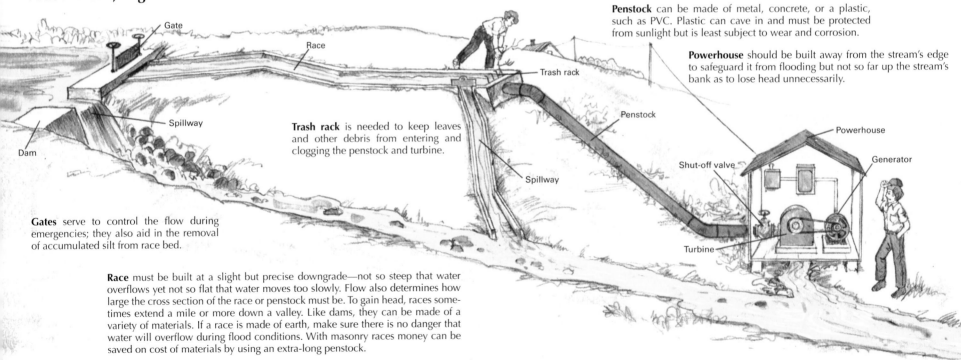

Penstock can be made of metal, concrete, or a plastic, such as PVC. Plastic can cave in and must be protected from sunlight but is least subject to wear and corrosion.

Powerhouse should be built away from the stream's edge to safeguard it from flooding but not so far up the stream's bank as to lose head unnecessarily.

Trash rack is needed to keep leaves and other debris from entering and clogging the penstock and turbine.

Gates serve to control the flow during emergencies; they also aid in the removal of accumulated silt from race bed.

Race must be built at a slight but precise downgrade—not so steep that water overflows yet not so flat that water moves too slowly. Flow also determines how large the cross section of the race or penstock must be. To gain head, races sometimes extend a mile or more down a valley. Like dams, they can be made of a variety of materials. If a race is made of earth, make sure there is no danger that water will overflow during flood conditions. With masonry races money can be saved on cost of materials by using an extra-long penstock.

Types of Dams

A dam impounds many tons of water. If its mass and strength are not sufficient, the weight of the water may be enough to topple the dam or slide it downstream. Also, water seepage under the dam can cause it to settle, crack, and eventually rupture. To protect against this, a variety of cores, barriers, and asphalt blankets are usually incorporated into the dam structure. Another hazard is the possibility of flood waters that may overflow a dam, eroding and disintegrating it as they pour downstream. To meet the danger, an overflow spillway should be built, either in the dam itself or as a separate pond-exit channel cut into the hillside to one side of the dam. On a site where the flood potential is great a spillway may be the dam's dominant feature.

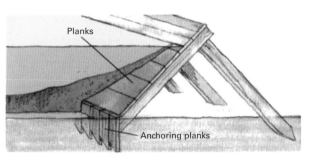

Frame dam is fabricated from planks that have been coated with such preservatives as creosote or pentachlorophenol to prevent rotting. To forestall seepage, face upstream side of dam with asphalt or a layer of fine silt or clay.

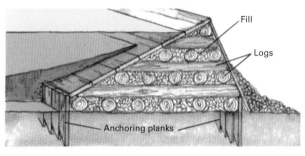

Log dam can be built of treated 6-in. logs, such as oak, with stone or gravel used as fill. Face the upstream side with seepage-proof planks. Wood dams do not last nearly as long as stone or earth dams and should not be more than 4 ft. high.

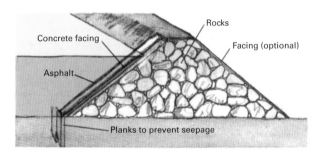

Rock-fill dam (and concrete dam as well) requires solid foundation of bedrock, compact sand, or gravel to prevent settling and rupture of watertight facing. When constructing on bedrock, anchor dam with bolts and seal joint with concrete.

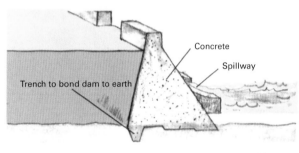

Concrete dam is preferred whenever overflowing is possible, since a spillway can easily be incorporated. To prevent erosion under the spillway, pile rocks at the base or shape the base to deflect the downward rush of water.

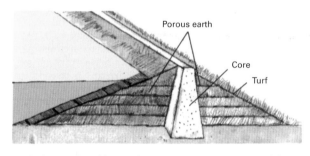

Earth dam is the oldest and most common type. For stability its slopes must be very gradual. To inhibit seepage, a core of impervious clay or concrete may be used. (See *Developing a Water Supply*, p.56, for more information.)

Bill Delp, Hydroelectric Contractor

Harnessing Stream Power Rocky Mountain Style

Bill Delp of Sandpoint, Idaho, once worked for a large public utility and had his own electricity and refrigeration company. When he realized two of the houses he was working on had streams on the property, he told the owners he could install hydroelectric power systems and save them money and trouble. Now he has his own water power business, one that has grown largely by word of mouth.

"I started out with cabins, and now we're installing equipment that's compatible with regular electric homes too. But the main problem with hydroelectric power isn't installing it. Anybody with a crescent wrench, a screwdriver, and a little elbow grease can do that. The pitfalls come before you get to the installation stage. With hydroelectric systems in Idaho and Montana, you first have to get the legal rights to use the water. Even if the stream is on your own property you have to get what is called a 'nonconsumptive beneficial use permit' from the state. Then if you are going to have lines that cross anybody else's property, you have to get a right-of-way. Once you get through the legal hassles and arrange the financing, the rest is easy.

"Maintenance isn't difficult. The waterlines are insulated in cold weather areas so you don't have to worry about freezing in winter. The major learning curve is realizing that you don't have unlimited power the way you would if you were hooked up to a big system. You're on your own, and if all the kids want hot showers and somebody is using the electric stove, you're headed for trouble. You have to make up an energy schedule so you can balance your use of power. Once you've done that, your major problems are solved.

"There's been tremendous interest in the hydroelectric power field. It's an immediately available technology on a large or small scale. It doesn't pollute, causes very little environmental disturbance, and it can be installed very quickly. Our only problem is figuring out how to handle the amount of growth."

A Power System For Hilly Areas

A high head system relies on a long vertical drop rather than a large volume of water in order to generate power. The minimum head needed is 50 feet, but even at that minimum surprisingly little flow is required to develop usable wattages. For example, with a 50-foot head a flow of only 1 gallon of water (1/8 cubic foot) per second will yield an average power output of 300 watts.

Energy storage is a key factor in many hydroelectric systems. In some, a pond or lake serves as the main storage element. In other systems, especially small ones like the one shown on this page, a bank of rechargeable batteries plays a similar role, helping the system to adapt to daily and seasonal variations in stream flow and power demand. Perhaps the most important function of the batteries is to store power during periods when little current is being drawn so that it can be tapped at times of peak usage. Demand is generally lightest after 10:00 P.M. and heaviest in the morning and between 6:00 and 8:00 P.M. in the evening.

The batteries in the system shown here will tolerate a power draw of up to 3 kilowatts. If peak demand exceeds this, or if the batteries become completely discharged, a circuit breaker discontinues service in order to protect them. A power outage will also occur if the waterline (penstock) becomes clogged. The inconvenience of an outage can be eased if there is an emergency backup system to switch on: either a small gasoline-powered generator or power from the local utility.

Clogging in the penstock is most likely to occur inside the turbine (the narrowest point along the line). To reach the nozzle and clean it, first close the shutoff valve and open up the turbine. Unclogging a plugged line is particularly important in winter, since the stopped-up water may freeze in the penstock and burst it. In cold areas of the country the safest procedure is to bury the penstock below the frost line.

Storage batteries currently on the market can last as long as 15 years if a somewhat reduced charging capacity toward the end of the period is not critical for the homeowner. Eventually, however, they must be replaced. The cost will not be out of line for a small system, but for a large system, such as the one described on the facing page, the number of batteries required would make replacement too expensive. For such a system a storage pond becomes the preferred alternative.

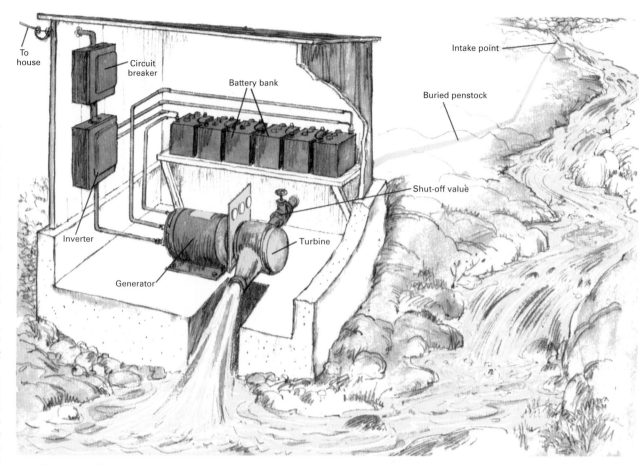

Powerhouse is built on concrete foundation to minimize vibration. Batteries are a special type that can withstand repeated charging and discharging; they are not conventional auto batteries. An inverter converts the 32 volts DC (direct current) delivered by the generator and batteries to the 60-cycle 115 volts AC (alternating current) on which most appliances operate.

Pelton turbine uses a 4-in.-diameter runner (left) with blades shaped in such a way that water striking them is deflected to the sides, where it will not interfere with the incoming jet. An access plate on the turbine (right) can be unbolted to permit access to the epoxy-coated runner for inspection and cleaning.

Intake to penstock includes a trash filter to keep debris out of turbine. Filter should be checked periodically, especially in autumn when leaves are apt to collect at intake.

Power Storage, Regulators, and Inverters

All but the simplest waterpower systems have some means of storing power to compensate for irregular stream flow and to hold power for periods of high user demand. It is also important to have some means of regulating the power output so that it matches the demand placed on the system. Power when it is generated has to be sent somewhere, whether to appliances, batteries, or the power company. If no loads of this type are present,

or if most or all of them happen to be switched off, the generating equipment may freewheel up to a point where it eventually burns out its bearings and self-destructs. The diagrams below show several methods to store and regulate power.

Where it is necessary to convert from DC to AC, an inverter is used. Inverters come in two forms. One is the rotary type, which consists of a combined motor and

generator plus built-in controls for maintaining a constant 60-cycle 115-volt AC output. The inverter motor is run electrically by the 32-volt turbine generator. The other type of inverter is electronic. It is less bulky than the rotary type and roughly 30 percent more efficient (the rotary type is only 60 percent efficient). In addition, electronic inverters consume much less power than rotary inverters when all the appliances are turned off.

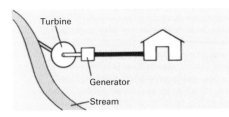

System without storage is the least costly to install but very limited in application. The output from the generator has a voltage that varies widely according to how much water is flowing in the stream and how many appliances happen to be switched on. Usually the only appliances that work well with such a system are ones with simple resistance elements for heating, such as hot water heaters and hot plates. The temperature of the heater's water may not be constant, but the arrangement is satisfactory if sudden demands on hot water are avoided.

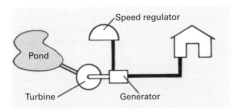

Pond formed by damming a stream is the traditional means for storing energy and smoothing the effects of erratic stream flow. A speed regulator, such as the hydraulic model in the installation shown below, is needed to take care of varying electrical demands as appliances are switched on and off. Hydraulic regulators are expensive, however, sometimes costing more than everything else in the powerhouse. Regulators currently being developed to accomplish the same task electronically may become a cheaper alternative.

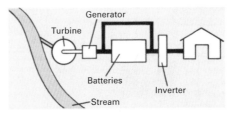

Battery storage works well for small systems such as the one shown on the facing page. Since batteries store and deliver DC electricity, an inverter is required to convert to AC. An attractive feature of battery storage is that it acts in part like a regulator, automatically diverting power into the batteries when house power demand is low and releasing it when demand is high. But to accommodate periods when the batteries have become fully charged, the turbine must be sufficiently rugged to withstand the resulting no-load condition.

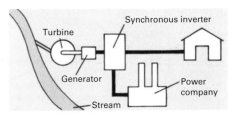

Local power utilities usually permit private citizens to sell their excess power to them. In this way the power company becomes a substitute for batteries or a storage pond. A device called a synchronous inverter automatically sends out the excess when the home system overproduces and draws power from the company when the home system underproduces. Power companies tend to pay less for your power than what they charge for their power. Even if they pay nothing, the arrangement still saves the cost of a regulator or batteries.

Quick mini-hydro power table: Use this table to estimate approximately how much power in watts you might expect from your water source if you know the total head and the flow rate. For example, 20 feet of head at 30 GPM equals 50 watts of continuous power.

Hydroelectric Power Output (in watts)

Head (Vertical distance, in feet)	Flow Rate (in GPM)									
	5	15	20	30	40	50	75	100	150	200
5			5	8	10	15	20	30	40	
10		7	12	18	23	30	45	60	80	100
15	5	15	20	30	40	50	75	100	125	150
20	8	25	32	50	65	85	125	170	210	275
30	12	35	45	70	90	120	180	240	300	400
40	16	48	60	95	125	160	240	320	450	600
50	20	60	80	120	160	200	300	400	600	
75	30	90	120	180	240	300	450	600		
100	40	120	160	240	320	400	600			

Something for Nothing: Water Pumping Itself

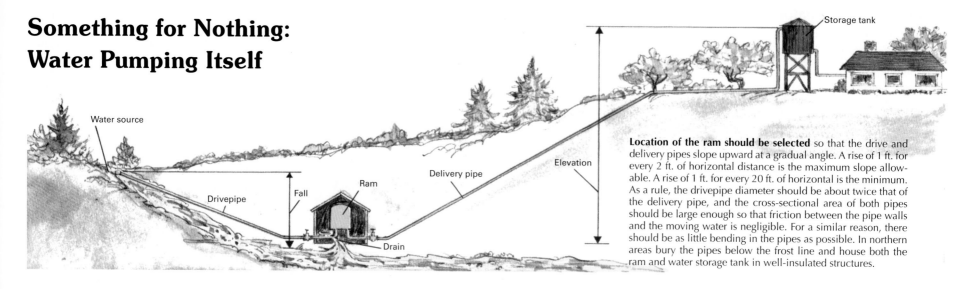

Location of the ram should be selected so that the drive and delivery pipes slope upward at a gradual angle. A rise of 1 ft. for every 2 ft. of horizontal distance is the maximum slope allowable. A rise of 1 ft. for every 20 ft. of horizontal is the minimum. As a rule, the drivepipe diameter should be about twice that of the delivery pipe, and the cross-sectional area of both pipes should be large enough so that friction between the pipe walls and the moving water is negligible. For a similar reason, there should be as little bending in the pipes as possible. In northern areas bury the pipes below the frost line and house both the ram and water storage tank in well-insulated structures.

Hydraulic Rams

Although a stream or other water source may be considerably below the level of your house, it can be tapped for fresh water without relying on electrical motors, windmills, hand pumps, or buckets. The trick is to use the water to pump itself. The Amish system on the next page is one method. A more common approach is to use a hydraulic ram, a century-old invention that at first glance seems to give something for nothing.

The heart of a hydraulic ram is a special pump, or ram, that uses the energy of a large mass of water dropping a short distance to raise a small amount of water far above its source level. A typical installation is illustrated at the top of the page. Ideally, for a fall of 10 feet and an elevation of 50 feet, 50 gallons per minute of water flowing down the drivepipe would be able to pump 10 gallons per minute into the storage tank, with the remaining 40 gallons being returned to the stream. In actual practice, however, rams operate at about 50 percent efficiency so that the water delivered would be half the ideal figure—5 gallons per minute in the example.

Rams pump at a cyclic rate of 20 to 150 times per minute. The ram shown at right has two built-in rate adjustments: a sliding weight that regulates spring tension and a bolt that limits valve movement. Increasing tension and restricting valve motion speeds the rate and decreases the amount of water pumped. Such a control is useful when waterflow in the stream drops off. If a ram's pumping capacity exceeds the stream's flow rate, intermittent and inefficient operation results.

The ram pumping cycle

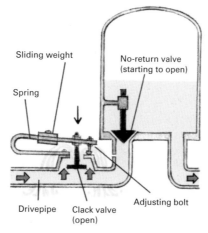

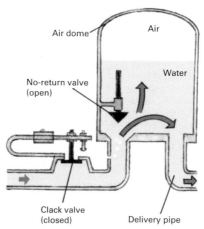

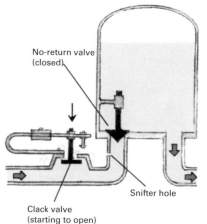

1. The cycle begins with the no-return valve closed and the clack valve open. Water starts to flow down the drivepipe, out of the clack valve, and onto the floor of the ram enclosure from which it is drained off and returned to the stream. As the flow builds up momentum, pressure against the clack valve increases. Within a second or so the pressure rises to a point where it overcomes the force of the clack valve's weighted spring. The valve closes and the water stops pouring out of it.

2. With the clack valve closed the water in the drivepipe begins to push against the no-return valve, opening it. Water now flows into the air dome, compressing the air trapped inside while at the same time forcing water into and up the delivery pipe. After about a second, the air pressure inside the dome becomes great enough to exert a counterpressure that closes the no-return valve again. With both valves closed waterflow down the drivepipe momentarily stops.

3. With the no-return valve closed, pressure in the dome continues to drive the water in the delivery pipe upward toward the storage tank. At the same time the clack valve's spring opens the valve again because the pressure of the now stationary water in the drivepipe has fallen off. At this point, the conditions are the same as in Step 1 and the cycle repeats. Note that the flow of water up the delivery pipe is continuous, largely because of the cushioning action of the air in the dome.

Waterwheels to Pump Water

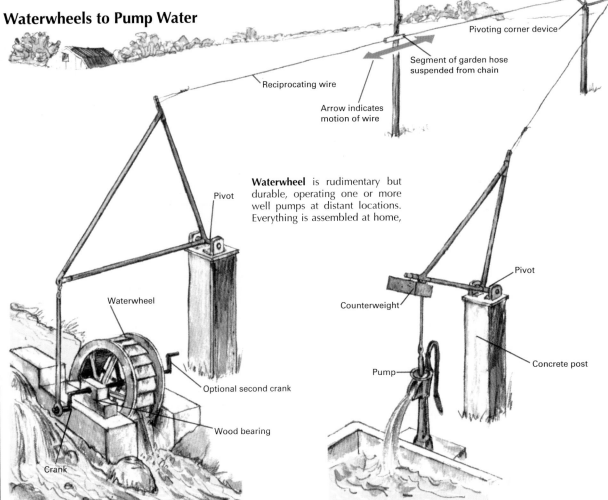

Waterwheel is rudimentary but durable, operating one or more well pumps at distant locations. Everything is assembled at home,

Commercially made rams can be purchased in a variety of sizes with drivepipes ranging from 1 1/4 in. to 8 in. in diameter. Or a person who has plumbing experience can actually build a ram at

Sources and resources

Books and pamphlets
Allen, Inversin. *Hydraulic Ram*. Mt. Rainier, Md.: Volunteers in Technical Assistance, 1979.
Design of Small Dams. Washington, D.C.: U.S. Department of the Interior, 1984.
Eshenaur, Walter C. *Understanding Hydropower*. Arlington, Va.: Volunteers in Technical Assistance, 1988.
Holland, Peter R. *Amazing Models: Water Power*. Blue Ridge Summit, Pa.: TAB Books, 1990.
Marier, Donald, and Stoiaken, Larry, eds. *Alternative Sources of Energy: Hydropower*. Melaca, Minn.: ASEI, 1988.
Naudascher, Eduard. *Hydrodynamic Forces*. Brookfield, Vt.: Ashgate Publishing, 1990.
Ovens, W.G. *A Design Manual for Water Wheels*. Mt. Rainier, Md.: Volunteers in Technical Assistance, 1988.
Rickard, Graham. *Water Energy*. Milwaukee, Wis.: Gareth Stevens, 1991.

Equipment
Aurelius Manufacturing Co., Inc. 222 S.W. 8th St., Braham, Minn. 55006.
Canyon Industries. 5346 Mosquito Lake Rd., Deming, Wash. 98244.
Cumberland General Store. Crossville, Tenn. 38555.
GSA Associates. P.O. Box 536, Croton Falls, N.Y. 10519.
Hydro-Air, Inc. 1275 Bloomfield Ave., Fairfield, N.J.
M.P. Sales Co. 70 Fort Point St., East Norwalk, Conn. 06855.
Small Hydraulic Systems & Equipment. 5141 Wickersham St., Acme, Wash. 98220.

Water resources district offices
For address of office in your area write U.S. Geological Survey, Department of the Interior, Washington, D.C. 20240.

The Amish people of Pennsylvania have for many years been applying stream power to pump water from their wells. Their method is to use small waterwheels that turn at 10 to 20 revolutions per minute located on streams as much as 1/2 mile away from the well. Power is transmitted between waterwheel and well by a wire, attached at one end to a crank on the wheel and at the other end to the pump handle. As the waterwheel turns, the crank translates its circular motion into reciprocating motion. The wire carries the movement to the pump.

Both undershot and breast wheels are used. The wheels are from 1 to 3 feet in diameter and are fabricated from steel sheet, with curved cups for blades. The length of the crank arm is critical; it must be just long enough to produce the back-and-forth motion needed by

the pump, usually 4 to 6 inches. The crank is connected by a rod to a triangular frame that pivots at the top of a post. The frame is made of 3/4-inch-diameter galvanized pipe welded or bolted together. A similar frame is used at the pump end of the system. A counterweight weighing about 100 pounds is attached to a corner of this frame.

The wire that connects the frames so that they move in tandem is smooth, galvanized 12-gauge fence wire. If the wire is very long, poles spaced 75 feet apart are used to support it. If the wire is to traverse a zigzag course around obstacles, a device for negotiating the corners, such as the one illustrated, can be constructed.

The system can also be rigged to operate an additional water pump by attaching a second crank to the opposite end of the waterwheel shaft.

Wind Power

Clean, Cheap Power From an Old Idea And a New Technology

Wind power has been used for hundreds of years to pump water and grind grain. Its use in milling grain was once so common, in fact, that all machines with blades turned by the wind became known as windmills, even though they were and are used for other purposes than milling. Traditional windmills of the type associated with Holland were ponderous and inefficient. As a result, wind power did not become popular in this country until mills with multiple metal blades were developed. Such mills performed admirably at pumping water from wells and proliferated rapidly after 1850, particularly across the Plains States. Millions of them were erected on farms and placed along railroad rights-of-way to supply water for the boilers of steam locomotives.

In the 1930s it became possible to buy a windmill that could generate electricity. This was a new development based on a mill using two or three propellerlike blades turning at high speed. The best of these wind-electric systems were made by Marcellus Jacobs, whose product is still admired today. Many of these depression era wind-powered generators, along with their water-pumping brethren, have fallen into disuse or been sold for scrap. But with the steady rise in the cost of electricity, wind generators may yet become a competitive alternative in areas of the country where the average yearly wind speed is high. However, it takes a very large wind plant to supply the entire power needs of a typical modern home, so unless the family is willing to budget its household electricity usage stringently, a wind plant can only act as a supplement or serve as an emergency backup during utility blackouts.

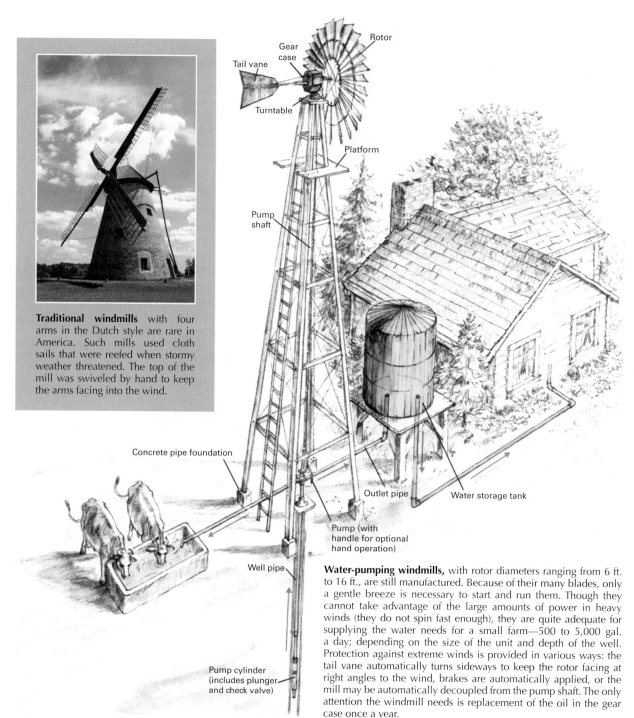

Traditional windmills with four arms in the Dutch style are rare in America. Such mills used cloth sails that were reefed when stormy weather threatened. The top of the mill was swiveled by hand to keep the arms facing into the wind.

Water-pumping windmills, with rotor diameters ranging from 6 ft. to 16 ft., are still manufactured. Because of their many blades, only a gentle breeze is necessary to start and run them. Though they cannot take advantage of the large amounts of power in heavy winds (they do not spin fast enough), they are quite adequate for supplying the water needs for a small farm—500 to 5,000 gal. a day; depending on the size of the unit and depth of the well. Protection against extreme winds is provided in various ways: the tail vane automatically turns sideways to keep the rotor facing at right angles to the wind, brakes are automatically applied, or the mill may be automatically decoupled from the pump shaft. The only attention the windmill needs is replacement of the oil in the gear case once a year.

Modern Windmills

Turning speeds of greater than 1,500 revolutions per minute are necessary to generate electricity. To attain these speeds, propellers with only two or three blades must be used. Traditional multibladed windmills do not work because they operate well only at relatively low speeds. At higher rates of rotation the blades spin so fast that the air cannot pass between them, and as a result the whirling blades act like a solid disc.

High-speed wind generators are subject to stresses that can quickly destroy them if they are not carefully designed and built. Exhaustive testing of a variety of prototypes has led to several key discoveries. The most important was that the propeller blades should have an aerodynamic design similar (although not identical) to that of airplane propellers. In addition, it was found that the blades should be constructed from a durable lightweight material such as Sitka spruce or carbon fiber. Finally, engineers determined that either two or three blades will work well. Wind generators in both styles are being produced in sizes over 1000 kilowatts—electricity for more than 400 U.S. homes.

High-speed windmills behave like gyroscopes. When the wind changes its direction and pushes at the tail vane to swing the mill around, the windmill balks and exerts a gyroscopic counterforce that can either break the blades or tear the entire propeller-generator unit off its base unless it is sturdily moored to the tower and cushioned at critical points by shock absorbers.

Windmills for residential installations that meet these requirements can be obtained from manufacturers in the United States, Europe, and Australia. The propeller diameters of the units (diameters of circles swept by the blade tips) range in size from 3 feet up to 30 feet, corresponding roughly to power outputs of 25 watts to 6,000 watts at a 25-mile-per-hour wind speed. Most of the plants are designed to run for 20 or more years with little or no attention. Lubrication is relatively permanent, parts are moisture-proof and noncorrosive, and some means is built into each unit to keep the windmill from running wild and destroying itself in extreme winds. Two such safety devices are illustrated below.

Wind-electric technology is no longer in its infancy, yet a variety of ways to tap the wind continue to be investigated. The Darrieus rotor shown at the right solves the problem of twisting stresses since it does not have to swivel its axis with each change in wind direction. A virtue of sailwing plants is that extreme winds are likely to do no more damage than rip the sails—a considerably safer consequence than a broken propeller blade flying downwind. They are also easier to repair.

Experimental designs

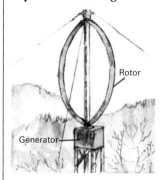

Darrieus rotor resembles a two- or three-bladed eggbeater. Because it spins on a vertical axis, it does not have to swivel into the wind to catch it every time the wind shifts direction. It does not start by itself, however, so a small motor is usually built on to get the unit going after each spell of no wind.

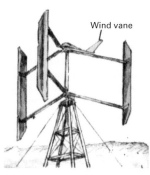

Variable-pitch blades on this type of Darrieus rotor give the unit a means to start by itself. A small wind vane on top of the rotor shaft makes starting possible by sensing any new direction from which the wind may be rising and altering the angle that the blades make with respect to the new direction.

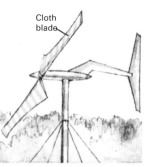

Sailwing windmills use blades made of nylon. The cloth is kept taut by a framework of aluminum poles and takes on the airfoil profile of a sail on a sailboat whenever the wind blows. Since the cloth is flexible, the blades bend with the wind and so are less likely than solid blades to break.

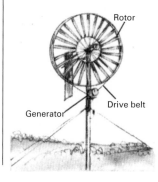

Bicycle-wheel rotor is a modern cousin to the old multibladed windmills. The rotors weigh very little. To operate a generator, the rotor perimeter is employed as a drive wheel in a pulley system with a large step-up ratio. Fair amounts of power can be produced in this way in the low wind-speed range within which these mills are most effective.

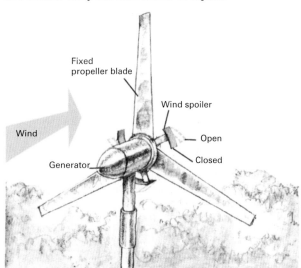

Wind-powered generators are manufactured in two configurations: with a tail vane and without one. Generators without a vane pivot on an off-center support point so that the force of the wind keeps them oriented toward the wind on the downwind side of the pivot. In heavy winds the generator shown with a vane has weights on each propeller shaft that turn outward like governor weights and "feather" the blades. (Feathered blades are edged into the wind; in this way they lose their propulsive power and keep the unit from overspeeding.) The wind spoilers shown on the downwind generator serve the same purpose, but instead of feathering the blades, the spoilers spread centrifugally outward in rising winds to act as a brake.

Measuring the Wind In Order to Reap It

Although the most accurate way to calculate the power potential of the wind in your area is to measure it yourself, a fair estimate can be obtained by using wind data accumulated by the government at over 270 locations around the country. It can be obtained by writing the National Climatic Data Center, Federal Building, Asheville, North Carolina 28801; ask for data collected by the station nearest you. Also check with your local newspaper and television and radio stations—they frequently maintain files on wind and weather dating back many years. The most useful information you can get is the average wind speed for each month of the year as well as for the year as a whole. For most parts of the United States the average falls between 8 and 12 miles per hour. Localities that have an average wind speed of more than 12 miles per hour are definitely worth considering for a wind power installation; areas with an average below 8 miles per hour are marginal at best.

What the Wind's Power Can Do

After an optimum location has been selected, use the wind speed measured at that location and the monthly power output chart (far right) to determine the number of kilowatt-hours available if a wind-powered generator is installed. The output will depend, of course, on the wind-plant model planned for the site. The manufacturer will probably specify a power rating that is the maximum power the wind plant will deliver—usually it will be the power generated when the wind speed is 25 miles per hour. Use this rating in the chart.

Having determined the expected monthly output in kilowatt-hours, you can estimate what value it can have for you. One way to do this is to compare the kilowatt-hours on your electric bill with the expected output of the wind generator. This will tell you how much of your electric power needs the wind plant will satisfy. For the comparison, use a bill that is typical of the year.

Alternatively, use a power capability chart like the one at the right for the estimate. The chart indicates in an approximate way the number and type of appliances that various monthly power outputs can handle. It is expected that the use of these appliances will be fairly evenly distributed over each month and that batteries are used to store power and absorb peak power demands.

If you make your own wind speed measurements, you should obtain periodic readings at a number of locations around your property, particularly at higher elevations, to find the optimum site. One shortcut is to measure for a week or two only; if the ups and downs of the data over this period are similar to those reported by the nearest weather station, you can assume that the station's readings for the remaining 11 months will also be similar. For example, if your measurements consistently turn out to be 10 percent higher than the station's reported wind speeds, augment the remaining reported figures by 10 percent to achieve a year-round estimate.

A variety of instruments are available for measuring wind speed. Some, costing only a few dollars, simply measure the speed at a given moment. To obtain a reliable average over a period of time with these devices requires that you make many observations, a chore that can quickly become tedious. At the other end of the spectrum are sophisticated instruments costing hundreds of dollars that automatically provide a complete printout of wind data over an extended period. The best choice for the individual homeowner may be a compromise, such as the semiautomatic anemometer-odometer arrangement shown at the right.

Low cost system to measure wind speed uses anemometer wired to odometer. Cups of anemometer are spun by wind; odometer (black box at base of mast) counts each revolution of the anemometer. To measure wind, set odometer counter to zero and note the time. After several hours, read number tallied by odometer and recheck time. Divide odometer reading by 60 and by number of hours elapsed to obtain average wind speed in miles per hour. For example, if odometer tally is 1,500 after an interval of 21/2 hours, the tally divided by 60 and then by 21/2 gives an average wind speed of 10 miles per hour.

Power capability

The amount of kilowatt-hours per month that can run the appliances listed is:

    150 kilowatt-hours will run all of those in A
    300 kilowatt-hours will run all of those in A and B
    700 kilowatt-hours will run all of those in A, B, and C

A		B	
Blender		Iron	
Mixer		Electric blankets	
Heating pad		Lights	
Vacuum cleaner		Television set	
Toaster		Refrigerator	
Washing machine			
Coffee pot		C	
Record player		Food freezer	
Humidifier		Clothes dryer	
		Electric range	

Average monthly power output

Output rating in watts	Blade diameter in feet	Kilowatt-hours at various wind speeds				
		8 mph	10 mph	12 mph	14 mph	16 mph
100	3	5	8	11	13	15
250	4	12	18	24	29	32
500	5	24	35	46	55	62
1,000	7	45	65	86	100	120
2,000	11	80	120	160	200	240
4,000	15	150	230	310	390	460
6,000	18	230	350	470	590	710
8,000	21	300	450	600	750	900
10,000	24	370	550	730	910	1100

Chart shows the output you can expect for a variety of generator sizes and wind speeds. To use the chart, locate the wind speed column most closely matching the average in your area, and read down the column. Each entry shows the kilowatt-hours (kwh) per month that will be developed by a particular generator-blade combination. For instance, if the average wind speed at a potential site is about 12 miles per hour, a 100-watt wind generator will turn out 11 kwh (scarcely worthwhile), but a 2,000-watt generator will produce 160 kwh and a 10,000-watt generator, 730 kwh.

Preferred Sites for Windmills

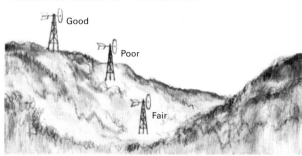

In hilly areas average wind speed can differ markedly according to location. As a guide when checking, hilltops are the best sites, hillsides are the poorest, while valley bottoms can do very well provided the direction of local prevailing winds is up and down the valley. But test each site to make sure.

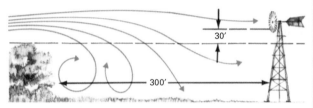

Nearby obstacles can be very detrimental to windmill power output. Even when a barrier is situated downwind from the mill it can produce enough turbulence in the area to interfere with the windmill's efficient performance. For best results, a windmill should be at least 30 ft. higher than any obstruction within a circle of a 300-ft. radius out from the windmill.

Height of windmill above the ground makes a substantial difference in power output, since wind speed in general increases with altitude. Also, windmills respond in exaggerated fashion to small changes in wind speed, their power output climbing 33 percent for each 10 percent increase in wind speed. The net effect is shown in the illustration. A wind plant that generates 100 kwh per month on a 10-ft. tower, for instance, will generate 240 kwh per month on an 80-ft. tower.

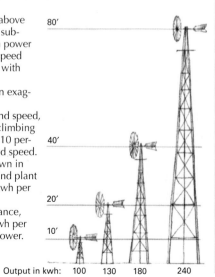

Output in kwh: 100   130   180   240

Selecting and Putting Up Towers

As towers rise in height, they also rise in cost, and eventually a point of diminishing returns is reached where added tower expense is not appreciably offset by added power output. Where to draw the line will depend on your power needs and the nature of the site. Factors to consider include average available wind speed, the type of tower used, and the cost of the windmill. For example, if a pole-type tower is to be erected, an array of at least five guy wires fanned out in different directions is preferable, an arrangement that requires more and more space as tower height increases.

It is easy to underestimate the twisting forces that a wind plant will exert in extreme winds, so it is best to use a commercial tower specifically engineered to support a windmill, especially for heights greater than 30 feet. The manufacturer will provide instructions concerning assembly and erection. You will need at least two helpers to put up the tower and install the windmill on it. The usual procedure is to prepare the foundation, assemble the tower on its side, and erect it by the gin-pole method (below). The mill is then installed part by part at the top. (Do not attach the generator unit before raising the tower; the added weight increases the tower's likelihood of falling down as it is being pulled up.) Towers can also be built vertically, section by section, but this is more hazardous. In general, erecting a tower or climbing one to install equipment can be dangerous work. Never work alone and always wear strong boots, gloves, sturdy clothing, and a hard hat—tools or construction debris falling from a structure can cause serious injury.

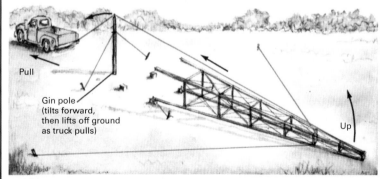

Gin-pole method for raising a tower depends for its success on carefully placed temporary guy wires that keep pole and tower from falling sideways during lifting. Wires at base of tower prevent it from sliding forward as vehicle pulls.

Temporary crane attached to top of tower is used to raise windmill parts—first the generator, then tail vane and blades. Man on ground guides each part with guy, helping it into place at tower top, where assistant installs it.

Pole-type tower must either be deeply anchored in concrete or supported by guy wires. Use a minimum of three guy-wire anchors (five are preferable). Set anchors at least one-half of tower height away from base of tower and use turnbuckles in the guy wires so that their tension can be adjusted. Some pole towers are hinged at the bottom to permit lowering for servicing and during gales.

Self-supporting tower does not need additional bracing but must have an adequate foundation—usually concrete piers in which the tower's legs are embedded or to which they are bolted. Self-supporting towers are delivered in segments by the manufacturer and must be assembled on location. They are about twice as expensive as pole-type towers of equivalent height but require no guy wires.

Homemade towers up to 30 ft. high, such as the wooden structure shown here, can be built by experienced do-it-yourselfers. They can be quite attractive (this one includes a small picnic platform in the base) but are more apt to be blown down in high winds. If you plan on building one, consult a structural engineer and site the tower in an area where danger to life and property due to the tower falling will be negligible.

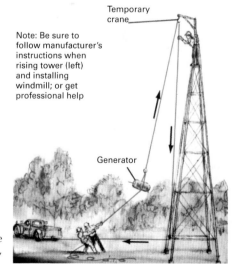

Note: Be sure to follow manufacturer's instructions when rising tower (left) and installing windmill; or get professional help

A Wind-Electric System For Household Needs

A system such as the one shown at right can supply a significant portion of the electrical needs of a one-family home. A bank of batteries installed in a well-ventilated shed (or basement of a house) stores excess power that the wind plant generates during low demand periods and releases during windless periods or times of peak demand. Operation is automatic. When the wind blows strongly and few appliances are on, or when the wind is down, the battery current reverses, sending just enough to the house system to make up the difference between windmill output and appliance demand.

Wind plants are generally rated according to their maximum output. The one illustrated here is rated at 2,000 watts, the rating corresponding to its power output when the wind is 25 miles per hour. Its actual output is considerably lower—in the 50- to 150-watt range for most places in the United States—since there are very few locations where wind speeds average 25 miles per hour.

The wind plant is built to stand up in winds of up to 120 miles per hour, but the propeller should be braked whenever winds above 80 miles per hour are anticipated. The brake, which is also useful for stopping the windmill for inspection and servicing, can be operated from the base of the windmill tower.

Sources and resources

Books and pamphlets
Bailey, Donna. *Energy from Wind and Water*. Chatham, N.J.: Raintree Steck-Vaughn, 1990.
Gipe, Paul. *Wind Energy Comes of Age*. New York: John Wiley & Sons, 1995.
Rickard, Graham. *Wind Energy*. Milwaukee, Ind.: Gareth Stevens, 1991.
Wind Energy Technical Information Guide. New York: Gordon Press, 1991.
Wind Power: A Source Guide. New York: Gordon Press, 1991.
Periodicals
Wind Power Digest, P.O. Box 700, Bascom, Ohio 44809.
Equipment
Northern Power Systems. 1 North Wind Rd., Moretown, Vt. 05660.
Omnion Power Engineering Corp. 2010 Energy Dr., East Troy, Wisc. 53120
Pease Windamatic Systems Inc., Huntertown, Ind. 46748.
Zephyr Wind Dynamo Co. 107 Bowery St., Bath, Maine 04530.
Organizations
The American Wind Energy Association. 1516 King St., Alexandria, Va. 22314.

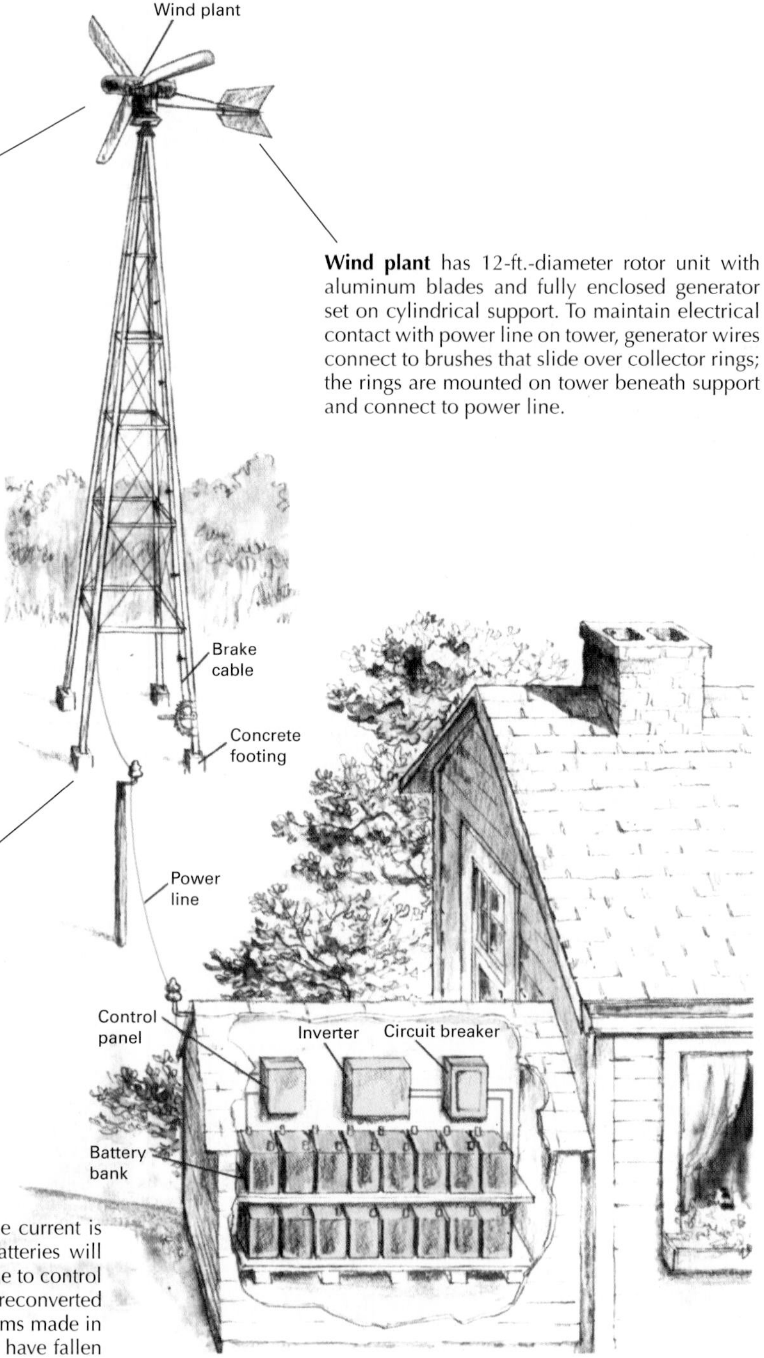

Propeller shaft drives generator through set of step-up gears inside generator housing. During gales the propeller blades are automatically feathered (turned edge-on into the wind) by a set of weights protruding horizontally from shaft of each blade. Cable under generator is part of brake cable running from tower base.

Wind plant

Wind plant has 12-ft.-diameter rotor unit with aluminum blades and fully enclosed generator set on cylindrical support. To maintain electrical contact with power line on tower, generator wires connect to brushes that slide over collector rings; the rings are mounted on tower beneath support and connect to power line.

Brake cable

Concrete footing

Foundation for each leg of tower is 1 cu. yd. of concrete extending down below frost depth. To protect generator against lightning damage, a 1/8-in.-diameter cable connects leg of tower to metal grounding rod inside concrete footing. Rod extends 8 ft. into earth below footing to provide safe path for lightning.

Power line

Control panel

Inverter   Circuit breaker

Battery bank

Wind-electric system includes an AC generator. The current is converted from AC to DC inside the generator (batteries will only charge on DC) and is then carried by power line to control panel in shed. There it may be stored in batteries or reconverted to AC for household use by the inverter. Older systems made in the 1930s and 1940s used DC generators, but they have fallen out of favor because of the extra maintenance they require.

Electrical Equipment

The amount of electrical energy that can be stored by a wind-electric system depends on the capacity of its batteries. A typical home system will store enough to carry a family through two or three windless days after which some type of alternate backup supply must be switched on. If more batteries were used, more windless days could be handled, but batteries are expensive, and it is generally cheaper to use an occasional backup.

Batteries come in various storage ratings and are priced accordingly. Those shown below have a rating of 270 ampere-hours. This means, for example, if an appliance draws 10 amperes of current from such a battery, the battery will become discharged after 27 hours (10 amperes times 27 hours equals 270 ampere-hours). Appliances such as electric irons and toasters each draw about 10 amperes. This calculation can be extended to any amount of current drawn provided it is not excessive. (For instance, the batteries will not deliver 270 amperes for one hour; they are not built for it.)

Properly maintained and operated, a battery will last about 10 years. Water should be added periodically, usually every one to six months, the battery terminals should be kept clear of corrosion, and the batteries must not be permitted to become more than 90 percent discharged. Maintain the batteries at room temperature or above, since cold reduces battery effectiveness. However, be sure to ventilate the room in which the batteries are placed; they can emit hydrogen, a highly flammable and potentially explosive gas.

The public utility or a standby gasoline-fueled generator can be used for backup power. A standby unit requires an engine no larger than a snow thrower's, but it has a limited life span. A better backup option may be photovoltaic (PV) cells. PV cells convert sunlight to electricity and can allow greater daytime electric use.

Inverters are employed to convert DC to AC. The inverter used with the batteries illustrated below has a 2,000-watt capacity and automatically adjusts to changing loads. Such a device is quite expensive, almost as much as the wind plant shown on the facing page. If DC can be used in the house, a mixed system—one that delivers both AC and DC—is preferable; the inverter can then be smaller and less costly.

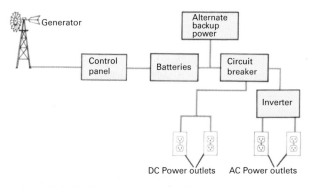

Typical wind-electric system has control panel to protect batteries from overcharging, an inverter to convert some of the DC output to AC, and a source of standby power. (Alternate systems, similar to some hydroelectric systems, can also be employed. See *Power Storage, Regulators, and Inverters*, p.101.)

Bank of 58 batteries produces 116 volts DC. Batteries are like those used in electric golf carts and can provide a steady output over long periods. Inverter is at far right on counter. Above it, on wall, are control panel and circuit breaker (partly hidden).

State of charge or discharge is indicated by ball-shaped battery floats. When left ball drops to level shown, battery has become 30 percent discharged; when center ball drops, battery is 60 percent discharged; when right ball drops, battery is 90 percent discharged. Battery water level can also be seen through glass and checked. The water, which must be distilled water, should never be above high mark or below low mark. At top is a capped opening for replenishing water.

Neil Welliver, Painter and Wind Enthusiast

Independence From The Local Power Company

Neil Welliver, of Lincolnville, Maine, is an internationally renowned artist who often paints his giant landscapes under floodlights powered by the two wind plants on his isolated farm. The plants serve his other electrical needs as well and have saved him thousands of dollars in utility costs.

"I suppose I first got interested in wind power as a child when I got my first pinwheel. Later I read a little about electricity and wind plants but, really, I was a rank amateur. I put up my first wind plant myself with the help of a local electrician. I sure learned a lot about electricity in a hurry.

"There's no problem in generating enough power for all our household activities from the 2- and 6-kilowatt plants we have. We're conscious of what we're using, but I've never even had a light flicker. I have a backup generator, but we hardly ever need it except for August and September during the doldrums—you know, the period when the wind really dies down. In the winter the wind up here is very strong, and I get more power than the batteries can store.

"There's been an enormous interest in wind plants in the last several years. I was one of the first people in the country to install one and a New York paper did a story on me. People drove from as far away as Louisiana to see the wind plant without so much as a call beforehand.

"Despite the interest, I should say that wind plants are not for everybody. First of all, you have to climb a 50-ft. tower to grease the equipment. And to use a wind plant effectively, you really have to know how the whole thing operates, how to check the machinery and the batteries to see if everything is in good shape. Then, remember, a wind plant produces direct current. That's all right for light bulbs, but for most electronic equipment you have to use an inverter to change that direct current to alternating current.

"Nonetheless, I hope more people will get the information on wind plants. It's madness not to use the wind as power. Look, 90 percent of my electricity I get free. I like to think of myself as a consumer with my own electric company."

Solar Energy

Earth's Private Star Holds Bright Promise For Abundant Energy

If you ever stepped barefoot on a sunbaked rock on a July afternoon, you know what solar energy is all about. Heat generated by the sun would melt a sphere of ice the size of the earth in 16.6 minutes. While only a small portion of that energy is intercepted by the earth, there is still enough to provide 646,000 horsepower for every square mile of its surface.

People have been trying to capture and use this enormous reservoir of free solar power since the dawn of history. The Greeks designed their houses around central sun-gathering courtyards 3,000 years ago. In pre-Columbian America, Indians of the Southwest carefully oriented their cliff pueblos to trap the warmth of the winter sun. During colonial times prudent homeowners built their homes with stove-warmed kitchens on the north side so that living areas would have sunny south walls. Thomas Jefferson, in designing Monticello, was keenly aware of the sun's potential for providing heat and used special windows to help trap its warmth.

Some of our most modern solar technology has its roots in the past. Functional solar systems were producing domestic hot water in 30 percent of the homes in Pasadena, California, before 1900, and by 1940 Miami had 60,000 of them. A flat-plate solar collector array built in 1907 used a sheet-iron absorber plate topped by glass. By 1914 solar collectors using copper tubes soldered to copper sheets were heating homes in California.

Today, solar systems for home heating are working almost everywhere in the country, not only in the Sun Belt but in the North too. Wherever local codes permit, you can save money and fuel with a do-it-yourself solar installation.

Montezuma Castle, a 1,200-year-old five-story pueblo cliff dwelling in central Arizona, is a classic example of passive solar design. Cliffs shade it in summer; in winter the sun pours in.

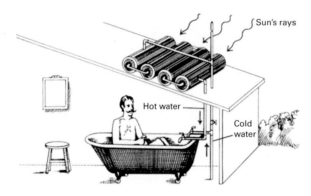

Climax solar collector, patented in 1891, consisted of a series of black tanks in a glazed box. Sun-heated water moved through tanks by convection for use in bath or kitchen below.

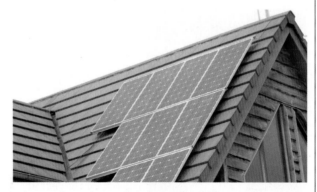

Solar panels on this south-facing roof and large windows on the east side allow the sun to warm the house during the day and provide consistent power. Costs for solar electric cells like these have dropped dramatically the last few decades and continue to become more affordable.

Where Solar Stands Today

The energy crisis of the 1970s spawned a kaleidoscope of dreams and schemes in solar home design. Some are solidly practical, some are innovative and radical, and a few resemble Rube Goldberg contraptions.

Among the most simple contrivances is a hot water system for a beach house. Tap water is run through 100 feet of black plastic hose coiled on the roof. The sun-warmed water feeds into an attic tank that is tapped as needed for showers or dishwashing. Almost as simple is a supplementary heating system that is not much more than a box sloping from the ground to the bottom of a south-facing first floor window. A black-painted divider of foam insulation suspended down the box's center permits cool air from the house to slip down the channel beneath the foam panel and up its sun-warmed topside.

At the other end of the technological scale are houses with towering glass walls and ingenious devices for trapping and storing the sun's heat. One New Hampshire home has two-story double-glazed plastic panels covering a black foot-thick concrete wall. During the day sun pouring through the panels heats the concrete. Ports at floor and ceiling allow cool interior air to circulate by convection up the wall and then reenter the building at the top after being warmed. At night and on cloudy days bushels of tiny plastic beads are blown into the space between the double glazing to prevent escape of stored heat. Come morning, the beads are sucked out by a vacuum pump to canisters in the garage until needed again. Another unique solar home in New Mexico has south-facing walls of water-filled drums stacked in racks like wine bottles. Ends facing outward are black to soak up sun and warm the water. At night windowless walls of insulating material hinge upward to seal in the heat.

Many technological improvements are on the way, including vacuum insulated collectors and cells that can convert sunlight into electricity. Engineers in New Mexico have built a "power tower," topped by a boiler located at the focus of almost 2,000 mirrors, which has produced temperatures of 3000°F.

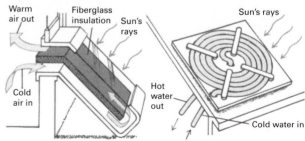

Window box collector (left) and simple hose water heater.

Will It Work in Your Home?

Solar water heaters have long been competitive with electricity, fuel oil, and natural gas in many parts of the country. Solar space heat is usually competitive wherever there is moderate to high solar radiation (see map). Even in low radiation locales, solar home heating can be a big money saver if fuel and utility costs are high.

Most successful systems take over part, not all, of the heating load. Such systems are cheaper to build and will usually pay for themselves sooner than those that rely exclusively on the sun.

For solar heating to be effective a house must have a large surface—typically a roof—facing within 10 degrees of true south. The building should also be well insulated (10 or more inches of high quality insulation in the attic and six inches in the walls for northern parts of the nation). Heating ducts or pipes should be wrapped with insulation. Storm doors and storm windows are important. All outside joints should be caulked and fireplace dampers snugly fitted and closed when not in use.

As a rule of thumb, solar heating makes good economic sense if it amortizes, or pays for itself, within 10 years.

In other words, your 10-year savings in home fuel consumption should equal or exceed the cost of installing a solar system. Generally speaking, solar heating will provide the biggest savings in homes with high fuel bills: if your fuel bills run more than $3,000 a year, a $15,000 solar system can be amortized in 10 years by cutting fuel consumption in half; but if you only spend $500 to heat your home, it is doubtful that solar heating will pay. Another consideration is the relative cost-effectiveness of a switch to solar versus a simple modernization of your present heating system. For example, you can often save more money by installing a fuel-efficient oil burner in place of an old one than you can by going solar.

The chart on this page can help you determine if solar energy is for you. However, a complete analysis of heating loads, site location, fuel consumption, house size, thermal efficiency, government tax incentives, and other variables is needed to make a precise appraisal. Information needed to determine the size, cost, and amortization time of a home hot water system may be available from your state energy office or public utility.

Solar radiation in the United States

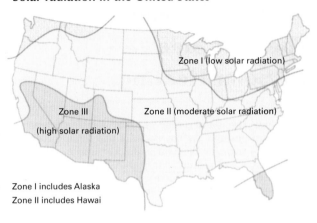

Zone I includes Alaska
Zone II includes Hawaii

Solar Water Heating System Characteristics: Factors Useful in Selecting System Type for Particular Situations

		Suitable system size	Cost/ft^2 for 40 ft^2 unless noted	Freeze tolerance	Hard water tolerance	Maintenance need
Low-Temperature Systems						
Unglazed		for pools	$10-$25 (400 ft^2)	none	good	very low
Passive Mid-Temperature Systems						
Integrated collector		small	$50-$75	moderate	minimal	very low
Thermosiphon	direct	small	$40-$75	none	minimal	low
	indirect	small	$50-$80	moderate	good	low
Indirect, Active, Mid-Temperature Systems						
Flat-plate, antifreeze	small		$50-$90	excellent	good	high
	large		$30-$50 (30,000 ft^2)			
Flat-plate, drain back		small	$50-$90	good	good	high
Direct, Active, Mid-Temperature Systems						
Drain down		small		corrections being developed	minimal	high
Recirculating		small			minimal	high
High-Temperature Systems						
Evacuated tube	direct	small	$75-$150	good	minimal	high
	indirect	large	$75-$150	excellent	good	high
Parabolic trough		large	$20-$40 (30,000 ft^2)	excellent	good	high

Sources and resources

Books and pamphlets

Anderson, Bruce, and Michael Riordan. *The New Solar Home Book.* Andover, Mass.: Brick House Publishing, 1987.

Bason, Frank C. *Energy and Solar Heating.* College Park, Md.: American Association of Physics Teachers, 1984.

Cooling Your Home Naturally. Washington, D.C.: U.S. Department of Energy, 1994.

Crowther, Richard. *Affordable Passive Solar Homes.* Boulder, Colo.: American Solar Energy Society, 1983.

DeWinter, Francis. *Solar Collectors, Energy Storage and Materials.* Cambridge, Mass.: MIT Press, 1991.

Energy Efficient Water Heating. Washington, D.C.: U.S. Department of Energy, 1995.

Freeman, Mark. *The Solar Home: How to Design and Build a House You Heat With the Sun.* Mechanicsburg, Pa.: Stackpole, 1994.

Guide to Making Energy-Smart Purchases. Washington, D.C.: U.S. Department of Energy, 1994.

Kubsch, Erwin. *Home Owner's Guide to Free Heat.* Sheridan, Wyo.: Sunstore Farms, 1991.

Reynolds, Michael. *Earthship: How to Build Your Own.* Taos, N. Mex.: Solar Survival, 1990.

Solar Electric Power Association, 1391 Connecticut Ave., suite 3.2, Washington, D.C. 2006. www.solarelectricpower.org.

Solar Water Heating. Washington, D.C.: U.S. Department of Energy, 1994.

Tomorrow's Energy Today. Washington, D.C.: U.S. Department of Energy, 1994.

Using the Earth to Heat and Cool Homes. Butte, Mont.: NCAT, 1983.

Organizations

American Solar Energy Society (ASES), 2400 Central Ave., Suite A, Boulder, Co. 80301. www.ases.org.

National Renewable Energy Laboratory, 1617 Cole Blud., Goledon, Co 80401-3393. www.nrel.gov.

Solar Energy Industries Association, 805 15th St., NW Suite 510, Washington, D.C. 2005. www.seia.org.

Passive Systems: The Soft Side Of Solar Heating

There are two basic types of solar heating systems: active and passive. Active systems use liquid or air to absorb and transfer the heat to its destination. They require pumps and piping or fans and ducts to do the job but are relatively easy to install in existing buildings as well as new ones. An active system is the type most often used when an older home is being remodeled and upgraded with energy-saving features.

Passive solar systems, sometimes referred to as the soft approach because they require little in the way of hardware, let nature do most of the work. They do not need pumps, blowers, or plumbing and usually have no leakage or winter freeze-up problems. They use large, heat-absorbing masses, such as concrete walls and water-filled drums, to trap solar heat as it passes through south-facing windows. Heat transfer can be by natural radiation or convection, or warmed air can be channeled to where it is needed with the help of vanes, dampers, and blowers. Because a passive system is a

Instead of a Furnace Try a Greenhouse

Greenhouses are among the oldest and most familiar solar heating devices, but because they warm vegetables and flowers rather than men and women, most people do not think of them as replacements for a conventional home-heating device. However, what warms a plant can also warm a house, and lean-to greenhouses are being used more and more as passive solar collectors in homes with unobstructed south walls. In a typical design, such as the one shown at right, the original frame wall has been replaced by a cinder block collector wall, painted black to improve heat absorption.

The greenhouse, made with double-glazed panels of transparent plastic, is butted directly against the wall. Vents cut through the cinder blocks allow the circulation of heated air. The vents have dampers, but under most conditions the dampers are left open: the small amount of heat that escapes from the main house on cloudy days or at night helps to keep the greenhouse—and the plants growing in it—at the proper temperature. During an excessively warm day the vents would be closed and the greenhouse itself shielded from the sun.

Water-filled oil drums and large pulley-operated shutters of lightweight insulating material form south wall of solar pioneer Steve Baer's house in Corrales, New Mexico.

basic element of the house, it works best when planned as part of a new construction. However, there are many features of passive systems that can be incorporated to advantage in any house. Large glass areas on a south wall (shaded by arbors in the summer) can cut heating bills substantially in locations with moderate solar radiation. A simple greenhouse (see below) can be an effective solar supplement to the home-heating system. Another passive heat collector is the thermosiphon air panel. Heat absorbed by a black metal sheet under insulated glass vents through a duct at the top. Cool room air enters the panel through a bottom duct.

Trapping and Storing the Sun

The simplest passive systems use double transparent glazing to admit sunlight, wall and floor masses to soak it up, and some sort of drapery or shutter arrangement to prevent the trapped heat from escaping through the glass at night or on cloudy days. Temperatures produced by such systems are relatively low, but heat builds up significantly in good storage materials, such as concrete, adobe, and ceramics, which release it slowly to the building's interior during nights and sunless days.

In more sophisticated passive systems the sun does not penetrate the deep interior of a building but is intercepted by a heat collecting-absorbing structure located behind large double-glazed window panels and backed up inside by an interior partition. Vents at top and bottom of the partition allow natural convection of house air to pick up the stored heat from the collector and move it to the living area. In the system shown below, low-powered fans blow cooled house air through a bank of water-filled black plastic columns that serve as the solar collectors. At night sliding foam panels are moved between the columns and the windows to prevent stored heat from escaping.

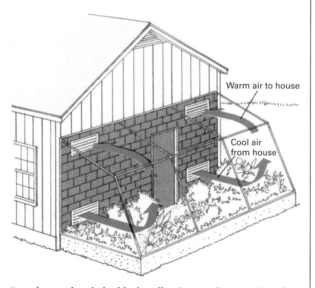

Warm air to house

Cool air from house

Greenhouse plus cinder block wall makes a collector and garden.

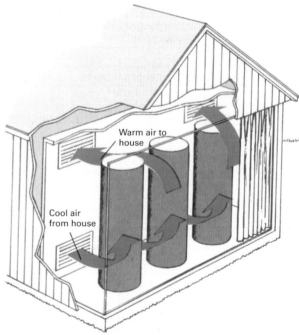

Warm air to house

Cool air from house

Black plastic columns filled with water collect and store heat.

Making the System Fit the Environment

A passive solar heating system must be carefully tailored to local conditions so that the best use is made of available sunlight. The key element in any passive system is the collector wall. The generally accepted rule is that the wall should face directly south, although some experts recommend angling it slightly to the east to catch more sun in the early morning when outside temperatures are lowest. The ideal collector should be aligned so that the rays of the sun strike it perpendicularly. At 40°N, which is roughly the latitude of New York, Philadelphia, Indianapolis, Chicago, Kansas City, Des Moines, Denver, and Salt Lake City, a solar wall sloping at an angle of 60 degrees to the horizontal comes close to the ideal. Farther north, the ideal angle is greater; farther south, it is smaller. Nevertheless, considerations involving snow accumulation, summer shading, high initial cost, and structural integrity generally lead solar architects to specify vertical walls despite the loss of about 10 percent in efficiency.

Collector walls are almost always sheathed in double-layered glass with an insulating airspace between the layers. This type of glass provides the best combination of transparency to sunlight plus the ability to insulate against the loss of house heat. Reflecting glass and heat-absorbing glass both provide relief from overheating in the summer but only at the cost of reduced heating ability in the winter. Intelligent landscaping and carefully designed top and side shading surfaces solve the problem even more efficiently and effectively. Proper planting can moderate summer and winter temperatures by as much as 20°F. A curving row of evergreens bracketing the north and northeast quadrants of a building will serve as a windbreak against winter gales. Tall deciduous shade trees with high canopies placed on the south and southwest sides of the house will form a parasol against searing afternoon sun in summer. During winter, when the leaves have fallen, the rays of the sun can penetrate to bathe the south wall.

In addition to the collector wall, the shape and design of the house are significant factors in passive solar heating. Not surprisingly, it has been found that a house that is elongated in the east-west direction is best for collecting solar energy, since this shape permits maximum exposure to the sun's radiation from the south. An intelligent choice of roofing and siding materials will also contribute to heating efficiency. The roof and outside walls, like the collector wall, should absorb the sun's radiation easily but reradiate little of the thermal energy from the home. Galvanized steel, black roofing material, and siding finished with flat black paint are among the most effective surfacing materials.

Reverse Flow: Controlling It and Putting It to Use

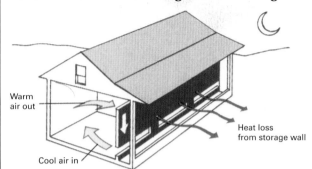

Storage walls of passive systems are often subject to an annoying reverse flow that causes cool night air to spill into the house through the floor vent while warm house air circulates out the top vent, radiating its heat to the outside.

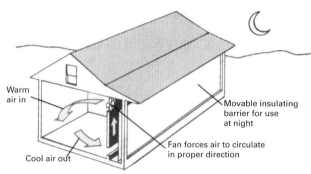

Most common way to prevent reverse flow is to install a fan in the top vent that blows air into the house, thus maintaining positive flow. Insulating curtains or shutters behind double-paned windows further cut down on heat loss.

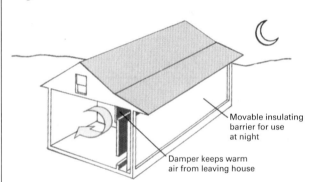

Reverse flow can also be controlled with a damper over the top vent. The damper is closed at night to prevent any circulation from behind the solar wall. This system is not as effective as a fan, since less heat is picked up from the storage wall.

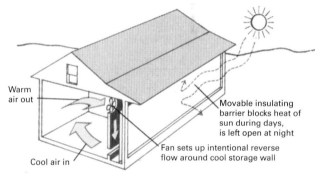

Where summer nights are cool, a passive system can double as an air conditioner. The collectors are exposed at night so they can cool off. During the day a deliberate reverse flow is set up that pulls house air over the cool collectors.

Shading the Solar Window

Concept of a "solar window" is important when designing shading for a collector wall. The window is shown at right on an imaginary dome around a house. Outlines of the window are the sun's path on December 21 and June 21, the winter and summer solstice respectively. As illustrated above, the roof overhang should block the midsummer sun but let the low slanting rays of the winter sun through. Upright sunshades contribute additional shading in early morning and late afternoon. During winter the solar window should be free from obstructions from one hour after sunrise to one hour before sunset.

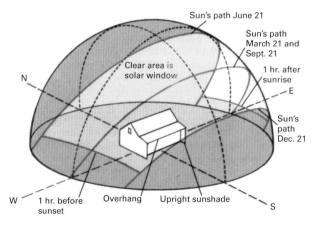

Active Solar Movers: Complex but Convenient

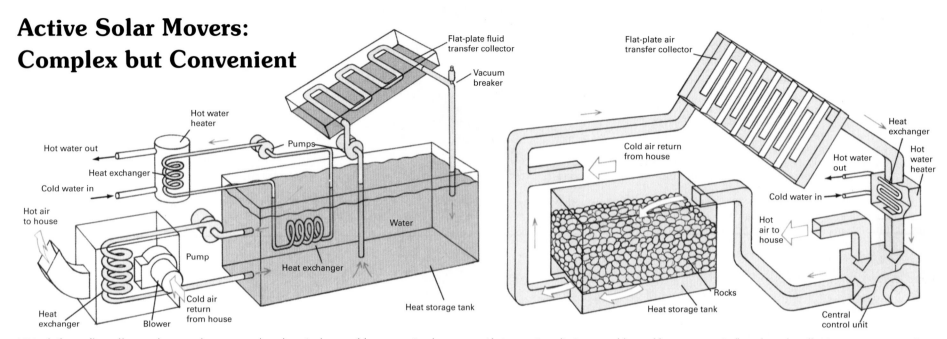

Flat-plate fluid transfer collector

Vacuum breaker

Hot water heater

Hot water out

Pumps

Heat exchanger

Cold water in

Hot air to house

Pump

Water

Heat exchanger

Cold air return from house

Heat exchanger

Blower

Heat storage tank

Flat-plate air transfer collector

Heat exchanger

Cold air return from house

Hot water out

Hot water heater

Cold water in

Hot air to house

Water

Rocks

Heat storage tank

Central control unit

Water is the medium of heat exchange and storage in this active solar heating system. An automatic draindown device removes water from collectors when there is danger of freeze-up. Another type of system circulates antifreeze solution instead of water through collectors.

Air-type system eliminates problems of freeze-up. Key to system is the central air control unit. It contains a blower and dampers that enable it to direct air flow through collectors, storage reservoir, or hot water heater according to heating needs and sun conditions.

Active solar heating is an indirect process. Radiation from the sun warms an intermediate medium (either liquid or air) rather than heating the house directly. The medium is then piped into the house where its heat is extracted by heat exchangers. Excess heat is generally stored in a water- or rock-filled reservoir from which the house system draws as needed. Active solar systems are almost always paired with a conventional system that switches on automatically to tide the house through spells of cold, overcast weather. Typically, a forced hot air system is used as the backup.

The operating temperature of a typical active system is in the 120°F to 160°F range—twice as high as most passive systems. As a result, active systems can easily be put to use to produce hot water. They are also preferred by many engineers for space heating because they perform better than passive systems in areas with low to moderate solar radiation. Their adaptability to existing homes and compatibility with forced air heating systems are added advantages. On the debit side are their relative complexity and high initial cost, medium, the heat storage facility, a circulating pump, flow controls, and heat exchangers. Storage of sun-warmed

water to supply heat at night and on sunless days requires a tank big enough to hold at least 1 1/2 gallons for each square foot of collector area plus an additional 2 percent allowance for expansion when the water heats up. The tank can be located in the basement, the garage,

or behind a fence in the backyard. It can be aboveground or buried. It must, however, be well insulated against heat loss. If the system is to be used for domestic hot water heating only, an insulated 80-gallon tank will do the job for a family of four or five.

Solar collectors are becoming more and more common as their prices go down and oil prices go up.

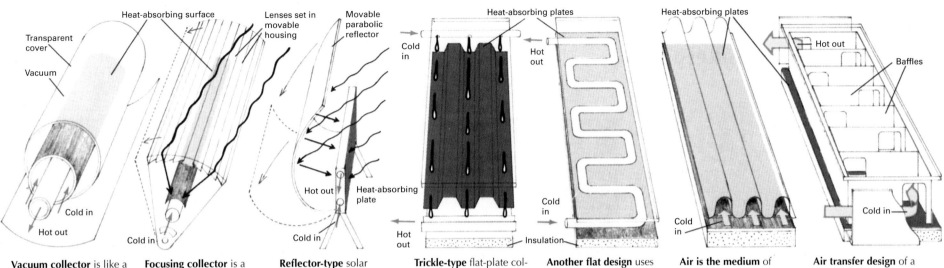

Vacuum collector is like a thermos bottle. Fluid-carrying pipes are surrounded by an evacuated insulating cylinder. Collectors can be placed on roof or against south wall.

Focusing collector is a trough, capped by lenses that bend the sun's rays so they concentrate on a water-carrying pipe along the trough's bottom. Unit swivels to track the sun.

Reflector-type solar collector has a curved mirrored surface that concentrates solar rays onto an absorber plate. The plate contains pipes that enclose liquid for heat transfer.

Trickle-type flat-plate collectors have channeled or corrugated absorber plates. Water is heated as it trickles from a pipe over the absorber to a trough at the bottom.

Another flat design uses water flowing through pipes either welded to the absorber plate or extruded as an integral part of it. As in other collectors, insulation forms the bottom.

Air is the medium of heat transfer in this flat-plate collector. Cool house air entering at the bottom warms as it passes through channels above a panel of black foam plastic.

Air transfer design of a different type warms cool house air by feeding it through a maze of baffled passages. Such baffled air systems can be driven either by a blower or by convection.

The Collectors Are the Key

The prime components of any active system are the collectors. These are the devices that trap the sun's heat and carry it into the building in a stream of moving air or water. There are three basic types of collectors: vacuum, focusing, and flat plate.

Vacuum collectors consist of three concentric tubes. The two inner tubes carry the transfer liquid. A vacuum between them and a transparent outer tube insulates the fluid against heat loss. The tubes are highly efficient, producing fluid temperatures over 300°F in commercial use. For domestic application, an automatic drainback system prevents overheating. The collectors work well in overcast, and are seeing increasing use in the far north where their superior fuel-saving capabilities compensate for their high initial cost.

Focusing collectors use lenses or mirrored surfaces to concentrate sunlight on fluid-carrying pipes. Such collectors can produce temperatures of several thousand degrees Fahrenheit. They are more efficient per square foot than flat-plate collectors but require a complex tracking system to keep them pointed at the sun. Not only is the tracking system expensive, but the reflectors themselves are two or three times as costly per square

foot as most flat-plate types. If they drift off the sun, or if skies are overcast, they stop working completely.

Flat-plate collectors are simple, inexpensive, and can be mounted on the roof or walls of an existing home or on the ground in angled frames. Most will collect some heat in light overcast.

For maximum heat production the surface area of an array of flat-plate collectors should be equal to about one-half the floor area of the house. However, a collector array with only one-third the area of the floor will handle 40 to 60 percent of the heat load in most regions, provided the house is well insulated and has a south-facing roof on which the collectors can be mounted. Most homeowners settle for such a system, since its lower cost results in faster payback of the investment.

The pitch, or slope, at which collectors are mounted depends on how far north the house is located. Ideally, the pitch should equal the latitude plus 15 degrees. Experience has shown, however, that tilts between 20 degrees and vertical are acceptable, provided the collectors face south. Flat-plate collectors are generally fastened directly to the roof rather than mounted on frames that can rip off in a severe storm.

What Happens in Freezing Weather?

Whenever water is used as the heat transfer medium, provision must be made to prevent it from freezing and bursting the pipes on cold winter nights or dark, frigid, snowy days. In regions where there is any chance of freeze-up, active systems using a water medium incorporate what is known as a draindown, or drainback, feature. At night or when ultralow temperatures are forecast, a valve opens that drains all the water out of the collector loop. Generally, the drained water is channeled into the main heat storage tank so that neither water nor warmth is wasted. The draindown feature can be made automatic by installing a temperature-sensitive device known as a thermistor inside the piping. The thermistor triggers the draindown valve when water temperature drops too low.

With the collector loop drained, heat from the sun is no longer delivered to the house, and the storage tank comes into play. A second loop, isolated from the collectors, begins to circulate warm water from the storage tank to the heat exchanger in the return air duct. In most systems the storage tank will hold enough heat to maintain moderate indoor temperatures for two or three days. After that, the backup furnace must take over.

Underground Residences And Backyard Cookery

Underground architecture is attracting more and more attention from solar heating experts and others interested in squeezing the last drop of heating potential from the sun's output. The temperature at a depth of 10 feet or more is a nearly constant 55°F summer and winter, day and night, in the cold north and the warm south. As a result, only enough energy is needed to raise indoor temperatures by 10 or 15 degrees in order to have a comfortable year-round living climate—a requirement that is well within the reach of even the simplest solar heating systems.

Architects employ a wide variety of techniques aimed at eliminating any dampness or a cavelike atmosphere in their underground dwellings. Skylights, dropped gardens, solaria, and light wells are common features. Two particularly successful approaches are illustrated on this page: a hillside house and an atrium-type house.

Solar homes that are built into a hillside almost always feature an exposed south side that accommodates, at the very least, double-glazed conventional windows or sliding glass doors. These south-facing expanses of glass serve as large passive solar collectors. Buried walls on the north, east, and west sides act as storage masses, soaking up solar heat during the day and releasing it to the house interior at night and on cloudy days, much as in any passive solar home. The more sophisticated and elaborate in-hill design shown at right, below, includes a broad sweep of south-facing glass along the roofline, windows backed by a concrete heat storage structure along the south-facing side of the second floor, and a solar greenhouse stretched out along the first floor's south wall. Concrete floors and walls inside the home store part of the sun's warmth; the excess is fanned through ducts to a bed of stone rubble beneath the ground floor. At night or on sunless days the same system of fans and ducts pulls stored heat from the rubble for use in warming the house. Shutters of insulating material hinge down from ceilings to prevent the loss of heat through the glass at night.

Cutaway view at top shows an atrium-type house on Cape Cod, where fuel savings of up to 85 percent are said to have been achieved. More than half the savings are attributed to the in-ground construction, the rest to 150 square feet of air-type solar collectors that circulate warmed air through tunnels in the concrete ceilings.

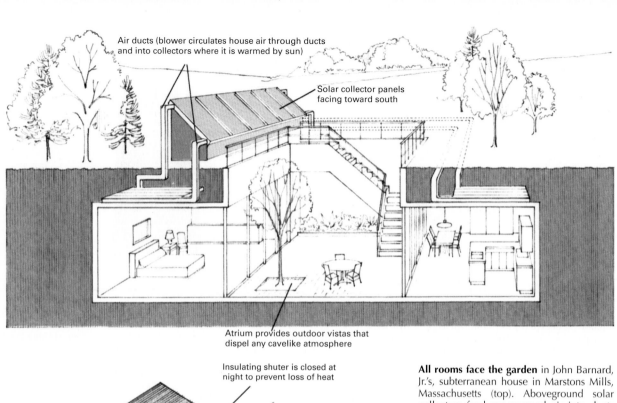

Air ducts (blower circulates house air through ducts and into collectors where it is warmed by sun)

Solar collector panels facing toward south

Atrium provides outdoor vistas that dispel any cavelike atmosphere

All rooms face the garden in John Barnard, Jr.'s, subterranean house in Marstons Mills, Massachusetts (top). Aboveground solar collectors feed sun-warmed air into ducts penetrating concrete ceiling panels. Large underground complex (bottom), known as Raven Rocks, was designed by architect Malcolm Wells. Located in east-central Ohio, the house backs directly into a hill. South-facing glass walls trap heat, which is stored in rock bed under slab.

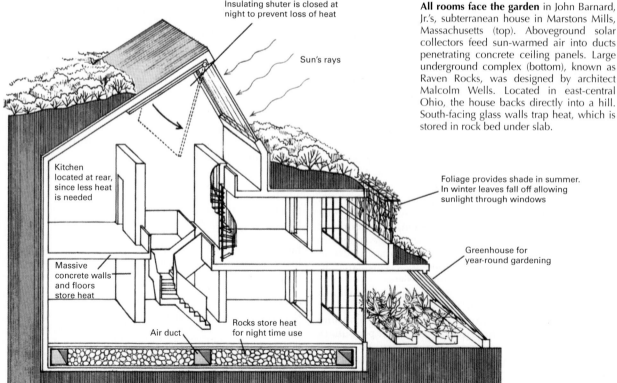

Insulating shuter is closed at night to prevent loss of heat

Sun's rays

Kitchen located at rear, since less heat is needed

Massive concrete walls and floors store heat

Air duct

Rocks store heat for night time use

Foliage provides shade in summer. In winter leaves fall off allowing sunlight through windows

Greenhouse for year-round gardening

Constructing a Solar Cooker

The backyard solar cooker described here is simple in concept and easy to build; all it takes is a sheet of reflective material mounted so that it focuses the rays of the sun on a spit. You will need the following materials:

2 feet of 1 × 3 clear pine for uprights
2 1/2 feet of 1 × 6 clear pine for side pieces
2 feet of 1 × 10 clear pine for base
two 2 1/2-inch bolts with wing nuts
four washers to fit the bolts
one 16- by 18-inch piece of reflective sheet aluminum
two dozen 1/2-inch aluminum brads.

The reflector is designed so that the sun's rays will focus along a line where the cooking spit is located. For proper focus it is important that the shape of the side pieces and positioning of the spit holes follow the given dimensions very precisely. Also take care to protect the mirror finish on the aluminum by taping tissue paper over it during assembly.

To construct the reflector unit, first mark and cut out the curved side pieces and plane and sand them to shape. Clamp the pieces together when shaping so that they will be identical. Next, bend the aluminum to fit the curve of the side pieces. Work carefully to avoid creasing

the sheet and be sure that the shiny side is on the inner side of the curve. Clamp the side pieces 18 inches apart on a level surface with the curved edges up. Then use the brads to tack the aluminum to the side pieces.

Assemble the rest of the cooker as indicated in the diagram. An old rotisserie skewer or a 1/4-inch-square steel rod filed to a point at one end will make a serviceable spit. Note that the notches in the side pieces should be square to hold the spit in position.

While in use, the reflector must point directly at the sun. To maintain this orientation, the tilt of the reflector and the position of the cooker should be adjusted from time to time. A small sun alignment hole is built into one of the side pieces as an aid in aiming the reflector. When rays of the sun impinge directly on the target spot, the cooker is in alignment. After the entire cooker is assembled, test it on a sunny day to make sure the alignment hole is properly located. It can be adjusted by shifting the aluminum tab. Choose a clear, sunny day for cooking (a strong sun is more important than outside temperature). Wrap the food in aluminum foil, dull side out, and turn the spit occasionally. The foil keeps grease from dripping and enhances heat buildup.

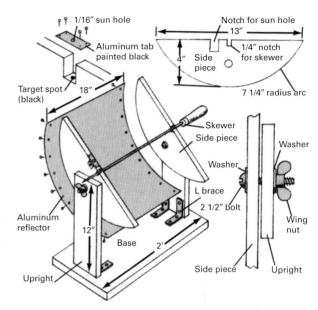

Solar oven, based on the focusing reflector principle, is easily constructed with common materials and is fun to use.

Malcom Wells, Architect and Author

It's Not Just How You Build It But What You Believe In Too

Malcolm Wells designs solar-heated structures from small homes to urban complexes. He is a specialist in what he calls gentle architecture. He would like to give the earth back to nature instead of covering it with subdivisions and blacktop.

"When it comes to designing a solar home, the amount of southern exposure and insulation quality are what count. We see solar domes, circular houses, capes, ranches, and so on. The best are simple rectangles, elongated east-to-west for southern exposure, with small windows on the north and large ones on the south. With insulating indoor shutters you can hardly miss. Winter performance of underground buildings is amazing the experts. Passive or active is a matter of choice, but if the basics are not right, you might as well give up.

"There's a few 'don'ts,' though. Stay away from L's, angles, and offsets: the more surface, the more heat loss. And let the landscape do double-duty, enhancing design and conserving energy. Planting windbreaks on the cold side and clearing branches on the south side will pay dividends. As for what type of system is best for an existing conventional home, well, assuming the house is already properly insulated and has a correctly oriented roof, I'd probably vote for rooftop collector panels using air or water. But now solar greenhouses covering south walls are producing heat *plus* vegetables. I have yet to see a split level behind a greenhouse, but I know I will soon, and the idea will spread. The nice thing about passive—windows or greenhouses instead of fans, pumps, machinery, and controls—is that there's nothing to break down.

"Assuming a flat roof, I would vote for the solar greenhouse. Rooftop collectors will work but I don't like punching holes in an existing roof and installing devices that expand and contract severely in zero degree weather. If the house has a large south wall, solar collectors can be installed there.

"Here's some more tips for people going solar. Safety. Don't create a hazard with a solar installation; conform to building codes. Second, inform yourself. Most libraries have good solar books. Talk to people who've built solar houses. The solar installation racket feeds on ignorance; your defense is good information. Also do as much as you can yourself. You'll make up for lack of experience by the care you put into the work. An outsider won't take the pains you will to prevent rain, water, heat, and air leaks.

"Of course, there are places you can't use solar heat. If your house is in the shadow of a high-rise or under a cliff or in a primeval forest, you're out of luck for solar heat. Usually, on the roof, in the yard, on the walls, there's at least room for a solar water heating panel. Remember, when you check on a summer day for sunlight exposure, the sun will be in a different place in winter. Remember, too, solar is simple.

"But, you know, the real secret to successful solar heating is your own attitude about things like nuclear power, pollution, and even the future of the human race. Unless you are what I call a solar family, any solar system will disappoint you. We are a nation of wasters. If we make token changes, we'll get token results. The successful solar houses we studied had concerned people living in them. The link between one-way bottles and fuel waste is stronger than you think."

Solar Water Systems: A Simple Design For Year-round Use

Solar-powered hot water systems are the most practical way for the average homeowner to take advantage of the sun's energy. They are easier to build and far less expensive than complete solar home-heating units. Moreover, since there is a year-round need for hot water, maximum use can be made of available sunlight. Complete solar water heating kits, ready to install in a new home or incorporate into an existing one, have been available for several years, and various designs have been developed to accommodate diverse conditions of weather, sunlight, and the amount of hot water needed by the user.

For families living in regions where freezing weather occurs frequently each winter, a system such as the one shown here is the best choice. It is an active system with a small electric pump to circulate the heat-transfer fluid. Instead of water, a nontoxic antifreeze solution is used for heat transfer, eliminating the need for draindown during freezing weather. To install the system yourself, you should have a sound knowledge of basic plumbing techniques and an understanding of how the system works. If your plumbing skills and technical expertise are limited, seek professional assistance.

Theoretically, it is possible to put together a solar water heating system that will completely supply your hot water needs no matter where you live. In practice, however, the amount of solar collector area required to achieve this goal is usually so great that total reliance on solar-heated hot water would be uneconomical. The solution for most families—unless they use very little hot water or live in a particularly sunny region—is a system that produces a large percentage of their hot water needs, the rest being supplied by a conventional backup heater. During the summer such a system may provide totally solar-heated water; at other times of the year the equipment will act as an economical preheating unit for a conventional hot water system. In this latter mode the solar collectors raise the temperature of the cold water part of the way, and a standard gas, oil, or electric heater finishes the job. In many cases, the secondary system is simply the hot water heater already present in an existing home. For new homes it is likely to be a built-in feature of a water storage tank that has been specifically designed for solar heating.

As a rule of thumb, a solar hot water heater should supply about 50 to 75 percent of your yearly water needs in order to make it worthwhile. The collector area required to achieve this depends on the amount of sunlight in your area and the amount of hot water your household uses—80 gallons a day for a typical family of four. Assuming 24-square-foot flat-plate collectors (a standard size) and a family of four, you will need the following number of collectors: Region I, five to six collectors; Region II, three to four collectors; Region III, two collectors. (See the map on page 111 to find the region in which you live.) These are rough approximations, since even adjoining areas can differ widely due to differences in cloud cover, topography, and wind patterns. Many references carry more precise figures (see *Sources and resources*, p.111), or consult a manufacturer of solar equipment.

Plumbing for solar hot water is easily integrated into standard home plumbing system. Tall tank at right stores solar-heated water, which is later transferred to ordinary electric water heater at left. Insulated pipes along back wall carry antifreeze to and from collectors; thermometers monitor entire system.

Solar water heaters will save energy all year round and are well suited for installation in existing houses. The panels can be mounted flush on the roof, provided the roof faces south and has a pitch of about 40° or more. Otherwise they must be mounted on raised metal brackets so that the sun will strike them directly. Sturdy bracing and positive anchorage is vital in case of high winds; roof mounting may even require that rafters beneath the panels be reinforced by doubling them. The panels can also be mounted on the ground. Generally, panels mounted on the ground are securely fastened to concrete piles sunk below the frost line.

How the System Works

The cutaway drawing at right shows the layout of a typical solar water heating system. All the parts can be purchased off the shelf: solar equipment manufacturers carry the collector panels, antifreeze, and the special stone-lined water storage tank with a built-in heat exchanger; the other units are standard fixtures available from plumbing suppliers. Copper piping is used throughout. Three primary subsystems constitute the overall system: the heat transfer loop, the hot water loop, and the electrical control loop.

Heat transfer loop circulates the antifreeze fluid through the solar collector panels and heat exchanger coil. Heat picked up by the fluid at the collectors is given off at the coil to warm the water in the storage tank. The loop contains an expansion tank with an air purger, plus an air vent at the highest point in the system. The expansion tank cushions pressure changes in the loop; the purger and vent bleed off any air bubbles that develop. Reverse flow of antifreeze is prevented by a check valve, and a relief valve guards against pressure buildup by providing an escape port for the fluid. A boiler drain located at the lowest point in the system is used for filling or draining the loop; gate valves at various points permit isolation of individual components for maintenance. A pressure gauge and two thermometers, one mounted on a pipe to the collectors and the other on the pipe from the storage tank, monitor the system.

Hot water loop starts at the point where the cold water enters the house from outside. A backflow preventer, expansion tank, and vacuum relief valve (positioned above the level of the water storage tank) are code requirements common to all home water systems, whether or not they are solar. Cold water feeds into the storage tank, is warmed by the heat exchanger, rises to the top of the tank, and is passed on to the auxiliary heating tank, usually a conventional water heater. For safety, a tempering valve and crossover pipe (fitted with a check valve) are installed beyond the second tank. If water should accidentally be heated above a safe temperature on a particularly sunny day, the tempering valve automatically mixes in cool water.

Electrical control loop automatically turns on the system whenever the sun is shining and shuts it off at night or on overcast days. The loop consists of a differential thermostat, plus two sensors, one that measures fluid temperature in the collector and one that measures water temperature in the storage tank. The thermostat compares the readings of the two sensors and automatically switches on the pump in the heat transfer loop whenever the water in the storage tank is more than a few degrees cooler than the collector fluid.

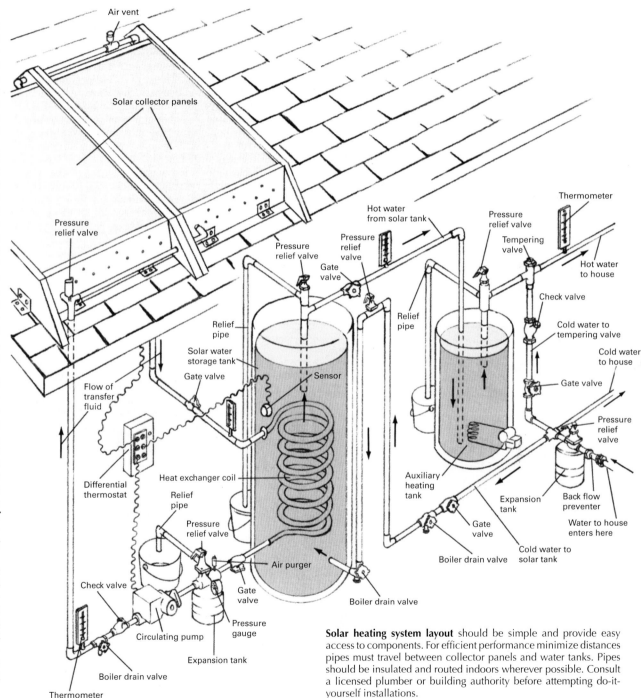

Air vent

Solar collector panels

Pressure relief valve

Flow of transfer fluid

Differential thermostat

Relief pipe

Check valve

Boiler drain valve

Thermometer

Circulating pump

Pressure gauge

Expansion tank

Pressure relief valve

Gate valve

Relief pipe

Solar water storage tank

Gate valve

Heat exchanger coil

Pressure relief valve

Gate valve

Air purger

Sensor

Boiler drain valve

Hot water from solar tank

Pressure relief valve

Gate valve

Relief pipe

Auxiliary heating tank

Expansion tank

Gate valve

Cold water to solar tank

Thermometer

Pressure relief valve

Tempering valve

Hot water to house

Check valve

Cold water to tempering valve

Cold water to house

Gate valve

Pressure relief valve

Back flow preventer

Water to house enters here

Solar heating system layout should be simple and provide easy access to components. For efficient performance minimize distances pipes must travel between collector panels and water tanks. Pipes should be insulated and routed indoors wherever possible. Consult a licensed plumber or building authority before attempting do-it-yourself installations.

Assembling the Units Into a Working System

Factory-built collector panels are available as complete units. However, you can save money by making your own either by assembling them from components or by making them from scratch with ordinary building supplies and hardware. The absorber plate is the most important and the most difficult part to build. Prefabricated plates are available from firms specializing in solar heating equipment, and their efficiency and durability make them well worth the investment. If you choose to construct your own, use 7-ounce (.01-inch-thick) copper sheeting and flexible copper tubing with 3/8-inch outside diameter. Form the tubing into a grid and attach it to the sheet with a high-temperature solder (plate temperatures can

reach 400°F on a sunny day). Coat the finished plate with high-carbon flat black paint.

The plate rests unanchored in the collector box on a rigid, resin-free duct insulation board (available at heating-supply outlets). A layer of soft fiberglass insulation is usually installed beneath the board. Allow a 3/4-inch airspace above the plate, then cover the collector box with one or two sheets of glass, polyester reinforced fiberglass, or plastic film. The most effective glazing is tempered iron-free glass. In most regions a single pane 3/16 inch thick is sufficient. In very cold areas use two 1/8-inch-thick panes with a 1/2-inch airspace between. A less expensive alternative is a sheet of .040-inch-thick polyester reinforced fiberglass above an inner glazing of 1-mil.-thick Teflon film, separated by an airspace of 1/2 inch. Drill 1/8-inch-diameter holes in the lower end of the collector box between the absorber plate and the glazing panel to prevent condensation. If double-glazing is used, also drill holes in the space between panes.

Installing the Panels

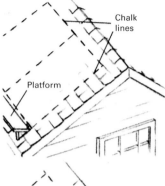

1. Lay out positions of panels using chalk line. Panel ends should be parallel to roof peak. Sides should lie along inside edges of rafters (usually spaced 16 or 24 in. apart center to center) so that they can be anchored with lag screws and angle brackets. Note platform is roof mounted to provide a safe working area.

2. Nail temporary 2 × 4 guide strip below the bottom chalk line to align the lower ends of the beveled collector box sides. Raise the panels onto the roof and position them so that they rest along the upper edge of the strip. The horizontal endpieces of the boxes should cover the top and bottom chalk lines.

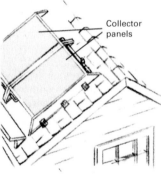

3. Attach the panels directly to the roof. Use 1/4-in. lag screws that are long enough to penetrate at least 2 in. into the rafters. Mount panels on 1/2-in.-thick neoprene washers to provide air circulation beneath collectors. Wrap screws with Teflon tape; coat heads with silicone sealant.

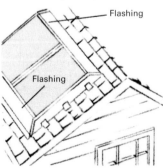

4. Solder headers to plate connections using high-temperature solder. Test and insulate plumbing (see p.120), then install aluminum flashing over headers to prevent debris accumulation. Flashing need not be weathertight. Screw or nail metal to sides and ends of box; fasten edges under shingles or with tar.

Labels (left illustration): Glazing · Glazing · Glazing · Copper sheeting · Copper tubing grid · Duct insulation · Fiberglass insulation · 2 x 6 redwood or cedar sides · Groove for top glazing (all four sides) · Marine grade plywood bottom · 2 x 6 · Weep holes

Labels (center illustration): 2 x 6 · Neoprene seal · Spacer · Absorber plate · Glazing · Wood spacers (1/2" x 3/4" parting stock) · Angle iron · Lag screws · Duct insulation · Grid · Header · Elbow with reducer · Neoprene washers · Fiberglass insulation · Bottom of panel

Labels (right illustrations): Chalk lines · Platform · Guide strip · Collector panels · Flashing · Flashing

Seal edges of glazing (either glass or synthetic) with a neoprene strip to keep out moisture while allowing leeway for expansion. Caulk all other seams with silicone sealant. Header pipes linking panels are made from rigid copper tubing with 1 1/8-in. outside diameter. Sweat-solder them in place after panels are attached to roof. Use torch carefully near combustible material.

Pipes and Plumbing

Use copper tubing—either flexible or rigid—for the plumbing in the solar water heating system. Rigid tubing is somewhat more durable; flexible (soft-tempered) tubbing is easier to work with, less expensive, and can be connected with flare fittings or by sweat-solder fittings. Both kinds of tubing are available in type K (thick wall) and type L (medium wall), but only rigid tubing is sold in type M (thin wall). The two kinds of tubing can be used together in a single installation. Employ the rigid style for long horizontal runs and in locations where the plumbing might be subject to denting; go to the flexible tubing in places where soldering is awkward, presents a fire hazard, or where complex situations would require an excessive number of connections and fittings if a rigid pipe were used. Drain the water from existing plumbing before soldering on additional piping—pipes containing water cannot be soldered.

After the plumbing has been connected, but before the system is put into operation, the entire assembly must be pressure-tested for leaks by the procedure described below. To avoid damage to air vents, expansion tanks, valves, and other components that are sensitive to excessive pressure, omit them when first installing the plumbing. Screw in a Schrader-type valve—the kind used in automobile and bicycle tires—in the opening where the pressure gauge would normally go, and insert plugs (available from plumbing suppliers) into all the other openings. When testing is completed, remove the valve and plugs and install the final components in their place. Then cover the pipes with closed-cell foam pipe insulation, available from air conditioning, refrigeration, and solar equipment suppliers. Use 3/4-inch-thick outdoor-grade foam for pipes exposed to weather and 1/2-inch-thick foam indoors.

The final step is to connect the differential thermostat and temperature sensors. Follow the manufacturer's instructions and be sure to locate the thermostat in a convenient spot (it serves as the system's control box). Add the antifreeze to the heat transfer loop and the system is ready to go.

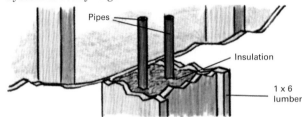

Exposed pipes can be enclosed within hollow columns built of 1 × 6 lumber filled with fiberglass insulation.

Joining techniques

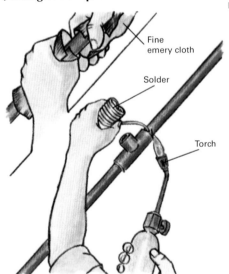

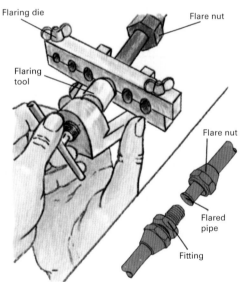

Sweat-soldering. Use 95-5 tin/antimony (high-temperature) solder throughout, especially at the collectors, to reduce lead leaching into the potable water. Scour parts to be joined with fine emery cloth until shiny, then apply thin coat of paste flux to each piece. Assemble joint, place asbestos pad behind for fire safety, and wrap nearby soldered joints with wet cloths to keep them from melting accidentally. Heat joint with propane torch until flux bubbles, then apply solder to the seam between fitting and pipe. The solder will flow into the fitting.

Flare fittings. These can be used only with flexible copper piping. Begin by cutting pipe ends square and removing any burrs. Slide flare nut onto pipe, and insert pipe into proper size hole in flaring die. Position pipe end even with face of die, then screw pointed flaring tool into pipe end, making certain tool is centered. Tighten tool until pipe end is flared to 45° angle. Insert fitting into flare and slide flare nut up. Tighten the nut to the fitting using two wrenches worked in opposition. Flare second pipe and attach to other end of fitting.

Testing the system

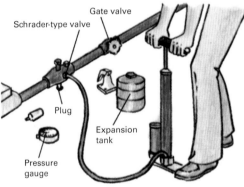

Adding the antifreeze

Locate leaks in finished plumbing by filling pipes with water, then raising pressure to 100 psi (pounds per square inch). With Schrader-type valve installed instead of pressure gauge, connect garden hose from main water supply to boiler drain located in heat transfer loop piping, and fill entire loop with water. Next, use high-pressure hand pump to pressurize the system; it should be able to hold the pressure for one hour. Check all connections and mark defective joints. Afterward, drain water and repair leaks. Measure water drained to determine amount of antifreeze needed.

Rent a portable electric pump to force antifreeze into heat transfer loop. Pressure inside loop should be 20 to 30 psi. Check operating pressure periodically against this initial figure; any drop in pressure may indicate a leak in the loop. To avoid water contamination, only non-toxic antifreeze should be used. Solar equipment dealers carry a safe blend containing propylene glycol, distilled water, a corrosion inhibitor to protect pipes, and a colored dye that helps in the detection of an accidental leakage of antifreeze into the water supply. Manufacturer's instructions usually suggest draining loop and replacing fluid every three years.

Other Energy Sources

From Pedal Power To Atomic Fusion

There are a great many ways to obtain energy, some old, some fashionable, some expensive, and a few still technological dreams. Several of the newest energy sources are inherently large-scale and can produce useful amounts of energy only at the industrial level. Others are of a scale small enough to be used by an individual household. These include such sources as bicycle power and methane digesters.

Bicycles have been with us for about a century and have proven to be the most efficient way to transport people. The intrinsically high mechanical efficiency of the cycle mechanism can be transferred to other activities in various ways, a few of which are shown on this page. Unfortunately, such pedal devices are limited by the comparatively small amount of power that humans can generate compared to the output of machines using fossil fuels or waterpower.

A new and promising source of energy, still in the experimental stage, is the methane digester. This device represents a kind of cooperation with billions of anaerobic bacteria: we feed them refuse, they provide us with methane. The process should not be confused with means for disposing of human wastes that use aerobic bacteria, as in some flushless toilets. Aerobic bacteria use oxygen to convert refuse into carbon dioxide, fertilizer, and water. Anaerobic bacteria, on the other hand, work in a tank that contains no air at all.

Ethyl alcohol—a superb, nonpolluting 115-octane fuel—can be made from sugarcane and other farm crops with the help of yeast cells. The process is the same as that used to make hard liquor. Although the basic technology is thousands of years old, it does not yet offer an economic alternative to other industrial fuels.

Muscle power

Machines that use leg power free the hands and triple the energy output of the human body as compared to arm power alone. Pedal operated jigsaws, like the one shown here, were being manufactured and sold long before the turn of the century. Sewing machines with treadles, dating from the same era, are still in use.

Animal power—not just horses and oxen but dogs as well—was widely used in America a hundred years ago. The treadmill is being used to run a cream separator but could be disconnected and attached to run the butter churn at center.

A homemade pedal machine

Versatile pedal machine can be made at home by following instructions given in the book on pedal power listed in *Sources and resources* on the next page. With appropriate attachments the machine can be used to polish, buff, drill, churn butter, peel potatoes, grind meat, knead dough, mill flour, and make ice cream.

Some Large-scale Prospects

Geothermal energy. Deep in the earth the temperature is very high. In some areas, such as California and Iceland, water has been trapped far below the surface and turned to steam. The steam can be tapped by drilling or by taking it from fissures and its energy used for heating or to run steam-electric generators. Rather than rely on natural water pockets, plans are underway to drill to the heat-bearing strata and pump water down so that it heats and returns as steam.

Waste conversion. Two high-temperature processes under development are hydrogenation and pyrolysis. Both require that an effective, large-scale system for collecting organic waste be devised. Either process will produce about 2 barrels of oil from 1 ton of manure, paper, wood, garbage, or agricultural refuse.

Magnetohydrodynamics. Conventional generators produce electricity by passing wires through magnetic fields. A magnetohydrodynamic generator replaces the wire with a current-conducting fluid pressured by heat to pass through the fields. Since no moving parts are used, the process is more efficient than conventional generators. In addition, less heat is wasted. Unfortunately, costly temperature-resistant materials are needed to contain the hot fluid.

Hydrogen fusion. The sun burns hydrogen as its principal fuel by a process known as atomic fusion. If fusion could be duplicated in a controlled fashion on earth, a millennium of endless energy would be at hand, since the fuel is available in seawater in almost limitless supply. The residue of the process is helium, which, unlike by-products of atomic fission, is nonpolluting.

Methane Digesters

A homeowner can manufacture his own natural gas with the help of a methane digester and the cooperation of vast numbers of bacteria that convert manure, vegetable matter, and other waste into methane, or marsh gas. The methane can be used for heating, lighting, and cooking. It can even power an internal combustion engine provided the engine is modified slightly. (During World War II in Europe, methane was frequently used to run automobiles; instead of a fuel tank the methane was stored in huge bags tied to the tops of cars.)

To produce methane in usable quantities, a large amount of animal waste is required. (The waste can be partly vegetable matter, but a greater portion of it should be manure; otherwise, a substantial percentage of the gas produced will be carbon dioxide, a product that is useless as a fuel.) For example, to make enough gas to meet the cooking needs of one family, the manure of one or two horses or cows, or of several hundred chickens, must be in steady supply. For this reason a farm is the best location for a methane digester. In addition, a farm will benefit from the sludge left over after the bacteria have finished digesting the manure—the sludge makes excellent fertilizer.

Operation of the digester itself is simple. The main job is to collect the waste to feed the digester and to dispose of the sludge that accumulates inside it. **Note, however, that a mixture of methane and oxygen can be explosive; for this reason the storage drum must be airtight and located far from any buildings.**

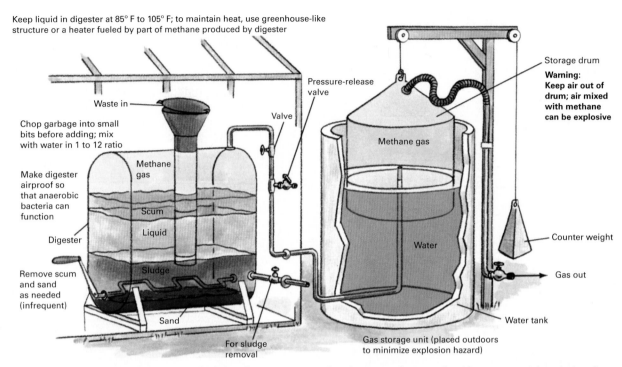

Keep liquid in digester at 85° F to 105° F; to maintain heat, use greenhouse-like structure or a heater fueled by part of methane produced by digester

Waste in
Chop garbage into small bits before adding; mix with water in 1 to 12 ratio
Make digester airproof so that anaerobic bacteria can function
Digester
Methane gas
Scum
Liquid
Sludge
Remove scum and sand as needed (infrequent)
Sand
For sludge removal
Pressure-release valve
Valve
Storage drum
Warning: Keep air out of drum; air mixed with methane can be explosive
Methane gas
Water
Counter weight
Gas out
Water tank
Gas storage unit (placed outdoors to minimize explosion hazard)

Digester converts waste to methane gas, which then flows via pipe to storage drum. The drum has no bottom, and as the gas gradually fills it, the drum rises farther and farther above the water. Pressure of methane at outlet is regulated by counterweight, which reduces pressure by offsetting the downward push exerted by the weight of the drum on methane inside it.

Alcohol as a Fuel

Alcohol offers a tantalizing prospect as a replacement for ordinary gasoline used in cars. It enhances performance, decreases pollution, and is gentler on engines. Its two most common forms are methyl alcohol (methanol) and ethyl alcohol (ethanol). Both can be produced from such organic materials as sugar, corn, and wood.

Of the two, ethyl alcohol is considerably more desirable as a fuel. Ethanol mixes readily with gasoline in any proportion; methanol does not. Ethanol works as well as gasoline in an internal combustion engine; engines using methanol as fuel are sometimes difficult to start. Ethanol can be made at home by fermenting and distilling agricultural products that contain sugar; methanol must be made in a commercial plant. As a result, the use of methyl alcohol as a power source is still in the experimental stage, while ethyl alcohol is already in wide use as "gasohol," a blend of ethanol and gasoline.

An interesting characteristic of ethyl alcohol is that you can "grow" it yourself. There are obstacles, however.

One is the fact that alcohol production is strictly regulated by federal law. Another is the relative inefficiency of small-scale distilling. Different crops will produce different yields of ethanol. An acre of sugarcane or sugar beets will yield about 500 gallons of alcohol; the same acreage of potatoes about 250 gallons; corn about 150 gallons; and wheat about 75 gallons. A great deal of labor is involved in harvesting these crops, then processing them batch by batch through a mash barrel and a still, with each batch requiring several days of fermentation. In addition, fuel is consumed in keeping the mash barrel heated to the optimum temperature of 172°F unless some alternative, such as solar heating, is brought into service. One hope, issuing from the laboratory, is a recently discovered fungus that can convert raw cellulose from such substances as wood and waste paper into the glucose (sugar) that the fungi in brewer's yeast subsist on. Fuel alcohol production from such a plentiful raw material will then be more attractive.

Sources and resources

Books and pamphlets

Carless, Jennifer. *Renewable Energy: A Concise Guide to Green Alternatives.* New York: Walker & Co., 1993.

Cole, Nancy, and Skerrett, P.J. *Renewables Are Ready: People Creating Renewable Energy Solutions.* White River Junction, Vt.: Chelsea Green Publications, 1995.

Collinson, Alan. *Renewable Energy.* Chatham, N.J.: Raintree Steck-Vaughn, 1991.

Fairmont Press Staff and Rosenberg, Paul. *Alternative Energy Handbook.* Needham Heights, Mass.: Prentice Hall, 1993.

Learning About Saving Energy. Washington, D.C.: U.S. Department of Energy, 1995.

Sharpe, Grant W., et al. *Introduction to Forestry and Renewable Resources.* New York: McGraw-Hill, 1995.

Swan, James A., and Swan, Roberta. *Bound to Earth.* New York: Avon, 1994.

Periodicals

Energy Magazine. Business Communications Co. 25 Van Zant St., Norwalk, Conn. 06855.

Home Energy. Energy Auditor and Retrofitter, Inc. 2124 Kittredge St., #95, Berkeley, Calif. 94704.

Part Three

Raising Your Own Vegetables, Fruit, And Livestock

The best fertilizer for a piece of land is the footprints of its owner.
—*Lyndon B. Johnson*

An 18th-century almanac cautions that "overplanted fields make a rich father but a poor son." This advice and its corollary—that good farmers are partners of the land, not exploiters—is as current now as when it was first written. Care, consideration, a little knowledge, and a lot of common sense: these are the ingredients that will ensure rich harvests year after year, whether your farm is a window ledge in the city, a backyard in the suburbs, or wide acreage in the country. *Raising Your Own Vegetables, Fruit, and Livestock* shows how to keep your land healthy while reaping bumper crops each year. It explains how to grow fruits and vegetables without resorting to expensive synthetic fertilizers or dangerous chemical pesticides. The old-time kitchen garden is treated at length, but other aspects of small-scale agriculture—some traditional, some quite modern—are also covered. Among these subjects are fish farming, keeping bees, growing grain, raising dairy animals, keeping chickens and rabbits, and using horses as draft animals.

The Kitchen Garden

Homegrown Produce: A Delicious Sense Of Self-sufficiency

It is easy to list the material benefits that a kitchen garden can bring. Your vegetables will arrive on your table garden fresh. They will probably be far tastier than the often days-old produce found on the shelves of food stores—and more nutritious too. And there will be impressive savings in your food dollar; experts say that for each $20 worth of supplies and labor invested, a return of more than $200 can be reaped.

But beyond such practical considerations are additional benefits: the pleasure of working with the soil, of watching seeds sprout and grow, and of knowing that the food on your table is a product of your own labor. It is these reasons, perhaps, more than mere economics, that account for the recent upsurge in home vegetable gardening.

The story of vegetable gardening in America goes back further than the current boom or even the victory gardens of World War II. The first gardeners, in fact, were the first Americans: the Indians who raised corn, beans, and squash in neatly tended plots. This food saw the Indians through the lean times of the year when game and fish were scarce. The colonists, like the Indians, depended on their gardens for survival. Life was hard, toil unending, and there was no room in the garden for any plant that was merely ornamental. What herbs and flowers were grown were used for flavoring, medicine, or dye.

For most people today, the home kitchen garden is no longer a necessity for survival. However, the garden still has an important role to play not only in economic terms but also in a well-earned sense of independence and accomplishment, as well as in the closer relationship with nature that working with the soil and its produce affords.

Garden goodies shown here are part of a bountiful harvest of delicious homegrown vegetables for freezing, canning, storage, and, of course, eating fresh. Even a small garden can make a big difference in your food budget, not to mention adding true garden freshness and flavor to your mealtimes. The only prerequisite is that you enjoy gardening.

Companion Planting

For centuries, observant gardeners have noticed that certain vegetables seemed to thrive in the company of one plant while doing poorly in the company of another. There is evidence that secretions given off by the roots of some plants are the cause of this effect. For example, the roots of black walnut trees exude a chemical that inhibits the growth of tomatoes. Onions apparently inhibit the growth of beans, peas, and several other vegetables. Tomatoes and basil, on the other hand, are believed to do well together, as are cucumbers and cabbage.

Another aspect of companion planting is that certain vegetables and herbs seem to repel the pests of other plants. Marigold roots, for example, exude a secretion that repels nematodes—tiny wormlike creatures that attack plant roots—and parsley is said to repel the carrot fly. Other plants lure pests away from their neighbors, as the eggplant lures Colorado potato beetles from potato plants. Although companion planting is a source of controversy among experts, it is certainly worth trying in your own garden.

Vegetable	Does well with	Does poorly with	Vegetable	Does well with	Does poorly with
Asparagus	Parsley, tomatoes	———	Lettuce	Carrots, cucumbers, onions, radishes	———
Beans (bush)	Beets, carrots, cucumbers, marigolds, potatoes	Fennel, garlic, onions	Onions	Beets, cabbage family, lettuce, tomatoes	———
Beans (pole)	Marigolds, radishes	Garlic, onions	Peas	Beans, carrots, corn, cucumbers, potatoes, radishes, turnips	Garlic, onions
Cabbage family	Beets, celery, corn, dill, nasturtiums, onions, sage, sunflowers	Fennel, pole beans, tomatoes			
Cantaloupe	Corn, sunflowers	Potatoes	Potatoes	Beans, cabbage, corn, marigolds, peas	Sunflowers
Carrots	Leaf lettuce, parsley, tomatoes	Dill	Pumpkins	Corn	Potatoes
Corn	Beans, cucumbers, peas, potatoes, pumpkins, squash	———	Radishes	Beets, carrots, spinach	———
			Rutabagas and turnips	Peas	———
Cucumbers	Beans, cabbage family, corn, peas, radishes	Aromatic herbs, potatoes	Squash	Nasturtiums, radishes	———
Eggplant	Beans	Potatoes (attacked by potato pests)	Tomatoes	Asparagus, basil, garlic, marigolds, parsley	Cabbage family, fennel, potatoes

The Gardener's Basic Tools

Surprisingly few tools are needed for a basic vegetable garden. To work a 15-by-20-foot plot, the only essential items are a spading fork, rake, hoe, watering can, and garden spade or round-point shovel. In addition, a string and two stakes are helpful for laying out rows, and a stout pair of gloves will protect your hands. Other useful tools are a trowel for transplanting, a mattock for dealing with rocks and roots, a hose, a soaker or sprinkler, a wheeled cultivator, and a cart for carrying sacks of fertilizer or other heavy loads. Power equipment is not necessary for the average kitchen garden except, perhaps, a rotary tiller, and this can be rented for the few days each year that it is needed.

Buy good quality tools; the extra expense will be worth it in the long run. Well-made tools last longer and are easier to use. Maintain your tools properly. Clean off soil and mud after each use and oil the tool lightly before putting it away. An occasional coat of linseed oil helps preserve wooden parts.

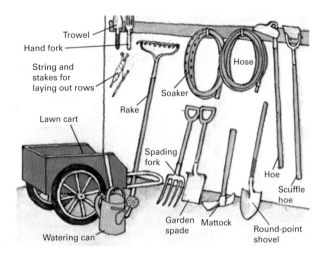

This assortment of tools will handle practically any job that needs to be done in the average home kitchen garden.

Old-time planting lore

Plant corn when the oak leaves are the size of a squirrel's ear or when the hickory buds are as big as a crow's bill (about 1 in. long). By then the danger of frost will be past.

Sprinkle plants with wood ashes or soot to keep bugs off.

Bury pieces of rhubarb in the row when planting cabbage to protect it against club root (a soil-borne disease).

To keep cabbage heads from splitting, give each young plant a half-twist in the ground.

When planting corn or squash in hills, be generous with the seed to allow for mishaps: "One for the woodchuck, one for the crow / One for the slug, and one to grow."

Much old-time lore involved astrological signs. Planting under Gemini—the sign of the Twins—was said to double the crop. As for the moon, farmers were enjoined to plant leafy vegetables when the moon was waxing and to plant root crops when it was waning. Such beliefs may be interesting, even charming, but their usefulness is dubious.

Gene Logsdon, Writer and Farmer

Whether It's Food Or Philosophy, He Grows His Own

Gene Logsdon, of Upper Sandusky, Ohio, is an organic farmer who puts into practice the ideas he has preached in his many books and articles.

"I've always gardened. I've left gardens all over America, just like Johnny Appleseed. But it wasn't until about 10 years ago that I got into organic gardening. I was an editor at a farm magazine and, to be honest, I used to ridicule organic gardening. I had the opinion that it was a bunch of malarky.

"But a lot of things began to disturb me about farming—the expansion of big agribusiness and the decline of the small farmer. And I got a bit fed up with big city life. I had visions not only of becoming self-sufficient but of farming the land the same way that my father and grandfather had farmed it.

"Organic gardening is no real problem other than it's a hell of a lot of work. You've got to be willing to put in the time if you want your garden to succeed. I don't spend my weekends golfing or traveling. I'm content to be here working my 22 acres.

"And I guess it's a truism, but you've got to do everything on time in gardening. There's a time when the ground is perfect to work and plant and that's when you should do it. When you see weeds, that's the time to pull them out—not to put it off for another weekend.

"It's very important to maintain a high level of organic matter and to fertilize the soil well. I've got animals, so I use manure. Some people swear by leaf mulch, but you have to use a lot of it if that's your only fertilizer.

"For organic farming on the scale I do it, green manuring—planting alfalfa in a field every three or four years and plowing it under—is very important. It puts nutrients back in the soil and it also helps keep the weeds at bay. The alfalfa hay is thick and it's hard for the weeds to get started. Big farmers think they have to use herbicides to control weeds. They've abandoned the old way—the irony is that they have more weeds than ever.

"When I started organic gardening, I read everything I could get my hands on. But you can't learn everything about farming from reading a book. You have to build on your experience. I think the secret of organic gardening is love of ecology, of seeing man blend with nature, of feeling the rhythm of the four seasons. Organic gardening is not just gardening; that's the real secret of the whole thing. It's bringing your life into mental and physical harmony with the world around you."

Sources and resources

Books

Arms, Karen. *Environmental Gardening*. Savannah, Ga.: Halfmoon Publishing, 1992.

Bartholomew, Mel. *Square Foot Gardening*. Emmaus, Pa.: Rodale Press, 1981.

Berry, Susan, and Bradley, Steve. *Plant Life: A Gardener's Guide*. North Pomfret, Vt.: Trafalgar Square, 1995.

Burke, Ken, and Walter Doty. *All About Vegetables*. San Francisco: Ortho Books, 1990.

Clevely, A.M. *The Total Garden: A Complete Guide to Integrating Flowers, Herbs, Fruits and Vegetables*, Avenal, N.J.: Random House Value, 1988.

Crockett, James. *Crockett's Victory Garden*. Boston: Little, Brown, 1977.

Engelken, Ralph, and Engelken, Rita, eds. *The Art of Natural Farming and Gardening*. Greeley, Iowa: Barrington Hall Press, 1981.

Loewer, Peter. *The New Small Garden: Plans and Plants That Make Every Inch Count*. Mechanicsburg, Pa.: Stackpole, 1994.

Raver, Ann. *Deep in the Green: An Exploration of Country Pleasures*. New York: Knopf, 1995.

Thomson, Bob. *The New Victory Garden*. Boston: Little, Brown, 1987.

Periodicals

Harrowsmith. Camden East, Ontario KOK 1JO, Canada.

The Mother Earth News. Box 70, 105 Stoney Mountain Rd., Hendersonville, N.C. 28791.

National Gardening Magazine. National Gardening Association, 180 Flynn Ave., Burlington, Vt. 05401.

Organic Gardening. Rodale Press, 33 East Minor St., Emmaus, Pa. 18049.

Seeds

George W. Park Seed Co. P.O. Box 31, Greenwood, S.C. 29647.

Gurney Seed and Nursery Co. 201 E. 2nd St., Yankton, S. Dak. 57079.

Henry Field Seed and Nursery Co. 415 N. Burnett St., Shenandoah, Iowa 51602.

Stokes Seeds. Box 548, Buffalo, N.Y. 14240.

W. Atlee Burpee Co. 300 Park Ave., Warminster, Pa. 18974.

A Successful Garden Requires Planning

To get the most out of your garden plot, it is necessary to plan ahead. Whether you have an established garden or are starting a new one, the best time to prepare is in the off season, well before planting time.

A good location is even more important than good soil. You can do a great deal to improve poor soil, but it is almost impossible to improve a bad site. The ideal kitchen garden should be sheltered from wind and have direct sunlight for at least six hours a day, preferably longer. It should be well drained; that is, the soil should not remain muddy after a heavy rain. It should be located away from trees, which can shade out light and whose roots may compete with vegetables for moisture and nutrients. Avoid locating your plot in a low spot where water and cold air tend to collect.

The garden should be near a tap, since watering will almost certainly be necessary at some time during the growing season. If you can manage to locate the garden close to the house, you will save many extra steps.

The site should be level or slightly sloping—if it slopes, a south-facing tilt is best, since it provides extra warmth in spring and fall. If the only available site is on a steep slope, terrace it to prevent soil erosion.

Another important decision is the size of the garden. This depends on the amount of arable land available and on how much of your own food you intend to grow. A garden to supply a family of two adults and two school-age children with staples the year round should cover at least 2,500 square feet (50 by 50 feet or the equivalent). However, a garden as small as 15 by 20 feet (300 square feet) can produce an amazing quantity of fresh vegetables. Even a 6- by 8-foot minigarden can add flavor and variety to your diet while reducing the food bill.

The traditional shape for a garden is rectangular—it is the easiest to plow and cultivate with horse or machine. However, free-form shapes are becoming popular and can be adapted to the conformation of your lot as well as to obstacles such as rock outcrops and structures.

When breaking new ground for a garden, be sure either to remove the sod or plow it under so it can decay and enrich the soil. Remove stones, roots, and debris. Soil improvement is also an important part of planning. Test your soil each spring to determine what needs to be done to improve it, then set up a schedule for preparing the soil, planting your seeds, and setting out transplants.

The Right Crops Can Make All the Difference

The most obvious rule is to plant vegetables that you and your family like—it is a waste of time, labor, and garden space to raise produce that goes uneaten. You should also select vegetables that are suited to your local climate and growing season. It is a mistake, for example, to try to raise okra (a tropical plant that needs a long, warm growing season) in Maine or to plant potatoes, which prefer cool weather, in the Deep South.

Once you have decided on what vegetables to grow, you are faced with the problem of selecting the proper varieties. Seed catalogs and garden centers offer many hybrids specially bred for disease resistance, productivity, size, and flavor, as well as for rapid development. Although hybrids are higher in price than standard varieties, their special bred-in qualities often make the extra investment more than worthwhile. Avoid so-called market or cropper varieties. These are for commercial growers who want crops that ripen and can be harvested at one time. If you plant one of these varieties, you will have a glut of beans, tomatoes, or cabbages for a few days and nothing for the rest of the season.

Plan your garden so that it will yield a steady supply of vegetables once it comes into production. Succession cropping and interplanting are two methods of getting more out of your garden space. Another device is to stagger your plantings to yield a steady supply of snap beans, radishes, and other vegetables in season. Sow small batches at one- to two-week intervals. An alternative is to plant early and late varieties together.

Remember to set aside time to care for your garden— you will need about three hours a week for weeding, cultivation, harvesting, and other chores. An untended garden usually fails; only weeds grow without help. Keep the rows short for easy maintenance. If you are a first-time gardener, plant only a modest plot; the smaller the garden, the simpler it is to manage.

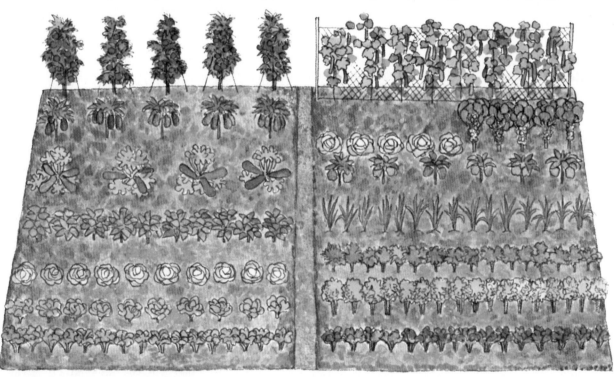

Vegetables should be placed where they will not shade each other. Plant tall vegetables, such as corn or staked tomatoes, on the north side of the garden or the side near a house or other light barrier. Low-growing vegetables such as beets and onions should be located on the side that gets the most light. Asparagus and other perennials should be planted out of the way of the annuals or in separate beds. So, too, should early crops such as peas; they can be plowed under and a new crop planted. The sample layout shown here can easily be expanded or altered or planted with other types of vegetables.

The Frost-Free Season, From Spring to Fall

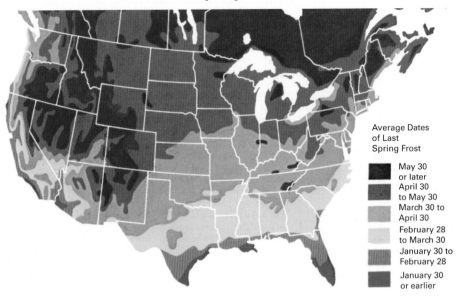

Average Dates
of Last
Spring Frost

	May 30 or later
	April 30 to May 30
	March 30 to April 30
	February 28 to March 30
	January 30 to February 28
	January 30 or earlier

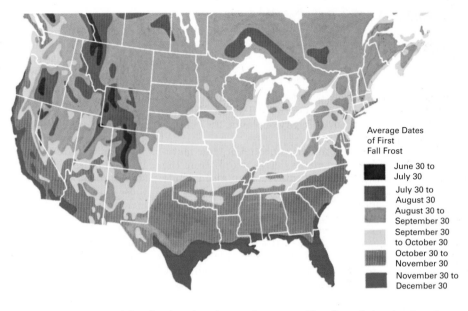

Average Dates
of First
Fall Frost

	June 30 to July 30
	July 30 to August 30
	August 30 to September 30
	September 30 to October 30
	October 30 to November 30
	November 30 to December 30

Last hard frost of spring and the first hard frost of fall mark the limits of the growing season for tomatoes, corn, melons, beans, and other tender vegetables. (A hard frost is one where the temperature falls significantly below the freezing point for several hours.) The dates shown in the maps represent averages over large regions. There is a wide variation in frost dates within each region and sometimes within the same neighborhood. Elevation, landforms, nearby bodies of water, and the proximity of big cities all affect the frost date. The presence of water and urban development both tend to increase temperature and therefore lengthen the growing season. The effect of elevation is to lower average temperatures by 3°F per 1,000 ft. of altitude. Allow a few days leeway when planting in the spring to make sure your young shoots will not be caught in an unexpected freeze. Your county agent is a good source of information on local frost-free dates. For greater precision, you can maintain your own temperature and planting records. For this purpose, special thermometers are available that record the daily highs and lows.

Shapes to Suit Your Site and Taste

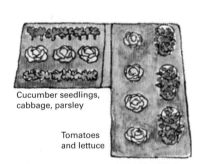

Cucumber seedlings, cabbage, parsley

Tomatoes and lettuce

An L-shape is well suited for a garden that must follow the side of a house or is to be placed in the corner of a lot. Each arm of the L can be extended as far as you wish to create a peripheral garden space around central lawn or patio. A path at the base of the L gives improved access to both areas of the garden.

Terracing is the answer to the problem of gardening on a steep slope. Make terraces 2 to 4 ft. wide; use a carpenter's level on a 2 × 4 when laying them out. Hold the soil in place with either railroad ties, boards supported by stakes, logs, or flat stones laid on edge. Terraces can be curved to follow natural contours.

The round garden, with corn, pole beans, and squash thriving together, is based on a traditional American Indian plan. Almost any combination of tall and low-growing plants can be used. Locate the tall plants in the center where they will not choke out or shade their smaller but still desirable companion vegetables.

Two harvests in the space of one

Succession planting is a simple idea that can enormously increase your harvest. One technique is to plant successive crops of the same vegetable at one- to two-week intervals. Another is to follow an early-maturing spring crop with a fall crop planted in midsummer. The chart shows some of the best combinations, but you should experiment with others yourself. In areas with mild winters you may even get three crops by following your fall crop with a hardy vegetable such as collards. A related technique is to interplant quick-maturing vegetables, such as radishes, with slow growers, such as carrots or beets.

Early crop	Late crop
Beets	Kale
Carrots	Brussels sprouts
Corn	Winter squash
Lettuce	Winter radish
Mustard greens	Bush beans
Peas	Fall cabbage
Spinach	Chinese cabbage
Turnips	Fall lettuce
Turnips	Tomato plants

129

A Life-Giving System Beneath Our Feet

Soil is a living, complex system to which our lives are linked in a very real sense. On the soil and its fertility depend the vigor and productivity of plants, the basis of our food chain.

Soil is composed of both inorganic and organic material. The inorganic components derive mainly from the slow breakdown of rocks and minerals but also include air and water held in the pores between soil particles. Organic material comprises both the remains of once-living plants and animals plus a multitude of simple life forms such as bacteria, fungi, algae, and protozoans.

Other life forms also dwell in the soil, among them insect larvae, microscopic worms called nematodes, and the familiar earthworms. Some, such as nematodes, can harm plants by attacking their roots; others, such as ants and earthworms, help plants by their constant tunneling, which aerates the soil.

Most soils are a mixture of sand, silt, and clay. Sand and silt are chemically the same as the rocks and minerals from which they are formed, while clay has undergone chemical changes that alter its properties. Clay attracts and holds water and many nutrient chemicals, while sand and silt do not. The varying proportions of sand, silt, and clay give soil its character, and soil classifications are based on which of these mineral substances predominates.

Organic matter supplies nutrients to the soil and improves soil consistency. It increases water-holding capacity and adds body to loose, sandy soils; it loosens dense, heavy clay soils, making them easier to cultivate and easier for plant roots to penetrate. Manure, compost, and mulches such as grass clippings, spoiled hay, and dead leaves are good sources of organic matter to add to your garden soil.

The ideal gardening soil is soft, loose, and crumbly. It should also be rich in organic matter and free from stones, roots, and debris. Even if your soil does not have these characteristics, you can tailor it to your requirements by removing debris and adding organic matter.

There are several simple ways to tell what kind of soil you have in your garden. One test is to place a small amount of soil—about a spoonful—in the palm of one hand. Mix it with water until it is thoroughly wet (but do not use so much water that it becomes runny). Then rub the wet soil out into a thin layer on your palm. Clay soil will feel slippery and look shiny. Sandy soil will feel gritty and look dull. Silty soil will feel slippery but will not shine. Another test is to roll the wet soil into a ball, then into a long, thin snake. Sandy soil is difficult to make into a ball; and when you roll it out into a snake, it will quickly fall part. Clay soil will hold its shape both as a ball and as a snake—the more clay, the thinner the snake that can be rolled. Silty soil will feel like clay but will not hold together.

Testing the soil

How can you tell whether your soil is acid or alkaline? In many cases the weeds and the wild plants that grow on it are natural indicators. Sorrel and knotweed, for example, thrive in acid soil; wild blueberries usually indicate a very acid soil. Sagebrush is a sign of alkaline soil. The familiar hydrangea bush blooms blue in acid soils, pink in alkaline. A carpet of moss indicates a damp soil that is poor in nutrients.

For a more precise analysis, simple and easy-to-use soil testing kits are widely available from seed houses and garden-supply centers. Such kits can measure the soil's nutrient content as well as its pH. For testing a large area of soil the most practical procedure may be to send soil samples to your Cooperative Extension Service to be analyzed by experts with sophisticated equipment.

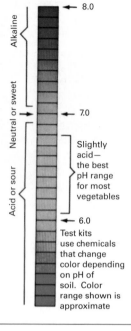

- 8.0
Alkaline

Neutral or sweet
- 7.0

Slightly acid— the best pH range for most vegetables

Acid or sour
- 6.0

Test kits use chemicals that change color depending on pH of soil. Color range shown is approximate

Acid or Alkaline—The Mysteries of pH

The health and vigor of plants depend to a great degree on how acid or alkaline the soil is in which they grow. This is because the degree of acidity or alkalinity controls the availability of important nutrients in the soil. If the soil is too acid or alkaline, the nutrients may be locked up in insoluble chemical compounds, and some may even become toxic to plants. Most plants do best in soil that is neutral to slightly acid, although some vegetables have different needs (see *Grower's Guide*, pp.138–145).

Acidity and alkalinity are measured by the pH scale, which runs from 0 to 14. Zero is extremely acid; 7 is neutral; 14 is extremely alkaline. Each point on the pH scale represents a factor of 10. A soil with a pH value of 5, for example, is 10 times more acid (10 times less alkaline) than soil that tests out at pH 6. A soil with a pH value of 9 is 10 times more alkaline (10 times less acid) than one with a value of 8.

For comparison, lemon juice, which is an acid substance, has a pH of about 3 and soapy water, which is alkaline, has a pH of 9. Most soils range from pH 4 to 8.5, and most vegetables thrive best between pH 6 and 6.8. Methods of correcting pH are suggested on page 131.

The Soil and Its Principal Constituents

Fill jar with one-third soil, two-thirds water. Shake well

Undecomposed organic matter floats at top

Clay
Silt
Sand

Fertile, humus-rich soil consisting largely of sand, silt, and clay is called loam. The ideal loam contains about 40 percent silt and 20 percent clay, with sand and organic matter making up the remainder. Such soils have a good balance between drainage, looseness, and retention of moisture and nutrients.

To determine the makeup of your soil, mix a cupful with water and shake well in a bottle. As shown at left, the soil will settle in distinct layers of sand, silt, and clay. The relative thickness of the layers indicates the proportion of each.

Sand particles are big enough to see with the naked eye and are gritty to the touch. Sandy soils are loose and porous, absorbing water readily but not holding it long. Plant roots penetrate them easily, making them suitable for root crops such as carrots and beets. Because sandy soils warm up and dry out quickly in spring, they usually can be worked several weeks ahead of the denser clay soils.

Clay particles are thin, flat plates, too small to see without a microscope. Clay is hard and bricklike when dry, greasy and plastic when wet. Clay soils absorb water very slowly but hold it for a long time. They also hold plant nutrients, a valuable quality in garden soils.

Silt falls between sand and clay in its properties. The particles are about as fine as sifted cake flour. Silt feels powdery when dry, slippery when wet. It adds bulk and moisture-holding capacity to soil.

Heavy clay soil can be lightened by digging in sand for drainage and peat moss or compost to keep the soil from compacting into a concretelike mass. However, for any type of soil the most important ingredient is organic matter.

Fertilizers for Productivity

Fertilizers are used to supply plants with nutrients that the soil lacks. Plants need at least 13 chemical elements for good health and growth. The big three—nitrogen, phosphorus, and potassium—are standard ingredients of almost all packaged garden fertilizers. Other necessary plant nutrients are calcium, magnesium, sulfur, and the so-called trace elements: iron, copper, manganese, zinc, boron, chlorine, and molybdenum.

The signs of a nutrient deficiency are often obvious. A lack of nitrogen, for example, shows up in the form of stunted growth and yellow leaves. Symptoms of a phosphorus shortage are stunted growth and leaves of a darker than normal green. A lack of iron appears as yellowing in new leaves. An excess of a nutrient can be bad too. An overdose of nitrogen often results in a lush growth of leaves but weak, brittle stems and little fruit. Large amounts of trace elements can be toxic to plants.

A fertilizer is considered organic if it is derived from naturally occurring materials, such as manure, dried blood, bone meal, rock phosphate, and green sand. Synthetic fertilizers are based on man-made chemicals. The numerals on a bag of fertilizer denote its percentage of nitrogen, phosphorus, and potassium, in that order. A 100-pound bag of fertilizer labeled 5-10-5, for example, contains 5 pounds of nitrogen, 10 of phosphorus pentoxide, and 5 of potassium oxide.

Organic and synthetic fertilizers both supply the nutrient chemicals that plants need. However, the trend among small-scale gardeners is toward the natural and the organic, and away from the synthetic. There are practical reasons for this trend. Organic fertilizers release their nutrients slowly and over a long time; synthetic fertilizers act quickly and must be renewed more frequently. Most organic fertilizers add organic matter to the soil; synthetic fertilizers do not. Organic fertilizers often improve soil texture as well as adding nutrients; synthetics do not. Organic fertilizers naturally contain trace elements and other necessary plant foods; synthetics do not. Earthworms and other beneficial organisms are sometimes harmed by synthetic fertilizers. Synthetics are more concentrated than organic fertilizers and so are more prone to burn delicate plant roots and destroy valuable soil organisms. Perhaps most important, however, is that more and more people are making their own compost, raising animals that provide them with manure, and otherwise finding or creating their own homegrown fertilizer.

Excellent results can be achieved with either type of fertilizer, however, provided the correct amount is used—neither too much nor too little. The art of efficient fertilization consists of feeding the plants, not the soil.

Improving the Soil

Garden soil is seldom ideal when first tilled. It may be too sandy, have too much clay, or be full of roots, rocks, and debris. The pH may be too low or too high and often the soil is deficient in organic matter.

The most important soil-improvement and conditioning task is usually to add organic matter to the soil. This is best done in fall, while the soil is still warm enough to promote the activity of bacteria and fungi and when the decay process will not use up the nitrogen needed by growing crops. Manure and compost are excellent additives, as are lawn clippings, dead leaves, and so-called garden trash—the leaves and stems of plants that have died or ceased producing. But do not use plants that are diseased or insect infested. They will contaminate the soil and cause problems in future years.

If you have used organic mulch on your garden during the summer, turn it under at the end of the season.

Green manure, a cover crop grown for the purpose of being added to the soil, is much used. Rye, alfalfa, and clover are favorites for this purpose, particularly alfalfa and clover, which have nitrogen-fixing bacteria growing on their roots. In addition to improving the structure of the soil, organic matter provides food for earthworms and other beneficial soil organisms.

Organic material should be thoroughly mixed into the topmost 12 inches of soil but no deeper—the roots of most common vegetables do not penetrate beyond this depth. Since organic matter is at a premium, it should be used where it does the most good.

Overly acid soil can be corrected by adding lime, which also contributes calcium—a major plant nutrient—and improves soil structure. Alkaline soils can be made more acid by adding powdered sulfur, which is slow acting but long-lived, or aluminum sulfate.

A catalog of organic fertilizers

Type	Contributes	Other things you should know
Bonemeal	Phosphorus, 20–25%	Very slow acting. Will not burn roots
Compost	Organic matter, varying proportions of all nutrients	The best all round organic fertilizer; should also be used with chemical fertilizers
Cottonseed meal	Nitrogen, 6–9%; phosphorus, 2–3% potassium, 1.5–2%	Low pH, good for acid loving crops
Dried blood and tankage	Nitrogen, 5–12%; phosphorus, 3–13%	One of the best organic sources of nitrogen, aids growth of soil organisms. Quick acting
Fish meal, fish emulsion	Nitrogen, 6–8%; phosphorus, 13%; potassium, 3–4%; trace elements	Quick acting
Horn and hoof meal	Nitrogen, 7–15%	Quick acting
Manure, cow (fresh)	Nitrogen, 0.6%; phosphorus, 0.15%; potassium, 0.45%; organic matter	Relatively low in nitrogen. Can be used directly on garden without aging
Manure, goat and sheep (dried)	Nitrogen, 2.5%; phosphorus, 1.5%; potassium, 1.5%; organic matter	Relatively high nitrogen content. Should be aged or composted at least three months before using on garden
Manure, horse (fresh)	Nitrogen, 0.7%; phosphorus, 0.25%; potassium, 0.55%; organic matter	As for goat and sheep manure
Manure, poultry (dried)	Nitrogen, 4.5%; phosphorus, 3.2%; potassium, 1.3%; low in organic matter	Very high in nitrogen. Should not be used on plants directly, as it may burn them
Manure, rabbit (fresh)	Nitrogen, 2.4%; phosphorus, 1.4%; potassium, 0.6%; organic matter	As for goat and sheep manure
Rock phosphate	Phosphorus, 24–30%	Slow acting, nonburning
Seaweed (dried)	Nitrogen, 1–2%; phosphorus, 0.75%; potassium, 5%; organic matter	A good soil conditioner because of its high content of colloids, which retain nutrients
Sewage sludge (sterilized)	Nitrogen, 4–6%; phosphorus, 3–4%; some potassium and trace elements; organic matter	May contain heavy metals that build up in the soil over the years
Wood ashes	Phosphorus, 1–2%; potassium, 3–7%	An old time standard. Has alkaline effect on soil

The Art and Science Of Soil Improvement

Composting is a method of converting garden trash, kitchen scraps, and other organic wastes into humus—a partly decayed form of organic matter that is an important ingredient of rich soils.

There are many variations in composting techniques, but the basic idea is to let the biological action of bacteria and fungi heat the interior of the compost pile to 150°F, killing weed seeds and disease organisms. The most efficient way to produce compost is in a bin or container to keep the material from spilling out.

A compost pile is built up like a layer cake with each layer watered as it is completed. Optimum height for a compost pile is about 4 feet. A lower pile loses too much heat; a higher one tends to pack down and interfere with the biological action. Length and width are optional, but remember that two small piles are easier to handle than one huge one. Start with a 2- to 3-inch layer of coarse materials, such as cornstalks, twigs, or straw (the purpose is to let air into the bottom of the pile). If coarse material is not available, you can use a layer of sawdust or other absorbent material or omit it entirely. In

any case, only one layer of coarse or absorbent material is necessary. Next, add a 3- to 6-inch layer of organic material, such as garden trash or dead leaves. Over this place 2 to 3 inches of manure (or a light sprinkling of synthetic fertilizer) to supply the nitrogen needed for the breakdown process. Other good sources of nitrogen are dog and cat droppings, feathers, hair clippings, and dried blood. The next layer should be a thin cover of topsoil or old compost. At this point some gardeners cover the heap with a sprinkling of lime. Repeat the process until the pile is about 4 feet high; then shape the top of the pile into a shallow saucer to let water soak in.

Moisture content is important for good composting. If the pile is too dry, the breakdown process slows to a halt; if too wet, undesirable biochemical reactions take place. The pile should be about as damp as a just-squeezed sponge. In dry weather water it every few days; in very rainy weather cover it with a tarp or plastic sheet.

The pile should be turned about once a week to aerate it. This procedure speeds decomposition, combats odor, and mixes the material so that it will decay at a uniform rate. To turn compost, take apart the old pile and put it together backward so that the material that was on the outside of the old pile is in the center of the new pile.

Compost is ready to use when the pile no longer gives off heat or odor when opened up and the material has turned brown and crumbly.

Refuse into compost, quickly and easily

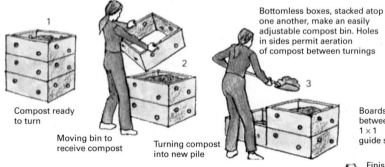

Compost ready to turn

Moving bin to receive compost

Turning compost into new pile

Bottomless boxes, stacked atop one another, make an easily adjustable compost bin. Holes in sides permit aeration of compost between turnings

Shredding and plenty of nitrogen are the keys to the fast 14-day method of compost making. The schedule: *1st day.* Shred the material and build pile. (Use a compost shredder or run a rotary mower over the material spread on the ground.) *2nd and 3rd days.* Check pile for heating and moisture (insert a kitchen thermometer to check temperature). If it is heating too slowly, add high nitrogen fertilizer. *4th and 7th days.* Turn pile; check temperature and moisture. *10th day.* Turn pile once more; it should be cooling off. *14th day.* Compost is ready for use.

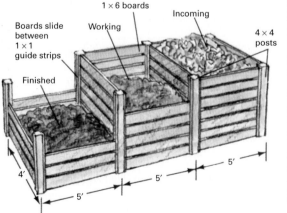

Three-stage bin turns out a near-continuous supply of compost. Removable slat sides make turning compost easy. Graded sizes allow for shrinkage as compost matures

Boards slide between 1 × 1 guide strips

Finished

Working

Incoming

1 × 6 boards

4 × 4 posts

4'

5'

5'

5'

Some easy-to-build compost bins

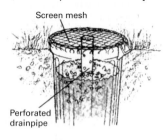

Screen mesh

Perforated drainpipe

Sunken garbage can makes convenient compost bin when space is limited. Punch holes in bottom of can for drainage and fill with alternating layers of material. Cover with screening to keep out insects and scavengers. Perforated drainpipe in center provides aeration.

Chicken wire

1 × 2 lumber

Screened compost bin is made of chicken wire and light lumber. It is easily disassembled for turning compost. Two L-shaped sections fasten with hooks and eyes. To use, simply unfasten hooks and eyes, remove sides, and set up in position to receive the turned compost. (The heap will remain standing when sides are removed.)

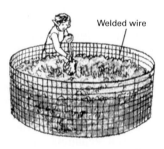

Welded wire

Wire mesh cylinder is one of the simplest of all compost bins to construct. Use mesh with heavy gauge wire; support with stakes driven into the ground. Often used for autumn leaves, it can handle any type of compost.

Rotating steel compost drum

Rotating steel drum tumbles compost each time drum is turned, mixing and aerating it. Material is loaded through a hatch. These compact, durable units are available commercially and can also be built at home using an empty oil drum and 2 × 4 lumber for frame.

Tilling the Soil

Since the beginning of agriculture, man has tilled the soil. Tilling serves several purposes. It breaks up and buries sod and weeds that would otherwise compete with cultivated plants for space, water, and nutrients. It loosens the soil, permitting water and air to reach the plant roots. It kills eggs and larvae of many insect pests. And it enriches the soil by turning under organic matter.

One of the oldest methods of tilling is with a spade and rake. The soil is first turned over with the spade (a broad-tined garden fork will also serve); then the rake is used to break up clods and level the surface.

Almost as old as the spade and rake is the plow, a laborsaving invention that is essentially a spade moved through the soil by man, animal, or machine. When a plow is used to till the ground, a harrow usually takes the place of a rake. There are two basic types of harrow: tooth harrows and disc harrows. A recent addition to the roster is the rotary tiller, dating from the 1950s. This motorized device combines the functions of plow and harrow and mixes the soil thoroughly.

For full-scale farming or for a very large garden (an acre or more) you will need a plow and harrow and either a tractor or draft animal to pull them. For plowing land that has been cleared of sod a small tractor of 12 to 16 horsepower may be big enough, but for breaking and plowing in sod a tractor weighing at least 1 ton and with at least 40 horsepower is necessary. It is often more practical to rent equipment or to hire someone to do the plowing and harrowing for you than to invest in expensive equipment. For an intermediate-sized garden (1/4 to 1 acre), a rotary tiller provides a good combination of high efficiency and low cost.

When tilling, go no deeper than the top 12 inches of soil. This leaves the fertile topsoil in place, where plants can utilize it. It also helps keep the soil structure, or tilth, in good condition (porous and crumbly).

The soil should be fairly dry, without any trace of muddiness or stickiness, before you work it. If the soil is worked when it is wet, soil particles will become packed together, damaging the tilth. Heavy equipment is the worst culprit in this respect, but even a man walking on the soil will cause damage if the earth is wet.

If you do not use mulch to keep the weeds down, you should till the soil lightly between rows with a rake, hoe, wheeled cultivator, or rotary tiller as the growing season progresses. This light tilling, or cultivation, should be no deeper than 1 or 2 inches. Cultivation kills weed seedlings and reduces evaporation of water by pulverizing the soil's surface (this blocks off pores through which water vapor escapes). Cultivation also makes it easier for rainwater to soak in rather than run off.

Labor savers for the garden

Wheeled cultivator, an old-time implement still sold by many supply houses, is valuable for cultivating between rows. Powered by hand, it gives the user more "feel" for the soil than the motorized cultivator.

Rotary tiller, driven by a small gasoline engine, is meant for land that has been cleared of sod. Rotary tillers can be either bought or rented. Type with power-driven front wheels handles best.

Device doubles as a harrow.

Harrows for the farm

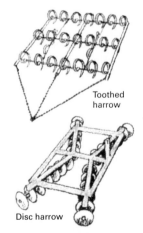

Toothed harrow

Disc harrow

Harrowing is done after land has been plowed. Purpose is to smooth and level the soil—the same job raking does. The toothed harrow is the simplest type. The more versatile—and usually costlier—disc harrow, which also improves soil by turning under crop residues, is widely used in commercial farming. Harrowing should be done at an angle to furrows made by the plow. Do not harrow unless soil is dry.

The standard plowing pattern

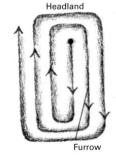

Headland

Furrow

Earth thrown off by plow should be directed to center of garden. Follow a clockwise pattern with plows that throw earth to right (as most of them do). Start at middle of one edge of field and plow from end to end. Use headlands—narrow strips of land at either end of field—for turning.

Horse vs. tractor

In recent years there has been a resurgence of interest in horses for farm work. A pair of good drafters can plow 3 acres a day. Although the rate is considerably less than a tractor's, horses provide many other benefits: they can work land too steep for a tractor, they supply manure, they are "fueled" with grasses and grains that you can raise yourself, they do not pollute the atmosphere, and they can be used for recreation and transportation. Of course, horses require daily care and skill in handling. Such massive, muscular breeds as Clydesdale, Belgian, and Percheron make the best draft horses, but any healthy horse can be used.

Contour plowing for sloping land

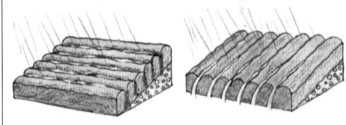

Plowing turns over a slice of soil with each pass of the plow, breaking up the soil as it goes. The result is the familiar pattern of ridges and furrows associated with newly plowed farmland. Hilly and sloping land should be plowed by a special technique known as contour plowing. As shown (above left), each ridge and furrow on contour plowed land stays at the same height across the slope. Such a pattern traps rainwater. letting it soak into the soil. The wrong way to plow (above right) leaves furrows running uphill and downhill. This directs the rainwater into channels made by the furrows, causing it to scour out gullies and carry off soil.

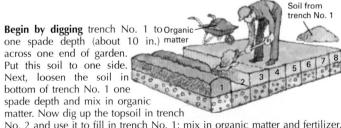

Soil from trench No. 1

Begin by digging trench No. 1 to one spade depth (about 10 in.) across one end of garden. Put this soil to one side. Next, loosen the soil in bottom of trench No. 1 one spade depth and mix in organic matter. Now dig up the topsoil in trench No. 2 and use it to fill in trench No. 1; mix in organic matter and fertilizer. Continue digging and filling until you reach end of garden. Use topsoil from trench No. 1 to fill in last trench. Double-digging is hard work, so spread it over several days.

Starting the Seeds For the Garden And for Your Table

You can gain weeks on the growing season by starting your vegetable seeds indoors, then setting out the seedlings when the danger of frost is past. Supermarkets and garden centers sell seedlings ready for planting, but serious home gardeners prefer starting their own. The cost is far lower, you can cull out all but the strongest seedlings, and you have a vastly greater choice of vegetables—typically, most outlets stock only the best-selling varieties, and some are limited to a few standbys such as tomatoes, peppers, and eggplant. Moreover, if you start your own seeds, you can be certain that no unwanted pesticides have been used. Perhaps most important, however, is the satisfaction you have of knowing that the vegetables you harvest are the products of your own labor, from seed to tabletop.

The only equipment you need to start seeds are some small containers, a suitable growing medium, and a sunny window. Vermiculite, a mineral product, is a popular growing medium because it is light, inexpensive, porous, and holds water well. Old-time gardeners often used sand, mixing it with sphagnum moss to improve its

moisture-holding ability. Commercial potting compounds are usually a mixture of vermiculite, sphagnum moss, and plant food. Compost from your compost heap is an almost ideal starting medium, but sterilize it first to kill disease organisms and insect eggs. To sterilize, bake the compost in a shallow pan in a slow oven until it reaches 180°F. You can check the temperature with a meat thermometer. Garden soil is also a satisfactory medium. It, too, must be sterilized before using it. Mix in vermiculite and sphagnum moss after sterilizing the soil in order to lighten it.

Unless the cost of seed is an important factor, do not use the tedious, old-fashioned method of starting seeds in flats (open trays) and transplanting them to pots. Instead, use small containers and sow three or four seeds in each. Although almost any small container will do, the most convenient devices in which to start seeds are peat pots, peat pellets, or fiber cubes. Since the seedlings' roots will grow right through the growing medium into the soil, there is no need to disturb the seedlings when they are set out by removing them from the container. When the true leaves appear (see below right), cut off all but the strongest seedling in each container at soil level. Do not pull up the unwanted seedlings, as this may injure the roots of the one you want to save.

Most seeds should be started in a warm room—the kitchen is often a good choice—since the soil must be fairly warm for the seeds to germinate. You can speed germination by keeping seeds in the dark; check them

daily for soil moisture and sprouting. When they have sprouted, move them into direct light.

The starting medium should be kept moist but not soggy. Excessive wetness may cause seedlings to die of damping-off, a fungus disease. A simple and efficient way to conserve moisture (and retain heat at night) is to make a mini-greenhouse by stretching plastic wrap over the seed containers. The plastic should be removed as soon as the seeds have sprouted.

When the seedlings have four to eight true leaves, they should be transplanted to the garden. If set out when older, they tend to be stunted and yield poorly. Before transplanting them, seedlings should be hardened off; that is, acclimated to outdoor conditions. About two weeks before planting time, begin putting them outdoors for short periods of time. Leave them out for about an hour the first day, gradually increasing the time until they are out all day. Protect the seedlings from the wind and do not expose them to the midday sun for the first few days. Do not feed them the last week.

Do the actual transplanting on a cloudy day or in late afternoon to avoid the drying effects of the sun. When transplanting from flats or containers with several seedlings, make sure that each seedling has as much soil as possible around its roots when you remove it. (A teaspoon makes a good digger for removing seedlings.) Give each seedling a thorough watering when it is placed in the ground. Many gardeners shade their seedlings from direct sun the first few days after transplanting.

Homemade Starting Containers

Almost any container that is waterproof will serve for starting seeds. Yogurt cups are convenient for individual seedlings; larger containers will hold peat pellets and peat pots, or they can be used as old-fashioned flats. You can make a miniature greenhouse from a plastic milk jug, with its midsection cut out, or by rigging a plastic cover, supported on wire hoops, to fit over a plastic egg carton.

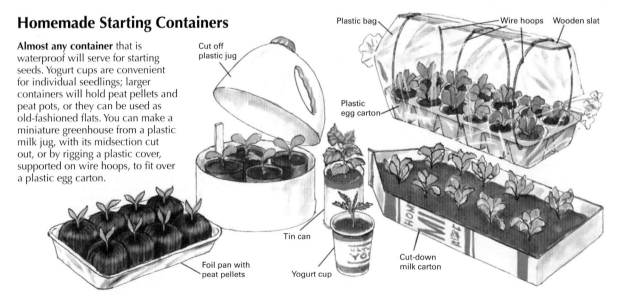

Cut off plastic jug

Plastic bag · Wire hoops · Wooden slat

Plastic egg carton

Tin can

Foil pan with peat pellets

Yogurt cup

Cut-down milk carton

From seed to seedling

Four stages in the growth of a seedling are shown below. Note the difference between seed leaves and true leaves: seedlings should be set out when four to eight true leaves appear. Seedlings do best in a window that faces south or east with at least six hours of sunlight a day; otherwise use 40-watt white fluorescent lights positioned about 6 in. above the seedlings.

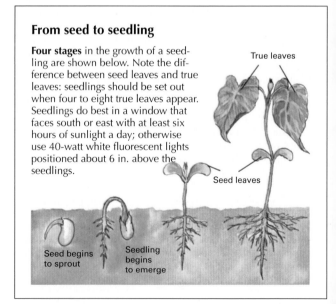

True leaves

Seed leaves

Seed begins to sprout

Seedling begins to emerge

Saving Seeds for Future Use

There are two aspects to saving seeds: collecting them and storing them. Collecting seeds from your own plants is a gamble because the seeds you harvest in the fall are likely to be hybrids, or crosses, between different varieties planted nearby. These natural hybrids are unpredictable and usually inferior to the parent varieties. Many of the most popular varieties of garden vegetables produced by seed growers are specially bred hybrids (specified on the seed packet). It does not pay to save seeds from such vegetables nor from plants grown in close proximity to another variety, such as two varieties of squash that have been planted side by side.

If you decide to try your hand at harvesting seeds from your own garden, the safest course is to take seeds only from nonhybrid varieties of tomatoes, peppers, and eggplant. These vegetables are self-pollinating, and their seeds are likely to come true to type. Let the fruit become overripe on the plant. Mash it, scrape the seeds out, and let them soak in water for a day or two until they begin to ferment. Discard the pulp and the light, infertile seeds that float to the top. Dry the heavy, fertile seeds that sink to the bottom on a sheet of paper. Peas and beans are also a reasonably good risk for seed saving. Simply let the pods dry on the vine, then shell them.

Proper storage of seeds is important whether they are those you collect yourself or leftover commercial seeds from the spring planting. The key to storing seeds is to keep them dry and cool. (Moisture and warmth activate a seed's biological processes, not enough for sprouting but enough to use up the seed's food reserves.) Put seeds you have collected yourself in envelopes, label each envelope with date and vegetable type, and seal with tape. You can leave commercial seeds in their original packets; simply fold over the open end and fasten it firmly with tape, then mark each packet with the year you bought it. Place envelopes and packets in a tight container, such as a jar with an airtight top, and store them in a cool, dry location.

The usable lifetime of common seeds

Vegetable	Yr.	Vegetable	Yr.	Vegetable	Yr.
Beans	3	Eggplant	4	Pumpkin	4
Beets	3	Kale	3	Radishes	3
Cabbage	4	Lettuce	4	Spinach	3
Carrots	1	Melons	4	Squash	4
Cauliflower	4	Onions	1	Swiss chard	4
Corn, sweet	2	Peas	1	Tomatoes	3
Cucumbers	5	Peppers	2	Turnips	5

Sprouting Seeds for the Dinner Table

Wide-mouthed jar makes a handy sprouter. Cover jar with cheesecloth held by rubber band or with wire mesh inside screw-on rim.

Rinse seeds by running water into jar and swirling it around. Method works well for small seeds, provided mesh is fine enough.

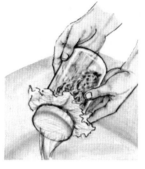

To empty rinse water, invert jar so that water drains out through mesh. Seeds should be kept constantly moist, but not wet or else they will rot.

Place sprouting jar at an angle of approximately 45° inside a large bowl to allow excess moisture to drain from sprouts between each rinsing.

Seed sprouts, easy to grow and rich in vitamins and proteins, take only three to five days to raise. The basic techniques and equipment are simple. Seeds can be sprouted in almost any kind of household container, and the only space they require is a dark niche in a warm place, such as a kitchen cupboard.

The best-known sprouting seeds are mung bean (the sprouts are often used in Oriental dishes), soybean, and alfalfa, but many other kinds can be used including wheat, corn, barley, mustard, clover, and radish. Most health-food stores carry seeds for sprouting. Even dried peas, beans, and lentils from the grocery or supermarket make tasty, nutritious sprouts. However, you should never eat sprouts from seeds that have been sold for planting in the garden; they are generally treated with a poisonous chemical fungicide. Also avoid tomato and potato sprouts, both of which are poisonous. In addition, the seed sprouts of many ornamental flowers, foliage plants, and wild plants are poisonous.

The first step in sprouting is to measure out the seeds. With most seeds 1/4 cup will yield 1 to 2 cups of sprouts—enough for four average servings. Rinse the seeds thoroughly in a sieve or strainer, then soak them overnight in cool water. Allow at least four times as much water as seeds, since the seeds will absorb a great deal of moisture. The following morning, drain the seeds and place them in a clean, sterile sprouting container, such as a bowl, wide-mouthed jar, or flowerpot. Keep the seeds damp—not wet—and allow air to reach them. A shallow layer of seeds in a wide container is better than a deep layer in a narrow container.

Very small seeds, such as alfalfa and clover, are more easily sprouted on a moist paper towel than in a jar.

Place the towel in a shallow bowl or dish, sprinkle the presoaked seeds onto it, and cover lightly with another paper towel. Sprinkle water over the towels from time to time to keep the seeds moist. For added flavor, give alfalfa and clover sprouts a few hours of light on the last day of sprouting.

Seeds should be rinsed in a strainer twice daily in cold water when they are sprouting. Discard any that

Damp paper towel is excellent for sprouting small seeds.

are not sprouting properly, drain the rest, and return them to the container. The seed hulls should come off and float away during the last few rinses. Chickpeas and soybeans should be rinsed four to six times a day.

Most seeds sprout well at room temperature (60°F to 80°F); soybeans and chickpeas do best at about 50°F. For use in salads most sprouts should be 1 to 1 1/2 inches long. Peas and lentil sprouts should be the length of the seed. As a general rule, the bigger the seed, the shorter the sprout should be for maximum flavor and tenderness. Sprouts are best when eaten fresh but will keep four to six days in the refrigerator.

Trapping the Sun For Winter Farming

Cold frames, hotbeds, and greenhouses are devices for trapping the sun's energy to grow plants in cold weather. The cold frame is the simplest of the three. Basically, it consists of a bottomless box with a movable top cover of glass. Sunlight passes through the transparent top, strikes the walls and soil inside, and is converted to heat. Most of the heat waves, however, will not pass back out through the glass and are trapped inside. This is known as the greenhouse effect. Transparent plastic can be substituted for glass.

The versatile cold frame has several uses. It can be used for starting seeds in spring or for hardening seedlings that have been started indoors. In fall and winter it can provide a steady supply of such cold-tolerant crops as lettuce, spinach, and cabbage. And by adding a source of warmth, such as an electric heater cable, a cold frame is quickly converted into a hotbed for starting seedlings of tender crops even in cold weather.

When building a cold frame, make the back several inches higher than the front so that the top is tilted.

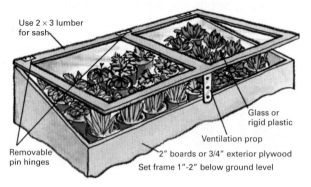

Use 2 × 3 lumber for sash

Removable pin hinges

Glass or rigid plastic

Ventilation prop

2" boards or 3/4" exterior plywood

Set frame 1"-2" below ground level

Cold frames are simple and inexpensive to build. Tailor the dimensions to fit your own needs or components at hand.

This, allows rain and melting snow to drain off and helps capture more rays from the low-angled winter sun.

For starting or hardening seedlings in a cold frame, it is easiest to have the seedlings in separate containers. For raising fall or winter vegetables dig out the bed of the cold frame to a depth of 4 to 6 inches and fill it in with good garden soil enriched with compost or manure.

A cold frame should face south for maximum exposure to winter sun. If this is not possible, east is the next choice, then west. The ideal temperature inside the cold frame is 65°F to 75°F during the day and 55°F to 65°F at night. Keep an inexpensive outdoor thermometer in a shaded spot inside the frame for quick reference.

On sunny spring days raise the sash for ventilation or the temperature may rise to a point that kills delicate seedlings. Do not forget to close the sash at night. On cold nights cover the glass with hay, burlap, or an old blanket to retain warmth. In wet weather add an additional cover of waterproof material, such as a canvas tarpaulin or sheet of plastic.

A typical cold-frame measures about 3 feet by 6 feet and is 9 inches high in front and 15 inches high in back. When building a frame, the best lumber to use is a rot-resistant species such as redwood or cypress, but most woods can serve if they are treated with copper naphthenate, a wood preservative that is not toxic to plants. (The commonly used wood preservatives creosote and pentachlorophenol are both toxic to plants and should be avoided.) For the top, glass is most durable, but fiberglass is a close second. Plastic film is cheap but short lived. Old storm windows make an economical and laborsaving cover. In fact, almost any kind of window can be recycled into a serviceable cold-frame top; some economy-minded gardeners even use old window screens with plastic film tacked to them. When constructing a cold frame out of old parts, it is a simple matter to tailor the dimensions of the frame to fit what is available.

Converting a Cold Frame Into a Hotbed

The simplest way to convert a cold frame into a hotbed is to install an electric heating cable equipped with a thermostat. Cables specially designed for this purpose are sold by many garden-supply centers and mail-order houses. First dig out the soil inside the cold frame to a depth of 1 foot. Put in a 4-inch layer of coarse gravel for drainage and lay the heating cable on this. Note: For safety and compliance with the law, make certain that your installation conforms to all local regulations governing outdoor electrical installations. Lay the heating cable in long, parallel U-shaped loops and cover it with 1/2-inch galvanized wire mesh to protect it from gardening tools. Over this goes 2 inches of builder's sand and then 6 inches of topsoil or planting medium. If you plan to plant in containers rather than soil, omit the planting medium. On sunny days the hotbed must be ventilated just like a cold frame.

You can heat a hotbed without electricity by using the warmth of fermenting organic matter. Dig a pit 3 feet deep inside the frame and fill it with a 2 1/2-foot layer of straw-rich horse manure or raw compost with a generous dose of nitrogen to speed bacterial action. Wet the organic material thoroughly and cover it with a foot of soil. It will heat up rapidly. Put in seeds or seedlings when the soil temperature drops to 75°F. The warming effect should last for several weeks.

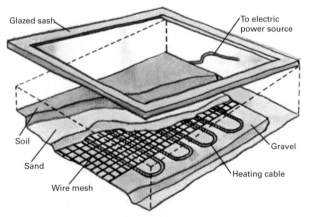

Glazed sash

To electric power source

Soil

Gravel

Sand

Heating cable

Wire mesh

You can convert a cold frame into a hotbed using materials readily available at hardware stores and garden centers.

A window greenhouse

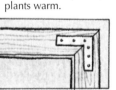

Window greenhouse at left is made out of an old storm window. (You can also make your own storm window or buy one.) Sides and floor are 3/4 in. exterior plywood fastened to the sash with 1 × 1 strips. Seal all edges with caulking compound. House heat helps keep plants warm.

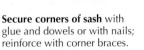

Secure corners of sash with glue and dowels or with nails; reinforce with corner braces.

A Do-it-yourself Greenhouse

A greenhouse is basically a giant cold frame designed to hold large numbers of plants, including ones of considerable size. In most parts of the United States greenhouses are equipped with heating devices so that even tender crops such as tomatoes and peppers can be raised in the coldest months. Greenhouses also need shading devices to protect the plants on hot, sunny days.

Ideally a greenhouse should face south to get maximum winter sunlight. If this is not possible, the next best choice is east (plants benefit from morning light). A western exposure is also satisfactory, but vegetables will not grow in a north-facing greenhouse.

Greenhouses can be bought or built in an almost infinite variety of sizes and designs, from a geodesic dome to a simple lean-to. Greenhouse manufacturers sell complete kits that the home handyman can assemble, but for economy and personal satisfaction many gardeners prefer to build their own from scratch. The simple greenhouse shown here is an economical design that uses materials available at local lumberyards.

The plans show a freestanding unit with a rear wall of weather-resistant exterior-grade plywood. The greenhouse can also be adapted to a lean-to design by butting the rear wall against the side of the house.

Note, however, that if the greenhouse is attached to the house in a region where winter temperatures drop below freezing, a concrete foundation should be laid that extends below the frost line. Otherwise frost heaving can distort the greenhouse's frame and cause glass breakage, structural damage, and even damage to your home.

If it is freestanding, the greenhouse can rest directly on the ground or on a base of 2-inch-thick patio blocks or 8-inch-thick concrete blocks. The sills should be of rot-resistant redwood or else treated with wood preservative, especially if the greenhouse rests on patio blocks or on the ground. The floor need not be paved.

In windy areas the greenhouse should be secured to a permanent foundation or else anchored to the ground. For anchors use rods extending through the sills to 4-inch-square steel plates buried 18 inches in the soil.

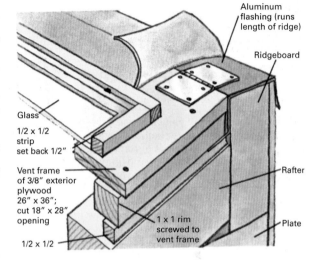

Aluminum flashing (runs length of ridge)

Ridgeboard

Glass

1/2" x 1/2" strip set back 1/2"

Vent frame of 3/8" exterior plywood 26" x 36"; cut 18" x 28" opening

1/2 x 1/2

1 x 1 rim screwed to vent frame

Rafter

Plate

Cross section shows construction details of rooftop vent.

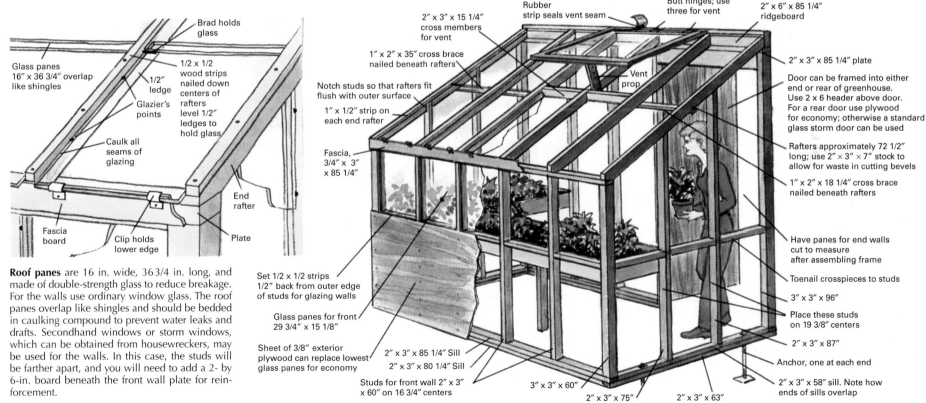

Brad holds glass

Glass panes 16" x 36 3/4" overlap like shingles

1/2 x 1/2 wood strips nailed down centers of rafters level 1/2" ledges to hold glass

1/2" ledge

Glazier's points

Caulk all seams of glazing

End rafter

Fascia board

Clip holds lower edge

Plate

Roof panes are 16 in. wide, 36 3/4 in. long, and made of double-strength glass to reduce breakage. For the walls use ordinary window glass. The roof panes overlap like shingles and should be bedded in caulking compound to prevent water leaks and drafts. Secondhand windows or storm windows, which can be obtained from housewreckers, may be used for the walls. In this case, the studs will be farther apart, and you will need to add a 2- by 6-in. board beneath the front wall plate for reinforcement.

Rubber strip seals vent seam

Butt hinges; use three for vent

2" x 6" x 85 1/4" ridgeboard

2" x 3" x 15 1/4" cross members for vent

1" x 2" x 35" cross brace nailed beneath rafters

Vent prop

2" x 3" x 85 1/4" plate

Notch studs so that rafters fit flush with outer surface

1" x 1/2" strip on each end rafter

Door can be framed into either end or rear of greenhouse. Use 2 x 6 header above door. For a rear door use plywood for economy; otherwise a standard glass storm door can be used

Fascia, 3/4" x 3" x 85 1/4"

Rafters approximately 72 1/2" long; use 2" x 3" x 7' stock to allow for waste in cutting bevels

1" x 2" x 18 1/4" cross brace nailed beneath rafters

Have panes for end walls cut to measure after assembling frame

Set 1/2 x 1/2 strips 1/2" back from outer edge of studs for glazing walls

Toenail crosspieces to studs

Glass panes for front 29 3/4" x 15 1/8"

3" x 3" x 96"

Sheet of 3/8" exterior plywood can replace lowest glass panes for economy

Place these studs on 19 3/8" centers

2" x 3" x 85 1/4" Sill
2" x 3" x 80 1/4" Sill

2" x 3" x 87"

Studs for front wall 2" x 3" x 60" on 16 3/4" centers

3" x 3" x 60"

2" x 3" x 75"

2" x 3" x 63"

Anchor, one at each end

2" x 3" x 58" sill. Note how ends of sills overlap

137

From Seed to Harvest:
A Grower's Guide
To Garden Favorites

Home gardeners today can choose from a greater selection of vegetables than ever before. A typical seed catalog offers more than 30 varieties of tomatoes, ranging from the tiny cocktail type to 1-pound giants, from genetically engineered hybrids to old favorites like Ponderosa and Rutgers. With so many special varieties available, you can grow virtually any vegetable you want no matter what the soil type, how long the growing season, or how arid or humid the climate.

The guide that follows provides the basic information needed to select, grow, and harvest all the standard vegetables. Suggestions are given on how many to plant. They are based on Department of Agriculture recommendations and do not take account of personal tastes. When a vegetable is suitable for canning or other home preserving, an extra quantity has been allowed.

In addition to the detailed information given for each vegetable, there are a few general pointers to follow if you want a bountiful harvest. One of the most important is to leave ample space between plants. A vegetable needs enough room so it can get its share of sunlight, water, and nutrients: it is better to raise two good heads of lettuce than three runty, undernourished ones.

Another point to bear in mind is that many pests and diseases attack all members of a plant family—not just one particular species. For this reason, you should not plant members of the same family in the same spot in the garden two years in a row. The three major groups of related vegetables are: (1) tomatoes, peppers, and eggplant; (2) cabbage, broccoli, cauliflower, radishes, turnips, rutabagas, kohlrabi, and mustard; and (3) melons, cucumbers, gourds, and summer and winter squash.

Also note the following when using the guide:

Days to harvest refers to the length of time between when a plant is set out in the garden and when it is ready to harvest. It does not include the number of days a plant grows indoors after being started from seed.

Planting depth is an approximate guide. If in doubt, it is best to err on the shallow side. A handy rule is to plant the seed three times as deep as its size.

Planting in hills, in modern parlance, means planting seeds in small, compact groups. Years ago, a hill was literally that—a low mound of enriched soil.

Asparagus. A hardy perennial that yields edible spears (young shoots) in spring and early summer. A well-managed asparagus bed will be productive for 20–25 years. Since asparagus needs a period of cold for dormancy and resting, it does poorly in areas that are warm the year round.

Asparagus can be started from seed, but the usual practice is to set out year-old roots in early spring or late fall. Start about 10 to 15 plants for each member of your family. The roots are planted in trenches 4–5 ft. apart. Dig the trenches 18 in. wide and 12 in. deep. Loosen the soil at the bottom and mix well with manure, compost, or fertilizer, then cover the bottom of the trench with 4–6 in. of good soil and rake level. Set the asparagus roots on this soil 18 in. apart. Cover them with soil up to the top of the trench; if there is any extra soil it may be mounded over the top. An older technique is to barely cover the roots and fill in the trench gradually as the shoots grow. Mulch is recommended for keeping the asparagus bed free of weeds because the roots are shallow, and deep cultivation can injure the roots.

Do not harvest the first spring. The next year, harvest lightly (for about two weeks). Thereafter, you may harvest freely until the spears become spindly, a sign that the roots are becoming exhausted. The harvesting season lasts six to eight weeks. Spears are ready to pick when they are tight, smooth, and about 6–8 in. tall. When they start to open up they are too old. Harvest by cutting or breaking the spears at ground level. Any surplus can be frozen or canned for an out-of-season treat.

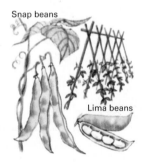

Snap beans

Lima beans

Beans. A warm-weather crop of tropical origin. Lima beans and snap (string) beans are the most popular types in American gardens. Each is available in pole varieties (requiring support) or in low-growing bush varieties. Limas are especially sensitive to cold and need a longer, warmer growing season than snap beans.

Lima beans should be planted when all risk of frost is past. (Some gardeners get a jump on the season by starting limas indoors two to three weeks before the last frost date.) For bush limas, plant seeds 1 in. deep and 2 in. apart in rows 2 ft. apart. Thin later to 8 in. between plants. For pole varieties set poles 3 ft. apart in rows 4 ft. apart. Plant about six seeds per pole and thin to three or four seedlings. About 5–6 ft. of bush limas (or 2–4 ft. of pole limas) per person is ample. Supply plenty of water in hot weather. Harvest when seeds begin to plump out the pods. Pick frequently to keep plants productive. Days to harvest: 70–90. For use as dried beans let limas mature and dry on the plants. Lima beans are also excellent for freezing and canning.

Snap beans are a high-yielding crop that is excellent for freezing and canning. Sow when soil is warm, after last frost date. Some gardeners gamble by planting an early batch about a week before the last expected frost.

Plant bush varieties 1/2–1 in. deep, 2 in. apart, and thin to 4 in. apart. For pole varieties set poles 3 ft. apart in rows 3–4 ft. apart. Plant six seeds per pole and thin later to the four strongest seedlings. You will need 5–6 ft. of bush beans or 3–6 ft. of pole beans per person. Harvest when beans are young and tender (3–4 in. long). For continuous yield plant a short row every week or 10 days, or select a variety that keeps bearing till frost. Wax beans, which are yellow instead of green, are a kind of snap bean and need the same culture. Days to harvest: 50–60 for bush varieties, 60–65 for pole varieties.

Beets. An easy-to-grow, dual purpose crop: both roots and greens (leaves) can be eaten. Beets are quite frost hardy and can be planted in spring as soon as the soil is ready to work. They do well in most types of soil except those that are highly acid. Plant 1/2 in. deep, 1 in. apart in rows 18 in. apart. Allow 3–5 ft. of row per person for the average family. Thin to 2–3 in. apart. For a fall crop, plant in late June or early July. Harvest when roots are 1–3 in. in diameter (pull up one or two to check). Beets that grow larger become tough and woody. Days to harvest: 50–70. The vitamin-rich greens may be cooked and eaten like spinach. In the warmer parts of the nation beets are often sown in early fall for a winter crop.

Broccoli. A member of the cabbage group raised for its flower buds, which are eaten before they open. (Broccoli is not edible after it goes to seed.) Broccoli prefers cool weather and can stand light frost. It will not bear in hot weather. In very mild areas it can be grown in winter.

Start broccoli indoors about six weeks before the average date of the last spring frost; set out in garden two weeks before the last expected frost date. Allow three to five plants per person. Space plants 15–18 in. apart in rows 2 1/2–3 ft. apart. Harvest while flower buds are tight and heads compact. Cut off about 6 in. below the head so as not to waste the tender, edible upper stem. After the center heads (the first to develop) are cut, side shoots will develop additional heads. One plant yields six to eight cuttings over a period of 8–10 weeks. Days to harvest: 55–60, 75 for fall crops. For a fall harvest sow directly in the garden around midsummer. Broccoli retains its flavor and texture well when frozen, and it is an excellent source of vitamins A and C.

Cabbage. A cool-weather crop that can be raised for spring or fall harvest. Cabbage is a good source of vitamin C and keeps well in winter. Types include the familiar green cabbage, the mild-flavored, crinkly-leafed savoy, and the colorful red cabbage. A heavy feeder, cabbage needs a rich, nearly neutral soil that contains plenty of organic matter.

For spring cabbage start seeds indoors about six to eight weeks before the last expected frost. Transplant to the garden after danger of frost is past—cabbage seedlings exposed to frost or cold grow slowly and tend to be fibrous and tough. Allow two to three plants per person for the average family. Plants should be spaced 12–18 in. apart in rows 2–3 ft. apart. For fall crops start seeds indoors in May and set out after midsummer, or sow directly in the garden June to August–the milder the winter, the later you should sow. For direct sowing plant seeds in groups of three or four, 1/2 in. deep at 1-ft. intervals in the rows; thin later to the one strongest seedling. Cabbage thrives with an insulating mulch of hay or straw to keep the soil cool. Harvest cabbage when the heads are tight and full. Days to harvest: 50–90. Fall cabbage develops larger heads and—many people think—better flavor than spring cabbage.

Several soil-borne diseases attack cabbage and its close relatives, such as broccoli, cauliflower, and turnips. To avoid infection, do not plant any member of the cabbage family in soil where any of them has been grown in the last two years.

Cantaloupe. An orange-fleshed melon with a netted exterior. Cantaloupe (a kind of muskmelon) needs a long, warm growing season and full exposure to the sun. Early-maturing dwarf varieties are recommended for northern gardens. Since cold is bad for melons (cool temperatures and rain lower the quantity of sugar), they should not be planted until dependably warm weather, several weeks after the last frost.

Like other melons, cantaloupes do best in sandy soil with plenty of manure and compost mixed in. To plant in rows, sow seeds 1/2 in. deep, 4–6 in. apart in rows 5 ft. apart and thin to 18–24 in. apart. Alternatively, plant three to a hill, with the hills 5 ft. apart each way. Figure on about four fruits per plant. In colder regions start the melons indoors three to four weeks ahead of planting time. Melons need ample water while the fruits are growing, but during the final ripening stage limiting the water is said to increase their sweetness. Cantaloupes are ready to pick when the fruit separates from the stem with a slight pull. Days to harvest: 60–90. If any fruits form after midsummer, pick them off the vine; they will not ripen and will take food from the others.

Carrots. One of the old standbys, high in vitamin A and with many culinary uses. Carrots are a hardy vegetable that can be planted in spring as soon as the soil can be worked. Since the seeds are slow to germinate, it is helpful to plant radish seeds along with them to mark the row. The radishes will be ready to harvest about the time the carrots start coming up. Carrots do best in rich, deep, sandy loam but will grow well in almost any soil that has been properly prepared. Dig up the soil to a depth of at least 1 ft., loosen it, and remove stones and other debris. This will allow the downward-growing carrot roots to develop properly. Heavy clay soils often cause carrots to fork. Lighten such soils by working in a goodly proportion of sand or humus.

Sow carrot seeds 1/4–1/2 in. deep, 15 to 20 seeds to the inch in rows 16–24 in. apart. Allow 4–5 ft. of row per person. Thin seedlings to 2 in. apart when they are 2–4 in. high or when the roots are about as thick as your little finger (pull up a few carrots to check root size). The tender baby carrots that have been thinned out make delicious eating. The remaining carrots may be harvested at any time, depending on how large you want them. Keep the soil moist until the seedlings have come up. For a fall crop sow in the garden in early July. Carrots keep well in the refrigerator or in winter storage.

Cauliflower. A "luxury" member of the cabbage group that is difficult for beginners to grow successfully. Cauliflower needs rich soil and constant moisture for best development. It is sensitive to heat, requiring a long, cool growing season to produce good heads. Cauliflower does best as a fall crop in most areas.

For a fall crop, seeds may be sown directly in the garden in June or July, 8–10 weeks before the first expected autumn frost date for your locality. Plant seeds three or four together, 1/2 in. deep and 18–24 in. apart and thin to the strongest single seedling. For a spring crop start indoors in February or March and set out a week before the last average frost date. Plants should be no older than six weeks when set out. Set seedlings 18 in. apart in rows 30 in. apart. Allow two to three plants per person. When heads are about 3 in. across, they should be blanched—that is, the leaves should be tied over them (this will produce white heads). Harvest while heads are compact and fairly smooth (two to four weeks after tying up, depending on the weather). Days to harvest: 50–95, depending on variety.

In addition to the standard white cauliflower, seed houses offer a purple-headed variety that turns green when cooked.

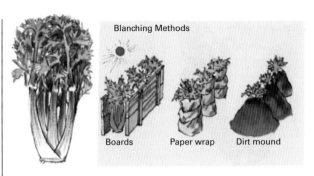

Blanching Methods

Boards   Paper wrap   Dirt mound

Celery. One of the trickier plants for the home gardener to raise. Celery is very sensitive to both cold and heat and requires a growing season of four months. Consequently, it must be started indoors in March or April and set out in the garden between June 15 and July 15. Plants should be 6 in. apart in rows 18–24 in. apart. Celery needs a constantly moist soil very rich in organic matter; muck soils are the best. For maximum growth celery should be fertilized every two weeks.

Celery stalks are naturally green but can be blanched (whitened) by various means. You can hill up dirt around the plants, place boards along the sides of the rows, or cover the plants with drain tiles, paper, or mulch. Blanching is not recommended for the home garden because of the extra space required and the danger of rot. Days to harvest: 115–135. Note: Celery may be harvested before fully mature. While celery is primarily raised for its crunchy stalks, the nutty root, or "heart," is a delicacy. The leaves are used for flavoring soups and stews.

Collards. A loose-leafed relative of the cabbage. A traditional southern favorite, collards thrive in almost every section of the country. They are an excellent source of vitamin A. Collards tolerate cold as low as 15°F, and frost actually improves their flavor. They also tolerate hot summers better than cabbage and will grow in relatively poor soil. In areas with short, cool summers sow collards in late spring. Elsewhere, sow them in midsummer for a fall crop. Plant seeds 1/2 in. deep and 1 in. apart in rows 24–30 in. apart. Allow 5–10 ft. of row per person. Thin so plants are 18–24 in. apart along the rows; the thinnings can be used as greens. Harvest by clipping the young leaves, including the stems. Be sure to leave six to eight leaves on the plant: they are needed to sustain growth. Do not harvest the central growing point or you will have to wait for side shoots to form to provide new leaves. Days to harvest: 75–80. In the Deep South collards are grown through the winter to furnish fresh greens. Collards can be eaten raw in salads or cooked in a variety of traditional methods,

particularly as an accompaniment to ham or pork. The flavor is similar to that of cabbage but richer.

Corn. A space-consuming crop but well worth growing for its fresh-picked sweetness. Corn needs a long, warm growing season, plenty of water, and rich soil. Varieties of sweet corn (the sortgrown for the dinner table) include yellow, white, and bicolored kinds, dwarf strains for the small garden, and quick-maturing hybrids for regions that have a short growing season.

Plant in either rows or hills. For rows sow seeds 1 in. deep, 4 in. apart in rows 30 in. apart, and thin later to 8–12 in. For hills plant three to four seeds per hill, 2–3 ft. apart. Old-time gardeners always planted extra seeds to allow for destruction by birds, bugs, and other pests. Corn should not be planted until the soil is warm and all danger of frost is past. Harvest when the silk of the ears turns dark brown and the kernels spurt milky juice when pressed with a fingernail. Each plant will produce one or two ears of corn. Corn is best when picked just before eating; once off the plant, the sugar in the kernels turns to starch, making the corn tough and pasty. Days to harvest: 62–94, depending on variety and weather.

For a continuous harvest, plant successively maturing varieties at the same time or plant successive batches of the same variety at 7-to 10-day intervals. Since corn is pollinated by the wind, it should be planted in compact blocks rather than long, thin rows. A block should have at least three rows to ensure pollination. Weed every week until the seedlings are tall enough to shade out weeds, or mulch when the corn is 3–4 in. tall. Corn plants often produce suckers–smaller extra stalks that do not bear ears. Old-time farmers removed the suckers, thinking them useless, but modern practice is to leave them, as they provide additional food for the plant and the growing ears.

Popcorn and the colorful Indian corn should be planted at least 300 ft. from sweet corn to avoid cross-pollination—corn is one of the few plants in which cross-pollination affects the current year's crop. Hybrid varieties should also be planted separately from other strains of corn.

Cowpeas. A favorite in the South. Cowpeas (also known as blackeyed peas or field peas) can be grown successfully in most sections of the country. Actually a type of bean, they can be eaten green or dried. Cowpeas need a long growing season with warm days and nights; the slightest touch of frost damages them. Sow when soil is warm and all danger of frost is past. Plant seeds 1/2–1 in. deep, 2 in. apart in rows 24–36 in. apart. Thin to 4–6 in. apart. Days to harvest: 85–90. A 10-to 15-ft. row will probably be enough for four people. Cowpeas come in varieties with green, white, or brown seeds.

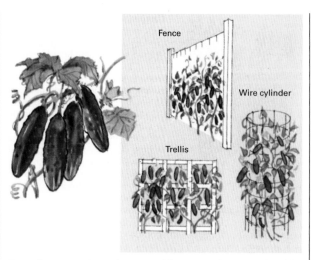

Fence

Wire cylinder

Trellis

Cucumbers. Not the easiest vegetable to grow but a good yielder with a long harvesting season. Sow outdoors when soil is warm and danger of frost is past. Plant seeds 1/2–1 in. deep, 4–6 in. apart in rows 5 ft. apart; thin 12–15 in. to give the vines room to grow. Cucumbers can also be planted in hills 5 ft. apart each way, 5 to 10 seeds per hill; thin later to three to four plants per hill. For a headstart plant seeds indoors four to eight weeks before the last frost date. Three to six plants should produce enough for the average family. For large-scale pickle making the Department of Agriculture recommends three to five hills per person.

Cucumbers need ample moisture and do best in a deep, rich, neutral soil. Well-rotted manure mixed into the soil is helpful. Plants should be watered throughout the growing season: insufficient water results in undersized, misshapen fruits. Mulching helps retain soil moisture and protects fruits by keeping them off the soil. Cucumber vines are eager climbers and may be trained on poles, fences, frameworks, or wire netting. These methods of saving space are preferable for the small garden.

Some cucumbers are bred for pickling, others for salad use. The difference is mainly in size and shape; in other respects pickling cucumbers are perfectly good in salads, and salad varieties make fine pickles. Pick salad cucumbers when 6–9 in. long; harvest pickling types at whatever size is convenient. Note, however, that cucumbers must be picked before they turn yellow–at this stage the seeds harden and the fruit loses its flavor. Keeping the vines picked stimulates them to produce until frost kills them; the presence of big, ripe cukes on the vines halts fruit production. Days to harvest: 50–70, depending on variety.

Each cucumber vine bears separate male and female flowers (except for certain all-female hybrids). No fruits are produced until the female flowers appear (identifiable by a tiny cucumber beneath the blossom). Since the vines grow from the tip only, do not break their tips off, as this will stop their growth. To avoid spreading disease, do not handle the vines or harvest the fruits when they are wet. Despite old wives' tales to the contrary, cucumbers do not cross with squash and melons.

Eggplant. A native of India related to the tomato and the sweet pepper. It is a staple of Middle Eastern cooking. The eggplant needs a long, warm growing season and will not sprout unless the soil is warmer than 75°F. Most gardening books recommend buying started seedlings.

Eggplant can be started indoors in warm soil 8–10 weeks before the last frost. Set in the garden 2–3 ft. apart in rows 3–4 ft. apart. Three to six plants yield an adequate supply for the average family. Eggplant can tolerate drought better than most vegetables. Harvest while fruit is plump and glossy; when it loses its sheen it is overripe and will taste bitter. Eggplant produces until frost. Days to harvest: 65–75.

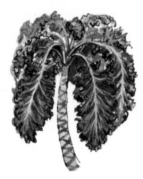

Kale. A nonheading member of the cabbage family often grown for its ornamental, curly foliage as well as for the dinner table. It is a good source of vitamin C and thiamin. Kale can tolerate summer heat and is extremely cold hardy. It can be raised as a spring or fall crop. Sow in spring as soon as soil can be worked, 1/4 in. deep, 1 in. apart in rows 20 in. apart; thin to 12 in. between plants. About 5 ft. of row per person should furnish an adequate supply.

For fall and early winter harvesting sow in midsummer. Harvest by taking entire plant or by cutting the outer leaves only, leaving the inner ones to develop. Days to harvest: 60–70, depending on variety. Kale can be covered with straw or burlap and kept fresh and green in the garden until very cold weather. South of Virginia, this protection is usually not necessary.

Kohlrabi. A cold-resistant member of the cabbage group raised for its turniplike, bulbous stem. Kohlrabi makes a good crop for both spring and fall. Sow in early spring as soon as the ground can be worked, 1/4 in. deep and 1 in. apart in rows 18–24 in. apart; thin to 3–4 in. apart. About 5 ft. of row per person should be sufficient for the average family. Kohlrabi can be eaten either raw for snacks and salads or cooked.

For a fall harvest sow in July or August. Harvest when the bulbs reach 2–3 in. in diameter. When larger, they become stringy and lose flavor. Days to harvest: 55–60.

Bibb

Iceberg

Oak leaf

Lettuce. A cool-weather crop available in either head or looseleaf types and in many varieties of each. All varieties will provide a bountiful harvest of salad greens until summer heat stimulates the plants to flower, which makes them tough and bitter. Lettuce can also be sown in late summer for a fall crop.

Lettuce is one of the easiest vegetables to raise from seed. Sow thinly in early spring, 1/4 in. deep in rows 16 in. apart. Thin gradually to 12 in. between plants for loose-leaf types, 16–18 in. for head types. (Head lettuce is often started indoors in flats and set out when the soil is ready to work.) Allow 4–5 ft. of row per person. Thin ruthlessly—lettuce needs a lot of room to grow in. Thinnings may be transplanted or used thriftily in a garden-fresh salad.

To be tender and free from bitterness, lettuce should grow quickly. It needs plenty of water and nitrogen. To keep leaf lettuce producing for a maximum length of time, harvest only the outer leaves so that the plant continuously produces new leaves for use. With head lettuce the entire head must be harvested. Head lettuce is more sensitive to heat than is loose-leaf lettuce. The growing season for both types can often be prolonged by planting them in a partly shaded area of the garden. Days to harvest: 40–83. For a fall crop sow in August. Lettuce seeds will not sprout when the soil temperature is more than 80°F, but they can be forced to germinate by chilling them in the refrigerator in damp peat moss and sand for five days.

Seeds

Mustard. Another southern favorite that can be raised anywhere that radishes will grow. Esteemed for its pungent green leaves, mustard is a fast-growing, frost-hardy, cool-season crop. Sow in spring as soon as the soil can be worked, 1/2 in. deep and 1–2 in. apart in rows 16 in. apart. A 20- to 25-ft. row provides ample supplies of mustard greens for the average family. Thin the plants to 4–6 in. apart. Harvest when leaves are 3–4 in. long (sooner if you like). Snap or cut off the leaves, leaving the growing point to produce more. For a fall crop sow in August or September. In areas with mild winters mustard can be grown for a winter supply of fresh greens. Days to harvest: 25–50. Pulverize the seeds, and mix with water to make fresh old-time mustard.

Okra. A tall warm-weather plant related to hibiscus and cotton that is raised for its edible pods. Although considered a southern vegetable, okra may, with luck, be grown as far north as southern Canada. It thrives in almost any fertile, well-drained soil.

Sow when soil is thoroughly warm, 1/2–1 in. deep and 18 in. apart in rows 3 ft. apart. To speed germination, soak the seeds in water overnight. Plant three or four seeds at each spot; when seedlings are 1 in. tall, remove all but one. Allow three or four plants per person. Okra may also be started indoors about a month before the last expected frost date. Harvest pods when they are 3 or 4 in. long or three to four days after the blossom petals fall off. For best flavor pick just before cooking. For continued production keep the pods picked. Days to harvest: 55–60. Okra is used in stews and in soups, especially the famous gumbo of New Orleans.

Young transplants

Ready to harvest

Young onions

Onions. Hardy members of the lily family raised for their pungent bulbs. Onions do best in loose, fertile soil. They are heavy feeders, so the soil should be enriched by digging in manure or compost before planting time.

Onions may be raised from seed, from immature bulbs called sets, or from young plants. Because onions have a long growing season, home gardeners generally prefer sets or plants over seeds. Whatever the choice, onions can be planted as soon as the soil can be worked. Place sets or plants 1 in. deep and 4 in. apart in rows 12 in. apart. If grown from seed, thin seedlings to 3–4 in. apart when they are 3 in. tall. The thinnings can be used as young green onions or transplanted. Allow 4–5 ft. of row per person for average use. Days to harvest: 80-110 from seed, 50–60 if sets or young plants are used.

To harvest onions for storage, bend the tops down to the ground when they start to go yellow. After the tops turn brown, pull up the onions and spread them out to dry for a week (longer if the weather is damp). Then braid the tops together and hang the onions indoors to store; or cut tops off an inch above the bulbs and store the onions in mesh bags or shallow open boxes in a cool, airy place. They should keep from two to four months.

Parsnips. A slow-growing relative of the carrot; resembles a large white carrot. Parsnips do best in fertile, loamy soils. Heavy clay soils and stony soils distort and toughen the roots.

Sow seeds in spring as soon as the soil can be worked. Since they may take several weeks to germinate, mark the row with radishes, which will be ready to pull when the parsnip seedlings emerge. Loosen the soil to a depth of 12 in. to let the roots grow properly. Plant seeds thickly 1/4 in. deep in rows 18 in. apart. Thin to 3–4 in. apart. Allow 4–5 ft. of row per person.

Parsnips can either be dug (not pulled) in fall and stored in damp sand, or they can be left in the ground for use as needed throughout the winter. Freezing temperatures improve their naturally sweet flavor. Days to harvest: about 100.

Peas. A cool-weather crop with both bush and tall (requiring support) varieties. Green peas (known in the South as English peas) are raised for their immature seeds. Snow peas, or sugar-pod peas, are eaten pod and all when very young. Peas do well in most kinds of soil as long as it contains plenty of organic matter.

Plant peas in spring as soon as the soil can be worked. Dig in compost, manure, or other organic matter. Plant seeds 1–2 in. deep, 1 in. apart in rows 3 ft. apart. If you plant double rows (8–12 in. wide), allow 40 in. between rows. Many authorities recommend planting peas in a shallow trench, which is filled in with soil as the pea vines grow, but this is not necessary. Give peas plenty of water. Mulch to retain water and keep soil cool. Allow about 10 ft. of row per person.

Tall-growing varieties should be supported on branches or brush stuck in the ground when the vines begin to get bushy. They can also be trained on wire, twine, or netting strung between stakes. Dwarf, or bush, varieties can be grown without support but are easier to care for and harvest if supported.

Pick green peas when the pods are well filled but the peas inside are not hard. Pick snow peas when the pods are just beginning to plump out. All peas are at their best if cooked within a few hours after picking. If left too long on the vine, peas become tough and unappetizing, so check the vines every couple of days. However, if you wish to dry peas for storage, let them mature on the vine until they are completely hard, then remove from vine, shell, and dry them in an oven at low heat. They make a hearty pea soup. Peas are also excellent for freezing fresh. Days to harvest: 55–78, depending on variety.

In areas with above-freezing winters peas can be sown from midsummer on for a fall or winter crop.

Hybrid bell pepper

Pimiento

Cubanelle

California Wonder

Sweet banana

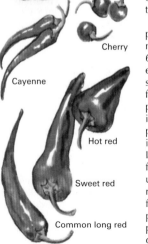

Cayenne

Cherry

Hot red

Sweet red

Common long red

Peppers. A frost-tender crop that needs a long, warm growing season. In their tropical home pepper plants are perennials and reach the size of small trees. In the mainland United States they are raised as annuals and grow about 2 ft. tall. There are sweet and hot types of peppers. All varieties have much the same cultural requirements as tomatoes, to which they are related. They do best on a slightly acid soil with full sun and plenty of moisture.

For most areas of the United States peppers should be started indoors about eight weeks before the last expected frost date and set out in the garden when the soil is warm. The plants should be 18–24 in. apart in rows 24–36 in. apart. Three to five plants per person are sufficient. The fruits of both sweet and hot peppers may be harvested at any stage of growth. Sweet peppers, also known as green or bell peppers, turn red or yellow at maturity. At this stage they are sweeter. Some hot peppers turn red or yellow soon after the fruits are formed. Be careful when picking peppers: the plants are brittle, and you may end up with a whole branch in your hand instead of a fruit. You can avoid the problem by cutting the fruits off, not picking them.

Peppers are temperamental plants. They set fruit only when nighttime temperatures are between 60° and 70°F. If they do not get enough moisture, they drop blossoms and fruits. However, under favorable conditions they bear plentifully. Sweet peppers are rich in vitamin C and freeze well; hot peppers can be stored by stringing them up and letting them dry. In fall sweet peppers can be kept for two to three weeks by pulling up the entire plant and hanging it, roots uppermost, in a cool (but not freezing) indoor location. Pepper plants can be grown indoors in pots in wintertime or where garden space is limited.

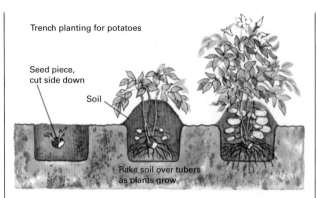

Trench planting for potatoes

Seed piece, cut side down

Soil

Rake soil over tubers as plants grow

Potatoes. One of the world's major food crops. Native to the bleak Andean highlands of South America, the potato is related to the eggplant, pepper, and tomato. Though killed by frost, potatoes do best in cool weather. They thrive in light, sandy, acid soil. If you can spare the space in your garden (potato plants are sprawling and take up a good deal of room), potatoes are well worth planting for the rewards of tender, young new potatoes or full-sized tubers from your own soil.

Potatoes can be raised from sets (small tubers) or seed potatoes (medium-sized tubers specially bred for propagation). A set is used whole; seed potatoes are cut into pieces about the size of a small hen's egg, each containing one or more eyes. Potatoes sold in food markets are not recommended as seed pieces—they are often contaminated with disease, and many are treated with chemicals that inhibit them from sprouting. If you are using seed potatoes, spread the seed pieces on a clean surface and allow the cut surfaces to dry out for 1 to 10 days. This permits the cut surfaces to heal over and reduces the chance of infection from decay organisms. The seed pieces can be dusted with a fungicide for further protection.

Potatoes should be planted in spring as soon as the soil can be worked–if late frosts are common in your area, plant them about three weeks before the last expected frost. Plant sets or seed pieces 3 in. deep and 12–18 in. apart in rows 24–36 in. apart. The tubers form close to the surface of the soil, so cultivate no more than an inch deep to avoid injuring them. As the vines grow, mound up soil, mulch, or compost around them to shield the tubers from light: sunlight not only turns potatoes green but generates a poisonous alkaloid called solanine in the green portions. If a potato should have a green portion, cut it away before cooking. For new potatoes harvest when vines blossom. For mature potatoes, intended for storage, dig up when vines have died. Dry tubers for several hours and store them in a cool, dark place, preferably between 40° and 45°F.

Another method of planting is to set the seed pieces directly on the bare, prepared soil, press them in lightly to ensure good contact, and cover them with a 12-in. layer of straw, salt hay, or other light organic mulch. When the mulch settles, add 6 in. more. Potatoes raised this way are cleaner and easier to harvest, since no digging is necessary. You need only pull the mulch away. Days to harvest: 100–120.

Potatoes will not form tubers when the soil temperature reaches 80°F. For this reason they do poorly in warm regions.

Mammoth Gold

Cushaw type

Cinderella

American

Pumpkin. A kind of squash first cultivated by American Indians. Whether they are the vine or bush type, pumpkins require a great deal of space; however, in a small garden they can be grown on a trellis with the fruits supported by slings. Pumpkins grow 7–24 in. in diameter, depending on type. In general, the smaller varieties are better for eating. Large pumpkins were used for stock feed on the old-time family farm. There are also special varieties that are raised for their tasty seeds.

Frost tender, as are all members of the gourd family, pumpkins should not be planted until all danger of frost is past and the soil is warm. They may be started indoors three to four weeks before the last expected frost date. For outdoor planting plant seeds in hills 8–10 ft. apart for vine types, 4–6 ft. for bush types. Plant six seeds to the hill; when seedlings are about 6 in. tall, thin out all but the two or three strongest ones. A shovelful of manure or compost mixed in with the soil will get the plants off to a good start. For pumpkins started indoors use two or three to a hill. Pumpkins may also be planted in rows, with 3–4 ft. of space between plants and at least 6 ft. between rows to allow room for the sprawling vines. Mulching is recommended to keep down weeds, conserve soil moisture, and keep the fruits off the dirt. On the old-time farm pumpkins were often planted with corn, a practice settlers had learned from the Indians.

To grow huge exhibition-type pumpkins, plant seeds of a large variety such as Big Max or Mammoth. Allow only one fruit to develop on each vine and water the plants heavily.

Pumpkins are normally left on the vine until the vine is killed by frost or deteriorates from age. (The fruits, with their thick skins, are not harmed by a light frost.) The best practice is to cut the stem a few inches above the fruit. Store pumpkins in a cool, dry place. Days to harvest: 100–120 for most varieties.

Radishes. A fast-growing, hardy, virtually foolproof cool-weather crop related to cabbages and turnips. Radishes are often sown together with seeds of other, slower germinating vegetables such as carrots and parsnips. This practice makes double use of the garden space, marks the location of the second vegetable, and loosens and aerates the soil when the radishes are pulled up for harvesting. Plant as soon as the soil can be worked, two or three to the inch, 1/2 in. deep. Rows can be as close as 6 in. apart. Thin seedlings to 2 in. apart soon after they emerge. Radishes become tough, pithy, and increasingly hot to the taste as they get old. Plant small batches at intervals of a week to 10 days to get a continuous supply of young, mild, tender radishes. Hot weather and lack of water also make radishes hot. Do not plant radishes in the hottest part of summer (when daytime temperatures average over 80°F). They will not bulb up. Sow them for a fall crop when the weather cools off.

Radishes are ready to harvest when the bulbs are about 1 in. in diameter, although some people prefer them smaller. If the top of the bulb shows above the ground, the radish is usually ready to pick. Alternatively, probe the soil at the base of the leaves with your finger to estimate the size of the bulb. Days to harvest: 22–30, depending on variety.

Winter radishes, much larger and slower growing than ordinary radishes, should be sown in early summer for a fall crop and around midsummer for late fall and winter use. Thin to 6–8 in. between plants. Dig in late fall and store in damp sand in a location safe from freezing. They will remain fresh and crisp for several weeks. Winter radishes may also be cooked using any recipe suitable for turnips. Days to harvest: 55–60.

Rhubarb. A hardy perennial raised for its tart, edible stalks. Rhubarb thrives in any deep, well-drained fertile soil as long as it has a good supply of moisture.

Rhubarb is almost always raised from roots, which are planted in early spring 3–4 ft. apart each way. (It does not come true from seed.) Do not harvest the first year. Thereafter, harvest when stalks reach 1 in. in diameter. **Caution: Do not use the leaves; they contain oxalic acid, a dangerous poison.** Pull stalks, do not cut them. Most varieties of rhubarb send up a seed stalk noticeably taller than the leaf stalks. It should be cut off at ground level to keep the plant producing.

Every five to seven years, when the stalks become markedly thinner, dig up the plants, split up the root clumps, and replant them. Where possible, select the plants that in past years have yielded the best stalks for replanting.

Spinach. A hardy cool-weather vegetable that yields both spring and fall crops. Spinach is rich in vitamin A and a good source of iron. Most spinach contains small amounts of oxalic acid, an agent that causes loss of calcium from the blood. New strains are available, however, that have almost none of this substance. Spinach thrives on well-drained, fertile soils with plenty of organic matter. The soil should be slightly acid; on very acid or very alkaline soils spinach does poorly.

Plant seeds four to six weeks before the last expected frost date, 1/2 in. deep and about 1 in. apart in rows 14 in. apart. Thin to 4 in. between plants. Plan on 5–10 ft. of row per person. Harvest spinach by picking the outer leaves as soon as they reach edible size. Should buds form at the center, it is a sign that the plant will soon bolt (send up its flower stalk) and its leaves will become tough and unpalatable. At the bud stage the plants are still good and can be salvaged by pulling them up or cutting them off at ground level. Long days and hot weather in combination stimulate spinach to bolt.

For a fall crop, plant in late August or early September. Because of its short growing life, spinach should be planted in small batches at two-week intervals. Spinach can be grown as a winter vegetable in areas where temperatures do not dip much below the freezing point. Days to harvest: 40–50. Spinach can be eaten raw as well as cooked and is excellent for freezing.

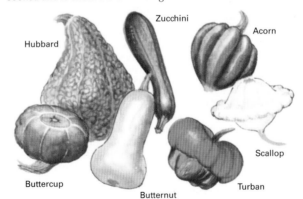

Zucchini

Acorn

Hubbard

Scallop

Buttercup

Butternut

Turban

Squash. A large group of vegetables belonging to the gourd family. Summer squash have soft skins and moist, succulent flesh; they are eaten while young and tender. Popular summer squash include zucchini, yellow straightneck, and scallop. Winter squash, which are picked in fall and eaten fully ripe, have hard, thick skins and a rather dry, fibrous flesh, a combination that helps them keep for months. Acorn, buttercup, butternut, hubbard, and turban are standard types of winter squash. Most summer squash are bush varieties; most winter squash grow on sprawling vines. All require a good deal of space, although bush kinds are more compact.

Cultural requirements are the same for all types of squash. Squash are frost tender and should not be planted until danger of frost is past and the soil is warm. Where the growing season is short, squash plants should be started indoors. Squash should have a rich, loamy, slightly alkaline soil and plenty of moisture; otherwise the fruits may be undersized.

Squash can be planted in hills or in rows. Plant seeds 1–2 in. deep. For hills plant five or six to the hill, thinning later to the two or three strongest seedlings. Hills should be 4–6 ft. apart in each direction for bush squash, 8–10 ft. for vine squash. When row-planting bush varieties, place seeds 24–30 in. apart in rows 36 in. apart; for vine varieties 2–3 ft. apart in rows 9–12 ft. apart. Plant three or four seeds together as insurance against cutworms, slugs, and other garden pests; thin later to the strongest seedling. Squash do well with mulch.

Summer squash are best picked when they are about 1–2 in. in diameter and while the skin can still be pierced with a fingernail. (Zucchini, however, can be allowed to grow much larger and still be used for baking.) Scallop squash can be picked when 3 or 4 in. across. Cut fruits off with a knife to avoid injuring plants. Days to harvest: 48–55. Keep plants picked for continuous production.

Winter squash should be picked in fall when their skin is so hard that it cannot be scratched by a fingernail. Harvest by cutting stems about 3 in. from the fruit. For maximum storage life cure in a warm room for about 10 days, then move to a cool, dry area (avoid freezing). Days to harvest: 80–115.

Sweet potatoes. Not a true potato but a member of the morning glory family. Sweet potatoes are a good source of many vitamins, particularly vitamin A. They need a very long growing season—four to five months without frost—and require warm temperatures. For this reason they are grown mainly in the South, where they are often known erroneously as yams.

Sweet potatoes do best in sandy soil that is low in organic matter. (Too rich a soil makes them run to vines instead of roots.) Once the vines are established, they are quite drought tolerant. In fact, too much moisture in the soil rots the tubers.

Sweet potatoes are raised from transplants (slips cut from sprouting tubers). The slips should be 8–10 in. long and have several leaves. Plant them 15 in. apart in rows 3–4 ft. apart. Set the slips about 6 in. deep, leaving at least two leaves aboveground, and water well. They will root quickly. Rooted plants are also available. In heavy, moist soils, the soil should be raised into flat-topped ridges 8–15 in. high—the wetter the soil, the higher the ridge. Harvest after the first frost blackens the vines. In frost-free areas harvest about four months after planting. Cure the tubers in a warm, dry place for about two weeks after picking them. Store in a cool, humid place with good air circulation (not below 50°F or they may spoil). Days to harvest: 120–150.

143

Swiss chard. A type of beet bred for its large, crisp leaves and fleshy leaf stalks rather than for its root. Chard is rich in vitamin A and a good source of vitamin C. It tolerates both frost and hot weather—a single planting can give a continuous yield from spring to late fall. The leaves of chard may be prepared like spinach, the stalks like asparagus.

White   Red

Plant Swiss chard in early spring as soon as the soil can be worked and there is little danger of a severe frost. Set the seeds 1/2 in. deep and 1–2 in. apart in rows 18 in. apart. Thin later to 12 in. between plants. Chard should be harvested while the leaves are still tender and succulent. Cut the outer leaves off with a sharp knife about an inch above the ground. Be careful not to injure the inner leaves and central bud, which produces new leaves. Harvest regularly throughout the summer and fall in order to keep new leaves coming. Days to first harvest: 50–60.

Tomatoes. Once shunned as poisonous but now the most popular garden vegetable in the United States. A member of the nightshade family, the tomato is closely related to eggplant, pepper, potato, and tobacco. Tomatoes are among the best yielders of all vegetables but need a long growing season with moderate temperatures—they will not set fruit when nighttime temperatures are below 60°F or above 75°F, to many a gardener's puzzlement and dismay.

Years of experimentation, research, and controlled breeding have resulted in a profusion of special varieties. Tomatoes are available that range in size from giant 1-lb. Big Boy hybrids down to tiny plum and cherry tomatoes. There are egg-shaped and pear-shaped tomatoes. In addition to the familiar red, there are orange, yellow, and pink tomatoes (orange and yellow types tend to be sweeter, with less bite). There are bushy dwarf strains that can be grown in a pot or window box.

Early, midseason, and late-ripening varieties have also been developed. Most early types are so-called determinate tomatoes—the vines grow to a certain length, bear their fruit over a short period, and then die. Midseason and late-season varieties are usually

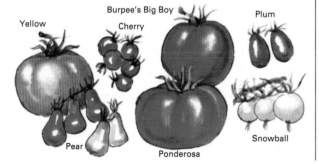

Yellow

Burpee's Big Boy

Cherry

Plum

Pear

Ponderosa

Snowball

indeterminate—the vines continue to grow and bear fruit until the onset of cold weather stops them.

Since tomatoes are killed by frost and grow poorly at cooler temperatures, they are usually started indoors in all but the warmest parts of the country. Start the seeds six to eight weeks before the last expected frost date, and set out when the weather is safely warm. To save time and trouble, you can buy ready-to-plant seedlings at most garden-supply centers and supermarkets and at many neighborhood stores as well. However, only the top-selling varieties tend to be available.

The number of plants you will want to grow depends on the type grown, the amount of canning you plan to do, and your family's appetite for tomatoes. Three to five plants each of early varieties and midseason varieties are enough for the average family. Tomatoes do best in slightly acid soil and need plenty of water. Before setting out the seedlings, dig compost, well-rotted manure, or damp peat moss into the soil to improve its moisture-holding capacity. Place the plants 2–3 ft. apart in rows 3 ft. apart. The vines may either be allowed to sprawl on the ground, which gives a higher yield, or trained on stakes, fences, or other supports. A popular method is to train the vines on a circular "tower" of heavy wire. The advantage of training is that the vines yield cleaner fruit and are easier to inspect and pick. Mulching is helpful, especially if the vines have been left to grow on the ground.

Trellis   Stake

Sucker

Sucker

Tomatoes that are trained above the ground should be pruned to one or two main stems. This is done by pinching or cutting off the suckers next to the main stems. (Suckers are shoots that grow in the joints where the leaf stems meet the main stem; if allowed to grow, they divert energy from fruit production.) Suckers should be pinched off throughout the growing season. However, do not remove foliage to let sunlight reach the fruits. Instead of aiding them to ripen, it causes sun scald, a discoloration and toughening of the skin.

Tomatoes are ripe when they separate easily from the stem. If cool or rainy weather delays ripening, they may be picked as soon as they start to change color and ripened on a sunny windowsill. To pick unripe tomatoes, twist them off the vine.

Tomatoes can be stored for several weeks in fall by pulling up the entire plant and hanging it upside down in a cool, shady place. The tomatoes will ripen slowly on the vine. Unripe tomatoes may also be picked and stored in a single layer. Rich in vitamins A and C, tomatoes are excellent for canning and freezing. Days to harvest: 52–90, depending on variety.

Turnips and Rutabagas. Two related root crops of the cabbage family. Most turnips have white flesh, while most rutabagas have yellow flesh. Rutabagas are larger than turnips and are often called yellow turnips or Swedish turnips.

Turnips are raised for their tops, or greens, as well as their roots. A quick-growing, hardy cool-weather crop, they can be planted for spring or fall harvest. Sow in spring as soon as the soil can be worked, 1/2 in. deep and two or three seeds to the

Turnip

Rutabaga

inch in rows 18 in. apart. Thin seedlings to 2 or 3 in. apart. Turnips should be harvested when they are about 2 in. in diameter. In most cases they get tough, pithy, and bitter if allowed to grow longer. For a fall crop sow in midsummer. Days to harvest: 35–60.

Rutabagas are slow growing and are planted for fall harvest. For table use, plant as for turnips about three months before the first expected fall frost date. Thin to 6 in. between plants. Harvest when roots are 3–6 in. in diameter (quality declines when they grow larger). Harvest rutabagas and turnips by pulling them up by their tops. Days to harvest: 90–100.

Super Sweet
seedless hybrid

Sugar Baby

Charleston Gray

Watermelon. One of the gourd family raised for its sweet, juicy fruit. Watermelons need a warm growing season, plentiful moisture, and full sun for proper growth and flavor (even a light frost can kill them). Standard melons reach sizes of 20 lb. and up and are best grown in the warmer sections of the country. For cooler regions midget varieties are available. They weigh 4–15 lb. and mature in a shorter time.

In all but the warmest areas watermelons should be started indoors about four weeks before the last expected frost date and set out when the nights are reliably warm (above 55°F). Watermelons are usually planted in hills, at least 6 ft. apart in each direction, two seedlings to a hill. If planted in rows, the plants should be 2–3 ft. apart in rows 6–7 ft. apart. Mulch is very helpful in preventing the fruit from rotting.

There is no sure way of telling when a watermelon is ready to harvest. One traditional method is to thump the melon; a hollow sound indicates it is ripe. Another is to examine the underside of the melon. When it turns yellow, the melon is probably ripe. Days to harvest: 70–95, depending on variety.

Out-of-the-Ordinary Vegetables

Many first-rate vegetables are seldom raised by American gardeners. Some are tricky to grow, others require special conditions, and a few are just not in style. But all can add variety, flavor, and nutrition to your diet—and also impart a touch of the exotic to your harvest.

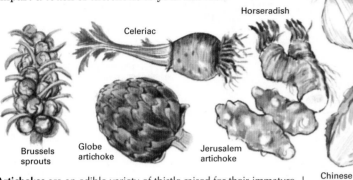

Artichokes are an edible variety of thistle raised for their immature flower buds. The plants, which are perennials, need cool summers and frost-free winters; as a result, they are difficult to raise outside a small area on the California coast. In many northern areas frost kills the plants before they can produce. Artichokes are normally planted as roots.

Brussels sprouts are a kind of cabbage. They grow as numerous small heads on a central stalk. A cool-weather crop, sprouts are usually planted in early June for harvest in fall. They can stand temperatures down to about 20°F—frost actually improves the flavor. In areas with short growing seasons, Brussels sprouts should be started indoors; where winter temperatures are mild, they can be grown as a winter crop.

Celeriac, or root celery, is raised for its large, bulbous roots (about the size of a grapefruit). It is usually eaten cooked. Its cultural requirements are the same as those of celery, and it has a similarly long growing season.

Chinese cabbage, a frost-hardy relative of cabbage, is a good source of vitamins A, B, and C and gives a high yield in limited space. It is sown in midsummer for a fall crop. Chinese cabbage keeps well in winter.

Florence fennel, or sweet fennel, is a variety of the popular herb and shares its delicate licorice flavor. Florence fennel is raised for its bulbous stem, which may be eaten raw or cooked. It is prepared like celery and is a staple of Italian cooking.

Horseradish is a hardy root vegetable used as a relish. It does best in a cool climate in rich, moist soil. Horseradish is raised from root cuttings—horseradish roots from the grocery store are a satisfactory source. Cuttings planted in spring will produce roots of a usable size by late fall.

Jerusalem artichokes, not artichokes at all but a type of sunflower, are raised for their edible tubers, which resemble the artichoke in flavor. Native to North America, these hardy, drought-resistant perennials can be left in the ground for winter storage. Once established, Jerusalem artichokes thrive with minimum care. Low in calories and sugar, they are recommended for diabetic persons. They are raised from tubers.

Leeks are a type of onion raised for their thick, fleshy stems. Milder than most other onions, they can be eaten raw or cooked. They are planted in early spring for harvest in late summer or fall. In most areas they should be started indoors.

Mushrooms can be raised wherever a constant temperature between 50° and 60°F can be maintained. They are raised from blocks of spores, called spawn, that are mixed with specially composted manure and kept continually moist. For growing mushrooms on a small scale ready-made compost can be obtained from seed houses and some garden-supply centers. Mushrooms thrive best in the dark but tolerate light. They are low in calories and a good source of B vitamins and iron. They may be cooked, eaten raw, or dried for future use.

New Zealand spinach, not a true spinach, is a low-growing, wide-spreading bushy plant that thrives in summer heat. The edible parts are the young leaves and tips of the branches, which are prepared like spinach and may be picked throughout the growing season. They may be cooked or eaten raw in salads.

Peanuts are a popular garden crop in the South and Southwest. Although they require a long, warm growing season (over 100 frost-free days), these protein-rich cousins of the garden pea can be grown in many parts of the North. Peanuts do best on a loose, sandy soil, where the developing seed pods can dig themselves into the ground.

Popcorn, developed by American Indians centuries ago, is easy to raise anywhere corn can be grown. The culture is the same as for ordinary corn. However, popcorn should not be planted close to ordinary corn or cross-pollination may give you unexpected and inferior results.

Salsify, or oyster plant (it resembles an oyster in flavor), is raised for its slender parsniplike roots and has the same cultural requirements as parsnip, although it needs a slightly longer growing season. Salsify may be left in the ground through the winter or dug and stored in damp sand.

Scallions, also known as bunching onions, are a fast-growing type of onion that does not form bulbs. They are used for seasoning, as an appetizer, and in salads. Scallions are sown in early spring and reach table size in about two months. Some varieties can be sown in the fall and harvested well into winter if the soil is protected from freezing. Ordinary onions can be used as scallions if pulled before their bulbs form and are commonly known as scallions at this stage.

Sunflowers, strictly speaking, are not vegetables, but these giant relatives of chrysanthemum, aster, and lettuce have been raised for centuries for their nutritious seeds. A single plant may yield several hundred seeds, which can be toasted for snacks, mixed with vegetables, made into flour, or used as bird food.

Tampala, a relative of both pigweed and ornamental amaranth, is cultivated as a hot-weather replacement for spinach. It yields heavily over a long season and bears until killed by frost. It is similar to the artichoke in flavor.

Vegetable spaghetti, or spaghetti squash, is a winter squash with a stringy flesh that becomes tender and flavorful when boiled. It is excellent with butter or spaghetti sauce.

Watercress is a pungent green related to cabbage and mustard. It grows naturally in clear, cold, flowing water but can be raised in the garden if the soil is kept constantly moist. Watercress can be started from seed or stem cuttings taken from bunches of cress sold at the supermarket.

Yard-long beans are actually a form of cowpea. This novelty vegetable may be grown wherever cowpeas succeed. They are eaten like snap beans in the immature stage. Yard-long beans are also used in Oriental cooking.

Mulch and Water: Helping Nature The Natural Way

Mulching is a traditional practice that has found new favor. Properly applied, a blanket of organic mulch smothers weeds, conserves soil moisture, and adds organic matter to the soil as it decomposes. Mulch insulates the soil, keeping the temperature even and aiding the growth of plant roots. It provides food and habitat for earthworms and burrowing insects, whose tunnels loosen and aerate the soil. It controls gullying and erosion. It prevents the rotting of fruit-type vegetables such as squash, melons, and cucumbers by keeping them away from ground moisture.

Mulch should be applied to the garden in the spring, after the soil has warmed up. Otherwise, by keeping the soil cold, it may retard plant growth. The thickness of mulch to be applied depends on the nature of the material. Loose, porous mulch such as straw should be 6 to 8 inches thick to keep sunlight from reaching weeds; denser materials such as sawdust need only be 1 1/2 to 2 inches thick. If possible, weeds should be removed before applying mulch, even though a thick layer of mulch will smother them. When placing mulch on the soil, be careful not to cover the vegetable seedlings.

It is best to turn the mulch under at the end of the growing season. If you wait until spring for this chore, be sure to add extra nitrogen fertilizer, since decay organisms, activated by warm weather, will rob the soil of much of its nitrogen as they break down the mulch.

A wide variety of materials can be used for mulch, ranging from hay and straw to chipped bark, ground corncobs, and cocoa bean hulls. Some of the best mulches cost nothing. Lawn clippings and leaves, for example, are both excellent; they function not only as mulches but add nutrients and humus to the soil when plowed under. In addition to organic materials, strips of black plastic film are often used as mulch.

Mulch is not entirely problem free. It may contain weed seeds and can also serve as a shelter for slugs, destructive insects, and field mice. (For dealing with these and other pests, see pp.168–171.) Mulch must also be replenished from time to time, since it breaks down gradually. Nevertheless, a properly applied mulch is one of the simplest and most effective ways for saving labor, improving the soil, and getting better crops.

A survey of mulching materials

Sawdust (1) can be obtained from lumberyards and sawmills. If you heat with wood, save the sawdust from your own wood-cutting operations. Let the dust rot until it is dark before use. Apply 1 1/2–2 in. thick.

Leaves (2) are abundant and easy to come by in most regions of the country. You can usually obtain additional supplies from neighbors or from your local park and highway departments. Apply 4–6 in. thick.

Pine needles (3) are cheap and plentiful in many areas. Their resin content makes them long lasting, and they have a neat appearance. Apply 4–6 in. thick.

Hay and straw (4) can be obtained from local farmers, garden-supply centers, or your own fields. Spoiled hay, which is unfit for animals, and salt hay, from tidal flats, make excellent mulches. Apply 6–8 in. thick.

Black plastic film (5) is sold by most garden-supply and hardware stores in 25-, 50-, and 100-ft. rolls of a standard 3-ft. width. Weed and till soil before spreading plastic on it. Bury edges of plastic film in shallow trenches to hold it in place, or weight edges down with stones or dirt. Leave a path for walking between plastic strips (never walk on the plastic itself, as it tears easily). Cut holes as needed to plant seeds. Also cut X-shaped slits at intervals to admit water. Black plastic warms the soil, aiding the growth of many crops.

Cocoa bean hulls (6) are attractive but expensive. They are alkaline and so help to sweeten soil; do not use on acid-loving vegetables. Apply 3–6 in. thick.

Old newspapers (7) can be recycled as mulch, but avoid colored newsprint—it may contain lead. Apply papers in layers at least six sheets thick, and weight them down to keep them from blowing. Paper is biodegradable.

Wood chips (8) can often be obtained from power or telephone companies, whose road crews chip up the brush and limbs they clear. Wood chips are durable and slow to decay. Apply 3–6 in. thick.

Lawn clippings (9), considered a problem by many homeowners, can be used productively as mulch. Clippings should be allowed to dry out before use as mulch, since they tend to mat together when fresh. Apply 3–6 in. thick.

Compost (10) is one of the best garden mulches. It supplies nutrients in addition to performing the other functions of a mulch. However, for maximum effectiveness compost for mulching should be only partly broken down; otherwise it may encourage, rather than deter, the growth of weeds. Apply 3–6 in. thick.

Wood chip mulch discourages weeds and keeps the dirt moist around this Gerber daisy. Mulch absorbs the energy of falling rain and permits the water to soak gently into the underlying soil instead of running off.

Surprising seaweed mulch

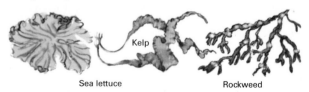

Sea lettuce   Kelp   Rockweed

Those who live near the shore can harvest their own supply of one of the finest natural mulches—seaweed. Rich in potassium and trace elements, seaweed is also a good fertilizer and a desirable addition to the compost pile. It should be dried in the sun before using in the garden.

Watering: How, When, How Much

Vegetables cannot live—much less grow and yield an abundant harvest—without water. If natural rainfall does not supply enough water, then the gardener must supply it. In the arid Southwest artificial watering or irrigation is a necessity. Even in the more humid Northeast dry spells of several weeks are not uncommon.

For large commercial farms, open irrigation ditches are one answer to the problem of delivering water to where it is needed. For the home gardener there are less costly, more efficient methods of supplying water. The familiar oscillating and spinning types of lawn sprinklers duplicate natural rainfall, as does a permanently installed overhead sprinkler system or even the simple hand-held garden hose. Perforated hoses are much more economical of water. Laid on the ground, they deliver a long, soaking trickle of water directly onto the soil with minimal loss from evaporation or runoff. A wide variety of such hoses are sold by garden-supply centers.

For the ultimate in water-saving efficiency there are buried plastic pipes, also perforated, that deliver moisture directly to the root zones, where it is most needed. (Water must reach the roots to be effective—a light watering that wets only the surface of the ground leaves plants thirsty.) Experts recommend a heavy watering once a week rather than a light one every day. The watering should be heavy enough to saturate the soil 10 to 12 inches deep. (Check the depth of water penetration by opening a slit with your spade.) Clay soil requires more time and more water to saturate it than sandy soil but also holds water longer and so needs less frequent waterings. Experiment with varying amounts of water to determine how much your garden actually needs. No matter what method you use to water your garden, the watering pattern should be spread evenly over the entire area. This is because water tends to move downward through the soil rather than sideways. Water has a limited sideways spread, ranging from about 1 foot in clay soils to 2 feet in sandy soils.

How do you tell when your garden needs watering? The simplest way is to watch your plants. If they wilt in the sun and do not recover when it cools off, they need watering. (Remember, though, that any vegetable may wilt temporarily on a hot summer afternoon, no matter how wet its roots are.) The best time to water is in late

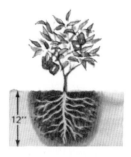

The roots of most vegetables grow in the top 8–12 in. of soil, although some, like tomatoes, may reach 4–5 ft. down in deep, loose soils. When watering, it is important to saturate the root zone about 1 ft. deep, not just wet the surface. Shallow watering encourages roots to grow close to the surface, where they are likely to dry out during hot spells with resultant damage to the plants.

afternoon, when little water will be wasted by evaporation and the air is still warm enough to dry the foliage. (Wet foliage is susceptible to fungus infections.) Early to midmorning is also a good time for watering. Avoid watering the garden in midday or after sundown.

Do not overdo it when watering. Overwatering wastes water, leaches nutrients out of the soil, damages roots, and encourages the growth of lush, disease-prone foliage. In arid areas it can also cause a buildup of salts in the soil: mineral-laden water, moving upward by capillary action, evaporates leaving a saline residue.

Water-saving drip irrigation

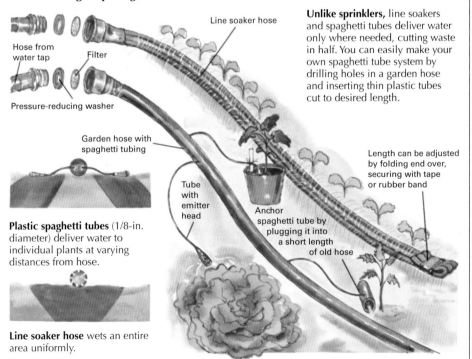

Hose from water tap

Filter

Pressure-reducing washer

Garden hose with spaghetti tubing

Tube with emitter head

Anchor spaghetti tube by plugging it into a short length of old hose

Line soaker hose

Plastic spaghetti tubes (1/8-in. diameter) deliver water to individual plants at varying distances from hose.

Line soaker hose wets an entire area uniformly.

Unlike sprinklers, line soakers and spaghetti tubes deliver water only where needed, cutting waste in half. You can easily make your own spaghetti tube system by drilling holes in a garden hose and inserting thin plastic tubes cut to desired length.

Length can be adjusted by folding end over, securing with tape or rubber band

Other ways to wet the soil

Connected saucers or basins for watering are a refinement of the traditional irrigation ditch. They confine water to root zones and also collect rainfall. The series of saucers should be graded to let water flow slowly down the whole length of the chain.

Perforated cans or milk cartons, placed in the soil at planting time, conserve water by letting it ooze slowly into the root zone. Fill them by hand or with a hose. A variant on this idea is a short piece of pipe inserted in the soil at a convenient angle for a hose.

Overhead sprinklers cover a wide area and can be fed by hose or buried pipelines. They are much used by commercial vegetable growers and their spray radius is easily adjusted. However, they waste much water through evaporation.

Gardening in Limited Space

For Big Results Think Small

High-rise living, cluster-zoned developments, and an increasing scarcity of land are giving rise to a new class of farmer: the urban gardener. Using simple space-saving stratagems, city dwellers and suburbanites are growing an impressive variety of vegetables. With the help of intensive culture (very close planting) the yield per square foot can be multiplied. Intercropping and succession planting can also bring impressive increases in crop

size. Where soil is poor or space extremely limited, you can get excellent results by raising vegetables in containers.

Lack of sunlight, as well as a shortage of space, often limits the kinds of plants an urban gardener can grow. Crops that are raised for their fruits, such as tomatoes and cucumbers, need at least six hours of sunlight a day. Root crops, such as beets and turnips, can get along with less. Lettuce and other leaf crops can be grown with as little as four hours a day of direct light. Best choices for the minigarden are plants that give a high yield and take little space: leaf and salad crops, plus those that can be trained vertically.

The French Intensive Method

Developed nearly a century ago by French truck farmers, the French intensive method combines special soil preparation with heavy feedings of organic fertilizers to support a dense planting of vegetables.

To prepare the soil, first rototill or double-dig it (see *The Kitchen Garden*, p.133). Then work compost or well-rotted manure into the soil until the top 12 inches are one-third to one-half organic matter. In clay soils build up the proportion of sand to one-third.

Adding these materials will increase the volume of your soil so that it forms a low mound, which aids drainage. Rake the mound smooth; then top it with a 2-inch layer of manure plus a light sprinkling of bone-meal and wood ashes. Work these into the top 3 or 4 inches of soil and rake smooth. (For succession crops repeat this feeding each time a crop is replaced.)

Soak the soil deeply a day or two before you sow seeds or set out transplants and mark off the areas where you plan to plant each vegetable. Spread seeds thinly in their designated areas. As the seedlings grow, thin them to about half the spacing recommended for an ordinary garden. A laborsaving trick is to drag a steel rake lightly across them when they are 1 inch tall; thin by hand later. Large seeds, such as peas and beans, can be sown so that no thinning will be necessary later. Transplants of tomatoes and other large vegetables should be set a little more than half as far apart as in an ordinary garden.

Leafy vegetables, such as lettuce and Swiss chard, should be left close enough for their leaves to form a continuous canopy over the soil, thus shading out weeds, conserving moisture, and creating a favorable microclimate for plant growth.

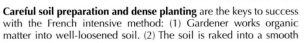

Careful soil preparation and dense planting are the keys to success with the French intensive method: (1) Gardener works organic matter into well-loosened soil. (2) The soil is raked into a smooth mound. (3) Seeds are broadcast thinly (not sown in rows) to cover the soil. (4) The resulting crop forms a soil-protecting canopy with its densely growing leaves.

Raised Beds and Planters

Raised beds, originally developed to cope with infertile or poorly drained soils, are increasingly popular. They are convenient for planting, weeding, and other garden tasks; they give excellent drainage; and they warm up, several weeks ahead of regular garden plots in the spring.

For best results, raised beds should be at least 12 inches high. Fill them with enriched garden soil or a special mix, such as the one described on page 149. If the soil level is kept 2 or 3 inches below the top of the beds, they can be covered with glass and made to serve as cold frames.

When a bed runs along a wall or is otherwise accessible from only one side, it should be no more than 3 feet wide so that you can tend it without having to step on the soil. When both sides are accessible, the width may be up to 6 feet. Raised beds may be any length desired, but they are easier to manage when they are short. Popular sizes are 4 by 4 feet and 3 by 9 feet.

Raised beds can be made of treated 2-in.-thick boards held in place by stakes or fastened at the corners with angle irons. If 2 × 12 boards are not available, combine narrower boards to gain the needed height. The higher the bed, the less stooping is required to tend the plants.

Stepped boxes, a variant of the raised bed, give plants better exposure to sunlight and can be tucked in a corner or against a wall. The separate levels are easy to tend. Boxes and stand can be made separately for easy disassembly and moving.

Narrow strip beside the house is thriftily utilized with a raised bed made of railroad ties. Pole beans or other climbers are trained up a trellis for maximum sunlight. The bed can also be made of brick, stone, concrete, or cement blocks. Whatever material is used, be sure drainage is adequate.

Farming in Containers

Container gardening is one of the most efficient methods for growing vegetables in limited space. Almost any vegetable can be grown in a container—even corn or pumpkins—although plants that take up a great deal of space are not practical. Miniature varieties of vegetables are especially suited to container growing: they require less space than full-sized varieties and mature earlier.

Many vegetables can be container-raised indoors as well as outdoors. Leaf crops can be grown indoors even in winter with the aid of fluorescent lights. Fruit crops, such as tomatoes, can be grown indoors but need warm temperatures and at least six hours of summer sunlight. Most root crops, however, are best grown outdoors.

Almost any sturdy, water-resistant receptacle can be used for container gardening: plastic or galvanized iron garbage cans, redwood planters, 2-gallon or 5-gallon buckets, even a plastic garbage bag. Of course, any type of container must be provided with holes for drainage. Recommended practice is to drill drainage holes just above the bottom rather than in it.

For best results, use an artificial planting medium rather than garden soil. Artificial mixtures do not compact, even after repeated waterings, and they are much lighter in weight than soil. As a result, it is much easier to move the containers, an important feature since one of the advantages of raising vegetables in containers is that they can be shifted indoors on a cold night or around the yard to follow the sun. A good homemade mix can be made from peat moss, vermiculite (or perlite), and fertilizer. To make 1 gallon of mix, use 1/2 gallon peat moss, 1/2 gallon vermiculite, 1 teaspoon lime, 1 1/2 teaspoons of 5-10-10 fertilizer, and 1/2 teaspoon superphosphate. About 9 gallons of mix will fill a bushel container.

Because of the intensive care they get, container-grown plants can be spaced much closer together than if they were planted in an ordinary garden. The chart at right gives recommended space and soil allowances for a number of popular vegetables.

Plants grown in containers need watering more frequently than they would in a garden—as often as once a day in hot, dry weather. To check for moisture, probe the top 2 inches of soil with your finger. If the soil is dry, soak it thoroughly until water runs out at the bottom of the container. You should also add fertilizer every three weeks. Use light doses, however; overfertilizing can damage or kill plants that are grown in containers.

Selected vegetables for containers

Vegetable	Minimum container size	Number of plants per container
Beans (bush)	2 gal.	6 plants; in larger containers space 2"-3" apart
Beans (pole)	4 gal.	6 plants
Beets	1 pt.	2-3 plants; in larger containers space 2" apart
Broccoli	5 gal.	1 plant
Brussels sprouts	5 gal.	1 plant
Cabbage	5 gal.	1 plant; in larger containers space 12" apart
Chinese cabbage	1 gal.	1 plant
Carrots	1 pt.	3-4 plants; in larger containers space 1"-2" apart
Corn	10 gal.	4 plants; space 4" apart. Plant at least 12 for pollination
Cucumbers	5 gal.	2 plants. Train vertically
Eggplant	5 gal.	1 plant
Kale	5 gal.	3-4 plants; in larger containers space 16" apart
Lettuce	1/2 gal.	1 plant; in larger containers space 10" apart
Mustard greens	1 pt.	1 plant; in larger containers space 4" apart
New Zealand spinach	2 gal.	1 plant (good for hanging basket)
Onions	1/2 gal.	16 green onions. For full-sized onions use larger containers; space 2"-3" apart
Peppers	2 gal.	1 plant
Radishes	1 pt.	4-5 plants per pot; in larger containers space 1" apart
Spinach	1 pt.	1 plant per pot; in larger containers space 5" apart
Summer squash and zucchini	5 gal.	1 plant
Swiss chard	3 1/2 gal.	4-5 plants; in larger containers space 8" apart
Tomatoes (dwarf)	5 gal.	1 plant
Tomatoes (standard)	1 1/2 qt.	1 plant

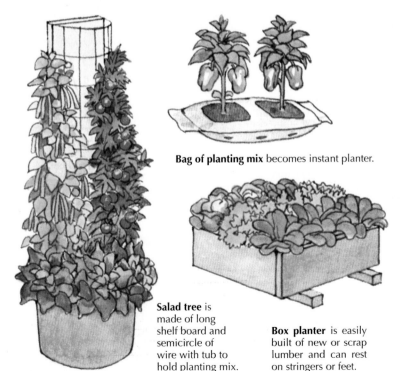

Bag of planting mix becomes instant planter.

Salad tree is made of long shelf board and semicircle of wire with tub to hold planting mix.

Box planter is easily built of new or scrap lumber and can rest on stringers or feet.

Many variations of the container idea are possible. The movable bookcase-type planter shown above holds several levels of plants growing in slits in its wire or plastic lining. Water and fertilizer are supplied through perforated pipes. Casters make the planter easy to move, an idea that is adaptable to other heavy, bulky containers.

149

Windowsill Farming Indoors and Out

Apartment dwellers can use windowsills, balconies, and rooftops to raise surprisingly large crops of homegrown vegetables. According to one expert, as many as 100 carrots, 50 beets, and 50 cherry tomatoes can be harvested from a dozen 8-inch pots.

The most practical vegetables for the windowsill farmer are those that need little space and give high yields. The nature of your space also determines what you can grow. If you have balcony or rooftop space, climbers—such as standard tomatoes, pole beans, and cucumbers—are practical. For a windowsill concentrate on such low-growing vegetables as lettuce, spinach, carrots, and dwarf tomatoes.

Daylight exposure is also important, since indoor plants have the same needs for light and warmth as those grown outdoors. For an east-facing window the choice is limited to leafy vegetables and radishes. Southern and western windows are suitable for most vegetables. Warmth lovers, such as tomatoes and beans, do best in a southern exposure. A northern window is unsuitable for vegetables unless artificial lighting is provided as a supplement.

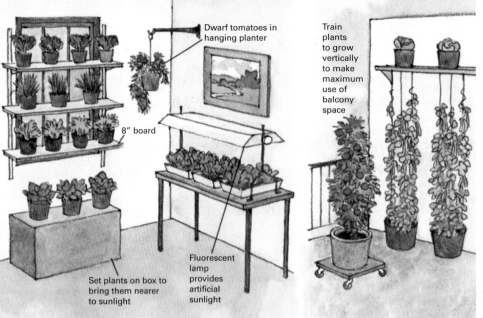

Dwarf tomatoes in hanging planter

Train plants to grow vertically to make maximum use of balcony space

8" board

Set plants on box to bring them nearer to sunlight

Fluorescent lamp provides artificial sunlight

Growing space can be increased by a number of simple expedients. You can widen a windowsill to hold more containers by adding an 8-in. board supported by brackets. Most windows can accommodate two or three boards placed across them, again supported by brackets. Hanging containers are fine for dwarf tomatoes, but be sure not to make them too heavy for their supports. Bulky plants can be placed on a table in front of the window or on an up-ended box on the floor to raise them to window level.

Unused bureau tops, tables, bookshelves, and even closets become planting areas with the aid of easily installed fluorescent light fixtures. On a balcony or other outdoor area you can make use of vertical space by training vegetables on stakes, strings, or against a wall as well as by using hanging containers and wall brackets.

What to grow where

For the windowsill:	
Carrots	Radishes
Cress	Spinach
Lettuce	Tomatoes
Mustard	Zucchini

For balcony, rooftop, or windowbox:	
Any windowsill vegetables plus:	
Beans	Peppers
Broccoli	Potatoes
Brussels sprouts	Squash
Cabbage	Tomatoes
Corn	Turnips,
Cucumbers	other root vegetables

Indoors under lights:	
Beets	Cucumbers
Carrots	Endive
Celery	Onions
Chinese cabbage	Radishes
	Watercress

Gardening Under Lights

Vegetables need ample light to flourish, especially rays from the blue and red ends of the spectrum. Normally these rays are supplied by the sun, but fluorescent tubes can take the place of natural sunlight. An equal number of cool-white (rich in blue) and warm-white or natural tubes (rich in red) seem to give the best result. Tubes especially designed for indoor gardening, high in both blue and red wavelengths, are also available.

Some growers use incandescent lamps to augment the red end of the spectrum, but these consume much more electricity for the light produced. In addition, they must be used with caution because of the heat they generate.

Fluorescent tubes should be positioned 6 to 12 inches above the plants: light intensity diminishes rapidly as distance increases. A fixture with four 4-foot tubes provides enough light for a 3- by 4-foot area.

Vegetables require 13 to 18 hours of artificial light per day. They also need a resting period of darkness. Leafy and root vegetables are easiest to grow under lights; tomatoes require extra care.

Sharon Kahkonen, Urban Gardener

A Farmer's Daughter In the Inner City

Sharon Kahkonen, Cornell graduate, teaches urban gardening in New York. She says, "It's nice to see how delighted people are when things begin to grow. It's therapy for emotional problems, no kidding about that."

"I grew up on a farm and I was out in the garden as soon as I could walk. We grew everything—peas, beans, corn, tomatoes. My mother put up a lot of our food. When I graduated from college, I taught high school biology, but now I'm teaching for a fed erally funded program in urban gardening. I like teaching gardening much better. People are so eager to learn and they get really involved with their plants; sometimes it changes a whole neighborhood. People really respond to growing things. Sometimes they come from rural areas and the gardening helps remind them of home.

"We're starting container gardening projects in elementary schools so city kids can get an idea of how things grow and how to take care of them. Did you know that you can grow nearly anything you can raise in a farm garden in a container? Tomatoes are the most popular because they're easy and they taste so much better than the ones in the store, but you can grow a whole salad in your apartment—a little lettuce, a few tomatoes, some peppers, and carrots. A lot of people think the containers have to be something special. They buy new pots, but there's so much thrown out in the city—fruit baskets, vegetable crates, old cans. You can use anything like that for a container. Some people turn a rubber tire inside out and use that for a planter.

"It's nice to see the relationship that develops between plants and people. I think watching things grow is a basic human need. It's exciting."

Herb Gardens

A Treat for the Eye As Well as the Palate

Herb gardening is at least as old as the earliest civilizations. In every age and every part of the world herbs have been valued in cooking, medicine, and the preparation of fragrances. Elaborate herb gardens were planted in Europe during the Renaissance as a result of a fascination with the medicinal qualities of herbs. The inspiration for these intricately designed gardens probably came from the Far East, which was then being explored for the first time by Europeans.

Early settlers in America carried the tradition of herb growing across the Atlantic. Initially, the settlers' herb gardens were modest affairs—a small plot adjacent to the house in which were grown such culinary staples as sage, dill, bay, rosemary, parsley, basil, and thyme. Occasionally, the herbs were planted between the rungs of an old ladder or the spokes of a wagon wheel. Where space was limited, a dirt-filled barrel with holes cut in its sides was used. Eventually, wealthier colonists planted formal herb gardens based on European designs. Nowadays, a growing appreciation of natural foods and seasonings, plus increased interest in the esthetic values of bygone days, has led to a revival of herb growing.

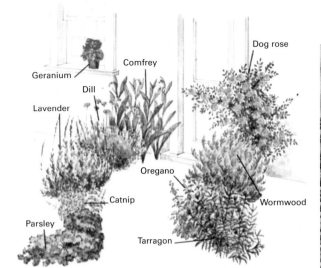

Herbs create an interesting, varied, and fragrant border along paths in large or small gardens. Landscape the herbs so that each plant receives full sun for at least five hours a day.

Lavender, like many herbs, can be used in aromatherapy, as well as for culinary and medicinal purposes.

Herbs are pictured in flower to aid in identification. In actual garden, flowering times vary. For best flavor and fragrance pick herbs just before they flower.

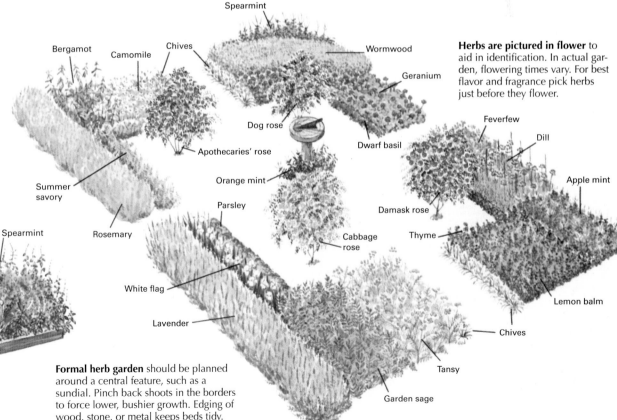

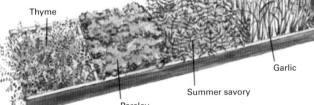

Plant culinary herbs in the spaces between the rungs of an old ladder for an attractive herb garden that is easy to tend.

Formal herb garden should be planned around a central feature, such as a sundial. Pinch back shoots in the borders to force lower, bushier growth. Edging of wood, stone, or metal keeps beds tidy.

151

Planting and Managing Your Herb Garden

The basic requirements of a successful herb garden are well-drained soil that is neutral to slightly acid and at least five hours of sunlight a day. A few herbs are exceptions to the rules. Mints, for example, do best in damp ground, while species such as basil and lemon balm prefer partial shade and should be planted near a shade tree or fence. To improve an area with poor drainage, excavate the site to a depth of 12 inches, carefully separating the rich topsoil from the subsoil. Then put down a layer of gravel or crushed stone and refill, adding sand or stones to the subsoil and compost to the topsoil.

Enrich the soil around the herb with fertilizer or compost after any major harvesting of leaves, and make sure that the soil never completely dries out. Roses benefit from a thick mulch that keeps down weeds and retains soil moisture. In areas with cold winters, tender perennials, such as rosemary and lavender, must be moved indoors for the winter. Hardier herbs can be left outside if they are properly protected. Cut back their dead growth in autumn. Later, when the ground has frozen an inch or two deep, cover the plants with a winter mulch of salt hay, evergreen branches, or straw.

Basket of herbs, fresh from the garden.

Culinary herbs

Basil, a tender annual, 12 to 15 in. tall. Seeds germinate easily; sow them outdoors when the weather is consistently warm in medium-rich soil in a sheltered sunny, or partially shaded, spot. Pinch off main shoots to make a bushy growth. Dwarf varieties (6 in.) make good edging plants. Basil grows well indoors.

Chives, a hardy perennial, 12 in. tall. Seeds germinate slowly but can be sown outdoors in spring or fall in medium-rich soil. Chives increase rapidly by bulb division, and clumps should be dug up and spaced out every few years.

Dill, a hardy annual, up to 3 ft. tall. It germinates easily and will often self-sow for the following season. Do not transplant; but thin and weed around plants and stake after 18 in. high. Dill grows well in a fertile, sandy soil.

Garlic, a semihardy perennial, 1 to 2 ft. tall. Plant single cloves 2 in. deep in early spring in moist, rich soil. Hoe soil at intervals and harvest as soon as leaves die in fall. Garlic repels many insect pests and is a good companion plant for a number of vegetables.

Mint, a hardy perennial, 2 to 3 ft. tall. There are many varieties of mint, but spearmint, the usual culinary variety, applemint, and peppermint are the most popular. Plant 6-in. pieces of root in spring or fall 2 in. deep in rich, moist soil and a semishaded position. Water thoroughly. To prevent mint spreading beyond where you want it, sink 12-in. boards around planted area.

Oregano, a hardy perennial, 2 to 3 ft. tall. Oregano, a species of marjoram, is also known as wild marjoram. Sow seeds in spring or fall in medium-rich alkaline soil. Oregano spreads rapidly.

Parsley, a semihardy biennial, up to 12 in. tall. In cooler climates it grows as an annual. Sow in spring or fall in medium-rich soil in sun or semishade. Do not transplant. Seeds are slow to germinate and can be soaked before planting to speed germination. Pinch out or clip new growth to give bushier growth.

Rosemary, a tender perennial, 2 to 6 ft. tall. It is a decorative, aromatic, and culinary shrub that can be used for hedges. Because seeds germinate slowly, buy young plants and propagate by cuttings or layers. Rosemary needs a sandy, alkaline soil and a sheltered, sunny situation. Add chalk or lime to the soil around the plant regularly. Winter the plants indoors in a cool climate.

Sage, a hardy perennial, 2 to 3 ft. tall. It is a small evergreen shrub with several varieties, including common or garden sage, generally used for cooking, and pineapple sage, which is aromatic but not good for cooking. Seeds germinate easily. Plant in moist soil and a sunny situation. Do not grow near annuals as sage inhibits their root growth.

Summer savory, an annual, 12 to 18 in. tall. It is a fine-leaved aromatic herb that spreads rapidly. Sow seeds in medium-rich soil and allow four weeks for germination. Summer savory is more valued for cooking purposes than winter savory.

Tarragon, a hardy perennial, 2 to 3 ft. tall. French tarragon has a much better flavor than Russian tarragon. It does not set seed, so buy young plants or propagate from cuttings or layers. Plant in a slightly sandy soil. Mulch with salt hay where winters are severe.

Thyme, a hardy perennial, 4 to 10 in. tall. Lemon and common, or garden, thyme are the most useful varieties for cooking. As thyme grows slowly, it is helpful to start with a young plant and propagate by cuttings and layers. Seed can also be sown in rows in spring. Plant in sandy soil with a little added lime. Thyme's fragrant purple blossoms yield a prized honey.

Fragrant herbs

Bergamot, a hardy perennial, 2 to 3 ft. tall. This native American species produces showy, fragrant flowers used in dried potpourris. Buy young plants and propagate by root division. Bergamot spreads rapidly if not restricted.

Geranium, a tender perennial, 2 to 4 ft. tall. Lemon-scented, roses-scented, and peppermint-scented varieties have highly fragrant leaves used for potpourris and culinary flavoring. Buy plants from a reputable nursery and propagate by stem cuttings, as seeds often fail to grow true to type. Plant in dry, sandy soil. The plants must be transplanted and brought indoors during the winter.

Iris Florentina, or white flag, a hardy perennial, 18 to 24 in. tall. The dried root, called orris root, makes a useful scent fixative for potpourris and sachets. (See *Household Recipes*, pp.336–337.) Flags produce showy white flowers in early spring. Plant rhizomes horizontally with the top side just above the soil surface. The roots multiply rapidly and should be dug up and divided every few years.

Lavender, a semihardy to hardy perennial, 1 to 3 ft. tall. Fragrant flowers and leaves are used in potpourris and sachets. As seeds are slow to germinate, propagate from cuttings or layers. Plant out in sandy, alkaline soil. Mulch English lavender to protect from cold winters. Other varieties should be wintered indoors in cold climates. Fertilize with lime occasionally.

Lemon balm, a hardy perennial, 2 to 4 ft. tall. Balm is highly fragrant and attractive to bees. As seeds are extremely slow to germinate, it is worth buying young plants and propagating by root division and cuttings. Balm grows best in sandy soil and in a semishaded position.

Rose, a hardy perennial, 2 to 5 ft. tall. The old varieties of cabbage, damask, dog, and apothecaries' rose have the most fragrant flowers; they have long been used for certain medicinal purposes. Buy young plants and establish in a bed free from other roots in a slightly clayey soil enriched with manure or compost. Propagate from stem cuttings. Mulch for severe winters.

Medicinal and decorative herbs

Camomile, a hardy perennial, 4 to 15 in. tall. The flowers of Roman camomile can be used to make a soothing sleep-inducing tea and for hair lightening and conditioning rinses as well. Camomile tea is also said to relieve headaches. Propagate from seed or root division. Camomile thrives in any well-drained soil.

Comfrey, a hardy perennial, 2 to 3 ft. tall. Rich in allantoin and vitamin B-12, it is a renowned healing herb often prepared as a tea. Propagate from root cuttings or by division; plant in rich, moist soil in sun or semishade.

Feverfew, a hardy perennial, 1 to 2 1/2 ft. tall. An infusion of this ornamental herb can be applied externally to repel insects and soothe insect bites. (See *Household Recipes*, p.343.) Propagate by seed or root division in spring. Plant out in rich, heavy soil in a sunny or semishaded position.

Wormwood, a hardy perennial, 2 to 14 ft. tall. This herb, an ingredient in absinthe, received its name from the days when it was popular as a remedy for worms. It makes a decorative contrast in any herb garden with its delicate silvery foliage. Propagate by root division or seeds sown in the fall. Cut back and mulch in the fall to protect from severe winters.

Propagation and Planting

Most perennial herbs can be grown from seed, but for quicker starts and surer true-to-type reproduction, stem cuttings, root cuttings, layering, or root division is advised. Set out cuttings or seedlings on an overcast day and provide shade for a few additional days. Sow annuals directly in the ground; thin later by pinching off extra plants. Start thinning when the seedlings are 2 inches high and have produced four leaves. Use the trimmings of culinary herbs in your cooking.

Cut stem here

Strip lower leaves

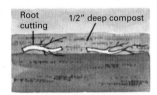

Root cutting   1/2" deep compost

Stem cuttings. Use 3- to 6-in. cuttings. Strip off lower leaves, dust ends in hormone powder, plant in vermiculite.

Root cuttings. Separate a large root and cut into 1- to 4-in. sections. Lay 1/2 in. deep in compost. Keep moist.

Staple

Root division. Cut back top growth in fall or early spring. Dig up roots, ease gently apart, and replant.

Layering. Cut or scrape stem on underside, dust with hormone powder, and staple into soil; add compost.

Growing Herbs Indoors

An indoor herb garden can provide city dwellers as well as countryfolk with a year-round supply of fresh herbs, even such tender types as parsley, basil, and rosemary. Keep the herbs in a moist atmosphere and make sure that they get at least five hours of direct sun each day.

Plant the herbs in containers with good drainage. Use either a mixture of four parts potting compost and one part sand or three parts loam and one part each of sand and compost. Herbs can be set singly in 4- to 5-inch pots or grouped in larger pots. Turn them from time to time so that they will grow evenly. Prostrate thyme and rosemary are particularly attractive in hanging pots. If you have a south-facing window, you can plant the herbs in a window box. Provide plenty of room for each plant to grow, and make some provision for turning them.

To assist drainage and provide a moist atmosphere for indoor herbs, set the pots in a tray of pebbles; add water to 1 in. below the tops of the pebbles.

For a small veranda, strawberry jar (right) makes an attractive planter. Put trailing herbs in outer pockets and upright herbs at top.

Harvesting and Storing

Drying is the traditional way to preserve herbs. For best results, pick the herbs at their peak of flavor, in midsummer just before they start to flower. Harvest by snipping entire sprigs or the top 5 or 6 inches of the stems. Do this in the morning as soon as the dew has dried off and before the sun's heat has driven off any of the essential oils. Wash the leaves gently and shake off the excess water, then pick the leaves off the stems and place them separately on screens or newspaper. Let the leaves dry until they are brittle and crumble easily. If the atmosphere is too humid for the herbs to dry at room temperature, put them in the oven on a very low heat (less than 150°F) for a few minutes, leaving the oven door open to allow moisture to escape.

Roots can also be dried. Collect them in fall or early spring, wash them thoroughly, slice them, and set them out to dry. When the roots are partially dry, they can be placed in a cool oven to speed the drying process—it can otherwise take up to two years. The roots are dry when they are brittle and snap when bent.

Once the herbs are dry, place them in airtight containers, such as glass jars with ground-glass stoppers. Check the jars after a few days to be sure no traces of moisture have condensed on the inside. If there is moisture, remove the herbs, dry further in the oven, and rebottle them. Store the bottled herbs in a cool, dark place to preserve their flavor and fragrance.

Herbs with fleshy leaves, such as parsley, basil, dill, chives, and the various types of mint, tend to lose much of their flavor when dried and are best preserved by freezing. Either put them in the freezer whole directly after washing, or chop them finely and freeze them in ice-cube trays filled with water.

Window screen covered with cheesecloth makes ideal rack for drying leaves, flowers, roots, and seeds. Set screen in a warm, dry area away from drafts and direct sunlight. Alternatively, hang herbs in bunches in a dry place. If the area is at all dusty, wrap them in cheesecloth as protection.

Sources and resources

Books

Bacon, Richard M. *The Forgotten Arts: Growing, Gardening and Cooking with Herbs*. Emmaus, Pa.: Yankee Books, 1972.

Beston, Henry. *Herbs and the Earth*. Lincoln, Mass.: Godline, 1992.

Bown, Deni. *Encyclopedia of Herbs and Their Uses*. New York: Dorling Kindersley, 1995.

Claiborne, Craig. *Cooking With Herbs and Spices*. New York: Harper & Row, 1984.

Garland, Sarah. *The Herb Garden*. New York: Viking, 1985.

Genders, Roy. *Growing Herbs as Aromatics*. New Canaan, Conn.: Keats Publishing, 1977.

Gilbertie, Sal. *Herb Gardening at Its Best*. New York: Atheneum, 1986.

Grieve, Margaret. *Culinary Herbs and Condiments*. New York: Dover, 1954.

Griffin, Judy. *Mother Nature's Kitchen: Growing and Using Herbs*. Fort Worth, Tex.: Herbal Essence Inc., 1993.

Herbs: *A Guide to Growing, Cooking and Decorating*. Lincolnwood, Ill.: Publications International Ltd., 1993.

Jacobs, Betty. *Growing and Using Herbs Successfully*. Charlotte, Vt.: Garden Way Publishing, 1981.

Lust, John. *The Herb Book*. New York: Bantam, 1983.

Miloradovich, Milo. *Growing and Using Herbs and Spices*. New York: Dover, 1986.

Owen, Millie. *A Cook's Guide to Growing Herbs, Greens & Aromatics*. New York: Knopf, 1978.

Segall, Barbara. *The Herb Garden Month-by-Month*. New York: Sterling Publishing, 1994.

Simmons, Adelma. *Herb Gardening in Five Seasons*. New York: Dutton, 1977.

Weiss, Gaea, and Shandor Weiss. *Growing and Using Healing Herbs*. Emmaus, Pa.: Rodale Press, 1985.

Suppliers of herb plants and seeds

Caprilands Herb Farm, Silver St., Coventry, Conn. 06238.

George W. Park Seed Co. P.O. Box 31, Greenwood, S.C. 29647.

W. Altee Burpee Co. Warminster, Pa. 18974.

Fruits and Nuts

Tree, Bush, or Vine: A Lifetime Harvest Of Fruits and Nuts

By raising your own fruits, you gain freshness and a range of flavor that cannot be matched by store-bought fruit, which is often limited to a few varieties more pleasing to the eye than to the taste. You can grow such historic favorites as the Spitzenburg apple, relished by Thomas Jefferson, and the famous Concord grape, plus fine modern varieties including the Reliance peach, so hardy that it defies the severe winters of New Hampshire. You can enjoy such unusual treats as yellow and purple raspberries or fresh currants and gooseberries, not to mention pies, jam, cider, or wine made with your own fruit. And fruits yield beauty as well as food: clouds of fragrant blossoms in spring, colorful clusters of fruit in fall.

Nut trees, while needing more space than fruit trees, thrive with minimal care and live for generations, often reaching giant size. They provide welcome shade in summer and valuable timber, as well as bountiful crops of nuts—a source of pleasure long after your own lifetime. As an added benefit, both nut and fruit trees provide food and habitat for many species of wildlife.

It is easy to grow your own fruit and nuts if you have enough space for a couple of trees or a few berry bushes. They need less care than flowers and vegetables; and although fruit-bearing plants take one to five years before they come into production, with care most of them will keep on producing for many years—even for generations.

Almond trees in full bloom. Fruit and nut trees can be beautiful as well as practical.

Hardiness Zones

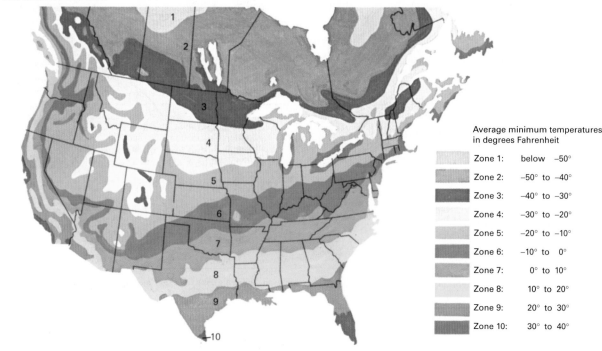

Average minimum temperatures in degrees Fahrenheit

Zone 1:	below −50°
Zone 2:	−50° to −40°
Zone 3:	−40° to −30°
Zone 4:	−30° to −20°
Zone 5:	−20° to −10°
Zone 6:	−10° to 0°
Zone 7:	0° to 10°
Zone 8:	10° to 20°
Zone 9:	20° to 30°
Zone 10:	30° to 40°

Climate is a critical survival factor for fruit trees, nut trees, bushes, and vines. Fruit- and nut-bearing plants vary widely in hardiness (resistance to subfreezing temperatures). Many require an extended period of chilling below 45°F to bear fruit. The map shows average minimum temperatures for winter over broad zones. Local features, such as hills and valleys, wind patterns, and urban areas, can cause sharp variations within each zone. Frost dates and length of growing season can also affect the kind of fruit or nuts that can be raised in your area. Contact your county agent for varieties that do well locally.

Starting Your Orchard

The most important step you can take for your newly purchased stock is to plant it properly. An old adage advises that you should plant a $5 tree in a $10 hole, meaning that the hole should be large enough to give the roots ample room to spread. Cramped roots grow poorly and may even choke one another.

If you buy a tree or bush from a local nursery, it is probably either growing in a container of soil or balled-and-burlapped. (Balled-and-burlapped, or B & B, means that the roots are embedded in a ball of soil and wrapped in burlap.) Stock from a mail-order nursery, which offers a far wider range of choices, will arrive with its roots bare, packed in damp moss or excelsior. For B & B or container-grown stock, planting is simple: make the hole as deep as the root ball and a foot wider, place the plant in position, loosen the top of the burlap, and replace the soil. Bare-root stock needs more care (see below).

Ideally, stock should be planted as soon as it arrives. If this is not possible, it can be stored. B & B stock can be held for several weeks by placing it in a shady location and keeping the root ball moist. Bare-root stock can be kept up to 14 days by opening the base of the package and keeping the roots moist. If kept over 14 days, it should be "heeled in" until you are ready to plant: remove the plants from their package, place them roots down in a shallow trench, and cover the roots with soil. Keep the plants out of the sun, and keep the soil moist.

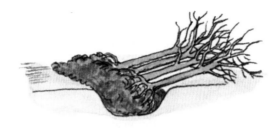

Heeling-in is a method of storing plants for up to a month.

When planting, do not expose bare roots to sunlight or air any longer than necessary. If they dry out, the plant may die. To avoid this, keep roots immersed in a pail of water or wrapped in a wet cloth until the hole is ready. Fruit or nut stock can be planted in either spring or fall provided the plants are dormant and the soil is not frozen. In Zones 3 and 4 and the northern part of Zone 5 spring planting is safer. Choose a site that has at least eight hours a day of full sunlight during spring and summer. The best locations are on high ground or on slopes to permit cold air to drain off. Avoid areas that are wet for most of the year.

If the soil is poor, mix peat moss or compost with it before planting the stock, but do not use fertilizer when planting: it may burn the roots and cause severe damage to the plant. Give newly planted stock plenty of water during the first growing season. If rainfall is insufficient, provide each young plant with a laundry pail of water once a week. Young trees have thin bark that is easily scalded (injured) by winter sun. To avoid sunscald, loosely wrap the trunks of newly planted trees from the ground to their lowest branches for the first few years. Use burlap, kraft paper, or semirigid plastic spirals (obtainable from nurseries). It may be removed in summer or left on year round as protection against deer, rodents, and farm animals.

Any vegetation close to the young tree, including grass, competes with it for water and nutrients. Therefore, the soil around the tree should be clean cultivated or heavily mulched from the trunk out to the drip line (the ends of the branches). If mulch is used, place a collar of hardware cloth around the base of the trunk to protect against field mice and other small nibblers.

After the first year, fruit and nut plants can be lightly fertilized. Overfeeding makes them produce a profusion of leaves and branches with fruit of poor quality. Manure, compost, wood ashes, and fertilizers high in nitrogen, phosphorus, and potassium are recommended.

Organic-minded fruit growers are usually willing to accept some blemishes and even the loss of some fruit as the price for avoiding sprays. However, in many areas spraying is necessary to get a crop at all. Organic insecticides include pyrethrum, rotenone, nicotine sulfate, and ryania. Also available are man-made insecticides that do not have a long-lasting toxic effect.

How to Plant a Tree

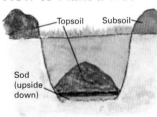

1. Dig hole at least 2 ft. deep and 2 ft. wide for nut trees, 1 1/2 ft. deep and 1 1/2 ft. wide for fruit trees, to give roots room. When digging hole, keep sod, topsoil, and subsoil separate. Loosen soil at bottom of hole and place sod upside down on it. Then make a low cone of topsoil in the center of the hole.

2. Prune broken or damaged roots with a sharp knife or pruning shears. Also remove roots that interlace or criss-cross. Shorten any roots that are too long to fit the hole. Do not allow the roots to dry out during this operation, and avoid crowding them into the hole when positioning the tree.

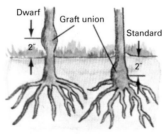

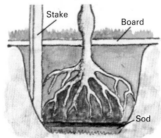

3. If tree is grafted, the graft union will appear as a small bulge near bottom of trunk. Standard trees should be planted so graft is about 2 in. below soil level. For dwarf trees the graft should be 2 in. above soil level to prevent the upper part of the tree from forming its own roots and growing to full size.

4. Newly planted trees need support. Set a temporary stake in hole before planting tree to avoid damage to roots. Place tree on cone of topsoil with roots spread out evenly. If necessary, adjust height of cone to bring graft union to proper level; a board laid across the hole makes a handy depth gauge.

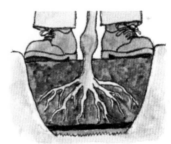

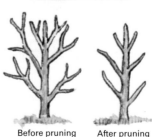

Before pruning   After pruning

5. Add soil until roots are covered, then work it around the roots with your fingers, leaving no air pockets. Fill hole almost to top and pack the soil by treading it. Gently pour a pail of water onto soil to settle it further. Fill in remainder of hole, leaving a shallow saucer for watering. Do not pack this soil.

6. Prune off all but the three or four strongest branches, and head these back a few inches to a strong bud. Lowest branch should be about 18 in. above soil. These "scaffold" branches will be the tree's future framework. Tie tree to stake with soft material, such as a rag, to avoid injury to the bark.

Less Means More: Pruning, Grafting, And Espaliering

Pruning, grafting, and espaliering are skills that will keep your plants productive, help you propagate special varieties, and enable you to shape your trees so they can be grown on a wall or along a fence.

Pruning is the art of selectively trimming or removing parts of a living plant. Properly done, pruning will promote the formation of flowers and fruit, eliminate dead and diseased wood, and control and direct the growth of the tree, bush, or vine. Pruning can also compensate for root damage at transplanting time. One of the most important rules is not to injure the bark when making a cut. The inner bark, or cambium, is the lifeline of woody plants, whether trees, bushes, or vines. This thin green layer of living tissue, only one cell thick, is not only the actively growing part of the tree, it is also the pathway that transports nutrients from the leaves to the roots. Whenever the cambium is injured or destroyed, the tissue around the injury will also die back.

When a limb is removed, the cambium forms a scarlike tissue called a callus and gradually begins to grow back over the exposed wood surface. A small wound often heals over in a single growing season, thereby excluding decay organisms. Wounds larger than a 50-cent piece should be painted to keep out rot, which weakens the tree and shortens its life, besides ruining the wood.

The traditional time for pruning is in late winter or early spring, while the tree is dormant and the weather is not excessively cold. (Pruning should not be attempted when the temperature is below 20°F, since dieback may result.) In general, summer pruning is not recommended, since it encourages plants to put out new growth to replace what has been removed. The new growth seldom has time to harden before frost comes; as a result, it is usually killed. The exceptions to the rule against summer pruning are dead, diseased, or damaged branches, and so-called water sprouts or suckers, which should be cut off as soon as they appear. Water sprouts are vigorous, vertical shoots that spring from a tree's trunk and limbs; suckers are similar but spring from the roots.

An important function of pruning is to keep branches from crowding one another; thus weak and interlacing branches should be removed regularly. A light pruning every year is better—and easier—than a heavy one every two or three years.

Pruning Tools for Every Job

One-hand pruning shears sever branches up to 1/2 in. in diameter and are handy for light work.

Small-toothed pruning saw can handle branches up to 5 in. thick if necessary.

Two-hand lopping shears are used on branches up to 1 1/2 in. in diameter and for extending reach.

Speed saw, with large teeth, cuts fast but coarsely; do not use it for branches under 3 in.

Pole saw is for work too high to reach without a ladder. Many models include cord-operated shears for twigs.

Fundamentals of Good Pruning

Wrong: stub remains **Right:** Flush with trunk **Wrong:** too far from bud, bad stub **Wrong:** too close to bud **Right:** a bit above bud

"Leave no stubs" is the pruner's first commandment. Stubs soon die, creating an entryway for decay organisms and harmful insects. Make your cut flush with the main stem or as close to it as possible without injuring the bark. Such a cut will soon begin to heal over. When heading back a branch, leave at least one strong bud to ensure that the branch survives. Use a slanting cut just beyond the bud to promote healing. Select a bud that points in the direction in which you wish to direct the growth of the branch after pruning.

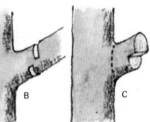

A B C

Pruning off large branches can injure trees if not done properly, since the weight of the branch may cause it to break loose when partly cut through, tearing away large areas of bark or even splitting the tree. To prevent this, first cut upward from the lower side of the branch, about 6 in. from the trunk or main stem (A). This undercut should go a third of the way through the branch. Then cut down through the branch an inch or two farther out (B). The undercut prevents tearing when the branch falls. The stub can now be removed with a cut flush to the trunk (C).

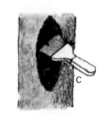

A B C

To speed healing, trim the bark around the edge of the wound with a sharp knife and smooth off rough spots and projections on the bare wood (A). If the wound is large, use a wood rasp for smoothing, and trim the bark lengthwise in a diamond shape (B). This eliminates bark that would die because sap cannot reach it. Wounds more than 1 to 1 1/2 in. in diameter (about the size of a 50-cent piece) should be painted with shellac or water-soluble asphalt-based tree wound paint to seal them against decay organisms and insects (C).

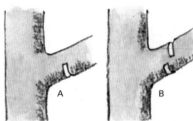
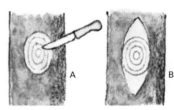

Espaliers for Fence or Wall

The ancient art of espaliering is finding new popularity with space-conscious modern gardeners. The technique, which dates back to ancient Rome, was revived in medieval times by monks who needed to utilize every inch of their cramped monastery gardens. It has also been part of the New World tradition since colonial days.

Despite its high-sounding French name, espaliering is simply a method of training fruit trees or ornamentals to grow flat against a wall or on supports. Espaliered trees occupy a minimum of space and can be planted in spots that would otherwise be unproductive. When grown against a wall, they benefit from reflected light and heat so that their fruit often ripens early.

Espaliering is most easily done with dwarf trees. They may be trained on trellises, on wires strung between spikes in a wall, or on fence rails. In the North espaliers should have a southern exposure; in the South and Southwest an eastern exposure is favored. Since a healthy tree needs balanced growth, espaliers are often trained in symmetrical geometric patterns that combine economy of space with beauty.

Shown below are the basic steps for training a one-year-old tree into an espalier. The pattern is the double horizontal cordon. A new tier of laterals can be added each year until the desired height is achieved; after that, keep the leader trimmed back.

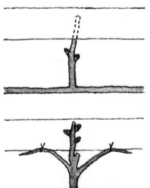

First year. At planting cut tree back to three buds just below bottom wire. One bud will form new vertical leader; the others will become lateral branches. Keep all other shoots that sprout later pruned back to 6 in. to encourage fruit buds to form.

Second year. Cut leaders back below second wire. Gently bend the two laterals and tie them to wire with a soft material such as twine. Remove all other first-year shoots. Leave three strong buds at top of leader to develop into new leader and new laterals.

Third year. Tie down second tier of laterals to wire. Cut back leader slightly below wire. Remove shoots from trunk and leader as before. Trim all side shoots on laterals to three buds. Do not cut back ends of laterals until they reach desired length.

Grafting for Propagation

Because of their complex genetic makeup, cultivated fruit and nut plants do not come true from seed, and the vast majority of seedlings are of poor quality. The only way to ensure that a young plant has all the desirable qualities of its parent is to propagate it nonsexually by grafting, layering, or division. Grafting is used principally with fruit and nut trees; layering (see p.165) is used to propagate grapes and some bush fruits; division (see p.167) is used with bush fruits.

Grafting is the most complex of these techniques but is still simple enough for amateurs to master. It has been practiced at least since the days of the ancient Romans. Grafting involves joining the top of one variety to the roots or trunk of another. Old-time farmers propagated their best fruit trees by grafting and gave buds and scions (young shoots) to their friends. The famous McIntosh apple was propagated in this way from a single wild seedling discovered on a pioneer farm in the Canadian bush in 1811. All McIntosh apples in existence today are descendants of that one seedling.

In addition to propagating desirable varieties, grafting is used to impart special characteristics such as hardiness, extra-small tree size, or disease resistance. Three common grafting techniques are shown below.

Bud grafting

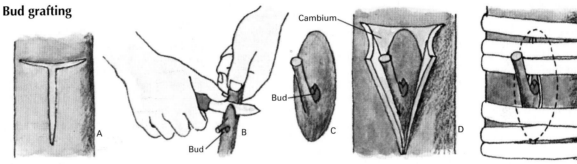

Bud grafting, or budding, is done in late summer. With a sharp knife or razor blade make a small T-shaped cut in the bark of the rootstock (A). Cut a twig from the tree you wish to propagate and snip off the twig's leaves, leaving about 1/2 in. of each leaf stem. At the base of each leaf stem is a bud that will produce the next year's growth. Cut toward the tip from just behind the bud (B). You should get a broad, shallow slice of bark and cambium and a little inner wood (C). Spread the flaps of the T-cut and insert the bud so that its cambium contacts that of the rootstock (D). Fasten tightly with soft twine or adhesive tape, leaving the bud and leaf stem exposed (E). This protects the graft from drying out. Remove the wrappings after three weeks. In the spring, when the bud sprouts, cut off the rootstock 1 in. above the bud.

Cleft grafting

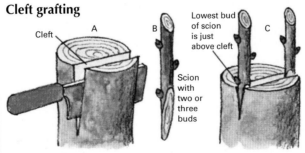

Cleft grafting, the simplest way to graft, is done in early spring before growth starts. Cut off the rootstock a few inches above the ground. With a cleaver, heavy knife, or wide chisel, split the rootstock stem near one edge 2 to 3 in. deep (A) and wedge the split open. Take a scion (a short section of a shoot with several buds) and cut one end to a wedge shape (B). Insert the scion at one side of the cleft so that cambium touches cambium (C). Cover all cut surfaces with grafting wax to prevent drying out. As insurance, use two scions: if both take, cut off the weaker one.

Whip grafting

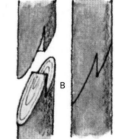
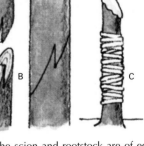

Whip grafting is used when the scion and rootstock are of equal size and less than 3/4 in. in diameter. It is done in early spring. With a sharp knife, cut off the rootstock diagonally about 6 in. above the ground (A). Make a matching cut on the scion. The cuts should be smooth and clean. Now cut a slanting tongue in the rootstock and another in the scion and fit the two pieces together so that cambium meets on both sides (B). Fasten firmly with twine, waxed thread, or adhesive tape and cover the top of the scion with grafting wax (C) to prevent it from drying out.

Apples and Pears Are Old Favorites

Apple and pear trees are closely related and have similar cultural requirements. Both grow best in a deep, rich, well-drained, slightly acid soil but can be grown in almost any type of soil that is not excessively acid or alkaline. The orchard should be sited on a north-facing slope if possible to delay blossoming and reduce the danger of frost damage.

Both apple and pear trees need a period of cold and dormancy to set flowers and fruit. Apples thrive best in Zones 5 to 7 (see map on p.154), although there are hardy varieties that succeed in Zone 4 and a few heat-tolerant ones that grow in Zones 8 and 9. Pears, more delicate than apples, do best in areas with mild winters and cool summers, such as the Pacific Northwest, but can be grown in Zones 5 to 7.

Most varieties of apples and pears are not self-fertile; that is, they need at least one other variety planted close by to set fruit. Even those listed in catalogs as self-fertile produce better when they are cross-fertilized by another variety. Standard apple trees should be planted 20 to 30 feet apart, with the same distance between rows; for standard pear trees the figures are 20 feet apart and 20 feet between rows. Dwarf trees can be planted as close as 10 by 10 feet or even 6 by 10 feet. Semidwarfs should be at least 12 feet apart.

Like other fruit trees, apples and pears are prey to a variety of diseases and insect pests. For a good crop of unblemished fruit, commercial growers must spray as often as 13 times a year. Home growers can get by with six sprayings—fewer if they do not mind a few blemishes.

Both types of trees bear fruit on spurs–short, gnarled twigs that grow from the branches and produce blossoms for several years in a row. Spurs can be identified in winter by their buds—fruit buds are plump and rounded, while leaf buds have a slenderer, more pointed shape. With a little practice it is not hard to tell the difference. For best results the fruit should be thinned three to six weeks from the time it first forms, after the early summer "June drop." First eliminate any wormy, diseased, and undersized fruits. Then space out the remaining fruits to 6 or 7 inches apart. Thinning produces larger and more flavorful fruit and also reduces the danger of branches breaking from too heavy a load. Be careful not to break off fruit spurs when removing the fruits.

The fruits are ready to harvest when their stems separate easily from the tree. Pears should be picked before they are ripe, when their color changes from deep green to light green or yellow. Apples should be tree ripened and have reached their mature coloration. Pears should be ripened in a cool, dark place for immediate use or held in storage in the refrigerator.

When picking fruit of any kind, try to keep the stem on the fruit—removing it creates an entry for rot. Place fruits gently in a basket or other container rather than dropping them in; bruises cause rapid spoilage.

Apples and pears should begin to bear at 5 to 10 years of age for standard trees and 2 to 3 years for dwarfs. Owners of commercial orchards replace their trees at 25 to 40 years, but with care a tree will survive, blossom, and bear fruit for as long as 100 years.

Both apples and pears have early, midseason, and late-ripening varieties. The early and midseason varieties do not keep well and should be eaten soon after picking or else be dried or canned. Late varieties are picked before they are fully ripe and attain peak flavor and aroma in storage.

Chenango Strawberry apple ripens early.

Rhode Island Greening, a cooking apple, dates from colonial days.

Rome Beauty is a large apple used for cooking.

Spitzenburg was the favorite apple of Thomas Jefferson.

Winesap is an old favorite cider apple.

York Imperial, an excellent keeper, comes from eastern Pennsylvania.

Grimes Golden is a richly flavored winter apple.

Roxbury Russet ripens late and gains sweetness in storage.

Jonathan apple, discovered in 1826, is good for eating and cooking.

Dwarf trees for efficiency

Where space is limited, dwarf trees can be the answer. Dwarf trees, produced by grafting standard varieties onto special rootstocks or by inserting a special stem section, bear full-sized fruit but seldom grow more than 8 to 10 ft. tall. Because of their small size, they are easy to prune and care for, and the fruit can be picked without climbing a ladder. Dwarf trees usually bear much sooner than standard (full-sized) trees, and as many as 10 dwarfs can be planted in the space required by one standard tree. This not only increases the yield but allows you to plant more varieties. On the debit side dwarf trees require more care than standards and must usually (except for interstem dwarfs) be staked permanently to prevent them from toppling under the weight of a heavy crop.

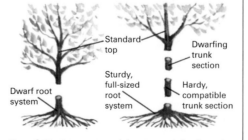

Dwarf trees are created by two methods: using dwarf rootstock or interstem grafting.

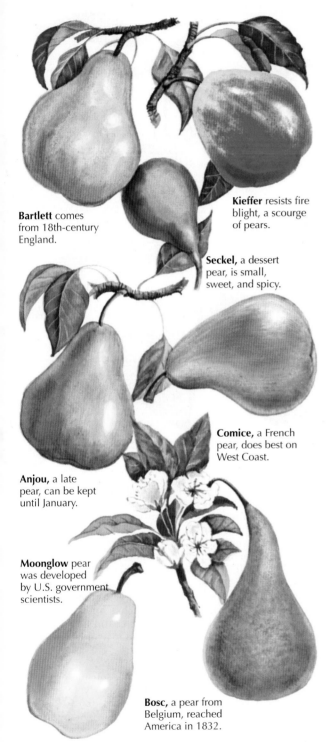

Bartlett comes from 18th-century England.

Kieffer resists fire blight, a scourge of pears.

Seckel, a dessert pear, is small, sweet, and spicy.

Comice, a French pear, does best on West Coast.

Anjou, a late pear, can be kept until January.

Moonglow pear was developed by U.S. government scientists.

Bosc, a pear from Belgium, reached America in 1832.

Training for Better Trees

Left to themselves, fruit trees grow into a nearly impenetrable jungle of branches that yield small, inferior fruit and leave the trees vulnerable to destruction in storms or under the weight of snow. The fruit grower's aim is to direct the growth of the tree into a shape that is structurally sound, easily cared for, and requires little pruning. This training should begin when the tree is two to four years old and the branches are still pliable. The best configuration for apple and pear trees, known as the central leader shape, features a tall main trunk surrounded by lateral, or scaffold, branches. The lowest scaffold branch should be 18 inches from the ground. Each succeeding scaffold branch should be at least 8 inches above the one below it. No two scaffold branches should be directly opposite each other.

Scaffold branches should grow at an angle between 45 and 90 degrees to the main leader; a narrow crotch is structurally weak, and vertically growing branches produce fewer fruit buds. If possible, select scaffold branches that grow naturally at this angle. If the tree has none—and many varieties are upright growers—you can force them to grow horizontally with the aid of spreaders (see illustration below). Prune the trees to maintain a Christmas-tree profile so light can reach the lower branches. The central leader should be headed back each year to encourage the scaffold branches to grow—the leader will produce new shoots to continue its own growth. Head back the laterals, too, to keep them within bounds and promote formation of fruit spurs.

Trees that naturally tend to produce more than one leader can be trained on the modified central leader plan. The traditional open-center plan should not be used for apple and pear trees. It tends to produce lots of water sprouts and makes the tree vulnerable to splitting.

Central-leader system produces a strong tree that resists breakage. The shape allows sunlight to reach the lower branches.

Modified central leader tree has a main leader that is headed fairly low and scaffold branches nearly as long as the leader.

Open-center system is best for peaches and other stone fruits but experts no longer recommend it for apple or pear trees.

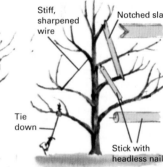

Stiff, sharpened wire

Notched slat

Tie down

Stick with headless nails

Train branches to the best growing position by tying them down to stakes or by using spreaders like the homemade types above.

Rejuvenating Old Trees

An old, overgrown apple or pear tree, picturesque but unproductive, can often be restored to fruitfulness by pruning and feeding. The first task is to head the tree back to a manageable height, such as 15 to 20 feet (some varieties may reach 35 to 40 feet), and to cut off all dead, diseased, and damaged branches. Next, eliminate branches that are weak, crisscross, grow downward, or have narrow crotches, and cut off water sprouts and suckers. Paint wounds with tree-wound compound.

If the tree has a major limb that can serve as a central leader, save it and try to select branches that form a natural scaffold. If there is no leader, prune the top into an open vaselike shape to let in light and air. In addition to pruning, a neglected tree almost certainly needs cultivation and feeding. Rototill or spade up the soil, starting near the trunk and moving out to the drip line of the branches. This frees the tree's feeder roots from the competition of sod and weeds. It is helpful to till in compost or rotted manure. Another way to feed the tree is by using a crowbar to make a circle of 12-inch-deep holes around the drip line 18 inches apart and filling them with 10-10-10 fertilizer. Apply a thick layer of mulch around the tree to keep down weeds, but leave an 18-inch circle clear around the trunk to discourage rodents.

The Stone Fruits: Cherries, Peaches, Apricots, and Plums

The stone fruits—cherries, peaches, nectarines, apricots, and plums—get their name from the hard, stony pits that encase their seeds. In general, the stone-fruit trees are smaller and come into bearing sooner than apple and pear trees. They are also shorter lived, although with reasonable care they can remain productive for 20 to 40 years, depending on type.

All the stone fruits need well-drained soil, and good drainage is particularly important for peaches and cherries. Like apples and pears, the stone fruits need a period of winter chilling to blossom and produce fruit. Plant standard-sized trees 20 feet apart and dwarfs 10 feet apart. Some dwarf varieties can be grown even closer together; the nursery from which you buy them should supply details on planting and care.

The stone fruits are highly perishable and keep only a few days in storage. However, they are excellent for canning, drying, and, in some cases, freezing. All of them make fine preserves.

Cherries. There are two basic types of cherries: sweet and sour. Sweet cherries can be eaten fresh or cooked; sour cherries, also known as pie cherries, are used mainly for pies and preserves, although some are sweet enough to eat from the tree. The black cherry, a wild native American tree, yields small, sour cherries that can be used in pies; they are also a favorite food of songbirds.

Sweet cherries are grown in Zones 5 to 7 (see map, p.154); pie cherries in Zones 4 to 7. Bush cherries, a different species, grow throughout Zones 3 to 7 and bear small, sour fruits. Sweet cherry trees are upright in form and reach 25 to 30 feet if not pruned back. Most sour cherry trees are spreading and reach 15 to 25 feet, although the black cherry, an upright tree, occasionally grows as high as 100 feet. Sweet cherries should be trained as central-leader trees (see p.159). Sour cherries do better on the modified-leader plan.

Sour cherries are self-fertile, but sweet cherries must be cross-pollinated by another variety of sweet cherry if they are to bear fruit. Check with your county agent for compatible varieties, since certain types are not mutually fertile. Bush cherries also require cross-pollination, but they are not as finicky as sweet cherries. Sweet cherries rarely cross-pollinate with sour varieties.

Black Tartarian, an early sweet cherry, is a long-time favorite.

Napoleon is a golden red sweet cherry.

Emperor Francis, a yellow cherry with firm flesh, is seldom harmed by birds.

Bing, a sweet cherry, ripens in midsummer.

North Star, a very hardy sour cherry, grows on a dwarf tree.

Commercial varieties of both sweet and sour cherries live 30 to 40 years; bush cherries about 15 to 20 years. Wild black cherry trees live much longer; individual trees that are 150 to 200 years old have been found. Sweet cherries begin bearing about five years after they are planted, sour cherries usually bear three years after planting, and bush cherries often bear after the first year. All of them produce their fruit on spurs. Thinning is seldom needed for cherries. Robbing by birds can be countered by covering the trees with netting.

Peaches and nectarines. Often thought of as warmth-loving southern fruits, the peach and its smooth-skinned variant, the nectarine, flourish in Zones 5 through 8. Several hardy varieties, such as the Reliance peach, produce fruit in Zone 4. Peaches and nectarines must have a substantial winter chilling period to blossom—the number of hours of chill required differs with the variety. A few recently developed varieties produce fruit in the cooler parts of Zone 9.

Peaches and nectarines grow best on slightly acid soil (pH 6 to 7), but their prime requirement is good drainage. Late spring frosts often kill blossoms; to avoid this danger, plant the trees on high ground.

Peach and nectarine trees should be trained to the open-center or modified-leader plan with three or four scaffold branches. They bear on shoots that were formed the previous year, not on spurs like apples, pears, and cherries. Most peaches and all nectarines are self-fertile. Thin the fruits to 6 to 8 inches apart. Thinning is especially important with peaches and nectarines to get fruits of good size and flavor and to avoid weakening the tree by overproduction.

Peaches and nectarines should ripen on the tree. They should be picked when they feel soft under gentle pressure and when they separate readily from their stems. They keep only a few days in cool storage but are excellent fruits for freezing and canning. The quality is better if they are frozen in syrup or sugar.

Elberta, a freestone peach, is considered by many the finest of all.

Moorpark is an old favorite of apricot lovers.

Santa Rosa is a red Japanese plum.

Moongold is a hardy apricot with small aromatic fruit.

Greengage plum, a European variety, makes delicious sherbet.

Reliance peach has produced good crops after winter freezes of −25°F.

Peach tree in bloom

Mericrest nectarine, from New Hampshire, is superhardy.

Shiro is a popular early-ripening yellow Japanese plum.

Damson plum is a traditional popular blue European type.

Apricots. Although little grown for home use, apricots are not difficult to raise. The prime requisite for success is protecting these early-blossoming trees from spring frosts. Planting them on a north slope or on the north side of a building helps by delaying blossoming. If the tree is small, it can be covered on a frosty night. Apricot trees themselves are quite hardy and can be grown in Zones 4 through 8.

Standard apricots, if left unpruned, will reach a height of 20 feet and a spread of 25 to 30 feet; dwarfs reach a maximum height of 8 feet and a spread of 10 feet. Both produce better when kept pruned back.

Apricots should be trained on the open-center plan (see p.159), with three or four main scaffold branches beginning between 18 and 30 inches from the ground. Each scaffold branch should have one or two secondary scaffold branches arising 4 to 5 feet above ground level.

Apricots bear fruit on short-lived spurs. Almost all apricots are self-pollinating and set heavy crops without the aid of another variety. The fruit should be thinned conscientiously to 6 inches apart. Apricots normally begin to bear two or three years after planting and can produce for as long as 70 years.

For eating fresh and for drying, apricots should be harvested when they are fully ripe and separate easily from the stem. For canning, harvest the fruit while it is still firm.

Some nurseries have developed strains of apricots with edible kernels. (The kernels of most varieties of apricots, like those of most stone fruits, contain enough cyanide to render them bitter and even poisonous if eaten in quantity.)

Plums. Plums fall into two major groups: European and Japanese. Japanese plums are mostly round and red; European plums are mostly oval and blue. There are also green and yellow varieties, such as the Greengage and Yellow Egg, both old European-type favorites. Most European plums are self-fertile; all Japanese plums require another variety of Japanese plum as a pollinator. Certain European varieties with a very high sugar content are called prunes, and dried prunes are made from their fruits. They are also delicious fresh.

Plums thrive on soils with a pH of 6.0 to 8.0. European plums do best in Zones 5 to 7; Japanese plums in Zones 5 to 9. A few hardy varieties, produced by crossing European or Japanese plums with native American species, will bear fruit in Zone 4.

Standard plum trees reach a height and spread of 15 to 20 feet; dwarfs reach 8 to 10 feet. European plums do best when trained on the modified-leader plan; Japanese plums on the open-center plan. Plums usually bear three to four years after planting. The fruit, borne on long-lived spurs, should be thinned to 3 or 4 inches apart.

For eating fresh or for drying, pick plums when they are soft and come away from the tree easily. For canning, pick them when they have acquired a waxy white coating and are springy to the touch but still firm.

The Warmth-Loving Citrus Fruits

Citrus fruits are semitropical plants requiring a warm frost-free climate the year round. They do best in Zone 10 and the warmer parts of Zone 9 (see map, p.154). The members of the genus vary in their resistance to cold. Limes are the most cold tender; tangerines are the hardiest. Kumquats, which belong to a related genus, are even hardier. Cold hardiness is influenced by the weather just before a freeze: cool weather makes the trees hardier. However, citrus trees rarely survive prolonged exposure to temperatures in the lower teens.

Citrus trees grow best in a slightly acid soil (pH 6.0 to 6.5). They can be planted at any time of the year, but the winter months are preferred because less watering is necessary then. No pruning is needed except to remove dead wood and to shape the tree to fit the available space. Citrus trees reach a height of 20 to 40 feet, with an equal spread; kumquats usually reach half this size.

Both grafted and ungrafted citrus trees are available. Most are sold in containers. Look for plants with large healthy leaves; reject any that are potbound, that is, whose roots have grown until they fill the containers.

Grafted citrus trees begin to bear when they are two to four years old. Ungrafted plants bear much later; in addition, they are quite thorny and tend to become very large. Citrus trees are long-lived—some that are more than 100 years old are still producing.

Most citrus trees produce fruit without pollination, although some of the tangerine hybrids do need cross-pollination. Citruses can be prolific bearers: a mature navel orange tree will yield more than 500 pounds of fruit per year, and large lemon trees can bear even more. The fruits should be allowed to ripen on the tree for the best flavor. Color is usually, but not always, a guide to ripeness. (Cool weather enhances color while delaying ripening.) The fruit also becomes softer as it gets ripe, usually about 8 to 12 months after bloom. In the cool coastal areas of California it can take 24 or more months for the fruit to mature, and three crops of fruit can be found on the trees at the same time. Tangerines should be harvested by clipping their stems to avoid tearing the loose rind; other citrus fruits can be pulled off by giving the fruit a slight twist. Citrus fruits keep well in cool storage. Most citrus varieties can be left on the tree for long periods without the fruit developing any symptoms of deterioration.

Grapefruit can have white, pink, or red flesh and is available in seeded and seedless varieties. Grapefruit trees tend to be larger than orange trees and need more warmth. When ripe, the fruit grows to 6 inches in diameter, usually with a thick, pale yellow rind. Best quality is reached after Christmas.

Kumquats are valued as ornamentals as well as fruit producers. The bright orange fruit is eaten whole, rind and all. Kumquats have a tart, spicy flavor and are commonly made into preserves. Limequats, a pale yellow lime-kumquat hybrid, are useful lime substitutes in climates where limes will not survive.

Lemons grow very vigorously and are thorny; thus they are suitable only for very large gardens. Their sensitivity to cold limits them to Hawaii, southern Arizona, coastal California, and the Gulf Coast. The Meyer lemon, a semihardy hybrid, is a good choice for home gardens. Lemons bloom and bear fruit the year round, but the main crop is usually set in summer.

Limes, like lemons, tend to fruit the year round. They are very cold tender and are common only in southern Florida. The Key lime is small, sour, and seedy and thrives only in the warmer areas of Florida.

Oranges are divided into early, midseason, and late varieties; these in turn can be subdivided into seeded and seedless types. The best-known early orange is the navel orange. The most common late variety is the Valencia.

Tangelos and tangors are common garden trees in the citrus belt. Tangelos are crosses between tangerines and grapefruits, tangors between tangerines and oranges. The temple orange is a well-known tangor.

Tangerines, also called mandarins, are hardier than most other citrus fruits. They have a loose skin that is easily peeled and are best when eaten fresh. As with oranges, there are early, midseason, and late varieties, most of which are well suited to home gardens.

Protecting trees from frost

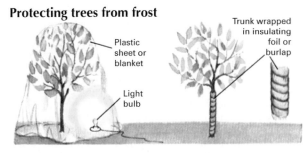

Plastic sheet or blanket

Light bulb

Trunk wrapped in insulating foil or burlap

When temperatures drop below 26°F, citrus trees need protection, either by covering them or providing artificial heat. Smudge pots—containers of burning oil—are seldom used anymore.

Temple orange, a Florida specialty.

Tangelo is a cross between a tangerine and a grapefruit.

Valencia, an orange good for juice and marmalade.

Lemon is a prolific bearer and yields tasty honey.

Lime gained fame as a scurvy preventive in Britain's navy.

Kumquats are hardy and easy to raise.

Grapefruit can have white, pink, or red flesh.

Long-lived Nut Trees For Food and Shade

Nut trees adapt to a wide range of climates and soils, although they prefer a deep, rich, crumbly soil that is neutral or slightly alkaline. (An exception is the Chinese chestnut, which does well in acid soil.) Nut trees even thrive in rough or otherwise uncultivatable land, provided the drainage is good. Full sunlight is needed for best results. Most nut trees do not succeed where minimum temperatures fall below −20°F, and they need a frost-free growing season of at least 150 days to produce a crop. Nut trees also need ample summer heat for their nuts to develop properly.

Nut trees are planted like fruit trees. However, walnuts and hickories have a single deep taproot rather than a branching root system. Since the taproot should not be cut back or bent, dig the hole deep enough to accommodate it. At planting time the top of the tree should be cut back by a third to a half to force it to grow a strong new sprout that will mature into the main trunk. Nut trees need little pruning except to maintain a strong central leader during the first years of growth and to remove dead and crisscrossing branches.

Nut trees can be propagated from seed, but in many cases the extraction of the kernels will be so difficult that it is hardly worth the effort. As a result, with the exception of Chinese chestnuts and Carpathian walnuts, only grafted trees of named varieties should be planted. However, seedlings can be grafted with buds or scions of named varieties after they have become established.

Well-cared-for grafted nut trees usually begin to bear at three to five years of age. For proper pollination it is advisable to plant two or more of each kind of tree. With cultivated strains plant at least two varieties. When mature, nuts will fall from the tree by themselves or with the aid of gentle shaking. For best quality they should be gathered as soon as they fall; when allowed to lie on the ground, they deteriorate rapidly if not eaten by squirrels and other wildlife.

The nuts should be husked and dried in a shaded spot until the kernels are brittle—usually about three weeks. The dried nuts, stored in a cool place, will remain in good condition for a year. Freshness can be restored by soaking them in water overnight. Shelled nuts will keep indefinitely if stored in a plastic bag in the freezer. (Chestnuts should be boiled for three to five minutes before freezing them.)

Almonds are grown mainly on the West Coast because of their climatic needs: a long, warm growing season with low humidity. For other sections nurseries sell hardy strains that can be raised where peaches succeed, but the kernels are toxic to some people.

Butternuts are a species of walnut and the hardiest of all native nut trees. They grow in Zones 4 to 8 (see p.154). The oil-rich nuts can be pickled when immature as well as eaten ripe. A gray-brown dye can be made from the bark. The nuts can be dried with their husks on.

Chinese chestnuts are resistant to the blight that wiped out the native American chestnuts. About as hardy as peach trees, they succeed in Zones 5 to 8. Chinese chestnuts yield large crops of high-quality nuts, borne in sharp-spined burrs that split open at maturity. Each burr contains from one to three nuts. When fresh, chestnuts are high in starch and low in sugar, which gives them a taste like potatoes. However, as the nuts dry out the starch changes to sugar.

Filberts and hazelnuts are closely related. (The name filbert is generally used for the European species, hazelnut for the native American species.) There are also numerous hybrid varieties. American hazelnuts grow in Zones 4 to 8; European filberts are hardy in Zones 5 to 8.

Hickory trees are native to North America and grow over most of the eastern half of the United States in Zones 5 to 7. Two species, the shagbark and the shellbark, produce edible nuts that are hard to crack. However, cultivated varieties with meatier kernels and thinner shells have been developed and are sold by nurseries.

Pecans belong to the hickory clan. Essentially a southern tree, the pecan's native range is the Southeast and lower Mississippi Valley. Paper-shell pecans grow in Zones 7 to 9. There are hardy northern varieties that grow in Zones 6 to 9, and even one that survives in Zone 5. However, pecans in the North often fail to produce nuts when summer is cool or frost comes early.

Walnuts include the native American black walnut; the English, or Persian, walnut native to Central Asia; and the heartnut, a Japanese walnut variety. The roots of black walnuts give off a substance that is toxic to apples, tomatoes, potatoes, and a number of other plants. Do not plant these susceptible plants within 30 feet of a black walnut. The black walnut can be raised in Zones 5 to 9. English walnuts reach a height and spread of about 60 feet. Easier to shell than black walnuts, they are hardy in Zones 5 to 9. Heartnuts are low, spreading trees that reach 30 to 40 feet in height. They are hardy in Zones 4 to 8. The nuts, which grow in clusters of 8 to 10, resemble butternuts in flavor.

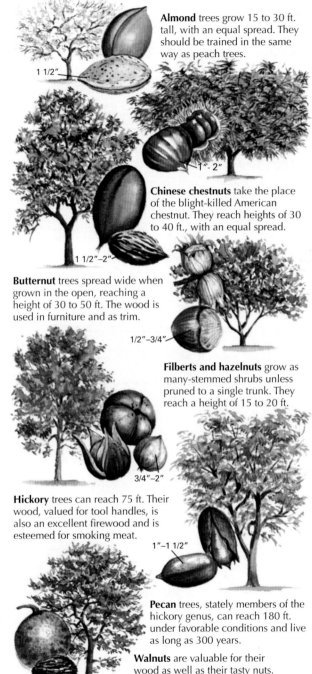

Almond trees grow 15 to 30 ft. tall, with an equal spread. They should be trained in the same way as peach trees.

1 1/2"

1"- 2"

Chinese chestnuts take the place of the blight-killed American chestnut. They reach heights of 30 to 40 ft., with an equal spread.

1 1/2"–2"

Butternut trees spread wide when grown in the open, reaching a height of 30 to 50 ft. The wood is used in furniture and as trim.

1/2"–3/4"

Filberts and hazelnuts grow as many-stemmed shrubs unless pruned to a single trunk. They reach a height of 15 to 20 ft.

3/4"–2"

Hickory trees can reach 75 ft. Their wood, valued for tool handles, is also an excellent firewood and is esteemed for smoking meat.

1"–1 1/2"

Pecan trees, stately members of the hickory genus, can reach 180 ft. under favorable conditions and live as long as 300 years.

Walnuts are valuable for their wood as well as their tasty nuts. Black walnut trees reach 100 ft.; English walnuts, 60 ft.

1"–2"

163

Tasty Strawberries Give Vitamin C Too

Sparkle, a late-blooming variety for northern gardens, escapes late spring frosts.

Ozark Beauty, an everbearer, keeps on producing until killing frosts.

Wild strawberries, small but prolific, are one of the ancestors of today's large succulent garden strawberries.

Strawberries, though short-lived, are one of the most adaptable of fruits. They can be grown from Florida to Alaska, and since the plants are small, they can be raised in containers, in ornamental borders, or among vegetables, provided they have full sunlight.

Once established, strawberries spread by sending out numerous slender stems, or runners, along the ground. When a runner is about 8 inches long, it bends sharply upward. At this bend the runner sends roots down into the soil and begins to form leaves. Once the new plant is formed, it sends out runners of its own.

The best planting time for strawberries is in the early spring, although in the South they can be planted in the fall. Plant them in well-tilled soil mixed with compost or rotted manure. Spread the roots out fanwise in the hole and pack the soil firmly around them. Some growers find that trimming the roots to 4 inches simplifies planting. Proper planting depth is critical for strawberries (see diagram). Spacing depends on which system of culture you choose: hill, matted-row, or spaced matted-row.

Most strawberries bear fruit in May or June, depending on the local climate. There are also so-called everbearing varieties that produce a crop of berries in early summer and another in late summer or early fall.

Strawberries will produce blossoms the year they are planted, but these blossoms should be pinched off to strengthen the plants and ensure a good crop the next year. The yield is greatest on two- and three-year-old plants. Production tends to drop sharply after three years, and the recommended practice is to replace the plants, preferably putting them in a new bed to avoid soil-borne disease. You can use runners that rooted the previous year in the old bed, but it is safer to order new certified virus-free plants from a nursery.

Strawberries thrive when mulched between the rows and under the plants. The plants should be covered with 6 inches of straw, leaves, or pine needles after the ground has frozen. Remove the mulch cover in late spring when new leaves are about 2 inches long.

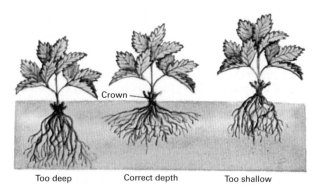

Too deep — Correct depth — Too shallow

Strawberries must be planted with their crowns level with soil.

Three Culture Systems

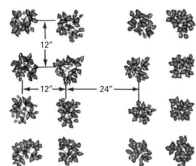

Hill system requires that all runners be kept pruned off the plants. Plants are spaced 12 in. apart. Growers usually plant double or triple rows with 12 in. between rows and a 24-in. alley between each set of rows. The hill system gives high yields and large berries, but it requires a great deal of labor and attention.

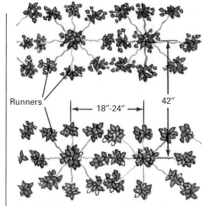

Matted-row system requires very little maintenance. However, the yields are lower and the berries are smaller than they are under other systems of culture. In the matted-row system almost all the runners are allowed to root. The plants are spaced 18 to 24 in. apart in single rows with about 42 in. between rows.

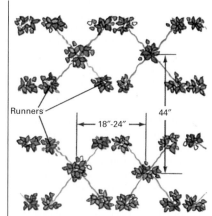

Spaced matted-row system is popular with home gardeners. It is a compromise between the hill and matted-row systems. The plants are spaced 18 to 24 in. apart in a single row; only four to six runners per plant are allowed to develop. The spaced matted-row system gives good yields and high quality.

Grapes: A Variety For Every Palate

Three types of grapes are raised in the United States. Labrusca grapes are descended from the native eastern wild grape. They are grown in the northern two-thirds of the country east of the Rockies in Zones 5 to 8 (see p.154). Muscadine grapes are grown in the Southeast, where they are natives, in Zones 7 to 10. Vinifera (European) grapes, the kind usually found at fruit stores, do best in Zones 6 to 9 and are raised mainly in California and Arizona (in other areas they are subject to disease and pests). In addition to the basic types there are many hybrids that combine the tastiness and the winemaking qualities of European grapes with the hardiness and resistance of American grapes. Most Labrusca and European grapes are self-fertile; most muscadines are not.

Grapes can be propagated easily by rooting cuttings of dormant stems in damp sphagnum moss or by layering—bending a shoot down and burying part of it in the soil, while leaving a few leaves or buds at the tip uncovered. This should be done in spring; roots will form along the buried portion during the growing season. Early the next spring, before growth starts, cut the newly rooted portion away from the parent vine and transplant it.

Grapes are produced on each year's new growth, and the best fruit is produced from the new shoots formed on canes from the previous year. The year-old canes are easy to recognize at pruning time: they are about as thick as a pencil and have light, smooth bark whereas older canes are stouter and have dark, fibrous bark. Remove blossoms and fruits from the vines the first two summers for a good crop the third year. Grapevines are long-lived and may produce for a hundred years. Although they will yield fruit in poor soil, they do better in fertile soil. However, overfertilization will produce masses of shoots and leaves with inferior fruit. The vines should be heavily mulched or clean-cultivated, since grass and weeds rob grapes of nutrients. Cultivate no deeper than 4 inches to avoid injuring the shallow roots.

Aurora, a French-American hybrid, makes delicate white wine and is also a good dessert grape.

Concord, the most famous American grape variety, is the standard for blue-black grapes.

Scuppernong, the most widely grown muscadine grape, thrives over most of the South.

Himrod grape, a hardy seedless variety, keeps until Christmas if refrigerated.

Catawba, a late-ripening American red grape, was developed over a century ago; an excellent keeper.

Planting and Training Grapes

Grapes grow in a wide variety of soils as long as the organic content is high. They should be planted in spring. Try to plant your vines on a slope so that cold air and water will drain off. Set new vines 8 to 10 feet apart in holes 12 inches wide and 12 inches deep. Trim the roots to fit the hole and prune off all canes (branches) but one. Prune that cane back to two buds.

Grapes must be trained on supports to keep the fruit off the ground and provide air circulation. A sturdy wire trellis is the most common form of support. Training should begin at planting time: the vine should be trained on a stake to form a straight main stem, or trunk. Training on the wire trellis begins the second year. While grapes can be trained in a myriad of forms, the most used system is the four-arm Kniffin (below). The first year, at pruning time, leave about three buds above

the lower wire and two buds below it. Remove all other buds and side shoots. Head the trunk back a few inches above the lower wire. As the new shoots grow from the buds, select the straightest one above the wire to be the main leader and tie it to the upper wire when it is long enough. Train the shoots from the two lowest buds along the lower wire to become the next year's fruiting arms. Train two shoots along the upper wire as they develop.

The third spring prune back the fruiting arms to 6 to 10 buds each. Remove other lateral canes, but leave two stubs, or spurs, near the fruiting arms to produce next year's fruit. Follow the same procedure each year for steady crops of fruit. Muscadine grapes, however, are treated slightly differently. They should have fruiting spurs of three or four buds left along the fruiting arms, which need to be renewed only every four or five years.

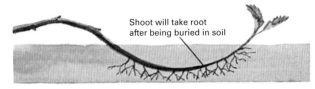

Shoot will take root after being buried in soil

Layering a grapevine, a simple means of propagation.

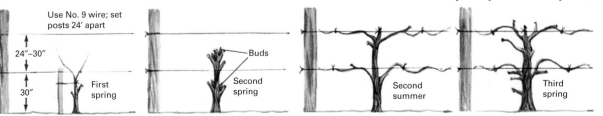

Use No. 9 wire; set posts 24' apart

24"–30"

30"

First spring

Buds

Second spring

Second summer

Third spring

Newly planted vine (left) should be tied to stake. After two additional springtimes vine will be well established on wire trellis.

165

Fast, Prolific Bearers: The Bush Fruits

Latham is a very popular red raspberry.

Bristol, a black raspberry, is a heavy bearer.

Darrow, an improved blackberry strain, bears inch-long fruit.

The cultivated bush fruits include raspberries, blackberries (and their relatives), blueberries, currants, and gooseberries. (There are numerous other fruit-bearing bushes, but they are not cultivated on any significant scale.) All are hardy and productive. Most are shallow rooted. All need to be pruned every year to keep them from becoming overgrown. All prefer well-drained humus-rich soil, and all need at least eight hours of sunlight. Although not as long-lived as fruit trees, most of the bush fruits can be kept going for several decades with a modest amount of care.

Raspberries are divided into two basic types: red and black. Yellow raspberries are considered a variant of red, and purple raspberries of black. Varieties of differing hardiness grow from Zones 3 to 8 (see p.154). Raspberries bear fruit the year after planting, and a raspberry bed will generally last for 7 to 10 years before production declines, usually due to one of the many viruses to which raspberries are susceptible. The plants should then be replaced with new ones, preferably in a different bed, and the old bed should not be used for raspberries or blackberries for at least five years.

Spring planting is best for raspberries, except in the South. The soil should be well cultivated and free of sod and weeds. Dig a small hole 4 inches deep for each plant, or plow a 4-inch-deep furrow. Set the plants with the crowns just below soil level. Cover the roots with loose soil and pack it down gently. Fill the remainder of the hole or furrow with loose soil. Space plants 3 feet apart in rows 5 to 8 feet apart.

Raspberries produce their fruit on two-year-old canes, that is, stems that sprouted the previous summer. In most varieties the canes die after one crop. The exceptions are the everbearing varieties, which yield a small crop in the fall on the tips of one-year-old canes and a second small crop lower down on the same canes the following summer. Once a cane has borne its full crop of fruit, it should be cut off at ground level and removed as a sanitary measure. Many growers prefer to treat ever-bearers as fall bearers only. They cut the canes down to soil level after the end of the growing season; the next year's new canes will then produce a heavy fall crop. Some growers use a rotary lawn mower at the lowest setting to cut down their old everbearing canes. Red and yellow raspberries produce numerous suckers from

their roots. Most of these must be pulled out to keep the bed under control, but a few of the strongest from each plant should be saved to become next year's bearing canes. Excess suckers can be dug up with a bit of root and replanted to become new bushes. As the plants fill in, they may be grown in clumps or in hills 3 feet apart, with 6 to 10 canes per hill. They can also be grown in hedgerows 1 to 2 feet wide with no more than five canes per square foot of row. Leave at least a handbreadth of space between canes to permit air circulation. Raspberries are most easily managed when wire trained.

Black and purple raspberries produce few if any suckers; they increase instead by tip layering. In late summer the bearing canes arch down to the ground and push their tips into the soil. The buried tips produce roots and new shoots that can be clipped free the next spring and replanted if necessary.

Although raspberry roots strike as deep as 4 feet, most of the roots are in the upper 12 inches of soil. Since so much of the root system is shallow, mulching is preferable to cultivation.

Prune red raspberry canes back to 4 or 5 feet in spring. The canes of black raspberries should be cut back to 18 to 24 inches their first summer. This stimulates them to form the lateral branches on which they will bear their fruit. Shorten the laterals to 8 to 10 inches the next spring. Black raspberries treated this way will not need a trellis for support.

Since raspberries bloom over a period of several weeks, the harvest season is correspondingly long. By planting successively maturing varieties you can extend the harvest season from midsummer to heavy frost. Raspberries are ready to pick when they separate easily from the stem, leaving the core of the berry behind.

Blackberries that are sold for cultivation are larger, juicier, sweeter cousins of the widespread wild blackberry. Not as hardy as raspberries, blackberries do best in the South, but there are varieties that are hardy as far north as Zone 3. Boysenberries, loganberries, and youngberries are hybrids of blackberries and either dewberries (another species of bramble fruit) or red raspberries. They are relatively cold tender and prosper best in Zones 7 to 9. Thornless blackberries are not reliably hardy north of Zone 5. Within their climate range they are a desirable choice because they lack thorns.

There are bush and vine types of blackberries. The bush types, which are hardier, are planted and propagated like red raspberries. Vine types are treated like black raspberries. Like raspberries, blackberries bear fruit on two-year-old canes. Bush-type canes should be pruned back to 5 feet at midsummer during their first year to aid in the formation of laterals. The next spring head back the laterals to 12 to 18 inches. Vine-type canes can be pruned like black raspberries. Blackberries should not be picked until they are dead ripe, separating from the stem at the slightest touch.

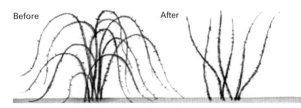

Pruning red raspberries keeps the bushes within manageable size, removes dead canes, and permits air circulation.

Before   After

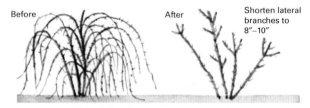

Before   After   Shorten lateral branches to 8"–10"

Black raspberries produce lateral branches where the fruits are borne. These branches should be headed back in spring.

Bluecrop is a hardy, dependable blueberry.

Wild blueberry is found in many areas.

Red Lake is the leading currant in the United States.

Pixwell gooseberry turns pink when ripe.

Blueberries thrive wherever their relatives, azaleas or rhododendrons, grow. They demand a very acid soil, ideally close to pH 4.8. Blueberries will not survive in alkaline soil. If your soil has a pH over 6.5, grow your blueberries in containers or raised beds filled with an acid soil mix. Do not plant blueberries in soil that has been limed in the last two years. Two species of blueberries are cultivated in the United States: the highbush blueberry in the Northeast, Midwest, upper South, and Pacific Northwest, and the rabbiteye blueberry in the Deep South. The highbush grows to 10 feet or taller if unpruned; the rabbiteye can reach 20 feet.

Highbush blueberries should be planted 4 to 5 feet apart in rows 8 to 10 feet apart; rabbiteye blueberries should be spaced 5 to 6 feet apart with 10 to 12 feet between rows. Dig a hole about 6 inches deep and 10 inches in diameter and set the plants with the crowns at soil level. If the soil is poor in humus, mix in compost. Be sure to keep the soil moist the first year—blueberries are very sensitive to drought. A 6-inch mulch of leaves or rotted sawdust will maintain soil moisture, add to the soil's organic content, and keep down weeds. Cultivation is apt to injure the shallow root systems of blueberries.

Rabbiteye blueberries very seldom need pruning except to remove weak or dead branches. Highbush blueberries should be pruned annually beginning the third year after planting. Remove old canes (stems) by

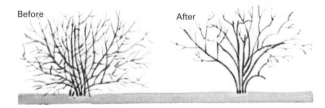

Before   After

When pruning highbush blueberries remove old canes and twigs that interlace. Crowded bushes produce poorly.

cutting them off at soil level when they become twiggy. New canes arising from the root system will take their place. The desired result is a bush with clean, sparsely branched canes with a few fat buds on each branch. If necessary, head back lateral branches to three buds each.

Commercial growers propagate blueberries by rooting cuttings in sand or sphagnum moss. Better systems for the home gardener are mounding (a form of layering) and division, a technique familiar to flower gardeners. In mounding, pile soil, compost, or a mixture of peat moss and rotted sawdust around the base of the blueberry bush about a foot deep. Keep the mound damp. New roots will form on the covered portions of the canes, which can be severed below the roots and replanted. In division, use a sharp spade to split the bush into two or more parts, each with its own roots and stems. Head back each portion about one-third and replant.

Highbush blueberries are moderately self-fertile but produce better crops if two or more varieties are planted together. In addition, by combining early, midseason, and late varieties, you can stretch out your harvest so that it lasts more than two months. Rabbiteye blueberries require cross-pollination. Blueberries are ready to harvest when they separate from the stem at a light touch and are sweet to the taste.

Currants and gooseberries, close relatives of each other, are the most cold loving of the bush fruits, thriving as far north as Zone 2 but doing poorly from Zone 7 south. Unfortunately, both species are hosts to white pine blister rust, and raising them is governed by strict regulations (check your own state's regulations with your county agent). Some states ban them entirely.

Well-drained soils are best for both currants and gooseberries, although they tolerate damp ground better than other bush fruits. They should be planted in fall in holes 12 inches across and 12 inches deep, with 2 to 4 feet between plants and 8 to 9 feet between rows. Bushes may be propagated by layering branches or by

taking 8- to 10-inch cuttings of the current season's shoots in fall and sticking them in the ground, leaving two buds exposed. Currants form roots in one year; gooseberries can take as long as two years.

Currants and gooseberries bear fruit the year after planting, and production is heaviest on two- and three-year-old canes. Canes more than three years old can be removed after harvest. The canes darken as they grow older, a clue to their age. Let a few new canes develop each year as replacements. Little pruning is needed except to keep the bushes open and to remove the nonproductive overage canes.

Many people find currants too tart to eat fresh, but they make excellent jelly, jam, and fruit syrup. Gooseberries can be eaten fresh, in pies, or as preserves.

Sources and resources

Books and pamphlets

Clarke, J. Harold. *Growing Berries and Grapes at Home*. New York: Dover, 1976.

Ferguson, Barbara J. *All About Growing Fruits and Berries*. San Francisco: Ortho Books, 1982.

Hedrick, U. P. *Fruits for the Home Garden*. New York: Dover, 1973.

Hessayon, D.G. *The Fruit Expert*. New York: Sterling Publishing, 1995.

Hill, Lewis. *Fruits and Berries for the Home Garden*. Pownal, Vt.: Storey Communications, 1992.

Kains, Maurice G. *Five Acres and Independence*. New York: Dover, 1973.

Seymour, John. *The Self-Sufficient Gardener: A Complete Guide to Growing and Preserving All Your Own Food*. Garden City, N.Y.: Doubleday, 1979.

Smith, Miranda. *Backyard Fruits and Berries*. Emmaus, Pa.: Rodale Press, 1994.

Van Atta, Marian, and Wagner, Shirley. *Growing Family Fruit and Nut Trees*. Sarasota, Fla.: Pineapple Press, 1993.

Stock for planting, including old varieties

Stark Bros. Louisiana, Mo. 63353.

Worcester County Horticultural Society, 30 Elm St., Worcester, Mass. 01608 (Scions for planting).

Pest Control

Protecting Your Crops Without Poisoning Them

Gardens and orchards are threatened by three enemies: disease, insects, and animals. During the last few decades the standard defense against most of these pests has been massive doses of man-made poisons. For large-scale farmers there may be no practical alternative, but the home gardener has an arsenal of nonchemical and organic methods from which to choose.

Some are as simple as picking pests off plants by hand or employing basic preventive hygiene to keep them from breeding; others are as sophisticated as electronic traps that lure insects, then electrocute them. Some strategies enlist the aid of nature herself to fight pests by encouraging natural predators or cultivating pest-repellent plants near valued crops. Fences bar the larger animals, while traps and barriers defend against a variety of insects and small animals. As a last resort there are organic sprays and dusts—naturally occurring insecticides usually derived from plants.

The underlying theme of natural pest control is the recognition that a garden or orchard is part of an ecological whole and that the entire system must be in balance for the garden or orchard to be healthy. Those who practice ecological gardening do not try to eliminate pests completely, since in so doing they will eliminate the food supply of many beneficial organisms. Instead, the aim of organic pest control is to keep the number of pests low enough so that they do not do serious damage, while at the same time maintaining the predator population that feeds on the pests.

Nonchemical controls entail more time and labor than chemical methods, and the nonchemical gardener must be prepared to lose some crops to "bugs." But an increasing number of people find this a price worth paying.

A Rogue's Gallery of Common Insect Pests

Aphids are probably the most common garden pests. They suck sap from leaves and stems, weakening plants. They also spread virus and fungal diseases.

Spotted or Striped cucumber beetles feed on every part of cucumber plants, including the roots, and spread bacterial wilt. They also attack squash, melons, beans, peas, and corn.

Codling moth larvae are serious pests to apples. They tunnel their way into the hearts of young fruits, emerging on the far side and leaving worm holes behind.

Colorado potato beetles attack potatoes, eggplant, tomatoes, and peppers. The adults and larvae both devour foliage and may kill entire plants if unchecked.

June beetles (also called May beetles in some locations) can cause extensive damage to the roots of lawns and shrubs.

Japanese beetles feed on leaves of fruit and shade trees and also destroy much fruit directly. The larvae, which feed on the roots of grass, are major lawn pests.

Plant louses feed on plant juices and can damage both indoor and outdoor plants.

Using Natural Controls

One of the easiest ways to combat pests is to protect and encourage such natural allies as birds, toads, spiders, nonpoisonous snakes, and insects that feed on other insects. In many cases this simply involves no more than tolerating the predator (such as a snake or spider) instead of killing it or destroying its habitat. With a little more effort you can provide suitable habitats for insect destroyers; for example, an inverted flower pot for toads or a special birdhouse for purple martins (see *Living With Nature*, p.445). Another solution is to stock your garden or orchard with beneficial insects. Ladybug and praying mantis eggs are sold by many garden supply houses; both insects prey on a variety of common pests. Another natural predator is the trichogramma wasp, which lays its eggs inside the eggs of many species of caterpillar. The wasp larvae feed on caterpillar eggs, destroying them.

The introduction of specific insect diseases is a proven biological method of pest control. Milky spore disease, available as a white powder, can be dusted on the soil to infect and kill the larvae of the Japanese beetle. Bacillus thuringiensis—BT for short—is a bacterium that infects many destructive caterpillars, including the cabbage worm and gypsy moth. It is applied as a spray and has an effective life of seven days. Both milky spore and BT are harmless to humans, domestic animals, and such beneficial insects as honeybees.

More sophisticated biological controls have been developed, although as yet they are practical for large-scale use only and are therefore beyond the scope of the home gardener. One such method is the rearing and release of huge numbers of sterile male insects. By competing with normal males in mating, these sterile insects reduce the number of offspring. Another technique is to spray caterpillars with juvenile hormones; the caterpillars never mature to have young, cutting down tremendously on the size of the next generation.

So-called trap crops take advantage of the food preferences of various insect pests by luring them away from more valuable crops. For example, nasturtiums lure aphids away from nearby vegetables, while Japanese beetles are attracted to white geraniums, white or pastel zinnias, and odorless marigolds. Radishes lure root maggots away from cabbage crops, eggplants draw flea beetles away from potato plantings, dill attracts tomato hornworms, and mustard greens are a good trap crop for harlequin bugs. Pests concentrated on the trap crop can be picked off by hand and destroyed, but this must be done regularly or the trap crop will not be effective. Kill the pests by dropping them into kerosene or into water that has a thin layer of kerosene on it.

Garden spider

Purple martin

Toad

Parasitic wasp

Lacewing fly

Parasitic wasp cocoons on tomato hornworm

Lacewing fly larva

Black snake

Ladybug larva

Ladybug

Praying mantis

Natural predators are one of the gardener's most powerful weapons for fighting pests; moreover, they require no care and need only be left alone to do their work. Some of the more commonly found predators that feed on insect pests are shown above. All are harmless to humans and should be encouraged in your garden, berry patch, or orchard.

Preventive measures stop trouble before it starts

Gardens, like human beings, can be kept healthy and productive more cheaply and more easily with an ounce of prevention than with a pound of cure.

Prevention begins with the soil. Till your garden in the autumn as well as spring to expose subsoil insects and larvae to predators and the weather. Since well-nourished plants have greater resistance than poorly nourished ones, keep the soil's organic content high. Compost, organic mulches, and well-rotted manure are excellent additives.

Sanitation is a simple but effective preventive technique, useful against both disease microorganisms and insect pests. Locate your garden in a spot with good drainage and air flow; quick drying discourages fungi. Disease organisms can be kept from spreading from sick plants to healthy ones by removing all sick plants from the garden, the orchard, and the surrounding area. The diseased material should be burned or buried—do not use it for compost. Branches and canes pruned from fruit trees, bushes, and vines should be disposed of in the same way. If they are left on the ground near plants, they can act as breeding grounds for boring insects and fungus disease. Fallen fruit should be picked up twice a week and buried or fed to livestock. Vegetable plants should be removed from the garden at the end of the growing season. They can safely be composted in a fast-acting compost pile (see *The Kitchen Garden*, p.132).

Crop rotation is an effective measure, especially against soil-borne disease. By shifting a crop to a new area yearly, pathogens and pests that may have developed the previous year are deprived of their host. In a small garden it may be difficult to rotate crops, but the same effect can be gained by changing the type of vegetables planted. For example, if squash is grown one summer, plant a member of a different family the next. If you are fond of a certain vegetable, plant different varieties each year and concentrate on pest-resistant strains.

Do-it-yourself Defenses For Foiling the Enemy

Repellents are often effective in deterring pests, thereby protecting crops without having to resort to poisons. Many gardeners report success with homemade sprays based on hot peppers, onions, and garlic. As with poison sprays, add a few drops of liquid detergent or 1/3 cup of soap flakes per gallon of spray to increase the spray's sticking power and effectiveness. Another type of repellent spray is made by liquifying the pests in a blender. It is said to be effective on slugs, snails, and insects, but each liquified pest repels its own species only.

Some plants are natural repellents. Mints and other aromatic herbs interplanted with vegetables discourage a number of insects, especially those that attack the cabbage family. Radishes have been successful in repelling pests of melons and other vine crops. Garlic is one of the most potent repellent plants and will protect nearby fruit plantings from Japanese beetles and aphids. If planted around fruit trees, it is said to keep borers away. (For more information on companion planting, see *The Kitchen Garden*, p.126.)

Tar paper repels cutworms by its odor. Use 3-inch squares of tar paper laid on the ground, with holes in the centers for the stems to pass through, to protect seedlings from these pests. Aluminum foil laid on the ground has been found to be effective against aphids and squash-vine borers. Plants also appear to benefit from the extra reflected light. A simple way to remove aphids from foliage is to knock them off with a jet of water from the garden hose; few return to the plants.

There are a number of botanical poisons—natural chemicals produced by plants for their own protection— that are deadly to many insects but virtually harmless to humans and other warm-blooded animals. These substances break down into harmless by-products soon after use. The best known are ryania, rotenone, and pyrethrum. Nicotine, another powerful natural insecticide, is very dangerous to humans, animals, and bees.

Diatomaceous earth is a different sort of pesticide, working mechanically rather than chemically. It is sold as a fine dust made up of the skeletons of tiny one-celled sea organisms. The dust particles have sharp spikes that pierce the skins of such soft-bodied insects as aphids, causing them to die of dehydration.

Harmless pest killers can be made from a number of common household substances. A safe old-time remedy for cabbage worms is to sprinkle flour on the developing cabbage heads. The worms ingest the flour, which swells up inside them and bursts their intestines. Finely powdered sugar sprinkled on the plants can kill cabbage worms by dehydration. Salt sprinkled on slugs causes them to exude masses of orange slime and die. Insect eggs on the bark of trees can be smothered by painting the bark with a mixture of old cooking oil and soapy water during the dormant season—a homemade variation on the standard dormant spray. A good dormant spray can also be made by adding one part superior oil (sold in garden stores) to 15 parts water. No detergent is needed to emulsify superior oil. (Vegetable oil can be used instead, but it needs an emulsifier.)

Countering the common insect pests

Pest	Control
Aphid	Spray with dilute solution of clay or quassia extract; soapy water is also effective, but be sure to rinse off plants immediately after application (kills)
Cabbage worm, imported	Apply sour milk in the center of the cabbage head (repels). Or dust with a mixture of 1/2 cup salt to 1 cup flour (kills)
Codling moth	Spray with ryania, fish oil, or soapy water (kills)
Colorado potato beetle	Dust plants with wheat bran while they are wet (kills). Or pick off by hand
Corn earworm	Apply mineral oil to the silk just inside the tip of each ear—use a medicine dropper or small oil can (repels)
Flea beetle	Dust with soot mixed with slaked lime or wood ashes (repels). Or spray with rotenone (kills)
Harlequin bug	Spray with pyrethrum (kills)
Mexican bean beetle	Spray with garlic or cedar extract (repels)
Tarnished plant bug	Dust with sabadilla, an organic insecticide (kills)
Thrips	Spray with rotenone, oil-water mixture, or tobacco extract (kills)

Formulas You Can Make at Home

Homemade pesticides and repellents tend to be safer than synthetic substances in terms of undesirable side effects. Nevertheless, they should be treated with respect. Wash fruits and vegetables before eating them, and use the sprays as sparingly as possible to avoid unnecessary ecological damage.

Biodynamic spray. Mix powdered clay and an organic insecticide such as rotenone with enough water to make a thin fluid. Spray on fruit trees in early spring before leaves appear to suffocate eggs of insect pests.

Buttermilk and flour spray. Mix 1/2 cup buttermilk and 4 cups wheat flour with 5 gallons of water; kills spider mites and other mites by suffocation.

Cedar extract. Boil 1/4 pound cedar chips or dust in 1 gallon of water for two hours; strain and dilute the liquid with three parts water; spray on plants to repel Mexican bean beetles and other troublesome beetles.

Garlic and hot pepper spray. Steep 1/2 teaspoon each of crushed garlic and crushed hot peppers in 1 gallon of water for 10 to 24 hours. Use full strength on woody plants; dilute 25 percent for annuals and vegetables. Spray repels many sucking and chewing insects.

Glue mixture. Dissolve 1/4 pound of fish or animal glue in 1 gallon of warm water. Spray trees and bushes to trap and kill aphids, spider mites, and scale insects. (It removes pests from trees when it flakes off on drying.)

Green soap spray. Mix 1 cup of green soap tincture with 3 gallons of water; kills nonfurry caterpillars on contact. Green soap is available in drugstores. Laundry soap can be used instead in the ratio of 1/2 cake of soap to 1 gallon of hot water. If used on nonwoody plants, rinse off with clear water immediately after applying.

Quassia spray. Boil 1/4 pound of quassia chips in 1 gallon of water for two hours, strain the liquid, and mix with three to five parts water. The spray poisons aphids and caterpillars but is harmless to ladybugs and bees.

Homemade organic sprays can also be made from infusions of larkspur seeds, rhubarb leaves, or tobacco. Such sprays are nonpersistent and are effective against a variety of insect pests—larkspur against aphids, thrips, and several species of chewing insects; rhubarb against aphids; tobacco against a wide assortment of soft-bodied insects. However, these preparations are highly poisonous to humans and animals. If you do use them, be sure to wash the produce thoroughly before eating it.

Traps and Barriers

Proper fencing and netting will protect fruits and vegetables against most of the larger animals, including deer, rabbits, raccoons, woodchucks, dogs, and birds. Raccoons can be a bother because of their ability to climb, but extra-high chicken wire or an electric fence line across the top will discourage them. Some simple yet effective barriers are shown at right.

Many of the smaller common garden pests can be caught in simple traps. A shallow pan filled with beer is deadly to slugs and snails: the odor of the beer lures the mollusks into the pan where they drown. Using flour to thicken the beer will increase its effectiveness.

Aphids are attracted by the color yellow. Fill a yellow plastic dishpan with a solution of soap and water and place it near infested plants. Other containers, such as a 5-gallon oil can, can be used; paint the inside bright yellow (the outside can be any color other than red, which repels aphids). Japanese beetles are also attracted by yellow. An effective Japanese beetle trap is a yellow container with a scent lure, such as geraniol or oil of anise. Another Japanese beetle trap consists of a glass jug containing an inch or two of a fermenting "soup" of water, sugar, and mashed fruit scraps. Japanese beetle traps should be placed well away from your plants, since they attract beetles from a wide area.

Codling moths, apple maggot flies, and many other flying orchard pests can be trapped in empty tin cans or glass jars filled with a mixture of one part molasses and 1 1/2 parts water, plus a little yeast. Hang the traps in the fruit trees when the moths or flies appear. To catch earwigs, use rolled-up newspapers or hollow bamboo tubes. The insects will seek shelter in the tubes toward evening. Shake them out into kerosene each morning.

Caterpillars can be trapped by smearing bands of Tanglefoot, a sticky commercial preparation, around the trunks of fruit and other trees. Experimenters have also found that destructive flying insects can be trapped on colored spheres 3 to 6 inches in diameter, hung from the trees and coated with Tanglefoot or homemade flypaper stickum (see *Household Recipes*, p.343). Construct the spheres of any lightweight material, such as small gourds or styrofoam, and paint them orange, dark red, or black.

The tomato hornworm and other destructive caterpillars, such as the armyworm, cutworm, peach borer, and corn earworm, are actually larvae. The moths are easily caught at night in traps that use an ultraviolet bulb to lure the moths into a container. Another version of this type of trap has an electric grid around the bulb that kills the insects on contact. Check such traps regularly; if too many beneficial insects are being caught, discontinue their use.

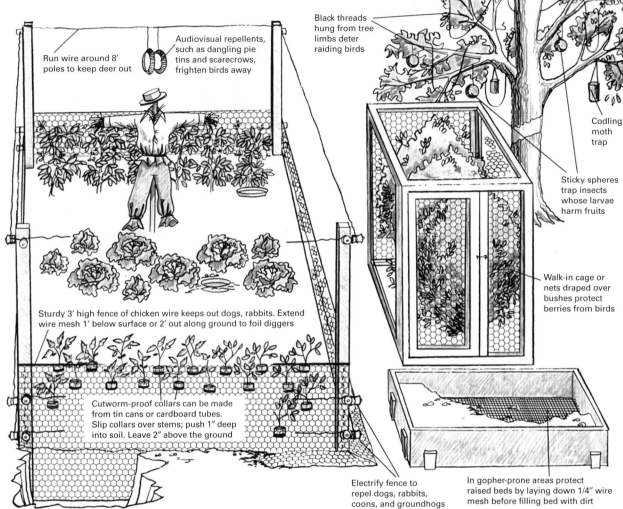

Run wire around 8' poles to keep deer out

Audiovisual repellents, such as dangling pie tins and scarecrows, frighten birds away

Black threads hung from tree limbs deter raiding birds

Codling moth trap

Sticky spheres trap insects whose larvae harm fruits

Sturdy 3' high fence of chicken wire keeps out dogs, rabbits. Extend wire mesh 1' below surface or 2' out along ground to foil diggers

Walk-in cage or nets draped over bushes protect berries from birds

Cutworm-proof collars can be made from tin cans or cardboard tubes. Slip collars over stems; push 1" deep into soil. Leave 2" above the ground

Electrify fence to repel dogs, rabbits, coons, and groundhogs

In gopher-prone areas protect raised beds by laying down 1/4" wire mesh before filling bed with dirt

Fencing, barriers, and traps prevent pests from reaching valuable crops. Fencing can be costly but is long-lasting and relatively trouble free if set up properly. Many traps can be made at home from scrap materials. All avoid the use of harmful chemicals.

Sources and resources

Books and pamphlets
DeBach, Paul. *Biological Control of Natural Enemies.* New York: Cambridge University Press, 1974.
Pleasant, Barbara. *The Gardener's Bug Book: Earth Safe Insect Control.* Pownal, Vt.: Storey Communications, 1994.
Yepsen, Roger B., Jr. *The Encyclopedia of Natural Insect and Disease Control.* Emmaus, Pa.: Rodale Press, 1984.

Sources of natural controls
Fairfax Biological Laboratory. Clinton Corners, N.Y. 12514 (milky spore disease).
Mellinger's, Inc. 2310 W. South Range Rd., North Lima, Ohio 44452.
Natural Pest Controls. Lexington Way, Sacramento, Calif. 95815.

Grains and Grasses

Raising Food and Forage For the Small Place

Grains and grasses were staples of the old-time self-sufficient farm. Grasses, in the form of hay or fresh pasturage, supplied the bulk of the diet for the farm animals. Grains provided flour for homemade bread, supplementary feed for the livestock, and raw materials for everyday needs. An acre of corn can fill a year's grain requirements for a pig, a milk cow, a beef steer, and 30 laying hens. Still another use for pasture plants and grains is green manure—crops that are raised for the purpose of being turned under the soil to improve it.

Raising grain or grass does not require large acreage or costly machinery. Indeed, if you can grow a lawn, you can raise grains and grasses as crops. A plot of land only 20 by 55 feet can supply all the wheat an average family of four will need in a year. The crop can be harvested, threshed, and winnowed with hand tools and ground into flour in a tabletop mill.

Like any other crop, grains and grasses require soil preparation, fertilization, and attention. However, they require much less care than a good-sized vegetable garden.

Grains are the seeds of certain members of the grass family, such as wheat, corn, and rye, that are used for food and animal feed. Buckwheat is also considered a grain, although the plant is not a grass but a member of the knotweed family.

Corn and wheat are the two most widely grown grains in the United States, accounting for hundreds of thousands of acres and millions of bushels. The major use of wheat is for flour; the major use of corn is for animal feed. Both also have many industrial applications. The other grains have more specialized uses, but all are nutritious, high yielding, and good for small-scale farming.

Planting rates

Type of grain	Amount of seed per acre	Land area needed to grow 1 bushel
Wheat	75–90 lb.	10' × 109'
Oats	80 lb.	10' × 62'
Field corn	6–8 lb.	10' × 50'
Barley	100 lb.	10' × 87'
Rye	84 lb.	10' × 145'
Buckwheat	50 lb.	10' × 130'
Grain sorghum	2–8 lb.	10' × 60'

Note: These figures are estimates; actual yields may be affected by weather, soil, and variety of seed

Sowing the Cereal Grains

The most important food plants in the world are the cereal grains. Whether eaten directly, processed into bread, or used as animal feed, they provide the basic nutritional needs of almost every man, woman, and child on the face of the earth. North America is particularly suitable for growing grain. Almost every one of the major grains flourishes over vast regions. The sole exception is rice, a crop whose cultivation is restricted to the Deep South and southern California.

Wheat, barley, and other hardy grains can be grown as either spring or winter crops. Winter crops are sown in early fall, grow a little, and then go dormant during the cold months. When spring returns, they shoot up and are ready to harvest in midsummer.

Spring crops are usually grown where winters are too severe for fall-sown grains. They are sown about the time of the last killing spring frost and are ready for harvest in early fall. In general, the winter crops yield more heavily. There are separate varieties for spring and fall sowing. Spring wheat will not survive the winter if planted in fall; winter wheat may not have time to mature before autumn frost kills it if it is planted in spring, especially if the growing season is short.

Most grains do best on well-tilled soil of average fertility—too much nitrogen makes them grow overly lush and topple over. Corn, however, needs highly fertile soil. Before planting, the soil should be plowed and disked or rototilled and lime and fertilizer added as needed. The seeds can be broadcast (flung out) by hand or with a hand-cranked seeder, as in planting a lawn. To ensure even coverage, go up and down the plot lengthwise as you sow; then go over it again at right angles to your first direction. After sowing, till or rake the soil to work the seeds in. If the plot is large, sow the grain with a drill, a mechanical device that spaces out the seeds in straight rows at precise depths. Except for field corn and sorghum, grains need virtually no care until harvest time. Corn and sorghum should be planted in widely spaced rows so that they can be cultivated while small.

To prevent soil depletion and the buildup of pests and pathogens, grain crops should be raised as part of a rotation system with other crops. Your county agent can advise you on the best rotation plan for your area. A typical plan might be corn the first year, followed by alfalfa, winter wheat, vegetables or soybeans, and pasture in succeeding years.

The Major Grains

Wheat, the world's leading bread grain, requires a cool, moist growing season and about two months of hot, dry weather for ripening. Wheat grows 3 to 4 feet tall and turns golden brown when ripe. It is ready to harvest when the grain is hard and crunchy between the teeth.

Wheat can be sown in fall or spring. Winter wheat should not be sown before mid-September: it may grow too much before cold weather arrives and be killed by freezing as a result. Early planting also exposes winter wheat to attack by the destructive Hessian fly.

Five kinds of wheat are commonly grown in the United States and Canada. They are hard red winter wheat, used for bread; soft red winter wheat, used in cakes and pastries; hard red spring wheat, the best for bread; white wheat, used mainly for pastry flour; and durum wheat, used for spaghetti. Wheat supplies the best-balanced nutrition of all the grains.

Oats are the highest in protein of all grains. They are a hardy crop that thrives in a cool, moist climate and cannot tolerate drought. Oats are sown as a spring crop except where winters are mild. A mature oat plant stands 2 to 5 feet tall. Oats can be harvested while they still have a few green tinges. They should be gathered into shocks and left to dry in the field.

Rye, once a major bread crop, is now grown mainly for stock feed and whiskey. It is also much used for green manure and as a cover crop. Rye grows 3 to 5 feet tall and is almost always sown in fall. Although its per-acre yield is less than that of wheat, it can produce crops on poorer soil than wheat and tolerates cold, drought, and dampness better. Most rye bread contains at least 50 percent wheat flour. Old-timers often mixed rye and corn flour to make a bread called Rye-and-Injun.

Buckwheat is raised for its nutlike, triangular seeds. Its dark, strong-flavored flour is excellent for pancakes. Buckwheat grows about 3 feet high; it prefers moist, acid soil and hot weather. Because it matures rapidly (60 to 90 days), buckwheat is often used as a second crop after winter wheat or early vegetables.

Barley does best with a long, cool ripening season and moderate moisture but adapts well to heat and aridity. It also tolerates salty and alkaline soils better than most grains. In warm regions barley is usually planted as a fall crop; in colder areas it is planted in early spring. Barley is used for animal feed, beer, and malt. It is also used in soup and as a whole-grain dish.

Sorghum resembles corn but with narrower leaves and no ears. There are four types of sorghum: grain, sweet, grass, and broomcorn. Grain sorghum grows to about 4 feet tall, and its seeds are used mainly for animal feed. They also make nutritious porridge and pancakes. Sweet sorghum is raised for syrup and silage, grass sorghum finds use as pasturage and hay, and broomcorn is valued for the long, springy bristles of its seed heads, used in making brooms. Sorghum tolerates heat and drought well. Plant it about 10 days after corn.

Corn: America's unique contribution is an Indian discovery

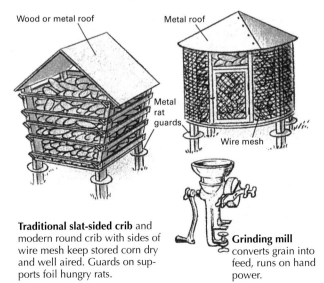

Traditional slat-sided crib and modern round crib with sides of wire mesh keep stored corn dry and well aired. Guards on supports foil hungry rats.

Wood or metal roof

Metal roof

Metal rat guards

Wire mesh

Grinding mill converts grain into feed, runs on hand power.

Corn, first domesticated by American Indians thousands of years ago, leads all other grains in the United States in acreage and harvest.

Corn raised for grain is not sweet; it is called field corn to distinguish it from the sweet corn we raise as a vegetable. Field corn is used for animal feed, cornstarch, hominy, grits, and a variety of breakfast cereals and snack foods. A limited amount is used for corn bread. Field corn is taller and yields more heavily than sweet corn but is planted and cultivated in the same way. It can be harvested easily after the plants are dead and dry by snapping the ears off the stalks. The ears of corn should be taken under shelter as soon as possible to protect them from rain and mold. The corn should be husked before storing.

Corn can be fed to animals while still on the ear, but for most purposes it should be shelled—that is, the kernels should be removed from the cob. Shelling can be done by rubbing an ear of corn briskly between your hands, or you can buy a hand-powered sheller.

From Field to Flour

Harvesting is the same for all grains other than corn. After the grain has been cut, gather the stalks into sheaves and stack them to dry in the field until no trace of green is left. To thresh the grain, lay the sheaves on an old sheet on a hard surface and hit the seed heads with a flail, broomstick, or baseball bat to knock the seeds loose. To separate the grain from the chaff, or loose husks, toss it in a sheet outdoors on a breezy day, or pour grain and chaff back and forth from one container to another. On a calm day a fan can supply the air current.

Store grain in covered metal trash can or a wooden bin that has been rat proofed with wire mesh. Stored grain must be kept thoroughly dry to prevent mold. Grain can be ground in a small mill designed for home use (some are equipped with revolving stones that duplicate the old-time stone-ground flour). Small batches can be run through a heavy-duty food blender.

1. Make a sheaf by tying an armful of grain stalks into a bundle. Use twine or twist grain stems into a cord.

2. Stack sheaves together to make a shock. Leave them outdoors to dry in the sun. Do not store damp grain.

Flail

Chaff

Grain seeds

3. Thresh the grain to separate the kernels. A simple flail can be made of two sticks joined loosely.

4. Final step is winnowing threshed grain by using the wind to blow away chaff and other small particles.

173

Grassland Management For Hay and Pasture

If you have a horse, a cow, or other livestock and an acre or two of unused land, an excellent way to put that land to work is by planting it to grass. In addition to providing essential pasturage and hay for the animals, grass protects the soil from erosion and furnishes a habitat for a myriad of small creatures.

Managing a grassland is like managing a small ecosystem. The trick is to keep various plant species—not just grasses but also such legumes as clover and alfalfa—in balance so as to provide a nutritious diet for livestock while at the same time maintaining or increasing the fertility of the soil. By regulating the intensity of grazing, by mowing, and by minor adjustments of the soil's mineral content, the landowner can favor the growth of one plant species or another and keep many troublesome weeds under control without resorting to chemicals.

Grasslands fit well into crop rotations, and for maximum production you may wish to establish a grassland on a cultivated field. Such rotation also prevents the buildup of pests and pathogens by depriving them of hosts. You may also decide to put steep, uneven, or rocky land into permanent grassland. The only prerequisites are sunlight for at least half the daylight hours and sufficient moisture. In areas of low rainfall moisture can be supplied by irrigation or sprinklers.

To establish a pasture on cultivated land, plow and harrow the soil and lime it, if needed, to bring the pH to between 6 and 7 (slightly acid). Till in manure, compost, or an all-purpose chemical fertilizer. The seed can be broadcast or planted in very close rows using a seed drill. For hay you may wish to plant only one crop, such as alfalfa or timothy. For pasture a mixture is preferable, since livestock suffer from bloat on a pure diet of fresh legumes. Consult your county agent for the best combination of forage plants. A mixed pasture is ecologically sound. A variety of plants lessens their vulnerability to pests and disease, and the legumes supply nitrogen, which the grasses need for good growth.

Do not let livestock graze in a pasture until the plants are well established and about a foot tall. This gives them time to build up food reserves in their root systems. Repeated grazing closer than 3 or 4 inches depletes the food reserves of the forage plants, so they grow back poorly. Eventually they die off, leaving the land open to invasion by weeds and brush. However, properly controlled grazing and mowing help keep weeds and brush under control.

To renovate an old or run-down pasture, plow it up thoroughly, apply lime and fertilizer, and reseed the land with desirable varieties. Grasses will often come back vigorously from their roots in the soil, so little reseeding may be required. Legumes, however, must usually be reseeded, sometimes every year. If the old pastureland is overgrown, as it often is, grub out brush and young trees or keep them mowed close to the ground. Eventually they will be starved out.

Legumes: green nitrogen factories

Legumes add nitrogen to the soil in which they grow by means of symbiotic bacteria that form nodules on their roots. These bacteria convert nitrogen from the air into forms that plants can use. However, each type of legume needs a different strain of bacteria, and the proper type may not be in the soil when the legume is planted. Legumes will grow without their bacteria, but they then take nitrogen from the soil instead of adding it. To ensure success, inoculate the soil with the proper bacteria, obtainable at most garden supply stores.

When scything, cut with a rhythmic, sweeping motion of the upper body. Stand with your feet well apart for balance. Keep the scythe blade sharp, and wear heavy work boots for greater safety.

Let hay dry partially on the ground after cutting; then rake it into long piles, or windrows, to complete drying in the open air. Windrows should be 6 to 12 in. high and loosely heaped so that air can circulate freely. Turn the windrows over periodically.

Grasses

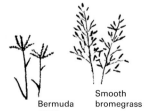
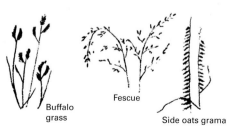

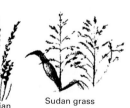

Bermuda grass   Smooth bromegrass   Buffalo grass   Fescue   Side oats grama   Kentucky bluegrass   Orchard grass   Redtop   Italian ryegrass   Sudan grass   Timothy   Wheatgrass

Hay and Haymaking

Although the terms "hay" and "straw" are often confused, the two are actually quite different. Hay is made from grass, legumes, or other forage plants that have been cut while young and tender and cured by drying. Straw consists of the stalks of grain after threshing or the dried stalks and stems of other farm crops. Hay is palatable, nutritious livestock feed; straw is useful as bedding but contains little food value. Legume hay is an excellent source of protein for livestock; clover and alfalfa are leading legume hay crops.

Whether made from grasses or legumes, the best hay comes from plants that are cut in the early blooming stage: at this point they have their highest nutritive value. If allowed to set seed before cutting, the plants become tough, dry, and woody, like straw. Hay can also be made from immature oats and other grains, which should be cut while the kernels are soft and milky.

It is important to cut your hay on a clear day so that the hay can dry on the ground in the sun's heat. After drying for a day or two, rake the cut hay into long parallel rows. These rows, known as windrows, should be turned over periodically with a pitchfork or by machine to expose all the hay to sun and air. The hay is ready to store when its moisture content is down to 15 percent. A simple way to judge its readiness is to pick up a handful of stems and then bend them in a U shape. If they break fairly easily, they are ready for storing. If they are pliable and take a lot of twisting to break, the hay is still too damp. If the stems are so brittle that they snap off easily, the hay is too dry—safe to store but with much nutritional value lost. Hay that is too dry is also subject to leaf shattering—the leaves, which are the most nutritious portions of the plants, break off and are lost.

Good hay often has a tinge of green even though thoroughly dry. (Alfalfa hay should be bright green.) Hay can be stored loose or in bales. In either case it should be protected from the weather. Wet hay may rot into good compost, but it makes bad feed. It can go moldy and may then poison the animals to which it is fed; in extreme cases it will ferment, and the heat produced will start a fire. If you have no barn or shed, a tarpaulin over the hay will provide a fair degree of protection from the effects of rain and snow.

Sources and resources

Books and pamphlets
Elkins, Donald M. and Darrel S. Metcalf. *Crop Production: Principles and Practices.* New York: Macmillan, 1980.
Nation, Allan. *Grass Farmers.* Jackson, Miss.: Green Park, 1993.
Willis, Harold L. *How to Grow Great Alfalfa . . . & Other Forages.* Wisconsin Dells, Wis.: H. L. Willis, 1993.

Selected forage crops

Variety	What you need to know
Alfalfa	Perennial legume; the leading hay crop in all sections but the Southeast. Grows 2'–3' tall; deep roots (8'–30') tap moisture in subsoil and make plant drought resistant. Tolerates alkali; fails on acid soils. Very rich in protein; raised chiefly for hay but also used in pasture together with grass
Bermuda grass	Perennial grass; grows best in Southeast. Forms sod. Primarily a pasture grass, though some strains grow tall enough to cut for hay; a good companion for legumes. Tolerates heat well
Bromegrass, smooth	Vigorous perennial grass; 3'–4' tall. Forms dense sod. Thrives in Corn Belt and Pacific Northwest; under irrigation on Great Plains. Used for pasture, hay, erosion control. Withstands drought, extreme temperatures
Buffalo grass	Low-growing perennial native to Great Plains; forms dense, matted turf 2"–4" tall. Noted for tolerance of drought, heat, cold, alkaline soil. Withstands heavy grazing
Bur clover	Annual legume related to alfalfa. Used for winter pasture; needs mild, moist winters
Clover	Important genus of legumes; five species predominate in United States: red, white, alsike, ladino (giant white), crimson. Height ranges from a few inches to 3'. May behave as annuals, biennials, or perennials depending on climatic variations and soil. Used for hay, pasture, silage, green manure
Fescue, tall	Perennial grass can be grown in most parts of United States; important in Southeast and Pacific Northwest. Used for pasture and hay; grows 3'–4' tall; very tolerant of wet soils
Grama grass	Perennial grass; native to Great Plains. Several species; height ranges from 2"–3". Primarily used for pasture
Kentucky bluegrass	Perennial grass; grows in most of United States except Southwest and at extreme elevations. From 12"–30" tall; best suited to permanent pasture. Leading pasture grass of Canada and United States
Lespedeza	A cloverlike legume. Two annual species important in United States. Height from 4"–2". Most important in southern Corn Belt and South. Used chiefly for pasture; in South grows tall enough for hay also
Orchard grass	Perennial grass; vigorous, long-lived. Tolerates shade and wide range of soil types; likes moisture. Forms bunches 2'–4' tall; used for hay and permanent pasture
Redtop	Perennial grass; tolerates heat, cold, acid, and run-down soils. Grows up to 3' tall. Used for hay and pasture; often sown with timothy
Ryegrass, Italian	Fast-growing annual, 2'–3' tall. Used for winter pasture in South; hay and pasture in Pacific Northwest. Excellent poultry pasture
Sudan grass	A grasslike sorghum; annual; reaches 3'–8' in height. Tolerates heat, drought. Used primarily for pasture and fresh chopped feed; also makes excellent hay. Most important in South but grows as far north as Michigan
Timothy	One of the oldest cultivated grasses; perennial. Thrives in cool, moist climate. Grows in bunches 20"–40" tall. Primarily used for hay, especially for horses
Trefoil, bird's-foot	Hardy perennial legume. Tolerates damp, acid, and infertile soils. Raised from Vermont to eastern Kansas, also Pacific Northwest. Grows 20"–40" tall; used for pasture and hay
Wheatgrass	Perennial grass; five important species, some native to West. Grows 2'–4' tall. Some types form sod; others are bunch grasses. Important in dry lands of West; used for hay and pasture

Legumes

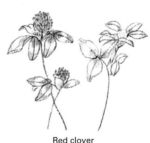

Alfalfa   Bur clover   Red clover   Lespedeza   Bird's-foot trefoil

Beekeeping

One Small Hive Can Keep You in Honey All Year Round

Few projects yield so much satisfaction in return for such a small investment in money and labor as beekeeping. Once the bees are established, a single hive can easily produce 30 pounds or more of delicious honey each year—enough to supply the needs of the average family of four or five plus plenty to give away or even sell. In return, bees need only minimal attention and a little feeding to carry them through the winter.

Bees gather food from an astonishing variety of plants. Wild flowers, fruit blossoms, shrubs, trees—even weeds—are sources of the nectar that the bees convert to fragrant honey and of the pollen that supplies their vital protein needs. Bees also perform the valuable service of pollinating many plants. So efficient are they that commercial fruit growers often import bees to pollinate their orchards.

Beekeeping in America dates back to the early colonial period when British settlers first brought honeybees to the Colonies (they are not native to the New World). Some swarms escaped and established themselves in the wild; these free-living bees spread slowly westward to the edge of the Great Plains, where the lack of hollow trees for nesting stopped them. It was not until the 19th century that bees reached the Far West, carried there in the wagons of homesteaders.

In colonial times, and long afterward, bees were kept in hives of straw, called skeps, or in hollow logs. Lacking scientific knowledge, beekeepers often found their hives wiped out by disease. Honey yields were often low. However, thanks to a series of advances since the 1850s, beekeeping today is a scientifically based, thoroughly up-to-date enterprise.

The Standard Hive

The beehive used by 90 percent of American beekeepers was developed in the early 1850s by Lorenzo L. Langstroth, a Philadelphia-born Congregational minister with a lifelong interest in bees.

Hives with removable frames in which bees could build combs already existed in Langstroth's time. However, the bees tended to fill up any space around the frames with combs and a sticky, gumlike substance known as propolis, or bee glue, which bees manufacture from plant resins. As a result, the frames became cemented in place and honey could be harvested only with considerable difficulty.

Langstroth's great contribution was the discovery that if the frames were separated from each other and from the sides of the hive by a gap of approximately 5/16 in.—just enough room for a single bee to pass through—the bees would leave the space free.

The discovery of this key dimension—Langstroth called it bee space—allowed him to design a hive with frames that almost never had to be cut free in order to remove them. Harvesting honey and inspecting the hives were enormously simplified.

The hive itself consists of open boxes called supers (a contraction of the word *superhive*) in which the frames are hung. When more room is needed for a growing bee population or for stores of honey, extra supers are stacked on top of those already in the hive.

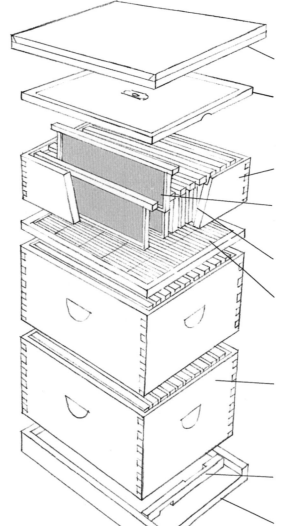

Outer cover, metal-sheathed for durability, protects hive from rain snow, and hailstones.

Inner cover has hole for ventilation.

Shallow super, usually employed for honey to be harvested, is lighter and easier to handle than a deep super (40 lb. versus 75 lb. when filled with honey).

Frames contain wax foundation sheets stamped with a honeycomb pattern to guide bees in building regular combs with uniform cells

Bee space, about 5/6 in., surrounds frames on all sides.

Queen excluder is a flat grille that prevents the queen from leaving her brood chamber to lay eggs in honey supers. Workers, being smaller, can pass freely through to all parts of the hive.

Brood and food chambers are deep supers in which the queen lays eggs to maintain and increase the hive's population. Food supplies for winter are also stored in these supers.

Entrance cleat, a movable wooden block with different-sized openings, allows entrance to be widened or narrowed.

Bottom board.

Early types of hives

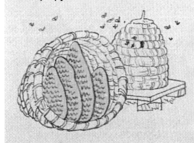

Straw skep is the traditional symbol of beekeeping. It is cheap and snug but unsanitary. The only way to remove honey from a skep is to kill the bees and cut the combs out.

Early settlers frequently used bee gums—hollow sections of the gum tree or tupelo—to hive their bees. Bears often raided these backwoods apiaries to feast on bee larvae and honey.

Choosing a Site for Your Hive

The right location will get your colony off to a good start and help ensure a productive future. One of the first things to look for is good drainage—dampness leads to disease and encourages the growth of mold. Ideally, the hive should be set on a gentle slope so that rain and melting snow can drain off rapidly. Avoid hollows or low spots where water can collect. Raising the hive above the ground on bricks, cinder blocks, or other supports helps to combat dampness.

The site should be sheltered from wind. Bees are susceptible to cold, and even a mild breeze can chill them enough to reduce their efficiency as honey collectors. Severe cold can kill bees, and in winter a good windbreak may mean the difference between survival and death for an entire colony of honeybees.

Another important factor is adequate sunlight to warm the hive. (To maintain the hive's normal inside temperature of 93°F, bees must "burn" honey, thereby reducing the yield.) Experienced beekeepers orient the hive entrance toward the east or south to take advantage of the warming effect of the morning sun. Afternoon shade is also important—especially in the hotter sections of the country—since excessive heat can be as deadly to bees as excessive cold.

Be sure there is a good supply of forage plants (sources of nectar and pollen) before setting up a hive. Since bees can easily forage as far as two miles from the hive, this is seldom a problem except in densely built-up areas.

If neighbors live close by, screen the hive with a tall hedge or board fence. This protects the hive from molestation and forces bees to fly high above passersby.

Identifying the bee castes

Queen: About 1 in. long (larger than drones or workers) with a long, shiny abdomen. Queens leave the hive only during mating or swarming. They lay as many as 2,000 eggs a day and live as long as four years. Queens develop from larvae that are fed royal jelly by nurse bees.

Worker: A bit over 1/2 in. long with furry abdomen and long tongue for collecting nectar. Carries brightly colored pollen in "baskets" on hind legs. Workers make honey, build the comb, and tend larvae. They live one month during honey flow, three in winter.

Drone: About same length as a worker but with larger eyes and thicker body. Drones buzz lo dly but harmlessly: they have no stingers. The drone's only function is to mate with the queen; it dies in the act. Drones still alive in late autumn are turned out of the hive by the workers. Unable to feed themselves, they die.

Birth of a bee

New larva

Eight-day larva ready to spin cocoon is 160 times the size of new larva

Egg, larva, pupa: A bee begins life as an egg about as big as the dot on an *i*. In three days the egg hatches into a wormlike larva. At eight days the larva spins a cocoon and nurse bees seal the cell. Workers emerge after 21 days, queens after 16, drones after 24.

Tools and equipment

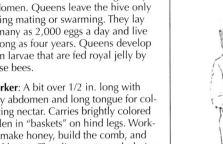

Hat and wire veil protect head, face, and neck, the body's most vulnerable parts.

White coveralls or light-colored clothing is recommended. (Dark colors irritate bees, making them likelier to sting.)

Loose-fitting gloves and stout boots protect hands and feet, which bees are apt to go for.

Smoker for quieting bees burns wood scraps (such as cedar pet litter) or rags.

Hive tool is used to pry hive open, loosen frames.

Uncapping knife is electrically heated, makes cutting easier by softening wax of comb.

Centrifugal extractor, hand or motor powered, removes honey without damaging combs.

Some favorite bee blossoms

Alfalfa
Light-colored honey with mild, delicate flavor. One of the major sources for commercial production.

Aster
White, minty honey; granulates readily. It is a major source of fall honey and pollen.

Basswood
Light, aromatic honey. Prolific nectar producer. Often mixed with other honeys for sale.

Clover
Light, delicate honey. Because of its abundance, clover is one of the leading sources of honey.

Dandelion
Important early spring source of nectar and pollen. Honey is yellow to amber, with strong flavor.

Goldenrod
Excellent fall source of pollen and nectar. Thick, golden honey mostly used as winter food for bees.

Orange and other citrus
One of the most popular honeys. Fragrant and mild. Often used for blending with other honeys.

Sage
Important in West. Light colored, mild in flavor. Most sage honey does not granulate.

Tupelo
Mild greenish-amber honey. Known for not granulating. A favorite in health-food stores.

Sources and resources

Books and pamphlets
Dadant, C.P. *First Lessons in Beekeeping*. New York: Scribner's, 1982.
Gojmerac, Walter L. *Bees, Beekeeping, Honey and Pollination*. Westport, Conn.: AVI Publishing, 1980.
Graham, Joe M., ed. *The Hive and the Honey Bee*. Hamilton, Ill.: Dadant & Sons, 1992.
Hubbell, Sue. *The Book of Bees and How to Keep Them*. New York: Random House, 1988.
Melzer, Werner. *Beekeeping: An Owner's Manual*. Hauppauge, N.Y.: Barron, 1989.
Morse, Roger, and Flottum, Kim, eds. *The ABC and XYZ of Bee Culture: An Encyclopedia of Beekeeping*. Medina, Ohio: A.I. Root, 1990.

Periodicals
American Bee Journal. Hamilton, Ill. 62341.
Bee Culture. P.O. Box 706, Medina, Ohio 44258.
The Speedy Bee. P.O. Box 998, Jesup, Ga. 31545.

How-to plans for hive and extractor
Garden Way Publishing, Charlotte, Vt. 05445.

Setting Up Shop As a Beekeeper

Start your colony in early spring so the bees can build up their numbers before the honey flow begins. Start on a small scale with one or two hives. Two hives have an advantage, since if one queen dies, the colonies can be combined. Of the various strains available, Italian bees are the best for beginners. They are gentle, good foragers, and disease resistant. Caucasian, Carniolan, and Midnite bees, also popular, tend to swarm and stray.

Major mail-order houses and bee-supply specialists offer complete beginners' kits, including bees, hive, tools, protective gloves and veil, and instructions. As the season progresses, you can purchase extra supers and frames. Bees need plenty of fresh water. A nearby stream or pond, a pan of water with a wooden float for the bees, or a slowly dripping hose will supply them.

Bees are shipped in packages with wire-screen sides, usually containing a mated queen, 2 1/2 pounds of bees (about 6,000 bees), and a can of syrup to feed them en route. The queen is in a small cage inside the package with several workers to tend her. The exit hole of the queen cage is usually closed with a plug of soft candy that the other bees will gnaw through to release her.

Check your bees on arrival to make sure that they are healthy and that the queen is alive. You should contact your county agent before ordering bees. He can advise you on diseases, parasites, pesticides, and regulations.

Once the bees have been installed, open the hive as little as possible; every one or two weeks is enough to check on your bees' welfare.

Bees sting only when they feel threatened. Nevertheless, it is important to wear protective gear. A hat and veil are basic; coveralls, gloves, and stout boots are recommended. However, many experienced beekeepers work without gloves for greater dexterity and because bee stingers left in gloves release a scent that stimulates other bees to sting. Move slowly and gently—violent or abrupt motions alarm bees. If you want to open the hive, quiet the bees first with your smoker.

When a worker bee stings, its barbed stinger becomes trapped in the skin and is torn loose when the bee escapes. (The bee later dies.) The venom sac remains attached to the stinger and continues to pump poison into the wound. Scrape off the stinger as quickly as possible with a fingernail or knife blade. Do not try to pull it out. You will only squeeze more venom into the wound. Ammonia or baking soda paste helps neutralize the venom. Most persons develop immunity after a few stings. However, those who have severe reactions should consult their physicians.

Swarming and How to Avoid It

Swarming occurs when the queen bee and a large number of workers abandon the hive to establish a new colony, leaving behind other workers, eggs and larvae, and a crop of contenders for the new queenship. In the wild, swarming spreads the bee population and prevents overcrowding the colony. For the beekeeper, however, it results in the loss of both bees and honey production.

By far the major cause of swarming is overcrowding although excessive heat, poor ventilation, or an over-anxious owner who opens the hive too frequently can also cause the bees to swarm.

One warning that bees are preparing to swarm is the near-cessation of flight in and out of the hive during honey season. The bees, instead of going out to gather nectar, remain in the crowded hive and gorge on stored honey in preparation for flight. Another sign is the presence of peanutlike cells on the brood combs, in which new queens are being reared.

A simple preventive measure is to give the bees more room. Add a shallow super early in spring and add extra supers as needed. Switching the two lowest supers every five to six weeks also helps. Bees tend to work upward; so by the time the upper chamber is filled with eggs and larvae, the lower chamber will be empty.

If you suspect the hive is overheating, rig a shade of boards or burlap. To improve ventilation, tilt the top cover up at one edge and remove the entrance cleat.

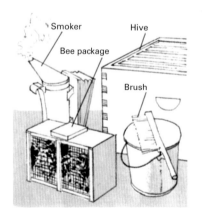

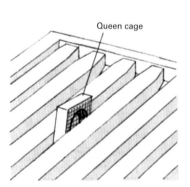

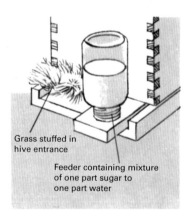

Smoker / Hive / Bee package / Brush

Queen cage

Several frames have been removed to make room for bees

Grass stuffed in hive entrance

Feeder containing mixture of one part sugar to one part water

1. The best time for hiving is late afternoon or early evening, when the bees are quietest and least likely to fly off. Place the package of bees near the hive, which you have assembled beforehand. Light the smoker and have a pail of syrup handy. Wear protective clothing for safety.

2. Lay the package on its side and brush or spatter some syrup on the wire mesh. The food will help to calm the bees and make them easier to handle. Repeat feeding until they stop eating. When they are full, rap the package on the ground to jar bees to bottom of package.

3. Pry cover off package with your hive tool; again jar bees to bottom. Remove queen cage and replace cover. Remove cover from candy plug and make a small hole in plug so that bees can gnaw through and release queen. Wedge queen cage between two frames in hive.

4. Knock bees down again and remove cover and syrup can from package. Pour half of bees over queen cage, the rest into empty space in hive. Place package on ground facing hive to let remaining bees make their way in. Replace all frames but one; replace it in a few days.

5. Place inner and outer covers on hive. Be careful not to crush any bees. A puff of smoke will send bees down between frames to safety. Fill feeder and place in position. Stuff entrance lightly with green grass to keep bees inside until they feel at home. Remove queen cage after a few days.

Harvesting Honey

An established hive will yield 30 to 60 pounds of honey a year. You will usually have to wait a year for your first harvest, however, since newly hived bees must build up the strength of the colony and rarely produce much honey beyond their own needs in their initial season.

Plants yield nectar in two main flows. The spring flow starts with the blossoming of dandelions and fruit trees and lasts into July in most parts of the country. The fall flow begins around September and ends when hard frost kills the last flowers. Honey can be extracted after each flow, but many amateur apiarists prefer to wait until the end of the fall flow.

One way to extract honey is to let it drip from an uncapped comb into a clean pan. Another is to crush the combs and squeeze the honey out through cheesecloth. However, bees must then build new combs, which takes time and honey (they consume 8 pounds of honey to make 1 pound of wax). Centrifugal extractors are widely available but expensive. One option is to build your own extractor (see *Sources and resources*, p.177).

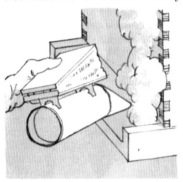

1. Choose a sunny, windless day for harvesting honey, since bees are calmest then. The first step is to drive the bees away from the honeycombs. Begin by blowing smoke through the hive entrance to quiet the bees. A few puffs are all that are needed; too much smoke may injure the bees.

2. Wait a few minutes for the smoke to take effect. Then pry the outer cover loose with your hive tool and lift it off. Blow more smoke in through the hole in the inner cover. Remove the inner cover and blow smoke across the tops of the frames to drive bees downward and out of the way.

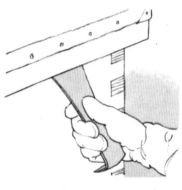

3. Instead of smoke, the bees can be cleared out with an escape board, which lets bees move down but not up. Using the hive tool, pry up the super you want to remove and slide the escape board beneath it. Install the board about 24 hours in advance to give the bees time to leave the super.

Bee escape

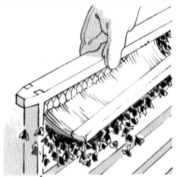

4. Remove the super and pry the frames loose with the hive tool. Be careful not to crush any bees (a crushed bee releases a scent that stimulates other bees to attack). Gently brush off bees that cling to the frames. A comb is ready to be harvested if it is 80 percent sealed over.

5. Uncap the combs in a bee-proof location, such as a tightly screened room. (If the bees can get at the honey, they may steal it.) Slice off the comb tops with a sharp knife warmed in hot water—a heavy kitchen knife is fine. It is best to use two knives, cutting with one while the other is heating.

6. If an extractor is available, place the frames of uncapped comb in it and turn it on. (If it is a manual model, turn the handle at moderate speed to avoid damaging the combs.) Return emptied combs to the hive for the bees to clean and use again. Combs can be recycled for 20 years or more.

Storing Honey

Newly extracted honey should be strained through cheesecloth to remove wax and other impurities. Let the strained honey stand several days so that air bubbles can rise to the top; then skim them off. To prevent fermentation and retard crystallization, heat the honey to 150°F before bottling it. To do this, place the honey container in a water bath on a stove. Check the temperature carefully with a candy thermometer, since overheating will spoil the flavor. Next, pour the honey into clean, dry containers with tight seals; mason jars or their equivalent are excellent. Store the honey in a warm, dry room (the ideal temperature is 80°F). If the honey crystallizes—a natural process—it can be liquified by heating in hot water and stirring occasionally.

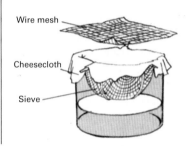

Wire mesh

Cheesecloth

Sieve

Double layer of damp cheesecloth in a wire sieve makes a good honey strainer. Use another sieve or a piece of window screen above strainer to catch larger bits of foreign matter, such as wax and dead bees.

Getting your hive ready for winter

The goal of winter management is to bring as many bees through the winter alive as possible. A good food supply is vital. Leave one deep super filled with honey and poller for the bees. (Bees need pollen as a protein source, and larvae will not develop without it.) Supplement with syrup; check feeder regularly. Bore a 1-in. hole in top super for ventilation—dampness can be fatal to bees. This will let out warm, moist air and provide an extra hive entrance.

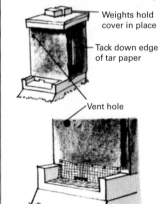

Weights hold cover in place

Tack down edge of tar paper

Vent hole

Wrap hive in a layer of tar paper to protect bees from sudden temperature changes. Fasten paper with tacks or staples. Leave vent hole and entrance open. Remove tar paper in spring.

Mice move into beehives in fall and nest in combs, destroying them. To keep mice out, bend 1/2-in. wire mesh into an L-shape, and tack or staple over hive entrance. Mesh lets bees pass but excludes mice.

Fish Farming

A King-sized Aquarium That Feeds a Family

Fish farming is starting to become a major industry in America just as it has long been in China and other parts of Asia. Fish produce more protein per acre than other kinds of livestock, they are more efficient at converting feed into usable meat, and they yield a higher proportion of meat than livestock.

You do not have to be an expert to raise fish successfully; basically, it is like managing an oversized aquarium. Fish are raised commercially in large artificial ponds or complex structures, but for individual homeowners and homesteaders a simple backyard tank can produce a significant proportion of a family's protein needs. An aboveground wading pool, 12 feet across and 2 feet deep, can yield 50 to 100 pounds of tasty trout, catfish, or other species in a single growing season of five to six months.

Good Water Is the Key to Productivity

The types of fish you can raise as well as the poundage you harvest depend on three factors: oxygen content of the water, water quality, and water temperature.

Oxygen content. Fish must have oxygen to survive. When oxygen dissolved in the water falls too low, the fish suffocate and die. Oxygen enters water by diffusion from the air and by the action of algae and other water plants. Oxygen content drops on a sunless day, when plants photosynthesize slowly, and in hot weather, because warm water holds less oxygen than cold water. The fish farmer can get around natural deficiencies by using an aerator to supply needed oxygen. In fact, constant aeration can double the fish harvest, since fish are healthier and grow faster when they have plentiful oxygen.

Many models of aerators are sold by aquaculture supply houses. Some bubble air up from the bottom via perforated pipes or hoses; others spray a fountain of water up into the air. The latter type of aerator has the advantage of providing circulation as it splashes down on the surface of the tank. For a small-scale home operation a sump pump with a short hose attached to jet the water back into the tank can serve as an aerator.

Water quality. The pH (degree of acidity or alkalinity) and the presence of such impurities as heavy metals and organic waste play a part in determining water quality. Fish will not thrive in water with a pH much lower than 6 (acid) or much higher than 8 (alkaline).

The ideal pH is 6.5 to 7. Check the pH of your water regularly: add lime to reduce acidity; add gypsum to reduce alkalinity. Before setting up your tank, have the water tested for such heavy metals as iron, lead, and copper. Even in concentrations as low as three parts per million these substances are toxic to fish. If your water supply chlorinated, filter it through charcoal before using it.

Fish give off nitrogenous wastes in large quantities. These must not be allowed to accumulate. Algae are effective purifiers in ponds and lakes; but if you are raising fish in a tank, particularly if you are raising trout you will need a recirculating filter. An efficient filter can be made at home from a clean 55-gallon drum filled with crushed rock, gravel, sand, seashells, or special plastic ringlets. Naturally occurring bacteria that grow on the filter medium convert the fish wastes to harmless substances. A small electric pump circulates water to the filter; gravity feeds it back to the tank.

Water temperature. Trout do best in water between 54°F and 56°F, but they can survive lower temperatures as long as the water does not freeze. If the temperature rises to 85°F they will die. A steady supply of water from a cold spring is close to ideal. Catfish, in contrast, thrive at 80°F to 90°F and become torpid below 40°F. If your climate permits, raise trout in the colder months and catfish in the warm season. For best results, match your fish to the climate and let nature work for you.

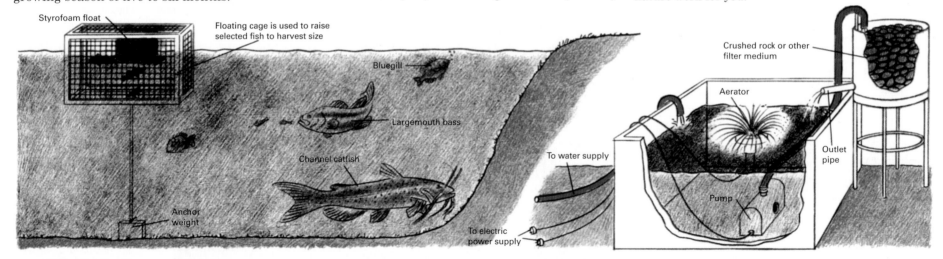

Self-sustaining fish pond contains a balanced mixture of life: algae and other plankton, tiny animals that feed on the plankton, small fish that feed on the plankton eaters, and so on up the chain to the big fish. The pond shown above contains a combination of fish species recommended by government experts: bluegill sunfish, largemouth bass, and channel catfish. Each fish utilizes a different source of food.

Backyard fish tank is easy to manage and produces plenty of fish for family use. The system requires few components. Tank can be built of cement block painted with waterproof epoxy compound. It can also be made from fiberglass or from wood lined with plastic sheeting. Even a standard child's wading pool will serve.

Setting Up a Backyard Fish Tank

Breeding your own fish entails an extra investment in equipment and labor. Most fish farmers, from large-scale trout ranchers to backyard hobbyists, find it easier to obtain their stock from commercial hatcheries. Fish are purchased as 2- to 6-inch fingerlings and harvested after one growing season (it is seldom economical to carry them longer). The bigger the fingerlings, the bigger the fish you will harvest.

During the growing season water must be added to the tank regularly to replace water lost by evaporation. When the time comes to harvest the fish, drain out most of the water and scoop the fish up in nets. The fish can be frozen, eaten fresh, or preserved in a variety of other ways (see *Preserving Meat and Fish*, pp.222–231).

If you lack experience in fish farming, plan on stocking about 1 pound of fingerlings for each cubic foot of water—more could overload the system. (Fish farmers think in terms of total fish weight, not numbers.) It is possible to stock more than one species together; in fact, studies show that polycultures outyield monocultures provided the species are selected so as not to compete with each other for food or living space. For a sustained yield in farm ponds experts recommend a mixture of 100 largemouth bass and 500 bluegill sunfish per surface acre. The bluegills feed on small water organisms, and the bass feed on the bluegills. Some pond owners, however, stock bass only, since bluegills tend to overbreed.

The leading types of fish raised in the United States are trout and channel catfish. Both are best raised in monocultures, since they do not compete effectively with other species for food and oxygen. Under proper conditions both gain weight rapidly, and both are excellent for eating.

A tropical fish, the tilapia, holds promise for tank culture in temperate areas, but providing warm water (75°F) for the five-month growing season they need to reach a half-pound size can be a problem. Tilapia are tasty, cheap to feed (they can live largely on algae and garden waste), and tolerant of less-than-perfect water quality. Because they are prolific and might pose an ecological threat if they escaped, tilapia are banned in some states. However, since they die when the water temperature falls to 50°F, they are no problem in northern states.

Carp are also an excellent fish for tank culture. They were among the first species to be raised by man (ancient Chinese records describe their culture as long ago as 500 B.C.), and they are mainly vegetarian. Israeli carp and several species of Asian carp do well in polycultures. Since carp are banned in many states, check with your conservation officer before stocking them.

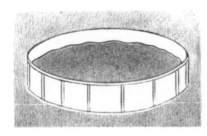

1. Set up your tank in a level area as close to a water outlet as possible. Fill the tank, then check that the filter and aerator are functioning properly.

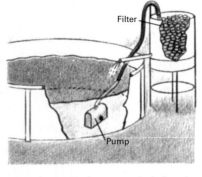

2. Run the system for two weeks before the fish arrive to condition the water and permit waste-neutralizing bacteria to become established in the filter.

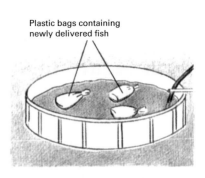

3. Fish will be delivered in water-filled plastic bags. To avoid thermal shock, place bags in tank until temperatures are equalized, then release fish.

4. Keep the water thoroughly aerated; a good oxygen supply is vital to the health of the fish. A small submersible fountain-type aerator is shown operating here.

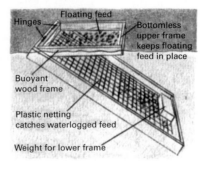

Floating feed
Hinges
Bottomless upper frame keeps floating feed in place
Buoyant wood frame
Plastic netting catches waterlogged feed
Weight for lower frame

5. Feed can be broadcast on the water, but a floating feed rack, easy to make at home, will provide better sanitation and will waste less feed.

6. Harvest fish with a dip net or by draining the tank. If the fish are in a pond, a drag net can be used to harvest large numbers of them at one time.

Feeding Your Fish

For intensive fish culture supplementary feeding is required. If the fish are to reach harvesting size (1/2 to 1 pound) in one growing season, trout and catfish need high-protein rations. Commercial feeds supply protein, vitamins, and minerals in the correct proportions; fish scraps are an acceptable substitute. Experimenters have devised mixtures of chopped earthworms, soy flour, grain meal, and midge larvae. Tilapia and carp have been raised successfully on a diet of algae and grass clippings fortified by small doses of animal manure. Feed your fish at the same time every day, gradually increasing the rations as they grow so that they receive about 3 percent of their body weight daily. (Estimate a gain of about 1 pound for every 2 to 3 pounds of feed.) When feed is left over, use less the next day. Overfeeding can cause sanitation problems.

Sources and resources

Books

Bardach, John E., John H. Ryther, and William O. McLarney. *Aquaculture: The Farming and Husbandry of Freshwater and Marine Organisms*. New York: John Wiley, 1974.

Bennett, George W. *Management of Lakes and Ponds*, 2nd ed. Melbourne, Fla.: Krieger, 1983.

Huet, Marcel. *Textbook of Fish Culture: Breeding and Cultivation of Fish*. Cambridge, Mass.: Blackwell Scientific Publications, 1994.

Spotte, Stephen H. *Fish and Invertebrate Culture: Water Management in Closed Systems*. New York: John Wiley, 1979.

Yoo, Kyung H., and Boyd, Claude E. *Hydrology and Water Supply for Pond Aquaculture*. New York: Chapman & Hall, 1993.

Periodicals

Aquaculture Magazine. Achill River Corp., Box 2329, Ashville, N.C. 28802.
Farm Pond Harvest. P.O. Box AA, Momence, Ill. 60954.
Organic Gardening. Rodale Press, 33 E. Minor St., Emmaus, Pa. 18049.

Hatcheries

Contact your local environment or fish-and-game commission.

Raising Livestock

Animals Pay Their Way With Meat, Milk, Eggs, And Heavy Work Too

Vast grazing lands, fertile soil for feed grains, and the demand for protein have helped make meat, milk, and eggs mainstays of the American diet. Our hunger for beef financed the railroads that opened the West to intensive settlement. Our love of pork and lard made the fast-growing hog the traditional "mortgage lifter" for on-the-move farmers.

To keep pace with America's demand for meat and dairy products, farmers have worked to find new ways to make animals grow bigger, gain weight faster, and produce more abundantly. But their advances have not been without some drawbacks. Animals that are scientifically fed for fast growth simply do not have the flavor of ones on a varied diet. Growth-stimulating hormones and medicated feed may have long-term side effects that are as yet unknown. And in spite of record-high productivity, meat, milk, and eggs are becoming increasingly expensive.

But you need not remain bound by the limits—and costs—of mass production. If you like animals, have a little extra space (a few square feet is all it takes to raise rabbits), and can put in a little time daily, you can have cream-rich milk, fresh eggs every day, and full-flavored, chemical-free meat that you have produced yourself. You can also learn to keep costs to a minimum—by feeding discarded greens, stalks, and bumper crops that would otherwise go to waste or by turning unused land into pasture.

Do not let anyone tell you that raising animals is easy. It may take only a few minutes a day, but you can never skip a day. Nonetheless, there is an abundance of rewards, not the least of which is the satisfaction of watching animals prosper.

Self-sufficient life-style of 19th-century farm families was based on the use of animals for heavy work as well as for food.

An Ounce of Cleanliness Is Worth a Pound of Cure

Cleanliness is the single biggest contributor to livestock health. Feeding and shelter requirements vary from one farm animal to another, but all require good sanitation to stay in top condition. Begin with good planning. Be sure the feeding and watering equipment is protected from contamination and that the shelter is easy to clean. If you have a pasture, it should be free of boggy areas, poisonous weeds, and dangerous debris. Use fencing and traps to protect your animals from rodents, and guard against flies by installing screens. Daily care is important too. Wash equipment after each use, keep bedding dry, and check animals daily for early signs of trouble.

Once or twice each year thoroughly scrub and disinfect your animals' shelter. Haul all the old bedding to the compost heap and replace it with some that is clean, new, and dry. Take all movable equipment outside, wash it thoroughly, and let it dry in the sun—sunlight is an excellent disinfectant. Scrub the inside of the house with a stiff bristled brush to remove caked dirt, then go over everything again with a disinfectant

formulated for use with livestock. Follow the directions that come with the disinfectant and allow adequate drying time before letting the animals back into the house. The same sanitary procedures should be followed in the event of an outbreak of disease or before bringing a new animal into the shelter—for instance, if you are putting a new feeder pig into the pen used by last year's feeder.

Try to keep strange animals away from your livestock. If you buy a new animal, keep it quarantined until you are sure it is healthy. If you take an animal to a livestock show, isolate it for awhile when you return before reintroducing it into the herd. Some farmers go so far as to pen new animals with a member of the established herd to be sure the new ones are not symptom-free disease carriers. If they are, only a single animal need be lost, not the entire herd. Many chicken raisers slaughter their entire flocks and start with a new batch of chicks instead of trying to introduce a few new birds at a time. Remember: a clean environment is the best way to guarantee healthy, profitable, attractive livestock.

Keeping Records of Productivity

Good records are essential if you want to know whether your animals are paying their way and how the cost of raising them stacks up against going to the supermarket. Keep track of all expenses, including veterinary bills, and write down exactly how much feed you provide each day. If possible, record the amount fed to individual animals. Keep track of productivity too. Note how many offspring each animal produces, whether the offspring survive to maturity, and how fast they gain weight. If you have dairy animals, weigh their milk at each milking. Count the number of eggs laid by each of your chickens, ducks, or geese and the percentage of the eggs hatched. Maintaining records is not a time-consuming chore. The most convenient system is to keep a looseleaf notebook or box of file cards near your animals' shelter. Carefully kept records will tell you which animals are producing efficiently and which should be culled. They will also increase the worth of any animals you choose to sell and help you decide which offspring will make the most valuable additions to your stock.

Learn Before You Leap

Before buying animals, learn as much as you can about keeping them. Books, breeders' magazines, and government pamphlets are helpful, but do not expect to become an expert just by reading. Talk to your county agent and other knowledgeable people. Attend shows and exhibits to learn what distinguishes good specimens. Check costs of feed, equipment, fencing, and building materials. And be certain there is a veterinarian available who will be able to treat your animals. If you are interested in selling produce, find out what markets are available, what laws restrict its sale (the sale of milk is particularly strictly regulated), and what price it is likely to bring. You might also want to make sure that there is someone in the area to slaughter your livestock—or to help you learn to do the job yourself.

Before you commit yourself to purchasing any animals, check at town hall to determine whether they are permitted in your area. Be sure that you have ample space as well as clean, sanitary shelter. If you plan to range-feed, make sure your pasture is of sufficiently high quality. It can take years to develop top-quality grazing land, and if yours is not, you will have to buy hay. Before the animals arrive you should have on hand all necessary equipment, such as feed pans, milk pails, watering troughs, halters, and grain storage bins. You should also be prepared to store what your animals produce. Milk and eggs must be refrigerated, and meat must be salted, smoked, or kept frozen until you are ready to eat it.

Sources and resources

Books and pamphlets

Poultry
Bartlett, Tom. *Ducks and Geese: A Guide to Management*. North Pomfret, Vt.: Trafalgar Square, 1991.
Mercia, Leonard S. *Raising Poultry the Modern Way*. Charlotte, Vt.: Garden Way Publishing, 1990.
Raising Geese. Washington, D.C.: U.S. Department of Agriculture, 1983.

Rabbits
Attfield, Harlan D. *Raising Rabbits*. Arlington, Va.: Volunteers in Technical Assistance, 1977.
Bennett, Bob. *Raising Rabbits Successfully*. Charlotte, Vt.: Williamson Publishing, 1984.

Hogs
Baker, James K., and Elwood M. Juergenson. *Approved Practices in Swine Production*. Danville, Ill.: Interstate Printers and Publishers, 1979.
Beynon, Neville. *Pigs: A Guide to Management*. North Pomfret, Vt.: Trafalgar Square, 1994.

Sheep
Simmons, Paula. *Raising Sheep the Modern Way*. Charlotte, Vt.: Garden Way Publishing, 1989.

Goats
Belanger, Jerome. *Raising Milk Goats the Modern Way*. Charlotte, Vt.: Garden Way Publishing, 1990.
Dunn, Peter. *Goatkeeper's Veterinary Book*. Alexandria Bay, N.Y.: Diamond Farm Books, 1994.

Jaudas, Ulrich. *The New Goat Handbook*. Waltonville, Ill.: Barton, 1989.
Luttmann, Gail. *Raising Milk Goats Successfully*. Charlotte, Vt.: Williamson Publishing Co., 1986.
Mackenzie, David. *Goat Husbandry*. Winchester, Mass.: Faber & Faber, 1993.

Cows
Etgen, William M., et al. *Dairy Cattle: Feeding and Management*. New York: John Wiley & Sons, 1987.
Juergenson, Elwood M., and W.P. Mortenson. *Approved Practices in Dairying*. Danville, Ill: Interstate Printers and Publishers, 1977.
Van Loon, Dirk. *The Family Cow*. Charlotte, Vt.: Garden Way Publishing, 1975.

Horses
Evans, J. Warren, and others. *The Horse*. San Francisco: W.H. Freeman and Company, 1995.
Lorch, Janet. *From Foal to Full Grown*. North Pomfret, Vt.: Trafalgar Square, 1993.
Telleen, Maurice. *The Draft Horse Primer*. Waverly, Iowa: Draft Horse Journal, 1993.

Periodicals
Country Journal. Cowles Enthusiast Media, 4 High Ridge Park, Stamford, Conn. 06905.
Harrowsmith. Camden East, Ontario KOK 1JO, Canada.

Sharon and Kenny Eastwood, 4-H Club Animal Raisers

Milk, Pork Chops, And Blue Ribbons

Pigs are one of the prize-winning animals the Eastwood kids raise at their local 4-H club.

The Eastwood kids—Kenny, 10, Carol, 13, and Sharon, 15—go to school, help out around the house, and also raise prize-winning animals at their local 4-H club in suburban Brewster, New York.

Kenny: "If you want to give a pig a bath, you've got to get more than one person. One person holds and the other one scrubs. You've got to be careful that the pigs don't get back into the pig house—if they roll over in the straw or in manure, then you have to start all over again. When you have more than one pig, it's really hard. While you're washing one, the others try to bite the hose.

"Giving pigs a bath—that's what you do when you get ready for a show. I got a pig trophy for bringing my pig to the Putnam County Fair, and then I got a herdsman trophy for having a clean pig and pen. It's really fun bringing the pigs to fairs. When you get ribbons and stuff, you really feel happy.

"It takes about an hour a day to take care of the pigs. I'm not afraid that they're too big for me. The only thing to watch out for is sometimes when you're climbing over the fence to the pen, they nibble your toes. But they don't try to eat you alive or anything like that.

"I help take care of chickens too, but I really like pigs better. When you butcher chickens, you get just one thing: chicken. But with a pig you get ham and bacon and pork chops."

Sharon: "We started out with one goat and then someone gave us another and pretty soon we had six. They're French Alpine goats, and their milk is very good and thick. We all drink it. We don't really do anything special to it before drinking it except to strain it to get all the dirt out. And also, you have to have your goats tested for tuberculosis.

"Goats are really not that hard to take care of. If they want food or water, they'll really let you know it. My sister and I have to go out and feed them in winter, give them water and hay. In the summer we stake them out on ropes and it's a lot easier. Milking takes about 10 to 20 minutes between us to do. We get 3 1/2 to 4 quarts of milk from each goat. It's just delicious.

"We belong to the Rockridge 4-H Club, and we've learned a lot about goats there, and my sister Carol belongs to a special 4-H dairy goat club. We've just started showing our goats. We never did that before. You have to brush them and clip them and really clean them up because cleanliness is one of the things they're judged on. We've gotten a couple of blue ribbons already, which really makes it worth the work."

Chickens: Best Bets For the Small Farmer

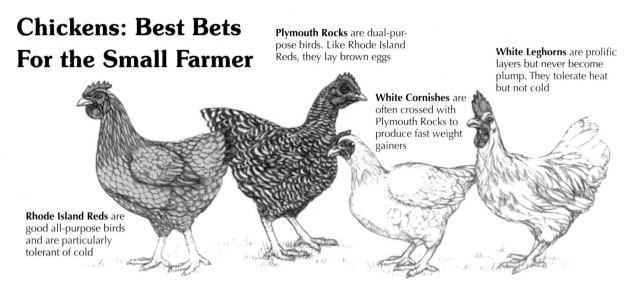

Plymouth Rocks are dual-purpose birds. Like Rhode Island Reds, they lay brown eggs

White Cornishes are often crossed with Plymouth Rocks to produce fast weight gainers

White Leghorns are prolific layers but never become plump. They tolerate heat but not cold

Rhode Island Reds are good all-purpose birds and are particularly tolerant of cold

Which breed of chicken you raise will depend on whether you want meat or eggs. Some dual-purpose breeds can provide both.

Most chickens are bred to produce either eggs or meat but not both. The best egg producers remain thin no matter how much they eat, while meat types become plump quickly but lay fewer eggs. There are a number of dual-purpose breeds and hybrids, however, that provide plenty of eggs as well as meaty carcasses.

You can buy chickens at almost any stage of their development, from day-old chicks to old hens who are no longer very productive. (You can even buy fertilized eggs, but they are unlikely to hatch successfully for a beginner.) If possible, obtain your birds from a local hatchery or breeder. However, buying chicks through the mail is very common and may be the only way you can get them. Purchasing started pullets—females about four months old that have just begun to lay—is an easy way for a novice to start a flock. Pullet eggs are small, but the birds will soon be laying full-sized eggs.

Day-old chicks are cheaper but require extra attention and special equipment until they are grown. They are available either sexed (that is, differentiated as to sex) or unsexed. If you are interested in egg production only, buy all females, since a rooster is not necessary unless you want fertilized eggs.

The number of birds you need depends upon the number of eggs you want. A good layer will produce an egg almost every day but none during the annual molt (shedding of feathers). If you want a dozen eggs a day, you will need about 15 birds. This allows for decreased productivity and for any deaths. If you buy unsexed

chicks, buy twice that number plus a few more to allow for higher mortality among the younger birds. Butcher the males for meat when they become full grown at about 5 to 6 pounds live weight.

Try to obtain birds that have been vaccinated against pullorum, typhoid, and any other disease that might be prevalent in your area. If the birds have not been vaccinated, have a veterinarian do the job. It is also advisable to buy chickens that have been debeaked to prevent pecking later in life. Most hatcheries routinely vaccinate and debeak all birds.

Whatever type of bird you decide to raise, be sure to make arrangements well in advance. Start by checking with your county agent; he will be able to advise you on what breeds are popular in your area and what diseases are prevalent. Send in your order early.

Troubleshooting

Symptoms	Treatment
Cannibalism (pecking)	Increase feed and space. Keep bedding dry and let birds scratch in it
Egg eating	Increase feed and calcium. Darken nest boxes. Gather eggs often
Lice	Dust birds and coop with louse powder
Change of habit, listlessness	Isolate sick bird. Call veterinarian. If bird dies, bury deeply or burn

Feeding Your Poultry

The quality, quantity, taste, and appearance of a chicken's meat and eggs depend on proper feeding and watering. Fresh water must be available at all times and must be kept from freezing in winter. Each bird will drink as much as two cups a day, particularly while laying, since an egg is almost entirely water.

Mash purchased from a feed supply store is the most commonly used chicken feed. It is a blend of many components: finely ground grains, such as wheat, corn, and oats; extra protein from such sources as soybean meal, fish meal, and dried milk; calcium from ground oyster shells and bone meal; and vitamin and mineral supplements. There are a variety of special mixes, such as high-protein mash for chicks and high-calcium mash for laying hens. There are also all-purpose mashes containing plenty of everything, but these are generally more expensive. On the average, each bird will eat 4 to 5 ounces of mash per day but will require more food during peak production periods or in cold weather.

You can save money by feeding your chickens with homegrown scratch (unground grain) and food scraps in addition to commercial mash. Most chicken raisers consider it wasteful to scatter scratch on the ground, where it gets dirty and is not eaten. Instead, load the feeder at one end with scratch and the other end with mash, or sprinkle the scratch on top of the mash. When scratch is used for feed, it is necessary to provide the birds with grit—bits of pebble and sand—that collects in their gizzards and helps them digest the grain.

Extra protein and calcium must also be provided when feeding scratch. (Protein should make up 20 percent of a chicken's total diet, but most scratch grains are only 10 percent protein.) Birds that can range freely get protein from bugs in the ground. Table scraps and dried milk are other good sources or you can use mash with an extra-high protein content. To supplement calcium in the diet, feed the chickens ground egg or oyster shells, but be sure to grind the eggshells thoroughly. Otherwise the birds may develop a taste for them and eat their own eggs. (Egg eating can also mean the birds lack calcium.)

Birds also like and benefit from very fresh greens, such as grass clippings and vegetable tops. Feed only as much of these greens as the birds will eat quickly—in about 15 minutes. Remember, scraps can affect the taste of eggs and meat. Do not feed anything with a strong flavor.

Most chicken raisers keep food available to the birds at all times but fill the feeders no more than halfway so that the feed is not scattered and wasted. Mash and grains may be stored in airtight, rodent-proof containers, such as plastic garbage pails. Do not store more than a month's supply of mash, since it quickly becomes stale.

A Shelter Planned for Comfort and Minimum Care

Whether you are converting an unused shack or starting with a new building, you will want a chicken house that is warm, dry, draft free, and easy to clean. It should have at least 2 square feet of floor space per bird. A dirt floor—the cheapest and simplest type—is adequate for a small flock. Concrete is easier to clean and gives more protection against rodents but is expensive. If the floor is wooden, it should be raised at least 1 foot off the ground (build it on cinder blocks) as a protection against rats as well as to reduce dampness.

Cover the floor with a litter of wood shavings, shredded sugarcane stalks, or other cheap, absorbent material. Start with about 6 inches. Whenever the litter becomes dirty, shovel away any particularly wet spots and add a new layer of absorbent material. The litter absorbs moisture and provides heat and natural antibiotics as it decomposes. It should be completely replaced at least once or twice a year. Add the dirty litter to the compost heap—it makes excellent fertilizer—then clean and disinfect the coop before spreading new litter.

Insulation in the ceiling and walls will moderate the temperature and help to keep it near 55°F, the level at which chickens are most comfortable and productive. Adequate ventilation is needed to cool the coop, dry the litter, and disperse odors. It can be provided by slots high in the walls, double-hung windows open at the top, or windows that tilt inward at the top. The windows should face away from the wind but in a direction where they can let in the winter sun.

You may want to let your birds out of their house during the day to range free on your land (be sure they are all safely inside at night), but they will be better protected against dangerous dogs, foxes, weasels, and rats in a wire-enclosed run. The run should have a wire-mesh covering or a fence high enough to keep the birds inside. (The smaller the breed, the higher the birds can flutter.) Birds allowed out-of-doors are less likely to develop boredom-induced problems, such as egg eating and pecking. They will also be supplied with plenty of free vitamin D from the sun.

Eggs and Meat

Most small flocks are kept primarily for their eggs, with meat as a valuable by-product. Eggs are less likely to crack or get dirty if they are gathered frequently—at least once a day or even twice a day if possible. Avoid washing the shells, since water removes the protective layer that slows evaporation and protects against disease. If you must wash an egg, use warm water (cold water will be drawn through the shell and into the egg), and eat the egg promptly. A fresh high-quality egg has a thick white and a yolk that remains at the center when hard-boiled. As the egg ages, water evaporates, the air pocket enlarges, and the albumen (white) breaks down.

When a hen is two or three years old, its laying rate falls off and it should be butchered. Be sure it has not had antibiotics for a week or two (check the instructions on the medicine) and that it has not eaten for 24 hours before it is killed. To kill the bird, hold legs and wings firmly with one hand while you chop off the head with the other. Then hang the carcass upside down by the feet for 10 minutes to let the blood drain. To loosen the feathers for plucking, scald the carcass briefly in 150°F to 190°F water. Start the butchering by slitting the neck skin open, cutting off the neck, and pulling out the windpipe and gullet. Eviscerate as shown below, and finish by thoroughly washing the carcass.

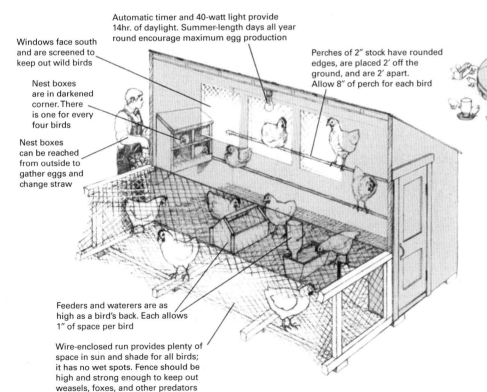

Windows face south and are screened to keep out wild birds

Nest boxes are in darkened corner. There is one for every four birds

Nest boxes can be reached from outside to gather eggs and change straw

Automatic timer and 40-watt light provide 14hr. of daylight. Summer-length days all year round encourage maximum egg production

Perches of 2" stock have rounded edges, are placed 2' off the ground, and are 2' apart. Allow 8" of perch for each bird

Feeders and waterers are as high as a bird's back. Each allows 1" of space per bird

Wire-enclosed run provides plenty of space in sun and shade for all birds; it has no wet spots. Fence should be high and strong enough to keep out weasels, foxes, and other predators

Chick brooder is needed to raise day-old chicks. The brooder should be draft free and very warm. Start with a temperature of 95°F, then reduce it 5°F each week for six to eight weeks. In warm weather a cardboard box with a lightbulb hung above it can be used as a brooder. Chicks will scatter evenly throughout the brooder if the heat is comfortable. Dip the chicks' beaks into water until they learn to drink.

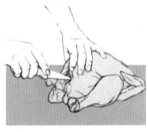

1. Insert finger to pry lungs and organs loose.

2. Cut around vent, being careful not to cut into it.

3. Carefully pull out vent and attached intestines.

4. Pull out entrails. Do not rupture gall bladder.

For Food Without Fuss
Try Geese and Ducks

Indian Runners are egg-laying ducks that gain little weight

Emden geese are excellent for meat and the 40 eggs per year each produces makes them among the best layers of any breed of geese

Khaki Campbell ducks can lay more then 300 eggs a year, rivaling chickens in productivity, but they grow to only 4 1/2 lb.

Pekin ducks are the most popular breed for meat thanks to fast weight gain and white feathers that leave skin clear and attractive once plucked

Choose the right breed: a small laying type of duck for eggs, a heavy breed of duck or a goose for rich, flavorful meat.

A simple shed with 5 to 6 sq. ft. of floor space per bird is all that ducks or geese need for shelter. Good ventilation and sanitation are necessities, and litter should be spread and tended as for chickens. The birds enjoy a place to swim, but a pond or other open body of water is not needed to raise them successfully.

Geese and ducks are extremely hardy and will forage for most of the food they need. They are also amusing pets and, in the case of geese, make excellent lookouts that squawk loudly whenever a stranger approaches. To start a small flock, raise day-old birds to maturity or buy young birds—ducks about seven months old or geese about two years old—that are ready to start breeding.

One male and six females is a good number of ducks to start with. Geese tend to be monogamous, so it is best to buy a pair. Buy the birds a month before breeding season (early spring) to give them time to adjust. By midsummer there should be plenty of fertile eggs.

Incubation. A goose can hatch only 12 of the 20 or so eggs it lays, while domesticated ducks (except the Muscovy breed) rarely sit on their eggs at all. Since machine incubation is difficult, use broody hens (ones that want to sit on eggs) as foster mothers. Dust the hen and nest with louse powder and put five eggs under the bird. Keep water and food nearby so that it will not need to leave its nest for more than a few minutes. The hen will turn the eggs daily if they are not too heavy; if this does not happen, turn them yourself to keep the yolks from settling. Mark one side of each egg with a grease pencil so that you can tell which need to be turned. Sprinkle the eggs with water every few days to maintain the high humidity that a duck or goose provides naturally with its wet feathers. About five days after incubation begins, hold each egg up to a bright light in a dark room and look for the dark spot inside, which means the egg is fertilized. Hatching takes 28 days for ducks, 30 days for geese.

Brooding. Newborn birds must be kept warm and dry until they grow protective feathers at about four weeks of age. For birds raised by their natural mothers, this is no problem, but if the young are raised by a hen, take special precautions. First, as each bird emerges, remove it to a warm brooder until all are born. Otherwise, the hen may think the job is finished and leave the rest of the eggs before they hatch. Then confine the hen and babies in a small area for the first few days.

If you are using a brooder like the one shown on page 185, provide 1 square foot of floor space per bird and keep it at 85°F. As the birds grow, gradually increase the floor space and reduce the temperature by 5°F a week for four weeks. Give starter feed and plenty of water to the newborns. If it is warm and dry outside, two-week-old goslings can be let out to eat some grass. After four weeks begin to shift the little ducklings and goslings entirely to range feeding.

Feed. At least 1 acre of range is needed for 20 mature birds. To prevent overgrazing, divide the area into three sections and shift the birds from one to the other as the supply of grass dwindles. Carefully fence any young trees on the range area, since geese love to eat their tender bark. You can supplement foraging with pellet feed placed in covered self-feeders right on the range. Supply laying birds with ground oyster shells to provide calcium, and provide plenty of fresh drinking water at all times or the birds will choke on their food. Water troughs must be deep enough that a duck can submerge its bill (to clear its nostrils) and a goose its entire head.

Eggs, Meat, and Down

Duck eggs are larger than chicken eggs and have a stronger taste but can be treated and used just the same way. Butchering too is the same, but be prepared to spend much more time plucking, especially with geese, since the feathers of waterfowl are harder to remove. If you are not planning to save the down, paraffin can be used to help remove the pin feathers. Melt the wax, pour it over the partially plucked bird, and then plunge the carcass into cold water to harden the wax. Many of the pin feathers will come out as you peel off the hardened wax. Ducks are ready to be butchered at 8 pounds live weight and geese at 12 pounds live weight.

Feathers and down tend to blow about, so do not pluck a bird in a drafty area or in a spot where you might mind finding feathers later. To save the down, stuff it loosely into pillowcases and hang them to dry. Down is the warmest insulator for its weight that is known. Once dry, it can be used as stuffing for soft pillows, comforters, and sleeping bags. You can even make your own feather bed.

Troubleshooting

Symptoms	Treatment
Droopiness, change in habit, diarrhea	Call veterinarian for diagnosis. Isolate bird. Improve sanitation
Slow weight gain	Check for worms and use dewormer if necessary. Improve sanitation
Lice, ticks, mites	Use appropriate insecticide. Follow directions carefully

Rabbits: Good Protein In a Limited Space

Rabbits are excellent animals to raise for meat. Not only are they delicious, prolific, and hardy, but they are also inexpensive to feed. In fact, they yield more high-protein meat per dollar of feed than any other animal.

Food. Specially prepared rabbit pellets provide the best diet. These can be supplemented with tender hay, fresh grass clippings, and vegetable tops—but greens should be fed sparingly to a rabbit that is less than six months old. Root vegetables, apples, pears, and fruit tree leaves are also favorites. Water is essential (change it at least once a day). Many raisers also provide a salt lick.

Mating. Medium-weight types, such as the New Zealand, are ready to breed at about six months old. Signs to look for in the female are restlessness, attempts to join other rabbits, and a tendency to rub its head against the cage. Once a doe has reached maturity, it is fertile almost continuously, with infertile periods lasting only a few days. Simply place the female in the male's cage; mating should take place immediately. If it does not, bring the doe back to its own cage, wait a few days, and then try again. Never bring the male to the female; fearing an intruder, the female may attack.

Birth. Ten days after mating, check for pregnancy by feeling the area just above the pelvis. Try to locate

New Zealand White, the most popular rabbit for meat, is a medium-weight breed of about 5 lb. Buy the best animals you can afford, since the quality of future litters will depend upon them. Be sure they are alert, bright-eyed, and clean, with dry ears and nose and no sores on the feet. Start with rabbits six months old. To pick up a rabbit, grip it as shown. Never hold it by the ears.

the small marble-shaped embryos. If you feel nothing, check again a week later and rebreed if necessary.

Birth—called kindling—occurs 31 days after conception. Five days before the young are due, put the nesting box—with a good supply of straw in the bottom—in the doe's hutch. The young will probably be born at night. Leave them alone for a day or two until the doe is calm. Then distract the mother with some food and look inside the nest to see if there are any dead or deformed babies that must be removed. Start feeding the doe a special high-protein nursing diet as soon as the young are born, and make sure that the family is not disturbed. Otherwise the doe may kill the young. The rabbits will suckle for about eight weeks.

A Basic Wire-Mesh Hutch

Housing can be very basic, since cold is no real problem for rabbits. A hutch should, however, provide protection against drafts, rain, and intense heat, and each rabbit should have its own cage. Individual cages can be hung in a garage or empty shed. Or build an outdoor hutch of lumber and 1 in. wire mesh or hardware cloth. Individual cages should be about 3 ft. wide by 3 ft. deep by 2 ft. high with mesh sides and floors. Set them up at a convenient height for feeding and cleaning. If the cages are not in the shade, they need to have a double roof to help keep them cool. For easy cleaning, place trays beneath the cages to catch droppings. Clean the trays regularly, and scrub and disinfect the cages between litters.

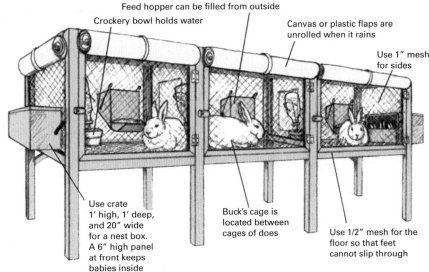

Feed hopper can be filled from outside

Crockery bowl holds water

Canvas or plastic flaps are unrolled when it rains

Use 1" mesh for sides

Use crate 1' high, 1' deep, and 20" wide for a nest box. A 6" high panel at front keeps babies inside

Buck's cage is located between cages of does

Use 1/2" mesh for the floor so that feet cannot slip through

Butchering a Fryer

When the rabbits are 8 to 12 weeks old, they are ready to be butchered as fryers. They should be about 4 pounds live weight and will weigh only about half as much after they are fully skinned and dressed.

For one day before butchering, do not feed the rabbit. To kill it, administer a sharp blow directly behind its ears. Use a heavy pipe or piece of wood, and hold the animal upside down by its feet or place it on a table to deliver the blow. Next, immediately hang the animal by its feet, cut off the head just behind the ears, and let the blood drain out. Cut off the feet, then follow the steps below to skin and dress the carcass. After dressing, immediately chill the meat, including the liver, heart, and kidneys, all of which are edible. Discard the other entrails or feed them to other animals.

1. Slit skin along back legs and center of belly.

2. Pull skin down toward the animal's front legs.

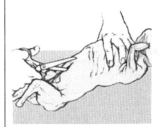 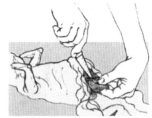

3. Slit carcass, being careful not to cut into anus.

4. Carefully remove insides. Do not cut into gall bladder.

Troubleshooting

Symptoms	Treatment
Refusal to eat	Check water. Call veterinarian if refusal persists
Runny nose, sneezing, diarrhea	Destroy sick animal or isolate it and call veterinarian
Sore hind feet	Keep floor of cage scrupulously clean and dry

Pork for the Year From a Single Hog

Chester Whites are always white. They are of medium size, weighing 600 to 700 lb. at maturity

Yorkshires are also white. Mature boars can weigh as much as 1,000 lb.

Durocs are noted for their red color. They are fast weight gainers, reaching a 200-lb. slaughtering weight in as little as five months

Hampshires are noted for a white band over shoulders and forelegs. Like Chester Whites, they are medium sized at maturity

Crossbred hogs—combining the best qualities of such pure breeds as these—tend to be the most vigorous and are thrifty to raise.

Pigs are the most intelligent of barnyard animals. They can be taught to perform as many tricks as a dog and even seem to be able to puzzle out answers independently—for example, the way to open a complicated gate latch. For anyone with a good source of leftover produce, pigs can be profitable as well as amusing animals to raise. They will eat almost any type of food, including table scraps, restaurant garbage, an unexpected bumper crop of vegetables, a summertime oversupply of goat's milk, or alfalfa and grain from the pasture.

Owning a sow and raising the two or three litters of 10 or so piglets produced each year is likely to provide too much pork for even a large family. Instead, buy a just-weaned pig, called a shoat, in the early spring and fatten it during the summer. When, in the fall, it reaches 220 pounds, it will be ready for butchering into 150 pounds of edible cuts. Your larder will be full and you will be free from the daily chores of animal tending.

Breeding for leanness

Fat type   Meat type

Modern hogs are bred to be lean and meaty, not fat like the ones popular 50 years ago when lard brought high prices. You can recognize a meat-type hog from its wide, straight stance; its long, lean, muscular physique; and its thick shoulders and hams (upper back legs).

In choosing a shoat, health and vigor are more important than breed. Buy from a reliable breeder who maintains a clean, healthy herd. Make arrangements with him well in advance, for his litters may be in great demand. When the time comes, pick the biggest and best of the litter. Look for an animal that is long, lean, and bright-eyed. Never accept a runt, even if it is offered at a greatly reduced price. It will take too much extra feed to fatten, since a runt needs extra food throughout its life.

The shoat should be six to eight weeks old at the time of purchase. A good rule to follow is to select one that weighs between 30 and 40 pounds; if it weighs less, it is either too young or a runt. If your shoat was not free to range for its food, it should have received an iron shot, since pigs born in confinement are anemic. It also should have been inoculated against hog cholera and any disease prevalent in your area (check with your county agent). If it is a male, be sure it has been castrated.

Troubleshooting

Symptoms	Treatment
Lice, mites	Apply disinfectant according to directions. Improve sanitation
Slow weight gain	Check for worms. Deworm regularly. Improve sanitation
Joint pain, skin blotches	Consult veterinarian. Move pig to new pen or pasture

Summertime Fattening

A pig must eat 3 pounds of feed to gain a pound of weight, or a total of 600 to 700 pounds to reach slaughtering weight. Commercial feeds provide the right balance of vitamins, minerals, proteins, and carbohydrates, but so do many less expensive substitutes.

One partial substitute is pasture. Up to six pigs can forage on 1 acre of such high-quality pasture as clover, grass, and alfalfa. Alfalfa, a legume, is especially valuable because it provides the precise amount of protein—16 percent—required in a pig's diet. In addition to eating plants, pigs on a range will get valuable minerals and trace elements when they root through and ingest the dirt in the field. Divide the pasture into three or more areas and rotate the animals from one to another to minimize the buildup of parasites harmful to pigs.

Range feeding must be supplemented with a small amount of coarsely ground grains, usually 2 to 4 pounds per animal depending upon the quality of the pasture. Traditionally, corn has been the most commonly used grain supplement, but oats, barley, and rye are also good. Despite their reputation, pigs will eat only as much food as they need, not enough to make themselves sick. This simplifies feeding, since the grain can be put into self-feeding hoppers set inside the grazing area.

If acreage is too scarce for foraging, raise the pig in a pen. Supplement grain or commercial feed with table scraps, garbage, and garden or orchard wastes, such as vegetable tops, stalks, and rinds. Discarded food from restaurants and school cafeterias can make an excellent feed supplement if it is properly prepared.

To process discarded garbage, sort through and remove inedible items. Also pick out all chicken bones (they will splinter and choke the pig) and pork scraps (a seemingly healthy pig can carry germs to which your animal is susceptible). Cook the remaining garbage at 212°F for 30 minutes to kill dangerous bacteria. If you must feed pork scraps, thorough boiling is especially important. Otherwise you risk the spread of trichinosis, a parasitic disease that is dangerous to humans. (The parasites live in the pig's intestines and muscles but are killed when heated to 137°F. Use a meat thermometer, and cook the pork slowly until the thermometer reads 170°F for small roasts, 185°F for thick roasts.)

If you have a goat or cow, its milk will provide an excellent source of supplemental protein. Up to 1 1/2 gallons of milk per day may be fed. To provide trace minerals, let the pig root through clumps of dirt or sod that you have carried to the pen. Be sure that the dirt does not come from a field fertilized with hog manure (it can contain harmful bacteria) or sprayed with chemicals. Provide plenty of fresh, clean water for your pig.

A-frame on skids is a popular hog shelter. Windows or doors are put at front and rear to provide maximum cooling and ventilation, since overheated pigs gain weight slowly. Skids permit the house to be moved to different parts of the pasture or pen.

Housing Should Be Cool and Sturdy

In summer almost any unused shed will make a good home for a pig, or you can build a simple A-frame, either permanently sited or movable like the one shown above. As protection from the sun's heat, the structure should be set under a tree or have a double roof with several inches of space between the two levels. Good ventilation will also help to keep the house cool.

To keep a 220-pound hog confined, strong fencing is essential. A wire fence usually proves the most practical for a range. Set the posts at least 3 feet deep to make the fence strong enough so that the animal cannot knock it over. A strand of barbed or electrified wire placed 3 inches above the ground may be needed to keep the hog from burrowing under the mesh.

If you are raising your pig in a pen, provide as much outdoor space as possible; the absolute minimum for a single pig is 100 square feet. Fence the pen with closely spaced boards so that the shoat cannot catch its head between them. The boards must also be strong enough to keep a grown hog inside. Nail all boards to the inside of the posts so that the pig cannot push them loose, and bury the bottom board several inches deep in the ground to keep the pig from burrowing underneath.

A hog has very few sweat glands to keep it cool and will appreciate a wallow in its pen or range area. Use a garden hose to make a big, muddy area or fit the hose with a spray nozzle to provide a light shower.

Careful Butchering Is Key to Quality Meat

The hog must be kept quiet and in a pen by itself for at least three days before slaughtering. Bruises, overheating, and excitement will damage the meat's flavor and texture and cause unnecessary spoilage during the butchering. For the last day before butchering, withhold food, but provide as much water as the pig will consume.

Sticking is the best method of killing. The animal can be shot or stunned first to make the job easier, but experts warn that this hampers efficient bleeding. Hang the freshly killed animal head downward, and collect the blood for use in sausage, as a protein supplement for other animals, or as fertilizer.

Once all the blood is drained, remove the hog's body hair as quickly as possible. To loosen the hair, immerse the entire hog in 145°F water for several minutes. An old bathtub set on concrete blocks and with a fire underneath is an easy way to heat the 30 to 40 gallons of water necessary for this task. After scalding, hoist the carcass onto a table where two or more people with special bell-shaped hog scrapers can scrape off the hair. Finally, rehang the carcass and butcher as shown below.

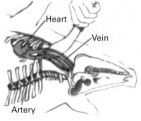
Heart
Vein
Artery

To stick a hog, hang it head down or flip it on its back. Insert knife under breastbone between ribs. Move knife up and down to sever main artery that comes out of heart. Do not damage heart, which must keep pumping to ensure proper bleeding.

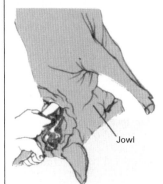

1. Remove head (except for jowl) by cutting from back of neck toward jawbone.

2. Slit carcass open by cutting upward from throat, downward from hams.

3. Cut circle around anus to begin removal of bung (lower end of intestine).

4. Pull bung away from body cavity. Bung must not be cut, torn, or punctured.

5. Use hand or knife to sever fibers joining entrails to body. Do not cut gall bladder.

6. Pull entrails out and place in cold water. Hose out body cavity with cold water.

7. Slit backbone, pull out lard, and hang carcass for 24 hours at 34°F to 40°F.

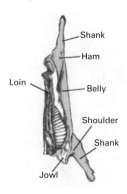
Shank
Ham
Loin
Belly
Shoulder
Shank
Jowl

8. Cut carcass into parts. Use innards and blood for sausage and scrapple.

Sheep: Gentle Providers Of Meat and Fleece

For homespun yarn, homegrown meat, lustrous shearling skins, and the companionship of a few amiable yet profitable animals, consider raising sheep. Their moderate size and gentle disposition make them easy to handle, their shelter needs are minimal, and they can graze for most of their food.

To start a small flock, buy grade (nonpurebred) ewes, but find out as much as you can about their background. If you can find a ewe that is a twin and born of a mother that is also one of twins, that animal is likely to bear many twins to build your flock. When purchasing a ram, pick the best purebred you can afford. The good qualities will gradually improve the overall excellence of the entire flock.

When shopping for sheep, go to a reliable breeder and select alert animals that are close to two years old (the age they begin to breed). Make sure they are free of any indication of disease, particularly sore feet, teats, or udders, and that they have no sign of worms. Color is another consideration. Sheep raisers have traditionally sought animals with pure white fleece that can be dyed a variety of colors. But many modern handspinners enjoy working with the fibers from their black and brown ewes.

Pasturage, Hay, and Grain

Sheep, like cows and goats, are ruminants whose stomachs have special bacteria that break down grass into digestible food. Unlike nonruminant animals that derive little food value from grass, sheep can get all the nutrients they need from good-quality pasturage.

A sheep pasture must be well fenced, as much to keep out predators as to keep the sheep inside. Build a 4-foot-high fence of medium-weight wire field fencing attached to heavy wooden posts. Set the posts at least 3 feet deep in the ground and no more than 15 feet apart. Install a strand of barbed wire at the bottom and another one or two strands at the top to protect sheep from dogs and other enemies. Barbed wire, however, will not prevent sheep from wandering through a broken fence. Their thick wool coats protect them against the barbs—and against electric shock as well if the fence is electrified. As a result, you must check the fencing regularly and repair any weak spots or holes through which the sheep can pass.

One acre of good-quality pastureland containing about half tender grass and half legumes will feed four sheep for most of the summer. To be sure that the animals do not overgraze and ruin the pasture, rotate the grazing area. Use at least three separate sections, and move the sheep from one to another when they have cropped the tops off the plants. The older, tougher parts—which the sheep dislike—will send up new shoots, so the pasture will regenerate. Another precaution that helps to keep the pastureland in good condition is to exclude the sheep in the very early spring before the new growth has had a chance to become well established.

When good pasture is not available or when extra demands are placed on a sheep's body during pregnancy and nursing, its diet must be supplemented with grain. In the spring, when the ewes are being prepared for breeding, begin giving them whole grains, such as oats, corn, and wheat. Feed them each 1 pound of grain per day. A mother nursing twins requires 1 1/2 to 2 pounds of grain per day. During winter provide each sheep with 1 pound of grain per day along with all the top-quality hay it will eat. The hay should be tender and green with plenty of legumes, and it should never be moldy. Put it in a hayrack, where it will stay fresh and not be scattered on the ground and wasted.

For good health and fast growth, feeding must be managed carefully. If a grain supplement is being used, measure it out carefully and give half the daily amount in the morning and half in the afternoon. Keep the feeding times constant, and make any change in diet extremely gradual, especially when changing from winter hay to summer pasture. Sheep unaccustomed to grass can develop bloat (excess gas in the stomach), which is painful and can cause death.

Whether they are grazing or being fed hay and grain, the sheep need salt (in the form of a salt lick). Medication for internal worms, a major danger to sheep, as well as extra minerals can also be supplied in the lick. Plenty of fresh water is also vital.

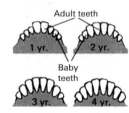

Teeth indicate age of sheep. When an animal is about one year old, it gets its first two adult teeth. It will add two more permanent teeth each year until there are eight in all. In old age, tops of adult teeth wear down to leave short, narrow bases with spaces between them.

Troubleshooting

Symptoms	Treatment
Weight loss	Check for worms, deworm regularly
Limping, inflamed feet	Check hooves and trim semiannually, avoid wet pasture, use footbath
External worms, ticks, mites	Dip, dust, or spray, especially after shearing
Change in habits, weakness	Consult veterinarian for diagnosis and proper medication

Corriedales are fast growing, easy to handle, and produce good spinning wool

Columbias yield good meat, and fleece that is easy to spin

Romneys are a favorite among spinners who like the long, silky fleece

Merinos are raised for their beautiful wool but are not desirable for meat production

When choosing a sheep, look for such traits as hardiness, fast growth, ability to forage, quiet disposition, and spinnable fleece.

Housing a Small Flock

Sheep thrive in cold weather and, as a result, their housing requirements are minimal. A three-sided shed is adequate in most climates unless there is to be a mid-winter lambing. In that case, you will need a warm place for the lambs. The shelter should be roomy enough to provide at least 12 square feet of space per animal and preferably 15 square feet or more. A wide door is another essential so that pregnant ewes will not be crowded as they enter and leave the building. Good ventilation will keep the shed cool and minimize dampness.

The floor can be dirt or concrete but not wood, and it should be covered with about 1 foot of litter. Sheep manure is normally dry and can be allowed to accumulate in the litter, where it will warm the floor. Remove the dirty litter once a year, and clean and disinfect the floor and building. If damp spots develop before the year is up, they must be removed and fresh litter added. Similarly, if the litter becomes wet and smelly, it should be changed.

At lambing time a few additions to the sheep shed are necessary. A fenced-off stall should be provided for each ewe—most sheep raisers keep a supply of gatelike panels that can be set in place at lambing time to create temporary stalls. A lamb creep—a small area with a barrier that permits the lambs but not the sheep to enter—is also needed to protect the lambs' special feed.

Shed must have ample space because sheep dislike crowding.

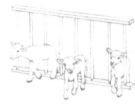

Lambs need a creep, an area only they can enter. To set up one install a fence diagonally across one corner of the shelter. The fence palings should be 9 in. apart—enough space for lambs, but not sheep, to get through. Use heat lamp to warm creep.

Shearing

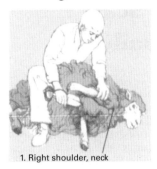

1. Right shoulder, neck

Shear sheep every spring. A good shearer will cut close to the skin and remove the entire fleece in one piece. Second cuts—made by going back over previously clipped areas—are not desirable. Use your knees to hold sheep in position and to keep the animal calm. Proceed to shear, following order shown in illustrations starting at left. Either electric or hand shears can be used.

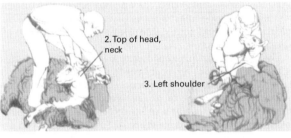

2. Top of head, neck
3. Left shoulder

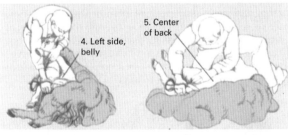

4. Left side, belly
5. Center of back

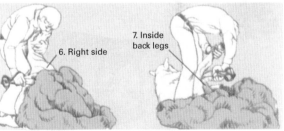

6. Right side
7. Inside back legs

The Breeding Season

Since most breeds of sheep mate just once each year, managing the breeding season is not difficult. The season begins in the fall. A few weeks before, check the ewes for worms, sore feet, and other problems. At the same time put them on a high-protein diet to bolster their health and improve their chances of bearing twins.

Lambing time is 148 days after mating. In the normal birth, feet come out first, followed by the head resting between the legs. A number of complications can arise, including breech birth (tail first delivery) and other positions that cause the lamb to get stuck in the birth canal. Until you accumulate enough experience to recognize signs of trouble, it is wise to seek the help of someone who is knowledgeable—either a veterinarian or a neighbor who has raised sheep for some time.

Be prepared to take good care of the lambs as soon as they are born. Wipe the lamb dry—particularly around the nose so that it can breathe—and put it in a small, warm box until its mother can tend it. Make sure that each lamb gets some of the ewe's first milk, called colostrum, which contains vital antibodies and vitamins. Occasionally a ewe will not feed its lamb. If this should

happen, you will have to bottle-feed it every two to four hours for the first few days. After that, bottle-feed the lamb twice a day until it is two months old; at that time it can be weaned. Use special sheep's milk replacer (from a feed supply store) rather than cow's milk, which has too little fat. You can also get another ewe to adopt the lamb. Disguise the lamb's smell by washing it in warm water and rubbing it with the afterbirth from the adoptive mother's own lamb. Or rub it with something tasty, such as molasses.

Keep each ewe and its lambs together in a separate stall for the first few days after birth or until they learn to recognize each other. Before the young are two weeks old, vaccinate them for tetanus and castrate any males that are to be used for meat. You may also want to remove, or dock, their tails to prevent dirt from collecting. A suckling lamb whose diet is supplemented with grain will gain about 5 pounds per week and is ready for sale at 40 pounds. Or a lamb can be gradually switched to grazing and fattened until it reaches about 100 pounds. Lambs are usually shipped live to market, but one or two might be butchered like pigs for home use.

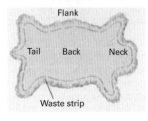

Flank
Tail Back Neck
Waste strip

Cleanest fibers are at the fleece's center—which was on sheep's back before shearing. Outermost 3 in. around edge of fleece comes from sheep's tail, legs, and belly. This strip is usually too dirty and matted to spin and must be cut off and thrown away.

Dairying on a Scale That Fits a Family

The easy-to-handle size, quick wit, excellent foraging ability, and moderate production level (3 to 4 quarts per day) of goats make them ideal dairy animals for a family or small farm. Their milk is fully comparable in flavor and nutritive value to cow's milk and, in fact, in some ways is superior. It is naturally homogenized—the fat particles are so small that they do not separate from the rest of the milk—and as a result is easier to digest. In addition, it is less likely than cow's milk to provoke an allergic reaction.

The most important consideration in buying a dairy goat is milk production. Several breeds of goat are available, all of them satisfactory producers, but it is not necessary to purchase a purebred to get good productivity. The surest course is to buy a milking doe (a female already producing milk) with a good production record. If you are buying a goatling (young female), the productivity of its mother and sisters will provide an indication of how much milk you can expect. Young kids, though inexpensive, are usually not a good choice for beginners, who do not have the expertise to raise them and who will probably have to purchase most of their feed—with no return of milk until the young goats give birth to kids.

A goat's appearance is indicative of good productivity. Look for an animal with a large well-rounded udder with smooth elastic skin and no lumps; a straight back and broad rib cage, which show that the doe can consume large quantities of feed for conversion into milk; and a long trim body, which indicates that the doe will convert most of its feed into milk, not body fat. But avoid does with any signs of disease or lameness. Bright eyes and a sleek coat are good signs of health. You should be sure the animal you buy has been tested for brucellosis and tuberculosis. Although both diseases are rare among goats in the United States, they are dangerous, since they can be transmitted to humans through milk. Annual testing of milkers is essential.

Before you buy a milking doe, make sure you know how to milk it correctly. If you fail to empty the udder completely at each milking, milk production will slacken and can even stop completely. Once this happens, the doe will give no more milk until it bears another kid. Many first-time goat owners buy a bred doe that has not yet borne a kid so that they can become accustomed to caring for the animal before having to milk it.

Bucks (male goats) are not usually kept by people interested in producing only a small quantity of milk. Bucks have a strong smell that can easily taint the flavor of the doe's milk and must therefore have separate quarters. Since it is easy enough to take a doe to a neighbor's buck for breeding, most small farmers avoid the added bother and expense of keeping a buck.

Feed According to Productivity

Good-quality forage will satisfy almost all the nutritional needs of dry (nonmilking) does. Unlike pasture for cows and sheep (which, like goats, are ruminants), a goat's pasture should include a variety of leaves, branches, weeds, and tough grasses to supply essential vitamins, minerals, and trace elements. Legumes are also needed, since they provide necessary protein. When pasturage is unavailable, feed well-cured hay. Goats will not eat hay off the ground; so place it in a rack or manger, or hang it in bundles from the walls.

Unlike a dry doe, a milking doe needs the additional protein of a mixed-grain supplement in its diet. Between 2 and 4 pounds of grain per day—in two evenly spaced feedings—is an average amount of grain to feed, although top producers need more than poor ones. A combination of corn, oats, and wheat bran with some soybean oil meal or cottonseed oil meal (for even more protein) is the most common supplement. Molasses is often added to this combination for extra moisture, sweetness, and vitamins. If a good-quality, fresh premixed feed is not available, buy a calf starter or horse grain mixture.

Overfeeding of grain is dangerous, since it can lead to less efficient digestion of roughage and in extreme cases cause bloat—a serious buildup of gases that can cause death. To prevent overeating, feed the grain only after the goats have eaten plenty of grass or hay. Place the goats in separate stalls or lock them in separate feeding slots in front of a common manger to be sure that each gets only its own ration. A goat's stomach can also be disturbed by changes in its diet, so feed your animals at the same time each day and make any dietary changes very gradually. This is especially important when changing from wintertime hay to spring pasturage.

Plenty of fresh, clean water is important to any milk-producing animal. The more a goat drinks, the more feed will be converted into milk instead of body fat. If you do not have an automatic waterer, change the water twice each day when you feed grain.

Troubleshooting

Symptoms	Treatment
Listlessness, weight loss	Test for worms, and deworm if necessary. Rotate pasture grazing
Pain, distended stomach, heavy breathing	Call veterinarian immediately to treat bloat. Massage stomach. Keep goat moving if possible
Flakes or clots in milk, hot udder	Have veterinarian treat for mastitis, an udder disease. Isolate goat, milk it last, and disinfect hands

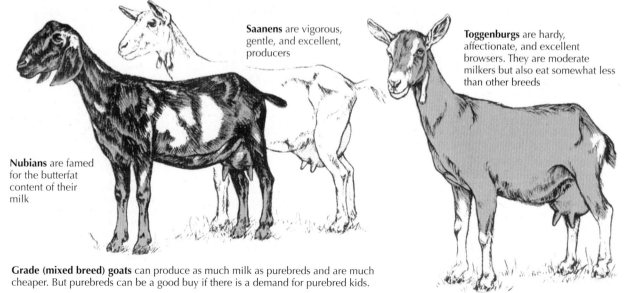

Saanens are vigorous, gentle, and excellent producers

Toggenburgs are hardy, affectionate, and excellent browsers. They are moderate milkers but also eat somewhat less than other breeds

Nubians are famed for the butterfat content of their milk

Grade (mixed breed) goats can produce as much milk as purebreds and are much cheaper. But purebreds can be a good buy if there is a demand for purebred kids.

The Goat Barn

Quarters for one or two milking does can be fairly simple, but their sleeping area should be draft free and well bedded. Goats do not mind cold weather, but they cannot withstand drafts on their skin. Overheating can be almost as bad; a goat that has been kept unnaturally warm for an extended period of time is likely to get sick if it is accidentally exposed to the cold.

Provide access from the barn to a fenced-in outdoor area for browsing and exercise. The fence must be at least 4 feet high—though even this may not be high enough for an unusually agile goat. If you cannot provide a fenced area, you can tether your goats, but tethering should be a last resort. It not only limits access to food and confines the goat close to its own droppings, but by inhibiting exercise it reduces milk production and increases the danger of disease.

Whether tethered or fenced, goats should be pastured on well-drained ground to avoid foot rot. They should also have access to shade and to temporary shelter in case of wind and rain. If possible, include a large boulder or other object for the goat to climb on within the exercise area. Rocks are especially valuable because they help keep the goat's feet trimmed.

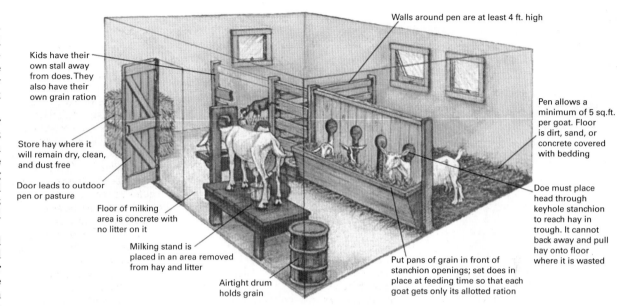

Walls around pen are at least 4 ft. high

Kids have their own stall away from does. They also have their own grain ration

Store hay where it will remain dry, clean, and dust free

Door leads to outdoor pen or pasture

Floor of milking area is concrete with no litter on it

Milking stand is placed in an area removed from hay and litter

Airtight drum holds grain

Pen allows a minimum of 5 sq.ft. per goat. Floor is dirt, sand, or concrete covered with bedding

Doe must place head through keyhole stanchion to reach hay in trough. It cannot back away and pull hay onto floor where it is wasted

Put pans of grain in front of stanchion openings; set does in place at feeding time so that each goat gets only its allotted ration

Ideal goat shelter provides a well-ventilated but draft-free stall and an easy-to-clean, dust-free space for milking.

Breeding and Milking

When does reach 18 months, they should be bred once each year to ensure a continuing supply of milk. They can mate as young as six months old, but waiting until they are fully developed guards against permanent stunting that the double burden of pregnancy and continuing maturation can cause. The breeding season for goats begins in the fall and lasts through early spring. During these months a doe will come into a two-day-long heat every 21 days until pregnant. Arrange well in advance for the services of a neighbor's buck. Then when you notice signs of heat—restlessness, tail twitching, bleating—take your doe to be serviced. At the end of five months watch for signs such as bleating, reduced feeding, engorged udder, and white vaginal discharge that mean the young are about to be born.

Newborn kids (goats often bear twins) must receive colostrum, the doe's antibody-rich first milk. After that they should be separated from their mother and fed from a pan or bottle. Give them 1/2 to 1/3 pint of milk three times daily for the first two weeks. Then gradually reduce the amount of milk and substitute grain and fresh green hay.

A doe freshens (begins producing milk) after giving birth. Rebreed the goat six months after freshening. You can continue to milk for three months longer, but then allow the doe to dry off by stopping the daily milkings.

Otherwise its strength may be overtaxed. Establish a familiar milking routine by spacing milkings as evenly as possible. A 12-hour interval is ideal but not vital. At milking time keep the atmosphere calm and allow the doe to settle down, then lift or walk it onto the milking stand. Put the doe's head in the stanchion, where a bucket of grain should be waiting. Next, wipe the udder with a warm, moist cloth. This cleans the area and stimulates secretion of a hormone that relaxes the muscles holding the milk in place. Milk each teat alternately, using the technique shown below. When the flow subsides, stop and gently massage the udder from top to bottom to stimulate the flow; then begin milking again.

For good-tasting milk, cleanliness is essential. Even a minute quantity of dry goat manure or dust will damage the milk's flavor if it should fall into the milk bucket. To prevent this, milk in an area that is easy to clean, has few ridges or niches to collect dust, and is separated from the feeding and bedding areas. Keep the hairs around the goat's udder clipped short to minimize the spread of dust that the doe may be carrying, and keep the doe's coat free of dirt by frequent brushing. The person who is doing the milking and the equipment that is used must be scrupulously clean. Clothes should be clean and hands well washed. (For more information on dairy hygiene, see *Making Your Own Dairy Products*, pp.232–241).

The technique of milking, step by step

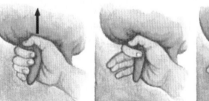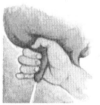

Milk by pressing gently upward against udder, then closing successive fingers; when flow decreases, massage udder.

Protein by the Gallon, Courtesy of Old Bossy

Jersey is the smallest breed, averaging 1,000 lb. Its milk is extremely rich in butterfat

Guernsey is also a relatively small breed. Guernsey milk has a slight yellowish tint

For a family cow avoid a glut of milk by choosing a modest producer—its feed requirements will probably be modest too.

The dairy cow was a nutritional mainstay of the 19th-century homestead, helping to fatten pigs and hens and feed the family. It can perform the same functions for modern homesteaders, exurbanites, and first-time farmers provided it is given the care and attention it needs.

A cow is a major responsibility. It is a big animal—often over 1,200 pounds—and requires relatively large quantities of food. Before obtaining one, be sure that you have at least 2 acres of high-quality, well-drained pasture, a well-ventilated, roomy shed, and a place to store several tons of hay and straw. Also, find out if artificial insemination is locally available; your cow will not continue to produce milk unless bred once a year.

The cow you choose should be gentle, accustomed to hand milking, and have several good years of milking ahead of it. A bred heifer—a cow carrying its first calf—is often an economical choice for a beginner. Since it cannot be milked until after the calf is born, the novice has a chance to adjust to other cow-tending chores. Another good choice is a four- or five-year-old cow in its second or third year of milking. If you have a source of feed and some experience nurturing young animals, you might try buying a three-day-old calf and raising it to maturity, but this is a demanding job.

The cow you buy should have a trim body, clear eyes, and a smooth, elastic udder. The udder should not be lumpy, but protruding veins are typical of a good producer. Try to see the cow milked several times and watch out for any signs of trouble, such as stringy milk or clots and blood in the milk. Some breeders will show you milk production records for their cows, while others will give only a general estimate. In either case buy from a reliable breeder with a reputation for standing behind his promises. He should have proof that his cow is free from tuberculosis and brucellosis, diseases that are rare today but are dangerous because they can infect humans. The breeder should also guarantee in writing that the animal he sells you is able to bear calves.

Troubleshooting

Symptoms	Treatment
Distended stomach, pain	Call veterinarian immediately to treat bloat. Keep cow moving
Clot or blood in milk, swollen udder	Discard milk. Consult veterinarian to treat mastitis. Improve sanitation. Disinfect hands after milking
Swollen feet, pain in legs (foot rot)	Clean foot thoroughly. Apply copper sulfate as powder or salve. Keep bedding and pens dry and clean

Feeding the Dairy Cow

Cows, like sheep and goats, are ruminants and can absorb nutrients from pasture grasses and leaves. Their pasture should also contain legumes, such as clover, alfalfa, or lespedeza, since grasses and leaves alone do not provide adequate protein and high-energy sugars for prolonged milk production. To get maximum food value from any plant, the cow must eat it when it is tender and green. Most dairy farmers turn their cows onto a pasture when the grass is 5 1/2 to 6 inches tall. After the plants are eaten, but before the land is overgrazed, the cows are moved to a new pasture so that the first area can rejuvenate itself. By rotating pastures, the cows are assured a steady supply of nutritious roughage.

During winter months cows must be fed hay. Like fresh pasturage, hay should be tender and green. It is best when cut just as it blooms. From 2 to 3 pounds of top-quality hay per 100 pounds of body weight will meet a cow's daily nutritional needs. When fed excellent hay or pasturage alone, most cows will produce 10 quarts per day during peak production months. This amount, which represents 60 to 70 percent of maximum capacity, should be more than enough for the average family. To boost productivity or to supplement average-quality hay or pasturage, feed a mixture of grain and highprotein meal. Ground corn, oats, barley, and wheat bran are the most popular grains. High-protein meal is the pulp left over after the oil has been extracted from cottonseed, linseed, soybeans, or peanuts. Feed stores sell these supplements already mixed in proper proportion for lactating cows. They also sell high-protein mixtures specially designed to be diluted with your own grain. Feed the high-protein mixture twice daily—it is usually fed during milking—in measured amounts, and make any changes in diet very gradually. Otherwise the cow may develop bloat, a dangerous stomach disorder.

Up to a point the more grain and meal you feed a cow, the more milk it will produce. Beyond that point the extra grain is wasted. To achieve maximum production, gradually increase the grain ration until the increase no longer results in higher productivity. Then cut the ration back slightly. Conversely, when grain rations are cut—or when pasture quality deteriorates—milk production will fall. A rule of thumb is to feed 1 pound of grain for every 3 pounds of milk the cow produces. When fed about half this grain ration, together with good-quality pasture, most cows produce 90 percent of their top capacity.

Besides good feed, the other essentials to top milk production are free access to salt and plenty of water. For best results provide a salt lick and water in the pasture as well as in the cow's stall. Change the water at least twice a day or else install a self-watering device.

Breeding and Milking

A cow must freshen, or bear a calf, in order to produce milk. Heifers (young females) can be bred when they are as young as 10 months old, but it is best to wait until they are 1 1/2 years old or weigh at least 600 pounds.

Today most breeding is done by artificial insemination. Your county agent will help you find a professional inseminator. Arrange well in advance for his services, since the cow will be fertile for only 12 hours after the onset of heat. Signs to watch for are restlessness, bellowing, a swollen vulva, and reduced milk flow. When 21 days have passed after the cow is serviced, watch again for signs of heat. If they reappear, the cow is not settled (pregnant) and must be serviced again.

Carrying a calf while producing 10 or more quarts of milk a day is a tremendous drain on a cow's system. Watch your pasturage carefully to be sure that it is tender, green, and rich in legumes. If the crop shows signs of browning off (as is likely to happen during a hot summer) or if the cow is losing weight, provide some high-energy food supplement. Avoid overfeeding, however, especially during the last months of pregnancy, since this too can cause illness. To keep from overtaxing the cow and to protect future milk production, stop milking two months before the calf is due; the cow will go dry for the remainder of its pregnancy.

The calf will be born 280 days after settling. Bellowing and restlessness are signs that freshening is imminent. Once actual labor begins, check its progress periodically but avoid disturbing the cow. If labor lasts for more than a few hours, call a veterinarian for help.

When the calf is born, be sure it begins to suckle and gets colostrum, the cow's first milk that is rich in vitamins and disease-fighting antibodies. The cow will produce colostrum—which humans should not drink—for five days after freshening. After the first two or three days separate the calf and mother. The calf's new quarters must be clean, dry, and draft free. Cold temperatures are not harmful, but dampness, drafts, and sudden exposure to cold can cause pneumonia. Teach the calf to drink from a bucket by pulling its mouth down to the pail when it is hungry. The calf should receive a daily ration of 1 quart of milk for every 20 pounds of body weight. Provide the milk in three or four equally spaced feedings. When a milk-fed calf is about eight weeks of age, it is ready to be sold as veal.

Begin milking as soon as the calf is removed from its mother. Cleanliness is essential. Keep the milking area free from dirt and sanitize all milking utensils. Pay attention to the cow too. Clip long hairs near its udder and brush the cow daily to remove dirt. (See *Making Your Own Dairy Products,* pp.232–241, for additional information on dairy hygiene.) It is important to maintain a relaxed atmosphere during milking: milk at the same times each day and avoid disturbances.

At milking time lead the cow to its stanchion, where a pail of grain should be waiting. Wipe the udder with a warm, wet cloth, then start to milk as you would a goat. The cow's teats are much larger and will require more strength to milk, but the basic action is the same. The first milk from each of the cow's four teats should be collected in a strip cup, a special cup with a filter on the top. If strings, clots, or blood spots appear on the filter, discard the milk and call a veterinarian.

After testing the milk proceed to milk two of the teats, holding one in each hand and squeezing them alternately. Eventually, their milk flow will slacken. When this happens, change teats and milk the other pair. (It makes no difference which two teats you milk together.) As you empty the second pair, more milk is secreted from the udder into the first pair. Work back and forth, milking one pair and then the other until they do not refill. Then rub the udder with one hand as you strip the teats with the other. To strip, close the thumb and forefinger tightly around the top of the teat, then continue to squeeze as you pull your hand down its length.

Milking Shed and Pens for Cow and Calf

Simple three-sided shed provides the healthiest environment for a cow. With the open front facing away from prevailing winds—usually toward the east or south—the shed ensures plenty of ventilation and allows warm, drying sunlight to reach all the way inside. Rotting, manure-laden bedding on a dirt floor supplies enough heat to keep a cow comfortable in climates as cold as North Dakota's.

The milking area needs careful planning. While a cow can be milked almost anywhere, a well-planned, easy-to-clean area close to the cow's sleeping shed will make the job easier and more sanitary. Floors should be concrete, sloping toward a drain or gutter. Running water is helpful for hosing down walls and floors. There should be ample room to store grain for feeding at milking time.

The same building might contain a calf pen or a spot where a temporary one can be constructed from movable panels when necessary. A lean-to on the cow's shed provides a place to store straw or other bedding material as well as hay, which must be kept dry to protect its nutritive value.

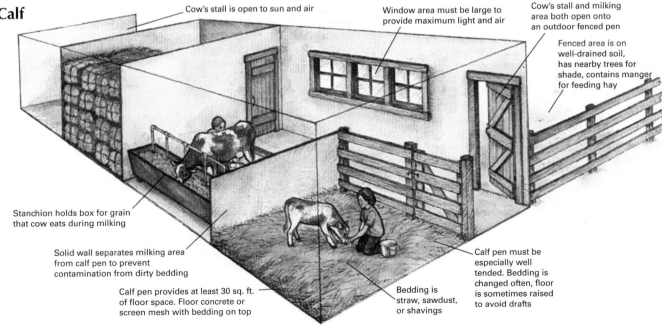

Cow's stall is open to sun and air

Window area must be large to provide maximum light and air

Cow's stall and milking area both open onto an outdoor fenced pen

Fenced area is on well-drained soil, has nearby trees for shade, contains manger for feeding hay

Stanchion holds box for grain that cow eats during milking

Solid wall separates milking area from calf pen to prevent contamination from dirty bedding

Calf pen provides at least 30 sq. ft. of floor space. Floor concrete or screen mesh with bedding on top

Bedding is straw, sawdust, or shavings

Calf pen must be especially well tended. Bedding is changed often, floor is sometimes raised to avoid drafts

Strong and Spirited, The Working Horse Will Pull Its Weight

For a small amount of acreage a horse can be an efficient substitute for a tractor. While the horse is slower, it is also much cheaper to buy, fuel, and repair. It does less damage to the soil, and it can work in areas too wet and hilly for a wheeled vehicle. Purebred draft horses are the ideal types for farm work. Used at one time to carry medieval knights in full armor, these horses have the size and strength necessary for long hours of strenuous labor. Buying a purebred Belgian, Percheron, or Clydesdale is an expensive proposition, however; a more economical alternative would be to purchase a crossbreed. One such cross would be a draft horse sire with a utility-type mare; such crossbreeds have the size—about 1,200 pounds—and steadiness for farm work, though they are not as powerful as drafters. The mule, a cross between a horse and an ass, is another good draft animal. Riding horses are too light for extensive plowing, but if properly taught, some can do light pulling.

Whatever horse you purchase, it should be trained for the work you expect it to do. As a beginner, you will almost certainly be unable to train the animal properly, and you can easily damage its personality by trying. A 7 to 10-year-old gelding or mare would be ideal, but an older horse is better than one that is too young and playful for hard work. Never buy stallions because they are too unpredictable for a novice to handle.

Buying from a reliable breeder is essential, but it is no substitute for close inspection. Examine the horse's stall for any signs of kicking or biting the walls. Watch as the horse is harnessed to be sure it is not head-shy or dangerous to approach. Before it has had a chance to warm up, look for indications of stiffness, such as shifting of weight from one front leg to the other or failure to rest its weight equally on both front feet. Next, see the animal doing the work you will be asking of it and make sure it neither balks nor is too frisky to handle the job. Its gait while working can provide clues to soundness. Shortened stride, nodding of hip or head, unusually high or low carriage of head, and unevenness of gait may mean the horse is lame. After watching the animal work, listen to its breathing to be sure it is not winded. Finally, examine the horse as it cools down; look for any signs of stiffness and for unusual lumps or knobs on the legs.

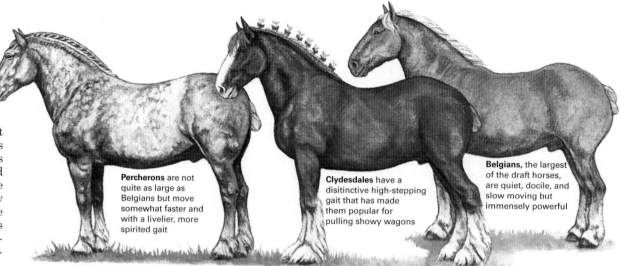

Percherons are not quite as large as Belgians but move somewhat faster and with a livelier, more spirited gait

Clydesdales have a disitinctive high-stepping gait that has made them popular for pulling showy wagons

Belgians, the largest of the draft horses, are quiet, docile, and slow moving but immensely powerful

Horses have filled so many different roles throughout history that there is amazing diversity among breeds. Drafters such as these, weighing 2,200 lb. and standing 17 hands to the top of the shoulder (a hand equals 4 in.), have provided pulling power for centuries.

Feed According to Work Performed

A top-quality, well-fertilized pasture can provide the nutrients an idle horse needs. Provide per horse 2 to 3 acres of grasses combined with high-protein alfalfa, clover, or birds'-foot trefoil. Since horses are destructive of turf, protect the pasture by practicing rotation and by closing off the land whenever it is wet or soggy. When pasturage is unavailable, feed 8 to 12 pounds per day of fresh, green, leafy legume hay.

A working horse—whether used for riding or pulling—needs more energy than can be provided by pasturage and hay alone. Oats are the best grain supplement to feed. They are high in protein, contain plenty of bulky roughage, and are unlikely to cake in the horse's stomach. Wheat bran is another high-protein, bulky feed. Corn is relatively high in carbohydrates but is not high enough in protein. If the grain is dusty, mix it with molasses to reduce dustiness, improve flavor, and provide extra energy. The exact amount of grain to feed depends upon the size of the horse, strenuousness and duration of work, and the quality of pasturage. An underfed horse will lose weight, but overfeeding on rich pasturage or grain can cause founder (laminitis), a painful inflammation of the lining of the hoof wall. For light work a daily supplement of 1/3 pound of grain per 100 pounds of horse is sufficient. This can be raised as high as 1 1/4 pounds of grain per 100 pounds of live weight during heavy work.

Horses have delicate stomachs and must be fed carefully. Eating and drinking while overheated from exercise—like overeating—can cause laminitis and colic. For best health, feed a horse at the same times each day—morning and evening for light work; morning, noon, and night for strenuous work. Make changes gradually, and avoid turning a horse suddenly into a lush pasture.

Fresh water should be available at all times—in the pasture as well as in the horse's stall. Change the water twice a day if you do not have an automatic waterer. A salt lick is also essential. Many owners provide one containing trace minerals especially balanced for horses.

Troubleshooting

Symptoms	Treatment
Upset stomach (colic)	Call veterinarian immediately. Keep horse standing. Improve feed
Sore feet (founder)	Consult veterinarian. Be careful not to overfeed or feed while hot
Hoof odor	Consult veterinarian. Treat with salve
Teeth worn to sharp edge	Have veterinarian file teeth so feeding is not disrupted

Shetland ponies stand about 10 hands. They descend from miniature drafters of Scotland's Shetland Islands

Morgans, a spirited breed averaging 14 to 15 hands, can do many kinds of farm work

Quarter horses, noted for dexterity and speed, are favorites for working cattle

Speed, agility, steadiness, and spirit are among the qualities that have been cultivated in horses of various breeds. Nonpurebreds, too, exhibit marked differences in personality and aptitude. Know which traits are important to you before you buy a horse.

Stabling Your Horses

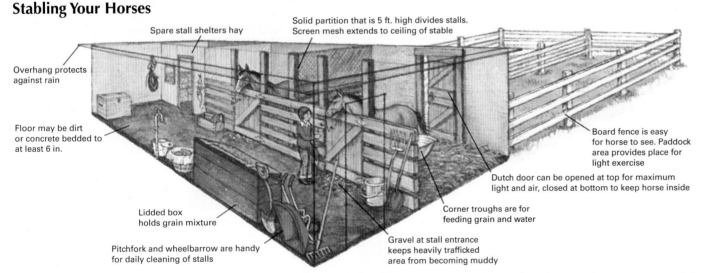

Spare stall shelters hay

Solid partition that is 5 ft. high divides stalls. Screen mesh extends to ceiling of stable

Overhang protects against rain

Floor may be dirt or concrete bedded to at least 6 in.

Board fence is easy for horse to see. Paddock area provides place for light exercise

Dutch door can be opened at top for maximum light and air, closed at bottom to keep horse inside

Lidded box holds grain mixture

Corner troughs are for feeding grain and water

Gravel at stall entrance keeps heavily trafficked area from becoming muddy

Pitchfork and wheelbarrow are handy for daily cleaning of stalls

Stall measuring 12 ft. by 12 ft. is ideal for a horse. A dirt floor is best; although it is more difficult to maintain than concrete, it is easier on a horse's feet. Make the floor several inches higher than the surrounding ground and rake it periodically to keep it level. From time to time dig out the dirt and replace it with a clean new layer. If you own more than one horse, each will need its own stall, with floor to ceiling partitions between stalls.

The horse should have access to a paddock or pasture. The more time it spends there, the better its muscle condition will be. The best pasture fences are of boards or the traditional post and rail (see *Fences*, pp.70–73); both styles are safe, secure, and highly visible. An electrified wire can be run along the top to discourage an especially spirited animal. If you use wire fencing instead, choose a small mesh size so that the horse's hooves cannot get caught, and tie rags to the top so the horse can see the fence. Avoid barbed wire, since it can damage your animal. Set windows high in wall and screen them against flies and other insects.

Checking teeth and conformation

Placement of legs beneath body, slope of shoulders, and slant of ankles are all aspects of a horse's conformation that affect leverage and, therefore, pulling power. Teeth give a general idea of a horse's age. In a young horse they are nearly vertical; in a 20-year-old horse they slant forward.

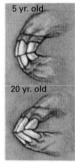

5 yr. old

20 yr. old

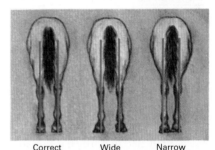

Correct · Wide · Narrow

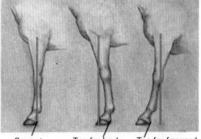

Correct · Too far back · Too far forward

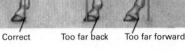

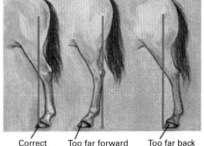

Correct · Too far forward · Too far back

Hardworking Drafters Need Considerate Care

Whether you intend to hitch your horse to a plow or show it in a ring, daily grooming is essential to good health as well as appearance. A good brushing before every workout prevents painful hard-to-cure skin injuries caused by dirt matted beneath the harness, saddle, or other tack. Another brushing is necessary after a hard day's work to remove the sweat and dust that will have accumulated in the horse's coat.

For proper grooming you will need a currycomb, a stiff-bristled brush, and a brush or comb for the mane and tail. The currycomb is used first. Rub it in a circular motion over the horse's neck and sides to remove dirt caked on the surface. Avoid using it near bony, sensitive areas, such as the legs, where a bump from its metal or rubber ridges would be extremely painful. After currying, brush the coat to remove embedded dirt and distribute the natural oils. Press the brush firmly enough against the horse's body so that the bristles penetrate the coat but not so hard that you hurt the tender skin beneath. Always brush in the direction of the coat hairs. Pay special attention to the lower legs and ankles—they get extremely dirty and yet are very sensitive. As a result, they need slow, gentle treatment.

Wipe the horse's face and then the area beneath its tail with a clean cloth wrung out in warm water. A bit of mild soap can be added to the water for washing the tail area if it is particularly dirty, but be sure to rinse the soap off thoroughly. Sponges are sometimes used instead of a cloth, but they are more likely to spread disease because they are difficult to sterilize. Gently comb or brush the mane and tail. When doing the tail, stand beside the horse, not behind where you can get kicked.

An acre per horse per day is an old rule of thumb that tells how much land a team of horses can be expected to plow. Few farm chores are harder. By way of comparison, a single horse can harrow, cultivate, plant, or mow as much as 7 to 10 acres in a day.

If the horse is confined in a paddock or stall, its hooves should be cleaned daily to remove any manure, debris, or stones embedded between the shoe and the frog (the sensitive pad at the back of the foot). At the same time check to be sure the shoes have not worked loose and that the hoof walls are not overgrown. Hooves should be trimmed and reshod every six to eight weeks. Like fingernails, they grow slowly—1/4 inch to 1/2 inch per month—but the toe grows faster than the heel. If the toe becomes too long, the horse's weight will be forced back toward the heel and its stance changed in a way that can damage its legs and feet. On an unshod horse an overgrown hoof can break off unevenly, causing a cracked hoof. A farrier will cut and file the hoof walls to just the right length and shape them before fitting a new set of horseshoes. Never try to do this job yourself. Proper shoeing can only be learned by years of training with an expert. Poor shoeing can permanently injure the horse.

A mule is the sterile offspring of a jack (a male ass) and a mare. Mules have more endurance than horses and are noted for being tough, strong, and surefooted. A female ass, or jennet, bred to a stallion produces a hinny. Jacks weighing 1,100 lb. and standing 15 to 16 hands tall can be bred to average-sized mares to produce mules strong enough for drafting. If they are to breed with mares, the jacks must be separated early from other asses and raised exclusively with young horses until thoroughly trained.

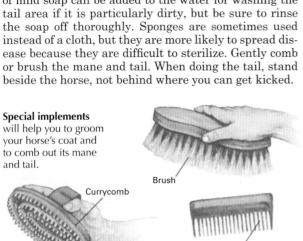

Special implements will help you to groom your horse's coat and to comb out its mane and tail.

Brush

Currycomb

Comb

Clean hooves regularly. To lift horse's foot, face toward rear of horse, run hand down its leg to ankle, and lift. (A horse will usually lift its foot.) Starting near hoof wall, run the hoof pick from heel toward toe to remove accumulated dirt. Check hoof wall for dryness and apply salve if it is needed.

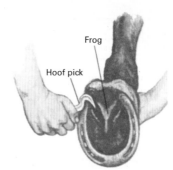

Frog

Hoof pick

Hitching a Team

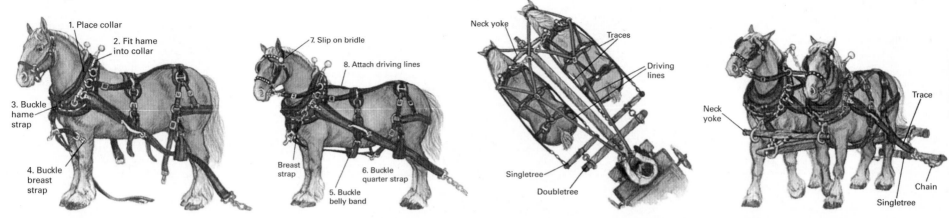

1. Place collar
2. Fit hame into collar
3. Buckle hame strap
4. Buckle breast strap

7. Slip on bridle
8. Attach driving lines
Breast strap
6. Buckle quarter strap
5. Buckle belly band

Neck yoke
Traces
Driving lines
Singletree
Doubletree

Neck yoke
Trace
Chain
Singletree

1. Start by putting collar on horse. Fit hame into collar, spread out harness, and buckle straps.

2. Buckle harness straps under horse's belly, then put on bridle and driving lines.

3. Arrange driving lines on a team as shown. For safety keep lines in top condition.

4. To hitch wagon, clip breast straps to neck yoke and attach chains to the singletrees.

Pulling and Plowing

The only sure way to learn to use a team for plowing is to be taught by someone with experience. Horses must be handled firmly and consistently; even a well-trained team can be ruined by a poor driver. Use the command words that your horses were trained to obey. In America standard commands are "whoa" (stop), "get up" (go), "gee" (turn right), and "haw" (turn left). Learn to maintain steady control of the reins; keep them taut, but never pull so hard that you damage a horse's mouth.

Be careful and considerate of your animals. Talk kindly and quietly to them so that they learn to recognize and trust your voice. During breaks in work loosen their collars so they can relax too. Never leave a hitched horse unattended. If you must tie it up temporarily, use the bridle, not the harness straps, and be sure it is tied securely to something immovable. A team that has been idle during the winter needs to get back into condition gradually. Start with small amounts of light work and build up gradually to such heavier jobs as plowing. Keep your equipment in top condition and do not let anyone inexperienced drive your team. With care you will avoid injuring either yourself or your valuable horses.

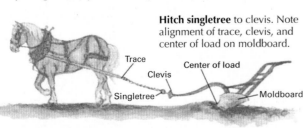

Hitch singletree to clevis. Note alignment of trace, clevis, and center of load on moldboard.

Trace
Center of load
Clevis
Singletree
Moldboard

Draft horses can also be trained to pull a sleigh in the wintertime.

Part Four

Enjoying Your Harvest The Year Round

Gather the gifts of Earth with equal hand;
Henceforth ye too may share the birthright soil,
The corn, the wine, and all the harvest-home.
—*E.C. Stedman*, The Feast of Harvest

Once the harvest is in, the next job is to make sure it does not go to waste. Countryfolk call this process putting by: storing up today's surplus against tomorrow's shortage. Putting by is a happy skill because most of the old-time methods of preservation add delicious flavors to the food. Nowadays, such products as cheese, yogurt, smoked meat, sauerkraut, pickles, and jams and jellies are prepared more for their taste than because they keep well on the shelf. In *Enjoying Your Harvest the Year Round* all the ways to put food by are explained along with dozens of delicious recipes that will add special tang to the preserved foods. There are instructions on maple sugaring too and detailed descriptions and recipes for making beers, wines, and a host of excellent nonalcoholic drinks. Finally, there is a collection of regional recipes followed by primers on two forgotten arts: cooking in a fireplace and cooking on a wood-burning stove.

Preserving Produce

One Harvest Can Provide A Year-round Feast For Your Whole Family

In the not too distant past, drying, salting, and live storage were the only ways known for preserving produce. The Indians of North and South America depended on sun-dried foods. American settlers survived bitter winters by eating salt-cured produce or vegetables stored live in root cellars. Caesar's army carried pickled food with it, and the builders of the Great Wall of China dined on salt-cured vegetables.

Nowadays we can choose among a much larger variety of processes, including canning, freezing, and jellying. Besides being more convenient, these newer methods have helped to transform the job of preserving food from a mere necessity into a full-fledged culinary art.

Red peppers, like mushrooms, peas, corn, and many other vegetables, can be dried in the sun. A few long, hot days with low humidity should do the trick.

A Survey of Ways to Preserve Fruits and Vegetables

Food spoils for two reasons: the action of external biological agents, such as bacteria and molds, and the digestive actions of naturally occurring enzymes. The art of "putting food by," as canning and other preserving methods were known in the old days, consists of slowing down or halting both types of spoilage while at the same time preserving nutritive values and creating food that tastes good. No system of preservation fully achieves all these goals, but no system fails to contribute something of its own—in taste, in food value, in convenience, in simplicity, in economy.

Live storage—either aboveground or belowground—preserves produce with minimum alteration in taste, color, and vitamin content. However, such storage requires certain temperature ranges: winters must be cold enough to slow down food deterioration, but food must not be allowed to freeze. In addition, only certain fruits and vegetables can be stored by this method, notably apples, pears, and root crops.

Canning involves heating to high temperatures, resulting in vitamin loss and changes in taste. Water soluble vitamins can be retained by conserving the cooking liquid, but some others are destroyed. If food is canned in jars, store it in a dark place to avoid loss of riboflavin by exposure to light. A cool area—below 65°F—also helps retain nutrients: at 80°F vitamin C will be reduced by 25 percent after one year, vitamin A by 10 percent, and thiamine by 20 percent.

Freezing, the most modern method of food preservation, has a minimum effect on flavor and food values if the food is properly prepared and carefully packaged. Only vitamin E and pyridoxine (B_6) are destroyed by the freezing process. For best results, frozen foods should be stored at 0°F or below. Vitamin C is easily oxidized and as much as half can be lost if food is kept at 15°F for six months. Length of storage time also affects nutrients. Even at 0°F, most of the vitamin C can be lost if produce is stored for a year.

Salt curing alters the taste of the food (although in the case of pickling and fermenting, the results are delicious). If salt curing is done in a strong salt solution, nutritional value is greatly reduced because the food must be thoroughly washed before it can be eaten, a process that will rinse away vitamins and minerals. A weaker salt solution will preserve more nutrients, but there will be a greater risk of spoilage. Nor is salt curing reliable for truly long-term storage: pickles, sauerkraut, and relishes must be canned if they are to be stored for more than a few weeks after the three- to five-week salt-curing process is finished.

Jellying changes the taste of the food because of the large amounts of sugar, honey, or other sweetener that are needed in order to form a gel. In addition, some vitamins are lost during the heat processing required to sterilize fruit and make an airtight seal.

Drying retains a high percentage of most vitamins. But if dried foods are stored for long periods, considerable destruction of vitamins A, C, and E can result because of oxidation, especially if food has not been properly blanched. In addition, vitamins A and E and some B-complex vitamins are broken down by light; as a result, considerable food value can be lost by drying outdoors in direct sunlight.

Choosing the right storage method

Almost every fruit and vegetable can be stored by one of the common preserving methods: live storage (root cellars and in-ground storage), canning, freezing, salt curing, jellying, and drying. The table gives the methods that are considered most successful in preserving flavor, texture, appearance, and nutrients in various produce.

Produce	Recommended storage methods
Apples	Live storage, canning, jams and jellies, drying
Apricots	Canning, jams and jellies, drying
Asparagus	Canning, freezing
Beans (green)	Canning, freezing, salt curing
Beans (lima)	Canning, freezing, drying
Beets	Live storage, canning, salt curing
Broccoli	Freezing
Cabbage	Live storage, salt curing
Carrots	Live storage, canning, freezing
Cauliflower	Freezing, salt curing
Celery	Live storage
Cherries	Canning, jams and jellies
Corn	Canning, freezing, salt curing
Cucumbers	Salt curing
Onions	Live storage
Parsnips	Live storage
Peaches	Canning, jams and jellies, drying
Pears	Live storage, canning, salt curing, jams and jellies, drying
Peas	Canning, freezing, drying
Peppers	Freezing, salt curing
Plums	Canning, jams and jellies, drying (prunes)
Potatoes	Live storage, canning
Pumpkin	Live storage, canning
Radishes	Live storage
Raspberries	Jams and jellies
Rutabagas	Live storage, salt curing
Spinach	Canning, freezing
Squash (summer)	Canning, freezing
Squash (winter)	Live storage, canning
Sweet potatoes	Live storage
Tomatoes	Canning, salt curing
Turnips	Live storage, salt curing

Maintaining a Winter Garden

The simplest method of preserving garden produce is to leave it right where it is—in the garden. The technique is particularly suitable for root crops, such as radishes, beets, carrots, and parsnips, but even tomatoes can be kept beyond their normal season. With little more than a covering of earth and straw to help maintain a temperature of 30°F to 40°F, many vegetables can be safely left in the ground from the end of one growing season to the start of the next. The main requirement for successful in-garden preservation is wintertime temperatures that are near or just below freezing.

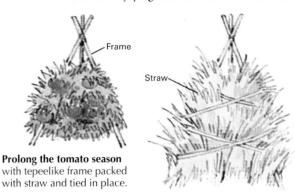

Prolong the tomato season with tepeelike frame packed with straw and tied in place.

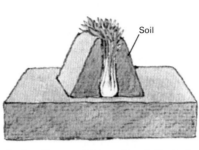
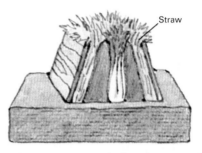
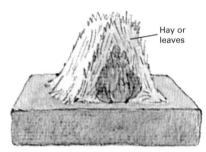

Bank soil around late celery (left). As temperature drops, cover plants completely. In near-freezing weather add straw held down by boards (center). Cover kale, collards, parsnips, and salsify with 2 in. of hay or leaf mulch (right).

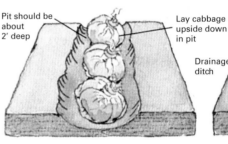

Cabbages can be stored in a long pit dug in the garden as well as in a root cellar (p.204) or conical mound (p.205). Dig storage pit about 2 ft. deep, pull cabbages out by the roots, set them upside down, and cover them completely with soil.

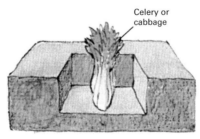
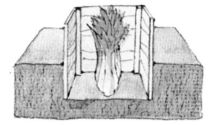
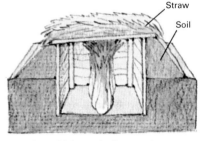

Trenching preserves both cabbages and celery. Dig shallow trench for cabbage, a deep one (2 ft.) for celery. Place plants, roots down, in trenches; then replace soil. Build frame high enough to cover plants, bank soil against it, and top with straw.

Keep Produce Fresh In Cold, Moist Air

If you live in an area where fall and winter temperatures remain near freezing and fluctuate very little, you can store root vegetables, apples, and pears in a wide variety of insulated structures and containers. These range from a simple mound in the garden to a full-fledged root cellar. In each case, the storage unit must maintain temperatures in the 30°F to 40°F range with humidity between 80 and 90 percent. The high mois-

ture content of the air prevents shriveling due to loss of water by evaporation. An old-fashioned, unheated basement is an ideal spot for a root cellar, but a modern basement can be used if a northerly corner is available. Construction details are given below. Root cellars can also be built outside the house, either above the ground or embedded in earth.

Different vegetables can be stored together in a single container, but fruits should never be stored with vegetables nor should different fruits be stored together. Be sure to check stored produce every week or two, and cull out any that is spoiling. The old saying "One rotten apple spoils the barrel" still holds true.

In addition to the basement, many warmer areas within the house can be utilized for preserving crops. Onions, pumpkins, and squash, for example, do best at temperatures between 50°F and 55°F with a humidity of 60 to 70 percent. An unheated attic or an upstairs room that is closed off for the winter months are excellent storage sites for these vegetables.

Onions and herbs can be strung and hung upside down above the hearth or in the kitchen for preservation. Tomatoes that have been picked green can be stored for several weeks by letting them ripen slowly. Set the tomatoes on a rack or shelf, spacing them 6 inches apart to allow for air circulation.

Setting Up a Simple Root Cellar

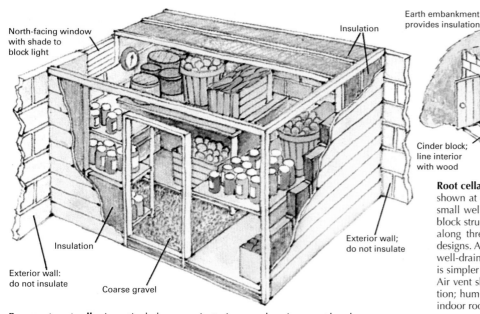

Basement root cellar is particularly convenient, since produce is near at hand.

Root cellars can be part of the house, as shown at left, or completely separate. A small well-insulated shed or a concrete block structure (above) with soil banked along three walls are both time-tested designs. A wood-lined excavation dug in well-drained soil with a hatch to get in is simpler yet and still quite serviceable. Air vent should be provided for circulation; humidity control is the same as for indoor root cellar.

An 8-foot by 10-foot root cellar will accommodate 60 bushels of produce, more than enough for most families. Indoor root cellars are the most convenient to use and easiest to build. Try to use a northeast or northwest corner of your basement that has at least one outside wall and is as far as possible from your oil burner or other heat source. One north-facing window is desirable for ventilation. The interior walls of the root cellar should be constructed of wood, and if the basement is heated, they should be insulated. The precise amount of insu-

lation needed depends on the average basement temperature, but standard 4-inch-thick fiberglass batting with a foil or plastic vapor barrier should be more than adequate. Install the insulation with the barrier against the wood. Add an insulated door and fit the window with shades to block out light. To keep humidity high, spread 3 inches of gravel on the floor and sprinkle it occasionally with water. You can also maintain humidity by storing the produce in a closed container, such as a metal can lined with paper.

Window Wells and Stairways

Basement window well can be used as a mini root cellar. Cover the well with screening and wood to keep in heat and keep out animals. When temperatures drop below freezing, open window so that heat from the house can warm the storage area. If outside temperatures rise into the 70s, open window to allow cool basement air to circulate in storage area.

Outdoor basement entrance can make an excellent root cellar. Install a door at the bottom of the steps to block off house heat. The top steps near the outside door are coolest, the bottom steps are warmest. Store root crops, such as potatoes, on top steps; warmth-loving pumpkins, squash, and onions at bottom; apples and pears in between. Place pans of water at the bottom of the stairwell to provide necessary humidity.

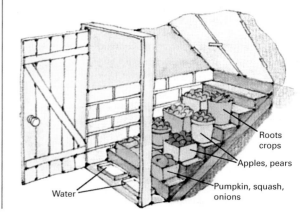

Heap up root crops and store them right in the garden

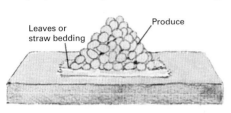

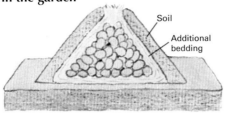

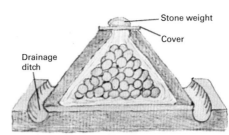

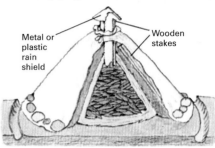

1. Spread several inches of leaves or straw as bedding. Stack produce in cone shape.

2. Cover produce with bedding and 4 in. of soil. Let bedding extend through soil for air.

3. Small drainage ditches and wood or metal covering protect cone from rainfall and runoff.

4. Cover large stacks with tarp; provide additional ventilation with wide central opening.

Create a storage chamber out of bales of hay

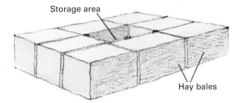

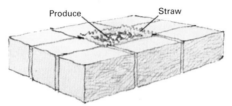

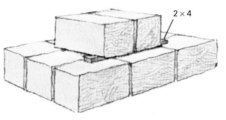

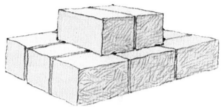

1. Form hay bales into rectangle. Central opening will be used as storage area.

2. Line opening with straw and stack produce. Spread hay over each item, then over stack.

3. Use additional bales as a lid over the opening. Raise bales on 2 × 4 for ventilation.

4. During periods of severe weather remove the 2 × 4 in order to seal opening.

Store apples in an upright barrel

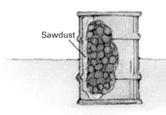

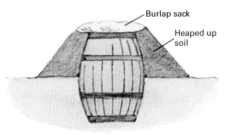

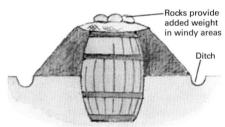

1. For apple storage, start by burying wooden barrel or metal drum halfway in ground.

2. If metal drum is used, line it with sawdust at bottom and between produce and sides.

3. Fill barrel or drum with apples. Cover with leaf-filled sack, then pile soil around sides.

4. Dig a 6-in. ditch around barrel for drainage; put rocks on sack to keep it in place.

Turn the barrel on its side and store other types of produce

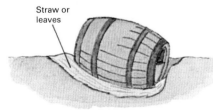

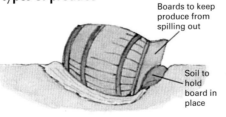

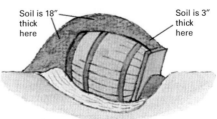

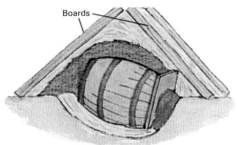

1. Dig space for barrel in well-drained area. Put bedding under barrel and fill with produce.

2. Slant open end down so any moisture will run out, then place board over the opening.

3. Cover sides and upper end of barrel with 18 in. of soil. Cover lower end with 3 in. of soil.

4. Cover everything with straw. Place boards on top to keep straw from blowing away.

205

High-Heat Processing Eliminates Spoilage

Canning has been one of the most popular methods of preserving food since 1809, when the technique was first developed by the Frenchman Nicolas Appert. Today over 40 percent of the families living in the United States do some home canning, and the percentage is increasing. The principle behind canning is simple: decay and spoilage are caused either by enzymes in the food itself or by bacteria and other microorganisms. During the canning process, food is heated to a high temperature to stop the action of the enzymes and to kill all decay organisms. The food is then stored in sterile, airtight containers to prevent contamination.

Different foods require different processing temperatures. Low acid vegetables—and this includes every type other than tomatoes—can harbor heat-resistant bacteria and must be heated to at least 240°F, a temperature that can only be achieved by pressure canning. High acid foods, including tomatoes and most fruits, can be processed at the temperature of boiling water—212°F—since the only spoilage microorganisms present in them will be destroyed at this lower temperature. Pickled vegetables can also be processed in a boiling water bath.

Cans and jars

Home canners generally do their canning in glass jars rather than tin cans. Jars are easier to use, cost less, and allow you to see the contents. In addition, they can be reused many times and are chemically inert with respect to all types of food. The tin can's immunity to breakage is its only significant advantage. Two commonly used jar designs are shown at right, along with an old-fashioned clamp-type jar. Jars—and tins as well—come in a variety of sizes ranging from 1/2 pint (1 cup) to 1 gallon and larger.

If you plan to can in tins, you will need to purchase a sealing device. To check that the sealer is properly adjusted, seal an empty can, then immerse the can in warm water for several minutes. No bubbles should rise from the can. When canning in tins, the food should be packed while it is hot (more than 170°F) or else heated to that temperature in the can. Seal the can immediately after heating, then process it by the appropriate method shown on the opposite page. Processing is similar to jar canning except that steam pressure can be reduced immediately after the heating period is completed.

Specialized Canning Utensils

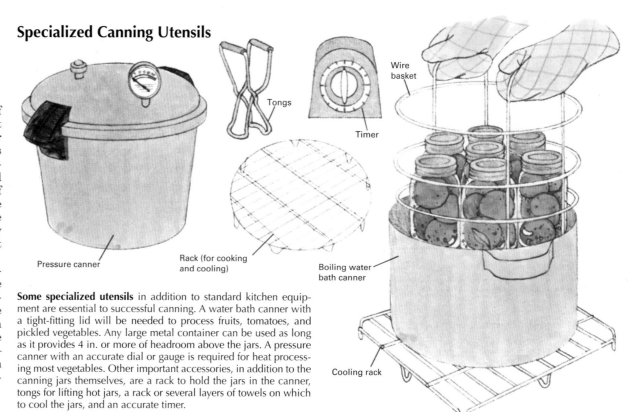

Tongs

Timer

Wire basket

Pressure canner

Rack (for cooking and cooling)

Boiling water bath canner

Cooling rack

Some specialized utensils in addition to standard kitchen equipment are essential to successful canning. A water bath canner with a tight-fitting lid will be needed to process fruits, tomatoes, and pickled vegetables. Any large metal container can be used as long as it provides 4 in. or more of headroom above the jars. A pressure canner with an accurate dial or gauge is required for heat processing most vegetables. Other important accessories, in addition to the canning jars themselves, are a rack to hold the jars in the canner, tongs for lifting hot jars, a rack or several layers of towels on which to cool the jars, and an accurate timer.

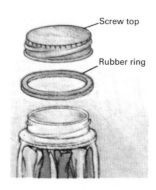

Screw top

Rubber ring

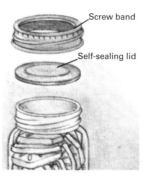

Screw band

Self-sealing lid

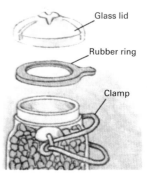

Glass lid

Rubber ring

Clamp

Canning machine

Porcelain-lined cap consists of screw top and rubber ring. To seal, fit wet ring against shoulder of jar, screw on cap firmly, then back off a quarter turn. When jar is removed from canner, immediately screw cap tight.

Self-sealing cap consists of lid with sealant around its rim and a screw-on band that holds lid against lip of jar. Tighten band firmly before processing and do not loosen again. Band can be reused but not the lid.

Bailed jar with glass lid and wire clamps is rarely sold now. Lid is held in place with long clamp during processing, then short clamp is snapped down for a tight seal. Decorative replicas should not be used for canning.

Tin cans are sealed by machine. Plain tin cans are safe for all foods, but to avoid discoloration of produce enamel-lined tins are used for corn, beets, berries, cherries, pumpkin, rhubarb, squash, and plums.

The ABCs of Canning

Vegetables and fruits must be pretreated before they are packed into jars for heat processing. Wash all produce, and cut vegetables into pieces. Berries and other kinds of small fruits can be left whole, but larger fruits, such as peaches, pears, and pineapples, should be pitted, if necessary, and sliced. Fruits are often dipped in ascorbic acid (vitamin C) and packed in sugar syrup to preserve their shape, color, texture, and flavor.

There are two ways to pack the produce into jars: raw (raw packed) or cooked (hot packed). To hot pack most fruits or vegetables, steam them, or heat them to boiling in juice, water, or syrup; then immediately pack them into the containers. (Tomatoes and some fruits can be cooked in their own juices.) For raw packing, load clean produce tightly into containers and pour on boiling juice, water, or syrup. The exact amount of space to leave at the top of the jar above the packed fruits or vegetables is specified on page 208. Wipe the rim and sealing ring to remove any particles of food, then close the jar and proceed with the canning process: boiling water bath for fruits and high acid vegetables, pressure canning for low acid vegetables. After canning, store food in a dark place, since light can cause discoloration and loss of nutrients. Be sure to date and label all jars.

Boiling water bath canning

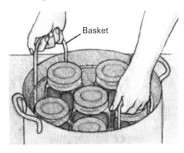

1. Fill canner halfway with hot water, load jars in basket, and put inside.

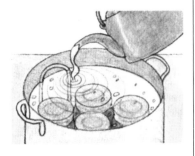

2. Add boiling water to 2 in. above jars. Do not pour directly on jars.

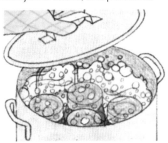

3. Cover canner. Bring water to rolling boil and start timing.

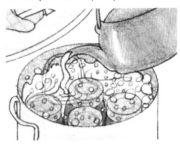

4. Reduce heat, but maintain rapid boil. Add boiling water if needed.

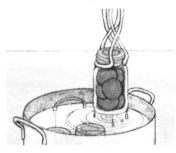

5. When processing time is up, remove jars immediately with tongs.

6. Tighten lids if needed. Set jars on rack, leaving space between them.

Pressure-cooker canning

1. Pour 2 to 3 in. of boiling water into bottom of pressure canner.

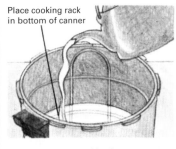

2. Place jars on rack set at bottom of canner. Jars must not touch.

3. Fasten lid. Turn heat to maximum. Let steam exhaust 10 minutes.

4. When the first inch of the steam jet is nearly invisible, close the vent.

5. At 8-lb. pressure lower heat slightly. Let pressure rise to 10 lb.

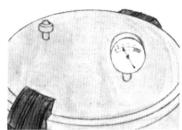

6. At 10-lb. pressure start timing. Hold pressure for full canning period.

7. Remove canner from heat and let cool. Do not pour cold water on it.

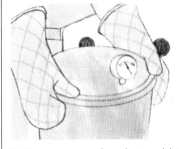

8. When pressure is zero, open vent, then lid. Tilt lid as shown for safety.

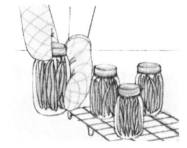

9. Set jars on rack leaving spaces between jars. Tighten lids if necessary.

It Pays to Be Careful When Canning Food

Canning must be carried out with scrupulous care if bacterial contamination and spoilage are to be avoided. Most types of spoilage cause only minor illness at worst, but one type—botulism—is extremely dangerous and often fatal. This form of food poisoning is caused by toxins produced by germs that multiply rapidly in the low-oxygen, low-acid environment of canned vegetables. To prevent botulism as well as other food poisoning, it is essential that care be taken at every step of the way.

The first rule is to can only perfect produce. Overripe or damaged fruits and vegetables are prone to spoilage. Inspect jars, lids, and sealing rings to be sure they are in perfect condition, then wash and scald them before use. Wash all produce thoroughly, and pretreat it according to a reliable recipe and the principles described on page 207. Be sure to use the correct time, temperature, and method of processing. (Because the spores that cause botulism are killed only at temperatures well above boiling, all vegetables except tomatoes must be pressure canned.) When canning with the boiling water bath method, use a lidded container and keep the jars totally immersed in rapidly boiling water. Before starting to pressure can, test the canner according to the manufacturer's instructions. After processing, check the seal on every jar: when you push down on a self-sealing lid, it should stay down. Test porcelain lids by turning jars upside down; if you see a steady stream of tiny air bubbles, the seal is not airtight.

There are further safety precautions to take after the processed food is on the shelf. Discard any jar whose contents appear foamy or discolored, whose lid bulges or is misshapen, or whose rim is leaking. Be sure that the canned produce is normal before you eat it; discoloration, odor, mold, and spurting liquid are all reasons to discard it. When disposing of suspect food, place it where animals or humans cannot accidentally eat it. Home-canned vegetables, except tomatoes, should be cooked before they are served. Bring the vegetables to a rolling boil, then boil an additional 20 minutes for corn or spinach, 10 minutes for other vegetables.

Store canned goods in a cool, dark place—a root cellar is ideal. Jars let you see all the produce easily, but they must still be dated either on the lid or on a label. Also list such additives as salt, sugar, and spices.

Choose the Proper Canning Method and Follow Procedures Exactly

The specifics of canning vary from one fruit or vegetable to the next. For high-acid produce, use the boiling water bath method; start to time only when the bath reaches a rolling boil. For low-acid produce, use a pressure canner. Let steam vent for 10 minutes to expel all air from the canner, then close the vent to let pressure build. Start timing after pressure in the canner reaches 10 pounds. If pressure falls below 10 pounds at any time during processing, start timing over again. Processing times for both methods depend upon the size of the jar used.

Adjustments for high altitudes

If you live in an area that is more than 1,000 feet above sea level, the reduced atmospheric pressure causes water to boil at temperatures lower than 212°F. To compensate, you must increase processing times for boiling water baths. You must also increase pressure settings for pressure canning to attain the required 240°F temperature. Add time or pressure according to the table.

Vegetable	Time to maintain pressure for pints	Time to maintain pressure for quarts
Asparagus	25 min.	30 min.
Beets	30 min.	35 min.
Carrots	25 min.	30 min.
Corn	55 min.	–
Cowpeas	35 min.	40 min.
Lima beans	40 min.	50 min.
Potatoes	35 min.	40 min.
Pumpkin	55 min.	90 min.
Snap beans	20 min.	25 min.
Winter squash	55 min.	90 min.

Fruit or vegetable	Time in boiling water bath for pints		Time in boiling water bath for quarts	
	Hot pack	Raw pack	Hot pack	Raw pack
Apples	15 min.	–	20 min.	–
Apricots	20 min.	25 min.	25 min.	30 min.
Berries	10 min.	10 min.	15 min.	15 min.
Cherries	10 min.	20 min.	15 min.	25 min.
Peaches	20 min.	25 min.	25 min.	30 min.
Pears	20 min.	25 min.	25 min.	30 min.
Plums	20 min.	20 min.	25 min.	25 min.
Rhubarb	10 min.	–	10 min.	–
Sauerkraut	15 min.	15 min.	20 min.	20 min.
Tomatoes	35 min.	40 min.	45 min.	50 min.
Tomato juice	35 min.	–	35 min.	–

Altitude above sea level	For boiling water bath: of 20 min. or less, add	of more than 20 min., add	For pressure canning, add
1,000'	1 min.	2 min.	1/2 lb.
2,000'	2 min.	4 min.	1 lb.
3,000'	3 min.	6 min.	1 1/2 lb.
4,000'	4 min.	8 min.	2 lb.
5,000'	5 min.	10 min.	2 1/2 lb.
6,000'	6 min.	12 min.	3 lb.
7,000'	7 min.	14 min.	3 1/2 lb.
8,000'	8 min.	16 min.	4 lb.
9,000'	9 min.	18 min.	4 1/2 lb.
10,000'	10 min.	20 min.	5 lb.

Simple Recipes With a Delicious Flavor Difference

Try a variety of flavorings and combinations when canning fruits and vegetables. Sugar or salt can be added or deleted from any recipe without changing the processing requirements; so too can vinegar, lemon juice, or spices. Tomatoes can be flavored in a number of ways to make condiments and sauces. But be careful when adding any other vegetable, such as onions, peppers, and celery, to tomatoes: the mixture will be less acid than tomatoes alone and *must* be pressure canned. In addition, changes in density can affect processing time, so do not try to mix a variety of vegetables unless you have a reliable recipe that includes canning instructions.

Fruit Puree

3 lb. Fruit	Sugar to taste

Wash and cut up fruit, remove any pits. Simmer fruit pulp until soft (about 15 min.), adding water as necessary and stirring frequently to prevent sticking. Put pulp through food mill or strainer. Add sugar to pureed pulp. Simmer pulp for five minutes more. Pack hot puree into jars, allowing 1/2-in. headroom. Adjust lids. Process in boiling water bath for 10 minutes for either pint or quart jars. *Makes 1 quart.*

Pear Honey

8 cups ripe pears, peeled and chopped	1 lemon, juice of and rind cut into pieces
5 cups sugar	

Put all ingredients into large heavy pot. Bring slowly to a boil and simmer until thick (about 45 minutes). Stir frequently to avoid burning. Pour boiling mixture into jars, leaving 1/2-in. headroom. Process in boiling water bath for 20 minutes for either quarts or pints. *Makes 1 quart.*

Applesauce

3 lb. apples, quartered and cored	1/4 tsp. cinnamon sugar to taste

Place apples in a saucepan with 1/2 cup water. Bring slowly to a boil, then reduce heat and simmer until soft (about 10 minutes). Add cinnamon and sugar and stir. Pack hot applesauce into jars, allowing 1/2-in. headroom. Insert knife to pierce any air bubbles. Adjust lids. Process in boiling water bath for 10 minutes for either pint or quart jars. *Makes 1 quart.*

Brandied Pears

1/4-1/2 cup sugar	2 cups water
1 tbsp. lemon juice	2–3 lb. perfect pears,
1 tbsp. lemon rind	peeled, halved,
2 cups brandy	and cored

Mix sugar, lemon juice, rind, brandy, and water, and bring to boil. Add pears a few at a time, and cook until tender (about 20 minutes). Pack pears in jars, leaving 1/2-in. headroom. After all the pears are cooked and packed into jars, return liquid to a boil. Pour liquid over pears, leaving 1/2-in. headroom. Adjust lids. Process in boiling water bath 20 minutes for pint jars, 25 minutes for quart jars. *Makes 1 quart.*

Cream-Style Corn

5 lb. fresh corn	1 tsp. salt

Husk and wash ears of corn. Cut kernels from cob, but cut far enough away from the cob that the knife blade slices through the center of the kernels. Scrape cobs with knife to extract juice and pulp from part of kernels still on cob. Add scraped pulp to cut kernels. Pack corn into pint jars, allowing 1 1/2-in. headroom. Add 1/2 tsp. salt to each jar. Fill to 1/2 in. from top with boiling water. Adjust lids. Process jars in pressure canner at 10 lb. for 95 minutes. Do not use quart jars to process corn. *Makes 1 quart.*

Beans in Tomato Sauce

1 lb. dry kidney beans	1 tbsp. chopped onion
1 qt. tomato juice	1/4 tsp. mixture of ground
3 tbsp. sugar	cloves, allspice, mace,
2 tsp. salt	and cayenne pepper

Rinse the beans, cover with boiling water, and boil for two minutes. Remove from heat and soak for one hour. Reheat beans to boiling just before you are ready to put them in jars. Mix together tomato juice, sugar, salt, chopped onion, and spices, and heat mixture to boiling. Fill jars three-quarters full of hot, drained beans. Pour in boiling sauce, allowing 1-in. headroom. Adjust lids. Processs in pressure canner at 10-lb. pressure for 65 minutes for pint jars, 75 minutes for quart jars. *Makes 2 quarts.*

Tomato Ketchup

1/2 bushel ripe tomatoes	1 whole nutmeg, grated,
1/3 cup salt	or 1/2 tsp. ground nutmeg
1 tbsp. whole cloves in spice bag	1/2 tsp. cayenne pepper
	1 qt. cider vinegar

Press the tomatoes through a sieve or food mill to remove seeds and skin. Cook the tomato pulp to boiling over low flame, stirring frequently to prevent scorching. Add salt, spices, and vinegar. Simmer over low heat, stirring often, until liquid is reduced by half (about 1/2 hour). Remove spice bag. Fill pint jars with tomato mixture, allowing 1/2-in. headroom. Adjust lids. Process in boiling water bath for 10 minutes. *Makes 3 quarts.*

Tomato Preserve

2 cups red tomatoes, peeled and chopped	1 small lemon, juice of and grated rind
2 cups sugar	1 stick cinnamon
	1/4 tsp. powdered ginger

Cover tomatoes with sugar. Let them stand for 12 hours. Drain juice and boil pulp until thick, stirring often to prevent scorching. Add lemon juice, grated rind, cinnamon, and ginger. Cook until thick. Pour into pint jar. Process in boiling water bath 15 minutes. *Makes 1 pint.*

Freezing Produce

Freezing is not only simple and reliable but also retains flavor and nutrients better than any other preservation method except live storage. It prevents deterioration by slowing enzyme action and halting bacterial growth. For best results, store foods in moisture-proof containers and cool the food quickly to 0°F or below. Rigid containers of glass, metal, and heavy plastic are impermeable to all moisture and vapor. Other products made especially for freezing are resistant enough to prevent deterioration. These include paper cartons lined with a heavy coat of wax, freezer paper, heavy plastic wraps, and heavy plastic bags. Waxed paper, cartons lined with only a thin layer of wax, and thin plastic containers, bags, or wraps should not be used.

For rapid freezing, pack produce that is already cool; work with small quantities, filling only a few packages at a time, and freeze the packages immediately. Place them against or as close as possible to the freezer coils, and allow ample air space around each package. Once the food is frozen, rearrange it to make the best use of freezer space. Put no more food into the freezer than will freeze within 24 hours.

Frozen produce will keep for as long as a year. Label and date all packages and make a list showing the kind of produce and the date frozen. Put the list near the freezer and cross off entries as food is used. Once frozen fruits and vegetables are thawed, they deteriorate rapidly; so use the thawed food immediately and do not try to refreeze it.

How to freeze fruits

1. To prevent discoloration, dip light-colored fruits in a solution of ascorbic acid (vitamin C) and water. Use 1 teaspoon per cup of water for peaches and apricots, 2 1/4 teaspoons per cup of water for apples.

2. For a dry pack, sprinkle fruit with 1/2 cup of sugar per pound of fruit. For a wet pack, make a light syrup by mixing 1 cup of sugar with 2 1/2 cups of water.

3. Pack fruit into rigid containers or plastic bags. In a wet pack, cover fruit with liquid; leave 1-inch headroom in glass jars, 1/2 inch in plastic containers.

4. Label and date containers, and freeze at 0°F.

How to freeze vegetables

1. Blanch vegetables in boiling water or steam to destroy enzymes that break down vitamin C and convert starch into sugar. (See p.218 for blanching instructions.)

2. Cool vegetables quickly by immersing them in cold water. Drain on absorbent toweling.

3. Pack and freeze as you would dry-pack fruit, but do not use any sugar.

Salt Enhances Flavor And Shelf Life Too

Salt was a treasured commodity in the ancient world not only for its flavor but also for its preservative properties. When produce is impregnated with salt, moisture is drawn out and the growth of spoilage-causing bacteria inhibited. There are four basic methods of salt curing: dry salting, brining, low-salt fermentation, and pickling.

Dry salting and brining require heavy concentrations of salt during processing. In general, the more salt used, the better the food is preserved, but the greater the loss in food value, particularly since heavily salted food must be soaked and rinsed to make it palatable—a process that further depletes vitamins.

Modern cooks are more likely to choose a salt-curing method for its distinctive flavor than for its preservative properties. As a consequence, low-salt fermentation (the process used to make sauerkraut) and pickling remain popular today in spite of drawbacks as means of preservation. In both methods bacteria convert natural sugars in the produce into lactic acid, a substance that enhances flavor, improves preservation, and is said to promote health. The chief difference between low-salt fermentation and pickling is the use of vinegar, herbs, and spices in the pickling process. In either method salinity is low enough for the produce to be eaten without first being freshened (rinsed in water).

Almost any vegetable or fruit can be preserved by one or more of the salt-curing methods. Once cured, the produce will remain fit for consumption for periods of up to three weeks, provided it is kept at a temperature of about 38°F. If you want to keep the produce for longer periods or if the 38°F storage temperature is impossible to maintain, can the food by the boiling water bath method as soon as possible after it is thoroughly cured. For salt curing, choose vegetables and fruits that are firm, tender, and garden fresh without any trace of bruises or mold. Store-bought produce can be employed, but avoid vegetables that have been waxed (cucumbers and rutabagas are frequently coated with paraffin), because the curing solution will not penetrate. Wash the produce thoroughly under running water, and scrub each fruit or vegetable individually. Curing containers should be enamelware, stoneware, or glass (avoid metal, since it may react with the brining solution). Do not cure with table salt—it contains additives that will discolor the food. Instead, use pickling or canning salt.

Pickling is an excellent way to preserve a small bumper crop and make it last for the first few months of the fall. If you want sharp, spicy pickles all winter, can them. Pickled foods are relatively easy to can because their acidity eliminates any chance of botulism growth. As a result, they can be processed by the boiling water bath method rather than the more complicated steam canning method required for unpickled vegetables.

Dry Salting

Severest method of salt curing is dry salting. Corn, beans, green vegetables, cabbage, and root crops are the foods most frequently dry salted. Use additive-free, finely granulated salt (coarse salt takes too long to dissolve) in the proportion of one part salt to four parts vegetables by weight. Produce must be "freshened" (thoroughly rinsed of salt) before it is eaten. To freshen, soak food for 10 to 12 hours in fresh water, changing the water every few hours.

1. Blanch vegetables in steam over rapidly boiling water (see *Blanching*, p.218). Cool by plunging into cold water.

2. Weigh produce and divide into batches that will make 1-in. layers. Weigh out 1 lb. salt per 4 lb. produce.

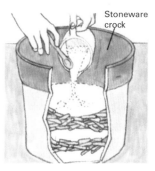

3. Fill crock with alternate layers of salt and 1-in.-thick layers of produce. First and last layers should be salt.

4. Leave 4-in. headroom above final salt layer. Cover with cheesecloth weighted down with a plate or board.

5. After 24 hours juice should cover produce. If it does not, add a solution of 3 tbsp. salt mixed into 1 cup of water.

6. Store container in cool area (38°F). Change cloth when soiled. Use glass or china cup to dip out food.

7. Before eating salted produce, soak and drain it in several changes of fresh water until saltiness is gone.

Brining

Salt solution is used to cure food by the brining method. Prepare the brine in advance by mixing 1 lb. salt per gallon of water. You will need 1 gal. of brine for each 2 gal. of produce. While the food is being brined, a process that will take four to eight weeks, keep it at room temperature (65°F to 70°F). Rinse food in several changes of cold water before eating it.

Food being blanched (see p.218)

Burner

1. Weigh and blanch food, then place in crock and add brine to 4 in. of top.

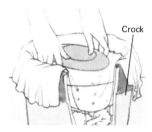

Crock

2. Cover produce with cheese-cloth; weight with plate to keep submerged.

3. The next day, add salt on top of cloth—1/2 lb. for each 5 lb. of produce.

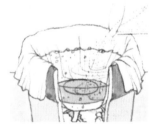

4. After one week add 1/8 lb. salt for every 5 lb. of produce. Repeat each week.

5. Check container every few days and remove any scum that appears on the surface.

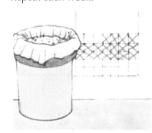

6. Maintain at room temperature until no bubbles rise (four to eight weeks).

7. Store brined food in cool area (38°F) in container covered with tight lid.

Low-Salt Fermentation

Do not blanch food when using the low-salt method, since fermentation organisms would be destroyed. Let the produce ferment at about 70°F, then store at 38°F in a tightly lidded container. For long-term storage, can by boiling water bath method (see p.207). Low-salt fermentation is particularly suitable for such vegetables as turnips and cabbage.

1. Wash and dry cabbage, then shred into small pieces so salt can penetrate.

2. Weight out 1 oz. salt per 2 1/2 lb. of cabbage. Thoroughly mix salt into cabbage.

3. Pack salted cabbage into container. Press down firmly to help extract juices.

4. Cover with cheesecloth weighted down with plate. Check after 24 hours.

5. If brine does not cover cabbage, and solution of 1 tsp. salt per cup of water.

6. Check fermentation regularly. Remove scum and change cloth if dirty.

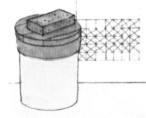

7. Keep at room temperature until no bubbles rise to surface (one to four weeks).

David Cavagnaro, Teacher and Farmer

His Garden Provides An Abundance of Pickles

David Cavagnaro is a Santa Rosa, California, writer, teacher, photographer, and homesteader. He and his family grow all the food they need and put by enough in autumn to tide them through the winter and into spring.

"Pickling is really the easiest way for us to preserve summer vegetables to have year round. We pickle a whole bunch of things—cucumbers, beans, cauliflower, broccoli, mushrooms, peppers, and artichoke hearts, for example. We even pickle eggs—they have a sharp, vinegary taste, but otherwise they're just like any other hard-boiled eggs. We also do relishes ourselves and make our own pimentos. We make vinegar from our own apples and we grow garlic, mustard, dill, horseradish, coriander, and even grape leaves, which we use in some of the pickling mixtures. The only thing we don't make is our own olive oil.

"Pickling is really very simple, except for the chopping you do for relishes. There's one I do, Grandma Mabel's chili sauce, that's very time-consuming. Like a lot of pickling recipes, that one has been handed down in the family. But once you get into it, you start making up recipes of your own.

"The most important thing in pickling is the strength of the vinegar. You see, you're working with vegetables that don't have a very high acid content, and if you're not careful, there could be a danger of botulism. You need vinegar that has an acid strength of 5 percent, like most commercial brands. If you make your own, you really should check the acid concentration, and if it's less than 5 percent, you should increase the proportion of vinegar.

"I like all the things we pickle, but I'm very, very partial to honest-to-goodness crock pickles—just the cukes in a salt brine pot. You make them the same way you make sauerkraut. The salt brine ferments the cukes, and you get a pickle that's hard to describe. You could never get anything like it from a jar. But to tell you the truth, simple as it is, we've had some real failures with crock pickles. You have to remember to skim off the brine once or twice a day. It takes regular vigilance, and with a busy family, it's awful easy to forget. Let me tell you, we have gotten some of the muckiest-looking crocks of pickles you can ever imagine."

For Unbeatable Taste Add Vinegar and Spice

Pickling serves two purposes: it preserves and it adds delicious flavor. Choose firm, fresh vegetables and fruit for pickling—green tomatoes and underripe fruit can be used for greater firmness—but avoid vegetables that have been waxed. (Wax prevents the pickling solution from penetrating.) Use only pickling-type cucumbers.

There are two methods of pickling—fresh-pack pickling and fermentation pickling. Both rely on brine and vinegar as the primary preservatives; sugar, herbs, and spices are often added for additional flavor. The vinegar should have an acid content of 4 to 6 percent. Either cider vinegar or distilled white vinegar is acceptable; the latter has a sharper, more acid taste. Do not use homemade vinegar unless you are sure of its strength. For sweeteners, honey or granulated white or brown sugar is generally specified. Salt should be the pure granulated variety (often sold as "pickling salt") with no additives. Herbs and spices should be fresh and the

water soft if possible. If the tap water in your area is hard, you can use rainwater or bottled soft water.

Pickled products should be heat treated (canned) unless they are to be consumed soon after pickling. The boiling water bath canning procedure described on page 207 can be used for all pickled products; processing times vary from recipe to recipe. The usual precautions should be followed during canning and afterward: the jars of pickles should be labeled, dated, and stored in a cool, dry location. If there is any sign of spoilage—a bulging lid, bad smell, poor pickle consistency, sliminess, discoloration—do not eat any of the food in the jar.

Making Dills by Fermentation Pickling

1. Line bottom of 1-gal. crock with half of dill and other spices, then add cucumbers.

2. Top cucumbers with the remaining dill and spices. Add brine to cover all ingredients.

3. Keep produce submerged with a heavy plate so that it is under at least 2 in. of brine.

Cucumbers and green tomatoes are the vegetables most frequently treated by fermentation pickling. The method is similar to low-salt fermentation (p.211), but a stronger salt solution is employed, and vinegar and spices are generally added. After pickling is completed (a matter of one to three weeks), the pickles can be stored for up to three weeks in a refrigerator or cool (38°F) location. For long-term storage, can the pickles with the boiling water bath method (p.207). If the pickling brine is cloudy, make a fresh one to use in canning. You will need the following ingredients:

1/2 gal. water
1/3 cup salt
1/2 cup vinegar
4 lb. pickling cucumbers (4 to 5 in. each)
15 sprigs dill
30 peppercorns
15 cloves garlic (optional)

Prepare the brine by mixing water, salt, and vinegar. Clean and scrub cucumbers (especially the flower end) thoroughly, and be sure the crock and all other utensils are clean.

4. Remove scum daily. When bubbles and scum stop forming, fermentation is completed.

Making Dills by Fresh-Pack Pickling

1. Soak cucumbers overnight in brine solution; then drain and pack into 1-qt. jars.

2. Divide spices among jars. Mix together vinegar, salt, sugar, and water, and bring to a boil.

3. Pour boiling mixture over cucumbers to 1/2 in. from top of jars. Put lids on jars.

Not only cucumbers but beets, cauliflower, green beans, pears, peaches, tomatoes, and watermelon rind are suitable for fresh-pack pickling. Each type of fruit or vegetable can be processed individually, or several can be combined to make a relish or chutney. Details of processing vary from recipe to recipe depending on the ingredients used. Vegetables are frequently marinated overnight in brine before being heat processed; fruits and relishes are often simmered in a syrup of sugar, vinegar, and spices before processing. The procedure shown here for making fresh-pack dills is typical. As for any pickle recipe, use only ripe, perfect produce, and wash it thoroughly. You will need the following ingredients:

4 lb. pickling cucumbers
1/2 gal. brine (1/3 cup salt in 1/2 gal. water)
4 cloves garlic (2 per qt.)
8 heads dill (4 per qt.)
4 tsp. mustard seed (2 per qt.)
11/2 cups vinegar
3 tbsp. salt
1 tbsp. sugar
3 cups water

4. Process jars in boiling water for 20 minutes. Set jars several inches apart on rack to cool.

Pickling Recipes

There are pickling recipes to suit every taste. All kinds of fruits and vegetables can be combined, and vinegar, salt, sugar, and spices can be adjusted in an almost endless variety of ways. The results are piquant relishes, chutneys, and sauces—as well as pickles with sweet, sour, or sweet-and-sour taste combinations. Although pickling is of limited use as a means of preserving fruits and vegetables—it prolongs shelf life only a few weeks—it does simplify long-term storage, since pickled produce has a high enough acid content to be processed by the boiling water bath method (see pp.206–209). The recipes given below include processing times.

Tomato-Apple Chutney

6 lb. tomatoes, peeled and chopped
5 lb. apples, peeled, cored, and chopped
2 medium green peppers, seeded and chopped
4-5 medium onions, peeled and chopped
2 cups seedless white raisins
1 qt. white vinegar
4 tsp. salt
2 lb. brown sugar
1 tsp. ground ginger
1/4 cup mixed whole pickling spices

Combine all ingredients except the mixed whole pickling spices. Put the spices in a spice bag and add to the mixture. Bring to boil and cook slowly, stirring frequently until mixture thickens (about one hour). Remove spice bag. Pack boiling mixture into sterile pint jars, leaving 1/2-in. headroom. Process in boiling water bath for 10 minutes. *Makes 7 pints.*

Pepper-Onion Relish

6-8 large onions, peeled and finely chopped
4-5 medium sweet red peppers, finely chopped
4-5 medium green peppers, finely chopped
1 cup sugar
1 qt. vinegar
4 tsp. salt

Combine all ingredients and bring to a boil. Simmer, stirring occasionally, until mixture begins to thicken (about 45 minutes). Pack into sterile half-pint jars, leaving 1/2-in. headroom. Process in boiling water bath for 10 minutes. *Makes 2 1/2 pints.*

Sour Pickles

3 tbsp. mixed whole pickling spices
3 tbsp. pickling dill
40 well-scrubbed cucumbers
2 1/4 cups salt
3 cups white cider vinegar
3 gal. hot water
9 horseradish roots and leaves, or to taste
9 garlic cloves, or to taste
9 peppercorns, or to taste

Put half the mixed whole pickling spices in the bottom of a large stone crock and cover with half the dill. Add cucumbers. Put remaining pickling spices and dill on top of the cucumbers. Make a pickling brine by dissolving 1 1/2 cups salt in mixture of 2 cups vinegar and 2 gal. hot water. Cool brine and pour it over the cucumbers. Cover with a plate weighted down to hold it beneath the brine. Keep crock at room temperature (68°F to 72°F) for two to four weeks. Remove scum daily.

When pickles are an even olive color without any white spots, they are ready for packing. Make a new brine of 1 gal. hot water, 3/4 cup salt, 1 cup white cider vinegar, horseradish roots, and peeled garlic; bring to boil. Pierce each pickle on the ends and once in the middle with a sterilized ice pick or knitting needle. Divide pickles among quart jars and add at least one peppercorn and one horseradish leaf to each jar. Pour hot brine over pickles, cover, and process by the boiling water bath method (p.207) for 15 minutes. *Makes 8 to 9 quarts.*

Pickled Green Beans

4 lb. green beans
1 3/4 tsp. crushed hot red pepper
3 1/2 tsp. mustard seeds
3 1/2 tsp. dill seeds
7 cloves garlic
5 cups water
5 cups vinegar
1/2 cup salt

Wash beans and remove ends. Cut beans into 2-in. pieces and divide among seven hot, sterile pint jars. Put 1/4 tsp. red pepper, 1/2 tsp. mustard seeds, 1/2 tsp. dill seeds, and 1 clove garlic into each of the jars. Combine water, vinegar, and salt, and bring quickly to a boil. Pour boiling liquid over beans, leaving 1/2-in. headroom. Process jars in boiling water bath for 10 minutes. *Makes 7 pints.*

Watermelon Pickles

6 lb. watermelon rind with green rind and pink meat removed
3/4 cup salt
3 3/4 qt. water
2 trays ice cubes
9 cups sugar
3 cups white vinegar
1 tbsp. whole cloves
6 1-in. cinnamon sticks
1 lemon, sliced thin

Cut rind into 1-in. squares (it makes about 3 qt.). Dissolve salt in 3 qt. water, add ice cubes, and pour over watermelon rind. Allow to stand five to six hours. Drain rind and rinse in cold water. Cover with cold water and cook until fork tender (about 10 minutes). Drain. Combine sugar, vinegar, and remaining 3 cups water; then add a spice bag filled with cloves and cinnamon sticks. Boil five minutes and pour over rind. Add lemon slices and marinate overnight. Boil rind in syrup until rind is translucent (about 10 minutes). Pack boiling pickles into hot, sterilized pint jars. Remove cinnamon sticks from bag and divide among jars. Cover with boiling syrup, leaving 1/2-in. headroom. Process in boiling water bath for 10 minutes. *Makes 6 pints.*

Sauerkraut

5 lb. tender young cabbage, washed and thinly shredded
3 tbsp. salt

Mix cabbage and salt in a large pan and let stand 15 minutes. Pack mixture into clean nonmetal container, pressing it down firmly with wooden spoon. Juices must cover cabbage. Allow 4 to 6 in. of headroom above cabbage. Cover cabbage with clean white cheesecloth tucked down inside container. Weight down the cloth with a flat, tight-fitting lid that is heavy enough for the juice to rise up to but not over it. The cabbage should not be exposed to any air. Ferment at room temperature (68°F to 72°F) for five to six weeks. Skim off any scum that forms, and replace cloth and lid if they are scummy. When fermentation stops (bubbles will no longer rise to the surface), cover container with clean cloth and sterile lid, and move sauerkraut to a cold area (38°F), or process it in boiling water bath. To process, bring sauerkraut to a simmer (do not boil), and pack it into hot, sterile jars, leaving 1/2-in. headroom. Process in boiling water bath 15 minutes for pints, 20 minutes for quarts. *Makes 1 to 2 quarts.*

Sauerruben

5 lb. white turnips, peeled and shredded
3 tbsp. salt

Mix turnips and salt, pack into clean nonmetal container, and tamp down. Cover and weight down as for sauerkraut. Ferment at room temperature for four to six weeks. Process in boiling water bath as for sauerkraut. *Makes 1 to 2 quarts.*

Homemade Horseradish Sauce

2-4 horseradish roots, washed peeled, and grated
1/2 cup white vinegar
1/2 tsp. salt

Mix ingredients, pack into a clean jar, and seal tightly. The horseradish sauce can be used immediately, or it can be stored in refrigerator for up to four weeks. (Heat processing destroys the sharp bite of homemade horseradish.) *Makes 1 cup.*

Spiced Peaches

2 cups water
5 cups sugar
3 cups apple cider vinegar
1 tbsp. whole cloves
1 tbsp. whole allspice
2 sticks cinnamon
1 piece gingerroot
6-8 lb. peaches, peeled and pitted

Combine water, 2 cups sugar, and vinegar. Put spices into a spice bag, add to liquid, and bring to boil. Cook peaches a few at a time until barely tender (about 5 minutes). When the last batch has been removed, add 2 more cups sugar to syrup, and return to boil. Pour syrup over peaches and let stand 12 hours. Reheat peaches and syrup, then pack peaches into quart jars. Add final cup of sugar to syrup, bring to boil, and pour over peaches. Process in boiling water bath for 20 minutes. *Makes 6 quarts.*

Spiced Pears

8 cups sugar
4 cups white vinegar
2 cups water
8 2-in. cinnamon sticks
2 tbsp. whole cloves
2 tbsp. whole allspice
8 lb. pears, peeled

Mix sugar, vinegar, water, cinnamon sticks, spice bag filled with cloves and allspice. Simmer 30 minutes. Add pears. Simmer 20 minutes more. Divide pears and cinnamon sticks among pint jars, and cover with boiling liquid, leaving 1/2-in. headroom. Process in boiling water bath for 20 minutes. *Makes 8 pints.*

Sweet and Savory Ways To Store Your Fruits

Homemade jams, jellies, and preserves, cooked from fresh fruit sweetened just to your liking, are a treat for just about everybody. For exotic flavors add herbs, spices, or wines to the fruit or combine several different types of fruit.

Just as salt and vinegar preserve vegetables and fruits through pickling, so sugar acts as the preserving agent in jellies, jams, conserves, marmalades, preserves, and fruit butters. Since most fruits are high in sugar to begin with, they are natural candidates for preservation in one of these forms.

In order to achieve proper gelling of a sugar-preserved product, three key ingredients must be present in correct proportion: sugar, pectin (the gelling agent), and acid. The best way to ensure good results is to follow a recipe and measure all ingredients carefully. All fruits need added refined white sugar or other mild-tasting sweetener, such as light corn syrup or honey. Very few recipes use brown sugar, molasses, or maple syrup because the flavors of these sweeteners are too strong and will overpower the taste of the fruit.

Many fruits contain sufficient natural pectin and acid for gelling, but others require extra amounts of one or the other. Some fruits have enough pectin or acid if they are sour or just barely ripe but not when they are fully ripe or overripe. To test for pectin, mix 1 teaspoon of cooked fruit with 1 tablespoon of rubbing alcohol. If the mixture coagulates into a single clump, there is sufficient pectin. (Do not taste the mixture, since rubbing alcohol is poisonous.) To check a fruit for acid, compare its taste to that of a mixture consisting of 3 tablespoons of water, 1 teaspoon of lemon juice, and 1/2 teaspoon of sugar. If the fruit is less tart than the lemon juice mixture, it needs more acid.

Pectin can be purchased in either liquid or powdered form, or you can make your own from apples (below right). A pectin substitute, low-methoxyl pectin, forms a gel when combined with calcium salts or bonemeal and lemon juice. It can be used to make jelly without any added sweeteners. If fruits lack sufficient acid, add lemon juice or citric acid when you add sugar.

Equipment for making jams and jellies

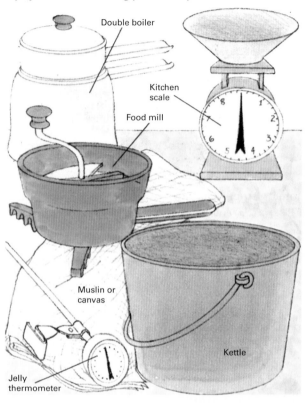

Equipment required for making jams and jellies includes all the standard canning supplies plus a few others. Buy a jelly thermometer, double boiler, and strainer. You will also need 1/2 yd. of a strong fabric, such as unbleached muslin or canvas, to make into a bag for straining jelly. A heavy kettle (less likely to let fruit scorch than a thin one), a food mill for pureeing, and a kitchen scale for precise measurement are also helpful.

Gelling properties of common fruits

Fruits with sufficient acid and pectin to gel		Fruits that may need added acid or pectin		Fruits that always need additional acid or pectin	
Apples (sour)	Gooseberries	Apples (ripe)	Grapefruit	Apricots	Pears
Blackberries (sour)	Grapes	Blackberries (ripe)	Grapes (California)	Figs	Prunes
Lemons		Cherries (sour)	Loquats	Grapes (Western Concord)	Raspberries
Crabapples	Loganberries	Chokecherries	Oranges		Strawberries
Cranberries	Plums	Elderberries		Guavas	
Currants	Quinces			Peaches	

Making and using pectin

To manufacture your own pectin, wash 10 lb. of tart apples, remove stems quarter the fruits (but do not core), and place in a kettle. Cover apples with cold water and bring to a boil over moderate flame. Then cover kettle and simmer until the fruit is soft (about 30 minutes). Drain fruit in jelly bag overnight (see p.215) and collect juice (there should be about 3 qt.). Boil down juice to make 1 1/2 to 2 cups pectin.

Adding liquid pectin to fruit. Cook fruit until it is soft, add sugar, bring to a full boil, then boil fruit and sugar together for one full minute. Add the pectin. No additional cooking is required.

Adding powdered pectin to fruit. Stir pectin into softened, cooked fruit, bring fruit and pectin mixture to a boil, and add sugar. Return mixture to a boil, then boil one minute. Jelly will then be ready.

Making Jelly Without Added Pectin

While any sugar-preserved product needs a good recipe, accurate measuring, and precise timing, nowhere is care more important than in the preparation of jelly without added pectin. The first requirement is that the fruit has enough natural pectin for gelling; either select a high-pectin fruit from the list on page 214 or test for pectin content as described on the same page.

To collect juice for jellymaking, cook the fruit, then hang it in a jelly bag made of muslin or several layers of cheesecloth. Squeezing the bag or pressing it with a spoon hastens the flow of juice but can cause cloudy jelly—it is better to let the juice drip naturally. If you do squeeze the jelly bag to collect extra juice, strain the juice a second time through a clean cloth.

Prolonged cooking turns the sweetened fruit juice into jelly by boiling away water until the sugar reaches just the right concentration. Timing is critical: overcooking leads to jelly that is stiff or full of sugary crystals; undercooking will produce thin, runny jelly. Because of the precision required in the process, work with the exact amounts specified in recipes: do not double a batch for extra jelly, make two separate batches instead.

An accurate thermometer provides the simplest and safest way to tell when the sugar has reached the proper concentration. Start by measuring the exact temperature at which the mixture first boils (it will vary depending on weather as well as altitude, so take a new reading each time you make a batch of jelly). As cooking progresses and water boils away, the sugar concentration will rise and the temperature go up. When the thermometer registers 8°F to 10°F above the initial boiling point, the jelly is done. As an additional test, dip a cold metal spoon into the mixture and hold the spoon away from the heat. If the jelly runs off in a sheet rather than individual drops, it is ready. A third test is to put a spoonful of jelly on a plate and put it in a freezer. If the sample becomes firm after one or two minutes, the jelly is ready. The freezer test can also be used for jams and preserves, the sheet test cannot.

The traditional way to seal jelly is with paraffin. Melt clean paraffin in a double boiler or small pan set in a larger wide-bottomed pan filled with water. (Do not melt paraffin directly over a flame or it may catch fire.) Prepare the paraffin in advance so that you can use it as soon as the jelly is done. Once the sealed jars are cool, put on lids to protect the paraffin from being accidently broken. For surer long-term storage, use canning jars and lids, and process the jars of jelly for 5 to 10 minutes in a boiling water bath (see p.207). For best retention of color and consistency, store the sealed jelly in a cool, dark place and use it within three months.

Blackberry Jelly Step-by-step

1. You will need 5 qt. of berries (about one-fourth should be underripe) to make 2 qt. of juice. Remove stems, wash fruit, and place in heavy kettle.

2. Crush berries with potato masher, add 1 1/2 cups water, cover, and bring to boil. Reduce heat and simmer, stirring occasionally, until tender (five minutes).

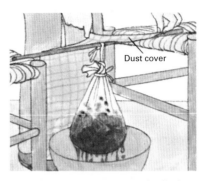

3. Pour mixture into dampened jelly bag, suspend bag over bowl or pan, and let juice strain overnight. Cover bag and bowl with cloth to protect from dust.

4. If you are going to seal with paraffin, cut fresh paraffin into chunks, and add a few at a time to double boiler until all are melted. Hold until jelly is done.

5. Pour 2 qt. of juice into heavy kettle and add 6 cups of sugar. Place kettle over a high flame and heat the liquid to a full rolling boil that cannot be stirred down.

6. Stir juice, insert thermometer so that bulb is covered but does not touch pan, and note temperature at which juice reaches full rolling boil.

7. Continue heating until temperature reaches 8°F to 10°F above initial boiling point. At this temperature sugar is concentrated enough for product to gel.

8. Pour jelly into hot, sterile jars, leaving 1/2-in. headroom. Process by boiling water bath method (p.207), or cover with 1/8 in. of paraffin, using pin to break bubbles.

9. Let jars stand undisturbed on rack overnight. Then put on lids over paraffin seal; label with name, date, and batch number; and store in a cool, dark place.

A Variety of Confections To Please Every Taste

Unlike jelly, which is made from fruit juice, other sugar-preserved foods contain parts of the whole fruit. Fruit-butter is mashed pulp simmered with sugar until the pulp is thick; in the other fruit products pieces of fruit float in a light gel. Jam consists of gelled, mashed pulp; preserves are made of fruit pieces in a thin gel; and marmalade contains bits of fruit and citrus rind in a stiff,

clear gel. Conserves contain a high proportion of mixed, chopped fruits in a small amount of gelled juice; nuts are often stirred into the gel just before it starts to set.

In all these products, with the exception of the fruit butters, the concentration of pectin, acid, and sugar are critical to proper setting, particularly if extra pectin is not being added. As in making jelly, best results are achieved by following a recipe carefully—do not double or triple ingredient measures to make a bigger batch. Instead, make several small batches. Be sure pectin and acid content are high enough by using plenty of underripe high-pectin fruit or by testing for pectin and acid as described on page 214. You can tell if the sugar concentration is correct by measuring the temperature of the sugar-fruit mixture as it cooks. First, find the

temperature at which water boils. Then cook the fruit and sugar until it reaches 8°F to 10°F above the boiling point of water. If you do not have a thermometer, use the freezer test described on page 215. When making jams or other fruit products with added pectin, you need not cook down the fruit mixture to make it gel, but precise measurements and accurate timing are still important.

Jams, marmalades, preserves, conserves, and butters must undergo further processing to eliminate spoilage-causing organisms if the product is to be stored for more than two or three weeks. Certain recipes specify freezing; all others require canning by the boiling water bath technique described on page 207. Use hot, sterile canning jars, and leave a 1/2-inch space above the fruit.

Jams, Marmalades, Preserves, and Conserves Without Added Pectin

1. Wash fruit, remove pits, and peel if called for in recipe. Cut up large fruits, such as peaches. Measure exact boiling point of water.

2. Put fruit into kettle, first crushing bottom layer. (Add water if fruit has little natural juice.) Cook according to recipe instructions.

3. Add sugar (and lemon juice if acid content is low). Insert thermometer. Return mixture to boiling, stirring constantly to prevent scorching.

4. Boil rapidly, stirring constantly, until temperature reaches 8°F to 10°F above boiling point of water. Remove from heat immediately.

5. To prevent fruit from floating in finished product, let mixture cool for about five minutes and stir several times during cooling.

Making Fruit Butters

1. Wash and cut up fruit, remove pits, and crush fruit into a pulp with potato masher. Measure pulp and put into a heavy kettle.

2. Add half as much water by volume as there is fruit pulp. Cook over low heat, stirring almost constantly to prevent scorching, until pulp is soft.

Food mill

3. Press fruit pulp through a colander or strainer to get rid of all pits and skin. Then put it through a food mill or blender to make a smooth puree.

4. With kettle removed from heat, pour pureed pulp back in, and stir in 1/2 cup of sugar per cup of fruit pulp. Return kettle to low heat.

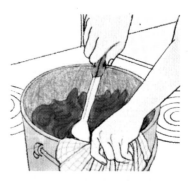

5. Cook mixture over low heat, stirring constantly and watching carefully to prevent scorching. Simmer until fruit is thick and glossy.

Apple Jelly

2 1/4 lb. just-ripe tart apples	2 tbsp. lemon juice (if apples
3/4 lb. underripe tart apples	are not sufficiently tart)
3 cups sugar	

Wash apples and cut into small pieces without paring or coring. Put apples and water into heavy kettle, cover, bring quickly to a boil. Reduce heat and simmer until apples are soft (about 20 minutes). Pour cooked apples into jelly bag and collect juice as it drips. Return 4 cups juice to heavy kettle, add sugar and lemon juice. Place over high heat, and boil rapidly until temperature rises to 8°F to 10°F above boiling point of water. Remove from heat immediately, skim, and pour into hot, sterile jelly jars. Seal. *Makes four to five 1/2-pt. jars.*

Grape Jelly

3 1/2 lb. underripe Concord grapes	1/2 cup water
1 tart apple, cut into eighths but not peeled or cored	3 cups sugar

Wash grapes and remove stems. Put grapes into heavy kettle and crush. Add apple sections and water, cover, and bring quickly to a boil. Reduce heat and simmer until grapes are soft (about 10 minutes). Pour grapes into a jelly bag and collect juice as it drips. Let collected juice stand in a refrigerator or other cool place for 8 to 10 hours, then strain juice through two layers of cheesecloth to remove any crystals.

Return 4 cups juice to heavy kettle, and add sugar. Place over high heat, bring to a full boil, and continue rapid boiling until temperature rises to 8°F to 10°F above boiling point of water. Remove from heat immediately, skim, and pour into hot, sterile jelly jars. Seal. *Makes three to four 1/2-pt. jars.*

Mint Jelly

1 cup tightly packed mint leaves	3 1/2 cups sugar
1 cup water	5 drops green food coloring
1/2 cup cider vinegar	3 oz. liquid pectin

Wash mint, remove stems, and coarsely chop leaves. Put mint leaves, water, vinegar, and sugar into heavy kettle, and bring quickly to a full boil, stirring constantly. Remove kettle from heat, add food coloring and pectin, return liquid to a full boil, then boil 30 seconds. Remove immediately from heat, skim, strain through two layers of damp cheesecloth, and pour into hot, sterile jelly jars. Seal. *Makes three to four 1/2-pt. jars.*

Apple Butter

8 cups applesauce	2 cups brown sugar
1/2 tsp. cloves	1/2 tsp. cinnamon
1/2 tsp. allspice	Grated rind of one lemon

Mix all ingredients and spread in shallow baking pan. Bake at 275°F, stirring occasionally, until thick (about four hours). Pack into hot, sterile canning jars. For long-term storage, process in boiling water bath for 10 minutes. *Makes two 1/2-pt. jars.*

Peach Jam With Powdered Pectin

3 lb. peaches	1 3/4 oz. powdered pectin
1/4 cup lemon juice	5 cups sugar

Wash, peel, pit, and crush peaches; there should be 3 3/4 cups. In a heavy kettle mix fruit, lemon juice, and pectin. Bring quickly to a full boil, stirring constantly. Add sugar. Return mixture to boil, then boil rapidly, stirring constantly, for one minute. Remove immediately from heat, skim, and pour into hot, sterile canning jars. For long-term storage, process 10 minutes in boiling water bath. *Makes six 1/2-pt. jars.*

Blueberry Peach Jam

4 lb. fully ripe peaches	1/2 tbsp. whole cloves
1 qt. firm blueberries	1/4 tsp. whole allspice
2 tbsp. lemon juice	5 1/2 cups sugar
1/2 cup water	1/2 tsp. salt
1 stick cinnamon	

Wash, peel, pit, and chop peaches; there should be 1 qt. Wash and sort blueberries. In a heavy kettle mix fruit, lemon juice, and water; then simmer, covered, until fruit is soft (about 10 minutes). Tie cinnamon, cloves, and allspice in a cheesecloth bag, and add bag, along with sugar and salt, to fruit. Bring mixture quickly to a full boil, and boil rapidly, stirring constantly, until mixture reaches 8°F to 10°F above the boiling point of water. Remove immediately from heat, skim, and remove spices. Pour jam into hot, sterile canning jars. For long-term storage, process in boiling water bath for 10 minutes. *Makes six 1/2-pt. jars.*

Uncooked Berry Jam

1 qt. fully ripe berries	1 3/4 oz. powdered pectin
4 cups sugar	1 cup water

Wash berries and remove stems. Place fruit in bowl and crush; there should be 2 cups. Add sugar, and let stand for 20 minutes, stirring occasionally. Meanwhile, mix pectin and water, bring to a full boil, then boil one minute. Pour pectin solution into berries, and stir for two minutes. Pour into sterile jars or freezer containers. Store in refrigerator for up to three weeks or in freezer for up to one year. *Makes five 1/2-pt. jars.*

Strawberry Preserves

2 qt. firm, tart strawberries	4 1/2 cups sugar

Wash berries and remove stems and leaves. Arrange alternate layers of whole berries and sugar in a large bowl, and let stand in refrigerator or other cool place for 8 to 10 hours to bring out juice. When juice has accumulated, place fruit-sugar mixture in heavy kettle over medium-high heat. Bring quickly to a boil, stirring gently so as not to break berries. Boil mixture rapidly; stir frequently to prevent scorching until temperature reaches 8°F to 10°F above the boiling point of water. Remove fruit mixture immediately from heat, skim, and pour into hot, sterile canning jars. For long-term storage, process 10 minutes in boiling water bath. *Makes four 1/2-pt. jars.*

Orange Marmalade

1 1/2 cups orange peel, cut into thin strips	6 oranges
1/3 cup lemon juice	1/3 cup lemon peel, cut
1/3 cup lemon peel, cut into thin strips	3 cups sugar

Cover orange and lemon peel with 1 qt. cold water and simmer, covered, until tender (30 minutes). Drain. Section oranges, remove filaments and seeds, and cut into small pieces. In a heavy kettle mix oranges, lemon juice, drained peel, sugar, and 2 cups boiling water. Bring quickly to a full boil, then boil rapidly, stirring often, until temperature reaches 8°F to 10°F above the boiling point of water. Remove immediately from heat, skim, and pour into hot, sterile jars. For long-term storage, process in boiling water bath for 10 minutes. *Makes three 1/2-pt. jars.*

Tomato Marmalade

5 1/2 lb. tomatoes	1 tsp. salt
3 oranges, thinly sliced	4 sticks cinnamon
2 lemons, thinly sliced	1 tbsp. whole cloves
6 cups sugar	

Peel, chop, and drain tomatoes. Cut fruit slices into quarters. Mix tomatoes, fruit, sugar, and salt in a heavy kettle. Tie spices in a cheesecloth bag and add. Bring mixture quickly to a full boil, and boil rapidly, stirring constantly, until thick (about 50 minutes). Remove from heat, skim, remove spices, and pour marmalade into hot, sterile canning jars. For long-term storage, process in boiling water bath for 10 minutes. *Makes nine 1/2-pt. jars.*

Apple Marmalade

3 lb. tart apples	5 tbsp. sugar
1 orange	2 tbsp. lemon juice
1 1/2 cups water	

Pare, core, and slice apples. Quarter and slice oranges. In a heavy kettle heat water and sugar until sugar dissolves. Add fruit and lemon juice. Bring quickly to a full boil and boil rapidly, stirring constantly, until mixture reaches 8°F to 10°F above boiling point of water. Remove immediately from heat and pour into hot, sterile jars. For long-term storage, process 10 minutes in boiling water bath. *Makes six 1/2-pt. jars.*

Apple Raisin Conserves

3 lb. tart red apples	1 3/4 oz. powdered pectin
1/2 cup raisins	5 1/2 cups sugar
1/2 cup water	1/2 cup nuts, chopped
1/4 cup lemon juice	

Wash, core, and chop apples fine; there should be 4 1/2 cups. In a heavy kettle mix apples, raisins, water, lemon juice, and pectin. Bring quickly to a full boil, stirring constantly. Add sugar. Return mixture to a full boil, then boil rapidly, stirring constantly, for one minute. Remove from heat, skim, and add nuts. Pour into hot, sterile canning jars. For long-term storage, process in boiling water bath for 10 minutes. *Makes six 1/2-pt. jars.*

Let Sun and Air Preserve for You

When 80 to 90 percent of the moisture in food is removed, the growth of spoilage bacteria is halted and the food can be stored for long periods of time. By exposing your produce to a flow of hot, dry air, you will not only remove moisture quickly but also concentrate natural sugars for a delicious, sweet flavor while reducing volume for easy storage. In addition, proper drying can preserve many of the natural nutrients in foods.

Careful preliminary treatment is an important contributor to high vitamin retention, good flavor, and attractive appearance. To fix the natural color in sliced fruits, dip the pieces of fruit in pure lemon juice or a solution of ascorbic acid (vitamin C) as soon as they are cut. You will need about a cup of lemon juice to process 5 quarts of cut fruit; or mix 3 teaspoons of pure ascorbic acid with 1 cup of water. Vitamin C tablets in

the proportion of 9,000 milligrams per cup of water can also be used to prepare the dipping solution, but the tablets are expensive and difficult to dissolve.

Sulfuring and blanching are the most common ways of preserving vitamin content and preventing loss of flavor in produce that is to be dried. Of the two techniques blanching is preferable, since sulfuring destroys thiamine (vitamin B_1). In addition, sulfuring may impart a sour taste to food. In general, the sulfur method is best for fruits, where the tartness may be an asset to flavor.

High vitamin retention also depends upon striking the right balance between the relatively fast drying made possible by exposure to heat and slower drying at lower temperatures. Generally, the faster the food is dried, the higher will be its vitamin content and the less its chance of contamination by mold and bacteria. Excessively high temperatures, however, break down many vitamins. Most experts recommend drying temperatures in the range between 95°F and 145°F; 140°F is the optimum suggested by the U.S. Department of Agriculture. Exposure to bright sun also speeds up drying, but sunlight is known to destroy some vitamins.

Blanching

Blanching—brief heat treatment in either steam or boiling water—helps preserve both color and vitamin content by deactivating plant enzymes. It also speeds the drying process by removing any wax or other surface coating on the produce and makes peeling easier by loosening the skins. Blanching in boiling water is recommended for fruits whose skins are to be peeled. Steam blanching is recommended for most other fruits and vegetables. Onions, garlic, leeks, and mushrooms should be dried without blanching.

Boiling water blanching. Immerse produce in boiling water for the time listed on the chart. Use your largest pot and add fruit a little at a time so that the water will return to a boil quickly. After blanching, immediately dip the produce in cold water to cool it, then either peel the skin or crack it by nicking with a knife in order to aid in evaporation during drying.

Steam blanching. Place a 2 1/2-inch layer of cut vegetables in a strainer or colander. Bring 2 inches of water to a boil in a large kettle. Set the strainer on a rack above the water, cover the kettle tightly, and process for the time specified on the chart.

Sulfuring Protects Vitamins and Bright Colors

Sulfuring should be done outdoors—the fumes are not only unpleasant but also dangerous. You will need a heavy cardboard box large enough to allow 6 to 12 in. of space on all sides of a stack of drying trays. Cut a flap at the bottom of one side of the box to aid in air circulation.

To prepare fruit for sulfuring, cut it up, weigh it, and spread it in single layers—with cut sides up and no pieces touching—in nonmetal trays (sulfur fumes will corrode most metals). Stack the trays 1 1/2 in. apart (set pieces of wood at the corners to keep trays separated), and support the stack on cinder blocks or bricks.

You will need about 2 tsp. of sulfur per pound of fresh fruit. Sulfur is sold at most pharmacies; a standard 2-oz. box contains about 16 tsp. Heap the sulfur about 2 in. deep in a clean, disposable container, such as a tuna fish can, and set it next to the stack of trays. Place the cardboard box over the trays and sulfur, then pile dirt around the box's edges to seal them. Light the sulfur through the flap and check frequently to make sure that it keeps burning. (If the sulfur will not stay lit, poke a venthole in the box at the top of the side opposite the flap.) When the sulfur is entirely consumed, seal both the flap and the vent and let the fruit sit in the fumes until it is bright and shiny. Dry the fruit immediately after sulfuring is completed.

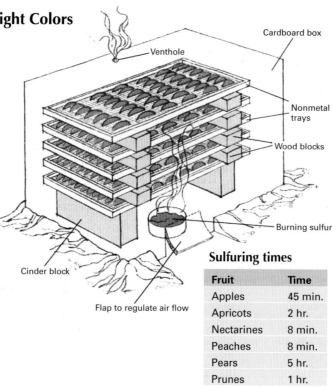

Cardboard box

Venthole

Nonmetal trays

Wood blocks

Burning sulfur

Cinder block

Flap to regulate air flow

Sulfuring times

Fruit	Time
Apples	45 min.
Apricots	2 hr.
Nectarines	8 min.
Peaches	8 min.
Pears	5 hr.
Prunes	1 hr.

Blanching: preparation and timing

Produce	Preparation	Steam	Boil
Apples	Peel, core, slice 1/8' thick	5 min.	2 min.
Apricots	Leave whole to boil; otherwise halve and pit	3-4 min.	4-5 min.
Beans	Cut into 1' pieces	2 1/2 min.	2 min.
Broccoli	Cut into flowerettes	3-3 1/2 min.	2 min.
Brussels sprouts	Halve lengthwise	6-7 min.	4 1/2-5 1/2 min.
Cabbage	Core, slice 1/8' thick	2 1/2-3 min.	1 1/2-2 min.
Carrots	Peel, slice 1/8' thick	3-3 1/2 min.	3 1/2 min.
Cauliflower	Cut into flowerettes	4 min.	3-4 min.
Celery	Remove leaves, slice stalks	2 min.	2 min.
Corn	Remove husks	2-2 1/2 min.	1 1/2 min.
Grapes (seedless)	Remove stems	No blanching necessary	
Nectarines, peaches	Leave whole; halve and pit after blanching	8 min.	8 min.
Pears	Peel, halve, core	6 min.	–
Spinach	Trim, wash leaves	2-2 1/2 min.	1 1/2 min.
Summer squash	Trim, slice 1/4' thick	2 1/2-3 min.	1 1/2 min.
Tomatoes	Peel, section or slice	3 min.	1 min.

Outdoor Drying

If you live in an area with clean air, a dry climate, and consistently sunny weather, the simplest way to dry produce is to do it right in the garden. Peas and beans can be left to dry on the vine if the growing season is long enough. Store vine-dried peas in mesh bags in an airy spot. When you are ready to eat them, whack the bag with a stick to remove the shells. Vine-dried green and wax beans must be blanched and then oven cured by baking them for 10 to 15 minutes at 175°F before storing. Oven curing will kill any insect eggs and ensure thorough drying. For long-term storage, string the beans together and hang them in a dry place, such as the attic. Onions can also be allowed to dry in the garden. Pull them up and let them lie on the ground in the sun for four to six days. When the tops turn stiff and strawlike, braid them together with a length of strong twine.

While outdoor drying is convenient, there are some drawbacks. The longer the fruits and vegetables are exposed to air and sunlight, the more vitamins they lose. Moreover, even mild air pollution can contaminate food—in rural areas the fumes from trucks and automobiles can be a serious problem.

Sun-dried tomatoes are delicious in pasta, salads, or on pizza.

Drying on trays

Produce that is not suited to garden drying can still be dried outdoors on trays made from parallel wooden slats or from nonmetallic screening. (Metal screening should not be used, since some metals are poisonous while others destroy vitamins.) The mesh should be tacked or stapled to wooden frames. Old metal window screens covered with brown paper are sometimes used for drying, but they are not recommended because the metal may still contaminate despite the paper.

When your food is ready for drying, spread it on trays in single layers so that the pieces do not touch one another. Choose a warm drying spot, such as a heat-reflecting driveway or a rooftop, and set the trays out, raising them on blocks to 6 inches above the ground for better air circulation. For even more heat tilt the trays so that they face the sun. To protect against insects, shield the food with cheesecloth placed above the tray. Drape the cloth over wooden blocks to keep it from touching the food, and weight its edges down with stones. Put out the trays as soon as the morning dew has evaporated. At dusk either bring the trays indoors or cover them with canvas or plastic.

Solar driers

Solar driers collect heat from the sun and use it to speed up air circulation and reduce the moisture content of the air. They are especially useful in areas, such as the Southeast, where there is plenty of sunlight but the humidity is relatively high. The simplest design has glass or plastic panels that trap sunlight to warm a box. A more elaborate drier, made from an oil drum, circulates sun-heated air around stacks of drying trays. The key to successful solar drying is to check the apparatus frequently. If sunlight is blocked even partially, the air inside the drier will cool, fail to circulate, and become damp. The result is increased risk of deterioration of food.

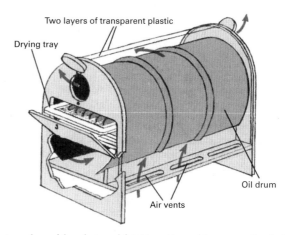

Ingenious drier designed by New Hampshire sun enthusiast Leandre Poisson uses curved layers of plastic as solar collectors. Heated air travels by natural convection into the oil drum, where food is spread on trays. Electric light bulb and small fan increase reliability by maintaining the temperature and a balanced flow of air if sun dims.

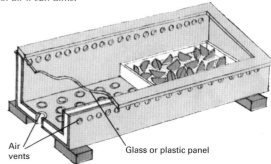

Simplest solar drier is like a cold frame with glass panels tilted toward sun. Specially placed vents maximize air circulation.

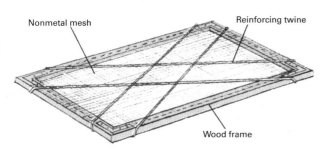

Make a drying tray from wooden slats or by stretching nonmetal mesh on a wooden frame. Reinforce bottom with twine.

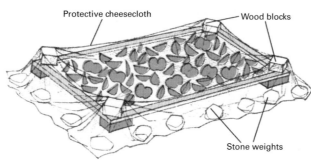

Cover trays with cheesecloth to allow maximum air and heat circulation while protecting against insects and birds.

Drying Indoors Is Most Efficient

In many parts of the country indoor drying is the most convenient and practical way to remove moisture from food. Not only is indoor drying independent of the weather, but it is faster than open-air drying because it continues day and night. As a result, vitamins are conserved and there is less chance of spoilage.

The simplest way to dry food indoors is in an oven. Start by preparing the food as described on page 218, including blanching or sulfuring. Next, preheat the oven to 145°F. (Buy an accurate thermometer to check the oven temperature.) Spread the pieces of fruit and vegetable in single layers on cookie sheets, making sure that the pieces do not touch one another. Place the sheets on racks inside the oven, leaving at least 4 inches above and below

Dried fruit or vegetables will be dramatically reduced in size and weight after drying but will maintain most of the flavor and color.

the trays for air circulation. With the oven door slightly ajar for ventilation, turn the temperature down to 120°F, then gradually increase it to 140°F. Be sure that the food is exposed to 140°F temperatures for at least half the full drying time. From time to time rearrange the trays and shift the food to ensure even drying. A number of commercial devices are available for drying food in the home, or you can make one of the simple driers shown on this page. Such driers generally do the job more slowly than an oven but have the advantage of using less energy. In addition, they free the oven for more routine tasks, such as cooking dinner or baking bread.

Easy-to-make indoor driers

Wooden box in which several trays can be stacked makes an easy-to-construct home drier. Some models are raised on legs to accommodate the heating unit underneath; in others the heater is held within the box itself. Hot plates, electric heaters in which the heating element faces upward—even ordinary light bulbs—are all possible sources of heat. (Long-life bulbs screwed into porcelain sockets are recommended for safety.) Devices that burn coal or oil should be avoided because their fumes are dangerous when concentrated in a small enclosed space. The simplest of all driers is a cardboard box lined with aluminum foil.

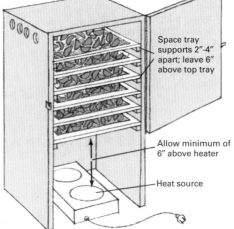

Space tray supports 2"-4" apart; leave 6" above top tray

Allow minimum of 6" above heater

Heat source

Home dehydrator (above) holds trays 2 to 4 in. apart and leaves 6 in. above top tray for circulation of heated air.

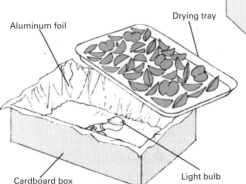

Aluminum foil

Drying tray

Cardboard box

Light bulb

For simple drier (left) line box with foil and place light bulb inside box, but not touching the box. Blacken bottom of tray and set on top of box. Spread food on tray.

Drying on top of the stove

Stove-top driers designed for wood-burning stoves can be used on gas and electric stoves as well. In this type of drier the drying tray is separated from the direct heat of the burner by a 3-in-deep reservoir of water. All burners are lit, but they are turned very low. As in other drying techniques, food must be spread in a single layer with space between pieces.

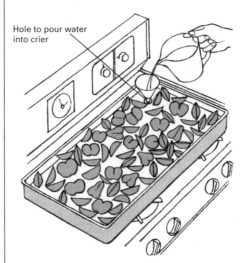

Hole to pour water into crier

Keep a watchful eye and add water to the reservoir as needed to prevent burning of food.

Tests for dryness

Drying times vary considerably depending on weather as well as size and moisture content of produce. Fruit is dry if it appears leathery and tough and no moisture can be squeezed from it. Vegetables should be so brittle and crisp that they rattle on the tray. Check weight too. If food has lost half its weight, it is two-thirds dry. The table gives approximate drying times.

Produce	Time in drier
Apples	6-12 hr.
Apricots	24-36 hr.
Beans	8-18 hr.
Broccoli	12-15 hr.
Brussel sprouts	12-18 hr.
Cabbage	10-12 hr.
Carrots	10-12 hr.
Cauliflower	12-15 hr.
Celery	10-16 hr.
Corn	12-15 hr.
Grapes (seedless)	12-20 hr.
Nectarines	36-38 hr.
Peaches	36-48 hr.
Pears	25-36 hr.
Spinach	8-10 hr.
Summer squash	10-12 hr.
Tomatoes	10-18 hr.

Storage and Rehydration

After food has been dried it should be pasteurized in an oven to be sure no insect eggs or spoilage microorganisms are present. Final pasteurization also helps ensure thorough drying. To pasteurize, preheat the oven to 175°F. Spread food 1 inch deep on trays, and put the trays in the oven for 10 to 15 minutes.

Even though a batch of fruit or vegetables may have been meticulously dried and pasteurized, small pockets of residual moisture always remain trapped. Additional conditioning helps spread this moisture evenly throughout the produce. The conditioning is accomplished by placing the cooled, dried produce in open enamel, glass, or ceramic containers, such as mason jars. The food is then stirred thoroughly twice a day to distribute any remaining moisture. If the food seems moist at the end of five days, return it to the drier.

After the fruits and vegetables have been conditioned, they are ready for long-term storage. Dried food is best kept in sterilized glass jars or plastic bags. Metal containers can be used, provided they are lined with brown paper—dried food should never be allowed to come in direct contact with metal. A perfect seal of the sort required in canning is not necessary, but the containers should have secure, tight-fitting lids to keep out dirt, dust, and insects. For best results, store dried food in a dark place where the temperature is below 60°F. Produce will sweat if stored in a warmer area, so refrigerate it during warm periods. Check periodically for condensation (it encourages mold), and return the food to the drier if any moisture is present.

Dried fruits may be eaten without reconstitution for snacks or in cereals, desserts, and salads. Vegetables, however, should be rehydrated by infusing them with enough water to replace the moisture removed during the drying process. Most fruits and vegetables can be rehydrated by pouring boiling water over them in the ratio of 1 1/2 cups of water to 1 cup of dried food and letting the food soak until all the water has been absorbed. Vegetables generally rehydrate in about two hours, but dried beans and fruits require overnight soaking. If all the water is absorbed but the food still appears shriveled, add more water a little at a time. Avoid adding excess liquid, however, since it will dissolve nutrients and waste them.

Rehydrated fruits need not be cooked, but vegetables must be. Cover the vegetables with any water left over from soaking and add fresh water if necessary to prevent scorching. Bring the water to a boil, reduce the heat, and simmer until the vegetables are tender. Reconstituted fruits and vegetables can be eaten plain or combined with other foods and flavorings.

Recipes

Substitute reconstituted dried food for fresh in almost any recipe (generally the volume of soaked food will be four times that of dried), or take advantage of the concentrated flavor of tomato paste and vegetable powder to enrich soups and stews.

Apple Leather

4 qt. apples, peeled, cored, and cut in pieces
1-1 1/2 cups apple cider
Honey to taste
Cinnamon, cloves, and nutmeg to taste
Cornstarch or arrowroot powder

Crush apples in a blender or food mill. Catch the juice and return it to mixture. Put ground apple mixture in a heavy kettle and add enough apple cider to prevent scorching. Bring mixture to a boil over low flame. Add honey and spices to taste. When mixture is as thick as apple butter, spread it in a 1/4-in.-thick layer on oiled cookie sheets or cookie sheets covered with freezer paper. Cover sheets with cheesecloth and place in a warm, dry area until dry (one to two weeks) or in a 120°F oven or a food drier. When fruit leather is dry enough to be lifted from sheets, lay it on cake rack so both sides can be dried at once. When leather is no longer sticky, dust with cornstarch or arrowroot. Wrap each sheet in freezer paper, wax paper, or aluminum foil, stack sheets, and cover with more paper. Store in a cool, dark place.

Apple Pie

1/4 lb. dried apple slices (3 1/2 cups)
2 cups water
1/3-1/2 cup sugar
1/2 tsp. cinnamon
One 9-in. unbaked pie shell

Cook apples in water until soft (one hour). Add sugar and cinnamon. Pour into pie shell. Bake at 350°F for one hour.

Sun-Cooked Preserves

4 cups mixed fruit, such as peaches, pears, and berries
1 cup honey

Wash fruit and cut large types into 1/2-in. chunks. Place fruit in saucepan, add honey, and bring to a boil, stirring constantly. Spread boiled mixture 1/2 in. deep in cookie sheets, making sure fruit is spread in a single layer. Cover trays with cheesecloth stretched taut, and put them in direct sun or drier for two to seven days to dry. When preserves are thick, pack into sterilized jars and refrigerate or freeze.

Vegetable Powder

Use any thoroughly dried vegetable for this recipe. Grind vegetables in blender and store. Add dried powder to boiling water to make instant vegetable soup, or add to stews and casseroles to enhance flavor.

Tomato Paste

Italian plum type tomatoes, which have less juice, are best for this recipe, but any type of tomato may be used. Put tomatoes into heavy kettle and crush to bring out juice. Cook until very soft (about one hour), then put through blender or food mill to puree. Return puree to kettle and simmer, stirring often, over very low heat until reduced by half (two to four hours). Spread puree 1/2 in. thick on cookie sheets and place in sun or drier until no longer sticky (about two days). Roll dried paste into 1-in. balls and let dry at room temperature for another one to two days. Store in airtight jars. Add balls of tomato paste to soups, stews, sauces, and gravies to enhance flavor, or add to cooked tomatoes to make tomato sauce. For variety add such herbs as basil and parsley when making tomato paste.

Sources and resources

Books and pamphlets
Bailey, Janet. *Keeping Food Fresh*. New York: Harper Collins, 1993.
Brennan, Georganne, and Kleinman, Katherine. *The Glass Pantry: Preserving Seasonal Flavors*. San Francisco: Chronicle Books, 1994.
Chesman, Andrea. *Summer in a Jar: Making Pickles, Jams and More*. Charlotte, Vt.: Williamson Publishing, 1985.
Chioffi, Nanci, and Gretchen Mead. *Keeping the Harvest*. Pownal, Vt.: Storey Communications, 1991.
Holm, Don, and Holm, Myrtle. *Don Holm's Book of Food Drying, Pickling and Smoke Curing*. Caldwell, Ind.: Caxton, 1978.
Home Canning of Fruits and Vegetables. Home and Garden Bulletin No. 8. Washington, D.C.: U.S. Department of Agriculture, 1983.
Home Freezing of Fruits and Vegetables. Home and Garden Bulletin No. 10. Washington, D.C.: U.S. Department of Agriculture, 1971.
Humphrey, Richard. *Saving the Plenty: Pickling and Preserving*. Kingston, Mass.: Teaparty Books, 1986.
Hupping, Carol. *Stocking Up*. New York: Simon and Schuster Trade, 1990.

Innes, Jacosta. *The Country Preserves Companion*. San Francisco: Collins Publishers, 1995.
Kinard, Malvina. *Well Preserved*. New Canaan, Conn.: Keats Publishing, 1994.
Lesem, Jeanne. *Preserving Today*. New York: Knopf, 1992.
Nichols, Naomi. *Food Drying at Home*. New York: Van Nostrand Reinhold, 1978.
Pyron, Cherry, and Clarissa M. Silitch, eds. *The Forgotten Arts: Making Old-Fashioned Pickles, Relishes, Chutneys, Sauces and Catsups, Mincemeats, Beverages and Syrups*. Dublin, N.H.: Yankee Books, 1986.
Stoner, Carol Hupping, ed. *Stocking Up III*. New York: Fine Communications, 1995.
U.S. Department of Agriculture. *Complete Guide to Home Canning, Preserving and Freezing*. New York: Dover, 1994.

Preserving Meat and Fish

The Old Methods Survive Not Just for Practicality But for Unsurpassed Flavor

The problem of storing meat and fish for use the year round is as old as mankind. Most of the traditional methods involve processing with salt, smoke, and spices that not only preserve but add flavor as well. Although modern refrigeration has made food storage simpler, many of the old ways are still popular, primarily because they make meat and fish taste so good.

Curing and smoking were once the standard ways of preserving, and many popular products—Smithfield hams, corned beef, lox, pastrami—are still made by one or both of these techniques. Sausages, too, were and are popular. The recipes by which sausages are made vary according to climate. In warm areas traditional recipes call for cured meat laced with plenty of herbs and spices; the result is sausages that tend to be hard and dry. In colder climates, where storage is less of a problem, sausages are generally milder and are made from fresh, uncured meat.

Some old-time methods of preservation are now all but forgotten. Poultry, cooked and deboned, was stored for months beneath a covering of lard or butter. Roasts were kept fresh for up to a week by immersing them in cold running water—when the meat began to float, it was time for it to go into the oven. Charcoal, a strong antibacterial agent, was often ground and rubbed into the surface of meat; fish would be kept fresh by replacing the innards with a lump of charcoal. American Plains Indians perfected the art of drying, or jerking, meat and then grinding the jerky to make pemmican; modern outdoorsmen have rediscovered this ancient food, and today a small jerky-making industry flourishes, catering to the needs of hikers, campers, and skiers.

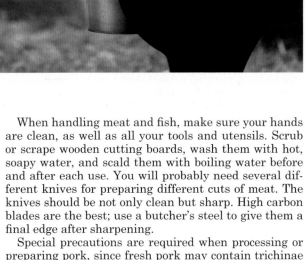

Smoking meat, fish, and poultry is much easier than it might seem. This unique smoker is crafted to look like a bull, but really no specialized equipment is required beyond a firepit, where the hardwood smolders, and a ventilated smoke chamber (a wooden crate or even a cardboard box could serve). The smoke helps to preserve meat, partly by coating it with smoke-borne preservative chemicals. Thoroughly cured and smoked meats, such as the South's famous Smithfield hams, can be kept for years. (Smithfields have reputedly been stored for as long as 25 years—from a girl's christening until her wedding.) Nowadays, many people use smokers to add a delicious woodsy flavor to a piece of fresh meat or fish.

Short-term Storage, Hanging, and Sanitation

Fresh meat (including poultry) deteriorates rapidly in temperatures above 40°F, so it is important to refrigerate it as soon as possible and to keep it under refrigeration until it is cooked or processed. In addition, a period of chilling, or hanging, can improve the flavor and texture of most meats by giving natural enzymes time to break down tough muscle fibers. The temperature range for hanging is 33°F to 40°F. Freshly killed poultry should be hung for 12 to 48 hours, depending on the size of the bird. Pork and veal should hang for one or two days; beef, mutton, and lamb for as long as a week. Game should be gutted first, and any scent glands should be removed. If you cannot maintain a temperature at or below 40°F, do not attempt to hang meat. Instead, cure it, freeze it, or otherwise process it for preservation immediately. Fish rots very quickly, so it should never be hung; process it immediately or else freeze it.

When handling meat and fish, make sure your hands are clean, as well as all your tools and utensils. Scrub or scrape wooden cutting boards, wash them with hot, soapy water, and scald them with boiling water before and after each use. You will probably need several different knives for preparing different cuts of meat. The knives should be not only clean but sharp. High carbon blades are the best; use a butcher's steel to give them a final edge after sharpening.

Special precautions are required when processing or preparing pork, since fresh pork may contain trichinae worms, which cause the disease trichinosis. These worms can be killed by heat or by cold. Always cook pork to a minimum of 137°F *throughout*. (To be safe, cook it to 145°F to 150°F.) For cuts of pork less than 6 inches thick the worms can also be destroyed by freezing at −10°F for 10 to 12 days or at 0°F for three to four weeks.

Freezing In Fresh Flavor

Since World War II freezing has become the most popular way to store meat and fish; it is quick and easy, and preserves both the nutritional value and flavor of the fresh food. The only drawback is that freezing is dependent on a consistent supply of electrical power. The best way to freeze meat and fish is to flash-freeze at –15°F, then store at 0°F. Most chest-style freezers have the capability of reaching –15°F, but some uprights may not. Set your freezer's control to its coldest setting several hours before using it as a flash-freezer. Shift the food that is already in the freezer to one side; try to leave about 1 cubic foot of freezer space for every 2 pounds of meat or fish to be flash-frozen.

Chill meat or fish before you freeze it to make it easier to cut and package and to decrease the chance of spoiling other food in the freezer. Wrap all pieces securely in individual moisture-proof packages to prevent freezer burn (caused by dehydration) and to avoid contaminating one meat with the odors of another. There are many brands of freezer wrap available that give durable protection for frozen goods. Label each package with the type and cut of meat or fish it contains and the date

it was frozen. Then load the packages into the freezer. To protect the frozen food, be sure to keep the unfrozen packages from touching any of the already frozen food. When all the food is hard frozen, return the control to normal (0°F). In the event of freezer breakdown or power failure, do not open the freezer—it will maintain its temperature for several hours. During longer breakdowns keep the empty space in the freezer packed with dry ice. Once meat is thawed, it should not be refrozen.

All meats begin to deteriorate if they are left in the freezer too long. Cured meats, such as ham and bacon, and very fatty meats, such as sausage, do not keep well under refrigeration and should not be kept frozen for more than a month. Ground meat, stewing meat, pork chops, liver, and kidneys can generally be left frozen for up to three months. Steak, chops, fish, and roasts will last as long as six months. The best way to thaw frozen food when you are ready to use it is to place it in the refrigerator, still in its sealed package, and let it warm gradually. For quick thawing run cold water over the package. You can cook frozen meat without thawing by allowing extra cooking time.

Wrapping meat for the freezer

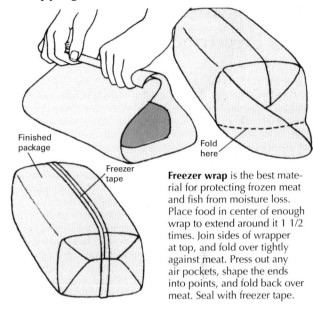

Finished package

Fold here

Freezer tape

Freezer wrap is the best material for protecting frozen meat and fish from moisture loss. Place food in center of enough wrap to extend around it 1 1/2 times. Join sides of wrapper at top, and fold over tightly against meat. Press out any air pockets, shape the ends into points, and fold back over meat. Seal with freezer tape.

Canning for Convenience

Canning is convenient and economical. Canned foods are not endangered by power failures, they are easy to transport, and they keep a long time. Both meat and fish can be safely preserved either in glass jars or in tin cans, but jars are generally recommended because they cost less, are more convenient, and do not require a mechanical sealing device.

The greatest danger in canning is botulism, a severe and often fatal form of food poisoning caused by bacteria that thrive in dark, airless conditions. To be sure of killing the bacteria, you must treat the food and containers for an extended time at 240°F. To reach this temperature requires a pressure canner with its control set for at least 10 pounds. (For instructions on pressure canning, canning terminology, and canning equipment, see *Preserving Produce*, pp.206–208.)

Meat, fish, and poultry can be canned by either the raw-pack or hot-pack method. Raw-packed food is put into containers before it is cooked; hot-packed food is cooked first. In both cases the presence of fat on the rim of the jar may spoil the canning seal, so it is safest to trim off as much fat as possible before packing. For raw packing cut the food into pieces, pack it loosely in sterilized jars, and add 1/2 teaspoon of salt per pint but no liquid. Place the uncovered jars in an open saucepan of water, and heat gently until a thermometer inserted in

the middle of the meat reads 170°F—the temperature at which air is driven out and all yeast and mold spores are killed. This process, known as exhausting, may take an hour or longer. Cap the jars immediately according to the manufacturer's directions; then process them in a pressure canner.

To hot pack, cook the food thoroughly in salted water, and pack it loosely into jars, leaving 1-inch headspace. Next, fill the jars to within 1 inch of the top with boiling water or cooking broth. Make sure the rims of the jars are clean and free of fat before putting the caps on, then carry out the standard pressure canning procedure.

After the jars have been pressure processed and allowed to cool, check for a perfect seal. Metal lids should be slightly concave and should give a clear metallic ring when you tap them. If one fails to do so, either discard it or open it and reprocess the contents from the beginning. After they are checked, label all jars with the contents and date. Store them in a cool, dry, dark location (direct light can discolor the contents).

If a lid bulges during storage, or if the contents spurt or show any sign of being under pressure when the jar is opened, do not use the food. Botulism is extremely virulent, yet affected food may not show the usual signs of spoilage. When disposing of the food, be sure it will not be eaten by an animal or other person.

A guide for canning

Meat	Preparation	Time at 240°F (sea level)	
Chicken, duck, goose, rabbit, squab, turkey, and other poultry and small game	Bone in: remove meat from breast; break legs and wings into short pieces	1-pt. jars . . . . 65 min. 1-qt. jars . . . . 75 min. No. 2 cans . . . . . . 55 min. No. 2 1/2 cans . . . 75 min.	
	Boneless: cut meat into chunks with skin attached	1-pt. jars . . . . 75 min. 1-qt. jars . . . . 90 min. No. 2 cans . . . . . . 65 min. No. 2 1/2 cans . . . 90 min.	
Beef, lamb, pork, and veal	Cut raw meat into strips or chunks, or grind and cook as patties	1-pt. jars . . . . 75 min. 1-qt. jars . . . . 90 min. No. 2 cans . . . . . 100 min. No. 2 1/2 cans . . . 135 min.	
Mackerel, salmon, trout, and other fish	Fillet large fish; for saltwater fish add 1 tbsp. vegetable oil per pt.	1/2-pt. jars . . . . . . 90 min. 1-pt. jars . . . . 110 min. 1/2-lb. flat tins . . . 90 min. No. 2 cans . . . . . 100 min.	
Smoked salmon	Use C-enamel cans	1/2-pt. jars . . . . . . 95 min. 1/2-lb. flat tins . . . 90 min. No. 2 cans . . . . . 100 min.	

Curing and Smoking For Lasting Flavor

Curing, the first step in the smoking process, is essential for good flavor. In the old days a strong brine cure was the rule—pioneer women judged that there was enough salt and other ingredients in the brine when a raw potato floated. Such a powerful mixture resulted in meat that had excellent keeping qualities but was extremely salty. Before the meat was eaten it was generally desalted by soaking in cold water. Modern refrigeration has opened the way for mild, sweet cures in which flavor is more important than long-term preservation.

Not only curing methods but smoking methods as well have changed over the years. In former times meat was kept for days or even weeks in chambers filled with cool, dense smoke (the temperature rarely topped 110°F). The result was strongly flavored meat that would keep for a very long period. Modern methods of hot smoking require temperatures of at least 170°F in the smoke chamber. In this heat the meat cooks as it smokes, and to prevent dehydration it must be removed from the smoke chamber after a relatively short time. The only purpose of hot smoking is to add flavor—hot-smoked meat does not keep significantly better than other cooked meat.

Hot smoking can be done all year round, but lengthy curing and cold smoking are best accomplished when the weather is cool enough to prevent the meat from spoiling but not so cold that the meat freezes. For these reasons the best time to start a cold-smoking project is in the autumn, when nighttime temperatures approach freezing and the days are consistently cool.

Nitrites and Nitrates

Sodium and potassium nitrite, and to a lesser extent sodium and potassium nitrate (saltpeter)—ingredients that have been used for many centuries in curing meats—have recently come under suspicion as possible cancer-causing agents. These additives have several purposes: they preserve the red color of meat, they are partly responsible for the distinctive flavor of many smoked foods, and they reduce the risk of botulism and other types of food poisoning. Meat that is cured without the use of either nitrites or nitrates must either be kept under refrigeration like any nonsmoked product or else cured with enough salt so that the fluids in the meat contain at least 10 percent salt.

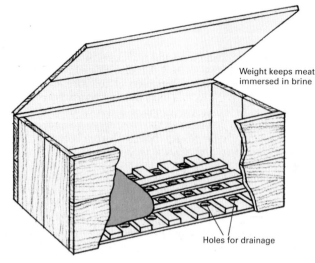

Weight keeps meat immersed in brine

Holes for drainage

Hardwood box for dry-curing has a wooden rack at bottom for drainage space. Holes drilled in the bottom allow the escape of juices drawn from the meat or fish by the salt.

Brine

Stoneware crock

Traditional crock made out of stoneware is ideal for brine-curing, but any large container of pottery, plastic, or glass—even a sterile plastic garbage can—will serve the purpose. Do not use a metal container: salt water is highly corrosive, and the meat or fish can be contaminated. A seasoned hardwood barrel is also good for the job; avoid barrels made of softwood, such as pine, because the resins in the wood will leach into the brine and impart a bitter flavor to the meat or fish.

How to Cure: Two Methods

Salt is the only essential ingredient for curing. It retards spoilage by drawing water out of meat or fish while simultaneously killing decay-causing microorganisms. Meat cured with salt alone will store well but will be tough and dry. Sugar or honey is often added for flavor as well as to keep the meat moist and tender. Herbs and spices can be included in the curing mixture according to personal taste, but do so cautiously; some combinations give unsatisfactory results. Garlic and pepper, for example, can overpower the flavor of a cure.

There are two curing methods: brine-curing and dry-curing. Dry-curing is faster, but many people prefer brine-curing because the results are more consistent and the flavor milder. In either case do not use ordinary table salt; the iodine it contains can discolor meat and fish. Pickling salt is the best type for curing. It has no additives, it is inexpensive, and since it is finely ground, it dissolves readily in brine cures and is quickly absorbed by the meat in dry cures. Other acceptable salts include rock salt, kosher salt, dairy salt, and canning salt.

Brine-curing. For a brine cure the curing mixture is dissolved in pure water. Boil questionable water first to kill bacteria and diminish chlorine, then let it cool. Lay larger pieces of meat or fish, skin side down, on the bottom of a watertight, nonmetal container, such as a stoneware crock, then pack smaller pieces on top. Fill the container with brine until the pieces start to shift. To keep the meat or fish submerged, cover it with a plate on which several weights have been placed; make

sure no air pockets are trapped under the plate. Maintain the brine at 36°F to 40°F. After three to five days remove the meat from the brine, spoon off any scum, stir the brine up, and repack the crock. This procedure need be done only once for most cuts of meat; but if the pieces are large (a whole ham, for example), it should be repeated once a week until the cure is complete.

To check progress, cut off a small piece of meat, wash it, cook it thoroughly, and taste it. When the meat is cured to your taste, remove each piece from the crock and rinse it first in warm water, then in cold. Use a scrubbing brush to remove any encrustations of salt, and hang the pieces in a warm place to dry. When dry, red meats will generally have a glossy film of dissolved protein that helps to preserve them.

Dry-curing. In this process the meat or fish is packed directly in a mixture of salt and seasoning. Start by coating each piece; rub it in well and press extra mix into the crannies on the cut ends, especially around projecting bones. Cover the bottom of the curing box with a thick layer of curing mix and place the pieces of meat (or fish) on it. Pack more mix on and between the pieces, making sure each piece is well covered, especially where chunks touch, then put down another layer of meat. Continue until the final layer of meat is packed and covered. After three days remove the pieces of meat and recoat any surfaces that are not well coated. This process of checking and replenishing should be repeated every five days thereafter.

Making and Using a Smokehouse

The difference between a smokehouse designed for hot smoking and one designed for cold smoking is largely a matter of the distance between the smoke chamber and the fire: the greater the distance, the cooler the smoke. Proper ventilation is important with either smoking method, since smoke that is trapped in the chamber too long becomes stale and gives food a bitter taste. Too much ventilation, however, dissipates the smoke. Your best guide is the temperature inside the chamber; install a thermometer that can be read from outside, then open or close the vents as needed.

Meats are cold smoked for flavor or for long-term preservation. When the aim is preservation, the temperature should be between 70°F and 90°F; the maximum is 110°F, although large hams are sometimes smoked at higher temperatures. Locate the fire pit about 10 feet from the smoke chamber on the side from which the prevailing winds blow. The top of the pit should be about a foot lower than the bottom of the chamber with a stovepipe or tile-lined tunnel between.

Hot smoking requires temperatures of 170°F to 210°F, so the smoke chamber should be insulated. Smoke is produced inside or directly beneath the chamber. If you use an electric burner to produce smoke and heat, the job of maintaining a proper temperature is made easier.

The flavor that smoke adds depends on the wood being burned. Softwoods should not be used—their resins are ruinous to smoked food—but almost any hardwood is usable. The best smoke is produced from hickory, apple, or cherry. To use an electric burner, fill a 1-pound coffee can with damp shavings or chips, and place it on the top of a burner set to *low*; you will need to replenish the fuel about once an hour. Otherwise, start a fire with dry hardwood and let it burn to a bed of glowing coals before adding damp chips or shavings (see *Wilderness Camping*, p.419, for fire-building tips). Do not use a chemical fire starter—the odor will linger in the smoke.

When the chamber is filled with smoke and the temperature is right, load in the meat or fish. The best method is to hang the food from crossbars near the top. It can also be placed on mesh shelves of stainless steel or aluminum—not brass, copper, or galvanized steel. During smoking, continue to add damp fuel to maintain dense white smoke; should the smoke turn blue, it means the fuel supply is running low. If your smoke chamber is lined with metal, it is important to avoid the buildup of smoky deposits that will make new batches of smoked food bitter; clean and scrub the walls of the smoke chamber after every third or fourth use. Wooden walls are more difficult to clean, but they absorb much of the deposits and need not be scrubbed as often.

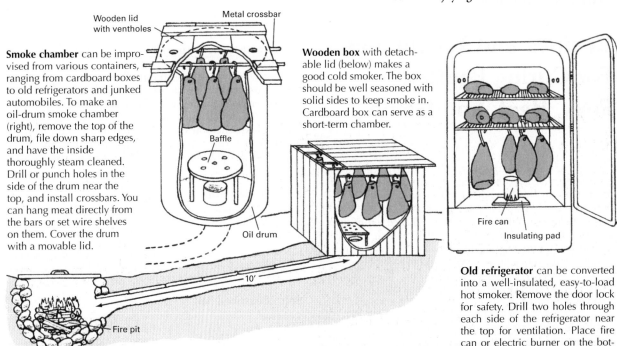

Smoke chamber can be improvised from various containers, ranging from cardboard boxes to old refrigerators and junked automobiles. To make an oil-drum smoke chamber (right), remove the top of the drum, file down sharp edges, and have the inside thoroughly steam cleaned. Drill or punch holes in the side of the drum near the top, and install crossbars. You can hang meat directly from the bars or set wire shelves on them. Cover the drum with a movable lid.

Wooden box with detachable lid (below) makes a good cold smoker. The box should be well seasoned with solid sides to keep smoke in. Cardboard box can serve as a short-term chamber.

Old refrigerator can be converted into a well-insulated, easy-to-load hot smoker. Remove the door lock for safety. Drill two holes through each side of the refrigerator near the top for ventilation. Place fire can or electric burner on the bottom atop an insulating pad.

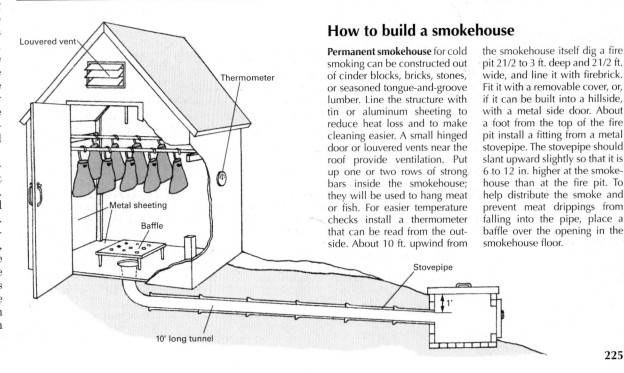

How to build a smokehouse

Permanent smokehouse for cold smoking can be constructed out of cinder blocks, bricks, stones, or seasoned tongue-and-groove lumber. Line the structure with tin or aluminum sheeting to reduce heat loss and to make cleaning easier. A small hinged door or louvered vents near the roof provide ventilation. Put up one or two rows of strong bars inside the smokehouse; they will be used to hang meat or fish. For easier temperature checks install a thermometer that can be read from the outside. About 10 ft. upwind from the smokehouse itself dig a fire pit 2½ to 3 ft. deep and 2½ ft. wide, and line it with firebrick. Fit it with a removable cover, or, if it can be built into a hillside, with a metal side door. About a foot from the top of the fire pit install a fitting from a metal stovepipe. The stovepipe should slant upward slightly so that it is 6 to 12 in. higher at the smokehouse than at the fire pit. To help distribute the smoke and prevent meat drippings from falling into the pipe, place a baffle over the opening in the smokehouse floor.

225

Recipes and Techniques For Curing Poultry, Pork, Beef, and Game

Curing and smoking are inexact arts, and any attempt at precise instruction concerning the strength and duration of the cure, or the time spent in the smokehouse, will be frustrated by variables. The type of meat and its weight, size, and quality are considerations. So are temperature and the density of the smoke, both of which vary with humidity and air pressure. The way the salt is ground makes a difference, as does the kind of wood burned for smoke. The greatest variables of all are the tastes and intentions of the person doing the smoking.

If your purpose in curing and smoking a piece of meat is to preserve it, use a strong, salty brine cure, and cold smoke for the full recommended time. If you are not interested in long-term storage but merely wish to add tenderness and flavor, soak the meat in a marinade, or dry-cure it briefly in seasoned salt before hot smoking. The length of time a piece of meat should be hot smoked

Country-Style Ham and Other Pork Cures

The majority of traditional curing recipes are designed for pork. One reason is that the meat's rich taste is ideally complemented by curing and smoking. Another is that pork was the staple meat among early settlers, and smoking was the most practical way to store hams, pork shoulders, sides of bacon, and other large cuts.

Long-term preservation of large pieces of pork calls for thorough curing and cold smoking. The process, known as hard-curing, can take from 10 to 90 days, depending on the size and cut of meat. The result is the familiar, rich flavor of country-style ham, pork shoulder, and bacon. Of the many old-time methods of preservation with all their regional variations, this is still the most popular. The chart at right gives curing and smoking times.

You can also cure and smoke pork for flavor alone rather than for preservation. Cut the meat into pieces of no more than 4 pounds. Dry-cure up to a week or brine-cure up to nine days, then rinse and scrub the pieces, and hang them to dry. Smoke for one to four hours at 110°F to 120°F.

The cure recipes given at right can be used for either type of smoking. Always cook pork well before eating it.

varies with temperature. The best guide is a reliable meat thermometer stuck deep into the meat.

Meat that has been cured and cold smoked for long-term preservation keeps best at 55°F to 60°F. It should be suspended to allow good air circulation, and pieces should not touch each other. Before storing smoked meat, clean the storage area thoroughly, and seal all cracks where dirt can collect or insects might breed.

The following basic curing recipes can be used with a variety of meats:

Sweet Pickle Brine

4 oz. pickling spices	3 cloves crushed garlic
2 1/2 gal. water	1 lb. sugar
2 1/2 lb. salt	

Simmer spices in a cup of boiling water for 10 minutes, then mix with remaining water and other ingredients. Chill brine to 35°F, and add meat. Maintain temperature throughout curing.

Spicy Seasoned Salt

1 cup salt	1 tbsp. celery salt
4 tbsp. sugar	2 tsp. onion powder
4 tbsp. black pepper	2 tsp. garlic powder
4 tbsp. white pepper	1 tsp. sage

Mix all ingredients and store for several days in an airtight jar to allow the flavors to blend before applying to meat.

Cut of meat	Type of cure	Quantity of cure	Length of cure	Smoking
Ham or shoulder	Dry	1 lb. for every 12 lb.	2 days per lb.	1–4 days at 100°F –120°F
	Brine	To cover meat	4 days per lb.; 28 days max.	
Bacon or loin	Dry	1/2 lb. for every 12 lb.	1 1/2 days per lb.; 25 days min. for cuts over 2" thick	
	Brine	To cover meat	15–20 days	

Brine Cure for Pork

2 gal. water
3 lb. salt
1 lb. brown sugar
2 tbsp. black pepper
5 crushed cloves
1 tbsp. white pepper

Dry Cure for Pork

3 lb. salt
1 1/2 lb. brown sugar
5 crushed cloves
2 tbsp. black pepper
3 crushed bay leaves
1 tbsp. cinnamon

Protection from insects

Insect infestation is a major enemy of stored meat. To protect a ham after it has been cured and smoked, first wrap it in heavy brown paper according to the numbered sequence shown above. Place the wrapped ham in a fitted bag of strong sackcloth, tie the top with string or wire, and suspend the sack in a cool place. Inspect regularly for signs of insects, such as greasy spots or holes in the sackcloth. If the meat has been attacked, trim away all affected parts and use the remainder as soon as possible. Remove all meat from the storage area and spray room surfaces with a methoxychlor solution (1/2 lb. powder per gallon of water). When you replace the meat, do not allow it to contact sprayed surfaces.

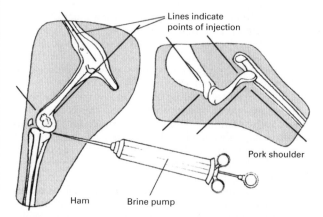

Pumping a ham. To prevent rot at the heart of a large piece of pork, inject brine cure close to the bone. A brine pump to do the job can be bought at most agricultural supply stores. Sterilize the pump and fill it with 1 oz. of brine for each pound of meat. Thrust the needle deep into the meat; then press the plunger gently and steadily as you withdraw it. Pinch the opening closed to prevent brine from oozing out. Make four or five separate injections to distribute the cure evenly.

Curing Beef

Any cut of beef can be cured and smoked for preservation, but only the cheaper cuts, such as rump, chuck, and brisket, are really improved by the process. To give a smoky flavor to steaks and other good cuts without losing too much moisture, cook them first, then cold smoke them for a short time to taste. In curing beef for preservation, avoid dry cures; use a brine cure that is rich in sugar or molasses.

Corned Beef

2 1/2 lb. salt	1 lb. brown sugar
10 lb. brisket of beef	4 cloves garlic
1 gal. Water	4 tbsp. pickling spices

Rub 2 lb. of the salt into the meat, then place meat in a clean container for 24 hours. Boil water, and mix in sugar and remaining salt. Let cool, then pour brine over meat. Add garlic and spices, weight meat down, and cure for 30 days in refrigerator at 38°F to 40°F, turning meat every five days. Remove meat as needed; rinse in fresh water for a few hours before cooking. Keep remaining meat submerged in brine at 38°F to 40°F.

Pastrami

1 1/2 gal. water	6 crushed garlic cloves
3 lb. salt	2 tsp. black pepper
3 cups brown sugar	1 tsp. onion powder
4 tbsp. pickling spices	1/2 tsp. cayenne
8 crushed cloves	Whole brisket of beef

Mix all ingredients except brisket. Submerge brisket in brine and cure three to four days for each pound. Rinse and dry. Cold smoke for four hours, then finish by cooking in slow oven until center of meat reaches 140°F. Store in refrigerator.

The Ancient Art of Jerking

The word "jerky" is an Anglicized version of the Spanish *charqui*, which itself comes from the Peruvian *ch'arki*, meaning "dried meat." Jerky is a product that is so hard as to be nearly indestructible. It was a staple of American Indians as well as the Incas, and frontiersmen were quick to learn jerking for their own survival. Today, jerky and its derivative, pemmican, are popular among campers and backpackers. The meat is nutritious, lightweight, and compact, and will remain edible for months or even years if stored in containers that have a bit of ventilation. Any meat can be jerked, but lean beef and venison produce the best results.

Brine-cured jerky. Cut lean meat into long, wide slabs about 1 inch thick, and cure for three to six days in the sweet pickle brine described on the opposite page. Then rinse and dry in a cool place. Use a very sharp knife to slice the meat lengthwise into 1/4-inch-wide

Curing Poultry

Large birds with a high fat content, such as ducks, geese, and capons, respond well to smoking. Turkeys and large chickens can also be smoked but tend to become dry and tough unless they are basted frequently either with cooking oil or with their own juices. Because dry cures tend to make the problem worse, they are seldom used with any poultry—and never with chicken or turkey. For flavor the bird can be rubbed with a basic seasoning mixture, such as the spicy seasoned salt on page 226. The more usual method is to brine-cure before smoking. Prepare the bird by cutting off its lower legs, head, and neck. Then remove the entrails and internal organs and wash the central cavity to remove all blood clots.

After brine-curing the bird, hot smoke it at 200°F to 225°F to taste, basting often to prevent drying. Alternatively, cold smoke until the skin turns a golden brown or deep reddish brown, then cook in oven. While cooking, keep the bird moist by wrapping it in tightly sealed aluminum foil along with a few tablespoons of water. Once the bird is smoked, use it immediately, since neither procedure contributes to preservation.

Brine Cure for Poultry

6 cloves	1 tbsp. onion powder
3 gal. water	1 tbsp. sage
3 lb. salt	Ginger, nutmeg, paprika
3 1/2 cups brown sugar	to taste (optional)
2 tbsp. dill salt	

Crush the cloves, and mix the ingredients in a crock. Submerge the bird in the mixture, and let it cure at 38°F to 40°F for 24 to 36 hours per pound. Rinse and dry the bird.

slices (it will help to chill the meat to near freezing first). Hang the slices on racks and cold smoke at 75°F to 85°F for 12 to 36 hours. If the jerky snaps when it is bent rather than merely folding, it is ready.

Quick-cured jerky. Cut lean raw meat into very thin slices. Dip into a dry-curing mix (pure pickling salt will do) and suspend from racks. Smoke at 100°F to 120°F for two to four hours. Rinse off any encrustation of salt, and dry the meat between paper towels; then lay flat in baking trays and place in a cool oven (175° to 200°F) until meat is stiff and dry. Leave the oven door open to allow moisture to escape.

Pemmican. Pound some jerky into a powder or run it through a meat grinder. Add nuts, seeds, or dried fruit that have been finely chopped or ground. Bind the whole mixture together with melted beef fat and roll it into balls. Store in a lidded container in a cool, dry place.

Dressing and Curing Game

All wild game should be field dressed as soon as it is killed. Start by removing any musk glands from the legs. Next, open the body cavity from the base of the tail to breastbone, cutting around the anus to free it. Remove the entrails, cut around the diaphragm and through the windpipe and gullet, and remove the heart and lungs. Roll the animal facedown to let the blood drain, then clean the body cavity by rubbing it with grass, paper, or cloth—do not wash it, since moisture speeds spoilage. Keep the carcass chilled if possible.

Bear. Use the same recipes and smoking techniques for bear as for pork. Bear meat, like pork, must be thoroughly cooked as a precaution against trichinosis.

Deer, elk, moose. Venison is even less fatty than beef. Use the sweet brine cure given below before smoking large pieces, or cut the meat into strips for jerky.

Sweet Brine Cure

3 gal. water	6 crushed bay leaves
5 1/2 lb. salt	3 tbsp. black pepper
3 1/2 cups brown sugar	

Small Game Marinade

1 cup wine	3 bay leaves
1 cup vinegar	1 tbsp. oregano
1/2 cup olive oil or	1 tsp. nutmeg
vegetable oil	2 cups water
1 medium onion, chopped	3 tbsp. sugar (optional)

Small game animals, such as rabbits and squirrels, are too lean to smoke well, but their flavor is enhanced by soaking in this marinade before cooking.

Jerking meat the American Indian way

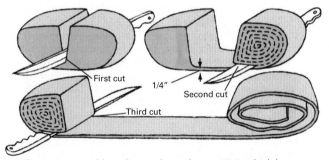

First cut
1/4"
Second cut
Third cut

Indian women could produce a sheet of meat 1/4 in. thick by several yards long from a single chunk of lean meat. The technique was to cut down through the center to within 1/4 in. of the bottom, then outward in one direction, unwrapping the meat as the cutting proceeded until half the chunk was sliced. The chunk was then reversed and the other half cut the same way.

Smoking and Drying Food From the Sea

Almost every type of fish responds well to curing and smoking. The flavor of oilier fish, such as salmon and eel, is particularly enhanced by the process. Less juicy fish, such as pike, should be basted often while they are smoking to prevent them from becoming dried out.

Because fish rot quickly, they should be cleaned and dressed as soon as they are caught, then kept on ice until they are processed. (For instructions in the standard methods of dressing fish, see *Fishing*, p.437.) The processes of curing and smoking are quicker and easier with fish than with most meats. Only a brief period in the cure followed by a few hours in the smokehouse is sufficient to add a delicious flavor; with slightly extended treatment you can achieve long-term preservation.

A fish that is to be cold smoked should first be cured to extract surplus moisture. Removing water firms the flesh and helps preserve the fish during smoking. First soak the dressed fish in a solution of 1 cup of salt per gallon of water for half an hour, then either dry-cure for up to 12 hours or else brine-cure for two to four hours (see p.224). After curing, rinse the fish in fresh water, removing any lumps of salt with a stiff brush, then hang it to dry in a warm, shaded, well-ventilated place.

When the surface of the fish is absolutely dry, put it in the smokehouse. How long you smoke the fish depends on your personal taste and on how long you intend to store it. If you plan to eat the fish within a week, 24 hours of cold smoking should be sufficient. If you intend to keep it for several weeks, smoke the fish for up to five days, depending on its size and thickness: fillets will be ready the soonest, but steaks may require a few extra days. In either case expose the fish to light smoke by keeping the vent open for the first third of the total smoking period, then increase the density of the smoke, but keep the temperature in the chamber below 90°F.

Fish that is to be hot smoked need not be cured first; in fact, the combination of curing and smoke cooking will probably make it dry and tough. If you wish to add flavor, soak the fish briefly in a marinade or rub it with seasoned salt before moving it into the smoke chamber. Smoke it at a temperature of about 100°F for the first two to four hours, then gradually increase the temperature in the chamber to 140°F until the flesh is flaky. Eat the fish immediately, or let it cool, wrap it in wax paper, and refrigerate it.

Dressing Fish for Curing and Smoking

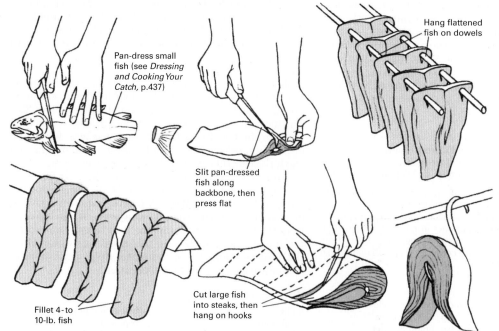

Pan-dress small fish (see *Dressing and Cooking Your Catch*, p.437)

Slit pan-dressed fish along backbone, then press flat

Fillet 4- to 10-lb. fish

Cut large fish into steaks, then hang on hooks

Hang flattened fish on dowels

Prepare small fish (up to 4 lb.) for smoking by splitting and pressing. Start by pan-dressing the fish (see *Fishing*, p.437); then carefully cut down the length of the backbone, and press the fish flat. Pierce the flattened body through the upper corners with dowels, and hang it for smoking.

Fillets and steaks. Fillet a 4- to 10-lb. fish (see *Fishing*, p.437), and hang the fillets over wooden bars in the smoke chamber. Cut larger fish into 1- to 2-in.-thick steaks. First, pan-dress; then use a sharp knife to slice the body crosswise. Hang on hooks or place on mesh grills as with red meat.

Two Cures and a Marinade

The three recipes given below are good, basic formulas for curing almost any type of fish. For more tang you can add dried mustard, bay leaf, or other spices. The marinade only adds flavor but does not aid in preserving. After either cure, the fish should be left to dry until a glossy layer, called the pellicle, appears on its skin.

Dry Cure for Fish

1 lb. salt	2 tbsp. white pepper
1 lb. dark brown sugar	1 tbsp. onion powder
1 tbsp. garlic powder	

Combine ingredients 24 hours before cure is needed, and store in airtight container to allow flavors to blend.

Fish Marinade

1 cup pineapple juice	1/2 tsp. black pepper
8 tbsp. lemon juice	1 crushed garlic clove
4 tsp. soy sauce	

Brine Cure for Fish

5 qt. water	2 tbsp. onion powder
3 lb. salt	2 tbsp. oregano
2 cups brown sugar	

Smoked Salmon

A salmon's large size and oily flesh make it a prime candidate for smoking, and there are nearly as many recipes for smoked salmon as there are for smoked ham. Lox, a traditional favorite, is thoroughly cured and cold smoked and eaten raw. Other recipes use hot smoking.

Dress the salmon by removing the strip of fat near the dorsal fin but not the rest of the skin. Clean the central cavity, then fillet the fish, or—if the salmon is large—cut it into thick steaks. The salmon can be dry-cured in the spicy mixture described below or brine-cured by submerging the fillets or steaks in a very salty brine for one to two hours, then letting them drain.

Spicy Dry Cure for Salmon

1 lb. salt	2 oz. mace
2 lb. sugar	2 oz. white pepper
2 oz. allspice	2 oz. crushed bay leaves
2 oz. crushed cloves	

Mix ingredients thoroughly. Pack salmon fillets or steaks in mixture and cure for 8 to 12 hours. Rinse and dry fish. Smoke at 90°F for eight hours in light smoke, then increase density of smoke for 18 to 48 hours, depending on the flavor you like. (Or you can hot smoke the fish at 170°F until the flesh becomes flaky.) Store the salmon in a refrigerator.

Drying Fish in the Open Air

In an area where warm sun and low humidity can be relied on for at least a week at a time, the flesh of lean fish can be preserved without smoking by air drying it. Properly dried, a fish will keep without refrigeration for a year or longer, provided it is protected from moisture. Drying is not practical for salmon, catfish, and other species whose oil content exceeds 5 percent.

The only cure that is needed before drying is packing in salt. Finely ground pickling salt is best for the job. Clean and dress the fish as soon as it is caught; split and press fish that weigh less than 2 pounds and fillet larger fish; if the fish is large enough to require steaking, it is probably too fatty to be dried. Rinse the meat in a brine made from 1 cup of salt per gallon of water, towel it dry, then coat in salt, allowing about 1 pound of salt for every 4 pounds of dressed fish. Spread a layer of salt on the bottom of a dry-curing box (see p.224), and place a layer of fish, skin side down, on it. Cover with more salt, then add more layers of fish in the same manner. The last layer of fish should be placed skin side up. A small batch of fish may cure in 48 hours in warm weather; allow up to seven days for a large batch in cool temperatures.

When the weather is right—warm and dry but not too hot—take the fish from the curing box, rinse them, and clean off all salt, scrubbing with a stiff brush to remove any visible salt encrustations. Hang the fish or lay them on racks in a shady, well-ventilated place (direct sun will cause spoilage). Bring the fish inside every evening and stack them one atop another, head to tail, with the skin side down, except for the top fish, which should be placed skin side up. Then cover them, and press them with a weight about equal to the weight of the stacked fish.

Six warm days are usually required for thorough drying. To test for dryness, push on the flesh with your finger; if the impression remains, the fish is not yet dry. Should the weather turn before drying is complete, take the fish inside and wait for another good day. They can be kept for up to two weeks in a cool, dry place, provided that every second day you restack them, putting the bottom fish on top and putting a little salt on each layer.

Preserving Fish in Brine

Oily fish that are not suitable for drying can be preserved without smoking by using their own juices to produce a strong brine. About 25 pounds of fish can be preserved in this manner in a 2-gallon stone crock.

Dress the fish according to size and score the flesh so the salt will penetrate faster. Soak them for an hour or two in a mild brine (1/2 cup salt to 1 gallon water). After draining, coat the fish with dry salt (allow about 1 pound for every 3 pounds of fish). Next, sprinkle a layer of salt in the bottom of the crock and place a layer of fish on top of it. Cover with another layer of salt, then another layer of fish. Continue in this way until the container is full. Weight the fish down. Within 2 to 10 days, depending on the size of the cuts, the salt and fish juices will have combined to make a thick brine. At this point remove the fish, rinse and brush them. Scrub the crock and replace the fish; then cover with strong brine (2 2/3 pounds of salt to 1 gallon of water). Store in a cool, dark place. Change the brine at least once every three months. If the weather is hot, change the brine more often.

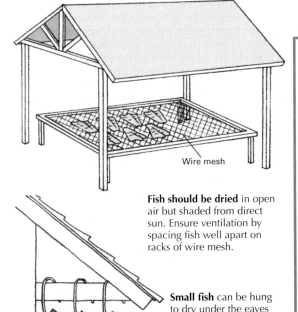

Wire mesh

Fish should be dried in open air but shaded from direct sun. Ensure ventilation by spacing fish well apart on racks of wire mesh.

Small fish can be hung to dry under the eaves of a house or barn. Suspend each fish on its own metal hook. Bring fish inside at night and stack in a location that is dry and well ventilated.

Smoked salmon is moist and full of rich flavor.

Bob McClement, Smoking Hobbyist

Smoking Meat for Fun, Producing Wood Chips For a Livelihood

Bob McClement, of Tacoma, Washington, runs a wood chip manufacturing operation for a firm that makes home smokers.

"There are an awful lot more people smoking food these days. I think they do it primarily for the flavor. You know, in the old days you could get charcoal in all different kinds of wood—oak, maple, hickory—and, of course, each one gave a different taste to what you were cooking. Now, with this homogenized charcoal, you don't get much taste at all, so people have gone in for smoking because they want to get that taste they remember from when they were kids.

"The smoking, you know, doesn't really preserve the meat. It's soaking the meat in the brine and drying it that does the preserving. Your basic brine can be salt, sugar, and water. Then you can add whatever spices you like, just like in a marinade. Your different flavors come from the brine and from the kind of wood chips you use. Fruitwood chips give a very different taste than hickory, for example. Applewood has a real nice flavor; and then there's cherrywood—that's got a very strong flavor so you would want to use that on deeper, redder meat.

"You've got to remember to keep the meat cold when it's in the brine. The meat isn't preserved at that stage and if you leave it out in the heat, it will just deteriorate. How long you smoke, of course, is a matter of taste, just the same as how long you boil an egg.

For myself, with something like a turkey, what I do is keep it in the smoker for maybe four hours and then finish it off in the oven. That way it doesn't get too dry.

"How long you leave things in the smoker depends on the weight and thickness of the meat and also on the amount of area exposed—the more area exposed, the more flavor the meat or fish will retain. With a roast, because of the thickness, I usually wrap it and put it in the refrigerator for a few days after it comes out of the smoker to let the flavor sink all through the meat.

"Of course, you can save a lot of money—look at the price of smoked salmon in the market compared to what it costs to do it at home—but that's not the only reason people get into smoking. With fish, chicken, or turkey you don't save money by smoking, you just get more enjoyment and flavor out of what you're eating. Once people have made something that's really well smoked, they tend to go the whole gamut. They develop their own recipes for pride and pleasure as much as anything. I think out here in the Pacific Northwest if you asked 200 people how they smoked salmon, you'd get 198 different replies."

Sausages and Scrapple: Delicious Techniques For Avoiding Waste

Autumn was the traditional time for slaughtering and putting up meat: the animals had been fattened during the summer, and cooler fall temperatures helped keep just-slaughtered meat fresh. Almost no part of a carcass was allowed to go to waste. Large joints of meat were carefully cured and smoked; organ meats were consumed immediately, and fat was rendered into lard for soap, candles, and shortening. Hides were fleshed and tanned, large bones used for broth, heads were boiled down to make headcheese, and the feet, or trotters, of pigs were stewed, jellied, or pickled. With all this accomplished, there were still many scraps of meat, fat, and innards that remained, waiting to be put to good use. Nowadays, such bits and pieces are discarded or ground up for pet food. In the old days, however, they were converted into sausage or scrapple with the intestine of a freshly slaughtered animal serving as casing.

Although sausages, scrapple, and headcheese are still produced commercially, traditional recipes and ingredients are seldom used. If you want to enjoy their special flavors, you will probably have to make them yourself—and when you make your own, you can include just the right blend of meats and spices to suit your own taste. The only special tool you will need is a meat grinder. Electric grinders do the job quickly and effortlessly but are expensive and, in general, designed for the processing of larger quantities of meat than you are likely to need.

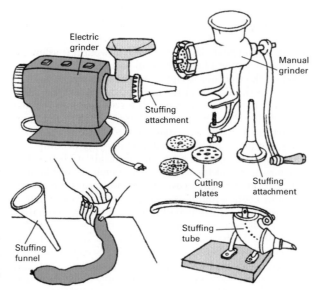

Manual and electric grinders usually come with a stuffing attachment. A variety of other sausage-stuffing devices are available, in-

Food processors can be used to grind meat but have only limited value, since they will only produce a fine grind. Old-fashioned hand-cranked meat grinders call for a bit of elbow grease but are still best for home use; they will not overheat the meat while it is being ground, and they come with several cutter plates for finer or coarser grinds plus an attachment for stuffing sausages.

Plastic casings and other types of artificial casings are available in various sizes but are difficult to use. For the home sausagemaker the best casings are probably those made from the small intestine of a hog or sheep. They can usually be bought from a butcher who makes

his own sausages. If you want to try making your own casings, you will need the intestine from a freshly slaughtered animal. Clean it thoroughly, scraping both sides to remove all traces of fat and mucus (this is a time-consuming job). Rinse the intestine in several changes of water, and store it in brine until it is needed. Hog casings can be used for sausages up to 1 1/2 inches in diameter; larger casings are commonly made of light weight muslin.

Any kind of meat, poultry, or game can be used for sausage, from the cheapest to the most expensive. The lower the quality of the meat, however, the poorer the sausage is likely to be. Although pork and beef are commonly used, lamb, veal, and poultry will also serve the purpose—and venison sausage is a rare treat. No matter what type of meat is employed, it is important to strike a balance between fat and lean meat: about two parts lean meat to one part fat is satisfactory in most cases. Too little fat results in hard, dry sausages; too much fat results in greasy sausages that shrink when they are cooked. When stuffing the sausage casings, it is important to avoid air bubbles, since they can become pockets of spoilage; if any exist in the finished sausage, prick them with a needle. To give a soft texture and consistency to the meat so that it will fill the casings easily, it is a good idea to add a little water or wine.

Many types of sausage and scrapple must be eaten soon after they are prepared or else stored in a freezer. Other types, such as hard sausages, benefit from aging and will keep unrefrigerated for considerable periods of time. If you plan to preserve your sausages by freezing there are certain seasonings to avoid: garlic loses its flavor, sage produces an off flavor if it is kept frozen too long, and salt may cause a rancid taste after about a month of freezing.

1. Meat grinder ensures that the meat is cut into fine ribbons rather than pulped. Use pusher, not your fingers, to press meat into the grinder.

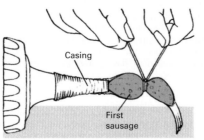

2. Rinse casing thoroughly. Place it over nozzle, stuff a small section, and tie off tightly in the middle in order to give an airtight seal to the first sausage.

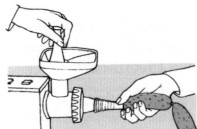

3. Continue stuffing, supporting casing with free hand to prevent kinks and bends. Tie off or twist each link. Tie off end, leaving a little meat outside.

Old-fashioned Pork Sausage

4 lb. lean pork	3 tsp. pepper
2 lb. pork fat	1 1/2 tsp. sugar
3 1/2 tsp. salt	3/4 tsp. ground clove
6 tsp. sage	2/3 cup cold water

Thoroughly chill meat and fat and put them separately through grinder with 1/2-in. cutting plate. Chill meat again. Combine all seasonings and mix into meat, then put through grinder with 1/8-in. cutting plate. Mix meat and fat in a bowl and add just enough water to make a soft dough. Stuff into casings of muslin or hog intestine, taking care to avoid air bubbles. Hang sausages in a cool, dry place (or in the refrigerator) for one to two days. These sausages gain from being cold smoked at about 80°F for 10 to 14 hours until they turn a deep, dark brown. Store under refrigeration. Cook before serving.

Traditional Recipes for Sausage, Scrapple, and Headcheese

The different regions of America developed sausage recipes tailored to local food resources and ethnic traditions. Another influence was weather: sausages that are stuffed with cured meat and then smoked afterward have superior keeping qualities in warm climates. Many sausages are made with uncooked pork; they must be thoroughly cooked before they are eaten (see p.222).

Indiana Farm Sausage

This herb-flavored sausage is delicious fried for breakfast, especially with eggs or pancakes and syrup.

4 lb. lean pork	2 tsp. thyme
1 lb pork fat	2 tsp. basil
2 cloves garlic, minced	4 tsp. salt
2 tsp. black pepper	2 tbsp. sage
2 tsp. chili powder	2 tbsp. parsley
2 tsp. cayenne	2 onions
2 tsp. marjoram	6 tbsp. iced water

Cut meat and fat into chunks, add seasonings, and grind with medium cutting plate. Grind onions. Knead ground meat and onion in bowl and add iced water to give a soft dough consistency. Stuff into hog casings. Store in refrigerator.

Southwestern Sausage

Although well-flavored and spicy, this Spanish-Indian sausage is not quite as hot as the Mexican *chorizo*.

2 1/4 lb lean pork	1 tsp. black pepper
3/4 lb. kidney suet or fat	1 tsp. ground coriander
5 cloves garlic, minced	1 1/2 tsp. cumin
4-6 chili peppers, chopped	Salt to taste
1/2 cup onion, finely chopped	1/2 tsp. Tabasco
1/4 cup brandy	1/2 cup vinegar
1/3 cup chili powder	

Grind lean pork and fat together with coarse cutting plate. Combine garlic, peppers, onion, brandy, and seasonings. Mix into meat along with Tabasco and vinegar. Stuff into casings, lying off each link at 4 in. Hang in a warm, breezy, insect-free place to dry for 24 hours. Store in refrigerator.

Summer Sausage

Although the traditional recipe contains some pork, beef and beef fat can be used throughout.

6 lb. lean beef	2 lb. lean pork
Sweet Pickle Brine	2 lb. pork fat
(see p.226)	8 whole black peppercorns
4 tbsp.salt	2 tbsp. coriander seed
4 tsp. garlic powder	Pinch mustard seed
3 tbsp. white pepper	2 1/2 cups dry red wine

Cut the beef into 2-in. chunks and place in a crock. Cover with brine; use weight to keep meat submerged. Remove the meat and stir the brine every four days. After 8 to 12 days remove beef, rinse

it, and place it in the refrigerator to drain for 24 hours; then cut it into smaller chunks, and mix with the salt, garlic powder, and white pepper. Grind the beef, pork, and pork fat twice through 3/16-in. plate, and mix. Mix in other seasonings and wine; let stand for 48 hours in refrigerator. Stuff into muslin casings. Cold smoke at 80°F for 12 to 14 hours until the skin turns dark brown (the sausage will dry and shrink by as much as one-third). Hang the sausage in a refrigerator or other cool place for at least two weeks. Use in salads and for snacks. Store in refrigerator.

For a faster recipe grind pork and beef through coarse cutting plate and mix in 14 oz. of Dry Cure for Pork (see p.226). Regrind through same plate, knead meat in a glass or plastic bowl, and place in the refrigerator for 48 hours. Then mix in salt and other ingredients and continue as with brine-cure recipe.

Old-Style Frankfurters

Turn of the century cartoonist Tad Dorgan deserves credit for the name "hot dog"; his drawing of a frankfurter as a dachshund encased in a bun inspired the term. Store frankfurters under refrigeration.

1 1/2 lb. pork loin or shoulder	1/2 tsp. coriander
1 lb. pork fat	1/2 tsp. nutmeg
2 tbsp. salt	1/2 tsp. cinnamon
1 tsp. white pepper	

Cure the meat for three days in the Brine Cure for Pork (p.226); then grind it two times, along with the fat, through a coarse cutting plate. Mix in salt and seasonings, and grind again through a medium-fine cutting plate. Slowly add 1 cup of iced water and mix thoroughly. Stuff into hog casings about 18 in. long. Secure at both ends and twist in the middle to make two long, thin sausages from each length of casing. Hang to dry for 24 hours; then cold smoke for eight hours or until sausages turn deep brown. To cook, simmer in boiling water for 10 minutes.

Scrapple

This Pennsylvania Dutch delicacy, once popular in many parts of America, has slowly lost favor; a shame because it is tasty, economical, and easy to make.

5 lb. pork scraps, including	3 cups cornmeal
bony meat, liver, kidneys,	Freshly ground pepper, sage,
and heart	thyme, and salt to taste
1 gal. Water	

Boil liver, kidney, and heart in salted water until tender. Remove from pot and cut into small pieces. Mix with other meat and return to water. Boil until meat shreds when tested with two forks (there should now be about 3 qt. of broth). Remove any bones, then slowly add cornmeal to pot, stirring constantly until the mixture starts to thicken. Continue to cook until the scrapple has a thick, mushy consistency. Season with plenty of pepper plus sage, thyme, and salt. Pour into greased molds and allow to cool. To cook, cut into 1/4- to 1/2-in. slabs, coat in flour, and fry in butter. Serve with eggs for breakfast or as a tasty trimming with roast game birds. Philadelphia scrapple is made the same way but only shoulder and neck meat is used. Store in refrigerator.

Headcheese

Sometimes called brawn, headcheese is the most popular way of preparing the various bits and pieces of meat from the head of a pig, calf, or lamb.

Head of a pig, calf, or lamb	1/2 tsp. hot pepper sauce
(for calf or lamb, use half	1 tbsp. ground mixed spices,
the quantities of spices)	such as garlic, onion
2 tbsp. salt	powder, sage, mace,
2 tbsp. black pepper	savory, and cloves
1 crushed bay leaf	

Split the head into halves or quarters (most butchers will do this for you). Remove the snout, eyes, brain, and any remaining bristles or extra fat. Soak in cold water for at least six hours to rinse out the blood. Then wash pieces under running water and put them in a heavy pot. Barely cover with water and bring to a boil; simmer until the meat slides off the bone. Separate meat from the bones and let it cool. Grind meat through 1/2-in. cutting plate. Add enough broth to the ground meat to make a soft batter consistency and discard the rest. Return mixture to pot and add seasonings. As soon as the mixture boils, pour it into molds of glass, china, or enamel. Cover with a cloth and plate, and put a few pounds of weight on top. Refrigerate until set. Remove from mold. Serve cold in thin slices. Headcheese can be kept in a refrigerator for two to three weeks.

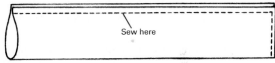

Making a muslin sausage casing

Sew here

To case extra-large sausages (more than 4 in. in diameter), fold and sew a piece of muslin into a tubular shape, turn it inside out, and dampen with water just before stuffing.

Sources and resources

Books and pamphlets

Ashbrook, Frank G. *Butchering, Processing and Preservation of Meat.* New York: Chapman & Hall, 1973.

Dubbs, Chris, and Dave Heberle. *The Easy Art of Smoking Food.* New York: Winchester Press, 1978.

Eastman, Wilbur F., Jr. *The Canning, Freezing, Curing & Smoking of Meat, Fish & Game.* Charlotte, Vt.: Garden Way Publishing, 1975.

Sleight, Jack, and Raymond Hull. *Home Book of Smoke Cooking Meat, Fish and Game.* Harrisburg, Pa.: Stackpole Books, 1982.

Stoner, Carol Hupping, ed. *Stocking Up III.* New York: Fine Communications, 1995.

U.S. Department of Agriculture Staff. *Complete Guide to Home Canning, Preserving and Freezing.* New York: Dover, 1994.

Making Your Own Dairy Products

Savory Dairy Treats Preserve Fresh Milk's Nutritional Values

Dairying—the collection and processing of milk into such foods as cheese, butter, and yogurt—has been practiced since man first domesticated wild animals. Cheese, in fact, is one of the first man-made foods: well-preserved cheeses were found in the tombs of the pharaohs, and in 1948 a 2,000-year-old cheese was discovered in Siberia—reportedly still edible.

The reason for most milk processing is preservation. Milk is an almost perfect food, containing most of the essentials for human nutrition: protein for growth and muscle development, fat for digestion and warmth, carbohydrates for energy, vitamins and minerals for general health and well-being. But milk spoils rapidly in its natural state. By converting it into dairy by-products, its nutritive value can be retained for long periods of time.

Different regions of the world have developed their own recipes and methods for handling milk. In Eastern Europe and the Middle East yogurt is particularly popular. Calabash, an African specialty, is a form of fermented milk named for the dried and hollowed gourds in which it is made and stored. In Europe and America more than a thousand varieties of cheese have been developed over the centuries.

If you have your own milk animals or a supply of raw milk or unhomogenized pasteurized milk, you can separate cream to use fresh or make into butter, buttermilk, and ice cream. The remaining skimmed milk can be converted into yogurt or cottage cheese. With a plentiful supply of raw milk you can also learn the intricacies of cooking, pressing, and aging your own cheeses.

Over the centuries a variety of butter churns were developed, all designed to ease the tedium and effort involved in the weekly butter-churning chore. The Victorian advertisement at left features the latest in 19th-century centrifugal churns, a sophisticated model that is geared for rapid churning and can be operated with only one hand. The drum of the churn is made of wood, a material that does not react with the lactic acid in milk. Many old dairying items are now sought-after antiques. Cheese presses, decorative butter stamps, molds, scales, and ice cream makers all command premium prices. In addition, a lively business has sprung up in working replicas of these old implements. As a result, almost any dairying tool you need is available in its old-fashioned form as well as its modern equivalent.

Good Milk Makes Good Dairy Foods

Almost all milk sold in supermarkets and grocery stores has been pasteurized to destroy bacteria and homogenized to break up butterfat particles. This commercial milk can be used for making yogurt and kefir but will only make soft low-quality cheeses and cannot be used at all for making butter, since the cream will not separate out. Reconstituted instant dried milk will produce a good soft cheese and some simple hard cheeses. However, to make a full range of dairy products, you will need a source of raw milk. If you do not have your own milk animals, you may be able to buy raw milk from health food stores or other outlets. In some states you can purchase raw milk direct from the farm, but be sure that the animals have been tested for disease and have been milked under hygienic conditions.

The diet of milking cows and goats will affect the quality and flavor of their milk. Goats should be allowed to browse over weeds and scrub, since such plants provide the extra minerals and proteins that the animals need. Cows will produce their best milk on rich pasturage. Any strong-smelling foodstuff, including turnips, wild onions, or garlic, can flavor the milk.

After an animal gives birth do not use its milk for four days (in the case of goats) or for two weeks (in the case of cows). During these periods the milk is of a special type called colostrum, high in protein, minerals, vitamins, and antibodies but low in sugar and fats. It is unsuited for most dairy uses. Moreover, colostrum is essential to the health of the newborn animals. You should also avoid using milk from cows or goats that appear to be sick. If an animal is treated with antibiotics or other drugs, wait at least three days after the treatment before using its milk. When processing or storing milk or cream, use wooden, glass, ceramic, enamel, or stainless steel equipment; milk contains lactic acid, a substance that reacts with many metals.

About 6 percent of Americans have difficulty in digesting cow's milk. In infants the problem is usually manifested by symptoms of stomach upset. As the baby grows older and its digestive system develops, the problem often disappears, but in some cases a more-or-less permanent allergy develops. If undetected, the allergic reaction can be severe, even fatal, particularly in infants less than six months old. Goat's milk is often helpful for children and adults who have problems digesting cow's milk. It is easier to digest and does not contain some of the complex proteins found in cow's milk, which are the usual causes of allergy.

Hygiene Is Vital When Processing Milk

All fresh milk contains bacteria, most of them harmless, some beneficial to the human digestive system, and others vital in the production of cheese and butter. Certain strains, however, are pathogenic and can transmit diseases, such as brucellosis (undulant fever) and tuberculosis. If you intend to use raw milk for dairying purposes, it is of the utmost importance that it be taken from cows or goats that have been tested and found free of disease. This is just as important whether the milk is from your own animals or has been purchased elsewhere.

Even though your milk may be good to start with, it can quickly go bad. Your dairy hygiene should aim to prevent contamination by pathogenic bacteria and inhibit the excessive multiplication of all bacteria. If you milk your own animals, maintain strict standards of cleanliness while milking, and take the milk from the milking shed to your dairy room as soon as it is collected. Once in the shed, cool the milk quickly to about 40°F and maintain it at that temperature until it is used. To eliminate any possibility of harmful bacteria, pasteurize your milk by heating it gently to 145°F for 30 minutes or to 158°F for 15 seconds. Cool it immediately after it has been pasteurized. Pasteurization, however, can interfere with some dairying processes.

Separating Cream From Milk

To extract cream from cow's milk, put fresh, chilled milk in shallow dishes in a cool place. After 12 to 24 hours the cream will have risen to the surface. Gently skim it off with a spoon or ladle until you come to the bluish "skim milk" underneath. Store the cream in the refrigerator in a clean, covered jar.

The cream obtained from goat's milk, unlike cow's cream, is pure white. It is also lighter, easier to digest, and whips to a greater bulk. Unfortunately, goat's cream is very finely emulsified within the milk and several days are needed for even a small amount to rise to the surface. During this period the cream, which picks up odors very easily, often takes on an unpleasant flavor. Although separation can be speeded by adding cow's milk, the best way to obtain significant quantities of goat's cream is to use a separator, a centrifugelike device that automatically splits whole milk into skim milk and cream. Separators are expensive, however, unless you are lucky enough to find a used one—even a low-priced separator will cost several hundred dollars if it is bought new. As a result, a cream separator is worthwhile only if you are milking several animals. If you are thinking of getting a separator, be sure it can be adjusted finely enough to work with goat's milk.

The dairying room should be cool, dust free, well ventilated, and well lit. All dairying equipment must be kept scrupulously clean and should be free from cracks, sharp corners, nicks, or other spots where dirt can collect. Clean the equipment immediately after it is used. First rinse it in cold water, then wash it in warm water with a dairy detergent. (Standard detergents may leave a residual flavor that will spoil the taste of the milk.) Next, scald the equipment by pouring boiling water over it. The equipment can then be left to air dry. Every few weeks, completely sterilize all your dairy implements by washing them in a chlorine solution or placing them in an electric oven at 250°F for 15 minutes. From time to time clean off any milkstone—a hard, transparent milk residue—that may have formed on your equipment. Use commercial milkstone solvent, a product that is available from dairy suppliers.

Keep milk away from any strong barnyard, household, or food smells, since milk, particularly goat's milk, absorbs odors very easily, and never use milk that seems abnormal. An unusual flavor in fresh milk can mean contamination and a high bacteria count. If fresh milk tastes off or sour, check your dairy hygiene and the health of your livestock as well as their diet.

One solution to the problem of getting cream quickly and easily is to make Devonshire cream. Set whole cow's or goat's milk in heat-proof pans for 12 to 24 hours, then warm the pans gently to 187°F. When the surface of the milk begins to wrinkle and crack, remove the pans from the heat. When the milk is cool, skim off the surface. This will produce a rich, delicious, thick-textured cream.

A time-honored way to get cream is to leave fresh cow's milk overnight in large, shallow pottery bowls. The next day the cream can be scooped off with a wooden or brass skimmer.

Devonshire cream is a clotted cream produced in Devon, Cornwall, and Somerset, England. It is traditionally served on scones with jam.

Cynthia Willis, Dairywoman

Dairying Can Be a Pleasure When You Love Your Goats

Nubian goats, like this one, produce rich, creamy milk. Cynthia Willis of Bantam, Connecticut, owns a heard of Nubians that produces up to 20 gallons of milk a day.

"Goat's milk has become unbelievably popular in the last couple of years. Up here, I can't possibly begin to satisfy the demand. I honestly think that some of the prejudice against goats is beginning to die out. Breeders are taking them to county fairs, and now people say, 'Hey, this animal doesn't smell bad.' Really, goats are extremely clean, and they're just beautiful animals.

"I think we've finally proven the point that goat's milk tastes good, not some smelly, awful concoction. I breed my own goats from Nubian stock to get the richest milk possible. Nubians are not the biggest producers, to be honest, but their milk has higher butterfat content than any other breed. It can go as high as 9 percent. Nubians are rather like Jersey cows in that respect; it's not the quantity they give but the quality.

"Besides tasting good, more and more doctors are discovering the medical benefits of drinking goat's milk. A lot of old-fashioned doctors knew how good goat's milk was for babies with digestive problems, but now some of the younger doctors are becoming convinced too. You can put a baby with stomach problems on goat's milk from earliest infancy, and it will thrive better than on most prepared formulas. And women who breast-feed can switch their babies to goat's milk without disturbing the child at all. Very often children won't make that kind of switch to cow's milk. Recently, I sold some milk to a cancer patient who was very thin. Her doctor recommended goat's milk and she was able to digest it very easily. Doctors also recommend goat's milk for people with ulcers because of its digestibility. The advantage of goat's milk, as I understand it, is that it breaks down in the stomach much more quickly and easily than cow's milk and is absorbed into the body much faster.

"I guess you can tell I'm really a goat person. I just love them. That's why I am in this dairy business. It's not really the money that's important. But if I can breed a goat that gives richer milk, that's what makes me happy."

Churning Fresh Butter Out of Your Cream

Butter can be made from cream that has been ripened (slightly soured) or from fresh cream. Ripened cream churns more rapidly and produces butter with more flavor; sweet cream butter is comparatively bland. To ripen cream, let it stand at room temperature for 12 to 24 hours until the surface appears glossy and the cream has a slightly acid taste. If it is allowed to stand longer, the butter may have a sour flavor.

Any form of agitation—the dairyman's term is concussion—that brings together the globules of butterfat that are suspended in cream will yield butter. The equipment need not be expensive. Even a hand whisk or an electric beater will work for small quantities of cream. Some people churn butter simply by shaking cream in a covered jar. In the Middle East butter was once made by filling leather bags with cream, then strapping the bags onto the backs of horses. If you intend to make butter for your family on a regular basis, however, it would pay to invest in a home churn. Most are powered by an electric motor and can process from 1 to 5 gallons of cream at a time, but several types of manual churns are available.

Bring the temperature of the cream to about 60°F before churning. This is an important step; if you churn cream at a higher temperature, the butter will be soft and keep poorly, while if you churn at a lower temperature, the butter will take much longer to form, or come.

After 15 minutes of churning, the cream should begin to feel heavy. If it does not, check the temperature. When using goat's cream, it helps to add a tablespoon or two of cold skimmed cow's milk at this stage. After another 10 to 20 minutes the cream should separate into buttermilk and grain-sized pellets of butter.

Once the granules have formed, stop churning, drain the buttermilk from the churn, and thoroughly rinse the butter with cold water. The buttermilk should be saved for later use—it can be used in baking or consumed directly by drinking it plain or in milkshakes. The butter can be rinsed in the churn, but a better way is to place it on a cheesecloth in a colander and let cold water run over it. Next, work the butter granules together with a butter paddle or wooden spoon. You will probably want to add salt at this time—1/4 to 1/2 teaspoon per pound of butter—since unsalted butter spoils quickly. Wrap the finished butter in wax paper and place it inside a refrigerator to protect it from light and air.

If you use ripened cream, you can avoid any risk of an unpleasant taste by pasteurizing it first. Heat the cream in a double boiler to a temperature of 180°F to 200°F for 40 minutes. Then let the cream cool for 12 hours, and add a small amount of starter, such as cultured buttermilk, sour cream, or yogurt, before churning. Follow the same procedure if the cream comes from an animal that is near the end of lactation; cream taken at that time will be difficult to churn into butter.

Old-fashioned wooden barrel churn allows more cream to be processed at once. Buttermaking equipment is available from mail order firms, online sources, and country stores.

Making Butter With a Hand Churn

1. Bring cream to temperature of 60°F before churning (a degree or two warmer if the dairying room is cold). Temperature can be adjusted by placing cream jar in warm or cool water.

2. Fill churn partway with cream (one-third for maximum concussion), and begin churning immediately. Butter should "come" within 30 minutes. If it does not, check temperature.

3. Pour off buttermilk, and rinse butter granules several times in cold water until the water runs completely clear. Any buttermilk left behind will make the butter taste sour.

4. Work the butter with a butter paddle to remove remaining moisture and to mix any salt that has been added. Put butter in molds or shape pats with paddles and stamps.

For Flavor and Health Try Fermented Milks

Any milk or cream that is allowed to stand at room temperature will soon ferment and curdle because of bacterial action. With careful timing, thorough sterilization of the milk or cream, and the use of pure cultures of desirable bacteria, this natural spoiling process can yield such healthful and delicious cultured milk products as yogurt, sour cream, buttermilk, and kefir.

Cultured milks not only taste good, but they are also easy on the stomach. Part of the reason is that lactose, a complex, hard-to-digest milk sugar, breaks down during fermentation. In addition, the bacteria used in making cultured milks help relieve certain stomach upsets and can restore the natural bacterial balance of the stomach after antibiotic treatments.

Raw milk, pasteurized milk, powdered milk, and homogenized milk can all be used to make cultured milk products. Raw milk must be pasteurized before it is used, but pasteurized milk need not be repasteurized if the containers are kept sealed until use.

In addition to the milk or cream that will form the base of your yogurt or other fermented product, you will need a starter—a culture of the proper strain of bacteria. The safest and surest way is to buy a fresh, unadulterated starter from a dairy supplier. You can also achieve good results, with less work, by using a portion of a store-bought fermented milk product as your starter, provided it does not contain flavoring or sweetener. Check to make sure that the product has not been repasteurized after culturing, since repasteurization destroys most of the desirable bacteria. Preservatives will also affect the bacteria adversely.

Once you begin producing a cultured milk, you can keep making it again and again by reculturing—using a portion of the old batch to begin a new batch. It is important to reculture within 10 days after the first batch has been made, since the bacteria will be destroyed by long refrigeration. Cover all containers tightly during culturing and refrigeration (except for kefir), and maintain strict hygienic standards to avoid contamination. Eventually, however, a starter will lose its vigor. If the flavor of a freshly cultured milk product appears to be inferior or the product takes longer to thicken, it is time to buy a new starter. The flavor and texture of cultured milk products will improve if they are refrigerated for at least a few hours after being cultured.

Buttermilk is a term applied to two different products. One is simply the milk fraction left over after butter is made; the other, cultured buttermilk, is produced like yogurt—by the fermentation of skim milk. Buttermilk from churned butter varies in taste depending on whether the cream was ripened or not and on which bacteria happen to develop. To make cultured buttermilk—a much more consistent product—allow 1 quart of low-fat milk to reach room temperature, then add 1/4 to 1/2 cup of previously cultured buttermilk and leave overnight in a warm place (80°F to 85°F). Refrigerate as soon as the milk reaches the desired level of acidity. Buttermilk adds flavor and lightness to baked goods and is useful as a starter for cheeses.

Yogurt, a centuries-old favorite of Middle Eastern peoples, has become the best known and most popular cultured milk product sold in America. By making your own yogurt, you can experiment with different milks, starters, incubation temperatures, and culturing times to produce the flavor you like best.

Begin by sterilizing a quart of low-fat milk by heating it briefly to 180°F. Allow the milk to cool to about 105°F (just above body temperature). Add 2 tablespoons of starter from a dairy supplier or 4 tablespoons of store-bought yogurt. Stir in thoroughly, then set the cultured milk to incubate undisturbed at 105°F to 112°F for two to three hours. Yogurt can be cultured at any temperature between 70°F and 120°F, but it takes longer to thicken at the lower temperatures and may have a sour flavor. As soon as the yogurt retains the impression of a spoon

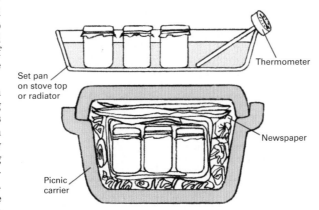

Set pan on stove top or radiator

Thermometer

Newspaper

Picnic carrier

Cultured milks must be kept warm while they develop. The top of a refrigerator or warming oven of a wood stove are good locations. A pan set on top of a radiator or stove-top pilot light also works well. Another method is to place the warmed containers in a picnic carrier filled with crumpled newspaper.

pressed into its surface, stop incubation and refrigerate. This will prevent the yogurt from becoming very acid and help it keep longer. If the yogurt is lumpy, it means too much starter was used.

For a richer, sweeter yogurt, use whole milk or a mixture of milk and cream. For a thicker curd, add up to 3 tablespoons of powdered milk per quart of milk. After the yogurt has thickened, you can add fresh fruit, fruit preserves, nuts, honey, maple syrup, or even a strong brew of sweetened coffee as flavoring.

Sour cream is thicker and stronger tasting than yogurt and is generally eaten in conjunction with other foods. It makes an excellent base for dips and goes well with salads, potatoes, and some soups. Use fresh, heavy cream that has been pasteurized at 150°F to 160°F for 30 minutes. Mix 1 cup of cream with 11/2 cups of pasteurized whole milk, then add 1/2 cup of cultured buttermilk. Raise the temperature of the mixture to that of a warm room (68°F to 70°F), and let it stand for 12 to 24 hours or until it is sufficiently sour and thick enough to cling firmly to a spoon. Keep it in the refrigerator until you want to use it. For a richer, heavier sour cream combine 2 cups of pasteurized heavy cream with 5 teaspoons of cultured buttermilk and incubate as before. For better texture refrigerate for 24 hours before serving.

Kefir, sometimes called the champagne of milk, is similar to yogurt but thinner, milder, and easier to culture. Kefir starter consists of individual grains made up of a combination of yeast and several strains of bacteria. The yeast gives kefir a slight fizz and a small alcoholic content. Kefir grains are difficult to obtain. Some firms sell them in a milk base or in freeze-dried form. The more widely available powdered cultures do not seem to produce as good results as the grains.

To make kefir, add 1/2 to 1 cup of grains to a quart of skim milk. Cover, but do not seal the mixture, and allow it to stand at room temperature for 12 to 48 hours until it has a mild acid taste and has achieved the desired degree of carbonation. Strain the grains from the milk and rinse them thoroughly in cold water, then add them to a new batch of milk. Refrigerate the cultured milk. To slow down the process, culture the kefir at a lower temperature of 55°F to 60°F.

The grains multiply rapidly, so some must be removed periodically to prevent the kefir from becoming too thick. To preserve grains that have been removed, wash them thoroughly, then let them dry between two pieces of cheesecloth in an airy location. To revive dried grains, place them in a cup of milk for 24 hours; drain, rinse, and add another cup of milk. After two days the amount of milk can be gradually increased to a quart.

Cheese: The Most Varied Of the Milk By-products

According to legend, cheese was discovered by a Middle Eastern traveler named Kanana, who was carrying milk in a bag made from a lamb's stomach. When Kanana paused to drink, he noticed that his milk had coagulated into a custardlike mass. More daring than most, he sampled this odd substance and found it surprisingly pleasant. What had happened was that rennin—an enzyme found in the stomachs of newborn lambs, kids, and calves—had transformed the milk into curds and whey. The process is known as curdling, and it is the fundamental step in the production of all cheeses.

There are two types of cheese: soft and hard. Soft cheeses are made from unpressed curds and must be eaten within a week or two. Hard cheeses take longer to prepare but keep better in storage. Cow's milk is the most popular base for both types of cheese. Goat's milk cheese can be quite mild when fresh but tends to develop a strong ammonia taste if kept for long. Sheep's milk is employed for genuine Roquefort, while traditional mozzarella is made from the milk of the water buffalo. The richest, creamiest cheeses are made from whole raw milk. However, skim milk and reconstituted dried instant milk can be used for most cheese recipes and are particularly suitable for cottage cheese. If you use pasteurized milk, ripen it by adding cultured buttermilk or a cheese starter. Do not use homogenized milk; it will produce weak curds and a watery cheese.

Rennet, the substance that contains the chemical agent rennin needed to curdle the milk, is available at dairy suppliers and some pharmacies, often being stocked as junket tablets. If you use junket tablets, be sure they are unflavored. Originally, rennet was simply dried pieces of stomach from newborn calves.

Cream cheese: an easy-to-make treat

Combine 2 cups heavy cream with 2 tbsp. buttermilk, then suspend the mixture in a clean piece of cloth over a bowl for 24 hours or until the cream thickens. (The longer you leave it suspended, the drier the cheese will be.) Season with salt and herbs to taste. For a tangy cream cheese with less fat, use yogurt in place of the cream and buttermilk.

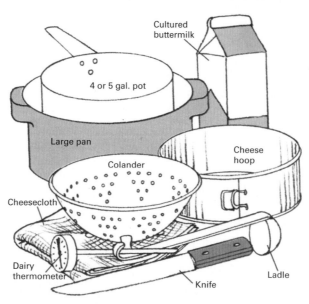

Cheesemaking implements should be made of stainless steel, enamel, glass, or wood and should be kept scrupulously clean. You will need a 4- or 5-gal. pot and a somewhat larger pan that can hold the pot. When heating the milk, fill the pan partway with water and set the pot in it so that the combination functions as a double boiler; leave enough space between to test the temperature of the water. Other useful supplies include a good dairy thermometer, a long knife for slicing the curdled milk, a large ladle, and several yards of cheesecloth. A cylindrical mold, or cheese hoop, and a cheese press—both required for making hard cheese—can be improvised or purchased.

Two presses you can build yourself

Simple cheese press is made from an empty coffee can. Use an awl to pierce the bottom and sides of the can. These are the holes through which the whey will escape. Pierce from the inside out so that metal will not project inward. Next, use a coping saw to cut a circular "cheese follower" out of 3/4-in.-thick wood. The circle need not be precise but the follower must be able to slide inside the can easily. Several bricks serve as weights to press the follower downward and squeeze the whey out of the curds. Sterilize the bricks first, then wrap them in foil. Place a smaller coffee can on the follower, then stack the bricks on it.

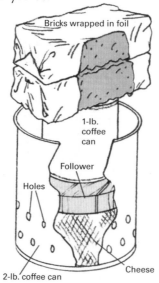

Traditional cheese presses differ little from modern versions. Whey is forced out and the curds consolidated by pressure from a cranking device. A bowl underneath collects the whey.

More elaborate press is made from 1 × 12 board and 1/2-in. dowel. Cut the board into two 12- × 12-in. squares. Clamp the squares together and drill 1/16-in. pilot holes centered 1 in. from the sides of each corner, then separate the boards and enlarge the pilot holes to 3/4 in. in one board and 1/2 in. in the other. Cut the dowel into four 10-in. lengths and glue them into each of the 1/2-in. holes. Slip the follower (the board with 3/4-in. holes in it) over the dowels to hold them in position while the glue dries. The follower should slide down the dowels easily when the press is completed. Sterilized bricks or stones can be used to provide pressure.

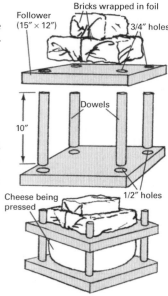

Making Basic Hard Cheese

Large cheeses tend to ripen better, so start with at least a gallon of milk–enough to make 1 1/2 to 2 pounds of cheese. Either raw milk or unhomogenized pasteurized milk is satisfactory. The ideal milk for making cheese is a blend of equal parts of raw morning milk (fresh milk that has just been collected) and evening milk (milk that was collected the night before and allowed to stand at room temperature overnight). If pasteurized milk is to be used, it must first be ripened. Heat the milk in a double boiler to 86°F and stir in 1 cup of unpasteurized, preservative-free cultured buttermilk per gallon of milk. Let the milk stand for 30 minutes if you want a mild cheese or up to three hours for a sharp, strong-tasting cheese.

Once the milk is ready, the next step is to add rennet to coagulate, or curdle, it. Rennet tablets are sold for use in junketmaking and, in more concentrated form, for cheesemaking. For basic hard cheese, use one-eighth of a cheese rennet tablet or 1 1/4 junket tablets per gallon of milk. Dissolve the rennet in 30 to 40 times its volume of cool water before putting it in the milk. Once the rennet is added, stir the milk thoroughly and place it in a warm location where it will not be disturbed.

After about 45 minutes a thin layer of watery whey will appear on top, while the firm, custardlike curds will form beneath. Cut the curds immediately, since they soon begin to deteriorate. Slice them into even-sized cubes so they will all cook at the same speed. Cubes measuring about 1/2 inch will produce a moist cheese; smaller 1/4-inch cubes will give a dry cheese. Next, mix the cut curds for 10 minutes, then start to heat the curds and whey very slowly. If the curds are heated too quickly, they will become tough on the outside but remain watery inside. When stirring the curds, do so gently to avoid crushing them.

After the curds are cooked (they will be slightly firm and will not stick together), strain off the whey and mix in approximately 3 teaspoons of salt per gallon of milk. Salt improves flavor while slowing the ripening process. Put the curds in the cheese press, applying gentle pressure for the first hour or two to avoid bruising them. Later, for a harder cheese with improved keeping qualities, add more weight. After the cheese has been pressed, allow it to dry in a cool, airy place for four to five days, turning it over twice a day. Next, coat the cheese with paraffin, butter, vegetable oil, or salt, and allow it to ripen in a cool, well-ventilated area. Most cheese will improve in flavor for several months. After a month, sample the cheese and reseal it if it is not ready. If mold develops, scrape off the moldy parts, rub with salt, and reseal. Date your cheeses, making a note of any special method used so that you can develop your own recipes.

Step by Step From Raw Milk to Finished Cheese

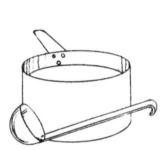

1. Allow milk to stand for a few hours at room temperature. Mix in rennet and leave milk to stand undisturbed in a warm place (86°F).

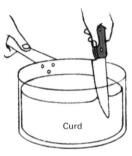

2. When the white curd can be separated cleanly from the side of the pot with a knife, the milk has coagulated and is ready for cutting.

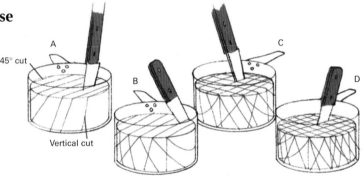

3. The cuts should be 1/2 in. apart across the curd. Make the first cut at a 45° angle, but change gradually so that final cut is vertical (A). Using the same surface marks, make similar cuts sloping the other way (B). Turn the pot and make similar cuts at right angles to the first two sets (C and D).

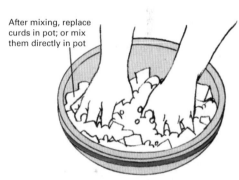

4. Mix the curds gently with your fingers to break up any large pieces.

5. Heat curds for about an hour to 102° F. Increase heat by no more than 2°F every five minutes and stir frequently. Remove from heat.

6. Leave curds in hot whey until they separate after being held together in your hand. Strain through cheesecloth and add salt a little at a time.

7. Leave curds in cloth, and either put into mold or bandage with a strip of strong material folded double. Push curds into shape to avoid airspaces.

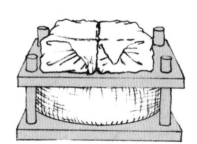

8. Fold cloth over top, put cheese in press, and weight lightly for about two hours. Turn cheese, and increase weight for another 12 hours.

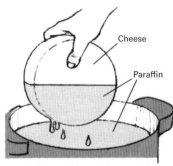

9. To prevent mold from developing, dry cheese for four days, then coat in hot paraffin. Dip one half, allow to dry, then dip other half.

237

Old-time Favorites For the Adventurous

Early settlers in America, more concerned with survival than with gourmet dining, made only simple cheeses. As the population grew and living conditions became less harsh, a number of entirely new cheeses were created, often inspired by recipes brought over by immigrants. Together with the nation's immense dairy production, these new local varieties have helped make the United States one of the world's major cheese producers.

One of the best known of the homegrown American cheeses is Monterey Jack, a descendant of a cheese developed by early Spanish settlers in California. Its name comes from a California Scotsman named David Jacks, who began manufacturing the cheese in 1916,

Cottage and Farmer Cheese

The key to success for both small-curd and large-curd cottage cheese is to warm the curds gently and gradually.

Small-curd sharp cottage cheese is made by allowing the milk to coagulate, or clabber, without rennet. Heat a gallon of skim milk to about 72°F and add 1/2 cup of buttermilk. Stir thoroughly. Cover the milk and let it stand undisturbed in a warm place for 16 to 24 hours until it coagulates. You can use raw milk, but because of the risk of unfavorable bacteria developing, you will probably have better results with pasteurized milk. Do not let the temperature drop below 70°F during clabbering, as this will slow the process, increasing the likelihood of bacterial growth.

When the milk has clabbered, cut the curds into 1/4-inch cubes, mix, and allow to rest for 10 minutes. Then slowly raise the temperature to 104°F, increasing it by 5°F every five minutes. Continue to cook at 104°F for 20 to 40 minutes or until the curds feel firm. The curds should not stick together when squeezed, and the inside of the curds should appear dry and granular. If necessary, raise the temperature as high as 120°F. When the curds are cooked, drain and rinse them. Add a teaspoon of salt for every pound of curd. For a creamed cottage cheese add 4 to 6 tablespoons of sweet or sour cream.

Large-curd sweet cottage cheese is made with rennet. Heat 1 gallon of skim milk to 90°F (no higher), and add 1/4 cup of buttermilk. Dissolve 1 1/4 junket tablets or an eighth of a cheese rennet tablet in a glass of cool water, add it to the milk, and let stand at 90°F. Test

the milk for coagulation after a few hours. When the milk has coagulated, cut the curd into 1/2-inch cubes, allow them to rest for 10 minutes, then heat to 110°F by raising the temperature 5°F every five minutes. Test as for small-curd cottage cheese, and raise the temperature as high as 120°F if the curds are not ready. Drain, rinse, and cream as for small-curd cottage cheese.

When rinsing cottage cheese, first remove cooked curds from heat. Drain through cheesecloth, allow to stand for a minute or two, then lift up the corners of the cheesecloth to make a bag. Dip the bag several times into warm water, rinse for two minutes in ice water to chill the curds, and let the water drain off.

Farmer cheese can be made by using either of the cottage cheese recipes, but use whole milk rather than low-fat milk. After coagulation cut curd into 1/4-in. cubes. Heat slowly to 104°F and continue to cook until curds retain shape after being pressed. Drain, rinse, and pour into oblong shape on a clean, folded cheesecloth. Wrap cloth over and press lightly with board.

exporting it from Monterey. In taste and consistency Monterey Jack is a member of the Cheddar family. Another cheese developed in America is Colby. The first Colby cheeses were manufactured in Wisconsin in 1882 by Ambrose and J. H. Steinwand. Colby is related to Plymouth cheese, a granular variety still produced in small quantities in Vermont. Liederkranz and Wisconsin brick are two entirely new cheeses created in America.

Cheesemaking is not an easy art, and homemade cheeses can vary from batch to batch depending upon temperature, humidity, and which bacteria are most active. However, with careful hygiene they should almost all be good tasting and long lasting. And if a cheese is not quite good enough to eat plain, it can be used for cooking, salad dressing, or in a cheese spread. If you are interested in trying your hand at cheesemaking, start with a simple hard cheese or cottage cheese. Once you feel confident with a basic cheese, try making Cheddar, Colby, or Wisconsin brick cheese.

Cheddar Cheese

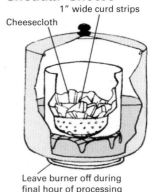

1" wide curd strips

Cheesecloth

Leave burner off during final hour of processing

Cheddaring imparts a characteristic nutty flavor and dense texture to cheese.

After the curds have been drained, return them to the double boiler and spread over a rack lined with cheesecloth. Cover and reheat at about 98°F for 30 to 40 minutes until the curds form one solid mass. Remove the curds, cut them into strips 1 in. wide, and return them to the pan. Turn the strips every 15 to 20 minutes for an hour.

The basic Cheddar recipe was developed in Somerset, England, four centuries ago as a way of reducing contamination in the local cheeses. The word "Cheddar" comes from Cheddar Gorge, where the cheeses were ripened, and the term "cheddaring" has come to mean the reheating process used in making the cheese.

To make a 1 1/2-pound cheese, combine 2 gallons of whole milk with 3/4 cup of buttermilk, and allow the mixture to ripen at room temperature overnight. The next day warm the milk gently in a double boiler to 86°F, mix in one cheese rennet tablet dissolved in a glass of cool water, and let the mixture coagulate undisturbed. When the milk curdles (about 45 minutes later), cut the curds into 3/8-inch cubes. Mix the curds and allow them to stand 15 minutes, then heat very slowly to 100°F. Cook for about an hour until a piece of cooled curd retains its shape when squeezed. If it crumbles, it needs more cooking. Drain the curds for a few minutes and rinse out the double boiler, then cheddar the curds as shown for two hours (longer for a strong flavor). After cheddaring, cut the resultant cheese strips into cubes and gradually mix in 1 tablespoon of salt, being careful not to bruise the curds. Let the curds stand for 10 minutes, put them into a cheesecloth, and press them with 15 pounds for 10 minutes, then with 30 pounds for an hour. Remove the cheese from the press, unwrap it, dip it in warm water, and fill in and smooth off any cracks or unevenness. Rewrap in a clean cheesecloth and weight with 40 pounds for 24 hours; then remove from the press and let the cheese dry for four to five days in a cool, airy location. Turn the cheese twice a day during this period, and wipe it dry each time with a clean cloth. When a hard, dry skin has formed, rub it with oil or seal it with paraffin. Cheddar can be eaten after six weeks but is best if aged six months or more. American cheese is actually a mild variety of Cheddar.

Colby Cheese

Making Colby cheese involves the unusual step of adding cool water to the curds after they are cooked. The result is a mild, moist, porous cheese. Because of its high moisture content, Colby does not keep well.

To reduce the risk of the Colby having an off flavor, use pasteurized whole or skim milk. Heat 2 gallons of milk to 88°F and add 1/2 cup of buttermilk. Stir thoroughly and allow to stand for 30 minutes. Dissolve 1/4 cheese rennet tablet or 2 1/2 junket tablets in a glass of water and add to the milk, stirring vigorously to mix it well. Allow the milk to coagulate (about 30 minutes), then cut the curds into 3/8-inch cubes. After mixing the curds for 10 minutes, heat them very gently to 98°F, increasing the temperature about one degree every three minutes. Continue to cook at this temperature for 40 minutes, then slowly add cool water until the temperature drops to 80°F and remains stabilized at that point. Turn off the heat and gently mix the curds for 15 minutes.

Drain the curds and gradually mix in 6 teaspoons of salt. Put the curds into a cheese hoop or mold and press them lightly for half an hour, then add more weight for an hour and a half. Coat with paraffin when the surface has dried, or rub with vegetable oil or salt. Ripen in a cool place (40°F to 45°F) for two to three months.

Wisconsin Brick Cheese

To make Wisconsin brick, first warm 2 gallons of whole, pasteurized milk to 90°F. Next, add 2 tablespoons of buttermilk. Stir thoroughly, and add half a cheese rennet tablet dissolved in water. When the milk coagulates, cut the curd into 1/4-inch cubes, and mix gently for 15 minutes. Then increase the temperature 1°F every five minutes to 96°F. Maintain this temperature for 20 minutes while stirring gently, then remove from heat, spoon out as much whey as possible, and transfer the curds into a mold with plenty of drainage holes. (A perforated bread pan will give the characteristic brick shape.) Add the follower and weight with a brick.

After 12 hours remove the cheese from the mold and weight it so it stays submerged in a salt solution (1 teaspoon of salt per cup of water). After 24 hours remove the cheese and rub its entire surface with rind from a piece of Wisconsin brick or Limburger. Each day for the next two weeks, rub the surface with a mild brine solution (1/2 teaspoon of salt per cup of water). During this period, keep the cheese at about 60°F in a very moist atmosphere. (Place it in a sealed container along with two or three bowls of water, sprinkling it with water occasionally.) The last step is to apply paraffin and age the cheese in a cool place (about 40°F) for eight weeks.

Making Cheese in Colonial Days

Before the development of thermometers, cheesemaking was a very inexact skill. Housewives heated their milk in large copper pots in front of an open fire until it was warm to the touch. For rennin they added either brine solution in which a calf's stomach had been kept or a fingernail-sized piece of dried calf's stomach. Another method was to use a little of the dried contents of a newborn calf's stomach. The cheese being made below follows a recipe that was used in the Hudson Valley in the late 18th century. The curds are pressed directly after being cut and drained. After several days in the press the cheese is removed and rubbed several times with salt before being stored on long benches in a cool dairy room. Cheese made this way did not have any distinctive flavor. Its main virtue was that it preserved the summer surplus of milk for use during the winter.

1. Rennet is added to a kettle of milk that has been warmed by an open fire.

2. Curdled milk is cut with a traditional five-pronged curd cutter.

3. Large, shallow ladle is used to remove as much whey as possible from curds.

4. Curds are transferred to old-style ash-splint basket lined with cheesecloth.

5. Curds are gathered up in the cheese cloth to put inside a cheese hoop.

6. Curds are gently pushed into the shape of the hoop to remove airspaces.

7. Extra cheesecloth is neatly folded over the curds before adding the follower.

8. Cheese is slid into an old-fashioned press. Note follower and wooden block.

9. Final step is to rub cheese with salt to prevent mold and help form hard skin.

Is Anything as Good As Homemade Ice Cream?

Although ice cream, like apple pie, has become a national symbol, it was for many centuries a luxury even for the very rich. George Washington, for example, once ran up a bill of several hundred dollars with a New York ice cream merchant in the course of a single summer. The transformation of ice cream from an occasional delicacy for the rich into an everyday treat for the common man dates to the invention of the ice cream freezer in 1846. By doing away with much of the labor required to make the dessert, this simple device lowered the cost of the storebought product and at the same time greatly simplified the task of making ice cream at home.

There are two basic ways to make ice cream. The first is simply to mix and then freeze the ingredients. The second method—stir-freezing—requires a hand-cranked or motor-driven ice cream freezer. In stir-freezing, an inner container, chilled by packed ice or placed directly in a freezer compartment, is loaded with the ingredients. These are then agitated, usually by means of a built-in rotary dasher, until they blend to a thick, creamy consistency. Such homemade ice cream benefits by being left to "ripen" in the bucket for a few hours; it can then be eaten or stored for future use in the freezer. Homemade ice cream is mellower and denser than the store-bought variety and can be difficult to dish out. It helps to move the ice cream out of the freezer and into the refrigerator compartment about an hour before you plan to serve it and to use a heated scoop to dish it out.

Philadelphia Vanilla

This famous recipe, named after the city that was once the ice cream capital of America, is simple to make and has a particularly delicate flavor. Its only ingredients are cream, sugar, and flavoring.

6 cups light cream	3 in. vanilla bean or
1 cup sugar	1 1/2 tsp. vanilla extract
	Pinch of salt

Heat cream until almost boiling. Remove from heat and add sugar. Stir until dissolved. Allow to cool, then scrape the seeds from inside the vanilla bean and add to the cream with the salt. Stir again. Chill the mixture, then pour into ice cream freezer and stir until very stiff. Leave in freezer to ripen for a few hours before serving. *Makes 2 quarts.*

Peach

Fresh fruits make healthful, delicious flavorings for homemade ice creams. Raspberries or other full-flavored fruit can be substituted for peaches in this recipe.

6 cups light cream	Pinch of salt
1 1/4 cups sugar	1–2 cups peach pulp

Heat cream to just below boiling point. Remove from heat, add sugar and salt, and stir until dissolved. Add peach pulp when cool. Chill and stir-freeze. *Makes 2 quarts.*

Blueberry

For delicate-tasting fruits with a high water content, such as pineapples or the blueberries used in this recipe, use 1 to 2 cups of sweetened fruit per cup of cream.

6 cups blueberries	Pinch of salt
1/3 cup water	1 1/2 cups sugar
Juice of 1 large lemon	3 cups light cream

Simmer blueberries with water in covered pan until soft. Mash and strain. Add lemon juice, salt, and sugar. Allow to cool, then combine with cream and stir-freeze. *Makes 2 1/4 quarts.*

Italian Chocolate

Whole eggs are added to Italian ice cream to give a richer flavor. The whipped whites, folded in just before freezing, provide a light, fluffy texture.

6 eggs	1 qt. whole milk
Pinch of salt	3 oz. unsweetened chocolate
1 1/2 cups sugar	1qt. heavy cream

Separate the egg yolks and whites into different bowls. Mix yolks, salt, and 1 cup sugar, and beat well. Heat milk until almost boiling, add lumps of chocolate and stir until melted. Slowly stir chocolate mixture into yolks. Allow to cool. Beat egg whites until thick, add remaining sugar, and continue beating until whites form peaks. Fold whites into cooled chocolate mixture, add cream, then chill and stir-freeze. *Makes 21/2 quarts.*

French Strawberry

French ice cream made with heavy cream and the yolks of several eggs is the most expensive recipe to make, but for many people its smooth, rich flavor is the best.

6 egg yolks	4 cups heavy cream
2 cups milk	2 cups crushed strawberries
1 cup sugar	1 tbsp. lemon juice
Pinch of salt	

Mix the egg yolks, milk, sugar, and salt in a double boiler and heat to make a thick custard. Cook until the mixture coats the back of a wooden spoon evenly. Allow to cool. Add heavy cream. Pour into ice cream maker and stir until half frozen. Add crushed strawberries and lemon juice and continue to stir-freeze. Allow to ripen a few hours before serving. *Makes 2 1/2quarts.*

Hand-Cranked Stir-Freezing

To make hand-cranked, stir-frozen ice cream, first crusl plenty of ice in a cloth bag or sack. Chill the innel cylinder, dasher, and all the ingredients. Then replace the cylinder and dasher, add the mixed ingredients to two-thirds full, and fit the lid and handle. Pack the outer bucket one-third full with crushed ice, and scatter 1/4 cup of rock salt over the ice. Add 2 inches of crushed ice, and scatter more rock salt on it. Continue packing alternate layers of ice and salt to the top of the inner cylinder, and begin cranking. Crank slowly at first and more rapidlyat the end to achieve the best texture; it will take about 25 minutes before the ice cream is ready. If you use more salt on the ice, the cream will freeze faster but will become granular. As the ice melts, drain the water off and add further layers of ice and salt. If you are going to eat the ice cream immediately, crank until the cream holds its shape in peaks. If you intend to freeze it, stop cranking as soon as the cream becomes thick and does not quite hold its shape.

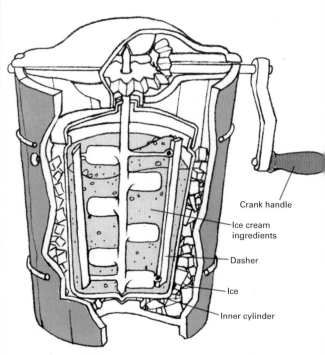

Crank handle

Ice cream ingredients

Dasher

Ice

Inner cylinder

Ice cream's immense popularity dates to 1846, when Nancy Johnson of New Jersey invented the hand-cranked ice cream maker. To this day ice cream connoisseurs maintain that hand cranked ice cream has a more perfect texture than ice cream made by any other method.

Frozen Desserts Without Stir-Freezing

Light, refreshing sherbets, frozen yogurt, rich fruit parfaits, and even some traditional ice creams can be made in a freezer compartment of your home refrigerator without using an ice cream maker or other special equipment. Set the freezer control to maximum cold an hour beforehand; when the dessert is frozen, return the control back to normal. Some recipes suggest restirring the mixture when it is half frozen to prevent any separation between the cream and flavorings. Water ices can be prepared by the same method to make low-calorie summer treats. The method works best if your freezer can reach a temperature as low as 0°F.

Traditional Lemon Ice Cream

Grated rind of 1 large lemon	2 cups light cream
3 tbsp. lemon juice	1/8 tsp. salt
1 cup sugar	

Mix the rind, juice, and sugar together and slowly add the cream and salt. Stir well. Pour into refrigerator or trays and freeze. When the outer edges are firm, remove from freezer and stir well with a wooden spoon; then cover and freeze. *Makes 1 1/2 pints.*

Chocolate and Cinnamon Ice Cream

4 oz. semisweet chocolate	1/2 tsp. cinnamon
4 egg yolks	Pinch of salt
3/4 cup white corn syrup	1 cup heavy cream, whipped

Melt the chocolate in a double boiler. Beat the separated egg yolks, and stir in corn syrup and the melted chocolate. Heat in a double boiler and stir until mixture thickens. Remove from heat and allow to cool. Add cinnamon and salt, and fold the mixture into whipped cream. Pour into refrigerator trays and freeze. *Makes 1 1/4 pints.*

Maple-Pecan Parfait

3 oz. pecans	1 1/2 cups maple syrup
2 1/4 tsp. gelatin	3 cups heavy cream
1/3 cup cold water	Pinch of salt
6 eggs, separated	

Chop or break pecans coarsely, and chill bowl for cream. Mix gelatin in cold water and set aside to dissolve. Mix egg yolks in a double boiler and add maple syrup. Heat, stirring constantly, to 180°F, or until mixture begins to thicken. Remove from heat and mix in gelatin. Allow to cool. Whip cream in chilled bowl until thick but not stiff. Beat whites with salt until thick. Fold cold yolk and syrup mixture into whites, fold again into whipped cream. Add nuts. Freeze. *Makes 2 quarts.*

Orange Sherbet

2 cups sugar	10 juice oranges
2 lemons	2 cups heavy cream

Stir sugar into the juice of lemons and oranges until dissolved. Whip cream and fold in fruit juice. Freeze. *Makes 1 1/2 quarts.*

Fresh fruit can be mixed into the ice cream or made into a sauce to be drizzled over the top. Any lightly sweetened fruit can be used, just be careful not to add too much sugar or honey to the ice cream, since this will prevent the cream from freezing.

Apricot Sherbet

1 cup water	1 cup light cream
1 cup sugar	3 tbsp. lemon juice
4 cups apricot juice	4 egg whites

Heat water and sugar until sugar dissolves. Remove from heat; add apricot juice. Allow to cool. Mix in cream and lemon juice. Freeze until thick and mushy. Combine with egg whites in chiled bowl and beat until thoroughly blended and light. Freeze. *Makes 2 quarts.*

Frozen Fruit Yogurt

1 qt. plain yogurt	Sugar to taste
cup fresh fruit	

This refreshing low-calorie substitute for ice cream is not only economical but also remarkably easy to make. Simply mix 1 qt. of plain homemade or store-bought yogurt with a cup of sweetened fruit. Freeze without restirring. *Makes 1 1/4 quarts.*

Cranberry Water Ice

3 cups cranberries	3 cups water
1 1/2 cups sugar	

Simmer cranberries, sugar, and water until cranberries soften and break open. Strain the mixture and freeze. Restir once or twice during freezing. *Makes 1 1/2 quarts.*

Old-fashioned ice cream makers require more work than modern types but can be fun and yield delicious results.

Sources and resources

Books and pamphlets

Baldwin, Jo G. *Let's Make Ice Cream.* Cisco, Tex.: Longhorn Press, 1977.

Carroll, Robert, and Ricki Carroll. *Cheesemaking Made Easy: 60 Delicious Varieties.* Charlotte, Vt.: Garden Way Publishing, 1982.

Duback, Josef. *Traditional Cheesemaking: An Introduction.* New York: Intermed Technology Development Group of North America, 1988.

Hobson, Phyllis. *Making Cheese and Butter.* Charlotte, Vt.: Garden Way Publishing, 1984.

Hunter, Beatrice Trum. *Fact Book on Yogurt, Kefir and Other Milk Cultures* New Canaan, Conn.: Keats Publishing, 1973.

Stoner, Carol Hupping, ed. *Stocking Up III.* New York: Fine Communications, 1995.

U.S. Department of Agriculture. *Cheeses of the World.* New York: Dover, 1972.

Suppliers of dairying equipment

Cumberland General Store. Crossville, Tenn. 38555.

Suppliers of yogurt, cheese starter, and rennet

Chr. Hansen's Laboratory. 9015 West Maple St., Milwaukee, Wis. 53214. (minimum order 300 rennet tablets)

Marschall Products. 3322 Vondron Rd. Madison, Wis. 53716.

Walnut Acres. Penns Creek, Pa. 17862.

Suppliers of kefir grains

International Yogurt Co. 628 N. Doheny Dr., Los Angeles, Calif. 90069.

Maple Sugaring

Two Quarts of Syrup From One Maple

The art of making maple syrup and maple sugar is uniquely American. In the days before the coming of the white man, Indians of the Northeast would cut slashes in the bark of the sugar maple, collect the sap that ran off, and boil it down in a hollowed-out cooking log by continually adding heated rocks. Early settlers in the New World soon learned the skill and improved on the Indian system by using iron drill bits to tap the trees and copper buckets to evaporate the sap into syrup and sugar. Small-scale family sugaring has long been an American tradition, and recently the rising cost of syrup has provided additional incentive for the backyard sugarer. A good maple will yield 15 to 20 gallons of sap during a single sugaring season—enough to make about 2 quarts of pure, preservative-free maple syrup.

Raw sap being harvested; soon it will be processed into syrup.

Stalking the sugar tree

For sugaring, the sugar maple and black maple are best, with the Norway maple a close third. Other maples can be used, but syrup production is lower. The sugar maple's ash-gray bark is often broken into hard flakes. The bark of the black maple is smooth and gray when young; scaly, furrowed, and darker when old. The range of both trees extends from New England west to Minnesota, north into Canada, and south to Tennessee. Identify trees in summer and mark them for spring tapping.

Very tight angle

Sugar maple

Tight angle

Black maple

Wide angle

Norway maple

The Tools and Techniques of Tapping

The larger the diameter of the trunk and the greater the spread of limbs at the crown, the more sap a healthy tree will yield. Trees with trunks smaller than 10 inches should not be tapped; the yield will be low and the tree may be injured. There are several sap flows, but by far the best time to tap is in late winter or early spring before the buds open: sugar content is high, flavor is at its peak, and the cool nights inhibit bacterial action.

Tap holes can be drilled on any side of the tree, although production from the south side is generally greater early in the season. Drill 2 to 3 inches into the sapwood—no deeper. Greater penetration will not produce much more sap and may injure the tree. Use a brace and bit and drill at a slight upward angle (10° to 20°). The hole diameter should be less than that of the spout, or spile, to be inserted: 7/16 inch for a standard 1/2-inch spout. Tap holes can be located anywhere from 2 to 6 feet above the ground. A big tree (over 2 feet in diameter) can be tapped in four or more spots. One or two taps is safer for a small tree. A new hole in a tree that has been tapped previously should be about 6 inches from tap scars.

As soon as a hole is drilled, the spile should be inserted. Do this by tapping the spile rather than hammering it; if excessive force is used, the bark may split, damaging the tree and creating a leaky tap. Metal spiles, tapered to fit snugly and with built-in bucket hooks, are widely available in rural areas, or you can make your own spiles by hollowing out 4-inch lengths of sumac with a heated awl or other reaming instrument. (Be sure to select only red-berried sumacs; white or light green berries indicate a poison sumac.) If you use a wooden spout, hammer a nail in the tree above it to support the sap bucket.

Collect the sap in covered containers. Galvanized 2- to 3-gallon buckets are traditional, but plastic 1-gallon milk containers serve well, and their narrow necks do away with the need for a cover. Clean the container thoroughly and suspend it beneath the spile by a wire or strong string. You can store sap outdoors in large containers, such as clean plastic trash cans, for up to three days as long as the weather remains cold. A warming trend is a signal to process the sap more rapidly and to remove the spiles. The tree will heal by midsummer.

Spile is gently driven into hold at slight upward angle. Gray, somewhat scaly bark is typical of black maple.

Sap Into Syrup

As soon as you have collected enough sap to make an appreciable amount of syrup, you should begin boiling it down. Almost any outdoor heating device will do, from a simple bonfire to a commercial evaporator working on bottled gas. Kerosene stoves, gasoline-fired camp stoves, and old coal-burning ranges have all been used successfully. Wood is the fuel of choice, however, since it is safe, inexpensive, and there is less risk of spoiling the taste of the syrup. If you have an outdoor barbecue pit, you can do your evaporating there. If not, you can construct a temporary evaporator out of cinder blocks. Do not boil sap down inside your house, however. The result will be a sticky deposit of sugar on walls, furniture, and floors. Whatever the fuel used, shield the evaporating device from the wind to conserve fuel.

Boiling down sap takes a lot of fuel, so be sure to have plenty on hand. If you are using wood, you will need about a quarter cord for every 4 gallons of syrup produced. The evaporator pan should be clean, have a large heating surface, and hold at least a gallon of sap, preferably more. A big roasting pan will do for small-scale sugaring. You will also need a stirring spoon, a candy thermometer, a 1- or 2-gallon "finishing" pot, and a kitchen strainer. In addition, have some heavy felt cloth or paper toweling on hand to filter the finished syrup.

Fill the evaporator pan about half full of sap and bring the sap to a boil over the fire. Unprocessed sap is mostly water, and its boiling point is the same as that of water (212°F at sea level, 1°F lower for each 550 feet of elevation). As the water vapor is driven off, the boiling point slowly rises. When the temperature reaches 7°F above the boiling point of water, the syrup is done.

During the course of the evaporation process, skim off surface froth with the kitchen strainer. Whenever the sap gets low in the pan, add more to prevent burning or scorching. As the syrup nears the ready stage, it tends to boil over, so most sugarers finish the syrup on a stove whose heat can be easily controlled. When the syrup is 6°F above the boiling point of water, it is ready for finishing. Remove the evaporator pan from the fire and pour the syrup into the finishing pot, at the same time filtering it through felt cloth or paper towels placed in the strainer. (Be extremely careful when handling the pan; hot sap will stick to the skin, producing severe burns.) The purpose of filtering is to remove any impurities, particularly the granular calcium compound known as sugar sand, which is found in all maple sap. Once the syrup is finished, it should be bottled immediately while still hot. Some sugarers filter the syrup a second time, as it is being poured into the storage jars, to remove any traces of sugar sand that may remain.

Storing and Processing Maple Syrup and Sugar

Pure maple syrup can be stored for extended periods of time without the addition of artificial preservatives. The most practical method for long-term storage is by canning in airtight glass, plastic, or metal containers. Of the three, glass containers, such as mason jars, are best because they do not rust, do not affect the flavor as some plastics do, and allow the syrup to be inspected without opening the container. Pour the hot syrup (it must be at least 180°F) directly from the finishing pot into the containers, seal the containers, and let the syrup cool slowly to avoid risk of contamination. Store the bottles of syrup in a cool, dark place such as a basement or pantry. Syrup will also keep in nonairtight containers for several months provided they are refrigerated. It can even be frozen, but this may result in loss of flavor and will also cause the syrup to crystallize and separate.

Soft maple sugar and hard maple sugar will both stay fresh for long periods of time if stored in moisture-proof containers and protected from contaminants. To make soft maple sugar, cook maple syrup in a pot to about 30°F hotter than boiling water, let it cool to 155°F, and stir until it becomes thick and viscous. Then pour into molds. Hard sugar is made by bringing syrup to 33°F above boiling water, cooling to 150°F, and stirring until crystals form. While you are sugaring, you can also enjoy an old-fashioned treat simply by pouring some of the hot syrup (about 230°F) on snow or crushed ice. The result is a taffylike confection known as Jack wax.

Highest grade syrup (left) is pale and delicately flavored; it is made from clear sap that has been boiled down quickly. Home sugarers, however, often prefer the richer-tasting, darker syrup.

Sugar shack in Nova Scotia, Canada is well-ventilated to allow steam from evaporator to escape. As the sap cooks, it is checked periodically with a candy thermometer. When temperature reaches 7°F above the boiling point of water, syrup is ready. About 1/4 cord of dry hardwood will boil down 200 gal. of sap.

Maple leaves turn vibrant colors in the autumn as the chlorophyll drains away and the stored glucose shows through.

243

Homemade Beverages

Potables Made at Home Not Only Taste Better, They Are Better

Almost every morning of his adult life President John Adams drank a tankard of hard cider. The reason, as he put it, was "to do me good." And, indeed, it seems to have done him considerable good, for he lived to be 91. Of course, making and drinking your own cider and other fruit beverages—whether soft, hard, or in between—may not guarantee longevity but they will make the years pass more pleasantly.

Almost anyone who can follow a simple recipe can make delicious fruit drinks and sodas. With a bit more care and effort alcoholic beverages, such as wine, beer, and hard cider, can be home brewed using simple equipment and ingredients. Lager, ginger beer, applejack, mead (honey wine), dandelion wine, and red table wine are all within the scope of the home beermaker and winemaker. In fact, almost any drink other than those whose alcoholic content is increased by distillation is not only easily made but is also sanctioned by law. (Federal regulations effective since 1979 permit adult citizens to make 200 gallons of beer or wine yearly for home consumption and all the hard cider they want. However, selling these beverages or distilling them to make hard liquors, such as whiskey and brandy, is illegal.)

The fundamental prescription for making safe, delicious beverages at home is similar to that for processing most other food products. Use the best ingredients available, pay scrupulous attention to cleanliness and hygiene, and do not be afraid to experiment; trying a new ingredient or a new mix of old ingredients is the best way to introduce your own tastes and personality into the beers, wines, and fruit drinks that you create.

Home cidermaking today is much the same as it was 150 years ago when cider was the most popular drink in America. Presses almost identical to the antique one shown here are still sold by country stores and mail-order houses. Do-it-yourself kits are also available. For still greater savings rig up your own press, or purchase plans that show how to build a traditional type.

Getting the Cider out of the Apple

Old-fashioned cidering is easy. Basically it is simply a matter of separating the juice from the apple. Start by deciding which apple varieties will give a flavor you like. Use a blend of tart and sweet, not just one kind. Fallen and bruised apples can be used, but avoid ones with worms, mold, or rot. A bushel will yield about 3 1/2 gallons of cider. Next, wash the apples thoroughly, and if they come from commercial orchards (which often use large amounts of pesticides), remove the stem and the end of the blossom. Chop or grind the apples into a fine pulp, or pomace. You can make or buy your own grinder or you can use almost any device that will aid in pulverizing them—a food chopper, food mill, food grinder, rolling pin, even a leaf shredder. Whatever you use, be sure to clean it carefully before you start and after you finish. Grind the pulp as finely as possible—twice if need be—and save any juice to add to the cider.

The pomace must now be pressed to extract the cider. Wrap the pomace in a clean pillowcase or cheesecloth and place it in a cider press—manufactured presses are widely available, or you can rig up one of your own. Do not rush the process. Apply pressure, wait until most of the juice stops dripping, then apply more pressure. Your patience will result in increased yields and clearer cider. The cider can be used at once or stored in clean glass bottles. Before pouring it into containers, filter the cider through several layers of cheesecloth to clarify it and improve its storage qualities.

The flavor of cider starts maturing the minute it is pressed, progressing from a sweet, tangy tartness to a more mellow, full-bodied, fruity taste. However, unless the cider is stored properly, the changes will continue until the cider becomes vinegar. Provided the fruit was healthy and well washed, the processing equipment clean, and the storage bottles sterile, cider will keep several weeks under refrigeration, frozen cider for a year or longer. Pasteurization improves keeping qualities but harms flavor. To pasteurize cider, heat it quickly to about 170°F, then immediately pour the hot cider into sterile canning jars, seal them, and set them in a water bath of 165°F for five minutes. Let the jars cool in lukewarm water for an additional five minutes, and then cool them completely in cold running water.

Variety makes the best cider

Cider should be made from a blend of apple varieties, each of which will contribute its own special taste and complement the others. The 12 most widely grown varieties fall into three main taste categories: sweet (Cortland, Delicious, Rome Beauty); mildly tart (Jonathan, Northern Spy, Rhode Island Greening, Stayman, Winesap, York Imperial); and aromatic (Golden Delicious, Gravenstein, McIntosh).

Use a sweet apple for the bulk of the cider, with a somewhat lower percentage of apples from each of the other groups. For an especially tangy cider, add a few crabapples.

Cider Recipes

Cider is a versatile mixer that can be used in both alcoholic and nonalcoholic drinks. It also can be fermented into hard cider, applejack, and cider vinegar. The latter is not so much a beverage (although it is used in a few drinks) as it is a general household do-it-all, serving as a flavoring agent, food additive, and cleanser.

Instant Apple Breakfast

1 cup chilled cider   **1 banana**
1 egg

Blend all the ingredients for a few seconds in an electric mixer. The flavor can be changed by blending the apple cider with other fruit juices, such as grape, cranberry, or prune. You can substitute a tablespoon of gelatin for the egg. *Makes 1 cup.*

Cider Syllabub

Syllabubs are frothy drinks made by combining milk with either cider, juice, or an alcoholic beverage. Old-timers used fresh unpasteurized whole milk in their syllabubs, preferably by milking the cow directly into the mix.

A typical syllabub recipe calls for mixing 1/2 lb. sugar, 1 pt. cider, and some grated nutmeg; 3 pt. milk is then poured in from a foot or two above the mixing bowl, the stream being directed in a circular motion to yield the maximum amount of froth. As the final touch, 1 pt. of heavy cream is poured over the top. For an alcoholic syllabub combine 1 pt. hard cider, 4 oz. brandy, the juice and the scraped outer rind of one lemon, and 1/2 cup sugar. Let the mixture ripen for one day; then whip 2 cups of heavy cream until stiff, beat the whites of two eggs until stiff, and fold both ingredients into the mixture. Syllabubs are excellent when served either hot or cold.

Mulled Cider

1 qt. apple cider   **4 cinnamon sticks**
10 whole cloves   **Nutmeg**
1 cup maple syrup

Bring the cider and cloves to just below a boil in a saucepan. Add the maple syrup and stir until thoroughly mixed. Serve hot in 8-oz. mugs with a cinnamon stick in each, and top with freshly grated nutmeg. A bit of rum will make the drinks even tastier. Some recipes for mulled cider recommend adding eggs. For this variation beat two eggs, and mix them into the warm cider, stirring constantly as you do. *Makes 4 cups.*

Hard Cider

Fill a used wine or whiskey keg with cider that is fresh and unpasteurized, leaving about a tenth of the container empty to allow room for expansion. (The keg should be clean but not new; new wood will impart an unpleasant flavor to the cider.) Cover the keg loosely and place it in a cellar or other cool, dark room where the temperature stays between 40°F and 50°F. Be sure to check the temperature frequently: high temperatures produce rapid fermentation and a bitter flavor; temperatures that are too cool may prevent the cider from hardening.

The cider should start fermenting in a day or less—you will hear hissing when you place your ear near it and tiny bubbles will appear in the liquid. If the cider seems to be fermenting too quickly—the hissing will be loud and the bubbles large—move the cider to a cooler place. If little or no fermentation appears to be taking place, dissolve a cup or two of sugar in some fresh cider and add it to the keg. A more scientific method for adjusting the sugar content is to measure it with a winemaker's saccharometer (see p.250). The instrument should indicate a sugar content of about 17 percent.

The cider is ready when the bubbling and hissing have completely stopped. Siphon it off carefully, leaving the residue in the bottom of the container, and bottle it in containers that are clean and airtight. The hard cider is ready to drink right away, but the benefits of delaying for several months until the cider has had an opportunity to age will be well worth the wait.

Applejack

Applejack is hard cider whose alcoholic content has been increased beyond what fermentation alone will produce. Commercially, this is accomplished by distillation, a process that is subject to government regulations, but you can achieve the same effect by putting a bucket of hard cider where it will freeze—outdoors on a cold night or in the freezer. Slushy ice will form on top. Remove the ice in order to concentrate the hard cider.

Cider Vinegar

One of the most valuable of all homemade concoctions, cider vinegar can be used for anything from a salad dressing to cleaning stove tops and removing stains. Open a bottle of sweet cider and let it stand at about 70°F. After about five weeks it will turn to hard cider, then to vinegar. You can speed the process by adding a little "mother" (the cloudy clump of bacteria that forms on the surface of natural vinegar) from a previous batch or from a friend's cider vinegar.

The Traditional Cider Press

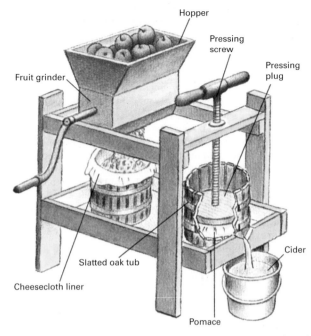

Hopper

Pressing screw

Pressing plug

Fruit grinder

Cider

Slatted oak tub

Cheesecloth liner

Pomace

Cider press design has changed little over the years. A slatted hardwood container holds the crushed apples (oak is the favored wood because it is strong yet does not affect the taste of the juice), and a center-mounted screw press forces out the juice. Presses are available at some country stores and from some mail-order houses as grinders for making the pomace. Wine presses are sometimes recommended for cidermaking, but they are too small—a cider press should be at least large enough to handle the pomace extracted from a bushel of apples.

Improvised presses

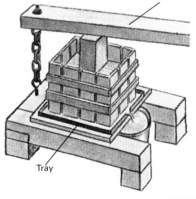

Lever

Tray

Lever press is simple in design and easy to build. Make the lever arm of strong, durable lumber—a 4 × 4 or even the trunk of a small tree can be used as a lever for a large press. Fashion the box and the follower (the piece that actually presses on the pomace) out of 2 × 4's. A long lever arm will make the task of pressing somewhat easier.

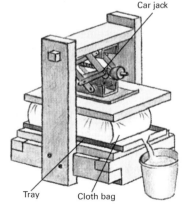

Car jack

Tray   Cloth bag

Car jack multiplies muscle power in this homemade press. Use scissors-type jack, and be sure the frame of the press is strong. You can do without a frame if you have an overhang to put the jack under, such as a crawl space beneath the house or a low branch. Apply pressure gradually, and wait until all the juice runs out before applying more.

Soft Drinks and Juices To Slake All Thirsts

Almost any garden fruit or vegetable will yield juice that can be used to make tasty, delicious drinks. Grains, flowers, roots, and barks also contribute flavorings, and you can even make your own soda pop by adding a little bicarbonate of soda or unflavored carbonated water.

The first step in making most juices is to reduce the fruit or vegetable to a pulp. (A frontier wife once described it as "beating the hell" out of the fruit.) A variety of common kitchen tools can be used for this purpose, including potato mashers, fruit blenders, juicers, food grinders, and food processors. You will need a strainer on hand to separate the juice from the pulp and a clean bowl to hold the juice after it is strained.

Clean and peel the fruit or vegetables and cut the larger produce, such as carrots, tomatoes, and peaches, into sections. In some cases, particularly for fibrous vegetables, such as celery, carrots, and beets, it is necessary to cook the produce for a few minutes over a low flame to aid the extraction. Once you have made the pulp, put it in a jelly bag, colander, or cheesecloth and let it stand for several hours over a clean container. Generally, this is all you need to do to get the juice out. Some fruits, however, notably grapes and apples, require extra force to extract their juice. Make a sack out of cheese-cloth or an old pillowcase, put the fruit in the bag, and squeeze it in a cider or wine press. Tighten the press about every half hour. Many fruit juices can be frozen into a frappe (the Italians call it *granita*). Simply freeze the mixture solid, then reduce it to slush by putting it in a blender. A little egg white or unflavored gelatin will thicken the potion. Bear in mind that coldness dulls the taste buds, so try to make your frozen drinks stronger flavored than their liquid counterparts. With citrus drinks you can add flavor by grating in some of the rind. Extra honey or sugar will also help.

Beverages that have been simmered a few minutes, then bottled in sterile, tightly capped containers, will keep well in the refrigerator. For long-term storage (up to a year), can or freeze the drinks. Vegetable drinks, with the exception of those based on tomatoes, should be canned by the pressure-cooker method (see *Preserving Produce*, pp.206–209). To freeze a beverage, pour it into clean plastic bottles, cover it securely, and store at 0° F. (Leave the upper fifth of each container empty to allow for expansion as the drink freezes.)

Homemade lemonade is a delicious summertime treat. Don't throw out the peels until you've extracted the lemon oil to mix with the juice.

Old-fashioned Concoctions

Hot summers and hard work produced some mighty thirsts in years gone by, and American inventiveness created the beverages to slake them. Some of these concoctions are as popular now as they have ever been. Others, however, such as shrubs, switchels, and syllabubs, have become as obsolete as their names—a pity, because many are delicious and all are healthful. The decline can be traced to an enterprising Philadelphia druggist named Hires, who in 1893 bottled and sold the first ready-made soda pop—Hires Root Beer.

Lemonade

Lemonade is synonymous with summer. The secret to making old-fashioned lemonade is to extract the aromatic lemon oil from the rinds, either by letting the sugar soak up the oil or by steeping the rinds in boiling water.

4 lemons	**1 qt. water**
1 cup sugar	

Peel the rinds from the lemons, put them in a bowl, and cover with the sugar for about 30 minutes. Then boil the water and pour it over the sugar and rinds. When the water is cool, remove the rinds. Squeeze the lemons, strain the juice, and add it to the mixture. Refrigerate until ice-cold. Pink lemonade can be created by adding the juice from half a bottle of maraschino cherries before serving. *Makes 1 qt.*

Mint Punch

James Monroe, our fourth president, is said to be responsible for this icy, clean-tasting concoction.

1/2 cup water	**1 cup grape juice**
1/3 cup sugar	**1 cup orange juice**
1/2 cup fresh mint leaves	**1/2 cup lime juice**

Warm the water until it just boils, turn off the flame, and add the sugar and most of the mint leaves (reserve a few leaves for a garnish). Stir the mixture until the sugar is dissolved. When the liquid cools, strain out the mint; add the grape, orange, and lime juices; place in the refrigerator. Serve the punch over ice with a mint leaf on top. *Makes six 4-oz. servings.*

Hay-Time Switchel

Switchel is a refreshing, energy-boosting drink used by farm-hands to slake their thirsts during the heavy work of harvest season, especially the backbreaking labor of haymaking. Long before refrigerators, or even icehouses, jugs of switchel were kept cool in the springhouse or by hanging them in a well.

2 cups sugar	**1 tsp. ground ginger**
1 cup molasses	**1 gal. water**
1/4 cup cider vinegar	

Heat ingredients in 1 qt. of water until dissolved, then add the remaining water, chill, and serve. *Makes 1 gal.*

Extracting Juice From Fruits and Vegetables

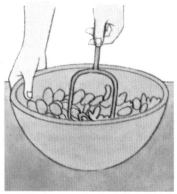

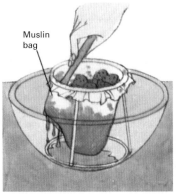
Muslin bag

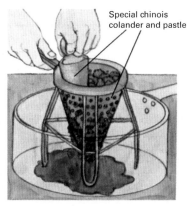
Special chinois colander and pastle

Mashing or crushing is the best way to juice berries and other small fruits such as grapes. A stainless steel potato masher can be used as a pestle and a large, heavy mixing bowl as a mortar. Warming the pulp in a large saucepan (do not boil it) will yield more juice. Strain leftover pulp through a sieve or a cheesecloth, and use it for pies and other fruit desserts.

Small pitted fruits, such as cherries, plums, and elderberries, should be strained through a jelly bag. Heat the fruits first in a little water until they burst; once again, take care not to boil the mixture, since it will damage the flavor and destroy nutrients. You can get the most juice out by letting the pulp drain for a period of several hours or overnight.

Squeezing is the best way to extract juice from most citrus fruits, especially when they are fully ripe. Remember that much of the distinctive citrus flavor is in the rind, so it is a good idea to squeeze some rind into the juice or to include a little grated rind. Add the oil or rind a bit at a time and sample the juice after each addition until the taste is right.

Pureeing is an effective way to prepare juice from hard fruits, such as peaches, pears, and pineapples. Chop the fruits into small sections, then force them through a sturdy colander. A chinois (a conically shaped colander with a matching pestle) makes the job easier. You can also use a food processor or blender. If the puree is too thick, add water.

Grinding and chopping is another method of juicing hard fruits. The job is most easily done with a food mill or food processor. Once the fruit is reduced to pulp, drain the juice off with a jelly bag or sieve. You can get extra juice by adding a little water to the pulp, letting it stand overnight, then extracting the juice by straining through a fine sieve.

Homemade Soda Pop

Nowadays we use artificial carbonation for our soft drinks, but years ago a mixture of bicarbonate of soda and tartaric acid was added to a drink to make it fizz.

1 qt. water	Whites of 3 eggs, beaten
4 cups sugar	until stiff
4 tsp. cream of tartar	Tartaric acid powder (available
1 tbsp. vanilla	from winemaking suppliers)
	Bicarbonate of soda

Heat 1 qt. of water to near boiling; dissolve the sugar and cream of tartar in it, and add the vanilla. When the syrup mixture has cooled, add the egg whites, stir thoroughly, then bottle and store in the refrigerator. To make the actual soda pop, dissolve 2 tbsp. of the syrup plus 1/4 tsp. tartaric acid powder per 8-oz. glass of ice cold water. Then add 1/2 tsp. of bicarbonate of soda and stir. Half a teaspoon of lemon juice per glass can be substituted for the tartaric acid, or simply eliminate the bicarbonate and tartaric acid and use carbonated water instead of ice water.

Ginger Beer

Root beer, ginger beer, lemon beer, and a host of similar drinks had little or no alcoholic content. Such beverages were fermented briefly with the same kind of yeast used for making bread, then bottled and stored: the fermentation served only to make them fizzy. Old-fashioned root beer is difficult to make because of the rarity of its ingredients: spice wood, prickly ash, and guaiacum, to name a few. The ginger beer given here is adopted from a Mormon recipe for Spanish gingerette.

4 oz. dried gingerroot	1 packet active dry yeast
1 gal. water	1/2 lb. sugar
Juice from 1 lemon	

Pound the gingerroot to bruise it, then boil in 1/2 gal. water for about 20 minutes. Remove from stove and set aside. Mix lemon juice and packet of dry yeast in a cup of warm water, and add to the water in which gingerroot was boiled. Pour in remaining water, and let mixture sit for 24 hours. Strain out the root and stir in sugar. Bottle and place in refrigerator. Do not store at room temperature; bottles may explode. *Makes ten 12-oz. bottles.*

Hot Chocolate

Despite its current reputation as the bane of dieters, chocolate is a highly nutritious food. This recipe derives from the Shakers.

2 oz. unsweetened	Pinch of salt
chocolate	1 tsp. cornstarch
1 cup water	3 cups milk
1/2 cup sugar	1 tsp. vanilla

Melt the chocolate in a double boiler. Boil the water, and stir in the sugar, salt, and cornstarch until dissolved. Pour over the chocolate and stir thoroughly. Scald the milk, pour it into the mixture, and add the vanilla. Then reheat mixture almost to boiling and whip it with an egg beater until frothy. *Makes 4 cups.*

Raspberry Shrub

Shrubs are effective hot weather coolers. Red raspberry shrubs were the most popular, but almost any fruit can be used, including black raspberry, orange, cranberry, strawberry, and currant.

1 qt. red raspberries	3/4 cup sugar
1 qt. water	1/2 cup lemon juice

Pour berries into a bowl and use a potato masher to reduce them to a pulp. Heat water to a boil, add sugar and lemon juice; continue to boil until the sugar dissolves in the water. Then pour the hot sugar water over the berries. When the mixture is cool, press it through a colander and refrigerate. Serve the shrub over ice cubes. For an alcoholic version of the same shrub, use a pint of water rather than a quart, and stir in 1 1/2 cups of brandy and 1/2 cup of rum before refrigerating. *Makes 1/2 gal.*

Fruit Syllabub

This semisoft Connecticut syllabub is of English ancestry. Although not truly a beverage, it still can quench a thirst as well as satisfy a palate. The juice of any berry can be used.

Sugar to taste	2 cups heavy cream
1 cup berry juice	

Stir sugar into juice until sweet, then continue stirring until all sugar is dissolved. Add cream, and whip mixture until it starts to stand in peaks. Serve cold or use as a topping. *Makes 3 cups.*

Home Brew: Fine Flavor At Modest Expense

Beer is one of the oldest and most popular drinks in the world, as much for the ease with which it can be made as for its good taste. And with today's inexpensive instruments for measuring both temperature and sugar concentration—the crucial factors in successful brewing—making home brew is more foolproof than ever. You will need the following equipment:

Bottles, caps, and capping machine. Beer is usually bottled in 12- or 16-ounce containers. You can buy new bottles or save empties, but do not use nonreturnable bottles—they are too fragile. Beermaking supply houses, some hardware stores, and several mail order houses sell caps and capping machines.

Brewing vessel. Use a 7- to 10-gallon food grade polyethylene pail with a tight-fitting lid.

Fermentation lock. This device mounts on the lid and allows carbon dioxide to escape from the fermenting beer while keeping outside air from entering.

Saccharometer. This instrument measures the level of sugar concentration. It is available at stores selling winemaking or beermaking supplies.

Thermometer. Any immersible thermometer that is accurate in the 50°F to 230°F range will do.

All items should be sterilized before use by soaking them for 10 minutes in a solution of 2 cups of chlorine bleach and 5 gallons of very hot water. Rinse everything thoroughly in more hot water after sterilizing.

The essential ingredients for making beer are brewer's yeast, sugar, water, malt, and hops. During fermentation the yeast consumes sugar and produces carbon dioxide and alcohol. Some sugar is naturally present in the malt, but more is generally added in the form of cane sugar or corn sugar. Good water is important in making beer, but almost any tap water will produce acceptable brew provided it is not heavily chlorinated and does not have a strong mineral taste.

Sweet-tasting malt (made from barley) and bitter-tasting hops (the female flower of the hop vine) give beer its distinctive flavor. Both are available in premeasured packets at stores selling beermaking supplies; beginners should use the packets to avoid disappointment. Making malt from barley corn is not difficult, however. The purpose of the process is to produce an enzyme, dia-stase, that converts the barley's starch into sugar—the raw material of alcohol.

The first step in making malt is to let the grains of barley sprout (see *The Kitchen Garden*, p.135, for information on sprouting seeds). When the shoots are as long as the kernels, the growth must be stopped—without destroying the diastase—by heating the barley to a temperature above 185°F but never any higher than 230.°F. (The higher the temperature, the darker will be the beer.) Once malted, the barley must be soaked in water so that the diastase can convert more of the kernel's stored starch into sugar. First crack the grain by grinding it very coarsely or rolling it with a rolling pin. Then put it into 150°F water and let it soak for about six hours. Strain the mixture through fine cheesecloth; the resulting liquid is the malt extract.

Hops cut the sweetness of the malt and also contain preservative oils. To bring out the oils, boil the hops in the malt for at least three hours. Because the prolonged boiling reduces flavor, many brewers reserve a small proportion of the hops until the last quarter hour of boiling. Proportions of water, malted grain, and hops vary according to recipe and personal taste, but an average formula is 2 bushels of malted grain and 2 quarts of dried hops to make 5 gallons of beer.

Basic Steps in Making Light Beer

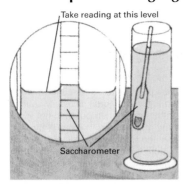

Take reading at this level

Saccharometer

Fermentation lock

Water

Siphon

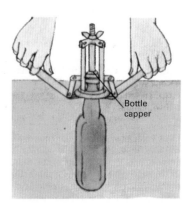

Bottle capper

1. Boil 2 1/2 gal. of water for five minutes and pour into polyethylene pail. Add 3 lb. hop-flavored malt extract, 3 lb. sugar, and 2 1/2 gal. cold water. To test sugar content, pour some brew into a glass cylinder, let it cool to 70°F, and insert saccharometer. Twirl meter to release any air bubbles that are clinging to it, and let float. For beer that will have 6 percent alcohol, reading should be 12 percent.

2. Dissolve 1 tsp. tartaric acid in a small quantity of brew and add to pail. When the mixture has cooled to about 70°F, sprinkle a package of brewer's yeast and a package of yeast nutrient (special vitamins and proteins that encourage yeast growth) over the brew; let stand three hours, then stir thoroughly into mixture. (Note: Temperatures over 80°F will harm yeast and slow fermentation.)

3. Cover pail with tight-fitting lid that includes a fermentation lock on its top to allow carbon dioxide gas to escape. After about five days (when the fermentation slows and the sugar falls to about 5 percent) siphon brew into clean polyethylene pail or 5-gal. glass bottle. Siphon from the top of liquid, being careful not to disturb sediment at bottom of fermenting beer. Replace cover on pail.

4. Check sugar concentration daily. When it falls below 1 percent, fermentation is complete, and liquid should be siphoned into the bottles at once. (Fermentation time depends upon proportions of ingredients as well as holding temperature but is usually from three to six weeks—most recipes give an approximate time.) Siphon carefully from top of pail; do not disturb sediment.

5. Many recipes call for addition of small amounts of sugar (about 1 tsp. per quart) to each bottle to ensure enough fermentation to carbonate beer. To avoid adding too much sugar to any one bottle (it could cause the bottle to explode), dissolve the total amount in a small quantity of malt, then divide malt equally among the bottles. Cap bottles and store at least three weeks before drinking.

Beer and Ale Recipes

The procedure for making dark beer is identical to that for light beer described on the previous page; the only difference is that darker malt is used. For ale, follow the basic beer procedure, but use more sugar for a higher alcohol content and more hops for a stronger taste.

Nowadays, most beer and ale is served cold and unmixed, but in times gone by beer was a basic ingredient in many mixed drinks. These ranged from spiced summer-time coolers to such hearty winter concoctions as the spectacular Ale Flip or the more prosaic but no less pleasing Mulled Ale, Posset, and Yard of Flannel.

Ale

3 lb. hop-flavored malt extract	2 1/2 gal. cold water
3 1/2 lb. sugar	1 tsp. tartaric acid
2 1/2 gal. water	1 package yeast
3/4-1 oz. Hops	1 capsule yeast nutrient

Stir hop-flavored malt extract and sugar into boiled water that has cooled for five minutes, as in making beer. Add extra ounce of hops and cold water, and measure sugar level—it should be 5 percent. Add tartaric acid, yeast and yeast nutrient, then ferment and bottle as for beer. *Makes 5 gal.*

Cold Spiced Ale

2 cinnamon sticks	1/4 cup sherry
2 whole cloves	4 cups ale
1 allspice berry	4 cups ginger beer
Pinch of grated nutmeg	(see p.247)

Soak the spices for several hours in room-temperature sherry, then strain into a pitcher. Add ale and ginger beer, chill thoroughly, and serve in well-chilled mugs. Or serve the spiced ale as it would have been drunk in the days before refrigeration—only slightly cooled. *Makes eight 8-oz. servings.*

Ale Flip

1 qt. beer or ale	Sugar to taste
1/4 cup rum	

Mix all ingredients in a stainless steel or other type of metal container. Heat a poker until red-hot, then insert it into the brew. In the 18th century ale flips were so popular that a special tool, called a loggerhead or flip dog, was kept by the fire ready to be heated to make a tankard of ale steaming hot. *Makes two to four servings.*

Mulled Ale

2 qt. ale	1/2 tsp. ground nutmeg
1 tsp. ground ginger	2 tbsp. sugar
1/2 tsp. ground cloves	1 cup rum

Mix together ale, spices, and sugar, and heat just to boiling. Add rum and serve hot. *Makes eight 8-oz. servings.*

Summer Refresher

3 cups ale	1 cup ginger beer (see p.247)

Mix the two ingredients together and serve well chilled. *Makes four 8-oz. servings.*

Ale and Sherry Posset

4 cups milk	1 cup sherry
1 cup ale	Grated nutmeg to taste
1 tbsp. sugar	

Heat milk just to boiling. Mix together ale, sugar, sherry, hot milk, and stir until sugar dissolves. Serve in mugs; sprinkle with grated nutmeg. *Makes six 8-oz. servings.*

Yard of Flannel

1/2 cup brown sugar	1/2 cup rum
3 eggs, beaten	4 cups beer or ale
1/2 tsp. nutmeg	

Beat sugar into eggs, add nutmeg and rum, and heat over very low flame or in double boiler. Heat beer or ale just to boiling. Pour ale slowly, beating constantly, into egg mixture. The traditional way to make this drink frothy is to pour it back and forth between mugs. *Makes 4 cups.*

Hop vines grow wild in many sections of the country. It is the female flowers that are used in beermaking (they look just like the males but in the fall contain seeds). Powdered hops and dried hop flowers are also available.

Pat O'Hara, Home Brewer

Brewing or Quaffing: Beermaking Satisfies Twice

Pat O'Hara, who runs a Bedford, Ohio, general store, loves his home brew.

"I've been making beer and wine since 1964. I saw a small article on winemaking in the newspaper and, believe it or not, that's all it took to start me. At first most people were interested in making wine, but more and more people are getting into brewing. Some people just like the fuller-bodied taste of home-brewed beer, and others are outraged by high prices in the market. And then there are folks who just like doing things for themselves. Once somebody starts making beer, pretty soon one of his friends will taste it and start beermaking too. Believe me, you can really make some terrific-tasting beer at home.

"We've got so many people interested in my area that we even have a beermaking club. We meet about once a month, 60 to 80 people, counting wives and a few folksingers. You can really learn a lot tasting the beer that other people make. Of course, some people have already drunk so much of their product that they don't have any beer to bring to the club.

"The biggest disaster in beermaking is the old story about grandpa who brewed some beer and the bottles all blew up. It's possible, of course, but I haven't heard of it myself in quite a while. Sometimes you get it with what I call these old Prohibition brewers. They brewed the beer, left it in a crock, and after four days bottled it and added a little sugar. The modern way is to leave the beer in the crock and then transfer it to a 5-gallon jug and let it sit until no more fermentation gas bubbles up. Then you add a specific amount of sugar to the brew and bottle it. If you do it that way, there's very little chance of accident.

"The other time I hear about problems is during the month of August. If it's too warm and if you leave the beer to ferment in an open crock, the air gets to it and it turns to vinegar. The only real nuisance job in brewing is washing all those 12-ounce bottles. You can get real tired of that. Some people are going to quart bottles to cut down on the work. I guess I probably brew about a case of beer a week myself. What's the most fun in the whole process? Just the joy of drinking it."

The Delicate Art Of the Home Vintner

Wine, like beer, is made by adding yeast to a sugar-rich solution; as the yeast cells grow, they convert the sugar into alcohol. But a wine's flavor does not come from any one ingredient; it comes from a complex chemistry that gradually transforms a pulpy concoction of fruit and yeast into a clear, flavorful wine.

The trick to making dry wine is to start with exactly the right amount of sugar: too little sugar and the yeast cells cannot produce enough alcohol; too much and they are poisoned before they can convert all the sugar. A saccharometer of the same type used in beermaking (pp.248–249) makes it easy to measure sugar content. There is more to good wine than dryness and alcohol, however. Start with good fruit, avoiding any that is old or overripe. To ensure a taste that is tangy but not too harsh, check your fruit's acidity with a vintner's acid-testing kit. For richness and body add tannin by mixing in 1/2 cup of strong tea per gallon of juice (note, however, that red wines need no extra tannin, since the grape skins supply enough). Yeast is another variable. Beginners should use an all-purpose vintner's yeast, but there are a wide variety of yeasts, such as those for making sherry and champagne.

Keep all equipment clean. You should also sterilize equipment by rinsing it in a solution of six Campden tablets (available at winemaking stores) per pint of water. These tablets inhibit the growth of unwanted, or wild, yeasts by liberating the gas sodium dioxide. They are also used during the winemaking process itself.

It is after fermentation that the real magic of winemaking takes place. In a process that can take as much as a year, dead yeast cells and other sediments gradually fall to the bottom of the fermentation vat. Whenever they accumulate, the wine is carefully racked off (siphoned) into a clean container. Many experts believe that the longer the wine is aged and the more often it is racked, the better it will taste. Only when it has become so clear that you can see the edge of a candle flame through it is it ready for bottling.

Once your wine is in the bottle, continue to treat it well. Stopper the bottles with new corks, and seal the corks with paraffin. After several days put the bottles on their sides in a cool, dark place to age, a process that takes at least six months but can continue for up to one year for wines made from high-quality grapes.

How to Make Red Wine, Step by Step

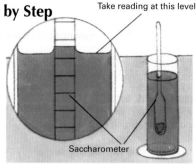
Take reading at this level

Saccharometer

Na OH 0.1M

1. Crush 70 lb. of unwashed wine grapes and stems with a crusher or potato masher. Put juice and crushed grapes into 7-gal. pail (it should be three-quarters full). Or fill pail three-quarters full of purchased grape juice.

2. Check sugar content. Pour juice (it should be 70°F) into glass cylinder. Twirl saccharometer to dislodge bubbles, and take reading. Add about 4 3/4 tsp. sugar for each percent needed to raise reading to 22 percent (for 11 percent alcohol).

3. Use acid-testing kit to check acidity. Juice should be .6 to .8 percent acid. If too acid, add cooled, boiled water; if not acid enough, add 1/2 tsp. acid blend per gallon for each .1 percent that acid must be raised. Retest acidity.

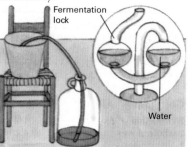
Fermentation lock

Water

4. Dissolve five Campden tablets in a small quantity of juice, add to pail, and stir. Wait four hours, then add yeast and yeast energizer (packaged nutrients that encourage yeast growth). Add tannin if using purchased grape juice.

5. Cover pail and place in 65°F to 70°F area to ferment. Stir several times daily to mix skins with juice. When fermentation has nearly stopped and sugar level is 3 to 5 percent (three to seven days), strain through nylon mesh bag.

6. Siphon juice into 5-gal. glass bottle, filling it to 1 in. from stopper. Fill smaller bottle with remaining juice. Close bottles with fermentation locks so that carbon dioxide can escape but wild yeasts and other contaminants cannot get in.

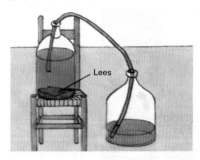
Lees

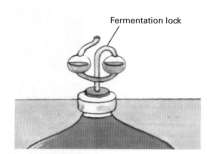
Fermentation lock

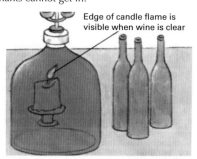
Edge of candle flame is visible when wine is clear

7. When fermentation stops (bubbling ceases and sugar level is almost at zero), rack the wine into a clean 5-gal. bottle. Do not disturb lees. Keep outlet end of siphon near bottom of bottle to avoid splashing and overoxidizing wine.

8. Dissolve 2 1/2 Campden tablets in some wine, add to bottle, then fill bottle to 1 in. from stopper with reserved juice or previously made wine. Insert fermentation lock and set bottle in 65°F to 70°F area for two to three months.

9. Rack wine into clean 5-gal. bottle whenever lees accumulate. When wine is clear (after two or more rackings), refrigerate for two days to stabilize. Let wine return to room temperature, then siphon into bottles, cork, and label.

Other Types of Wines

The best-known wines are made from grapes, but there are hundreds of other excellent wines based on an amazing diversity of ingredients. Honey is used to make a wine known as mead; the flower heads of the lowly dandelion make an excellent spring wine; and almost any pit fruit, including cherries, plums, peaches, and apricots, can be converted to wine.

White Wine

70 lb. white wine-type grapes or 5 gal. juice	Tartaric acid
	1 package vintner's yeast
10 or more Campden tablets	5 capsules yeast energizer
Sugar	

Crush grapes and stems in grape crusher or with potato masher, taking care not to crush seeds. Strain pulp immediately through nylon mesh bag, but do not squeeze; squeezing may result in cloudy wine. Add sugar to adjust content to 21 percent, and use tartaric acid to adjust acidity to .7 to .9 percent. Add five Campden tablets that have been dissolved in a small amount of juice. After 4 to 12 hours add yeast and yeast energizer and stir thoroughly. Siphon into 5-gal. glass bottle and fill smaller bottle with any excess. Stopper bottles with cotton, and let stand in 55°F to 60°F area.

When fermentation action calms (about five days), fill 5-gal. bottle to within 1 in. of stopper with reserved juice or with previously made white wine, replace cotton with a stopper that has a fermentation lock, and let fermentation continue until bubbling ceases and sugar content is near zero (one to two weeks). Rack wine into new bottle, add 2 1/2 dissolved Campden tablets, fill bottle to 1 in. from stopper with reserved wine, and insert stopper with fermentation lock. Rerack wine as often as necessary until clear, adding 2 1/2 Campden tablets and filling bottle to 1 in. from stopper each time. Stabilize by refrigerating for two days, then let wine return gradually to room temperature. Bottle and cork as for red wine. *Makes 5 gal.*

Dessert-Type Fruit Wine

12–15 lb. ripe perfect pit fruit (cherry, peach, plum, apricot)	1 capsule yeast energizer
	1 Campden tablet
4 pectic enzyme tablets (to destroy pectin that would otherwise cloud wine)	Tartaric acid
	1 package vintner's yeast
	4 cups sugar

Peel and pit fruit, then crush it. Place pulp and half the pits in large plastic pail. Test acidity and adjust with tartaric acid to about .5 percent. Crush and dissolve pectic enzyme, yeast energizer, and Campden tablet in a little warm water and add to fruit. Cover the container with a sheet of plastic or cloth, and tie sheet tightly in place to keep out insects. Let stand overnight.

Stir in yeast, re-cover container, and place in 70°F area to ferment. Four days after fermentation starts, strain mixture through nylon mesh bag, squeezing to extract juice. Add 2 cups sugar, stir to dissolve, and siphon liquid into glass bottle that is 2 gal. or larger. (Or divide between two 1-gal. bottles.) Seal with fermentation lock and hold at 70°F to ferment.

When fermentation calms (about seven days) test sugar level and adjust to 22 percent—about 2 cups sugar per gallon of juice is usually required. Replace fermentation lock, and let fermentation continue. When fermentation slows again, rack wine into 1-gal. glass bottle, and add fruit wine or brandy to bring level of liquid to within 1 in. of stopper. Rack as often as necessary until wine is clear. Bottle and cork as for grape wine and age for at least six months. *Makes 1 gal.*

Dandelion Wine

1 gal. dandelion flower heads	5 1/2 cups sugar
3 oranges	1 package vintner's yeast
3 lemons	1 capsule yeast energizer
1 gal. boiling water	1 tbsp. strong tea

Wash flower heads thoroughly in cold water, pull off stalks and other green parts, and place petals in a large plastic pail. Chop fine the colored outer rind of oranges and lemons, add to petals, then cover with boiling water. Drape pail with sheet of plastic or cloth, and tie sheet tightly in place to keep out insects. Stir mixture twice

Siphon enables winemakers to rack homemade wine into bottles. The wine should be chilled to stabilize it, then allowed to return to room temperature so that expansion of cool air in the bottles will not cause corks to pop.

daily for three days. After three days strain the juice into a large kettle, squeezing or pressing to extract as much liquid as possible. Add sugar, to bring its level to about 21 percent, and cook juice at medium boil for 30 minutes. Let cool to 70°F, and mix in yeast and yeast energizer. Divide mixture between two 1-gal. bottles, and seal the bottles with fermentation locks. When fermentation slows (one to three days), siphon all the liquid into one bottle, filling it to within 1 in. of stopper. Add tea. Reseal with fermentation lock, and let ferment at 70°F until the bubbling stops (one to four weeks). Rack as often as necessary to clear wine, adding enough liquid each time to fill bottle to 1 in. from stopper. When wine is clear (usually after three rackings), bottle and cork as for grape wine. *Makes 1 gal.*

Mead

1 Campden tablet	1 1/2 tsp. strong tea
1 capsule yeast energizer	1 package vintner's yeast
6 lb. mild-flavored hone	or special mead yeast
3/4 oz. acid (citric, tartaric, malic, or a blend)	

Crush Campden tablet and yeast energizer, and stir into 3 lb. of honey, then pour the honey slowly into 2 cups of warm water, stirring constantly until honey is completely dissolved. Stir in the acid and tea. Cover the mixture and leave it in a warm area (about 70°F) for one day. Stir in the yeast. Cover mixture, fit with a fermentation lock, and let it ferment for five days. On fifth day dissolve remaining honey in 2 cups warm water and add to the original mixture. Refit lid and fermentation lock, and let mixture continue to ferment for another two days. One week after initial fermentation began, rack liquid into a clean 1-gal. plastic pail or glass bottle, being careful not to disturb sediments at bottom of honey mixture. Fill new container to within 1 in. of stopper by adding 70°F water if necessary. Seal with fermentation lock and allow fermentation to continue. Rack fermenting liquid into a clean container whenever sediments collect. When mead stays completely clear, bottle it; store in cool, dark area. *Makes 1 gal.*

Sources and resources

Books and pamphlets

American Homebrewers Association Staff and National Conference on Quality Beer and Brewing Staff. *Just Brew It!* Boulder, Colo.: Brewers Publishing, 1992.

Boulton, Roger B., et al. *Principles and Practices of Winemaking.* New York: Chapman & Hall, 1995.

Brown, Sanborn C. *Wines & Beers of Old New England.* Hanover, N.H.: University of New England Press, 1978.

Burch, Byron. *Brewing Quality Beers.* Fulton, Calif.: Joby Books, 1993.

Cox, Jeff. *From Vines to Wines.* Pownal, Vt.: Storey Communications, 1989.

Johnson, Hugh. *Wine.* New York: Simon & Schuster, 1987.

Orton, Vrest. *The American Cider Book.* New York: Farrar, Straus & Giroux, 1995.

Turner, Paul, and Turner, Ann. *Traditional Home Winemaking.* Santa Rosa, Calif.: Atrium Publishing, 1990.

Baking Bread

First Master the Basics And the Rest Is Easy

Nothing smells quite so good as the aroma of bread baking in the oven. And the incomparable taste and texture of a loaf of wholesome, home-made, preservative-free bread is well worth the effort, especially since breadmaking is not nearly as time-consuming as many people believe. Measuring, mixing, kneading, and shaping can be accomplished in 30 minutes or less. Rising takes longer; but this is a process that occurs by itself, leaving you free to handle other chores or simply to sit back, relax, and contemplate the warm, fresh bread you will soon be enjoying.

Tools and ingredients for making bread are simple. Start with a basic bread recipe and then experiment by using different grains, nuts, seeds, fruit, etc.

Ingredients and Supplies: What Goes Into a Loaf of Bread and Why

Bread is a simple food. Few ingredients and little equipment are required to make it. The basic components of bread are yeast and flour: yeast to make the dough rise, flour to provide substance and structure.

Yeast. When yeast, a plant with millions of living cells, is placed in warm water and is fed sugar and flour, it grows and multiplies, giving off the carbon dioxide gas that makes dough rise. Yeast adds vitamins, gives bread its airy texture, and contributes to aroma and flavor.

You can buy yeast in two forms: active dry and compressed. Active dry yeast is granulated and will remain fresh for months without refrigeration. Before it is used, it is generally dissolved in warm (110°F) water or milk. However, it is sometimes added directly to the other dry ingredients and then mixed with the water or milk at a somewhat higher temperature—120°F to 130°F.

Compressed yeast in cake form is more perishable: it should be refrigerated or frozen immediately. Refrigerated, it will keep about 10 to 14 days. Frozen, it can be stored for much longer periods. When you are ready to make bread, thaw the yeast at room temperature and use it immediately by dissolving it in water or milk that has been warmed to no more than 95°F.

You can also make your own yeast as old-time homesteaders did. Mix together 1 cup of cooked mashed potatoes, 1/4 cup sugar, 2 teaspoons salt, and 1 cup of warm water (105°F to 115°F). Pour the mixture into a 1-quart glass jar, cover with a cloth, and leave in a warm place (80°F to 85°F) for two days or until it ferments and bubbles up. One cup of this mixture is equivalent to one package of active dry yeast or one cake of compressed yeast. Every time you use a cupful, replenish the starter by stirring in 3/4 cup of flour and 3/4 cup of potato water, water, or milk. Allow to ferment for a day or so and return, covered, to the refrigerator. It is best to use the starter once a week. If you do not, stir it down after three or four weeks, discard half of it, and replenish the balance with flour and one of the liquids.

Flour. The gas emitted by the growing yeast must have a framework that will hold it. This structure is provided by the flour, more strictly by gluten, a sticky combination of proteins that is developed by stirring and kneading moistened flour. The gluten traps the minute pockets of gas given off by the yeast, causing the bread to rise. Hard-wheat flour, also known as bread flour, is the richest in gluten and produces loaves of greater volume than other flours. Neighborhood bakeries sometimes sell hard-wheat flour, or you may be able to purchase it from a health food store. So-called all-purpose flour is widely available and is satisfactory for both yeast and quick breads. Buy it unbleached—it gives the bread a better texture. Rye, whole wheat, and buckwheat flour are low in gluten and must be combined with all-purpose flour. Used alone, they produce heavy, compact breads.

Other ingredients. In addition to yeast and flour, salt, sweetener, shortening, and eggs are often used in bread recipes. Salt adds flavor and controls the yeast action. Sweeteners add flavor, help in browning, and provide food for the yeast. White cane sugar is the type most often used, but brown sugar, honey, and molasses can be substituted in many recipes. Shortening, generally butter or lard, provides additional flavor, makes bread more tender, improves keeping quality, and helps form a brown crust. Eggs give yeast breads color, texture, and flavor. However, dough that has been enriched with shortening or eggs takes longer to rise.

Special equipment. Several bread pans and, perhaps, a heavy-duty mixer are the only special implements you will need. The size of the pan is important, so be sure to use the one specified in the recipe. If the pan is too large, the dough will rise properly but will not expand over the top of the pan to make a dramatic-looking loaf. If the pan is too small, the dough will rise too high and slide over the sides of the pan. As a rule of thumb, the dough should fill two-thirds of the pan.

Some experienced bakers prefer dark-colored bread pans to help absorb heat and give a browner crust. Special black steel pans are best, but aluminum pans are satisfactory. Darken aluminum pans before using them by heating them in a 350°F oven for five hours. Pans of heat-resistant glass are also popular.

Basic White: Template for Breadmaking

The instructions for making basic white bread can be used as a guide for almost all other yeast breads. Master it and you will be on the way to mastering the entire art of breadmaking from the simplest recipes to the most complex. You will need two 9- by 5- by 3-inch bread pans plus the following ingredients:

2 cups milk	1/2 cup warm water
1 tbsp. salt	(105°F-115°F)
2 tbsp. butter	2 tbsp. sugar
1 package active	6-7 cups unsifted hard-wheat
dry yeast flour	or all-purpose flour

Making the dough. Heat the milk, salt, and butter in a saucepan until bubbles appear around the edges of the pan. Remove from the heat and let cool to about 110°F.

Sprinkle the yeast over the warm water in a large mixing bowl. Make sure the water is not more than 115°F: higher temperatures will kill the yeast. To test the temperature touch a drop of water to your wrist; it should feel only slightly warm. Now add the sugar, stir well, and set aside for 5 to 10 minutes to "proof" the yeast; that is, to

test it to see if it is alive (if it is, small bubbles will appear on the surface). Once the yeast is proofed, stir in the mixture of milk, salt, and butter.

Add 3 cups of flour. Stir to mix, then beat with a wooden spoon until smooth—about two minutes. Gradually add more flour, mixing it in with your hands until the dough tends to leave the sides of the bowl. The secret of making bread is to use as little flour as possible and still be able to handle the dough; any flour beyond this amount will tend to make the bread heavy and tough. Remember that the amount of flour given in a bread recipe can only be an approximation, since flours vary greatly in their ability to absorb moisture, differing from one locale to another and from batch to batch. Experience will help you judge the correct amount.

Kneading the dough. The purpose of kneading is to distribute the yeast cells throughout the dough and to develop the gluten in the flour, which traps the gas produced by the yeast, causing the bread to rise. Turn out the dough onto a lightly floured board, marble slab, or countertop. Sprinkle the dough lightly with flour. As shown in the

illustration at bottom left, knead by folding the dough toward you, then push down with the heels of your hands. Fold the dough over again, give it a quarter turn, and repeat the kneading; try to develop a rhythmic motion. Continue kneading and turning for 10 minutes or until the dough is smooth and elastic. To test the dough to see if it has been kneaded sufficiently, press two fingers into it about 1/2 in. deep; the dough should spring back. Form the dough into a ball.

First rising. Grease a large mixing bowl with about 1 tbsp. of softened butter. Place the ball of dough into the bowl and roll the dough around to cover it with butter. This will keep the surface from drying out and cracking as the dough rises. Cover with a kitchen towel or plastic wrap, and let rise in a warm, draft-free place (80°F to 85°F) for 1 to 1 1/2 hours or until doubled in bulk. If the room is cold, put the dough in a bowl, cover, and place the bowl in a pilot-lighted oven, or on a rack over a pan of hot water, or near (not on) a radiator. If you have a wood stove, the warming oven over the range is ideal for rising.

To test if the dough has risen sufficiently, make an indentation by pressing two fingers into the dough about 1/2 in. deep. If dough does not spring back, it is ready. If the dough has risen a little too much, it will not be seriously affected; however, excessive rising can change the texture and flavor of the finished product.

Punch the dough down with your fist to deflate it. Turn it out on a lightly floured board, then knead well about two minutes. Cut the dough in half with a sharp knife and shape each half into a smooth ball. Cover with a towel and let rest about five minutes.

Shaping the dough. Use a rolling pin to shape each ball of dough into a 9- by 12-in. rectangle, then roll the dough up tightly from the short sides (above left). Next, press the ends together to seal them, and fold the ends so that they are underneath the rolls (above right). Lift the loaves carefully and place them in the greased pans with their seam sides down.

Second rising. Brush the top of each loaf with 1/2 tbsp. melted butter. Cover pans with a towel. Let rise as before in a warm, draft-free place until the dough has doubled in volume or when a finger pressed lightly near the edge leaves a dent. The purpose of the second rising is to give the dough a finer grain. This rising will take less time than the first rising; 3/4 to 1 1/4 hours is typical.

In case of an interruption. If at any time during the first or second rising you cannot complete the breadmaking, punch the dough down as you did after the first rising, and place it in a buttered bowl. Set a clean plate on top of the dough, weight it down with a brick or other heavy object, and place the bowl in a refrigerator. The cold plus the weight will bring the action of the yeast almost to a halt.

Baking the bread. For glazed loaves, gently beat one egg yolk with 1 tbsp. of milk. Lightly brush the top of each loaf with this mixture just before putting the bread in the oven.

Bake the loaves 40 to 50 minutes on the lower rack of an oven that has been preheated to 400°F. Place the bread pans so that their tops are as close to the center of the oven as possible. In order to permit adequate circulation of hot air, however, the pans should

not touch each other or the sides of the oven. To check if the bread is ready, tap the top of a loaf with your middle finger (left). If it is done, the bread will sound hollow. To test further, take a potholder in each hand, turn the loaf out of the pan, and tap the bottom of the bread with your finger (right); it should sound hollow. If it is soft on the bottom, return the loaf to the pan, bake an additional 5 to 10 minutes, and test again.

Remove the pans from the oven, turn the loaves on their sides on a rack, and place in a draft-free location. For easy slicing, the bread should cool completely—about two to three hours. To store the bread, put it in plastic bags and tie securely or keep it in a bread box or freezer. Bread will keep at least a month in the freezer. If you use only a small amount of bread at a time, slice the loaf before freezing and remove slices from the freezer as needed. For quick thawing of a whole loaf, wrap it in aluminum foil and heat in a 300°F oven about 25 to 40 minutes.

Bread Names Preserve History and Folklore

Sourdough Bread

Prospectors who went to Alaska in the 1890s to seek their fortune in gold took sourdough starters with them in their knapsacks. These miners ate so much of the bread that they came to be known as sourdoughs, a term now associated with backwoodsmen in general.

1 1/2 cups sourdough starter (see recipe below)	2 tbsp. butter
3/4 cup milk	1 package active dry yeast
2 tbsp. sugar	1/2 cup warm water (105°F-115°F)
2 1/2 tsp. salt	4-5 cups all-purpose flour

The sourdough starter must be prepared three days before the bread is to be made.

Scald the milk. Stir in the sugar, salt, and butter. Cool to lukewarm. In a large mixing bowl dissolve the yeast in the warm water. Add the milk mixture, the starter, and 3 cups of flour. Stir with a wooden spoon to mix. Turn the dough out on a lightly floured board, and work in one more cup of flour. Then add only enough flour to make a soft dough. Knead 10 minutes.

Place the dough in a buttered bowl, turning the dough to grease it all over. Cover and let rise in a warm, draft-free place for about an hour or until doubled in bulk.

Punch the dough down. Divide into three equal pieces. Form each piece into a smooth, round ball or a 14-in. tapered roll, and place on buttered baking sheets. With a sharp knife make several diagonal cuts about 1/4 in. deep on the tops of the long loaves. Cover and let rise in a warm, draft-free place until doubled in bulk (about one hour).

Bake in a preheated 400°F oven 25 minutes or until the bottom of the loaf sounds hollow when tapped. Cool on wire racks. **Makes three round or one large tapered loaf.**

Sourdough Starter

3 1/2 cups flour	2 cups warm water (105°F-115°F)
1 tbsp. sugar	
1 package active dry yeast	

Combine the flour, sugar, and undissolved yeast in a large glass or ceramic bowl. Gradually add the warm water to the dry ingredients, beating until smooth. Cover with cheesecloth and let stand in a warm place three days.

After the amount needed for the recipe is removed, replenish the starter by adding 1 1/2 cups flour and 1 cup warm water to remaining starter. Beat until smooth and let stand in a warm place until mixture bubbles well, at least eight hours. Store, loosely covered, in the refrigerator and use and replenish at least once every two weeks.

Sourdough loaf, resting on a bread peel, hot from the oven.

Kolaches

This sweet bread is attributed to immigrants from Bohemia (a region of Czechoslovakia) who emigrated to America in the 1860s, settling in Nebraska.

1 package active dry yeast	1/4 cup sugar
2 tbsp. lukewarm water (105°F-115°F)	2 egg yolks
1 cup lukewarm milk	Melted butter
4 cups all-purpose flour, approximately	Confectioners' sugar
1 tsp. salt	PRUNE FILLING
1/2 cup (1 stick) soft butter	1 1/2 cups dried prunes
	1/4 cup sugar
	1/2 tsp. cinnamon

In a large bowl sprinkle the yeast over the warm water and stir to dissolve, then add the milk. Sift the flour with the salt. Work in half the flour and beat until smooth.

Cream the butter, gradually adding the sugar. When light and fluffy, blend into the first mixture. Add the egg yolks, one at a time, beating well after each addition. Work in the remaining flour by hand. Add only enough flour to make a light dough.

Place the dough in a greased bowl. Grease the top of the dough with some melted butter, cover, and let rise in a warm, draft-free place until doubled in bulk, about 2 to 2 1/2 hours.

Punch the dough down, then turn out on a lightly floured board and roll to 1/4-in. thickness. Cut into circles with a 2-in. cookie cutter and place about 1 1/2 in. apart on buttered baking sheets. Cover and let rise until doubled in bulk, about 1/2 hour.

With the thumb make a deep depression in the center of each roll and fill with prune filling. Let rise 10 minutes.

Bake in a preheated 400°F oven 10 to 15 minutes or until golden. Transfer to wire racks and brush the buns with melted butter. Dust with confectioners' sugar. **Makes about 36 buns.**

To make the filling, cook and drain the prunes. Pit and mash with a fork. Stir in sugar and cinnamon.

For a cherry filling fill each depression with cherry preserves.

Anadama Bread

The story goes that this bread was invented by a New England fisherman who was angry at his wife, Anna, for serving cornmeal and molasses day after day. One night, in an attempt to create a new dish, he mixed flour and yeast into the cornmeal and molasses and placed the mixture in the oven to bake. While eating the bread, he constantly mumbled to himself, "Anna, damn her!"

1/2 cup yellow cornmeal	1 package active dry yeast
3 tbsp. butter or shortening or shortening	1/4 cup warm water (105°F-115°F)
1/4 cup dark molasses	1 egg, lightly beaten
2 tsp. salt	3 cups sifted all-purpose flour
3/4 cup boiling water	

Combine the cornmeal, butter or shortening, molasses, salt, and boiling water in a small bowl. Cool until lukewarm. Sprinkle the yeast over the warm water in a large bowl. Let sit five minutes. Add the egg, cornmeal mixture, and half the flour. Beat with wooden spoon until well mixed. Stir in the remaining flour. Use hands toward the end to mix well. Shape into a ball, put in a buttered bowl, and turn to coat the surface. Cover; let rise until doubled in bulk. Punch down.

Turn into a well-buttered 9- by 5- by 3-in. loaf pan. Cover with a towel and let rise until doubled in bulk. Sprinkle the top of the dough with cornmeal. Bake in a preheated 350°F oven 40 to 45 minutes. Cool the bread on a rack. **Makes one loaf.**

Sally Lunn

One of the popular theories of the name's origin is that the bread was once baked as buns. The golden tops and white bottoms of the buns resembled the sun and the moon, or *soleil lune*, as it was called in French.

1 package active dry yeast	1/2 cup (1 stick) butter, melted
1/3 cup sugar	1 tsp. salt
1/2 cup warm water (105°F-115°F)	3 eggs, slightly beaten
1/2 cup warm milk	3 1/2-4 cups all-purpose flour

In a mixing bowl combine the yeast, sugar, and warm water. Stir to dissolve. Add the milk, butter, and salt. Add the beaten eggs and mix well with a wooden spoon. Add about 1 cup of flour at a time, beating well after each addition. Add enough flour to make a stiff batter.

Place in a clean, well-buttered bowl, cover with a damp cloth, and let rise in a warm, draft-free place until doubled in bulk. Beat the dough hard with a wooden spoon for about one minute. Transfer to a buttered 9-in. angel food pan, and let rise in a warm place about 45 minutes or until the dough has doubled in bulk.

Bake in a preheated 350°F oven 45 to 50 minutes until golden brown on top and hollow sounding when tapped. A toothpick or metal skewer inserted into the bread will come out clean and dry. Unmold and serve hot or warm. Cut into wedges with lots of butter. **Makes 8 to 10 servings.**

A Collection of Quick Breads for Hurry-Up Baking

Quick breads are just that; they can be made in much less time than yeast breads because they do not require kneading or rising and can be cooked as soon as they are mixed. The leavenings used in these breads—baking powder, baking soda, steam, or air—raise the bread after it goes into the oven or onto the skillet and work much faster than yeast. Quick breads do not keep as well as yeast breads and taste best when they are eaten hot.

Steamed Boston Brown Bread

This truly American bread was created by the early settlers to accompany Boston baked beans.

1 cup yellow cornmeal	1 tsp. salt
1 cup rye flour	2 cups buttermilk
1 cup whole-wheat flour	3/4 cup molasses
2 tsp. baking soda	1 cup chopped raisins

Combine the cornmeal, rye flour, whole-wheat flour, baking soda, and salt in a bowl. Then combine the buttermilk, molasses, and chopped raisins in a separate bowl. Add the buttermilk mixture to the dry ingredients, stirring only enough to moisten. Do not overmix.

Pour the batter into two well-buttered 1-lb. coffee cans about three-quarters full. Cover the cans with aluminum foil well buttered on the underside. Make sure the seal is tight. Place the cans on a rack or trivet in a large kettle. Pour in enough boiling water to come halfway up the sides of the cans, adding more boiling water if needed. Cover tightly and steam two hours. Keep the water boiling gently at all times.

Lift the cans from the kettle, remove the foil, and run a knife around the insides of the can to loosen the bread. Unmold on a wire rack. To cut without crumbling, wrap a tough string around the loaf, cross the ends, and pull the strings to slice. Serve warm with butter. **Makes two loaves.**

Cranberry Nut Bread

This delicious bread is lighter in texture than many other fruit breads of this type.

2 cups sifted all-purpose flour	1 tsp. grated orange peel
1 cup sugar	3/4 cup orange juice
1 1/2 tsp. baking powder	1 egg, well-beaten
1 tsp. salt	1 cup fresh cranberries,
1/2 tsp. baking soda	coarsely chopped
1/2 cup chopped pecans or	1/2 cup chopped pecans or
1/4 cup shortening	walnuts

Sift together the flour, sugar, baking powder, salt, and baking soda. Cut in the shortening with a pastry blender or a large fork. Combine the orange peel, orange juice, and egg. Add to the dry ingredients, mixing just to moisten. Fold in the cranberries and the chopped nuts.

Turn into a buttered 9- by 5- by 3-in. loaf pan. Bake in a preheated 350°F oven one hour. Cool. Wrap and store overnight before serving. **Makes one loaf.**

Blueberry muffins are especially delicious made with freshly picked berries.

Blueberry Muffins

The extra butter and the addition of cinnamon in this recipe make these muffins especially delicious. They are best served hot with plenty of sweet butter.

2 cups sifted all-purpose flour	3/4 tsp. cinnamon
4 tsp. baking powder	1 cup milk
3 tbsp. sugar	1 egg, well beaten
1/4 tsp. salt	1/2 cup melted butter
	1 cup blueberries

Combine the sifted flour, baking powder, sugar, salt, and cinnamon, and sift again. Mix the milk, egg, melted butter, and add to the dry ingredients all at once. Stir only enough to moisten—a few swift strokes. The batter should be lumpy. Do not overmix or the muffins will be tough. Fold in the blueberries.

Butter muffin tins (bottoms only, not the sides), and fill each two-thirds full. Bake immediately in a preheated 400°F oven 25 minutes or until golden. **Makes 12 muffins.**

Tortillas

A favorite bread of the Southwest, the tortilla is often eaten plain, but it is also used as the foundation for many of the best-known Tex-Mex dishes, such as tacos, enchiladas, tostados, burritos, and nachos. Tortillas can also be made with wheat flour.

2 1/3 cups masa harina	1 tsp. salt
(corn flour)	1 1/2 cups warm water

Mix the *masa harina* (available in specialty stores, Latin and Mexican groceries, and some supermarkets) with the salt. Add 1 cup warm water gradually, stirring constantly. Knead the dough on a lightly floured board, adding enough of the remaining water by tablespoonfuls until the dough becomes smooth and firm and no longer sticks to the fingers.

Divide the dough into 12 equal portions and form these into balls. Place the balls between sheets of oiled paper and press them into thin, round pancakes about 5 in. in diameter. They can be pressed with a rolling pin, or use a tortilla press—a clamshell-like device with two metal plates that automatically flattens the balls of dough into tortillas.

Cook one tortilla at a time on a moderately hot ungreased griddle or skillet, about two minutes on each side, turning once with a spatula when the bottom is very lightly browned. As the tortillas are cooked, stack them on a large sheet of aluminum foil. When all are done, wrap the foil over the stack and warm the tortillas in a 300°F oven five minutes. **Makes 12 tortillas.**

Johnnycakes

Some authorities believe that this thin, flat bread was originally called journey cake because it was the staple food of circuit riders as they preached the Gospel from settlement to settlement.

1 cup stone-ground	1 cup boiling water
white cornmeal	1 tbsp. sugar (optional)
1 tsp. salt	1/4-1/2 cup milk
1 tbsp. butter	Bacon drippings

Combine the cornmeal, salt, butter, boiling water (and sugar if desired) in a small bowl. Add the milk and mix well. Batter should be a little thicker than pancake batter.

Drop the batter by tablespoons onto a hot griddle well greased with bacon drippings. Press the batter to about 1/2-in. thickness using a greased pancake turner. Cook a few at a time over moderate heat until brown and crisp, about 5 to 10 minutes. Turn and brown on the other side 5 to 10 minutes. If the batter gets too thick before all the cakes are done, just add a few tablespoons of warm water to it. Serve very hot with butter and maple syrup or molasses. **Makes about four servings.**

Green Pepper and Cheddar Cornbread

Records show that as early as 1612 Indians were making a type of corn cake that the white settlers called cornpone—the origin of the cornbreads we make today.

1 cup finely chopped	4 tsp. double-acting
green pepper	baking powder
1/2 cup chopped onion	1 stick (1/2 cup) butter, melted
3 tbsp. butter	2 eggs, well beaten
1 cup yellow cornmeal	1/4 lb. sharp Cheddar cheese,
1/2 tsp. salt	very finely diced
1 cup plain yogurt	

Cook the green pepper and onion in the 3 tbsp. of butter over moderate heat until tender—about 10 minutes, stirring occasionally. Transfer to a mixing bowl and add the remaining ingredients. Mix just until moistened. Pour into a well-buttered 8-in.-square baking dish. Bake in a preheated 350°F oven 25 to 30 minutes or until a toothpick or cake tester inserted in the center of the bread comes out clean. Cut into squares. Serve very hot. **Makes nine servings.**

Regional Cooking

American Cuisine: The Splendid Variety Of a Bountiful Land

America's rich and complex culinary heritage reflects the many nationalities and races that settled the continent, from the American Indians, who taught the colonists how to grow and cook the strange foods of the New World, to the waves of immigrants who brought with them their own unique cultural traditions.

The evolution of New England cooking is typical: an established European tradition adapted to the needs and resources of a new land. Foods unknown to the settlers—cranberries, turkey, pumpkin, maple syrup, and corn—were put to good use by early New England cooks. The ocean's bounty was also a key factor in the evolution of the local cuisine. Clams, lobsters, scallops, oysters, and cod, available in seemingly limitless profusion, were quickly integrated into the Yankee menu. The heavy physical demands of a settler's life and the rugged New England winters were important influences, combining to place a premium on simple, hearty, energy-giving foods, such as potatoes, beans, molasses, milk, chicken, lamb, and beef.

In addition to New England, five other major American culinary regions can be identified: the Middle Atlantic, the Plains and Midwest, the Old South, the Southwest, and the Mountain and Pacific states. Each has local subdivisions, some with cooking styles that are so narrowly specialized as to be unique—Creole cooking, for example, or Pennsylvania Dutch, or the hundreds of different ethnic cuisines. The recipes included are a sampling of what the nation has to offer. All of them are traditional, all are based on locally grown foods, all have historical interest, and, of course, all are pleasing to the palate.

One of the most appetizing and most convivial American traditions is the New England clambake.

An Old-fashioned New England Clambake

The American custom of steaming clams over hot stones covered with seaweed originated with the Indians. The early white settlers quickly picked up the technique and embellished their clambakes with other types of shellfish as well. Modern clambakes are prepared much as they were in colonial times, but New Englanders now include such foods as corn, potatoes, and chicken in the feast.

4 bushels seaweed, preferably rock seaweed	5 lb. small white onions
	40 ears fresh corn
5 (2 1/2- to 3-lb.) chickens, quartered	20 dozen steamers or cherrystone clams, well scrubbed
Salt and pepper	
Paprika or herbs, such as thyme or rosemary	20 (1 1/2-lb.) lobsters
	2 lb. butter, melted

Setting up in advance. Collect sufficient driftwood to keep a fire going for three hours. Search for large, smooth rocks about 1 ft. in diameter. You will need enough to line a 4-ft.-wide pit with two layers of rocks. Gather 4 bushels of rock seaweed. It is best to soak the seaweed in seawater 45 minutes before the bake begins. Have on hand two tarpaulins large enough to cover the food and to extend over the edges of the pit by 1 ft.

Digging the pit and building the fire. Start preparations about five hours before time to serve. Dig a saucer-shaped pit about 1 ft. deep and 4 ft. wide. Line it with two layers of stones. Build up the wood directly on top of the stones to a height of several feet. Keep feeding the fire until it is time to assemble the clambake.

Preparing the food. The chicken will have more flavor if it is seasoned and partially cooked before adding it to the clambake. Rub the chicken with salt, pepper, and either paprika or herbs, such as thyme or rosemary. Next, set up a charcoal fire and grill the chicken over it until the chicken is slightly charred on both sides. Let the chicken cool; it will finish cooking later. If you do not wish to partially cook the chicken, just rub it with salt and pepper. Tie the cooled chicken into cheesecloth bundles, four pieces of chicken to the bundle.

Peel the onions and tie them in two bundles of cheesecloth. Husk the corn, removing all but the last two or three layers. Pull these layers back far enough to remove the silks, and then replace them to cover the corn kernels completely. Tie the clams in cheesecloth, putting about 12 in each bundle.

Assembling the clambake. After the fire has burned for about three hours, rake the burning wood and coals from the stones. Working quickly to keep the stones from cooling, place about 6-in. of wet seaweed on top of the stones. Cover with a large, damp bed sheet or a large piece of cheesecloth.

Put the clams around the perimeter of the sheet, then add the chicken in a circle next to the clams. Distribute the corn inside this circle and on top of the food. Place the onions and lobsters on top of everything and cover with a second layer of seaweed.

Cover the mound with another damp bed sheet or cheese cloth, then with the two wet tarpaulins. Shovel about 5 in. of sand over the tarpaulins and weigh them down around the edges with heavy rocks.

Steam the food for one to two hours. The length of cooking time will depend upon the number of rocks and how hot they are. To test, carefully lift a corner of the tarpaulin so that no sand will get in the pit. If the clams have opened, the food is done.

Serving. Remove the sand from the tarpaulin, then remove the tarpaulin, and finally take off the bed sheet. Pour melted butter into individual cups for the guests. Eat the clams as a first course, then the lobster, chicken, corn, and onions. Serve cold beer and soft drinks, and watermelon for dessert. ***Makes 20 servings***.

Fourth of July Salmon With Egg Sauce

Salmon with egg sauce on the Fourth of July has been a delicious tradition for many years. Midsummer is the time that Atlantic salmon begin to run and that new potatoes and peas are ready for harvest.

	EGG SAUCE
4 qt. water	1 stick butter
1 small onion, peeled and chopped	1/2 cup flour
1 stalk celery, chopped	1 qt. milk
1 large bay leaf	1 tsp. salt
1/2 tsp. black peppercorns, crushed	1/2 tsp. white pepper
1 tbsp. salt	8 hard-cooked egg
3 slices lemon	yolks, crumbled
1 (6–7 lb.) fresh salmon, cleaned	
with head and tail left on,	
or 1 (6–7 lb.) piece of fresh salmon	

Bring the water, onion, celery, bay leaf, peppercorns, salt, and lemon slices to a boil in a large saucepan. Reduce the heat and simmer 15 minutes. Strain the liquid into a 12-qt. fish poacher, large oval kettle, or a large, deep roasting pan.

Rinse a double thickness of cheesecloth in cold water and wrap the salmon in it, leaving enough cheesecloth at each end to use as handles for lifting the fish out of the liquid.

Measure the fish at its thickest point. Lower the fish into the liquid, cover, and simmer 10 minutes per measured inch.

While the fish is poaching, make the egg sauce. Melt the butter in a large saucepan. Stir in the flour. Remove from heat, then gradually add the milk, stirring constantly. Return to the heat and cook, while continuing to stir constantly until the sauce thickens. Stir in the salt and pepper. Reduce the heat and simmer 10 minutes, stirring occasionally. Remove from the heat and gently stir in the hard-cooked egg yolks.

Lift the fish from the liquid and lay it on a platter. Open the cheesecloth and carefully peel away the skin and fat, and scrape off any brownish bits of flesh. Using the cheesecloth, turn the salmon over on the other side and remove the skin and fat. Reheat the egg sauce. Serve the sauce separately or pour it over the salmon. The salmon is traditionally served with fresh green peas and boiled new potatoes. *Makes 8 to 10 servings.*

New England Boiled Dinner

This excellent beef and vegetable dish has been popular in New England for 250 years. It was a one-pot meal ideal for fireplace cookery, since it could be left to simmer unattended for hours while the colonial housewife performed other duties in and around the house.

5 lb. corned beef brisket	8 medium potatoes, peeled
1 large rutabaga, peeled and cut into 6 pieces	1 medium green cabbage, cut into 8 wedges
8 onions of uniform size, peeled	10 beets of uniform size
8 carrots, scraped	Cider vinegar
	Mustard

Rinse the meat. Place it in an 8-qt. pot and cover with cold water. Bring to a boil and skim off material that collects on the top of the

New England Boiled Dinner, a hearty old-time Yankee classic.

water; then cover and simmer three to four hours until the meat is tender. Remove the meat from the pot.

About 1 1/4 hours before time to serve, start cooking the vegetables. As each vegetable is added, turn up the heat and bring the liquid quickly to a simmer. Add the rutabaga to the pot. After 25 minutes add the onions and carrots. Cook 25 minutes more and add the potatoes and cabbage. Continue to simmer 20 more minutes, then add the meat to reheat five minutes. Add water to the pot if necessary to keep the vegetables covered. If any of the vegetables are done before the allotted times, carefully remove them from the pot and return them to the liquid to reheat later with the meat.

Cook the beets separately in salted water, then peel. Start them about 1 to 1 1/2 hours before serving time.

Remove the brisket from the pot and slice across the grain. Arrange the meat and vegetables on a platter. Sprinkle the beets with vinegar. Serve with mustard. *Makes six servings.*

Leftovers can be used for Red Flannel Hash: Cook 1/3 cup finely chopped onion in bacon fat five minutes. Add 3 cups diced leftover potatoes, 1 cup diced leftover beets, 2 cups finely chopped leftover beef, 1/2 tsp. salt, and 1/4 tsp. pepper. Toss to mix. Place the skillet under a broiler to brown. Spoon 2 tbsp. melted butter over hash. *Makes four servings.*

Boston Baked Beans

The Puritan religion restricted work on the Sabbath, which began at sundown on Saturday and lasted until sundown on Sunday. Baked beans were a salvation because they could be cooked on Saturday and served cold or reheated for breakfast or lunch the next day.

1 lb. dried peas or navy beans	1/2 tsp. pepper
1/3 cup molasses	1/4 lb. salt pork
1 tsp. dry mustard	1 medium onion, peeled
1 tsp. salt	

Wash and drain the beans. Place the beans in a large saucepan, cover with 2 in. of water, and bring to a boil. Boil two minutes. Remove from the heat, cover, and soak one hour.

Replace water to cover the beans. Simmer about one hour or just until the beans are done, adding more water as necessary to keep beans covered. Drain, reserving the liquid.

Put the beans in a 2-qt. bean pot or casserole. Combine the remaining ingredients and 1 cup of the bean liquid. Pour over the beans. Cut the salt pork into 1/2-in. slices up to but not through the rind. Bury the onion and pork in the beans. Add more bean liquid to cover the beans if necessary.

Bake covered at 250°F five hours, adding more liquid or water if necessary to keep the beans from drying out. Uncover for the last half hour of baking. *Makes six servings.*

Hartford Election Cake

This spicy cake, studded with fruit, was served in March at town meetings that often lasted all day. The recipe was first published in 1800 in Hartford, Connecticut, in the second edition of Amelia Simmons' *American Cookery*. Later the cake became known as Hartford Election Cake and was eaten while waiting for returns or to celebrate a victory. It was one of the first foods to be associated with American politics.

1 cup milk	1/4 tsp. mace
1 tbsp. sugar	1/4 tsp. nutmeg
2 packages active dry yeast	1 tsp. grated lemon rind
3 1/4 cups sifted all-purpose flour	1 cup seedless raisins
1/2 cup butter	GLAZE
1 cup sugar	1 cup confectioners' sugar, sifted
3 eggs	2 tbsp. lemon juice or orange juice
1 tsp. salt	
1 tsp. cinnamon	

Scald the milk. Add the sugar and let cool to lukewarm. Mix the yeast with the milk. Let stand five minutes. Gradually add 1 1/2 cups of flour, beating well after each addition. Cover the bowl with a kitchen towel or plastic wrap and let rise until doubled in bulk, about 45 minutes.

Cream the butter, then cream the sugar until light and fluffy. Add the eggs, one at a time, beating well after each addition. Beat in the yeast mixture.

Sift the remaining flour with the salt, spices, and lemon rind; mix in the raisins. Beat this gradually into the creamed mixture.

Pour the batter into a buttered 9-in. tube pan. Cover with a towel or plastic wrap and let the dough rise 1 to 1 1/2 hours until it has doubled in bulk.

Bake in a 350°F oven 35 minutes. Cool on a wire rack 10 minutes, then invert on another wire rack to cool completely. Transfer the cake to a plate.

Mix the confectioners' sugar and lemon or orange juice until smooth. Spread over the top of the cake, letting some of the glaze dribble down the sides. This cake is even better the next day. *Makes a 9-in. tube cake.*

Middle Atlantic

Outstanding among the food resources of the Middle Atlantic region are the dazzling varieties of fish and shellfish—ranging from striped bass, flounder, and riverspawning shad to oysters, crabs, and littleneck and cherrystone clams. The region is also famous for its dairy industry and truck farms, the latter producing enormous quantities of asparagus, tomatoes, potatoes, cauliflower, mushrooms, corn, and beets. Superior orchards and thriving livestock, poultry, and duckling industries round out the area's bounty. Prominent among the local cooking specialties are the famous dishes of the so-called Pennsylvania Dutch, descendants of immigrants from Switzerland and Germany who settled in the vicinity of Lancaster, Pennsylvania, in the 17th and 18th centuries. Their cooking is based on a wide range of locally produced foods, including chicken, pork, cabbage, potatoes, corn, buckwheat, and apples.

Philadelphia Pepper Pot

Some sources attribute this soup to the success of the American Revolution. At Valley Forge, during the severe winter of 1777–78, George Washington ordered his cook to prepare a good meal to cheer up his disheartened troops. With only tripe, peppercorns, and a few meager scraps, the cook improvised this soup and named it in honor of his hometown.

1 lb. honeycomb tripe	1 large carrot, chopped
1 veal shank, sawed into 2- or 3-in pieces	1 bay leaf
	2 springs parsley
2 qt. water	1/2 tsp. thyme
2 tbsp. butter	1 tsp. salt
1 large onion, peeled and coarsely chopped	1/2 tsp. pepper
	1/2 tsp. crushed red pepper
1/2 cup celery, chopped	3 medium potatoes, peeled
1 green pepper, chopped	and cut into 1/2-in. cubes

Wash the tripe. Place it and the veal shank into a 4-qt. pot. Add the water and bring to a boil, skimming off any scum that forms. Cover and simmer two hours until the tripe is tender.

Strain the broth into a bowl. Measure and, if necessary, add enough water to make 6 cups of broth. When the meat is cool, cut the tripe into 1/2-in. squares. Strip the veal from the bone and then cut the meat into 1/2-in. pieces.

Melt the butter in the same pot and cook the vegetables at high heat five minutes or until the vegetables are golden. Add the strained broth, bay leaf, parsley sprigs, thyme, salt, pepper, crushed red pepper, tripe, veal, and potatoes. Simmer one hour. Taste for seasoning, and add more salt and pepper if needed. Serve in large soup bowls. *Makes six servings*.

Maryland Crab Cakes, a treat from the Chesapeake Bay area.

Chicken Pot Pie

The Pennsylvania Dutch no doubt made this dish from an old hen instead of a young and more useful egg-laying bird. Squares of egg noodle dough called pot pies were poached along with the chicken. A crust as we know it today never covered the pie.

1 (3–3 1/2 lb) chicken	Chopped parsley
2 1/2 tsp. salt	4 hard-cooked eggs, cut into wedges
1/4 tsp. pepper	
1 stalk celery, chopped	DOUGH
1 medium onion, chopped	2 cups sifted all-purpose flour
1/2 tsp. saffron	2 eggs
4 medium potatoes, peeled and cut into 1/2-in. slices.	1/2 tsp. salt
	4–6 tbsp. water
4 stalks celery, thinly sliced	

Place the chicken in a 4-qt. pot or Dutch oven. Add the salt, pepper, celery, onion, and saffron. Add water to almost cover the chicken. Bring to a boil, reduce the heat, cover, and simmer about one hour or until the chicken is tender. Do not overcook.

Remove the chicken from the broth. Strain the broth, skim off as much fat as possible, and return the broth to the pot. When the chicken is cool, remove the meat from the bones and cut it into bite-size pieces. Discard the skin and bones.

To make the dough, place the flour into a mixing bowl. Make a well in the center of the flour and add the eggs and salt. Gradually work the eggs into the flour, adding only enough water to make a soft but not sticky dough. Knead five minutes. Cover the dough with a cloth and let it rest on the kneading board 30 minutes.

Divide the dough in half. Roll out each half as thinly as possible into a 15-in. square and cut each square into 2-in. squares with a sharp knife or pastry wheel.

Add the potatoes and celery to the broth. Simmer 25 minutes until the vegetables are tender. Taste the broth and add more salt or pepper if needed. Add the chicken pieces and bring to a boil. Slide the squares of dough into the broth, a few at a time, pushing them down gently. Cover with a tight-fitting lid and simmer 20 minutes.

Ladle the pot pie into large soup bowls and garnish with chopped parsley and the wedges of hard-cooked eggs. *Makes six to eight servings*.

Maryland Crab Cakes

Crabmeat dishes have been a specialty of Maryland and other areas bordering the seafood-rich Chesapeake Bay since the 18th century. The key to making good crab cakes is to handle the mixture lightly when shaping it into cakes and to go easy on the bread crumbs.

1 lb. fresh cooked lump or backfin crabmeat	1/2 tsp. salt
	1/4 tsp. pepper
2 tbsp. finely chopped parsley	1 cup soft, fresh bread crumbs
1 tbsp. minced onion	
1 tsp. spicy brown mustard	1 egg, slightly beaten
1 tsp. Worcestershire sauce	4 tbsp. butter

Pick over the crabmeat and remove all bits of shell. Mix the crabmeat with the remaining ingredients except the butter. Shape into eight cakes about 1 in. thick. Cover. Chill the cakes at least one hour.

Heat the butter in a heavy skillet with a nonstick coating. Cook the cakes over moderate heat about three minutes on one side. Turn carefully and brown three minutes on other side. Makes *four servings*.

Apple Pandowdy

Could the word *dowdy*, usually applied to a person with a shabby appearance, have derived its meaning from this famous Pennsylvania Dutch dessert? When the dish is removed from the oven, the crust is dowdied, that is, stirred or pushed down into the apples, making the dessert look quite untidy indeed.

CRUST	1/4 tsp. cloves
1 1/2 cups sifted all-purpose flour	1/4 tsp. salt
	9 medium apples, peeled, cored, and cut into 1/2-in. slices
1/2 tsp. salt	
1/2 cup vegetable shortening	
3–4 tbsp. cold water	1/2 cup light molasses
FILLING	4 tbsp. butter
1 tsp. cinnamon	1 cup heavy cream, whipped, or vanilla ice cream
1/4 tsp. nutmeg	

To make the crust, sift the flour with the salt into a bowl. Cut in the shortening with a pastry blender or two knives until the mixture resembles cornmeal. Add only enough cold water to hold the dough together. Form the dough into a ball, wrap it in wax paper, and chill one hour.

To make the filling, mix the spices and salt in a large bowl. Add the apple slices and toss to coat them with the spices. Place the apples in a buttered 13- by 9- by 2-in. baking dish, then pour the molasses over them and dot the apples with butter.

Roll out the pastry to a 13- by 9-in. rectangle and place on top of the apples. Bake at 400°F for 10 minutes. Reduce the heat to 325°F and bake 30 minutes more. Break the crust with a spoon and push a few of the sections down into the apples. Serve warm with unsweetened whipped cream or vanilla ice cream. *Makes six to eight servings*.

Plains and Midwest

Corn, wheat, and other grains play key roles in the cuisine of the central United States, the breadbasket not only of America but of the world. Beef and pork—animals largely sustained on grain and grain by-products—are also important in the region's cooking. So too are freshwater fish from the Great Lakes and the Mississippi River watershed. Ducks, geese, pheasants, and deer rank high among the wild game. Also important are the dairy, poultry, and egg industries as well as the large apple, peach, and cherry orchards.

Königsberger Klopse

Our German heritage in the Midwest rewards us with this different but delectable recipe for meatballs. The meat is poached—not browned in fat—and is served with a slightly tart lemon-caper sauce.

MEATBALLS	POACHING LIQUID
1 medium onion, finely chopped	2 qt. water
2 tbsp. butter	1 medium onion, peeled and sliced
1/2 lb. ground beef	1 bay leaf
1/2 lb. ground veal	1 tsp. salt
1/2 lb. ground pork	SAUCE
4 anchovy fillets, mashed	4 tbsp. butter
1 egg, slightly beaten	4 tbsp. flour
1 cup soft, fresh bread crumbs	1–2 tbsp. lemon juice
1/4 cup milk	2 tbsp. capers, drained
1/4 tsp. salt	1 egg yolk, well beaten
1/4 tsp. pepper	1 tbsp. heavy cream

Cook the onion in the butter about 10 minutes until soft. Mix in the remaining meatball ingredients and gently shape the mixture into 2-in. balls.

Bring the 2 qt. of water, onion, bay leaf, and salt to a boil. Boil 10 minutes, then add the meatballs and simmer uncovered 20 minutes or until the balls rise to the surface. Remove the meatballs to a platter, cover them with aluminum foil, and keep warm in a 250°F oven. Strain the liquid and reserve 2 cups for making the sauce.

To make the sauce, heat the butter in the skillet, add the flour, and cook slowly one minute. Remove the skillet from the heat. Gradually stir in the reserved liquid and cook, stirring until the sauce thickens. Add the lemon juice and capers. Cook slowly for five minutes.

In a small bowl mix the egg yolk with the heavy cream. Stir a few tablespoons of the hot poaching liquid into the egg mixture. Return this to the hot liquid.

Add the meatballs, cover, and simmer about five minutes to cook the egg yolk. Do not boil. *Makes six servings.*

Japanese Persimmons are delicious made into a pudding.

Pheasant in Sour Cream

Many of our pioneers owed their survival to the abundance of game in America. Surprisingly, however, these settlers never saw or ate the majestic pheasant until a large shipment of them was brought from China in 1880.

2 pheasants, about 2 1/2 lb. each, cut into serving pieces	4 tbsp. bacon drippings
2/3 cup flour	1 cup chopped onions
2 tsp. salt	1 cup finely diced celery
1/2 tsp. pepper	1 cup sour cream
2 tsp. paprika	1 cup light cream
	Lemon juice

Shake the pheasant in a paper bag with the flour, salt, pepper, and paprika. Shake off the excess flour from the pheasant.

Heat the bacon drippings in a skillet, and brown a few pieces of the pheasant at a time on both sides. As they brown, transfer them to a baking dish just large enough to hold the pieces in one layer.

In the same skillet cook the onions and celery five minutes. Cover the pheasant with these vegetables. Mix the sour cream and light cream together and pour over the pheasant. Cover the dish with aluminum foil and bake in a 275°F oven 1 to 1 1/2 hours until tender. Skim off the fat and add a few drops of lemon juice to the sauce to taste. *Makes six servings.*

Scalloped Corn

The Indians taught the Pilgrims how to cultivate corn, a grain unknown in the Old World. They would first gird any trees in the planting area by removing a strip of bark from around the circumference of the trunk. The trees soon died, permitting the sun's rays to reach the ground where the corn seeds were planted.

1/3 cup finely chopped onion	2 large eggs, lightly beaten
1/2 cup chopped green pepper	10 saltine crackers, coarsely crumbled
2 tbsp. butter	3/4 tsp. salt
2 cups fresh corn kernels	1/4 tsp. pepper
1 cup milk	
1 cup light cream	

In a small skillet cook the onion and green pepper in the butter over moderate heat 10 minutes. Combine with the remaining ingredients. Pour into a buttered 1 1/2-qt. baking dish. Place the dish in a large pan and pour in enough hot water to come halfway up the sides of the baking dish. Bake at 350°F for 45 minutes, then test by inserting a knife in the center. If the knife comes out clean, the dish is done. *Makes six servings.*

Wilted Lettuce Salad

This unusual salad, tossed with a dressing that is hot rather than cold, deserves its long-standing popularity not only because of its good taste but also because of its practicality. Almost any leafy green can be used, few ingredients are needed to make the dressing, and during the pioneer days it could be rustled up in minutes in a covered wagon along the trail.

2 heads leaf or Boston lettuce	1 tsbp. sugar
6 slices bacon, cut into pieces	1 tsp. salt
6 scallions, thinly sliced	1/4 tsp. pepper
4–6 tbsp. cider vinegar	

Wash, drain, and dry the lettuce leaves and tear them into bite-size pieces. Cook the bacon until crisp. Drain the bacon on paper towels and reserve.

Add the remaining ingredients to the bacon drippings and simmer until the sugar has dissolved. Pour this dressing over the lettuce in a large salad bowl and toss lightly. Sprinkle the bacon bits over the salad and serve at once. *Makes four servings.*

Persimmon Pudding

Like tomatoes, persimmons were not greatly appreciated in the early part of America's history. In fact, they did not achieve even their present modest popularity until the Japanese persimmon was introduced by Commodore Matthew Perry. If you have never enjoyed persimmons, this dish may change your mind.

2 lb. wild or Japanese persimmons	2 tsp. soda
2 cups sugar	1 tsp. cinnamon
8 tbsp. butter, melted	1 tsp. ginger
1 cup seedless raisins	1/2 tsp. nutmeg
2 cups sifted all-purpose flour	1 cup milk
1/4 tsp. salt	4 tsp. vanilla
	1 cup heavy cream, whipped

Wash, peel, and remove the seeds from the persimmons. Puree the fruit through a sieve or use a blender or food processor. Stir in the sugar, melted butter, and raisins.

Sift together the flour, salt, soda, and spices. Add the flour alternately with the milk and vanilla. Spread the batter evenly in a buttered 2-qt. casserole and bake in a 350°F oven 50 minutes or until a toothpick inserted in the center comes out clean. Top with whipped cream and serve hot. *Makes nine servings.*

Apricots may be substituted for persimmons. Drain two 17-oz. cans of apricot halves and puree them.

The Old South

The Old South has a great variety of culinary patterns, but generally much of the cooking is based on pork and corn, especially white corn, cornmeal, and grits. All parts of the pig are used, from the snout to the tail. Bacon, sausages, pork chops, and Smithfield and country hams are popular throughout the region. The favorite greens—collards and turnip greens—are flavored with fatback or country ham bone. Chicken, especially fried chicken, and a myriad of seafoods grace many southern tables, along with an assortment of hot breads and such vegetables as sweet potatoes, black-eyed peas, corn on the cob, butter beans, okra, tomatoes, and cucumbers. Pecans and peanuts are important crops in addition to peaches, canteloupes, watermelons, and citrus fruits. Among the famous Creole dishes of Louisiana, bouillabaisse, gumbo, and jambalaya are perhaps the best known. Some of the meats, vegetables, and spices used in these dishes are seafood (including crayfish), ham, bacon, onions, green peppers, okra, tomatoes, rice, garlic, and filé powder, a seasoning and thickening agent produced from dried young sassafras leaves.

She-Crab Soup

This renowned delicacy from Charleston, South Carolina, has become a favorite throughout the South. If female crabs with roe are not available, use fresh blue crabs, and substitute hard-cooked egg yolks for the roe.

12 live blue she-crabs (female crabs with roe) or 1 1/2 cups fresh cooked lump or backfin crabmeat and 2 hard-cooked egg yolks, crumbled	1 tbsp. flour
	2 cups milk
	2 cups light or heavy cream
	Dash of Worcestershire sauce
	Cayenne pepper
	3/4 tsp. salt
2 tbsp. butter	1 tbsp. dry sherry
1/4 cup minced onion	Chopped parsley

Cover the she-crabs in salted water and simmer 15 minutes. Cool and remove the crabmeat or use the lump or backfin crabmeat, but be sure to pick over the crabmeat carefully in order to remove as much shell and cartilage as possible.

Melt the butter in a saucepan and cook the onion slowly for five minutes. Stir in the flour and cook one minute. Remove from heat and gradually add the milk, stirring constantly. Add the cream, crabmeat and roe, or the lump or backfin crabmeat, the Worcestershire sauce, a few grains of cayenne pepper, and salt to taste. Simmer the soup 15 minutes, stirring occasionally. Stir in the sherry and crumbled eggs if lump or backfin crabmeat was used. Ladle the soup into individual bowls and sprinkle with chopped parsley. **Makes four servings**.

Roast Pork With Sweet Potatoes and Apples. Each ingredient in this dish sets off and emphasizes the flavor of the others.

Roast Pork With Sweet Potatoes and Apples

For many years the South has enjoyed a well-deserved reputation for its delicious pork dishes, particularly barbecued pork and country ham. Records show that pork and bacon were shipped from Virginia to New England as early as 1639, and it is reported that Queen Victoria once placed an order for six hams a week to be sent to her from Smithfield, Virginia. A succulent roast pork with sweet potatoes and apples is a hallmark of the very best in southern cookery.

1 (5-lb.) Pork loin	1/3 cup light brown sugar
1 tsp. salt	1 tsp. cinnamon
1/2 tsp. pepper	1/4 tsp. nutmeg
2 lb. sweet potatoes, peeled and cut into 1/2-in. slices	1 tbsp. flour
	1 cup beef broth
1 1/2 lb. apples, peeled, cored, and cut into 1/4-in rings	

Have the butcher saw lengthwise through the backbone of the loin and tie the bone back on the roast in several places. The bone will add flavor to the meat, and the meat will be easier to cut when the bone is removed before serving.

Preheat the oven to 350°F. Rub the meat all over with the salt and pepper. Insert a meat thermometer in the thickest part of the meat but not touching the bone or fat. Roast about 30 minutes per pound or until the thermometer reaches 170°F.

While the pork is roasting, boil the sliced sweet potatoes in salted water until tender but not falling apart. Drain.

Remove the pork from oven 30 minutes before it is done, and skim off most of the fat from the roasting pan, leaving the pork drippings behind. Place the cooked sweet potatoes and the raw apple rings around the pork. Mix the brown sugar and spices, and sprinkle them over the apples and sweet potatoes. Spoon the reserved pork fat over the apples and sweet potatoes.

Return the pork to the oven and bake about 30 minutes until the apples are tender. Place the pork on a platter and surround with the sweet potatoes and apples. Keep warm.

Again skim off most of the fat from the roasting pan, leaving the pork drippings behind. Add the flour to the contents of the pan. Cook over low heat on top of stove two minutes, stirring constantly. Remove the pan from the heat and gradually add the beef broth, stirring constantly until the gravy is well blended. Return gravy to the heat and cook, stirring until it thickens. Serve gravy separately. **Makes six servings**.

Baked Grits With Cheese and Garlic

Hominy, like so many other traditional American dishes, is attributed to the American Indian. It was an important staple of the early settlers and is still prepared in much the same way: by soaking corn in a weak lye solution to dissolve the hulls and then washing and cooking the corn until tender. Grits are simply coarsely ground dry hominy.

The following method of baking grits with cheese and garlic may be a pleasant revelation to those who have an aversion to the popular boiled grits so often served for breakfast in the South.

1 cup quick-cooking grits	1/2 cup chopped scallions, including green parts
1 1/2 cups sharp, grated Cheddar cheese	2 eggs, slightly beaten
1 tsp. minced garlic	3/4 cup milk
4 tbsp. butter, melted	

Cook the grits according to the package directions. Stir in the cheese, garlic, butter, and chopped scallions. Pour the mixture into a buttered 2-qt. casserole, and allow to cool. Preheat oven to 375°F. Mix the eggs and milk and pour over the grits. Bake one hour. **Makes six servings**.

Barbecued Chicken

As early as 1607 colonists were raising chickens for meat, eggs, and mattress feathers as well. It is believed that chicken was one of the dishes served to Lafayette at Mount Vernon. Most people find this old-fashioned, slightly tart barbecue sauce for chicken to be a welcome change from the heavy tomato-based sauces so frequently used today.

1/2 tsp. salt	1 medium onion, finely
1 (3-lb.) chicken, cut into	chopped
serving pieces, or 3 lb.	1/2 cup chicken stock
chicken parts, such as	1/3 cup white vinegar
legs and thighs	1 tbsp. sugar
SAUCE	1 tbsp. Worcestershire sauce
4 tbsp. butter	1 1/2 tsp. crushed red pepper
1 garlic clove, minced	1 tsp. paprika

Salt the chicken pieces and place them in a baking dish large enough to hold them in one layer. In a saucepan add the remaining ingredients and bring to a boil. Boil one minute. Pour the sauce over the chicken and bake uncovered at 350°F for 1 1/2 hours, basting occasionally with the sauce.

Remove the chicken from the baking dish and place it on a hot platter. Tilt the casserole, skim off the fat from the sauce, and serve the sauce separately. **Makes four servings**.

Squash and Onion Casserole

The mild-flavored yellow squash can be transformed into an especially savory vegetable when cooked with its perfect companion, the lowly onion.

2 lb. yellow squash	2 eggs, slightly beaten
3 medium onions, chopped	TOPPING
1/2 cup water	1/2 cup finely crumbled
1 tsp. salt	saltine crackers
1/4 tsp. pepper	2 tbsp. butter
2 tbsp. bacon drippings or	
butter, melted	

Scrub the squash with a vegetable brush and trim the ends, but do not peel. Dice the squash into 1/2-in. pieces. Place the squash, onions, water, and salt into a large saucepan. Cover and cook about 20 minutes until the squash is tender. Drain well, reserving 1/2 cup of the squash liquid.

Return the squash to the saucepan. Mash the squash lightly with a fork. Mix in the reserved liquid, pepper, bacon drippings or butter, and eggs. Spoon the mixture into a buttered rectangular 1 1/2-qt. baking dish.

For the topping scatter the 1/2 cup of crumbled crackers evenly over the top. Cut the butter into small pieces and distribute them evenly over the cracker crumbs.

Bake in a 350°F oven 25 minutes. If the top has not browned slightly, place the dish under the broiler, about 3 or 4 inches from the flame, for a few minutes. Watch carefully to make sure the crackers do not burn. **Makes six servings**.

Jambalaya

Historians disagree over the origin of this Creole classic. Some believe the recipe was introduced to New Orleans by the Spanish during the late 1700s. Others hold that it dates back to the Acadians of Nova Scotia who settled in Louisiana after the 1750s. In either case, the name derives from the word for ham: *jamón* in Spanish, *jambon* in French.

Jambalaya is an ideal dish for a buffet because much of it can be prepared in advance in large amounts and simply served.

1 (2 1/2-lb.) chicken, cut into	3 cups tomatoes, peeled,
serving pieces	seeded, and chopped
2 tbsp. bacon drippings or	2 cups chicken stock
butter	1 cup uncooked rice
2 medium onions, chopped	2 cloves garlic, minced
2 tbsp. flour	1 medium green pepper,
1 1/2 cups smoked country	diced
ham, cut into 1/2-in. by 2-in.	1/2 tsp. thyme
strips, or 6 highly seasoned	1 tsp. crushed red pepper
pork sausages, cut into	1 1/2 lb. raw shrimp, peeled
1-in. pieces	and deveined

Brown the chicken on all sides in the bacon drippings or butter in a large, heavy skillet. Remove the chicken to a platter. Cook the onions slowly in the fat remaining in the skillet five minutes. Stir in the flour and cook, stirring until the flour turns a light brown. Add the ham or sausages, chicken, and tomatoes. Cover tightly and simmer 20 minutes.

Add the chicken stock, rice, garlic, green pepper, and seasonings. Cover tightly and simmer 20 more minutes. Do not stir. Gently push the shrimp down into the rice and simmer two or three minutes until the shrimp turn pink. If the jambalaya seems dry when done, add a few tablespoons of hot chicken stock. **Makes eight servings**.

Key Lime Pie

The invention of condensed milk in the 1850s was a godsend to the South after the destruction caused by the Civil War. In Key West, Florida, sweetened canned milk became the inspiration for this famous pie. Because the traditional crust becomes soggy when refrigerated, many cooks today prefer to use a crumb crust.

CRUST	1 (14-oz.) can sweetened
1 1/3 cups graham	condensed milk
cracker crumbs	1/2 cup fresh Key lime juice or
6 tbsp. butter, melted	other fresh lime juice
FILLING	1 tsp. grated lime rind
3 egg yolks	1 cup heavy cream

Mix the crumbs and butter until the crumbs are evenly coated with the butter. Press the mixture against the sides and bottom of a 9-in. pie plate. Bake in a 350°F oven five minutes. Set aside to cool completely.

Key Lime Pie, a smooth dessert from southernmost Dixie.

To make the filling, beat the egg yolks with a rotary or electric beater until thick, about four minutes. Beat in the condensed milk, the lime juice, and grated lime rind. Pour into the cooled pie shell. Cover and refrigerate at least four hours.

When ready to serve, beat the heavy cream until stiff (do not sweeten it) and spoon over the pie. **Makes eight servings**.

Fried Peach Turnover

Fried fruit pies have been made in the South for almost two centuries. In the early 1800s these delicious, chewy turnovers were commonly called crab lanterns, but the reason for the unusual name remains a mystery.

2 cups all-purpose flour	1/3 cup milk
1/2 tsp. salt	2 1/2 cups peaches, peeled and
1 tsp. baking powder	finely chopped
1/2 cup sugar	1/4 tsp. cinnamon
6 tbsp. butter	Vegetable oil for deep frying
1 egg yolk, slightly beaten	Confectioners' sugar

Sift the flour, salt, baking powder, and 1 tbsp. of the sugar into a bowl. Cut in the butter with a pastry blender or two knives until the mixture resembles coarse crumbs. Mix the egg yolk with the milk and stir into the flour mixture, adding only enough to hold the dough together. Shape into a ball, wrap in wax paper, and chill one hour.

Meanwhile, cook the peaches with the cinnamon and remaining sugar in a saucepan five minutes, stirring occasionally. Cool.

Roll out the pastry on a lightly floured surface to a 1/16-in. thickness. Cut into 4 1/2-in. rounds. Place about 1 1/2 tbsp. of the peach mixture in the middle of each round. Moisten the edges of each round with cold water and fold in half. Press the edges together with the tines of a fork dipped in flour to seal.

Heat the lard or oil to 375°F. Deep fry a few turnovers at a time until light brown (about two to three minutes), turning once. As they brown, place them on a platter lined with paper towels to drain and keep warm in a 200°F oven. Sprinkle them with confectioners' sugar. Serve hot. **Makes about 16 turnovers**.

The Southwest

"Tex-Mex" dishes are the distinctive foods of this region: chili con carne, tortillas, tacos, enchiladas, frijoles refritos, and guacamole are particularly famous. Barbecues are also popular. The fare may range from barbecued quail and wild turkey to chicken, beef, pork, and kid (cabrito). Southern dishes, such as sweet potatoes, black-eyed peas, and pecan pie, are also popular.

Frijoles Refritos

It is interesting to note that refried beans are not refried at all but fried only once. According to a leading authority on Mexican cooking, the word *refrito* should be translated as "well fried" not "refried."

1 lb. dried pinto beans	2 cloves garlic, minced
1/2 lb. finely diced salt pork	1/2 cup bacon fat or lard
1/2 cup finely chopped onion	

Pick over the beans, removing any that are shriveled or discolored. Next, wash the beans, cover with water, and bring to a boil. Boil for two minutes, cover, turn off the heat, and let the beans soak one hour. Drain.

Add the salt pork, onion, and garlic. Cover with water and simmer the beans two to three hours until very soft, adding more water if necessary to keep the beans moist. Do not stir during this time. Add salt to taste. Drain.

Heat a tablespoon of bacon fat or lard in a large skillet. With the heat on add a heaping tablespoon of the beans and mash them with the back of a fork into the fat until the beans and fat are well blended. Continue to add fat and beans, mashing them together after each addition until all the fat and beans are used. The beans should be fried until they are crisp at the edges of the skillet, creamy inside. *Makes four servings.*

For variety stir in 1/2 cup finely diced Monterey Jack or mild Cheddar cheese, or 1/2 cup cooked tomatoes and 1 tsp. chili powder just before serving.

Huevos Rancheros

These country-style eggs provide an excellent change of pace for breakfast, and they make a fine brunch or lunch when accompanied with frijoles refritos.

3 cups peeled, chopped tomatoes	1/2 tsp. cumin
1 canned jalapeño pepper	2 tsp. chili powder
2 cloves garlic, minced	1/4 tsp. oregano
1 onion, finely chopped	Additional peanut oil for frying the tortillas and eggs
1 sweet green pepper, finely chopped	8 frozen or canned tortillas
1/4 cup peanut oil	8 eggs
1/2 tsp. salt	1 cup grated Monterey Jack cheese

Frijoles Refritos are the base for many "Tex-Mex" meals, such as these nachos.

Puree the tomatoes, jalapeño pepper, and garlic in a blender. Cook the onion and green pepper in the oil five minutes. Add the blended ingredients and the salt and cook over high heat five minutes. Add the cumin, chili powder, and oregano. Taste for salt and add more if necessary.

In a large skillet briefly fry a few tortillas at a time on both sides in a teaspoon of the oil. They should not become crisp. When all the tortillas are fried, cover them with aluminum foil and keep them warm in a 250°F oven.

Fry the eggs in the oil on one side only. Lay the tortillas on an ovenproof platter. Place each egg on a warm tortilla and cover with some of the sauce. Sprinkle the cheese over the eggs and place the eggs under a broiler for a few seconds until the cheese begins to melt. *Makes four servings.*

Chili con Carne

Some experts claim that this dish originated in Texas and is not Mexican at all. According to the story, a German in New Braunfels, Texas, developed chili powder in 1902 and later opened a chili con carne canning business in San Antonio.

3 lb. top round or rump of beef, cut into 1/2-in. cubes	2 tsp. salt
	4 tbsp. chili powder
1/4 cup bacon fat or corn oil	2 tsp. ground cumin
2 cups finely chopped onions	1 tsp. oregano
3 cloves garlic, finely chopped	1 tsp. crushed red pepper
	Beef stock

Dry the meat on paper towels. Heat half of the bacon fat or oil in a large skillet and brown the meat over high heat. Remove the meat from the skillet and set aside. Heat the remaining bacon fat or oil in the same skillet, and cook the onions and garlic over moderate heat five minutes. Remove the skillet from the heat and add the salt, spices, and browned meat. Add enough beef stock to cover the beef. Stir thoroughly.

Cover and simmer 1 to 1 1/2 hours or until the meat is tender. Stir the chili occasionally to prevent sticking. Carefully skim off the fat. *Makes six to eight servings.*

Tamale Pie

The ancient Aztecs made tamales by wrapping corn husks spread with cornmeal batter around a spicy filling, such as chopped chicken, beef, or pork; then they steamed the dish. This is a simpler version baked as a pie.

2 medium onions, chopped	1 1/2 cups fresh corn kernels
1 green pepper, cored, seeded, and chopped	1/2 cup sliced, pitted ripe olives
1 cup finely chopped celery	2 medium tomatoes, peeled and chopped
2 tbsp. bacon drippings	
1 lb. lean ground beef	CRUST
1 tbsp. chili powder	3/4 cup yellow cornmeal
1/4 tsp. oregano	1 tsp. salt
1 tsp. salt	2 cups water
2 cloves garlic, minced	2 tbsp. butter

Cook the onions, green pepper, and celery in the bacon drippings in a large skillet over moderate heat 10 minutes until the vegetables are tender. Add the meat and cook until the meat loses its red color. Drain off the fat. Stir in the remaining ingredients of the filling and simmer 30 minutes. Spoon the mixture into a buttered 2-qt. baking dish.

To make the crust, stir the cornmeal and salt into the water in a saucepan. Cook, stirring occasionally, about five minutes. Stir in the butter. Spoon this mixture over the meat mixture. Bake at 350°F for 40 minutes. *Makes six servings.*

Pollo en Salsa

The cumin used in this dish is one of the most distinctive seasonings in Southwest cookery and, along with chili, one of the most widely used. It is native to Egypt and other Mediterranean countries and was prized by the ancient Greeks, Persians, and Romans.

1 (3–3 1/2 lb.) chicken, cut into serving pieces	2 garlic cloves, minced
	1 tsp. cumin
2 tbsp. oil	1 tsp. chili powder
1 medium onion, finely chopped	2 medium, ripe tomatoes, peeled and chopped
1 medium green pepper, chopped	1/2 tsp. salt
	1/4 tsp. pepper

Brown the chicken in the oil. Remove the chicken from the skillet. Pour off all but 2 tbsp. of the fat from the skillet and cook the onion and green pepper five minutes. Stir in the garlic, spices, tomatoes, salt, and pepper. Return the chicken to the skillet and spoon the sauce over the chicken. Cover and simmer 45 minutes. *Makes four servings.*

Mountain and Pacific

From Alaska to California and from Wyoming to the Hawaiian Islands, almost every imaginable food resource can be found in this enormous region. Game abounds in the far north and in the Mountain States, ocean and freshwater fish are plentiful throughout the area, and Hawaii contributes its tropical specialties: pineapple, guava, papaya, coconut, and bananas.

Kalua Pua'a for Sixty

The Hawaiian luau was originally a religious ceremony created to appease and honor the gods. No women were allowed to take part in the ritual or to eat the foods served during it. King Liholiho changed this tradition in 1819 by sharing his food with the women. A feature of the traditional luau was kalua pua'a: *kalua* meaning "to bake in the ground" and *pua'a* meaning "pig."

1 pig, cleaned and drawn, about 90 lb. (dressed weight)	Several bushels of banana leaves or fresh corn husks
Coarse salt	60 bananas
Soy sauce	60 sweet potatoes
	60 fish fillets

Dig an imu (pit) the length of the pig and about 18 in. deep. Save the leftover dirt in a pile nearby for later use.

In the pit build a fire of hardwood logs, enough to last two to three hours. Place about two dozen smooth, porous stones in the fire. The stones should be about 3 to 4 in. in diameter.

Slit the hams so that the heat can penetrate, and slit through the underside of the skin and meat of the pig in several places to make room for the hot stones later. Thoroughly rub the pig inside and out with salt and soy sauce.

When the fire has burned down and the stones are red hot, place the pig on a square of chicken wire large enough to form a cradle for lowering the pig in the pit and for removing the pig later. Lift a few of the hot stones with tongs from the fire and insert a few in the throat cavity and in between the legs and body. Tie the front legs and the back legs together. Wrap the wire over the pig and fasten it to make a compact bundle.

Rake the embers from the pit and level the remaining stones in the pit. Line the pit with banana leaves or corn husks several inches deep. Put the pig on the leaves or husks, back down and feet up. Wrap each banana (unpeeled), sweet potato, and portion of fish in leaves, corn husks, or aluminum foil, and place them around the pig. Cover several inches thick with additional leaves or husks to form a steam-proof covering. Cover the mound with water-soaked burlap bags. The bags should reach to the ground so that they can be tucked in around the mound.

Shovel earth on the mound, starting from the bottom edges and building up the dirt to the top, making certain that no steam escapes. Dampen the dirt slightly to hold it in place.

Cioppino, a savory seafood stew popularized by San Franciscans.

After about four hours, carefully remove the dirt, burlap bags, and banana leaves or corn husks. Begin the luau with the fish, then follow with the sweet potatoes, bananas, and the pig, in that order. In keeping with tradition, all luau foods should be eaten with the fingers. ***Makes 60 servings.***

Cioppino

A specialty of San Francisco, this famous fish stew has been attributed to Portuguese, Italian, and French settlers, but no one really knows who started cooking cioppino or the origin of the name.

2 lb. striped bass, sea bass, or halibut fillets	3 cloves garlic, peeled and finely chopped
1 lb. raw shrimp	3–4 tomatoes, peeled and chopped
24 clams or mussels	
1 Dungeness crab or 1 (1 1/2-lb.) lobster	2 cups red wine
	1/4 tsp. oregano
2 medium onions, peeled and chopped	1/4 tsp. basil
	1 tsp. salt
1 green pepper, chopped	1/2 tsp. pepper
1/4 cup olive oil	1/2 cup chopped parsley
1/3 cup tomato puree	

Cut the fish fillets into serving pieces. Shell and devein the shrimp. Scrub the clams or mussels under cold running water. If mussels are used, cut off the tuft of hairs that cling to the shells with a sharp knife. Clean and crack the crab or cut the lobster into serving pieces and crack the claws.

Cook the onions and green pepper in the oil five minutes. Add the remaining ingredients except the seafood and parsley. Cover the pot and simmer 30 minutes.

In a large nonaluminum pot, arrange the fish, shrimp, and crab or lobster in layers. Pour the sauce over all, cover, and simmer 20 to 25 minutes until done. Add the clams or mussels and simmer five minutes or until the shells open. Serve in large soup bowls and sprinkle with parsley. ***Makes six servings.***

Roast Leg of Venison

Venison has been prized for centuries around the world. The Indians valued it for making pemmican, a dried meat concoction, and Europeans wrote home extolling the succulent venison dishes served in America.

1 (6–8 lb.) leg of venison	1/2 tsp. pepper
3 cloves garlic, finely chopped	4 tbsp. butter
1 tsp. dried rosemary or thyme	1 1/2 tbsp. flour
1 tsp. salt	1 cup beef stock
	1/2 cup Madeira or sherry

Rub the meat with the garlic, rosemary or thyme, salt, and pepper. Let the meat stand two hours. Rub in the butter. Place the venison on a rack in a shallow roasting pan. Insert a meat thermometer halfway down into the thickest part of the venison but not touching the bone.

Roast 15 minutes at 450°F, lower the heat to 350°F, and continue to roast until the thermometer registers 140°F for medium rare or 150°F for medium. Baste the roast every 20 minutes with the drippings in the bottom of the pan. Remove the venison to a serving platter and let it rest 10 to 12 minutes while preparing the sauce.

Remove all but 1 tbsp. of fat from the pan. Place the pan over low heat. Add the flour and cook, stirring one minute. Remove the pan from the heat and gradually add the stock and Madeira or sherry, stirring constantly with a wooden spoon to remove all the brown bits in the bottom of the pan. Return pan to the heat and cook until the sauce thickens. Taste for salt and pepper. Serve the sauce separately. ***Makes 10 to 12 servings.***

Blueberry Buckle

This delicious cakelike dessert comes from Alaska, where, despite the fierce climate, blueberries grow in wild profusion in fertile coastal valleys.

4 tbsp. butter	2 cups blueberries, rinsed
1/2 cup sugar	**CRUMB TOPPING**
1 egg	4 tbsp. butter
1 tsp. vanilla extract	1/2 cup sugar
1 cup all-purpose flour	1/2 tsp. cinnamon
1 tsp. baking powder	1/3 cup all-purpose flour
1/4 tsp. salt	Sweetened whipped cream
1/3 cup milk	

Cream the butter and sugar until light and fluffy. Beat in the egg and vanilla extract. Sift together the flour, baking powder, and salt. Mix the flour mixture alternately with the milk into the creamed mixture, beginning and ending with the dry ingredients. Pour the batter into a buttered 8-in.-square baking dish. Cover evenly with the blueberries.

To make the topping, combine the butter, sugar, cinnamon, and flour. With a pastry blender or two knives, cut in the batter until the mixture resembles coarse cornmeal. Sprinkle the topping over the blueberries. Bake 40 minutes in a 375°F oven. Serve warm with the whipped cream. ***Makes six to eight servings.***

Cooking With Wood

Hearth or Range: Food Tastes Better With Wood as Fuel

Until a century and a half ago almost all cooking in America was done over an open fire, a method of preparing food that dates back to prehistoric times when freshly killed game was roasted over campfires. As man became more civilized, the campfire was abandoned in favor of large indoor fireplaces, most of them spacious enough to roast a whole pig.

Fireplace equipment evolved gradually. Spits, for example, which were originally long poles or iron bars turned by hand, were replaced in richer households by multiple spits turned by clockwork. In some cases the power of hot air rising in the chimney was used to turn the spit, and a few were run by small dog-powered treadmills. Roasting on a spit is unique to open-fire cooking and cannot be duplicated on modern stoves. Properly done spit-roasted meat develops a flavorful crust but remains extremely tender and juicy inside.

The open fire is an amazingly versatile cooking device. One fire can be used to boil water, simmer a stew, bake pies, bake flat loaves of soda bread, and roast several pieces of meat. At the same time, sausages and hams can be hung nearby to be smoked slowly by the fire day after day.

With the coming of the Industrial Revolution, low-cost cooking ranges made of cast iron became available. Although they were being sold in America as early as 1830, housewives were slow to abandon the hearth in favor of the newfangled "iron monsters." This resistance to change stemmed partly from the fact that all the traditional recipes were devised for the fireplace. By the turn of the century, however, almost every household had a cast-iron range and the age of fireplace cooking was over.

Cast-iron pot hangs over a hot fire. Other traditional cookery implements include spider pots (with three legs and a handle), grills, pothooks, spatulas, ladles, kettles, Dutch ovens, and toasting racks.

Utensils for the fireplace

Most of the basic gear needed for fireplace cookery, including cast-iron ware and a small reflector oven, can be purchased from dealers specializing in camping goods. You can also make some of the equipment yourself, such as the spit shown on the next page or the portable reflector oven whose construction is described in *Metalworking* on pages 348 and 349. Fireplace cranes, vital accessories for full-scale fireplace cooking, are not easy to come by, but they are still being manufactured and advertisements for them appear in country magazines. All cast-iron ware should be seasoned before it is used. Wash and dry the implement, then grease it thoroughly with lard or vegetable oil and place it in a 300°F oven for two hours. Apply more oil or fat when the previous coating has been absorbed. Old or rusty ironware should be soaked and then scrubbed clean with steel wool before it is seasoned. The surface should be slightly shiny after seasoning. If it is not, season it again. Ironware should be reseasoned whenever it shows signs of rust.

Shelf brackets

Two important implements not widely available are the pothook (left) and fireplace trivet (center). The pothook is used to lift hot lids. The trivet is a three-legged stand for supporting a cook pot. Both items can easily be made by any ironworker. You can also put together a trivet from three sturdy shelf brackets and some nuts and bolts (right). For convenience, make several sizes.

The Cooking Fire

The key to a good cooking fire is establishing a bed of hot coals, or embers, that will produce a steady, long-lasting heat with almost no smoke. The quantity and quality of coals that a fire will produce is determined by the wood burned. Fruitwoods make the best cooking fuel and provide the most coals, but many hardwoods, including elm, ash, and oak, will yield sufficient coals and produce a good, steady fire. Hickory, another well-known hardwood, makes an excellent fire, but it should be remembered that hickory smoke tends to impart its own flavor to food. In contrast, the aromas that apple and cherry wood give off blend pleasantly with almost any dish.

Softwoods make few coals and burn rapidly. Many of them produce creosote, which not only makes pots hard to clean but can give food an unpleasant turpentine flavor. They are best reserved for use in starting fires. (For directions on starting a fire, see *Heating With Wood*, p.92.) Bellows are useful for reviving a fire.

The Basic Techniques of Fireplace Cookery

It takes time and experience to be able to judge the heat of a cooking fire and know when to add more fuel, when to improve the draft, and where to place the cooking pots so that the food will cook at the right temperature. With a good bed of coals, cooking times are roughly the same as for a modern stove, but timing is not precise and will depend on your fireplace, the wood you are using, and other variables. Cooking a full meal on an open fire should be planned in advance, particularly because only one pot can be hung over the center of the fire at one time. For safety, wear clothing of either wool or cotton (both of these materials are less flammable than synthetics, even when the synthetics have been treated).

Stews, soups, and boiling. To bring a pot to the boil, remove some coals from the center of the fire with a shovel or peel, and pile them under a trivet; then place the pot on top. For longer, slower cooking the back of the fire is an ideal place to simmer large pots of stew, soup, or stock, or even just to keep a supply of hot water. Once a pot is somewhat removed from the center of the fire, the heat is slow and gentle; this is one of the great bonuses of cooking over a fire.

Cooking in the ashes. Baked potatoes, chestnuts, and even fish can be cooked in the ashes at the side of the fire. Put them into gray ashes well in advance of mealtime and scatter hot coals over the top. Before serving, wipe the potatoes with a damp cloth to remove the ashes. Wrap fish in a double layer of foil.

Dutch oven. Made of cast iron, a Dutch oven can be used for any baking except yeast breads. First, place some crushed aluminum foil or a small, flat trivet in the bottom of the oven to keep food from scorching. Next, stand the oven near the fire to warm, then put an oven-proof dish containing the pie, cake, bread, casserole, or other food inside it. Put the lid on and suspend the oven from a crane over the fire, or position it to the side over some coals. Use a peel or fireplace shovel to pile hot coals on the lid. (Note that the lids of Dutch ovens are either concave or are turned up at the rim in order to hold the coals that are laid on them.) Replace the coals from time to time during cooking. The food must be checked periodically. Initially, the lid should be lifted every 15 minutes to see if the food is cooking too fast or too slowly; add or remove coals from the lid accordingly. When removing the lid, clear its edges of ash with a brush or shovel to keep ashes from getting in the food.

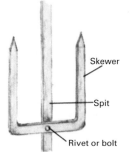

Roasting on the spit. Impale the meat lengthwise on a spit, making sure it is secured to the skewer. Next, place the spitted meat close to the fire to seize, or seal in, the juices. (Some cooks sprinkle a little flour over the roast to help seal it.) When the meat is light brown all over, move it further away to finish cooking more slowly. Small pieces of meat, such as chicken, are best cooked by a hot (fast) fire that seizes and cooks them simultaneously. Large roasts, stuffed poultry, and all pork should be cooked more gently by a cool (slow) fire. As the meat cooks, catch the fat and juices in a drip pan so that you can baste and enrich the roast with its own juice. To avoid a

grease fire, tilt the drip pan away from the fire so that hot coals cannot fall in. Keep some baking soda or dry chemical fire extinguisher close at hand.

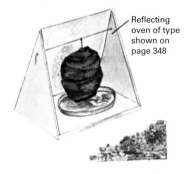

Reflecting ovens. Tin reflecting ovens provide a simple and effective method of baking or roasting without the use of large spits or Dutch ovens. Reflecting ovens can be used in front of small fires and campfires. Different models are available for either roasting or baking.

Frying and broiling. Frying is best done over a "clear" (vigorously burning) hardwood fire. A hanging griddle is good for frying, but if you cannot find one, you can support a cast-iron griddle on a rack or grating across the fire. The same technique can be used for simmering over gentle heat or broiling over hot coals.

A roasting spit you can make yourself

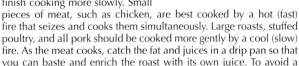

Fireplace spit is made from standard pipe fittings, hook bolts (commonly used for clotheslines), and brass lamp finials. Pipe lengths and diameters shown are for an average unit. For small fireplaces reduce pipe diameters by 1/4 in. To conceal screw holes in flanges, fill them with furnace

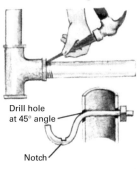

cement. Lock all threaded connections in position by hammering with a center punch at each pipe juncture at several points (top left). To keep hook bolts from turning, file or drill front mounting holes at 45° angles (bottom left). Note notch in hook to hold square spit rod (available from ironwork shops) in set position.

A dangle spit almost makes itself

Attach meat to strong cord and secure other end of cord to fireplace so that the meat hangs by the fire. If the cord is twisted from time to time, the meat will revolve slowly. A reflector, made from board faced with foil, helps the meat cook faster and more evenly.

265

Versatile Cookery On a Wood Stove

A wood cookstove demands time and patience–it may need encouragement, it may need damping, it may be hard to start. Some owners say that owning one is like having another child in the family. But once you have learned the ways of your particular stove, you can produce a remarkable variety of excellent dishes—as many as or more than with a gas or electric range.

Bread baked in the oven of a wood burner is considered by almost everyone who has tasted it to be better than bread prepared in a modern oven. Stews and casseroles develop their full flavor when simmered for hours on a wood range. Soups and stocks also benefit from the slow-cooking capability of wood stoves. (In the old days almost every housewife kept a stockpot toward the rear of her stove into which she put leftover scraps of meat and bones. The stock was later used as a base for soup or, with a few additions, made into a hearty casserole.)

Wood-burning kitchen stoves have recently come back into demand not only for their cooking abilities but also because they can double as heating stoves during the winter. Ornate cast-iron models, similar in design and appearance to those used in the 1890s, are still being manufactured, and you can occasionally find antique ones in working condition. New designs are also available, some with enamel finishes, others incorporating the latest advances in fuel-saving construction.

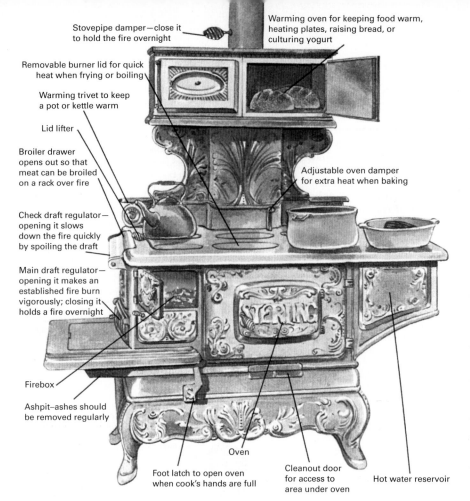

Stovepipe damper—close it to hold the fire overnight

Warming oven for keeping food warm, heating plates, raising bread, or culturing yogurt

Removable burner lid for quick heat when frying or boiling

Warming trivet to keep a pot or kettle warm

Lid lifter

Broiler drawer opens out so that meat can be broiled on a rack over fire

Adjustable oven damper for extra heat when baking

Check draft regulator— opening it slows down the fire quickly by spoiling the draft

Main draft regulator— opening it makes an established fire burn vigorously; closing it holds a fire overnight

Firebox

Ashpit–ashes should be removed regularly

Oven

Foot latch to open oven when cook's hands are full

Cleanout door for access to area under oven

Hot water reservoir

Housewife's pride of years gone by, the ornate cast-iron stove of the past is reappearing in kitchens around the country, not just for its cooking ability but for its decorative value and for the savings on heating bills as well. Modern wood-burning stoves differ little in performance from the older stoves—they only look different and weigh less (a woodburner like the one at the left tips the scales at about 500 lb.). At the peak of their popularity cast-iron ranges served as complete home energy centers, providing heat for cooking, hot water, and home heating. The model shown has a simple hot water reservoir; others had a water jacket inside the firebox: cold water entered at the bottom and hot water was piped out the top, much as a modern hot water system. Wood-burning stoves do have a few drawbacks, however. One well-known problem is that when the stove is in use it gets quite hot. The expression "slaving over a hot stove" had real meaning to a farmwife cooking on a woodburner during a summer heat wave.

Temperature Management: The Key to Successful Cooking

The heat of a wood-burning stove depends on how well the fire is established, what type of wood is being burned, and how the draft regulators are set.

It is important to have a good supply of dry wood close at hand as well as some slightly green wood for slowing down a fast-burning fire. Hardwoods burn slowly and throw off an even heat, making them good for cooking. Ash is particularly suitable, as it produces a hot, longlasting flame. Softwood should be used only for kindling and building a quick, hot fire.

A series of dampers and draft regulators permit rapid and accurate heat adjustments. Most stoves have two dampers and two draft regulators. The oven damper, when open, allows hot air to pass straight from the firebox into the stovepipe. Set it open when the fire is being lit, but close it down as the stove gets warm so that the hot air is redirected around the oven. The stovepipe damper controls the flow of hot air up the chimney. It is generally left open except when the fire is banked.

Below the firebox is the main draft regulator. When open, it allows air to flow into the firebox to increase combustion; when closed, little air reaches the fire, and the fire dies down. Above the firebox is the check draft regulator. When it is open, the draft through the firebox is reduced and the fire will slow down.

To make a hot, or fast, fire, stoke the firebox full of dry wood and open all dampers and regulators wide except for the check draft regulator. Use narrow split wood for a quick fire and whole logs for a long, steady fire suitable for baking. To drop the temperature, simply stop fueling the firebox and allow the fire to die down. For a steady baking fire, add a slightly green log to a fast-burning fire. If the oven gets too hot during baking, open the check draft regulator a crack.

Some stoves have a thermometer in the oven door, but the readings tend to be unreliable: a small oven thermometer placed on the oven shelf is better. Most cooks eventually learn the difference between a warm oven (250–325°F), a moderate oven (325–400°F), and a hot oven (400–500°F). However, in the past cooks improvised many methods for testing their ovens. One was a sort of pain test: if you could hold your hand in the oven for 20–25 seconds, the oven was hot; 35–45 seconds, the oven was moderate; 45–60 seconds, the oven was warm. Another test was to leave a piece of white paper in the oven for five minutes. If it turned chocolate brown, it meant the oven was right for baking cookies; if dark yellow, it was right for bread; if pale yellow, it was right for a sponge cake. Another prescription called upon the housewife to insert her hand inside the oven. If her hairs started to burn, the oven was ready for baking.

The Basics of Wood Stove Cookery

Baking. The dry, radiant heat of a wood stove's oven is especially good for baking bread, which develops a thick, crisp crust. The oven should be hottest when the loaves are first put in, then cooled down by slightly opening the check damper.

To brown baked goods, move them to the top of the oven; if a dish is cooking too quickly, move it down to the floor of the oven. If your baked food should fail to brown evenly, the flues probably need to be cleaned. Most wood stove ovens have hot spots and cool spots in them, so it is wise to shift the cakes or pies occasionally as they cook. If your oven seems very uneven, put a large sheet of cookies into the oven, then examine the whole sheet after they have cooked to find out where the temperature is most reliable for baking.

Small articles, such as potatoes, fish, and stuffed peppers, can be baked gently in the ashpit under a hot fire. Potatoes need only be greased before being put in to bake. Wrap fish and peppers in double layers of foil before placing them in the ashes. Cook peppers until they are tender and the stuffing begins to shrink.

Frying. Any kind of frying is possible on a wood range. For stir frying make a fast fire to cook the finely shredded meat and vegetables in the shortest time possible, and place the wok or skillet in an open burner directly over the firebox. Such meats as bacon and chops are especially good if fried very slowly over one of the cool burners. Bacon cooks to a crisp without charring, and chops are tender and juicy after cooking for an hour or more in fat that is barely popping.

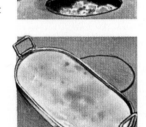

Soapstone griddle. The broad surface of a cookstove is perfect for making hotcakes, particularly if you can obtain a soapstone griddle. These remarkable griddles have nature's own nonstick coating-they never need to be greased, and food will never stick to their surface. For breakfast cooking leave the soapstone on the stove to warm overnight. Then, in the morning, heat it over a hot fire until a splash of water skitters off. Skillet breads, such as johnnycakes, can also be cooked on a soapstone. (See *Baking Bread*, p.255.)

Stews, soups, and casseroles. These dishes are particularly tender and well flavored when allowed to simmer gently at the back of a wood stove all day before an evening meal.

For bean soups boil the dried beans in plenty of water on the stove in the evening, then set in a cool place overnight and return the pot to the stove the following morning. Add a bone or joint of ham for extra flavor and nourishment. Simmer until lunchtime; then add a mixture of chopped vegetables including onions and carrots; season and continue cooking until suppertime. The beans can then be served as a main dish with the ham joint or mashed and strained to make a thick soup.

Broiling. Most stoves have a broiler door above the firebox into which a grill can be inserted; grooves in the firebox will support the grill. If your stove does not have such an arrangement, you can remove the burner covers over the firebox and set a rack across it. Before broiling allow the fire to burn down to a bed of glowing coals, then open both dampers so that smoke will go up the chimney. Put the meat on a grill, brush it with oil, and place the grill across the fire. Do not baste the meat while it is cooking.

Warming oven. This unique feature of a wood stove can be used to preheat plates, keep pies or other dishes warm, dry herbs, culture yogurt, and raise bread dough. For making yogurt and raising yeast dough, the warming oven should be about 110°F. To cool the oven, leave the door slightly ajar.

Overnight cooking. If you have been using the stove in the evening, and especially if you are banking the fire overnight, there is a variety of breakfast and other dishes that can be left to cook in the oven and on the stove for the next day.

Apple and rhubarb sauce is particularly easy. Simply put a mixture of sliced apples and rhubarb in a casserole with a little water, cover, and set in the oven overnight. Sweeten to taste.

Old-fashioned oatmeal is an almost legendary wood stove dish. In a heavy saucepan mix 1 cup of rolled oats with 2 cups of water, add a pinch of salt, and bring to a boil. Cover and set the pan at the back of the stove overnight. Oatmeal is usually served with either milk and honey or molasses and cream.

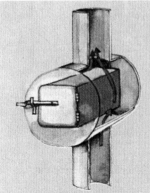

Stovepipe oven. If you have a heating stove but not a cookstove, this small, inexpensive oven can improve the heating efficiency of your stove and provide a cooking facility as well. It fits directly into the chimney and warms up with the first flames in the firebox, soon getting hot enough for most baking recipes.

Care and Maintenance

Wood stoves are not difficult to maintain. The most important task is to empty the ashpit daily; if the ashes get too high, they can choke the fire and damage the grate through overheating. Do not throw the ashes away. If they are kept dry, they can be plowed into the garden to sweeten the soil or scattered over the garden to deter slugs. They can also be used for making soap.

Clean the stove top after each meal by rubbing it with a handful of newspapers. Sprinkle salt or baking soda on messy spills, and use a scraper to remove the residue. Some cooks wipe their iron stoves or stove tops with waxed paper or an oiled rag once a week to keep the surface shiny and rust free. Enameled stoves can be washed with warm water and detergent.

About every two weeks, clear out soot and ashes from beneath the oven and under the lids. The cleaned surfaces will conduct heat more effectively. Wood stoves are fitted with cleanout doors so that hard-to-get-at spots can be reached with special L- or T-shaped cleaning rods. A wire clothes hanger can be made to serve almost as well. After the bulk of the ashes has been removed, use a vacuum cleaner to pick up the last traces.

Stove black should be applied to cast-iron stoves occasionally to improve the stove's appearance and to retard rust. Stove black is sold in most hardware stores. It comes either as a paste or a liquid. The liquid is easier to apply, especially on highly ornate surfaces.

Minor cracks, chips, and gaps between parts can usually be plugged with oven putty, available at stove suppliers. If a crack is too large to be repaired, replace the damaged part. A few companies still supply spare parts for some old stoves, and a number of others will cast new parts for you if you send them the damaged part as a pattern. For more information on stove care, see *Heating With Wood*, pp.86–93.

Sources and resources

Addkison, Andrew R. *Cooking on a Woodburning Cookstove: 150 Down Home Recipes*. Rolling Hills Estate, Calif.: Jalmar Press, 1980.

Cooper, Jane. *Woodstove Cookery: At Home on the Range*. Charlotte, Vt.: Garden Way Publishing, 1977.

Glasse, Hannah. *The Art of Cookery Made Plain and Easy* (facsimile of 1796 edition). Schenectady, N.Y.: U.S. Historical Research, 1994.

Hogencamp, Robert. *Heating With Wood*. Washington, D.C.: U.S. Department of Energy, 1980.

McLaughlin, Doris. *Cooking on a Wood Stove*. Austin, Tex.: Eakins Publications, 1983.

Ritchie, Ralph W. *All That's Practical About Wood: Stoves, as a Fuel, Heating*. Springfield, Oreg.: Ritchie Unlimited, 1992.

Sunset Magazine and Book Editors. *Fireplaces and Wood Stoves*. Menlo Park, Calif.: Sunset Books, 1989.

Weddon, Willah. *How to Heat and Eat with Woodburning Stoves*. East Lansing, Mich.: Eberly Press, 1980.

Part Five

Skills and Crafts
For House and Homestead

It is my special pleasure to behold the lines of hand-made things and to see the patina of seasoned wood and to feel a patriotic pride in the good workmanship there.
—*Eric Sloane*, Diary of an Early American Boy

Handicrafts were once part of everyday life. People thought no more of making their own candles, spinning their own yarn, or mixing their own paints and glues than modern folks think of vacuuming a rug or screwing in a new light bulb. In those days crafts were not just for artists and hobbyists—they were the survival skills of average men and women. Today, Americans are beginning to rediscover these old-time home skills: for fun, for economy, but most of all for the feeling of independence that comes when one makes do for oneself. Some topics covered in *Skills and Crafts for House and Homestead*, such as patchwork quilting, rug hooking, and scrimshaw, have evolved into full-fledged folk arts. Others, such as tanning, soapmaking, and blending homemade cosmetics, can be practical money savers. And a few, among them furnituremaking, blacksmithing, and weaving, yield satisfaction on many levels: pride of accomplishment, pleasure in artistic creativity, and the gratification of doing something with your own hands.

269

Natural Dyes

A Rainbow of Color From Common Plants

Indigo blue and madder red were the favorite colors of early migrants to the New World. Both had to be imported, but the permanent, deep shades they produced made them worth the expense. Experimentation did occur, however, and settlers learned to create rich yellows and beiges from natural dyestuffs native to America. The bark of the American black oak tree became a particularly valuable source of bright yellow and was eventually used by commercial dyers throughout Europe. When home dyers needed mordant (one of several chemicals that make dye colorfast), they turned to an apothecary or tanner. In areas lacking these suppliers, settlers relied on the metal leached from the copper or iron pot in which the dye was cooking or else employed a concoction of stale urine and ashes. Then, as now, color results varied from batch to batch—but, with luck and skillful use of dyes and mordants, the tones were rich, mellow, and durable.

Start by Scouring

Because all fibers contain oils that keep mordants and dyes from penetrating, it is necessary to clean or scour them before beginning the dye process. To scour 1 pound of fiber takes about 3 gallons of water. As with all dyeing procedures, soft mineral-free water is best. If the tap water in your area is hard, use rainwater instead or add commercial water softener to the tap water. To scour grasses, do not use any detergent or soap; simply soak them in water until they are soft. For other fibers, once the water is softened, add enough mild detergent to make it sudsy, then immerse the yarn and gradually raise the temperature. Silk should be allowed to simmer for 30 minutes and wool for 45 minutes. For cotton or linen, also add 1/2 cup of washing soda to the detergent solution to make the scouring bath, and boil the fibers rather than simmering them for one to two hours. When scouring is completed, allow the bath to cool, then rinse the fibers in soft water until no suds remain.

Naturally dyed yarn at a market. Marigolds and dahlias are among the several kinds of flowers that give bright, long-lasting dyes. Most flower heads will produce a shade of yellow no matter what color their petals.

How to Prepare and Use a Dyebath

A dyebath is prepared by soaking and cooking the raw dyestuff in water. Use either an enamel or stainless steel pot (unlike aluminum, copper, and cast iron, these materials will not give off chemicals that affect the dye). Your dye pot should be large—4 gallons or more—and you will also need a wooden spoon or dowel for stirring and some cheesecloth in which to wrap the dye substance.

Prepare the dyestuff so that as much color as possible can be extracted. Leaves and blossoms should be shredded. Twigs, bark, and roots should be cut up into small pieces, and nut hulls should be crushed. Pick out foreign particles and remove extraneous parts of plants.

Wrap the dye substance in cheesecloth, put it into the pot, and cover with water. (Some dye materials must first be soaked in cold water.) Cook until the dyebath becomes richly colored, adding more water as needed to keep the dye substance covered. After cooking, remove the cheesecloth bag and its contents or strain the liquid

Collecting and Storing Dyestuffs

The first step in making your own dyes is to gather the dyestuffs. The chart on pages 272–273 is a guide to common, naturally occurring sources of dyes and to the colors they will produce. In general, the plants are easy to identify; if you need more information, consult a good botanical guide that illustrates leaves, flowers, bark, buds, and other distinctive characteristics.

You not only need to collect the right plants, you also need to collect them at the right times. Flowers should be picked just after they reach full bloom. Roots, bark, and branches should be from mature plants—do not pick new branches. Nuts should be fully ripe and even a little aged (but should not have lain on the ground through the winter). Acorns, for example, are best just after they have fallen from the tree, while black walnuts benefit from lying on the ground until they become spotted. Berries make the best dyes when picked fully ripe.

Although fresh dyestuffs produce the strongest dyes, most plants can be stored for later use. Twigs, leaves, nuts, blossoms, bark, and roots can be dried. Spread them in a single layer in a shady, well-ventilated spot, turning them occasionally for faster drying. A window screen set on bricks makes a good drying rack because it lets air circulate underneath as well as on top. Plants with stems may be hung in bundles to dry. Once drying is complete, store the dyestuffs in brown paper bags or other containers through which air can circulate. Berries should not be dried but can be kept for several months if frozen. Freeze them unwashed, either whole or pulverized into juice.

through a sieve. To the concentrated dye, add enough cold water to make a bath in which the yarn can float freely—4 gallons is adequate for 1 pound of wool. Wet the fibers, add them to the bath, and bring slowly to a simmer for animal fibers or to a boil for plant fibers. Cook until the desired shade is reached, turning the fibers occasionally with the wooden spoon or dowel so the bath penetrates evenly. Then allow the fibers to cool, either in or out of the bath, and rinse until the water runs clear. You may also cool the yarn by rinsing it in successively cooler baths. After gently squeezing out excess moisture, hang the skeins to dry.

If there is any color left in the dyebath, you may reuse it to produce lighter shades. A dyebath can be stored for several days by refrigerating it. Freezing will keep it for several months, and by adding 1 teaspoon per gallon of the preservative sodium benzoate, you can preserve the dye for a month without refrigeration.

Mordants: The Stuff That Makes Dyestuffs Colorfast

Mordants are chemicals that help to keep dyes from fading, changing color, washing out, or rubbing off. They may also affect the final color so that a single dye can produce a variety of shades depending on what mordant is used with it. Textiles may be mordanted either before or after dyeing, or the mordant may be added directly to the dyebath. It is simplest to do the mordanting first. Once the fibers are mordanted, you can soak them in the dyebath for as long as necessary to achieve the desired shade without worrying that long exposure to the mordant will damage the yarn.

For mordanting, use an enamel or stainless steel pot for cooking and a wooden rod or spoon for stirring. Dissolve the chemical in about 4 gallons of lukewarm soft water (use commercial water softener if necessary), then thoroughly prewet the textile and immerse it in the mixture. Bring the bath slowly to a simmer or boil. Once mordanted, the yarn may be dyed immediately or dried and saved for future use.

The most commonly used mordants are alum, blue vitriol, chrome, copperas, tannic acid, and tin.

Alum (aluminum potassium sulfate) causes least change in color. Use 1 ounce per gallon of water and simmer one hour to mordant wool, silk, or other animal fibers. For cotton or linen use 1 1/3 ounces of the mordant per gallon of water and boil the fibers for one hour.

Blue vitriol (copper sulfate) sometimes colors fibers green. Use 1/4 ounce per gallon of water and simmer one hour to mordant animal fibers. For cotton and linen use 1 ounce per gallon and boil for one to two hours.

Chrome (potassium dichromate) often strengthens colors. Use 1/8 ounce per gallon for animal fibers and simmer for one hour. With linen or cotton use 1/2 ounce per gallon and boil for one to two hours. Because chrome mordanted fibers are turned brown by exposure to light, keep mordant pot covered and dye the yarns immediately or store them in complete darkness. Keep the pot covered when dyeing the chrome-mordanted fiber.

Copperas (iron sulfate) grays colors. For wool use 1/8 ounce per gallon of water and simmer for 30 minutes. For linen or cotton use 1 ounce per gallon and boil for one hour. For greater color fastness add 3/4 ounce of oxalic acid, dissolved in water, to the mordant bath. Some dyers sadden colors (dull them) by adding 1/8 teaspoon of copperas to 4 gallons of dyebath for the last few minutes of dyeing premordanted fibers. Dissolve the mordant in a little water and remove the fibers from the bath before adding the solution.

Tannic acid tends to turn fibers brown. For animal fibers use 1 1/4 tablespoons per gallon of water and simmer one hour. Use 2 1/2 tablespoons per gallon for plant fibers and boil them for one to two hours.

Tin (stannous chloride) brightens colors, particularly reds and yellows, but it can easily damage fibers. To prevent damage, mordant fibers for as short a time as possible and wash them thoroughly after mordanting. For both animal and plant fibers use 1 ounce per gallon of water and simmer for one hour. Some dyers use tin in combination with another mordant by adding 1/8 teaspoon of tin to 4 gallons of dyebath for the last few minutes of dyeing. As with copperas, remove fibers, add the tin in solution, then replace the fibers.

Mordants are sold by most pharmacies and chemical supply houses. They are available in a range of purities. The so-called chemical grade, which is less expensive than purer grades, is sufficient for dyeing purposes. **Mordants are strong chemicals and must be handled carefully. Use them in a well-ventilated place and keep the mordanting pot covered to prevent chemicals from escaping into the air. Never use mordant pots to cook food. Chrome requires particular care since it is highly poisonous.**

General Tips on Textiles, Fibers, and Dyes

Fibers derived from animals, particularly wool from sheep, tend to take dye more easily than either plant fibers or synthetics. In addition, the colors you get with wool and other so-called protein fibers will be darker and brighter than any you could obtain with plant fibers.

Animal fibers must be treated carefully during the dyeing process. Cooking time is shorter than for vegetable fibers. Yarns should be simmered in the dye solution, not boiled, and should be handled as little as possible when wet. Turn them over gently in the water to keep them from settling to the bottom of the pot and avoid wringing or twisting them. Wool will shrink if subjected to abrupt temperature changes. Always immerse it in room-temperature water, then raise the temperature slowly, allowing at least half an hour to reach a simmer. Be sure that dye and mordant baths are the same temperature if you move yarn from one to another.

Plant fibers such as cotton and linen do not absorb color easily and must be scoured and mordanted at higher temperatures and for longer periods than those from animals. They must then be boiled for as long as one to two hours in the dyebath. Grasses can also be dyed but must be treated gently. To minimize handling, mordant and dye them in the same bath.

Yarn is the easiest textile to dye since slight unevenness of color is unnoticeable. To keep yarns from tangling during dyeing, loop them into skeins, then tie the skeins with string at various points. Make the ties very loose so that dyes and mordants can reach the yarn. To store yarn between steps, you may either wrap it wet in a towel and keep it for a day or two (or for as much as a week if refrigerated) or dry it and keep it indefinitely. To dry, gently squeeze out excess moisture, then hang the skeins. Turn the yarn several times during the drying so that it will dry evenly. Before immersing dry fibers in a mordant or dye, rewet them in clear water to promote deep, even penetration.

No two dyebaths made from natural dyes are quite the same. Colors made from identical plants will vary according to when and where they were collected, the chemistry of the water in which they were cooked, and even the weather conditions during their growing season. The chart on pages 272–273 gives formulas and cooking times for a variety of colors from several popular, widely available dye materials. While these recipes provide good guidelines, the colors you create will be your own and, as you gain experience, you will enjoy experimenting with other recipes.

Dyeing with indigo

Because indigo is not water soluble, special techniques are employed to dissolve it and to use it as a dye. Start by mixing 1 oz. of washing soda in 4 oz. of water, then add 1 tsp. of indigo paste. Shake 1 oz. of hydrosulfite (available from a pharmacy) over the solution and stir gently. Next add 2 qt. of warm water, heat to 350°F, and let stand for 20 minutes. To complete the dyebath, shake another ounce of hydrosulfite over the top and stir gently again. Immerse wet yarn in the yellow-green solution for 20 minutes. When the yarn is removed from the bath and exposed to air, it will turn blue.

Sources and resources

Books and pamphlets

Adrosko, Rita J. *Natural Dyes and Home Dyeing.* New York: Dover, 1971.
Bemiss, Elijah. *The Dyer's Companion.* New York: Dover, 1973.
Dye Plants and Dyeing. Portland, Oreg.: Timber Press, 1994.

Periodicals

Fiberarts. Lark Communications. 50 College St., Asheville, N.C. 28801.
Shuttle Spindle & Dyepot. Handweavers Guild of America, Inc. 65 La Salle Rd., West Hartford, Conn. 06107.

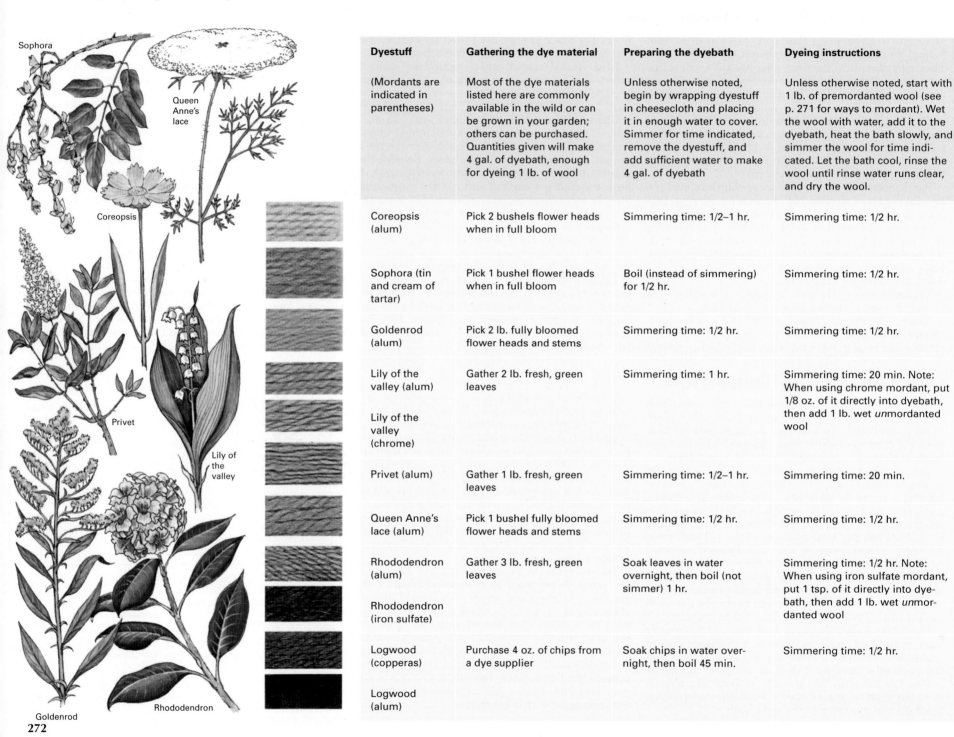

Sophora

Queen Anne's lace

Coreopsis

Privet

Lily of the valley

Goldenrod

Rhododendron

Dyestuff	Gathering the dye material	Preparing the dyebath	Dyeing instructions
(Mordants are indicated in parentheses)	Most of the dye materials listed here are commonly available in the wild or can be grown in your garden; others can be purchased. Quantities given will make 4 gal. of dyebath, enough for dyeing 1 lb. of wool	Unless otherwise noted, begin by wrapping dyestuff in cheesecloth and placing it in enough water to cover. Simmer for time indicated, remove the dyestuff, and add sufficient water to make 4 gal. of dyebath	Unless otherwise noted, start with 1 lb. of premordanted wool (see p. 271 for ways to mordant). Wet the wool with water, add it to the dyebath, heat the bath slowly, and simmer the wool for time indicated. Let the bath cool, rinse the wool until rinse water runs clear, and dry the wool.
Coreopsis (alum)	Pick 2 bushels flower heads when in full bloom	Simmering time: 1/2–1 hr.	Simmering time: 1/2 hr.
Sophora (tin and cream of tartar)	Pick 1 bushel flower heads when in full bloom	Boil (instead of simmering) for 1/2 hr.	Simmering time: 1/2 hr.
Goldenrod (alum)	Pick 2 lb. fully bloomed flower heads and stems	Simmering time: 1/2 hr.	Simmering time: 1/2 hr.
Lily of the valley (alum) Lily of the valley (chrome)	Gather 2 lb. fresh, green leaves	Simmering time: 1 hr.	Simmering time: 20 min. Note: When using chrome mordant, put 1/8 oz. of it directly into dyebath, then add 1 lb. wet *un*mordanted wool
Privet (alum)	Gather 1 lb. fresh, green leaves	Simmering time: 1/2–1 hr.	Simmering time: 20 min.
Queen Anne's lace (alum)	Pick 1 bushel fully bloomed flower heads and stems	Simmering time: 1/2 hr.	Simmering time: 1/2 hr.
Rhododendron (alum) Rhododendron (iron sulfate)	Gather 3 lb. fresh, green leaves	Soak leaves in water overnight, then boil (not simmer) 1 hr.	Simmering time: 1/2 hr. Note: When using iron sulfate mordant, put 1 tsp. of it directly into dyebath, then add 1 lb. wet *un*mordanted wool
Logwood (copperas) Logwood (alum)	Purchase 4 oz. of chips from a dye supplier	Soak chips in water overnight, then boil 45 min.	Simmering time: 1/2 hr.

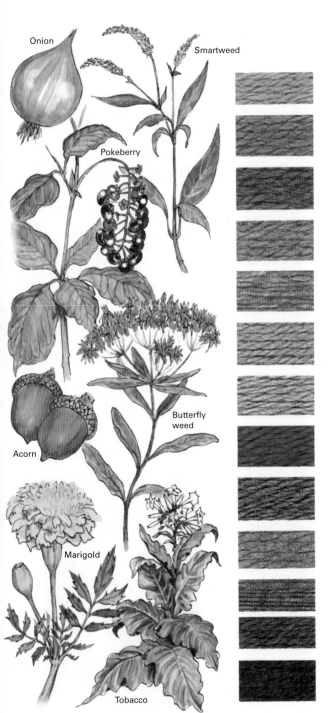

Dyestuff	Gathering the dye material	Preparing the dyebath	Dyeing instructions
Onion skin (alum)	Collect 2 lb. dry outer skins	Simmering time: 20 min. Do not overcook	Simmering time: 20 min.
Smartweed (tin)	Gather 2 bushels fully bloomed whole plants except roots	Boil (instead of simmering) for 20 min.	Simmering time: 1/2 hr.
Marigold (alum)	Pick 2 bushels flower heads when in full bloom	Simmering time: 1 hr.	Simmering time: 1/2 hr.
Pokeberry (alum)	Gather 16 qt. fully ripe berries	Boil 1/2 hr. in water to which 1 cup of vinegar has been added	Simmering time: 1/2 hr.
Madder (alum)	Purchase 1 oz. dried root from a dye supplier	Soak dried root in water overnight, then simmer 1/2 hr.	Simmering time: 1/2 hr.
Butterfly weed (alum)	Pick 1 bushel blossoms when in full bloom	Soak blossoms in water for 1 hr., then boil 1/2 hr.	Simmering time: 1/2 hr.
Tea (no mordant)	Purchase 1/4 lb. dried leaves	Cover leaves with boiling water, then steep for 15 min.	Simmering time: 20 min. Use unmordanted wool
Cochineal (alum)	Purchase 1 1/2 oz. dried powder from a dye supplier	Soak powder in water to dissolve (about 30 min.), then boil 15 min.	Simmering time: 1/2 hr.
Coffee (no mordant)	Purchase 1/2 lb. grounds	Boil (instead of simmering) for 15 min.	Simmering time: 1/2 hr. Use unmordanted wool
Tobacco (alum)	Purchase 1 lb. cured leaves	Boil 1/2 hr. in water to which 1 oz. cream of tartar has been added	Simmering time: 1/2 hr.
Acorn (alum) Acorn (copperas)	Gather 7 lb. nuts that have already fallen to ground	Soak nuts in water overnight, then boil 2 1/2 hr.	Simmering time: 1 hr.
Indigo (alum)	Purchase 1 oz. of prepared paste from a dye supplier	Prepare dyebath by special technique given on page 271	Gradually heat wool, then immerse and simmer in dyebath for 20 min.

273

Spinning

The Relaxing Art Of Twisting Fleece Into Yarn

The basics of spinning are easy to learn, especially if you begin with a drop spindle; a flick sets the spindle whirling, then your fingers draw out the fleece into yarn. A bit more persistence will be needed to learn the hand and foot motions of the treadle wheel, but once they are mastered, you can concentrate on making fine thread and specially textured yarns; or you can simply relax, daydream, chat with neighbors, and delight in the feel of the fleece as it slips through your fingers.

In preindustrial America a homestead wife was more likely to spin her own thread than to perform any other traditional craft. Not only was spinning a virtual necessity of life, but the equipment required was small, light, and easily accommodated in a corner where it could be turned to in free moments. The craft even became fashionable among rich upper-class ladies, many of whom not only owned elegant parlor wheels but also had special visiting wheels to take with them when paying social calls on their neighbors. In the East, where sheep were scarce, linen was the most commonly spun thread. In the Southwest, wool yarn was the staple. A little cotton was sometimes spun, and occasionally someone experimented with silk.

Wool is by far the easiest fiber to spin. You may be able to buy fleece from a local herder; ask your county agent where one can be found. Otherwise, contact spinning supply companies and stores (check advertisers in spinning magazines) for fleece as well as for more exotic fibers. Other spinnable fibers that may be locally available are angora rabbit fur, goat hair, wild cotton, and dog hair. It is surprising how many spinners treasure a sweater made of hair combed from a favorite pet.

Low wheel twists fleece into yarn and winds it onto spindle in a continuous sequence. Many spinners enjoy the relaxed rhythm of treadling almost as much as the yarn that results.

Preparing the Fleece

Many spinners prefer to spin "in the grease"—that is, with unwashed fleece—because the natural lanolin coating lets the fiber slide more easily through the fingers, making spinning faster and more comfortable. In addition, garments knitted from yarn that still contains lanolin from the sheep are naturally waterproof.

However, if a fleece is very dirty it must be washed. You will need a large basin for the job (two would be better) or a large sink. For 1 pound of fleece, fill the basin with 4 gallons of lukewarm soft water and add mild soap. Lay the fleece on the surface of the water (do not pour water over it); submerge and squeeze the fleece gently. When the first bath is dirty, make a second, similar bath and shift the fleece to it. Most of the dirt tends to collect at the tip of each lock of sheep's wool. Gently scrape with your thumbnail to remove the dirt lodged there. Rinse the wool and dry it on a rustproof window screen.

Washed fleece should be sprayed lightly with thinned lanolin oil to recondition it. A good recipe is one part of any lanolin-containing hand lotion to five parts water. Spray one or two squirts of the mixture over each 1/2 pound of fleece and let it stand overnight.

Doloria Chapin, Spinner

Lamb to Llama: She Grows What She Spins

Doloria Chapin, a Fabius, New York, writer, and mother of eight, turns to her spinning wheel for peace and quiet when things get too hectic.

"We're antique buffs, and my husband once bought me an old spinning wheel. I always wanted to use it but I had no idea how to spin. When a neighbor told me she was going to spinning class, I was only too happy to go along with her, but we moved the very next week from Michigan to upstate New York. So I am really a self-taught spinner, at least mostly self-taught.

"Now I teach spinning myself, I write, and I've just designed a new type of spinning wheel. We live on a 65-acre farm, and we also raise animals and use the wool for spinning. I started with angora rabbits. We used to have angora goats but we've sold them, and now we have sheep and a llama. The llama fiber is lovely—light and fluffy, but honestly, I think we're going to have to do something about that llama. He butts people and he could knock them down, stand on them, and suffocate them. He's a big animal and hard to handle.

"When we shear the sheep, we don't use electric shears, we use hand clippers. The clippers give you better wool for spinning, without any short ends. My daughters and I usually do the shearing.

"Once you've caught on to it, spinning is just a delightful craft. It's a comfortable skill and fairly easy to attain. The wonderful thing is that you can see the product of your efforts as you work. It's something that you can create for yourself in these days of rush, rush, rush, when everything is done for you.

"Once you get into spinning, it's as natural as walking and very soothing. I just love the feel of the wool playing through my hands. It's very therapeutic. Everyone you ask about it will tell you the same thing, that if you go in all shook up, after a half hour of spinning you'll come out smiling. I know that's true. I have eight children, and there have been times when I really needed the spinning just to keep me level."

Carding the Fleece

Wool, as it comes from the sheep, is kinky, matted, and may contain dirt and burrs if it has not been washed. To prepare the wool for spinning, the fibers must be separated from one another and the foreign matter removed. The method by which this is accomplished is called carding, after the pair of paddle-shaped wire brushes, or cards, that are used in the process. (Long fibers can also be separated and cleaned by combing with a metaltoothed dog comb or even an ordinary hair comb, but working with these tools is too tedious for anything except a small quantity of fleece.)

Cards are rated by fineness. The finer the card, the thinner the wires in the mesh and the tighter the mesh itself. As a rule, No. 8 cards are adequate for wools of medium weight. For lighter wools use a finer (higher numbered) card; for heavier wools use a lower numbered card. When you buy your cards, it is a good idea to mark one card for the right hand and one for the left. Then as you use them, the pitch, or angle, of their teeth will adjust to your particular stroke. Prepare the fleece for carding by teasing it apart with your fingers. Then follow the steps for carding.

1. Start carding by pulling fleece across a card so that fibers catch on teeth. Spread fleece evenly across card.

2. Pull upper card gently across fleece. Stroke several times until half the wool is distributed on each card.

3. Transfer fleece from top card to bottom one by first reversing top card, then pulling it across bottom one.

4. Stroke the fleece several more times, repeating Steps 2 and 3 until fibers are evenly distributed and fluffy.

5. Remove fleece from cards by first transferring all to bottom card, then pulling top card across as shown.

6. Shake wool from card, then roll between palms to form a "rolag" (long roll of evenly distributed fiber).

Using the Drop Spindle

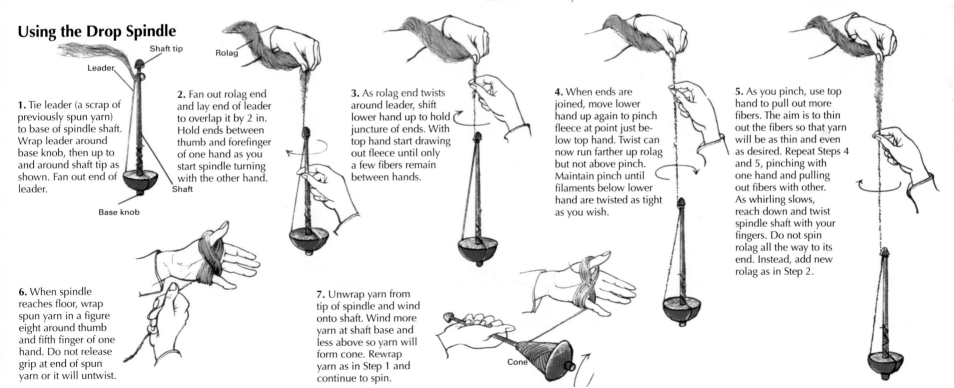

1. Tie leader (a scrap of previously spun yarn) to base of spindle shaft. Wrap leader around base knob, then up to and around shaft tip as shown. Fan out end of leader.

Shaft tip

Leader

Rolag

Shaft

Base knob

2. Fan out rolag end and lay end of leader to overlap it by 2 in. Hold ends between thumb and forefinger of one hand as you start spindle turning with the other hand.

3. As rolag end twists around leader, shift lower hand up to hold juncture of ends. With top hand start drawing out fleece until only a few fibers remain between hands.

4. When ends are joined, move lower hand up again to pinch fleece at point just below top hand. Twist can now run farther up rolag but not above pinch. Maintain pinch until filaments below lower hand are twisted as tight as you wish.

5. As you pinch, use top hand to pull out more fibers. The aim is to thin out the fibers so that yarn will be as thin and even as desired. Repeat Steps 4 and 5, pinching with one hand and pulling out fibers with other. As whirling slows, reach down and twist spindle shaft with your fingers. Do not spin rolag all the way to its end. Instead, add new rolag as in Step 2.

6. When spindle reaches floor, wrap spun yarn in a figure eight around thumb and fifth finger of one hand. Do not release grip at end of spun yarn or it will untwist.

7. Unwrap yarn from tip of spindle and wind onto shaft. Wind more yarn at shaft base and less above so yarn will form cone. Rewrap yarn as in Step 1 and continue to spin.

Cone

Wheels to Speed The Spinning

You can spin yarn six times as fast on a low wheel as on a drop spindle, primarily because the spun yarn is wound onto the bobbin automatically. The other great advantage of this wheel is its foot-powered treadle, which turns the flyer, the whirling mechanism that twists fibers into yarn and winds it onto the bobbin.

Handling the fleece is almost the same as with a drop spindle, but coordinating the hand and foot movements takes practice. You should familiarize yourself with treadling before you try to spin yarn. First, adjust the tension of the drive band by turning the tension screw. The band must be almost—but not quite—tight. If it is too loose, it will slip; if it is too tight, it will turn the flyer very fast and the yarn will be kinky. When the band is

adjusted, start the wheel turning clockwise by pushing it gently with your right index finger, then treadle as slowly and smoothly as you can without letting the wheel stop or go backward. Many spinners remove their shoes to increase control over the treadle. Others chant a simple song or recite a nursery rhyme as they work to help maintain the slow, steady rhythm that is required.

When you are ready to begin spinning, arrange several rolags side by side over one knee. Tie a leader to the bobbin—a beginner will find it easiest to use a 2-foot-long leader—and start spinning as shown below. When you have spun almost to the end of the first rolag, attach a new one just as you attached the first one to the leader.

As the spindle fills with yarn, you will need to tighten the drive band occasionally to keep the flyer turning as fast as it did when empty. This is accomplished by turning the tension screw. As you work, strive for yarn of even thickness and uniform twist. This will be difficult to accomplish at first, but in the meantime take satisfaction in the rich character of your homespun.

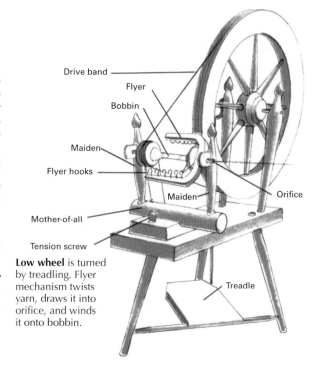

Drive band
Flyer
Bobbin
Maiden
Flyer hooks
Maiden
Orifice
Mother-of-all
Tension screw
Treadle

Low wheel is turned by treadling. Flyer mechanism twists yarn, draws it into orifice, and winds it onto bobbin.

Using the Low Wheel

1. Tie leader to back of bobbin, then pass it over flyer hooks. Draw leader through orifice with crochet hook or with hook made of bent wire.

2. Fan out ends of rolag and leader and hold them together with one hand. Use other hand to start wheel by pushing a spoke clockwise.

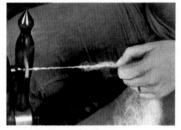

3. Treadle slowly and evenly. Allow rolag end to twist around leader so that they are joined. Meanwhile, leader is drawn toward orifice.

4. Pinch juncture of leader and rolag with right hand. Use other hand to draw out fleece to thickness appropriate to the size of your yarn.

5. When rolag and leader are joined, move right hand to pinch drawn-out fibers at a spot farther back on rolag. Twist can now run farther up fleece.

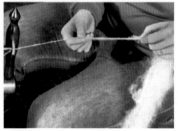

6. As yarn spins to tightness that you desire, continue to draw out fibers between left and right hands. Spun yarn is drawn into orifice.

7. When enough fibers are drawn out, open fingers to let twist travel farther up rolag. Continue to draw out fibers; add new rolag as needed.

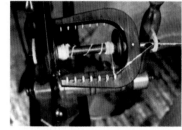

8. Flyer hooks determine where yarn winds onto bobbin. First wind yarn at ends of bobbin, then move it from hook to hook to build even layers.

Sources and resources

Books and pamphlets

Hecht, Ann. *The Art of the Loom: Weaving, Spinning and Dyeing Across the World.* New York: Rizzoli, 1990.

Hobdeen, Eileen. *Spinning and Weaving: A Practical Guide.* Portland, Oreg.: International Specialized Book Services, 1987.

Hochberg, Bette. *Handspinner's Handbook.* 33 Wilkes Circle, Santa Cruz, Calif.: Bette Hochberg, 1980.

Leadbeater, Eliza. *Handspinning.* Newton Centre, Mass.: Charles T. Branford Co., 1976.

Ross, Mabel. *The Essentials of Handspinning.* McMinnville, Oreg.: Robin & Russ Handweavers, 1988.

Simmons, Paula. *Spinning and Weaving with Wool.* Petaluma, Calif.: Unicorn Books for Craftsmen, 1991.

Periodicals

Shuttle Spindle & Dyepot. Handweavers Guild of America, Inc., 65 La Saile Rd., West Hartford, Conn. 06107.

SpinOff. Interweave Press, 306 North Washington Ave., Loveland, Colo. 80537.

Materials

Clemes & Clemes Spinning Wheels 650 San Pablo Ave., Pinole, Calif. 94564.

Spinning on a High Wheel

When using the high wheel, the spinner keeps the wheel constantly turning with one hand while drawing out the fleece with the other. As on the low wheel, the drive band must be adjusted to the proper tension and a leader ttached before starting. Then when the rolag fibers are wrapped around the tip of the spindle and pulled away from it at just the right angle, the whirling spindle can twist the fibers into yarn. As it does, the spinner pinches the rolag until fibers between fingers and spindle are spun to the desired tightness. Then additional fleece is allowed to slip through the spinner's fingers so that it can be spun. As the fleece slips through, the spinner must step back from the spindle in order to draw out even more fleece. Eventually, when the wheel can barely be reached, the spinner walks forward to wind the yarn onto the spindle. Because the spinner must continually walk back and forth alongside the wheel—as much as 20 miles in a day during colonial times—the high wheel is sometimes called a walking wheel. It is also known as a wool wheel, since it is so often used to spin wool.

High wheel is turned by hand. Spindle tip twists yarn, then spinner unwinds yarn from tip and winds it up on back of spindle.

Drive band

Pulley

Maiden

Maiden

Spindle

Mother-of-all

Tension screw

1. Tie leader yarn at back of spindle. Then hold yarn parallel to wheel, turn wheel clockwise, and wind leader onto spindle in even layer.

2. Wrap leader around spindle tip, pull leader away from spindle at angle shown (approximately 120°), and hold ends of leader and rolag together.

3. Turn wheel clockwise with free hand in order to start spindle turning. End of rolag twists around end of leader so that the two will be joined.

4. Keep turning wheel and slide hand farther back on fleece. Pull out fibers, then pinch so that fleece in front of hand is spun. Then slide hand back again.

5. When a length is spun, turn wheel counterclockwise to free yarn. Hold yarn parallel to wheel and turn clockwise to wind into cone on spindle.

6. Return yarn to spinning position and draw out fibers again. When necessary, add new rolag by holding ends together and joining as in Step 3.

After the yarn is spun

The spindle or bobbin must be emptied periodically whether you use a drop spindle, low wheel, or high wheel. To unwind yarn from either type of wheel, you must first take off the wheel's drive bands. Next, the yarn is wound onto a wooden frame called a niddy noddy. Do not unwind all the yarn. Instead, leave the last few feet on the spindle to use as a leader. The distance around a niddy noddy is about 2 yd., though the size varies from one to another. You should wrap 40 lengths before unloading it. This is about 80 yd., or 1 knot, of yarn. (A skein contains 560 yd., or 7 knots.)

When you have wrapped a knot of yarn, tie cotton string around it at several points before taking it off the niddy noddy. Now wet or steam the entire knot, tie a 1/2-lb. rock or similar weight at one end, and hang the knot up by its other end to dry. This will set the twist of the yarn. To store a knot or skein of yarn, twist it as shown at far right.

To wind yarn on niddy noddy, tie end of yarn to a crosspiece, grip shaft, and wrap in path shown above.

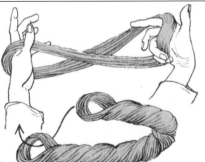

Store wound yarn by twisting it several times, then pulling loop at one end through loop a other end.

Weaving

A New Generation Rediscovers the Joys Of the Weaver's Art

When the first European colonists came to the New World, they brought with them a type of loom that had been in use in Europe since before the 1300s. This was the horizontal frame loom; handweavers use the same basic type today.

In the South, plantation owners built weaving shops and set slaves and servants to producing cloth for bed ticking and simple garments. A few estates even began turning out elegant silks and fine linens. Textiles, however, were of little value compared to tobacco, and most planters preferred to import their cloth from England, leaving them free to concentrate on their cash crop.

New Englanders could grow neither tobacco nor an equivalent crop to trade and so were forced to rely almost exclusively on their own weavers for their cloth. In some towns, such as Boston and Salem, bounties of free land and homes induced professional weavers to set up shop. Many an impoverished Englishman earned passage to New England by indenturing himself as an apprentice weaver, then later became a wealthy citizen through his trade. But many families, particularly rural settlers, had to weave for themselves.

In the Southwest, Spanish settlers brought sheep as well as floor looms to their frontier outposts. Through division of labor—some family members worked as carders, others as spinners, and others as weavers—they were able to make wool cloth for export by mule train to mining camps in northern Mexico.

Producing large quantities of cloth on a handloom was a formidable task in those days. It could take an entire day merely to fill enough bobbins with weft (the thread that is passed back and forth across the stretched warp threads) to

Intricately patterned scarf takes time and patience to weave, but will be cherished by whomever wears it.

weave a 5-yard length on a large loom. And the warp string itself had to be measured and put on the loom, a job that could take days.

Most of the cloth produced was simple and sturdy: plain-woven wool and linen for clothing; coarse homespun made from the part of the flax, called tow, left over after making linen; linsey-woolsey, with its linen warp and woolen weft. But some homemade cloth was beautiful as well. Hope chests were filled with finely woven bed linens, towels, and curtains. Beds were covered with intricately patterned woven coverlets. In the Southwest, Spanish caballeros dressed themselves in elegant serapes.

To produce fine fabric with straight selvages and parallel, evenly spaced weft required care, patience, and a steady rhythm perfected through years of practice. Good weavers were justifiably proud of their work and must have considered it more than just another chore to be completed. They probably shared the feelings of many contemporary handweavers who speak of the joy with which they watch a complicated pattern grow before their eyes and of the day-to-day cares they forget as they work at a loom.

Rag carpets were popular 18th-century floor coverings. This one was woven on a simple, inexpensive loom (pp. 280–281).

Sources and resources

Books

Black, Mary E. *The Key to Weaving*. New York: Macmillan, 1980.

Bridgman, Rosemary. *Weaving: A Manual of Techniques*. North Pomfret, Vt.: Trafalgar Square, 1992.

Davison, Marguerite P. *The Handweaver's Pattern Book*. P.O. Box 263, Swarthmore, Pa.: Marguerite P. Davison, 1977.

Drooker, Penelope B. *Samplers You Can Use: A Handweaver's Guide to Creative Exploration*. Loveland, Colo.: Interweave Press, 1986.

Oelsner, G.H. *Handbook of Weaves*. New York: Dover Books, 1915.

O'Reilly, Susie. *Weaving*. New York: Thomson Learning, 1993.

Regensteiner, Else. *The Art of Weaving*. West Chester, Pa.: Schiffer Publishing, 1986.

Periodicals

American Craft. American Craft Council, 401 Park Ave. South, New York, N.Y. 10016.

Fiberarts. Lark Communications, 50 College St., Asheville, N.C. 28801.

Shuttle Spindle & Dyepot. Handweavers Guild of America, Inc., 65 La. Salle Rd., West Hartford, Conn. 06107.

Organizations

Handweavers Guild of America, Inc., 2402 University Ave. W, Ste 702, St. Paul, Minn. 55114.

Preparing the Warp

The threads that are tied onto the loom before weaving begins are called the warp. The total length of warp thread that will be needed depends on the particular weaving project and the type of loom being used. (For a discussion of how to compute total warp length, see *Calculating the Warp's Dimensions*, p.280.) Whatever the amount of warp needed, the warp string must be carefully and systematically measured beforehand and bundled neatly so that it does not become tangled.

The warping board is a simple device for measuring off the individual lengths of string that make up the warp. Each time the string is wound from the first peg to the last or from last to first, another warp length is measured. The process is repeated until a length of warp has been measured for each strand to be placed on the loom. To keep the strands in order, the warp threads are wound on the board so that each crosses over the one below at a certain point (between pegs A and B in the board shown at right). The cross ensures that one thread will not slip down beneath another and thus be out of order.

As the threads pile up on the board, the weaver usually attaches threads of a color that contrasts with the warp, gathering every 20 strands into a separate group. Before taking the warp off the board, the weaver ties string around the cross to keep it intact. The warp is then removed by a process known as chaining.

Tying a slipknot

Use slipknot to tie end of string to warping board peg.

A Warping Board Makes Your Measuring Job Easy

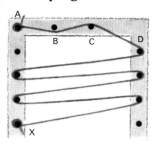

1. Cut a guide string 8 in. longer than the required warp and tie one end to peg A with slipknot. Stretch string over to peg D, keeping it inside of peg B and outside of peg C, then back and forth across board until entire string is used. Tie with slipknot to last peg that string reaches (peg X).

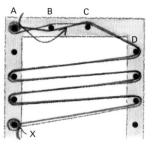

2. Tie end of warp string with slipknot to peg X and wrap it around other pegs, following guide string until you reach peg B. Pass warp outside peg B, then toward center of board and inside peg A. Wrap string around peg A and pass it inside peg B so that warp crosses over itself between pegs A and B.

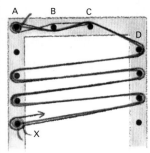

3. Bring warp to outside of peg C and then over to D, following guide string around all pegs until you are back to peg X. From this point until you have completed as many circuits of the warping board as you need, wind the string along the same route, always making the cross between pegs A and B as shown.

Counting strings (top left of board) are used to keep track of how much warp you have measured. Each time you place 20 strands (not counting guide string), tie them in a bundle with counting string of contrasting color. After entire warp is measured, tie other strings around it at last peg (X) and at several other points to prevent tangling when warp is chained.

Once the entire warp has been measured off on the warping board, the cross (between pegs A and B in the diagrams at left) must be tied to prevent it from coming apart after the warp is removed from the board. Two ties are made: one faces the inside of board, the other faces the outside. The diagrams above show the steps in making one tie. The knot can be a square knot (two overhand knots tied in opposite directions) or any simple knot that will not come apart easily.

Chaining the String Into a Bundle

1. Pull warp off last peg of warping board, insert hand through loop that wrapped around peg, and grasp bundle of threads in front of loop.

2. Use free hand to hold loop away from wrist while pulling bundle of thread back through loop with other hand. Bundle forms new loop.

3. Take new loop in one hand and insert other hand through. Grasp thread bundle and pull through loop. Repeat steps to chain entire warp.

4. When warp is fully chained and removed from board, open up the cross by tugging gently on the two tie threads that keep it in place.

5. Insert lease sticks (special sticks that come with loom) into holes made by cross. Tie stick ends together. Remove ties from cross.

Learning the Ropes
On a Simple Loom

A rigid heddle loom is compact, inexpensive, and simple to use—an excellent tool for learning the fundamentals of weaving. With it you can make modestly sized items, such as place mats, pillow covers, small rugs, and ponchos. The rag rug whose construction is described here is a particularly good project because the bulky rag weft fills the relatively wide spaces between warp strands, which are parcel post twine. The rug is made of three 12- by 50-inch strips sewn together into a single 36- by 50-inch piece. Calculate the warp length as explained below, then measure it off on a warping board (see p.279). Note that enough string should be measured so that the loom need be dressed only once to make all three strips. When a strip is completed, cut it loose, retie the warp to the loom, and weave the next strip.

Calculating the Warp's Dimensions

The amount of string needed for the warp depends upon the number of warp strands and their length. To calculate the number of strands, multiply the strands per inch by the fabric width. The loom shown here allows four strands per inch. Since a 12-inch strip is being woven, a total of 48 strands are needed. To calculate each strand's length, you must allow not only for fabric length (three strips of 50 inches each, or 150 inches in all for the rug shown on these pages) but for three other factors as well: shrinkage, tie-on or fringe allowance, and warp lost. Calculate these allowances as follows:

Shrinkage. This is the amount the warp is shortened as it goes over and under the weft. Expect 20 percent shrinkage with rag weft, 10 percent with yarn. For the rag rug, shrinkage is 20 percent of 150, or 30 inches.

Tie-on or fringe allowance. Even for a fringeless rug, 4 inches are needed to tie each end of the warp to the loom, or 8 inches for each of the three strips (24 inches in all). However, the rug shown will have 8-inch fringes, so the allowance must be increased to 48 inches.

Warp lost. This is the extra warp needed so that the strands can be separated for a shuttle to pass through. For the rigid heddle add 8 inches. (For a multiharness loom, as shown on page 282, allow 4 inches per harness.)

To find the total length of warp string needed for the rag rug, add together all the allowances (150 + 30 + 48 + 8 = 236) and multiply by the number of strands (48). The result is 11,328 inches, or 944 feet of warp.

First Steps in Threading

Warp must be centered on the loom so that the heddles will be easy to balance as you weave. To center the warp, subtract the number of warp strands from the total number of sticks and spaces; then divide the result by two to find how many sticks and spaces must remain unused on each side of the warp. Next, count over to find the place where the leftmost warp strand should be inserted. Mark the point with string. You can determine the order in which warp strands must be inserted by the way they cross each other between the two lease sticks. (See p.279 for a discussion of preparing the cross and inserting lease sticks.)

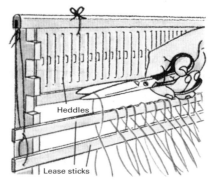

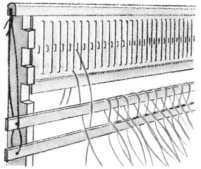

Suspend lease sticks—which hold warp—in front of heddles. Lift up leftmost loop from lease sticks and cut its top, separating it into two strands.

Insert end of left strand through farthest left space you are using. Insert end of right strand through hole in stick just to the right of that space.

Completing the Dressing Operation

1. After first warp strands are threaded as described above, continue cutting loops and inserting ends in spaces and holes. Pull ends far enough through heddles so that they will not slip out.

2. When you have inserted about six warp strands, tie their ends together in a loose slipknot. Continue across heddle, inserting threads and tying ends until all strands are threaded.

3. Place back apron bar on back beam. Undo first slipknot. Take six threads, divide into two equal groups, and tie with a square knot (p.281) to bar. Continue until all threads are tied.

4. While helper pulls to keep warp taut, wind it onto back roller. After two turns, start inserting paper continuously to keep layers of warp separated so that they pile evenly on roller.

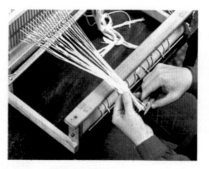

5. When 16 in. of warp remain unwound in front of heddles, cut loops of warp at front of loom. Now move heddles to rest position where all threads are at same level; then remove lease sticks.

6. Use first part of square knot to tie threads to front apron bar. Work from outer warp to center in groups of six as in Step 3. Adjust so that strands are equally taut, then finish tying knots.

The Rigid Heddle Loom

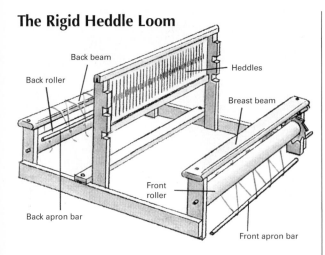

Back beam

Back roller

Heddles

Breast beam

Front roller

Back apron bar

Front apron bar

Rigid heddle loom is named for the flat, evenly spaced sticks, or heddles, that hold and separate the warp threads. Each heddle has a hole in it. Half the warp passes through the holes and half between the heddles. When heddles are raised or lowered, warp in the holes rises or falls to let weft pass through.

Preparing the Weft

The weft is the thread or other material that is woven between the warp strands to produce the finished cloth. The rag rug shown here has a weft made of strips of washable cotton calico. To prepare the strips, fold uncut pieces of cloth diagonally to the grain and cut along the fold lines. Next, make cuts parallel to the first cut to create 1-inch-wide bias-cut strips. Sew the strips together end to end and wind them into balls. The next step is to load the shuttles. One should be loaded with doubled

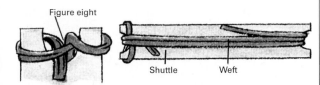

Figure eight

Shuttle   Weft

string to be used as heading (the first few rows of weaving). Load any others with rag strips. To load weft on a shuttle, first wrap one end in a figure eight around either double-pronged end of the shuttle (do not tie it). Then wind the weft lengthwise around the shuttle.

How to tie a square knot

Tie two opposite overhand knots to make a square knot.

Weaving a Rag Rug

   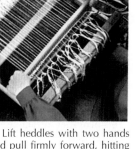

1. With heddles in bottom slot, pass shuttle through warp from left to right. Note that shuttle carries heading (string folded double) for first two rows. After that, use rag.

2. Hide weft end by pulling it around outside warp string and laying it alongside first row of weft. Do the same whenever weft runs out or new weft is added.

3. Lift heddles with two hands and pull firmly forward, hitting the heading weft several times to pack it. This is called beating. Beat after each pass of shuttle.

4. Place heddles in highest slot. Unwind one length of weft from shuttle and pass shuttle through warp from right to left. Each pass of shuttle is called a pick.

5. To be sure outer warp will not be pulled inward when weft is beaten, "bubble" weft by pushing some spots toward loom front. Work across loom toward shuttle as you bubble.

6. After inserting heading rows, weave with rags in same way. Add new weft by laying new end on old. Roll finished material onto front roller as weaving progresses.

7. When woven strip is 50 in. long, weave two rows of heading as at start of rug. Then cut warp strands 8 in. beyond heading. (Extra warp length is for fringe.)

8. Unroll woven strip and untie from front apron bar. Retie warp threads to front apron bar, and weave two more strips. Match color bands in all strips.

Applying the Finishing Touches

1. Sew strips together with warp string. Work back and forth, sewing under turn of weft at end of each row.

2. To make fringe, remove some heading, take two warp strands in each hand, and twist tightly clockwise.

3. As you twist string, wind twisted strands around each other counterclockwise to prevent their unwinding.

4. Knot ends when twists are 5 in. long. Remove heading a bit at a time as you work across end of rug.

To Clothe a Family Takes a Big Loom

The floor loom is the ultimate tool of the home weaver. A full-sized model is bulky and expensive, but with it an experienced weaver can turn out an almost infinite variety of beautiful patterns and textures. Although floor looms today are largely the province of those interested in weaving as a creative and artistic craft, they were once among the most practical of necessities; before the Industrial Revolution the floor loom was an irreplaceable implement for manufacturing the cloth needed for everyday living.

In design the floor loom is basically a larger, more sophisticated, and more versatile version of the rigid heddle loom described on pages 280 and 281. Instead of stick heddles, each strand of warp is held in the eye of a wire or string heddle, the eye being a loop in the center of the heddle. The heddles are suspended from two or more harnesses that, in turn, are connected to foot treadles. By pressing on the appropriate treadle, a particular harness, along with its set of heddles and threaded warp strings, can be raised or lowered.

To make plain weave, every other warp thread is raised and the shuttle passed between the raised and unraised threads just as with the rigid heddle loom. On larger looms with four or more harnesses the weaver can vary the number and sequence of warp strands lifted and so create an amazing variety of patterns.

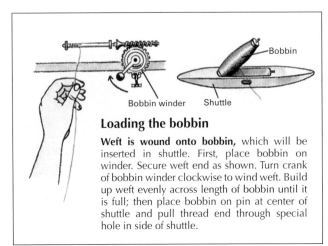

Loading the bobbin

Weft is wound onto bobbin, which will be inserted in shuttle. First, place bobbin on winder. Secure weft end as shown. Turn crank of bobbin winder clockwise to wind weft. Build up weft evenly across length of bobbin until it is full; then place bobbin on pin at center of shuttle and pull thread end through special hole in side of shuttle.

Dressing a Floor Loom

Dressing a floor loom with warp is much the same as dressing a rigid heddle loom, but the increased number of strands and their greater length make the job slower and trickier. First, the chain of warp is laid over the harnesses, and the lease sticks are tied to the top of the back harness. Next, the warp is centered and tied in evenly spaced groups across the back apron bar. To help apportion the strands, a comblike raddle is temporarily tied to the back beam. Small groups of warp strands are laid between teeth in the raddle, then tied to the apron bar. Next, the warp is wound onto the back roller (the bar is attached by straps to the roller). Paper is inserted on the roller as the warp is wound, just as with the rigid heddle loom. Finally, the warp is threaded through the heddles and beater and tied to the front apron bar.

Weaver works from edges to center, laying warp strands in raddle and tying strands with square knots to apron bar.

To wind warp on roller, have helper pull warp tight while you slowly wind. To untangle strands, slap warp sharply against harness tops and gently poke through warp strands with your fingers.

To thread heddles for plain weave, place one strand in frontmost heddle, one in next heddle back, one in third back, one in fourth back. Fifth strand goes in front heddle. Continue across loom.

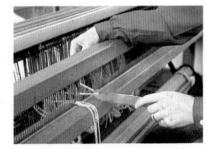

Special sleying hook is used to pull warp strands through beater after they have been threaded through heddles. Strands are then tied to front apron bar, and the raddle and lease sticks are removed.

Weaving With the Floor Loom

By pushing down on a foot treadle, the weaver raises the harnesses attached to it along with the warp threads held by the harnesses. The shuttle is then thrown between the two rows of threads and the beater pulled sharply forward to pack the weft tightly together. Next, the weaver presses a different treadle and throws the shuttle in the opposite direction. The shuttle is always thrown at an angle so that the loose weft does not lie perpendicular to the warp. The angle serves the same purpose as bubbling on the rigid heddle loom—it provides enough extra length so that the weft, when beaten into place, will not pull the cloth edges inward.

With harnesses raised, warp threads are divided into two groups. Weaver is about to throw shuttle between them.

Patterns Require Multiple Harnesses

Most home-woven cloth made in preindustrial America was an unpatterned plain weave used for suits, dresses, sheets, and other necessities of life. However, special cloth, such as linen for a young girl's hope chest or decorative wool weaves to brighten a bedstead, called for something more elaborate. A pattern of tiny diamonds might be woven from sun-bleached linen to make a delicately textured christening towel; or wool, home dyed with madder and indigo, might be combined in a bold geometric motif for a bed coverlet.

When making plain woven cloth, two sets of warp threads are raised alternately so that the weft always goes under every other thread. To create a pattern, the weaver has to be able to vary the order and number of warp threads that the weft skips under as the shuttle is passed across the loom. The multiharness loom provides the flexibility necessary to do this.

With multiple harnesses a limitless variety of patterns are possible. The pattern made depends on three things: the order in which the harnesses are tied to the treadles, how the warp is threaded into the heddles, and the order in which the weaver presses the treadles.

Any combination of harnesses can be controlled by each treadle, but one arrangement is used so often that it is considered standard. For a four-harness loom the standard tie-up is as follows: the first treadle is tied to the first and second harnesses, the second treadle is tied to the second and third harnesses, the third treadle is tied to the third and fourth harnesses, and the fourth treadle is tied to the first and fourth harnesses. The diagram in the upper right-hand corner of the page shows a standard tie-up on a four-harness loom.

An almost limitless variety of patterns and designs can be woven on a loom set in the standard tie-up. The key to all this variety lies in the way that the warp is threaded through the individual heddles. For example, the loom can be threaded so that a single harness controls intermittent pairs of warp threads, or intermittent trios of threads, or any other arrangement of threads across the loom. For anything but the simplest textures a plan (called a pattern draft) is needed. It specifies where each warp strand is to be threaded. In days gone by, these drafts were handed down from generation to generation, treasured and traded as one might today trade prized recipes. With them weavers created the large-scale patterns of circles, rectangles, stars, and pine trees that are so admired. Nowadays many books on weaving provide a selection of pattern drafts along with directions for tying treadles to harnesses and for the order of pressing the treadles to make a wide variety of favorite traditional designs.

The Jack Loom and How It Works

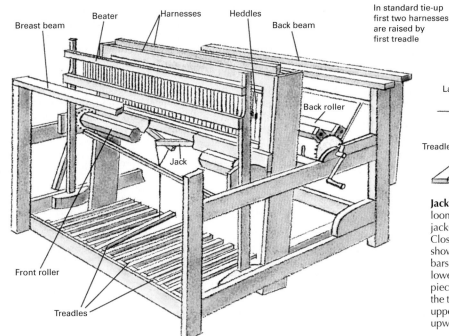

Breast beam · Beater · Harnesses · Heddles · Back beam · Back roller · Jack · Front roller · Treadles

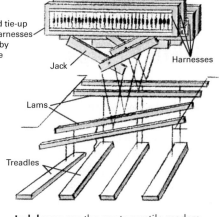

In standard tie-up first two harnesses are raised by first treadle · Jack · Harnesses · Lams · Treadles

Jack looms are the most versatile modern looms. The name comes from the rods, or jacks, that move each harness up or down. Close-up view (above) of standard tie-up shows that each jack consists of crossed bars held together by a pivot pin. The lower ends of the bars are tied to crosspieces, or lams. These in turn are tied to the treadles. When a treadle is pressed, the upper ends of the jacks linked to it pivot upward to raise their harnesses.

The pattern draft

Pattern draft is the weaver's guide for dressing a loom to make a particular pattern. Each column of the draft represents one strand of warp. Each horizontal row represents one of the four harnesses. A dark square (there is one in each column) indicates that the warp strand represented by that column should be threaded through a heddle of the harness represented by that row. The example at right provides the instructions for threading only the first eight strands of warp. Read it from right to left. A draft for a bed coverlet would be several inches long and give instructions for threading several hundred warp threads.

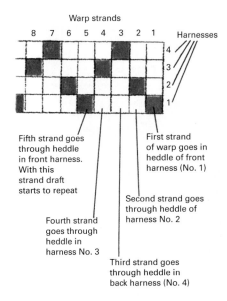

Warp strands
8 7 6 5 4 3 2 1 · Harnesses
4
3
2
1

Fifth strand goes through heddle in front harness. With this strand draft starts to repeat

First strand of warp goes in heddle of front harness (No. 1)

Second strand goes through heddle of harness No. 2

Fourth strand goes through heddle in harness No. 3

Third strand goes through heddle in back harness (No. 4)

Traditional patterns

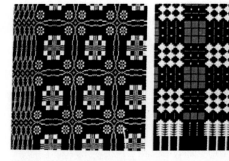

Colonial overshot coverlets have been colorful additions to American homes for centuries. Hundreds of different designs are in existence, many with picturesque names such as Whig Rose (left) and Pine Tree (right). In an overshot pattern, brightly colored wool weft skips over, then under, groups of undyed warp threads. Alternating with the bright weft are rows of undyed weft, called tabby, that go over one thread and then under the next to hold the overshot rows in place.

Hooked Rugs

Practical Artistry With Scraps and Rags

Hooked rugs became popular in the middle of the 19th century when burlap and machine-made cloth were first available in the United States. The early designs were home drawn, many with such charm and originality that they have become prized as works of art. Made from scraps, the most treasured rugs are richly textured with varied and inventive use of color.

After printed patterns and chemical dyes for home use were introduced in the 1860s, rugmakers began to create more realistic designs using finely cut strips and many gradations of color (10 shades might appear in a single flower). Though these rugs lack the boldness of earlier creations, they were crafted with enviable skill.

Preparing the Backing

While a few early rugs were backed with homespun or linen, burlap became the traditional and by far the most popular backing material. Much of the early burlap came from empty grain sacks, and even today, if you have no other source, you might consider using an old grain sack for a small project. However, the burlap sold by suppliers of rug-hooking equipment is stronger, wears longer, and has holes that are properly spaced for easy hooking. Before you buy, hold the cloth up to the light to see if there are any broken threads that could cause gaps in your rug. Monk's cloth is another durable backing, but its softness makes it difficult for beginners to use.

Whatever backing you choose, the edges must be bound. Use 1 1/4-inch cotton twill tape that will match the background color of the finished rug. You may want to dye the tape to obtain the correct shade. Attach the tape before you begin hooking so that you can hook right up to the edge where the tape is sewn to the rug. When your rug is completed, fold the tape back and hem it in place so that no backing will show.

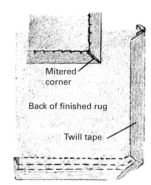

To prepare rug backing so that it will not fray, first make two lines of running stitches 1 in. beyond edge of rug pattern all the way around the perimeter (stitch on diagonal at each corner). Next, place cotton twill tape on front of rug just inside rug-pattern edge. Sew tape to backing by stitching 1/8 in. in from tape's outer edge. Tape must be gathered slightly to ease it around corners.

The final step in binding takes place after all hooking is completed. Cut off backing just beyond outermost stitches. Miter each corner by folding tape on the diagonal 1/4 in. from the corner of the hooked area, then fold tape along each side to back of rug. Leave 1/4 in. of tape showing on front. Use overcast stitches to sew tape to back of rug and to sew folds together at the corners of design.

Attaching the burlap to the frame

Though it need not be fancy—an inexpensive canvas stretcher from an art-supply store will do—you will want something to keep your rug taut as you work. You may eventually need a standing easel-type frame, but many experienced rugmakers are happy with a simple lap type that leans against the edge of a table. Choose a frame made of softwood so that it will be easy to tack the burlap to it. Keep a metal nail file handy to pry the tacks loose when you want to remove the rug. If your rug is larger than your frame, get extra-long tacks to go through completed parts of the rug when you reposition it on the frame to work on new sections.

The back of a well-made rug can be as attractive as the front. The strips lie flat, do not cross one another, are evenly spaced, and are packed tightly with no bare spots or gaps. This tight packing serves to hold the strips in place when the rug is being used.

Use thumbtacks to hold burlap on frame. First tack burlap at one corner, then pull one side tight. Now tack adjacent corner and insert tacks at 2-in. intervals along taut side. Fasten other corners and sides in same manner.

Sources and resources

Books

Beatty, Alice, and Mary Sargent. *Basic Rug Hooking*. Harrisburg, Pa.: Stackpole Books, 1990.

Book of Rug Hooking. New York: Dover, 1989.

Kopp, Joel, and Kate Kopp. *American Hooked and Sewn Rugs*. New York: E. P. Dutton, 1985.

Turbayne, Jessie. *The Hooker's Art: Evolving Designs in Hooked Rugs*. Atglen, Pa.: Schiffer Publishing, 1993.

Materials

Braid-Aid. 466 Washington St., Pembroke, Mass. 02359.

Craftsman Studio and W. Cushing Company. North St., Kennebunkport, Maine 04046.

Dorr Woolen Company. Guild, N.H. 03754.

Pearl K. McGown Hooked Rugs. W. Cushing Co., 21 North St., Kennebunkport, Maine 04046.

Carefully crafted rag rug demonstrates how fabrics of different colors can be used to create a unique design.

Choosing and Preparing Your Fabric

A hooked rug is an excellent way to recycle your torn or moth-eaten woolen clothing and blankets. Medium-weight, tightly woven fabrics, particularly flannels, are easiest to hook; but as you become expert, you will be able to incorporate different weights and weaves to produce a variety of textures.

Collect only all-wool fabrics; they wear best and are resistant to soiling. To prepare cloth for hooking, remove linings, facings, and other nonwool parts and wash the remaining woolen material in warm water and detergent. It is best to wash even new or freshly dry-cleaned woolens in order to shrink them and tighten their weave.

After washing, remove seams, buttonholes, and other stitching and discard any parts of the material (such as knees or elbows) that have worn very thin. If you wish, you can dye your material. Tweeds and plaids can be lightly overdyed (tinted) with a single color to impart a unifying cast to them. Bright colors can be toned down by dyeing with a complementary hue. For example, red cloth dyed green becomes a mellow brown.

After washing and dyeing, the fabric must be cut into strips that parallel the grain of the weave. To do this, first tear the material into 2-inch widths, then carefully cut these into much narrower strips. For medium-weight flannels 1/8 inch is usually about the right width. Light-weight fabrics should be cut a bit wider in order to make a heavy pile that does not pull out of the burlap backing. Heavy fabrics must be cut narrower or they will be difficult to pull through the burlap and may strain its threads. If you plan to do a lot of hooking, you may want to buy a mechanical cutter that can produce many strips at one time and make the job go more quickly.

The ABCs of Hooking: A Repetition of Simple Steps

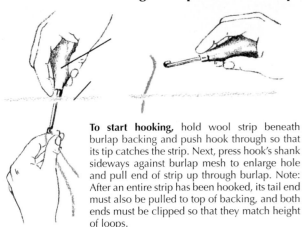

To start hooking, hold wool strip beneath burlap backing and push hook through so that its tip catches the strip. Next, press hook's shank sideways against burlap mesh to enlarge hole and pull end of strip up through burlap. Note: After an entire strip has been hooked, its tail end must also be pulled to top of backing, and both ends must be clipped so that they match height of loops.

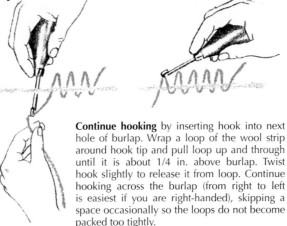

Continue hooking by inserting hook into next hole of burlap. Wrap a loop of the wool strip around hook tip and pull loop up and through until it is about 1/4 in. above burlap. Twist hook slightly to release it from loop. Continue hooking across the burlap (from right to left is easiest if you are right-handed), skipping a space occasionally so the loops do not become packed too tightly.

Making curved rows

Once you learn to hook straight rows, try your hand at meandering ones. Draw large, sweeping S-shaped curves on your backing and follow them as you hook. Make each row parallel to the one before. Fill leftover spaces with shorter rows. With practice you will not need to draw lines to follow. Unless you are striving for a special effect, as with the background stripes in the brown rug above, you should use curved rows to give rich texture to the background. Also use curved rows to fill and outline any design, following its contours as you hook. When you begin a rug, start by filling in the design; then outline the area with background color. Next, hook along the rug's outer edge and fill in the background.

Brightly colored rugs can add life to any room.

How to Make Your Own Pattern

Printed patterns have been available since rug hooking first became popular, and many experts urge that beginners avoid disappointment by using them. Most people, however, eventually want to make rugs that display their own artistic talents.

The simplest way to create a pattern is to draw free-hand on the burlap with indelible ink. Another method is to trace around cardboard cutouts. You can also plan a rug on paper, then transfer the design. One way to make the transfer is to place netting of the type used for bridal veils over the completed design and then trace the design onto the netting. Next, place the netting on the burlap and retrace the design, using ink that will bleed through onto the burlap. As an alternative, prepare your design on tracing paper, turn the paper over, and trace the lines with an iron-on transfer pencil (available in art-supply stores). Pin the paper to the backing so that the transfer marking lies against it and then iron over the design to transfer the markings.

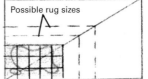 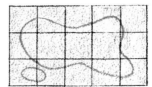

You can plan a scaled-down design, then enlarge it to full size. To find the right proportions, first draw a diagonal line on the backing between two corners of the planned rug. Next, on tracing paper, draw a smaller rectangle, two corners of which fall on the same diagonal. Plan your design on the paper, then transfer it to the backing using the squares of a grid as a guide.

Braided Rugs

Transforming Wool Into Sturdy Rugs

Although we associate braided rugs with colonial furnishings, the colonists had neither time nor material to make them. Instead, they used sand or rushes as floor covering. In the 1830s, however, machine-made carpeting became widely available, and people soon came to favor rugs and carpets on their floors. At the same time, the introduction of machine-made yard goods reduced the cost of material and provided a source of leftover scraps and rags. Thrifty homemakers put these scraps to use by braiding them into small mats for hearth and bedside. Interest in the rugs revived in the 1920s when interior designers, wishing to create a rustic atmosphere in their clients' country homes, suggested the use of room-sized braided rugs.

Colorful hand-braided rug radiates 19th-century aura of hominess and simple elegance.

Sources and resources

Books
Cox, Verna. *Illustrated Braiding Instructions: Braided Rug Manual.* Verona Island, Maine: Cox Enterprises, 1967.
Sturges, Norma. *The Braided Rug Book: Creating Your Own American Folk Art.* Asheville, N.C.: Lark Books, 1995.
Materials
Braid-Aid. 466 Washington St., Pembroke, Mass. 02359.

Left-handed braiding

The braiding instructions given here are for right-handed people. If you are left-handed and find it awkward to fold and braid as indicated, reverse directional instructions. In particular, keep center folds to the right, make corners that turn to left, and lace from left to right around the rug.

Collecting and Preparing Wool

A multicolored "hit-or-miss" rug is the easiest, most traditional, and most economical type to make. You will need about 1 pound of heavy, tightly woven all-wool fabric per square foot of rug. Collect a variety of colors—bright, dull, neutral—in solids and patterns so that you can use some of each throughout your braid.

Used woolen clothing is the traditional source of braiding material, but you can also buy wool by the pound at low rates from mill outlets. To prepare clothing for braiding, first remove linings and other nonwool parts and cut the garments apart along the seams. Then wash the wool in hot water to soften and shrink it. The next step is to tear the wool into strips that can be folded into cables for braiding. It is extremely important to use the proper strip width because the rug quality depends upon the plumpness and uniformity of these cables. To determine the correct width, tear a test strip about 1 1/2 inches wide from your heaviest wool and fold it as illustrated at right. It should form a plump, round cable. If the cable is wide and flat, try a narrower strip. Once the width of the test strip has been determined, use the cable it forms as a model. Fabrics that are lighter in weight will need to be torn into proportionately wider strips and their edges overlapped to form cables of the

proper thickness as you braid. When tearing the strips, start each tear with scissors, then rip the rest of the way along the fabric grain. Weave a test braid with a few strips before tearing up all your fabric to be sure that the final strips make a firm and full braid.

After the strips are torn and joined, wind them into 5-inch-diameter rolls for storage. Before you start a roll, lay a 3-foot piece of string across one end of the strip, then roll up the strip around the string. Tie the string with a bowknot around the completed roll in order to keep the roll from unwinding.

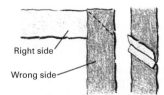

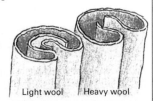

To join two strips, place them at 90° with right sides together; stitch on diagonal with matching thread, then cut off outer corners. Joined pieces open into straight strips.

Heaviest wool determines cable plumpness. Fold strip so edges meet, then in half again to form cable. Tear thin wool into wider strips, overlap edges for equally fat cable.

Getting Ready to Braid

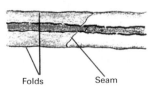

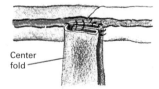

1. Join, with bias seam, the ends of two different colored strips. Fold edges inward so they meet at center of strip.

2. Fold a third strip into a cable. With its center fold to left, place on center of strip to form a T. Stitch in place.

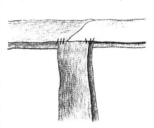

3. Fold crossbar strip in half lengthwise to enclose end of third strip. Stitch at inner corners of T.

4. Fold right arm of crossbar down and to left so it lies between two other strips and its center fold faces left.

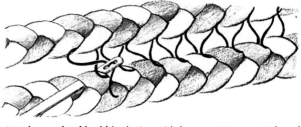

Attach rounds of braid by lacing with heavy cotton carpet thread and a blunt needle. Insert needle under braid loop and draw thread between loops and out top of braid. Work back and forth between loose braid and core of rug, lacing through each loop and pulling each stitch down into crevice of braid. Always lace on what will be back of rug because lacing will create a somewhat flattened look.

Skipped loop

You must occasionally skip a loop on the braid you are lacing because each successive round is longer than the preceding one. When a loop of the braid being added falls opposite another braid loop (instead of in a notch between two loops), do not lace the outer loop. Skip it and lace next loop instead. Skip only on shoulders (where the rug curves) and only one loop at a time. Mark skips with pins to avoid skipping at same point in successive rounds. If the rug edge ripples, you are skipping too often; if rug edge turns up, you are skipping too seldom.

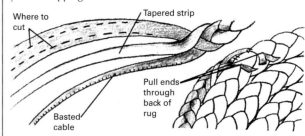

Where to cut   Tapered strip   Pull ends through back of rug   Basted cable

Final step is to taper last braid around a shoulder. Start by cutting off strips so they are 1 1/2 times as long as the distance around the shoulder; then use scissors to taper strips along each side. Strips should be barely wide enough to fold at their ends, widening gradually to full width at top of shoulder. Fold and baste tapered strips into cables, then braid and lace. Pull braid ends through loops on rug edge, sew into place, and trim excess.

1. Grip braid start in left hand, keeping center folds facing left. Fold right-hand strip to make cable. Note: Strips are folded as you braid.

2. Bring right-hand cable over center cable, twisting it as you go so that center fold stays to left. Push cable snugly against one above.

3. Shift already braided cables to right hand and use right little finger to help fold edges inward on left strip, forming more cable.

4. Bring left-hand cable over one in center, twisting to keep center fold left. Continue bringing cables over, pushing each against completed braid.

Forming the central braid

The length of the seam between the two central lengths of braid determines the size of the finished rug. Once you know the size you want, subtract the width from the length to find out how long to make the center seam. For example, a 4- by 6-foot rug needs a 2-foot-long seam.

Start your rug by making a braid length equal to the center seam. Next, make two corners in your braid (a braided corner is shown at right) to bring the braid back on itself. Continue braiding until the two lengths are equal, then sew and lace together as shown (below right).

Once the braid lengths are joined, you can easily see where to make a third corner so that when you braid further, the new braid will fit snugly against the old. After the third corner, braid only enough so that when you make a fourth corner it, too, will fit snugly. Sew and lace both corners in place. From this point lace as illustrated at far right.

A continuous spiral of braid, laced together, forms the rug.

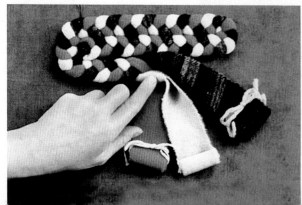

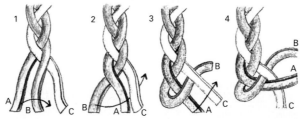

To make a corner in braid, start as shown above left. Step 1: Bring strand A over strand B and into center. Step 2: Bring B over A and under C. Step 3: Pull entire braid to right, and resume regular braiding by bringing A over C. Step 4: Hold C against A and B to maintain corner as you continue to braid.

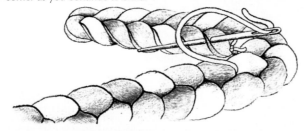

Use sew-and-lace technique to join central braid lengths. First turn braid over so side that faced you as you braided now faces away. Then knot end of thread and stitch so knot is hidden between two corners you have made in braid. Pass thread under first strand of cable on near arm of braid and pull thread tight; then stitch through the inward-folded edges of cable directly across from braid loop that has just been laced. Lace on near arm and sew on far arm for entire length.

Patchwork Quilting

An Art Spawned By New England's Frigid Winter

The history of patchwork quilting in America dates back to the first New England colonists. Most had brought quilted coverlets with them, but they quickly discovered that the harsh winters demanded far more substantial blanketing. Fabric was scarce and the women stitched together whatever bits and scraps were at hand to create larger pieces of cloth. These early patchworks were probably sewn randomly, in the style known as crazy quilt, but as fabric became more available simple geometric motifs were developed, and patchwork quilting began to evolve into a genuine American art form.

As patterns grew more elaborate, certain designs became popular and were christened with names such as Drunkard's Path, Sunshine and Shadow, and Wild Goose Chase. The patchwork block system also came into use, which broke the quilt design down into smaller units that were set together to make the whole quilt.

When a top was completed, it was the practice to hold a quilting bee to stitch together the top, bottom, and stuffing. These bees were social events as well as work sessions and were attended by menfolk and children as well as women.

Anything from dried leaves to pieces of rags, old blankets, and cotton batting were used to stuff a quilt. Nowadays polyester batting has become the most popular choice for a quilt stuffing. It is warm, resilient, and holds up well in laundering. Early patchwork quilts were sewn entirely by hand, but today a sewing machine can be used to stitch the patches together and even do some of the quilting. Purists, however, insist that only by hand stitching can the true spirit of the patchwork quilt be captured.

Quilting bees were occasions not only for work but also for socializing—as witness the couple holding hands at right.

A variety of quilt designs can be made based on the patterns in the next several pages.

Sources and resources

Books

Bolton, Janet. **Patchwork Folk Art: Using Applique and Quilting Techniques**. New York: Sterling Publishing, 1995.

Green, Marcy. **The Classic American Quilt Collection**. Emmaus, Pa.: Rodale Press, 1995.

Hanson, Joan, and Hickey, Mary. **The Joy of Quilting**. Bothell, Wash.: That Patchwork, 1995.

Ickis, Marguerite. **Standard Book of Quiltmaking and Collecting**. New York: Dover, 1949.

Landman, Annlee. **Learning to Quilt the Traditional Way**. New York: Sterling Publishing, 1994.

Martin, Judy. **Patchworkbook: Easy Lessons for Creative Quilt Design and Construction**. New York: Dover, 1994.

Savonen, Robby. **Nostalgia Patchwork and Quilting**. Des Moines, Iowa: Meredith Books, 1994.

Walker, Anne. **The Patchwork Pocket Palette: A Handy Visual Guide to Mixing and Matching Colored Fabrics**. San Francisco: Chronicle Books, 1995.

Tools and Supplies

Little in the way of special equipment is needed for patchwork quilting. Standard sewing tools and a few art supplies suffice. Fabrics used for the patchwork top should be light to medium in weight; cottons such as broadcloth, muslin, or percale are excellent, as are similar weaves of cotton-polyester. Avoid very heavy or very light fabrics as well as stretchy fabrics such as jersey.

When selecting fabrics of different colors for use in a quilt, be aware of the interplay between them in the finished pattern. Generally, you will want strong contrast between lights and darks. Also, small prints usually work better in patchwork because large-print designs are lost when cut into pieces. The backing fabric should be the same type used on the top. You may want to select a solid coordinating color or perhaps choose one of the prints used on the patchwork top. Bed sheets are excellent for backing, since they come in a variety of colors and prints and are large enough so that they do not need to be joined. The filler of a quilt is usually polyester batting in sheet form. The batting is sold in different sizes; try to purchase a batting sheet that is large enough for your particular quilt without having to be pieced together. Cotton batting can also be used; so too can old blankets. But for ease of working, ease of care, insulation value, and low cost, polyester is hard to beat. Plus it tends to hold together in one piece so that less quilting is required to prevent shifting or shredding.

To hand-stitch patchwork pieces together, use regular sewing needles, called sharps (size 8), and an all-purpose thread. When quilting, use needles that are slightly shorter: quilting needles or "betweens" (size 8–10). Special quilting thread is available that has a glazed surface. You can also use any all-purpose thread, but first run it through beeswax. Straight pins are handy to hold the patchwork pieces in place before they are sewn together. A good pair of scissors is a necessity; so too is a thimble to protect the middle finger of your sewing hand.

Art supplies that are useful in patchwork quilting include a hard lead pencil that does not smudge, graph paper, tracing paper, sturdy cardboard for making templates, a ruler, a compass for working circular designs, and a set of coloring pencils or pens.

If the quilt is large, a quilting frame that provides even tension and holds the three layers together while you work on them is very helpful. It also allows several people to work on the quilt at the same time. You can obtain quilting frames at most needlework stores or through large mail-order houses. If you wish, you can construct your own frame as shown at right. For smaller quilting projects a quilting hoop, similar to an embroidery hoop only larger, can be used.

Selecting Patchwork Designs

Most patchwork quilts are formed by setting individual square blocks together. When selecting a block design, you must know what the overall effect will be: a pattern that creates one impression in a single block may appear quite different once the blocks are set side by side.

Each block is usually made up of smaller square units called patches. Depending on the design, the block is generally broken into 4, 9, 16, or 25 patches. These patches themselves consist of the basic patchwork units: triangles, rectangles, circles, parts of circles—even trapezoids—cut from various fabrics and sewn together. You will find that you can change the look of a particular block simply by interchanging the elements within the patches, by rearranging the patches within the block, or by varying the color scheme. Before picking a design, first sketch out the possibilities on graph paper. For each design being considered you should draw out at least four full blocks. Because differences in color can change the whole look of a design, color the experimental blocks on a tissue paper overlay.

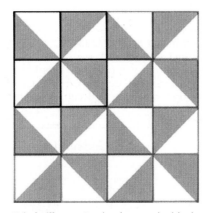

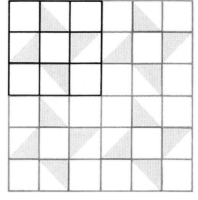

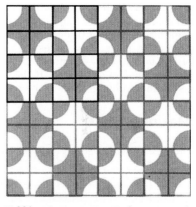

Windmill, a simple four-patch block, is created by dividing each of the four patches into triangles. Every other triangle is colored with a dark value.

Friendship Star, a typical nine-patch block, alternates plain patches with patches divided into triangles. Simple colors emphasize the star motif.

Robbing Peter to Pay Paul, a 16-patch block, is a variation of Drunkard's Path. New colors and new layout yield a repetitive, circular motif.

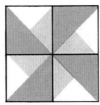

Variation on the windmill is achieved by dividing every other triangle into two smaller ones and adding another color.

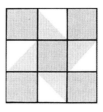

Adding another color to the block design achieves a slightly more intricate look without altering any of the basic pieces.

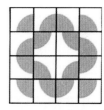

Changing colors and arrangement slightly but using identical cutting patterns achieves an entirely different, more diffuse effect.

A do-it-yourself quilting frame

Quilting frame shown here is easy to make and easy to disassemble for storage. Dimensions can be adjusted to suit your needs. Make the rails long enough to accommodate the entire width of the quilt plus an extra 12 in. at each end. When using the frame sew or staple the ends of the quilt to the rails, put one rail in its slots, roll up the quilt on the other rail until it is taut, and insert the second rail in its slots. Quilters often lace the sides of the quilt to the crosspieces with carpet thread to achieve more uniform tension.

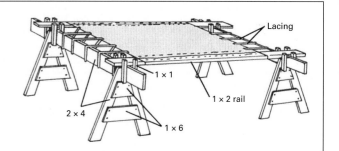

Lacing

1 × 1

1 × 2 rail

2 × 4

1 × 6

The Patchwork Top: Start to Finish

Once you have worked out the quilt's design, the next step is to make a draft of the quilt to serve as a guide during its construction. First, determine the overall dimensions of the quilt. These depend upon the size of the bed on which the quilt will be used and on how much overhang you would like at the sides and foot. Start by making up the bed fully with all blankets, sheets, and pillows in place. Now measure the length and width of the bed and the length of the hang on each side as well as the foot of the bed. If the quilt is to be a coverlet, it should hang down to the top of the box spring. A

coordinated dust ruffle is generally added to cover the box spring. A full bedspread, on the other hand, covers the entire bed and falls to 1/2 inch above the floor at the foot and sides. If a pillow tuck is desired, an additional 14 inches or so should be added to the length. Formulas to compute quilt size are as follows:

Length = Bed length + Hang at foot + Pillow tuck
Width = Bed width + Twice side hang.

As a rough guide you can use the following standard mattress sizes to estimate quilt dimensions:

Crib: 27 inches by 52 inches
Twin bed: 39 inches by 75 inches
Double bed: 54 inches by 75 inches
Queen-size bed: 60 inches by 80 inches
King-size bed: 72 inches by 84 inches.

The quilt measurements that you calculate should be looked on as approximations that can be varied somewhat to accommodate the size of the individual patch-

work blocks. Blocks can range from 10 to 16 inches for full-size quilts and from 8 to 12 inches for smaller quilts. Select a size that is appropriate for your design and that will allow the top to be pieced together entirely out of complete blocks. Fit as many full blocks as possible into the desired quilt dimensions. If, on the first try, the quilt dimensions are not an exact multiple of block size, adjust block size or quilt size until they are. You can also add strips or borders to make up the difference.

When choosing block size, keep in mind that block measurements should be easily divisible by the number of patches in the block. In other words, the patches should be in whole inches rather than inches plus odd fractions. For example, the Friendship Star block is made up of nine patches. If the block is a 12-inch square, each patch will be a conveniently sized 4-inch square, but if the block is a 10-inch square, each patch will be a hard-to-measure 3 1/3-inch square.

Making a Draft

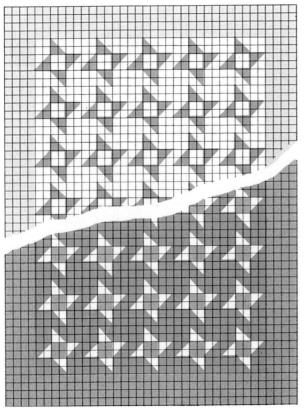

Before cutting any fabric or starting any other work on a quilt, draw the entire quilt design to scale on graph paper. Such a drawing serves as a guide for you as you work. It will also give you an overall view of your proposed quilt design. It is at this stage that you can start determining the colors. Lay tracing paper over the graph-paper drawing and experiment with different color combinations until you come upon a combination that pleases you. Use colored pencils or felt-tip pens to color in your choices. The two color schemes shown here illustrate that profoundly different results can be achieved in a quilt by altering its coloring. Remember that the colors you plan are simply preferences; the actual color scheme will vary according to how closely the fabrics you eventually find match those shown on your drawing.

Strips and borders

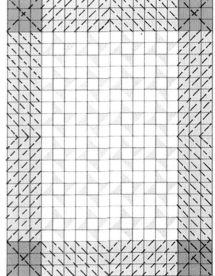

Patchwork blocks can be separated from each other with fabric strips to keep blocks from clashing, to increase quilt size, or simply to add more variety to a pattern. Strips can be in one piece or patched. Small, square patches are often introduced at intersecting corners, as shown, for additional design interest.

Borders around a quilt are quite common. They frame the patchwork design as well as adding width and length to the quilt. Borders can be made of solid fabric or of small patch designs. If a solid-color material is used for a border, it is usually decorated with additional and often elaborate quilting designs.

Cutting the Fabric Pieces

The pieces of material that will be sewn together to make the patchwork top must be cut out carefully and joined with precision in order for them to fit in the blocks as planned. Templates are used to ensure accuracy. You will need two templates for each different shape in the block—one for cutting the fabric and one for marking seams. Since the templates are used over and over again, they should be made of sturdy cardboard.

Once the templates are made, use your plan to determine how many pieces of each shape must be cut from each fabric. Before cutting all the pieces, test the accuracy of your templates by stitching or pinning an entire block together. Once you are satisfied that the pieces fit properly and the block size is correct, cut out the remaining pieces you will need for the quilt. Take your time when working; accuracy is important, especially if you have an intricate design. Sort the pieces by color and shape, and store them in separate envelopes.

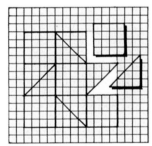

1. Draw block design to true size on graph paper. Cut out each different shape in the design, then use the cutouts to outline the shapes on cardboard. Make two outlines for each shape.

2. Mark off 1/4-in. seam allowance around one outline in each pair and cut out. Cut other templates along original outlines. Smaller templates are for marking, larger ones for cutting.

3. Lay cutting template on right side of fabric and mark around it with a sharp pencil; then move template along fabric and mark off new piece. Each marked shape should be flush against the previous one.

4. After patchwork pieces are cut out, mark stitching lines on each by centering appropriate marking template on wrong side of piece; then trace around template with a sharp pencil.

Assembling the Pieces to Complete the Top

When sewing the sections of a block together, be sure every seam joining two pieces is worked precisely. To stitch a simple straight seam, place the two pieces together, right side against right side, making sure the stitching lines of each piece are aligned. Use straight pins if necessary to maintain the alignment.

If you are sewing by hand, use a very fine running stitch and reinforce the seam by taking three or four overcast stitches at the start and end of the seam. If you use a machine, set the stitch length to 10 per inch.

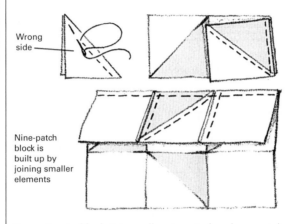

Wrong side

Nine-patch block is built up by joining smaller elements

To construct a block, join smaller pieces to form larger patches, then connect the patches. In the example shown, triangles are joined to form squares; squares are joined to form rows; and rows are joined to form blocks.

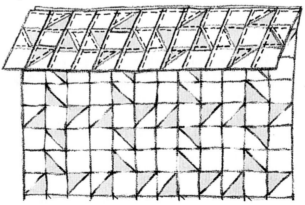

When all the rows are completed, stitch them together to form the patchwork top. Again, keep all matching seam crossings carefully aligned. Press the completed patchwork top with an iron to take out wrinkles, folds, and creases.

After a seam is stitched, press the seam allowances to one side with an iron before attaching another piece. Stitching a curved seam is a bit trickier, since the seam allowances bunch up when flattened.

Quilters generally prefer to complete all the patchwork blocks before they set them together to form the completed quilt top. Consult your initial plan at this point to avoid any mishaps. It would also pay to check the block arrangement by laying all the blocks out on the floor before stitching them together.

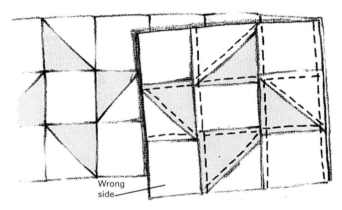

Wrong side

In order to join two blocks, lay one on top of the other, right sides facing and seam crossings aligned; then sew together. Keep adding blocks until a row is completed. Stitch the other blocks together into rows the same way.

Joining curved seams

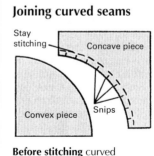

Stay stitching — Concave piece

Convex piece — Snips

Before stitching curved pieces together place a row of stay stitching just within the seam allowance of the concave piece. Make a series of snips in the seam allowance every 3/4 in. just up to the stay-stitching line.

Place concave piece on top of convex piece, right sides facing. Working from the center out to the edges, match and pin them along seamlines. Concave piece uppermost, sew the seam from one edge to other.

Joining the Layers To Finish the Job

The primary function of quilting (sewing together the top, filler, and backing) is to hold the three layers in place. However, quilting can also provide an additional decorative touch to the patchwork top. Most patchwork quilts are put together with simple outline quilting that follows the borders of individual motifs. When quilting in this manner, lines of quilting are stitched approximately 3/8 inch from seam lines; this avoids stitching through seam allowances. Experienced quilters can judge the distance by eye; beginners should mark quilting lines lightly with a ruler and hard lead pencil.

Decorative quilting is generally employed to adorn plain strips, plain borders, and large open spaces within blocks. Traditional designs range from elaborate feathers and scrolls to simple straight-line patterns. For more elaborate quilting motifs select one of the special designs that are available from mail-order firms or some needlework shops. When decorative quilting is to be done, mark the top with the quilting lines before you place it on the filler and backing.

The filler and backing are usually cut to the same size as the top. However, if you plan to finish the edges by the extended binding method (p.293), cut the backing a little larger. If the backing fabric must be pieced to bring it up to size, try to avoid having a center seam. For example, use a full fabric width down the center and partial widths on either side to make up the desired length. Press the backing to remove wrinkles.

Assemble the quilt by spreading the backing, wrong side up, on a clean floor and laying the filler on top of it; be careful not to crease the backing. Next, place the patchwork top over the filler, right side up. Again, smooth out any wrinkles. Then baste all three layers together and set them into a quilting frame so that they are taut but not drum tight. To quilt, thread the needle with a single strand of thread about 18 inches long and make a knot in one end. Insert the needle from the top, pull through to the backing, and gently tug the thread so that the knot pops through the top layer and lodges in the filler. Quilt with small, even stitches. To end a line of quilting, tie a knot in the thread close to the top of the quilt and make the final stitch by running the needle through the filler, bringing it up again. Then gently tug the knot so that it pops through the top layer and lodges in the filler. Cut off the thread end.

Assembling the Parts and Quilting Them Together

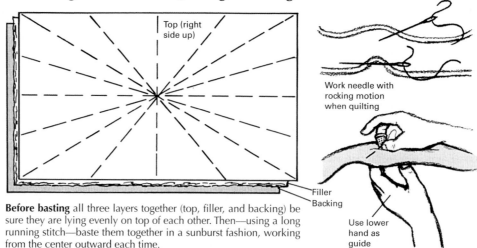

Work needle with rocking motion when quilting

When quilting, hold needle securely and use a rocking motion to pick up three or four stitches on needle before pulling it through. Keep one hand below the quilt to act as a guide and to ensure that you are sewing through all three layers consistently. The needle should graze your index finger with each stitch. Your aim should be to develop a fine quilting stitch, about 12 stitches per inch; long stitches break more easily than small ones when the quilt is being used or laundered.

Use lower hand as guide

Filler
Backing

Before basting all three layers together (top, filler, and backing) be sure they are lying evenly on top of each other. Then—using a long running stitch—baste them together in a sunburst fashion, working from the center outward each time.

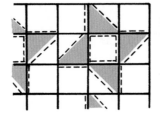

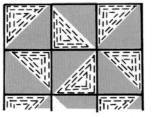

Quilting generally follows seam lines—it is a matter of choice which seam lines are quilted and which are not. At left, quilting is used to emphasize star motif. Use of "echoing," at right, adds dimension, texture, and interest.

Plain borders and strips are ideal areas on which to carry out decorative quilting designs. Even a grid of simple diagonal lines or a series of clamshell motifs are effective. Traditional designs include elaborate scrolls, feathers, medallions, and pineapples.

Tying a quilt

Another way besides quilting to hold the three layers together is to tie them at designated points, using one or more strands of decorative embroidery floss or yarn. This method is much quicker and easier to accomplish than actual quilting and is especially effective for very puffy batting. Use the patch design as a guide to select the tie points. You can place ties at each corner of small blocks or within different points of each block to form a pattern. In order to keep the stuffing from shifting, be sure not to leave an untied area greater than a 7-in. square. For variation, tie a bow or sew a button at tying points.

Ties

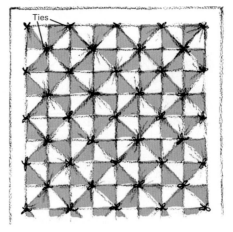

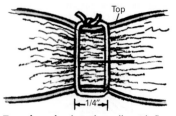

Top

⊢1/4"⊣

To make a tie, thread needle with floss or yarn, but do not knot ends. At each tie point bring needle down to backing side, leaving about 6 in. of thread on top. Push needle back up about 1/4 in. from original entry point, leave another 6 in. of thread on top, and cut. Tie the ends together securely in a square knot or decorative bow, and trim off excess.

Binding the Quilt

The finishing step on a patchwork quilt is to bind the edges, using either a separate binding strip or an extension from the backing fabric or the top. Bindings are usually narrow—about 1/2 inch wide—but can be broader if desired. If you plan to bind with extended backing, you must cut the backing a little larger beforehand. The extra fabric you will need consists of the desired binding width plus 1/4 inch along each edge. For a standard 1/2-inch binding this comes to an extra 3/4 inch at each end and each side. If you intend to bind with an extended top, make the patchwork top the larger piece.

For the separate binding method, cut 2-inch-wide strips of fabric (either matching or contrasting) and join them together until their length equals the quilt perimeter plus an extra 6 inches. If the quilt has square corners, cut the fabric strips along the straight grain. For rounded corners cut the strips on the bias; the binding will turn the corners more easily.

Extended backing method

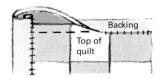

Use iron to press under 1/4-in. seam allowances all around the backing. Next, fold backing over edges of quilt and around to front. Then slip-stitch it to front of quilt.

Separate binding method

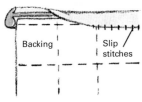

1. With right side of binding facing quilt top, position binding along one end of quilt. Stitch through all layers about 3/8 in. from edge of quilt. Turn binding up and iron along stitch line.

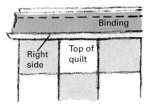

2. Bring binding around to back of quilt. Turn under raw edge of binding, iron it flat, then slip-stitch the binding to the backing. Cut off unused binding. Bind other end of quilt in same way.

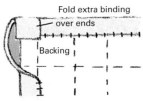

3. Bind sides of quilt in similar fashion, only leave the binding extended 1/2 in. beyond ends. Fold extensions over ends as shown, then turn down the binding and slip-stitch it in place.

Shoofly quilt

Fabric requirements for 86- by 100-in. quilt

- 2 3/4 yd. of 45-in. green fabric
- 4 yd. of 45-in. yellow fabric
- 2 1/3 yd. of 45-in. coral fabric
- 6 yd. of 45-in. coordinated fabric for backing
- 86- by 100-in. sheet of polyester batting

From the green fabric, cut 168 triangles, 42 large squares, and 56 small squares. Cut 168 triangles and 168 large squares from the yellow fabric. Cut 97 coral rectangles. Make 42 blocks by piecing the large green and yellow squares and the triangles together as shown in the design plan. To make a strip row, alternately join seven small green squares and six coral rectangles together, starting and ending with a square. Make eight strip rows. Next, set six blocks and seven rectangles together in a row, placing a rectangle between each block and at the start and end of the row. Make seven rows with the blocks and rectangles in this manner. Now join the strip rows to the block rows, setting a strip row at top and bottom. Cut backing fabric so that it extends 3/4 inch beyond top at sides and ends. Cut the batting to the same size as the quilt top. Baste the three layers together and quilt as shown. Bind the edges with extended binding. An illustration of part of the finished quilt is on page 288.

Drunkard's Path quilt

Fabric requirements for 84- by 96-in. quilt

- 5 1/4 yd. of 45-in. white fabric
- 2 5/8 yd. of 45-in. blue fabric
- 2 5/8 yd. of 45-in. brown fabric
- 6 yd. of 45-in. coordinated fabric for backing
- 84 1/2- by 96-in. sheet of polyester batting

Cut 448 quarter circles and 448 corner pieces from white fabric, 224 quarter circles and 224 corner pieces from each of the blue and brown fabrics. Join all blue and brown quarter circles to white corner pieces and all white quarter circles to the blue and brown corner pieces. To keep track of the stitched patches, make four piles: brown quarter circles together, blue quarter circles together, brown corners together, and blue corners together. Study the block design and carefully join patches to match it. Make 56 blocks. Set blocks together (seven in each row) so that the blues run diagonally in one direction and the browns in the opposite direction. Cut backing fabric for an extended binding, and cut batting to same size as top. Baste all layers together and quilt as shown. Bind edges with extended binding. A photograph of the finished design is on page 288.

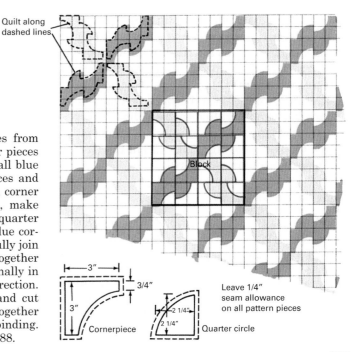

Quilt along dashed lines

Strip row

Block

Leave 1/4" seam allowance on all pattern pieces

4"   4"   12"   2"   2"

Quilt along dashed lines

Block

3"   3/4"   3"   Cornerpiece   2 1/4"   2 1/4"   Quarter circle

Leave 1/4" seam allowance on all pattern pieces

Rope and Twine

A Few Simple Knots For a Fine Hammock

The art of netmaking, perfected by fishermen over the centuries, can be put to an almost limitless number of uses. Once the fundamentals are mastered, you will be able to make netting that is strong enough to catch a tuna or delicate enough to wear as lace. The sturdy, attractive hammock whose construction is shown here illustrates the basic netting knots. With the same techniques a string bag can be crafted that will haul bulky objects but collapse into almost nothing when empty. Or by employing velvety chenille yarn, you can make a dramatic net shawl.

Filling the netting needle

Loop yarn back and forth around spike until needle is full.

294

A Gallery of Fishermen's Knots

One basic knot and two variations are needed to create net mesh. Start by winding twine onto a netting needle. Next, tie the end of the twine to a shower curtain ring and clip the ring to a heavy piece of furniture or other solid object. The ring can then serve as an anchor, allowing you to keep the net taut as you work. You will also need to cut out a netting gauge—a rectangle of plastic, wood, or cardboard—to help maintain uniform mesh size. To use the gauge, hold it firmly against a just-completed loop, then wrap the twine around it to make the next loop. When a length of twine runs out, use a square knot to tie on new twine at the end of a row.

Basic knot. Bulk of netting is accomplished by using this simple knot over and over.

Increase knot. To make one row longer than the previous row, use this knot.

Decrease knot. To make one row narrower than the previous row, use this knot.

New row. To start new row, turn mesh over, make first knot in last loop of old row.

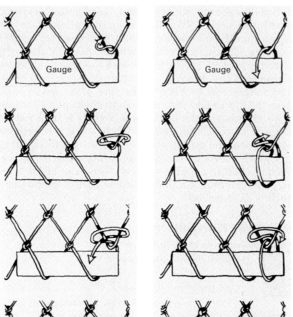

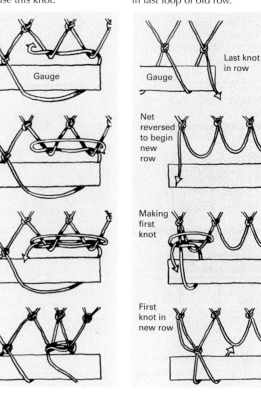

Starting the net

Use square knot to tie twine to shower curtain ring. Then clip ring onto convenient, nonmovable object, such as heavy furniture, so that you can pull mesh taut while working.

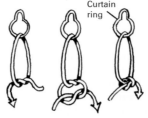

Curtain ring

Tying the final loop

When net is completed, tie last two loops together. Pass twine through both, then tie double knot in twine end.

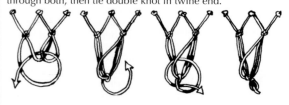

Solid 2-inch-diameter metal rings are available at marine and hardware stores.

Making Net for the Hammock Bed

The simple netting techniques shown on page 294 are all employed in constructing the bed of the hammock shown here. Use a gauge that is 2 inches wide to control mesh size (6 inches is a convenient length for the gauge). You will need three 2-pound cones of 30-ply butcher's twine or other strong, nonscratchy string. Such large cones of twine are available at office supply and stationery stores and are usually less expensive than smaller balls. To give the hammock additional texture and strength, wind the needle with doubled strands of twine; then use them as one when making the net.

Start the hammock by making a single loop. Move to the next row and increase to make two loops in that row.

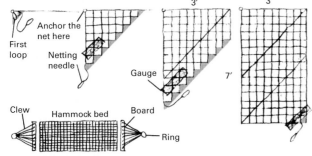

Build up bed of hammock in stages, then add clews at ends.

Increase at the end of every following row until the bed is 3 feet wide. Then start increasing at the end of one row and decreasing at the end of the next row until the bed's longest side measures 7 feet. (A ribbon tied at the short side will help you remember to decrease in rows ending there.) When one side is 7 feet long, begin decreasing at the end of every row until only two loops remain. Tie these loops together and clip off the excess twine.

Preparing Clews to Support the Hammock

In order to hang the hammock, supports, called clews, must be made for each end of the bed. You will need 40 yards of additional twine, a pair of 2-inch-diameter solid metal rings (available at marine and hardware stores), and two 1- by 3- by 29-inch boards. Drill twelve 3/8-inch-diameter holes in each of the boards, beveling the edges of the holes so that they will not cut into the clew strings. Place board and ring 24 inches apart and secure them in place before you start threading. Thread with doubled twine. Construct two clews, then attach the bed. Skip a loop now and then when threading the bed to the clews so that it will be evenly spaced.

Threading

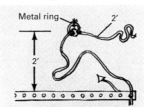

1. Tie 10 yd. of doubled twine to ring, leaving 2-ft. tail. Thread into hole.

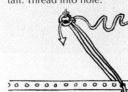

2. Thread from bottom to top of ring, then from top to bottom of board.

3. Continue threading from board to ring and back until all holes are used.

4. Working from tied end to free end, pull each strand taut. Tie twine end to ring.

Weaving

1. Prepare to weave twine through clew strands by first weaving ruler through.

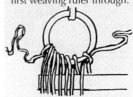

2. Strands under ring go on top of ruler; strands on top of ring go under ruler.

3. Turn ruler on edge, pass two tails between separated strands and pull tight.

4. Weave ruler through again so strands above ruler in Step 2 now go below.

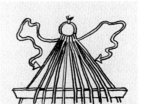

5. Again, as in Step 3, pass tails through but leave outermost strands free.

6. Continue, leaving one strand unwoven at each side of each successive row.

7. When two strands remain unwoven, cross tails over them, then push to back.

8. Cross tails again under last two strands, bring back to top, and tie square knot.

Attaching net

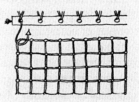

1. Knot end of 4-ft.-long twine. Thread up through board, then through mesh.

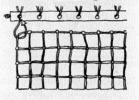

2. Pull twine through net mesh and insert end back into first hole in board.

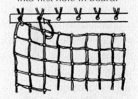

3. Push twine up through second hole, then through mesh and back into hole.

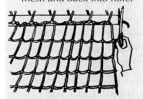

4. Continue until net is attached to top of board. Knot end behind last hole.

Tanning and Leatherwork

A Sensible Craft Whether for Necessity Or Just as a Hobby

Tanning and leatherwork call for a comparatively small investment in tools but can yield a great amount of satisfaction. There is a real sense of achievement in converting a rabbit skin, which a hunter might otherwise throw away, into a soft, lustrous fur and then into warm mittens or a fine hat. With experience, tanning and leatherwork can also become profitable sidelines. Hunters are frequently glad to pay to have the pelt of an animal made into pliable leather, a fur rug, or a trophy to hang on the wall.

The craft of tanning is older than civilization itself. Chemical tanning, as it is practiced today, existed at least 5,000 years ago—there are Egyptian wall paintings showing tanners at work with their tubs and mixing vats. Long before that, our prehistoric ancestors used the hides of animals to clothe themselves. At first, they must have worn the skins just as they came from the animal. Untreated hides, however, are stiff, crack easily, decompose rapidly, and, in addition, may emit an obnoxious odor. Eventually it was discovered that a hide could be treated to make it durable as well as comfortable. The earliest leather-conditioning methods probably involved nothing more than scraping off all the flesh and hair from the hide. The result must have been close to rawhide, a material the American Indians used to make drumheads, lashings, saddles, knife handles, sandals, and snowshoe thongs. The next development probably involved the application of animal fat or other substance—the Indians used animal brains—to soften the leather and make it more water resistant. Other skin-dressing procedures included smoking, soaking in urine, and rubbing with plant or animal oil.

American Indians were skilled leatherworkers. Here an Indian chief dries a rawhide in traditional fashion.

Different Leathers and Where to Get Them

Hunting, trapping, or raising your own livestock are the most direct ways of obtaining the hides you need to make fur or leather. Remember, however, that there are strict regulations governing where, when, and how you may hunt and trap game. There are also endangered species that must not be taken at any time of the year.

Another potential source of hides, especially for rabbit skins, is your local butcher. He may also be able to obtain cow, goat, sheep, and pig hides from a local slaughterhouse, or you can try the slaughterhouse yourself. Some hunters and trappers will sell animal pelts at relatively low prices; a hunter may even let you have them for free, since many hunters are more interested in an animal for sport or food than for its hide. A farm that slaughters its own animals can be another economical source of untanned leather. If you do not care to do the tanning yourself, you can obtain leather from stores listed in the classified telephone directory. Many of these stores cater to the hobbyist and carry a wide variety of hides. Generally, they will also stock a complete line of leatherworking equipment, such as needles, heavy thread, awls, and punches, as well as buckles, lacing, snaps, dyes, leather lubricants, and varnishes.

Animal	Use	Comments
Bear	Rugs	Hard, durable
Beaver	Coats	Wears well
Calf	Slippers, purses, wallets	Soft, durable
Cow	Jackets, gloves, belts, luggage, shoes	Rough, wears well
Deer	Gloves, moccasins	Soft, pliable, wears very well
Fox	Fur coats, jackets	Fairly durable, warm
Goat	Purses, wallets, gloves	Very fine leather
Muskrat	Fur coats	Wears well
Pig	Wallets, gloves	Wears well
Rabbit	Gloves	Delicate fur
Raccoon	Hats, coats	Fairly delicate
Sheep	Gloves, slippers, rugs	Soft, warm
Squirrel	Fur coats	Wears well
Wolf	Coat trimming	Warm, sheds snow
Woodchuck	Gloves	Delicate

The First Step Is to Remove the Hide

The object of skinning is to remove the animal's pelt cleanly, neatly, and with minimum damage to either hide or fur. To skin an animal perfectly requires experience. The first time, you are almost certain to damage the hide by slicing too close or else by cutting too cautiously and leaving large chunks of flesh that will mean extra work during the fleshing operation.

Practice skinning a few times with an inexpensive hide before trying your hand on more costly leather. A chipmunk, or even a mouse, is suitable for your first attempts, especially since they are more difficult to skin than larger specimens and so help attune you to the fine points of the skinner's craft. Another good choice for a first attempt would be a freshly killed rabbit from the butcher; if you slash through the hide, you can at least console yourself with a rabbit dinner.

The best tool to use is a skinning knife, an implement with a thin, curved blade specially designed for the job. However, good results can be obtained with almost any blade, provided it is razor sharp. For this reason, keep a sharpening stone handy, particularly since even the best edge will dull during the skinning operation. Note that while a single-edge razor blade can be used for making the first incisions, it should not be employed for the actual skinning: there is too much risk that the blade will slip, cutting either you or the hide.

Once the incisions are made, pull the skin gently away until you run into resistance. When this happens, it means the skin is being held by a membrane or other tissue. Use the knife to cut restricting tissue loose, then resume pulling. Throughout the skinning operation the animal must be held tightly to keep it from shifting.

All animals are skinned in much the same fashion. Generally, the skin on the animal's head and paws is not removed. Instead, incisions are made around the neck and feet, and the rest of the pelt is pulled off. Large animals, such as a bear whose skin is to be made into a rug, may have the head and paws left on the hide.

Once the skin is off the animal, the next step is to flesh it; that is, to remove bits of fat and meat that still adhere to the underside. To make fleshing easier, first soak the unfleshed skin in a solution of either salt or borax to loosen the clinging bits of flesh. Instructions for pre-soaking as well as for fleshing are given at the right. To make a salt solution, dissolve 1 pound of ordinary table salt per 2 gallons of soft water. For a borax solution dissolve 1 ounce of borax per gallon of water. Use hot water when dissolving the borax, but let it cool off before immersing the skin. An agitator-type washing machine will speed the soaking process and also help reduce hair loss from the pelt by avoiding oversoaking.

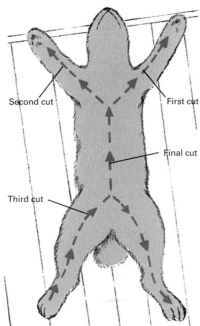

Make the first incision at the breastbone. Starting at this point, cut to the heel of one front leg and then to the heel of the other front leg. Next, cut from the heel of one back leg to the other. Now make one long incision joining both leg cuts as indicated in the drawing. Be sure to use a knife that is razor sharp.

Skin can be pulled off a rabbit with little additional cutting. However, with most other animals the skin must be pulled off a bit at a time, as though it were a very tight glove, until the hide resists further pulling; then use the knife to free the hide. Cut close to the skin, but be careful not to cut into the hide.

Last step in skinning is to free the pelt by incising a circle around the neck and around each leg near the paw. After the skin is off, use a dull knife or the back of the skinning knife to scrape off any flesh or fat that can be removed easily. Leave on pieces that adhere tightly; they will be removed in the fleshing operation.

Fleshing the hide

Before you flesh the hide, soak it in a brine or borax solution to make the flesh easier to remove. Let the hide soak about 12 hours—overnight will do. The next morning, rinse the hide in fresh water and let it drain. Then, while it is still moist, rub in salt until the flesh side is completely covered (avoid getting salt into the fur side). When the first application of salt has been absorbed, apply a second. Fold the hide in half lengthwise, flesh side to flesh side, roll it up, and place it on a slanting surface so that it can drain. Begin fleshing the next day. Place the hide on a smooth log, fur side down, and scrape away fat and gristle with a fleshing knife, butcher's knife, or drawknife. The log should be about 4 ft. long and 8 in. in diameter. Split it so one side is flat and work on the other side, which should be very smooth. Scrape carefully and evenly. The membrane on the hide's inner surface must be removed for tanning to be successful. Scrape with the blunt edge of the knife blade occasionally to help soften the leather. After fleshing is complete, wash the hide in a soapy solution, then rinse quickly and thoroughly.

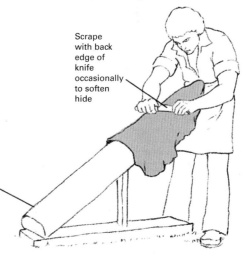

Scrape with back edge of knife occasionally to soften hide

Tanner's log: split 8" diameter log in half for use in fleshing. For small pelts substitute a 2 x 4 whose edges have been rounded

Converting a Hide Into Leather

There are almost as many formulas for tanning solutions as there are tanners, each one swearing by his own mixture. The recipe given here has two advantages: it will not overtan and it has no dangerous acids or toxic vapors. Nevertheless, when working with this tanning solution, as with all others, always use rubber gloves; tanning chemicals are not good for the skin. Use a large plastic or wooden container or nonmetallic washbasin for both mixing and tanning. To make the tanning solution, add 5 lb. of ordinary salt to 10 gal. of warm water. The water should be soft—rainwater will do. Next, mix 2 lb. of alum in enough hot water to dissolve it, then combine both solutions, stirring with a wooden paddle until the ingredients are thoroughly mixed. The solution can be used cold or warm but not hot.

Immerse the hide into the tanning solution and stir gently about twice a day with a wooden paddle. For a perfectly tanned piece of fur or leather make certain the tanning solution reaches every cranny and wrinkle in the hide. The larger the hide, the longer it takes to tan it. A rabbit skin will take about two days, a raccoon about three days. A deer may take from six to eight days, while a sheepskin may take a little less.

The ABCs of Tanning

Tanning converts an animal hide, which would otherwise decompose rapidly, into fur or leather that will stay soft and odor free for years. Originally, tanning was accomplished using tannic acid obtained from trees and vegetables, but most tanners today employ alum. To do a professional job, you must take time to tan the hide thoroughly and to work it until it is pliable.

After the hide has been soaked in the tanning solution for several days, cut off a tiny piece near one edge. If the color is uniform all the way through, then the hide is tanned. But if there is a difference in color between the center and edges, return the skin to the solution for an extra day or two. The most common mistake is to take a pelt out before tanning is complete.

Tanning procedures are the same whether you are processing leather or a fur. However, if the hair is to be removed, it must be removed from the hide before tanning takes place. The easiest way to get the hair off is to start by soaking the hide in a dehairing solution. Use 1 pound of hydrated lime per 8 gallons of soft water and soak for about five days (longer in cool weather) in a wooden container. Move the hide around occasionally with a wooden paddle. (Lime is caustic, so avoid contact with it.) When the hair is loose, rinse the hide, then place it fur side up on a smooth log, and scrape off the hair and loose surface skin with the dull edge of your fleshing knife. Use the same log or type of log that was employed for fleshing (see *Fleshing the hide,* p.297).

1. After the hide is tanned, remove it from the solution; then rinse it with a garden hose or in a sink with many changes of water.

2. Hang the hide fur side up over a railing. It should be out of direct sunlight, and air should be able to circulate around the hide.

3. After several days, while the hair and hide are still slightly damp, fold the hide flesh side to flesh side, roll it up, and leave it overnight.

4. If the hide has dried before you are able to roll it up, use a wet sponge to dampen the flesh side. Then fold it as described in Step 3.

5. Work the hide by stretching it, pulling it over a smooth edge, and twisting it with your hands. Continue working until it is pliable.

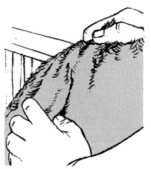

6. Use the tips of your fingers to rub in neat's-foot, cottonseed, corn, or leather lubricating oil. Warm the oil to speed up the work.

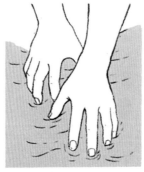

7. To clean the matted fur, fill plastic bag with dry oatmeal or hardwood sawdust. Then place hide in bag and shake until fur is clean.

8. Brush and comb fur until it is entirely fluffed up. Go over rough spots on underside of leather with coarse sandpaper wrapped around a block.

Rawhide: A Material for All Seasons

Rawhide is untanned leather—usually dehaired—that has been cured by being stretched and dried. To the Plains Indians, buffalo rawhide was a vital all-purpose material, serving as lumber, nails, cord, and cloth. Nowadays rawhide is commonly made from deer or cow skin and can be used for moccasin soles, knife handle grips, boxes, construction lashing, lacing for snowshoes, and drumheads for tom-toms. A special quality of rawhide is that it shrinks as it dries, tightening and forming itself around any object to which it is attached.

Use a fresh pelt when making rawhide. Skin and flesh the animal in the usual fashion, but do not salt the pelt. The next step is dehairing. You can use a dehairing solution of lime and water (see *The ABCs of Tanning*, p. 298) or one of wood ash and water, which combine to form lye. For the latter method make a paste of hardwood ashes and water, spread it on the hair side, then roll the skin up over the paste and place the roll, weighted down with a rock, in an ash and water solution. Wear rubber gloves as you work, since the water and ash mixture is caustic. Leave the hide in the dehairing bath until the hair can be pulled out easily—usually several days—then scrape off the hair with a blunt knife. Finally, rinse the hide thoroughly, wring it out, stretch it on a frame, and set it out to dry in a shady spot. It will dry into a hard, flat, platelike sheet.

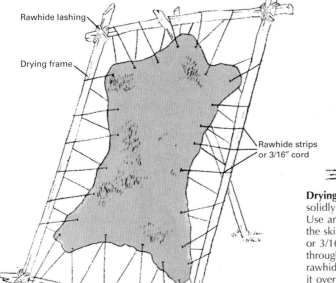

Rawhide lashing
Drying frame
Rawhide strips or 3/16″ cord

Rawhide lacing—or any type of leather lacing—is made by cutting a spiral in the hide. Place the leather on a board and drive a nail through, near the center, pinning the leather to the board. With a very sharp knife held vertically, cut a circular spiral. Start from the outside and work in toward the nail. When the nail is reached, remove the leather strip and stretch it out.

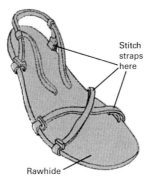

Stitch straps here

Rawhide

Moccasins with soles made of rawhide rather than tanned leather were used by some High Plains tribes. An equivalent contemporary use would be sandals—some believe rawhide to be the best sandal material. The width of the sandal should be 1/2 in. wider than the foot all the way around. Straps can be sewn, stapled, riveted, or simply laced through slots. Make them of soft leather.

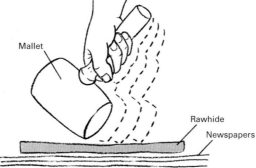

Mallet

Rawhide

Newspapers

Drying frame for rawhide should be built of stout branches lashed solidly together. Make the frame considerably larger than the hide. Use an awl or leather punch to make holes around the edge of the skin, then lash the skin to the frame by lacing rawhide strips or 3/16-in. cord through one hole, around the frame, and back through the next hole until the hide is stretched taut. After it is dry, rawhide can be lightened in color and made pliable by pounding it over its entire surface with a heavy, smooth implement, such as an ax, small sledgehammer, or mallet. Lay the hide on a thick mat of newspapers over a hard, smooth surface and strike it with short, glancing blows.

Skin dressing, Indian fashion

American Indians did not tan animal skins. The use of tannin—an extract from the bark of certain trees, among them hemlock, oak, sumac, and spruce—was unknown to them before the arrival of the white man. Nevertheless, they were able to create soft, pliable, durable leathers. Unlike modern commercial processes, which rely on chemical tanning agents, the Indians made their hides supple through laborious rubbing, stretching, and scraping.

There were six steps in the Indian system of dressing skins: fleshing, dehairing (or scraping), braining, stretching (or stripping), graining, and working. In some cases there was a seventh step: smoking. A fresh hide would be staked out on the ground, flesh side up, and stripped of flesh and fat with bone scraping implements. The hide would then be reversed so that the fur side was up, and the hair would be scraped off. Next came the application of the dressing agent, usually a mixture of animal brains, liver, and tallow, followed by an overnight soaking in water. The hide was wrung out the next day and stretched on a rectangular frame similar to the one shown at lower left on this page. Working together, two women would squeeze out the remaining moisture with wide-bladed squeegee-like stripping tools. The next step, graining, took place after the skin had been allowed to dry out thoroughly in the frame. Graining consisted of sanding the hide to a uniform thickness with a rough bone tool or pumice stone. The skin's final softness was provided by working it back and forth over a sharp edge or rough surface. Some tribes drew the skin across a taut rope made of animal sinew. Others worked it to and fro over the rough bark of a tree. A common system was to pull the hide back and forth across a sharpened post that had been stuck in the ground.

To smoke a deerskin the Indian way, dig a hole about 2 ft. across and 1 ft. deep. Burn enough hardwood to make a thick bed of ashes and coals. Build a support of four green boughs, and drape the already scraped hide over it (make certain the hide is not so close to the fire that it will burn). Add green wood—damp hickory or fruitwood chips are excellent—to make thick smoke, and leave until the desired color is reached. Move the hide occasionally so that it smokes evenly.

Coonskin for Heads
Cowhide for Feet

How to Make a Coonskin Cap

The coonskin cap has been an American favorite from pioneer days to the age of television. Like the moccasins shown on the next page, its origins predate the arrival of the white man—the oldest painting of an American Indian shows an aborigine wearing a round hat with a raccoon tail attached to the crown. By the time pioneers were beginning to settle Kentucky and Tennessee, the coonskin hat had evolved into the hunting cap that we associate with Daniel Boone and Davy Crockett.

When making a coonskin cap, use a large skin, free of blemishes and bald spots, with a tail that is full and well marked. Cut the pattern out of a heavy grocery bag, baste it together, and check to make sure you have the fit you want. The crown should be somewhat elongated—about an inch longer than it is wide. When cutting the leather, use a razor-sharp knife and cut on the skin side.

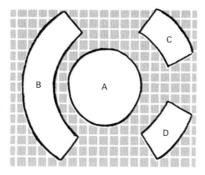

1. Pattern consists of four pieces. Crown (A) is the size and shape of the head at its widest. Headband is in three pieces (B, C, D), each about 4 in. wide.

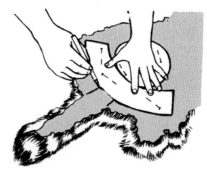

2. Join pattern pieces A and B with pins and place them on flesh side of skin close to tail. Use felt-tip pen to mark pattern. Cut A, B, and tail as one piece.

3. Place pattern pieces C and D on flesh side of skin near where A and B were cut; mark with pen and cut. Grain and color of new fur pieces should match piece B.

4. Use knife to slice base of tail one-third of way in at each side, then use blanket stitch to sew tail together into a tubular shape all the way down its length.

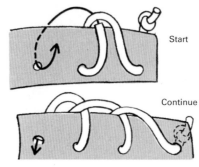

5. Blanket stitch is often used for joining pieces of fur. Use fine needle and nylon thread. Do not pull thread too tightly or you may cut the leather.

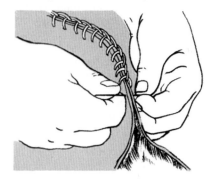

6. Bring edges of fur together when sewing, then stitch through. Be careful that hair is not gathered into seam, otherwise seam will be visible.

7. After tail is sewn, join rear part of headband (B) to crown. Sew on the skin side, and make stitches close so that joined fur looks like a single piece.

8. Add pieces C and D to headband and continue sewing to crown after testing for fit. Pieces C and D may need to be trimmed a bit so that the cap fits properly.

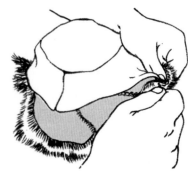

9. Satin lining can be added. Use same pattern except cut C and D as one piece. Turn cap inside out, then join lining to leather along lower edge only.

Finished cap should look like a single piece of fur without any seams showing.

Making Your Own Moccasins

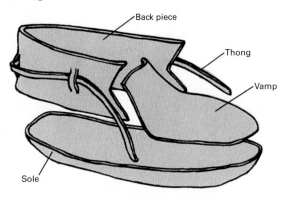

Each moccasin consists of three pieces: vamp, back, and sole. To add thong, cut slits at sides and rear of back piece.

Moccasins, in one form or another, were used as footwear by North American Indians from Mexico to beyond the Arctic Circle. Although styles varied from tribe to tribe and region to region, almost all moccasins shared certain characteristics: the upper parts were made of tanned leather, the leather was usually smoked to improve its resistance to water, and, except for moccasins made by a few western tribes, the soles were soft.

The three-piece moccasin shown here is based on an Apache design. Use heavy-weight, oil-tanned leather (oil tanning makes the leather moisture resistant) and cut the pattern pieces out of heavy paper (a heavy-duty grocery bag will do). Make separate patterns for each foot—right and left foot sizes are rarely the same—and baste the patterns together so that you can try them for fit before cutting the leather. Note that pattern shapes shown are for the left foot; reverse them for the right foot. Since the leather is heavy, holes must be punched before the seams are sewn, either with an awl (as shown) or a very fine drive punch or rotary punch (standard tools sold at leathermaking stores). Use the saddle stitch for all seams. Draw the thread tight after each stitch so that it bites into the leather; this will produce a strong yet attractive seam that will stand up under heavy wear. Note that the stitch holes punched around the soles are spaced slightly farther apart than the corresponding holes around the vamps and back pieces. The difference in spacing compensates for the longer perimeter of the sole piece and also produces a gathering effect. The final step in making the moccasins is to add a thong. Cut the thong from the same leather used for the moccasins, and thread it through slits in the back piece. Be sure to make the thong long enough to tie a bow.

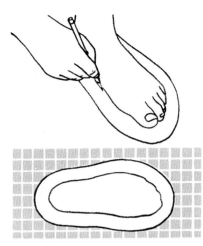

1. Place foot on paper, draw outline around it with pencil held vertically. Sketch pattern for sole by allowing additional 1 1/4 in. at heel and toe, 1 in. elsewhere all the way around outline.

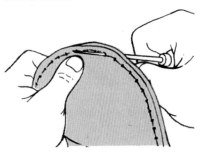

4. Use awl to punch holes 1/4 in. from edge around the soles, back pieces, and fronts (toes) of vamps. Holes are about 3/16 in. apart on vamps and back pieces; matching holes in soles are about 1/4 in. apart.

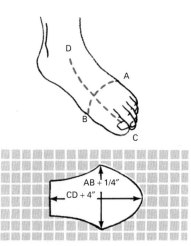

2. Make vamp pattern about 1/4 in. wider than widest part of foot (line AB). To estimate length of vamp, measure distance from back of big toenail to just above instep (line CD) and add 4 in.

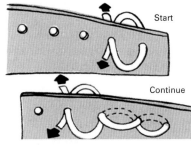

5. To join vamps to sole, begin by saddle stitching from center of vamp. Stitch along one side, then along the other. To join back to sole, start from center of heel. Sew one side, then the other.

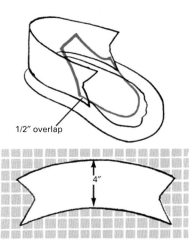

3. Pattern for back piece should be 4 in. high and long enough to wrap around heel of foot and overlap vamp by about 1/2 in. on each side. Check back piece using foot outline from Step 1.

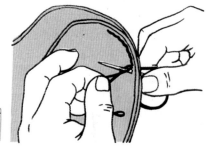

6. Easiest way to make the saddle stitch is with a needle at each end of thread. Even thread off at first hole, insert needles through succeeding holes in opposing directions. Finish with knot hidden in seam.

Sources and resources

Books and pamphlets

Farnham, Albert B. *Home Tanning and Leathermaking Guide.* Columbus, Ohio: A. R. Harding, 1950.

Hobson, Phyllis. *Tan Your Hide.* Charlotte, Vt.: Garden Way Publishing, 1977.

Hunt, W.B. *The Complete How-to Book of Indian Craft.* New York: Collier Books, 1973.

Ickis, Marguerite, and Reba S. Esh. *The Book of Arts and Crafts.* New York: Dover, 1965.

Seymour, John. *The Forgotten Crafts.* New York: Knopf, 1984.

Finished moccasins can be beaded if desired.

Woodworking

Re-creating the Designs Of America's Country Carpenters

Among the thousands of anonymous carpenters, joiners, and cabinetmakers who made the bulk of America's furniture during the frontier years were many whose skills equaled those of their rich and famous contemporaries. They worked in small shops all across the land, using hand tools and native lumber to produce furniture that was functional and affordable by the common people. Their work is now called country furniture by antique dealers to differentiate it from the intricately fashioned, highly polished products of such masters as Duncan Phyfe, Chippendale, Sheraton, Hepplewhite, and their colleagues and imitators. (The term "country furniture" has nothing to do with quality of workmanship or grace of design—or even whether or not a piece was made in the country. A city chair was sold as a work of art and as an expensive status symbol. A country chair was to sit on.) Much country furniture was, in fact, quite beautiful despite—or perhaps because of—its simplicity of design and lack of modish ornamentation. The best was so well made that it exists in usable condition today, having grown more beautiful with the passage of years. To study its workmanship and attempt to duplicate its design is to learn a great deal about the nature of fine woodworking—a lesson that will carry over to any craft you undertake.

In this section you will find eight examples of well-made country furniture, along with instructions for re-creating each by time-honored techniques. Every one is a unique creation whose parts are interchangeable with no other piece; all are typical of the kind of craft that only hand workmanship can produce.

Handmade chairs can be both practical and attractive when made with care. Rocking chairs are an American invention, credited by some to Benjamin Franklin. At first, curved rocker slats were simply attached to legs of existing chairs. In later designs the legs were splayed outward and were often wider at the bottom than at the top to accommodate notches for rocker slats. In this elegant chair (right) the legs are mounted on top of the rockers.

Work With Wood, Not Against It

Wood is organic, and every board has its own personality—the record of events in the long lifetime of a single tree. Examine your wood before you begin to work it. Perhaps you will spot a large heartwood knot marking where a branch began to form—a distinctive figure for a tabletop but a distinct problem for the carpenter. Or you might find a tight, dense series of annual rings, the remnant of a long-ago drought. The wood inside those rings will shrink differently than the wood nearby. It will respond differently to the cutting edge of a chisel and accept a finish less thirstily. In shaping a piece of wood, you need not know the cause of such personality quirks, but if you ignore them your work will suffer.

Like the wood from which it is made, every piece of handmade furniture is unique—an intimate collaboration between the woodworker and his material. Perhaps, having chosen one piece of wood over another because of its attractive figure, you will discover a knot where you had planned to cut a mortise. To follow your plan in defiance of the nature of the wood is foolish; the joint will be weak at best. You must make a decision: to use a different piece of wood, to make a different joint, or to position the joint differently than you had planned. Similar, more subtle decisions are made with each touch of a tool, and to achieve your original conception requires a finely tuned sensitivity to the many variations of grain and texture in the wood you are using. It is by no means impossible to maintain such sensitivity while working with power tools, but it is difficult; when using hand tools, however, it is hard not to be sensitive. The beginner, just learning how to work with wood, benefits from using hand tools as the old-time craftsman did.

The Workshop

A well-organized working space is important. The ideal shop contains a good, solid workbench; a softwood table for assembling and gluing large pieces; plenty of floor space; a storage area for lumber, sorted into kinds and sizes; another storage area for usable scraps, bits, and pieces; and a handy but unobtrusive place for every tool. Such a shop is the dream of nearly every woodworker.

In setting up your work space, however limited or temporary it might be, keep in mind the ideal from which to compromise. A big workbench is a fine thing, but if space is a problem, do not fill up your workroom with a larger bench than you really need; floor space is vital for laying out and working on large pieces. It is better to settle for a narrow bench and, when necessary, use sawhorses and 2-inch planks as a working surface.

A good place to keep your basic tool kit—those tools you are likely to need for almost any project you undertake—is right on the wall behind the workbench. Simply nail up a 1/8-inch pegboard framed with wood, and use metal hooks or your own homemade brackets to hang each tool in its place. (Make it a point to replace each tool after using it.) Other tools can go in a toolbox to be brought out when needed. For small tools, accessories, and hardware, a small chest with several drawers is handy. If you must store even your basic tool kit between work sessions, make an upright toolbox in two sections hinged to open like a steamer trunk. Mount it on casters for mobility, and install 1/8-inch pegboard for hanging tools on both inside surfaces.

Avoid the clutter of a large scrap pile. Store scrap in bins where it can be seen. That way you are more likely to use it than to cut into new lumber unnecessarily.

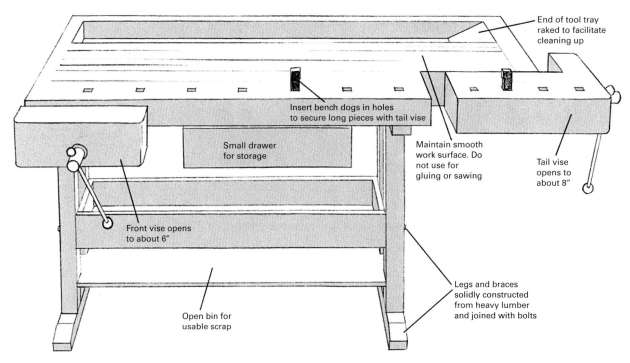

Heart of a workshop is a good workbench. Important considerations in choosing or building a bench are sturdiness, capacity to hold work firmly in a variety of positions, a large, smooth work surface, sufficient storage space, and a handy tool tray. This classic design is solidly built of hardwood and is heavy enough not to need securing to the floor. Front vise holds work for edge-planing; tail vise can be used in conjunction with bench dogs (pegs placed in holes in bench) to secure longer pieces for surface-planing. The tops of both vises should be flush with the bench top. If steel vises are used, line their faces with hardwood to prevent marring wood. Tool tray at rear is deep enough that tools are out of the way when not in use. Storage space consists of small tool drawer in center and bin beneath for scrap wood; some benches include cabinets and many drawers.

Kinds of Wood

In carpenter's parlance, hardwood is wood from deciduous trees; softwood is from evergreens. Typically, hardwood is heavier than softwood, firmer in texture, more difficult to cut, more likely to split while being worked, and less subject to warping and shrinkage. There are, however, exceptions. Some softwoods, such as yellow pine, are harder than most hardwood; and some hardwoods, such as poplar and tupelo, are extremely soft. Structurally, the difference is a matter of the kinds of cells that conduct and control the flow of sap in the two types of trees. In softwoods the cells are called thin-walled tracheids and resemble tiny sponges. They form in the early part of each growing season; later in the season thick-walled tracheids form around them to support the tree. In hardwoods sap flows through pipe-like vessels, which appear as pores among the supportive wood fibers; in most hardwoods these pores are distributed fairly evenly. In a few—called ring porous—they are concentrated in the early-season growth.

As far as the woodworker is concerned, the most important distinction is that softwood tends to splinter, while the longer, finer fibers of hardwood are more likely to split. Also, there is usually a greater variance of texture within a piece of softwood than of hardwood.

Popular American softwoods include white pine (the most commonly used wood in many places), western pine, white cedar, western red cedar, Douglas fir, yew, and sequoia (redwood). The orange-hued wood known as pumpkin pine is actually the heartwood of white pine. Hardwoods include ash, beech, yellow birch, maple, cherry, white oak, red oak, walnut, and hickory. (See also *Converting Trees Into Lumber*, pp.22–25.)

Grain, texture, and figure

Grain is a term that is often misused. It refers to the direction and alignment of the long fibers that run up and down the trunk of a tree and along its branches, not to the pattern made by the annual rings. The grain in most trees is more or less straight, with waves and irregularities caused by stresses in growth.

Texture depends on fiber density, particularly the contrast in growth layers, or rings, and in the size and distribution of pores. White oak, for example, has large pores and is coarse textured; cherry is fine textured.

Figure refers to the pattern on the surface of a piece of wood. It is the result of many structural elements, including grain and texture, conformation of annual rings and rays, color variation, and the angle at which the wood is sawed. To judge the figure of an unfinished surface, wet it with paint thinner; it will dry harmlessly.

Good Workmanship Begins With Good Tools Properly Used

To speak of handmade wood furniture is not strictly accurate. You need tools to work with wood, and nothing—save your own skill—is more important to the work than the quality of those tools. Always get the best you can afford. This is not to suggest that the best tool is always the most expensive, merely that cheap tools are seldom adequate. As a rule of thumb, shop for tools that are above average in price but not in the luxury class.

Chisels. Look for a blade of finely tempered steel, capable of taking and holding a razor-sharp edge, and for a handle of durable hardwood or plastic that will stand up under punishment. In the best chisels either the handle is set into a socket welded to the blade, or a tang on the end of the blade is inserted into the handle and a washer of leather or plastic absorbs the force of blows.

Clamps. You cannot have too many 2- to 8-inch C-clamps. For general use, simple, solidly built steel clamps will outlast costlier kinds. Also of great value are variable hardwood hand screws with jaws 10 to 12 inches long capable of holding oddly shaped pieces at various angles. Pipe or bar clamps are valuable for large jobs, although substitutes can be improvised (see *Putting on the Pressure: Three Methods*, p.306).

Coping saws. A firm steel frame is important. In a good saw the blade can be turned to face either side, and the tension adjustment will not loosen as you work.

Drawknives. A keen edge is all that is really vital; look for high-quality tempered steel. Try before you buy to be sure the tool is comfortable in your hands.

Drills. You can do anything with a brace and bit that you can with a power drill—it just takes longer. Choose a steel-shanked ratchet brace with an 8- to 10-inch sweep (the circle made by a full revolution of the handle). Auxiliaries include an assortment of double-twist steel auger bits, 1/4 to 1 inch in diameter; an expansive bit for cutting holes up to 3 inches across; a countersink; and plug cutters and matching counterbores of various sizes. Also invaluable is a small hand drill with a set of twist bits up to 1/4 inch in diameter.

Hammers and mallets. If you were to be restricted to only one hammer, your best choice would be a 10- to 12-ounce bell-faced, adz-eye claw hammer with

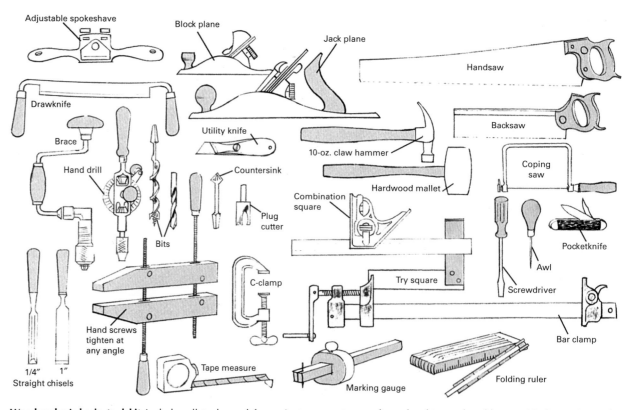

Woodworker's basic tool kit includes all tools used for projects described on pages 308–329 (hatchet, ax, and frame saw are needed for *Rustic Furniture*, pp.330–331). It is by no means a complete assortment of woodworking tools; add more chisels, carving tools, dovetail saws, mitering equipment, rabbet planes, and other special tools as they are needed.

a hickory handle that is comfortable to your grip. For light work and for shaping hardware, an 8-ounce ball peen is a good second hammer. To drive chisels, pegs, and wedges, use a mallet of hardwood or plastic. Many woodworkers fashion their own mallets from oak, applewood, lignum vitae, or other durable hardwood.

Handsaws. High-carbon tempered steel is vital for a thin, supple blade that will hold its edge. The teeth should be precision ground, all the same height, all sharpened to the same angle, and all set at the same degree. A good saw is almost certain to be expensive. Teeth of a cheap saw might look the same at a glance, but close examination usually reveals irregularities that result in slower, sloppier workmanship.

Knives. Dedicated whittlers maintain that time, patience, and a good knife are all you really need to make anything at all from wood. A knife is the most personal of tools; when you have found yours, treasure it.

Planes. Iron planes usually cost less than wooden ones, but many carpenters prefer the weight and solidity of the latter type. In either case, sharp blades and precise mechanical control are the vital elements.

Rulers. A 6-foot folding ruler and 12-foot steel tape measure are both valuable. Neither need be expensive.

Screwdrivers. You need several sizes. Tempered steel shanks and blades are the key to quality.

Scribers. Some woodworkers prefer to use an awl, some an ice pick, some the blade of a penknife.

Spokeshaves. For general use, the best of the many forms available is the adjustable type with a flat blade about 2 inches wide, the depth and angle of cut being controlled by means of two adjusting screws.

Squares. The adjustable combination square measures right angles and 45° angles and can serve as a marking gauge, ruler, or depth gauge. Most have built-in spirit levels, some may also contain a scriber.

Cutting Wood With Handsaws

The coarseness of a saw blade is expressed in points (number of teeth per inch). The lower a blade's point count, the faster and rougher the cut; the higher the point count, the slower and smoother the cut. Most crosscut handsaws are 8 to 12 point; most ripsaws, 5 to 7 point. Both kinds cut on the downstroke, and both operate most efficiently when they go through wood at a 30° to 45° angle. Cut a little to the outside of the guideline, leaving some wood for finishing. First make a groove with two or three backstrokes, then proceed with long, even strokes, using the full length of the blade.

A backsaw is a 12- to 16-point crosscut with a reinforced back to keep the blade rigid. With it you can cut closer to a line than with a handsaw. Even more precise is the dovetail saw, like a small backsaw with a very thin rip-sharpened 22- to 26-point blade.

Shaping Wood With Drawknives, Spokeshaves, and Planes

A drawknife is nothing but a long blade, sometimes hollow-ground like a straight razor, with a handle on each end. It is best used by pulling the cutting edge toward you to shave layers of varying thickness from the wood's surface. Because the depth and angle of cut are controlled only by the way the tool is held, its use requires skill and practice. When mastered, it is a versatile tool for shaping curves and irregular surfaces. The blade's bevel should be up when shaping convex curves, down for concave ones.

Spokeshaves are also usually used by pulling. Their narrow blades protrude through a flat base to ensure an even cut; thus they work like small planes for smoothing round surfaces—as in shaping wagon spokes, the job for which they are named—and for working inside curves. When using a spokeshave or a drawknife on a curve, employ a slicing motion, and always try to cut "downhill," that is, following the direction of the grain.

Planes are pushed rather than pulled. The most generally useful of the many types available is the bench plane. It comes in four sizes: smoother, jack, fore, and jointer. Smoother planes, 7 to 10 inches long, are used for finish-planing; jack planes, 12 to 17 inches long, are the rough laborers among planes, used for reducing the size of a piece of wood and creating a fairly even surface; fore planes, 18 inches long, serve much the same purpose for long boards and can be used in place of jointer planes in flattening shorter pieces; jointer planes, 22 to 36 inches long, are used to produce the flattest possible surface on large pieces of wood. Block planes, only 5 to 7 inches long, are used for shaping and smoothing small pieces as well as for trimming end grain.

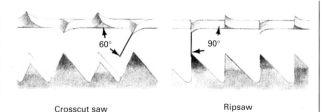

Crosscut saw   Ripsaw

Teeth of a crosscut saw are like a series of little knives slicing across the grain of a piece of wood. Those of a ripsaw are like chisels, gouging out a path along the grain. In both types the teeth are set—that is, bent outward in alternate directions so that they make a cut, or kerf, that is slightly wider than the thickness of the blade itself. This reduces friction on the blade and keeps it from binding. A blade with an uneven set is harder to use and will tend to veer to one side as it cuts.

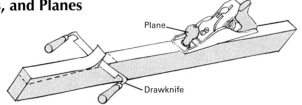

Plane

Drawknife

For best results in using plane, drawknife, or spokeshave, try to hold tool at slight angle to direction of cut so that blade slices through, rather than chops at, the grain of the wood.

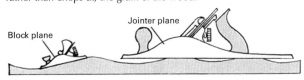

Block plane   Jointer plane

Short plane, riding over irregularities in wood like a small boat over ocean waves, smooths but does not flatten. Longer plane spans waves and cuts down high spots to make flat surface.

Edge-planing. To flatten and trim the edge of a board, be sure the work is held securely, as nearly level as possible. Apply even pressure throughout long, straight strokes to produce a continuous shaving. Use knob to support nose of plane at end of strokes to prevent chopping or rounding corners.

Surface-planing. To flatten the surface of a large piece, particularly one that has been formed by edge-gluing, first plane diagonally to eliminate high spots, then straight along the grain in long strokes.

Trimming end grain. With a block plane, work from the edges inward, then level the hump in the middle.

Drilling clean holes

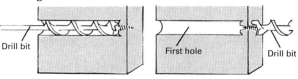

Drill bit   First hole   Drill bit

To prevent splintering, drill from one side until tip of bit emerges. Then bore back from the other side to clear hole.

The essential chisel

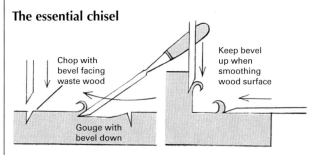

Chop with bevel facing waste wood

Gouge with bevel down

Keep bevel up when smoothing wood surface

Straight chisel, also called a firmer chisel, is a woodworker's most versatile tool. It is driven with a mallet to chop through the grain of wood, used like a knife to carve wood, or manipulated in many ways to gouge out waste wood and to shave, shape, and smooth wood surfaces. Dozens of other kinds of chisels, including rounded gouges, V-shaped parting tools, and skew chisels with angled blades, exist to perform specific tasks.

Keeping tools sharp

Use figure-eight motion to sharpen

Hold blade flat to remove burr

30°

Benchstones, to maintain the critical fine edge of straight blades, are perfectly flat. They come in varying degrees of hardness; the harder the stone, the finer the edge it can impart—and the longer it takes. The best natural stones, quarried in the Ozark Mountains of Arkansas, are quite expensive and so high in quality that they are used for sharpening surgical instruments. Artificial stones, such as carborundum, emery, and India stone (oil-filled fused alumina), are cheaper and do an adequate job for most wood-working needs. To sharpen a blade with one beveled edge, first lubricate the stone with water or fine oil; then hold the bevel at the proper angle (30 degrees in most cases) and stroke back and forth evenly over the stone's surface in a figure-eight motion. A burr will be raised on the flat side; remove it by gently rubbing the blade back and forth on the stone. Clean your stone with kerosene after each use, and keep it in a fitted box with a cover that can be removed.

The Art of Joinery: Putting Pieces Together So They Stay Together

Joinery is the woodworker's basic craft. The soundest joints are made by shaping pieces of wood to interlock firmly. They may be further secured by inserting wooden pins through the joint, by driving wedges into it, by applying glue, or by using such mechanical fasteners as screws or nails. The essence of the craft lies in designing each joint to withstand the specific stresses that will be put upon it. The joiner must understand the nature of each piece of wood. Its grain and texture and its strengths and weaknesses must be taken into account, the pieces must be made to fit as nearly perfectly as possible, and the inevitable shrinkage and movement that will occur over time must be anticipated.

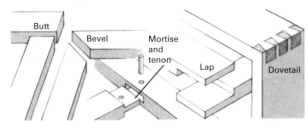

Five types of joints are used in the projects on the following pages. Practice with scrap wood before attempting each joint.

Kinds of glue

A wide range of liquid adhesives is available in ready-to-use form, including many brands of white glue, the somewhat harder drying yellow glue (aliphatic resin), two-part waterproof glue (resorcinol), and liquid hide glue. All work well for specific jobs.

The country carpenter's old standby, hide glue, prepared from the skin, horns, and hooves of cattle and horses, is almost a thing of the past—along with the mess and stench of the bubbling glue pot that was once a fixture in any woodworking shop. It is still available in flake form, however, and it has two advantages: it is inexpensive, and it will keep indefinitely. It is not a bad idea to keep a pound or two of dry hide glue on hand for use in case of emergencies.

Types of Joints

Butt joints. One piece of wood fits squarely against another and is secured by glue, nails, screws, pins, or other means, such as the metal braces used with the Shaker firewood carrier (pp.308–309). In several of the projects illustrated on the following pages, butt joints are used when edge-gluing narrow boards together to make a wider surface, such as a tabletop.

Bevel joints. Instead of fitting squarely, as with a butt joint, two pieces are beveled to fit at an angle, as in building the colonial cradle (pp.314–315). When both pieces are cut at 45° to form a square corner, the result is called a miter joint.

Lap joints. Two pieces are notched to fit one atop the other, forming a double layer that is the same thickness as each piece. This can be done on the ends of boards or it can be internal, as in joining the feet of the candlestand (pp.316–318). It is important that the notches run across the grain of both pieces and that the fit not be so tight that it puts undue stress on the joint.

Mortise-and-tenon joints. A tongue (the tenon) cut into the end of one piece fits precisely into a hole (the mortise) cut into another. There are countless variations on the theme. Of the several mortise-and-tenon joints employed in the projects, no two are quite the same. Some are "through joints"—the tenon pierces the mortise piece. In others the mortise is blind—only deep enough to accommodate the tenon. Some are secured by pins, some by wedges, some permanently, some temporarily, and some not at all. (See also p.311.)

Dovetail joints. Fan-shaped tails in one piece fit between matching pins in another. Although the joint is occasionally glued or even secured with nails or wooden pins, it is at its best when it is self-securing. For instructions on dovetail joinery, see p.313.

Edge-gluing

Whatever kind of glue you use, do not expect it to make up for a poorly fitted joint. Wood surfaces must be flush and clean; joints must be firmly clamped until the glue has set. When edge-gluing, plane both edges square; with long boards, plane to a slight concave curve so that the centers of the boards are 1/16 inch apart. Apply glue lightly to one edge, then clamp with even pressure until a bead of glue emerges along the entire length of the joint.

Before edge-gluing two or more boards, look at curve in end grain caused by circular conformation of annual rings. To control warping, place boards side by side so that curves alternate.

Putting on the Pressure: Three Methods

Bar or pipe clamps. Use enough clamps to apply pressure evenly over full length of joint. To prevent buckling, place clamps alternately, one above boards, the next below. With all methods apply C-clamps to ends of joints to keep boards even.

Frame and wedge. Make frame slightly wider than combined width of boards. Apply pressure with pairs of wedges driven together between boards and frame. Diagonal batten prevents buckling. Wax paper under joint prevents gluing to frame.

Tourniquet. Cut two battens as thick as and slightly longer than the boards being joined. Wrap 1/4-in. rope twice around ends of battens and tie. Apply pressure by winding hardwood spindles. Cross-members hold spindles in place until glue sets.

Using Nails and Screws

Fastidious cabinetmakers scorn the use of metal joining devices, but for ordinary folk—and that includes most of the old-time country carpenters and furniture-makers—nails and screws are reasonable compromises with perfection. If you strive for authenticity in making such pieces as the Shaker firewood carrier (p.308) and the colonial cradle (p.314), use old-fashioned cut nails, available with or without hand-wrought heads from specialty hardware suppliers—or make your own (see *Metalworking*, p.355). Modern wire nails come in three forms that are most useful in furnituremaking: common nails, with broad, flat heads; box nails, also flat-headed but lighter in weight than common nails; and finish nails, with very small heads for countersinking (brads are small finish nails). Nail size is expressed in terms of pennies (d), which once signified the price per hundred in old England. A 2d nail is 1 inch long; a 4d, 11/2 inches; a 6d, 2 inches; and so forth. Cut nails are less likely to split hardwood than are wire nails, provided they are driven with their flat sides parallel to the grain. To prevent splitting with wire nails, blunt the points before driving them so they do not act as wedges; in hardwood drill a pilot hole slightly smaller than the thickness of the nail.

Wood screws are threaded for about two-thirds of their length. The thickness of the shank above the thread determines screw size. To drill a pilot hole for screwing into softwood, select a bit about the same diameter as the inner core of the thread (hold the screw up to the light, hold a bit in front of it, and choose one that allows you to see all the thread on both sides of the bit). For hardwood first drill with a slightly larger bit—one that can barely be seen when held behind the core of the thread. Then enlarge the upper third of the hole with a second bit the same thickness as the shank.

Laying out patterns

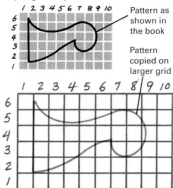

Pattern as shown in the book

Pattern copied on larger grid

Patterns are given in 1- or 2-in. scale on the following pages. To use them, make grid with lines 1 or 2 in. apart on heavy paper, then copy pattern on grid, using a straightedge where needed. Hold pattern on surface of wood and trace over lines with scriber, or use carbon paper beneath the pattern.

Making Pins and Wedges

Dowel shaper is metal plate with graduated holes; drive pin through one hole at a time to diminish size. Next, use dowel shaver; its holes are slightly tapered to compress pin driven from wide side and to shave excess when driven back.

To make wedges, start with length of hardwood of right width and thickness for butt of wedge. Use block plane to taper to desired degree, then cut off with backsaw. Make wedge a little longer than needed to allow for driving.

Fox wedges are used to secure tenons and pins in blind mortises where wedges cannot be driven from outside. Cut slot in tenon or pin, insert fox wedge, and drive into blind mortise. Wedge will be forced back into the tenon or pin.

The mortising gauge

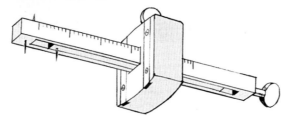

Marking gauge has only one point, for scribing a single line parallel to edge, face, or end of board. Mortising gauge has an additional pair of points—the inner one is adjustable—for scribing two parallel lines a given distance apart.

Finishing

The most important factor in finishing is preparing the wood. Country furnituremakers seldom used sandpaper, relying instead on their skill with planes, spokeshaves, drawknives, and scrapers to achieve a smooth surface. Their usual finishing materials were milk-based paint or boiled linseed oil mixed half-and-half with turpentine. A few suppliers carry old-fashioned milk-based paint in powdered form; if you want to try mixing your own, see *Household Recipes*, p.343. To apply linseed oil, brush the mixture of oil and turpentine on freely and let it soak in until the wood cannot absorb any more. Wipe off the excess, then rub with a clean linen pad—hard and long enough to generate heat. Let the finish dry for two days and apply another coat. Four or five coats will accent the wood figure with a lustrous sheen.

Sources and resources

Books
Alexander, John D., Jr. *Make a Chair From a Tree: An Introduction to Working Green Wood*. Mendham, N.J.: Astragal Press, 1994.
Feirer, John L. *Basic Woodworking*. Peoria, Ill.: Bennett Publications, 1978.
Margon, Lester. *Construction of American Furniture Treasures*. New York: Dover, 1975.
Moser, Thos. *How to Build Shaker Furniture*. New York: Sterling, 1980.
Seymour, John. *The Forgotten Crafts*. New York: Knopf, 1984.
Spence, William P., and Griffiths, L. Duane. *Woodworking Basics: The Essential Benchtop Reference*. New York: Sterling Publishing, 1995.
Stickley, Gustav. *Making Authentic Craftsman Furniture*. New York: Dover, 1986.
Underhill, Roy. *The Woodwright's Shop: A Practical Guide to Traditional Woodcraft*. Chapel Hill, N.C.: University of North Carolina Press, 1981.
Watson, Aldren A. *Country Furniture*. New York: New American Library, 1976.

Periodicals
Fine Woodworking. Taunton Press, P.O. Box 355, Newtown, Conn. 06470.
Woodshop News. Sounding Publications Inc., 35 Pratt St., Essex, Conn. 06426.
Woodworkers Journal. Madrigal Publishing, 517 Litchfield Rd., New Milford, Conn. 06776.

Tools and materials
Big Tool Box, Inc. 200 South Havanna St., Aurora, Ga., 80041.
Bimex, Inc. 2687 McCullum Pkwy., Suite 206, Kennesaw, Ga. 30144.
Frog Tool Co., Ltd. 700 West Jackson Blvd., Chicago, Ill. 60606.
Garrett Wade Co., Inc. 161 Avenue of the Americas, New York, N.Y. 10013.
Leichtung, Inc. 4944 Commerce Pkwy., Cleveland, Ohio 44143.
Tremont Nails. 8 Elm St., Wareham, Mass. 02571.
Woodcraft Supply. 313 Montvale Ave., Woburn, Mass. 01888.
Woodworker's Supply. 5604 Alameda NE, Albuquerque, N. Mex. 87112.

A Shaker-Style Firewood Carrier Is Made to Last

An important tenet of the Shaker religious communities that flourished in isolation during this nation's first century was the sanctity of good workmanship. Each community made its own furniture, tools, and implements of daily life in a style that is instantly recognizable for its uncompromising practicality. "All beauty that has not a foundation in use," the Shakers believed, "soon grows distasteful and needs continual replacement." The things designed by the Shakers seldom needed replacement. Their unornamented beauty is that of the perfectly functional, and they were built to last.

This firewood carrier embodies Shaker craftsmanship at its best. The design problem is simple: how to make a container strong enough to hold a load of heavy firewood yet light enough to carry. The fact that so many examples of the design still exist more than a century after they were made and used is testament to how well the Shakers solved the problem.

Three kinds of wood are used for this carrier: the sides, ends, and battens are of white or red oak; the bottom is of white pine; and the handle is of clear hickory or ash.

Firewood carrier is joined by corner braces of 20-gauge mild sheet steel (about 1/32 in.) lightly planished with ball peen hammer. For an authentic look use hand-forged nails to secure braces and to join handle to sides. Paint exposed metal in flat black to protect it and to simulate the look of wrought iron.

Preparing the Pieces

1. Saw side and end pieces roughly to size, allowing an extra 1/4 in. in each dimension for finishing. Surface-plane all pieces, then edge-plane to exact dimensions. Stop and clamp the unit together from time to time as you work to ensure square joints.

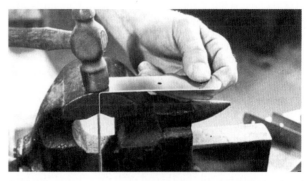

2. Use tin snips to cut corner braces from sheet steel. Before bending them, scribe center lines along length of each strip and drill nail holes 3/4 in. and 1 3/4 in. from either end. Bend 6-in. braces 90° across middle; bend 9-in. braces 5 in. from one end.

3. A dozen 6-in. corner braces are needed to assemble carrier frame. Begin by positioning three braces on each corner joint and marking for nail holes. To ensure tight fit, mark outer edge of holes, not center. Label all pieces for reassembly.

Materials needed

Part	Pieces	Size
Sides	2	3/8″ × 12″ × 21″
Ends	2	3/8″ × 12″ × 10 1/2″
Battens	2	1/4″ × 1″ × 11 1/4″
Bottom	1	1″ × 10 1/2″ × 20 1/4″
Handle	1	1/4″ × 1″ × 48″
Corner braces	16 small	20-gauge × 1 1/8″ × 6″
	4 large	20-gauge × 1 1/8″ × 9″
Nails	100	2d (1″) headed hand-forged mild steel or equivalent
Nails	8	2d (1″) finish nails

It may be difficult to find 3/8-in. oak. Planing heavier lumber to size is both tedious and wasteful. The alternative is to halve 1-in. stock with a two-man saw or frame saw, as early craftsmen did, and then plane to thickness.

Nailing It Together

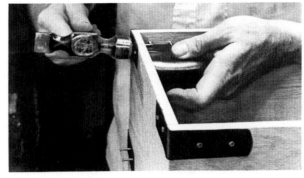

1. Using a bit slightly smaller than shank of nails, drill a pilot hole at each mark. To be certain of proper positioning, pin each brace in place with nails, but do not drive them home.

2. When all holes are drilled and all braces in position, drive nails. Use steel block or heavy hammer to back up wood while driving, but do not attempt to clinch nails.

3. Hammer points of nails over and down; flatten across the grain. With softwood, such as white pine, you could clinch nails as they are driven (Step 2), but this can split oak.

The fine art of making do

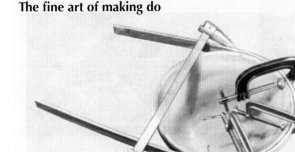

4. Cut bottom piece to fit snugly inside frame. Position two 9-in. braces on each side, about 3 1/2 in. from corners; center the four remaining 6-in. braces. Mark, drill, and drive nails as above.

5. Batten strips must be installed on bottom to prevent braces from scuffing floor. Chisel out center of battens (left) to fit over braces; secure with four counterset 2d finish nails.

Necessity may be the mother of invention, but simple convenience often gives birth to some pretty good improvisation. If you were to make a regular practice of building firewood carriers, it would be well worth your while to construct a jig, such as that shown in Step 6 at right, for forming the handles. But to build just one carrier, you may find it easier, and just as effective, to improvise. Look around your house, shop, garage, or toolshed for a makeshift mold of the appropriate size, such as this mixing bowl. (To lessen the risk of breakage, use a sturdy bowl and take care in tightening the clamps.) Other possible molds might include a metal wastebasket, a hubcap, the back wheel of a tricycle, a piece of clay drainage pipe, or a large flowerpot. A potential mold that is a little too small can be padded with the addition of two or three layers of flexible 1/8-in. hardboard.

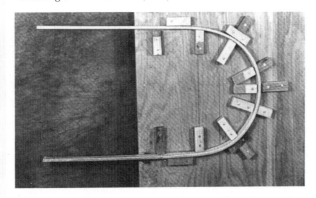

6. Lightly chamfer edges of handle. Steam handle or keep in hot water until supple. Then carefully bend to 5 5/8-in. radius and allow to dry overnight. Wood for handle must be free of knots.

7. When handle dries, clamp it in place. Mark position of six nail holes on each side, using staggered pattern to prevent splitting. Drill through, drive nails, and bend them over inside.

309

This Walnut Bench Has Moravian Roots

To enter the *saal*, or chapel, where the Moravian villagers of Bethabara (now Winston-Salem, North Carolina) met to worship, is to sense something of the devout heartiness of their lives. The furniture consists of 20 long black-walnut benches, simple in design, rich and graceful in appearance, upon which the villagers sat—strictly segregated by age, sex, and marital status—while singing rousing, even lusty, anthems of religious praise.

Original 18th-century bench upon which this adaptation is based is 10 ft. long and 15 in. wide and stands on three legs. Like this bench the original has a front side, the side with the apron. You can easily alter the design to suit your own needs. For a bench more than 7 ft. long, add a middle leg. For a bench with two fronts, or to further strengthen the seat, add an apron to the other side.

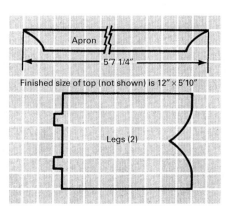

Use 2-in. gridded paper to make templates for cutting out legs and apron piece.

Finished size of top (not shown) is 12" × 5'10"

Apron

5'7 1/4"

Legs (2)

Materials needed

Black walnut is often available only in the form of rough lumber, sawed but not planed. If you buy finished stock, it will be 3/4 to 7/8 in. thick rather than 1 in. as listed below. Because black walnut tends to warp a great deal in drying, look for well seasoned stock. Wide boards are often hard to find and always expensive if you find them, so plan on edge-gluing for the top and legs.

Part	Pieces	Size
Top	1	1" × 13" × 6"
Legs	2	1" × 13" × 18"
Apron	1	1" × 3" × 6"
Wedges and pegs	1	1"×11 1/2"×12" or odd 1" scraps

Preparing the Pieces

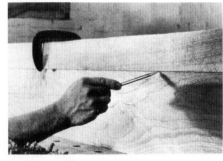

1. Before edge-gluing, surface-plane unfinished lumber until figure shows. Match figures for pleasing effect and mark both pieces lightly with pencil. Edge-plane and glue (see p.306).

2. While glue is drying on large boards, cut apron piece roughly to length, and edge-plane to width. Use template to scribe curve on both ends; cut 1/4 in. outside line with coping saw.

3. Use a straight chisel with the beveled side down to trim both coping-saw cuts to scribed line. To avoid chipping or splitting, carve wood in the direction of grain, not against it.

4. When edge-glued boards dry, plane flat. Saw wood to length for top and legs. Scribe legs with template; then use coping saw to rough-cut curved feet. Trim with straight chisel.

5. Make vertical cuts and outside cuts on both tenons with backsaw. To remove section between tenons, use coping saw first; finish by chopping with straight chisel and mallet.

6. To position mortises in top piece, first use square to scribe two lines across underside 7 in. from ends. Center legs inside these lines and scribe around tenons. Label for reassembly.

Fitting the Joints

1. With 5/8-in. bit, drill out most waste wood for mortises. Finish with 1/2-in. and 1-in. chisels. To prevent splintering wood, first cut from top, then from bottom.

2. When legs fit snugly into top, clamp apron in place and mark the spot where its bottom edge crosses the front of both legs. Use gauge to scribe depth of apron on legs.

3. Make a series of backsaw cuts to within 1/16 in. of depth line on both legs. Chisel away waste. Trim so that apron fits snugly into notch and is flush with front edge of legs.

4. Clamp legs securely in vise, and use backsaw to make two diagonal cuts, in the form of an X, to the full depth of each tenon. Assemble legs and top, but do not drive wedges.

5. Clamp apron in place. With 5/16-in. bit, drill seven 2-in.-deep holes to pin apron to top and two to pin apron to each leg. Start drilling in center of top and space holes 10 in. apart.

Mortise-and-tenon joints

Consult a dozen master woodworkers on the best technique for making a mortise-and-tenon joint and you will probably receive a dozen differing sets of instructions. None is wrong if it works. All will have in common a concern for precise measurement and careful fitting. A loose tenon means a wobbly joint; a tight one can mean split wood. A tenon with uneven or out-of-square shoulders will form a joint with gaps at the edges. A mortise whose sides are not cut straight (or at the same angle as the tenon) will form a crooked joint. Each craftsman eventually devises his own system for preventing these errors. The method outlined here is a conservative one by which the beginner can be fairly sure of achieving a snug and secure fit. Practice it a few times with scrap wood before undertaking a project involving mortise-and-tenon joinery.

Begin with the tenon. Scribe the desired size on the tenon piece's end grain—ideally, it should divide the narrow measure of the piece into equal thirds. For longer dimension scribe lines the same distance from the top and the bottom as the first lines are from the sides. With a mortising gauge or square extend the marks onto both faces of the piece. Then use a square to scribe the depth of the tenon on all four faces of the piece and deepen these lines a little with a straight chisel. Working on one face at a time, make a series of absolutely square backsaw cuts about 1/4 in. apart to within 1/16 in. of the scribed lines. Chisel away the waste wood to form the tenon.

Use the tenon itself to outline the mortise, and with a square extend the marks onto all faces of the mortise piece; this will give you a guide to help ensure a straight cut. Drill out most of the waste wood from inside the marked area (see *Drilling Clean Holes*, p.305). Then remove the remaining waste wood with a straight chisel and mallet, cutting just inside the scribed lines. Finally, test the joint and shave the tenon or the sides of the mortise as needed for a snug but not overly tight fit.

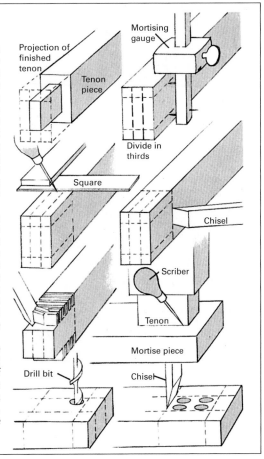

Projection of finished tenon

Tenon piece

Mortising gauge

Divide in thirds

Square

Chisel

Scriber

Tenon

Drill bit

Mortise piece

Chisel

Pinning, Wedging, and Finishing

Make 11 pegs 5/16 in. thick by at least 3 in. long and 16 wedges 1 1/2 in. long tapering from 1/8 in. thick to a dull point. (See *Making Pins and Wedges*, p.307). Make wedges wide enough so that two will fit into each diagonal cut in tenons. Position them all. Then remove pegs one at a time, dip in water, and quickly drive with mallet. Use mallet and wood block to drive wedges.

Taped hacksaw blade is useful to saw off pegs and wedges without scarring surface (see *Trestle Table*, Step 6, p.321). Trim with block plane. Then use smoother plane to lightly surface-plane top and apron. Chamfer all exposed edges slightly. For a traditional finish begin with a mixture of equal parts turpentine and boiled linseed oil. Apply several coats at two-day intervals, rubbing each in well and taking care to fill all exposed end grain. As a final step, apply one coat of pure boiled linseed oil. Occasional applications of boiled linseed oil will maintain finish over the years.

An Open Cupboard For Your Kitchen Or Living Room

This project is inspired by a cupboard dating from the early 1800s that stands in the kitchen of the Van Cortlandt Manor Restoration in Croton-on-Hudson, New York. To build it is equivalent to completing a capsule course in simple joinery. Having mastered the mortise-and-tenon joints for the shelves and the through dovetails for the top, you can use them for many other projects, including cupboards of your own design.

Cut pieces from No. 2 or better white pine, avoiding knots at joints. Dimensions given are not absolute; adjust them to suit your own needs. Finish with linseed oil or paint (see *Finishing*, p.307).

Cutting and Joining the Sides and Shelves

1. With rip and crosscut saws cut all pieces roughly to size, allowing an extra 1/8 in. all around for finishing. When cutting board for top piece, use template to scribe approximate bevel on front edge and saw at that angle, leaving extra wood for final fitting. Lightly surface-plane all pieces.

2. Sandwich sides and shelves in vise and plane edges simultaneously to ensure equal width. To scribe tenons on shelves, first find center of boards and measure 16 in. in both directions. Use combination square to scribe lines across boards, then to scribe 2-in.-wide tenons 2 in. from edges.

3. Use backsaw to cut straight sides of both tenons to within 1/16 in. of lines and to remove outside waste. Cut out waste wood between tenons with coping saw. Make all saw cuts to within 1/16 in. of lines, then finish shaping tenons by trimming flush to lines with straight chisel.

4. Scribe lines for shelves across both side pieces, 11 in. and 24 in. from top. Position shelves squarely on lines and scribe around tenons. Because tenons will vary slightly, label each joint for reassembly. Drill mortises with 11/16-in. bit and cut with chisel. (See *Mortise-and-tenon joints*, p.311.)

5. Assemble sides and shelves. On sides scribe a straight line from a point 6 3/4 in. from rear corner to a point level with front edge of upper shelf. At the same time check the angle of bevel on top piece. (Note that when joined, upper edge of top will drop down flush with upper edge of side.)

6. Disassemble. Use ripsaw to rough-cut slanting line on both sides. Edge-plane simultaneously. Plane bevel on front edge of top to fit. Then, from center point of bottom edge of both sides, scribe an arc with a radius of 3 3/4 in. Cut out with coping saw; finish with drawknife and spokeshave.

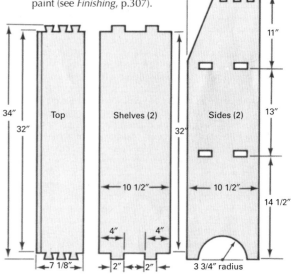

Materials needed

Part	Pieces	Size
Top	1	1 1/4″ × 8″ × 34 1/2″
Shelves	2	1 1/4 × 11″ × 34 1/2″
Sides	2	1 1/4 × 11″ × 39″
Hardwood wedges	1	1″ × 6″ × 7″ or available hardwood scrap

Making Dovetails to Join the Top Corners

There is no stronger or more attractive way to join the ends of two boards than with well-made dove-tails. Although instructions are specific to this project, they embody principles that apply to any dovetailing you might undertake. For safety's sake, make some practice joints with scrap before you start work on the cupboard.

Begin by making a pattern to serve as a guide. A traditional angle of rake is 1:5 (1-in. rake over 5-in. length). Make the pins about half as wide as the tails, and always arrange the pattern so that a half-pin (so called because it is angled on only one side) is on both ends.

Set a marking gauge to 1 1/6 in. more than the thickness of the wood.and use it to scribe a depth line around the ends of the top board and upper end of side pieces. (The scribed lines should be 32 in. apart on the top board; if they are not, trim the board to size.) Scribe

pattern on end grain of side pieces (Step 1, below) and use a square to extend lines down to depth line (Step 2). Shade tails as waste to be cut away. Use the same template to scribe pattern on upper face of top board, its edge flush with depth line (Step 3). Extend lines onto end grain, shade pins as waste, and compare markings to ensure an exact match (Step 4).

Cut pins into side pieces, using backsaw or dovetail saw to cut on shaded side of vertical lines to just short of the depth line (Step 5). Remove waste with coping saw, then trim with straight chisel (Step 6). Cut tails in top the same way (Step 7), using backsaw to remove outside waste and coping saw for waste between tails. Compare the pieces; if you have cut and trimmed precisely to the waste side of each line, they will match but not quite fit together (Step 8). Mark and trim a little at a time until they fit snugly together. To prevent offsetting the top forward or backward, trim both pieces equally.

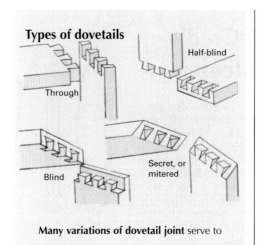

Types of dovetails

Through

Half-blind

Blind

Secret, or mitered

Many variations of dovetail joint serve to

Putting It Together

1. Use backsaw to make two diagonal cuts in each tenon to receive the wedges that will secure the joints. Cut slots with the grain, stopping about 1 1/6 in. before you reach the full depth of the tenons.

2. Make 16 hardwood wedges about 6 in. long, tapered from 1/4 in. to a dull point (see *Making Pins and Wedges*, p.307). Clamp cupboard together and drive wedges. (Shave sides of wedges to fit inside mortises.)

3. Tape hacksaw blade to prevent scratching wood, and trim wedges. Use block plane to smooth off protruding tenons and dovetail joints. Then finish-plane all surfaces and lightly chamfer all edges.

Pattern at right can be traced for use as a template to scribe tails and pins on wood surfaces for open cupboard.

| Half-pin | Tail | Pin | Tail | Pin | Tail | Half-pin |

Put this side against depth line of top

Put this side against outer face of sides

1. Scribe pattern on end grain of sides. Verify angles with bevel gauge.

2. Extend lines to depth line. Use pencil to crosshatch waste wood.

3. Scribe pattern on top piece, the wide part of tails toward ends.

4. Extend lines onto end grain; crosshatch pins for waste. Compare marks.

5. Cut pins into side pieces. Saw on the waste side of all lines.

6. Use scrap wood as backing while trimming with straight chisel.

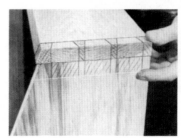

7. Cut tails into top piece, sawing on waste side of lines. Trim with chisel.

8. Mark and trim evenly until pieces can be tapped snugly together.

A Snug Colonial Cradle To Rock Baby Asleep

This charming project involves no mortise-and-tenon joints, no dovetails, no pins, and no wedges. All joints are planed for a flush fit and nailed. This seeming simplicity is deceptive, however. Because there are no square corners, at least two edges of each piece of the frame must be beveled at various angles. Some bevels are indicated at right, but for best results do not rely on patterns. Cut each edge square and a little outside the lines, then carefully fit the pieces together, marking and planing a little, refitting and planing some more.

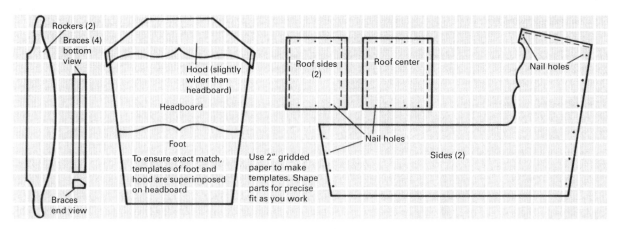

Rockers (2)
Braces (4) bottom view
Braces end view
Hood (slightly wider than headboard)
Headboard
Foot
To ensure exact match, templates of foot and hood are superimposed on headboard
Roof sides (2)
Roof center
Nail holes
Use 2" gridded paper to make templates. Shape parts for precise fit as you work
Nail holes
Sides (2)
Nail holes

American infants slept snug and warm in cradles like this during the colonial period and Revolutionary War.

Materials needed

Wood (clear white pine)
Needed to make the roof: 1/2" × 10" × 30"
Needed to make the frame, rockers, and bottom: 3/4" × 2' × 10'6"
Needed to make the braces: 1 1/4" × 5" × 12 1/2"

Nails (handmade mild steel if possible)
Needed to make the roof: 20 2d (1") brads
Needed to make the frame: 24 4d (1 1/2") wrought-headed
Needed to make the bottom: 48 6d (2") fine finish

Fitting the Frame Takes a Delicate Touch

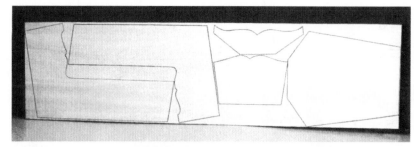

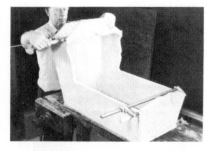

1. A single piece of 3/4-in. pine 10 1/2 ft. long by 2 ft. wide can yield all parts of the cradle except braces and roof pieces with very little wood wasted. (A 3-ft. section has already been sawn off the end of this board for making the bottom and rockers.) Use 2-in. grid to scribe patterns. Use rip and crosscut saws to rough-cut all pieces; cut scrollwork with a coping saw. Do not saw bevels but allow stock for them.

2. Edge-plane footboard and headboard, comparing to ensure identical angles. Do the same with side pieces. Assemble with bar or pipe clamps. Plane ends of hood to fit and clamp it in place.

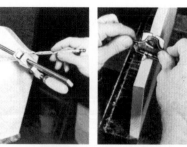

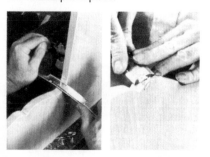

3. Begin the marking and fitting process with sides of footboard. Use straight edge to scribe junctures; loosen clamp, remove footboards, and edge-plane lightly. Reassemble often to check fit.

4. When joints are flush, mark top edge of footboard for bevel. Using a spokeshave, drawknife, and chisel, finish scrollwork so that the entire edge is slightly beveled inward to match upper edge of sides.

5. To finish sides, first plane ends to match line of footboard and headboard. Next, plane long edge to a slight inward bevel. Finally, finish trimming scrollwork with spokeshave, drawknife, and chisel.

Fitting the Roof and Nailing It Together

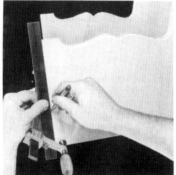

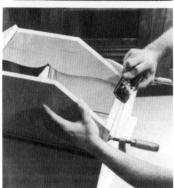

1. With rip and crosscut saws, rough-cut the three roof pieces from 1/2-in. stock, leaving 1/8 in. all around for fitting and beveling. Label each piece. To find bevel for the top edges of sides of frame, extend lines along slope of headboard and hood to the outer face of each side. Remove clamp that secures the hood while you scribe a straight line between the two points. Then clamp the hood back in place and use a block plane to bevel the edges of both side pieces so that the roof sides will sit flush. Secure the roof sides to the hood with C-clamps so that they overhang the frame slightly all around.

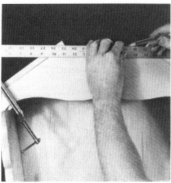

2. On the bottom of the two roof side pieces scribe the outline of the frame. Use a straightedge to find the angle of bevels across the top and along the sides, and scribe lines across the upper surfaces. Undo clamps and remove both pieces. Then sandwich them in vise with upper surfaces together and plane to the lines scribed on the undersides. Next, clamp the pieces together, underside to underside, and plane the bevels, double-checking the fit often. When both pieces fit properly, clamp them to the hood and place the center roof piece in position on top. Mark it, plane it to size, and bevel its two outer edges.

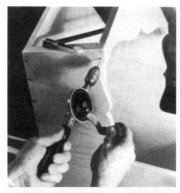

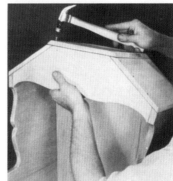

3. Use template to mark placement of nails on sides and roof pieces. Join frame with 4d wrought-headed nails. Clamp frame together and use a bit that is slightly smaller than the upper shank of nails to drill through sides and 1/2 in. into foot and headboard. Drive nails. Then drill through sides and 1 in. into hood for 6d fine finish nails; drill at upward angle for secure joints. (If you are using round nails, blunt the ends slightly before driving to prevent splitting wood; with cut nails be sure the wide edge is parallel to the grain.) Position roof pieces and drill for 2d brads 1/4 in. into hood and headboard. Secure roof side pieces first, then roof center.

Now All It Needs Is a Bottom With Rockers Attached

1. Place assembled frame on flat surface and mark a line for beveling about 1/4 in. up all around its lower edge. Turn frame upside down on bench and plane its bottom edge to the scribed line for a flat, even surface. Set the bottom piece on this surface and scribe the outline of the frame on it. Saw roughly to size. Edge-plane and surface-plane.

2. Rough-cut the two rockers with a coping saw. Clamp them together in vise for a close match, and use chisel, block plane, and spokeshave to trim and finish them. To make the braces, first rip a 5-in. board into four equal widths; saw to length and edge-plane square. Then plane a long bevel into one edge of each. Plane off corners at ends of beveled edge.

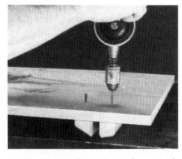

3. Position rockers 4 in. from each end of bottom and outline them on its upper and lower surfaces. Position braces on both sides of each rocker and outline braces as well. Within outlines of braces on upper surface of bottom, mark the placement of four nail holes. Set braces in place and drill through bottom piece into braces for 6d fine finish nails.

4. Drive nails partway into braces, then position rockers. If they fit snugly, remove rockers and drive nails into braces. Then reposition rockers and mark placement of three nail holes for each. Drill for and drive 6d fine finish nails into rockers. To prevent splitting, blunt the ends of round nails; place square nails with long side parallel to grain.

5. Position bottom on frame. Mark placement of four nails in each end, seven along each side. Drill for and drive 6d fine finish nails into frame at slightly outward angle to match angle of frame pieces. With chisel, plane, spokeshave, and scraper, finish and lightly chamfer all edges. Finish with penetrating varnish and well-rubbed coat of wax.

A Handy Stand For Candles, Lamps, And Knickknacks

The term candlestand applies indiscriminately to a wide variety of stands and small tables, most of which have only a central leg, or stem. While it is certainly true that these portable pieces of furniture were commonly used as pedestals for candles and candelabra, they were not limited to this practical function. In early American households, from log cabins to palatial mansions, you would have been as likely to find a bowl of fruit or flowers, an oil lamp, a birdcage, or the family Bible atop a candlestand as you would a candle.

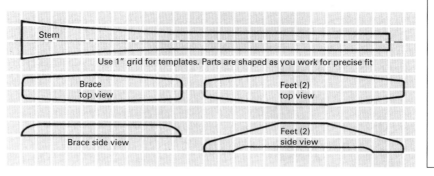

Use 1" grid for templates. Parts are shaped as you work for precise fit

Stem

Brace top view

Feet (2) top view

Brace side view

Feet (2) side view

Materials needed

Part	Pieces	Size
Stem	1	2 1/2" × 2 1/2" × 24 1/2"
Brace	1	3/4" × 2" × 10 1/4"
Feet	2	2" × 2" × 13 1/4"
Top	1	1" × 13 1/4" × 13 1/4"

Clear white pine is probably best for this project. Such hardwoods as walnut, cherry, or oak make very attractive candlestands but are more difficult to work with and can split when wedges are driven. Use ash or other hardwood for pins and wedges.

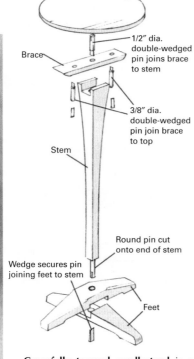

Top

Brace

1/2" dia. double-wedged pin joins brace to stem

3/8" dia. double-wedged pin join brace to top

Stem

Round pin cut onto end of stem

Wedge secures pin joining feet to stem

Feet

Gracefully tapered candlestand is a copy of a late-17th-century original made in or around Boston. It looks delicate but is solid and strong due to artfully hidden pins and wedges.

Shaping the Tapered Stem

1. Edge-plane stem piece to 2 3/8 in. square. Draw center line on all sides and across end grains. On two opposing sides align template to center line and scribe its outline.

2. With ripsaw make diagonal cuts from one end of piece to the other, outside of scribed lines. Plane square, redraw center lines, mark and saw the other two sides.

3. Plane these two sides square and redraw center lines using crossed lines on end grain as a guide. On two opposing sides align template with center and scribe its outline.

4. Use backsaw to make a series of cuts about 1/4 in. apart to within 1/16 in. of scribed lines. To be sure that saw cuts are square and level, use scribed lines on both sides as guides.

5. Clamp the stem piece firmly in vise while you use the widest chisel you have to remove waste wood from between the saw cuts. Hold chisel with the beveled side down.

6. Trim both sides to size with spokeshave. Then lightly redraw center lines and scribe outline of template on finished sides. Shape the remaining two sides in the same way.

Forming the Interlocking Feet

1. Use template to scribe side view of feet on 2-in. by 2-in. pieces. Cut roughly to shape, excluding hollows in bottom, with rip and crosscut saws. Clamp feet side by side in vise, and plane top surfaces to precise shape.

2. Use backsaw to cut the ends off square. Then clamp feet bottom side up in vise and make a series of absolutely level backsaw cuts across both to (but not through) the scribed lines that define the hollows in the bottom surfaces.

3. To shape sides of feet, scribe outline of template on bottom. Use drawknife to trim almost to line, then clamp feet together in vise and plane for exact match. Finish separately by shaping hollows in bottom with 1-in. chisel.

4. To locate lap joint, cross one foot squarely over the other at midpoint; scribe outline on top of lower foot and on bottom of upper foot. Use square to extend lines around both feet. Compare to be certain lines are centered.

5. Stand lower foot on bench and scribe horizontal line 3/4 in. down from top. Use backsaw and chisel as in shaping stem to cut notch in top just short of line. Insert upper foot, scribe across, and cut similar notch from bottom.

6. Join the notches. Fit should be snug, not tight, but joint should not yet fit flush. Gradually increase depth of notches (tapering both inward slightly for tightness) until tops are flush and both feet sit evenly on flat surface.

7. Mark center of joint on top and bottom with crossed pencil lines. Make a pilot hole through center using 1/4-in. or 5/16-in. bit in eggbeater drill. To ensure straight hole, drill halfway from bottom, then drill back from top to meet.

8. For final hole use 13/16-in. bit. To help keep hole straight, clamp brace in vise with bit vertical, and turn foot assembly on it. Bore from the bottom until tip of bit emerges, then bore from top (see *Drilling clean holes*, p.305).

9. Use straight chisel and spokeshave to lightly chamfer upper edges of foot assembly. Finish surface of feet with scraper, leveling off any unevenness in the joint and smoothing away any remaining nicks and blemishes.

Giving the stem a round pin

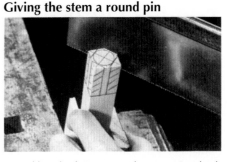

1. Find length of pin on stem by measuring depth of foot assembly at center hole; then scribe depth line around stem. Draw 7/8-in. circle on end grain of stem. Use backsaw to cut away corners to depth line, leaving octagonal pin slightly larger than scribed circle.

2. With a small chisel carefully trim pin down to a circle until it fits snugly into the hole through the foot assembly. Be sure that shoulder around pin is cut evenly for a flush fit against the upper surface of the feet. Use plane or spokeshave to lightly chamfer all four long edges of the stem.

3. Make a 3-in. hardwood wedge 1/4 in. thick on top and same width as pin. Use backsaw to slot pin lengthwise along the grain. If stem leans slightly when inserted in foot assembly, locate slot off center. Later, when wedge is driven, stem will adjust toward side with the slot.

317

Topping Off the Stand And Pinning It Together

Make the top from 1 1/4-inch stock, planed to 1 inch. Scribe a circle 13 inches across and rough-cut it with a coping saw 1/8 inch outside line. Trim to line with a block plane. For a delicate look plane a 1/4-inch bevel around the underside, extending inward 1 1/2 inches. The joints are made with double-wedged pins; fox wedges (p.307) secure the hidden half. Saw slots in both ends of all pins almost to the center at right angles to each other.

The Brace and Its Joint

  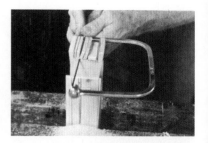

1. Scribe outline of brace from template. Rough-cut with rip and crosscut saws; use block plane to taper sides to scribed lines. Round off both lower corners with block plane and spokeshave.

2. Center the brace on upper end of stem, across the main grain line, and scribe its outline. Then scribe its thickness on sides of stem and use square to extend lines from end to this depth line.

3. Use dovetail saw or backsaw to make a series of cuts to depth line. Remove waste with coping saw rather than chisel to avoid danger of splitting end grain. Then use chisel to trim for snug fit.

Joining It All With Pins and Wedges

1. Drill 1/2-in. hole through center of brace and 3/8-in. holes 2 3/4 in. from both ends. Position center hole over center of notch in stem and drill 1/2-in. hole 1 1/2 in. deep in stem.

2. Make 1/2-in. pin 2 1/4 in. long; slot ends 1 in. deep in opposing directions. Insert 7/8-in. fox wedge in one end; drive so that wedge runs across grain of stem. Drive second wedge.

3. Center the brace on underside of top, with its grain running opposite to the grain of the top. Mark its outline in pencil, and mark centers for the two 3/8-in. holes.

4. Drill two 3/8-in. holes in underside of top no deeper than 9/16 in. (Bit must not break through upper surface of top.) Use small chisel to smooth and clean out bottom of both holes.

5. Make two 3/8-in. pins 1 1/2 in. long; slot both ends in opposing directions 11/16 in. deep. Insert 5/8-in. fox wedges. Drive with mallet so that wedges run with grain of brace across top grain.

6. Insert both second wedges and drive with hardwood mallet. Trim with taped hacksaw blade and chisel; finish with block plane and spokeshave. Chamfer edges of brace.

7. Insert stem pin into center hole in feet, and drive 3-in. wedge (p.317). Trim excess with taped hacksaw blade and spokeshave. Chamfer top of stand slightly. Finish with scraper.

The Trestle Table: A True Trencherman's Groaning Board

A trestle table in its most rudimentary form is nothing but a long board set across two or three sawhorses, inelegant but functional, with the clear advantages of easy storage and portability. The design shown here and on the following pages—a scaled-down version of a 12-foot-long 18th-century banquet table belonging to New York's Metropolitan Museum of Art—has the same practical virtues and is good looking as well.

In taverns and inns, homes and churches, wherever many people might gather to eat and drink together, trestle tables were used by early Americans. Like today's folding card tables, they took up little storage space and were easily transported—even through narrow doorways.

Materials needed

The best wood for the tabletop and all parts of the trestle structure is No. 2 white pine, although any good soft pine will do. The pins and wedges for the original were probably made of white oak; however, various light-colored hardwoods, such as white ash or beech, are satisfactory. (See *Making Pins and Wedges*, p.307.)

Part	Pieces	Size
Top	3	1 1/4″ × 11″ × 6′1″
Trestle structure (all parts)	4	3 1/2″ × 3 1/2″ × 5″
Pins and wedges	1	3/4″ × 11 1/2″ × 1″ or odd scraps 3/4″ thick

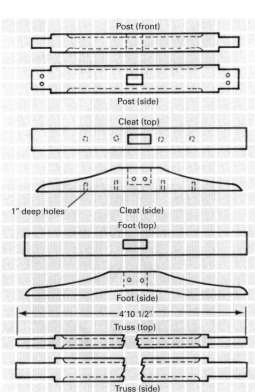
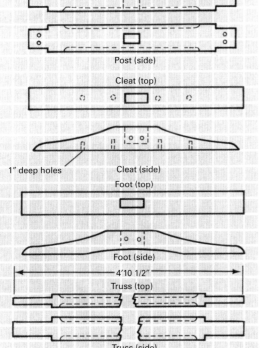

Post (front)

Post (side)

Cleat (top)

1″ deep holes

Cleat (side)

Foot (top)

Foot (side)

◄——— 4′10 1/2″ ———►

Truss (top)

Truss (side)

Use 2-in. gridded paper to make patterns for truss, feet, cleats, and posts. Scribe patterns on wood, avoiding knots where mortises are to be cut. Saw to length. Cut pieces roughly to width with ripsaw; then

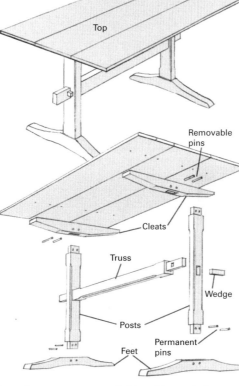

Top

Removable pins

Cleats

Truss

Wedge

Posts

Permanent pins

Feet

surface-plane truss, posts, and sides of feet and cleats to within 1/8 in. of finished size. Rescribe patterns. Cut tenons on truss and posts with backsaw and chisel (see *Mortise-and-tenon joints*, p.311).

Forming the Feet and Cleats

1. To shape curved surfaces on feet and cleats, begin by making a series of backsaw cuts about 1/4 in. apart to within 1/8 in. of scribed lines. Be certain cuts are absolutely square and level. Remove waste wood with 1-in. straight chisel.

2. Clamp both cleats firmly together and trim them simultaneously to size, using a block plane first, then a spokeshave or drawknife for a finished appearance. Next, clamp both feet together and trim them in the same way.

3. Cleats have blind mortises: they go only partway through. Use post tenons as guides to scribe mortises on center of cleats (see *Mortise-and-tenon joints*, p.311). With 5/16-in. bit, drill holes 1/16 in. deeper than length of tenon.

4. Trim mortises with straight chisel so tenon fits snugly. To remove waste wood from bottom of mortise, make a series of cuts across grain by tapping chisel with mallet; then scrape out. Drill and trim foot mortises all the way through.

Pins and Wedges: Some Are Permanent, Some Are Not

Four kinds of hardwood pins are needed to join the table's parts. To secure the feet permanently to posts, use four 1/4-inch dowels. For the removable pins joining the posts and cleats, fashion four round pins 41/2 inches long, tapering from 5/8 to 3/16 inch thick. For holding the truss in place, make two wedges 2 5/8 inches long by 3/4 inch wide, tapering from 5/8 to 5/16 inch thick. The cleats are affixed to the tabletop with eight fox-wedged pins that measure 7/16 inch square at the top, tapering to 5/16 by 3/8 inch. (See *Making Pins and Wedges*, p.307.)

The tabletop consists of three 11/4-inch-thick boards edge-glued to form one wide plank. To give the glue plenty of drying time, apply glue and clamp before starting on the frame. (See *Edge-Gluing*, p.306.)

Preparing the Pieces for Pinning

1. Assemble leg systems and stand them on flat surface. Clamp truss tenons to posts, as indicated by post templates, and scribe outlines. Extend lines around posts. Then butt tenons against inner face of each post, centered between lines, and scribe width. Use gauge to mark width on outer face. Drill and cut mortises (see *Mortise-and-tenon joints*, p.311).

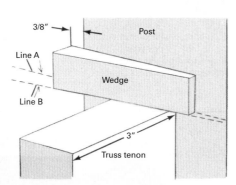

2. Insert truss tenons through mortises (they should protrude about 3 in.), and scribe line A across upper face of each to mark its exit from post. Place wedge atop tenon flush with post, its thick end extending 3/8 in. beyond front face of post, and scribe line B on tenon. Withdraw tenon and use combination square to scribe line C 1/8 in. closer to shoulder than line A.

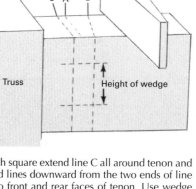

3. With square extend line C all around tenon and extend lines downward from the two ends of line B onto front and rear faces of tenon. Use wedge itself to scribe height of wedge mortise, yielding two rectangles on opposite sides of tenon, one broader than the other. The inner edge of both rectangles should be 1/8 in. inside post mortise when tenon is in place.

4. To cut wedge mortises, begin by drilling from small side with 5/16-in. bit, at angle indicated by line B on sides of truss tenon, until point of bit protrudes. Then bore back to clear hole. Next, use 1/4-in. and 1/2-in. chisels to trim remaining waste. (The extra width of wedge mortises will leave a 1/8-in. gap inside posts to allow for future tightening as trestle table ages.)

5. Using templates as guides, mark truss and both posts for 1/2-in. chamfers on all long edges. Cut ends of each chamfer with a chisel; then use plane or spokeshave for long, flat sections. To avoid cutting too deeply, always go with the grain, never against it. Specially designed chamfering planes, spokeshaves, and draw knives are available to make this job easier.

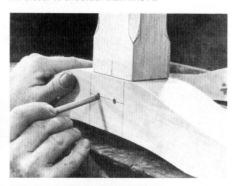

6. Locate holes for pinning foot permanently to post 1 in. down from top of foot and 3/4 in. in from sides of mortise. Drill 1/4-in. hole through foot at each mark. Insert tenons and mark top edge of holes on posts; then withdraw tenons and drill 1/4-in. holes centered on these marks. Since holes are offset, tenons will be drawn tightly down when pins are inserted later.

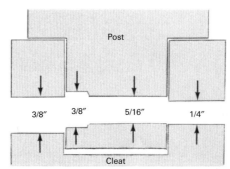

7. To make offset holes for removable pins that will join cleats to posts, begin with same hole-locating procedure as for Step 5. Use 3/8-in. bit to drill through one side of cleat into empty mortise. Place cleat on bench with mortise up, insert post tenon, and make a mark slightly above center point of the hole. Remove tenon and use 3/8-in. bit to bore 1/4-in.-deep holes in it at

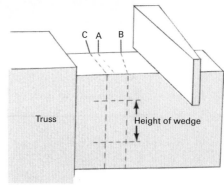

these marks. Change to 5/16-in. bit and continue through tenon until tip emerges, then bore back to clear hole. Replace tenon in mortise and, with 1/4-in. bit held against lowest surface of inside of hole, drill through other side of cleat until tip emerges. Bore back to clear hole. When tapered pin is inserted, tenon will be drawn tightly down into mortise.

Putting It Together and Taking It Apart

1. Remove clamps from tabletop after glue has set. Surface-plane to about 1 in. thick. Plane ends to size. Then draw a line on underside 2 in. from each edge, another on all edges 3/8 in. up from underside. Bevel edges for a graceful appearance by planing to these lines.

2. Assemble and pin together cleats, posts, and truss. Place top upside down on bench and center this trestle structure on it. Outline cleats. Within outlines use template to mark positions of pins for joining top to cleats. Drill through top with 3/8-in. bit. (See *Drilling clean holes*, p.305.)

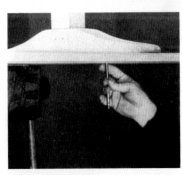

3. With the end of tabletop overhanging bench, replace trestle structure with cleats once again in their outlined positions. Mark center of each hole on cleats. Then shift top so other end overhangs bench, check position of cleats, and mark center of these holes.

4. Use piece of tape to mark depth of 1 in. on 3/8-in. bit. Drill holes in cleats to that depth, centered on marks. Reposition cleats on tabletop and insert pins to check hole alignment. Label all joints for reassembly, then take trestle structure apart and lightly chamfer all exposed edges.

5. To join feet and posts permanently, insert each post tenon into the mortise that was made to fit it. With knife or block plane, whittle slight bevel on one end of each pin so it can work its way through offset holes and draw tenons down. Then use mallet to drive all pins firmly home.

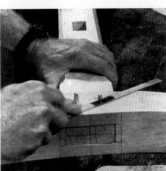

6. Drive pins all the way through legs so that beveled ends protrude, then use hacksaw blade to saw both ends of pins flush with sides of feet. Ends of hacksaw blade are taped to prevent marring wood surface. Finish trimming ends of pins with block plane.

7. Reassemble trestle and secure top to cleats with 2 1/4-in. fox-wedged pins (see *Making Pins and Wedges*, p.307). Pins should have 1-in. slots. Make fox wedges 1 in. long by 5/16 in. wide, tapering from 3/16 in. to 1/16 in. thick. Insert so wedges run across grain of cleats. Support cleats while driving pins.

Use taped hacksaw blade and block plane, as in Step 6, to trim pins off level with surface of tabletop. Then use jack or smoother plane to lightly finish the whole top and to chamfer all edges a little. It is almost certain that the original table upon which this design is based was left unfinished or, at most, treated with an occasional application of linseed oil (for instruction in applying linseed oil, see *Finishing*, p.307). A coat of penetrating varnish followed by a thin layer of wax, carefully rubbed with a soft cloth, is a good way to give your table more protection without destroying its natural look.

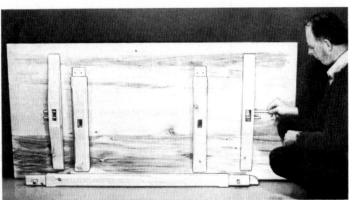

To disassemble table for storage, first use hardwood mallet to loosen all four tapered pins that secure the post-and-cleat joints. Then remove pins and lift off top. Next, use mallet to remove wedges from their mortises in the truss. When both wedges are out, pull posts straight off truss tenons. To prevent loss of pins and wedges, always tap them into their appropriate holes while table is in storage. Store parts in a warm (not hot), dry place to minimize the risk of warping.

The Hutch Table:
A Rural Space Saver
Made From Pine

In the crowded confines of old farmhouses and home-steads the versatile hutch table was a valued piece of furniture. It was a combination table and storage chest with a top that tipped back so the piece could be pushed flat against a wall—in which state it could also serve as a chair. The original of this charming example of the genre, dating from about 1700, was made from white pine by methods very like those illustrated on the following pages. White pine is still the ideal wood to use, although any soft pine will do. It was finished with a milk-based blue paint, so long-lasting that much of the original coat remains. A simple and attractive alternative, albeit inauthentic, is to apply a wipe-on, penetrating resin finish, such as those manufactured by Watco, Minwax, or Dupont, to highlight and protect the natural wood grain. The finish used here is clear, with a slight tint of light walnut stain added for accent.

The seat of this hutch table is a little high for comfort, a problem that is easily solved with the help of a small footstool. In other common designs—called, naturally enough, chair tables—storage space was sacrificed for the sake of a lower chair seat, with the arms of the chair serving to support the tabletop. Some featured pull-out drawers beneath the seat.

This hutch table is similar—but not identical—to project. Tool resting on it is a niddy-noddy. (See *Spinning*, p.277.)

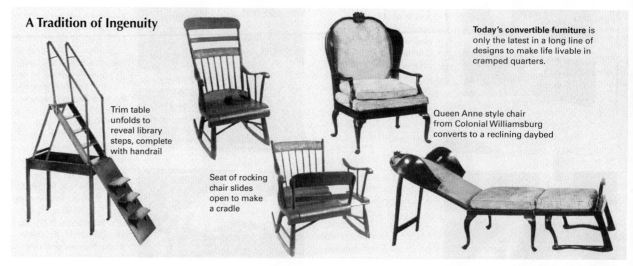

A Tradition of Ingenuity

Trim table unfolds to reveal library steps, complete with handrail

Seat of rocking chair slides open to make a cradle

Today's convertible furniture is only the latest in a long line of designs to make life livable in cramped quarters.

Queen Anne style chair from Colonial Williamsburg converts to a reclining daybed

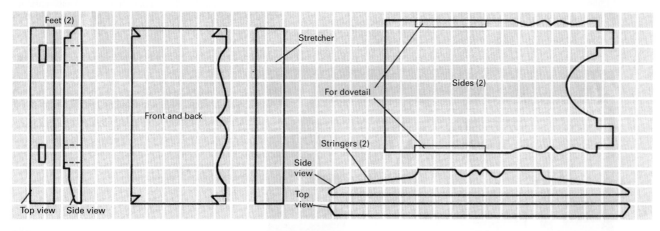

Feet (2) | Stretcher | Sides (2)

For dovetail

Stringers (2)

Front and back

Top view | Side view | Side view | Top view

Materials needed

Part	Pieces	Size
Tabletop	1	3/4" × 12" × 43"
Tabletop	2	3/4" × 16" × 43"
Sides	2	3/4" × 15" × 27 5/8"
Front and back	2	3/4" × 12" × 19 3/4"
Feet	2	2 1/4" × 2 3/4" × 20"
Top stringers	2	1 1/2" × 3" × 36"
Foot stretcher	1	3/4" × 4" × 20"
Hutch lid	1	3/4" × 15" × 18 1/2"
Hutch bottom	1	3/4" × 13 3/4" × 18 3/4"
Battens	4	3/4" × 1" × 14"
Hardwood pins	2	5/8" dia. × 4"

Use 2-in. gridded paper to make templates for all parts of hutch table.

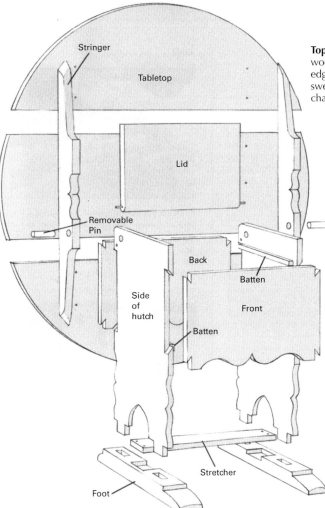

Stringer

Tabletop

Lid

Removable Pin

Back

Batten

Side of hutch

Front

Batten

Stretcher

Foot

Top is joined to stringers with wood screws. Boards are not edge-glued, so wood can swell and shrink in response to changes in humidity.

Stand assembly comprises front, back, and two side pieces joined with large dovetails and secured by wood screws. Top pivots on removable pins joining its stringers to sides. Lid pivots on permanent pins. Battens supporting lid and bottom are screwed to sides.

Foot assembly consists of two feet joined by a stretcher. Stretcher is recessed into half-mortises and is secured by screws. Mortise-and-tenon joints between stand and feet can be secured with pins or left loose for disassembly.

Shaping the Parts for the Stand

Use rip and crosscut saws to cut front, back, and two side pieces roughly to size. Allow 1/4 to 1/8 in. all around for shaping and finishing. If wide boards are not available, turn to edge-gluing (see p.306). To obtain an exact match, clamp the two side pieces together with hand screws and cut both at once with a coping saw. Saw along the outside of the lines scribed on one piece. (Do not at this time cut out the section marked on template "For dovetail.") Use your straight chisel and drawknife to trim the edges of both pieces simultaneously.

You will find that holding these tools at a slight angle and using a slicing motion will produce an attractive faceted effect, provided that your tools are sharp, your touch is light, and you never attempt to go against the grain of the wood—which means cutting downhill on almost all curves and angles. To smooth some of the marks left by the chisel and drawknife without losing this handmade quality, do as old-time craftsmen did and use a thin piece of steel as a scraper rather than using sandpaper.

Finish the side pieces by shaving about 1/16 in. from both sides of each tenon. When the time comes for fitting them into their foot mortises, the resultant overlap will cover any open space that may exist.

Clamp front and back pieces together and cut and trim them in the same way. Do not cut the dovetail sections at this time; the proper angles will be cut separately later.

The hutch table has three component assemblies, each permanently joined. For best results, make the stand assembly first, then fit the top and foot assemblies to it, as demonstrated on the following pages. This will allow you to make creative adjustments as you go along, just as the old-time furnituremakers did, in response to the demands of the wood, a passing inspiration, or even a slight error of craftsmanship. For the same reason, do not make any permanent fastenings until you know that all the parts fit together properly. For example, when the dovetail joints of the stand assembly are finished, use a light string to tie the unit together. The action of moving the stand assembly around while you use it to help set up all other parts of the table will increase the tolerance of the joints a little. As a result, the finished table will be better able to adjust to atmospheric changes.

Joining the stand with large dovetails

1. Cut male portions of dovetail joints first. They will serve as patterns for female parts. Use template to scribe the 45° angles of dovetail sections on both ends of front and back pieces. Cut just outside the scribed lines with a backsaw. Finish trimming to the lines with a 1-in. straight chisel.

2. Use hand screws as stands to hold sides upright on edge. Position pieces carefully on bench so they are properly spaced and parallel to each other. Lay front piece on them and scribe outlines of dovetail on edge of both side pieces. Scribe line for depth of female dovetail equal to thickness of front piece.

3. Rough out female dovetails by making a series of backsaw cuts about 1/4 in. apart to within 1/16 in. of depth line. Chisel out waste wood between them. Trim with straight chisel until front fits snugly into both sides. Then, with front in place, turn sides over and repeat the process with dovetails of back piece.

Feet on the Bottom And a Top That Pivots Finish the Job

For this project we have used 1 1/2-in. No. 8 flat-headed wood screws to secure all permanent joints. This is not strictly authentic. The original was probably joined with fox-wedged pegs like those used for the top of the trestle table (p.321) or the candlestand (p.318). The only way to know for certain is to take the original apart, and that has not been done for nearly 300 years. An alternative joining method is to drill 3/8-in. holes 2 in. deep at each spot where a screw is called for, apply glue, and drive in 3/8-in. hardwood pegs. Be sure to cut a small lengthwise groove in each peg to allow air to escape.

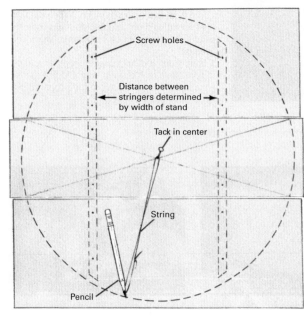

Edge-plane boards for tabletop. Find center of 12-in. board by drawing two diagonals, corner to corner. Place 16-in. boards alongside and scribe circle with 21-in. radius from center point. Cut all three boards with coping saw (old-time country carpenters would have used a frame saw), leaving 3/8 in. outside scribed lines for finishing. Surface-plane to flatten top and bottom surfaces. Store boards in plastic bags to forestall warping.

Foot Assembly

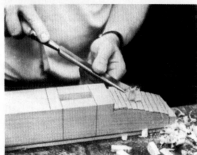

Use template to scribe the outline of both feet on 2-in.-thick lumber, then saw the pieces roughly to length. Locate the stand assembly carefully on both foot blanks and scribe around all four tenons. With a square transfer these mortise lines to sides and bottom of feet. (See *Mortise-and-tenon joints*, p.311.) To start mortises, drill three 7/16-in. holes in each marked area; bore from top until the point of the bit emerges, then bore back from bottom for a clean hole. Finish cutting with 1/2-in. and 1-in. straight chisels until tenons fit snugly. (To prevent breaking edges of mortises, chisel outline about 1/4 in. deep on top and bottom surfaces before driving with mallet.) To shape the feet, make a series of absolutely square backsaw cuts about 1/4 in. apart to within 1/16 in. of scribed lines, and chisel out between them with a broad, straight chisel. Use the chisel to carve away the resultant steplike surface, then use a drawknife or spokeshave to trim to the scribed line. To avoid splitting or splintering wood, always work downhill in direction of grain.

Cut foot stretcher to length, and plane its edges and top and bottom surfaces. To ensure a tight fit when joining it to the feet, do not plane edges square but bevel them about 1/16 in. narrower at the bottom than at the top. To locate half-mortises, center the stretcher across feet and scribe its lower outline on them. Set mortising gauge to the thickness of stretcher, and use it to scribe notch's depth on inner surface of feet. On one foot piece, make a series of slanting backsaw cuts to within 1/16 in. of both lines and chisel away waste wood, leaving a smooth beveled section where notch will be cut. Then use 1-in. chisel to carve this section out square so that end of stretcher fits snugly into it, its upper surface raised about 1/16 in. above foot. Assemble structure and use the stretcher to double-check marking on the other foot; then cut second notch in the same way. Finally, carefully shave the bottoms of the half-mortises in both feet so the stretcher fits down tightly. The "gaining fit" caused by beveling the edges of the stretcher ensures a secure joint.

Top

1. To shape top stringers, use template to scribe pattern and proceed as with shaping feet (left) by making a series of backsaw cuts to within 1/16 of line, chiseling out waste wood and finishing with chisel, drawknife, and spokeshave.

2. To locate position of stringers, assemble top facedown on flat surface and position stand assembly upside down on it. Place stringers across grain of top boards, 1/16 in. from sides of stand. Scribe around stand and both stringers.

3. Mark placement of six screws within each stringer area and drill 1/8-in. holes. Turn top over and rest it on stringers, using scribed lines as guide. Drive nails 1/2 in. into stringers to secure top while you drive screws one at a time.

Attaching the Top With Removable Pivot Pins

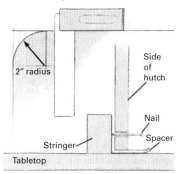

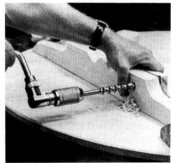

1. To locate pivot point, measure 2 in. down and in from rear corner of each side. Scribe arc and round off corners. Drill 1/8-in. hole at pivot points. Then place top facedown, position stand between stringers, and drive 6d finish nails into them. (To ensure clearance, use cardboard spacer.)

2. Stand table upright and pivot the top back and forth to be sure it moves freely—you may have to shave the rounded corners a little. Then pull out nails, remove top, and drill 5/8-in. holes through sides at pivot points. Back up work with scrap wood while drilling to prevent splintering.

3. Carefully drill 5/8-in. holes through stringers at point where nails were driven. Make two 5/8-in. hardwood pins 4 in. long for pivots (see *Making Pins and Wedges*, p.307). Finally, using same technique as in Step 1, round off front corners of both side pieces to 1-in. radius.

Final assembly

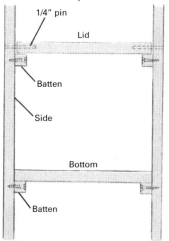

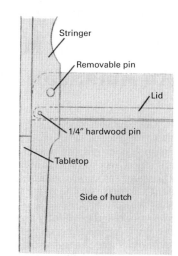

Join stand and foot assemblies with 1 1/2-in. No. 8 wood screws, countersunk and plugged (see below left). Cut and plane hutch lid, bottom, and four battens. Make two 1/4-in. hardwood pins 3 in. long for lid pivots. Lid should fit between sides of stand with 1/8-in. total clearance; use plane to round its front and rear edges. Place lid on stand, its front edge barely overhanging the front piece, its rear just resting on back, and scribe its outline on sides. Remove lid and drill 1/4-in. hole through both sides, centered within scribed outline, its edge 3/16 in. from rear of outline. Replace lid and drill back into it through these holes 2 in. deep. Drive 3-in. hardwood pins and trim. Install supporting battens beneath lid with three No. 8 screws per batten (because these battens are hidden, screws need not be plugged). To install bottom, screw battens to sides and simply set bottom piece on them.

Countersinking and plugging for screws

To simulate pegged joints, screwheads can be countersunk and the holes filled with wood plugs. The first steps in joining two pieces with screws are to mark placement of the screws on top piece and to drill 1/8-in. hole at each mark. Next, position the pieces and drive small finish nails through all holes about 1/2 in. into lower piece to hold it firmly in place. Remove one nail and drill pilot hole into lower piece, using appropriate bit for screw size (for No. 8 screw, use 1/16-in. bit in softwood, 3/32 in. in hardwood). Then use a larger bit (3/8 in. for No. 8 screw) or a fluted counterbore to countersink for screwhead. In 3/4-in. wood, such as that used for hutch table, countersink 1/4 in. to 3/8 in. deep. Drive screw, then repeat the process for the next hole. When all screws are driven, plug holes with pegs of the appropriate size. For authentic-looking peglike plugs, take them from end grain of a piece of scrap with a plug cutter. Lacking this special tool, shape them as you would any peg (see p.307). Trim with chisel and block plane.

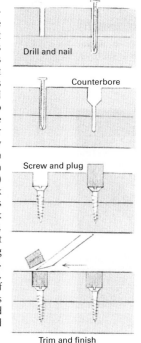

To finish table, use plane and drawknife to trim top evenly round. Lightly surface-plane to remove blemishes incurred in construction and to smooth over end grain of pegs and plugs. Correct other imperfections with scraper. Finally, chamfer top and all sharp edges.

From the Queen Of Spanish Missions: An American Chair

In the Spanish missions of the American Southwest there developed a unique style of furniture, clearly Spanish in origin, often with a hint of Dutch or Flemish influence, yet unmistakably American in character. The chair pictured below right, from the Mission of Santa Barbara on the coast of southern California, is at once typical of the style and exceptional in the way its elements blend gracefully together. The scrolled form of the skirt, for example, as well as the decorative carving on it and along the upper edge of the back are hardly as ornate as the work found on much Flemish furniture, but the slight adornment serves to allay the rigidity of the basic Spanish design.

Generally speaking, mission furniture was not overly comfortable. The Franciscan monks who manned the missions considered love of comfort an insidious vice. Yet this chair, with its raked back and gently tapered arms, is quite pleasurable to sit in—although modern taste might dictate a cushion upon the bare wooden seat. With this in mind, the copy described here was designed with the seat 1 inch lower than that of the original.

A Leg Jig to Guide Construction

The mission chair's construction involves 22 mortise-and-tenon joints. Each must be individually formed and fitted into its proper place in the assembled frame if the chair is to be structurally sound. As a result, you will find yourself devoting a great deal of time and effort to the process of disassembling and reassembling the developing piece as you mark, measure, cut, and fit each element in its turn. To make this repetitive chore easier and more accurate, begin by constructing a leg jig.

As a base for the jig, use 3/4-inch plywood that measures 24 inches wide by at least 30 inches long. For the sides of the jig use two strips of 3/4-inch plywood or stock lumber 4 1/2 inches wide by 24 inches long. All three pieces must be finished on one side and free from warp. Next, cut four hardwood blocks to the approximate dimensions given below. All edges must be square. Glue and nail a block to both ends of each 4 1/2-inch strip so that the strips are held upright at a 90° angle. Blocks should be glued to the unfinished sides of the strips, with the notched ends flush with the ends of the strips. Then use a framing square to place the strips 23 inches apart on the base. Clamp all four blocks down, being certain that the upright faces of both strips are square to the base.

Use the side view pattern (below left) to scribe the positions of the legs on the base and on the upright sides of the jig. Note that the rear legs slant slightly forward; the marks should reflect this. To use the jig, clamp each leg within its mark.

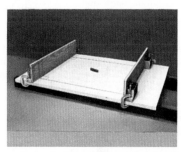

Make leg jig from 3/4-in. plywood and four blocks. Glue and nail blocks to side pieces, then clamp to base.

Space upright side pieces 23 in. apart. Scribe outlines of all four legs on base and on both side pieces.

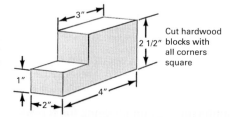

Cut hardwood blocks with all corners square

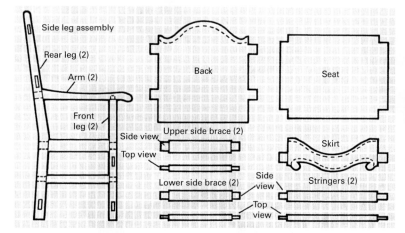

Use 2-in. grid to make templates for all pieces, including those that make up the side leg assembly. Mark mortises and tenons for guidance but do not cut from patterns.

Side leg assembly
Rear leg (2)
Arm (2)
Front leg (2)
Side view
Top view
Back
Upper side brace (2)
Side view
Lower side brace (2)
Top view
Seat
Skirt
Stringers (2)

Original Santa Barbara mission, where this chair was built, was founded in 1786 but was later destroyed by an earthquake. The present building, called Queen of the Missions for its great beauty, dates from 1815.

Legs, Braces, and Stringers Make a Frame

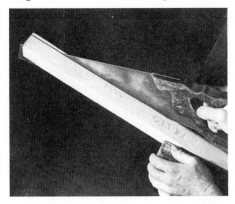

1. Use template to lay out side view of all four legs and both arms on 2-in. stock. Cut them roughly to size with a ripsaw, allowing about 1/8 in. extra for finishing. Cut rear legs so that the grain of the wood runs lengthwise along the center of the curve, not along either end. Cut stringers and side braces from 3/4-in. stock.

2. Use jack plane and spokeshave to trim the legs, stringers, and side braces to the scribed lines. Compare the pieces often as you work in order to achieve the closest possible match between the two front legs, the two rear legs, and among all six braces and stringers. (For instructions in shaping the arms, see p.329.)

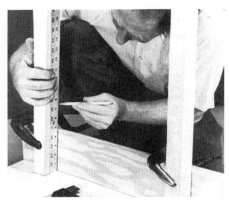

3. Clamp a front and rear leg in place on one side of the leg jig. On both legs make a pencil mark 7 1/4 in. up from base and another 16 1/4 in. up. Clamp side braces to legs, the bottom edge of the lower brace on the 7 1/4 in. mark, the top edge of the upper brace on the higher mark. Do the same with the other two legs.

4. Because the rear legs slant, side braces will not be quite level. Adjust positions on rear legs to correct. Scribe outlines of braces on all four legs and scribe outlines of legs on all braces. Disassemble frame after labeling both parts of all joints for reassembly. With a square extend scribed lines all around each piece.

Materials needed

Original of this mission chair was made of clear western pine, an ideal choice for the project because of its sharp, distinctive figure. Any clear soft wood, such as white pine, will do nicely, however—especially recommended is pumpkin pine, the orange-hued heartwood of white pine. For the leg jig use AD plywood (finished on only one side). Blocks can be made from construction-grade 2 × 4.

Part	Pieces	Size
Skirt, seat, back	6	3/4″ × 8″ × 23″
Side braces, stringers	1	3/4″ × 6″ × 42″
Legs, arms, wedges	2	2″ × 4″ × 7″
Leg jig	1	3/4″ × 24″ × 40″
Blocks	1	1 1/2″ × 2 1/2″ × 20″

Joining the Frame One Step at a Time

Before cutting tenons into the side braces, lay out the marked pieces on the side leg assembly template in order to double-check your marks. Make whatever adjustments are needed and replace the assemblies in the leg jig. If the two front legs and the two rear legs are exact duplicates, you can then clamp the two matching pairs of side braces together and cut tenons into the ends of each pair in one operation. If, as is more likely, the legs vary somewhat, the tenons must be cut separately. When all tenons are cut, clamp them to the outsides of the legs to scribe for mortises. (For further instructions in forming mortise-and-tenon joints, see p.311.)

Scribe mortises by extending lines onto all four sides of legs to serve as a guide in cutting. This is especially important with rear legs, as tenons pierce them at a slight angle. Center tenons between lines to scribe width of mortises. Use 3/8-in. bit to drill out waste wood before cutting mortises with 1/4-in. and 1-in. chisels.

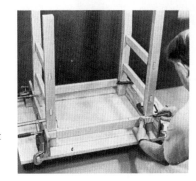

Assemble finished leg systems in jig and position stringers. Clamp front stringer to front of legs, rear stringer to back of rear legs, with bottom edges of both 2 1/4 in. up. Mark and cut tenons; if legs are of equal width, stringers can be formed in duplicate. Mark and cut mortises as for side braces.

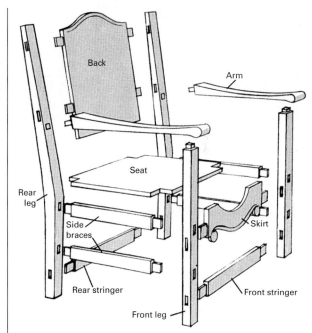

Build the mission chair from the ground up. First make frame; then shape skirt, seat, and back to fit; finish by forming arms. Only when all joints are fitted should wedges be driven, beginning with the fox wedges that secure arms to front legs.

Making the Seat, Skirt, And Back Fit the Frame

While it may be possible to find pieces of 3/4-inch clear pine that are wide enough for the seat and back and yet are not exorbitantly priced, the odds are not good. You will more likely have to resort to edge-gluing. That is why the list of materials on page 327 calls for six 8-inch-wide boards to make these two parts and the skirt. Use one board for the skirt. Rip one into two pieces, 2 inches and 6 inches wide. Then join two boards to the 2-inch width for the seat and the remaining two to the 6-inch width for the back. (For instructions in various methods of edge-gluing, see p.306.)

Scribing and Cutting the Back

When 3/4-in. stock has been edge-glued, plane surfaces smooth and flat for back, seat, and skirt. Use templates and straightedge to scribe patterns. Lay out patterns so that when chair is assembled wood grain will run side to side on all three pieces.

Check the width of the back against the assembled frame before cutting it out. Then use crosscut, rip, and coping saws to cut it roughly to size, including the tenons as marked. Allow about 1/8 in. extra in all dimensions for finishing. With straight chisel, drawknife, and spokeshave, trim the top and bottom edges to the scribed lines, always working downhill on curves to avoid digging into the grain of the wood.

Putting the Pieces in Place

1. Rough-cut seat to within 1/8 in. of the scribed lines. Use chisel to trim notches in all four corners so seat fits easily into frame. Fit should not be tight, as frame will be squeezed somewhat together when joints are secured.

2. Trim sides of back and skirt to fit frame; then cut tenons to size. For a neater fit give all tenons four shoulders; make a series of backsaw cuts 1/8 in. deep on front and rear surfaces and, with bevel down, chisel away waste.

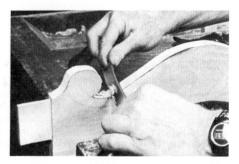

3. Plane upper edge of skirt to fit flush beneath seat. Clamp all tenons in place and scribe for mortises. Position mortises so that when assembled, front face of back and skirt will be parallel to and recessed 1/8 in. from front of legs.

4. Disassemble frame to cut out mortises (see *Mortise-and-tenon joints*, p.311); reassemble to fit each joint. Edge-plane seat flush with outside of legs. Then use coping saw to cut scrollwork in skirt. Trim with chisel and drawknife.

Adding the decorative touch

A woodcarver's V-shaped parting tool is designed for just such jobs as gouging out the grooves in the back and skirt; next best is a skew chisel. These are special carving tools available from some tool supply houses. You can also do the job with a narrow straight chisel and a sharp knife. First use the templates to scribe a line 5/8 inch below the upper edge of both pieces and 5/8 inch up from the long center arc on the lower edge of the skirt; continue the skirt's lower line freehand around the scrollwork. Cut along all three lines with a knife, about 1/8 inch deep. Use chisel first to carve steep grooves, then to diminish the inner side of each to a gentle bevel.

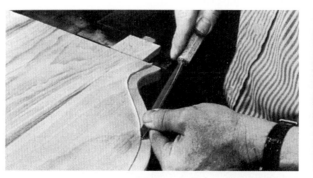

Cut line with knife; then carve V-shaped groove with chisel.

Carve inner side to blend gradually into center surface of piece.

The Arms Come Last

1. Begin by making a series of backsaw cuts squarely across top and bottom of arms to within 1/16 in. of scribed lines. To aid in making level cuts, scribe pattern on both sides.

2. Use 1-in. straight chisel to remove waste wood, and smooth surface. Trim to lines with drawknife and spokeshave, comparing arms often as you work to be sure of a good match.

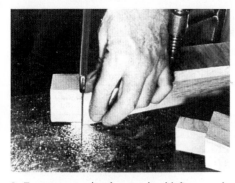

3. Tenons on ends of arms should fit squarely through front edge of rear legs. Use leg assembly template to scribe side view; for top view use mortising gauge to scribe tenons 7/8 in. wide.

4. Shoulders of tenons on top of front legs should be 26 5/8 in. from ground. Make tenons 7/8 in. square and 5/8 in. high. Scribe with mortising gauge; cut with backsaw and chisel.

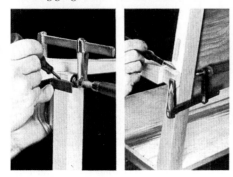

5. Reassemble frame and, using the side view template, clamp arms in place. Mark and trim shoulders of all tenons to fit flush, then scribe for mortises on arms and rear legs.

6. Disassemble. Lay pieces on flat surface to scribe width of mortises. Cut blind mortises in arms, and through mortises in rear legs. (See *Mortise-and-tenon joints*, p.311.)

Wedging and Finishing

1. Make two 3-in. wedges for each through tenon as wide as the tenon and tapering from 3/16 in. thick to a dull point. Also make four 1/2-in.-long fox wedges 3/16 in. thick on top.

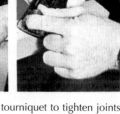

2. Saw two slots across each through tenon 5/16 in. from top and bottom to a little less than the full depth of the tenon. Assemble chair and insert, but do not drive, 3-in. wedges.

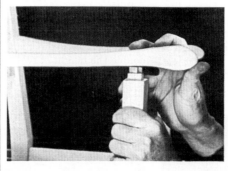

3. Remove arms while you saw two diagonal slots parallel to grain of each blind tenon. Insert fox wedges, and secure arms by driving mortises firmly into tenons with mallet.

4. Use pipe clamp or tourniquet to tighten joints of chair one side at a time, and drive all wedges home. Trim excess from end grain of tenons with chisel and block plane.

First step in finishing the mission chair comes before final assembly. Chamfer all outside edges slightly, then use a block plane, spokeshave, or scraper to remove any dents or blemishes that may have occurred in construction. Next, wedge the joints together as shown above. If one of the wedges starts to split as you are driving it, drive it no farther, but do not be concerned—the splitting means that the wedge is solidly seated. The original chair was probably left unfinished; certainly no sign of a finish remains. To protect and highlight the natural wood, use a mixture of linseed oil and turpentine (see *Finishing*, p.307).

Hearthside or Campsite: Rustic Furniture Fits in Everywhere

Whether you are outfitting a rustic vacation retreat or furnishing a suburban patio, you can do it quickly and easily by rough-hewing your own rustic furniture. The results can be every bit as attractive, practical, and satisfying as furniture shaped and joined from finished lumber. You can walk into a wooded grove in the morning, carrying only a knife, saw, drill, and hatchet, and emerge before the end of the day with a solidly built table, chair, or stool that will last the rest of your life, enduring extremes of wind and weather that would ravage a more delicately structured piece. Moreover, the simple mortise-and-tenon joints, if properly made, will grow tighter and tighter as time goes by.

The fundamental technique involves forcing square pegs into round holes. This is not as foolish as it seems.

If the hole is drilled in green wood and the peg is made of dry wood, the resultant joint needs no wedging and will grow firmer as the green wood's flexible fibers dry, contract, and harden around the peg. In the basic project demonstrated on these pages—a simple campstool—this principle is applied in two ways: 1-inch-square dry wood tenons are tapered slightly and driven into round mortises of the same diameter, and 3/8-inch-square dry pegs are driven through 3/8-inch round holes to pin green wood in place. In both cases the sides of the pegs must align with the grain of the wood to forestall splitting.

A calibrated ruler is not among the essential tools for rustic carpentry. Like old-timers, you can make a measuring stick from a long rod. Cut a notch to record each measurement; then your only problem in matching sizes will be remembering which notch to use.

With a little imagination the design can be adapted for any number of projects. For a table, build the frame to whatever size suits your needs and make the top from split stock with the flat side up. For a straight chair double the height of two posts to provide the stiles for a ladder back—if you can find wood with a natural curve to make the back more comfortable, so much the better.

Set up shop in the woods around a solid improvised workbench. The crossed poles at end, one secured to a post driven into the ground and anchored by rocks, make an adjustable sawbuck.

Footbridge over stream was built using techniques of rustic joinery.

Start Your Campstool by Cutting Down a Tree

1. Live aspen with trunk about 3 in. thick provides green wood for legs of campstool. Birch, poplar, pine, and ailanthus are among many other suitable woods. Taking a single tree from among a cluster is usually good ecological practice.

2. Saw eight 2-ft. stretchers from standing dead trees of slightly less girth. Then, 3 in. from both ends of each stretcher, make four saw cuts just deep enough to form center tenon sections 1 in. square. Note use of measuring stick.

3. To make 1-in. tenons, hold stringers firmly upright against a solid surface and carefully lop off slabs of waste wood with sharp hatchet. Use knife to trim knots and other irregularities so that tenons are straight but not undersized.

330

Constructing the Stool Quickly and Easily

1. Cut four 18-in.-long posts from green wood to serve as legs. Use 1-in. bit to drill parallel mortise holes 3 in. from both ends of each post. Then drill two more 1-in. mortises perpendicular to the first two, 5 in. from the ends.

2. Assemble one side of stool by driving tenons of two stretchers into innermost mortises of one post (chamfer ends of tenons to get them started). Drive another post into other end. Assemble second side of stool the same way.

3. Join the two sides with four stretchers. Drive tenons of all stretchers into mortises of one side first, then align mortises of other side with appropriate tenons and drive them down carefully, a little at a time, to avoid breaking tenons.

4. Whether to remove the bark or leave it on is a matter of personal taste. There are, however, advantages to be gained by stripping it—the green wood dries faster, and insect pests are denied a good hiding place.

5. Make the seat from 18-in. lengths of green wood, each 1 1/2 to 2 in. across. Strip bark and trim pieces to fit snugly without forcing. Use hatchet carefully to shape the undersides of both ends of pieces to sit flat on stretchers.

6. From dry wood whittle two 6-in.-long pegs for each seat piece, tapering from about 7/16 in. by 3/8 in. down to 1/4 in. square. Position all seat pieces on stretchers, and drill holes for pegs with 3/8-in. bit all the way through both pieces.

Rustic furniture made of twigs and branches fit perfectly in a garden or patio setting.

With rustic joinery you can make anything out of twigs and branches

Alternate direction of holes for pegs

To ensure tight joints when wood has dried, drill holes in opposition—both raked toward or both away from center of piece—at an angle of about 15° from vertical. Alternate the direction of rake from piece to piece.

Insert pegs so that the long side runs parallel to the grain of seat pieces, and drive them down into and through stretchers. With saw and knife trim pegs and tenons. Chamfer tops of posts. Saw ends of seat pieces off evenly and chamfer.

331

Broommaking

Working With Broomcorn, Birch, and Corn Shucks

Time was when almost every farm family grew broomcorn and made brooms. Making brooms was one of the more pleasurable chores. It was usually done when the weather was bad or in the evening while relaxing in front of a fire. Man-made fibers have largely replaced natural fibers in today's market, and vacuum cleaners have put a dent in the entire industry, but a comparison shows that nature can still hold her own. Natural-fiber brooms are more flexible, more durable, and sweep up dust and litter as well as or better than their artificial replacements; and they do the job without electricity and without petroleum-derived synthetic fibers.

In the past brooms have been made from a variety of plant materials other than broomcorn. Hickory twigs were bundled around a handle to form a besom, or witches' broom. Birch saplings were delicately shredded at one end to form a brush. In the Appalachian Mountains mops and sweepers were created from corn husks. And in warm coastal areas where palm trees grew, palm fronds were bound together and used as brooms.

Nowadays, the craft of broommaking is enjoying a comeback as modern housekeepers discover that old-style brooms do a better job than their short-bristled synthetic cousins. A growing appreciation of hand-crafted wares in general and the fact that homemade brooms can be attractive decorations in the home have also contributed to renewed interest in broommaking.

Sources and resources

Books
Foxfire 3. Garden City, N.Y.: Anchor Press, 1975.
Johnson, Doris, and Alec Coker. *The Complete Book of Straw Craft and Cork Husk Dollies.* New York: Dover, 1987.
Shaw, Robert. *America's Traditional Crafts.* Southport, Conn.: Hugh Lauter Levin Associates, 1993.

Handcrafted brooms are decorative and useful.

How to Make a Broom From a Sapling

Yellow birch sapling is the traditional wood for making a whittled broom, but good results can also be obtained with oak, ash, or maple. Cut straight, smooth saplings in the middle of spring, when the bark is soft and easy to remove and the high sap content of the wood makes it pliable and resilient. The saplings should be trimmed into 5-foot poles and their bark peeled off. To make the bristles, shave the wood into fine splints with a sharp knife. The finished broom, trimmed and bound, is strong enough for heavy-duty jobs.

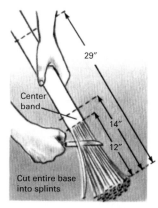

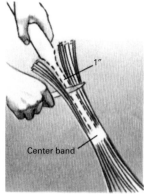

1. Peel bark from 5-ft.-long, 2-in.-thick pole. Mark at 12, 14, and 29 in. from one end; make splints by slicing from base to 12-in. mark.

2. Slice down from topmost mark to top of center band. Try not to cut off any splints. Keep slicing until handle is about 1 in. thick.

3. Fold top splints down over bottom splints. Gather them just below center band, and bind tightly with twine or rawhide thong.

4. Shave excess wood from upper handle, then smooth with sandpaper. Finish broom by trimming the splints to make ends even.

A Homemade Sweeper: From Broomcorn Seed to Finished Broom

Broomcorn belongs to the same family as sorghum and millet and is cultivated in much the same way. Locate it well away from related plants to avoid cross-pollination. Plant the seeds 5 to 6 inches apart in rows that are 30 inches apart. A plot of two 10-foot rows will yield enough corn for two to four brooms. When the plants are about 6 inches tall, thin them out to 8 to 12 inches apart. The broomcorn will be mature by late summer and will have developed its characteristic seed heads.

For the sturdiest brooms harvest the broomcorn when the seed heads are still green. If you are more interested in decorative effect than toughness, wait until the tassels ripen to a yellow or reddish color. To harvest, bend the stalks down 2 to 3 feet below the seed heads and let them hang in the field for three or four days to dry. Then cut them off for curing. Strip off the leaves, and spread the harvested broomcorn on a screen rack or boards to dry in the sun. Move the tassels indoors at night or when rain threatens, since moisture will cause mildew.

When the tassels are thoroughly dry (they will spring back to shape when gently bent), they are ready to be made into brooms. Trim each unit of broomcorn to approximately equal size (4 to 8 inches of stalk should remain in addition to the tassels), and shave the stalks flat on one side to reduce bulk in preparation for binding.

Broom handles should be 4 to 5 feet long. New handles are available at hardware stores, or you can use a discarded broom or mop handle. To make your own handles, select straight, smooth saplings, preferably of ash, hickory, or poplar, and whittle them to size—about 1 inch thick. You can also make a hearth broom by binding the stalks together without a handle.

If you do not plan to make your broom immediately, store the cured stalks flat in a dry place to keep the bristles straight. Hanging the broom by a loop when it is not being used will increase the life of the bristles.

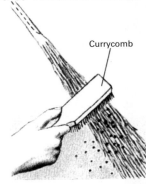
1. Select about 30 equal-sized lengths of broomcorn for each broom. Comb seeds out with currycomb or small saw.

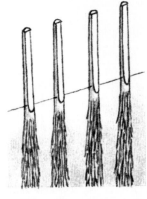
2. Shave stalks to reduce bulk, then thread them on twine just above tassels. Flat sides should all face same way.

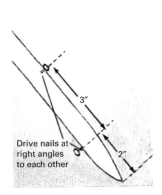
3. Hammer two small nails partway into handle, one 2 in. from tip, another 5 in. from tip, to anchor the stalks.

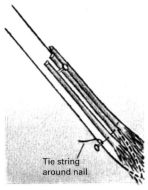
4. Fasten twine to lower nail, and wrap stalks snugly around handle. Flat sides should be against handle.

5. Tie stalks temporarily in place. Soften by pouring boiling water over them; let soak for a few minutes.

6. Rig up tying rope. Make loop in one end, tie other end to overhead support so loop is 6 in. from ground.

7. Twist rope once around the stalks, press down loop with foot to make tight, then bind with strong twine.

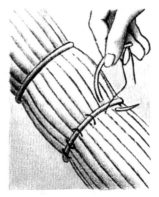
8. Bind at two or three points, remove nails, and sew bottom binding loop in place. Trim tassel ends to equal length.

Fashioning an Efficient Mop From Leftover Shucks

Mops and brushes were among the many household implements that early homesteaders made from corn husks. Today, corn-shuck products are still fashioned in parts of the Appalachian Mountains region.

To make a corn-shuck mop choose about 20 whole husks and let them dry thoroughly for several weeks. Soak the husks for a few minutes before making the mop so they will be soft and pliable. For the base use a 14-inch piece of 2 × 6 lumber (actual size is 1 1/2 by 5 1/2 inches). For the handle whittle one end of a pole to a blunt point and drive it into a hole in the base. If the handle works loose, wedge it or toenail it to the base.

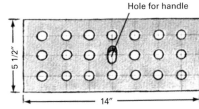
1. Drill twenty-one 1-in. holes into base centered 2 in. apart. Drill middle hole at a slant—it will accommodate handle.

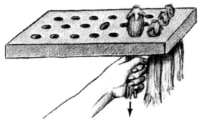
2. Push loose ends of husks down through holes, then pull husks firmly into place from beneath.

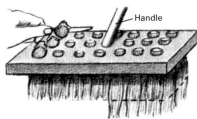
3. Cut off shank ends of husks with a sharp knife or saw, and trim loose ends. Press handle into center hole.

Scrimshaw

The Yankee Whaler's Art and Pastime

Scrimshaw—the etching, carving, and coloring of teeth, ivory, and bone—was invented by American whaling men as a way of whiling away the long days and weeks between whale sightings. Whenever a whale was caught, the creature's jaw was hoisted to the deck with block and tackle and its brown, ridged teeth doled out to the crew. Bone was carved into umbrella handles, canes, pie crimpers, and corset busks—complete with pictures and intimate quotations. Wives or sweethearts often received them as gifts.

Modern scrimshanders, concerned with the fate of the world's whale population, are turning to new materials, often bringing to them a level of artistic ability that few whaling men could match. But as one visit to a whaling museum's scrimshaw collection will show, a leisurely pace and an eye for detail can be more important "than artistic sophistication in this most American of crafts.

Antique scrimshaw picture, inscribed on the tooth of a sperm whale, shows a fully rigged ship—a difficult design but a favorite among whaling men.

Antique poker chips are made of ivory and feature a simple scrimshaw design.

Getting and Preparing the Raw Materials

In recent years whales and ivory-bearing mammals, such as elephants and walruses, have become increasingly scarce, and the importation of teeth, bone, or ivory from many of these animals has been restricted. As a result, whale teeth, the most traditional medium for scrimshaw, are not available, while ivory must be gleaned from secondhand odds and ends: piano keys, knife handles, old billiard balls, and similar remnants.

In place of traditional materials scrimshanders are now relying increasingly on other substances. The most widely available material is beef bone; with the right preparation its outer surface can make an excellent medium for scrimshaw. Ivory nuts—compact nuts with hard white centers—are highly satisfactory for small scrimshaw items, such as jewelry. Teeth, antlers, and horns from nonendangered species also make very good surfaces as do many types of seashells.

Preliminary preparations. Animal bones should be boiled several hours to remove scraps of meat. If you are using ivory nuts, bake them for 15 minutes at 300° F to harden them, then remove the brown outer shell. Ivory, antlers, and teeth need no preliminary preparation.

Cutting and drilling. The scrimshaw material should be cut to size before it is etched. Place the bone, ivory, or nut in a vise and cut it with a sharp fine-tooth hacksaw. Cut off a large chunk if you plan on making a freestanding display or a thin slab if you intend to create a pendant or earring. If the finished piece is to be worn on a chain, you should install a metal loop in its top before you proceed further. Use a pair of sharp-nosed pliers to bend the end of a piece of 18-gauge wire into a small circle, then clip the wire off, leaving a short length for insertion into the material. Next, drill a hole in the material, insert the wire, and glue in place with epoxy cement. A finished loop is shown on the next page.

Polishing. The final step in preparing the material is to polish it. The more highly polished you make the surface, the easier it will be to wipe off excess ink after coloring. Use two or three grades of sandpaper, starting with very fine (No. 220) and finishing with superfine (No. 400 or higher). Sand carefully by hand, then buff to a high gloss with the finest grade of steel wool (No. 4/0) or a gentle polishing compound such as jeweler's rouge. Sailors used sharkskin for sanding and their own rough hands for the final buffing.

When you are sanding and polishing, work in a well-ventilated location and avoid inhaling the dust; a mask is recommended if you are doing extensive polishing. Care is particularly important when working ivory, since ivory dust does not break down after entering the lungs. Many professional scrimshanders—especially those who use motor-powered polishing wheels—have special exhaust systems that suck the dust away from them.

Animal bones are more absorbent than whalebone or ivory. After polishing them, coat them with butcher's wax or polyurethane varnish to keep the coloring agents from soaking into the unscribed surface.

From Sketch to Finished Piece: Creating a Scrimshaw Picture

After the bone has been cut and polished, the next step is to create the decoration. Beginners should choose a simple design with gently curving lines (geometric shapes and straight lines are difficult to carve). If you have a flair for drawing, you can sketch the design directly on the polished surface, but use a soft pencil to avoid scratching. Do not include every last detail, just draw the basic outlines. You can also use paper to plan the design, then transfer it to the blank with carbon paper. Another way to transfer the drawing is to glue the sketch onto the bone with some flour-and-water paste, then use a sharp-pointed scribing tool to make tiny pricks through the design outline onto the bone. Many experienced scrimshanders carve directly on the surface without making a preliminary sketch. A particularly convenient system is to paint the entire surface with black ink before beginning a design. To plan the design, gently scratch away the black coloring with your scribing tool, but be careful not to cut into the material. You can also draw or trace the design on the blackened bone with a light-colored pencil, by using the pinprick method, or by employing orange-colored carbon paper.

Scribing. Almost any sharp-pointed implement can be used; for example, a craft knife or engraver's tool, both of which are available at art and hobby supply stores. Sailors often inserted a sail needle in a wood or bone handle. An ordinary nail can be used in the same way. Pound the nail into a wooden stick, cut off the nail's head with wire cutters, then sharpen the end to a point with a file.

You will also need something to hold your piece of scrimshaw as you scribe. To make a simple holder, tack two strips of wood on a small board so that they form a V as shown at right. You can slip a small scrimshaw piece between the strips and hold it there as you work.

When scribing, hold the tool like a pencil and cut into the surface slowly and firmly. The deeper the cut, the more color the scribed line will retain; with experience you will learn how deep to cut to achieve a desired effect.

Begin by scribing the design's outline, then fill in the detail. To create shaded areas, etch many close parallel lines. The closer the lines, the denser the tone will appear when colored. For deeper shading crosshatch the area by scribing a series of parallel lines in one direction, then topping with others at right angles to the first. The curve, direction, and density of the lines all influence the final appearance of the design. Study old black-and-white engravings and expertly carved scrimshaw pieces to see the range of effects that can be achieved.

Coloring. Color must be applied with care and patience. Popular coloring agents include oil paint, water color paint, dye, and indelible ink (it is better than India ink since it is more permanent). One of the whaler's favorite agents was tobacco juice. The traditional way to apply the color is by rubbing it on with your fingers. This method works especially well for oil paint. Ink, water color, or liquid dye can be applied with an artist's brush or the end of a toothpick.

The next step is to remove the excess color. This can be accomplished by wiping it off with a damp cloth, by scraping it away with the moistened end of a toothpick, or by buffing the surface with No. 4/0 steel wool. Because the dye is absorbed into the etched lines but not into the polished surface, the result is a strongly colored design in the areas that you have etched.

When creating a scrimshaw piece of more than one color, you must be careful not to let different tints run together. The recommended procedure is to scribe lines for the predominant color first, tint them, and remove excess color from the polished surface. Next, scribe lines that are to be a second shade and paint over them carefully with a fine brush or toothpick, being careful that the new color does not run into the first. Then use a toothpick to remove the second shade from the polished surface with as little smearing as possible. Additional tints are added in the same way.

After coloring, the scrimshaw piece is complete, though you may wish to polish the piece once more. If the piece is ivory or whalebone, this final polishing can be followed with a light coat of linseed oil. The oil can be reapplied every six months to protect the surface.

Sources and resources

Books and pamphlets
Collins, Blackie, and Michael Collins. *How to Scrimshaw and Carve Ivory.* Knoxville, Tenn.: Knife World Publications, 1978.
Hellman, Nina, and Brouwer, Norman. *A Mariner's Fancy: The Whaleman's Art of Scrimshaw.* New York: Balsam Press, 1992.
Lawrence, Martha. *Scrimshaw, the Whaler's Legacy.* Atglen, Pa.: Schiffer Publishing, 1993.
Linsley, Leslie: *Scrimshaw: A Traditional Folk Art, a Contemporary Craft.* New York: NAL-Dutton, 1979.
Shell, Harvey. *Scrimshaw and Ivory-Working Techniques.* Tulsa, Okla.: Ahio Publishing Co., 1986.

1. Blacken surface with indelible ink, then scratch very lightly to plan design.

2. Press firmly with sharp tool to etch lines deep into the material.

3. Brush black or colored ink over entire etched area to fill lines with color.

4. Let ink dry, then use No. 4/0 steel wool to rub off ink and to polish surface.

5. Wipe with clean cloth to provide a final shine. Note wire loop for chain.

6. Ink remains only in etched lines, but not on polished surface of piece.

Household Recipes

Perfume, Pot Cleaner, Lotion, or Lip Balm: Make Them Naturally

Most Americans are accustomed to going to the drugstore for their cosmetics and medicines, to the supermarket for their kitchen cleansers and pesticides, and to the hardware store for their paints and glue. But it was not very long ago that all these products, and most other necessities of life, had to be made in the home.

The making and using of simple recipes and remedies today provide an excellent way to save money and at the same time to learn old-time lore that was once common knowledge. In addition, when you prepare a household recipe yourself, you have the satisfaction and reassurance of knowing that your product contains only natural substances. Of course, no recipe or remedy should replace the advice and services of a doctor; and since an allergic reaction is always possible, you should be cautious when first using any recipe.

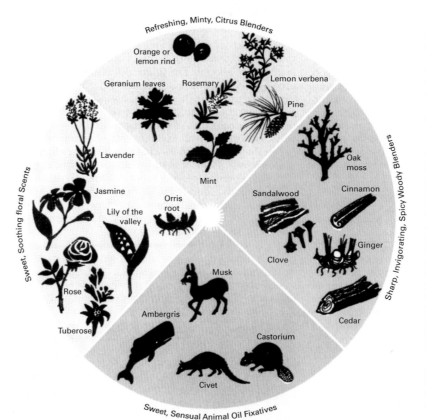

An aromatic mixture must be composed carefully to achieve a harmonious blend. Either choose one ingredient for the primary scent and add a small amount of blender from the same or neighboring category, or mix equal amounts of several similar ingredients.

Almost any fragrant flower or herb can be used for moist potpourri. Flowers that retain their aromas when dry should be the basis for dried flower potpourris. Lavender and rose—especially old-fashioned rose varieties such as damask and cabbage—are traditional. For color, use hollyhock, nasturtium, marigold, aster, and the everlastings. In enfleurage use highly scented flowers such as jasmine, lily of the valley, orange blossom, and rose. Mint, citrus peel, woods, and spices are good secondary blending materials for both potpourris and enfleurage.

Fixatives are needed to hold a scent. Animal-oil fixatives are best, but orris root, oak moss, gum benzoin, and cedar and sandalwood oils can be used.

Flowers in History

Flowers and other aromatic substances hold an important place in folklore and tradition. Before the discovery of bacteria and viruses, when diseases were thought to be transmitted through bad odors, flowers and scents were used to purify the air and ward off illness. Well-to-do members of society carried orange pomanders to hold to their noses whenever they encountered a bad odor.

In religious ceremonies incense made of herbs and resins has been used since Egyptian times, when it was believed to carry human souls to heaven. In classical times incense was considered to be one of the best offerings to the gods. In the Middle Ages a practicing "witch" would burn more sinister ingredients to summon devils or conjure up a spirit, and young girls would burn incense at night to ward off the advances of lecherous incubi. Incense has been used in Hindu monasteries as an aid to meditation and is still used in various rituals in the Roman Catholic Church.

Over the centuries, various flowers took on special meanings. A single rose, for example, represented silence, and roses were often sculpted on dining room ceilings to indicate that whatever was said there—particularly if the wine had been flowing freely—was *sub rosa* ("under the rose") and not to be repeated. Roses also became emblems for love: a white bridal rose signified happy love, a yellow rose indicated waning affection, and a deep red rose stood for bashfulness. Eventually nearly every flower and herb acquired a meaning—daisy for innocence, rosemary for remembrance, and so on—so that a lover could convey his feelings by sending a bouquet of the appropriate flowers. An inverted flower indicated the opposite of the normal meaning.

Flowers and herbs have been used since time immemorial to sweeten the air and perfume the body. In the Victorian era housewives placed bowls of potpourri around the house much as we use room deodorants today.

The name *potpourri*, which means "rotten pot" in French, derives from the fact that old-time potpourris were prepared by the moist method, in which the ingredients were allowed to stew, or rot, for months to develop a powerful, lasting fragrance. Nowadays potpourri is usually prepared by the simpler dry method.

Master perfumers today use a tremendous array of bottled fragrances (most of them synthetic) to create their perfumes. Their finished fragrances can be likened to pieces of music, with a main scent (the theme) and blending fragrances (the variations) that accent the theme and give it richness and staying power. The same principle—a symphony of aromas—applies to homemade potpourris, flower perfumes, and other fragrant concoctions. With a careful blend of ingredients, plus a little fixative to ensure the gradual release of fragrance over a long time span, you will be able to make your own natural, sweet-smelling scents.

336

Potpourri: Putting Summer in a Jar

The fragrances of summer can be captured for the winter with a potpourri—a sweet-smelling blend of preserved flower petals and other aromatic plant parts. There are two types of potpourri: dry and moist. Dry potpourri is easier to make and more decorative, since it preserves the form and color of the flowers. Moist potpourri bleaches color but creates a stronger fragrance.

To make dry potpourri, gather the flowers just after they have opened, as soon as the dew dries off in the morning. Pluck the petals from each flower and spread them out on newspapers or a window screen made of fiberglass or other nonmetallic screening. A few flowers, particularly rosebuds, can be dried whole to add visual interest to the finished potpourri. Place the screens in a warm, dry place away from drafts and direct sunlight. Shift the petals every day or two to speed the drying.

When the petals are completely dry and crisp, select a mixture that produces an agreeable blend of scents. Add several aromatic herbs, some bark or spices, a little aromatic oil (see p.338), and a drop or two of fixative (about 1 teaspoon for each 2 cups of petals). Let the mixture age in a covered crock for four to six weeks before setting the potpourri out in smaller jars and bowls. Cover the containers when their scent is not needed; this will preserve the fragrance longer. The scent can be revived from time to time with a few drops of aromatic oil or good brandy. Dry potpourri can also

Open bowls or jars are perfect for holding dry potpourri. Moist potpourri is traditionally kept in china jars with pierced lids.

be converted into a sachet by grinding or crumbling the blended ingredients into a coarse powder, then sewing them into a small bag made of tightly woven fabric.

For moist potpourri, let your newly collected petals dry until they are leathery—about two to three days. Load a large wide-mouthed crock with alternating layers of petals and noniodized salt. When the crock is two-thirds full, place a weighted plate on top to compress the petals. Stir the pot every few days, breaking up any crust that forms on the top. After two weeks or more have gone by (the longer the potpourri is left standing, the stronger and more lasting the fragrance will be), mix the petals thoroughly and add spices, roots, and aromatic and fixative oils. (The choice of additives depends on the potpourri's basic scent and your own taste; experiment with different combinations.) Mix again and allow to mature for another two weeks. The scent will be a little raw at first but should soon mellow.

Enfleurage: Extracting Perfume From Flowers

Genuine flower perfume is expensive and hard to come by. However, by using the technique known as enfleurage, you can extract the scents of flowers yourself.

Melt enough lard or other completely odor-free fat to cover the bottoms of about 10 large, shallow plates to a depth of 1/2 inch. The pairs of plates must be matched so that one can be placed upside down on another with

Aroma of fresh flowers can be preserved when absorbed by lard and held by alcohol.

almost no gaps at the rim. Allow the lard to solidify, then score it in a crisscross pattern. Fill the space between each pair of plates with the petals of a highly scented flower, and add a little spice, herbs, or citrus peel to accent the scent further. Be careful not to let any other plant parts drop into the plates; they may introduce fungi that will spoil the perfume. Next, seal the plates together with tape and set them aside. After one or two days remove the wilted petals and repeat the process with fresh, unblemished petals. When you have made seven or eight changes of flowers, cut up the lard, half fill several small, sterile glass bottles with it, and top off with alcohol. (Pure ethyl alcohol is best, but rubbing alcohol will do.) Close the bottles tightly, shake them well, and put them in a dark place for 8 to 12 weeks. During this time you should shake each bottle periodically—once each day if possible.

When the time period is up, pour the perfume into clean bottles using a funnel with a piece of muslin in it to strain out the fat globules. Now add a very small quantity of fixative oil (about two drops per 1/4 cup of perfume) as a preservative.

Four flower recipes

Aromatic rose beads. Pick 30 to 40 blooms on a dry day and cut the petals very fine. Place in a pot and barely cover with water. (If you want dark red beads, use an iron pot.) Heat gently for an hour, adding water as necessary. A day later heat again. Then strain the pulp and roll it into beads. Thread the beads onto fine string with a heated needle and dry for a day or two, moving the beads occasionally. When you wear the beads around your neck, your body warmth will cause them to release a sweet rose scent.

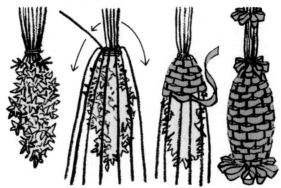

Lavenderette. By enclosing lavender flowers within a basket of their own stems, the fragrant blossoms are prevented from shedding. Tie an odd number of fresh lavender spikes together just above the flowers, bend the stems down, and weave ribbon to form basket. Cinch with bows at top and bottom. Place on bed, table, or among clothing.

Orange or lemon pomander. Take a fresh, unflawed fruit with a thick rind and push in cloves over the whole surface; then roll the studded fruit in a mixture of cinnamon, nutmeg, and orris root plus a few drops of lemon or orange oil. Wrap in tissue paper and dry in a warm place for a few weeks. Pomanders sweeten the air and also help to repel insects.

Crystallized flowers. Spread fresh violets, lilacs, or mimosa on a sheet of wax paper and dampen with a solution of 2 oz. gum arabic (available at specialty apothecaries) in a cup of water. Let the flowers dry for a day, then place them in oven-proof glass dishes. Mix 1 cup of water with 2 cups of sugar and heat to 250°F. Add food coloring, skim off surface froth, and pour the mixture over the flowers. After 24 hours place the uncovered dishes in a very slow oven until the flowers are dry. Crystallized flowers make bright and colorful decorations on frosted cakes and creamy desserts.

The Ancient Science Of Herbal Medicine

According to an Irish folk legend, the medicinal herbs sprang from the buried body of a fallen hero. The curative powers of each herb applied to the particular region of the hero's anatomy from which it grew. The legend goes on to say, however, that through carelessness the herbs were mixed up and that mankind has been trying to sort them out ever since.

Fanciful though the tale may be, there is no doubt that centuries of effort and experimentation have been expended, on the scientific level as well as the folk level, in trying to determine the efficacy of herbs in treating sickness. Many of the successes are well-known. Quinine, digitalis, rauwolfia, and the vitamins were all derived from botanicals. Even today, with our ability to synthesize so many drugs, about 40 percent of our pharmaceuticals are obtained from natural sources.

In America herbal medicine began with the Indians. They knew how to treat scurvy centuries before the discovery of vitamin C, and during the Indian Wars there were dozens of well-documented reports of their ability to heal gravely wounded warriors. Their medical reputation was so great that they sometimes served as doctors in isolated frontier areas. Indian lore was particularly important to the early settlers, since they were unfamiliar with New World plants and the traditional European herbs had not yet been introduced.

Many herbal remedies are safe and may help ease minor ailments. However, never substitute one for the advice of a doctor, and do not attempt self-medication without a doctor's approval.

Obtaining Herbs and Preparing Them for Use

Growing your own herbs is the best way to obtain ingredients for herbal mixtures, since the effectiveness of most herbs is highest when the leaves are fresh. You can collect herbs in the wild, but be careful to identify them correctly; many wild plants are quite poisonous. In addition, you should be sure the plant you pick is not a protected species and has not been sprayed. Herbs that are available commercially are usually in dried form. Health-food stores stock many of the standard herbs, or you can order less common herbs from specialist companies. (For information on growing and harvesting herbs, see *Herb Gardens*, pp.151–153.)

Herbs should be stored in a cool, dark place in airtight jars. When storing or preparing herbs, use china, glass, or unchipped enamel utensils. Avoid nonstick pans and metal, particularly aluminum. The shelf display above contains a few of the most useful ingredients for home remedies and cosmetics. Other valuable herbs include thyme, marjoram, tarragon, and peppermint.

There are any number of traditional ways to prepare herbs for medicinal and other purposes. The most useful are infusions, decoctions, ointments, and oils.

Infusions. An infusion is a strong tea. To make one, pour 1 pint of boiling water over 2 tablespoons of dried herbs. Steep for 10 minutes if the infusion is to be used internally, three hours if it is to be used externally.

Decoctions. Simmer 2 tablespoons of dried herbs in 1 pint of water in a covered pan for 5 to 10 minutes.

Ointments. Mix one part of powdered herbs with four parts of heated lard or other fat and stir thoroughly. Add a few drops of tincture of benzoin as a preservative.

Aromatic oils. Steep fresh flower petals or other aromatic substances in a pure, odor-free oil for one to two days, then discard the petals, and replace them with a new batch. Keep repeating this procedure until the aroma of the oil becomes as potent as that of the flowers themselves—seven or eight times should be enough.

Infusions and decoctions should be stored in a refrigerator and used within three days. Ointments and oils should be stored in a cool, dark place and will last for several months. Certain other herbal preparations, such as tinctures, elixirs, and spirits, are made with pure ethyl alcohol and will keep indefinitely.

The following labels appear within the illustration:

Rosemary. Used by the Romans to improve the memory. Applied as an infusion, it helps remove dandruff and increase hair luster

Aloe. Used by Indians of Southwest against both wrinkles and baldness. The juice of a cut leaf soothes minor burns and insect bites

Basil. Its strong scent, valued by monks in India as an aid to meditation, repels insects. Infusions may relieve certain types of headache

Camomile. An infusion of flowers soothing for insomnia and toothache and makes lightening rinse for blond hair. Sweet-smelling camomile lawns were once popular

Comfrey. Sometimes known as knitback through its reputation for helping to mend broken bones. A healing herb that can be used in creams and poultices

Ginseng. Believed to promote youth and long life. Considered an aphrodisiac in the Orient. In wide use as an appetizer and mild stimulant

Clove. Employed by the Chinese as a breath freshener. Clove oil has antiseptic and anesthetic properties and helps relieve toothache and nausea

Rose water. Long believed to promote and maintain a youthful skin, it makes a useful moisturizing ingredient for face creams and masks

Almond. Sweet almond oil makes a nourishing ingredient in cosmetics. Ground almonds can be used as a gentle cleansing facial scrub

Garlic. Used worldwide since the days of ancient Egypt for a host of illnesses including earache, low blood pressure, and diarrhea. Garlic has antiseptic and stimulant properties

Cider vinegar. Praised since ancient times for its many medicinal virtues. Reputed to increase energy and help sleep. Added to a bath, it can relieve skin itchiness

Lanolin. An extract from sheep's wool. Anhydrous (waterless) lanolin is beneficial for dry skin and finds use in many cleansing creams

Honey. A mild sedative and a quick source of energy. Applied externally, honey is soothing and nourishing to the skin

Coughs and colds

Soothing cranberry soup. Heat 1 cup of cranberries in 2 cups of water until the skins pop open. Strain and add honey to taste. Heat almost to boiling and remove from heat. Mix 1 tbsp. of potato starch in 2 tbsp. cold water and add slowly to the cranberry juice while stirring vigorously. Bring pot to the boil and continue to stir until the mixture thickens and becomes a little transparent. Serve warm with sugar and cream. This traditional Finnish recipe for colds makes a delicious dessert and at the same time supplies plenty of vitamins B and C.

Sore throat infusions. Drink infusions of comfrey root, camomile, or rosemary with honey and lemon. A cup of warm water water 2 tsp. vinegar can also help.

Herbs for smokers. Chew camomile flowers when you feel the desire to smoke. Camomile is reputed to alleviate the need for tobacco. If the urge to smoke becomes overpowering, try an herb recipe instead of tobacco: mix 1 ounce each of red clover tops and coltsfoot with a pinch each of lavender, yerba santa, and rosemary. Adjust the mixture to suit your personal taste. Crumble the dried mixture to make fine tobacco-sized shreds and roll your own cigarettes.

Glycerine-lemon cough syrup. Heat a lemon by boiling it in water for 10 minutes or roasting it in front of the fire. Cut open and squeeze out the juice, then add 2 tbsp. each of glycerine and honey. Take a teaspoonful at intervals whenever needed.

Headaches and nerves

Peppermint tea for mild depression. Drink a cup of peppermint or papaya mint tea and do something active such as jogging, hiking, weeding the garden, or playing tennis.

For nerves. Drink camomile tea or just a glass of milk. Camomile is very soothing. It can also relieve the pain of a toothache.

For headaches. Try to counteract the cause. If you have been in the sun, move into the shade and put a damp, cool cloth on your forehead. If you are tired, it may help to eat something to restore your energy or to move away from what you are doing, get some fresh air, and relax. It has been suggested recently that vigorous exercise may alleviate migraine attacks. Even at nighttime you can try jogging in place. For a soothing headache sachet put 4 tbsp. each of dried lavender, marjoram, betony, rose leaf, and rose petals, plus a few cloves, in a sachet. Whenever you have a headache, hold the sachet to your nose and breathe in its scent.

Fatigue and sore feet

Honey-vinegar energizer. A popular recipe for increased energy is 2 tsp. vinegar and 2 tsp. honey in a cup of water. Drink once a day for best results.

Bathing in vinegar. If the natural acidity of the skin has been reduced by too much highly alkaline soap, you can add vinegar or lemon to the bath water to restore the acidity. This may relieve skin itchiness and is reputed to increase your energy. (For other refreshing and soothing herbal baths, see p.341.)

Witch hazel for aching muscles and backs. Soothe tired or sore muscles by massaging gently but firmly with a mixture of 1 cup of witch hazel extract and 1/4 cup of rubbing alcohol.

Lavender footbath. Bathing the feet in warm water to which a few drops of lavender oil have been added is said to provide quick relief from foot fatigue.

Walker's remedy for foot fatigue. When suffering from foot fatigue on a long walk in the country, pick some ferns and stuff these into your boots. This provides quick, refreshing relief for tired or sore feet.

Athlete's foot vinegar bath. Vinegar is reputed to help by restoring the acid antibacterial surface of the skin. Steep 1 oz. each of sage and agrimony in hot apple cider vinegar. As soon as the vinegar has cooled sufficiently, place the affected foot in it. Soak for 30 minutes and repeat three times daily. Give the affected foot as much fresh air as possible. Bathing the foot three times a day in water as cold as the foot can stand is also said to help destroy the athlete's foot fungus.

Indigestion and stomach problems

Herbal teas and fruit for indigestion. Some Indian tribes drank mint tea for indigestion. A tea of peppermint or papaya mint tea may help to settle an uncomfortable stomach. Clove tea is held to be useful for allaying more acute cases of nausea. To stimulate the digestive juices, eat a dried fruit or drink some fruit juice as an appetizer before eating a meal.

Soda drink for acid stomach. Mix 1/2 tsp. baking soda and a few drops of lemon juice in 1/2 cup warm water and drink immediately. If your symptoms include vomiting, omit lemon juice from the mixture and rinse out your mouth with some of the soda drink before slowly sipping the remainder of the drink.

Garlic seasoning for intestinal infections. Garlic is an old and much used aid for a wide variety of intestinal disorders. It is also an effective stimulant for digestion. Include a clove or two of garlic in your cooking when you are troubled with minor stomach upset. To minimize the smell of garlic on your breath, eat a few sprigs of fresh parsley after eating garlic.

For gas and hiccups. After eating any meal that tends to cause stomach gas, chew candied ginger, fennel, caraway, or dill seeds. For hiccups eat a teaspoon of peanut butter.

Burns, insect bites, and skin irritation

Jewelweed for poison ivy. Indians crushed the leaves and stems of jewelweed, a variety of impatiens, also known as touch-me-not, to relieve the itch and rash caused by poison ivy, poison oak, and poison sumac. Jewelweed often grows near poison ivy, a fortunate coincidence since it is most effective when applied soon after contact. Drinking milk and eating fruits high in vitamin C also helps, and it is always good practice to wash affected areas very thoroughly with cold water and soap as quickly as possible after contacting poison ivy.

Some pleasant chapped-lip balms. Add a few drops of rose water to 1 tbsp. honey and apply to the lips or hands as often as necessary. Honey attracts water and will provide moisture for dry skin. Both honey and rose water are said to have healing properties that help new skin grow. In addition, a mixture of glycerine and rose water is a good moisturizer for lips that are chapped

Bathing in tea for sunburn. Drop two or three tea bags into the water near the tap while the bath is filling. Tannic acid in the tea will help to take the heat from your burn. Alternatively, a strong solution of tea or even a wet tea bag can be dabbed over the affected parts. A decoction of comfrey root added to your bath will also provide relief.

Two simple sunburn lotions. Mix 2 tbsp. vinegar in 1/2 cup water, or mix equal parts of vinegar and olive or vegetable oil.

An herbal lotion for minor burns. Crush together 2 tbsp. each of marshmallow and comfrey root and heat gently in mixture of 1 cup olive oil and 1 cup wine for 30 minutes. (The wine takes away any burned odor.) Cool and strain. Marshmallow and comfrey are reputed to have excellent skin healing properties.

Aloe remedy for minor burns and insect bites. Break off the largest leaf of an aloe plant and rub the jellylike sap over the burn or bite. The leaf can be wrapped and stored in the refrigerator. It can also be used for minor skin irritations and poison ivy rash.

Caution

Any natural or synthetic substance may cause an allergic reaction in certain people. If you are not sure of a substance, test a minute quantity and wait for up to three days to check for a reaction. Herbal remedies should only be prepared where identification of the plants is certain. Apparently unimportant symptoms may be caused by a serious illness for which a doctor's advice should be sought. Consult a doctor for any serious or persistent complaint.

Natural Cosmetics From the Kitchen

Unlike commercial beauty aids, homemade cosmetics take a bit of time and trouble to prepare and will generally spoil more quickly. However, what is lost in convenience is gained back in other ways: you save money, you are free to experiment with different ingredients to find ones that suit you best, and you know that the ingredients used are fresh and natural.

When making cosmetics at home, be sure that your equipment is absolutely clean. For instructions on preparing herbs, see page 338. **To avoid the possibility of an allergic reaction, test a small quantity of any unfamiliar substance on the underside of your arm, and wait 24 to 48 hours to see if a rash develops.**

The health of your complexion is the product of many factors including your diet, your age, the amount of exercise you get, and your sleeping habits. Factors that can upset the skin's balance include tension, lack of moisture in the air, overexposure to the sun, and too much of the wrong foods. Although some complexion problems require a doctor's care and others are not easily correctible, there are many simple topical treatments you can make yourself to cleanse, stimulate, and nourish the skin, and help preserve its youthful bloom. The health of the hair is also affected by diet. The condition and texture of the hair is generally improved by taking supplements of vitamins A and D and eating a teaspoon of brewer's yeast daily.

Fruits and Vegetables for Every Skin Type

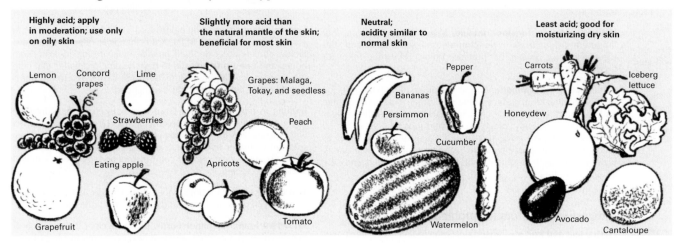

Highly acid; apply in moderation; use only on oily skin
Lemon — Concord grapes — Lime — Strawberries — Eating apple — Grapefruit

Slightly more acid than the natural mantle of the skin; beneficial for most skin
Grapes: Malaga, Tokay, and seedless — Peach — Apricots — Tomato

Neutral; acidity similar to normal skin
Bananas — Persimmon — Pepper — Cucumber — Watermelon

Least acid; good for moisturizing dry skin
Carrots — Iceberg lettuce — Honeydew — Avocado — Cantaloupe

Feeding the face. Any of these fruits and vegetables can be applied directly to the face; for example, a slice of tomato or cucumber can be used as a simple cleanser. Fruits and vegetables can also be blended and combined with one or more binders to make a complete natural facial to nourish and stimulate your skin. For dry skin, use lanolin, sour cream, honey, or egg yolk as a binder. If possible, add a few drops of liquid lecithin as a moisturizer. For oily skin, yogurt and egg white make drying binders. People with normal skin can use binders from either group and whole eggs and whole milk as well.

Before using a mask, thoroughly cleanse your face. Smooth the mask on gently, avoiding the area immediately around the eyes. Rinse off after 30 minutes or as soon as the mask dries. First use warm water and a clean facecloth, then splash with cool water to close the pores. Rinse off the mask immediately if there is any irritation.

For a peaches-and-cream complexion. Blend one ripe peach with enough heavy cream to make a soft cream, and massage into the skin once daily. Keep the mixture under refrigeration. This stimulating, rich moisturizer should help your skin achieve a legendary, soft peaches-and-cream complexion.

Brewer's yeast face mask. Yeast can brighten a sallow complexion (it is rich in B-complex vitamins, which improve blood circulation). Mix yeast powder with a little water to make a soft paste and smooth over the face, avoiding the eyes. Allow to dry before rinsing off with warm water. For best results use the mask once or twice a week and take a few teaspoons of brewer's yeast daily in orange juice or milk. This mask is also beneficial for oily and dry skins, as vitamin B helps to regularize the secretion of skin sebum. Do not use this mask just before going out; it may bring skin impurities to the surface temporarily. If you have a dry complexion, add a tablespoon of wheat germ oil or an egg yolk.

A deep-cleansing clay mask. This mask will cleanse the skin and leave it soft and glowing. Melt 1/4 oz. beeswax with 2 oz. lanolin in a double boiler, then add 1/2 cup rose water while stirring constantly. Remove from heat and work in 8 oz. of fuller's earth. For a simple cleansing mask for oily skin, mix a little fuller's earth with water to a milky consistency, smooth over the skin, and wash off after 15 minutes. This mask stimulates circulation but has a drying action and should not be used too frequently. Apply a light moisturizer after rinsing off the mask.

Papaya peeler for flaky skin. When the weather changes, some people suffer from a flaky complexion. An application of papaya quickly removes the dead flaky skin. Smooth the pulp of a fresh papaya over your face, wipe off the papaya with a facecloth after a minute or two, and splash cool water over your skin to close the pores. You may need to apply a moisturizer afterward, since papaya is a drying agent. For a milder peeler, steep a bag of papaya mint tea in half a cup of boiling water and apply with a facecloth while hot. Rinse off as above.

Mint and ice summer freshener. Blend a few sprigs of mint with finely crushed ice and apply as a quick freshener that will not dehydrate the skin. For a moisturizer rich in vitamins A, B, and C, blend ripe cantaloupe with a few mint sprigs.

Mayonnaise skin food. Simple mayonnaise with eggs, vegetable oil, and vinegar—but no salt—provides a handy blend of several useful skin nutrients. Use your own recipe or buy a good salt-free mayonnaise and massage into the skin as a night cream.

Comfrey and almond oil for wrinkles. With the passing years, the fatty tissue under the skin grows thinner, leaving the skin loose. This condition, together with the reduced elasticity of the skin, contributes to the formation of face lines and wrinkles. Comfrey is reputed to help preserve the youthfulness and elasticity of the skin. Add 1 tbsp. of an infusion of the leaves or 1 tbsp. of a decoction of the roots to a facial mask, or blend into milk or simple cold cream and apply to the skin for several minutes. Almond oil wrinkle cream is a rich moisturizer that boosts the water-holding capacity of the skin and helps plump out wrinkled areas. Melt 1 tbsp. of lanolin with 2 tsp. sweet almond oil in a double boiler. Add 2 tsp. water and allow the mixture to cool, then add in 2 tsp. cod liver oil.

Note: To help delay the formation of wrinkles, apply facial creams and masks very gently. This will preserve the cushion of fatty tissue and avoid stretching the surface skin.

Shampoos and rinses

Whole egg shampoo for dry hair. Beat two eggs until frothy and massage well into scalp. Leave on for a few minutes and rinse off with warm water. (Hot water will cause the eggs to congeal.) To cut the film left by a real egg shampoo, add 2 to 3 tbsp. vinegar to the rinse water if your hair is dark or the juice of half a lemon if your hair is fair.

Rum and egg shampoo for oily hair. Beat together three eggs, 3/4 cup rum, and 3/4 cup rose water and massage thoroughly into scalp and hair. Rinse with vinegar or beer if your hair is dark or the juice of half a lemon if your hair is fair.

Mayonnaise conditioner. After shampooing, apply any good quality mayonnaise as an excellent hair and scalp conditioner. Massage thoroughly. Leave for 1/2 hour and rinse off with a rosemary infusion or lemon or vinegar solution.

Rhubarb root golden hair coloring. This is a fairly strong dye that can create a more golden hair color for persons whose hair is blondish or light brown. Simmer 3 tbsp. of rhubarb root in 2 cups of water for 15 minutes, set aside overnight, and strain. Test on a few strands to determine the effect, then pour through the hair as for camomile rinse.

Sage infusions for darkening gray hair. Make a strong infusion of sage (1/2 cup of dried sage per cup of boiling water) and add to your shampoo or apply to the hair with a wad of cotton after you have shampooed and rinsed your hair. To build up a long-lasting color, mix a cup of sage infusion with a cup of bay rum and 1/2 oz. glycerine and apply to the hair, particularly the roots, each night until you achieve the color you want.

Rosemary as a versatile hair aid. Add an infusion of rosemary to the final rinse after a shampoo to prevent oiliness and give sheen to dark hair. A rosemary rinse also makes hair more manageable and easy to set and is said to help control dandruff.

Highlighting with henna. Henna is a strong vegetable dye that will produce different results on different hair pigmentations. It is more suited to persons with dark hair; on blond or gray hair it may produce a harsh red color. Be sure to test it on your hair before a full application. For auburn highlights in brown hair, first shampoo your hair and apply a light covering of safflower oil over the scalp (henna has a slightly drying effect). Put on plastic gloves to avoid staining your hands and fingernails, then mix pure henna powder with an infusion of sage to make a thin paste and add a few drops of cider vinegar. Use the paste by combing it through the hair and then wrapping the hair with a hot, wet towel and some plastic covering to hold the moisture in. (A gentler, more natural effect can be achieved by separating your hair into groups of strands, applying the paste to every other group.) Leave for 15 to 30 minutes depending on the intensity of color you want. Rinse with very warm water until the water runs clear. Towel dry. You can combine three parts of camomile infusion with one part henna paste for a soft golden highlighting. Specially prepared and mixed henna products are available with manufacturer's instructions at many pharmacies.

Camomile lightening rinse for blond hair. Gently heat a pot with 1 cup of camomile flowers and 2 cups of boiling water for 30 minutes. Do not bring to a full boil. Set the infusion aside for a few hours, strain and then pour through your hair several times, catching liquid in a bowl. The lightening effect will be increased if you dry your hair in full sunlight and use the rinse regularly. Prepare the infusion in an enamelware pot rather than one of aluminum, and filter out the flowers with a nylon mesh strainer.

Yogurt for dandruff. Yogurt is reported to help even difficult cases of dandruff. Work a liberal quantity into the scalp and hair and leave for an hour before shampooing as usual.

Gelatin as a setting lotion. Gelatin gives lifeless hair added body and weight. Simply dissolve a packet of fruit-flavored jello in a little boiling water and add to your rinse water. Select the flavor that is closest to your natural color. The sugar in the gelatin makes this setting lotion more effective.

Bath preparations

Herbal baths. Add herbs to your bath for their soothing, healing, stimulating, or aromatic properties. Camomile is soothing and cleansing; comfrey has a great reputation as a rejuvenating herb; lovage has deodorant properties; lady's mantle is considered helpful for skin irritation; and lavender, mint, and many others can be added to the bath water for their special aromas. To prepare an herbal bath, either make a strong infusion, strain, and add to the bath water, or tie a muslin bag of mixed dried herbs to the tap as the bath is filling.

Bath oils. Turkey-red oil, a derivative of castor oil, acts as an emulsifying agent for other oils so that they will not coat the skin or bathtub. Mix three parts turkey-red oil with one part of your favorite aromatic oil and add a few drops to your bath.

Milk baths. Cleopatra was famed for maintaining herds of animals that were used exclusively to provide her with fresh milk for her baths. Today, you can easily add a packet of dried milk to create your own softening and soothing bath.

Oatmeal scrubs. Oatmeal makes an excellent nonalkaline soap substitute. Wrap a handful of dry oatmeal in a washcloth, dampen it, and rub it over your body in place of soap when you take a bath or shower. Oatmeal is a soothing, softening cleanser. If your skin is dry, use ground almonds in place of oatmeal; they are particularly moisturizing.

Hand care

Bran water for smoother hands. To make your roughened hands smooth, simply dip them in bran water and dab dry three or four times a day, especially after washing dishes. To prepare bran water, add 1 cup of boiling water to 1/2 cup of natural bran and allow to steep for 15 minutes before straining the bran out. Leave a small bowl of the water by your sink and keep the remainder refrigerated. You may want to put on a simple moisturizer afterward. Oatmeal is another soothing and nourishing wash useful for irritated or sore hands. First simmer one part of old-fashioned, noninstant oatmeal in two to three parts of water until the meal swells and becomes soft. Then strain into a container and use as bran water.

Honey and almond cream. This traditional recipe makes a very moisturizing night cream for dry hands. Melt 2 oz. of honey in a double boiler and mix in 4 oz. lanolin until thoroughly combined. Remove from heat and allow to cool before stirring in 2 oz. sweet almond oil and a few drops of your favorite perfume.

Toothpastes, breath fresheners, and deodorants

Simple toothpastes. Benjamin Franklin used a mixture of honey and ground charcoal, which is said to leave teeth shining white. Thick pastes of salt or bicarbonate of soda are simple, effective toothpastes. For a smoother blend, combine three parts bicarbonate of soda with one part salt. Then add 3 tsp. of glycerine for every 1/4 cup of salt and soda mixture and combine with enough water to make a soft paste. To improve the taste and leave your mouth feeling clean, add several drops of peppermint oil.

For brown stains on the teeth, rub teeth with lemon rind and rinse the mouth thoroughly afterward. One of the pleasantest tooth cleaners is a fresh strawberry; simply rub the fruit against your teeth and into all the cracks.

Breath fresheners. Eating green vegetables, especially parsley and watercress, is helpful for simple breath odor. Use undiluted rose water for a fragrant mouthwash and gargle.

Natural deodorants. Eat plenty of green vegetables, as the chlorophyll they contain is helpful in reducing body odor from perspiration. A simple deodorant can be made from a few drops of lavender oil in a teaspoon of lavender water or plain water. Apply lightly to the freshly washed underarm area. A strong infusion of lovage or sage can be applied to the armpits or added to the bath water. Fresh crushed chrysanthemum or lovage leaves applied gently to the underarm area are additional natural deodorants. Some people use cider vinegar diluted or full strength; the vinegar smell disappears in a few minutes. Note that none of these simple deodorants act as antiperspirants.

Some Practical Formulas For Around the Home

Of necessity, country people used to be amateur chemists, making their own cleansers, glues, inks, polishes, and paints out of common household substances. Some of their concoctions were the products of experimentation; more often they were recipes handed down in the family or community for generations.

Old-time paintmaking methods illustrate the ingenuity of farmers in adapting materials they produced on the farm or could find nearby. As a binder to hold the pigment, they used sour milk, buttermilk, eggs, rice, sugar, linseed oil, or hot freshly slaked lime. Chalk improved covering ability by making the mixture more opaque. Colors were provided by anything from charred potatoes to berries, herbs, barks, and local clays.

Today, many of the old farm and homestead formulas are still useful. Some are the basis of products that are now manufactured, others work as well or better than commercial products, and almost all are less expensive than their hardware store equivalents.

Stain removers

When a stain occurs, act immediately to blot up any staining material not yet absorbed. Gently pat the stained area with a clean absorbent cloth or tissue or else scatter talc, flour, or baking soda on the stain. Be careful not to press the stain further into the fabric. Once the excess stain is removed, proceed with further stain removal. It is helpful to know what caused the stain. There are many substances that must be removed with dry cleaning fluid or other special treatment, and inappropriate action will only make the stain permanent. For stains on suede, velvet, or other sensitive fabrics, consult a professional.

Nongreasy stains on washable fabrics. Soak the material in a mixture of 2 pt. of lukewarm water, 1/2 tsp. dishwashing liquid, and 1 tbsp. of white vinegar or ammonia. After 15 minutes gently rub and rinse the fabric. If the stain persists, apply vinegar or rubbing alcohol with a clean cloth. Work gently from the center of the spot toward the edges to remove rings, and work at the edge unevenly to disperse the line. This formula is useful for removing stains made by coffee, tea, wine, vinegar, beer, mixed drinks, soft drinks, fruit juices, jellies, and maple syrup.

Wax, oil, and grease spots. Place paper towels or absorbent material on either side of the spot and apply a hot iron. Replace the absorbent material as soon as some of the stain has been absorbed and repeat the process until all the substance has been taken out. If the spot is stubborn, apply slightly diluted ammonia, and iron again as above.

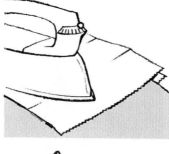

Grease stains can be removed by placing paper towels or absorbent material on both sides of fabric and applying a hot iron (upper left). With stubborn old stains (left) it may help to work the stain with the edge of a spoon. Use the back of a bowl for a convenient, stainproof work surface (above).

For ink and ball-point-pen marks. It usually helps to dissolve the spot in warm glycerine, apply absorbent material, and rinse with water. Then use the recipe given for delicate fabrics.

Potato starch for grease spots. Put finely grated raw potatoes into a pot of water. After 15 minutes, strain off the potatoes, allow any remaining particles to settle, and pour the liquid into a bottle. Apply the liquid only to the grease spot, since it may alter the color of the surrounding fabric.

For stains on delicate fabrics. Mix one part glycerine with one part mild dishwashing liquid and eight parts water. Dab the mixture onto the spot, then blot with cloth or tissue, changing it as soon as some of the stain has been extracted.

Metal cleaners

Cleaning copper and brass. Plain tomato juice, catsup, hot vinegar, hot buttermilk, or a mixture of equal parts of salt and vinegar all make effective cleansers for unlacquered brass and copper. For a stubborn tarnish, cut a lemon in half and dip it in a solution of equal parts of salt and vinegar and rub energetically. To make a cleaning paste, heat 10 oz. of liquid soap in a double boiler and add 1 1/2 tbsp. each of cream of tartar, jeweler's rouge, and magnesium carbonate, plus 3 tbsp. whiting (finely powdered chalk). Allow the mixture to cool before using it as a polish.

Ornamental copperware that is coated with lacquer should be rinsed in warm soapy water and wiped dry. To remove lacquer, submerge the pot in boiling water. Allow to cool until the lacquer peels off easily.

Removing rust from iron pots and kettles. Fill the kettle with as much hay as it will hold, add water to the brim, and boil for several hours. If some rust remains, repeat the same process.

Cleaning silver and silver plate. Moisten a soft cloth in ammonia, then dab it in some whiting and polish the silver with it. Another good polish can be made by mixing 2 oz. of soap flakes and 4 oz. of whiting into 2 cups of warm water, then adding 1 1/2 tbsp. ammonia when the mixture is cool. Store in an airtight bottle. If you are cleaning silver plate, do not rub too vigorously, since the plating is pure silver, which is softer than sterling silver.

Cleaning aluminum. Aluminum has a relatively porous surface, which stains and darkens easily. To restore a stained pot, immerse the discolored portions in several inches of water, add a few tomatoes or stalks of rhubarb, and bring to a boil. Wiper dry with a soft cloth. Alternatively, boil in a solution of equal parts water and vinegar and wipe dry.

Furniture polishes

Beeswax for wood. Beeswax is one of the best polishes for furniture and floors. It gives a good shine and helps furniture develop an antique patina. Melt down 2 oz. of grated beeswax in a double boiler. Turn off the flame, remove the melted beeswax from the stove, and stir in 2 cups of turpentine. Keep the mixture away from flames; turpentine fumes are highly inflammable. Apply sparingly to furniture and floors and polish energetically.

To brighten unpolished wood furniture. Wipe over with cold tea. This brings out the grain and slightly darkens new wood.

Carpet cleaning

Cleaning a wool rug with snow. For this cleaning method the temperature must be well below freezing and there should be at least 4 in. of clean, dry, fresh powder snow on the ground. Place the rug outside for half an hour to allow any grease particles to solidify, then lay the carpet on the snow and walk or jump back and forth over its entire area. Shake the rug out and repeat the process on the other side. Continue until the rug is clean. The same method can be used for wool blankets. The procedure does not remove the wool's natural oils.

Cleaning a carpet with potatoes. An old recipe for cleaning a dirty carpet recommends scattering grated raw potatoes over it followed by a vigorous brushing with a new broom. The carpet should be beaten or vacuumed thoroughly before putting down the potatoes and again after the job is finished.

Sweeping with tea leaves. If you are sweeping a dusty floor, first sprinkle damp tea leaves, damp bran, or fresh grass cuttings over the floor. They will settle and collect the dust.

Pest destroyers and deterrents

Flypaper. Combine equal parts of melted resin and castor oil, then spread over long strips of stiff writing paper with a knife warmed in a jug of hot water. For ease of handing, do not coat the edges of the paper. Thread string through one end of flypaper and hang the paper near light fixtures or windows. For a saucer of flykiller, mix an egg yolk with 1 tbsp. molasses and 1 tbsp. black pepper. Set it on windowsill or shelf.

Peppermint to discourage mice. Mice are reputed to dislike the smell of fresh peppermint. Grow your own peppermint and leave fresh sprigs wherever you see evidence of mice.

Tansy for moths. Tansy has long been used to keep rooms and food free of insects. To use it as a moth repellent, make sachets containing the crushed dried leaves. Distribute the sachets among clothing and bedding in chests, and hang them in closets.

Feverfew insect repellent. Make an infusion of feverfew by adding 1 oz. of the herb to 2 1/2 cups of boiling water. Apply to the skin when cool.

Glues and pastes

Flour paste. Flour and water make an excellent paste for gluing paper and light objects together. This paste is still used in bookbinding and mounting prints. Blend some whole wheat flour with cold water to make a liquid paste and beat until free of lumps, then heat gently to boiling, stirring all the time. Allow to cool before using. If paste hardens before use, it can be softened with water.

Wallpaper paste. Gradually mix cold water with 4 lb. of white flour to make a stiff paste, beating the mixture until the lumps are removed. Next, add more water until the paste has a creamy consistency; then stir in 2 oz. of powdered alum. Finally, stir vigorously while adding enough boiling water to make about 1 1/2 gal. of paste. Allow to cool before using. This paste will keep for several weeks.

White china cement. Make a strong solution of gum arabic by adding only enough water to dissolve it, then add plaster of Paris to produce a stiff paste. Apply to the broken edges of the china. If the china is colored, you can add pigment to match the color or paint the surface when the cement has dried. If applied skillfully, it can make an almost invisible repair. This glue is very strong but is soluble in hot water.

Wood-ash stove putty. To fill cracks in a cast-iron stove, mix equal parts of fine powdered wood ash, powdered fire clay, and salt; then add enough water to make a paste. Although this mixture dries hard, it still has to be replaced from time to time.

Fireproof cement for cast-iron stoves. Add enough egg white to some hydrated lime to make a paste, then mix in iron filings. Apply to the crack or broken pieces. Allow plenty of time to dry before using the stove. This cement becomes progressively stronger and more durable with repeated heating. **Caution: Lime is a highly caustic substance. Rinse skin immediately in the event of contact with skin.**

Paints, whitewashes, and inks

Simple black paint from potatoes. Bake several potatoes in a slow oven until they are cooked, then turn the oven to *hot* and let the potatoes continue cooking until they are completely black and dried out. Grind them up thoroughly in a mortar and pestle, and add enough linseed oil to give a runny consistency. For a durable green paint add yellow ocher.

Old-fashioned milk paint. To make a quart of paint, add 3 tbsp. vinegar to 4 cups of milk and heat gently until the mixture curdles. This creates sour milk. Then mix in 1 oz. of slaked lime. For a long-lasting paint, make sure that your mixture is pH balanced by testing with litmus paper from a pharmacy. If the paper turns red, the mixture is too acid and you should add more lime; if the paper turns dark blue, the mixture is too alkaline and you should add some sour milk. Next, mix in 2 to 2 1/2 lb. of whiting to achieve the proper consistency. Stir thoroughly and slowly sprinkle in some dried pigment. The paint will produce a soft, flat finish suitable for any antique-style wall or furniture decoration. Milk paint is not as durable as modern paint and should be protected with a coat of shellac if used on furniture.

New England glazed whitewash. Boil 3/4 lb. rice and 1/2 sugar in 7 pt. water until the rice has dissolved. Remove from heat and add 1 pt. raw skimmed milk, then mix in hydrated lime until the consistency is that of thin paint. This whitewash is best applied with a soft-bristled brush. Many other whitewash formulas exist. Almost all are based on slaked (hydrated) lime, and many employ zinc sulfate as the whitening agent. The mixture given here produces a finish with a soft, satiny sheen.

To make your own pigments. Any attractively colored earth can be used. Boil up a few spadefuls in plenty of water for several hours. Strain out the organic matter and stones and allow the sediment to settle. Pour off the water and set the residue to dry in shallow pans. Pound finely in a mortar and sift again before adding to paint. A few companies still supply earth pigments and other natural coloring agents.

To remove the smell of paint. Take a few handfuls of dry hay, the older the better, and immerse it in water. Shake out the excess moisture and set the hay in shallow pans around a freshly painted room. Dampen the hay as soon as it dries out. The moist hay will absorb the oily vapor.

To make Prussian blue ink. Dissolve enough Prussian blue, available as laundry bluing, in water to give the color intensity you want. Prussian blue makes a rich blue ink.

To make permanent black ink. Mix 8 oz. honey with 1 egg yolk and 1/4 oz. gum arabic. Then add enough lamp black to give a stiff paste. You can collect your own lamp black on a plate held over a candle flame or buy it in a tube. Store the paste in a jar. For use, mix a little paste in just enough water to make a fluid.

To make brown ink. For an easy to make brown ink, simply add 1/2 cup boiling water to four tea bags or 4 tsp. of loose tea. Steep for 15 minutes and stir to extract as much tannic acid as possible. Strain and allow to cool before bottling.

Sources and resources

Books and pamphlets
Botchis, Lilli. *Plants in the Light of Healing.* Fairfield, Iowa: Time Portal, 1995.
Buchman, Dian D. *Herbal Medicine: The Natural Way to Get Well and Stay Well.* New York: David McKay, 1979.
Coon, Nelson. *Using Wild and Wayside Plants.* New York: Dover, 1980.
Decorso, Dorothy. *Herbal Health.* Cincinnati, Ohio: Seven Hills Books, 1995.
Evelyn, Nancy. *The Herbal Medicine Chest.* Trumansburg, N.Y.: The Crossing Press, 1986.
Fettner, Ann Tucker. *Potpourri, Incense and Other Fragrant Concoctions.* New York: Workman Publishing Co., 1977.
Genders, Roy. *Growing Herbs as Aromatics.* New Canaan, Conn.: Keats Publishing, 1977.
Hayes, Elizabeth. *Spices and Herbs: Their Lore and Use.* New York: Dover, 1980.
Jacka, Judy. *A-Z of Natural Therapies.* Cincinnati, Ohio: Seven Hills Books, 1995.
Jarvis, D.C. *Folk Medicine.* New York: Fawcett Book Group, 1985.
LeArta, Moulton. *Nature's Medicine Chest.* Provo, Utah: Nature's Medicine Chest, 1990.
Ley, Beth. *Natural Healing Handbook: Get Back to Health . . . Naturally.* Newport Beach, Calif.: BL Publications, 1994.
Lust, Benedict. *About Herbs: Nature's Medicine.* Greenwich, Conn.: Benedict Lust Publications, 1983.
Mayer, J.E. *The Herbalist.* New York: Gordon Press, 1992.
Rose, Jeanne. *Herbs and Things.* New York: Grosset & Dunlap, 1972.
Schar, Douglas. *The Backyard Medicine Chest: A Herbal Primer.* Washington, D.C.: Elliott & Clark, 1995.

Periodicals
Prevention. Rodale Press, Inc., 33 East Minor St., Emmaus, Pa. 18049.

Suppliers of herbs and potpourri ingredients
Caswell-Massey Co., Ltd. (Mail Order Department). 111 Eighth Ave., New York, N.Y. 10011.
Indiana Botanic Gardens, Inc. 3401 W. 37th Ave., Hobart, Ind. 46342.
Kiehl's Pharmacy, Inc. 109 Third Ave., New York, N.Y. 10003.
Nichol's Garden Nursery. 1190 Old Salem Rd. NE, Albany, Oreg. 97321.
Pickity Place. Box 303, Nutting Hill Rd., Greenville, N.H. 03048.

Suppliers of pigment for paint
Johnson Paint Company. 355 Newbury St., Boston, Mass. 02215.

Metalworking

Tinsmithing and Blacksmithing: Forging the Implements Of a Self-sufficient Life

Metallurgists divide all the metals on Earth into two categories: ferrous and nonferrous—which is to say, iron and everything else. This is no exaggeration of the importance of iron and its derivative, steel, to our lives. It is, of course, possible to survive without it. The peoples of North and South America did so for centuries, some using nonferrous, or soft, metals, most using no metal at all. But living was difficult and individual survival by no means secure.

European settlers brought with them tools of iron and steel—sharp axes and knives; hammers, nails, and saws for building; rakes, hoes, shovels, and plows for tilling the soil; lamps and stoves and kettles and teapots and a thousand other implements of daily life—and they brought with them the knowledge of how to make more. The establishment of a blacksmith shop, or smithy, was a vital step in creating a viable frontier community. Almost as important was the tinsmith, also an ironworker despite the name. The raw material of his craft, tinplate, is actually sheet iron coated with a thin layer of tin (tin by itself is too soft and weak for practical use).

The soft metals, too, played their parts in the settling of America. Items of copper, lead, brass, and pewter were fairly common in early American homes. But for the most part they were luxuries, almost in a class with silver and gold, fashioned by specialists and sold in shops or by itinerant peddlers for impressive prices. Iron and tinplate were the stuff of everyday life, and knowing how to use them was a vital skill to a settler or frontiersman, as it is today to anyone seeking a degree of self-sufficiency.

Ornamental weather vanes were once used by businessmen to advertise their trades. A rooster might indicate a chicken farmer, where as a cow would indicate a dairy farmer. Now, however, weather vanes are most often simply for decoration.

Working With Tinplate and Sheet Steel

You can buy tinplate in most large hardware stores—if they do not have it on hand, they will generally order it for you. Sheet steel is even easier to find. When ordering sheet steel for handwork, be sure to specify hot-rolled stock. The alternatives, cold-rolled steel and galvanized iron, are rigid and hard to work with.

The thickness of sheet metal is expressed in terms of gauge numbers—the higher the number, the thinner each sheet. Thus 1-gauge sheet metal is .2893 inches thick, 14 gauge is .06408 inches, 26 gauge is .01594 inches, 32 gauge is .00795 inches, and 40 gauge (the thinnest of all) is .00314 inches. Most tinsmithing requires metal in thicknesses ranging from 14 gauge to 32 gauge.

So-called tin cans are a fine source of material. Most of the billions of tin cans produced annually in the United States are not tinplate at all but steel lined with a thin lacquer coating. This includes cans that contain corn, peas, fish, sweet potatoes, tomatoes, and most acidic fruits and vegetables. The lacquer makes for a tough, good-looking surface but it inhibits soldering. Before using solder on such a surface, remove the lacquer with steel wool. Restaurants, bakeries, fish markets, school cafeterias, and the like generally receive their supplies in 5-gallon cans, which are emptied and thrown out. Do not overlook this rich source of supply.

To reduce a can to a flat sheet, first remove the top and bottom, rim and all, by inserting it into a can opener sideways. Next, use tin snips to cut the can lengthwise along the seam and then to remove the seam entirely. Place the can on a flat hardwood surface and push it open as far as you can without buckling it. Begin hammering on the inside of the can with a hammer that has a flat face—the hammer causes the surface to spread slightly, hence the material curves upward. Finish by flattening both sides with a mallet.

Stretching Out a Pattern

Tinsmithing, like most sheet-metal work, usually involves making a three-dimensional object from flat materials. The first step is to make an accurate pattern, or stretch-out. Nearly anything you might choose to make is an adaptation of one or more of four basic forms: the box, the cylinder, the cone, and the pyramid.

You can make all the stretch-outs using only a compass, ruler, right-angle square, and sharp pencils. When working out a new design, first make a model from heavy paper or poster board, allowing edges for wiring, hemming, and joining. Several such models may be needed before all the design problems are solved.

Box

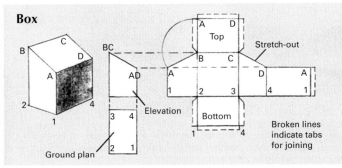

Ground plan

Draw ground plan and label corners. Directly above it, draw elevation (side view) and label top corners. Extend base of elevation to become the base line of stretch-out and mark off points 1, 2, 3, 4, 1 by taking measurements from ground plan. At each point draw a perpendicular. Mark off points A,B,C,D,A on the perpendiculars by extending the points from the elevation. Note that A and D coincide on this elevation as do B and C. Connect the lettered points with straight edge to give pattern. Add top and bottom if desired as well as allowances for joining and edging.

Mitered cylinder

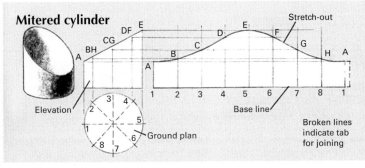

Elevation / Ground plan

Divide ground plan into eight equal parts and label. Draw elevation directly above and extend its base to form base line of stretch-out (length of base line = ground plan diameter × 3.14). Divide base line into eight equal parts and label. Draw a perpendicular at each labeled point. From labeled points on ground plan, draw vertical lines to meet top line of elevation. Then from each of these intersections extend a line parallel to base line, and mark where it crosses the matching vertical lines on stretch-out. Connect with freehand curve; add allowances for edging.

Truncated cone

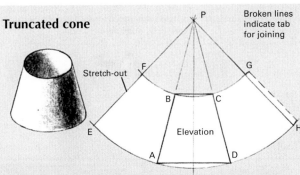

Making exact stretch-out of cone is difficult. For approximation, first extend sides AB and CD of elevation until they meet at point P. From P use compass to draw arc through A and D. Set compass to length AD and mark points E and H along the arc. Draw lines EP and HP for stretch-out of cone. For truncation set compass to radius BP and swing arc FG.

Pyramid

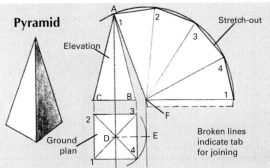

Ground plan

With point of compass at D (centerpoint of ground plan), swing arc upward from point 4 until it intersects center line of ground plan (point E). From E draw line up to a point level with base of elevation (point F). Next, draw line AF, then draw arc at that radius. Set compass to length of side of base (CB) and mark points 1,2,3,4,1 along arc.

Special Equipment for Tinsmithing

Small bending brake handles sheet metal up to 18 in. wide. Aluminum folding bar is held in place with C-clamps. Slots cut into bar with hacksaw allow 90° bend all around a sheet.

The shop of a working tinsmith usually contains several impressive-looking machines. These include at least one bending brake for making sharp, even folds; straight shears and circular shears for cutting; a roller for curving sheets; and several jennies—machines that look like large can openers—for hemming, forming flanges, wiring edges, and performing similar operations. These are all laborsaving devices for doing jobs that can be done by hand. Similarly, the same shop probably contains a wide selection of stakes and mandrels over which metal is hammered into special shapes. As demonstrated on the following pages, substitutes can usually be made from hardwood blocks, poles, dowels, and even tin cans.

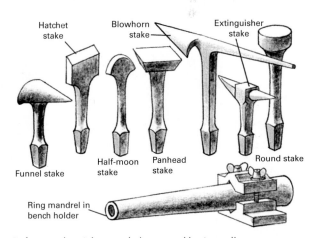

Stakes stand upright; mandrels are used horizontally.

345

A Full Kit of Tools For the Tinsmith

The tools at right make up a basic kit with which to begin tinsmithing. Although the set is by no means complete, it does provide a good foundation on which to build. If you should get serious about tinsmithing, you can add other, more specialized equipment as you go along. Some of the items shown are optional. The electric soldering gun, for example, is a modern convenience that many working smiths do not bother with, preferring instead the old-fashioned soldering iron, which they heat in a small gas oven like the one shown (also not essential). Another alternative is to use a propane torch with a soldering iron attachment for the head.

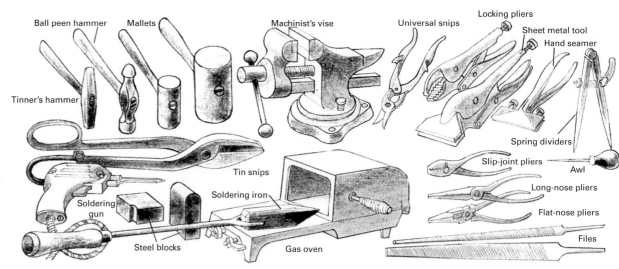

Most tools that a tinsmith needs are to be found in the average household tool chest. Exceptions include the 4- to 6-oz. tinner's hammer, assorted wooden and rawhide mallets, soldering equipment, spring dividers (for scribing arcs on metal surfaces), and, of course, the locking sheet metal tool and its hard-to-find but very useful ancestor, the adjustable hand seamer.

Edging and Joining Without Solder

There are some tricks of the tinsmith's trade that will be useful for many projects. All involve the knack of hammering, the tinsmith's single most important skill. Most beginners show their inexperience in the form of impatience: they hammer too hard and leave an irreparable rash of dents and dimples. Whether you are flatting a hem or tapping out a flange, wield the hammer with your wrist, not your elbow, and never do in one blow what you could do in three. Pass the work back and forth under a steady rain of light blows until the shape is formed. Then use a mallet to smooth it out, or place a block of wood on it and hit that as hard as you like.

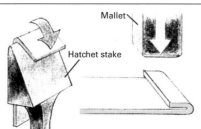

Hemmed edge gives a neat appearance, lends strength, and prevents injury from sharp metal. Scribe line 1/4 in. from edge. Use hatchet stake to bend at line to 70° (bending brake or sheet metal tool can also be used). Flatten with mallet.

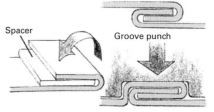

Grooved seam joins two pieces on single plane. Begin as though hemming edges, then flatten both over scrap metal spacer and hook together. Use groove punch to secure joint. Note that top piece needs twice as much extra material as bottom.

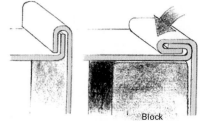

Corner seam is made by using spacer to form hook on one piece as with grooved seam and bending the other to 90°. Join as shown and flatten on block. Note that the hooked edge requires about twice as much material as does the bent edge.

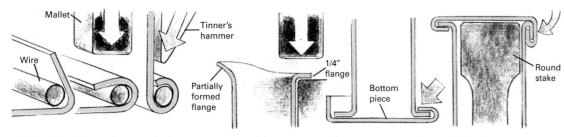

Wired edge adds rigidity. Bend edge (2 1/2 times diameter of wire) to 70° and insert wire. To secure, hammer metal over ends of wire first, then hammer middle and work outward. To finish rolling metal down, use cross peen of tinner's hammer.

Capped bottom is used for canisters and other cylindrical pieces. In making pattern, add 1/4 in. to height of cylinder and 1/2 in. to radius of bottom piece for joining. Use mallet to form 1/4-in. flange around bottom of cylinder. Then use tinner's hammer to turn up 1/4-in. edge around bottom piece, as in making scoop (p.347), and to flatten raised edge over flange. Finally, invert cylinder on round stake and flatten seam with mallet.

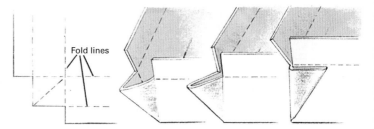

Leakproof corner is often needed for square containers, such as cake pans or the reflector oven shown on page 348. Cut pattern and scribe fold lines. Bend one side to 45°, and use sheet metal tool to start reverse crease in corner tab. Bend other side to 90° by stages, sharpening corner crease as you proceed. Then finish bending first side to 90° and flatten tab. Invert pan over square block and hammer tab down.

Bright tinplate scoops in various sizes are useful and attractive.

Making a Set of Scoops From Tinplate

The scoop that is shown being made below is the middle of the three at left. The others are made in the same way, except that mandrels and stakes vary in size as needed. The diameter of each scoop was determined by the size of the tin can that was used in place of a stake in edging its back. Thus the large scoop is 4 1/4 inches in diameter (No. 5 can), the small one 2 1/8 inches (frozen juice can). (For the method of laying out the body patterns, see *Mitered cylinder*, p.345). Note, however, that the mitered face of each scoop forms an S-curve, which must be drawn freehand on the elevation before the stretch-out is made. The large scoop is 6 inches long, the small one 3 3/4 inches. Handle pieces are 6 inches and 3 inches long, respectively; all are 1 1/2 inches wide.

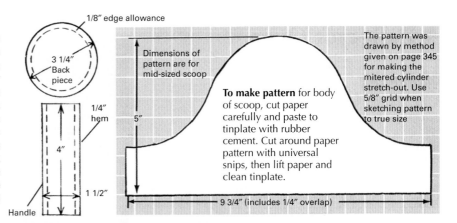

1/8" edge allowance
3 1/4" Back piece
1/4" hem
4"
1 1/2"
Handle

Dimensions of pattern are for mid-sized scoop

To make pattern for body of scoop, cut paper carefully and paste to tinplate with rubber cement. Cut around paper pattern with universal snips, then lift paper and clean tinplate.

5"

9 3/4" (includes 1/4" overlap)

The pattern was drawn by method given on page 345 for making the mitered cylinder stretch-out. Use 5/8" grid when sketching pattern to true size

Joining with solder

Molten solder works like glue, flowing between pieces of metal, then hardening to. secure them. To make a firm joint, the work itself, as well as the solder, must be heated. Flux is also needed to facilitate the flow of solder and to prevent the formation of oxides on the metal; acid-based flux such as zinc chloride or an organic substance such as tallow, rosin, or olive oil can be used. Acid fluxes are more certain to work, organic ones safer to use.

The surfaces to be joined and the tip of the soldering iron must be clean. Insert the tip into the flux, then heat it over a gas jet or charcoal fire. When a green flame shows above the soldering iron (which is actually made of copper not iron), brush a coat of flux along the edge of the seam to be soldered. Dip the heated iron into the flux again and touch it to the end of some wire solder. The solder will flow onto the iron. Next, press a face of the iron (not just the pointed end) firmly against the upper surface of the seam. When the metal is hot enough, the solder will flow down into the joint. At that point, begin "leading" it by slowly drawing the iron downward along the seam. Solder tends to flow downward and toward heat.

1. Use scriber and spring dividers to mark out all patterns on 28-gauge tinplate. Cut with universal snips. Use right-hand snips when waste is on right side of cut, left-hand snips when it is on the left.

2. Using standard No. 2 1/2 can (3-in. diameter) as stake, turn down 1/8-in. edge all around back piece. To ensure even edge, first tap down four equidistant points around the circle, then complete the edge a little at a time.

3. Form body of scoop over 2 1/2-in. wooden mandrel. First use mallet to curve both ends gently downward, then work by hand, forcing material down gradually to avoid sharp bends and to maintain an even curve.

4. Fit curved body into raised edge of back piece and mark overlap at base. Then use spring dividers as shown to scribe overlap line parallel with inside edge. This will ensure straight body when seam is soldered.

5. To spot-solder body to back, hold pieces together with one hand and apply flux to three points inside. Then pick up some solder on tip of heated iron and touch each spot until a little solder flows into seam.

6. Align overlap with scribed line on body and clamp in place with locking pliers. Apply a flux and solder the seam closed. Then apply some flux all around the outside of the back piece and solder body to back.

7. Use sheet metal tool to hem both edges of handle piece. Then, using 1 1/2-in. dowel as mandrel, shape into ring with hem on inside. Bend back both ends of the handle so it will fit flush against back of scoop.

8. Draw center line on back (do not scribe it or it will rust) and position handle along it. Apply flux and solder. Finish the scoop by filing the front edge lightly and applying a fine layer of solder to prevent rust.

A Reflector Oven
For the Fireplace
Or the Campfire

Reflector ovens—ranging from simple tin boxes in which to bake a single loaf of bread to intricate structures large enough to accommodate a whole suckling pig or joint of venison—were common utensils in the old days. Some larger models, with their gracefully hooded backs, turning spits, and built-in spouts for draining grease, were the work of master tinsmiths. Others could be, and often were, homemade. The ingenious oven shown below was designed for roasting small birds and game before a fireplace or open fire. Its reflector hangs from a wire; when the meat is done on one side, the oven is turned and the reflector flipped over to cook the other side.

Three game hens roast before an open fireplace in homemade reflector oven. Legs are trussed with heavy twine, and birds are suspended from lower rod on hooks fashioned from coat-hanger wire. Larger items can hang from upper rod.

Shaping the Pieces

1. Cut out body, scribe all fold lines, and punch 1/8-in. holes as indicated on pattern. Then fold ends up to 45°. To make bending brake from two 15-in. lengths of hardwood, first bevel edge of one piece. Next, place beveled edge on fold line and clamp second board beneath so metal is sandwiched between. Lift to bend.

2. Use sheet-metal tool to establish reverse crease in all four corner tabs for making leakproof corners (p.346). Do not bend back too far—just enough to ensure that crease will be straight. Round-nose pliers are also handy tools for shaping the corner tabs.

3. Once again using 15-in. hardwood boards and C-clamps as bending brake, bend sides up to 90° along fold line (boards must fit inside measurement of pan exactly). Bend in stages, using sheet-metal tool to sharpen reverse creases in corner tabs as you proceed.

4. To sharpen fold along both sides, use block of steel or hardwood to give solid backing, and tap lightly with tinner's hammer just above the bottom. To flatten bottom surface, simply strike downward on block with hammer.

5. Saw 15-in. hardwood boards to 10 in. (to fit inside measurement of pan crossways), and use them as bending brake to finish folding ends to 90°. Sharpen folds as in Step 4. Then hammer all four corner tabs out flat. Do not bend the corner tabs over yet.

6. In preparation for wiring, use sheet-metal tool (or adjustable hand seamer as shown) to bend all edges outward along scribed lines. Work across each edge three or four times, bending a little further each time until 90° angle is achieved. Then hammer out any irregularities against steel block and bend to 70°.

7. Using steel or hardwood block for backing, hammer the corner tabs over and down to complete all four leakproof corners. Note that top edge of tabs must be 1/8 in. below folded edge to allow for wiring. If necessary, trim them with universal snips before hammering down against the sides of the pan.

8. Cut reflector piece with tin snips. Scribe fold lines all around according to pattern. Then bend all edges to 70° with sheet-metal tool. Hem bottom edge and both sides (p.346). Do not hem top edge—it will be rolled around top wire of oven body later.

Pattern for oven body should be drawn on paper, then pasted to 26-gauge sheet steel with rubber cement. Cut out with tin snips (long, straight cuts) and universal snips (inside corners), and scribe all fold lines. Remove paper and clean sheet metal. For reflector, scribe rectangle directly on sheet steel and cut with tin snips. Scribe fold lines with spring dividers, then cut off corners at 45° angle to depth indicated. You will also need 101 in. of 14-gauge steel wire (.08-in. diameter) for edging and 34 in. of 10-gauge wire (.125-in. diameter) to make rods.

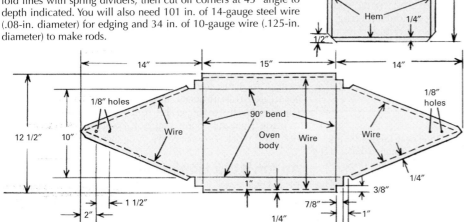

Putting It Together With Wired Edges

1. The first step in wiring edges of the oven body is to attach the top wire, which completes and strengthens entire structure. Cut a 29-in. length of 14-gauge steel wire and use sheet-metal tool or ordinary pliers to make 90° bend 7 in. from each end of wire. This will leave center section 15 in. long to bridge the space across top of oven body. This measurement is important; double-check it with a ruler before proceeding.

2. Left: Support oven body on hardwood block; place 7-in. end section of wire into fold along one edge of end of oven and bend fold over to form wired edge (p.346). Then put other end of oven on block, and wire the corresponding edge in the same way. Right: After raising top wire 1/4 in. by tapping it upward, bend the protruding section a bit so that it is centered over oven. This will allow reflector to swing freely.

3. Continue wiring all edges of oven body. First use another 29-in. length to complete the face of oven that was begun with top wire; place it end to end with existing wire and roll remainder of metal edge over it before bending it into fold across bottom. Then roll that edge over it before bending again. Trim excess wire with cutters. Use a 43-in. length to wire edges of remaining face of oven in the same manner.

4. To attach reflector, roll its upper edge, already bent to 70° but not yet hemmed, over top wire. Before you hammer edge down over wire, be certain reflector corners are trimmed enough to allow reflector to swing easily and that top wire is still raised 1/4 in. and centered. Then tap bent edge down over wire at both ends to hold it in place and finish as with other wired edges. Polish both reflector surfaces with steel wool.

5. Cut two 17-in. lengths of 10-gauge wire to serve as rods for supporting meat. Make 90° bend 1 in. from one end and a slight bend 1 in. from the other. Put the slightly bent end into 1/8-in. hole on one side of oven and pull it through. Then work it through the corresponding hole in the other side. Use a steel block for backing inside oven while hammering end of wire until it is bent to 90°. Insert second wire in the same way.

Iron and Steel: Forging and Shaping The Black Metals

Before the turn of the century most farmers, and many townsfolk as well, had their own anvils and small forges for making simple repairs and for turning out essential household tools and hardware. In those days one's childhood was enlivened not by the glow of the television tube but by the ringing anvil and flying sparks of the smithy. Youngsters grew up understanding the nature of forge work, and few skills contributed more to the American family's self-sufficient lifestyle.

Recently there has been a revival of interest in blacksmithing. Beginners find they can quickly achieve satisfying results. Skilled artisans are fascinated by the new forms and techniques they discover. In addition, forge work provides good exercise and a sense of independence from the vagaries of the commercial world.

The principles of forging are simple. Iron melts at 2802°F, just as ice does at 32°F. As it approaches this temperature, it becomes relatively soft and malleable; if it is then cooled quickly, it will "freeze" as hard or harder than before. The basic idea of forge work is to heat the iron to the proper temperature and then reshape it with hammer blows before it cools.

If you have never tried your hand at the forge, do not expect to start out doing fancy work. Begin by using scrap metal to practice basic techniques. Once you get the feel of the work, go on to a simple project, such as making a chisel. Soon you will be able to tackle more involved work and to create your own designs.

An Anvil Is a Lifetime Investment

In time of need a smith can use a steel plate, a piece of railroad track, even a convenient boulder, as a working surface. But on a regular basis, there is no substitute for an anvil; it is a masterpiece of efficient design.

The anvil's carbon steel face is hardened, tempered, and polished to make a smooth, solid working surface. In old anvils, this face was welded to a body of wrought iron: modern anvils are usually cast as a single piece of steel with the face specially treated for hardness. At one end the face forms a square overhang called the heel. At the other end is the horn of annealed steel. Between the face and the horn is a ledge, known as the table, also annealed. The softer annealed surfaces are used whenever a tool (for example, a chisel) is likely to penetrate through the work and hit the anvil; annealed surfaces will dent, but not chip, and are easy to re-dress.

Anvils are priced according to weight; about $2.50 per pound is average for a new one. Used anvils are cheaper but no longer easy to find. With luck and persistence you may unearth one at a country auction, flea market, or salvage yard. New or used, a good anvil will last a lifetime, so choose carefully. Test the face by striking it with a hammer; if it is properly tempered and undamaged, it will ring like a bell and the hammer will bounce back. (This resilience makes forge work easier. Hitting hot iron is like jumping on a feather bed; the force is absorbed. Tempered steel, by comparison, is like a trampoline. Experienced smiths "ring the anvil" every third or fourth blow to give their arms a rest.)

A 45- to 60-pound anvil is adequate for most uses. If you plan to do heavy work such as fire welding, and you can set up a permanent shop, a 100-pounder is better.

Steel post vise, in which force of blow is taken by post seated in floor, is best for forge work. Heavy machinist's vise of cast steel with quick release action is a suitable alternative. Mount it securely on solidly built workbench.

Safety goggles

Hood

Hood over forge is both a safety precaution and a convenience. Indoors, it draws smoke and fumes into chimney or vent; outdoors, it shades forge so color of heated metal can be clearly seen.

Leather apron

Hand-cranked blower

Tong holder used as blacksmith's helper to support long bar

Steel post vise

Table

Horn

Face

Forge

Heel

Pritchel hole

Hardie hole

Quenching bucket

Round pritchel hole in heel of anvil is for punching; square hardie hole receives shank of anvil tools. Use bolts or heavy staples to secure anvil to large log, wooden block, or frame of lumber or steel. Face of anvil should be level with knuckles when your arm hangs loosely at your side.

Arrange shop for economy of motion, with all equipment no further than a step or two from forge, so hot metal will not cool in transit. If you are right-handed, blower should be at your left as you face forge, anvil at your right with horn pointing toward forge. Quenching bucket must be near at hand to both. If you are left-handed, shop should be arranged as mirror image of illustration. Always set up all tools you will need for a project before heating metal.

Blacksmithing Begins With the Fire

No skill is more vital to the blacksmith than knowing how to build, tend, and use the fire in the forge. There is no need for a roaring blaze: it only dissipates heat. The ideal is a concentrated fist-sized fire pocket of intensely hot coke (partly burned coal) enclosed by a supply of fresh fuel and fed a steady flow of air. The metal is heated by being thrust deep into this pocket rather than being roasted over it like a marshmallow.

A good fire requires good fuel. Bituminous coal is best. It forms dense, long-lasting coke and is low in contaminants. Ask your dealer for blacksmith's coal, soft pea coal, or cannel coal (in descending order of preference). Charcoal, of the type used in barbecue grills, is usable, but it forms no coke and is hard to manage. Anthracite, or hard coal, is not suitable for the home blacksmith. Start the fire by filling the forge with a layer of fuel,

pushing any old, partly coked fuel toward the center. Then scoop out a depression over the air grate and clear all air holes. Place burning cardboard or other kindling over the grate and provide a gentle air flow as you rake coal around and over it. There will be a lot of smoke at first; it will diminish as the coal turns to coke.

Like smoking a pipe, tending the fire requires almost constant attention. If the air flow stops, the fire dies; and the harder you puff it, the hotter it burns. In addition, to prevent the fire pocket from burning hollow, the coke around it must be regularly moved into the fire and fresh coals banked up in its place. Impurities collect over the grate in the form of slag and must be removed from time to time. When it is hot, slag looks like glowing red putty; when cool, it is metallic and responds to a tap of a poker with a dull clink—hence its name: clinker.

Portable hand-cranked forge is practical for most home blacksmithing. To keep air grate from clogging, maintain air flow whenever you adjust fire or take work in or out.

Labels (top diagram): Hand-cranked blower · Fire pocket · Air grate · Air flow · Ash gate

Building a Forge out of a Brake Drum

A new coal-burning forge, complete with hand-cranked blower, can cost as little as $150. With luck, you may find a used one for considerably less, or you can make your own for next to nothing.

The basic parts of a forge are a fire pot with an air grate in the center, a blower with regulated air flow, a pipe connecting them, and a system for removing any ashes that fall through the grate.

A truck brake drum makes a good small fire pot. Other possibilities include the wheel of a car, a cut-down oil drum, or a heavy-duty barbecue grill. Pots made of sheet metal must be lined with fire clay.

Bolt a flange to the brake drum beneath the center hole to receive a threaded 2-inch pipe, then make further connections as shown. Air can be supplied by a portable hair dryer, car heater fan, vacuum cleaner exhaust, hand-cranked blower, or even an old-fashioned bellows. In general, manually operated blowers offer better and more precise control than motor-driven blowers. They are also safer to use and more portable.

Brake drum forge can be mounted on legs of steel pipe, or you can build a frame of steel, heavy lumber, or brick. Firm mounting is required if air is supplied by hand-cranked blower.

Labels (right diagram): Removable sheet steel grate fits into bottom of brake drum · Cast-iron brake drum from truck · 1/4" bolt · 3/16" bolt · 3/4" flange · 2" flange · 2" nipples · 2" T-coupling · 2" cap · 2" pipe connects to blower · 3/4" pipe legs

Assembling requires no welding or riveting. Holes must be drilled in drum bottom to bolt leg flanges in place. Center flange is bolted through existing holes; all other couplings are threaded. Removable cap at bottom acts as ash gate. Use snips to cut sheet steel, such as the top of an oil drum, to inside dimension of brake drum; punch center area over air grate with 1/8-in. holes and set in place. Sheet steel will have to be replaced occasionally.

How not to get burned: seven safety precautions

1. Be sure you have adequate ventilation.
2. Always keep a working fire extinguisher handy.
3. Wear a leather apron, safety glasses, and heavy-soled shoes or boots when forging. Do not wear gloves: they encourage careless habits.
4. Maintain a clean, organized shop. Piles of rags, paper, or wood chips are dangerous—and so are loose tools that you can trip over while carrying red-hot steel.
5. If a piece of work falls from the forge or anvil, resist the impulse to catch it. Let it fall.
6. Always be sure a piece of metal is cool before touching it. When in doubt, use tongs. More burns are caused by metal that looks cool than by glowing red metal.
7. If your forge has an electric blower, never turn your back on it without switching it off. Better still, get a blower with a variable-speed foot switch that cuts off automatically.

Tools and Materials For Setting Up Shop

The blacksmith's basic hand tools are his hammer and tongs. Other tools can be bought or made as they are needed. The economic benefits of making your own tools are obvious; even more valuable is the pleasure of using a tool that you have crafted with your own hands.

Hammers. The face should be of smooth, unchipped tempered steel. Most smiths have two hammers: a 40-to 48-ounce cross peen for regular work and a 32- to 40-ounce ball peen (the peen is the back side of the head opposite the face). You may want to start lighter.

Tongs. For simple work you can make do with locking pliers or long-handled channel-type pliers. For advanced work you will need a variety of tongs (see p.353).

Chisels. Cold chisels are thick, built for strength. They are designed to cut cold metal but can also be used on hot metal. Hot chisels are thin, to slice through hot metal, and long, to protect the hand from heat. Some are fitted with handles. Do not use them for cold work.

Punches. The points of most punches are either round or square. Decorative patterns such as heart shapes or other special forms are also available.

Hardies. Technically, any anvil tool whose shank fits into the square hardie hole is a hardie; in practice, the term applies only to those with a chisel edge.

Fullers. A top fuller is like a chisel with a rounded edge; a bottom fuller is a rounded hardie. Fullers are used separately or together to draw out metal by forging a series of dents, which are then flattened.

Flatters. A flatter is held on top of the metal and struck with a hammer to smooth out rough surfaces.

Swages. These are shaping tools, which are generally sold in matching top and bottom pairs. They can be used individually or in tandem.

Swage block. This heavy cast-iron block serves as an all-purpose bottom swage. It has an assortment of half-round and V-shaped notches in its sides plus holes and depressions of various shapes and sizes in its face.

Beaks. Many small special-purpose anvils can be devised to fit into the hardie hole. The simplest is the beak—a miniature horn for making small bends.

Holdfast. The square end of the holdfast wedges into the hardie hole, the flattened end secures the work.

Such common tools as files, hacksaws, and tin snips are also useful. Do not use tempered edges with hot metal, however, or the temper will be ruined.

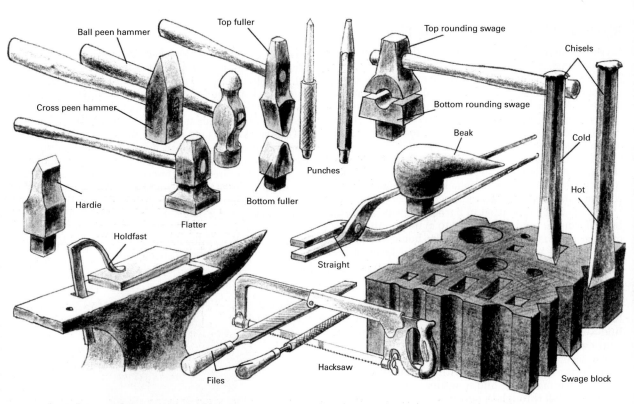

Among the blacksmith's large assortment of tools, only the hammers are used to strike a direct blow on heated metal. Most of the other implements—chisels, flatters, punches, fullers, swages (even those that look like hammers)—are held in place and struck.

Iron and Steel: Where to Find Them

Iron is available in four forms, based on carbon content; the more carbon it contains, the harder and more brittle it is and the more difficult to work with.

Wrought iron (up to 0.2 percent carbon) is very malleable, easily fire welded, and virtually rustproof, but it cannot be hardened or tempered. Its structure is somewhat fibrous because it contains silica slag. The old-time blacksmith's staple, and still best for most forging, it has become expensive and hard to come by. Most of what is now called wrought iron is mild steel.

Mild steel (0.2 to 0.3 percent carbon) is technically not steel at all but high-quality iron (true steel has at least 0.3 percent carbon). It is fairly malleable and can be hardened somewhat but not tempered. Though not impervious to rust, it can be protected by heating to blood red and quenching in oil. This is a touchy and potentially dangerous procedure, however (see cautionary note under *Tempering Carbon Steel*, p.361). Use hot-rolled rather than cold-rolled stock for forging—the best is sold as hot-rolled 1020.

Carbon steel (0.3 to 2.2 percent carbon) is malleable only within a narrow temperature range and is almost impossible to fire weld. It can be finely tempered and so is used in many tools. Note: Alloy steels (carbon steel to which other metals, such as chromium or tungsten, have been added) are seldom useful for forging.

Cast iron (over 2.2 percent carbon) is useless to the smith since it will never soften enough to be forged.

To buy iron and steel, look for a small steel yard or a scrap-metal dealer in your community. You may also be able to find what you need in the form of scrap. Junkyards are excellent sources of supply. When rummaging, keep an eye out for genuine (pre-1910) wrought-iron objects, such as fences, door hardware, kitchenware, axheads, and farm implements. For tool-quality carbon steel try an automobile graveyard. Look for axles, push rods, torsion bars, bumpers, stick shifts, steering crossarms, and springs of all kinds.

Caution: Never forge galvanized iron; the zinc with which it is coated will emit toxic gas.

Making Your Own Chisel

The total investment in the chisel shown on this page was one scrap piece of 3/4-in. carbon steel reinforcing rod and about 15 minutes of labor. (A beginner should allow a half day for the project and be proud to finish it within an hour or two.) It is not essential to use reinforcing rod. Any 3/4- to 1 1/4-in. carbon steel rod will do. As a general practice, it is better to use rod of a specific shape—either hexagonal or octagonal—for such tools so they can be easily identified when you need them while working.

The tool shown here is a cold chisel, useful for cutting hot as well as cold metal. A hot chisel, which slices more easily through heated metal but should not be used for cold work, can be made using the same tools, materials, and techniquesw—with the following exceptions: first (Step 1) cut rod to 1 ft. long rather than 9 in. Then (Step 2) taper the end to a longer, steeper angle than that shown, holding the rod about 20° from the horizontal and working back 4 to 5 in. In addition, although a cold chisel can be allowed to flare as the end is being tapered, a hot chisel must be dressed from the sides or it will spread too wide. Finally (Step 6), sharpen the cutting edge to an angle of 30°.

To see the cold chisel in action, turn to pages 358 and 360.

1. Heat rod to orange (see *Color guides*, p.361) 9 in. from end. Place heated spot on hardie and hammer first one side then the other until rod is cut almost through. Then break off by hand to avoid damaging edge of hardie.

2. Reheat end of 9-in. piece to a bright cherry red and hold it flush with far edge of anvil face at angle of 30° to the horizontal. Draw out end to a flat taper, then extend taper back toward handle about 2 in., turning to work both sides.

3. When rough form is achieved, reheat end of chisel to bright cherry red and use hardie to cut edge off square. Once again, to avoid damaging edge of hardie, cut steel almost through, then break end off by hammering over edge of anvil.

4. Reheat to bright cherry red and return to far edge of anvil face, as in Step 2, to forge cutting edge of the chisel. Be sure to remove from fire as soon as bright cherry-red glow appears on sharp edge; thin steel may burn if overheated.

5. Because of the many reheatings involved, handle of chisel may become too hot to hold while edge is being formed. If this occurs while you are performing Steps 3 and 4, hold heated end with tongs and quench handle in water to cool it.

6. Quench entire chisel in water, then clamp it upright in vise and use file as shown to sharpen cutting edge to angle of 60° for cold work—a little sharper if tool is to be used for hot work. (For instructions in tempering, see p.361.)

The blacksmith's tongs—form follows function

A vast array of tongs are likely to be found in a working smithy, and for good reason: a firm grip is vital when you are forging hot iron, and this requires tongs that conform to the shape of the work—whatever that may be. The village blacksmith's solution was often to heat the jaws of any handy pair of tongs and forge them around an object at the precise angle needed. As a result, antique hunters often turn up old tongs whose function remains mysterious. Another example of creative design is the pair of lockgrip tongs at far right, forerunners of today's locking pliers, made with a strip of steel band.

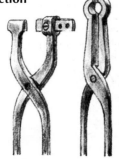

Adjustable   Link   Hollow bit   Farrier's   Side   Bolt   Hoop   Box   Lock-grip

A glossary of techniques

Annealing. Softening iron or steel by heating and allowing to cool slowly.

Bending. Forging an angle or curve in a bar or rod, usually over the edge of the anvil face or the horn. Can sometimes be done cold (p.359) or without hammering (p.357).

Collaring. Joining two or more pieces by forging a metal band around them.

Cutting. Severing a bar or rod crosswise with a chisel or hardie.

Drawing out. Making a piece of metal thinner, thus increasing its length and breadth by forging.

Dressing. Forging for the purpose of smoothness, alignment, or trim.

Fire welding. Joining two pieces of iron or steel by hammering them together at white heat (p.354).

Forging. Any operation that involves heating metal to a malleable state and shaping it with hammer blows.

Hardening. Solidifying the crystalline structure of steel by heating to its critical temperature and quenching (see *Tempering Carbon Steel*, p.361).

Heading. Upsetting to form a head, as with a nail or bolt.

Punching. Hammering a punch into heated metal to make a hole.

Quenching. Cooling heated metal by immersion, usually in fresh water or brine. Oil rather than water is sometimes used for special purposes (see *Tempering Carbon Steel*, p.361).

Riveting. Joining two or more pieces by heading both ends of a heated rod that pierces them.

Splitting. Severing a bar or rod lengthwise with a chisel or hardie.

Swaging. Forging heated metal into the recessed pattern of a swage, between two swages, or between a swage and a swage block.

Tapering. Drawing out to a point. It can be round or square, as with a nail or punch, or flat, as with a chisel.

Tempering. Removing some of the brittleness of hardened steel by reheating to a given temperature, then quenching quickly (p.361).

Upsetting. Making a heated bar or rod shorter and thicker than it is by striking it on the end.

Welding a Chain And Making Nails Are Basic Skills

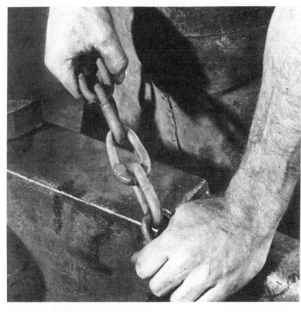

New, welded link repairs old chain, makes long chain of two short ones. Use mild steel rod of same diameter as chain links.

Repairing a Broken Chain With a New Link

1. Heat end of rod to cherry red (see *Color guides*, p.361). Then hold flat on face of anvil and draw out 1 1/2-in. bevel on one side. Measure circumference of existing link and cut rod 1/2 in. longer.

2. Bevel other end to match, on opposite side of rod. Reheat and bend both ends over a beak so that arcs match that of chain link. Note that arc is formed perpendicular to flat side of bevel.

3. Heat rod to cherry red in center and quench both ends. Then bend rod double so flat side of bevels overlap. Adjust curves for exact fit. Leave slightly open to insert existing chain links.

4. Insert links being joined and hammer new link almost closed. From this point on you must handle chains along with new link; support their weight on tong rack or have someone help.

5. Move anvil as close as possible to forge and place hammer on it. Build clean welding fire and use tongs to hold new link deep within it. Now bring metal slowly to white heat as described below.

6. When welding heat is reached, move new link quickly to anvil face. Pick up hammer and strike link firmly along weld, first at center of curve, then on each side (see diagram below).

Fire Welding: An Ancient Technique for the Modern Blacksmith

Since long before the invention of the acetylene torch, fire welding has been an important part of the blacksmith's craft. The simple concept behind the technique can be illustrated with a pair of ice cubes. If the cubes are warmed until their surfaces begin to melt, then squeezed together and refrozen quickly, the result will be a solid chunk of ice, not just two cubes glued together. The same is true of iron, except that it must reach white heat (about 2500°F) before its surface begins to melt, and the pieces must be joined by hammering before they cool.

The difficulties of working at such temperatures are complicated by the presence of carbon in the metal: the higher the carbon content, the lower the burning point; and when the surface burns, it leaves a scaly oxidation coating that inhibits welding. Wrought iron burns at 2790°F, mild steel at about 2650°F, carbon steel at lower temperatures. Thus the working range between white heat and the burning point is narrow—and for steels with high carbon content almost nonexistent.

A good way to learn the technique of fire welding is to join the ends of two bars with a simple lap, or scarf, weld. First heat the end of each piece to cherry red (see *Color guides*, p.361), hold it flat on the anvil face, and draw out a 2- to 4-inch-long bevel on one side. The bevels should match exactly, and each should be slightly convex.

Next, remove all clinker from the forge and prepare a deep fire, rich in coke and tightly enclosed with coal that has been dampened with water to form a sort of oven. Heat the end of both bars to cherry red, remove them from the fire, and sprinkle a flux—either borax or a commercial preparation—evenly on both beveled surfaces. This will curb the formation of surface oxidation.

It is at this point that the beginner is likely to make the mistake of trying to reach welding heat too quickly. The metal must be heated as bread is baked—slowly enough to be done throughout. Provide a steady air flow, not a blast, and be patient until white heat is reached and the metal begins to throw off tiny white sparks. Then there is not a second to waste. Place both pieces on the anvil with the bevels overlapping and strike three hard blows. Dress the weld with a series of quick, light blows.

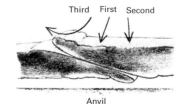

Place first three blows as shown: first blow joins center, driving out flux and surface oxidation; second joins lower lip before it cools on anvil; third blow secures weld.

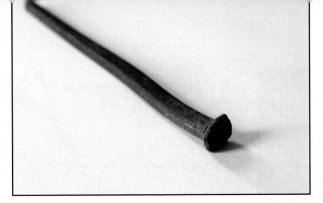

The ability to forge nails like this antique one can be an invaluable asset to a homesteader in time of need, particularly when a specific size is required.

The Handmade Nail

Nails of all styles and dimensions were, for centuries, important stock-in-trade to the blacksmith. An apprentice was expected, when not busy with other tasks, to produce as many as a thousand nails a day. For American settlers nailmaking was an essential skill; frontier children often spent long evenings before the fireplace at the task, using rod thin enough to be heated without a forge.

Nailmaking is good practice. From the moment a rod comes glowing from the fire, the nailmaker has 15 to 20 seconds in which to perform five tasks before the rod becomes too cool to be worked. Once the point is formed, it cannot be reheated without burning.

After you have made your first batch of nails, try driving a few into hardwood. It will not be easy but will help you to improve your technique. Once you have acquired sufficient skill, your nails will lend a personal touch to such woodworking projects as the firewood carrier on pages 308-309.

To make nails you must first make a nailheader

1. Cut 3/4-in. mild steel bar 18-20 in. long. Heat end to cherry red (see *Color guides*, p.361) and use edge of anvil to forge 90° bend 2 in. from end of bar.

2. Reheat to orange and upset bent end until it is almost flush with bar. Dress head by striking sides from time to time to maintain square shape.

3. Reheat as necessary to finish shaping head of tool. Finally, turn it face down on anvil and strike from rear, just below head, to offset handle slightly.

4. Heat head of tool to orange and punch it almost through from rear, or offset side. Then turn and punch smaller hole from front, where dark spot is.

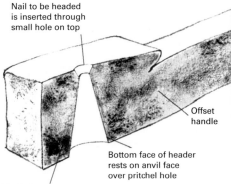

Nail to be headed is inserted through small hole on top

Offset handle

Bottom face of header rests on anvil face over pritchel hole

Vertical cross-section of tool showing tapered hole

Nailheaders were once standard tools in any smithy and on most farms and homesteads. They are now all but impossible to buy. Happily, they are easy to make. The one shown here is designed to produce round nails of the kind pictured at top left on this page. For square nails, make the smaller hole in nailheader with a square-ended punch. Note that the handle of the header is offset slightly so it can be held at a comfortable angle while the lower face sits flat on anvil. Headers are often made with a head on each end for forging nails of different sizes and shapes.

Making a nail in five steps and 15 seconds

1. Put hardie in hardie hole and keep header close by. Heat end of 1/4-in. rod to bright cherry red. Hold at 30° angle, flush with far edge of anvil face as shown, and taper to point.

2. Shift rod to near edge of anvil and hold it level while drawing out to length and thickness desired for shank of nail. Test by inserting in smaller hole of header.

3. Place rod over edge of hardie 1/4-1/2 in. above top of drawn-out shank (depending on size of nailhead desired) and hammer hard enough to cut rod only partway through.

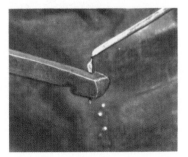

4. Insert shank of nail in small hole on upper face of header and twist rod back and forth to break it off cleanly at the point where you have scored it over the hardie.

5. Place header on anvil with nail point in pritchel hole. Use ball peen to upset nailhead. Quench in water, header and all, and tap nail loose (it will shrink a little when quenched).

Fireplace Tools:
A Pleasure to Behold
As Well as to Use

A matching fireplace set, consisting of poker, shovel, tongs, and log holder, is decorative as well as utilitarian. The basic material for the set is 1/2-inch-square mild steel bar. You will need four such bars for the tools, each about 5 feet long. Two of the bars are for the shovel and poker. The other two bars are for the tongs whose construction is described on page 358. The log holder (p.359) requires an additional 27 feet of 1/2-inch-square bar.

The first step in making the poker, shovel, or tongs is to forge the decorative ring by which the implement can be hung. The technique for making these rings is shown on page 357. It is best to make the rings (there are three, one for each tool) one after the other during a single session at the forge; this will make it easier to produce an attractive matching set.

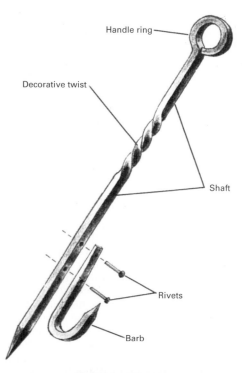

Labels: Handle ring, Decorative twist, Shaft, Rivets, Barb

Let personal taste and dimensions of your fireplace determine size of fireplace set. Give complete set protective finish with flat black spray paint.

Begin by Making the Poker

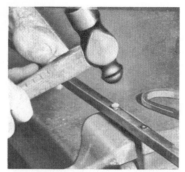

1. After forging rings (p.357), cut bar to length you have chosen for shaft of fireplace poker; save excess to make barb. Heat end of bar to bright cherry red (see *Color guides*, p.361). Hold on anvil at 30° to horizontal with tip of bar flush with far edge of face. Taper to a square point, rotating work a quarter-turn back and forth between blows so that hammer flattens two sides, the anvil the other two. Cut 7-in. piece for barb and taper to matching point in the same way.

2. Quench point of barb and heat other end to bright cherry red. Hold as shown and draw out 3-in. flat taper; dress sides often to maintain 1/2-in. width. Reheat and punch 1/4-in. hole near end and another hole 2 1/2 in. farther up. Quench entire barb. Then use tongs to hold flattened end while heating point to cherry red. Forge hook over horn of anvil in same way rings are forged (p.357). Finally, heat entire barb to cherry red and quench in water to harden.

3. Position barb on shaft while cold and use punch to mark placement of top hole; then heat shaft to orange at that spot and punch 1/4-in. hole. To avoid ragged edge, punch partway through from top, reverse bar over pritchel hole, set point of punch on dark spot, and punch again. Quench. Insert 1/4-in. rod to hold barb in place while marking lower hole; reheat shaft and punch in the same way. Protect point of punch by quenching after each use.

4. To form rivet, heat one end of short length of 1/4-in. rod to bright cherry red, then clamp tightly in vise with heated end protruding up 3/4 in. Slip hole in shaft over heated rod and use ball peen hammer to upset head. Remove from vise and, with rod still piercing shaft, clamp shaft upright in vise. Slip hole in barb onto other end of rod. Use hacksaw to sever rod, leaving 1/4-in. protrusion for heading back of rivet. Set first rivet aside and form second in the same way.

5. Heat one rivet to bright cherry red, then remove from forge with tongs; insert quickly through holes in barb and shaft. Turn poker over on face of anvil and head rivet with ball peen hammer. Quench quickly; rivet will shrink to form tight bond. Heat second rivet, insert in remaining holes, and head it in the same way. Do not apply decorative twist to handle until shovel is completed; then do both handles, one right after the other (see *Forming a decorative twist*, p.357).

Forging the Rings

1. Heat bar to cherry red 8 to 10 in. from end. Bend to about 30° from vertical by using hardie hole as shown, or forge over anvil. Quench.

2. Reheat just above bend. Forge first arc of circle over horn as shown; then reheat, quench completed section, and forge next part of arc.

3. Continue reheating and forging until circle is completed, each time quenching already completed arc section to preserve shape.

4. When first ring is completed, use it as pattern for other two. Allow extra material and cut it off when finished rather than risk running short.

An Oil Drum and a Steel Bar Make a Shovel

1. Use of forge is unnecessary in making blade of shovel from sheet steel. Material shown is from top of 55-gal. oil drum, the underside of which was steam-cleaned of oil residue. Mark out 6- by 8-in. rectangle (exact outside dimensions are not important) with the help of a straight edge and framing square. Use soapstone, chalk, or tempered point of punch. Be sure corners are exactly square. Cut out rectangle with tin snips.

4. Use finished poker to determine length of shovel handle. Lay out the two pieces side by side on floor or workbench. Slide shovel blade beneath bar so that edge is flush with end of poker, and use soapstone or chalk to mark spot where bar crosses back edge of blade. Make another mark 3 in. down. Reinforce marks on anvil, using cold chisel, then heat bar to bright cherry red and cut off over hardie at lower mark.

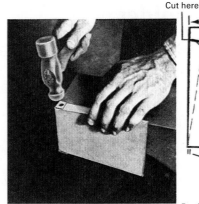

2. Use straight edge to mark out on rectangle the pattern shown at far right (exact interior dimensions are important). Score each fold line deeply with tempered point of punch, awl, or chisel. Use tin snips to cut two rear slots at angle indicated on drawing. Fold both diagonal side panels to 90° by bending in vise or hammering cold over edge of anvil. Then fold rear panel up so that it is flush with rear edge of sides.

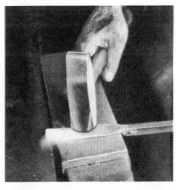

5. Heat end of bar to bright cherry red and place on anvil face with marked spot flush with near edge. Hold bar level and strike squarely with hammer to draw out entire end section to thickness of 1/8 in. Begin at edge of anvil and work toward end of bar. Do not dress sides but allow entire section to spread to width of 1 1/2 to 2 in. or more; it will also stretch to about 6 in. long, forming a fitted bed with notch for shovel blade.

3. Hammer protruding lips of rear panel over side panels and punch through both thicknesses. To rivet, cut points off two standard roofing nails and insert in holes so that nailheads are on inside surface of shovel and at least 1/4 in. of shank protrudes on outside. Place panel over heel of anvil, as shown, and head with ball peen hammer. Roofing nails are soft enough to form secure rivets for use with sheet metal without heating.

6. Reheat flattened section and punch two small holes through it for riveting. Quench. Place shovel blade tightly against notch at end of flattened section and use these holes as guides to mark riveting holes in blade. Roofing nails can again be used. Insert them from inside shovel blade and head them cold on back. Apply 10- to 12-in. decorative twist to center of handle as shown at right. Twist poker handle to match.

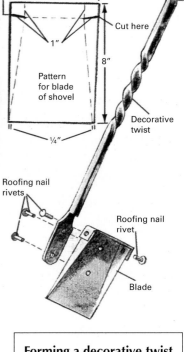

Cut here — Handle ring
6"
Cut here
1"
8"
Pattern for blade of shovel
Decorative twist
1/4"
Roofing nail rivets
Roofing nail rivet
Blade

Forming a decorative twist

Mark top and bottom of section to be twisted with cold chisel. Heat evenly to bright cherry red, then clamp bar in vise with jaws on lower mark. Grasp with tongs at top mark and apply steady pressure through one revolution (for a full twist) while keeping bar straight. Twist must be done in one heat, since it is very difficult to reheat and adjust.

Tongs and Log Holder Complete the Set

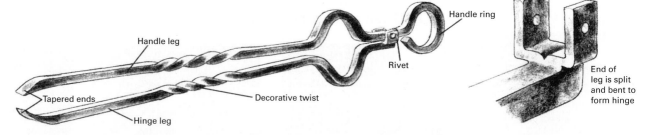

Handle leg

Handle ring

Rivet

Tapered ends

Decorative twist

Hinge leg

End of leg is split and bent to form hinge

First Forge Two Matching Legs for Tongs

1. Form handle leg of tongs first, then forge hinge leg to match. Make first bend on handle leg about 7 in. below ring base; on hinge leg about 1 ft. from end. Begin each bend by heating to cherry red (see *Color guides*, p.361); then forge rounded 60° angle over horn. Dress to maintain width.

2. Heat bar to cherry red 2 1/2-3 in. above peak of 60° bend toward handle of tongs. Dip first bend in water to harden it, then forge sharp reverse angle in bar over near edge of anvil face. When working on hinge leg, keep comparing it with handle leg to assure a good match.

3. Heat bar to cherry red 2-2 1/2 in. below 60° bend. Quench existing bends to preserve them; then forge sharp reverse bend, using horn of anvil as shown. Note that first arm of finished U-bend is longer than second so that legs of tongs will be slightly apart when they are closed.

4. Mark top of hinge leg even with base of handle ring. Then heat to orange at that spot and cut. Reheat and use chisel to make 1-in. split by cutting halfway through from one side; then turn and finish from the other. While some heat remains, pry open split with chisel.

5. Heat split end to cherry red and forge over far edge of anvil face so that both halves of split are bent back 90°, forming a pair of flattened wings. These will become hinge of tongs. Perform entire operation in one heat if possible to keep from burning thin wings of hinge.

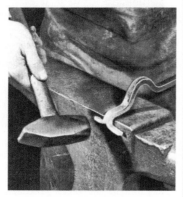

6. Reheat to bright cherry red. Quench just the face of flattened wings, then forge a perpendicular right-angle bend, as shown, as close as possible to point of split. Start bend by clamping flattened wings in vise and bending bar down, then finish by hammering over edge of anvil.

Then Join at the Pivot and Taper the Ends

1. Heat flattened wings to bright cherry red and place both legs of tongs together so that semicircles match; hold legs firmly, or use locking pliers or lock-grip tongs to secure them. Next, wrap flattened wings loosely around handle with tongs or pliers. Then hammer them into final shape. Quench in water without separating.

2. Heat both legs together at hinge until wings are bright cherry red, then punch in three steps: first, through one wing deep enough to mark shaft; then through other wing; finally, separate legs and punch through shaft as with poker (p.356). Rejoin legs and quench. Rivet as with poker; do not hammer rivet down too hard or it will prevent movement of tongs. Cut excess from wings with hacksaw.

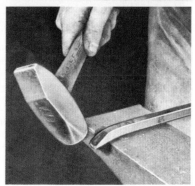

3. Measure tongs for length against poker; cut both legs evenly. Heat ends of legs to bright cherry red and taper to flat point, as with chisel (p.353), dressing sides to maintain width; bend chisel ends inward so they meet when tongs are closed. Quench. Apply decorative twist (p.357) halfway between end of each leg and U-bend. Make twists in opposite directions for more symmetrical appearance.

A Two-Hoop Log Holder

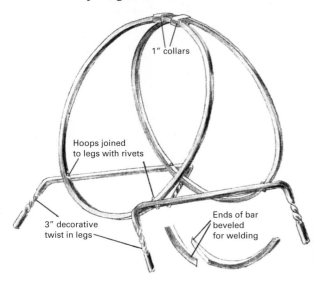

1" collars

Hoops joined
to legs with rivets

3" decorative
twist in legs

Ends of bar
beveled
for welding

Fireside log holder in style of matching fireplace tools requires welding. To make hoops measuring 3 ft. in diameter, you will need two 1/2-in.-sq. mild steel bars, each about 9 1/2 ft. long. Forge 3-in. bevels on the ends of both on opposite sides of bars (see *Fire Welding*, p.354). You will also need two 4-ft. bars for legs, a few inches of banding material for collaring, and enough 1/4-in. rod to make four rivets.

1. After bevels have been forged for welding, hoops are formed without heating. First, place two solid objects of equal height, such as cement block and anvil, about 15 in. apart. Lay bar across them with flat face of bevel vertical, and strike firmly with hammer. Move bar 6 in. and strike again. Continue to end of bar, then work back, striking between first blows.

2. Keep passing bar back and forth, striking at regular intervals until hoop is formed. (Job is easier if a helper holds end of bar.) As arc grows tighter, move blocks closer together. Check from time to time that circle is forming evenly, and correct any flat spots. When hoop is finished, beveled ends should overlap on flat plane as shown in drawing so that weld can be made flat on the anvil face.

3. Prepare clean fire in forge for welding (p.354). Overlap ends of hoop with beveled faces on top and bottom, not together; place in fire. Bring to cherry-red heat (see *Color guides*, p.361), then remove from fire and sprinkle flux evenly on both beveled surfaces. Commercially prepared fluxes are available, or use borax or a mixture of borax and clean sand. Replace in fire.

4. Bring slowly to white heat, turning occasionally to heat both beveled faces evenly. When welding heat has been reached, quickly spring one end over the other so beveled faces are joined; then place on anvil and weld with three hard blows (see *Fire Welding*, p.354). Dress weld with a series of short, sharp blows. Make second hoop the same way, using first as pattern.

Putting the Pieces Together

1. To make legs, form 90° bend 5-6 in. from each end of both 4-ft. bars; forge on anvil face or use hardie hole, as with rings (p.357). Apply 3-in. twist in each leg (see *Forming a decorative twist*, p.357)—vise shown is a hardie tool. Join hoops to legs with rivets, as with poker (p.356).

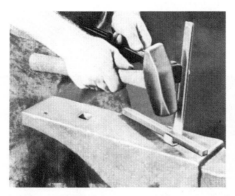

2. For collaring hoops use two short strips of 1/8- or 3/16-in. mild steel band about 1 in. wide. (A single band 2-3 in. wide can also be used but is hard to shape around arc.) First heat one end to cherry red, then forge into squared hook by bending around scrap piece of 1/2-in.-sq. bar.

3. Cut band, allowing enough material to form identical hook at other end. Heat band to bright cherry red and quench the hooked end. Force hoops together at top and hook band over one hoop as shown. Pull toward you with tongs, bend down sharply, and hammer corner square.

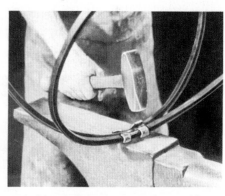

4. Bend band all the way around second hoop, hammering each corner square as you go and maintaining tension with tongs. Finally, place log holder on anvil and hammer band down from underneath. When quenched, heated band will shrink slightly to form tight joint.

Decorative Door Knocker Tests Your Skills

Blacksmithing is as much an art as it is a craft. The smith's artistry begins, of course, with his design for a piece; but even given the same design, no two smiths are likely to execute a job in exactly the same way. Each blow of the hammer is as personal an act as a painter's brushstroke. Each represents a creative decision.

To nail your own hand-forged knocker to your front door is to display both your craftsmanship and your creativity to the world. Consider the design well and give careful thought to all the steps involved in implementing it. Begin with sketches of the finished product, as you envision it, and graduate to a full-scale drawing. A model can be valuable too; bending a coat hanger with pliers, for example, gives some idea of what it will take to form the same shape from an iron bar.

The materials needed to make the knocker pictured at the right are one 20-in. length of 1/2-in.-sq. mild steel bar and one 4- by 10-in. piece of 1/4-in. mild steel plate.

Begin by shaping the knocker handle. First draw out both ends of the bar to 1/2-in. round pegs 1 in. long. You can do this by forging directly on the anvil face, but the job is more easily and neatly done by the use of top and bottom swages (Step 1). Unless you have three hands, however, you will need another person to help with the swaging operation. Heat the end of the bar to bright cherry red, position it in the bottom swage, place the top swage over it, and have your helper strike with a heavy hammer—a sledgehammer is best if you have one. Give the bar a quarter-turn and signal for another blow. Continue this way until the reduction is complete.

Next, heat one peg to cherry red and bend it 90° (Step 2); quench. Then heat the other peg and bend it in the opposite direction. When you have applied a half-twist (Step 3), the pegs will face the same way.

Shape one side of the ring first (Steps 4 and 5), quenching each bend to preserve it while you are working on the next one. Then shape the other side to match (Step 6). Dress the piece often on the anvil face to correct distortions and to maintain 1/2-in. thickness of bar. Finally, use a hacksaw or

Handmade knocker can be attached to door with hand-made nails, which are shown on page 355.

chisel to cut any overlap off the pegs. Hammer them so the ends meet flush.

Mark out the pattern for the doorplate with chalk or soapstone, and score the marks with a cold chisel. Cut the lower part of the pattern first by heating to cherry red and chiseling (Step 7). Forge the flares over the anvil horn (Step 8) and quench. Then cut out the top part of the pattern and punch the two nail holes. (If you are going to do any decorative work on the plate—cutting out a diamond, for example, or engraving initials—do it now.) Finally, bend the tab at the top of the plate around the top of the ring (Step 9), tipping it forward slightly so that the ring will hang loosely in front of the plate.

Mark pattern of doorplate with soapstone or chalk on 4- by 10-in. piece of 1/4-in. mild steel.

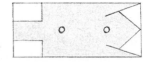

1. Swage ends of bar to 1/2-in. round pegs, or forge on anvil face.

2. Use pritchel hole to bend pegs 90° in opposite directions.

3. Heat 3-in. section in center of bar and apply half-twist (p.357).

4. Forge 90° bend over edge of anvil face, 11/2 in. from bent peg.

5. Forge arc over horn, quenching existing bends as you proceed.

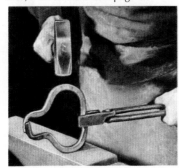

6. Repeat Steps 4 and 5 to shape other half of knocker handle.

7. To facilitate handling, cut out lower part of doorplate first.

8. Forge flares outward at cherry-red heat. Quench. Cut top and punch.

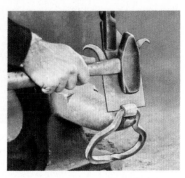

9. Form hinge at top of handle by bending tab down around pegs.

Tempering Carbon Steel

When iron is heated, the crystals that make up its structure expand, leaving spaces in their centers. When enough carbon is present in the iron to constitute carbon steel, and a certain critical temperature is reached, some of the carbon atoms are squeezed into these spaces. (You can find the critical temperature of steel with a magnet: when the crystals change form—usually at cherry red—the metal loses its magnetic attraction.) If the steel is quenched at this point, the crystals shrink, trapping carbon atoms inside and creating a condition of great stress. The steel is at its hardest and quite brittle; a sharp blow can crack it. If it is allowed to cool slowly, however, the atoms rearrange themselves to their least stressful relationship. The steel is annealed for softness.

To temper carbon steel, start by hardening it. Next, reheat it just enough to remove some stress, thus restoring a degree of flexibility. Then quench again.

To temper the chisel on page 353, for example, heat the cutting edge and 2 to 3 inches of the body to cherry red, then quench the cutting edge about 1 inch deep in water until the glow fades from the body. Now, quickly polish the beveled face with a file. Watch carefully; as the reserve heat still in the body moves downward, its progress will be marked by bands of colors as shown at right. Each indicates a degree of tempering. When the desired color (in this case full blue) touches the cutting edge, plunge the tool into the water and move it back and forth to ensure even cooling. The colors will remain.

A thin knife blade can be tempered by resting its back on a piece of blood-red iron. The spectrum will move upward toward the knife edge. Quench at dark straw or bronze. Quenching in oil rather than water is usually better for thin pieces because the cooling occurs more slowly, minimizing the danger of warping and cracking.

Caution: When quenching in oil, there is danger of a "flashback," or surface flame-up. Always submerge the heated metal entirely, and always have a lid handy with which to smother the flame.

Color guides

White
2500°F

Yellow
2000°F

Orange
1800°F

Bright cherry red
1600°F

Cherry red
1400°F

Blood red
1200°F

Dark red
1000°F

Incandescent color spectrum for forging iron and steel is best seen in semidarkness.

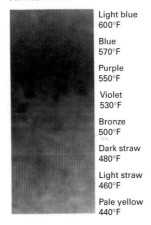

Light blue
600°F

Blue
570°F

Purple
550°F

Violet
530°F

Bronze
500°F

Dark straw
480°F

Light straw
460°F

Pale yellow
440°F

Oxidation color spectrum, a guide to tempering, appears on surface of polished steel.

Sources and resources

Books

Abraham, Fern-Rae. *Tin Craft: A Workbook.* Santa Fe, N.M.: Sunstone Press, 1994.

Austin, Catherine. *Making Country Classic Tinware.* New York: Sterling Publishing, 1993.

Bealer, Alex W. *The Art of Blacksmithing.* Edison, N.J.: Book Sales, 1995.

Blandford, Percy W. *Practical Blacksmithing and Metal Working.* New York: McGraw-Hill, 1988.

Handberg, Ejner. *Shop Drawings of Shaker Iron and Tinware.* Lee, Mass.: Berkshire House Pub., 1993.

Richardson, M.T. *Practical Blacksmithing.* Avenal, N.J.: Random House Value, 1991.

Untracht, Oppi. *Metal Techniques for Craftsmen.* New York: Doubleday, 1968.

Vosburgh, H.K. *The Tinsmith's Helper and Pattern Book.* Mendham, N.J.: Astragal Press, 1994.

Watson, Aldren A. *Blacksmith: Iron Worker and Farrier.* New York: W.W. Norton, 1990.

Working With Metal. Alexandria, Va.: Time-Life Books, 1990.

Kathy Henebery, Farrier

Shoeing Horses: Bread and Butter For the Blacksmith

"I started being a blacksmith mainly so I could shoe my own horses. I got my first horse at 11, and I had six by the time I was 16. My parents weren't too happy about my decision to become a farrier. They said: 'Why don't you go to college first, and then be a blacksmith?' But I graduated high school early and went to farrier's school in Phoenix, New York, a small town outside Syracuse. Now I've been a blacksmith for six years, and my parents can tell I'm serious. They're a lot happier about it.

"Shoeing horses is hard work, something you really have to build yourself up to physically. At first, I could only do one horse a day; now I usually do seven or eight. The muscles have really developed in my arms and back—but I don't find it unfeminine. It really doesn't alter you that much.

"I haven't found much comment because I'm a woman—not among horse people. If you do the job well, they don't care who you are. Anyway, I think that women have a better way with animals. Honestly, sometimes I've had horses that no blacksmith has been able to get shoes on. When I begin to work on them, they just behave like pussycats. Of course, you've always got to be aware of everything when you're shoeing horses—after a while you develop a sixth sense about what's coming. I've never been kicked. All I've ever gotten is a few scratches when I've driven a nail through a hoof and the horse has withdrawn his foot.

"To tell the truth, owners can be more of a problem than the horses. If you have to tap a horse to get him to move, they get all upset that you're mistreating their pet. I sometimes get rid of them while I'm working-tell them to go have a cup of coffee or something. They usually understand.

"Shoeing horses is almost like performing surgery. It should definitely be left to a pro. The most important part is trimming the hooves correctly. If you leave a spot too high or too low, the shoe won't fit and the horse won't be able to walk properly. It's also important to get the nails in right. If you drive the nail too far to the outside, you can break the wall of the hoof, and if you drive it in too far, you can lame the horse for life. Also, horses can have the same kinds of foot problems people have; they can be pigeon-toed or have their feet hit one another when they walk. You try to fix those things with corrective shoeing.

"I like working with iron, shaping the shoes. I feel like it's a chance for me to be creative in solving each horse's problems. And I like to study the finished job. No job is like any other, and I don't think you ever do a perfect job of shoeing. I look for tiny mistakes and I correct them next time.

"Sometimes I do artwork on the forge, making tables and lamps out of horseshoes, but I have to be in a special mood. I couldn't do that all the time. It's not like shoeing horses—that I can do seven days a week."

Shaping horse shoes is an art and a science. Kathy Henebery, of Salt Point, New York, earns her living as a farrier—a blacksmith who specializes in shoeing horses.

Stenciling

Cutouts and Colors To Brighten the Home

The art of stenciling—reproducing a design by painting over a cutout pattern—flourished in America during the 18th and 19th centuries, primarily in rural New England and among the Pennsylvania Dutch. Although "fancy painting," as stenciling was called, went into a decline in the late 1800s, it is becoming popular again. Stencils provide the means by which everybody—even someone with little artistic talent or sophistication—can create imaginative, attractive decorations for walls, floors, and furniture.

Wall stenciling can be as simple or ornate as you like. To create a "weathered" look like this, use a sponge to dab paint over the stencil, being careful not to fill it in entirely. To avoid drips, squeeze the sponge to get rid of excess paint before using. Remember when cutting a stencil to leave "bridges" between parts—uncut sections that will hold the stencil together (once you remove the stencil you can fill in these sections with a paint brush). Use masking tape or drafting tape to secure the stencil to the wall.

To see beautiful examples of traditionally stenciled walls, visit the so-called Stencil House in Shelburne Museum in Vermont. The walls in the cottage, which was moved from its original location in Columbus, New York, convey the charm and innocence of a quieter, more gracious age. Such stenciling was usually the work of itinerant artists who traveled from town to town with their paints and stencils. Most of these artists had distinctive styles, and the territories they covered can sometimes be traced from samples of their work that are still in existence.

Stenciling was in vogue in New England during the early 1800s; motifs shown above are typical of the period. By repeating individual designs, the effect of wallpaper can be achieved.

Tradition and Technique in Stencil Design

Early American wall stenciling usually took the form of vertical and horizontal borders arranged to give the effect of paneling. Later, as wallpaper from France became popular among the well-to-do, stencils were applied in broad area designs in imitation of the new and costly product. Fruit, stars, American eagles, and delicate semiabstract flowers were among the most popular motifs. Many traditional patterns can be seen at historic sites and museums in New England. Most of these designs have been reproduced in books on stenciling.

When designing your own stencils, remember that the outline is the most important element. It should be strong and attractive as an abstract shape and easy to recognize if it represents an object. Also bear in mind that details inside the outline must either be supported by ties (strips of stenciling material that hold the stencil together) or else applied with a second stencil.

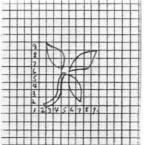   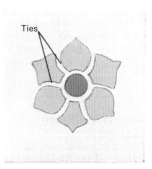

To enlarge a design draw an evenly spaced grid over it. Then make a second, larger grid on a separate piece of paper, and use it to sketch in the same design by following the pattern in each square of the smaller grid. The size of the new design will be larger than the original in proportion to the increase in grid size. Designs can also be enlarged by photocopying methods.

To convert a line drawing into a stencil, determine the outline and expand the major structural lines to a width of 1/8 in. Make sure that each line, or tie, connects to the outline to hold the stencil together. Intricate outlines and long, thin shapes, such as flower stems, should be broken up by ties into smaller areas so that the stencil does not warp when painted.

Stenciling Materials and How to Cut Them

Stencil board (oaktag) and waxed stencil paper are the standard stenciling mediums, but any stiff plastic, paper, or board resistant to water can be used. Stencil paper is best for intricate designs that will only be used a few times. Stencil board is more difficult to cut but much more durable; use it for simple repetitive designs. Architect's linen, a strong, flexible substance, makes a durable stencil. For floor stenciling and simple designs, .005-gauge acetate can be used.

Except in the case of architect's linen, use a craft or utility knife for all stencil cutting. It is important to keep the blade keen either by sharpening it frequently or replacing the blade as soon as it fails to cut smoothly.

To cut stencils, hold a craft knife so that it is almost perpendicular and apply enough downward pressure to make a clean cut. Use your free hand to keep the stencil and design flat and prevent them from moving.

Architect's linen can be cut into very intricate designs with fine manicure scissors.

To cut a stencil from a transparent or semitransparent medium, lay the design on a piece of heavy cardboard and tape the stencil material over it. Allow at least a 2-inch margin around the design. Cut toward yourself, shifting the cardboard and design as needed to maintain a comfortable cutting direction. If you are working with stencil board, you will have to transfer the design by retracing the outline over carbon paper before cutting it. After the design is cut, trim any ragged lines so that they are perfectly smooth. Pay particular attention to corners: scraps or uncut paper often cling there.

Broken or cut ties can be repaired with a strip of masking tape. Apply the tape to the top surface of the stencil, then turn the stencil over and carefully trim the excess tape from the backside with a craft knife. (Do not bend the extra tape over.)

Applying Multicolored Designs

For complex motifs in which colors overlap or meet, make a different stencil for each overlapping or abutting color. If designed carefully, this method will eliminate the need for stencil ties.

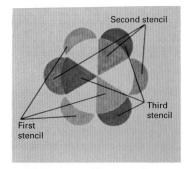

First stencil
Second stencil
Third stencil

When cutting stencils for multicolor work, allow a 1/8-in. overlap between colors that meet in order to get a neater join. Paint in light-colored areas first; overlapping dark colors will mask them out.

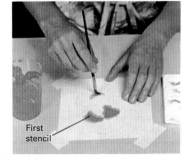

First stencil

Paints, Brushes, and Brushwork

Homemade milk paint (see *Household Recipes*, p.343) gives a soft, authentic touch to traditional wall and furniture stenciling. Japan colors, used by sign painters, are available in many of the traditional muted stenciling shades. These paints are fast drying, an advantage since the risk of smudging is lessened; however, they should not be used with stencils made of architect's linen. Acrylic paints come in a wide range of colors, dry quickly, and are easy to use. They make bold, sharp images that are suited to modern designs. Latex and oil paints dry slowly and tend to smudge.

Whenever possible, stenciling paint should have the consistency of thick pea soup. For a faded effect add a little white pigment. To soften a color, mix in raw umber. The best brushes for most stencil work are

stencil brushes or glue brushes; they have thick bundles of soft squared-off bristles. You can also wrap a piece of velour or other soft material around your finger and use it as a brush to produce lighter variegated effects.

Before you try stenciling walls, floors, or furniture, first experiment with different color combinations on scrap paper. Once the colors are chosen, position the first cutout on the surface to be stenciled and tape it firmly in place with masking tape. You can now brush on the paint. Use very small quantities to prevent running and to obtain clear outlines and an even texture. Each time you dip the brush, dab it on newspaper afterward to remove excess paint. Clean the stencils regularly during use so that paint does not build up around the edges, spoiling the outline.

Small cutouts allow alignment of stencils when opaque stenciling material is used. To make cutouts, trace outline of first stencil on second. Snip out triangles along outline just inside it. Points of triangles should face inward.

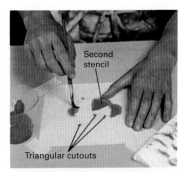

Second stencil
Triangular cutouts

Several stencils can be applied, one after the other, each in a different color. Quick drying paints, such as japan colors, are useful for this work, since the previous coloring must be dry before a new stencil is applied.

Third stencil

When painting the outline of a design, apply only a little paint and brush from the outside toward the center of each cutout area. Press down on the surrounding stencil to give a crisp, clear outline. Then fill in the center of the design. Brush gently across small cutout areas.

Antique effects and delicate shading can be created by wrapping a piece of velour or similar soft fabric around your index finger. Dip the material in the paint, dab dry, then wipe gently across the cutout areas. Alternatively, use a 1- by 1- by 6-in. strip of sponge as a paintbrush.

Decorating Your Home Floor to Ceiling

Start by measuring the piece of furniture carefully so you can draw full-scale patterns of the parts to be stenciled. This will allow you to plan the border stencils and to experiment with arrangements and colors. Plan the entire border before cutting any stencils, since border stencils should be designed and spaced so that the pattern either ends or turns neatly at each corner. One attractive way to turn a corner is to design a special corner motif or arrangement. If your border patterns are large and detached, space them evenly between corners by measuring with a ruler.

Before stenciling, make sure the surface is clean and dry. If the surface is smooth and shiny, use japan colors, since most other paints will not adhere to slick surfaces. After stenciling, you can either apply a transparent finish, such as shellac to seal and preserve the stenciled colors, or you can allow the paintwork and stenciling to age naturally to create a more antique look.

A Chest of Drawers, Yankee Style

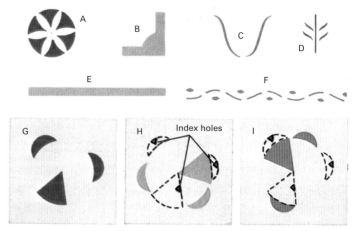

Paint the chest with two coats of dull yellow paint. Apply stencil F down each side of the chest front. Measure and mark the front and sides of the base to ensure that stencils will form a complete motif at each corner, then apply stencil C. When the paint is dry, apply stencil D. Remove the drawers and apply corner stencil (B) and border stencil (E) to each edge. Use stencil A around each handle, then apply stencils G, H, and I in sequence. Finish by painting the knobs.

Pennsylvania Dutch Dower Chest

Any low chest or blanket box can be decorated. After the chest is measured, stencils cut, and colors selected, you should stencil the borders. Start by applying stencil G in the two lower corners of each panel, followed by the border stencil (F) and panel head (H). Next apply the sunburst designs (D and E) with several coats in a contrasting light color on the panel head and a contrasting dark color along the top of the panel. Now apply stencils A, B, and C in sequence in the middle of each panel. Be sure to let the paint dry before applying an overlapping stencil.

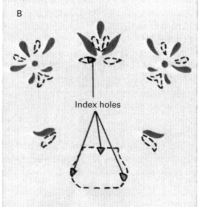

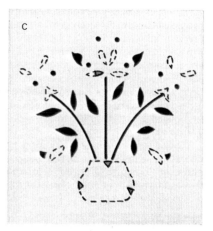

Stenciling Walls and Floors

When planning wall or floor stenciling, start by studying the room to decide which features you want to emphasize and what atmosphere you wish to create. If the room has a number of windows and doors, a simple border around each opening will help create a sense of unity. If there are large blank wall areas, an interestingly patterned design will help relieve the monotony of the open spaces. High points and special features in a room, such as a fireplace or sloping wall, can be set off by one or two large designs; for example, a vase of flowers over a mantelpiece or a geometric canopy design for a sloping ceiling over a bed.

Repetitive patterns with a strong geometric theme are often used for floor stenciling, but almost any design that is suitable for walls will also work on the floor. Broad, open patterns or simple repetitive designs, like those shown below, were popular in post-revolutionary homes. Many motifs suggest tiling or carpeting.

For wall stenciling, select designs that balance each other—one strong and heavy against another that is light and delicate. Bold designs, when repeated, stand out and attract attention; delicate designs, spaced to form an open lattice, retreat and create a passive, restful atmosphere. Designs applied on white walls tend to stand out strongly. The effect can be moderated by mixing a few drops of one of the main colors in the design into the white background paint. If you are mixing your own colors, make plenty of each in individual jars or plastic containers so that you do not have to remix and match the colors later on.

Once you have developed a scale plan of your design, mark out vertical and horizontal guidelines with chalk to help you keep the stencils in alignment. For a full traditional design apply the frieze border (top design) first, followed by the vertical designs, and then the surbase (lower horizontal motif) or base along the foot of the wall. The final step is to measure out the spacing and apply the separate panel designs.

For floor stenciling, simple patterns applied in black oil or japan paint over a varnished floor will produce a subtle hand-painted effect. Usually, floor stencils are applied on a base coat of off-white deck or patio paint. Both these paints wear well but are slow drying. If you use them, remember that you will not be able to walk on the floor for two to three days. One way around this problem is to apply the design in two sections so that one can be used while the other is drying. Apply one to two coats of paint, then when the floor is dry, mark it with chalked guidelines. You can stencil your designs with a paint roller or glue brush. Acetate is a good material for floor stencils, since it stands up well under repeated use; stencil board can also be used. Transparent varnish, either natural or synthetic, is often applied over a stenciled floor to preserve it.

To position stencils accurately, establish verticals and horizontals with a weighted plumb line and mark with chalk or else measure carefully using room corners as reference. An easy way to make a chalk line is to tack a chalked string so it is taut, then pluck it.

Traditional wall designs often included frieze and surbase borders that ran around the top and middle of the walls. Vertical lines of design broke the walls into separate panels in which large, individually stenciled designs were applied.

Another popular technique was to apply stencils as simple borders outlining the features of a room with or without a field pattern of larger stencils. For the floor a pattern of many interlocking stencils suggested a tile or carpet design.

Borders are the trickiest part of wall stenciling. Use one motif as a guide for the next. Either stop pattern before corner or make a duplicate stencil and cut it to fit the corner exactly. The stencil can be taped together and used again.

1. Use previously stenciled unit as a guide to align the stencil as you proceed around the border

2. Corner of border can be turned by interrupting pattern before corner is reached, resuming it on other side of corner at an equal distance away. Spacing variations from one corner of room to another may result

3. Best way to turn corner is by continuing pattern without interruption. When corner is reached, simply cut stencil to fit corner exactly

Sources and resources

Books
Grafton, Carol, ed. *Authentic Victorian Stencil Designs*. New York: Dover, 1982.
Hall, Katrina, and Llewelyn-Bwen, Lawrence. *Decorative Workshop: Stenciling*. New York: M. Friedman Publishing Group, 1995.
St. George, Amelia, and David, Penny. *The Stencil Book*. New York: NAL-Dutton, 1989.
Stencil It! Book and Kit. New York: Sterling Publishing, 1993.
Waring, Janet. *Early American Stencils on Walls and Furniture*. New York: Dover, 1968.

Flower Drying and Pressed Flowers

Preserving the Beauty Of Summer's Blossoms

Natural beauty of flowers in full bloom can be preserved indefinitely with only a modest expenditure of time and effort.

A Homemade Flower Press

A simple, inexpensive flower press can be made from two 12-inch-square pieces of 1/2-inch-thick plywood, four 3-inch bolts with wing nuts, six pieces of cardboard, and 12 sheets of blotting paper. Flowers can be put in the press along with leaves and stems, but be sure to keep them on separate sheets of blotting paper. The petals of bulky flowers, such as roses and peonies, should be removed and pressed individually. If the flower has a thick center, flatten it with your thumb before putting it in the press.

Arrange compatible plant parts on a sheet of blotting paper, and cover with a second sheet. Place a piece of cardboard on top, then arrange additional layers in the same way. Put the stack between the two pieces of plywood, insert bolts, and tighten wing nuts firmly. Leave press in a warm, dry place for about four weeks.

The colorful blooms of spring and summer need not fade with the passing season; instead, they can be gathered and preserved for year-round pleasure. Almost every type of plant can be preserved—from the most delicate flower to the hardiest grain and shrub—either by pressing, air drying, or using a drying agent.

Proper harvesting is the key to rich, bright, long-lasting colors. Ideally, flowers should be

How to Dry Flowers

Because of differences in structure and texture, the leaves and stems of plants usually must be dried separately from the flowering parts. The three basic ways to dry plants are hanging (air drying), impregnating with a glycerine solution, and burying in a granular desiccant, or drying agent.

Hanging is the easiest method and requires no special equipment. It is most successful with flowers that have tiny clustered petals, such as baby's breath and goldenrod. Tie the stems of a small bunch together with twine, hang them with their heads down in a warm, dry, dark place for three to four weeks.

Grasses and leaves dry best when their stems are placed in a solution of one part glycerine and two parts very hot water. (If there is bark on the stem, strip it away until about 4 inches of the stem is bare.) Split the ends, and stand the plants in 4 inches of solution. Remove them when their colors start to change and all brittleness has disappeared—usually within one to three weeks.

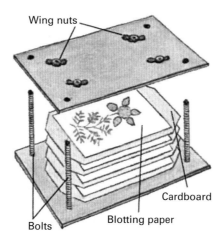

A simple press is all that is needed to preserve flowers for decorative purposes.

Labels: Wing nuts, Cardboard, Blotting paper, Bolts

gathered when the weather is dry, just before the peak of bloom. If an extended run of inclement weather forces you to cut the flowers while they are wet, blot away the moisture with absorbent tissues to prevent mold from forming.

Dried flowers lend themselves to a number of uses, including flower arrangements, pictures made of pressed flowers, and decorations on stationery, bookmarks, and greeting cards.

For such large, delicately petaled flowers as roses, carnations, and peonies, granular desiccants produce the best results. Three standard desiccants are perlite, silica gel, and borax mixed with cornmeal or sand. Spread an inch or two of the desiccant on the bottom of a box and lay the flowers on it. Then cover the flowers thoroughly with more desiccant, making sure to fill spaces between petals. The treatment takes two to four days.

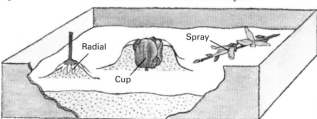

Labels: Spray, Radial, Cup

Position flowers according to shape when using desiccants—faceup for cups, facedown for radial shapes, flat for sprays.

Different methods for different plants

Air drying	Drying agent	Pressing
Amaranth	Azalea	Beech leaves
Artemisia	Carnation	Bluebell
Baby's breath	Chrysanthemum	Ferns
Butterfly weed	Daffodil	Galax
Celosia	Dahlia	Ginkgo
Chinese lantern	Daisy	Hickory leaves
Cockscomb	Dogwood blossom	Liriope leaves
Feverfew	Geranium	Maple leaves
Goldenrod	Larkspur	Oak leaves
Heather	Lilac	Pansy
Hydrangea	Peony	Poppy
Scotch broom	Rose	Rose leaves
Sumac	Snapdragon	Violet
Yarrow	Zinnia	Vitex leaves

Gourd Craft

Ready-made Pottery Growing on the Vine

There are two types of gourds—ornamentals and lagenarias. Ornamentals are soft skinned and have brightly colored patterns of orange, green, and yellow. Lagenarias, also called hard shells or calabashes, dry to a natural yellow or tan.

Gourds can be cultivated in much the same way as squash and pumpkins. Plant the seeds in a sunny, well-drained area and provide a trellis for the vines. When the stems become dry, the gourds are ready to be picked and cured. Ornamentals can simply be waxed and polished, but hard shells must be scraped and cleaned.

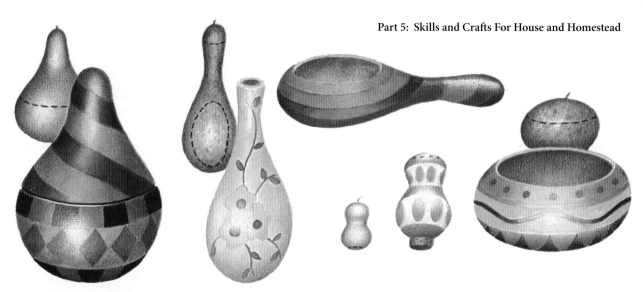

Let the form of the gourd suggest its function when creating gourd containers. The names of the gourds, derived from their shapes, include bottle, club, dumbbell, penguin, and ball. Uncured hard shells have an outer skin and crust that must be removed before they can be crafted. Decorations depend on personal taste and range from simple polishing and waxing to intricate carvings and appliqués. Gourds are vulnerable to cracking, but with care they can last for years.

Prepare ornamental gourds by letting them dry for several days after picking; then use steel wool to remove waxy outer layer.

Sources and resources

Books

Bauzen, Peter, and Suzanne Bauzen. *Flower Pressing*. New York: Sterling Publishing, 1982.

Hamel, Esther. *Creativity With Gourds*. Colorado Springs, Colo.: Ponderosa, 1977.

Laking, Barbara, ed. *Dried Flower Designs*. New York: Brooklyn Botanic Gardens, 1989.

Mierhof, Annette. *The Dried Flower Book: Growing, Picking, Drying, Arranging*. New York: Dutton, 1981.

Curing and Carving Hard-Shell Gourds

Hard-shell gourds require preliminary preparation before they can be cut open and made into utensils. The first step is to remove the outer skin. Once this is accomplished, the gourd will dry out rapidly. Start by wrapping the gourd in a towel soaked with a solution of liquid household cleanser. After several hours, when the outer skin is softened, remove the towel, scrape the outer skin off the gourd, and place the gourd in a warm, dry location for several days or until it is thoroughly dry.

There are no restrictions, other than your own ingenuity, on how you cut and decorate a gourd. The tools needed for cutting and carving hard shells include a fine-toothed saw (a hacksaw will serve the purpose), a knife with a sharp tip, a metal cooking spoon or spatula for scraping, steel wool, and sandpaper. (For more sophisticated work use a hobbyist's drill with interchangeable saw, sanding cylinder, ball tip, and buffer.)

When you have decided what you want to make (tureen, ladle, planter, sugar bowl, scoop, birdhouse) draw a cutting line in pencil on the gourd. Carefully saw along the line until the gourd is cut through, then remove the pulp and seeds. If some fibers cling to the inside, soak them with water and scrub them off with steel wool. If the gourd is to hold food or liquids, waterproof its inner surface with paraffin. Gourds can be decorated with carvings, appliqués, paints, and stains or left unadorned and simply coated with lacquer.

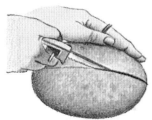

To cut open a gourd, first draw the cutting line in pencil. Start the opening by puncturing one spot with a pointed object, then continue cutting with a fine-toothed saw. If the skin feels resistant, exert steady pressure on the saw.

Remove pulp and seeds with scraper, and scrub insides with steel wool. If the shape of the gourd makes it difficult to scrape (for example, a long narrow gourd to be used as a vase), fill it with water for a few hours, then scrape out with a hooked wire.

Before decorating a gourd, draw the pattern on the shell with a pencil. Almost any type of paint or stain can be used. The design can be carved with an engraving tool or sharp knife. Finish by applying a coat of shellac or lacquer over the entire shell.

Soapmaking

A Simple Miracle To Perform Yourself In Your Kitchen

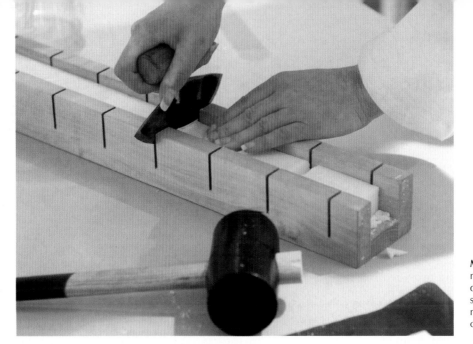

Making soap can be very simple or more involved depending on the desired product. For very evenly shaped and sized bars, a basic mold with slits like this one can be constructed.

According to Roman legend, soap was discovered after a heavy rain fell on the slopes of Mount Sapo (the name means "Mount Soap" in Latin). The hill was the site of an important sacrificial altar, and the rainwater mixed with the mingled ashes and animal fat around the altar's base. As a result of this fortuitous coincidence, the three key components of soap were brought together: water, fat, and lye (potash leached from the ashes). As the mixture trickled down to the banks of the Tiber River, washerwomen at work there noticed that the mysterious substance made their job easier and the wash cleaner.

Over the centuries the basics of soapmaking have remained essentially unchanged from the Roman prescription. To this day in parts of rural America soap is being made much as it was in ancient Rome: out of potash, rainwater, and animal tallow. Even commercial soap is manufactured by much the same process. Other than obvious differences in the scale of the operation and the use of automated equipment, the chief innovations in the commercial product are the substitution of sodium hydroxide for potash and the use of a variety of vegetable oils as supplements to the animal fats.

Homemade soaps can duplicate or improve on the commercial product, usually at considerably less cost. Scents, coloring agents, and decorative effects are all within the scope of home soapmakers who also have the advantage of knowing exactly what ingredients are in the soaps that they produce. The result is that more and more people are trying their hand at making soap, often experimenting with ingredients to devise their own favorite blends.

One Substance, Many Varieties

Although, by definition, every soap is made by the saponification (chemical combination) of lye, water, and fat, one soap will differ from the next depending on the kind of fat, the kind of lye, and how much of each is used. Lye made from wood ash, for example, produces soft soap, so-called because of its jellylike consistency. In contrast, soap made from commercial lye (sodium hydroxide) will be hard. Soaps containing coconut oil tend to lather well in cold water but may have a drying action on the skin. Superfatted soaps, such as castile, that contain excess amounts of unsaponified fat are particularly gentle and make excellent toilet soap.

For the sake of convenience or for some special use, soap can be altered in consistency and appearance. Jellied soap for doing the dishes is obtained by slicing off shavings of hard soap and boiling them in water until they dissolve; about 1 pound of shavings per gallon of water should be used. To produce soap flakes for laundry use, simply grate any ordinary hard soap, then add a few tablespoons of borax to improve water softening ability and quicken sudsing action. The preparation of liquid soap is somewhat more complicated. It is generally based on vegetable oils rather than animal fats and requires the addition of glycerine and alcohol during the soap-making process, followed by filtering. If you want soap that floats, gently whip the warm soap solution with an egg beater just before pouring it into molds; when the soap hardens, the trapped air bubbles will make it float.

Some plants are natural cleaners

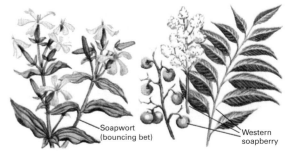

Soapwort (bouncing bet)

Western soapberry

American Indians and early settlers were familiar with a number of plants whose roots, leaves, or berries contain saponin, a natural ingredient that foams and cleans like soap. The best known and most frequently used of these plants is soapwort, or bouncing bet, a pink-blossomed perennial that grows wild throughout most of the United States; the juice from the root produces a lather when mixed with water. Another soap plant is the yucca found in Mexico and the Southwest. Its roots, broken into pieces and mixed with water, form a gentle soaplike compound for the skin and hair. California soap root, a member of the lily family, contains a liquid in the middle of its bulb that makes an excellent antidandruff shampoo; simply crush the bulb center and mix it with water. The fleshy berries of both the southern soapberry tree, found in southern Florida as well as South America, and the western soapberry tree of the American Southwest contain seeds that produce lather in water and closely duplicate the cleansing action of soap.

The Basics Are the Same No Matter What the Soap

The three ingredients needed to make soap—fat, water, and lye—are all readily available. Lye in the form of sodium hydroxide is sold as dry crystals in many supermarkets and hardware stores, while lye in the form of potash can be made at home from wood ash (see p.370). Because all types of lye are highly caustic substances that react with plastic, aluminum, and tin, soapmaking utensils should be made of wood, glass, enamel, stainless steel, or ceramic. Fat for soapmaking can be almost any pure animal or vegetable oil from reclaimed kitchen grease to castor oil. (See *Rendering and Clarifying*, p.370, for more information.) The water should be soft. If you are in a hard water area, treat the water with a commercial softener or add a few tablespoons of borax to it. You can also collect rainwater and use it to make soap. The following equipment is needed for soapmaking:

1. A container to hold the lye solution. A 2-quart juice bottle will do. Punch two holes in the cover, one on the opposite side from the other, so you will be able to pour the lye over the fat later on.
2. A 10- to 12-quart pot to hold the fat and lye.
3. A wooden spoon to stir the lye solution and fat.
4. A candy or dairy thermometer that is accurate to within 1°F in the 80°F to 120°F range. For convenience you may want to have two such thermometers.
5. Rubber gloves. Wear these as a precautionary measure, since lye will burn if it touches the skin.
6. Molds for the soap. Prepare the molds by lining them with plastic or greasing them with Vaseline.
7. Insulation to keep the soap warm after it is poured into the molds. Cardboard, styrofoam, or an ordinary blanket can be used.

8. Enough newspapers to cover work surfaces and floor areas where you will be working.

Prepare the lye solution before beginning the soapmaking process so that it will have a chance to cool. To make the lye solution, pour cold water into an enamelware pot, then add the lye slowly while stirring the solution steadily with a wooden spoon. The reaction between the lye crystals and water will generate temperatures over 200°F. The container can be placed in a basin of cold water to hasten cooling. Once the solution has cooled, pour it carefully into the 2-quart glass container. If you are going to use animal fat for your soap, you should also prepare it in advance to allow it to cool down (the rendering process takes place at well above the temperatures needed to make soap). Fats can be refrigerated and then brought to soapmaking temperature by warming in a basin of hot water. The type of fat you should use and the relative amounts of fat, lye, and water that should be combined depend on the particular type of soap being made. The standard recipe calls for 6 pounds of beef fat, 2 1/2 pints of water, and 13 ounces of lye crystals. (See p.371 for other recipes).

Saponification is the chemical process by which soap is formed from lye, water, and fat. In order for saponification to take place, the temperature of the lye solution and fat has to be carefully controlled. The simplest method is to bring both the lye and the fat to a temperature of 95°F to 98°F before mixing them together. Some experts recommend that the fat be at a higher temperature than the lye: about 125°F for the fat and 93°F for the lye when beef tallow is used, 83°F and 73°F when lard is used, 105°F and 83°F for half lard, half tallow.

Occasionally, saponification does not take place and the soap mixture separates into a top layer of fat and a bottom layer of lye solution. Generally, the mixture can be reclaimed by heating it to about 140°F while gently stirring with the wooden spoon. Then remove from the heat and keep stirring until the mixture thickens into soap. To test your soap solution, spoon up a bit and let a few drops fall on the surface of the soap; if the surface supports the drops for a moment or two, the soap is ready for the molds.

Caution: Lye is highly caustic and should be washed off immediately with cold water if it comes in contact with the skin. Avert your face to avoid inhaling the fumes while mixing lye. Always mix lye with cold water, and pour the lye into the water rather than the water into the lye.

The single bar method

If you want to experiment with a variety of scents, colors, and ingredients, the simplest and most economical way is to prepare a single bar of soap rather than a large batch. You will need the following ingredients:

1/2 cup cold soft water	1 cup melted beef tallow
2 heaping tbsp. commercial lye	

Slowly add the lye to the water, then bring both lye solution and tallow to about body temperature. Combine the two in a glass bowl and mix slowly and steadily with an egg beater until the consistency is that of sour cream. Pour mixture into mold and age according to standard procedure.

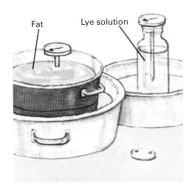

1. Bring both fat and lye solution to between 95°F and 98°F by placing their containers in basins of hot or cold water, depending on whether they need to be warmed or cooled.

2. To ensure thorough mixing, stir the fat before the lye is added. Pour in the lye solution in a steady stream while continuing to stir with an even, circular motion.

3. The mixture will turn opaque and brownish, then lighten. Soap is ready when its surface can support a drop of mixture for a moment; consistency should be like sour cream.

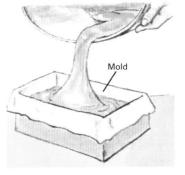

4. Add colorants, scents, and other special ingredients (adding them earlier would probably have interfered with saponification). Pour liquid into molds and place in warm location.

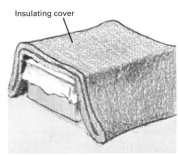

5. Cover molds with cardboard, styrofoam, or blankets. Soap should be removed from the molds after 24 hours, then left uncovered in freely circulating air for two to four weeks.

From Humble Origins Of Fat and Potash Come Fancy Soaps

Dried fruit or flowers can be pressed into soap while it's hardening for a decorative and aromatic touch.

Making Your Own Lye the Old-time Way

From pioneer times to the present the traditional way to make lye has been to leach it from wood ashes. Lye produced in this manner is known as potash and consists mostly of potassium carbonate, a less caustic substance than commercial lye. Any large wooden container can be used for the lye-making process—the bigger the better, since the more ashes the water seeps through, the more concentrated will be the lye solution. A barrel or large tub with a hole drilled as near to the bottom as possible is excellent for leaching.

Place the barrel on cinder blocks or other supports so that a crock or enamel pot can be placed beneath it to collect the solution as it seeps out. Set up the barrel at an angle, with the opening at the lowest point, so that the lye will run out of it and into the crock. Line the bottom of the barrel with straw to prevent ashes from sifting into the lye solution and pack the barrel with ashes—almost any hardwood will do, but oak, hickory,

Rendering and Clarifying

Any animal fat and most vegetable oils can be used in soapmaking. A combination of rendered beef fat (tallow) plus pig fat (lard) makes a most satisfactory basic soap and is the mixture most commonly recommended in books, pamphlets, and by manufacturers of lye. Poultry fat alone is too soft but may be used in combination with other fats, and so can most vegetable oils. Coconut oil produces high-quality kitchen and toilet soaps, while palm oil soap is gentle and pleasant smelling. Soy bean, cottonseed, corn, and peanut oils all yield low-foaming, medium-quality soap. The whitest, best-smelling soaps are made from pure rendered fats and oils. However, reclaimed kitchen grease and drippings from the frying pan if properly treated make good soaps.

Rendering is the process of melting and purifying solid fats. Start with twice the weight of fat called for in the soap recipe. Cut the fat into small pieces, and heat over a low flame. Do not let the fat burn or smoke. Although most of the fat will liquify, solid particles called cracklings will remain. After rendering, strain the liquid into a clean container and refrigerate until it is needed.

Grease and drippings can be reclaimed for soapmaking by clarifying them. Place the fat, an equal amount of water, and 2 tablespoons of salt in a pan and bring to a boil. Remove from the fire, cool slightly, and add cold water—about 1 quart per gallon of hot liquid. The mixture will separate into three layers: pure fat at the top, fat with granular impurities next, and water at the bottom. Spoon off the pure fat and save it for soapmaking. Even if the unclarified drippings were rancid, they can

be rescued by using a mixture of one part vinegar to five parts water in the clarifying process instead of plain water. To deodorize fat, cook sliced-up potatoes in the clarified fat. Use one potato for each 3 pounds of fat. To bleach fat, mix it with a solution of potassium permanganate, a powerful oxidizing and bleaching agent; then warm and stir. Use 1 pint of solution for each pound of fat. To make a pint of solution, dissolve a few crystals of potassium permanganate (available at some hobby supply stores) in a pint of soft water.

Soap as Art

For centuries soap has been a medium of artistic expression. It has been carved, painted, sculpted, packaged, and inlaid with pictures and patterns. Soap decoration begins with the mold. Almost any conveniently sized container can be used; for example, custard cups, cake pans, boxes of all sorts, jello molds, and ashtrays. Once the soap has set, designs can be pressed or cut into the surface of the individual bars, or the soap can be carved into almost any conceivable shape. The only equipment you need for carving is a small, sharp knife. If the soap is relatively soft, it can be worked like dough. Roll it into balls, or flatten it with a rolling pin, and cut shapes out of it with cookie cutters. An unusual decorative technique is to embed a picture or decal in the top of a bar of soap, then cover the picture with a thin layer of melted paraffin. The paraffin protects the design from water, keeping it intact as the soap wears away around it.

sugar maple, fruit woods, beech, and ash produce the strongest lye. Finally, scoop out a depression at the top large enough to hold 2 to 3 quarts of water.

To make the lye, fill the depression with rainwater heated to boiling, and let the water seep down through the ashes. When the water has all seeped away, add more. It will be a while before the lye begins to trickle out the bottom—perhaps as long as several days if the ashes have been packed tightly—but do not try to hurry the process by adding extra water prematurely.

Although soap can be made directly from the lye solution, it is often convenient to have the lye in crystalline form, since crystals permit more precision in the soapmaking process. To extract crystalline potash from lye water, boil down the solution in a stainless steel or enamelware pot. At first a dark residue called black salts will form. By maintaining heat, additional impurities can be driven off, leaving the grayish-white potash.

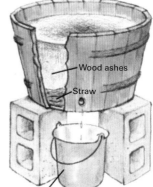

Wood ashes

Straw

Enamel pail

After lye is made test it by cracking in a raw egg. If the egg barely floats, the lye is good for soapmaking.

Sources and resources

Books

Bacon, Richard M. *The Forgotten Arts*. Book 1. Dublin, N.H.: Yankee, Inc., 1975.

Bramson, Ann. *Soap: Making It, Enjoying It*. New York: Workman Publishing, 1975.

Cavitch, Susan M. *The Natural Soap Book: Making Herbal and Vegetable-Based Soaps*. Pownal, Vt.: Storey Communications, 1995.

Seymour, John. *The Forgotten Crafts*. New York: Knopf, 1984.

White, Elaine C. *Soap Recipes: Seventy Tried and True Ways to Make Modern Soap with Herbs, Beeswax and Vegetable Oils*. Starkville, Miss.: Valley Hills Press, 1995.

A Survey of Soap Recipes

The standard batch recipe makes an excellent hard soap for laundry and bathing. The recipe calls for one can (13 ounces) of commercial lye, 2 1/2 pints of water, and 6 pounds of fat. About 9 pounds of soap result, enough to make 36 bars of toilet soap. These can be molded separately, or the soap can be poured into a large container, such as a shoebox, and later cut into bars. A combination of half tallow and half lard is usually suggested. Most other soaps—and there are as many formulas as there are soapmakers—are variations on the standard recipe. A number of attractive recipes are given here, but much of the fun in making soap comes from experimenting with your own combinations of fats, oils, and additives. Except where noted, the soaps are prepared by the procedure described on page 369.

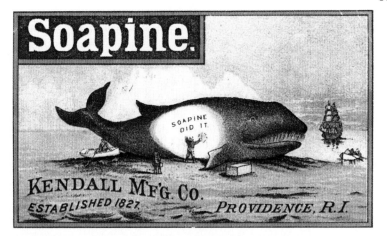

Colorful cards touted the virtues of cleansers in the days before soap operas.

Beauty soaps

Beauty soaps are made by adding scents, oils, and special purpose substances or by replacing some of the water and fat in the standard recipe with new ingredients. The most popular variation is in the amount and type of fat or oil used. Extra fat or oil makes the soap superfatted—that is, the soap becomes enriched with excess fat left unaffected by the saponification process. The result is an especially gentle soap suitable for delicate complexions.

Trade card from 1884 indicates that Acme soap will float even though child may sink.

Avocado soap. For sensitive skin. Use the recipe for castile soap but substitute 6 oz. of avocado oil for an equal amount of olive oil.

Castile soap. Simple but expensive with a hard consistency that is good for carving; named for the kingdom of Castile in north-central Spain where it was first produced.

1 lb. 9 oz. olive oil	10 1/2 oz. lye
3 lb. 10 oz. tallow	2 pt. water

Coconut and olive soap. Cream colored with rich, gentle lather, even in cold water.

1 lb. 7 oz. olive oil	11 1/2 oz. lye
1 lb. 7 oz. coconut oil	2 pt. water
1 lb. 7 oz. tallow	

Cold cream soap. Thoroughly mix 2 oz. of commercial cold cream into standard soap just before pouring it into molds.

Lanolin soap. Recommended for dry skin. Add 2 oz. pure liquid anhydrous lanolin to the standard recipe before pouring into molds.

Milk and honey soap. Nourishing for the skin. Thoroughly mix 1 oz. each of powdered milk and honey into any soap while it is still in liquid form, then pour it into molds.

Palm soap. For dry skin. Substitute 3 lb. lard, 1 lb. bleached palm oil, and 2 lb. olive oil for the tallow-lard mixture in the standard recipe.

Rose water soap. Slightly astringent for oily skin. Substitute 4 oz. of rose water for plain water when mixing the lye.

Scented soaps

Essential oils—powerful aromatic substances extracted from flowers, herbs, and animals—can be obtained from specialty druggists and added in small amounts to your soap before it is poured. Popular fragrances are bayberry, rosemary, jasmine, carnation, and musk. You can also make your own infusions, or strong teas, from various herbs and flowers. Steep the plant in boiling water, strain off the solids, and substitute the infusion for some of the water in the recipe. If the infusion is strong enough, you can get the same result by adding it to the soap mixture just before pouring it into molds. However, do not add over-the-counter perfumes or toilet waters: the alcohol they contain will interfere with saponification. (For more information on herbs and fragrances, see *Household Recipes*, pp.336–343.) Generally, 6 tsp. of scent mixture will be sufficient for the standard batch. *Savon au bouquet* and cinnamon are among many old-time scent mixtures. You can experiment with other combinations yourself.

Cinnamon. Traditionally, cinnamon soap was colored with yellow ocher. A few drops of oil of lavender can also be added.

6 tsp. oil of cinnamon 1/2 tsp. oil of bergamot
1/2 tsp. oil of sassafras

Savon au bouquet. In French the name simply means "perfumed soap." A 19th-century recipe for *savon au bouquet* advises: "The perfume, and with it the title of the soap, can be varied according to the caprice of fashion."

4 1/2 tsp. oil of bergamot	1/2 tsp. oil of thyme
	1/2 tsp. oil of sassafras
1/4 tsp. oil of clove	1/2 tsp. oil of neroli

Colored soaps

Roots, bark, leaves, flowers, fruits, and vegetables can be used for colorants. Spices such as turmeric and natural dyes such as chlorophyll can be added directly to the soap mixture before pouring into molds. Candle dyes and liquid blueing also work well. Food coloring, however, does not mix well with soap. To obtain your own dyes, make an infusion by pouring boiling water over dyestuff until a deep color is achieved. Strain out the solid pieces and use 4 to 10 oz. of the liquid in the standard recipe as a substitute for an equal amount of water when mixing up the lye solution. Or add the dye just before pouring the soap into the molds. (See *Natural Dyes*, pp.270–273, for more information.) A marbleized effect can be obtained by gently swirling the colorant into the mixture.

Shampoo soap for blonds. Add 3 oz. each of infusions made from camomile, mullein flowers, and marigolds before pouring into molds.

Shampoo soap for brunettes. Add 3 oz. each of infusions made from rosemary, raspberry leaves, and red sage before pouring into molds.

Special purpose soaps

Old-time soap recipes included special formulas for almost every conceivable purpose—insect repellent soaps, antiseptic soaps, medicinal soaps, abrasive soaps, dandruff remover soaps, louse-killing soaps, fungicide soaps. Some were useful, many were not, and several were downright dangerous, such as soaps containing mercury chloride for "the itch." Kerosene was a favorite additive but did little except make the soap harsh. Below are two safe and useful recipes.

Grease remover. For use on hands with ground-in dirt and grease. Add 1 oz. of almond meal, oatmeal, or cornmeal to the castile recipe before pouring into molds.

Vegetable soap. For strict vegetarians; reddish in color, soft enough to mold into balls. Vegetable soap is extremely mild and gentle. It can also be used as a base for a dry hair shampoo soap. Simply add a mixture of 1 1/2 oz. glycerine and 1 1/2 oz. castor oil to the liquid soap just before pouring it into molds.

2 lb. 10 oz. olive oil	2 pt. water
1 lb. 7 oz. of solid-type vegetable shortening	1 lb. coconut oil
	10 1/4 oz. lye

Candlemaking

Time-tested Methods Of Working With Wax

Autumn was candlemaking time in early America. Housewives spent long hours boiling down the fat of newly slaughtered beef and sheep into tallow. Not only was the job hot and sweaty, but the odor of the rendering fat was also unpleasant and the product was far from perfect: the candles burned too rapidly, buckled in warm weather, and gave off fumes and smoke.

Other sources of wax were available—notably bayberry and beeswax—but both were expensive, and candles made from them were reserved for special occasions. It was not until the discovery of paraffin in the 1850s that the average family could enjoy the luxury of bright, steady, smokeless illumination.

Hand-dipped candles are beautiful but time consuming to make. Dipping several wicks at once helps to hasten the process; another way is to add alum to the mixture, since alum will cause the wax to form thicker layers.

Candles from beeswax sheets

Sheets of beeswax that are used to start new hives can be rolled into candles without being melted. Buy sheets from suppliers of beekeeping equipment or from craft shops. Sheet widths vary, but the standard length is about 16 in. On a warm day your hands will provide enough heat to make the sheets pliable. In cold weather set the sheets in a warm (80°F to 85°F) spot to soften before shaping. Cut a sheet so that the top edge slants downward about 1 in. from corner to corner. Then roll up the sheet around the wick.

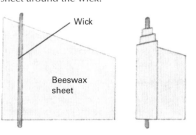

Roll beeswax sheet around wick to make a sweet-burning candle.

Waxes

Paraffin has come to be the chief ingredient in almost all candles. Beeswax is expensive, and tallow, a staple in years gone by, is seldom used today because of its many drawbacks: there are few more effective ways to dampen enthusiasm for the "good old days" than to spend a chilly winter's evening in the smoky, sputtering glow of an old-fashioned tallow candle.

Paraffin, a petroleum by-product, comes in five grades, the hardest of which is sold by craft shops for use in candlemaking. One 10-pound slab, the usual size, makes about 4 quarts of liquid wax. For firmer, brighter burning candles add 3 tablespoons of powdered stearin per pound of paraffin.

Beeswax, always a scarce commodity, is in shorter supply than ever, primarily because modern hives allow honey to be harvested without harvesting the comb in the process (see *Beekeeping*, pp.176–179). However, you can still buy beeswax at craft stores or you can make your own if you have a hive and are willing to sacrifice some honey (bees use up 10 pounds of honey to make 1 pound of comb). First extract the honey from the comb. Rinse the empty comb in cold running water, and place it in a pan along with 2 cups of water to prevent the wax from catching fire. Gently heat the comb until it is melted, and continue cooking for an hour. Pour the still-molten wax onto cheesecloth above a tub of cold water, and press the wax through the cloth to remove any impurities. If you are economy minded, use the beeswax as an additive only. Candles with as little as 10 percent beeswax have a better aroma and are harder than ones made entirely of paraffin or tallow.

Tallow for candlemaking is obtained by rendering animal fat (see *Soapmaking*, p.370). Beef fat is best, but sheep fat can also be used. To harden the candles and make them burn cleaner, add 1/2 pound of alum and 1/2 pound of saltpeter to each pound of melted tallow.

Bayberry candles, a Christmas favorite, are made from the tiny gray-green, wax-coated fruit of the bayberry, a spicy, woody shrub that grows in sandy soil along the New England coast. Old-timers gathered the berries in autumn, then sorted them to remove leaves and twigs. Next, the berries were boiled in hot water for two hours, and the muddy green fat that floated to the top was skimmed off, reboiled, and strained. Today, most bayberry bushes are protected by law and the berries cannot be picked, but artificial colors and scents can be used instead to make paraffin candles that look like and smell like the old-fashioned bayberry ones.

Wicks

Wax is the fuel of a candle, and the wick is its burner. The wick must blot up the molten wax, provide a surface for the wax to burn on, and yet not burn up too quickly itself. To make wicks the colonial way, soak heavy cotton yarn for 12 hours in a solution of 1 tablespoon salt plus 2 tablespoons boric acid in a cup of water. (A mixture of turpentine, lime water, and vinegar will also serve.) After the yarn is dry, braid three strands together to form the wick. Wicks can also be purchased. Be sure that any wicks you buy fit the candles you plan to make as indicated in the chart: too large a wick will cause a smoky candle; too small a wick and the flame will be doused in melted wax.

Wick types and their uses

Kind of wick	Wick size	Candle diameter
Flat-braided wick	15 ply	1"–21/2"
Square-braided wick	24 ply	3"–4"
Square-braided wick	30 ply	More than 4"
Metal-core wick	Small	Less than 2"
Metal-core wick	Large	2"–4"
Metal-core wick	Extra large	More than 4"

The Basics of Paraffin Candles

Candlemaking is a simple job requiring little in the way of special equipment. You will need an accurate candy thermometer to measure the temperature of the molten wax and plenty of newspaper (spilled wax is difficult to clean up). Whether you are making dipped candles or molded ones, the first step is to melt the wax. Wax is flammable, so never try to melt it in a container set directly over a flame. Instead, fill a wide-bottomed pan (one that is large enough to cover the burner completely) half-full of water, and place it over a low flame. Then put several chunks of wax in a can, and set the can in the center of the water-filled pan. As the chunks of wax melt, add additional pieces. If, despite your precautions, the wax should catch fire, douse the flames by covering the can with a lid or by pouring baking soda over them. Do not use water, since wax floats on it.

Once the wax is melted, add stearin (3 tablespoons per pound) and coloring. Use a liquid, solid, or powdered dye made especially for candles. Add it a little at a time, and test the color by dripping a bit on a white plate.

Sources and resources

Books
Constable, David. *Candlemaking*. Woodstock, N.Y.: A. Schwartz & Co., 1993.
Guy, Gary. *Easy-to-Make Candles*. New York: Dover, 1980.
Ickis, Marguerite, and Reba S. Esh. *The Book of Arts and Crafts*. New York: Dover, 1965.
Innes, Miranda. *The Book of Candles*. New York: Dorling Kindersley, 1991.
Meldrum, Sandie. *Traditional Candlewicking*. Cincinnati, Ohio: Seven Hills Books, 1994.
Seymour, John. *The Forgotten Crafts*. New York: Knopf, 1984.

Making dipped candles

Two cans are needed for candle dipping—one to hold molten wax, the other to hold cool water. The cans must be taller than the candles you wish to make; 48-ounce juice cans are a convenient size. Keep the melted wax at 150°F to 180°F during the dipping procedure. The water in the cooling can should be about room temperature.

Cut wicks 4 inches longer than the finished candles, and tie a washer to the lower end of each wick for weight. Dip the wicks individually or tie several to a dowel and dip them together. After cooling the first dip pull the wicks straight. It will take 30 to 40 dips to make a candle 1 inch in diameter. To harden the candle's outer layer and make the candle dripless, add an extra tablespoon of stearin per pound of wax for the final dip. After dipping is complete, cut the candle base straight with a sharp, heated knife, and trim the wick to 1/2 inch.

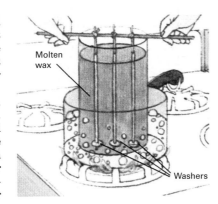

1. Dip wicks in hot wax held in tall can set in hot water. Remove wicks; let drip.

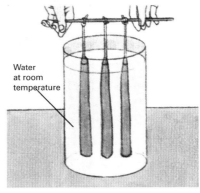

2. Dip in water, blot with paper towel, and lay on waxed paper 30 seconds.

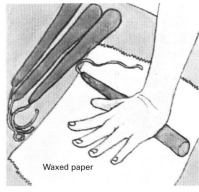

3. Dip repeatedly; roll candles on level surface occasionally to straighten them.

Making molded candles

Milk cartons, jars, cans, plastic cups, cardboard rolls, and many other common containers make interesting candle molds. Start by coating the interior of each mold with cooking oil or silicone spray to prevent sticking. (Waxed containers need not be coated.) If the mold is cardboard, wrap string around it so that it will hold its shape when filled. Next, prepare the container for the wick by one of the methods shown at right.

Use a coffee can for melting wax. Bend its rim to form a spout. Heat the wax to 130°F for cardboard, plastic, or glass molds; 190°F for metal molds. Turn off the flame, lift the can with potholders, and pour the wax into the molds. Let the molds cool overnight, then refrigerate them for 12 hours. Cardboard or plastic molds can be peeled off. Turn glass or metal molds upside down and tap until the candles slide out. If the candle sticks, dip the mold briefly in hot water. Smooth rough spots on the candles by rubbing with a nylon stocking. Candles should age for at least a week before use.

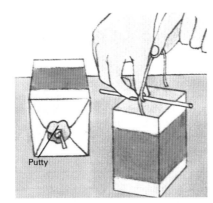

Wick-in-mold method. Cut hole in center of mold, tie washer to wick bottom, and thread wick through hole. Hold wick end in place; plug hole with putty. Pull wick taut and tie around pencil resting on top.

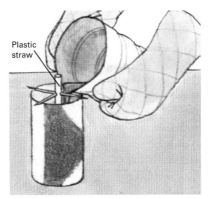

Plastic straw method. Stand straw in mold, then fill mold with wax. After wax hardens, pull out straw, tie foil to one end of wick, and thread other end through. When candle is lit, wax will fill hole.

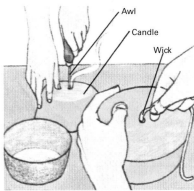

Hot-awl method. Bore hole in hardened candle with heated awl or metal knitting needle. Knot one end of wick and thread other end through hole. When the candle is used, melted wax will fill in hole.

Basketry

Beautiful and Versatile: There Is a Basket Style For Almost Every Job

Basketmaking has proven itself an invaluable skill to Americans from pioneer times to the present. Few tools besides a sharp knife are needed to make a basket, the basic techniques can be easily adapted to whatever materials are locally available, and an endless variety of basket shapes and sizes can be created to fill almost any need that may arise. A soft, lightweight willow basket can serve for gathering eggs or one of sturdy splint-work for apples. A big, flat-sided basket can be strapped onto a horse to carry major loads, while a large, lidded basket—designed to let in air but keep out sunlight—will store dried fruits and vegetables all winter long. An open weave makes a good strainer; a tightly wrapped coil can be virtually watertight.

Old-time basketmakers often specialized in just one technique and handed down its secrets from one generation to the next. Modern practitioners see basketry as an art form. They explore a variety of approaches and strive for imaginative combinations of colors, textures, and forms. They also take advantage of the wide availability of basketry materials, combining everything from wire, string, and feathers with the traditional splints and grasses. Craft stores supply an abundance of imported and machine-milled splints and reeds, whose uniform size and flexibility make them easy to manipulate. There is also a nearly limitless supply of free basketmaking materials growing in the countryside. Tall grasses and weeds alongside a highway, honeysuckle that has overgrown its boundaries, and thin shoots pruned from a tree or bush all make beautiful, serviceable baskets.

Brand-new or centuries old, all baskets are handmade because no way has yet been found to weave them by machine. While many modern baskets are primarily decorative, the old ones were absolute necessities. Settlers in isolated areas, working with homegrown or locally gathered materials, used baskets in place of scarce metalware and pottery.

How to Use Easy-to-Find Materials

Some of the most useful and widely available natural basketry materials are listed in the chart on the opposite page, but these represent only a few of the many possibilities for making beautiful baskets. Experiment with whatever vines, grasses, and leaves are available to you and try all the different methods of preparing them.

The easiest materials to work with are ones that are long and pliable: grasses and leaves that are mature but have not yet started to brown off, first-year branches and saplings, and spring or fall vines in which the sap is running. However, the rich colors of hard-to-handle dried grasses, leaves, and vines make them well worth learning to use too. The chart gives special instructions for preparing plants gathered after they are dry.

Most of the materials you collect will need some preliminary preparation to strengthen and preshrink them, since any shrinkage after a basket is finished tends to loosen the construction. Once the preparatory steps are completed, materials can either be used immediately or dried and stored. Dry the plants slowly in a cool, dark place unless you want to achieve the bleached effect of drying in full sun. To prevent mildew and general deterioration, store dried material in a location that is cool, airy, and free of moisture. Brown paper bags are good for storing small leaves and grasses. Vines can be coiled. Long grasses should be tied into loose bundles and hung.

When you are ready to make a basket, soak the dried material in water until it is pliable. Soaking time varies greatly. In general, the thicker and harder the plant is, the more soaking it will require. To avoid oversoaking, wrap the soaked material in a damp towel rather than letting it sit in water as you work.

Gathering and Preparing Natural Basketry Materials

Material	What to gather	When to gather	Preliminary preparations	Soaking instructions
Blackberry, raspberry (green)	Shoots, 1–2 yr. old	Late fall	Strip off thorns by pulling through heavily gloved hand. Use at once	20 min. in lukewarm water
Blackberry, raspberry (brown)	Any older canes	Anytime	Dethorn as for green shoots, but boil 3–4 hr. as for honeysuckle	20 min. in lukewarm water
Cattail leaves	Fully grown leaves	Early fall	Clean off slime at base and spread or hang leaves to dry	5–10 min. in lukewarm water
Cattail stalks	Fully grown stalks	Early fall	Remove top, clean base, split in half to dry, then in quarters	5–10 min. in lukewarm water
Corn husks	Pale green inner leaves	When corn is ripe	Spread or hang to dry slowly. Drying should take 1 wk.	1–5 min. in lukewarm water
Grasses (green)	Ripe green grasses	Spring or summer	Hang or spread to dry in cool, dark place or spread in sun	1/2 hr. in cold water
Grasses (brown)	Dry brown grasses	Late summer or fall	Use immediately or store in cool, dry place	1/2 hr. in cold water
Honeysuckle	Vines, 1–2 yr. old	Late fall to early spring	Boil for 3–4 hr. Rub briskly with towel to remove bark	20 min. in lukewarm water
Iris, crocus, daffodil (green)	Full grown green leaves	Late spring through summer	Spread to dry in sun to bleach or in darkness to retain color	Dip in water or spray lightly
Iris, crocus, daffodil (brown)	Brown, wilted leaves	After 1st frost	May be used immediately or spread to dry in shade	Dip in water or spray lightly
Maple, dogwood, other hardwoods	Thin 1st-yr. growth	Spring or fall	Use immediately, either peeled or unpeeled. May be split	Most shoots need not be soaked
Pine needles (green)	Long, green needles	Anytime	Hang branch full of needles upside down or spread on ground to dry	Until pliable in lukewarm water
Pine needles (brown)	Long, brown needles	Any dry day	No preliminary preparation except cleaning is necessary	Until pliable in lukewarm water
Straw	Nearly ripe stalks	Late summer or early fall	Spread on ground or hang upside down to dry slowly	10–20 min. in lukewarm water
Willow (green)	Green 1st-yr. growth	Spring	May be used immediately or dried for future use	1/2-hr. in warm water
Willow (brown)	Older growth	Late fall or winter	Boil 4–6 hr. or soak for 3–4 days. Peel off bark	1/2-hr. in warm water
Wisteria, ivy, grape	Any long, pliable vines	Fall or early spring	Hang to dry in cool, dark place. Peel off bark if it is loose	Overnight in lukewarm water

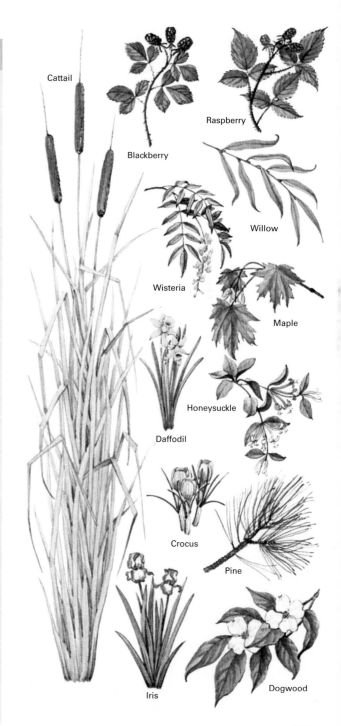

Cattail

Blackberry

Raspberry

Willow

Wisteria

Maple

Honeysuckle

Daffodil

Crocus

Pine

Iris

Dogwood

Constructing a Basket From Coils of Straw

Even a weak and brittle material, such as straw or grass, can be made into a strong basket when it is coiled. Gather 1 to 2 pounds of straw and 75 to 100 willow branches to use as wrapper for the straw. Choose long, straight first-year willow shoots with no side branches. Weeping willow is good if gathered in winter, or gather shoots from a basket willow anytime.

When you are ready to make a basket, soak the willow in water overnight and split it as shown below. Prepare the straw by removing short, broken pieces. The easiest way to do this is to take a small handful at a time (a bunch about 1 1/2 inches in diameter is easy to handle), slap it against your knee, and comb your fingers through so that the broken pieces fall out. Soak the straw for 10 minutes to make it pliable enough to coil. Keep it wrapped in a damp towel as you work so it does not dry out. As you coil the basket, strive for evenly spaced willow stitches and straw bundles of uniform thickness.

Bread basket is made of bundles of broom straw that were wrapped with strips of willow as they were coiled into a spiral. Grass or pine needles could be used instead of straw. The coils are 1/2 in. thick and the willow turns are 1/2 in. apart.

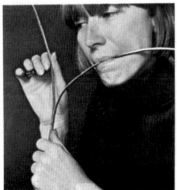

To split willow, cut with a sharp knife 2 in. into end of branch and pull halves apart with exactly equal force. Pull one side with teeth; use free hand to help control force. It takes practice to keep split centered so that one of the halves does not tear off in a short piece. After splitting, shave any lumps off split side of each half, and cut small end to a point.

Basic Coiling Techniques

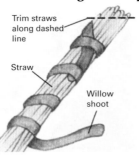
Trim straws along dashed line
Straw
Willow shoot

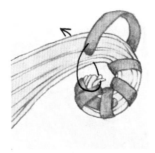

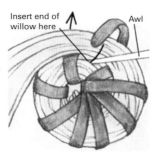
Insert end of willow here
Awl

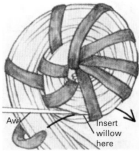
Awl
Insert willow here

1. Wrap a willow strip around its own end to anchor it to top of straw bundle. Trim off ends of the straws close to willow.

2. After four wraps, curl straw bundle into spiral, draw willow through center, and pull tight. Repeat five times.

3. Open a hole with the help of an awl, then stitch willow through straw under a wrap made in Step 1. Pull tight.

4. Continue wrapping willow strip around straw and stitching through straw bundle to make a continuous coil.

Making the Basket

1. As basket grows, add more straw by interweaving new ends among old.

2. To add more willow, draw new strand through, then hide ends between coils.

3. When base measures 6 in., gradually curve spiral upward to form bowl.

4. When sides of bowl reach a height of 5 in., cut off ends of straw at an angle.

5. Wrap tapered ends of straw with closely spaced willow stitches.

6. Reinforce rim by overstitching in direction opposite to first round of stitches.

Use Corn-Husk Braids To Make a Place Mat

Corn husks, braided into a long rope and sewn into a spiral, make a sturdy, heat-resistant place mat. Use the husk's soft inner leaves or buy packaged husks at a Mexican grocery. Sew with raffia (available at craft shops), cotton thread, or narrow strips of leather.

To make a corn-husk mat, you will need husks, raffia or other stitching material, a blunt needle, and a place to anchor the braid. For a good anchor, hammer a nail at one end of a plank, hook your braid over the nail, sit on the plank's other end, and pull the braid tight.

Dry the corn husks according to directions in the chart on page 375. A screen makes an excellent drying rack, or spread the leaves on a tabletop or board. Drying will take two to four days, depending on the weather. Prepare the husks by clipping off the ends to make them straight and even. Then soak them for five minutes. Finish the mat with a row of fringed braid.

Making the Mat

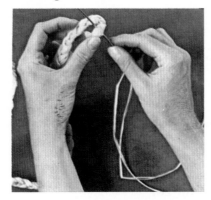

1. To start spiral, curve braid around and stitch through knot in end with raffia.

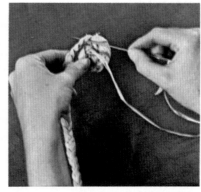

2. Secure center by stitching downward through section of braid opposite knot.

3. Continue sewing braid into a spiral. Stop as necessary to make more braid.

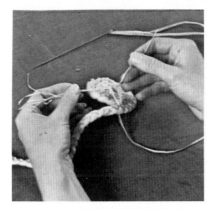

4. Add new raffia by joining ends of new and old strands with square knot.

5. When mat measures 12 in., braid the fringe using technique shown below.

6. Sew fringe to mat, cut end, bind with raffia, and sew bound end in place.

Braiding the husks

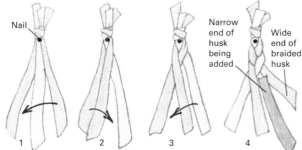

Narrow end of husk being added | Wide end of braided husk

Nail

To start the braid, tie together narrow ends of three husks. Hook knot over nail and pull husks taut as you braid. Add new husk by laying its narrow end inside wide end of braided husk.

How to make the fringe on the final row

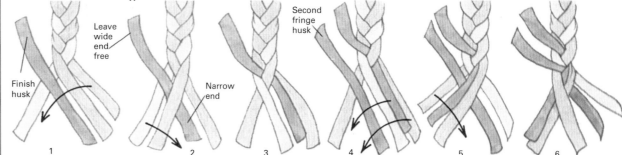

Leave wide end free

Finish husk

Narrow end

Second fringe husk

Finish mat with a decorative fringe. Add husks one at a time to the braid. Incorporate the narrow end of each husk you add into the braid; let the wide end stay free to form the fringe. Husks are shown in color to aid in identification.

Weaving Strong Baskets Out of Wood Splints

Black, or basket, ash is the ideal tree for making splints because it has tough annual growth rings separated from one another by relatively soft, spongy layers. The tough rings are torn apart into long, thin strips to make splints. Red maple, white maple, hickory, elm, poplar, and sassafras are other sources of splints, but they are more difficult to process than ash.

Whatever tree you choose, it should be 4 to 6 inches in diameter with at least 6 feet of straight, branch-free trunk. (Branches produce knots, which interfere with splintmaking.) One processing method is to soak the whole log in water for a month or longer and then pound it with a club to break up the spongy layers so that the tough rings will separate from one another naturally. In another method the log is first split into eighths using hardwood wedges and a froe, an old-fashioned homesteading and carpentry tool that was used to make shakes, shingles, and clapboards. The eighths are then cleaved into splints. Froes can still be purchased from specialty-tool mail-order houses. A sharp ax or cleaver makes a good substitute for starting the split in the log. Splints made by either method are fairly rough. They can be used as is or smoothed with sandpaper or by scraping with a sharp knife.

Drawknife

Drawknife is used to peel bark from whole log or from sections of a log that have been split into eighths.

Sources and resources

Books
Allen, Laura G. *Basket Weavers: Artisans of the Southwest.* Flagstaff, Ariz.: Museum of Northern Arizona, 1993.
Hart, Carol, and Dan Hart. *Natural Basketry.* New York: Watson-Guptill, 1978.
Harvey, Virginia I. *The Techniques of Basketry.* Seattle, Wash.: University of Washington Press, 1986.
Hoppe, Flo. *Wicker Basketry.* Loveland, Colo.: Interweave Press, 1989.
Mason, Tufton O. *American Indian Basketry.* New York: Dover, 1988.
Pollock, Polly. *Start a Craft: Basket Making.* Edison, N.J.: Book Sales Inc., 1994.
Tod, Osma G. *Earth Basketry.* West Chester, Pa.: Schiffer Publishing, 1986.
Tod, Osma G., and Oscar H. Benson. *Weaving With Reeds and Fibers.* New York: Dover, 1975.

Splints From a Whole Log

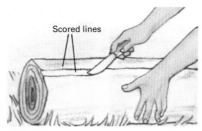

1. Score parallel lines along trunk of log that has first been soaked for one month and then stripped of bark.

2. Pound log end vigorously with wooden club until strip ends separate, then pound between score lines all along log.

3. Pull up strips. When necessary, repeat pounding at any spots where strips fail to separate easily from trunk.

Splints From a Split Log

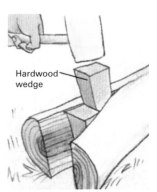

1. Stand 6-ft. log on end, and place froe or other blade so that it cuts directly across centermost growth ring. Pound froe into log.

2. Pull handle of froe toward you to pivot blade and split trunk, then work froe down; repeat until froe is worked several inches into log.

3. Remove froe and lay log on ground. Insert tip of wedge into split opened up by froe. Pound wedge all the way into the tree trunk.

4. Pound in second wedge. Work wedge over wedge down log, then repeat process to split halves into quarters and then eighths.

5. Remove dark heartwood. First cut partway down line where dark wood meets light, then pull sides apart with hands. Peel off bark.

6. Remaining light outer wood must be split exactly in half, repeatedly, to make splints. Start split by cutting into center of end.

7. Complete the split by pulling halves apart with equal force. If split drifts off center, recenter by pulling down harder on thinner half.

8. Resplit halves again and again to make successively thinner splints. For very thin splints control force with thumb and fingers.

A Square Basket Made From Ash Splints

To make a 10-inch by 12-inch yarn basket, you will need 1-inch-wide ash splints cut to the following lengths: 9 splints that are 22 inches long, 11 that are 20 inches long, and 7 that are 6 feet long. You will also need cane to reinforce the rim and two 1/4- to 1/2-inch-diameter hickory shoots for handles. Prepare the handles in advance by soaking the shoots overnight, then bend them into U-shapes. Finish the basket body, then fit the handles.

Before starting to weave, cut three 6-foot-long splints in half lengthwise. The halves will be used to create varied texture in the basket sides. Next, find the rough sides of the splints by bending them first one way, then the other. Splinters will be raised on the rough side when you bend a splint with its rough side facing out. The rough side will form the basket interior. Finally, soak the splints for 20 minutes in room-temperature water.

Ash splints make a lightweight basket that is excellent for storing balls of yarn. You can make your own splints or buy machine-made ones from a craft shop.

Weaving Splints to Form the Basket Body

1. With smooth sides up weave a 20-in. splint through three 22-in.-long splints.

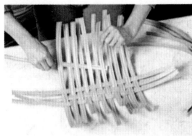
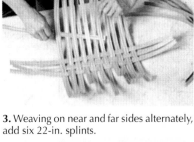

2. Weaving on right and left sides alternately, add ten 20-in. splints.

3. Weaving on near and far sides alternately, add six 22-in. splints.

4. With a sharp knife score splints lightly along edge of woven portions.

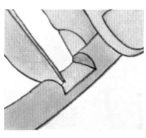

5. Turn basket over, bend up splints, and weave circumference with 6-ft. splint.

6. Weave half-width splints for next five rounds, then finish with a wide splint.

7. Cut off ends of all splints that are on the inside of the top round.

8. Cut half the width from each splint that comes up on outside of top round.

9. Cut half-width splints to a point, fold over, and tuck point into weaving.

Steps for making a hickory handle

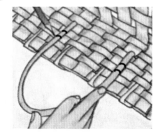

1. Tie 10-in.-long soaked shoots into U-shape. Let dry.

2. Mark width of splint on each side of hickory handle.

3. Cut notches between lines marked on handle.

4. Sharpen handle ends and insert into side of basket.

Finishing the edge

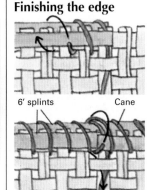

6' splints · Cane

Reinforce rim with two 6-ft.-long splints lashed in place with cane. On inside of basket insert cane end through weaving. Then lay a 6-ft.-long splint against each side of upper edge (top left), and lash with cane all the way around rim. (Long splints can be held in place temporarily with clothespins.) When you reach handles, lash around them and continue. Where splint ends meet, double-wrap with cane (bottom left).

Before Making Cheese, Make a Cheese Basket

An openwork basket lined with lightweight cloth makes a perfect strainer for draining liquid whey out of semi-solid milk curds. Traditionally, these baskets were constructed of splint, but they can also be made of flat reed, a material that is considerably easier to handle. Since openwork is a difficult technique to master, beginners should make their first baskets with reeds. For a 12-inch-diameter flat-reed basket, you will need eighteen 30-inch-long reeds, four 50-inch-long reeds, and 18 to 20 feet of cane to stitch the rim. Soak the reeds for 15 minutes in lukewarm water before using them. Then find their rough sides by bending them to see on which side splinters appear. The rough sides will face the interior of the finished basket.

Flexible flat reeds, available in hobby shops, are perfect for weaving the open hexagonal pattern of a traditional cheese basket. For the finishing touch, a reinforced rim, you will need strands of cane.

Weaving a Pattern of Diagonals for a Hexagon-Shaped Bottom

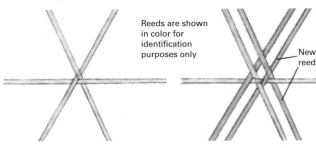

Reeds are shown in color for identification purposes only

New reeds

New reeds

1. Arrange three 30-in.-long reeds, rough sides up, with their centers crossing to form a small triangle.

2. Add a pair of crossed reeds to right of first group. All reeds should have rough sides up.

3. Place another pair of crossed reeds on the left. Note that the diagonal reeds are not interwoven.

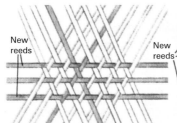

New reeds

New reeds

New reeds

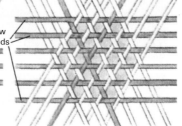

4. Add three more pairs, two at right, one at left. Keep spacing as uniform as possible throughout.

5. Weave two reeds horizontally—one above and one below center reed—through crossed diagonals.

6. Add three more horizontals, two above, one below. Large hexagon will be basket's bottom.

Finishing the Sides and Rim

1. Turn up edges of hexagon; use 50-in. reed, rough side in, to weave sides. Use same weave as horizontals in bottom.

2. Overlap and cut off ends so that they lie behind diagonal reeds. Start next row on opposite side of basket.

3. After two rounds cut off ends of all diagonal reeds that come up on the inside of top round of weaving.

4. Fold remaining reeds down to the inside of the top round and trim ends. Hold reeds in place with clothespins.

5. To reinforce rim, set one 50-in. reed against the inside of top round and another one against the outside.

6. Insert end of cane down through the center of the reeds in the top round. Stitch all the way around rim with cane.

7. Stitch around again, working in direction opposite to original stitching so that cane crosses itself on top of rim.

8. Draw end of cane through crossed reinforcing stitches to anchor it, then cut off any excess cane.

Twining Honeysuckle Into a Huge Carryall

Picnics, fresh garden vegetables, or even laundry can be packed in this large rustic basket. It is made by twining, a technique where two strands, called weavers, are woven simultaneously around a framework of vines known as spokes.

Almost any vine—blackberry, bittersweet, ivy, morning glory, honeysuckle—can be used to make a twined basket. Honeysuckle, the vine used in the basket shown here, is popular because it is strong, abundant, easy to handle, and has an attractive gnarled texture. Imported reed sold in hobby shops is also good. Experiment with vines of different sizes, but be sure to choose the thickest ones for the framework. In the basket shown the spokes are about 3/8 inch thick, and the weavers are about 1/4 inch thick. You will need at least six 5- to 6-foot-long spokes to start the basket and fifteen to twenty 4-foot-long spokes to fill in the gaps that develop as the basket gets bigger. You will also need a minimum of 200 feet of weavers, but it is a good idea to have plenty of extras, since some may break while you are weaving. Find at least one 3-foot-long extra-thick vine to use for a handle.

Look for vines that are straight and of uniform thickness, because they will be easiest to control as you shape your basket. Gather and prepare them according to the instructions in the chart on page 375. Weave the body of the basket using the techniques shown at right, then finish off with the sturdy rim and handle shown below.

Twining Techniques to Make the Body of the Basket

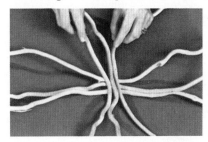

1. Lay three 6-ft. spokes on three others to form cross. Fold a long, thin weaver so that one leg is shorter than the other.

2. Loop weaver around top spokes, then twine it so it goes over and under bottom spokes. Repeat three times around cross.

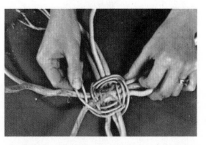

3. Begin twining weavers around individual spokes, crossing after each spoke. Yarn marks point where the twining starts.

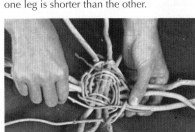

4. Add new weaver whenever necessary by inserting sharpened end alongside spoke in space between weavers.

5. As twining progresses, spaces between spokes enlarge. These must be filled by inserting new spokes among original ones.

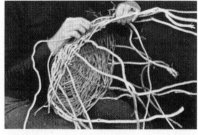

6. When base measures 1 ft. across, start turning spokes upward. Wet them first, if necessary, for greater flexibility.

7. When sides are 8 in. high, weave spokes to form rim (see pattern below left). Then insert handle into rim.

8. Insert thin vines on either side of the handle. They should protrude 2 ft. into basket. Ends will anchor handle.

9. Wrap thin vines, one at a time, around handle until it is covered. Leave 2-ft.-long ends to anchor handle as shown below.

Weaving the rim

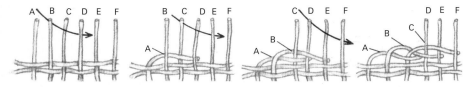

To make a sturdy rim for a twined basket, bend spokes over and weave them around one another as shown (the view is from inside the basket). Cut off ends on outside of basket.

Joining the handle to the rim

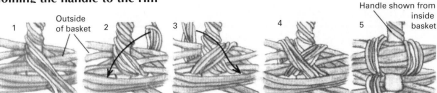

After wrapping thin vines around the handle, use the 2-ft.-long ends to anchor it to rim. Lash each handle end to rim, then push them both down into the inside of the basket's body.

Part Six

Recreation at Home And in the Wild

Leisure pastime in this country has become so complicated that it is now hard work. . . . We are not far from the time when a man after a hard weekend of leisure will go thankfully off to his job to unwind.
—*Russell Baker*, The New York Times

It often seems that the true purpose of recreation—refreshment of body and mind—has been lost somewhere along the road from primitive society to industrial civilization. Instead of simple fun, we now have motorized sports, electronic music, commercialized holidays, physical fitness fads, and television. The result, as columnist Baker points out, is that the pleasure has vanished from our leisure. Fortunately, the process is reversible, and in *Recreation at Home and in the Wild* an array of down-home entertainment ideas are presented that can help put us back on the track to enjoyment of our off hours. The sports and amusements range from strenuous (backpacking and cross-country skiing) to sedentary (cat's cradle and Easter egg decorating) and appeal to kids (street games and kite flying) as well as grown-ups (boating and square dancing). But most important, all the pastimes have withstood the test of time; for if something has been enjoyed for hundreds of years, it is almost sure to be enjoyed for hundreds more.

Old-time Good Times

Foot-stomping Dances And Fast-paced Games

Before television and radio, Americans created their own entertainment. Rough-and-tumble outdoor sports, homemade toys, and old-time games kept the kids busy. Among adults the art of conversation flourished and so did Saturday night square dances. Though times have changed, old-time amusements are still going strong.

Boys in knickers and jeans play crack the whip in front of their one-room schoolhouse in this 1870 painting by Winslow Homer.

Square Dancing

Instead of memorizing long, elaborate dances like the quadrille, Americans relied on a prompter to remind them of what steps came next. The square dance was born when some innovative prompters took to calling out whatever steps came to mind.

There are more than 2,000 different calls, as the steps are known, and it is doubtful if any one person can dance them all. Beginners should learn about 75 basic calls; old-timers master as many as 400. Each dance begins with a standard call, "Square your sets," in which pairs of dancers form into groups of eight to create the basic squares. From the first "Honor your partner," a good caller keeps the dancers continuously on the move and challenges their skill with the variety of figures (combinations of steps) that he calls.

Fiddles traditionally accompany the square dance calls.

384

Some basic calls

Square your set. Four couples form a square with women standing to their partners' rights. First couple is the one whose backs are to the caller. Others are numbered counterclockwise from first. First and third couples are head couples; second and fourth are side couples.

Honor your partner. Bow to partner.

Honor your corner. Men bow to women on their left, and women bow to men on their right.

Circle left, or right. All dancers face toward the center and join hands to circle in direction called.

Promenade. With men on inside of the square, couples interweave arms and circle counterclockwise around square.

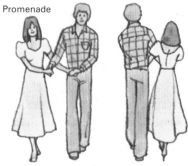

Promenade

Balance your partner. Partners face and hold hands, then hop on their left feet and kick out with right, and hop on their right feet and kick out with left.

Swing your partner. With hips side by side, and facing in opposite directions, partners pivot clockwise.

Swing your partner

Do-si-do. With hands on hips, partners face each other, then they circle around each other—without changing the direction they face. First, they move shoulder to shoulder, then back to back, then shoulder to shoulder again, then finally back to their original positions.

Do-si-do

Four hands round. Two couples named by caller join hands and circle either to the left or to the right.

Three hands round. One man and a couple join hands and circle.

Right-hand star. Dancers named by the caller step into center, face clockwise, join right hands together and circle.

Right-hand star

Allemand left. Dancers turn toward their corners and join left hands, then turn back and stand beside their partner.

Grand right and left. Dancers face their partners and join right hands, then move forward, each dancer passing on partner's right. Everyone extends left hand to next person in circle and moves to pass on that person's left. Dancers continue around circle, weaving in and out, passing to right of those to whom they extend their right hands, to the left of those to whom they extend their left.

Grand right and left

Tag Games

Tag requires no equipment, can be played almost anywhere, and has an amazing number of challenging variations. Most games start with one person who is "It," usually chosen by a counting-out rhyme. Whoever is It tries to tag someone who then becomes It in his place or else joins in the chase until all are caught.

Fox and Geese

Japanese tag. When a player becomes It after being tagged, he must keep one hand on the part of his body where he was tagged until he is able to tag someone else, who then becomes It.

Shadow tag. Players tag other players by jumping on their shadows.

Chain tag. Mark off an area about 50 ft. by 50 ft. The person who is It tries to tag others within the area; anybody who steps over a boundary line is also considered tagged. Everyone who is tagged joins hands to form a chain with the person who is It, and the entire chain must remain linked while the people on each end try to tag the other players in order to make them join the chain. The first person who was tagged by the It becomes It for the next game.

Ring-a-lievo. Any number—the more the better—can play this city variation of tag. Two equal sides are chosen, one is a team of "Hunters," the other is a team of "Hunted." A central stoop or area of sidewalk is set aside as home base for the Hunters and jail for anyone they capture. To start the game, Hunters gather at the stoop and count to 10 while the other side scatters. Then the chase begins. If a Hunter can catch and hold onto a Hunted long enough to shout "Ring-a-lievo-one-two-three," the victim is considered captured and is taken to jail where one of the Hunters stands guard. Members of the Hunted team can rescue the captives by kicking the stoop (or running into the sidewalk area) and shouting "Freed." The game ends when all the Hunted are captured.

Fox and geese. This is a good game to play in the snow, where it is easy to mark out a huge wagon wheel. The outer circle should be about 50 ft. in diameter with eight spokes across it and a small circle in the center. The central circle is home base for the geese. Players race along the rim and spokes as the person who is It (the fox) tries to tag the others (the geese). Any geese who are caught must help to tag other geese.

Blindman's buff. If you are It, you are blindfolded while everyone else forms a circle around you. As the others circle, you clap three times, then point. The person you point to must enter the circle. If you can catch and guess the identity of your prey, you join the circle and your prey becomes the blindman for the next game.

Turn cap tag. You can only be tagged—and thus become It—if you are holding the old cap after which this game is named. If you are about to be tagged, you toss the cap to someone else, but if the person who is It catches the cap, you become It anyway.

Ball Games

Games played with a ball are among the universal constants of human activity. Two favorites among kids are stoopball and dodge ball. The former, a city game, seems to have as many versions as there are stoops.

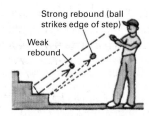
Strong rebound (ball strikes edge of step)
Weak rebound

Stoopball. In this street version of baseball the "batter" hurls a high-bouncing ball at a porch or stoop. In a typical variation the batter is out if the fielders catch the rebound on the fly; otherwise he is awarded a single, double, triple, or homer depending on how many times the ball bounces before it is caught.

Dodge ball. One team forms a circle while the other scatters inside. Players on the outside try to hit those inside with a ball. Anyone hit is out and the last remaining player wins. In chain dodge ball, team members inside the circle hold hands as the other team tries to hit and eliminate players at the ends of the chain.

Jump Rope and Children's Rhymes

Rhyming games, passed along for centuries by the play-yard grapevine, are favorite methods of designating who will be It. ("It" is the last one to be "O-U-T, out.") Rhymes are also used to challenge the skill of rope jumpers who act out such lines as "Hop on one foot."

Counting-out rhymes

Intry, mintry, cutry, corn,
Apple seed and apple thorn,
Wire, briar, limber lock,
Three geese in a flock:
One flew east, one flew west,
And one flew over the cuckoo's nest,
O-U-T, out!

Ibbity, bibbity, sibbity, sab,
Ibbity, bibbity, cannaba,
Cannaba in, Cannaba out,
Cannaba over the water spout,
O-U-T, spells out!

My mother, your mother,
Live across the way,
Every night they have a fight,
And this is what they say:
Hinkey, dinkey,

Soda crackers,
Hinkey, dinkey, boo,
Hinkey, dinkey,
Soda crackers,
Out goes you.
Onery, twoery, Ickory Ann,
Fillison, Follason, Nicholas John,
Queevy, Quavy, English Navy,
Stinkalum, Stankalum, Buck!

Bee, a bee, a bumble bee
Stung a man upon his knee
And a hog upon the snout
I'll be dogged if you ain't out!

Teacups and saucers,
Plates and dishes,
All little boys
Wear calico britches,
Out goes Y-O-U, sky blue!

Rope-jumping rhymes
Johnny over the ocean
Johnny over the sea
Johnny broke a milk bottle
And blamed it on me.
I told Ma
Ma told Pa
Johnny got a lickin'

Ha! Ha! Ha!
I love my Papa, that I do
And Mama says she loves him too
But Papa says he fears some day
With some bad man I'll run away.
Whom will I marry?
Rich man, poor man, beggar man, thief,
Doctor, lawyer, Indian chief!

Teddy Bear, Teddy Bear, turn around,
Teddy Bear, Teddy Bear, touch the ground
Teddy Bear, Teddy Bear, shine your shoe,
Teddy Bear, Teddy Bear, that will do,
Teddy Bear, Teddy Bear, go upstairs,
Teddy Bear, Teddy Bear, say your prayers,
Teddy Bear, Teddy Bear, turn out the light,
Teddy Bear, Teddy Bear, say goodnight,
Teddy Bear, hop on one foot, one foot,
Teddy Bear, hop on two feet, two feet,
Teddy Bear, hop on three feet, three feet,
Teddy Bear, hop right out!

One, two, tie your shoe,
Three, four, shut the door,
Five, six, pick up sticks,
Seven, eight, lay them straight,
Nine, ten, a big fat hen.

Time-tested Games That Never Grow Old

Many favorite children's games date back centuries, and some even echo themes and rituals from ancient religions. (London Bridge, for example, derives from an ancient pagan practice of offering a human sacrifice when a bridge was built.) The games that have stood the test of time generally require skill. Children have been working at ringers and one-through-sixes since colonial days. Making cat's cradles and other intricate string figures is an age-old pastime that exists in almost every culture. Some of these games are competitive, others are not, but all are fun at every level of proficiency.

Jacks

To start a game, hold the ball and jacks together in one hand, toss the ball up, scatter the jacks, then catch the ball on one bounce. To start play, toss the ball in the air, pick up one jack, and catch the ball on one bounce. In one-through-sixes you must pick up the jacks one at a time, then two at a time, then three at a time. Next, pick up four jacks, then two jacks; then five jacks and one jack. Finally pick up all six jacks at once.

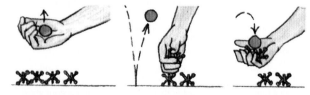

Crack the egg. Pick up more and more jacks as in one-through-sixes, but after each pick-up tap the jacks against the playing surface before catching the ball.

Pigs in a pen. Cup one hand and rest it on the playing surface to form the pen. Play one-through-sixes, but sweep the jacks into the pen instead of picking them up when you toss the ball.

Sources and resources

Books
Alderson, Frederick. *Outdoor Games*. Chester Springs, Pa.: Dufour Editions, 1980.
Anness Publishing Staff. *Parlour Games: Traditional Indoor Games to Amuse and Delight*. Boston: Bullfinch Press, 1992.
Boyd, Neva. *Handbook of Recreational Games*. New York: Dover, 1975.
Brock, Ray. *Go-Fly-a-Kite*. Freeport, Maine: Bookstore Press, 1976.

Marbles

Playing marbles reached a height in the 19th century when "playing for keeps" was the way to build a prized collection of shooters. Accuracy was essential, and the call to "knuckle down" (put your knuckles on the ground in order to shoot) meant to get ready for serious play.

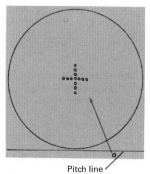

Pitch line

Ringers. Draw a 10-ft. circle and place 13 marbles, spaced 3 in. apart, in a cross. Players take turns trying to knock marbles out of the ring. Take first shot from pitch line, and keep shooting until you fail to knock out a marble. If your shooting marble lands within circle, shoot from where it lies; if it lands outside, shoot from any point outside. To win, knock out seven marbles.

Tops

Perfecting the launch is the key to success in the many games that can be played with tops. A top may be set spinning several ways; the most common are the underhand throw (the easiest) or overhand throw (it makes the top spin faster). Length and weight of the launching string both affect the launch's success. Generally, the longer the string, the faster the top will spin. String lengths vary from 45 inches to 60 inches. Most players experiment with various lengths and weights until they find a good combination.

Games with tops

Henckel, Mark. *Outdoors Just for Kids*. Billings, Mont.: Billings Gazette, 1992.
Timed spinning. Players take turns, timing their tops to see whose keeps spinning longest. Each player gets three chances. The best time of the three is pitted against the others' times.

Target shooting. Draw concentric circles 1 ft. and 3 ft. in diameter. Players take turns launching tops. If a top lands in the inner circle, spins, and comes to rest there, whoever launched it gains 15 points. If the top comes to rest between the inner and outer circles, it is worth 5 points. The first player to reach 100 wins. Sometimes a saucer is added in the center of the ring; if the top spins and falls on the saucer, it is worth 25 points.

Chipstones. This game was popular in colonial times. Everyone places a small, flat stone inside a 5-ft. circle, then takes turns launching tops into the circle. As the top spins, the player slides a small shovel or plank under it, carries the spinning top to a chipstone, and tries to drop it so that the top hits the chipstone's edge and flips the stone out of the circle. The player can keep trying as long as his top keeps spinning. If a stone is flipped out of the ring, the player gets to launch his top again and take another turn. Whoever moves the most chipstones wins.

To knuckle down properly, lay a marble in crook of index finger, place knuckles on ground, take aim, and flick thumb to send marble shooting forward.

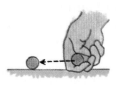

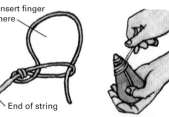

Shooter

2   Start along   3
           this line

                 5

1   4

Old bowler. Place one marble at each corner of a 2-ft. square and one in the center. Then take turns shooting the marbles away from the square in the order indicated. Start from the position shown, then shoot from where your marble stops. If you miss, all the marbles you have hit out go back to their original positions, and the next player takes a turn. The first to shoot out all five marbles wins.

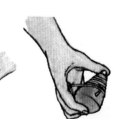

Insert finger here

End of string

Winding the top. Tie a loop, pull additional string through to form a slipknot, and put it on your middle finger. Right-handers generally wind clockwise for underhand launch, counterclockwise for overhand; experience will show what is best.

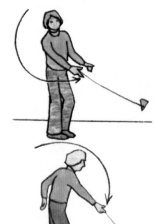

Underhand launch. Grasp top, point upward, between thumb and forefinger, and swing your arm forward in an underhand motion. Release the top at the peak of the forward motion, then whip your arm back so that the unwinding string sets the top whirling. Top will turn over in midair and drop, spinning, onto the floor.

Overhand launch. This is a difficult launch but sets the top spinning faster. Hold top, point upward, between thumb and forefinger, and extend arm back behind your head. Keeping arm and wrist rigid, throw top out in front of you, then pull back sharply on string.

Tangram

The object of tangram is to arrange seven simple geometric shapes into silhouettes of animals, people, structures, or any other objects the imagination can conceive. The only rules are that all pieces must be used and none must overlap. The game was introduced from China early in the 19th century and soon became a fad, with books and magazines being published on the subject.

To make tangram set, divide cardboard square as shown, and cut the pieces apart.

Cut on heavy lines

Five tangram figures—more than 1,500 are known—are pictured below.

Blowing Bubbles

Bubble blowing, an innocent recreation that almost every child has indulged in at one time or another, also holds its fascination for adults. By making wire frames of different shapes, you can enjoy the bubbles' iridescent beauty in a fantastic array of shapes and surfaces. For a good soap bubble mixture, add one part of mild liquid detergent to three parts of water and stir gently. Or dissolve 2 tablespoons of glycerine and 2 tablespoons of soft (green) soap in a pint of warm water.

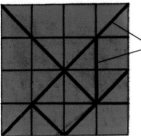

Wire loop

Straw

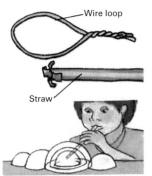

Bubble loop. Twist ends of 12-in. wire together for handle, then shape middle into circle.

Straw pipe. Cut several 1/2-in.-long slits at one end, then fold back cut sections.

Bubble city. Pour soap solution onto smooth surface, such as formica. Place one end of straw into solution and blow gently to form mound of bubbles.

Bubble soccer. Players divide into two teams. Make a wicket by bending a 3-ft. wire and setting the ends in bottles about 15 in. apart. Each player gets three chances to blow bubbles through the wicket. The team that blows the most through wins the game.

How to Play Cat's Cradle

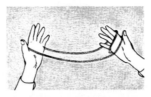

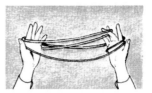

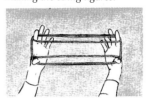

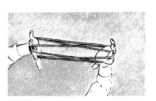

1. Tie a 6-ft. length of string into a loop, and stretch loop between hands.

2. Curl one hand around front string to wrap string around palm. Repeat with other hand.

3. With middle finger pick up string lying across opposite palm. Repeat with other hand.

4. *Cat's cradle* is formed. From now on, players take turns making the string figures.

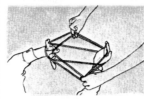

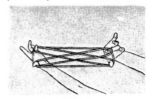

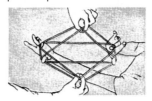

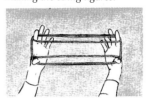

5. Pull crossed strings out, above parallel ones, then push up through center.

6. Stretch thumbs and fingers apart and pull string taut to form *soldier's bed.*

7. Pull crossed strings out, above parallel ones, then push up through center again.

8. Stretch thumbs and fingers apart and pull string taut to form *candles.*

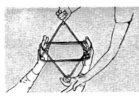

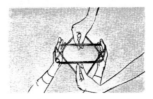

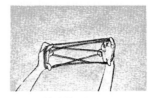

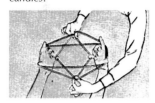

9. Use fifth fingers (pinkies) to pull inner strand to opposite sides of figure.

10. Hold strands against palms; scoop under double strings with thumb and finger.

11. Hold fifth fingers against palms and pull string taut to form *manger.*

12. Pull crossed strings out under parallel ones, then over and down through center.

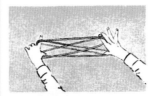

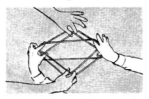

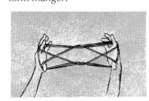

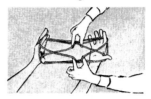

13. Stretch thumbs and fingers apart and pull string taut to form *diamonds.*

14. Pull crossed strings out above parallel ones, then under and up through center.

15. Stretch thumbs and fingers apart and pull string taut to form *cat's eye.*

16. Pinch intertwined strings from top, then pivot hands so thumbs and fingers point up.

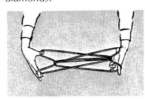

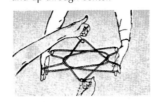

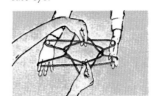

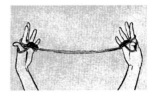

17. Stretch thumbs and fingers apart and pull string taut to form *fish in a dish.*

18. With fifth fingers pick up center strings and pull them out above other strings.

19. Pinch crossed strings and pivot hands so that fingers and thumb point upward.

20. Stretch thumbs and fingers apart and pull string taut to form *clock.*

Fun and Fascination With Homemade Toys

Anyone who has seen a three-year-old scold a doll in a disturbingly accurate imitation of Mommy or Daddy knows that toys can stimulate the minds of youngsters as surely as sports can help to develop their bodies. Kites become space shuttles, whistles become marching bands, and sandboxes are transformed into highway networks. But toys are not just for children. Turning a shriveled apple into a Victorian matriarch or building a fast, maneuverable box kite from sticks and paper is a challenge no matter what your age.

Apple-Head Doll

Use a firm apple, such as a not-quite-ripe Delicious, to make an Appalachian apple-head doll. For the head, peel a whole apple; for hands, use two slices from another apple. Dip fruit into lemon juice as soon as it is peeled to keep it from turning brown while you work.

1. Use hobby knife or sharp paring knife to carve eyes, nose, ears, and mouth in whole peeled apple. After carving, dip apple into lemon juice, insert thin stick through center, and tie string to stick. Hang apple in a warm, dry, draft-free place until it is dry and shriveled (about four weeks).

2. Carve the apple slices into mitten shapes for hands. Insert toothpicks at wrists, tie string to toothpicks, and dip in lemon juice. Allow to dry four days, then cut slits in each mitt to make fingers. Hang hands with head to finish drying. Make extras, so you can select the best.

3. For the body bend 24-in.-long wire in half and set 12-in. wire across it for arms. Wrap masking tape, adhesive tape, or strips of cloth around wires. Insert wire through head, and tape toothpick ends of hands to arm wires. Dress the doll in clothing made from scraps of fabric.

Rag dolls and other homemade toys can be as much fun to make as they are to play with.

Rag Doll

Rag dolls can be made from a single piece of cloth or a combination of colorful scraps. Make large patterns,

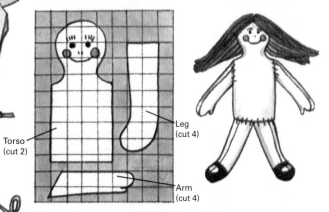

Torso (cut 2)

Leg (cut 4)

Arm (cut 4)

Pattern pieces, sewn together and stuffed, form rag doll.

using the ones shown on the grid as a guide, but add a 1/4-inch seam allowance around each part. Then cut out two torsos, four arms, and four legs from the material. Put the torso pieces together with their right sides facing each other, and stitch around, leaving the bottom edge open. Turn the torso right side out, stuff it with rags, foam rubber, cotton, or old nylons, and stitch the bottom opening. Make two arms and two legs in the same way, and attach them to the torso. Use embroidery floss to stitch the features of the doll's face, and sew strands of yarn to the top of her head for hair. Braid the yarn and tie the braids with ribbons. You can make the doll's dress plain or fancy, or deck her out in overalls.

Slip-Bark Whistle

A smooth, blemish-free branch from a striped maple or willow is all that is needed for an old-fashioned slip-bark whistle. The branch should be about 3/4 inches thick and is best cut in the spring, when the sap is running. Cut out a straight 7-inch section from the branch. The narrow end will be the whistle's mouthpiece.

Narrow half

1. Peel a 1/8-in.-wide ring of bark from center section of branch. Loosen and remove bark around narrower half of branch by tapping thoroughly with knife handle, then twisting bark off.

1"

2. Replace bark, grip it firmly to keep it in place, and shape mouthpiece by making upward-curving cut on underside of narrow end. Then cut wedge-shaped piece 1 in. from end.

1 1/2"

3. With bark removed, whittle out wood from base of wedge to within 1 1/2 in. of handle. Groove should extend halfway through the branch. Next, slice flat sliver from top of mouthpiece.

4. Dip whistle core in water to lubricate, then carefully replace bark in original position. Test whistle; if necessary, remove another sliver from top of mouthpiece.

Optical Toys

Optical gadgets were great favorites for parlor entertainment in the days before motion pictures. Especially popular were devices that provided an illusion of movement or position, such as the fancifully named thaumatrope and phenakistoscope described below.

Thaumatrope

Thaumatropes superimpose two pictures to give an illusion of a single picture. Cut a 3-inch circle out of strong heavyweight cardboard and draw two pictures, one on each side, that together will form a single scene (a fish in a bowl, a prisoner behind bars, a bird in a cage). Then punch a pair of holes in the disk, and tie string to each. To work the thaumatrope, wind up the strings and pull them taut so that the disk spins.

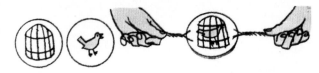

When thaumatrope spins, you see both pictures at once.

Phenakistoscope

A phenakistoscope is actually a simple motion picture machine. You can construct one from an 8-inch circle of cardboard tacked to a popsicle stick, dowel, or pencil.

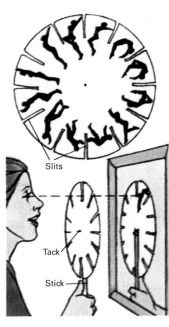

Divide 8-in. circle of cardboard into 16 equal wedges, and cut a slit 1 in. long by 1/16 in. wide at each dividing line. Draw a series of pictures in the spaces between slits that show consecutive steps of continuous motion, such as jumping rope or dancing. Next, tack the center of the disk loosely onto a dowel so that the disk can spin freely. Note that the picture sequence should close on itself, the final step blending smoothly into the first. To use the phenakistoscope, hold it in front of a mirror, then spin the disk, and look through the slits. You will be able to see a continuous moving picture reflected in the mirror.

Kitemaking

Box kites should be half as wide as they are high; diamond-shaped kites should be two-thirds as wide as they are high. On a windy day use a long tail and attach the kite string near the top of the bridle; on a calm day use a short tail and a lower point of attachment. Make the kite of strong lightweight paper (it can be taped together out of separate sheets if necessary). The frame pieces can be sawed from wooden screen beading.

Box kite

For a box kite you will need the following materials:

Parts	Number	Dimensions
Uprights	4	30″ × 1/4″ × 1/4″
Cross braces	4	16 3/4″ × 1/8″ × 3/8″
Sheets of paper	2	12″ × 50″

1. Fold over and glue down a 1-in.-wide strip along the long sides of both sheets of paper. Mark long sides at intervals of 12 in., leaving 2 in. at one end of each.

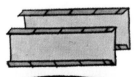

2. Make a loop from each sheet of paper by pasting its short ends together. The ends should overlap each other by exactly 2 in. to form a 48-in. loop.

2″ overlap

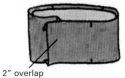

3. Notch ends of cross braces. Set uprights inside paper loops, aligning the ends with markings. Have helper insert cross braces and adjust them so frame is square. Braces should fit snugly; if they are too tight, shave the ends a bit.

Cross brace

Upright

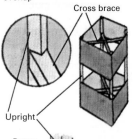

4. Glue a strip of paper near end of each upright to hold it in place at corner of kite. Lash braces together where they cross at center of kite, and add a dot of glue at each point where a cross brace joins an upright.

Paper strip

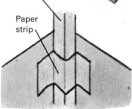

5. Glue 1-in. patch to top loop of paper. Patch should be in the middle of the loop directly over an upright. Poke holes in patch on either side of upright. Thread end of 70-in. string through holes and around upright, then tie it. Tie the other end to bottom in same way. Attach kite string.

1″ patches

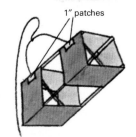

Diamond kite

For a diamond kite you will need the following materials:

Parts	Number	Dimensions
Upright	1	54″ × 1/8″ × 3/8″
Crossbar	1	36″ × 1/8″ × 3/8″
Sheet of paper	1	3″ × 4 1/2″

1. Make small slots in ends of sticks, then tie sticks together so that short one forms crossbar 14 in. below top of upright.

Crossbar

Upright

End of stick

String

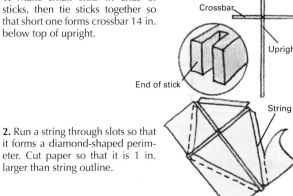

2. Run a string through slots so that it forms a diamond-shaped perimeter. Cut paper so that it is 1 in. larger than string outline.

3. Snip off corners of paper diamond to allow sticks to protrude. Fold edges over string, then tape or glue them in place.

4. Tie a string to the back side of the crossbar, then pull the string tight so that the crossbar bows out about 3 in. from the taut string at its center.

3″

5. Glue patch to paper where the sticks cross, and poke a hole in it near crossbar. Tie one end of 7-ft. string to cross. and other end to bottom of upright. Knot 2-in.-wide rag strips together for a tail and attach to bottom of upright. Attach end of kite string one-third of way down bridle.

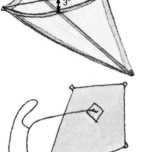

Crafting a Dulcimer

Sweet Accompaniment For Country Ballads

The dulcimer is one of our oldest folk instruments. There is evidence that, like many other things American, it is a product of several cultural influences. The Germans had similar instruments, and the French épinette is basically a dulcimer that is played either by plucking the strings or striking them with small mallets.

A dulcimer consists of a sound box, a fingerboard, and three or four strings that are strummed to create the instrument's sound. The name—from the Latin *dulce*, meaning "sweet," and the Greek *melos*, meaning "song"—is a fitting appellation for this soft-toned instrument that is so well suited to accompany the human voice.

A simple and attractive design

A three- or four-stringed dulcimer has several traditional shapes. The one shown here is not only the easiest to make but because of its simple and pure lines is one of the prettiest designs as well. Most of the tools and supplies you will need are available in any lumberyard or hardware store; they include a crosscut saw, a coping saw, a backsaw, an assortment of files, sandpaper (grades 80, 150, and 200), extra-fine steel wool, and strong white glue. The tuning head, fret wire, guitar strings, and nut and bridge can be bought at a music store.

As a rule, the body of the dulcimer—the sound box—is made entirely or in large part from such close-grained, knot-free hardwood as cherry, black walnut, butternut, or maple. Buy 3/16-inch-thick lumber. The top of the sound box (the soundboard) should be planed and sanded to a little less than 1/8 inch; the bottom (the back), sides, and ends need only be sanded smooth. Sometimes a combination of softwood and hardwood is used. A soundboard made of cedar (a softwood) will give the dulcimer a mellow tone, while a back, sides, and ends of hardwood, such as cherry, will ensure resonance, strength, and beauty. Other combinations include chestnut and rosewood, and gum (tupelo) and black walnut.

A dulcimer can be made very simply or with more ornate details, like this one. To play a dulcimer, place it across your lap or on a table, tuning pegs to the left. Hold fret positions with the fingers of your left hand while strumming with your right thumb or a pick.

Inside and Outside the Dulcimer: Parts, Patterns, and Dimensions

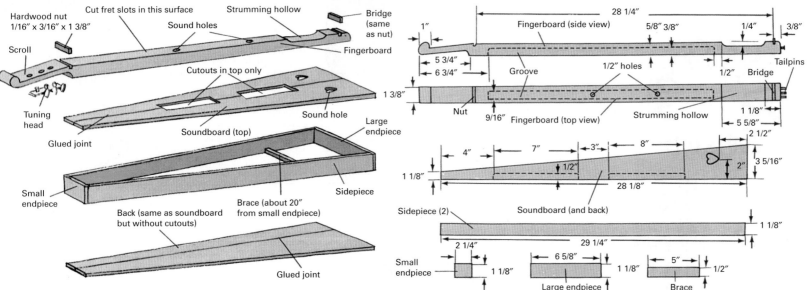

Essential parts of the dulcimer are the fingerboard with its frets, the sound box, and the tuning head. The sound box acts as an amplifier; its size and shape determine the quality of the sound. The shapes of the sound holes are a matter of personal choice.

Cut templates from construction paper or cardboard. Scribe outlines on wood, then saw out parts slightly oversize to allow for finish planing and sanding. Be sure to use wood that is thoroughly cured and dried.

Placing the frets

Distances in inches from nut to frets	
Frets	**Distances**
1st	3 5/64
2nd	5 13/16
3rd	7 5/64
4th	9 13/32
5th	11 7/16
6th	12 13/32
7th	13 9/32
8th	14 1/8
9th	15 11/16
10th	17 1/32
11th	17 21/32
12th	18 13/16
13th	19 55/64
14th	20 5/16
15th	21 3/16
16th	21 61/64

Putting the Pieces Together

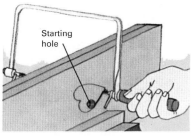

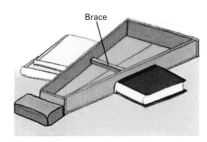

1. To get perfect matches clamp paired parts together when shaping them (the sidepieces and the halves of the soundboard and back). To make sound holes, drill starter hole, cut out with coping saw, finish with sandpaper.

2. Join halves of soundboard and back by edge-gluing (see *Woodworking*, p.306). Rest work on a firm, flat surface with waxed paper beneath to avoid sticking. Apply pressure with heavy books or bricks. Allow glue to dry 24 hours.

3. Plane and sand sidepieces, brace, and endpieces for exact fit, and glue them to the back. Clamp joints until dry, or use books as weights to hold the pieces in place. Scrape off excess glue when dry, and smooth any uneven edges.

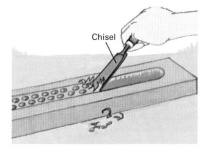

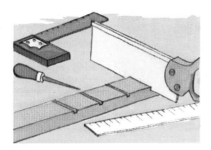

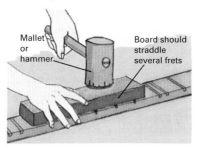

4. Use coping saw to cut scroll and strumming hollow in fingerboard. Smooth both with sandpaper. Next, carve 3/8-in.-deep groove down the underside as shown above as though making a blind mortise (see *Woodworking*, p.311).

5. Use backsaw to cut slots at each end of fingerboard for nut and bridge. Scribe fret positions with a try square and awl (see table on opposite page for precise location of each fret). Cut 1/16-in.-deep slot at each line with a backsaw.

6. Cut lengths of fret wire to the width of the fingerboard, and tap them into slots. To avoid damage and ensure that all frets are the same height, do not strike frets directly; instead, place a board on them and tap the board.

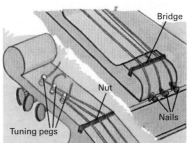

7. Tuning head is mounted on underside of scroll. Drill holes for the pegs and fit pegs through. Install nut and bridge so that strings are 1/8 in. above fingerboard. Make evenly spaced notches in nut and bridge to hold strings.

8. Drill two 1/2-in. sound holes in fingerboard, then glue fingerboard to center of soundboard. After glue dries, sand dulcimer with successively finer grades of sandpaper. Brush on shellac or lacquer, rub with extra-fine steel wool when dry.

9. Insert small nails or screws (tailpins) at the end of fingerboard near bridge. (Stagger nail positions to avoid splitting wood.) To thread string, loop one end over tailpins, wind the other end onto tuning pegs, and tighten.

Tuning Up and Playing

Correct tuning is essential to enjoying the dulcimer. There are several methods of tuning, but the most accurate for the amateur is with a piano or pitch pipe. First, make sure all the dulcimer's strings are threaded correctly. Use E guitar strings for the first two (or three) strings nearest you and a G guitar string for the third (or fourth) string. Wind the strings onto the tuning pegs to create enough tension to eliminate buzzing, then pluck each one to make sure it is free of the frets; it should produce a clear note.

To tune the dulcimer, place it in playing position. The string closest to the body is the melody string; the others are harmony strings. Start by tuning the string farthest from the body—the bass string—to middle C on a piano or pitch pipe by plucking it with the right hand while tightening or loosening its peg until the correct pitch is achieved. Pluck it at its midpoint in order to get the strongest and clearest note. Tune the other strings to G, adjusting the pegs in the same way.

Below is a simple score. The melody to which the words are sung is shown in standard musical notation. The fret positions are given immediately below and refer to the melody string only—the other strings are strummed without fretting. Press your left forefinger to the left of the desired fret and strum across all three or four strings with your right thumb each time a small mark is shown above the fret number. When the fret numbers are joined by a curved (slur) line, keep the string pressed down, but strum two times; otherwise, lift your finger between strums.

Amazing Grace

A-	maz-	ing	grace	how	sweet	the	sound	that	saved	a
8	11	13 11	13	12	11	9	8	8	11 13 11

wretch	like	me;	I	once was	lost,	but	now	I'm
13	12	15	15	13	15 13 15 13	11	8	9 11 11 9

found,	was	blind,	but	now	I	see.
8	8	11	13 11	13	12	11 — 11

Sources and resources

Books

Benade, Arthur H. *Horns, Strings, and Harmony*. New York: Dover, 1992.
Botermans, Jack, et al. *Making and Playing Musical Instruments*. Seattle: University of Washington Press, 1990.
Foxfire 3. Garden City, N.Y.: Anchor Press, 1975.

Celebrating Holidays

Our Holiday Heritage: Old-fashioned Sentiment Plus Just Plain Fun

To make up for long months of hard work, Americans have always enjoyed to the fullest the noise, laughter, games, and conviviality of holiday celebrations. Food was a highlight of most old-time celebrations, and preparations for a holiday dinner were often begun weeks in advance. Band music, sermons, and orations were featured during many holidays. Sometimes a dance floor was specially built—for there was nearly always a holiday dance; and if there was to be a parade, townsmen pitched in to build a reviewing stand. In the West, with its vast open spaces where isolation could be particularly demoralizing, families gathered from hundreds of miles away to enjoy the holiday festivities of a tiny dirt-street town. They would celebrate all day, dance all night, and pile into wagons at dawn to begin the long homeward trip.

Of course, not all holidays were boisterous. Many began as religious observances marked by prayer, special sermons, and a day of rest and meditation. Some religious groups, notably the Puritans, not only frowned on dancing and drinking but considered the very concept of honoring a day to be a form of paganism.

As the 19th century wore on, however, traditions intermingled, and celebrations born in isolation and tinged with old-country mores gradually evolved into amalgams of diverse customs. Most of the holidays that we celebrate today began to take their present form after the Civil War. Old patterns had been broken, the population was on the move, and the tide of European immigration was cresting. For those far from family and home, holidays provided not only a welcome diversion but also a link to the past.

May Day was more popular than Christmas to colonial Americans who spent the day playing and decorating the Maypole.

Lace and embroidery feature in this vintage handmade valentine. Eighteenth-century Americans bought books of amorous verses written especially for Valentine's Day and copied choice selections to sent to sweethearts and lovers. The words were flowery, but the paper was plain. Not until the 19th century did valentine cards become elaborate creations of satin, feathers, and lace. To make your own, use dried flowers, cutout paper figures, lace doilies, and gold braid—all glued to stiff paper or cardboard.

Independence Day

Church bells, bonfires, and a 13-gun salute marked the first Independence Day in Philadelphia, the nation's capital. Philadelphians proclaimed their support for the revolution by placing lighted candles in their windows. As John Adams described the spectacle, "It was the most splendid illumination I ever saw—a few surly houses were dark, but the lights were very universal. . . . Had General Howe been here in disguise, or his master, this show would have given them heartache." As the country grew and prospered, the Fourth of July became its most important national holiday. Every town had a parade and a huge communal picnic, such as the outing shown in this American primitive painting. Rural settlers traveled for hours to participate. Orations were the highlight of the holiday, which inevitably culminated in a night-long cotillion or a square dance in a barn or in the open air.

Easter Means Spring Has Arrived

The earliest American settlers paid little attention to Easter, but by the mid-19th century the holiday had started to gain wide popularity. It was about this time that wealthy New Yorkers began riding or strolling along Broadway to display their Easter finery—and observe one another's—in what came to be known as the Easter parade. In the 1880s the Easter lily was introduced. No one in this country had known of a white lily that bloomed so early in the spring until a traveler brought back a variety that grew abundantly in Bermuda. William Harris, an industrious Philadelphia nurseryman, propagated and popularized the plant.

The most widespread of all Easter symbols is the egg. In ancient Persia, eggs were exchanged as springtime gifts, and the Egyptians colored eggs as part of their celebration of the season. Europeans probably learned of the custom during the Crusades of the Middle Ages. In Eastern Europe, egg decoration by the wax-resist method was elevated to an art form. It was the Germans, however, who evolved the now familiar story of a rabbit who leaves colored eggs and other goodies in a secret nest for children to find on Easter morning. Until the 19th century eggs were colored with natural dyes (for information on dye plants, see *Natural Dyes*, pp.272–273). The shades produced resemble the muted, mottled coloring of wild birds' eggs. Later, aniline dyes were developed; their vivid, uniform colors were perfect for making the elaborate designs of the wax-resist method.

Tradition of leaving a nest or basket to be filled with eggs by the Easter bunny spread throughout the nation after the Civil War.

Decorating Easter eggs by the wax-resist method

Wax-resist dyeing, a technique used in batik as well as egg decoration, reached its highest development in the Ukraine. The method is based on the fact that dye will not penetrate through wax. Areas of an egg that are to remain undyed are coated with beeswax, the egg is dipped into a dyebath, then more wax is applied and the egg dipped into another dye. Aniline dyes are used because they provide brilliant hues even when applied over an underlying lighter color. (Green is an exception; it must be applied only to areas that are to remain green, since dyes applied over it will not hold their true colors.) The anilines are toxic, however, and eggs colored with them should not be eaten.

Beeswax, dyes, and other supplies are available in craft shops. Buy the beeswax in cake form. A stylus—a small funnel attached to a stick—is used to apply the wax. Get several with different-sized openings. Use raw white eggs with no bumps, cracks, or transparent spots, and make a nail board to support the eggs while they dry. Space the nails 1 to 1 1/2 inches apart—close enough to keep the eggs from touching the board. Clean the eggs in a solution of 2 tablespoons of white vinegar and 1 cup of cool water, then let the eggs dry while you prepare the dyes according to package instructions. After applying the colors, remove the wax and varnish the eggs. As time passes, the raw egg will evaporate.

1. Draw design guidelines faintly in pencil (do not erase; mistakes will be covered by dye). Warm an empty stylus over a candle, scoop up wax, and hold stylus over flame to melt wax. Make a few test strokes, then apply wax to egg with long, even strokes. Cover all areas that are to remain white on the completed egg.

2. Soak egg in lightest color (usually yellow), then remove and blot dry with paper towel. Next, wax over areas that should retain first color and dip egg in next dye. If green is to be used, paint it on with a brush. Wax over areas to remain green and dip egg in next color. Continue until all dyes are used.

3. To remove wax, warm egg carefully over flame until wax glistens, then wipe with tissue. Reheat wax as often as necessary until all is removed. To melt wax on several eggs at once, stand them on a nail board and place in a 150°F oven for 15 minutes. Finish by applying a thin coat of varnish to protect the colors.

Egg rolling, a popular American tradition, came to the nation's capital when James and Dolley Madison were in the White House. Children were invited to bring decorated eggs to roll on the lawn. The first child who managed to coax his egg to the bottom of the hill, without breaking the shell, won the contest. Today, thousands of children carrying baskets filled with decorated eggs gather on the White House lawn each year. Adults are barred unless accompanied by a child.

393

Gatherings of Friends And Family Cap The Harvest Season

Halloween: An Irish Import

Irish immigrants brought the Halloween tradition to America. The ancient Celtic tribes had considered All Hallows' Eve, when the souls of the dead revisited the earth, to be the start of the new year. To protect themselves from the wandering spirits, the tribesmen lit huge bonfires and paraded in grotesque costumes. According to legend, the jack-o'-lantern was invented by an Irish ghost named Jack who lit his way back from hell by carrying one of its embers in a hollowed-out turnip. From the Irish custom of carving out turnips, rutabagas, and potatoes come our glittering carved pumpkins.

Children's parties, featuring fortune-telling and boisterous games, have long been part of the Halloween tradition in America. Bobbing for apples is a familiar Halloween party game. For an old-time variation, suspend a 2-foot-long stick from the ceiling with an apple tied to one end and a cloth bag full of flour to the other. Set the stick swinging back and forth, and let the players try to catch the apple in their teeth.

Another Halloween game is played with a lit candle. Place the candle on a table, blindfold a player, and spin him around several times. Then let him try to blow out the candle as everyone cheers him on.

Autumn Husking Bee

Corn was the staple of the American pioneer diet. Many families subsisted almost entirely on corn mush, corn cakes, corn dumplings, corn gruel, and corn on the cob for many months of the year. There was even a recipe for coffee made from parched corn. To ease the drudgery of husking all this corn, neighbors would join with neighbors for a community-wide husking bee that turned tiresome work into a festive occasion.

Husking bees, like quilting bees and barn raisings, were opportunities for good fellowship and fun. With the labor of the harvest almost over, the husking bee became a social highlight of October. The work was accomplished quickly when it was turned into a contest featuring two enormous piles of corn with teams racing to finish shucking them. Husks and ears flew as youths stripped off leaves and tossed the cobs into waiting bins. The lucky lad who found an uncommon red ear was rewarded with a kiss from the lady of his choice. As a climax to the festivities, a supper featuring nothing but food made from corn might be served, or the meal might be potluck, with everyone contributing a dish. Dinner was often followed by a square dance in a barn decorated with bunches of maize. Even toys were made from corn; a particular favorite was a corn-husk doll of the type shown on the next page.

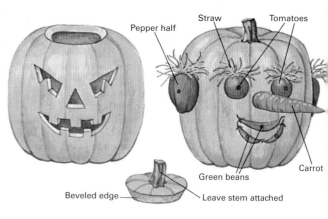

To carve a pumpkin, cut a circular piece out of the top, being sure to bevel the edge so that the top will not fall through when it is replaced after the pumpkin is carved. Scoop out seeds and stringy membranes. Use a crayon to sketch the face; then carve with a sharp paring knife. For a three-dimensional variation use long, thin nails to attach vegetables and fruits so that they look like facial features on the jack-o'-lantern. Save the seeds you scoop out of the carved pumpkin; pull off most of the membranes; salt the seeds; bake for 10 to 15 minutes at 350°F until crisp and brown; and serve as a healthy, tasty snack.

Bobbing for apples is always a fun harvest game.

Caramel apples are a favorite autumn treat. To make, bring 11/2 tbsp. butter, 11/2 cups brown sugar, and 6 tbsp. water to a boil and stir for three minutes. Remove from heat, dip 8 to 10 apples, roll in nuts, additional sugar, or candy and refrigerate 1 to 2 hours.

Scene from an 1858 engraving in *Harper's Weekly* shows that husking bees were far more than mere work parties. Young men and women courted and flirted, children frolicked, and neighbors exchanged pleasantries and renewed acquaintances.

Thanksgiving: A Homegrown Holiday

We celebrate Thanksgiving today much as the Pilgrims celebrated the first one in 1621. The Pilgrims' first year in America had been unremittingly harsh. Lacking adequate food and shelter, 47 men, women, and children died before the year's end. In contrast, the second year was one of vast accomplishment: seven homes were built and 20 acres of corn were harvested. To celebrate, colonists and Indians joined together for games, races, displays of marksmanship, and a parade led by Miles Standish. But the highlight of the event was the abundance and variety of fruits, vegetables, breads, seafood, and fresh-killed game that made up the week-long feast.

After that original celebration each of the colonies took to declaring days of thanksgiving whenever an occasion seemed suitable. With the exception of 1789, when George Washington declared a nationwide day of thanks, Thanksgiving remained an essentially local holiday until the Civil War. Then, on October 6, 1863, President Lincoln gave the celebration permanent status when he declared the last Thursday in November to be an annual day of national thanksgiving. The date remained unchanged until 1939, when Franklin Roosevelt altered it to the third Thursday in November. Two years later Congress changed it to the fourth Thursday in November. While some communities mark the day with parades, Thanksgiving dinner remains the main event. Turkey has replaced the wild fowl of the Pilgrims, but the rest of the meal revolves around traditional harvest foods—fruits, nuts, squash, turnips, sweet potatoes, and pies of mincemeat, apple, and pumpkin.

Pumpkin Pie

3 cups pumpkin, canned or steamed and pureed	1 tsp. ginger
1 cup light brown sugar	1 tsp. salt
1 cup white sugar	4 eggs, slightly beaten
2 tbsp. molasses	2 cups scalded milk
1/4 tsp. powdered cloves	Two 9-in. unbaked
1 tbsp. cinnamon	pie shells

If canned pumpkin is used, cook until thick before measuring. Combine ingredients and mix thoroughly. For variation, stir in 1 tbsp. grated orange rind. Pour mixture into pie shells. Bake at 450°F for 10 minutes. Reduce heat to 375°F, and bake 40 minutes more or until knife inserted between center and edge comes out clean. Cool. Serve topped with whipped cream, pecan halves, or a drizzle of caramel syrup. *Makes two 9-in. pies.*

Thanksgiving preparations in old-time kitchens began weeks in advance with everyone in the family lending a hand. Pies and breads were baked early in the week, fruits and vegetables were brought up from the root cellar, and the farm's best chicken or turkey was killed, plucked, and roasted for the occasion.

How to make a corn-husk doll

To make a corn-husk doll, use the pale inner husks from six ears of corn. Dry the husks between layers of newspaper for about one week or until they are a light straw color; then sprinkle them with water and place them in a plastic bag to soften overnight. You will also need dried corn silk, a 5-inch length of wire for the doll's arms, beige carpet thread for tying the husks together, several 1/4-inch-wide strips of husk to hide the thread ties, and three 3/4-inch-wide husk strips to make the doll's shawl and waistband. Form the doll's body, then let it stand for several days to dry. Afterward, glue the corn silk in place for hair and draw the face with pen and ink.

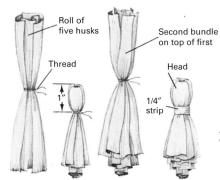

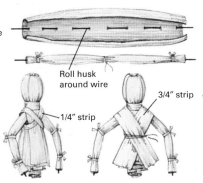

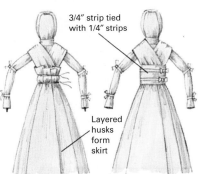

1. Roll five husks together and tie at the center, peel top half down, and tie 1 in. below top to make head. Tie a second bundle, set it atop first, peel down, and tie. Hide thread with 1/4-in. husk strips tied at back of head.

2. Thread arm wire through one husk, then roll husk around wire. Tie at center and wrists. Tie husk strips around wrists and elbows. Lash arms onto body with 1/4-in. husk strips, then cover with 3/4-in. strips tied at waist.

3. Wrap layers of husks—wide ends down—around waist for skirt, and tie in place. For extra strength tie twice around final layer. Trim husk tops, then hide waist with a 3/4-in. husk strip tied in place with two 1/4-in. strips.

Finished doll has hat cut from dried corn husk.

Sources and resources

Books and pamphlets

Austin, Catherine. *Christmas Past and Christmas Presents*. New York: Sterling Publishing, 1993.

Bacon, Richard M. The *Forgotten Arts*. Emmaus, Pa.: Yankee Books, 1975.

Boteler, Alison. *The Country Fair Craft Book*. Hauppauge, N.Y.: Barron, 1995.

Corwin, Judith H. *Easter Crafts*. Culver City, Calif.: Watts Publishing, 1994.

Corwin, Judith H. *Thanksgiving Fun*. Morristown, N.J.: Silver Burdett Press, 1984.

Echols, Margit. *A Patchwork Christmas*. New York: Macmillan, 1987.

Johnson, Doris, and Alec Coker. *The Complete Book of Straw Craft and Corn Dollies*. New York: Dover, 1987.

McCleeve, Carol. *Christmas Crafts*. New York: Sterling Publishing, 1995.

Christmas Season Magic And New Year's Cheer

The traditional American Christmas is actually a blend of Old World customs adapted to New World life. The Christmas tree and its ornaments grew out of a German custom of decorating an evergreen with candles. Americans were cautious about lighting candles on their Christmas trees for more than a moment—and then only if all adults were armed with buckets of water. Instead, they trimmed their trees with homemade ornaments—plain or fancy depending on the means of the family. Popcorn, a marvel discovered in the New World, was particularly popular for streamers.

Christmas carols are an ancient English tradition, but some of the best—"It Came Upon a Midnight Clear" and "Oh Little Town of Bethlehem," for example—were written by Americans. Ale-based wassail, too, was brought here from England but was soon replaced by eggnog laced with stronger spirits, such as Kentucky bourbon. Sinterklass, a stern but just and generous saint loved by Dutch children, reappeared here, transformed into a fat, jolly Santa Claus dressed in red.

As the nation grew, magazines and newspapers began to feature regional Christmas customs from around the country. Many were eagerly adopted throughout America, helping to transform our Christmas celebration into the present mixture of ritual and tradition.

Christmas trees, introduced to America by the Pennsylvania Dutch, had gained nationwide popularity by the 1850s. Ladies' magazines published patterns for all kinds of ornaments, and family gatherings to make them became favorite holiday events. On Christmas Eve the tree was trimmed. In addition to the handmade ornaments a few expensive glass balls were often hung from the tree. Fruits, nuts, strings of popcorn and cranberries, and such gifts as dolls, candy, and gloves completed the trimmings.

Christmas Tree Ornaments to Make at Home

Thomas Nast's cartoon gave the world its first glimpse of Santa Claus as we know him today. The good saint had come to America as a tall, stately gentleman. Then, in 1822, Clement Moore wrote his classic, "A Visit From St. Nicholas," describing Santa as a "jolly old elf." Nast, long renowned as a political cartoonist, published his first picture of Santa Claus in *Harper's Illustrated Weekly* in 1863. From then until 1886 Nast spun out images of Santa's busy workshop, lists of good and naughty children, and stacks of mail addressed "Santa Claus, North Pole."

Angel ornament can be made by soaking straw in warm water, bending it into shape, and tying it with red yarn or string. Shells, scraps of ribbon, lace, or fabric, clothespins, or pinecones can all be used in creating unique ornaments.

Gingerbread ornaments can be made by mixing 16 oz. applesauce, 1 cup cinnamon, and 2 tbsp. allspice. Mix all the ingredients thoroughly, roll dough to 1/4 inch thick, and cut out, piercing a small hole in the top of each ornament to hang it by. Bake at 150°F for 90 minutes, turn ornaments over, and bake for another 90 minutes. Cool for 1–3 hours before decorating with frosting or acrylic paint.

Christmas Trees and Greenery

Balsam, Douglas fir, and Scotch pine are the most popular trees for Christmas use, but you do not need to cut down a tree to display decorative ornaments. If you know a spot on your property where you would like to see a towering evergreen someday, you can buy a live Christmas tree from a local nursery and plant it after the holiday is over. Prepare for the planting in the fall by digging a hole before the ground gets hard. To keep the ground from freezing, fill the hole with leaves, and cover it over with a tarp or plastic sheet. The tree will arrive with burlap wrapped around a ball of earth that covers the roots. To prevent the tree from drying out, plan to keep it indoors for no more than 10 days, mist it before decorating, and water it daily with 1 to 2 quarts of water. Do not let the tree lights scorch the needles, and do not use artificial snow or any other spray that will coat the needles or bark.

If you have your own woodland or know a spot where you can cut your own tree, you can capture some of the old-time flavor of Christmas. (Check your local paper for Christmas tree ads—many growers let you cut your own for a small fee.) To carry a fresh-cut tree on top of your car for a long distance, wrap it in burlap to keep it from drying out, and tie it on the car roof with its base toward the front of the car. Before you set up the tree in your house, cut off a few inches at the bottom of the trunk to improve the tree's ability to absorb moisture. Stand the tree in water, and add water daily until you take it down.

Long before Christmas trees were popular, Americans made tabletop trees. This one is made of gingerbread, but greenery and fruit arranged around a wooden pyramid also creates a beautiful centerpiece. Poorer families would traditionally use stacked-up cabbages held together with knitting needles.

If cutting your own tree, look for one with full branches and measure it to be sure it will fit well where you plan to display it. Leave 6–8 inches of trunk (trim off bottom branches if necessary) so that it will fit securely in the stand.

Weaving an evergreen wreath

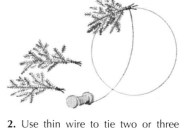

1. Cut evergreen branches 12 in. long and set in water for one or two days. Make wire ring from coat hanger or buy one from florist.

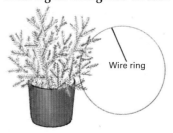

2. Use thin wire to tie two or three springs together, then wire springs to ring. Turn ring over and wire three more spings to back.

3. Wire another bunch of sprigs together and attach them to ring so that their tips cover base of first bunch. Continue around ring.

4. Finished wreath should be evenly and completely covered with greens. For decoration, add ribbon, fruit, Christmas balls, or herbs.

Seeing In the New Year

New Year's Day traditionally capped the Christmas season with a round of parties where friends, neighbors, and relatives could pay their respects and renew old acquaintances. George Washington adopted the custom of the open house in his first year as president when he invited not only members of the government but all citizens to a New Year's afternoon reception. In the social whirl of the East, hostesses tried to outdo one another with the lavishness of their entertaining. The successful ones became well known for their speciality dishes, such as a particularly rich eggnog or an exceptionally succulent turkey. As the tradition spread, party givers started to announce calling hours in the local newspaper. Guests arrived in all their finery to place calling cards on a special tray left in the front hall for the purpose. After a hostess's own guests had taken leave, she was free to galavant to other homes and parties. It became a challenge to attend all the open houses during a single day. The tradition faded, however, when hostesses found their homes invaded by party crashers.

In the Old West the start of the new year was heralded with even more revelry by enthusiasts shooting off guns and firecrackers. Large formal balls given by the rich were the social events of the year. Today the spirit of these traditions is carried on with the aid of noisemakers, toy horns, and popping champagne corks by celebrants and friends gathered to ring in the year.

Eggnog

8 eggs	1 pt. milk
3/4 cup sugar	5 oz. rum
1 pt. heavy cream	8 oz. rye

Separate eggs. Beat whites until stiff, gradually adding 1/4 cup sugar while beating. In a separate bowl beat yolks, then slowly add the remaining 1/2 cup sugar, stirring continuously to dissolve it. Add cream, milk, and rye to yolks and stir together until smooth. Stir beaten egg whites into mixture, then place in refrigerator until thoroughly chilled. Sprinkle with nutmeg before serving. *Makes 2 1/2 quarts.*

Canoeing and Kayaking

A Sport for All Seasons From White-water Rapids To Crystalline Lakes

Perhaps the British say it best: "There's nothing quite so much fun as messing about in boats." Boating seems to answer an inner human longing, and when necessity does not make us venture out on water, we do it anyway—just for pleasure. Children instinctively improvise rude rafts and embark on make-believe voyages; as adults, we daydream of romantic excursions.

Different boats are suited for different kinds of boating. A Polynesian outrigger canoe can master mountainous surf; the American Indian's bark canoe is most at home on inland waterways. The ingenuity of modern boat builders has created designs that are even more specialized: surf kayaks that can handle waves beyond the ability of an outrigger or decked white-water canoes that will wend their way through rapids that would make a salmon hesitate. With so many styles available, the cardinal consideration for successful and enjoyable boating, particularly for newcomers to the sport, is to choose the right craft for the boating you want to do. For example, a large guide-type canoe can take a family and its gear on an extended camping trip or a pair of experienced paddlers down a fairly rapid river. But it would be foolhardy to use it against a roaring Western river.

If you want to try different boating experiences, you can turn to rentals. Drive a short distance and rent an inflatable raft for a bouncing gorge trip one weekend. Drive the opposite direction the next weekend and try your hand at canoeing on a placid lake. Soon you will get a feel for what kinds of boats and boating are most to your liking. With the right craft and waterway, the trip of your dreams can become a reality.

White-water thrills await seasoned boaters on rivers across the continent. Although the roughest waters are the province of experts, anyone from a raw novice to a top pro can find a waterway that will match his skill, experience, and type of craft.

When day is done, canoe campers are ready for a warm campfire, a meal of freshly caught fish, and a good rest in tents and sleeping bags. Start scouting for a campsite several hours before dusk; otherwise night may fall before you have had time to beach the boat, unload gear, gather firewood, and set up camp.

Canoe camping lets boaters explore vast, virtually untouched natural regions all across the continent. The key to such extended trips is logistics: you must take everything with you that will be needed but still not overload the canoe. You must also carefully plan the itinerary. If you have to make a portage, your gear should be light. Nevertheless, occasions may arise when you will have to fall back on the old army axiom: "When in the field, improvise."

Planning Your Boat Trip

Choose a watercourse that matches your boat and your skills. Otherwise you might get in over your head—literally. A stretch of river that would delight a white-water enthusiast would not be a good choice for boaters on their first canoe outing. Many boating books and magazines describe suggested trips tailored for boaters with various types of boats and various degrees of experience. Local boating clubs and outfitters can usually furnish maps and suggest watercourses in their particular area that would fit your interests and proficiency. In addition, the same clubs and outfitters often sponsor group trips and provide equipment and transportation to and from the site. Trips like these, led and organized by experienced boatsmen, are probably the safest and least expensive way to get started in boating.

Never plan to go boating alone, and never go without first telling a friend or relative what your planned route is and when you expect to return. Then, should you get in trouble, searchers will know when and where to start looking. Timing is also important. A body of water may be placid in summer, dried up in the fall, and a raging torrent in spring. Boating conditions may change drastically with a change of only a few feet in water level. Snags and bars you skimmed over without noticing in April may be hazardous or impassable a few months later. A lake that is smooth paddling in the morning may be windswept and choppy by midafternoon. When inquiring of local boaters about a trip you are planning, always mention when you intend to go. Another general safety rule: if the water temperature is much below 60°F, either plan to wear an insulated wet suit or else postpone your trip to a warmer time of year. Should you get dumped, cold water will quickly sap your strength and deaden your reflexes. Many boating and swimming fatalities occur in spring when the air may be an inviting 75°F but the water is still numbing cold.

Selecting Supplies and Equipment

Choosing equipment for a boat trip is a compromise between necessity and weight. An overweight boat is hard to handle and difficult to portage, but omitting a vital item, such as dry socks, a life jacket, kneepads, or suntan oil, may destroy much of the pleasure of a trip or even endanger your life. Usually, you can find a lightweight version of the piece of equipment you need rather than leaving it out altogether.

Proper clothing and accessories will keep you warm and dry.

Take along clothing that can be worn in layers; then as the temperature or your level of physical exertion changes, layers can be added or taken off. In cool weather many boaters routinely wear woolen union suits and socks, since wool will retain its warmth even when soaking wet. A long-sleeved shirt, long pants, and a wide-brimmed hat will help protect against sunburn—a major hazard of boating—and annoying insects as well. Sunglasses, particularly ones with polarizing lenses, greatly diminish glare from the water. Canvas sneakers with rubber soles grip wet surfaces, do not trap water, dry out quickly, and will not slip off your feet as easily as moccasin deck shoes. Hooded rain suits are generally better than conventional raincoats or ponchos, which tend to become unwanted sails in strong winds. On all but the shortest trips be sure to take along a complete change of dry clothes.

Food is the fuel of a paddled boat. Backpacker's dried foods and other trail foods made especially for camping provide tasty, nutritious food without undue weight. Packing the food containers on the bottom of the hull out of the direct sun will help keep them cool. Water-treatment pills or chlorine bleach (three drops per quart and wait 30 minutes) will purify drinking water. Most small, light tents suitable for backpack camping will work well for boat camping.

"Keep it dry" is the first rule when packing a boat. Waterproof your supplies by tying them up tightly inside food or garbage bags made of heavy-duty plastic, then put the plastic bags into duffel bags or knapsacks to prevent tearing. Most boat campers use a few large packs rather than many small ones and lash each of them down to prevent them from shifting in rough water or floating away should the boat capsize.

Whether you are loading a canoe or kayak, stow the heaviest cargo centrally, as close together and as deep in the hull as possible, in order to keep the craft's center of gravity low. In a kayak, which cannot be unpacked easily, load the gear you need most near the openings.

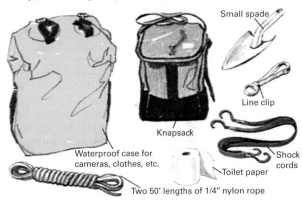

Other gear is needed for comfort, camping, and emergencies.

Special items include boating gear and sanitation supplies.

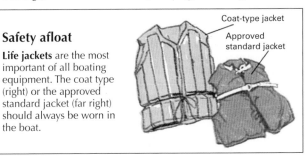

Safety afloat

Life jackets are the most important of all boating equipment. The coat type (right) or the approved standard jacket (far right) should always be worn in the boat.

Canoes: From Showroom, To Car Top, to Water

There are many types of canoes, each with specific advantages and disadvantages. If you plan to use your canoe for overnight camping on lakes, you should choose a different style than if you intend to specialize in one-day river trips. Let experience be your guide. Rent before you buy, and discuss your needs with veteran canoeists to get a range of opinions.

All canoes resemble a peapod opened at the top—but the pod can be rounded, widened, sharpened, or flattened. Each design change influences handling. When selecting a canoe, look it over carefully and weigh the design factors in light of your boating preferences. As a rule of thumb, canoes with flat bottoms and flat keel-lines, strong tumble home (side curvature), gradually tapering hulls, and moderate peaks are best suited for general cruising and camping. Round-bottom hulls, with less tumble home, more rocker (more arc in the keel line), and low peaks are best for white-water paddling. For easy handling and portaging, a general-purpose canoe should not weigh much more than 80 pounds. Many medium-sized canoes of various construction meet this guideline. A majority of canoeists find that the best all-around canoe is a 17- or 18-foot guide model.

Canvas-covered wooden canoes are lightweight and quiet in the water but are easily punctured and require frequent repainting. Aluminum canoes (about two-thirds of those sold) are strong and durable but are noisy and cold. Fiberglass canoes require little maintenance but are subject to puncturing. Newer plastic materials, including plastic laminates and polyethylene, combine many of the advantages of other materials without their drawbacks. They require little in the way of maintenance and are light, strong, and quiet; some of them even have a "memory"—after being dented or bent, they will return to their original shape either by themselves or with the help of a few minutes under a heat lamp.

When it comes to paddles, bigger is not better. The best all-around paddle is one with a moderate blade width of about 6 inches. The man in the bow should have a paddle that reaches from the ground to his chin; the sternman's paddle (or a paddle for a solo paddler) should be slightly longer, with a shorter, wider blade. Whether the paddle is made of wood, aluminum, or fiberglass, it should flex slightly when used: this springiness imparts more power to the stroke and provides more control.

Design Features

Bottom roundness refers to the degree of curvature of the underside of the hull. Standard profiles (left to right) are rounded, V-shaped, and flat. Flatness adds stability; round and V-shaped bottoms are faster and more maneuverable.

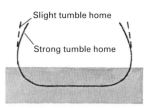 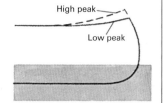

Tumble home is the inward curve of the sides of the hull. Tumble home adds strength and makes paddling easier, but waves can slop over the gunwales more readily.

Peaks are the top points of the canoe's bow and stern. High peaks make the boat more graceful but more susceptible to buffeting by strong winds.

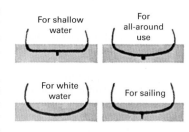

Keels are ridges along hull bottoms. A prominent keel helps the canoe steer straight but decreases maneuverability and increases the tendency of the boat to be caught in crosscurrents.

Keel line refers to the profile of the keel viewed lengthwise from the side. A boat with a flat keel line is easier to paddle in a straight line in crosswinds and crosscurrents, but a rocker keel (upswept keel line) makes for quicker turning.

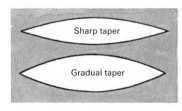

Hull taper describes the shape of the hull as seen from above. A gradually tapered hull can carry more weight. A sharply tapered hull is easier to paddle and faster in the water.

Transporting a Canoe

Boating trips start on land, so the first task is to get the boat to the water. Standard cartop carriers work well for transporting a canoe. The craft should be inverted on the carriers and lashed down securely with bow and stern lines made tight to the car's front and rear bumpers. Some useful knots for lashing, as well as for general boating, are shown below. Plastic hooks attached permanently to the lines make the job faster and surer. Elastic shock cords can be run over the hull laterally to prevent the canoe from shifting on the carriers. You should check the lines several times during a long haul, especially on a windy or rainy day.

Most river trips require at least two vehicles, one to take the canoeists to the start, the other to be left downstream for use at the end of the run. An alternative is a nonparticipating driver who is willing to drop off the canoeists at the starting point and then pick them up at a prearranged time at the end of their run downstream. Another solution is to use rented canoes: many outfitters provide a livery service for their customers, picking them up at the terminus and transporting them and their gear back to the starting point.

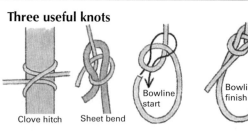

For long-distance hauls canoes and kayaks should be carried on the roof of the car. Crossing the bowlines on two canoes adds stability. Kayak mounts must be cut to fit the boat's deck.

Three useful knots

 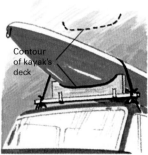

Clove hitch   Sheet bend   Bowline start   Bowline finish

Clove hitch will secure rope to pier. Use sheet bend for joining ropes of unequal thickness. Bowline is valuable in rescues, since it does not slip under tension.

Principles of Propulsion and Steering

Practice the basic paddling strokes—back, draw, pry away, J, and cruise—until they become second nature. Once mastered, they will enable you to overcome almost any boating problem and let you paddle tirelessly for hours without wasting motion or energy. You will gradually learn that a little twist here and a little cross thrust there will easily accomplish what at first required frantic effort. Good paddlers make paddling seem effortless, but do not expect to achieve this exalted state quickly; it takes time and training.

Some basic rules apply to all the strokes. First, make sure that only the blade of the paddle is submerged; a paddle that is too deep or too shallow wastes energy. Lean into each stroke slightly so that the muscles of your back and shoulders, as well as your arm muscles, get into the stroke. Pushing against the paddle grip with the heel of your hand provides most of the thrust. Your lower hand, which grips the paddle's throat, serves mainly as an oarlock or fulcrum. Avoid using too much body English; it wastes energy and causes you to lose control over the stroke. Begin your recovery when the paddle nears your hips, lifting the paddle and bringing it into position for the next stroke. Hesitate a moment between strokes. This brief rest will allow you to paddle much longer without tiring. The hesitation will also give your paddling a beat or rhythm. The rhythm is especially important when two boaters are paddling together. Otherwise their paddling is haphazard and the boat is much more difficult to control.

When practicing the strokes, try to get a feel for how they affect the boat's movements so that you will know what strokes are necessary to turn the boat, slow it, or move it sideways. Then when you encounter a situation that requires skillful maneuvering, such as an obstruction, a crosscurrent, or rapids, you will be able to use the stroke that will keep the boat moving where you want it to. After a few trips you will find yourself switching strokes automatically as the situation demands.

The stern paddler handles most of the steering and captains the canoe by giving orders to the bow paddler, after sizing up the situation and deciding what strokes are necessary. The bow paddler helps by serving as a lookout for hazards. When one of the paddlers wants to paddle on the opposite side, the stern paddler calls out a signal, such as "shift," and counts down with each stroke to ensure that both switch sides on the same stroke. The exact signals used are not important as long as some system is agreed on. Changing sides without signaling can result in a capsized canoe. Close friendships and even marriages have been strained during a canoe trip because of failure to arrange signals before setting out.

Cruise stroke moves the canoe in a straight line. Bring the paddle up and forward, dip it with the blade at a right angle to the hull, and draw it straight back. Apply the power while the paddle is vertical—a relatively brief period. The follow-through is quite short, since little power is produced after the paddle passes the hips. Lift the paddle and swing it forward in a wide, low, outward arc until it is in position for the next stroke. When moving the blade forward, feather it to cut through the air.

J-stroke enables a solo paddler to steer. Start a cruise stroke, but just before the end turn the paddle and push it away from the boat, making a hook, or J. By varying the hook, the boat can be made to turn toward or away from the stroking side.

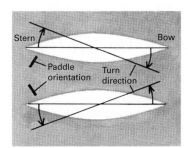

Steering a canoe requires cooperation. To turn the boat, the sternman uses his paddle as a rudder; the bowman paddles on the side opposite the turn. To go straight, the bowman uses the cruise stroke; the sternman, the J-stroke.

Back stroke slows, stops, or holds the canoe still in a current. Occasionally you can even use it to back the canoe up. The stroke is the reverse of the cruise stroke; start it on a line with your hips and push the blade steadily forward.

Poling a canoe enables you to move upstream against a strong current. Keep the pole close to the gunwale. Move the canoe forward by pushing the pole downward. Maintain the motion by pushing hand over hand up the pole.

Draw and pry strokes for quick turns

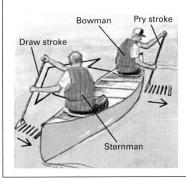

Draw and pry strokes are opposites. In both strokes move the paddle at right angles to the hull. The draw stroke pushes water under the hull and moves the canoe toward the stroke. The pry stroke pulls water from under the hull and moves the canoe away from the stroke. Both strokes are useful to shift the canoe quickly to avoid an obstacle. Used in combination by both paddlers, they can sideslip the canoe to avoid danger.

Using draw strokes on opposite sides, two paddlers can turn a canoe on a dime to change direction or avoid a hazard. Similar effect can be accomplished with bow paddler using draw stroke and stern paddler using pry stroke on same side.

In Order to Master a River Learn to Read the Water

The sport of canoeing has its cerebral aspects as well as its physical ones. To run a river successfully, you must be able to read the water as if it were a book—observing its features, interpreting what they mean, and knowing how to handle them. Canoeists' maps are available that spell out a river's special problems and rate their difficulty, but the real interpretation must be done on the spot. And for this task there are no substitutes for experience, good judgment, and a cool head.

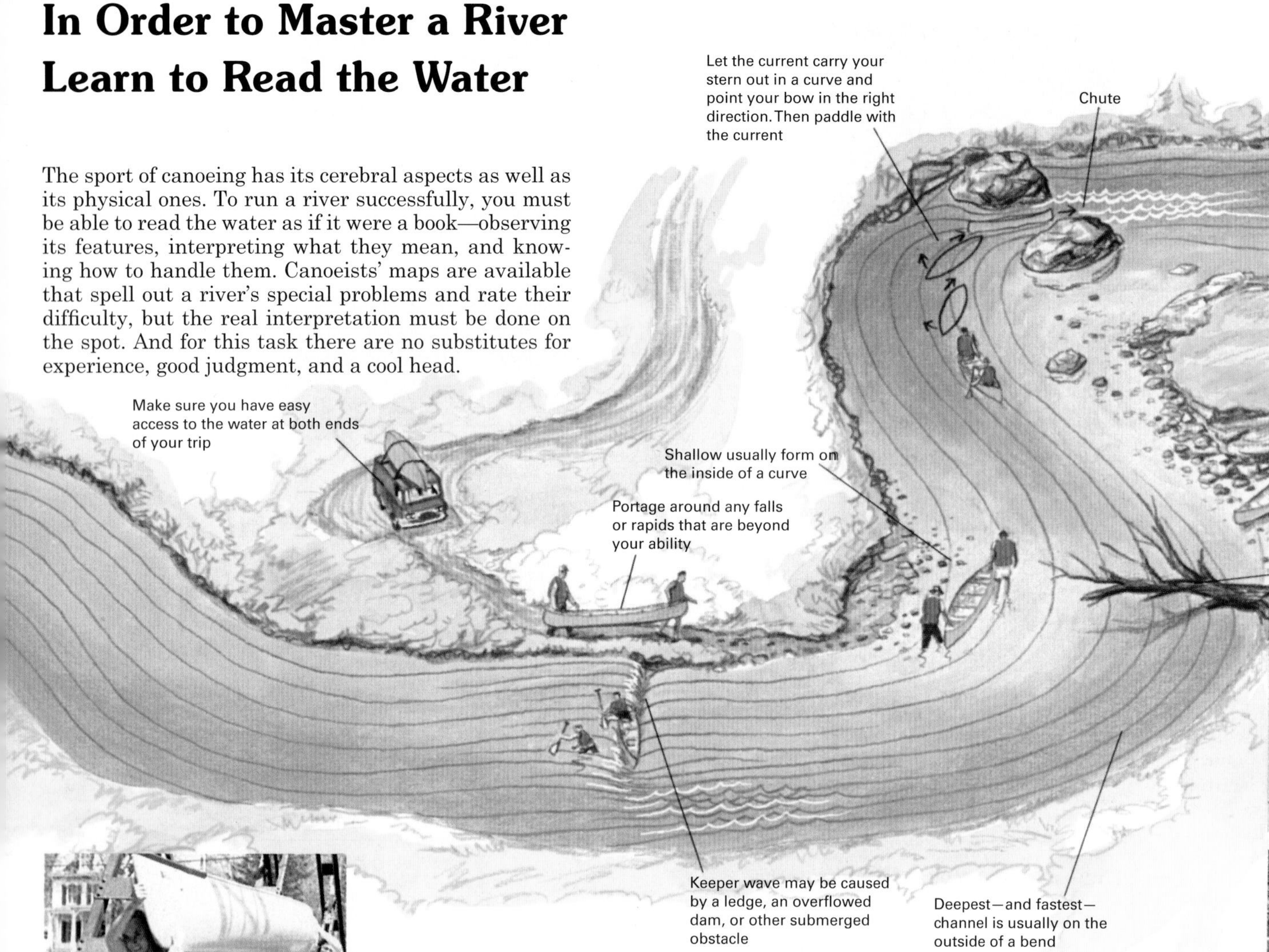

Let the current carry your stern out in a curve and point your bow in the right direction. Then paddle with the current

Chute

A combination draw and push stroke moves the canoe sideways while keeping it parallel with the current

Make sure you have easy access to the water at both ends of your trip

Shallow usually form on the inside of a curve

Portage around any falls or rapids that are beyond your ability

Keep your eyes peeled for low-hanging branches

Vs are signposts in a river. Vs that point upstream mark visible or submerged obstacles. Vs that point downstream usually show the way to clear, safe water between rocks.

Keeper wave may be caused by a ledge, an overflowed dam, or other submerged obstacle

Deepest—and fastest—channel is usually on the outside of a bend

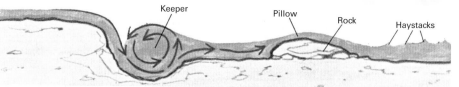

Keeper

Pillow

Rock

Haystacks

Portaging a canoe is often the only way to get around an obstacle, such as a waterfall or rocky shallows. A two-man, right-side-up carry is one of the easiest methods, since bulky gear can be carried in the canoe.

Keepers, pillows, and haystacks are signs of hidden obstacles. Swift current over a deep hole produces a keeper wave that can upset and trap a canoe; avoid it or meet it at a slight angle with speed to carry through. A pillow—a smooth surface hump—means a rock below. Haystacks—standing waves that form when swift water slows—usually provide a safe, exciting ride.

Draw strokes push water under the side of the canoe, moving it sideways. Contrary to what you might expect, the strokes tilt the boat *away* from the paddle. They help to counteract crosscurrents and provide control in avoiding obstacles.

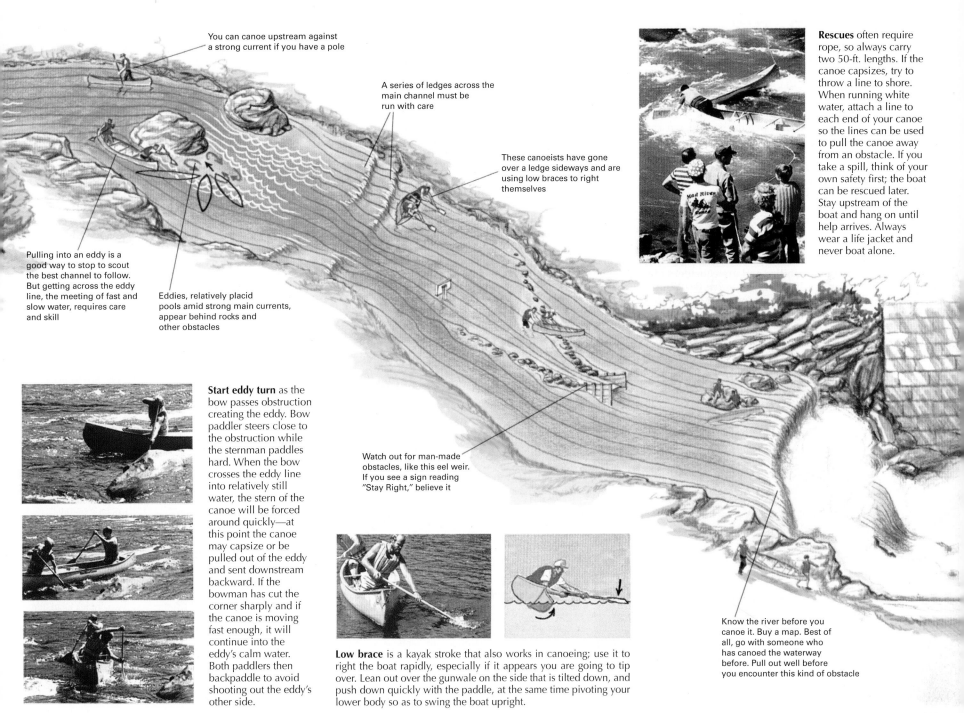

You can canoe upstream against a strong current if you have a pole

A series of ledges across the main channel must be run with care

These canoeists have gone over a ledge sideways and are using low braces to right themselves

Rescues often require rope, so always carry two 50-ft. lengths. If the canoe capsizes, try to throw a line to shore. When running white water, attach a line to each end of your canoe so the lines can be used to pull the canoe away from an obstacle. If you take a spill, think of your own safety first; the boat can be rescued later. Stay upstream of the boat and hang on until help arrives. Always wear a life jacket and never boat alone.

Pulling into an eddy is a good way to stop to scout the best channel to follow. But getting across the eddy line, the meeting of fast and slow water, requires care and skill

Eddies, relatively placid pools amid strong main currents, appear behind rocks and other obstacles

Start eddy turn as the bow passes obstruction creating the eddy. Bow paddler steers close to the obstruction while the sternman paddles hard. When the bow crosses the eddy line into relatively still water, the stern of the canoe will be forced around quickly—at this point the canoe may capsize or be pulled out of the eddy and sent downstream backward. If the bowman has cut the corner sharply and if the canoe is moving fast enough, it will continue into the eddy's calm water. Both paddlers then backpaddle to avoid shooting out the eddy's other side.

Watch out for man-made obstacles, like this eel weir. If you see a sign reading "Stay Right," believe it

Low brace is a kayak stroke that also works in canoeing; use it to right the boat rapidly, especially if it appears you are going to tip over. Lean out over the gunwale on the side that is tilted down, and push down quickly with the paddle, at the same time pivoting your lower body so as to swing the boat upright.

Know the river before you canoe it. Buy a map. Best of all, go with someone who has canoed the waterway before. Pull out well before you encounter this kind of obstacle

403

Kayak or Raft: Different Paths to Freshwater Fun

Kayaks are light, fast, and maneuverable; a beginner cannot just jump into one and paddle it off down the river. But once you master a few basic techniques under the eye of an experienced teacher, new worlds of boating will open up—from mountainous surf to roaring rapids—that would be off limits with any other kind of craft. And yet not all kayaking is so fast paced. Some two-place kayaks are designed for cruising and camping in flat water; and if your taste is for serenity, a kayak will serve just as well as a canoe in a tranquil pond or placid lake.

Most modern kayaks are made from fiberglass or other reinforced plastic. Slalom kayaks have a wide, nearly flat hull for high stability and are considered by many boaters to be the best all-around type. Whitewater kayaks have V-shaped hulls and rakishly pointed bows and sterns for speed and for breaking through standing waves. Both types are available in one-cockpit or two-cockpit models. Some two-place kayaks have a mid-deck hatch for easy stowage of gear.

One almost wears a kayak, rather than rides in it, so it is important to choose a boat that fits. Generally, low-volume kayaks are unsuitable if you weigh more than about 150 pounds or intend to carry a lot of gear. A high-volume design is a poor choice if you weigh less than about 120 pounds. Before buying or renting any kayak, try it on to see if you can get in and out easily.

A kayak paddle has a blade at either end of its shaft. In use, one hand serves as a fulcrum while the other turns the paddle with a rotary motion. Paddles come in left-and right-hand models. The designation refers to the hand you prefer for rotation, not to whether you are a natural left-hander or right-hander. Quality in a paddle is vital; an inexpensive paddle is likely to break just when you need it most. Two- or three-piece paddles serve well as spares carried beneath the deck or taped to it. Most kayakers prefer paddles with curved blades, since these furnish more thrust. Paddle size depends on your height. If you are 6 feet tall, the paddle length generally recommended is 87 inches. For every 2 inches of height above or below 6 feet, add or subtract 1 inch of paddle.

If you are new to kayaking, practice a wet exit (getting out of a capsized kayak) before anything else—you will need the skill often. With someone standing by in waist-deep warm water to offer help if you need it,

"Wearing a kayak" is how kayakers describe boating in these ultramaneuverable craft. An elasticized, waterproof spray skirt fits snugly around the boater's waist and the rim of the cockpit to keep out water, even if the boat capsizes.

take a deep breath and capsize the kayak. Unfasten the spray skirt by pulling the front loop, place both hands on the gunwales beside your hips, and push the boat away from you as you bend your hips to free your legs. Many beginners make the mistake of trying to get to the surface before they leave the boat. The secret is to get out of the boat first, then surface. Once you have the hang of it, practice the exit with your paddle. Do not let the paddle go, and do not lose contact with your kayak. Practice holding the paddle and the bow or stern grab-loop in one hand and swimming with the other. Three more safety tips that can save your life: (1) Never go kayaking without a safety helmet and life jacket. (2) Make sure your kayak has been fitted with secure flotation bags. (3) Always wear a wet suit in cold water.

Double-bladed paddle helps give an experienced kayaker control over his kayak in all kinds of water, even boiling rapids like those at left. The paddle blades are set at right angles so that while one is pushing the water broadside, the other is slicing through the air edgewise. The circular motion of each blade (above) and the paddler's leaning and twisting enable him to maneuver the kayak quickly in any direction, even sideways, making the boat an extension of the boater.

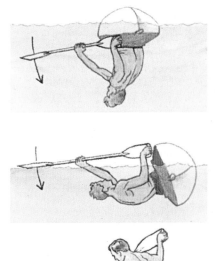

Eskimo roll maneuver lets the kayaker right a capsized craft without leaving it. Upside down and underwater, the boater grips the paddle at the throat and at one blade (top), while pushing hard with the opposite blade. Halfway righted (middle), the boater swings the paddle from the boat in a wide arc, keeping the blade horizontal to prevent it from diving. When the blade is out of the way of his head, the boater pushes it hard into the water again. Finally, he rights the kayak with a hip snap, then swings his head and shoulders up and out of the water (bottom).

Rafts—For the Tom Sawyer in You

Rafts are versatile, stable, and inexpensive. They are also fun to design, fun to build, and fun to use. You can make a serviceable raft out of almost anything that floats: logs, oil drums, plastic jugs, inner tubes. Whatever materials you use, build the raft as close as possible to the water—so you will not have far to drag it—and observe all the rules of boating safety.

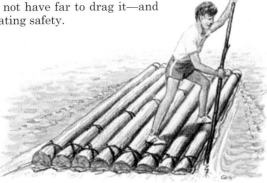

Log raft requires dry, buoyant wood. Lash smaller logs on top with strong cord. Always lash one strong log diagonally to keep the raft from getting "whopperjawed."

Notch logs log-cabin style to give the craft additional rigidity. Use an ax or saw to cut out matching slots on facing sides of the logs, and lash with cord across and diagonally.

Oil-drum raft is relatively light and very buoyant. Bore holes in planks, then pull strong cords through the holes and around the drums to bind both drums and planks together. Check the rigging after it gets wet, and tighten if necessary.

Sources and resources

Books and pamphlets

Beasley, Bob. *Whitewater Kayaking*. Birmingham, Ala.: Menasha Ridge, 1995.

Davidson, James W., and John Rugge. *The Complete Wilderness Paddler*. New York: Random House, 1982.

Evans, Jay. *The Kayaking Book*. Brattleboro, Vt.: Alan C. Hood, 1993.

Glaros, Lou. *Tandem Canoeing on Quietwater*. Birmingham, Ala.: Menasha Ridge, 1995.

Kalman, Bobbie. *A Canoe Trip*. Federal Way, Wash.: Crabtree Publishing, 1995.

Mason, Bill. *Path of the Paddle: An Illustrated Guide to the Art of Canoeing*. Minocqua, Wis.: North Word Press, 1995.

McNair, Robert E. *Basic River Canoeing*. Martinsville, Ind.: American Camping Association, 1968.

Mead, Robert D. *The Canoer's Bible*. Garden City, N.Y.: Doubleday, 1989.

Teller, Walter M., ed. *On the River: A Variety of Canoe and Small Boat Voyages*. Dobbs Ferry, N.Y.: Sheridan, 1988.

Ziegler, Ronald M. *Wilderness Waterways: The Whole Water Reference for Paddlers*. Kirkland, Wash.: Canoe America Association, 1992.

Maps of coastal and inland waterways

Defense Mapping Agency. Combat Support Center, Washington, D.C. 20315-0020.

National Ocean Service. Distribution Branch N/CG 33, Riverdale, Md. 20737. Request free map catalog by number. No. 1: Atlantic and Gulf Coast. No. 2: Pacific Coast. No. 3: Alaska and Aleutians. No. 4: Great Lakes waterways.

Henri Vaillancourt, Canoe Builder

Preserving a Vanishing Art

"I can't really explain what got me started on birchbark canoes. I was always interested in Indians and the way they built boats. I was about five years old the first time I tried to make a birchbark canoe, but I had an attention span of about a half-hour. I didn't succeed until I was 15 or so. I had an excellent book on bark canoes but a lot of what I did was trial and error. I work in the traditional Indian way, doing everything from scratch, or almost everything. I prepare the birchbark, the frame, and the root material that's used when you sew the joints. That's the whole joy of the thing, to see the canoe develop from the raw materials.

"I make about five or six canoes a year. Each one takes more or less a month to complete, depending on the length of the canoe; I've made canoes up to 24 feet long. I guess there's no common denominator among the people who buy the canoes except that they like traditional things. Some are canoers, some aren't. Some of the canoes even go to museums.

"I don't really know anybody else who makes birchbark canoes these days, or at least anyone who makes so many of them. There are some Indians in Quebec making canoes, but even they are making them from canvas. But the Indians still make snowshoes out of birchwood with traditional techniques. In the winter I make snowshoes myself, the very fanciest of the traditional Indian kind.

"There are a lot of people interested in the techniques I use, and information about them is very scarce. I'm doing research and making videotapes on Indian craftsmanship, not just snowshoes but kayaks, clothes, sleds. The tapes will be available for people who want to find out about native manufacturing techniques. It's urgent to get these things recorded; if we don't do it now, in 20 years it will be too late."

Dugout canoes can be made by chopping down and scooping out large tree trunks. American Indians would sometimes hollow out the trunks by burning them with controlled fires and removing the charred wood with an adze.

Wilderness Camping

Making Your Way In Nature's Domain

"The only inducements I can think of for making a ten days' journey through a strong wilderness, solitary and alone, were a liking for adventure, intense love of nature in her wildest dress, and a strange fondness for being in deep woods by myself." —Nessmuk

"Nessmuk" was the pen name of George Washington Sears (1821–90), eloquent outdoorsman and author of the classic book *Woodcraft*. In it he described a 60-mile trek through the wilderness of central Michigan at a time "when the Indians had left and the whites had not yet got in." For meat he shot deer, taking what he could use and "leaving the balance to the wolves, who never failed to take possession before I was out of earshot." He drank from streams and lakes and slept each night before an open fire on a fragrant bed of fresh-cut hemlock browse.

Today the old woodsman's inducements are still strong, but the wilderness has shrunk. (His 10-day trip is now a one-hour drive on U.S. Highway 10.) Millions converge yearly on America's parks and national forests, hiking trails, and wilderness areas for a taste of nature in her wildest dress. Because comparatively few venture from the beaten path, there are still vast areas accessible only on foot, where backpackers can enjoy the beauty and solitude that earlier generations took for granted. Most of these are in rugged country—mountains, deserts, and arctic wastes—where survival takes skill and where nature's balance is precarious. Today's camper must walk more carefully than Nessmuk did.

Head for the hills. When backpacking into high altitude, it pays to take it easy and enjoy the scenery. Thinner air means less oxygen per lungful; your head gets light, your legs grow heavy, and your heart works harder—and it takes time to acclimatize. Body moisture is lost faster than at sea level, so carry plenty of water and drink it often. When camping, remember that water boils at lower temperatures (–1°F for each 500-ft. rise in elevation), so cooking takes longer.

Compass and map are necessary tools for any wil outing.

A good campfire is a welcome treat after a long day of hiking. Fires are banned in many wilderness areas, but in places where fallen wood is plentiful and the danger of forest fire minimal, responsible campers need not forego its comforts.

Home for the night. Tarp and stout rope are shelter for this autumn family outing—not so luxurious as a geodesic dome, perhaps, nor so weathertight as a mountain tent, but also not so heavy. Making camp early leaves daylight hours for preparing food and enjoying woodland surroundings, an important consideration when young children are along. This campsite was chosen for its level ground where sleep was comfortable and erosion minimal.

For Well-Dressed Hikers Fashions Never Change

Being well dressed in the wilderness has nothing to do with how you look but a great deal to do with how comfortable you are, how warm, how dry—and perhaps how alive. In general, old clothes are better than new as long as they are in good repair, and loose-fitting garments are preferable to tight ones provided they do not bunch up. Dress in layers—several lightweight shirts will insulate better than one heavy one. Layering also lets you attune your attire to the changing weather: three layers for a chilly morning, one during a warm afternoon, two for a cool evening by the campfire.

Underlayer. Avoid tight straps, elastic bands, and anything that binds or constricts; irritations intensify quickly on the trail. Cotton T-shirts prevent sunburn and protect against chafing from pack straps on hot days. Fishnet undershirts are good for all seasons—worn beneath a shirt they trap warm air, worn alone they allow ventilation. Thermal underwear and woolen long johns are warm in winter and comfortable on chilly evenings but can get steamy inside while hiking.

Basic clothing layer. Many backpackers swear by army-style fatigue trousers with large cargo pockets; any loose-fitting cotton or woolen work pants are good. The problem with western-style jeans is that, like cowboy boots, they are designed for horseback riding, not walking—the tight crotch, especially with a new pair, can restrict movement, even to the point of being painful. Avoid bulky belt loops, big buckles, and similar items around the waist—they can be instruments of torture under the waistband of a heavy pack. Bring a work shirt that is made of cotton, wool, or a moisture wicking fabric like polypropylene, depending on climate. Carry one or two woolen or fleece sweaters for extra layers of insulation when needed.

Outer layer. A lightweight (5- to 6-ounce) water-repellent nylon parka shell is a good windbreaker and fair protection from rain. A zippered neck opening allows you to let heat out and fresh air in without removing an entire layer. Down-filled shirts, vests, and jackets are unbeatable insulation as long as the down remains dry. They require the same care as filled sleeping bags (p.411). Bulky down-filled parkas are hardly needed except in near-arctic conditions (see *Outdoors in Winter*, p.431). A rain poncho can cover both you and your pack and can double as a tarp. To keep it from flapping in the wind, sew cloth strips on it to tie around your waist.

Sequence illustrates the principle of layering. Summer hiker at left dresses for cool comfort. As temperature drops, more layers of clothing are added. Warmth is trapped between layers.

Why wear a hat?

Tiny blood vessels on top of the head keep the brain cool by continuously giving off heat. When the sun is beating down—even if the air is cool at higher elevations—this ventilating system can be thwarted. The body compensates by cutting down the blood supply to the brain. Mental activity is slowed, and the rest of the body overheats, perhaps resulting in sunstroke. Guard against this danger by wearing a head scarf or lightweight hat.

In cold weather the body sacrifices the hands and feet for the sake of the brain. When the demand for warmth is great, blood vessels in these extremities constrict, forcing blood up into the head. Because heat continues to be lost from the top of the head, the process can escalate, possibly leading to hypothermia or frostbite (see *Outdoors in Winter*, p.431). When your hands and feet start to get cold, therefore, put on a wool hat to help conserve your body's warmth.

Cotton, Wool, and Synthetic Fabrics

Clothing does not generate heat; it conserves the heat your body produces by surrounding you in dead-air space. Complications arise because the skin also expels about a quart of water a day—even more when you are active. If this moisture remains next to the skin, it drains body heat away through conduction and evaporation. Both cotton and wool absorb moisture but in different ways. Cotton fibers swell, eventually closing the spaces between them to form a solid, soggy wall; the wetter cotton becomes, the poorer the insulation it makes. Wool fibers, on the other hand, act like conduits or wicks, carrying water away from the body while preserving their own shape and texture. Even when soaking wet, wool maintains a good insulating air layer. For warmth, wear wool next to your skin. To keep cool, wear a light layer of cotton.

Synthetics, such as nylon, do not absorb moisture; they are of value as insulation only if no water collects between the fibers. Tightly woven, they may be almost impermeable, making for good protective outer wear. However, a fabric that keeps rain out also keeps water in. Though protected by a rainproof jacket, you can still find yourself and your clothing sopping wet. Materials like polypropolene or capilene help to solve this dilemma by wicking moisture away from the body.

A Good Boot Is Hard to Find

In Nessmuk's words: "Light boots are best. Not thin, unserviceable affairs, but light as to actual weight." The advice is still good—walking a mile means lifting each boot as many as 1,000 times, and the ounces add up. But it is hard advice to follow. A cobbler by trade, Nessmuk made his boots to his own specifications and advised others to do the same. The old woodsman never dreamed what a profusion of ready-made footwear would one day confront his readers. To single out the right pair for your feet and your purposes is no small task.

Most people tend to buy boots that are too heavy. Think about how you plan to use yours. For day hiking in summer along an established trail with fairly even terrain, 2- to 3-pound trail or work boots may be sufficient; they are light, their soles are flexible, and they give better support and protection than sneakers. For an assault on a major peak you need rugged mountaineering boots, solid and heavy (5 pounds is the minimum) with rigid lug soles and many layers of insulation. In between there exists a wide range of medium-weight hiking and climbing boots made for backpackers. The good ones have full-grain leather uppers, high enough and tough enough to protect and support your ankles; durable soles that can be replaced when needed; and firm internal support that prevents your arches from breaking down under the extra poundage of a full pack. To make waterproofing more effective, boots should have few seams, none of them sewn through, and the tongue should be gusseted at the sides to keep moisture out. Such niceties as interior padding and scree collars (they seal the top of the boots, making gaiters unnecessary) are matters of personal preference. Each has potential drawbacks: padded boots can become very hot on a long hike, and scree collars sometimes put strain

on the Achilles tendons. Good boots do not solve every problem. Whatever boots you wear, keep your feet dry with wool socks, even in summer. If wool irritates you, wear inner socks of silk—never cotton. Two pairs of socks insulate better than one if boots are not tight.

Kinds of boots

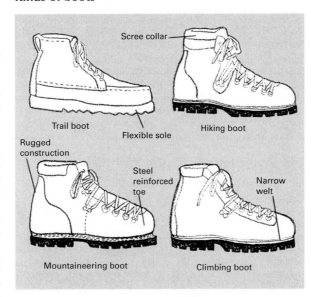

Trail boot · Scree collar · Flexible sole · Hiking boot · Rugged construction · Steel reinforced toe · Narrow welt · Mountaineering boot · Climbing boot

Shoelike trail boots have flexible soles but give little support. Hiking boots are tougher and stiffer, a bit heavier. Mountaineering boots are heavy, well insulated, and very rugged. Climbing boots have rigid soles and narrow welts for support on tiny footholds; walking any distance in them can be uncomfortable.

Caring for your boots

New boots are best broken in gradually by walking; for a quick job, fill boots with water and let them soak for a few minutes. Put them on wet, and walk for an hour or two so that leather will conform to your feet. To dry, stuff boots with paper and put them in a warm—not hot—place.

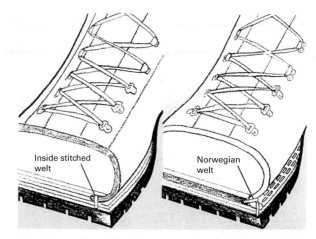

Inside stitched welt · Norwegian welt

Welt of boot, where sole joins uppers, is a vulnerable area. Inside stitching is durable but must be done by hand, so it is expensive. In Norwegian welt, stitching is exposed and water can seep through; protect the welt with epoxy sealer. Bonded welts (not shown) are waterproof, but soles cannot be replaced.

How to buy a pair of boots that fit

Among the many styles of hiking boots made by the dozen or so top manufacturers, there is almost sure to be a pair just right for your feet. Your second day in the wilderness is too late to discover that you failed to find them. The average shoe store does not stock a wide selection of hiking boots, so seek out shops catering to backpackers. Plan to visit several and be ready to make a pest of yourself. Try on as many boots as necessary until you find a proper fit: snug enough to prevent your feet from moving inside (which is how blisters are born) but not so tight as to constrict circulation. Try on both boots of each pair over wool hiking socks, and do not buy until you have walked around in them for 15 to 20 minutes.

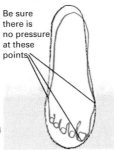

Be sure there is no pressure at these points

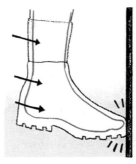

1. Before lacing, push foot forward. One finger should fit behind heel.

2. Lace boots and stand. Wiggle your toes; they must not be cramped.

3. Kick a wall. Your toes should not touch the end of the boot.

4. Rock up and down; squat and bounce. Heel should not move in boot.

5. Stand on sides of feet to test for ankle support and painless flexibility.

Get a Good Night's Sleep In Fair Weather or Foul

"I have suffered enough in close, dark, cheerless, damp tents."
—Nessmuk

Next to a clear, starry sky, the old woodsman's favorite shelter was an open-faced shanty made of cotton, which he waterproofed himself. It was stretched over a frame of freshly cut saplings. The front was open "to admit of a bright fire" and the roof slanted "to reflect the fire heat on the bedding below."

In his day, cotton and heavy canvas were the only choices for portable shelter. Today's camper has the additional options of lightweight nylon and the somewhat heavier and costlier "breathable" resin laminates. The latter keep out rain while allowing water vapor to escape (see *Cotton, Wool, and Synthetic Fabrics*, p.408). You can accomplish the same end by stretching a rain-fly over your tent; this is a waterproof tarp fashioned to fit a few inches above the tent's contours, repelling the rain while allowing water vapor to escape.

Tent designs have also progressed over the years. Campers can choose among many spacious shapes and sizes, most of them with easily erected, lightweight frames. Some are quite practical, some are worth carrying only in rigorous climates, and some are little more than pretty fantasies. Many are expensive, although you can cut costs by making your own from a prefabricated kit. Kits make the job easier than starting from scratch, but a lot of work is still involved—much of it requiring a heavy-duty sewing machine. Kits are also available for making down sleeping bags and garments.

The first question to ask in choosing a tent is: How much does it weigh? Put the answer on one side of a mental balance sheet. On the other side, consider your needs: Is it waterproof? Is it well ventilated? Is it fire retardant? Does it keep out insects? Is there space enough inside? How sturdy is it? Can it be put up in the dark? In a rainstorm? On a mountain slope?

Consider where you will be going and how long you plan to stay. For overnight summer bivouacs along a hiking trail, a tarp or tube tent might be all the shelter you want to carry. Even a tarp could be more than you need for a trek across the Arizona desert, where a poncho may be more valuable for shade than for rain protection. (The American desert is not the Sahara, however; sudden thunderstorms and even rainy weeks do occur.) In the damp Pacific Northwest or in the high Rockies, a warm, dry tent with a closable entrance and a rainfly is well worth its weight.

Tent Styles and the Knots to Tie Them

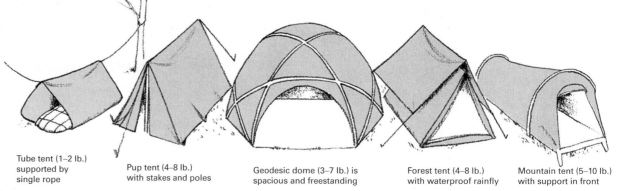

Tube tent (1–2 lb.) supported by single rope

Pup tent (4–8 lb.) with stakes and poles

Geodesic dome (3–7 lb.) is spacious and freestanding

Forest tent (4–8 lb.) with waterproof rainfly

Mountain tent (5–10 lb.) with support in front

Two-man tent with low profile is best for warmth and wind resistance. High ridgeline makes for headroom and ventilation.

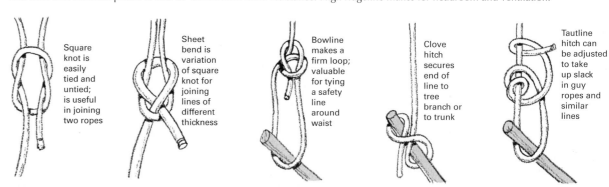

Square knot is easily tied and untied; is useful in joining two ropes

Sheet bend is variation of square knot for joining lines of different thickness

Bowline makes a firm loop; valuable for tying a safety line around waist

Clove hitch secures end of line to tree branch or to trunk

Tautline hitch can be adjusted to take up slack in guy ropes and similar lines

Knot tying is an important skill for erecting tents and other purposes. Practice these knots until they are automatic.

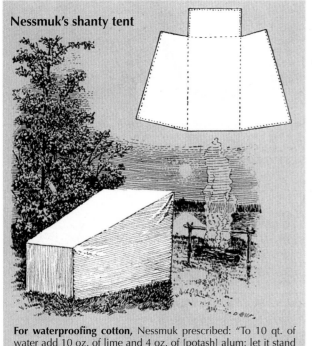

Nessmuk's shanty tent

For waterproofing cotton, Nessmuk prescribed: "To 10 qt. of water add 10 oz. of lime and 4 oz. of [potash] alum; let it stand until clear; fold the cloth snugly and put in another vessel; pour the solution on it, let it soak for 12 hr.; then rinse in lukewarm rainwater, stretch and dry in the sun."

Bedding for Comfort and Warmth

Sleeping bags are graded according to the lowest temperature at which they will keep you warm. The lower the temperature, the warmer the bag and the more expensive it is likely to be. Try to purchase a bag that matches your anticipated needs—sleeping in an overstuffed bag can be almost as uncomfortable as sleeping in one that is too light. Some campers own several bags for different seasons and climates and use them singly or in combination for various weather conditions. A less expensive solution is the three-layer combination: one lightweight bag with an insert for use in colder weather and an outer shell of waterproof nylon or breathable resin laminate for foul weather use.

Most sleeping bags are filled either with down or synthetic fiber. The purpose of both is to maintain a layer of dead air between you and the outside. The thickness of this layer is called the loft: the more inches of loft, the warmer the sleeping bag. Goose down—the most expensive filling for sleeping bags—provides more loft per pound than any material known, but it packs together when wet and dries slowly. Although the synthetics do not give as much loft as down, most of them hold it better when damp. They tend to deteriorate with time—a drawback that is offset by their comparatively low initial cost.

A comfortable night's sleep in cold weather depends on more than a good sleeping bag, however. An air mattress or, better yet, a foam pad—either closed cell or open cell—will not only cushion you but also insulate you from the cold ground. This is especially important because your body weight squashes the sleeping bag's insulation beneath you, all but eliminating its loft. Other factors influencing nighttime comfort in cold weather are your own metabolic rate (some people are simply warmer than others), the relative humidity, the altitude, and the quality of tent you are using.

Skillful use of a tarp

Many backpackers carry only a length of 1/8-in. nylon cord and a nylon tarp (total weight about 2 lb.) equipped with a dozen or so strategically placed grommets or tie lines, from which they rig shelter for various situations. Setting up a tarp is harder than it looks; practice before depending on it for survival.

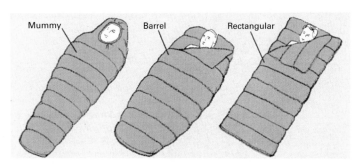

Choose bag for warmth, weight, and to suit your sleeping style. Mummy bag is warmest for its weight if you do not thrash about; heat is lost wherever elbows or knees compact filling. Rectangular bag is least efficient, but two bags can be zipped together for sharing.

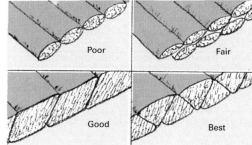

To keep filling in place, sleeping bag walls are joined to form chambers or tubes. When the stitching goes straight through, warmth is lost at each seam; for better insulation, baffles between walls are offset.

Caring for your down-filled bag and garments

Make every effort to keep your sleeping bag clean and dry. Do not roll it for storage, but push it loosely into a waterproof stuff sack. Sleep with your nose and mouth outside the bag so your moisture-laden breath does not condense inside the bag. Let the bag air dry after the trip is over, and repair all rips and holes promptly before filling is lost.

Never dryclean a sleeping bag or any other filled garment—the cleaning fluids will damage both down and synthetic fillings. Instead, wash by hand in a large tub, using warm water and mild nondetergent soap. Prescrub dirty spots, then submerge in soapy water and pump up and down. Do not wring or twist—baffles can be torn loose—and do not lift bag soaking wet. Rinse several times by draining the water, adding fresh water, and pumping some more. After the last rinse, when the water remains clear, gently press out all the water you can and gather the bag in your arms to support its weight. Spread the bag in the sun to dry (it will take several days), turning and fluffing it occasionally, or use a commercial dryer set at *Low*.

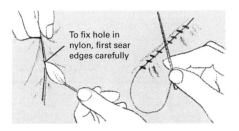

Carefully sear edges of small holes to prevent unraveling, then sew with nylon thread.

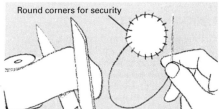

Patch large holes with pressure-sensitive rip-stop tape. Press in place and sew around edges.

All Your Essential Gear Will Fit Into One Pack

"It may be remarked that man is a vertebrate animal and ought to respect his backbone."
—Nessmuk

The human backbone is a remarkable but troublesome part of our anatomy. To use it for standing erect is in itself an amazing feat—but to hang weights upon it that pull it backward, or even to apply very much weight pushing straight down, is to treat it with disrespect. The best result you can look for is quick exhaustion; the worst, a disabling back problem. That is why pack frames were invented, to transfer as much weight as possible from the shoulders to the hips and to hold the rest as close as possible to the line of the spine.

A pack and frame is a personal thing. If it is to do its job properly, it must be fitted to your body as carefully as a suit of clothes. The most important dimension to consider is the length of your back from shoulder to hip. The pack's waistband should rest comfortably on your hips and the straps must be high enough to hold the frame securely to your back without putting weight on the shoulders. Equally important and almost as personal is the method of organizing gear inside the pack. Some people are happiest with a pack that is divided into several compartments; others prefer a single large bag. In either case, the load must be well balanced with the bulk of the weight held close to the body and fairly high in the pack. Never select a pack based on how it fits when empty—the addition of a 50-pound load will change things considerably. One good way to find the right pack for yourself is to rent a few different kinds from specialty shops so you can make comparisons in the field.

Pick the pack that suits your needs

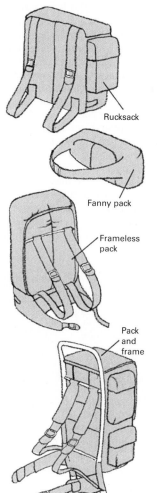

Rucksack

Fanny pack

Frameless pack

Pack and frame

Day packs. For a short hike or side trip with loads up to 25 lb., a rucksack strapped to the shoulders or a fanny pack strapped around the waist may be enough. Look for double stitching where straps join pack and around pack bottom.

Soft packs. Climbing and scrambling in forest and rough country is easier with frameless pack. Fewer protrusions mean less snagging on underbrush. Some soft packs have internal frames; others feature design innovations to eliminate the need for a frame altogether. Both must carry close to capacity for effective weight distribution.

External frame. Most comfortable way to carry heavy loads over long distances is in a pack attached to a rigid frame. Pack should attach to at least three points on each side. Padded straps should be firm, not spongy, be securely attached to frame, and have adjustable front buckles.

Fitting and loading for comfort

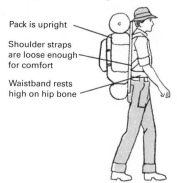

Pack is upright

Shoulder straps are loose enough for comfort

Waistband rests high on hip bone

Try on pack loaded with 30 to 50 lb. Tighten waistband; it should fit snugly around top of hipbone and relieve weight from shoulders. Then adjust straps so you can slip two fingers easily between them and shoulders. Make sure all buckles are secure and that waistband can be released quickly in case of emergency.

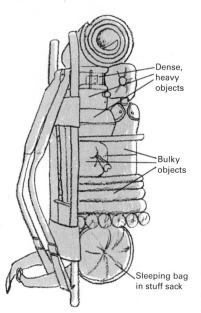

Dense, heavy objects

Bulky objects

Sleeping bag in stuff sack

Organize your pack so everything has its place and stick to your system. Put dense, heavy objects high in the pack and close to your spine, with sharp corners padded. Make sure all weight is well balanced. One way to keep things separated is with plastic bags, making your pack a bag full of bags; coding the bags by color can help in identification. Use outer pockets for trail food, first aid kit, toilet paper, and other potentially urgent items. Lash sleeping bag in stuff sack to lower part of frame; in some soft packs waistband doubles as a stuff sack.

Easing the weight

Getting a pack on and off can be more of a strain than carrying it. When taking a short break on the trail, leave your pack on; just lean back against a convenient tree or rock. When you take it off, put it down gently—lightweight frames damage easily. Two common techniques for putting on a heavy pack are shown at right. You will likely develop your own style.

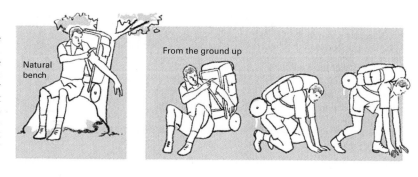

Natural bench

From the ground up

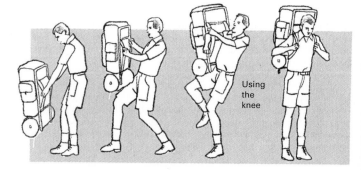

Using the knee

Hope for the Best and Prepare for the Worst

The best way to cope with an emergency is to anticipate and prevent it; the best time to do that is before you leave. Talk over every detail of the trip with your companions and reach agreements about your route, how fast to travel, what you will eat (meal by meal), what pieces of equipment are worth carrying and which are not, how early you intend to get started, how late in the day to stop. Decide on an equitable division of labor: who cooks, who cleans up, who pitches tents, who builds fires, who carries which piece of shared equipment, who knows about gathering wild food, who fishes, who is the best pathfinder, who leads on a rough trail, who has what talent or limitation that may be important later on. Discuss philosophy: Why are you going into the wilderness? For adventure? For peace and quiet? For exercise? How important is comfort? How important is schedule? If you arrive at a particularly attractive campsite, will you stay a day or two, or take a few pictures and keep moving? What happens on a rainy day? If you are not compatible, do not put your lives in each other's hands.

Learn all you can about the area where you are going. If it is a place with which you are unfamiliar, talk to people who have been there. Read books and magazine articles about the region. Send for topographical maps and study them carefully (see *Sources and resources*, p.429). Use them to plan your route, selecting a place for each night's campsite—you may not be able to stick to your plans, but they will provide a framework to keep track of your progress. Find out about the climate—average high and low temperatures, precipitation, possible extremes—and check on weather predictions, both short range and long range. Learn about the area's plant and animal life, especially what is edible and what is dangerous during the season when you will be there. Make sure you know about local licensing and conservation laws as well as land-use regulations.

Gather together all your equipment and check it out. Set up the tent and wet it down to see if it leaks. Go over seams on packs, sleeping bags, and clothing, looking for weak spots and signs of wear. Condition and waterproof your boots. Make sure your compass is in working order.

If you or any of your companions is a minor, be sure to carry a medical permission slip, signed by a parent or guardian, giving any doctor permission to treat illness and injury. Finally, make a copy of your itinerary, including a map, and leave it with someone dependable so that if you fail to show up when and where you should, people will have some idea where to start looking.

Getting in shape

Wilderness backpacking is a demanding sport, and your life may depend on your strength and endurance. You can build endurance by running long distances with your boots on. ("Running a stadium" is popular among back-packing college students—you can see them on spring mornings racing heavy booted up and down the steep aisles of football stadiums.) A daily regimen of sit-ups, push-ups, and pull-ups strengthens the arms and upper body. Climbing a 15-foot rope wearing a full pack is another good exercise. For the torso, try the trunk-twister. Stand with feet apart, arms out, and knees straight; pivot to grasp the right ankle with the left hand; pull a little, release, stand straight, and repeat on the other side. Work up to 50 of these per day.

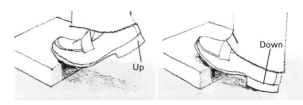

To stretch leg muscles, stand on edge of a thick book. Rise up on toes, then touch heels to floor. Repeat 40 to 50 times.

Equipment—the lighter the better

Nessmuk's key rule in selecting his equipment was "commence by studying to ascertain just how light one can go without especial discomfort." To follow this rule, first make a list of everything you might need, noting the weight of each item; then eliminate, ounce by ounce and item by item, until the list has been honed to essentials. The sample list at right totals about 45 lb.; if pack, tent, sleeping bag, boots, clothing, and food are added in, you would have a load worthy of a healthy mule. Some items, however, are redundant—the cook kit, for example, is an alternative to the frying pan, billy pots, and cup. And other supplies and equipment, such as stove, fuel, tent, lantern, repair supplies, and first aid kit, are generally shared by the group as a whole.

oz.	Item
25 oz.	Air mattress
3	Altimeter
2	Bags, plastic
1	Bandanas
4	Batteries
8	Binoculars
6	Book, paperback
2	Bowl, plastic
40	Camera and film
14	Camp shoes
2	Candles
6	Canteen
3	Compass
6	Cord, nylon (1/8")
20	Crampons
3	Eyeglasses, extra
8	Fanny pack
7	First aid kit
26	Fishing gear
4	Flashlight
4	Foot powder
16	Frying pan

Balaclava hat 4 oz.

Sierra cup 3 oz.

Candle lantern 4 oz.

Collapsible cup 3 oz.

oz.	Item
4 oz.	Gaiters
3	Gloves or mittens
8	Grill
8	Guide book
10	Hammock
4	Hat or balaclava
2	Insect repellent
16	Knapsack
3	Knife
1	Laces, extra
18	Life jacket
16	Long johns
2	Magnifying glass
1	Map, topographic
2	Notebook and pencil
45	Oven, reflector
14	Pad, foam
18	Parka shell
32	Parka, mountain
14	Poncho
36	Pots, billy
2	Pot lifter (pliers)

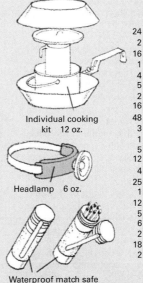

Individual cooking kit 12 oz.

Headlamp 6 oz.

Waterproof match safe 4 oz.

oz.	Item
24 oz.	Rope (1/4")
2	Salt tablets
16	Shorts, hiking
1	Snakebite kit
4	Soap
5	Socks, extra
2	Sponge
16	Staff
48	Stove and accessories
3	Sunglasses
1	Suntan lotion
5	Survival kit
12	Sweater, extra
4	Swimsuit
25	Tarp
1	Thermometer
12	Toilet kit
5	Toilet paper
6	Underwear, extra
2	Watch
18	Water filter kit
2	Whetstone

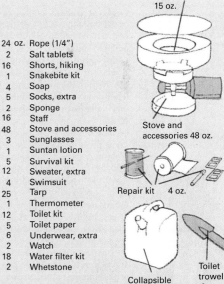

Over for stove 15 oz.

Stove and accessories 48 oz.

Repair kit 4 oz.

Collapsible 1 gal. water bottle 2 oz.

Toilet trowel 2 oz.

Getting There on Foot And Enjoying the Trip

"We do not go to the green woods and crystal waters to rough it, we go to smooth it. We get it rough enough at home."
—Nessmuk

The key to walking long distances over rough ground with a pack on your back is maintaining a comfortable, steady body tempo (not to be confused with a steady pace; drill sergeants may march their units in cadence, uphill and down, but for them hiking is a job, not a pleasure). The best gauge you have of your body's tempo, short of monitoring your pulse, is your breath rate. Establish a steady rhythm of deep breathing on level ground, taking three or four steps for each intake of air and three or four on each exhalation, and adjust your pace as needed to maintain the rhythm. On an uphill pull, for example, reduce the count to two steps before you get short of breath; a real climb may dictate one step per breath or less. At first you will probably have

to discipline yourself to slow down (beginners tend to go uphill much too quickly). Eventually, a well-established body tempo will tend to take care of itself.

Be economical with your energy; spend it only on necessities. A springy step takes energy, so walk flat-footed, using the large thigh muscles. Energy is wasted stepping up onto a rock or log, so step over or go around such obstacles. Energy is depleted by chills or overheating; add or remove a layer of clothing before discomfort demands that you do so (often it is enough to open the top of your jacket in order for trapped air to escape). Make a rest stop every hour or so, but not for too long—getting started is hard once you have cooled off. Eat a little high-energy trail food, such as chocolate "gorp" (see *Campfire Cookery*, p.420), whenever you feel hungry. Prevent dehydration by sipping water often.

Take good care of your feet. They are your only means of transportation. Remove your boots and socks at rest stops to let your feet cool off and air out; when you have the chance to soak your feet in a cool stream or lake, take it. If you feel the beginning of a hot spot—a point of irritation—do not be heroic. Stop and cover the spot with a piece of moleskin or a bit of masking or adhesive tape before it becomes a blister. (For treatment of blisters,

see *First Aid in Emergencies*, p.426.) When fording a stream, remove your socks and put your boots back on, lacing them tightly. Afterward, drain the boots and replace your socks; if they are wool, they will absorb the remaining moisture in your boots safely.

If you are part of a group (and two or three people is a group), gauge your pace to the slowest and the weakest. If you are the slowest, or if you develop a problem, such as blisters or a muscle pull, do not hesitate to make your needs known—better to slow the group than to be carried out. (But avoid idle complaints; everyone is enduring the same weather and being bitten by the same bugs.)

There are courtesies that backpackers observe. If you are following an established trail, stay on it; switchbacks are there to prevent erosion—do not shortcut them. If you find a shortcut developing, block it with brush. On a steep trail, descending hikers have right-of-way; clear the trail for them. Parties with pack animals always have right-of-way; move off trail on the downhill side and stand still (a horse spooked by your presence is easier to control and less likely to be injured if he shies uphill). Do not intrude on other campers unless invited, and then do not stay long. Do not accept food even if it is offered unless your need is very great.

The Fine Art of Walking

Level ground

Hillside

On level ground. Within the limits of comfort, long strides are more efficient than short ones. Keep heavy items high in pack and close to body so that the weight is centered over your hips.

Going uphill. Short steps minimize the struggle against gravity; so does the use of a staff or alpenstock, which also helps maintain balance. Stand straight rather than leaning forward (it will feel at first as though you are tilting backward) to keep your weight centered—and so that you can regain your balance in case of a slip before landing on your face. The best place for heavy items on a long climb is in the middle of the pack, close to your body. When climbing a very steep slope, use the mountaineer's rest step: pause briefly and exhale with each step after placing your front foot and before transferring your weight from the rear foot.

Going downhill. Stress is on toes, soles of feet, and knees. Tighten boot laces so feet do not move inside. Take short steps with knees slightly bent to cushion impact of each step. Lean slightly forward to help keep balance in case of a slip.

Traversing hillside. Lean away from hill, not toward it, to minimize stress on ankles, knees, and spine and so that body will be thrown into an upright position in case you slip. Use of staff or alpenstock helps to equalize weight and maintain balance.

Water Crossings Are Always Risky

Downstream

Safety line

Rock at water surface may be icy

Try to keep dry by boulder hopping or using a foot log. Ford a large stream at a wide spot where water moves slowly; undo waistband so pack can be shed quickly, face upstream, and sidestep across. If stream is deep or if you must swim, use safety line secured upstream; place heavy waterproof items in bottom of pack, the remainder in a plastic bag for buoyancy. Snow-fed streams are fullest late in the day, lower and slower in the early morning.

Keeping a Weather Eye

Professional weather forecasters arrive at their predictions with the assistance of such instruments as barometers, hygrometers, and thermometers, each of which measures some aspect of the ever-changing atmosphere: air pressure, humidity, and temperature, respectively. The wilderness is filled with indicators every bit as accurate, if not so nicely calibrated. Knowing how to read them is one of the skills of outdoorsmanship.

Masses of cold and warm air move across the earth from west to east at a rate of about 600 miles a day, propelled into and around pools and eddies of high and low pressure. Air blows clockwise away from the center of a high pressure area and counterclockwise toward the center of a low pressure area, where it escapes upward, cooling as it rises and leaving behind the moisture it contains. Thus a drop in air pressure (a falling barometer) generally indicates the arrival of a pocket of humid air, clouds, and, often, rain or snow, particularly when the low pressure area is at the front of an air mass. There are many signs of an approaching low pressure area: smoke hovers and turns downward; birds tend to roost; swallows and bats swoop low; ground odors arise from ditches and marshes; clouds form at low altitudes; the rising humidity makes hair limp, causes distant objects to appear closer (because the usual evaporation haze is missing), and precludes the formation of morning dew. These signs are all prominent among folklore's favorite foul weather warnings.

Other bits of weather lore are also firmly based in fact. Take, for example, the expression "Red sky at night, sailors' delight. Red sky at morning, sailors take warning." (The setting sun shines through tomorrow's air, 500 to 600 miles westward; the laws of light refraction are such that if that air is dry and cloudless, the sky will be red just after sunset. The same laws decree that a red sky before sunrise means the air that has passed to the east is clearer and drier than where you are.)

There are three basic cloud types: cirrus (wispy), stratus (layered), and cumulus (puffy). Each is produced by a specific air pattern, and each may presage a particular kind of storm. Learn to read the early steps of these developments. Fluffy white cumulus clouds, for example, are formed by warm updrafts called thermals. They are common on clear days and generally foreshadow more of the same, but they are also the stuff of which thunderstorms are made. When a thermal is intensified by the moist updraft of a low pressure area, the result is a huge, billowing thunderhead (cumulonimbus), bringing strong winds, thunder, lightning, and a downpour of rain. The telltale step in this pattern is when fair weather cumulus clouds begin to puff upward like the turrets of a castle. Such towering cumulus clouds are not always followed by thunderheads; but when they occur in the west or northwest sky, a little darker and lower than other cumulus clouds, the wise camper begins to make preparations for a sudden storm.

Cirrus clouds are made of ice crystals, formed when warm air suddenly meets cooler air (the way your breath forms vapor on a cold day). Often they signify nothing more than a high altitude wind pattern, but when they begin to form a thin, icy layer (cirrostratus)—causing the appearance of a halo around the sun or moon—it is probably the first warning of an approaching warm air front, with a long, steady siege of rain or snow.

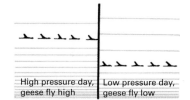

Migrating geese maintain their altitude by sensing air pressure; the more the pressure, the higher they fly. Low-flying geese mean a falling barometer, an omen of bad weather.

High pressure day, geese fly high | Low pressure day, geese fly low

Learn to Read the Language of the Clouds

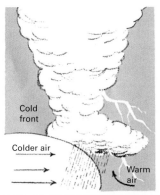

Cold air is heavier than warm, so the front of a cold air mass (left) hugs the ground as it moves eastward, pushing warm air upward like wood shavings before the blade of a chisel. Cold fronts give little warning: winds may change to easterly or northeasterly, often creating a squall line (a band of high winds and short-lived thundershowers) a few minutes before their arrival. Layers of cumulus clouds (cumulostratus) or thunderheads may accompany the front itself. Warm fronts (below) move more slowly and give 10 to 15 hours warning. Wispy cirrus clouds accumulate and grow steadily lower, and winds often shift to easterly or southeasterly; long, steady rain from low stratus clouds presage and accompany the front itself. When a cold front overtakes a warm front, the result is called an occluded front; the sky grows dark, and heavy weather, snow, or violent winds often result.

Cold front / Colder air / Warm air

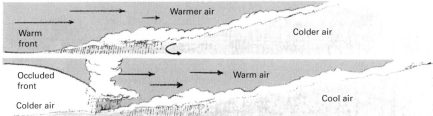

Warm front / Warmer air / Warm air / Colder air / Occluded front / Warm air / Cool air / Colder air

Cumulus clouds, fed by warm updraft of cold front, develop towering form, warning of approaching thunderstorms or snow.

Cirrus clouds form wispy mares' tails before warm front hits. Next comes cirrostratus, then "mackerel sky," then rain.

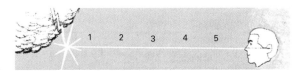

Sound travels a mile in about five seconds; light arrives almost instantaneously. To find how many miles away a thunderstorm is, count the seconds between a lightning flash and the thunderclap that follows it, and divide by five.

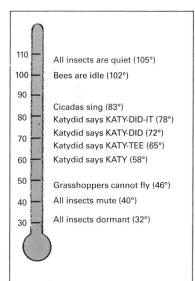

All insects are quiet (105°)
Bees are idle (102°)
Cicadas sing (83°)
Katydid says KATY-DID-IT (78°)
Katydid says KATY-DID (72°)
Katydid says KATY-TEE (65°)
Katydid says KATY (58°)
Grasshoppers cannot fly (46°)
All insects mute (40°)
All insects dormant (32°)

To find temperature in Fahrenheit, count a cricket's chirps for 14 seconds and add 40. Other insects indicate readings as shown above.

With a Map and Compass You Are Never Lost

Tales abound of frontiersmen plunging into unmapped wilderness and homing in with pinpoint accuracy on some far-off cabin or clearing in the woods. Today's camper, equipped with topographical map and compass, should have an advantage over the old-timers, yet many succeed in getting lost—some permanently. Why? For one thing, not everyone carries these vital tools at all times; for another, many do not know how to use them; and finally, there is more to finding your way than reading a map and knowing which way is north.

A topographical map, or "topo" in backpacker's parlance, is a picture of the landscape drawn with contour lines, each of which represents a constant plane of elevation above sea level. Because the picture is a bird's-eye view, the closer together the lines are, the steeper the slope they show, while the wider the space between lines, the more gradual the change in elevation. With practice you can learn to visualize any terrain from its depiction on a topo—at least in terms of its larger features. Then if you are in a position to see major landscape features around you, it is possible to orient the map to the real world and to find your position upon it.

Topos exist for all areas of the continental United States in several scales, or series. The most valuable of these for campers are the 7 1/2-and the 15-minute series. Each map in the 7 1/2-minute series covers 7 1/2 minutes (1/8 degree) of longitude (about 7 miles) at a scale of 1:24,000, or about 3/8 mile to the inch. A 15-minute map covers an area four times that size at a scale of 1:62,500, or about 1 mile to the inch. Contour intervals vary from 80 feet of elevation between lines on some 15-minute maps to 10 feet on some 7 1/2-minute ones. Each series has its advantages, each its pitfalls. Because 15-minute maps depict a larger area, they are easier to orient to large landscape features, and you need not carry so many of them. On the other hand, 7 1/2-minute maps show details that could be vital; it is possible, for example, for a sheer 150-foot cliff not to show at all on a topo with 80-foot contour intervals. Moreover, some of the older 15-minute maps are out of date or, worse yet, inaccurate.

Camping supply stores, sporting goods stores, and some bookshops often carry topos. Or you can write to the U.S. Geological Survey Office for a free index map of any state, from which you can select the topos you need (see *Sources and resources*, p.429).

The Map

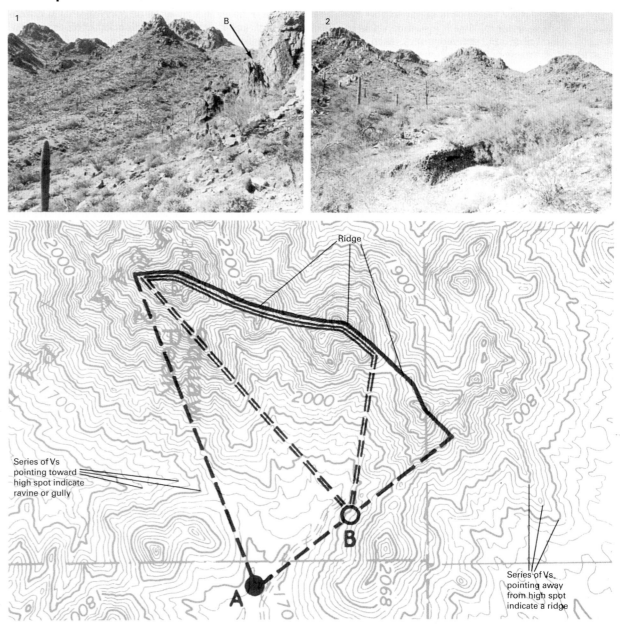

Series of Vs pointing toward high spot indicate ravine or gully

Ridge

Series of Vs pointing away from high spot indicate a ridge

Terrain features take on very different appearances when viewed from different angles. Photo 1 (left above), taken from point A on the map, shows the same mountain ridge as seen in photo 2 (right above). Photo 1 also shows the spot (point B) from which photo 2 was taken. The contour interval on the map is 20 ft. Note that every fifth contour line is heavier than the others and its elevation is labeled; the exact elevations of high points are labeled as well. On a standard topo map contour lines are brown; man-made features, such as roads and buildings, are black; and forested or overgrown areas are shaded green.

The Compass

The compass needle is a small magnet that points not toward the North Pole but toward magnetic north. The difference between the two, known as the angle of declination, varies with location and changes slowly with time. (There is a line, running more or less through Savannah, Georgia, and Gary, Indiana, along which they are currently the same.) The exact angle of declination for an area is given in the legend of a topo. If your compass has a movable collar, set it to reflect this declination, and align the compass so that the needle points to N on the collar; then move the map so that its north-south axis aligns with the north-south axis of the compass. If your compass has no collar, spread the topo out flat and place the compass on it so that its north-south axis aligns with true north on the map. Then turn map and compass together until the angle between the needle and true north matches the angle of declination. Next, look for a terrain feature that you can identify on the map. Take a reading on it and draw a line on the map along this bearing. If you cannot locate your position by studying the nearby terrain, sight on another landmark. Where the two lines intersect is your position.

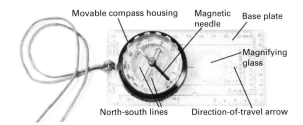

Orienteering compass (shown above) has inner scale for angle of declination and movable casing for direction finding. Another popular style—the sportman's compass—has a movable inner disk with an arrow that can be used for either purpose.

Deciding which way to go

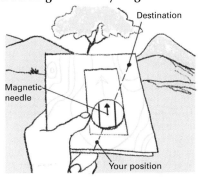

1. Orient map and use compass to find your position on it. Draw line on map from your position to destination.

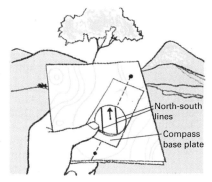

2. Place compass base plate on this line. Rotate compass housing so north-south lines match magnetic north on map.

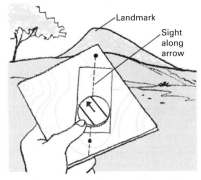

3. Hold compass and map steady, and view along direction-of-travel arrow to sight a landmark (hill in distance).

How to get there from here

Having sighted a landmark, you theoretically need only hike to it and take another reading. Or, having set your compass, you could keep the needle pointing to north on the dial and follow the direction-of-travel arrow to your destination. In fact, you can seldom do either: obstacles, ranging from bramble thickets to mountains, will probably cut off sight of your landmark; they may also obstruct progress. Some obstacles can be anticipated by studying the topo; others will be surprises. If you find you must go far out of your way, take a reading of 45 degrees and follow it, counting your paces, until you have gone far enough to clear; then take a reading of 90 degrees in the other direction and count the paces back; finally, take one more reading of 45 degrees to resume your original line of travel.

If you find yourself close to an objective—a wooded campsite, for example—but unable to locate it, make a methodical search pattern. Walk a set distance (20 paces, perhaps, depending on how far you can see) in any direction; then turn 90 degrees and walk the same distance. Turn 90 degrees again, and so forth, adding 20 paces every second turn.

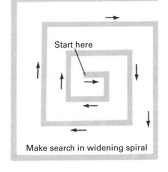

Make search in widening spiral

Finding Yourself

The best advice about getting lost is: do not. Follow your progress on the topo and use your compass to stay oriented. Be aware of landmarks and their relation to one another; look backward from time to time to memorize the terrain from the other direction.

But suppose you do become disoriented? As Nessmuk observed: "It has a muddling effect on the mind, this getting lost in the woods. But if you can collect and arrange your gray brain matter and suppress all panicky feeling, it is easily got along with." Resist the impulse to panic. Resist all impulses. Stop, relax for a while, and think. You have three choices: you can retrace your steps, stay where you are, or reorient yourself and proceed. If you have become separated from a group, stay where you are, signal your position in some way, and wait to be found. If you are alone, or if the whole group is lost with you, first orient yourself to north and south. Look for landmarks—if you can see none, seek high ground or climb a tree. Then decide whether to go back or go forward. At the very least, use the knowledge of which way is north to move in a straight line.

Orienting yourself without a compass

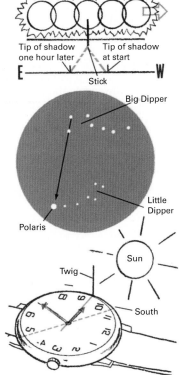

Sun or moon. Insert a short stick in the ground and mark where the tip of its shadow falls. One hour later, mark again. The line between these marks is roughly east-west; the stick is on the south side of the line.

North Star. First find the Big Dipper. Trace an imaginary line between the two stars that form its front lip and extend this line five times its own length to locate Polaris—never more than one degree from true north.

Watch. Insert twig into level ground. Place watch with hour hand pointing toward twig, aligned with its shadow. If watch is set to standard time, halfway between hour hand and 12 o'clock is south.

Midafternoon Is the Time To Pick a Campsite

"If there is a spot on Earth where trifles make up the sum of human enjoyment it is in a woodland camp."
—Nessmuk

Nessmuk's "trifles" were mostly examples of old-time woodcraft—pillows stuffed with hemlock browse or fire pokers and tongs fashioned from green hickory sticks—but the crux of his advice holds true for today's campers who carry their trifles with them.

The ideal campsite is on bare and level ground well off the trail, about 100 feet from fresh water (no closer), with plenty of dry wood scattered handily about. It is sheltered from wind but not in a hollow where damp air collects. It is not in a gully or natural runoff (in case of rain), and it offers esthetic pleasures: a nice view, the fragrance of surrounding pines, the murmur of a stream, the warmth of the rising sun. It is worthwhile to search out such a spot for a long-term campsite. For

an overnight bivouac you may have to be satisfied with considerably less. To hold out for the perfect campsite can lead to such joyless feats as pitching a tent in the dark on top of what you later discover to be an anthill.

The first important trifle—if it is neither raining nor threatening to start—is to spread and fluff your sleeping bag. Then get water on to boil for coffee, tea, soup, or whatever pick-me-up you fancy. Relax awhile and enjoy; change your boots for soft camp shoes if you carry them (another trifle well worth the weight). Then there is work to do—gear to unpack, shelter to set up, water to haul, dinner to cook and to clean up after, food to store, firewood to protect for morning—all before nightfall if possible. Before turning in, be sure that you have a water bottle handy as well as a flashlight, first aid kit, toilet paper, and shovel or toilet trowel.

In foul weather, shelter obviously comes first—a good reason to pack your tent on top. If yours is a floorless pup tent, erect poles, then stake the sides to the ground; if it has a built-in floor, drive stakes first. Freestanding tents need not be staked at all in calm weather or, in any case, only after they have been erected.

Protecting food from animals

Food attracts animals from chipmunks to bears. Do not keep it in your pack or in the tent overnight. Store food bags in one large plastic bag suspended from a tree limb or crossbar. In parks and along trails, where bears are consummate thieves, use two ropes as shown; bags must be at least 15 ft. high and 6 ft. from tree. Black bears usually flee loud noises—bang pots and pans, and yell. If they do not go away, do not argue further. Grizzlies are less timid; keep still. If they charge, lie down and play dead.

Purify Water Before Drinking

You cannot count on drinkable water from even the clearest stream. If you are not certain of the water quality in the place where you plan to hike, either bring the water you need or carry a method of purifying what you find. Halizone tablets do not always do the job, and they deteriorate with age; iodine is more dependable.

An iodination kit consists of a 1-ounce clear glass bottle with a tight-fitting cap and about 5 grams of USP-grade resublimated iodine crystals (available from pharmacists). The crystals can be reused up to a thousand times. Filtration devices are also available to remove pollutants and diminish the iodine flavor of purified water.

Sanitation and cleanliness

If toilet facilities exist, use them. They mean that the area is used by too many people for any other solution. If not, dig a hole 6 to 8 inches deep (not below topsoil, however), use it, burn the used toilet paper and drop it in. Cover your leavings with a little soil. Before abandoning the campsite, fill in the hole with the soil you took out and tread it down firmly. If you are part of a group, designate one person to choose and prepare the latrine site—it is as important as any other aspect of camp life. Its distance from camp must be a compromise between convenience and common sense. Do not dig it on rocky ground and never within 100 feet of any watercourse—even a dry bed. Do not pick a place that might otherwise make a good campsite for someone else.

Do not carry detergents into the wilderness. Wash dishes, clothes, and yourself with soap. (Actually, cleanliness is generally overdone by neophyte campers—in Nessmuk's words: "Don't fool with soap and towels where insects are plenty.") In any case, do not use soap directly in a lake, stream, or other water source. Nor should used wash water be dumped into such a place. Carry water to your campsite, heat it over the fire or stove, then take it farther away from the source before you use it. Dig a sump hole (following the same rules as digging a latrine) in which to dump it.

1. To kill amoeba, bacteria, viruses, and other microbiota, place about 5 grams iodine crystals in 1-oz. glass bottle and fill the bottle with water. Screw the top on tightly and shake for one minute.

2. Allow crystals to settle. Saturated solution (not crystals) is added to drinking water. The strength of the solution depends on water temperature: the colder the water, the weaker the solution.

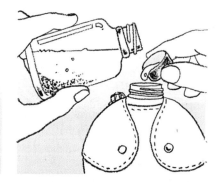

3. If water is 75° F, add 2 tsp. solution to 1 qt. water; at 40° F add 31/2 tsp. (bottle cap usually holds 1/2 tsp.). Let stand 15 minutes. For milder iodine taste use half as much solution; let stand 30 minutes.

Making and Managing a Fire

If you are camping in a heavily used area or in a place where trees are scarce, use a portable stove for cooking. But in a lowland forest where deadwood is plentiful and campers are few, there is no good reason to deny yourself the pleasures of a cooking fire.

Gather the wood you need while it is still daylight; foraging is difficult in the dark. Collect fallen wood only. A standing tree, no matter how dead it looks, is not fair game. Locate your fire on bare ground (preferably sand, rock, or gravel)—never on forest duff, humus, grass, or peat, all of which could smolder for days before bursting into flame; and never next to a tree, log, boulder, or rock face. (The tree can be killed, the log may be ignited, and the rocks will be defaced by scorch marks for decades or longer.) Clear a circle about 10 feet across of all burnable debris and in the center construct the simplest fireplace that will serve your needs, either by arranging flat rocks or by digging a shallow hole. If another camper has left behind a fireplace, do not build a new one.

The fire itself has three components: tinder, kindling, and fuel. Tinder is any such easily ignited material as paper or the dry tops of some plants (goldenrod, cattail, milkweed, Queen Anne's lace). The bark of a dead birch or aspen and pitch gathered from bends and knots of pine trees will burn even when wet. The best kindling is small twigs, especially from evergreens, willows, and poplar; its purpose is to generate enough heat to ignite the fuel. In case of difficulty whittle shavings from any dry stick. In wet weather you can use the heartwood of dead logs, litter from inside a hollow tree, pine cones, and abandoned bird or squirrel nests. For fuel the best cooking coals come from hardwood sticks 1 to 2 inches thick. The wood of conifers, pine in particular, ignites quickly and burns brightly because of the pitch it contains—another wet weather stratagem—but it burns out fast, imparts an unpleasant flavor to broiled meat, and throws off dangerous sparks.

When you are done with a fire, put it out thoroughly and completely. Douse the ashes with water, stir them around, and douse them some more. Before you move on, dismantle the fireplace. Put the rocks back where you got them, scorched side down, and scatter the dead ashes far and wide; if you dug a hole, fill it in with the dirt you took out. Distribute leftover bits of food for small creatures to dispose of. Any other trash that cannot be reduced to ashes, carry away with you.

Keeping Food Cool

Picnic coolers and thermos jugs are far too weighty for backpacking, so fresh meat and other perishables are out of the question as regular provisions on a long hike. For the first day or two, however, or for a weekend jaunt, you can improvise a lightweight cooler from three plastic bags and a towel or cotton cloth. Fill one bag with ice and seal it tightly. Place it, along with your perishable goods (a steak, perhaps, or a pound of hamburger), in a second bag; seal it and wrap it in the cloth. Then seal the whole package in yet another plastic bag and place it in the bottom of your pack. At the end of your first day on the trail—a time when morale is often in need of a boost—you will have fresh meat to enjoy and a bag full of cool water. (If you start with frozen meat and do not open the sealed bags, this makeshift thermos should keep the meat fresh for two days on the trail.)

To keep foodstuffs cool overnight, seal them in a waterproof bag along with a rock for weight, and immerse it in a stream or lake; attach a safety line with which to retrieve it. If you are not near a body of water, make an evaporative cooler: put perishables in a light-colored cloth bag and hang it in a shady, breezy place. Keep it damp; evaporation will cool the contents.

Stoves, Fires, and Fireplaces

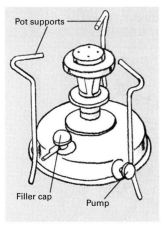

Most cookstoves are fueled by butane or white gas. Butane cartridges are safe and convenient but inefficient in very cold weather. White gas gives more heat per ounce, but it is volatile. Accessories include fuel container, funnel, and eyedropper for priming.

Tepee pattern concentrates flame at the high point and consumes fuel quickly; use it to ignite kindling, to boil water, to heat a reflector oven, and to dry damp wood. Arrange kindling over tinder, leaving plenty of space for air circulation. Light tinder from upwind side. When kindling has begun to burn well, add sticks for fuel until fire is the desired size.

Log cabin pattern burns more evenly; use it to make a bed of coals. Place two large sticks parallel for a base. Between them arrange kindling over tinder in tepee fashion, then place kindling across base. Put several larger sticks across these and continue to build crisscrossed layers, leaving enough space between sticks for air to circulate freely.

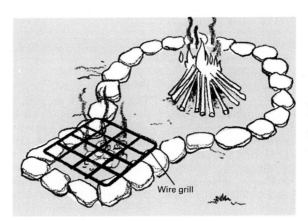

Keyhole fireplace is ideal for base camp or long-term campsite where much cooking will be done. Use flat rocks to enclose cooking slot, making it just large enough to be spanned by wire grill if you have one, narrow enough for pots and pans to rest across if you do not. Wood is reduced to coals in round area, giving light and warmth in the process; for cooking, rake the coals into slot. For overnight bivouac, fireplace can be made from three flat rocks or by digging a narrow trench. Heap soil from trench in one spot so you can replace it before breaking camp and moving on.

419

The Joy of Cooking Over an Open Fire

The biggest difference between cooking over a campfire and on a stove is that you can adjust a stove's burner at will, but you must use a fire when the fire itself is ready. The usual beginner's mistake is to immolate a meal by trying to cook over too hot a blaze. Reflector ovens need an open flame, but frying, broiling, stewing, or baking in closed containers calls for a bed of glowing coals. Water boils faster over an open fire, but rigging tripods, trapezes, dingle sticks, or other improvised devices for suspending a pot is a risky business—the odds are good that the whole contraption will collapse about the time the water gets hot. Compromise by putting a pot of water on to boil as soon as you have raked the cooking slot of your keyhole (see p.419) full of coals, while tongues of flame still lick upward. Use your largest pot—there are plenty of uses for hot water. Save any hot water that is left over from making coffee, tea, soup, or your preferred end-of-the-trail revivifier. If you need the pot for preparing the meal, pour the water into another container. Then after you have cooked your meal, use this water to rinse out the pot. Then rake a few fresh coals into the cooking slot, and while you eat, let some more water boil for cleaning up.

One-pot cookery is mostly a matter of stew, soup, pasta, and rice-based dishes, with protein provided by cheese, sausage, jerky, and various dried meats. Too often the result is nourishing but dull. This need not be so—a little imagination in packing provisions and a little more at the cookfire can turn even a steady diet of macaroni and cheese into a series of varied repasts. Add tomato crystals, garlic, oregano, and foraged burdock leaf stems for a zesty Italian dinner; the addition of margarine, dried milk, powdered eggs, dried mushrooms, wild onions, and watercress produces a flavorsome casserole with French overtones.

Gorp. In backpacker's parlance, "gorp" is a catch-all word for several high-energy trail foods that you can carry in your pocket. You can buy packaged gorp of various descriptions or you can make your own—everyone seems to have his own recipe, most of which are based on chocolate, nuts, and raisins. Start with a block of sweet or semisweet chocolate; melt it down in a double boiler and throw in handfuls of peanuts, raisins, chopped walnuts, dried fruit, berries—whatever pleases you. Let it cool and break it into pieces.

Food to Carry Into the Wilderness

Three basic questions to ask in deciding what food to carry: How much does it weigh? How much energy will it provide? What is its nutritional value?

Food energy is measured in calories. Most healthy people burn about 4,000 calories a day on the trail; if you pack 2 lb. of food for each day, it must deliver an average of 125 calories per ounce to replace this expenditure. Only dry foods and oils are so rich.

About 10 percent of the food energy should be in the form of protein (P) to rebuild body tissue, and at least 20 percent should be fat (F) for long-lasting energy. Carbohydrate energy (C) is readily available but short-lived; that which is not quickly used is stored as body fat—a problem for sedentary dieters but of no concern to a hardworking backpacker. In the listing at right, each food's major nutrients are given according to the order in which they predominate; minor nutrients (less than 25 percent) appear in parentheses. Seasonings and spices have little or no food value, but do not ignore them; flavorful food can be a great morale booster.

Most camping supply stores stock a variety of freeze-dried meals in foil packets. They are lightweight, nutritious, and easy to prepare but quite expensive.

Provisions	Calories per ounce	Major nutrients	Provisions	Calories per ounce	Major nutrients
Bacon	177	F	Milk (soy)	122	PC(F)
Beans, (navy, dried)	97	C(P)	Oatmeal	111	C(P)
			Oil (cooking)	250	F
Beef (chipped)	58	P	Peanuts (roasted)	166	FP(C)
Bouillon cubes	34	P			
Cheese (Cheddar)	113	FP	Peas (dried)	99	C(P)
Chocolate	147	CF	Pork (salt)	213	F
Coconut (dried)	188	FC	Potatoes (dehydrated)	103	C
Cornmeal	103	C			
Drink mix	168	C	Prunes (dried, pitted)	73	C
Eggs (powdered)	168	PF			
Flour (soy)	120	PC(F)	Pudding mix	102	C
Flour (wheat)	100	C(P)	Raisins	82	C
Fruit (dried)	100	C	Rice (brown)	102	C(P)
Gelatin (dry)	95	P	Sausage	110	F(P)
Honey	86	C	Soup (dehydrated)	105	CP
Jerky	102	PF			
Macaroni	105	C(P)	Sugar	109	C
Margarine	204	F	Sunflower seeds	159	FP(C)
Meat bars	171	FP	Tomato crystals	86	C(P)
Milk (dried whole)	142	CFP	Walnuts	159	F(C)(P)
			Wheat germ	103	CP(F)

Breakfast

You may make do with toast and coffee at home, but a day of packing a load in the wilderness should start with a hearty, well-balanced meal. The old standby, bacon and eggs, provides fat and protein. Stewed fruit and foraged berries are for vitamins, quick carbohydrate energy, and a taste of sweetness. Oatmeal or other hot cereal, biscuits, and pancakes provide additional carbohydrates and help keep your digestive system functioning smoothly. Coffee or tea serve as psychological and physiological pick-me-ups to get you started.

For buckwheat pancakes for two mix:

1 cup buckwheat flour	1/2 cup whole dry milk
1/2 cup wheat flour	2 tbsp. powdered egg
1/2 cup cornmeal	2 tsp. baking powder
1/2 cup wheat germ	1 tsp. salt

For convenience, premix the ingredients at home and pack in a labeled plastic bag. Add 2 tbsp. of oil and 2 to 3 cups cool water; then beat to a thin batter. Cook in a hot, oiled pan.

Cooking with foil

Foil

Aluminum foil has many uses. Bake a potato, yam, or wild root by wrapping it in foil and burying it among hot coals for half an hour. Turn a wire grill into a griddle with a sheet of foil turned up around the edges. Line a leaky pot with foil, or with the help of a few short sticks improvise a reflector oven. (For use of oven, see *Baking Bannock Bread*, p.422.)

Spark Your Diet With a Free Feast of Wild Greens

To pack a head of lettuce into the wilderness is inefficient and unnecessary. Not only is there an abundance of edible wild greenery, but much of it is tastier and more nutritious than its cultivated counterparts. You need not become a field botanist to recognize such commonplace delicacies as dandelions, chickweed, and clover, but the more you know the wider your choice will be. And be sure to carry a clearly illustrated plant identification guide, since some plants are poisonous.

Among the raw greens that are savory in salads or refreshing to munch on the trail are the young leaves of chicory, mint, mustard, orach, purslane, rock cress, several kinds of sedum (especially *Sedum rosea*, known as roseroot for the odor of its thick root), sheep sorrel, shepherd's purse, spring beauty, watercress, wild lettuce, and any of the several plants known as scurvy grass because of their high vitamin C content. Each has its own special flavor and texture. The older leaves of many of these plants are equally appetizing when cooked and served like spinach. Some—such as shepherd's purse, chicory, and mustard—become tough and bitter with age; to correct this fault, boil the leaves until tender, drain, and boil again in fresh water. Other plants whose leaves need this double cooking include burdock, jewelweed, marsh marigold, milkweed, and pokeweed. Cook the leaves of the remaining plants mentioned above— as well as those of coltsfoot, dock, plantain, and the wild spinach known as lamb's quarters (*Chenopodium album*)—just once, quickly, in a little boiling water.

Dandelions grow almost everywhere. The tender young leaves and unopened buds, delicious raw or steamed, are among the richest sources of vitamins A and C. Older leaves, boiled twice to remove bitterness, taste like Swiss chard but are somewhat more flavorful. To make a delicate tea, drop only the petals from 10 flowers into a cup of boiling water; let them steep until the tea's flavor pleases you.

Common chickweed is found in moist meadows, fields, and woods throughout North America. Its small, sharp-pointed leaves, rich in iron and vitamin C, stay fresh and green beneath winter snow. These leaves and the tender tips of the plant's long, sprawling stems are year-round food sources. They may be eaten raw or steamed—do not overcook or the delicate flavor may vanish completely.

Clover is protein-rich but difficult to digest raw. Indians dipped its leaves and flowers in salted water to prevent flatulence; boiling is a surer way. To make a tasty clover dish for four, melt 4 tbsp. margarine or butter in a frying pan; stir in 6 cups clover greens and flowers; add 1/2 cup water; cover and cook until wilted, stirring occasionally. For a chewy texture include sweetish clover roots as well.

Wild onions—including leeks, chives, and garlic (shown here)—can be prepared and eaten in all the same ways as their civilized cousins-. Flavor and potency vary tremendously; sample a small amount before deciding whether to use a plant as food or for seasoning. **Caution: Eat nothing that looks like a wild onion but does not smell like one–it could be either of two very poisonous plants, death camas or fly poison.**

Roots, Shoots, Stems, and Fruits

In spring the tender young shoots of calamus, catbrier, evening primrose, and wild asparagus are good cooked or raw—as are rose hips and the juicy berries of the wintergreen, left on the plants from the season before. Milkweed shoots can double for asparagus; the fat flower buds of summer make a broccolilike dish; young seed pods can serve the same culinary purposes as okra. Summer and fall offer a vast array of fresh fruits, nuts, and berries to fill out a meal or munch on the trail.

The only totally inedible part of the burdock is the familiar brown burr that sticks to your clothes, although most of the rest is enclosed in a bitter husk. Peel and cook first-year roots (those without flower stalks) as you would parsnips. Peel the rhubarblike leaf stalks in spring and eat them like celery, raw or stewed; unlike rhubarb, the leaves can also be eaten without fear of poison. In summer the white inner pith of the thick flower stalk makes an excellent replacement for potatoes. Slice the stalk crossways and bake, fry, boil, or roast.

Other potato substitutes include the peppery roots of the evening primrose, turnip-flavored groundnuts, the tiny chestnutlike tubers of spring beauty, and the giant wild potato (actually a wild yam), whose tuber may weigh 20 pounds or more. The starchy roots of such aquatic plants as arrowhead, bulrush, and water lilies are best gathered during the colder months, although Indians harvested them with their toes in summer by wading among the plants and collecting the firm young tubers that bobbed to the surface.

Salsify roots taste surprisingly like oysters. For a landlubber's oyster stew, scrub and scrape several tender first-year roots and slice them crosswise into 1/4-in. pieces. Barely cover with milk or soy milk; add salt and seasoning; cover and stew until tender.

Tea and coffee substitutes

Fresh wintergreen leaves steeped in boiling water make a fragrant tea. Strangely, however, black birch twigs are richer in wintergreen oil than wintergreen is; pour hot (not boiling) water over about a quart of them broken into 1-inch lengths, let steep until cool, then strain and reheat. The leaves of all members of the mint family, including catnip (you can recognize them all by their square stems), can be brewed fresh for an invigorating tea; just pour boiling water over them and let steep until the flavor pleases you. Brew coltsfoot leaves the same way. Leaves of Labrador tea, New Jersey tea, and two evergreen hollies—cassina and inkberry—must be dried before a fire or in a reflector oven before they are crumbled and brewed like tea. (The hollies are among the few North American plants that contain caffeine.)

For a caffeineless coffee, roast the roots of chicory, chufa, dandelions, or salsify over a low fire; grind and brew. Sunflower seeds can be used too, as can the fruits of cleavers, picked and roasted in early to midsummer.

Foraging for Flour And Emergency Rations

It takes time and energy to prepare flour from any wild source except cattail pollen. If you are in no rush, it is time well spent, both for the unusual flavors of foraged flour and to save packing pounds of processed flour. Easiest to prepare is flour made from the tubers of such plants as arrowhead and chufa. For immediate use, crush them and put the pulp in a container of cold water. Seal it and shake vigorously, then filter out the fibrous waste and allow the starchy residue to settle. Pour off the water, add more cold water, and repeat the process. Continue until the water no longer feels slimy. You can drain and use the flour as is (allowing for the water it contains) or dry and grind it for future use.

To make a flavorful meal—and simultaneously obtain cooking oil—from walnuts, butternuts, hickory nuts, or others, smash them with a rock and boil slowly, shell and all. A mixture of meats and oil will rise to the top; skim it off and filter or pick out the meats. Dry the meats before a fire and grind them to the consistency of cornmeal. (For nut butter, crush the meats into the oil.)

To grind flour from seeds is a hard job even with a mortar and pestle. Doing it between two rocks leads one to marvel that primitive peoples ever got around to baking at all. The result, however, is the closest wild approximation to conventional flour, in texture if not taste. For a hint of wild flavor, grind just a handful of bulrush, dock, or lamb's quarters seeds, and mix with wheat flour. First thresh the seeds to remove them from their husks; then winnow to get rid of the chaff. Threshing methods vary. Some seeds, such as green amaranth, require nothing more than rubbing them briskly between your hands. Others, including purslane and shepherd's purse, must be treated more roughly, up to and including beating them with sticks and treading them underfoot. In order to winnow the threshed seeds, pour them back and forth between two containers and let the breeze carry off the chaff.

To grind flour from seeds, nuts, or roots, look near running water for a large, nonporous rock that has been hollowed out to the shape of a bowl. For a pestle choose a smooth, round stone that fits your hand comfortably.

Using the Fruit of the Bountiful Oak

The plentiful acorn was a dietary staple of several native American cultures. To shuck acorns for use, crack the thin shells lengthwise (pliers facilitate the job), then squeeze the tips to pop the meat out whole. To leach out the bitter tannin, boil the meats for about two hours, changing the water whenever it turns yellowish; then dry and pound into fine meal. Or you can dry and pound the meats first, place the meal in a porous cloth bag, and pour boiling water through it. Use as you would cornmeal, or mix into any flour for a nutty flavor.

Bannock Bread

Nothing is more welcome at a fireside meal than fresh bread. Happily, baking it is one of the easiest jobs of campfire cookery. Start with the following ingredients:

1 cup flour (wheat or foraged)	1/2 tsp. salt
	1 tsp. sugar or honey
1 tsp. baking powder	2 tbsp. cooking oil
1 tbsp. whole dry milk	

Mix the ingredients gently with enough water (about 3/4 cup) to form a firm dough. Mold quickly and with as little handling as possible into a loaf 1 in. thick. Dust the loaf with flour, then cook it by any of the three following methods.

Covered pot. Place loaf in pan. Put a few stones in bottom of large pot and set loaf on stones. Cover pot and place on hot coals; heap more coals onto lid. Bake 30 minutes or until done. Test by inserting a twig; if dough adheres, bake longer.

Frying pan. Place loaf in prewarmed, greased pan. Hold over fire until crust forms on bottom; then flip and brown the other side. Place over coolest part of cooking slot and turn loaf from time to time until done.

Reflector oven. Put loaf on foil sheet and set on base or shelf of oven; place oven about 8 in. from fire. Maintain steady flame for 20 to 30 minutes, turning loaf occasionally until it is brown all around and done inside.

Easy Acorn Cakes

2 cups acorn meal	3/4 cup water
1/2 tsp. salt	

Combine ingredients and beat to stiff batter. Let stand one hour; then heat 3 tbsp. cooking oil in frying pan. Drop batter into pan to form cakes about 3 in. across. Reduce heat (or put pan at edge of cooking slot), and brown cakes slowly on both sides. Eat hot or cold. Acorn cakes will keep for days.

The cornucopious cattail

There is an old saying that you can use every part of a pig but the squeal. Cattails are even less wasteful—they have no squeal. All four native American cattail species are edible, and all were regularly used by Indians and early settlers as year-round sources of food and fiber. They are easily recognized by their tall, stiff flower stalks, which arise among clusters of sword-shaped leaves. The flowers at the tops of these stalks form two sausagelike sections—pollen-bearing male flowers above and seed-producing female flowers below. Cattails grow in marshes and in the shallows of lakes, rivers, and estuaries throughout the country.

In fall and winter gather fluffy white seed heads to use as insulation, tinder, or soft stuffing in pillows

In early summer cut young flower heads just as they are turning from green to yellow. Remove husk, boil, and eat them as you would corn on the cob

From midfall to midspring starchy rhizomes (underground stems connecting plants) make good potato substitutes or can be dried and ground for flour. To harvest, dig between plants with a hoe or sharp stick and break off section of rhizome. Sever the tiny green sprouts—known as Russian asparagus—and boil in salted water. Peel away the rhizome's spongy outer husk and use only the pithy white inner core

Throughout summer flower heads of an acre of cattails produce three times as much flour as an acre of cultivated wheatland. To gather the tasty, yellow, protein-rich pollen, put a plastic bag over the flower head and shake. It needs no grinding or processing; use as is, or mix with wheat or other flour for baking

Leaves are not edible but are useful year round for weaving mats and baskets and making thatched shelters

In spring cut young (18") sprouts close to the rhizome. Peel and eat raw, or slice and boil like green beans. The texture is carrotlike, the taste resembles cucumbers

In Case of Need

Cactus. All fruits and fleshy parts of all cacti are edible; some are quite tasty. The best part is the fruit, or tuna, that grows from between the pads of prickly pears (*Opuntia*). Slice off ends, open husk lengthwise, and scoop out pulp. Protect your hands from the spines while working. To eat pads themselves, first burn off spines, then slice through husk; pulpy core is good raw or cooked. Get water from cactus with the aid of a solar still (p.424).

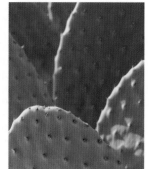

Thistle. This common biennial is a fine source of food from spring through fall. In its first year the plant forms a rosette of tender but spiny leaves; trim the spines and eat the leaves raw or steamed. During the second year a purple flower appears on the plants atop a spiny stem that tastes rather like an artichoke; peel, slice, and boil it. The root is more nutritious than tasty; eat it raw or cooked. First-year roots are best.

All parts of chicory are edible. The young leaves can be eaten as a salad or boiled. The roots can be cooked like a vegetable or used as a coffee substitute when roasted until dark brown and then pulverized. Look for chicory in fields, weedy lots, or along roads.

Poplar. The inner bark of poplars—including trembling aspens of the Rocky Mountains and cottonwoods of the South and Midwest—kept many a frontiersman alive for weeks at a time. It can be eaten fresh, brewed into tea, cut into strips and cooked like noodles, or dried and ground into flour. All are nourishing, as is the inner bark of the willow, a close relative. Pines, birch, and juniper also have edible inner bark.

Sources of Meat When Survival Is in Doubt

The meat of all healthy birds, insects, and mammals is edible. So is that of most reptiles and amphibians. The fat and protein they contain could mean the difference between life and death for one who is lost or stranded in the wilderness for a long time. If you are proficient in the use of a throwing stick, bolo, sling, spear, or bow and arrow, you will probably have little trouble improvising your weapon from natural materials and hunting with it. If not, it is too late to start practicing—you will do better to spend your energy gathering insects and grubs, fishing, or trapping reptiles, birds, and small game.

Grasshoppers, locusts, katydids, crickets, and cicadas are all excellent protein sources and good fish bait. It is easiest to catch them in early morning, while they are still sluggish from the nighttime chill. Like all insects they must be cooked before they are eaten to rid them of parasites. Pull off the wings, legs, and head and roast or steam the bodies. To gather a meal of ants, sink a steep-walled container, such as a cup or jar, into the top of an anthill so its rim is level with the surface of the mound, then use a stick to stir up the den. Hundreds of ants will fall into the container. Grubs and caterpillars are also rich food sources, but avoid caterpillars bearing hair or fuzz—many are poisonous.

Lizards are hard to catch, and few are meaty enough to be worth the effort. Snakes, however, are almost all meat and are easily clubbed or caught with a long stick. Cut off the head; skin and eviscerate the body. Cook by roasting or boiling—the flavor is not unlike catfish. Poisonous snakes are as edible as any other (the poison is all in their heads), but unless you are an experienced snake hunter the danger can be greater than the reward. Frogs are easily caught with a long, sharp stick (notch a barb onto the end) or even with your bare hands, particularly if you hunt at night using a head-lamp or flashlight. (Note, however, that light-hunting is illegal except in case of a real emergency.) Skin the frogs before cooking them. Avoid toads; their irritating skin secretions can easily spread into the meat.

It is also illegal to hunt with snares or traps except in emergencies. You may be able to club such slow-moving animals as porcupines, opossums, or groundhogs, but if your life hangs in the balance it is permissible to set traps. The simplest of these are deadfalls, in which a flat rock, large enough to kill a small animal, is supported by a baited trigger mechanism made from sticks. Snares made from wire or cord can be set for rabbits, squirrels, or other small game along paths that they normally follow in the course of their day-to-day lives. (For the finest source of protein, see *Fishing*, pp.436–441.)

To cook small game, such as rabbits or squirrels, first skin and eviscerate animal. Spread the carcass flat on a large rock or piece of hardwood, lash it in place with wire or green vines, and prop it up before an open fire. Another method is to pack the carcass in clay and bury it in hot coals to bake for an hour or so.

Traps and snares

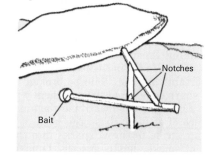

Figure-4 deadfall is a good trap for such foragers as ground squirrels and other large rodents. Use a flat rock or log heavy enough to kill prey. Be sure bait is securely attached to trigger.

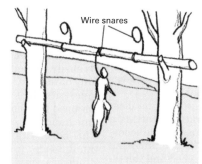

Squirrels are adventuresome. Rig up wire noose snares firmly along pole and place between two trees where you have seen squirrels at play. Always remove traps when you no longer need them.

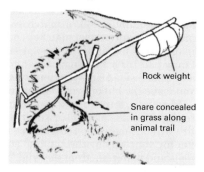

Rabbits tend to follow the same route daily. Rig a lift snare along their customary path. Fashion a noose from wire, cord, green vines, or twine made by twisting tough fiber of thistle stems or milkweed.

How to Survive The Unexpected

"Nature is stern, hard, immovable, and terrible in unrelenting cruelty [but] she has in store food, fuel, and shelter which the skillful, self-reliant woodsman can wring from her savage hand with ax and rifle."
—Nessmuk

If by some mischance you are separated from your equipment in the wilderness, you may find nature as terrible as the old woodsman did. Moreover, lacking his ax and rifle, your tools will be those of Stone Age man. One way to give yourself better odds of living through such an emergency is to carry your own survival kit.

Two kits, in fact, are better than one: a basic kit small enough to fit in a shirt pocket and a larger, more complete kit. You should never be without the small one, though its contents are never used except in case of emergency. They include a means of signaling, such as a whistle and signal mirror; a way to start a fire, such as waterproof matches or flint and steel; something to use in constructing shelter, such as a pocketknife and a length of picture wire; a few bouillon cubes for nourishment; a small compass; a few safety pins; and two or three adhesive bandages. These all fit into a metal box like the kind in which adhesive bandages are sold. The box can also serve as a container for boiling water.

Items to put in the larger kit include a sweater, such emergency rations as dried meat bars and rice, first aid supplies, signal flares, a 50-foot length of 1/8-inch nylon rope, a lightweight tarp, fishhooks and leader, a square foot of aluminum foil, a match safe containing waterproof strike-anywhere matches, paper and pencil, and in dry areas materials for a solar still. Keep this kit in a fanny pack or small knapsack, and take it with you on day hikes, side trips, and short excursions—whenever you leave the bulk of your equipment behind.

More important than the contents of any kit is mastering the skills of outdoor survival. Practice starting a fire without matches, recognizing and using wild foods, finding your way by the sun and stars, and improvising tools and materials from the wild. Milkweed and thistle stems, for example, yield fibers that are easily twisted into strong twine, but proficiency at this skill, like most skills, comes as a result of trial and error. Take the time to learn how to do it before you find yourself in a position where an error might be fatal.

Warmth and Shelter

To survive in the wilderness you need three things: food, water, and protection from the elements. You can live for weeks without food and many days without water, but death from exposure to wind, rain, and cold can happen overnight. In a survival situation your most urgent concerns must be shelter and a fire.

Look for a site that is naturally shielded from prevailing nighttime winds. A shallow cave with a southern

Poor placement of fire; camper does not get benefit of reflected heat

Good placement of fire; camper is warmed front and back

A fire's warmth rises along a rock face, drawing cold air from the open side. Later, the rock itself radiates extra warmth.

exposure beneath a rock overhang is ideal; the rock will hold the sun's warmth long into the night. Build a fire at the mouth of the cave, not against the rock face—the warmest place to be is between a fire and a nearby wall. In other situations a stand of shrubs may serve as a windbreak, or the drooping boughs of a lone evergreen might offer a place of refuge.

The simplest shelter to construct is a lean-to. This might be nothing more than a few evergreen branches propped against a fallen tree, adequate for a night's rest. Or it could be a more elaborate structure in the shape of a tepee or of Nessmuk's shanty tent (p.410), enclosed on three sides and open to the warmth of a fire. Make the framework for such a lean-to by lashing together three or more stout poles. Stack more poles and branches against this frame until you have a wall capable of supporting a thatching of grass, leaves, bark, evergreen boughs, or even dirt. The decision of how sturdy and weatherproof a shelter to build depends on the harshness of the environment. (For instructions on building cold weather shelters, see *Outdoors in Winter*, p.434.)

Starting a Fire Without Matches

There are two skills requisite for starting a fire without matches: preparing a nest of fluffy tinder and striking a spark to ignite it. Excellent tinder can be made from the downy seed heads of cattail, thistle, and milkweed or by pounding the stalks of these plants or those of nettle, yucca, and dogbane. Other sources of tinder include dead leaves; blades of dead grass; the outer bark of birch, juniper, and sagebrush; and the cambium layer (just beneath the bark) of aspen, poplar, willow, or pine. Shred the material and form a bundle, then rub it between your hands to make a light, fluffy nest.

The easiest way to strike a spark is with flint and steel. True flint is a hard brownish-gray variety of quartz that is easily shaped by flaking. It is the best rock to use, but any hard silica stone will do, including agate, jasper, and quartzite. It is important that the stone be broken or chipped to expose a sharp edge. Hold the rock firmly in one hand and strike a glancing downward blow against this edge with a piece of steel, such as the back of a knife blade. Aim your strike to throw sparks into the tinder. A thin wisp of smoke signals success. Quickly pick up the tinder and blow gently with short puffs until the spark spreads and bursts into flame.

Another way to obtain a spark is with a bow drill. This tool can be made from hardwood and a strip of twine or leather thong. Heat is generated by friction as the tip

of the drill turns rapidly back and forth in a notched depression in a piece of dry wood, called the fireboard. The notch fills up with charred dust, which eventually begins to smoke. At this point, the spark within the dust must be lightly fanned to life, then quickly placed in the tinder and blown into flame.

Tinder can sometimes be ignited by focusing the sun through a lens. Strong glasses with convex lenses can serve this purpose, as can a convex watch crystal.

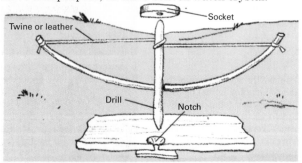

Socket

Twine or leather

Drill

Notch

Make the drill and fireboard from a single type of dry, seasoned hardwood, such as aspen, cottonwood, or poplar. For the bow use a strong green branch; for the socket, any piece of hardwood or stone that fits your hand. Lubricate the socket by rubbing the top of the drill through your hair or along the side of your nose.

Obtaining Fresh Water

Water exists everywhere on the surface of the earth, even in places where it does not run freely. It is in the air, beneath the ground, part of every living thing. With skill you can obtain it in drinkable form. To get clear water from a muddy river or lake, dig a hole a few feet from the bank and let water filter in. If you are close to an ocean beach, try using the first water that seeps into such a hole; it may only become salty later. Purify all questionable water by boiling for 10 to 15 minutes—longer at high altitudes—or with iodine crystals (see p.418).

Early morning dew is a good water source. Use a cloth to soak it up from grass and other vegetation, then wring it out into a container. Or you can scoop out a shallow hole, cover it with a tarp, and fill the depression with stones. After dawn, dew will form on the stones and collect in the tarp. In hills or mountains follow dry gulleys to the source. There you will often find a trickle of water that disappears within a few feet. Use a sluice made from a hollowed-out plant stem or stick to divert this trickle into a container. Sometimes you may find only a clump of greenery; the roots are deriving water from

beneath the soil. Dig for it. Water can often be found near the surface of dry river beds, at the base of cliffs, on the shady sides of sand dunes, and any place where willows or elderberries grow.

In the desert look for sandstone ridges along which pockets form where water can remain for months. The pulp of some large cacti yield water, but you have to work for it; cut off the top, mash and stir the pulp with a stick, then wring water from it. A better way to get water from cactus is to make a solar still from an unperforated piece of thin, transparent plastic. Whenever you camp in arid regions, include the materials for such a still in your basic survival kit. With it you can draw pure water not only from plant material but also from polluted or salty water—including your own body wastes—and from the soil itself. Conserving water is as important in the desert as finding it. Travel at night and rest in shade during the day. Eat only if you have water; digestion uses up moisture. Do not put faith in such fabled tricks as buttons or pebbles in the mouth—they alleviate thirst but do nothing to stop dehydration.

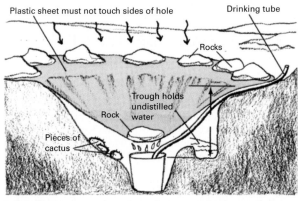

Solar still can extract about 1 qt. of water per day from soil alone—up to 3 qt. if plants or polluted water are added. Dig hole in low, sunny spot. Tape end of tube inside container. Spread 6-ft.-square sheet of clear plastic over hole, weight down edges, and seal with dirt. Put a stone in the center so that condensing water will run down into container. Water will begin to collect in about an hour; drink it through the tube.

Signaling for Help

Three of anything is the universal distress signal: whistles, gunshots, flares, or fires. The shrill sound of a whistle carries further than the human voice and indicates direction more clearly. It is wise to carry a whistle at all times. To call for help, give three long blasts at regular intervals. Two answering blasts mean that someone has heard you; stay where you are and repeat the signal to guide the search.

Fire is an effective signal. Lay out three tepee-style fires in the form of a triangle 50 to 100 feet across, and wait for an opportune moment to light them. A clear, still day is such a moment; throw green wood, wet leaves, or grass on the flames to make columns of smoke. At night listen for the sound of a plane, then use dry wood to make bright flames. Other ways to catch the attention of someone in a passing plane include flashing with a mirror and constructing huge signs or markers. Make signals from brightly colored strips of material, brush piles, or anything that contrasts with the surrounding terrain. If snow is on the ground, tramp trenches and line them with ashes, bark, or pieces of dark wood. The best signal mirrors are of highly polished metal, reflective on both sides, with a hole in the middle for sighting. Any reflective surface can be made to serve, including aluminum foil. Flash at any airplane, no matter how high, and occasionally flash toward different points on the horizon, even if a plane cannot be seen or heard.

International ground-to-air symbols

Carry a copy of these symbols when venturing into the wilderness. Make the marks at least 10 ft. across—50 ft. would be better—from material that contrasts sharply with the ground. If brush is used, pile it high enough to cast a shadow.

I Serious injury, need doctor	**II** Need medical supplies
X Unable to proceed	**F** Need food and water
Need compass and map	**→** Am proceeding in this direction
LL All is well	**N** No
Y Yes	Not understood
Probably safe to land here	**K** Which way should we go?

Using a signal mirror

Sight plane through hole in mirror. If plane is fairly near the sun, light coming through hole will fall on your face and you will see the reflection in the mirror (left). While continuing to sight on plane, adjust mirror until reflected spot seems to disappear into hole (right); at that point, mirror will flash sunlight at plane. (If plane is far from sun, move your free hand so spot falls on it, then adjust mirror.)

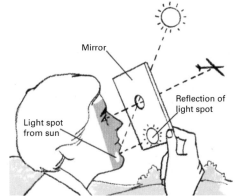
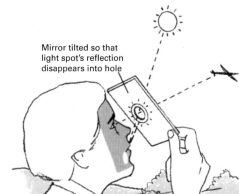

First Aid in Emergencies: Fast Action Saves Lives

The three sudden killers to watch for after any injury are asphyxia, bleeding, and shock. Asphyxia—cessation of breathing—may be caused by drowning, lightning, a bad fall, sudden pain, and even fear. If your companion stops breathing, act quickly. Within five minutes his brain will be damaged; after 10 minutes he will be dead. Remove obstructions, including dentures and bridgework, from the mouth and throat. Tilt his head back and raise the back of his neck with one hand to open the air passage. (If you suspect a neck injury, simply pull the lower jaw forward.) If this alone does not restore breathing, administer mouth-to-mouth resuscitation.

The only way to stop bleeding is to cut off the flow of blood in the severed vessel until clotting happens. Direct pressure on the wound is usually enough. Elevate the wound if possible to reduce blood pressure; then apply sterile pads or the cleanest cloth you have, and press hard for about five minutes. If severe bleeding persists, pack the wound with sterile gauze and wrap it tightly with a bandage. (Sanitary napkins make good packing.) If arterial bleeding continues despite direct pressure, the next step is to apply force at a pressure point (see below). A tourniquet is a last resort, since it will probably lead to gangrene and then to amputation. To make a tourniquet, wrap a broad cloth around the affected limb above the wound. Use a short stick to wind the tourniquet only tight enough to stop bleeding. Tie or tape the stick in place. Do not loosen the tourniquet; to do so is to risk sending a blood clot into the victim's heart or lungs.

Shock often follows an injury. Its symptoms, caused by constricted blood vessels and reduced flow of blood to the brain, include pale and clammy skin, cold sweat, trembling, thirst, dizziness, disorientation, and sometimes unconsciousness. The best treatment is prevention. After any injury to yourself or others assume that shock will ensue and treat it as described below until you are certain that the danger has passed.

Treating Common Injuries and Illness

Altitude sickness. At higher elevations the blood carries less oxygen. Your body requires several days to adjust to this deprivation. Drowsiness and yawning are common, but sleep may be sporadic. You may suffer headaches, nausea, shortness of breath, and flulike aches. Forgetfulness, anxiety, and hallucinations may occur, and physical coordination may suffer. To push on despite these symptoms is to risk serious damage, including pulmonary edema and retinal hemorrhage. The treatment is gradual acclimatization: avoid exertion, drink extra fluid, eat a light diet of carbohydrates, and do not use any drug except aspirin.

Blisters. Do not open a blister. Wash the area and cover the blister with moleskin, tape, or a donut-shaped piece of felt. Treat a broken blister as an abrasion.

Burns. To stop and perhaps reverse tissue damage, quickly immerse burn in cold water until the sensation of heat has passed. For first-degree burns (red skin) or second degree (blisters), keep the skin cool and wet until it stiffens; then lubricate with petroleum jelly or antiseptic cream. Clean third-degree burns (cooked flesh) gently, using boiled water that has been allowed to cool, soft soap, and sterile cotton. Cover lightly with gauze. Drink liquids and increase salt intake.

Cuts and abrasions. Infection is a danger when any break in the skin occurs. Wash the wound with soap and clean water and cover with a sterile dressing until a protective scab forms. To avoid destroying healthy tissue, use only the mildest antiseptic, such as highly diluted hydrogen peroxide, in open wounds; apply stronger antiseptic, such as iodine, to surrounding skin. Close a large gash with a butterfly closure or adhesive bandage. Cover abrasions with a single sheet of gauze impregnated with petroleum jelly or antiseptic cream, then bandage with several layers of sterile gauze.

Heat exhaustion. Exertion in hot weather may cause the tiny blood vessels in the skin to dilate to the point that the brain's blood supply is diminished. The result is dizziness, nausea, rapid heartbeat, and sometimes fainting. The skin feels cool to the touch; there may be cold sweat. Treatment involves resting in the shade, drinking nonalcoholic fluids, and increasing salt intake.

Heat or sun stroke. It is possible for the sweat glands to exhaust themselves. When this happens, body heat builds up quickly to 104°F or more. The victim may collapse or become delirious; his skin will be hot to the touch. Without quick action brain damage is imminent. Immerse the entire body in tepid (not cold) water, or cover the body with soaking cloth and fan the victim to promote evaporation. Massage the hands and feet at the same time to encourage circulation of cooled blood.

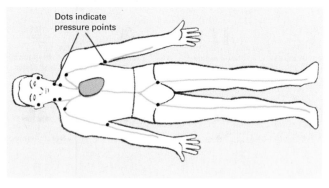

Lift neck up, tilt head back

Mouth-to-mouth technique can help asphyxia victim. Thrust the jaw forward and pinch the nose. Take a deep breath and exhale into victim's mouth until his chest rises. Repeat at 12 to 14 breaths per minute until the victim can breathe on his own.

Dots indicate pressure points

Pressure points are spots where an artery passes close to the skin and can easily be squeezed shut. If arterial bleeding (recognizable because it squirts in rhythm with the heartbeat) is not stopped by direct pressure, locate the nearest pressure point between the wound and the heart and push the artery shut until clotting takes place.

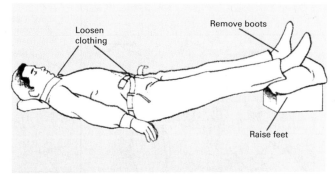

Loosen clothing

Remove boots

Raise feet

Treat for shock after any injury, particularly if burns, fractures, or loss of blood are involved. Lay the victim on his back, his feet higher than his head (unless there is a head injury). Remove boots and loosen all constrictive clothing. Keep the victim warm with blankets, sleeping bag, or your own body. Give plenty of warm, salty fluids.

Checklist for a first aid kit

Adhesive bandages, several sizes
Antacid tablets
Antihistamines
Antiseptic cream
Aspirin
Butterfly closures
Disinfectant or antibacterial soap
Elastic bandage, 3″
First aid manual
Gauze pads, 4″ × 4″
Gauze roll, 2″ × 30′
Insect repellent
Mobile phone

Moleskin, with foam backing
Needle and thread
Pencil and paper
Prescription medicine
Razor blade
Safety pins
Salt tablets
Sanitary napkins
Scissors, small
Snakebite kit
Tape, 2″ × 30′, nonwaterproof
Thermometer
Triangular bandage

In case of snakebite

If bitten by a poisonous snake, try to stay calm and motionless—activity and panic increase the rate at which the venom spreads. Tie a narrow constriction band around the limb 6 in. or so above the bite; snake venom spreads through the lymph system just beneath the skin, so the band need not be so tight as to cut off blood circulation. With a sharp, sterile blade make a straight incision about 1/4 in. deep across both fang marks. Apply suction to these incisions for about one hour. Use suction cups if possible, since using your mouth risks infecting the wound. There is also the chance that venom may enter your system via cold sores, chapped lips, or a bad tooth. Get the victim to a medical facility as soon as possible.

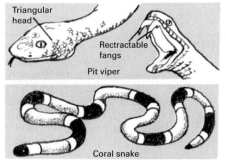

Pit vipers, such as rattlesnakes, inject venom through retractable fangs. Coral snakes chew with tiny needle-sharp teeth.

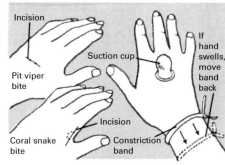

Tie constriction band above the bite, and make incisions over fang marks or across bite of coral snake. Apply suction for one hour.

Choking

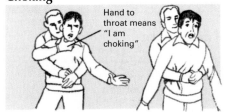

Hand to throat means "I am choking"

If a piece of food lodges in someone's throat, the victim may be unable to speak or even to cough. Do not pound his back. Grab him from behind with both arms, make a fist, and use your other hand to pull your fist sharply upward into the victim's diaphragm, just below the breastbone, to force the food out of the throat.

Transporting an injured person

Move a seriously injured person only if absolutely necessary—and then only after breathing is stable, bleeding is under control, shock is past, wounds have been treated, and fractures have been immobilized. It is generally best to leave the victim where he is. Make him as comfortable as possible and signal for medical aid or evacuation (see p.425). If you must evacuate the victim yourself, do so with extreme care. Stretcher-type litters improvised from two poles and a blanket or sleeping bag are only satisfactory if strong stiffeners, such as pack frames, are lashed between the poles to make a firm base. Pad the base and place the victim on it; lash him down to prevent him from being jostled. Use padding, such as rolled-up clothing, to cushion and immobilize his head.

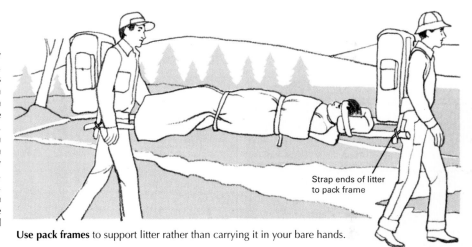

Strap ends of litter to pack frame

Use pack frames to support litter rather than carrying it in your bare hands.

Treating fractures and sprains

Fractures and sprains both cause swelling, discoloration, and pain. When the symptoms occur in a joint, it may be difficult to tell which injury is the cause. If in doubt, treat the problem as a fracture. Do not attempt to set a broken bone; its jagged ends can do great damage to soft tissue. Instead, immobilize the fracture with a splint or by binding it to the body. A broken leg can be lashed to the other leg. If the jagged end of a broken bone protrudes through the skin, do not try to push it in—stop the bleeding, dress the wound, treat for shock, and immobilize the fracture just as it is. A sprain is a torn tendon; it is painful but not as liable to further damage as a fracture is. Use cold water or ice to reduce swelling for the first day or two; then wrap tightly and keep warm.

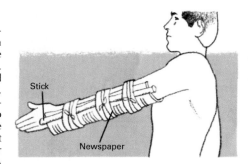

Stick

Newspaper

Use splints to immobilize fractured arm or leg; include the joints below and above the break. Improvise splints from wood or any rigid material, or use rolled-up blankets or newspapers.

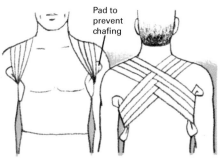

Pad to prevent chafing

Figure-eight splint supports shoulders to immobilize a broken collarbone. Pass rope or bandage around the shoulder, across the back, then around the other shoulder.

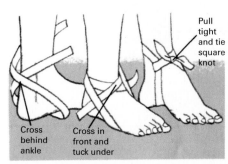

Pull tight and tie square knot

Cross behind ankle

Cross in front and tuck under

Sprained ankle can be walked on insofar as pain permits. Immobilize the joint by looping bandana or rope around heel, crossing the ends in front, and pulling the loop tight.

Sports and Activities For Outdoor Adventure

"In these days there are quite as many hunters as deer in the woods."
—Nessmuk

Between 1867 (18 years before Nessmuk wrote the above words) and 1946, 57 people are known to have survived the run down the raging Colorado River Rapids. In the decade between 1970 and 1980 the number was about 150,000. As the wilderness becomes more and more accessible, the popularity of many outdoor sports and activities also blossoms. Some of these, such as mountaineering, spelunking (caving), and rock climbing require special training and equipment and should not be undertaken unless you are in superb physical condition. Organizations exist throughout the country to help beginners get started in these sports.

There are also organizations devoted to the less hazardous pursuits of nature study and conservation. They range from bird watching clubs to volunteer labor corps that maintain thousands of miles of hiking trails. Finally, there are the competitive outdoor sports such as ridge running—for long-distance runners who specialize in traversing mountain terrain—and orienteering.

One of the essential skills of rock climbers and mountaineers is rappelling—the technique of descending a cliff or steep slope by sliding down a rope. The skill can be of equal value to a backpacker. A hiker with a good rope and the knowledge of how to use it will often find the direct route down a cliff to be faster, easier, and a great deal more exhilarating than spending hours in the bush finding a way around. **Caution: Rappelling must be mastered under the tutelage of an experienced climber before you attempt it on your own.**

The principle of rappelling is to wrap the rope around the body in such a way that it supports the rappeller in an upright position, while its friction against his body allows him to control his rate of descent. The rope must be long enough to hang double from the top of the cliff to the bottom, with plenty to spare to wrap around the body and loop around an anchor point on top. Only the best-quality climbing rope (minimum test strength 5,000 pounds) is used. The anchor must be totally secure and the rope should track around it easily so it can be retrieved from the bottom. Because the rope slides through the rappeller's hands and around his body as he descends, gloves and padding are important—it is not for nothing that the popular Dülfersitz technique is also known as the "hot-seat rappel."

Modern harnesses give added security and control to rappellers.

The Dülfersitz rappel

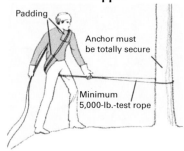

Padding
Anchor must be totally secure
Minimum 5,000-lb.-test rope

Body stays perpendicular to slope
Upper hand is used only for balance and to guide rope
Lower hand is used to control descent rate

1. Rappeller faces anchor and straddles rope. Right-hander wraps rope around right hip and over left shoulder.

2. Rappeller leans backward against rope, gripping with lower, stronger hand as he steps back over the edge

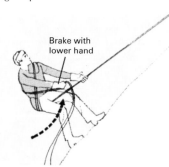

Brake with lower hand

3. To slow descent, rope is brought up across the surface of the back; at the same time lower hand squeezes rope.

4. To speed descent, rope is moved outward and behind with lower hand, reducing friction against back.

The sport of orienteering

Orienteering is like a cross-country race through unfamiliar terrain. Prior to a meet, checkpoints are set up along a route, then marked on topographic maps. Armed with the maps and nothing else except compasses, the contestants must reach each checkpoint in sequence and return to the start. Orienteering is more than a test of speed and stamina. In rugged country the shortest distance between two points is seldom a straight line; so map reading, direction finding, and woodsmanship are the true keys to excellence in the sport.

Lowell Thomas, Jr., Outdoorsman

Adventure Runs In the Family

Indus River Valley

In 1954, Lowell Thomas, Jr., and his wife, Tay, lived and traveled with a nomadic tribe during the tribe's autumn migration from the mountains of Afghanistan to Pakistan's Indus River Valley, covering 10 to 15 miles per day on foot and camelback.

"I've been hiking ever since I was a wee little fellow. I remember my dad taking me out camping with my own sleeping bag and what a thrill that was—but I don't think there was any particular parental pressure, even with my father's reputation as an explorer, to enjoy the outdoors just because it was expected of me. Of course, exploring has given me some really exciting moments. In the summer of 1949 my dad and I made what still has to be the most exciting trip of my life—an expedition across the Himalayas to visit the Dalai Lama in Tibet. It took so long to get there, over the mountains on little ponies, that it was really like arriving on another planet. I've also spent a good bit of time in Arctic exploration, on ice floes, and even living in ice houses. My wife and I have also spent some time living with pygmies in African rain forests. Now I do a fair amount of what we call ski mountaineering. I usually fly my own plane and we land on a glacier in the Alaska range. Then we get onto our skis, and we're off for two or three days. We pitch our tents right in the snow and it's very exciting, but it does take quite a bit of preparation.

"Preparation is really the most important thing for newcomers to the wilderness. To start off with, you ought to be in good physical shape, and then you should have the right gear, including footgear that protects the ankle. You also need the right clothing, medicine, and food. If you are really leaving the beaten track, you should leave information on where you're going and when you'll be back, just like a pilot's flight plan.

"Hordes of people pose a great threat to the wilderness. Up here [in Alaska] people cut down trees for firewood and use motorized equipment to tear up the tundra. But people don't have to cause destruction. They can ski or snowshoe into the woods or just walk in good weather. And it's important to respect the wildlife—not to frighten animals or shoot at them, particularly in the calving season. Up in Alaska, that is particularly important when the caribou are calving. It's a good idea though, if there are bears around, to make a little noise to let the animals know you're coming; whistle or rattle some branches every once in a while. The one thing you never want to do is sneak up on a bear. A friend of mine was once going along very quietly and he stepped on a sleeping bear. Well, the bear rose up, but then he turned and ran. Believe me, if he had heard the man coming, the bear would have been long gone before the man got there. It's always a good idea to let a bear know you're in the neighborhood."

Sources and resources

Books

Angier, Bradford. *Living Off the Country.* Old Tappan, N.J.: Macmillan, 1962.

Auerbach, Paul S., M.D. *Medicine for the Outdoors.* Boston: Little, Brown, 1991.

Bean, L.L., Staff and Riviere, William. *The L.L. Bean Guide to the Outdoors.* New York: Random House, 1981.

DeBairacle Levy, Juliette. *Traveler's Joy.* New Canaan, Conn.: Keats Publishing, 1994.

Dunn, John M. *Winterwise, a Backpacker's Guide.* Lake George, N.Y.: ADK Mountain Club, 1995.

Fletcher, Colin. *The Complete Walker III.* New York: Knopf, 1984.

Follett, Robert. *What to Take Backpacking—And Why.* Oak Park, Ill.: Alpine Guide, 1978.

Getchell. *The Essential Outdoor Gear Manual.* New York: McGraw-Hill, 1995.

Gibbons, Euell. *Stalking the Wild Asparagus.* New York: David McKay, 1975.

Greenspan, Rick, and Kahn, Hal. *The Camper's Companion: The Pack Along Guide for Better Outdoor Trips.* San Francisco: Foghorn Press, 1994.

Hart, John. *Walking Softly in the Wilderness.* San Francisco: Sierra Club Books, 1984.

Huggler, Tom. *The Camper's and Backpacker's Bible.* Garden City, N.Y.: Doubleday, 1995.

Jacobson, Don. *The One Pan Gourmet: Fresh Food on the Trail.* Camden, Maine: International Marine, 1993.

Lund, Duane R. *Camp Cooking.* Cambridge, Minn.: Adventure Publications, 1991.

Mason, Bernard S. *Woodcraft and Camping.* New York: Dover, 1974.

Mears, Raymond. *The Outdoor Survival Handbook: A Guide to the Resources and Material Available in the Wild and How to Use Them for Food, Shelter, Warmth, and Navigation.* New York: St. Martin, 1993.

Mendenhall, Ruth D. *Backpack Cookery.* Glendale, Calif.: La Siesta, 1974.

Miller, Dorcas S. *Good Food for Camp and Trail: All Natural Recipes for Delicious Meals Outdoors.* Boulder, Colo.: Pruett Publishing Co., 1993.

Mueller, Betty, ed. *Packrat Papers*, Vols. I and II. Lynnwood, Wash.: Signpost Publications, 1977.

Newman, Bob. *Commonsense Outdoor Survival: How to Survive in the Wilderness for Five Days.* Birmingham, Ala.: Menasha Ridge, 1994.

Olsen, Larry D. *Outdoor Survival Skills.* New York: Simon and Schuster Trade, 1990.

Olsen, Larry Dean. *Outdoor Survival Skills.* Buhl, Idaho: Salmon Falls, 1988.

Petzoldt, Paul. *The Wilderness Handbook.* New York: Norton, 1984.

Reidel, Arthur. *Fundamental Rock Climbing.* Cambridge, Mass.: MIT Outing Club, Massachusetts Institute of Technology, 1973.

Ruffner, James A., and Frank E. Bair, eds. *The Weather Almanac.* Detroit: Gale Research Company, 1991.

Silverman, Goldie. *Backpacking with Babies and Small Children.* Berkeley, Calif.: Wilderness Press, 1986.

Wilkerson, James A. *Medicine for Mountaineering.* Seattle: The Mountaineers, 1992.

Wright, Don, and Wright, Pam. *Camping with Kids.* Elkhart, Ind.: Cottage Publications, 1992.

Periodicals

Backpacker. Outdoor Adventure Group, CBS Magazines, 1515 Broadway, New York, N.Y. 10036.

Topographical maps

All maps should be ordered from U.S. Geological Survey, 12201 Sunrise Valley Dr., Reston, Va., 22092.

Outdoors in Winter

Sports and Games In the Cold Season

Before jet aircraft provided quick access to the tropics, most Americans spent their winters right where they were. As a result, cold weather sports and games played a major part in their winter entertainment. Ice-skating, sledding, snow sculpture, sleigh rides, and winter sports, such as curling and ice hockey, enjoyed wide popularity. Today, a growing movement back to traditional values—plus a booming interest in physical fitness—has made winter recreation into a major growth industry, especially the energetic sports of snowshoeing and cross-country skiing.

Traditional igloos are constructed from blocks of compact wind-slab snow.

Preparing for a Trip in Snow Country

Of all cold weather recreational activities, a winter backpacking trip is probably the most challenging. Cold weather camping is like summer camping only more so. You carry greater loads, expend more energy, and require more food. Your shelter must be sturdier, your physical condition better, and your route-finding abilities more accurate. In return for your effort, you will gain entry to a world that very few men or women ever have the good fortune to visit. It is an uncrowded world of remarkable beauty; a world of pure and brilliant color where the humdrum of everyday life quickly vanishes.

Careful preparation is the key to a safe and pleasurable winter excursion. There should be at least four members in your party (two of them experienced winter backpackers), so that if someone is injured, one member can stay behind to help while two go back for aid. Go over the itinerary carefully well in advance of the trip, and be sure each participant knows it thoroughly. Settle on the route to be followed, the overnight bivouac sites, and the overall goals (a circuit through a wilderness, attaining a particular peak, a traverse of a ridgeline). Such a plan will be important on the trip, since it will let you measure your progress against the rate at which you are consuming food and fuel.

Weather is of vital importance on any winter trip. Check the forecasts thoroughly before starting out. If reports indicate that severe weather is in the offing, let discretion be the better part of valor—disappointment in the form of a delayed or canceled trip is preferable to disaster. As an added margin of safety, take along a small portable radio capable of receiving weather reports from the local station.

Whether you use skis or snowshoes, the distance you will be able to travel each day will be considerably less than in summer. There are fewer hours of daylight, the packs are heavier (70 pounds or more), and the going, particularly uphill, is more difficult. Your schedule should take account of this and also allow time for relaxation and sightseeing. Also bear in mind that choosing a route along a marked trail is no guarantee against getting lost—the trail will probably be buried under several feet of powder snow, and even if the trail markers are not buried too, they are likely to be hidden under a crust of hoarfrost. Although maps and compasses can help, the only sure method of finding your way in the winter is to know the topography of the area and have the sense and experience to recognize important features in the field.

The final step before setting out on the trip is to divide up the load. There is always a great deal of communal equipment—food, fuel, cooking gear, tent, first aid kit, spare ski tips, extra snowshoe bindings—and it must be apportioned equitably, with due regard for the varying physical abilities of the party members.

A note on equipment

Most of the camping gear used in summer is also satisfactory in winter. Subzero conditions place greater demands on equipment, however; and at the same time there is less margin for error, so reliability becomes all-important.

Tent. Use a wind-resistant, freestanding tent with a snow-shedding fly. Total weight should be less than 3 lb. per man. A-frame, dome, or pyramid tents are all acceptable.

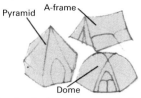

Sleeping bag. Down bags are by far the best: they weigh the least, take up the least space, and provide the most warmth. Be sure to get a bag that is rated below the coldest temperature you are likely to encounter; or take along two bags and use one inside the other. A closed-cell foam ground pad will provide insulation where you need it most—beneath your sleeping bag. A 3/8- by 21- by 72-in. pad should suffice.

Stove. A small stove that burns unleaded gasoline is easily the best choice, since butane stoves are inefficient in cold weather. Buy one that has a mini-pump—it will simplify cold weather operation. Carry extra gasoline in an aluminum fuel flask.

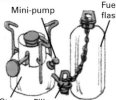

Food and Water

The food you consume on a winter backpacking trip must provide an enormous amount of energy—up to 6,000 calories per day for uphill travel in deep powder conditions compared with a normal daily requirement of one-third that amount. A balanced cold weather diet consists of 40 percent protein, 40 percent fat, and 20 percent carbohydrates; and the food should be lightweight, compact, easy to cook, and immune to freezing.

Dehydrated foods provide the most food value for the least weight. Preparing them takes time, however, and such ready-to-eat items as jerky (see *Preserving Meat and Fish*, p.227), canned sardines, and dried fruits are valuable for quick-energy snacks. One-pot meals—planned and tested in advance of the trip—are the rule for both breakfast and dinner. For dinner, freeze-dried trail meals make cooking easier, but many campers prefer creating their own glop out of such staples as instant potatoes, instant rice, cheese, canned tuna, soup mix, and dehydrated meat. Some campers forego a hot breakfast, preferring instead a simple meal of such foods as crackers, sardines, and dried dates, so that they can get moving as soon as possible. Others insist on the psychological and physiological benefits of hot cereal and eggs, plus tea, coffee, or cocoa.

Wintertime trail cooking consists in large part of melting down snow. It takes a great deal of heat to melt a small amount of snow, so be sure to take plenty of unleaded gasoline; 2 quarts should be sufficient for a three-day, two-night excursion involving four people. Set up the stove in a spot that is thoroughly sheltered from the wind, such as the entranceway to a tent or the cooking pit in an igloo. Fill a pot with snow (be careful not to get any on the outside of the pot so as not to douse the flames) and stir frequently—snow and steam are excellent insulators, and failure to stir will result in a small layer of boiling water on the bottom of the pot capped by a mass of unthawed snow. As soon as most of the first batch of snow is melted, spoon in more. Have a second pot of snow ready to put on the stove when the first is ready, and add water from the first pot to it as a starter. Do the bulk of your cooking and rehydrating in a third pot. The fundamental idea is to conserve precious fuel by keeping the flame continuously at work.

Fires are difficult to get going in the winter, so a stove is preferable. If you do try to build a fire, have plenty of dry wood and shavings on hand before you light it. Set the fire up on a platform of large logs to keep it from sinking in the snow.

Clothing

Food supplies heat, and clothing provides the protection that keeps it from being wasted. As in summertime, the layering principle applies: several light layers of comfortably fitted clothes are preferable to a single heavy layer. From the inside out, the three main layers are the under, mid, and outer. Many winter sportsmen wear wool or down garments. Down provides maximum warmth at minimum weight; wool has the important advantage of retaining its warmth even when wet.

Underlayer. Two-ply long johns and undershirts (cotton on the inside for comfort, wool on the outside for warmth) are warmer than thermal-knit underwear. Two pairs of socks—a thin pair of cotton socks beneath a heavier wool pair—are warmer and more comfortable than a single thick pair.

Midlayer. For warmth plus ventilation, wear a tightly woven wool shirt that opens down the front and a quilted jacket over it that also opens in the front. Your pants should be of tightly woven wool, cuffless, with plenty of room in the seat and legs, and flaps over the pockets to help keep snow out. For added ventilation use suspenders rather than a belt. A woolen stocking hat or a balaclava (a cap that can be pulled over the face like a mask) will stem heat loss from the head.

Outer shell. The main job of the outermost layer is to protect against wind, rain, and snow. A parka that covers the hips and has a hood and a full-length zipper is best. You will also need a windproof face mask if your route takes you above the timberline or along windswept ridges. Down pants, down mittens, and down booties are luxuries around camp but are too warm for use on the trail. Two-piece mittens—a wool liner and a nylon outer shell with a leather palm—are better than gloves.

You will also need a good pair of boots. Double boots—a felt inner liner and high-top outer boot—are warm and comfortable but are extremely expensive. A rugged mountaineering boot has many of the advantages of the double boot at considerably lower cost. Even cheaper are pac boots with rubber bottoms and leather or nylon uppers; they are a good choice for snowshoeing. Foam-insulated rubber boots will keep your toes warm in the coldest weather but may also make your feet perspire. In addition to boots you will need gaiters to prevent snow from sifting in as you travel. Or you can achieve the same result by installing metal grommets in the bottom of your pants, then lacing the pant legs snugly to the boots. Crampons are an important accessory if you venture above the timberline—their sharp points give your boots purchase on glare ice.

Footwear (left to right): double boot, mountaineering boot, pac, insulated rubber boot with gaiter and crampon.

Frostbite, hypothermia, and snow blindness

Frostbite is the freezing of body tissue, usually due to a combination of wind and cold. The first stage is frostnip—white patches of superficially frozen skin that appear on the fingertips, ears, toes, nose, chin, and cheekbones. Keep an eye on one another during a winter trip. If frostnip appears, warm the affected areas immediately by holding the palms of your hands over white spots on your face, tucking your fingers into your armpits, or warming your toes against a companion's body. Deep frostbite is a serious condition whose symptoms include loss of sensation and whitening and hardening of the affected areas. Quick warming in 105°F water is the best treatment, but frostbitten feet should not be thawed until civilization is reached, since the victim will be unable to walk afterward. Never rub snow on a frostbitten area, and avoid chafing.

Hypothermia occurs when the body is unable to maintain its normal temperature. Lethargy, intense shivering, and loss of coordination are early symptoms. The primary treatment is warmth: build a fire, have the victim drink hot liquids, get him into a sleeping bag with one or two other campers. Nourishing food and adequate clothing will prevent hypothermia.

Snow blindness is the result of ultraviolet glare from snow. It can be avoided by wearing dark goggles or sunglasses. Should these become lost, improvise a pair of Eskimo goggles by cutting 1/16- by 1 1/2-in. slits in cardboard, plastic, or tree bark. Symptoms of snow blindness take up to eight hours to appear. They include a gritty feeling in the eyes, loss of visual perception, swelling of the eyelids, and loss of vision. Darkness is the only cure; if possible, keep a blindfold over the eyes of the affected person during the day.

1/16" wide slits

Traveling Over Snow By Snowshoe or Ski

It is almost impossible to progress more than a few hundred feet in deep powder snow without the proper equipment. But with skis or snowshoes on, winter travel can be an exhilarating pleasure. Choose your equipment to suit the purpose: narrow, lightweight touring skis for cross-country; wide, sturdy alpine skis for ski mountaineering; and snowshoes for winter hiking. For the beginner a good way to start is by renting. Complete snowshoe or ski touring packages are available at camping goods stores throughout the country.

Types of Snowshoes

Snowshoes, an invention of the American Indian, let you "float" on snow. White ash frames and rawhide lacing are traditional, but tubular aluminum and neoprene-coated nylon are becoming popular. (Nylon lacing is stronger and more durable than rawhide and requires little maintenance.) The maneuverable bear-paw is the most popular style of snowshoe; the elongated Michigan and Alaskan are better when heavy loads are carried. When using snowshoes, step out far enough for the forward shoe to clear the edge of the rear shoe. Hesitate between strides to let the snow compact to give you a firm foundation for the next step.

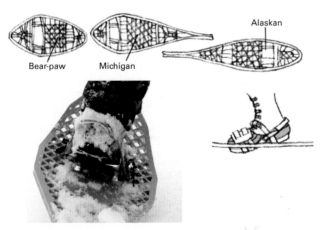

Bear-paw   Michigan   Alaskan

Bindings, sold separately from snowshoes, must allow boot to pivot. Note that toe penetrates snowshoe (above) for ease of walking and traction on hills.

Some Basic Maneuvers

Stationary shoe

Basic step is made with feet spread no farther apart than as for normal walking. Lift one shoe up and over other far enough to completely clear the stationary shoe.

Step turn is simply walking in a tight circle. Tail of inner snowshoe remains almost stationary while its tip pivots in direction of turn. Outer shoe follows.

Pivot tip so that it faces to rear

Kick turn is more acrobatic than step turn. Lift inside shoe until it is vertical, plant heel, and pivot it 180 degrees. Then swing other shoe around in pirouette movement.

Press here to keep tail up

Backing up is next to impossible without ski poles. The trick is to keep the tail from digging in by pressing down the tip of the snowshoe as you step backward.

Improvising in an emergency

If an unseasonable snowfall catches you unprepared, you can rig a pair of emergency snowshoes. Make the frames of strong, flexible 6- to 8-ft. branches. Shave the branch ends flat, and lash them together with twine. Notch and tie on cross members, and weave twigs lengthwise through them. Finish by stretching a cloth over each shoe, or weave evergreen sprigs in and out. In a severe emergency, especially when you are short of time, equipment, and supplies, evergreen branches lashed to your feet can function as crude snowshoes.

Backpacking on skis

Skis are an attractive alternative to snowshoes for winter backpacking. Although their elongated form can make them awkward to maneuver in tight turns or when sidestepping up a densely wooded slope, skis have the invaluable compensating advantage of allowing you to ski down slopes instead of being forced to walk down.

Skis used for backpacking should be wider and stronger than cross-country skis, lighter in weight than standard downhill skis, and should have steel edges to provide a grip on icy spots. Special dual-purpose bindings are needed that can be set for either hiking or skiing. When set for hiking, boot heels are free to rise; in the skiing position the heels are locked to the skis. The boots themselves are not critical. Any good mountaineering shoe will do, provided it has a notch or welt for the binding to grip. Standard ski boots can be used, but their extreme rigidity is likely to cause discomfort on extended trips.

The longer the ski, the more flotation it will provide, but the harder it will be to maneuver. If you are of average weight, select skis that reach the fingertips of your outstretched hand. The poles should have large baskets and should reach from your shoe sole to your shoulder. Mohair climbing skins that attach to the bottom of your skis are essential accessories for moving up long, moderately steep slopes.

Fibers grip snow for uphill travel

Fibers flatten on downhill runs

Climbing skins have a one-way nap like a cat's back. When a ski slides forward, the fibers flatten, permitting the ski to slide easily. When you are climbing, the fibers on the stationary ski dig in to prevent it from sliding backward.

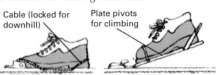

Cable (locked for downhill)   Plate pivots for climbing

Dual-purpose bindings are necessary when skis are used for backpacking in hilly terrain. Several styles are available. Binding at left has a cable that can be locked in place for downhill runs or left free for hiking. Step-in design at right has hinged metal plate that is locked for downhill and released for hiking and uphill work.

Cross-country Skiing

Cross-country skiing, long a major sport in the Nordic countries, is fast becoming one of America's favorite winter recreations. It is a sport that takes you out into nature's wilderness at its loveliest and most unspoiled, it can be enjoyed even by novices, and, unlike downhill skiing, there are no long lift lines to contend with or expensive lift tickets to buy.

In addition to the equipment shown below, take along the normal items that you would on any winter outing. Dress warmly (in layers, so you can shed clothing as you warm up), and carry along a first aid kit, trail food, and a thermos of cocoa or other hot drink. Remember to treat cold weather with respect—do not go out alone, and be sure to guard against frostbite, hypothermia, and snow blindness (see p.431).

More than any other single topic the cross-country enthusiast talks, thinks, and worries about wax. The right wax will give the ski good purchase for a strong push-off when the ski is standing still, but allow the ski to glide almost without friction once it is sliding forward. A base wax is generally applied first, followed by a final, or kicker, wax. As a rule, the colder the temperature, the harder the wax should be. When the temperature is above freezing, a sticky liquid wax called klister is used. An alternative to waxing, particularly appropriate for novice skiers, is the use of so-called waxless skis. These skis have special patterns on their running surfaces, such as diamond, fish scale, and stepped, or else have mohair strips embedded in their running surfaces.

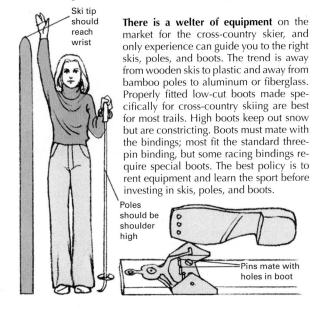

Ski tip should reach wrist

There is a welter of equipment on the market for the cross-country skier, and only experience can guide you to the right skis, poles, and boots. The trend is away from wooden skis to plastic and away from bamboo poles to aluminum or fiberglass. Properly fitted low-cut boots made specifically for cross-country skiing are best for most trails. High boots keep out snow but are constricting. Boots must mate with the bindings; most fit the standard three-pin binding, but some racing bindings require special boots. The best policy is to rent equipment and learn the sport before investing in skis, poles, and boots.

Poles should be shoulder high

Pins mate with holes in boot

Some Basic Techniques

Thrust with pole

Kick with leg

Diagonal stride is the cross-country skier's basic step. First practice shuffling forward without poles. After you gain confidence, try "hopping" from one ski to the other as you transfer your weight. This hop, or kick, as skiers call it, will provide enough thrust to let you glide forward on your other ski. Full diagonal stride, shown sequentially, combines a kick with a simultaneous pole thrust on the opposite side. The movement is easy to learn because the arms and legs move as in natural walking. This skatelike stride, once mastered, has been said to give one the sensation of flying along the snow.

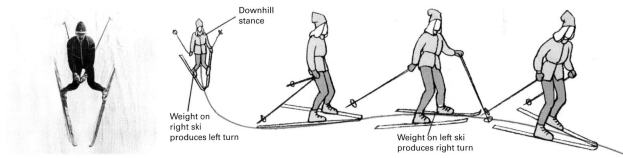

Downhill stance

Weight on right ski produces left turn

Weight on left ski produces right turn

Snowplow and snowplow turn are downhill braking maneuvers particularly suitable for beginners or those carrying heavy packs. To do the snowplow, assume an exaggerated knock-kneed stance, and form the skis into a wedge with their inner edges digging into the snow. To make a snowplow turn, shift your weight to the ski on the side opposite the direction you want to turn—to the right ski for a left turn, to the left ski for a right turn. The arcs of snowplow turns are wide and sweeping. To slow down your descent, make the angle of the wedge wider; to speed it up, make the angle narrower.

Cross-country skis allow you to explore places you might never see in the winter otherwise.

For Winter Comfort Build It From Snow

Of the various shelters that can be improvised for winter camping, igloos—an Eskimo invention—are probably the most luxurious. They take time to construct (two or three hours for an experienced team working together), but for an extended stay in the wilderness the effort is very worthwhile. Igloos are cozy and weatherproof, and the only supplies you need to build one are some well-compacted snow and a tool such as a machete or ice saw to cut it into blocks. The ideal snow for igloos is the wind-packed powder found in open terrain or above timberline. Other snow can frequently be used if it is first tramped down with skis or snowshoes. Fresh powder snow, however, does not have sufficient strength for use in constructing an igloo. Select a level site for your igloo, build up the main dome first, then construct the entranceway. Finish off the job by chinking all gaps and glazing the interior. (To glaze the igloo, warm the inside with a stove for about 15 minutes, turn off the stove, and pull out a base block to freeze the softened snow with cold outside air.) Keep the ceiling vent open when you cook, and avoid raising the interior temperature too high lest the igloo melt.

Three Snow-Country Shelters

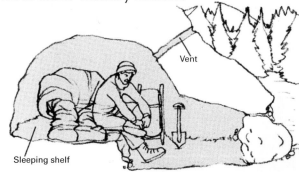

Snow cave resembles an igloo, but instead of being built of blocks, it is scooped out of a snowbank. Design shown has a rear sleeping shelf. Another style has a central cooking area with two-person sleeping shelves on each side. The roof should be at least 2 ft. thick with a sloping venthole. Check the venthole before cooking to make sure it is clear of snow. The preferred site for a snow cave is on a steep hillside in deep snow. A lot of digging is necessary, so snow shovels are a must.

Raising an Igloo From the Ground Up

1. Lay out a circle about 10 ft. in diameter to mark the interior boundary of the igloo. Pile up a mound of snow inside the circle for use as a sleeping shelf when the igloo is completed.

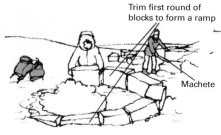

2. Use a machete or ice saw to cut 1/2- by 1 1/2- by 2 1/2-ft. snow blocks. Each block weighs about 40 lb., so get them from a nearby area. Place blocks around the circle, then trim to form a spiral ramp.

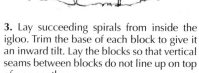

3. Lay succeeding spirals from inside the igloo. Trim the base of each block to give it an inward tilt. Lay the blocks so that vertical seams between blocks do not line up on top of one another.

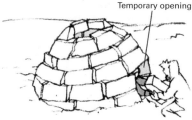

4. When walls are 3 to 4 ft. high, cut a temporary opening so blocks can be slid in. When shaping blocks, aim for a dome that will provide headroom for the tallest member of your group.

5. Final hole in roof is plugged with wedge-shaped block that serves as keystone. Chink roof and walls both inside and out with snow. Replace block in temporary opening and chink in place.

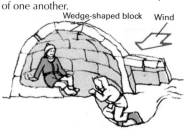

6. Build a permanent entranceway by tunneling under the igloo at a point that is 90 degrees from the prevailing wind. Finish by erecting a protective arch over the entrance tunnel.

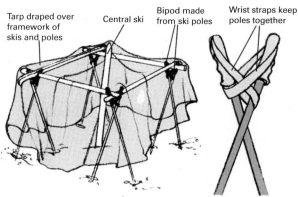

Large, lightweight nylon tarp can replace a tent at considerable savings in weight for a group traveling on skis, since skis and ski poles form the framework of the tent, eliminating the need for tent poles or stakes. Form bipods from ski poles by interlocking their straps, then plant them in the snow and hang skis between them. Drape tarp over this framework and pack snow around the base to keep snow from sifting inside. Ground cloths and a central ski that functions as a tent pole complete the shelter.

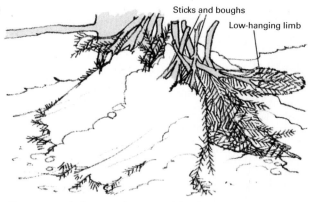

Emergency shelter can be created by forming a double lean-to from tree boughs, weeds, bushes, and sticks. A sturdy, low-hanging limb can serve as a ridgepole. Layer the sticks and boughs to provide maximum wind protection and fill the chinks with packed snow. Keep the entrance low and small to trap warm air inside, and build a windbreak of snow, sticks, or rubble in front of the entrance. The best place for such a shelter is on the lee (downwind) side of cliff.

Enjoying Wintertime In Your Own Backyard

While the more ambitious may prefer a holiday at a ski resort or a cross-country excursion through the wilderness, the traditional locale for wintertime recreation is no farther away than the backyard or at most the immediate neighborhood. Sleigh rides, tobogganing, snow sculpture, and such games as ice hockey and curling can be enjoyed almost anyplace where the weather is cold enough and the snow is deep enough.

Ice lends itself to a variety of winter sports and games. If no handy ice-skating rink or frozen pond exists nearby, you can still enjoy ice-skating by setting up your own backyard rink. A spell of cold weather, a little snow, and a level plot of ground are all you need. Scrape the snow away from a rectangular area (about 15 feet by 25 feet or larger), then pack up snow around the border of the cleared area to a height of a foot or so. Wait for a good, cold night (20°F or lower), hook up a garden hose, and cover the area with about an inch of water. The next day, when the water has frozen, set the hose on spray, and add another 1/2 to 1 inch. After several such treatments, the ice will be ready for skating. Keep the rink in good shape by clearing off new-fallen snow and by resurfacing the ice with more water when it becomes rutted. Be sure to drain the hose and bring it indoors after each use: in cold weather a hose can freeze and crack in minutes.

A frozen pond, of course, can make an excellent natural skating area as well as a likely spot for ice fishing, but the only way to be certain that the ice is strong enough to support your weight is if a responsible authority tests it and guarantees its safety. The general rule is that 2 inches of solid, hard, compact ice will be marginally safe for one person on foot, 3 inches will support a single

A homemade sled run

If there is a nearby hill and a foot or two of snow, you can rig up a run that will make sledding more fun than ever for the kids. Set out a curving downhill course by packing a pathway several feet wide through the snow. Smooth out large bumps, and build up snowbanks along the outer edges of curves. Any flat-bottomed sled can be used for the run—a plastic roll-up, an aluminum saucer, or even a sheet of corrugated cardboard. The run will improve with use provided it is kept in repair by filling holes and packing down new snow.

Skating and sledding will never lose their appeal for winter sports lovers.

person safely, and 4 inches will be safe for general pedestrian (not vehicular) use. Ice thicknesses may not be uniform, however, and ice that is tested and found safe in one location may be unsafe in a spot nearby. Springs and currents produce weak spots, and ice near the shore is almost always thinner than it is farther out. Moreover, ice that has thawed and refrozen is not nearly as strong as ice that has formed on still water and never thawed. Snow is another consideration: snow is an insulator, and ice that lies for a time beneath a covering of snow is likely to be weak, mushy, and honey-combed with air bubbles.

If you are ever in a situation where someone falls through the ice, it is imperative to get him out as soon as possible—20 minutes in freezing water can be fatal. Do not go near the edge of the broken area. Instead, throw the victim a line, or lie flat on the ice and slide a board, tree branch, ski, ladder, or even one end of a coat to him, then pull him toward you. Instruct the victim to remain calm—thrashing about will only cause his garments to soak through more quickly, thereby reducing their buoyancy as well as their insulating ability. The victim should help by pulling his torso onto the ice, swinging one leg at a time onto its surface, then rolling away some distance from the weak ice before attempting to stand.

Sources and resources

Books
Caldwell, John. *The New Cross-Country Ski Book.* Gloucester, Mass.: Peter Smith, 1988.
Conover, Garrett, and Conover, Alexandra. *Snow Walker's Companion: Winter Trail Skills from the Far North.* Camden, Maine: International Marine, 1994.
Edwards, Sally, and McKenzie, Melissa. *Snowshoeing.* Champaign, Ill.: Human Kinetics, 1995.
Gamma, Karl. *The Handbook of Skiing.* New York: Knopf, 1992.
Paul, Stephen L. *Ski Now.* Indianapolis: Masters Press, 1995.

The fine old sport of curling

Curling is a centuries-old Scottish sport that resembles shuffleboard on ice. The object of the game is to slide curling stones—smooth, loaflike 40-lb. rocks with handles on top for gripping—down a 138-ft. rink in such a way that they come as close to a tee, or marker, as possible. A distinctive feature of curling is sweeping (see photo below): the players have brooms with which they control the movement of the stones by sweeping the ice in front of the stones.

There are two teams, each with four players: Lead, Two, Three, and Skip. A match consists of 10 to 17 ends, or innings. During an end each player delivers two stones, alternating throws with his opposite on the other team; the Leads throw first, the Skips throw last. The stones are delivered from the hack, a foothold at the end of the rink, and must slide beyond the farther hog line before sweeping can begin. All the stones of one side that are closer to the tee than any of the opponents' stones score one point, provided they are within or touching the house circle.

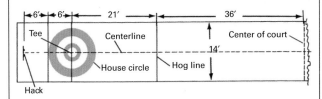

Diagram shows layout and dimensions of half a curling rink.

Fishing

Freshwater Angling Means Catching Fish With Hook and Line

Fish are notoriously brainless creatures against whom anglers have been matching wits with varying degrees of success for ages. Three distinct skills are involved in winning this contest: attracting the fish to take the bait, setting the hook, and landing the fish.

Though blessed with little intelligence, all fish are experts at recognizing two things: food and danger. The longer a fish has lived, the more expertise it is likely to possess. They are seldom fooled by things that move unnaturally in the water, although they may strike at lures that in no other way resemble anything that ever lived. Whether you are using live bait or lures fashioned from wood, cloth, feathers, metal, plastic, rubber, or hair, study what the fish are feeding on and try to match it. If this does not work, try something else; fish are creatures of habit, but their dietary habits often change without notice.

Setting the hook takes a delicate touch, particularly if you are using artificial lures. Most fish taste-test a bit of food before swallowing it. You must sense the moment when your quarry has taken the bait firmly in its mouth, then give a slight jerk on the line—too soon and you will snatch the bait away, too late and the fish may become suspicious and reject it.

Finally comes the part of the contest that most fishermen consider the height of the sport—playing the fish. Usually this is just a matter of reeling in a small or medium-sized fish, but when you hook a big one the fight can last for quite a while. The trick is to maintain enough tension on the line so the fish cannot throw the hook but not to exert so much stress that the line will part or the fish's flesh will be torn.

"Waiting for a Bite" by Winslow Homer. The fisherman's cardinal virtue—patience—is more important than fancy equipment.

Angling With Live Bait

The novice fisherman's first mistake often comes in baiting the hook—fearful of losing the bait, he impales it so securely that it cannot move and dies quickly. Whatever bait you are using, insert the hook carefully, so as to do the least damage and to allow free movement in the water. Do not bother to conceal the point of the hook; the fish has no idea what it is.

Earthworms are so successful at attracting fish that they have earned the common name angleworms. Pass the hook once through the clitellum, the tough collar near the head, and let the worm sink naturally to the bottom. When fishing for bass, lake trout, and other large fish, night crawlers are better than plain worms. Stalk these largest members of the earthworm family at night with a flashlight. If you find a night crawler half in and half out of its hole, hold it down with a finger, and with the other hand pull gently where it emerges from the ground. The worm will contract and pull back; wait until it relaxes, then pull again. Two or three such maneuvers should win the whole worm.

Nymphs are the underwater larval stage of many insects. They are a large part of the diet of rainbow and brook trout. Dobsonfly nymphs, known as hellgrammites,

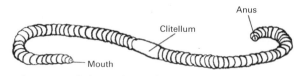

Earthworms, including night crawlers, are the commonest bait.

are a favorite of bass; they are about 2 inches long and are armed with sharp little pincers. Collect nymphs with a fine-mesh net from the shallows of lakes or gravelly areas of fast-moving streams. Hook them through the wide part of the body just behind the head.

Grasshoppers and crickets are good late summer bait. Insert the hook under the mouth of either insect and pass it beneath the hard ventral plate so that it emerges just in front of the large rear legs.

Minnows, frogs, and crayfish are the preferred food of most large lake fish. Hook a minnow through the lips and let it swim, pulling it toward you from time to time in a series of short, darting motions. Hook a frog through both lips or through the tough skin at the base of the back. Crayfish are best hooked through the tail.

Fishing Through the Ice

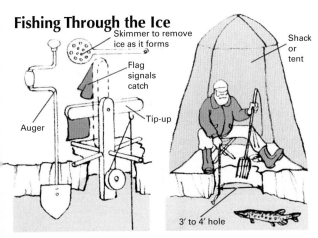

Skimmer to remove ice as it forms

Flag signals catch

Shack or tent

Tip-up

Auger

3' to 4' hole

Tip-up's balanced crossarm signals a bite. Most fish feed in schools, so several holes may be struck at once.

Spearfishing for pike takes patience. Use decoy minnow to lure fish. Inside a dark tent you can see into water.

When ice forms, large fish move to the bottom. They continue to feed, but for the most part they eat what comes to them rather than hunting for food—an exception is the northern pike, which often prowls the shallows in search of prey. Use an ice auger or spud (a heavy long-handled chisel) to make a hole in the ice about a foot across. Test the depth with a weighted line, then bait a hook with a minnow, meat, or lure. Use monofilament line to drop the bait to within a foot or so of the bottom. You can fish one hole with a short rod and bobber, but for best results make several holes and rig each with a tip-up device. Waiting is more bearable in a plywood shed or tent equipped with a small stove. (For tips on ice safety, see *Outdoors in the Winter*, p.435.)

Improvising equipment

Bent safety pin

Parts of belt buckle

Stone sinker

Ancient bone fishhook

Tin-can casting reel

Stick

Brightly colored yarn

Emergency hooks can be made from pieces of bone, as the Indians did, or from safety pins or belt buckles. Lures can be fashioned from feathers, fur, yarn, and bits of foil.

Dressing and Cooking Your Catch

A fish should be dressed for cooking as soon as possible after it is caught. Kill it with a sharp blow behind the head; then wash it in cold, salted water (about 1 tablespoon of salt per quart). Scrape off the scales with a sharp knife or scaler, working from the tail forward. To whole-dress, slit the fish's belly lengthwise and remove the entrails. To pan-dress for frying, continue by cutting out the pelvic fins (beneath and behind the head). Cut through the backbone and down behind the pectoral fins (behind the gills) to remove the head. Cut along each side of the dorsal (back) fin and jerk it out by the roots, pulling toward the head. Rinse the dressed fish in cold, salted water. Skin catfish and eels before dressing. Slice around the neck behind the pectoral fins, secure the head on a nail or with a piece of cord, and use pliers to peel the skin whole, like turning a glove inside out.

To broil a fish over a fire, whole-dress it (no scaling is necessary) and season the cavity with salt, pepper, and herbs. Spit the fish on a green stick or metal rod and suspend it over hot coals.

To fry a fish, first pan-dress or fillet it. For a crunchy outer crust, dip the fish in milk, then in beaten eggs, and roll it in bread or cracker crumbs. Heat fat or oil in a frying pan to just short of smoking (salt pork makes an excellent frying medium), and drop in the fish. Turn when the batter becomes brown. A simpler method is to drop unbreaded fish chunks into hot fat, frying them as briefly as possible.

To poach a large fish, place it whole-dressed in a baking dish. Add chopped, sautéed carrots, onions, and tomatoes. Dissolve a bouillon cube in enough hot water to barely cover the fish. Cover and bake at 350°F. For a similar result at a campfire, wrap the fish in waxed paper, then in several sheets of well-soaked newspaper. Bury the bundle in hot coals for about 20 minutes.

Planking a fish

This favorite northwoods method of cooking whitefish works for any slightly oily fish. Make a plank by splitting a piece of hardwood that is as long as the fish and about twice as wide. Smooth its surface. While you are scaling the fish, let the plank heat near the fire.

Any size fish	Salt
Butter, oil, or	Pepper
bacon grease	Herbs

Dress the fish by splitting it down the back so the belly skin is whole. Tack it or tie it flesh side up on the hot plank, and prop the plank up before the fire. Baste with butter, oil, or bacon grease; add salt, pepper, and herbs to taste. Turn the board occasionally to ensure even cooking.

How to fillet a fish

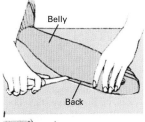

Belly

Back

1. To fillet a large fish, first whole-dress it. Then use a razor-sharp knife to make a cut along the backbone from head to tail. Next, remove the head, cutting behind the gills.

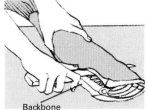

2. Hold the knife flat. Starting at the head end, slice along the upper edge of the backbone to the tail, running the blade over the ribs.

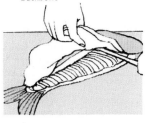

Backbone

3. Lift the boneless fillet whole from the tail end; use the knife to free any ribs that are not completely separated. Turn the fish, and fillet the other side.

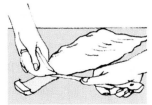

4. To skin a fillet, lay it flat with the skin side down. About 1/2 in. from tail end, cut through the flesh to the skin; then flatten the knife and slide it forward along the skin.

Baking a fish in hot coals

This is a simple way to cook a fish in a campfire without dirtying a pot or a pan. Whole-dress the fish; no scaling is necessary. The head may be cut off or left on.

Salt	Soy sauce and seasonings
Pepper	(optional)
1- to 3-lb. fish	Butter or oil
Bacon or salt pork	

Rub salt and pepper in the cavity (along with other seasonings if you wish). Wrap a slice of half-cooked bacon around fish, or use salt pork. For an extra tang, sprinkle on a few drops of soy sauce. Place the fish on heavy-duty aluminum foil, and put a little butter or cooking oil on top. Wrap tightly and bury in hot coals. Check after four minutes to see if it is done.

Going After Fish With Artificial Lures

You can hunt fish—rather than wait for them to seize your bait—by fly casting, trolling, or surf casting. The art of fly casting is a difficult technique to master. It calls for a long, flexible rod and a very light line, both of which allow even a small fish to put up a battle that it has a fairly good chance of winning.

Dry flies float on the water; wet flies sink beneath the surface. Both are made from bits of feather, fur, twine, and tinsel wrapped around a hook. Dry flies simulate an insect on the water's surface. Some wet flies are meant to imitate drowned insects; others mimic nymphs or shrimp; and some, called streamers or bucktails, look like minnows in the water.

The secret of casting a dry fly is to drop it so gently on the water that nothing disturbs the surface except the fly's bristly hackles, which look to a fish like an insect's feet rippling the mirror that is his sky. If there is a current, cast the fly upstream and let it ride the water down

while you keep the line out of the water. In a lake with no current, let the wind move the fly a little, then pull it back and cast again. A fish may leap from the water to take the lure, or the lure may disappear in a slight splash. In either case, the hook must be set quickly, before the fish has a chance to realize that he has only a mouthful of feathers rather than an insect.

Cast a wet fly across the current or slightly downstream, and let it run in the water until it reaches the end of the line; then retrieve it and cast again. Before you retrieve a bucktail or streamer, let it "swim" minnowlike against the current for a while.

Fly Casting Is All in the Wrist

1. Before casting, take back a few feet of line with your hand. To add line, take it from reel.

2. Bring the rod to vertical with your wrist. Hold extra line in your other hand.

3. Flick the rod forward just as the line is extended straight out behind you.

4. Release slack line as the spring of the rod sends the lure to settle gently on the water.

Fly rod and reel
Fly rods are generally 6 to 9 ft. long and made of light, flexible split bamboo or fiberglass. Reel can be hand operated or spring driven for automatic take-up.

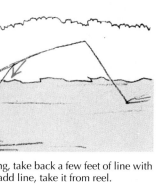

Single action click reel

Automatic reel

Trigger

Four types of flies

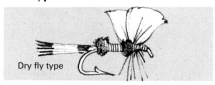
Dry fly type

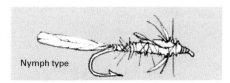
Nymph type

Fan-wing royal coachman is an adaptation of a fly first tied in the 1830s by Tom Bosworth, coachman to Britain's royal family.

Damselfly is made of reddish-brown fox fur and feathers of English grouse to simulate nymph stage of real insect.

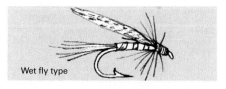
Wet fly type

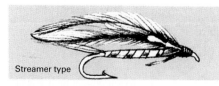
Streamer type

Professor was first tied around 1800 by Professor John Wilson, of Edinburgh University, using a buttercup for the yellow body.

Golden darter simulates a minnow in the water. A bucktail is a streamer with wings of animal hair instead of feathers.

Attaching a transparent leader

Leader

Use turtle knot to tie 3- to 5-ft. nylon leader to fly. Half-hitch at the end of the line prevents the knot from working loose.

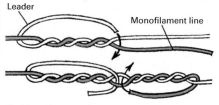
Leader

Monofilament line

Tie blood knot as shown or twist lines together, then pass ends through center. Finish knot by pulling ends tight.

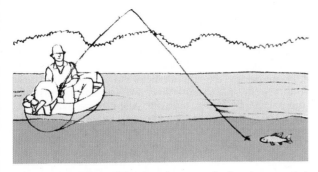

Fish may be frightened by the vibrations of a boat's motor. It is usually best to use the motor to reach your fishing spot, then proceed by paddling or rowing. If you are alone, the best alternative may be to drift and cast your lure.

Trolling for the Big Ones

Trolling means dragging a lure through water to simulate a minnow or other tasty morsel. It is generally done from a boat, either by pulling the lure behind or by casting from a stationary boat and reeling the lure in. When fishing strange waters, it is a good idea to pull the lure behind you through some likely places until you find out where the fish are, then drop anchor and cast. Because trolling is the way to go after big fish, such as musky and lake trout, which lurk in deep water, it calls for a heavy-duty line, a strong reel, and a stout rod.

Lures range from highly realistic plastic reproductions of living creatures to bizarre shapes and forms that resemble abstract sculptures to which feathers and beads have been added as decorations. Some ride beneath the water and some skim the surface. Some are designed to zigzag from side to side like darting fish. Others bob up and down like frogs or aquatic animals. Still others, known as wobblers, have a lurching action that suggests tipsy or injured fish. The simplest lures are shiny oblong bits of metal, known as spoons because of their concave shape. Spoons are wobblers that attract fish by reflecting light in all directions as they spin and gyrate; they can be used alone, in conjunction with another lure, or even with live bait.

Trolling rod and reel

Medium-weight spinning rod 5 to 7 ft. long is best for most trolling. For muskies and other big fish, use long, sturdy rod with flexible tip. Adjustable drag setting on reels allows you to vary the amount of pull needed to take out line.

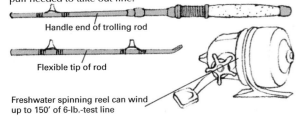

Handle end of trolling rod

Flexible tip of rod

Freshwater spinning reel can wind up to 150' of 6-lb.-test line

How to make two spoon lures from a real spoon

You can turn a teaspoon into a spinner by breaking off the handle and wiring a swivel onto the spoon. Use it to enhance another lure, or wire a hook on and use it alone. The handle becomes a minnow when you wire a swivel to one end; add a hook to one end and double hooks to the bottom.

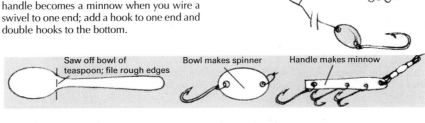

Trolling rig using minnow lure near surface and spinner at some depth

Saw off bowl of teaspoon; file rough edges

Bowl makes spinner

Handle makes minnow

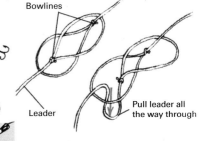

Bowlines

Leader

Pull leader all the way through

To attach leader to line, tie a bowline in each (see *Wilderness Camping*, p.410) and engage loops.

Surf Casting From the Ocean Shore

Surf casting is a way to go after ocean fish without using a boat. It involves the use of a heavy rod, a large spinning reel, and a long, strong line to reach fish hundreds of feet out. The technique varies, depending on whether you are using live bait or artificial lures. With live bait a heavy sinker is attached to the line to hold it to the bottom; you throw the sinker and bait as far as you can and then wait for a fish to accept the offering. Artificial lures are used in the same way as in trolling. Cast as far out as you can, then reel in slowly and steadily to keep the lure moving like a small fish swimming in the water. The lures are larger than freshwater lures, and spoons and spinners are almost always attached.

The best times for surf casting are during the first two hours of an incoming tide and the last two of an ebbing tide. When either condition coincides with a full moon, the situation is ideal; small fish are drawn closer to the shore, and they are followed by the large, hungry predators that are your prey.

Surf-casting rig for live bait

Attach a heavy pyramid sinker about 3 in. from the end of the line. Use a swivel to attach a 12-in. leader of wire or leather with a large single or double hook at the end. For bait use shrimps, crabs, or other bottom dwellers that are common in the area where you fish. Insert hooks carefully to allow the freest possible motion.

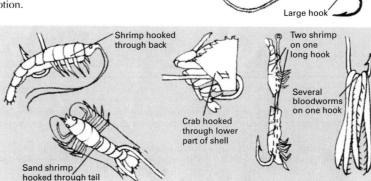

Swivel

Leader

Pyramid sinker

Large hook

Shrimp hooked through back

Two shrimp on one long hook

Crab hooked through lower part of shell

Several bloodworms on one hook

Sand shrimp hooked through tail

Rod and reel for surf casting

Surfcasting rods are heavy, 8 to 12 ft. long, and made of fiberglass or split bamboo. Heavy-duty spinning reel with adjustable drag should be able to wind 400 to 500 ft. of 18- to 22-lb.-test monofilament line.

Surf-casting rod in two parts

Spinning reel for surf casting

A Gallery of Favorite Fish And Water Creatures

Wherever water flows, a human being has no excuse for starving to death. At least some of the fish and aquatic animals listed on these pages are to be found in almost any permanent body of water in the country. The trick is to know which fish are likely to inhabit the waters where you are and to find the best way to go after them.

In mountain streams trout are the best bet. In slow-moving rivers of the Midwest and South catfish are the surest food source. In northern lakes pikes and lake trout are the sportsman's favorite, but sunfish, crappies, and perch are easiest to catch. Along the seashore wait for low tide and gather a feast of shellfish.

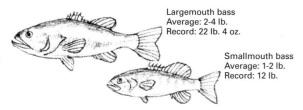

Largemouth bass
Average: 2-4 lb.
Record: 22 lb. 4 oz.

Smallmouth bass
Average: 1-2 lb.
Record: 12 lb.

Bass. Largemouth bass frequent lakes with heavy vegetation and the backwaters of slow-moving rivers. They eat almost anything that moves; try various live bait, lures, and flies. Cast near weeds, lily pads, and stands of cattail early and late in the day; troll in deep water in midday heat.

Smallmouths are prevalent in cold, clear lakes and cool, rocky streams. They are also omnivorous but prefer smaller prey. Flycast with wet or dry flies, troll with lures and spoons, or use live bait. Both types of bass strike quickly and fight to the end. The meat is flavorful broiled, baked, grilled, or fried.

Carp
Average: 2-5 lb.
Record: 55 lb. 5 oz.

Carp. This slow-moving bottom feeder thrives in many polluted waters where other fish cannot survive. Still-fish or troll with earthworms, pieces of meat, or doughballs. Carp may mouth and drop a piece of food several times before finally accepting it, so wait to set the hook until the bite is firm. Skin a freshly caught carp with a sharp, razor-thin blade by shaving off both the scales and skin from the tail forward. Fry, bake, broil, or—in the case of a very large fish—poach your catch.

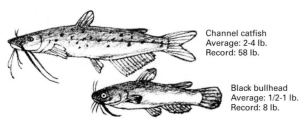

Channel catfish
Average: 2-4 lb.
Record: 58 lb.

Black bullhead
Average: 1/2-1 lb.
Record: 8 lb.

Catfish. These bottom-feeding scavengers detect food with their long whiskers. One or more of the many catfish and bullhead species exist in nearly every body of water in the country. Troll or still-fish for them, using a stout pole and live bait or a piece of dead meat. They have also been known to bite on blobs of dough, cheese, chewing gum, and laundry soap. Skin before cooking; bake, grill, panfry (dredge in flour or cornmeal), or cut into 1-in. cubes and make chowder or gumbo.

Black crappie
Average: 1/2-1 lb.
Record: 5 lb.

Crappie. Look for crappies near weedy shallows of streams and ponds in the Midwest, South, and East. They travel in schools, so where you catch one there will be more. Use live bait; or cast dry flies, nymphs, and small streamers. They may also strike small spoons and spinners. The delicate meat is best panfried.

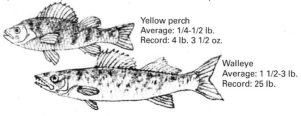

Yellow perch
Average: 1/4-1/2 lb.
Record: 4 lb. 3 1/2 oz.

Walleye
Average: 1 1/2-3 lb.
Record: 25 lb.

Perch. Schools of yellow perch swarm in lakes, ponds, and rivers in all but the warmest states. Still-fish for them with live bait, or cast wet flies and small streamers. Pan-dress and fry in butter.

The walleye, often called a walleyed pike, is the largest of the perches. Walleyes school in cold lakes and rivers. In warm weather, troll deeply during the day with live minnows or lures; in the evening, cast large streamers, lures, or live minnows into shallower, weedy waters. In winter both walleyes and yellow perch are popular with ice fishermen.

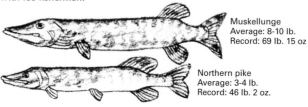

Muskellunge
Average: 8-10 lb.
Record: 69 lb. 15 oz

Northern pike
Average: 3-4 lb.
Record: 46 lb. 2 oz.

Pike. Northerns and muskies are solitary predators that attack their prey with a swift lunge from the side and run a short distance with it before they turn it in their mouths to swallow it. Wait to set the hook until this first run is over.

Muskies dwell in the deep waters of cold northern lakes. Use a strong rod, 25-lb.-test line, and wire leader (because of their sharp teeth), and cast for them with large lures or live bait. The meat is dry and bony but flavorful; marinate it in a mixture of oil, lemon juice, and salt before cooking.

Northerns lurk among weeds and reeds in clear, cold lakes. Cast or troll with lures or live bait, such as frogs or large minnows. Bake, fillet and fry, or poach the meat.

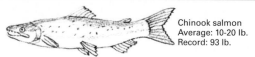

Chinook salmon
Average: 10-20 lb.
Record: 93 lb.

Salmon. These ocean fish return to freshwater rivers to spawn. Atlantic salmon enter rivers mostly in spring or fall; Pacific species, such as the coho and chinook, during late summer and fall. Cast for Atlantic salmon with wet or dry flies. For Pacific salmon troll deeply with lures or live bait. Landlocked salmon are Atlantics that never go to sea; they do not reach the same size as the ones that do. (For instruction in curing and smoking your own salmon, see *Preserving Meat and Fish*, p.226).

Bluegill
Average: 1/2 lb.
Record: 4 lb. 12 oz.

Sunfish. Bluegills, green sunfish, longears, pumpkinseeds, red-ears, and rock bass are among the many popular kinds of sunnies. They are found in the warm shallows of ponds and lakes everywhere, living on worms, insects, and nymphs. Still-fish for them with live bait, especially small earthworms; or cast small wet or dry flies. Broil them whole over a fire; or pan-dress, dust with cornmeal or flour, and deep fry in fat or oil.

Rainbow trout
Average: 1-2 lb.
Record: 42 lb. 2 oz. (steelhead)

Lake trout
Average: 2-6 lb.
Record: 65 lb.

Trout. Brook trout, cutthroats, goldens, and rainbows inhabit fast-moving streams and clear lakes, living largely on insects, nymphs, and small minnows. They are the dedicated fly caster's favorite opponents, often taking the lure with a spectacular leap and always putting up a momentous fight. The meat is sweet and tender, whether broiled whole, planked, or panfried.

Lake trouts are the giants among trout. They live in the deep waters of large northern lakes—the bigger the lake, the larger the trout—always seeking a water temperature of 40°F to 45°F. In summer troll for them at a depth of 50 ft. or more; in spring and fall they may be near the surface; in winter they are caught through the ice at various depths. Use large bait fish or lures sparked with spoons. The meat is rich in flavor. Fillet for frying, or whole-dress and bake or poach.

Shellfish for Good Eating

Some of the most prized gastronomic delicacies are shellfish found in shallow waters and along the shores of oceans, lakes, and streams. Many can be eaten raw; others should be cooked, both for digestibility and to bring out the flavor. Before you forage for any clams, oysters, or other shellfish, however, check local ordinances; the taking of many of these creatures is regulated by law. The easiest cooking method is simply to bring a pot of water to a boil and throw the shellfish in. A lobster will be done in about 10 minutes; crabs take about 20 minutes. Streams and lake shores are the home of the crayfish, or crawdad. Set traps for these small cousins of the lobster or, if you are quick, catch them by hand. Cook them as you would lobster; they will be done within five minutes. Of the many freshwater turtles found in lakes, ponds, and slow-moving rivers, the most flavorful are the snapping turtles. Kill them by turning them on their backs and chopping off their heads, or poke a sharp stick in through the openings of the shell. Cook them in their shells over a bed of coals; or open them up, take out the meat, and make a soup; or you can also simmer them in a pan with onions and carrots.

You can often find clams, mussels, abalone, and scallops clinging to rocks at low tide. Or explore tidal flats for these creatures as well as for conches and crabs.

To make traditional creamy New England clam chowder, use the following recipe:

1 2-in. cube salt pork	Pepper
1 large onion, minced	1 qt. chopped clams
1 cup diced potatoes	(quahogs, surf clams, or
2 cups boiling water	razor clams are favorites)
Salt	4 cups hot milk

Sauté salt pork in a deep pan until crisp. Add minced onion and cook until brown. Remove pork and set aside. Add potatoes, boiling water, salt, and pepper to taste; simmer about 20 minutes—until potatoes are done but firm. Add chopped clams, salt pork, and hot milk; simmer about three minutes. Pour melted butter over the top. *Makes six servings.*

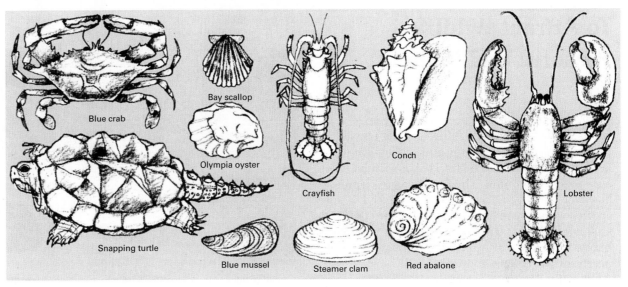

Many kinds of shellfish and turtles are delicious to eat. The shells of abalone and conch also make beautiful decorations.

Some common shellfish and where to find them

All healthy shellfish are edible if they are taken alive and consumed quickly before spoilage begins. There is danger, however, in taking shellfish from polluted waters or waters affected by microorganisms responsible for the "red tide."

Abalones. Large univalve (single-shell) mollusks cling to rocks in Pacific coastal waters. Pry off with tire iron or large chisel.

Clams. Bivalve (double-shell) mollusks burrow in sand. Many types are edible, including the quahog, razor clam, soft-shell (steamers), and geoduck (a Pacific Coast species that reaches 12 lb.). Look for tiny holes in sand and dig at once on seaward side; or use rake or bare feet to locate clams in shallow water.

Conches. Large spiral univalves of southern waters; catch by diving in shallow salt water or by exploring tidal flats.

Crabs. Crustaceans found in all coastal waters. Blue crabs are favorite, especially in the soft-shell stage when the shell is being shed. Catch in traps or nets, or tie a piece of rotting meat to a line and drop it to the bottom from a pier at high tide.

Crayfish. Crustaceans found in fresh and brackish waters, hiding beneath rocks and logs. Trap them, or catch by hand.

Lobsters. Spiny crustaceans caught in deep Atlantic coastal waters with the aid of traps called lobster pots.

Mussels. Bivalves that cling to rocks, jetties, and even fallen trees in fresh and salt water. Gather them at low tide.

Oysters. Rough-shelled bivalves inhabit coastal waters. Becoming scarce due to pollution but worth looking for at low tide.

Scallops. Small saltwater bivalves with distinctive "scalloped" shells. Gather them like clams at low tide in bays.

Turtles. Shelled reptiles that live in fresh and salt water as well as on land. Freshwater snapping turtles are tasty but dangerous; catch them by grasping the shell behind the head.

A trap for crayfish

Trap crayfish in a cylinder of 1/2-in. wire mesh with two conical entrances. For bait use dead fish or even a can of fish-flavored cat food punctured at both ends. When the trap is ready, weight it with rocks, and set it out overnight in a stream or lake. Attach a buoy to the trap or tie it to shore to aid in retrieval.

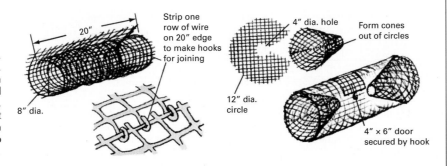

Sources and resources

Books

Bettell, Charlie. *The Art of Lure Fishing.* North Pomfret, Vt.: Trafalgar Square, 1995.

Evanoff, Vlad. *Freshwater Fisherman's Bible.* Garden City, N.Y.: Doubleday, 1991.

Fox, Charles K. *The Book of Lures.* Richmond: Freshet Press, 1975.

Jorgensen, Poul. *Poul Jorgensen's Book of Fly Tying: A Guide to Flies for All Game Fish.* Boulder, Colo.: Johnson Books, 1988.

Kugach, Gene. *Fishing Basics: The Complete Illustrated Guide.* Mechanicsburg, Pa.: Stackpole, 1993.

Leiser, Eric. *The Book of Fly Patterns.* New York: Knopf, 1987.

Living With Nature

To Attract Wildlife: Preserve and Plant

Before North America was settled by Europeans, it was said that a squirrel could travel the treetops from the mountains of New England to the banks of the Mississippi without once touching ground. The forests were cleared, however, and the native wildlife displaced. Some species were wiped out, others were threatened, and everywhere nature retreated from areas inhabited by man. Later, pesticides, trapping, and overhunting took an additional toll.

On a smaller scale the same story is often repeated today each time a tract of virgin land is turned into a home or farmstead. A young couple moving into the country hopes to enjoy much of what nature has to offer, but all too often the very qualities that attracted them in the first place are destroyed in the process of development. Yet, with a little care, concern, and common sense, it is possible to coexist with nature in a mutually beneficial relationship.

Preservation is one key to coexistence. If you are moving into the countryside, destroy as little as possible. Leave as many trees in place as you can, including dead trees—they serve as homes for owls, woodpeckers, and other animals. If you are thinking of draining a marsh, bear in mind that wetlands are rich sources of wildlife and major attractions for migrating waterfowl. And make a point of protecting your crops with fences and organic methods rather than poisons and pesticides. The other key to coexistence is encouragement: put in plantings that will attract animals, set up nesting sites for birds, and provide winter feeding stations for deer and small mammals. Wildlife has many benefits to offer, practical as well as esthetic. With very little effort you can enjoy them in your own backyard.

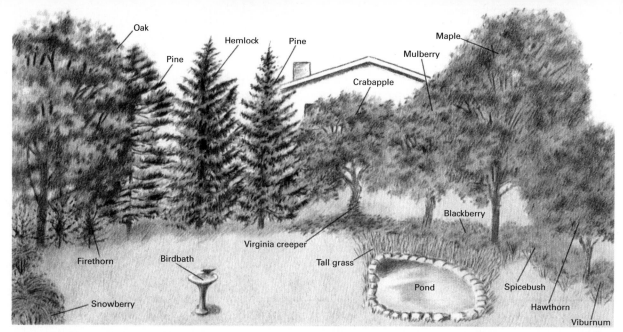

Careful planting can make a backyard into a wildlife sanctuary. Certain kinds of plants are particularly favored by animals for food; others provide nesting sites, cover, and protection. Put in a variety of trees, shrubs, vines, and flowers; a typical assortment should include 8 to 12 species in each category. Plants should be distributed equally for a balanced appearance.

Plantings to Attract Birds and Animals

Flowers and grasses aster, marigold, sunflower, columbine, delphinium, snapdragon, zinnia, verbena, panic grass, pokeweed, timothy	Some flowers and some species of grass produce large amounts of seeds that are especially attractive to seed-eating birds—many of them songbirds. Depending on when they ripen, the seeds will furnish food for such songbirds as finches, juncos, cardinals, and towhees from midsummer through winter. Columbine, delphinium, and snapdragon provide nectar for hummingbirds
Groundcovers knotweed, snowberry, blackberry, sagebrush, spicebush, Virginia creeper, viburnums: highbush cranberry, mapleleaf, nannyberry	Low-growing shrubs and vines provide a vital niche for many animals that live close to the ground. The intertwining vines and clustering leaves give year-round cover from predators and harsh weather, and the fruits and berries provide food. Planted close together they make attractive borders for hedges, driveways, and fencerows. A variety of these plants will attract more than 50 different species of birds, including such game birds as grouse and pheasants. Reptiles, amphibians, and small mammals, such as rabbits, will also benefit
Small trees and shrubs sumac, firethorn, hawthorn, tartarian honeysuckle, crabapple, flowering dogwood, red cedar, cherry, mulberry, elderberry	Small flowering trees and shrubs offer a wide range of attractions for wildlife. Their colorful blooms attract pollinating insects, which in turn attract birds including grosbeaks, vireos, bluebirds, and catbirds. The fruits provide food from spring through early winter. Wide-spreading boughs offer nesting areas, and in winter they give cover and roosting sites
Tall trees boxelder, white oak, birch, white pine, sugar maple, pinyon pine, colorado spruce, beech, elm, holly, hemlock	Tall trees can be the most valuable assets to wildlife on your property. They soften and camouflage the harsh lines of rooftops, pavements, and open fields and are like magnets to migrating birds that stop to feed and rest. They provide permanent homes and foraging perches for animals whose habitats are high off the ground. Conifers are especially attractive to nuthatches, waxwings, and crossbills, among others. Evergreen foliage is a winter haven

Providing Shelter and Food for Birds

Success in attracting birds depends on your ability to provide food, water, and cover. Such devices as feeders, birdbaths, and nesting boxes, plus intelligent landscaping and planting, can supply these necessities. Once you begin feeding birds, however, it then becomes your obligation to continue providing them with food, especially in the winter. Otherwise, the result may be a swollen population one year and famine the next.

Put out a variety of foods for your birds. Yellow corn, rice, millet, hemp, and sunflower seeds are high in carbohydrates (for body heat) and provide vitamins, minerals, and protein. Buy the grains and seeds separately and mix them yourself; your feed will cost less and be more nutritious. You can also save money by buying in quantity; 50- and 100-pound bags of seed are available at feed stores and supermarkets. For additional protein, plus fat for energy, supplement the grains and seeds with beef suet and peanut butter, particularly if there are insect-eating birds in your area, such as nuthatches, finches, and woodpeckers. Mix the peanut butter thoroughly with cornmeal before putting it out; peanut butter straight from the jar can stick in a bird's throat. Grit is also necessary to help birds digest their food. Many people provide sand, meal, and crushed eggshells. Other suitable foods include stale bread, crackers, nuts, and leftover dinner meats. Make sure water is always available; in winter it can be kept ice-free with an aquarium heater.

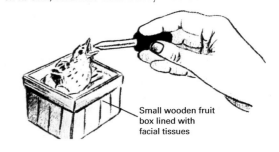

Bird feeders need not be elaborate, but they must match the feeding habits of the birds that are to be attracted. Place feeders near trees for easy escape but not directly under them. Birdbaths serve for both drinking and bathing. Any broad, shallow container will do—from a pie pan to an ornate fountain.

Caring for a baby bird

Occasionally a fledgling falls from its nest or is orphaned. If you find a young bird on the ground, try to return it to its nest or a nearby perch. Should this prove impossible, the first thing to provide is warmth—tiny birds are very susceptible to pneumonia. A small box of the type in which strawberries are sold, lined with tissues, makes a good emergency nest. If the bird's feathers have not come in yet, place the box on a heating pad set to *Low*. Begin feedings as soon as the chick is set up in its new nest. Start with warm milk sweetened with a bit of sugar and thickened with baby cereal. Feed with a medicine dropper at 15-minute intervals until the bird regains its strength, then about once each hour. Night feeding is not necessary. When the bird is old enough to swallow easily, change the diet to bits of mashed fruit, hard-boiled egg yolk, and lean ground beef. Never feed a young bird water—it could choke. When the bird can eat on its own, set a little water nearby in a saucer.

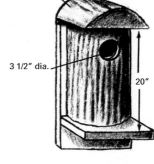

Small wooden fruit box lined with facial tissues

Make the Birdhouse to Suit the Bird

The style and location of birdhouses determine their ability to attract birds. Tailor each house to a particular species, and put them in the birds' favored areas.

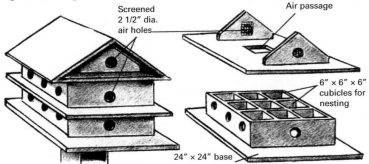

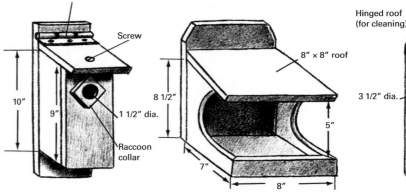

Purple martins are colony nesters, so houses with multiple dwellings are needed for them. To accommodate their swooping flight patterns, put the house in an open area away from trees and buildings on a pole 15 to 20 ft. high. Paint the house white to prevent overheating.

Bluebirds are rare because their nesting sites are used by sparrows. Make bluebird houses of wood with entrance holes 1 1/2 in. wide, and 7 to 8 in. from the base. The floor should be about 4 in. by 4 in. Place houses on posts near open fields.

Robins and phoebes prefer to nest on open platforms, so bracketed shelves and open boxes are best for them. Make the shelves from weathered wood, or paint fresh wood with a dull color. Place them under the eaves of a garage, barn, or porch.

Screech and saw-whet owls frequent orchards and will nest in hollow logs or boxes covered with bark. Nail the box directly to the main trunk of a tree at least 10 ft. off the ground. Flickers and nuthatches occasionally use the boxes if there are no owls.

Making Your Backyard Into a Wildlife Haven

In order to attract wild animals you will have to forego some of the manicured look of a perfectly groomed lawn. Nevertheless, the pleasure of seeing a deer browsing in your yard or watching a mother possum walk by your window with her young clinging to her back can make the trade-off more than worthwhile. And there are many practical benefits as well. Each animal plays a role in the balance of nature, preventing any one species from multiplying excessively. The predators keep the rodent population under control, while the rodents, along with birds, amphibians, and reptiles, help hold down the insect population.

Most animals prefer natural food supplies. Smaller mammals, such as chipmunks and possums, nibble buds, tender twigs, and seeds from the tops of trees and shrubs; rabbits and many other rodents are fond of low-growing vines. By leaving some fruit on trees and on the ground, you can keep animals coming to your yard even in winter. Raccoons are an exception to the rule, having a definite preference for human fare. A few table scraps (or an open garbage can) are apt to bring more of them around than you might care to have. Setting up a salt lick is another way of attracting wild animals. (An old farmer's trick is to put salt on a tree stump that must be removed; it will soon be gnawed to the ground.)

To reach your yard, animals need safe access routes or corridors. If there are any overgrown gullies or culverts on your land, leave them as they are; they will function as natural highways for wild animals. Establish connected strips of unmowed lawn, evergreen hedges, and ground-covering vines (try to enlist the cooperation of your neighbors in this endeavor). The animals also need hiding places from their enemies; an occasional thicket or a fallen tree or two will generally serve the purpose.

Domestic pets rank among the most serious deterrents to wildlife. Cats, whose predilection for catching mice makes them invaluable around the farm and homestead, will also hunt almost any small animal they spot. Dogs, allowed to run free, often form packs, bringing down deer as well as smaller game. In addition, the scent of a dog, or its barking, will frighten many animals away. The solution is to put reasonable restraints on your pets. A bell on the cat will warn birds and other animals of its approach. A dog can be kept indoors at night—when most animals are active—or else tied up or fenced in.

Providing food, especially in the winter, is one of the most effective ways to attract wildlife to your land. But winter feeding is a serious commitment; once started, the animals will quickly develop a dependence on your hospitality, and failure to continue throughout the winter can lead to disease and famine. Check your feeding stands frequently, replenish them if necessary, and keep them free of snow.

Winter Care and Feeding

One of the most effective ways to increase the wildlife population in your area is to help animals survive the rigors of winter by providing them with food and cover. Many mammals eat almost the same kinds of food as birds—seeds, grains, fruit, and. table scraps. For small mammals baskets made from chicken wire that are then attached to trees can be filled with corn; or stake ears of corn onto feeder boards. Raw vegetables, bits of fruit, and table scraps scattered under trees and near bushes will be eaten by rabbits, deer, and other species. A supply of water will also help. Keep it ice-free with an aquarium heater, or put out warm water daily.

Lack of cover is another winter hazard. Make brush piles by tying used Christmas trees onto small trees or by leaning several of them across a stretch of wire or rope. Cover log piles with brambles and fallen branches.

Safety and First Aid

A child's pleading question "I found him, can I keep him?" is often the beginning of a backyard first aid station for wildlife. However, before you try to help a lost or injured animal, even one on your own property, you should consult the U.S. Bureau of Sports, Fisheries, and Wildlife or your state health department about laws concerning the confinement of animals. Many states require special permits to keep or treat wild animals.

In addition to the legal questions, there is the matter of safety. An injured animal is often a dangerous animal, and it has no way of knowing that you are there to help it. Even such small creatures as squirrels and chipmunks can cause serious injury if you get too near to them. There is also the danger of rabies, or hydrophobia, a disease that is as deadly to humans as it is to animals. Never approach a wild animal that exhibits such unusual behavior as convulsions, lack of coordination, or loss of its natural fear of humans; even a spray of saliva from a rabid animal is infectious. Instead, notify the local police or health department.

If the animal's injury is minor, such as a case of shock after an attack by a predator, the most important aids you can give are warmth, food, and quiet. Should it appear that the animal has broken bones, special care may be needed; call a veterinarian or nature center for assistance. Injured animals can be transported in a simple litter made from a cardboard box lined with newspapers and soft cloths. Feed the animal what it normally eats. Most will accept unpeeled fruits, raw vegetables, and nuts. Carnivores will eat high-protein dog food and lean, raw meat.

A baby animal requires special care. If it is still hairless, constant warmth is vital; keep the litter near a stove or fireplace, or put it over a heating pad set to *Low*. Feed young animals frequently. In most cases warm milk, cooked or raw eggs, and baby cereals are safe. Mix an all-purpose vitamin supplement—liquid or powder—into the food. Use a plastic nursing bottle or plastic medicine dropper for feeding, since glass might shatter. Once the animal is well and active, return it to the wild by allowing it to wander from the house for longer and longer periods of time.

Making Waterfowl Feel at Home

The kind of water birds that will visit an area, as well as the number that will come there, depends on three key factors: regional location, type of water resource available (pond, lake, stream, seashore, marsh), and the nature of the surrounding topography. Since waterfowl have distinctive habitat requirements with respect to food, shelter, and reproduction, the more closely you can come to meeting their needs, the more likely you will be to attract the birds.

Although there is nothing you can do to create a seashore or to alter migratory patterns, there are other steps you can take to attract waterfowl. The most obvious, perhaps, is to build a pond. However, before embarking on pond construction you should check with local, state, and federal agencies concerning the use of wetlands, the damming of streams, and the maintenance of migratory

A Pond for Your Backyard

If you lack the space for a full-sized pond, an easy and inexpensive substitute can be made by sinking several wooden barrels into the ground. Put about 6 inches of soil mixed with a little fertilizer at the bottom of each barrel, and saturate the soil with water. Plant the roots of aquatic plants, such as pondweed, lotus, lily, eelgrass, arrowhead, water hyacinth, umbrella plants, and water lettuce, at a slanting angle in about 2 inches of the soil. Add a 1-inch layer of sand, then fill the barrels with water until the leaves float. Spread gravel on the ground surrounding the pond, and arrange a few stone heaps for animal perches and rock gardens. Plant a protective covering of such marsh plants as cattail, rushes, and pickerelweed around the perimeter of the barrels. After a few days, when the plants have taken root, stock the pond with goldfish, minnows, tadpoles, and even a turtle or two (not snappers, however, they are voracious predators and will eat up all the fish and frogs). Other animals, from dragonflies to raccoons, will soon be attracted. There will, of course, be seepage and evaporation, so check regularly and replenish the water supply from a garden hose. If you wish to keep the pond ice-free in winter, use a livestock immersion heater.

Sources and resources

Books

Cortright, Sandy, and Pokriots, Will. *Attracting Backyard Birds: Inviting Projects to Entice Your Feathered Friends.* New York: Sterling Publishing, 1995.
Dennis, John V. *A Complete Guide to Bird Feeding.* New York: Knopf, 1994.
Hickman, May, and Maxine Guy. *Care of the Wild Feathered and Furred.* New York: Kesend Publishing, 1993.

wildlife: in many areas even water that is entirely on your property is subject to regulations.

The type of watering area that is most attractive to the greatest variety of waterfowl is one that has both deep and shallow portions and is surrounded by an abundance of marshy vegetation, such as cattails, reeds, pickerelweed, rushes, and arrowheads. These plants provide food, protective covering, and nesting sites. In addition, many species of waterfowl feed on aquatic plants, such as duckweed, plantains, pond millet, and watercress. If the pond is large enough it should have a few sandbars and grassy islands—the preferred nesting sites for mallards, black ducks, and most species of geese. One or two partially submerged branches are useful as places for birds to preen. If you have cattle, fence the pond to prevent it from being trampled.

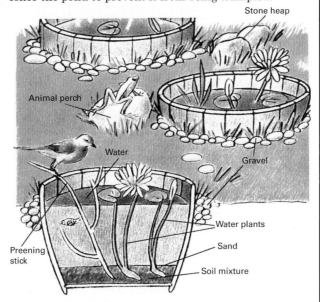

Sunken barrels filled with water take the place of a pond where space is limited. So too can a child's fiberglass wading pool. Another approach is to dig a shallow hole (about 2 ft. deep and 4 ft. wide) and line it with polyethylene sheet.

McElroy, Thomas P., Jr. *The New Handbook of Attracting Birds.* New York: W.W. Norton, 1985.
Stokes, Donald W., and Lillian Q. Stokes. *The Bird Feeder Book.* Boston: Little, Brown, 1987.
Terres, John K. *Songbirds in Your Garden.* Chapel Hill, N.C.: Algonquin Books, 1994.
Witty, Helen, and Witty, Dick. *Feed the Birds.* New York: Workman Publishing, 1991.

Fujico Matsumoto, housewife and bird lover

Mealworms And Suet Bring Birds To Her Home

Fujico Matsumoto, of Pawling, New York, boarded bluebirds for 30 years.

"I've had bluebirds in the backyard for years, ever since we moved from the city to the country. Some are nesting out there right now. Once I even raised a baby bluebird indoors. My husband put boughs and branches all over the living room to help teach the bird how to fly.

"I guess what some people consider very unusual is that I've managed to attract bluebirds to a feeder. That began early one spring at the end of a bad storm when the birds were desperate for food. I opened the back door and threw some mealworms on the porch floor, and the bluebirds began to eat them, and from then on they seemed to come to the feeder. Bluebirds are insect feeders and they love the mealworms (those are insects that turn into beetles as adults). I usually order them from California. To keep the bluebirds through the winter, you'll need some suet in addition to the mealworms. I always chop it up when it is frozen and then put it out for the birds. If it's in large lumps, it's difficult for them to eat.

"Bluebirds aren't the only birds that we have here. I also fed scarlet tanagers for about 10 years. The tanagers are summer birds, they migrate from South America. Four or five came, but only one learned to eat from the feeder. And then one winter a dozen white-winged crossbills came to the feeders. They're very northerly birds, and it's the kind of event that people tell me happens only once every 50 years or so.

"If you want to start having birds, the best way to begin is with an ordinary feeder, the kind you put sunflower seeds in. And then nearby you want to have a suet bag for birds like woodpeckers, chickadees, and nuthatches. And scatter some seed on the ground for ground feeders. You don't want the feeders to hang out in the open or in a windy place. The birds like a place with plenty of cover.

"No matter how busy I am, I never forget the birds, and these days it's really a lot of work because I have to keep my cats away. We've got some wire around the porch and the birds can hear the cats jumping on it, so it gives them time to fly away. Sometimes I've taken pictures of the birds, but for me the greatest pleasure is just watching."

Appendix

Organized Assistance: The Extension Service And Other Groups

If you have a question about what to raise on your land or how to raise it, your most reliable source of free information is your local county agent. The county agent is the direct link between the public and the government's agricultural experts. His job is to answer questions from individuals or, if he cannot answer them directly, to pass them on to appropriate specialists at the state or federal level who can. There is hardly a county in the United States where there is not at least one county agent, and the system extends to the associated commonwealth of Puerto Rico and to the various territories, including the Virgin Islands.

The county agent system was created by an act of Congress in 1914 to bring the services and knowledge of the land-grant colleges to the doorsteps of the nation's farmers. Officially called the Cooperative Extension Service, the system has a branch at each land-grant college and can call upon their agricultural experiment stations, animal and plant pathology labs, and other facilities for information and assistance. The county agent can also draw on the U.S. Department of Agriculture for information and diagnoses of every kind of problem from poultry disease to soil deficiencies.

Although the original purpose of the Cooperative Extension Service was specifically to serve full-time farmers, the great shift of population away from the farm to cities and suburbs did not spell its doom by any means. Instead, the county agents accepted the task of serving a new constituency with a different set of problems and concerns. (There are, of course, plenty of county agents who still serve professional farmers.)

A county agent's office usually includes experts whose specialties are keyed to local needs. These vary widely between city and country and from region to region, even within the same state. Along with the specialists almost every county agent's office includes a generalist—someone with a wide knowledge of many different types of crops and animal husbandry. For the homeowner, the part-time farmer, the city gardener, the neophyte homesteader, or anyone who is uncertain about what to raise and how to go about it, whether for a cash crop or for self-sufficiency, the generalist is the person to consult. His knowledge of local soil conditions,

Norman Rockwell immortalized the extension service in this painting of an Indiana agent at work checking the calf of a 4-H'er.

water availability, capital costs, government loans, and market possibilities makes him an invaluable resource for the inexperienced and the uncertain.

The functions of the Cooperative Extension Service go far beyond the farm, orchard, and garden. Most offices include a home economist and a youth worker whose main responsibility is advising the local 4-H clubs. On the statewide level nutritionists and psychologists are available to counsel families and individuals.

All Cooperative Extension Service agents are college trained and have one or more degrees in their specialties. All have a continuing university affiliation through the state land-grant colleges. (Established in 1862 with large grants of federal land to the states, the land-grant colleges are centers of research and development in agriculture and other practical arts and sciences.) In some states the county agents are full-time faculty members of the land-grant institutions, teaching courses there and in their communities. Among other duties the agents run local meetings, discussion groups, and field demonstrations. They work with local organizations, such as the dairymen's association, the nurserymen's league, gardening clubs, and other social or educational groups. To disseminate the most up-to-date information, county agents may run their own local radio and television shows where they lecture on specific subjects, answer inquiries, and interview guest experts.

A visit to the county agent's office—or better, a series of visits—is strongly recommended to anyone planning a farming operation of any size, especially for beginners or those unfamiliar with local conditions. One of the agents will almost certainly be familiar with the piece of property the would-be farmer has bought or is thinking of buying. He can recommend crops and livestock that are likely to thrive and warn against projects likely to fail. In addition to firsthand advice, county agents can arrange get-togethers with local growers, husbandry associations, and agricultural organizations; all are valuable sources of information on raising and marketing farm products. The agent also has an extensive library of material published by the Cooperative Extension Service and by the U.S. Department of Agriculture that provides detailed information on almost every subject of interest to a parent, homeowner, apartment dweller, farmer, suburbanite, or countryman. A list of the publications and a catalog of available extension courses can be obtained without charge.

In most communities the telephone number and address of the local Cooperative Extension Service office can be found under the county government heading in the white pages of the phone book. (In a few states it is known as the Agricultural Extension Service.) They are also available at www.csrees.usda.gov/extension/index.html.

Other Helpful Organizations

There are hundreds of organizations offering aid on matters of concern to the homeowner, apartment dweller, housewife, farmer, consumer, and small businessman. Some of the larger groups with more general appeal are listed below. In addition to these there are numerous special-interest groups ranging from the American Rabbit Breeders' Association and the Pinto Horse Association of America to the Appalachian Mountain Club, the American Canoe Association, and the Sierra Club. For a rundown of all organizations—along with descriptions of their activities—ask for the *Encyclopedia of Associations* at your local library. It is published by Gale Research Company, 835 Penobscot Building, Detroit, Michigan, 48226.

Farm Service Agency furnishes information on federal farm programs, cost-sharing assistance for soil and water conservation, and loans for farm-storage facilities. It also makes disaster payments to farm families. The FSA may be listed under its own name in the telephone directory or in the U.S. Government or county listings. www.fsa.usda.gov.

American Forests, P.O. Box 2000, Washington, D.C. 20013. A national non-profit citizen conservation organization, founded in 1875. Its Global ReLeaf campaign helps people improve the environment with trees and forests by restoring damaged ecosystems in urban and rural areas. www.americanforests.org.

American Rivers, 1101 14th Street NW, Suite 1400, Washington, D.C. 20005. Founded in 1973. Works to protect and restore America's river systems and to foster a river stewardship ethic. www.americanrivers.org.

Energy Information Administration, Furnishes current information on energy saving devices to consumers and businesses. www.eia.doe.gov.

Rural Housing Service, U.S. Department of Agriculture, Room 5037, South Building, 14th Street and Independence Avenue SW, Washington, D.C. 20250. Makes loans for home ownership, improvements, and business to farm and nonfarm families alike. Maximum income and certain other limits apply. RHS offices may be located in the telephone directory under their own names or under the U.S. Government listings. www.rurdev.usda.gov.

National Garden Clubs, 4401 Magnolia Ave., St. Louis, Mo. 63110. Seeks to protect and conserve natural resources through environmental education workshops for teachers; assists in establishing botanical gardens and horticultural centers. Grants scholarships in horticultural education, conservation, and landscape design. www.gardenclub.org.

National Grange, 1616 H St. NW, Washington, D.C. 20006. A fraternal organization of rural families, the National Grange promotes general welfare and agriculture through a variety of programs, including social, educational, home economics, youth, cooperative, and insurance and credit-union programs. www.nationalgrange.org.

Seed Savers Exchange, 3094 North Winn Road, Decorah, Iowa, 52101. Maintains and distributes "heirloom" varieties of vegetables and fruits for dedicated gardeners. Seed Savers publishes a yearbook through which members make available some 11,000 varieties of rare and endangered vegetables to interested gardeners. It also publishes Seed to Seed, a how-to-guide describing specific seed saving techniques for 160 different vegetable crops. Headquarters at Heritage Farm maintains 17,000 heirloom vegetable varieties as well as an historic orchard containing 700 varieties of old-time apples. www.seedsaves.org.

Natural Resources Conservation Service, Attn: Legislative and Public Affairs Division, P.O. Box 2890, Washington, D.C. 20013. Furnishes information on natural resources and how to improve them. It also helps restore wetlands, improve water quality, and enhance wildlife habitat. Offices are located in most counties and listed in the telephone directory under U.S. Government, Department of Agriculture. It works closely with local conservation districts and encourages voluntary conservation partnerships. www.nrcs.usda.gov.

National Gardening Association, 1100 Dorset Street, South Burlington, VT 05403. Works to sustain the essential values of life and community, renewing the fundamental links between people, plants, and the earth. The group promotes environmental responsibility, advances multi-disciplinary learning and scientific education. It also creates partnerships that restore and enhance communities. The association serves as a clearinghouse for home and community gardening information. Programs are conducted that provide technical assistance, material and grants to children's gardens nationwide. http://assoc.garden.org.

Additional Resources

Land: Buying It—Building on It

Ching, Francis D. K. and Cassandra Adams. *Building Construction Illustrated, 3rd Edition.* Indianapolis: Wiley, 2000.

Clark, Sam. *Independent Builder: Designing & Building a House Your Own Way.* White River Junction, VT: Chelsea Green, 1996.

Smith, Mark A. and Elaine M. *The Owner-Builder Book: How You Can Save More Than $100,000 in the Construction of Your Custom Home, 4th Edition.* Provo, UT: Consensus Group, 2007.

Thallon, Rob. *Graphic Guide to Frame Construction: Details for Builders and Designers.* Newtown, CT: Taunton, 2000.

Energy From Wood, Water, Wind, and Sun

Chiras, Daniel D. *The Homeowner's Guide to Renewable Energy: Achieving Energy Independence Through Solar, Wind, Biomass and Hydropower.* Gabriola Island, BC: New Society Publishers, 2006.

Freeman, Castle and Dirk Thomas. *Woodburner's Companion: A Practical Guide to Heating with Wood.* Chambersburg, PA: Alan C. Hood & Co., 2006.

Kemp, William H. *The Renewable Energy Handbook: A Guide to Rural Energy Independence, Off-grid and Sustainable Living.* Tamworth, Ontario: Aztext Press, 2006.

Raising Your Own Vegetables, Fruit, and Livestock

Bridgewater, Alan and Gill. *The Self-Sufficiency Handbook.* New York: Skyhorse, 2007.

Otto, Stella. *The Backyard Orchardist: A Complete Guide to Growing Fruit Trees in the Home Garden.* Maple City, MI: OttoGraphics, 1995.

Seymour, John. *The Self-Sufficient Life and How to Live It.* New York: DK Publishing, Inc., 2003.

Smith, Edward C. *The Vegetable Gardener's Bible.* North Adams, MA: Storey Books, 2000.

Thomas, Steven and George P. Looby. *Backyard Livestock: Raising Good, Natural Food for Your Family.* Woodstock, VT: The Countryman Press, 2007.

Enjoying Your Harvest The Year Round

Fisher, Dennis and Joe. *The Homebrewer's Garden: How to Easily Grow, Prepare and Use Your Own Hops, Malts, Brewing Herbs.* North Adams, MA: Storey Books, 1998.

Kingry, Judi and Lauren Devine. *Ball Complete Book of Home Preserving.* Richmond Hill, Ontario: Robert Rose Inc., 2006.

Kingsolver, Barbara. *Animal, Vegetable, Miracle: A Year of Food Life.* New York: HarperCollins, 2007.

Kitchen, Leanne. *Produce Bible: Essential Ingredient Information and More Than 200 Recipes for Fruits, Vegetables, Herbs and Nuts.* New York: Stewart, Tabori & Chang: 2007.

Skills and Crafts for House and Homestead

Buchanan, Rita. *A Dyer's Garden: From Plant to Pot, Growing Dyes for Natural Fibers.* Loveland, CO: Interweave, 1995.

Hasluck, Paul N. *The Handyman's Book: Tools, Materials, and Techniques for Woodworkers.* Berkeley: Ten Speed Press, 1987.

Lovelady, Donna. *Rug Hooking for the First Time.* New York: Sterling Publishing: 2005.

McCreight, Tim. *The Complete Metalsmith.* Worcester, MA: Davis Publications, 2005.

Recreation at Home and in the Wild

Albright, Barbara. *The Natural Knitter: How to Choose, Use, and Knit Natural Fibers from Alpaca to Yak.* New York: Crown Publishing Group, 2007.

Seton, Susannah. *Simple Pleasures of the Home: Cozy Comforts and Old-Fashioned Crafts for Every Room in the House.* Newburyport, MA: Red Wheel/Weiser, 1999.

Wiseman, John. *SAS Survival Guide: How to Survive in the Wild, in Any Climate, on Land or at Sea.* New York: HarperCollins, 2006.

Index

Index

Index

454

Index